THE LANGUAGE OF
THE PEOPLE

Etiquette has in the past tended to discourage the uttering, writing and studying of certain prohibited words and subjects—usually associated with sex and the bodily functions. For this reason, dictionaries of the standard language have for the most part been careful to omit these terms.

Now, at last, this indispensable resource book fills this vast linguistic gap by cataloguing and explaining these prohibited words and subjects, thus opening the way to a clearer understanding both of the living, evolving language and of the people who speak it.

Slang and Euphemism

"Try 'Slang and Euphemism' if you want a good knowledge of contemporary cussing"
     —William Safire, in *The New York Times Magazine*

RICHARD A. SPEARS *began collecting words at the age of eight and dictionaries at fourteen. This love of language eventually led to a Ph.D. from Indiana University and an appointment as Associate Professor of Linguistics in the Department of Linguistics at Northwestern University. He has written on West African languages and nonstandard English, including pidgins and creolized languages, and teaches courses in slang and unconventional English.*

More MENTOR and SIGNET Reference Books

(0451)

☐ **ALL ABOUT WORDS by Maxwell Numberg and Morris Rosenblum.** Two language experts call on history, folklore, and anecdotes to explain the origin, development, and meaning of words. (620712—$3.50)

☐ **WORDS FROM THE MYTHS by Isaac Asimov.** A fascinating exploration of our living heritage from the ancient world. Isaac Asimov retells the ancient stories—from Chaos to the siege of Troy—and describes their influence on modern language . . . and modern life. (123778—$1.95)

☐ **INSTANT WORD POWER by Norman Lewis.** A fast, effective way to build a rich and dynamic vocabulary. Entertaining exercises and challenging self-tests enable the student to master hundreds of new words and polish spelling and grammar skills. (117913—$3.50)*

☐ **MASTERING SPEED READING by Norman C. Maberly.** Basic steps and drills with illustrations, charts and tests provide self-instruction in speed reading. (098579—$1.75)

*Prices slightly higher in Canada

Slang and Euphemism

A dictionary of oaths, curses, insults, sexual slang and metaphor, racial slurs, drug talk, homosexual lingo, and related matters

---

ABRIDGED EDITION

by
Richard A. Spears

ASSOCIATE PROFESSOR OF LINGUISTICS
NORTHWESTERN UNIVERSITY

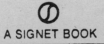

A SIGNET BOOK

NEW AMERICAN LIBRARY

Copyright © 1981, 1982 by Richard A. Spears

All rights reserved. No part of this book may be reproduced in any manner
without written permission from the publishers. For information address
Jonathan David Publishers, Inc., 68-22 Eliot Avenue, Middle Village,
New York 11379

Library of Congress Catalog Card Number: 82-81670

Published by arrangement with Jonathan David Publishers, Inc.

SIGNET TRADEMARK REG. U.S. PAT. OFF. AND FOREIGN COUNTRIES
REGISTERED TRADEMARK—MARCA REGISTRADA
HECHO EN CHICAGO, U.S.A.

SIGNET, SIGNET CLASSIC, MENTOR, PLUME, MERIDIAN AND NAL BOOKS
are published by New American Library,
1633 Broadway, New York, New York 10019

First Printing, November, 1982

3   4   5   6   7   8   9   10   11

PRINTED IN THE UNITED STATES OF AMERICA

For
JACK BERRY

ACKNOWLEDGMENTS

My heartfelt thanks go to:

Sally Reyering for proofreading various stages of the manuscript for the last two years.

Nancy Spears for her help with proofreading.

Professor Morris Goodman for his help with the material in French, Hebrew, and Yiddish.

Professor B. Claude Mathis for providing space for this project in its early stages.

Professors Rae Moses, Robert Gundlach, and James Wertsch for reading parts of the manuscript.

Alice Thompson, Manager, Language Laboratories, for a painstaking check of the entries.

And to M. Dwass, P. Heller, B. Litowitz, N.N. New, J.L. Wagner, J. Yozallinas.

INTRODUCTION

Slang and Euphemism

This dictionary deals with words and topics that have been ta-booed or suppressed by speakers of the English language. It lists, dates, and defines the slang, colloquial, standard, dialect, euphemis-tic, technical, medical, and legal terms for matters usually avoided in polite company.

This is not a collection of popular slang, nor is it a list of classical euphemisms. "Slang" is used here in the widest possible sense to refer to frivolous language of all types: cant, jargon, spoonerisms, double entendre, parody, nonce, malapropisms, backslang, rhyming slang, memorable dialect and colloquial terms, dysphemisms, pig Latin, and tabooed words. "Euphemism" refers to the processes of avoiding, disguising, mincing, abbreviating, lexical up-grading, and metaphorizing. Lexical up-grading includes the use of foreign lan-guage equivalents and the use of standard, technical, legal, or medical terms in place of more common terms. Slang and euphe-mism, broadly defined, are the two major mechanisms employed in the avoidance of taboo subjects.

The subject matter covered in *Slang and Euphemism* embraces death, deities and spirits, drugs and alcohol, fears and obsessions, derogatory terms for males and females, punishment, race, nationali-ty, occupation, scatology, sex, and verbal weapons. Any term that expresses any aspect of these topics is eligible. A few non-taboo words which serve as the etymological roots of other entries are included as well.

It may be surprising to learn that the majority of the terms in this dictionary are humorous word-play rather than vile epithets. It will be no surpise to find that sexual terms make up the bulk of the entries. The relative abundance of these terms is attributed to the teasing nature of sexual word-play, rather than to taboo. The real taboo areas in Western culture—incest and cannibalism—have prac-tically no slang terms or synonyms at all.

The sources listed in the bibliography were used to compile the collection on which this dictionary is based. That collection was supplemented by the author's own data, which include contributions from colleagues and students over the years. This collection mixes all levels of usage (formal, informal, slang, taboo) and brings together material from the major English-speaking countries—Britain, Australia, Canada, and the United States. In this way, the themes and imagery of the words, as well as their antiquity and ubiquity, are apparent. From the collection of words and meanings, new definitions were written; and the entries were given an approximate dating and geographical domain. The definitions are the focus of the study. It is almost impossible to assign accurate dates or locations to spoken taboo language. Crucial written citations simply do not exist.

Verbal taboos are caused by many different cultural phenomena. Throughout the twentieth century, we have assumed that Victorian prudery is the primary cause of verbal taboo. This is much too simple an explanation for such complex behavior. Victorian prudery does not begin to explain similar verbal taboos found before the Victorian Era or in cultures untouched by Victorianism. The remainder of the Introduction provides a basis for explaining the various causes of verbal avoidance.

This abridged edition of *Slang and Euphemism* is approximately three-quarters the length of the original edition. Terms for occupations, fears, obsessions, deities, spirits, the occult, and punishments have been reduced in number. In addition, obscure medical terms and some standard English terms have been omitted. The long lists of synonyms which are an important feature of this work are retained unaltered. Most of the entry words that have been eliminated still appear in the appropriate list of synonyms or related terms.

What Is Slang?

"Slang" was not originally a label for individual words. It was a term for British criminals' jargon, which was called "cant" or, in the jargon itself, "flash" or "slang." In addition to meaning "cant," the word slang also means "deception" and "chain." The latter is clearly derived from the Dutch word *slang*, "snake."

"Slang" originally referred to the patter of criminals, the entire semisecret idiom and vocabulary of the British underworld. By the 1800s "slang" was used outside of the underworld to label cant or cant-like words which crept into the speech of otherwise honest citizens. Like any of the habits of the lower classes, the use of slang was unwelcome in the company of ladies and gentlemen.

There is no sure test for deciding when an expression is slang or something else. From the point of view of standard English, slang is an intruder. Over the years the term "slang" has broadened to embrace all sorts of verbal intruders such as jargon, colloquialisms, dialect, and just plain vulgar words. Although in its original sense "slang" referred only to criminal jargon, in its expanded sense it can include any nonstandard or unpleasant word or phrase.

Despite the fact that "slang" means many things to many people, some general comments can be made about the types of language called slang.

1. Slang is not considered suitable for formal or serious matters.
2. Slang terms are usually synonyms for standard terms.
3. Slang terms and slang speech symbolize a lack of allegiance to social conventions.
4. Slang terms and slang speech flourish in nonliterate affairs; slang is a spoken phenomenon.
5. Slang and the standard language are at odds by nature. Slang is used defiantly by young people whom society is attempting to make respectful of literacy.
6. Slang is used to indicate membership in, and the integrity of, social groups which do not conduct their business in the standard language.
7. Slang that changes meaning or form fairly rapidly is often used by the young, who also change rather rapidly.
8. Slang is used by "outsiders" to indicate empathy with subgroups, especially with the young.
9. The use of slang is avoided when speaking to a person of a higher status.
10. Slang that can be subclassified as aggressive, rude, bawdy, or scatalogical serves additional functions in channeling aggression, establishing and maintaining rank, and in virility affirmation in groups of males.

What Is Euphemism?

The term "euphemism" refers to the substitution of a milder expression for a harsh or unacceptable one. This includes classical euphemisms, such as "pass on" for "die," but also refers to any circumlocution of a prohibited word or phrase. "Crap" is readily recognized as a euphemism for the word "shit." Other words such as "dung," "excrement," or "alvine dejections" are used to avoid all of the lowly and common words for this topic. The process of making topics presentable for more formal or polite situations is also part of euphemizing. Euphemisms and the process of euphemizing have the following characteristics.

1. A euphemism is an expression substituted for another expression which has acquired a negative connotation.
2. A euphemism is an expression which is a synonym for a word or phrase of lower status.
3. A euphemism is an expression deliberately created to raise the status of a concept.
4. Euphemism is used to protect oneself or one's audience from embarrassment or other emotional discomfort.
5. In the area of sexual taboo, euphemism signifies that the speaker is avoiding sexual overtures.
6. Euphemism is used in polite, sexually mixed company to avoid the coarse terms of all-male groups.
7. Euphemism is used in polite company to avoid the typical speech of lower levels of society.

The keys to understanding euphemism are the concepts of *avoidance* and *etiquette*. When people euphemize, they are avoiding giving offense. The culture defines the areas which are to be avoided, but it is the rules of being polite—etiquette—which motivate people to euphemize.

This dictionary includes many terms that are not recognized as classical euphemisms, *i.e.*, expressions whose sole use is euphemistic. There are times when the formality of a situation seems to require extremely polite language. In those cases, speakers often employ what can be called "lexical up-grading." This use of standard or technical terms in place of common terms, even acceptable common terms, is a type of euphemizing. This kind of stylistic leaning toward the most polite (or perhaps the least recognizable) expression for an avoided topic is a major part of the euphemism recorded in this dictionary. It contains, in addition to the rudest possible expressions, all of the levels of polite and evasive words that have been used for taboo topics for the last 900 years.

Slang and euphemism are related when they deal with tabooed subjects. This dictionary is about those words and subjects.

What Is Taboo?

"Taboo" is a Polynesian word for any of a number of religious prohibitions which forbid specified behavior usually under the threat of some kind of punishment. Many of the taboos of this type are absolute, that is, they are always in effect regardless of the situation. Many of them involve offenses toward the spirit world and religious custom. The term "taboo" is often used for any prohibition imposed by social convention. Although some Western taboos are supported by law, few of them are codified as specific laws. This dictionary is partly concerned with verbal taboos, that is, prohibitions against the use of specific words or the discussion of certain subjects.

Verbal taboos are selective in Western society, and they are not usually absolute. Taboos against profanity are observed both publicly and privately among devoutly religious persons, but most taboos are observed only in public and are clearly linked to the social setting, the sex, the age, the status of the speaker, and the audience. Included among the expressions usually prohibited are profanity, curses, oaths, discussions of sexual matters, and terms for excrement, prostitution, death, homosexuality, and mental illness. Most verbal prohibitions are supported by little more than the traditions of etiquette. They are defied often and with little if any punishment, and not all levels of society observe these taboos.

Human fears of human sexuality have long borne the blame for the prohibition of sexually-oriented speech. Sexual joking and sexual verbal play are less restricted than similar joking about feces, urine, nasal mucus, or putrid sweat, however. Mention of these and similar excrements are far more offensive than verbal sexual play. Certainly the area of sexual and excremental meaning has played a major role in developing and sustaining verbal taboos, but once a social convention is established, breaking it is a *social violation* and nothing more serious. It is not always clear, however, whether a person is avoiding taboo terms in response to social convention or for psychopathological reasons. The results are the same.

For some people certain words assume a kind of magical or mystical power. Words about death and some of the best-known "dirty words" seem to have that kind of power for some people. Personal prohibitions against certain words and concepts are quite complex and are due to different causes in different individuals. The basis for most of them is acquired at an early age.

Protecting Children

A reason frequently cited for censoring language is the protection of children. Western society hopes to improve itself by controlling very carefully the training and education of its children. Parents try to keep children from cursing and swearing in order to protect them from the social condemnation heaped on indiscriminate users of low language. Some people take considerable pains to keep children from hearing bad language, and children become the source of difficulties if they use bad language. For instance:

1. They will embarrass their parents by using bad language publicly.
2. They will embarrass their parents by asking the meaning of sexual or excretory terms.
3. They will develop a bad reputation due to their low language.
4. They will adopt the lifestyle associated with the free use of profanity and vulgarisms. In general the use of such language is a sign of resistance to socialization.

For many members of the middle class and above, most of these dangers are real. Even so, the degree to which all public communications can be regulated for the sake of children is a matter of constant dispute that will never be resolved to everyone's total satisfaction. Many of the notions that people have about the use of taboo words are instilled when they are children. Like so much of one's early training, especially that in cleanliness and grooming, these patterns persist into adulthood.

Current attitudes about prohibited topics are to some extent moral leftovers from the Victorian Period. Certainly, middle-class Victorians observed strong verbal restrictions, but the restrictions were not based totally on the Victorians' repugnance toward sex and excrement. The social structures that account for verbal prohibitions were in effect long before the Victorian Era and are still in effect now.

Victorianism

Queen Victoria ruled Great Britain from 1837 until her death in 1901. Her reign is remembered today for such things as tight corsets, bustles, styles of architecture, and above all an extraordinarily rigid moral code. People usually think of this moral code as being primarily one of sexual repression, but in fact the middle-class Victorian's concerns with propriety also embraced manners, dress, religion, personal habits, and possessions. The model Victorian is always clean, well-dressed, and a prude of the first water. Although a number of Victorians certainly did fit that description, a very large number were poor, dirty, ignorant, alcoholic, diseased, unskilled, exploited, immoral, amoral, vulgar, dishonest, unsuccessful, and, in present day terms, discriminated against. Persons who possessed one or more qualities on this long list of social woes had formed a substantial part of the English population for centuries.

Nineteenth-century England offered many people the opportunity to achieve a level of prosperity and a degree of economic independence never before known in the general populace. For many it meant not just an increase in income but a fairly rapid alteration of behavior and attitudes, invariably to a more genteel state. Books of etiquette, elaborate lists of table manners, and religious tracts of all types were available for the instruction of those aspiring to respectability. The values of the times were characterized by self-satisfaction, exaggerated delicacy, bourgeois opulence, and a moral complacency built on a conviction that progress was the reward of virtue and poverty was the penalty of sloth and vice. Victorian standards were not imposed by the queen or by the ''gentry.'' They were eagerly sought after and self-imposed by a middle class working to create an orthodoxy of gentility on a massive scale.

A major characteristic of this social development was the rift between the lower classes and the rapidly expanding middle class. This middle class seemed to have a commitment to being as unlike the laboring and serving classes as possible. Some of the most conspicuous class markers of this period were found in language usage, in particular, the use of verbal ''distancing'' by the middle class. Whereas a member of the laboring class could say ''bloody'' with every other breath, the proper Englishman would not utter it except under the most dire circumstances, if ever. The ''dropping'' of an H, as in 'at (hat) or 'otel (hotel), was an indelible sign of lowness, and although this extracted no new penalties for the lower-class speaker, it was an unspeakable lapse on the lips of the middle-class Victorian. The public utterance of low language regardless of content was simply not to be done.

It can be assumed that the lower classes also developed behavioral distancing to avoid looking foppish, prudish, impotent, weak, educated, or effeminate. This only served to widen the distance between the haves and the have-nots. This pattern can be observed today in the lower socioeconomic levels. It accounts in part for the perpetuation of nonstandard English varieties despite free public education.

There is no question that sexual behavior was included in the rigid orthodoxy of the middle-class Victorian, especially as it related to feminine chastity. Sloppy dress and manners were a sign of sloppy morals. Unattached women in the lower classes were assumed to be sexually free. The sight of a slatternly, drunken prostitute on the streets of the poorer neighborhoods was very common. The notion of unmarried cohabitation was repugnant to the prosperous Victorians, and the vocabulary of sexual intrigue was, like the intrigue itself, out of place in polite society.

Among the poor, common-law unions frequently began at puberty, and there was little restriction on what could be discussed in mixed company and little mention of what "nice girls" should or should not do. On this point, like so many others, the freedom of the lower classes shaped the etiquette of the prospering middle class. The middle class did not live up to its standards, and the term "Victorian" for some has a strong connotation of hypocrisy. Essentially, the period contained the economic and social adjustments that Western society made to the Industrial Revolution, capitalism, and the growth of science, technology, and wealth.

Apart from Victorianism, some aspects of contemporary Western social behavior are related to attempts to identify with some groups by adopting behavioral patterns of that group. People also avoid behaving like members of groups with which they do not wish to be associated.

Identification and Distancing

To some extent, people show identification with one another by using one another's vocabulary. This is parallel to showing identification through dress, residence patterns, and diet. History is filled with examples of persons identifying with the rich by affecting the speech and dress of wealthy society, and within the last decade young people have been seen affecting the speech and dress of poverty and the underworld. This identification accounts for the spread of certain speech patterns.

Some of human social behavior can be described in terms of "oppositions." For instance, some aspects of the behavior and attitudes of rural persons are the opposite of those of urban persons. When these differences are the basis for conscious or unconscious avoidance behavior in either group, it is called "social distancing." Social distancing is responsible for a wide variety of verbal avoidance. Prohibitions against dirty words, street talk, drug slang, or black slang, for example, are reinforced by (or caused by) negative feelings toward the people who typically use them. It must be emphasized that these are widespread tendencies, not hard and fast rules.

People may also avoid characteristic verbal signs of antireligiousness, poverty, sex, political philosophy, youth, age, and level of education. At some levels of society, there is distancing from Victorianism. The niceties of Victorian euphemism are ignored for more frank terms, perhaps to make clear the speaker's feelings against Victorian prudery.

A major arena for sexual and scatological patter, including the creation and use of sexual metaphor and "dirty words," is found in groups of men. This patter is characterized by talk that treats women as sex objects, mock-aggressive curses, threats, sexual boasting and challenging, and all of the rest of the verbal behavior frowned on in the presence of women and refined men. For the males this activity has values for interpersonal bonding, masculinity affirmation, and identity, and if done in a group, group integrity and strength. This type of male agressiveness also serves as a protective barrier against the real or imagined threats of female aggressiveness. At lower socioeconomic levels, women may witness this behavior, but in general it is avoided in their presence. Normally, women do not participate in this activity at any socioeconomic level. For the males it provides an outlet for the masculine behavior which is usually repressed in contact with women.

The use of "dirty words" in other settings can serve as masculinity affirmation. To some extent the male's public oaths, curses, and the use of "dirty words" are denounced as juvenile behavior or taken as evidence of sexual insecurity. Such acts of masculinity affirmation are considered to be exhibitionistic, and males are encouraged to suppress such behavior.

Another major area of male verbal behavior concerns the use of alcohol, although the drinking of alcoholic beverages is by no means an all-male activity. Being able to drink heavily is equated with "taking it like a man." One finds a vast number of terms for degrees of inebriation, most of which reflect the ill effects of overindulgence. The ability to withstand or recover from overindulgence in alcohol may be analogous to withstanding or recovering from physical damage. Most drinking slang comes directly from male-to-male usage.

Verbal Aggression

Verbal aggression is known in every human society and is totally absent in all other animal societies. Verbalizing hostilities obviously serves a valuable social purpose if it attenuates aggression and lessens the chance of injury or death among the populace.

Verbal aggression is not only symbolic of physical aggression, it is often an essential adjunct to physical aggression, a sign of impending physical aggression, or a cause of physical aggression. A society's general prohibition against aggression or violence applies also to verbal aggression. The typical tools of verbal aggression— oaths, curses, etc.—all have negative connotations. Verbal aggression depends on impact for its effectiveness, and it is suppressed except when tensions seem to justify its use.

Derogatory nicknames are also a type of verbal aggression. Terms for persons of different classes or races make up the bulk of these words. Derogation is completely opposite of identification and is meant to offend. (In some cases, however, the same term—for example, nigger—can serve both purposes, depending on who is using it.) Terms exist for stupid men and slovenly women as well as for specific races or nationalities. Many of the latter terms are known to be deeply resented by the recipients of the names, and this makes them even more effective as verbal weapons. Even polite and standard terms are used as modifiers meaning "wretched" in compounds such as "Irish fortune" or "Mexican mud."

A common form of defense or aggression in many species of animals is dung-throwing. This is not frequently practiced by humans (see the entry **flying pasty**) but is analogous to scatological epithets. Often the use of such terms as verbal aggression accounts in part for the strength of the prohibition against them. Human association with any fecal material, including one's own, is strongly prohibited.

Male-to-male behavior includes elements of mock-aggressive verbal behavior. This is no stronger than the level of physical activity observed when boys or men jostle and strike one another in rough play. It is clearly a part of group identity (as described above) and is analogous to physical jostling. The mock-aggressive expressions have the same impact as physical jostling. In certain all-male situations (for example, the battle-front, drinking sessions, locker-room sessions), this can involve crude terms ("ass-hole buddy," "old sod," "son of a bitch"), and this behavior along with the harsh vocabulary which accompanies it is prohitited in polite mixed company.

To some extent, males use prohibited language among themselves for male sexual identification. Females may avoid using prohibited language for female sexual identification.

Not surprisingly there are other sexual factors contributing to verbal sexual taboos between men and women.

Male and Female

Part of the human sexual negotiations which may lead to copulation are conducted verbally. These interchanges include a range of activities from teasing through courting and the "proposition." The initial "inquiry mode" of verbal sex-play or verbal seduction involves casting the bait and watching very carefully for negative or positive responses in the other player. Verbal sex-play and double entendre are also used by both sexes as an affirmation of male or female sexuality (as appropriate). One can find class differences in the kind of vocabulary employed and the directness of approach of the players, and like verbal aggression verbal sex play is effective only if it is reserved for the appropriate setting. At a very basic level, prohibitions against sexual terms or graphic sexual joking serve to protect strangers from unwanted sexual overtures or the embarrassment of responding to verbal sex-play misinterpreted as a sexual overture. These prohibitions are by no means found at all levels of society, and they are frequently ignored.

It is often said that women do not use foul language, dirty words, and profanity. If one is speaking of the middle class (and above), especially what a society might define as the respectable middle class, this is true to some degree. If one is speaking of all women, it is false. Whether or not a woman (or a man) uses prohibited language is very much dependent upon socioeconomic factors, age, personality, and the specific situation. Nevertheless, decency in womanhood in many areas of contemporary society in determined in part by whether a woman uses foul language. Ladies are not expected to swear like harlots even if they feel like it. This prohibition is linked to the avoidance of all aggressive or low behavior. The motivation for enforcing the prohibition is linked to feminine sexual identity and to a woman's class status. In general, modern educated adults do not usually use low language in the company of strangers, in particular strangers of the opposite sex. Nevertheless males are regarded as more frequent users of taboo language.

Traditionally, taboo subjects tend to be euphemized by both sexes in the presence of women and in polite mixed company. At the other end of the scale, all-male groups, especially groups which would not be considered refined, tend to use slang and ruder terms for taboo subjects. Women, at the extremes of their traditional roles, are the designers, arbiters, and enforcers of etiquette, including verbal etiquette. Often, again in the extremes of the role, women are expected to be perfect examples of the etiquette which they espouse.

The differences in the prohibitions on the behavior of males and females are the result of a widely recognized double standard. Males are regarded as having a variety of behavioral options, including the privilege of the free use of taboo words. The notion that this is a privilege of which females are deprived is not a recent one. The gay nineties and the flapper era of the twenties were both times of less restraint in language and sexual matters for women, at least on the level of fashionable social behavior. In the 1970s and early 1980s both sexes were uttering things in public which the preceding generation would not have permitted. Even a limited number of idioms containing "fuck" and "shit" can be heard in fashionable social gatherings. It should also be noted that many people are appalled and disgusted at the public use of these words.

Whether or not the public use of taboo words lasts, there still remains the problem of verbal sexual play being interpreted as sexual overtures or signs of sexual availability. The need for the two sexes to move freely in society and associate with one another on an asexual basis will probably serve to maintain existing prohibitions against casual verbal sexual exchanges in sexually mixed groups.

Much of this discussion has been based on a notion of "polite" society and the recognition that there is a range of vocabulary items and language style which correlates to polite behavior. As pointed out before, this discussion does not describe what all people actually do linguistically or otherwise. This is an attempt to go beyond the traditional assumption of sexual prudery being the cause of the repression of public sexual matters. The societal restrictions placed on children's language sustain verbal prohibitions until adult restrictions take over. Part of the restrictions establish an asexual social setting wherein men and women may interact socially and transact business relatively free from sexual signals. Where verbal prohibitions are observed, it is due to a combination of the factors described above.

Real Words, Nonce Words, and Synthetic Slang

The words found in dictionaries of standard English are supported by "citations." These are bits of written evidence that a given word was used in the past by a reputable person who was consciously attempting to write acceptable standard English. Standard English tends to remain stable because educated people have "agreed" to try to use the language the way it has been preserved in dictionaries and grammars, and they have been trained to avoid (and even condemn) other uses of the language. Much of the material in this dictionary does not appear in the writing of reputable authors (except for effect) and, in fact, much of it is avoided in writing and speaking by users of the standard language. The attestations for slang, colloquial, and dialect terms are very often found in word lists or dictionaries written by persons who got the word from spoken rather than written sources. Even where a word has been collected from a written source, the writer may have made up the word and perhaps it was never used after that.

A word created for and used on one particular occasion (*e.g.*, "logolatry," meaning "word-worship") is called a "nonce word." Although nonce words which are humorous, clever, or of learned derivation are sometimes preserved in dictionaries, particularly nonstandard dictionaries, it is very difficult for an average person to get away with creating new words for use in formal writing. Well-known writers such as Anthony Burgess and Vladimir Nabokov are highly praised for verbal innovation; the average college freshmen would probably get flunked for making up new words.

Many individuals have their own clever nicknames and private words for things. These prize euphemisms are occasionally picked up by a word collector and are recorded in a dictionary of slang or cant. They survive not because their use is widespread but because they are clever and interesting examples of word play.

It is possible to create slang which sounds quite authentic and is as effective as any other slang (*e.g.*, "renovate," meaning "to divorce"), but which is never used by most speakers of English. This can be called "synthetic slang." In addition, authors sometimes reintroduce old slang or other archaic material directly from slang or dialect dictionaries. This is particularly true in underworld matters and other areas where authors may not have firsthand experience. It is virtually certain that lexicographers do not collect all of their low-life words firsthand. The likelihood of unwittingly collecting nonce words and synthetic slang is therefore quite high.

Dating

Some words can be accurately dated, most cannot; only a very few words have memorable beginnings. It is known that "streak" in the sense "run about in public totally nude" originated in December 1973 because there are dated newspaper reports which describe the act and use the word. In general, when a word appears in writing and the date of the writing is known, it is certain that the word was in existence at that time. In the case of words which have social taboos attached to them or words which are not normally written down, accurate or meaningful dating is all but impossible.

An example of the problem of dating is seen in the *Oxford English Dictionary* in its treatment of the word "mubble-fubbles," meaning "melancholy." There are four citations for the word; the earliest is

1589, the latest is 1654. Since there is no reason to believe that
anyone has falsified any of these dates, one might assume that the
word was in use from 1589 to 1654 and probably for some time
thereafter. It is not known (a) whether the word was in spoken use
before 1589, (b) whether the first writer created the word or picked
it up in conversation, (c) whether the word was ever in widespread
use or whether it was copied from the first citation to the second and
so forth, (d) whether the word had use restrictions such as primarily
juvenile, primarily female, primarily upper-class, primarily lower-
class, primarily youth, (e) whether the word had survived (or was
revived or "recoined") since 1654. This is not a criticism of the
dictionary's treatment of the word; rather it means that it is not
accurate to say "They said 'mubble-fubbles' to mean 'melancholy'
between 1589 and 1654," if by "they" you mean a substantial
percentage of the population.

What Is Standard English?

Standard English dictionaries have for more than two centuries
been concerned primarily with the written language of educated
people. In his *Dictionary of the English Language* (1755), Samuel
Johnson abandoned his predecessors' practice of entering words
simply because they were interesting or because they had appeared
in older dictionaries. Johnson's famous dictionary was a collection
of the words used by "the best writers" excepting those whom he
knew personally, because he did not want his friendships to preju-
dice his choice of words. At this point in the history of the English
language the style and vocabulary of the literate language began to
be codified. This standardizing toward a *norm* was accomplished
carefully, consciously, and persistently over a long period of time,
and it has become a part of what is called standard English.

Dictionaries and Authority

Along with the development of a literate form of English in the
last three centuries, a kind of ethic in the "rights" and "wrongs" of
language use has developed. The literate language is considered
"right" or even "good," and all other varieties are "wrong" or
"bad." On another scale, literate languages are praised while
nonwritten languages (sometimes derogatorily called "primitive dialects") are looked down upon. Logic is often brought into the
argument when people claim that standard English is "logical."
Actually, people can be logical or illogical in any variety of any

language. Logic is a means of evaluating propositions, not a means of evaluating natural languages.

The standard language is very much a thing of tradition. The grammatical features are maintained as received from the previous generation, and the situations which call for the use of the standard language are the same as in previous generations. The primary component of standardization is the regularization of the form and meaning of words and sentences. One is "correct" if one conforms to the traditionally recognized linguistic forms. One is "incorrect" when one innovates forms or uses forms not recognized as part of the standard. Dictionaries of the standard language are usually well respected, and they are thought to be authoritative in matters of correctness. As noted above, the scholars who write dictionaries collect citations of the use of English words, and when it is evident that consciously careful writers are using words in new or different ways, the next revision of the dictionary reflects that fact. In addition to keeping an eye on careful writers, dictionary makers also consult other dictionaries.

The traditional standard language remains stable because careful writers consult good dictionaries; careful dictionary-makers consult the work of careful writers and existing dictionaries. The decision as to who the careful writers are and when a change is sufficiently widespread for it to be recognized as standard is one of well-informed scholarly judgment. This really is not "authority" at work; it is a very slow procedure for achieving concensus relating to change in the standard language.

Nonstandard varieties of a language have no officially recognized grammars or dictionaries. When people use slang they do not consult dictionaries or grammar books to determine whether they are using it correctly. Being "correct" is not part of the game of slang. Being up-to-date, clever, and innovative is the game of slang.

Why a Dictionary of This Type?

Although the twentieth century has seen major advances in explaining the social and psychological ramifications of fear, guilt, and sexuality, one of the richest sources of date—our language—has been grossly neglected. Lexicography—the science of writing dictionaries—has always had as its major concern the proper or correct way of using language. Since etiquette tends to discourage the uttering, writing, or studying of prohibited words and subjects, dictionaries of the standard language usually omit impolite and frivolous expressions. As long as "politeness" and "correctness" are equated by the writers and users of standard dictionaries, these dictionaries cannot provide data on impolite language and its use in society.

This dictionary is a comprehensive resource for persons working with verbal taboo and verbal avoidance in the areas of anthropology, communication studies, comparative literature, drug abuse, English, folklore, history, law, linguistics, medicine, psychology, sexual harassment, and sociology. It also servers as a valuable reference for physicians, lawyers, writers, or anyone else needing to interpret different social levels of taboo expressions.

There are a number of very specific dictionaries which concern themselves in some way with nonstandard words. These dictionaries are usually national in scope, that is, American, British, or Australian, and they deal with slang, colloquial, or dialect terms. It is virtually impossible to explain the themes, origins, and symbolism of nonstandard terms without looking at as much of the English-speaking world as possible. This dictionary incorporates material from many sources, covering nine centuries and all major English-speaking regions.

Owing to the nature of slang and colloquial terms, it is not likely that a single individual will ever know all of the current slang and colloquial words. Like most of one's knowledge, linguistic knowledge is limited to one's experience and reading. There are over 900 terms for degrees of drunkenness in this dictionary, and certainly no human being has a vocabulary including all of them. A collection of this size makes available far more data than any person or contemporary group of persons is likely to know. This dictionary is the only suitable source for the diachronic study of prohibited words.

The reader will be surprised not only at the antiquity of many of the terms but also that the Victorians created some of the ''ripest'' of the sexual metaphors. Anyone willing to wander through these pages is certain to learn something about Anglo-American culture as well as its vocabulary.

There are three cautions, however. The first concerns the interpretation of the time and place indicated in brackets. The time shown is the best possible approximation. The word may not be limited to the place indicated, and it is not always known how widespread the use of a word was in any particular population.

The second concerns interpreting the thematic content of the words. It should be remembered that some of the material is taken directly from the jargon of criminals, a very large amount is from bawdy male-to-male talk, and some is everyday slang or standard English. Still other entries are extremely polite and euphemistic. The long lists of synonyms found within some entries represent a variety of conflicting attitudes and should not be assumed to represent what "society believes." Many different levels of society and many different periods are represented in the various entries.

Lastly, many of the words entered here have additional, non-taboo meanings in standard English. One should consult a dictionary of standard English for those meanings.

GUIDE TO THE DICTIONARY

Order

Main entries are arranged in absolute alphabetical order. All spaces and punctuation (except commas) are ignored in alphabetizing. Except for a few entries, such as **Bob, Harry, and Dick** and **hanged, drawn, and quartered,** a comma indicates that prepositions or other short single syllable words have been shifted from the beginning of the entry to the right of the comma. Thus, **I'll be switched!** will appear as the entry **switched, I'll be.** Single syllable words which are always shifted are: a, an, at, be, by, for, I, I'll, in, it, my, off, old, on, the, to, up. Prepositions and short words which are not shifted are: after, between, do, get, go, have, over, under, upon, with. The sole purpose of alphabetization in this dictionary is to provide a means for finding a word; semantic relationships are indicated through cross-referencing.

The Entry

Each entry consists of an entry word and its variants, followed by a definition or other identification. Parts of the definition or identification are separated by commas or semicolons and definitions or identifications are followed by a period. Following the definition, there may be statements concerning the derivation of the word (if it is English) and cross-referencing directions. The last part of the entry, which is enclosed in brackets, gives information such as location of use, foreign language etymology, type of use, period of use, and a source for the entry word.

Main Entry Words

Main entries and their variants appear in boldface roman type. Foreign words which are often italicized in written English are followed by an asterisk. Variants and closely related synonyms which apply to the entry and all of its senses follow the main entry in parenthesis, for example, **phooey** (also **fooey**). Spelling variants

applicable to only one sense of a word with numerous senses are
listed after the applicable sense. Whenever main entries or their
variants are cited elsewhere, they appear in small capitals. Some of
the words that appear in the long lists of synonyms are not entry
words in the abridged edition.

Definitions, Identifications, and Senses

Each main entry is followed by one or more definitions or identifications. Definitions are synonyms or phrasal equivalents of the
main entry. Identifications are translations of foreign words, the
spelling out of acronyms and initialisms, and indications of broad
areas of meaning or function, such as oath, curse, or nickname.

Where there is more than one sense to a word, the senses are
numbered if they appear to have distinct periods of usage or otherwise need to be referred to separately. Where a word has a range of
related meanings, those meanings are separated by semicolons rather
than numerals. Numbered senses are often listed in chronological
order, but this is not an implication than the senses were derived in
that order or are necessarily related unless that fact is specifically
stated.

Parts-of-Speech

Part-of-speech is indicated by the grammatical form of the definition or identification. Where words, compounds, or phrases have
uses or restrictions which are not evident from the definition, an
example of usage is given. It should be noted that a lack of rigidity
in the use of words in their usually assigned part-of-speech is a
major characteristic of slang and jargon.

Pronunciation

There are no standards of pronunciation for slang, colloquial, or
jargon. Much of the slang and colloquial material gathered before
1900 did not have its pronunciation recorded in any form. Where
pronunciation must be indicated, it is done either with rhyming
words (for example, "tear," which rhymes with "bear" or with
"beer") or with phonetic respelling ("jee-ho-suh-fat").

Source and Etymology

Due to the limitations of space, the dictionary contains only very brief etymological notes. Some of the entry words are borrowed from languages other than English, but most slang, colloquial, and euphemistic words are reinterpretations of existing English words. When an entry word has as its source a foreign language or a specific dialect of English, that information is included in brackets at the end of the entry. When slang, colloquial, and euphemistic terms are derived from other slang, colloquial, or euphemistic terms, that fact is stated explicitly or is indicated through the cross-referencing. Many of the words have extremely long and complex etymologies, and many of those etymologies are in doubt. The exact origin of some of the dialect terms is totally unknown.

The final element in the bracketed material is sometimes a book title or an author's name. These titles and names refer to material listed in the bibliography. Where a title or author's name appears in parentheses, that means that the word in question was used rather than defined in the work listed. In a few instances, a listed source is the sole source for an entry. In most cases it is difficult if not impossible to tell what the very first attestation of a word is. The locations and dates listed in the bracketed material are not necessarily the same as those given by the source cited.

Geographical Domains

The specification of a country within the brackets at the end of an entry indicates the location(s) where an entry word has been recorded in its greatest use, or where it originated. It should be assumed that the knowledge and usage of many words extends beyond the country mentioned. It should not be assumed that all speakers in a particular country know a particular word. People sometimes think of slang as known on a national basis, but most slang is used locally and regionally. It is impossible to know where, when, and how frequently much of the colloquial and slang terms are used. The geographical domains listed are based on information found in the works listed in the bibliography.

It should be assumed that "British" refers to England and various parts of the Empire or Commonwealth (depending on the date specified). "British use, 1600s-1700s" includes the thirteen American colonies. The "1700s-1800s" could include the English spoken in Africa, Australia, India, and the United States. "British dialect" refers only to England. It can be assumed that "U.S." refers to North American use in general. It is certain that much of the twentieth-century slang listed as "British" or "U.S." is known and used in Australia and Canada. It is certain that there has been a far greater exchange of slang betwen Great Britian and the United States than is indicated here and that the U.S. and Canada share a far greater vocabulary than is indicated here. Since the World Wars, the exchange of slang in the English-speaking world has increased at a high rate.

The term "widespread" is used instead of a geographical location to indicate that the word probably has global distribution in English-speaking countries.

When no country is named, that indicates that no conclusive evidence exists as to whether the term is of British or U.S. origin. In most such instances, the word can be assumed to be common to both countries to some degree at one time or another.

Periods of Usage and Dates

The dates shown are in some cases speculative and in a few cases educated guesses. The dating period specified for a word is intended to mark the outside boundaries of the period of "greatest usage" of the word. No claim is made that the word was universally known during the period or when a period of "lesser usage" might have begun or ended. The dating period means that "during the period specified, the available attestations indicate that the word was created by someone, used by a large population or one of its subgroups, or known to, or remembered by, one or more persons." Most of the words with only one (early) date listed are still preserved in some fashion.

"Recurrent nonce" refers to a word that has probably been "coined" hundreds or even millions of times over the centuries. In phallic nomenclature alone, metaphorical nicknames such as "carrot," "post," "snake," and "rod" have been created independently by millions of persons. Such words are certainly older than their earliest attestations. The study of ancient languages indicates that this type of naming is extremely old.

In assigning dates, each century is divided into thirds. Even these divisions may be interpreted generously. It is quite certain that word use is in no way keyed to the turn of a century. Therefore, early 1900s could be 1890-1940 or 1910-1925; late 1700s could be 1775-1810. Mid 1800s could be a period as long as 1820-1880.

Usage Domains

Many words have more than one class of usage, and many of the older words were not recorded with any indication of usage domains. The terms used are explained in the section Terms and Abbreviations.

All of the labels are very broad and must be interpreted carefully. For instance, "prostitute's argot" means that the word is attested as having been used by prostitutes. It does not mean that it is known to all prostitutes, and there is also a high probability that the word is known to persons other than prostitutes.

Virtually all of the sexual metaphors, swear words, and drinking terms are in the domain of male usage. Many of the definitions reflect this. Explanations and definitions assume an orientation of traditional sex roles and attitudes. Definitions of sexual matters should be assumed to refer to heterosexual matters unless indicated otherwise.

Punctuation and Spelling

Most of the spelling up to the 1700s has been modernized. Most of the British spelling has been Americanized if the term is known in the U.S.

Acronyms and other initialisms are regularized. Acronyms appear capitalized and do not have a period after each letter, for example, **AWOL,** pronounced "ay-wall." Other initialisms are capitalized, and each letter is followed by a period, for example, **A.W.O.L.,** pronounced "ay-double-u-oh-ell." This applies only to entry words in this dictionary and is not necessarily the way the acronyms and initialisms are found in writing.

The problem of hyphenization is one which plagues even the standard orthography. Many compound words could appear in any one of three ways, for example, **blubber brain, blubber-brain, blubberbrain.** The hyphenization of nonstandard material in written attestations is completely chaotic. In general, words like "housepainter" are hyphenated; beyond that, the chaotic hyphenation and spacing found in written attestations is used here. If written attestations were not available, words of the compound are separated by a space. Although this has been done "carefully," it has not been done "authoritatively," that is, this dictionary is not the ultimate authority on the hyphenation and spacing of compounds, and indeed it contradicts standard dictionaries in some cases.

Oaths and exclamations and other entries which constitute complete sentences begin with a capital letter and end with the appropriate punctuation.

Main entry words which often appear italicized when used in written English are printed in boldface roman type and are followed by an asterisk.

CROSS-REFERENCING

There are four terms used in cross-referencing: *cf.*, *q.v.*, "see," and "see also." *Cf.* means "consider the following word as you ponder the meaning of the entry word." The word following *cf.* may be a synonym of the entry word or simply a related form. *Q.v.* after a word or series of words is used here as a stylistic variant of *cf.* For instance, HOUSE (*q.v.*) is the same as *cf.* HOUSE. When one is referred to a specific sense of a word, the *q.v.* is omitted; thus, HOUSE (sense 3) is the same as HOUSE (*q.v.*, sense 3). In both cases one is not obliged to look up the word or words in question if one is satisfied with one's understanding of the definition. "See" on the other hand, indicates that one should look up the word after "see" in order to have all of the information available concerning the entry word. In some cases, "see" will lead to the definition, the date, or some other relevant piece of information.

A variant of "see" is "see also," which refers to *unrelated* entries which are similar in some way to the entry word in question. These references are for convenience and do not lead one to any additional information pertaining to the entry in which they occur.

Many of the topics covered in this work have generated long lists of synonyms or related subjects. Generally, cross-referencing will lead the reader to the appropriate list. Some are to be found at familiar terms. Others are to be found at euphemisms. Here is a directory for these listings.

alcohol	**booze**
amphetamines	**amp**
anus	**anus**
backside	**duff**
barbiturates	**barb**
bastard	**accident**
belly	**belly**
black (person)	**ebony**
bloody	**bloody**

booze (strong) . . . . embalming fluid
break wind . . . . gurk
breasts . . . . bosom
brothel . . . . brothel
bull . . . . bull
bull (nonsense) . . . . bullshit
butt . . . . duff
castrate . . . . castrate
Caucasian . . . . peckerwood
cemetery . . . . cemetery
cocaine . . . . nose-candy
coffin . . . . coffin
condom . . . . eel-skin
copulate with . . . . occupy
copulation . . . . smockage
corpse . . . . corpse
crazy . . . . daft
cunnilingus . . . . cunnilingus
dame . . . . bird
damn . . . . damn
damned . . . . damned
dead . . . . done for
death . . . . demise
defecate . . . . ease oneself
deflower . . . . deflower
delirium tremens . . . . ork-orks
devil . . . . fiend
diarrhea . . . . quickstep
die . . . . depart
doctor . . . . doc
drunk . . . . woofled
drunkard . . . . alchy
dung (animal) . . . . droppings
dung . . . . dung
effeminate male . . . . fribble
ejacualte . . . . melt
erection . . . . erection
fellator . . . . piccolo-player
fondling . . . . firkytoodle
fool . . . . oaf
gadget . . . . gadget
gay (noun) . . . . epicene
genitals . . . . genitals

prostitute . . . . harlot
pubic hair (female) . . . . Downshire
pudendum . . . . monosyllable
rape . . . . assualt
rascal . . . . snoke-horn
scrotum . . . . tool bag
semen . . . . mettle
sexually aroused . . . . humpy
syphilis . . . . specific stomach
sodomite . . . . sodomite
sodomy . . . . sodomy
stupid . . . . stupid
sychophant . . . . acquiesce-man
testicles . . . . whirlygigs
toilet . . . . W.C.
trousers . . . . galligaskins
underwear . . . . nether garments
urinate . . . . retire, whiz
urine . . . . tea
V.D. . . . . social disease
vagina . . . . passage, monosyllable
vomit . . . . york
vulva . . . . monosyllable
whorehouse . . . . house, brothel
wife . . . . warden
woman as sex . . . . lay, tail

TERMS AND ABBREVIATIONS

The following terms and abbreviations are used in the dictionary. Cross-referencing refers to terms in this section.

abbreviation a shortening of a word or phrase by cutting the word(s) down to one syllable or initial(s), *e.g.*, **A.**, meaning "amphetamine." See ACRONYM, INITIALISM.

acronym an abbreviation of a phrase where the initial letters are pronounced as if they were a single word. Acronyms are capitalized, but the letters are not followed by periods, *e.g.*, **AWOL,** meaning "absent without leave." See INITIALISM.

all senses when introducing a comment, this means the comment applies to all of the senses listed above the comment in a particular entry. See BOTH SENSES.

also 1. "also" enclosed in parentheses immediately after the entry word introduces spelling variants and closely related synonyms which correspond to all senses of the entry. **2.** "also" followed by a word or phrase in boldface type introduces a spelling variant or closely related synonym corresponding only to the numbered sense in which the "also" appears.

Anglo-Saxon a language spoken in England from about 800-1300; the basic Germanic component of English. Also called OLD ENGLISH.

argot the French equivalent of CANT (*q.v.*). Also, any slang or jargon. See CANT, JARGON, SLANG.

asterisk (*) indicates an entry word which is usually italicized in written English.

attested as introduces a location, date, or usage domain which may appear to be questionable.

backslang refers to the reversal of the letters of a word, *e.g.*, "mur" for "rum."

based on means that the entry word is related semantically or formally to the form or forms specified after "based on."

B.E. the initials of the author of a cant dictionary printed in about 1690. His full name is unknown.

because some entry words and their definitions constitute a riddle. For instance, "Because she is open to all parties" explains why the entry **public ledger** means "prostitute."

black slang refers to words which are currently or originally American Negro slang.

black use refers to words which are currently or originally used by black people. The same as NEGRO USE (*q.v.*).

Boontling a collection of slang, jargon, and catch phrases spoken by the population of Boonville, California between 1880 and 1920.

both senses refers to a comment which applies to the two senses listed immediately above the comment in a particular entry. See ALL SENSES.

cant British criminal and underworld jargon which flourished from the 1600s to the 1800s. See ARGOT, JARGON.

catch phrase a frequently repeated phrase which attracts attention to the speaker or some activity being performed.

center slang a type of permutation where the spelling of a word is turned inside out, *e.g.*, "oolfoo" for "fool."

cf. an abbreviation of Latin *confer*, "compare." The word following *cf.* should be considered as one ponders the meaning of the entry word. It does not mean that one must look the word up in order to understand the meaning.

Cockney pertains to the pronunciation and dialect of the working class residing in the East End of London.

cognate related in form to the specified word or the ancestor of the specified word.

coit See COIT in the dictionary. The term is borrowed from the works of Eric Partridge where it is used as a transitive or intransitive verb. It replaces cruder terms such as "fuck" or "screw" for the actions of the male in copulating with a female. Standard English lacks a transitive verb for this action.

college slang a word or phrase typical of the very informal colloquial patter used on campus among college students.

colloquial pertains to words which are used everyday in informal speech but which are not written as formal English. Some taboo words are traditionally considered colloquial. SLANG (*q.v.*) and colloquial are similar, and a word may be used as slang in some domains and colloquial in others

corruption pertains to words which have been formed by either accidentally or purposefully distorting another word. *E.g.*, **Cheese and Crust!** is a corruption of "Jesus Christ!" See MINCED OATH.

costermonger's slang the jargon of the London pushcart hawker of fruits and vegetables.

derogatory pertains to terms of address or words derived therefrom which are deliberately insulting to the addressee.

dialect pertains to nonstandard words used in a specific region of a country.

double entendre refers to ambiguous words or phrases which have at least one taboo or indelicate meaning in addition to the standard meaning.

drug culture pertains to a word or phrase which is typical of the jargon of drug users and addicts since the mid 1900s.

dysphemism pertains to a word which has been deliberately degraded to having unpleasant or taboo connotations.

Egan's Grose refers to Pierce Egan's version of Grose's *A Classical Dictionary of the Vulgar Tongue.*

elaboration a word or phrase which is built on another expression, *e.g.,* **Bessie Smith** is an elaboration of **B.S.,** both signifying "bullshit."

euphemism a relatively mild or vague phrase substituted for a harsh or specific word or phrase, or the process of making such substitutions.

eye-dialect the use of spelling to signify dialect pronunciation, *e.g.,* "shore" for "sure," or illiteracy, *e.g.,* "sez" for "says."

fad word a word which quickly becomes known in a specific geographical area and becomes disused or obsolete just as quickly.

from 1. derived from; borrowed from a foreign language. **2.** derived from a particular sense of an English word.

generic pertains to a term for a group or type as applied to an individual or used as a nickname.

homosexual use pertains to terms originated by or used primarily by homosexuals.

initialism an abbreviation consisting of the intial letter(s) of a word or phrase in which each letter is pronounced separately and followed by a period, *e.g.,***A.W.O.L.,** "absent without leave."

jargon a specialized vocabulary used by a well-defined group of people. See ARGOT, CANT, SLANG.

jocular deliberately humorous; joking.

juvenile pertains to terms typically used by children or adults speaking to children.

literary pertains to any writings in standard English regardless of merit.

malapropism a ridiculous misuse of a word. Usually a deliberate misuse.

medical pertains to words used primarily in the physical health sciences.

military pertains to a term originated in or primarily or originally used in any military organization.

minced oath a disguised or euphemized profane oath, *e.g.*, **Egad!** meaning "By God!"

mock in imitation of a particular language or style. Typically "mock-Chinese" or "mock-Latin."

nickname a familiar name substituted for the proper name of a group or of an individual.

nonce pertains to a word which was made up for use on a particular occasion. See RECURRENT NONCE.

Old English See ANGLO-SAXON.

onomatopoetic pertains to a word whose phonological form is suggested by the sound of the thing for which it stands, *e.g.*, YORK, meaning "vomit."

orthography the standard spelling system.

phonological refers to the actual sounds (not the spelling) of words or to characteristic sound patterns of words.

Pig Latin a type of play language used in the U.S., *e.g.*, *air-chay*, "chair."

play on punning on; based on in a jocular fashion.

pres. the present time.

q.v. an abbreviation of Latin *quod vide*, "which see." The word preceding *q.v.* should be considered as one ponders the meaning of the entry word. It does not mean that one must look the word up in order to understand it. "Both *q.v.*" means consider both of the preceding words or phrases.

recurrent nonce pertains to a word or phrase which has been coined afresh numerous times by different individuals over the years.

reinforced by pertains to the semantics of a word or phrase. Indicates a secondary or supporting etymology. For example, the word **bomphlet,** meaning "propaganda leaflet dropped from the air," is a blend of **bumf** (from **bumfodder**) and "pamphlet," reinforced by "bomb."

rhyming slang the word represented by a and b (or just a) in the pattern a and b = c, *i.e.*, needle and pin means gin, (a = needle, b = pin, c = gin). Also called "Cockney rhyming slang."

rural pertains to farming and country life. See also DIALECT.

see indicates that the reader should look up the word which follows it in order to have all of the available information about the entry word.

see also refers to unrelated entries which share a key word with the entry in which the "see also" appears. This cross-referencing does not lead to any new information about the entry word.

slang pertains to a word or phrase which is known to always be used as slang, has been observed to be used as slang, or appears to have all of the characteristics of a slang word or phrase. Slang and COLLOQUIAL (*q.v.*) are similar, and a word may be used as slang in some domains and colloquial in others.

spoonerism pertains to an exchange of initial consonants in a pair of words, such as "blushing crow" for "crushing blow."

synonym a word or phrase having essentially the same meaning as another.

taboo pertains to an expression which has prohibitions against its utterance under certain situations.

truncation refers to a shortening of a word or phrase. Technically, abbreviations are truncations.

ultimately from refers to the probable original language source regardless of the route taken into the English language.

underworld pertains to the specialized vocabulary used by thieves, convicts, prostitutes, con-artists, and tramps. It is sort of a twentieth-century cant. Terms relating to mid 1900s dope use and the youth-drug cult are classified as DRUG CULTURE. (*q.v.*).

widespread indicates that the entry word probably has global distribution in English-speaking countries. It usually indicates attestations for Australia, England, and the U.S. with the assumption that it occurs elsewhere.

word-of-choice pertains to a word or phrase which is the most likely expression used in a given setting.

Slang and Euphemism

A

A. 1. an abbreviation of AMPHETAMINE (*q.v.*). *Cf.* AMP (sense 2). **2.** the drug L.S.D. (*q.v.*); an abbreviation of ACID (*q.v.*). [both senses, U.S. drug culture, mid 1900s-pres.]

Aaron's rod the penis. *Cf.* STAFF OF LIFE. For synonyms see YARD. ["Aaron's rod" is from the Old Testament (Numbers); British, 1800s]

abandoned woman a woman who has been seduced, impregnated, and abandoned by a man.

abbess the procuress or madam of a brothel. *Cf.* ABBOT. [British, late 1700s]

Abbie (also **Abe, Abie**) a nickname for a Jewish male. From the proper name "Abraham." Derogatory when used as a generic term. For synonyms see FIVE AND TWO. [U.S. slang and colloquial, 1900s and before]

abbot 1. a PONCE (*q.v.*), an abbess' favorite man. [British slang and cant, 1800s] **2.** Nembutal (trademark), a barbiturate. From the manufacture's name, "Abbott Laboratories." [U.S. drug culture, mid 1900s-pres.]

Abe a nickname for a Jewish male. See ABBIE.

ability a euphemism for "sexual potency." [implied in the 1300s (*Oxford English Dictionary*) and appears in *Troilus and Cressida* (Shakespeare)]

A-bomb a marijuana cigarette containing heroin or opium. [U.S. drug culture, mid 1900s]

A-bomb juice MOONSHINE (sense 2); inferior or strong liquor. [U.S. slang, mid 1900s]

about gone intoxicated with alcohol. For synonyms see WOOFLED. [U.S. slang, early 1900s-pres.]

about right (also **about done**) intoxicated with alcohol [U.S. slang, mid 1900s-pres.]

about to find pups pregnant; about to give birth *Cf.* CAST (sense 2), DROP (sense 1), FIND. [U.S., 1900s and before]

Abraham 1. the penis. For synonyms see YARD. **2.** the female genitals. For synonyms see MONOSYLLABLE. [both senses, 1900s and before]

Abraham's bosom the Biblical "heaven." [based on a Biblical reference in Shakespeare's *Richard III*]

Abraham's bosom, in engaged in coition, "in heaven." ABRAHAM (sense 1) is the penis. *Cf.* HEAVEN (sense 2). [British euphemism, late 1800s, Farmer and Henley]

Abram naked; nude. For the Hebrew proper name. [cant, late 1600s-1700s]

abso-bloody-lutely (also **abso-bally-lutely**) absolutely; emphatically. [widespread slang, 1800s-1900s]

abso-fucking-lutely absolutely; without a doubt. [U.S. slang, 1900s]

abuse 1. to cheat; to make a cuckold of. From an earlier sense meaning "cheat." [late 1400s] **2.** to ABUSE ONESELF (*q.v.*); to masturbate. See SELF-ABUSE. [since the late 1500s] **3.** masturbation. A truncation of SELF-ABUSE (*q.v.*). [since the late 1500s]

abuse oneself to masturbate. [widespread euphemism]

abyss hell; the insides of the earth. Especially the abyss. [since the 1300s]

academician a prostitute; an inmate of an ACADEMY (*q.v.*). [cant, 1800s or before]

academy a bawdy house; a brothel. [British, late 1600s, B.E.]

Acapulco gold (also **Acapulco**) high-quality marijuana grown in Mexico. *Cf.* GOLD. [U.S. drug culture, mid 1900s-pres.]

accident 1. a bastard. [colloquial and nonce since the early 1900s or before] Synonyms: ADULTERINE, ADULTERINE BASTARD, ADULTEROUS BASTARD, AVE-TROL, BABE OF LOVE, BACHELOR'S BABY, BACHELOR'S SON, BANTLING, BAR STEWARD, BASE-BEGOTTEN CHILD, BASEBORN, BASE-SON, BAST, BASTARD, BASTARDA, BASTRICH, BELL-BASTARD, BLANKARD,

BORN OUT OF WEDLOCK, BRAT, BUSH CHILD, BUSH COLT, BY-CHOP, BYE-BLOW, BY-SCAPE, BY-SLIP, BY-SPELL, CATCH-COLT, CHANCE-BAIRN, CHANCE-BORN, CHANCE-CHILD, COME-BY-CHANCE, FILIUS NULLIUS, FILIUS POPULI, GRASS COLT, HASTY PUDDING, HYBRID, ILLEGITIMATE, INCIDENT, LOVE-BEGOTTEN CHILD, LOVE-BRAT, LOVE-CHILD, MERRY-BEGOTTEN CHILD, MISBEGOTTEN, MOMZER, MON-GREL, NATURAL, NATURAL-CHILD, NEPH-EW, NIECE, NON-WEDLOCK, NULLIUS FIL-IUS, OFF-GIRL, OF UNKNOWN BIRTH, OLD FIELD COLT, OUT-CHILD, OUTSIDE, OUTSIDE CHILE, OUTSIDER, SIDE-SLIP, SIDE-WIND, SIDE-WIPE, SINGLE CHILD, SON OF A BACH-ELOR, SON OF A BITCH, SQUEAKER, STALL WHIMPER, UNLAWFULLY BEGOTTEN, WHORE'S-KITTLING, WHORESON, WOODS-COLT, YARD-CHILD. **2.** an unplanned conception, specifically a failure of a birth control device. [U.S., mid 1900s-pres.] **3.** a loss of control of the bowels or bladder, said primarily of young children.

accommodate to copulate; to fit oneself to another; to serve another person sexually. For synonyms see OCCUPY. [colloquial since the 1800s]

accommodation house a brothel. [British slang, early 1800s]

accost for a prostitute to solicit someone to an act of sexual immorality. [U.S. euphemism, early 1900s-pres.]

accounts vomitus, in the expression CAST UP ONE'S ACCOUNTS (*q.v.*). [British, late 1600s, Dekker]

A.C.-D.C. (also **A.C./D.C.**) **1.** BISEX-UAL (sense 2). [U.S. slang, mid 1900s-pres.] **2.** pertaining to a homosexual male who is ambivalent to the choice of male or female sex roles. [slang, mid 1900s-pres.]

A.C.-D.C. bar a bar offering sexually oriented entertainment appealing to both male and female sexual interests. Usually considered appealing to a BISEX-UAL (sense 3) person. [U.S., mid 1900s-pres.]

ace 1. a marijuana cigarette. [U.S. drug culture, mid 1900s-pres.] **2.** the female genitals. From ACE OF SPADES (sense 1) and the darkness of the pubic

hair. For synonyms see MONOSYLLABLE. [British slang, late 1800s] **3.** a sarcastic term for an oaf or jerk. [U.S. slang, mid 1900s]

ace of spades 1. the female genitals. From the color or shape of the pubic hair. [British slang, late 1800s, Farmer and Henley] **2.** a Negro. Potentially derogatory. Also in the phrase ''as black as the ace of spades,'' referring to a very dark Negro. For synonyms see EBONY. [U.S. before mid 1900s]

achieve to achieve coition with a woman. Also ''win the heart of.'' *Cf.* SCORE. [from *Othello* (Shakespeare)]

acid lysergic acid diethylamide, the drug L.S.D. [U.S. drug culture, mid 1900s-pres.] Synonyms: A., BIG-D., BLOTTER, BLUE ACID, BLUE CHEER, BLUE FLAG, BLUE HEAVEN, BLUE MIST, BROWN DOTS, CALIFORNIA SUNSHINE, CANDY, CHERRY TOP, CHOCOLATE CHIPS, CLEAR LIGHT, COFFEE, CONTACT LENS, CUBE, DOMES, DOTS, FLATS, HAZE, INSTANT ZEN, L.S.D., LUCY IN THE SKY WITH DIA-MONDS, MELLOW-YELLOW, MICRODOTS, ORANGE MUSHROOMS, ORANGE SUNSHINE, ORANGE WEDGES, OWSLEY, PAPER ACID, PEARLY GATE, PINK, PINK SWIRL, PURPLE FLATS, PURPLE HAZE, PURPLE MICRODOTS, ROYAL BLUE, STRAWBERRY FIELDS, SU-GAR, SUGAR LUMP, SUNSHINE, THE CHIEF, THE HAWK, TICKET, WEDDING BELLS ACID, WEDGES, WHITE LIGHTNING, WINDOW PANE, YELLOW, YELLOW SUNSHINE, ZEN.

acid-head (also **acid-dropper, acid-freak**) One who uses the drug L.S.D. regularly and is frequently under its influence. [U.S. drug culture, mid 1900s-pres.]

acid pad a place to consume the drug L.S.D. in safety and seclusion. [U.S. drug culture, mid 1900s-pres.]

acne an inflammation of the skin of the face and sometimes the back and chest, usually with noticeable pustules. A truncation of ACNE VULGARIS. [since the early 1800s]

acne-type surface blemish a euphemism for ''pimple.'' [U.S. advertising, mid 1900s]

acquiesce-man a sycophant. Punning

on "yes-man." [U.S. slang, mid 1900s]
Synonyms: ARSE-CRAWLER, ASS-KISSER,
ASS-SUCKER, ASS-WIPE, BOOT-LICK, BOOT-
LICKER, BROWN-NOSE, BROWN-TONGUE,
BUM-LICKER, BUM-SUCKER, BUTT-WIPE,
CATCH-FART, CLAWBACK, COCK-SUCKER,
CRAWL, EGG-SUCKER, FARTLICKER, FART-
SUCKER, FOOTLICKER, GRAECULUS ESU-
RIENS, GREASE-BOY, GREASER, HAIRY
BELLY, KISS-ASS, LICKDISH, LICKSPIT,
LICKSPITTLE, PAPELARD, PICKTHANK,
SCRAPE-SHOE, SLAP-SAUCE, SOAP-CRAWL-
ER, SPANIEL, STROKER, SUCK, SUCK-ASS,
SYCOPHANT, TOAD-EATER, TOADY, TRUCK-
LER, TUFT-HUNTER, YES-MAN.

act, the copulation. A truncation of
"the sexual act." For synonyms see
SMOCKAGE. [euphemistic since the 1600s
or before]

action 1. coition; sexual activity; intrigue with the opposite sex. [since the
1600s or before; U.S. euphemism and
slang, early 1900s-pres.] **2.** excitement,
especially from gambling. [U.S., early
1900s-pres.]

active citizen a louse. Usually in the
plural. [British and U.S. slang, early
1800s]

active sodomist an active homosexual;
an active pederast; an INSERTOR (*q.v.*).
Cf. PASSIVE PEDERAST. [since the 1800s]

activity booster an amphetamine tablet; a PEP PILL (*q.v.*). [U.S. slang and
drug culture, mid 1900s-pres.]

act of androgynation a euphemism
for "copulation." For synonyms see
SMOCKAGE. [mid 1600s, (Urquhart)]

act of darkness a euphemism for
"copulation." [from *King Lear* (Shakespeare)]

act of generation (also **act of sport**)
a euphemism for "copulation." [Brit-
ish, late 1800s]

act of kind a euphemism for "copulation." *Cf.* DEED OF KIND. [British, 1800s]

act of love a euphemism for "copulation." [1800s-1900s]

act of shame (also **act of sport**)
coition; an act of copulation. [from
Othello (Shakespeare)]

actus coitu, in* "in the act of copulation." [Latin]

A.D. an abbreviation of "drug addict." [U.S., mid 1900s-pres.]

Adam, the old 1. original sin; male
and female lust; human sexuality. [from
Henry V (Shakespeare)] **2.** the penis.
Cf. ADAM'S ARSENAL. [both senses,
British, 1800s, Farmer and Henley] **3.**
lust; male sex drive and potency.

Adam-and-Eve it 1. to copulate. *Cf.*
WHAT EVE DID WITH ADAM. [British
slang, late 1800s, Farmer and Henley]
2. to be in a state of nudity; to practice
nudism. [U.S., mid 1900s]

Adam and Eve's togs (also **Adam
and Eve's clothes**) nakedness; nudity.
[British and U.S., early 1900s]

Adamatical naked; nude. For synonyms
see STARKERS. [implied in the 1600s,
Oxford English Dictionary]

Adamize to copulate, from the male
point of view. *Cf.* PHALLICIZE. [British,
1800s]

Adam's arsenal the male genitals,
the penis and testicles. For synonyms
see VIRILIA. [British, late 1800s, Farmer
and Henley]

Adam's own the female genitals. [Brit-
ish, 1800s]

Adod! (also **Adad!, Agad!, Ecod!,
Egad!**) an exclamation and a minced
oath from "Afore God!" and "By
God!" [late 1600s-1700s]

Adonis a fop or dandy; an extremely
good-looking or "pretty" male. [from
the proper name "Adonis" in Greek
mythology; U.S., early 1900s-pres.]

adrip sated and intoxicated with alcohol. [U.S. colloquial, 1900s]

Ads- "God's" in oaths dating from
the late 1600s. Found in compounds
such as: Ads-bled! (blood), Ads-bobbers!
(body), Ads-bud! (blood), Ads-buntlines!
(rope), Ads-flesh!, Ads-heart!, Ads-
heartlikins! (little heart), Ads-heart's-
wounds!, Ads-wauntlikins! (little
wounds), Ads-zookers! (nails). For synonyms see 'ZOUNDS! [1600s-1800s]

adult pertaining to publicly available
material (*i.e.*, books and films) containing excessive violence or excessive
and unusual sex. *Cf.* FRANK. [U.S.,
mid 1900s-pres.]

adultery an act of sexual intercourse where at least one partner is married to someone else. [since the 1300s] Synonyms: COMARITAL SEX, CONJUGAL INFIDELITY, EWBRICE, FLESHLY TREASON, FOUL PLAY, INFIDELITY, MARRIAGE-BREACH, SMOCK-TREASON, SPOUSE-BREACH, TREASON.

Adzooks! an oath and an exclamation, "By God's hooks!" (nails). *Cf.* GADZOOKS! For synonyms see 'ZOUNDS! [mid 1700s-1800s]

a- -e "arse," the posteriors; the anus. See ARSE, ASS. [British, late 1700s, (Grose)]

affair 1. a romantic or sexual relationship of a brief duration, especially an illicit one. [U.S., 1900s or before] Synonyms and related terms: AFFAIRE D'AMOUR, AFFAIRE DE COEUR, AMORETTE, AMOUR, AMOURETTE, CARRY ON, ENTANGLEMENT, EXTRA-CURRICULAR ACTIVITIES, FLING, FOOL AROUND, INTRIGUE, SMOCK-SECRET, TRYST. **2.** the male or female genitals. Sometimes in the plural. Used jokingly in double entendre. [since the late 1500s]

affaire d'amour* a "love affair"; an AFFAIR (sense 1). [French]

affaire de coeur* an "affair of the heart"; a love affair as opposed to a purely sexual matter. [French]

afflicted intoxicated with alcohol. For synonyms see WOOFLED. [slang since the early 1700s]

affy lustful. [U.S. slang, 1900s, Berrey and Van den Bark]

afgani the alcohol extract of CANNABIS SATIVA (*q.v.*). For synonyms see OIL. [U.S. drug culture, mid 1900s-pres.]

afgay a homosexual male. From AGFAY (*q.v.*), which is Pig Latin for FAG (sense 2). For synonyms see EPICENE. [British backslang, early 1900s, *Dictionary of the Underworld*]

afloat intoxicated with alcohol; drunk. *Cf.* AWASH. [British and U.S., late 1800s-1900s]

Aframerican an American Negro. [U.S., 1900s]

African black a variety of marijuana said to be from Africa. [U.S. drug culture, mid 1900s-pres.]

Afro 1. an American negro. [U.S., early 1900s-pres.] **2.** a hair style worn mostly by blacks of both sexes. [U.S., mid 1900s-pres.] **3.** Negroid; African. [U.S., early 1900s-pres.]

Afro-American 1. an American Negro. For synonyms see EBONY. [U.S., early 1900s-pres.] **2.** pertaining to the American Negro. [both senses, U.S., early 1900s-pres.]

Afro-Saxon a Negro who behaves like or aspires to be like Caucasians. *Cf.* OREO. [U.S., mid 1900s-pres.]

after dinner man a SOT (*q.v.*) or drunkard; someone who drinks after the noon meal and well into the evening. *Cf.* MEALER. [British, early 1800s]

after hair chasing after women, especially for sexual purposes. Refers to the pubic hair. *Cf.* HAIR. [since the 1800s]

after one's greens in pursuit of sexual release or satisfaction, usually said of men. [British, 1800s]

ag-fay a homosexual male. Pig Latin for FAG (sense 2). *Cf.* AGFAY. [U.S., early 1900s-pres.]

aggressor in homosexual practices, the party assuming the more masculine or less submissive role; in male homosexuality, the INSERTOR (*q.v.*). *Cf.* ACTIVE SODOMIST. [nonce and euphemistic, 1900s]

A-head a frequent user of amphetamines. A. (sense 1) refers to amphetamines. [U.S., mid 1900s-pres.]

A-hole 1. the anus. **2.** a term of contempt. Both are from ASS-HOLE (*q.v.*). [both senses, U.S., 1900s]

air one's pores to be naked; to become naked, partially or completely. [British, 1900s]

airs, in one's intoxicated with alcohol. [U.S. slang, early 1700s, Ben Franklin]

ajax a PRIVY (*q.v.*). A jocular variation of "a JAKES" (*q.v.*), an outhouse. From *The Metamorphosis of Ajax*, by Sir John Harington. [British, late 1500s; U.S. slang, 1900s] Synonyms: BACK, BACKHOUSE, BACKY, BANK, BOG, BOGGARD, BOG-HOUSE, BOG-SHOP, CACATOR-

IUM, CAN, CHAPEL, CHAPEL OF EASE, CHIC
SALE, CLOSET, CLOSET OF EASE, COFFEE
HOUSE, COFFEE-SHOP, COMMONS, COM-
POST HOLE, COTTAGE, COUNTING-HOUSE,
CRAP-HOUSE, CRAPPER, CRAPPERY, CRAP-
PING-CASA, CRAPPING-CASE, CRAPPING
CASTLE, CRAPPING-KEN, CROPPING-KEN,
DILBERRY CREEK, DONAGHER, DONEGAN,
DONIGAN, DRAUGHT, DUNAGAN, DUN-
NAKEN, DUNNAKIN, DUNNY, DUNNYKEN,
FORAKERS, FORICA, GARDEN-HOUSE,
GONG, GONG HOUSE, HONEY-HOUSE,
HOOSEGOW, HOPPER, HOUSE OF EASE-
MENT, HOUSE OF OFFICE, IVY-COVERED
COTTAGE, JACQUE'S, JAKE, JAKE-HOUSE,
JAKES, JAQUES, JOHN, KYBO, LEAK-
HOUSE, LIBRARY, LITTLE HOUSE, NEC-
ESSARIUM, NECESSARY, NECESSARY
HOUSE, NECESSARY VAULT, OFFICE, OUT-
DOOR PLUMBING, PARLIAMENT, PETTY-
HOUSE, PLACE, PLACE OF CONVENIENCE,
PLACE OF EASEMENT, PLACE OF RESORT,
PLACE WHERE YOU COUGH, PREP CHAP-
EL, PRIVATE OFFICE, PRIVY, QUAKER'S
BURYING-GROUND, REAR, RELIEF STATION,
SCOTCH ORDINARY, SHACK, SHIT-HOLE,
SHIT-HOUSE, SHITTER, SHOUSE, SIEGE,
SIEGE-HOLE, SIEGE-HOUSE, SIR HARRY,
SMOKEHOUSE, SPICE-ISLAND, STOOL OF
EASE, TEMPLE, THE PATH, UNCLE, UN-
FLUSHABLE, VANDYKE, WARDROBE.

A.K. **1.** an "ass-kisser." **2.** an ALTE
KACKER (*q.v.*), an old man; an "old
shitter." [possibly from German *alte
Knacker*, "old fogey"; both senses,
U.S., early 1900s-pres.]

alchy (also **alki, alky**) **1.** alcoholic
beverages; any kind of alcohol. [U.S.,
mid 1800s-1900s] **2.** a drunkard. [U.S.,
early 1900s-pres.] The following terms
apply to men unless indicated other-
wise: AFTER DINNER MAN, ALCOHOLIC,
ALE-KNIGHT, ALE-WISP, ALKI STIFF, ALKY
BUM, BANG-PITCHER, BAR-FLY, BARREL-
HOUSE BUM, BAT, BEER-JERKER, BEER-
SLINGER, BEER-SWIPER, BELCH-GUTS,
BEZZLER, BIB-ALL-NIGHT, BIBBLER, BILED
OWL, BILLY-BORN-DRUNK, BIMMY,
BINGO-BOY, BINGO-MORT (female),
BLACK-POT, BLOAT, BLOATER, BLOKE,
BLOMBOLL, BLOTTER, BOOSEY-COCK,
BOOZE ARTIST, BOOZE-FIGHTER, BOOZE-

FREAK, BOOZEGOB, BOOZE-HEISTER,
BOOSE-HOUND, BOOZE-KING, BOOZER,
BOOZICIAN, BOOZINGTON, BORACHIO,
BOTTLE-BABY, BOTTLE-MAN, BOTTLE-
SUCKER, BRANDY-FACE, BREWER'S HORSE,
BROTHER-WHERE-ART-THOU?, BUBBER,
BUBBING-CULL, BUBSTER, BUDGER, BUM-
BOOZER, BUMPER, BURSTER, BUSTHEAD,
CADGER, CAGER, CATERPILLAR, COD,
COMPOTATOR, COPPER-NOSE, CROCK,
CROW, DEHORN, DIPS, DIPSO, DISTILLERY
STIFF, DRAINIST, DRAMSTER, DRINKSTER,
DRUNKARD, D-T-IST, ELBOW-BENDER,
ELBOW-CROOKER, ENSIGN-BEARER, FID-
DLE-CUP, FLUFFER, FUDDLE-CAP, FUDDLER,
FUDDLING FELLOW, FUNNEL, GARGLER,
GEEK, GIN DISPOSAL UNIT, GIN-HEAD,
GLOW WORM, GRAPE-MONGER, GRAVEL-
GRINDER, GROGHOUND, GULLION, GUTTLE,
GUZZLE-GUTS, GUZZLER, HAIL-FELLOW-
ALL-WET, HISTER, HOISTER, HOOCH-
HOUND, HOOTCHER, INEBRIATE, JAG, JERK-
ER, JICK-HEAD, JOB, JOLLY NOSE, JUICE-
HEAD, KENNEDY ROT, KENNURD, LAPPER,
LAPPY CULL, LARGE-HEAD, LEANAWAY,
LICK-SPIGOT, LICK-WIMBLE, LOVE-POT,
LUG-POT, LUSH, LUSH-COVE, LUSHER,
LUSHING MAN, LUSHINGTON, LUSH MER-
CHANT, LUSHY, LUSHY-COVE, MALT-BUG,
MALT-HORSE, MALT-WORM, MOIST 'UN,
MOONER, MOP, NAZY-COVE, NAZY-NAB,
OENOPHILIST, OILER, ONE OF THE FAITH-
FUL, PEGGER, PHILISTINE, PINT POT, PISS-
HEAD, PISS-MAKER, PISSO, PISSY-PAL,
PITCHER-MAN, PLONK-DOT, PLONKO, POT,
POT-FURY, POT-KNIGHT, PUB-ORNAMENT,
QUARTER POT, REEL-POT, ROB-POT, RUM-
BAG, RUM-DUMB, RUMMY, RUMPOT, RUM-
SUCKER, SCHICKER, SCOWRER, SHAKER,
SHICK, SHIFTER, SHIKKER, SIPSTER, SOAK,
SOAKER, SOD, SODDEN BUM, SOT, S.O.T.,
SOUSE, SPIGOT-SUCKER, SPONGE, SQUIFF,
STEADY-LAPPER, STEW, STEW BUM, STEWIE,
SUCK-BOTTLE, SUCK-PINT, SUCK-SPIGOT,
SWELL-HEAD, SWILL-BOWL, SWILLER,
SWILL-POT, SWILL-TUB, SWIPER, SWIPPING-
TON, SWIZZLE-GUTS, TAVERNER, THIRST-
INGTON, TICKLE-BRAIN, TICKLE-PITCHER,
TID, TIGHT SKIRT (female), TIPPLE-ARSE,
TIPPLER, TOAST, TODDYCASK, TOOTER,
TOPE, TOPER, TOSS-POT, WASSAILER, WET-

HAND, WET-QUAKER, WETSTER, WET-SUBJECT, WET-'UN, WHIPCAN, WINE-BAG, WINEBIBBER, WINO.

Al Cohol alcohol; alcohol personified. *Cf.* JOHN HALL. [U.S. slang, early 1900s]

alcohol abuse the excessive drinking of alcohol; alcoholism. *Cf.* DRUG ABUSE. [U.S., mid 1900s-pres.]

alcoholic 1. pertaining to alcohol. [since the 1700s] **2.** originally a drunkard, now a person suffering from the disease of alcoholism. [1900s]

alcoholic hallucinations the DELIRIUM TREMENS (*q.v.*). For synonyms see ORKORKS. [medical]

alcoholic seizure the DELIRIUM TREMENS (*q.v.*). [U.S., 1900s]

alcoholism 1. drunkenness. [mid 1800s] **2.** a physical, emotional, and social disability characterized by the excessive ingestion of alcohol. [1900s]

alcoholized saturated with alcohol; drunk. For synonyms see WOOFLED. [U.S. slang, early 1900s or before]

alcove the female genitals. *Cf.* CRANNY, NICHE-COCK. [British, late 1800s]

alecie (also **alecy**) intoxicated with ale. A play on "lunacy" and an old nonce word preserved in dictionaries. [late 1500s]

ale-knight (also **pot-knight**) a tippler; a drunkard. For synonyms see ALCHY. [British, late 1500s-1800s]

ale-wisp a drunkard. [British slang, 1800s or before, Farmer and Henley]

Alice B. Toklas a BROWNIE (sense 4) with marijuana baked into it. Named for Gertrude Stein's companion in the 1920s who is said to have devised the recipe for brownies containing marijuana. [U.S., mid 1900s-pres.]

alimentary canal the food and waste passage from mouth to anus; sometimes euphemistic for "bowels" or "gut." [since the mid 1800s]

Al K. Hall a jocular nickname for liquor based on "alcohol." [U.S. slang, 1900s]

alkied-up (also **alkied**) intoxicated with alcohol. For synonyms see WOOFLED. [U.S., 1900s]

alki hall alcohol. [U.S. slang, early 1900s]

alki stiff a hobo drunkard; any drunkard. [U.S. underworld, early 1900s]

alky bum a hobo drunkard; any drunkard. [U.S., 1900s]

all at sea intoxicated with alcohol. [nautical, 1900s or before]

alley apple 1. a piece of horse manure. *Cf.* HORSE APPLE, ROAD APPLE. [U.S. slang, early 1900s] **2.** a stone used as a missile. [U.S. slang, 1900s]

alley cat 1. a prostitute, especially one who prowls in the night. *Cf.* MOONLIGHTER. [U.S., early 1900s] **2.** any person who is loose in sexual matters. *Cf.* TOMCAT. [U.S. slang, mid 1900s-pres.]

all face naked; nude. [British and U.S. slang, late 1800s]

all-fired (also **jo-fired**) a euphemism for "hell-fired," damned. [U.S. colloquial, mid 1700s-pres.]

all get-out a euphemism for "hell" in "it's as hot as all get-out." [U.S., 1800s-1900s]

all gone intoxicated with alcohol. For synonyms see WOOFLED. [U.S. slang, 1900s]

alligator bait 1. poor-quality food or disliked food **2.** a Negro, especially a Negro child. Derogatory and jocular. [both senses, U.S. slang, early 1900s or before]

alligator bull nonsense; BULLSHIT (*q.v.*). A play on "bull alligator," the mature male alligator.

all-night trick a prostitute's term for a customer who pays for the entire night. [U.S., 1900s]

all over one, be to be in close bodily contact, *i.e.*, fighting, necking, or fondling. [U.S. slang, mid 1900s-pres.]

alls-bay nonsense; BALLS (sense 4). Pig Latin. [U.S., 1900s]

all's not quiet on the waterfront a catch phrase pertaining to a woman's state when menstruating.

all the way copulation, especially in

"go all the way." *Cf.* LIMIT, THE. [U.S. slang, mid 1900s-pres.]

almanach the female genitals. Possibly having something to do with MONTHS (*q.v.*). For synonyms see MONOSYLLABLE.

almond rock (also **almond**) the penis. Rhyming slang for COCK (sense 3). *Cf.* DICKORY DOCK. For synonyms see YARD. [British, late 1800s]

Alphonse a pimp; a PONCE (*q.v.*); a generic nickname for a pimp. Possibly rhyming slang for "ponce." For synonyms see PIMP. [British, late 1800s, *Dictionary of Rhyming Slang*]

altar a toilet; the water-flush toilet bowl; a chamber pot. [U.S. slang, early 1900s-pres.]

altar of Hymen the female genitals. *Cf.* TEMPLE OF LOW MEN. [Brtish, late 1800s]

altar of love the female genitals. For synonyms see MONOSYLLABLE. [British, late 1800s]

altar room a W.C.; a bathroom. *Cf.* ALTAR. [U.S. slang, early 1900s-pres.]

alte kacker* (also **alter cocker, alter kocker, alter kucker**) a dirty old man; a seasoned lecher. [possibly from German *alte Knacker*, "old fogey"; U.S., early 1900s]

alter to castrate a male animal. *Cf.* CHANGE. [U.S. colloquial, late 1800s-pres.]

altitudes, in one's intoxicated with alcohol and in an elevated mood. [British colloquial, 1600s-1700s]

altogether, in the naked; nude. [colloquial, late 1800s-pres.]

altogethery intoxicated with alcohol. For synonyms see WOOFLED. [British slang]

Amanita muscaria* the scientific name for a mushroom known to produce hallucinations; a highly poisonous substance known as fly agaric. [U.S. drug culture, mid 1900s-pres.]

amateur night 1. refers to an instance of copulation involving a woman who is casual about sex but not a prostitute. **2.** a specified night at an entertainment establishment featuring nude entertainment in which the patrons are invited to participate. [both senses, U.S. slang, mid 1900s-pres.]

Amazon 1. a mythical, warlike woman found in Greek mythology. The notion that the word is from the Greek for "without a breast" is doubted. (Amazons were supposed to have cut off their right breasts in order to facilitate drawing the strings of their bows.) [in English by the 1300s] **2.** an extremely masculine woman; a virago. [since the mid 1700s] Synonyms for sense 2: ANDROGYNE, BELDAME, BOON-DAGGER, BOY, BRIMSTONE, BULL BITCH, COTQUEAN, HORSE-GODMOTHER, JEZEBEL, MUSCLE MOLL, OGRESS, QUEER QUEEN, VIRAGO.

ambidextrous bisexual. See AMBISEXTROUS. [British, early 1900s, *Dictionary of Slang and Unconventional English*]

ambisextrous pertaining to a bisexual person. A jocular play on AMBIDEXTROUS (*q.v.*). [U.S., early 1900s]

ambulance-chaser a lawyer who seeks out clients from persons who are in trouble or injured. [U.S., early 1900s-pres.]

amen-snorter a religious person, especially a clergyman. For synonyms see SKY-PILOT. [since the late 1800s]

amies See AMY.

ammunition 1. toilet tissue. [British and U.S. slang, 1800s-pres.] **2.** a perineal pad, sanitary pad, or napkin. For synonyms see MANHOLE COVER. [slang, early 1900s, *Dictionary of Slang and Unconventional English*]

among one's frills copulating; the act of copulating. *Cf.* FRILLS. [British, 1800s, Farmer and Henley]

amor (also **amour**) passion; love, especially sexual love.

amoret (also **amorette**) **1.** an amorous female; a passionate woman. [1400s] **2.** a love affair.

amorosa 1. a female lover or sweetheart. **2.** a wanton woman; a harlot. [both senses, early 1600s]

amoroso a male lover or sweetheart. [early 1600s]

amorous 1. pertaining to lovemaking, usually with sexual implications. **2.** pertaining to a person, presumably a male, who is sexually aroused; occasionally a euphemism for "having an erection." [both since the 1300s]

amorous congress an old euphemism for "sexual intercourse." For synonyms see SMOCKAGE. [late 1700s]

amorous rites lovemaking; coition. [from *Romeo and Juliet* (Shakespeare)]

amp 1. an ampule of a drug. **2.** an amphetamine tablet or capsule. Usually in the plural. [both senses, U.S. drug culture, mid 1900s-pres.] Synonyms for sense 2: A., AMPHETAMINE, BAM, BLACK BEAUTIES, BLACKBIRD, BLACK MOLLIES, BOTTLE, BROWNS, BUMBLEBEE, CARTWHEEL, CHALK, CHICKEN POWDER, COASTS-TO-COASTS, COCKLE BURR, CO-PILOTS, CRANKS, CROSSROAD, CRYSTAL, DOLL, DOUBLE-CROSS, EYE-OPENER, FIVES, FOOTBALLS, FORWARDS, GREEN DRAGON, GREENIE, JELLY BABY, JELLY BEAN, JOLLYBEAN, JUG, L.A. TURNABOUTS, LIDPOPPERS, LIGHTNING, METH, MINI-BENNIES, NUGGETS, PEACH, PEP PILL, RHYTHMS, ROOT, ROSES, SKYROCKET, SPARKLE PLENTY, SPECKLED BIRD, SPEED, SPLASH, SWEET, TENS, THRUST, THRUSTERS, TRUCK-DRIVER, TURNABOUTS, UP, UPPER, UPPIE, WAKE-UP, WEST-COAST TURNAROUNDS, WHITE CROSS, WHITES, WHITEY, ZOOM.

amped intoxicated with amphetamines. From AMP (*q.v.*) with reinforcement from "ampere." For synonyms see TALL. [U.S. drug culture, mid 1900s-pres.]

ampersand the posteriors; the buttocks. A compressed form consisting of "and-per-se-and," represented by the symbol "&" (which is the last symbol in children's alphabets, thus "the end"). This was a way of indicating that one was talking about the word "and" and not using it as a conjunction. Whenever letters were recited or words were spelled out, they were cited in the form "a per se a," and "o per se o," (Nares). [British, 1800s and before]

amy 1. an amyl nitrite ampule. This appears frequently as "amyl nitrate"; the plural is "amies" or "amys." *Cf.* PEARL (sense 2), SNAPPER (sense 5). **2.** an Amytal sodium (trademark) tablet or capsule, one of the barbiturates. [both senses, U.S. drug culture, mid 1900s-pres.]

Amy-John a masculine lesbian. A play on AMAZON (*q.v.*). *Cf.* JOHN-AND-JOAN (sense 2). [U.S., mid 1900s]

amyl amyl nitrite. See AMY (sense 1).

anatomical a euphemism for "lewd" or "sexually oriented"; explicit about the breasts or genitals. *Cf.* ADULT. [early 1900s-pres.]

anatomy one's body, especially the parts which are not visible in public; specifically the POSTERIORS (*q.v.*). [U.S., 1900s or before]

anchored in Sot's Bay intoxicated with alcohol. For synonyms see WOOFLED. [nautical, 1900s or before]

angel 1. a male homosexual pederast; an INSERTOR (*q.v.*) who supports one or more other homosexuals. *Cf.* SUGARDADDY. [U.S. slang, early 1900s] **2.** a passive pederast; a RECEIVER (*q.v.*); a catamite. *Cf.* ANGELINA. For synonyms see BRONCO. [U.S. slang, 1900s] **3.** cocaine. For synonyms see NOSE-CANDY. [U.S. drug culture, mid 1900s-pres.]

angel dust (also **angel hair**) **1.** powdered P.C.P. (*q.v.*), an animal tranquilizer. *Cf.* HEAVEN DUST. **2.** synthetic heroin. [both senses, U.S. drug culture, mid 1900s-pres.]

angel hair See ANGEL DUST.

angelina a hobo's catamite or any passive pederast; a RECEIVER (*q.v.*). *Cf.* ANGEL (senses 1 and 2). [U.S., 1900s]

angie cocaine. From ANGEL (sense 3). [Australian, mid 1900s, Baker]

angle the penis. *Cf.* YARD. [British slang, late 1800s]

Anglo-Saxon pertaining to words (usually "dirty words") which are assumed to be Old English. See PARDON MY FRENCH.

anilingism See ANILINGUS.

anilingus (also **anilingism**) the use of the mouth or tongue to stimulate the anus of another person.

animal 1. a euphemistic nickname for a bull. [U.S. rural colloquial, 1900s] **2.** nonsense, *i.e.*, BULLSHIT (*q.v.*). [U.S. slang, 1900s] Synonyms for sense 2: ALLIGATOR BULL, ALLS-BAY, AP-CRAY, APPLESAUCE, ARGLE-BARGLE, BALDER-DASH, BALDUCTUM, BALLOCKS, BALLOON JUICE, BALLS, BALLYHOO, BALLY HOOEY, BALONEY, BATSHIT, BEANS, BIBBLE-BAB-BLE, BILGE, BLAH, BLARNEY, BLATHER, BOSH, BOVRIL, BULL, BULL-FEATHERS, BULL-FODDER, BULLO, BULLONEY, BULL-ISH, BULLSHIT, BULL'S WOOL, BUM-FLUFF, BUNCOMBE, BUNK, BUNKUM, BURMA SHAVE, CHAFF, CLACK, CLAPTRAP, CLISH-CLASH, COBBLER'S AWLS, COBBLER'S STALLS, COCK, CODDING, COD'S WALLOP, CORRAL DUST, COW-CONFETTI, COWSH, COWYARD CONFETTI, CRAP, DRIP, DRIVEL, DURHAM, EYEWASH, FADOODLE, FAL-DERAL, FIBLE-FABLE, FIDDLE-CUM-FAD-DLE, FIDDLEDEEDEE, FIDDLE-FADDLE, FIDDLESTICKS, FLAMDOODLE, FLAPDOO-DLE, FLAP-SAUCE, FLUMMADIDDLE, FLUM-MYDIDDLE, FOLDEROL, FOOEY, FOR THE BIRDS, FUDGE, GAMMON, GAS, GIBBER-GABBER, GIBBERISH, GILHOOLEY, GOBBLE-DYGOOK, GUFF, HOKUM, HOOEY, HORN-SWOGGLE, HORSE, HORSE APPLE, HORSE FEATHERS, HORSERADISH, HORSESHIT, HORSH, HOT AIR, HOT COCK, HUMBUG, JACK SHIT, KIBOSH, MACARONI, MA-LARKY, MEADOW DRESSING, MEADOW-MAYONNAISE, MIFF-MAFF, MOONSHINE, MUMBO-JUMBO, MUSH, NERTS, NURTS, OIL OF TONGUE, PALAVER, PARSLEY, PHOOEY, PIFFLE, PIGWASH, PILE OF SHIT, PISS AND WIND, POPPYCOCK, PRIZE BULL, RATS!, RIMBLE-RAMBLE, ROT, SHIT FOR THE BIRDS, SHUCK, SKIMBLE-SCRAMBLE, SLOBBER, SLUDGE, SONG AND DANCE, TITOTULAR BOSH, TOMMY-ROT, TRIPE, WHANGDOODLE, WHIFFLE-WHAFFLE, YAWP. **3.** a term of contempt for a person implying nonhumanness. **4.** a fool; an oaf. [since the late 1500s] **5.** an athlete, especially if big, clumsy, ugly, or smelly. *Cf.* JOCK (sense 5). [U.S., mid 1900s-pres.] **6.** a sexually aggressive male; a STUD (sense 2) or an extremely uncouth male. [U.S., mid 1900s-pres.] **7.** a prostitute. Essentially a contemptuous term for any person of low character and habits. [U.S. underworld, 1900s]

animal magnetism sex appeal; pertaining to physical sexual attraction, usually said of males but also of females. [U.S., 1900s]

animal tranquilizer the drug P.C.P. (*q.v.*). *Cf.* ELEPHANT. [U.S. slang, mid 1900s-pres.]

ankle an attractive young woman or girl. [U.S. slang, mid 1900s] See also SPRAIN ONE'S ANKLE.

Anne's fan a rude gesture, thumbing the nose. Touching the tip of the thumb to the end of one's nose and spreading the fingers wide. It can be made worse by wiggling the fingers. This is similar to giving someone the FINGER (*q.v.*). [British, 1800s]

anonyma a prostitute. [British, mid 1800s]

answer nature's call to retire to the W.C., specifically to defecate or urinate: [colloquial euphemism, 1900s and before]

answer the final summons to die. For synonyms see DEPART. [late 1800s-pres.]

ansy-pay a homosexual male. Pig Latin for PANSY (*q.v.*). *Cf.* AG-FAY. [U.S., 1900s]

anti-bod a scrawny or underdeveloped male or an ugly, overweight woman. *Cf.* BOD. [U.S. slang, mid 1900s]

antifreeze 1. liquor. For synonyms see BOOZE. [U.S., 1900s] **2.** heroin. From sense 1. [U.S. drug culture, mid 1900s-pres., Wentworth and Flexner]

antipodes, the the female genitals; the "exact opposite" of the male genitals. For synonyms see MONOSYLLABLE. [British, 1800s or before]

ant-mire an avoidance for "piss-ant." See PIS-ANT. [U.S. euphemism, 1800, Read]

anus the posterior opening of the alimentary canal. [since the mid 1600s] Synonyms: A- -E, A-HOLE, ARS, ARSE, ARS MUSICA, A-S, ASS-HOLE, BACKDOOR, BACK-DOOR TRUMPET, BACK-WAY, BLIND-EYE, BLOT, BOGEY, BOGY, BOODY, BOTTLE AND GLASS, BROWN, BROWN BUCKET, BROWNIE, BRUNSWICK, BUCKET, BUM, BUNG, BUNG HOLE, BUNKEY, CHUFF, CORN HOLE, CRACK, CRACKER, CULO, DATE, DILBERRY-MAKER, DINGER, DIRT-CHUTE, DIRT-ROAD, DOPEY, DOT, ELEPHANT AND CASTLE, FARTING-CLAPPER, FEAK, FUGO, FUN, FUNDAMENT, GIG, GIGI, GONGA, GOOSEBERRY-GRINDER, HIND-BOOT, HINDER-ENTRANCE, HOLE, JACKSIE, KEESTER, KHYBER PASS, MEDLAR, MONOCULAR-EYEGLASS, NOCKANDRO, NORTH POLE, PERVY, PODEX, POOP-CHUTE, PORT-HOLE, RINCTUM, RING, RIP, ROUNDEYE, ROUND-MOUTH, SEWER, SHIT-HOLE, SIEGE, SLOP-CHUTE, SPICE-ISLAND, TAN-TRACK, TEWEL (horse), THE BROWN WINDSOR, TIB, TOKUS, TRILL, WIND MILL, WINDWARD PASSAGE.

ap-cray nonsense. Pig Latin for "crap." For synonyms see ANIMAL. [U.S. slang, 1900s]

ape 1. a derogatory nickname for a Negro. [U.S., 1900s or before] **2.** a hoodlum or strong-arm man. [1900s] **3.** any ugly man, especially if large. *Cf.* BABOON. [U.S. slang, 1900s]

aped intoxicated with alcohol. For synonyms see WOOFLED. [U.S., early 1900s-pres.]

ape-shit the state of being obsessed with a person or thing, as in the expression "go ape-shit" or "be ape-shit." [U.S., mid 1900s]

aphrodisiacal tennis court the female genitals. [1600s, (Urquhart)]

apparatus the male genitals; the VIRILIA (*q.v.*). *Cf.* EQUIPMENT. [U.S. slang, 1900s]

appetent pertaining to sexual desire; lustful or aroused. Extended from the standard meaning relating to craving. [since the early 1400s]

apple and pip urine; to urinate; an act of urination. Rhyming slang for "sip,"

which is backslang for "piss." [British, 1800s, *Dictionary of Rhyming Slang*]

apple dumpling shop a woman's breasts, especially if fat and partially exposed. [British slang, late 1700s-1800s]

apple-jack 1. brandy made from apples. **2.** any alcoholic liquor. For synonyms see BOOZE. [both senses, U.S., early 1800s-pres.]

apple palsy drunkenness from APPLE-JACK (*q.v.*). [U.S., late 1800s-early 1900s]

apples 1. a woman's breasts. See CAT HEADS. [U.S., 1900s or before] **2.** the testicles; the same as LOVE-APPLES (*q.v.*). For synonyms see WHIRLYGIGS. [slang, 1800s-1900s] See also ALLEY APPLE.

apple-squire (also **apron-squire**) **1.** a kept man. **2.** a pimp. [both senses, British, 1500s-1700s]

approachable 1. of easy morals; sexually easy. **2.** pertaining to a person who will take bribes.

appurtenances a woman's breasts. For synonyms see BOSOM. [U.S., 1900s]

apron-up pregnant in "have one's apron-up." Refers to the bulge of the abdomen. *Cf.* SHORT-SKIRTED. [British, late 1800s, Farmer and Henley]

ap-say an oaf; a dullard. Pig Latin for SAP (*q.v.*). [U.S., 1900s]

arbor vitae* "tree of life," the penis, especially when erect. *Cf.* STAFF OF LIFE. For synonyms see YARD. [Latin; British, 1700s-1800s]

ard hot; sexually aroused. From ARDOR (*q.v.*), possibly reinforced by HARD (sense 1). [British, 1600s-1800s]

ardor (also **ardour**) very strong lust; heated passion. [1300s-pres.]

area the pubic or genital area. *Cf.* PARTS, PLACE (sense 2). [U.S., mid 1900s-pres.]

areola the relatively darker area surrounding the nipple in humans. *Cf.* HALO. [since the early 1700s]

arf an arf 1. "half and half," lightly intoxicated with alcohol. For synonyms see WOOFLED. [early 1800s] **2.** an equal mixture of ale and porter. [British slang, 1800s]

arfarfanarf "half, half, and half," very drunk. [Cockney, late 1800s-early 1900s, Ware]

argle-bargle the throwing about of words; nonsense. [British, 1800s]

arm the penis. *Cf.* SHORT-ARM, SMALL-ARM. For synonyms see YARD. [U.S., mid 1900s-pres.]

armour a condom. For synonyms see EEL-SKIN. [late 1700s, Grose]

armour, in angry and fighting drunk; courageous due to liquor. *Cf.* POT-VALIANT. [British, 1600s-1700s, B.E.]

army form blank toilet paper. For synonyms see T.P. [British military, mid 1900s]

around the world a variety of sexual acts performed with the tongue and lips, including licking and sucking the penis, testes, and anus of a man, or licking the entire body. [originally prostitute's argot; U.S. slang, 1900s]

arousal sexual stimulation; sexual excitement or interest. Synonyms and related terms: CHARGE, CONCUPISCENCE, ERETHISM, FIRE, TENTIGO.

arouse to cause someone to become sexually interested, stimulated, or ready for copulation. *Cf.* AWAKEN THE LIBIDO.

arrange to castrate. [U.S. euphemism, 1900s]

arse (also **a-**, **-e**, **ars**, **a-s**) **1.** the posteriors or the anus. *Cf.* BOTTOM (sense 1). [since *c.* 1000, *Oxford English Dictionary*] **2.** the bottom of anything. [British dialects, 1800s and before] See also ASS.

arse-king a pederast, especially one who is notably proficient. For synonyms see SODOMITE. [British, early 1900s, *Dictionary of Slang and Unconventional English*]

arse-opener the penis. For synonyms see YARD. [British slang, 1800s, Farmer and Henley]

arse-rug trousers; breeches. For synonyms see GALLIGASKINS. [British, 1800s, Farmer and Henley]

arse-wedge the penis. For synonyms see YARD. [British, 1800s, Farmer and Henley]

arsey-versey (also **arsey-varsy**, **arsy-varsey**) topsy-turvy, head over heels. *Cf.* BASSACKWARDS. [British dialects, mid 1500s-pres.]

ars musica* the anus, specifically when it is crepitating, *i.e.*, when one is breaking wind. [a play on *ars musica*, Latin for "art of music"; British, 1700s, Grose]

arsworm (also **arseworm**) a small or insignificant fellow; an oaf. For synonyms see OAF. [British slang, 1600s, B.E.]

arsy-farcy ass-ended; vice-versa. *Cf.* ARSEY-VERSEY. [British colloquial, 1700s or before]

arsy-tarsy backwards; ass-ended; BASSACKWARDS (*q.v.*). *Cf.* ARSEY-VERSEY. [British]

artichoke 1. a debauched old woman, especially a hideous old prostitute. [underworld slang, 1800s-pres.] **2.** a hanging, *i.e.*, a "hearty choke." [British, 1800s]

article 1. a wench, woman, or prostitute. *Cf.* LEADING ARTICLE. [British, 1800s] **2.** a CHAMBER POT (*q.v.*). For synonyms see POT. [British, 1800s] See also ARTICLES.

article of virtue a virgin, usually said of a female. [British, mid 1800s, Farmer and Henley]

articles breeches, trousers, and possibly underwear. [British, late 1700s-1800s]

artillery man a drug addict who injects narcotics directly into a vein; one who shoots (drugs). [U.S. underworld and drug culture, mid 1900s-pres.]

art of pleasure the techniques of lovemaking; a euphemism for "copulation." *Cf.* DEED OF PLEASURE. [British, 1800s]

a-s "arse," the posteriors; the anus. *Cf.* ARSE, ASS. [British, mid 1700s]

asafetida (also **asafoetida**) the resinous gum of a plant having the odor and taste of garlic. *Cf.* DEVIL'S DUNG, RUMPITYFETIDA. [since the 1300s]

ashes marijuana. For synonyms see MARI. [U.S. drug culture, 1900s]

asleep in Jesus a euphemism for "dead." For synonyms see DONE FOR. [U.S., late 1800s-1900s]

aspro an experienced male homosexual, especially a pederast; a male homosexual prostitute. From "ass prostitute." *Cf.* ARSE-KING. [British slang, mid 1900s, *Dictionary of Slang and Unconventional English*]

ass 1. a donkey. Sometimes taboo in this sense. *Cf.* JOHNNY BUM. [since the 1200s, *Oxford English Dictionary*] **2.** the rectum, anus, or posteriors. For synonyms see DUFF. [U.S. from a British dialect variation, 1800s and long before] **3.** the female genitals; women considered sexually. [1800s-pres.] **4.** a fool; an oaf. See also ARSE.

ass!, My a vulgar oath and an exclamation; an expression of complete disbelief. [U.S., 1900s]

ass, on one's 1. depressed; broken; down-and-out. [U.S., 1900s] **2.** intoxicated with alcohol. [U.S., mid 1900s-pres.]

assault 1. to ravish or rape forcibly. A truncation of "sexual assault" or of "an assault with intent to commit rape." **2.** an act of forcible rape. These synonyms for both senses refer to women unless indicated otherwise; ANAGRIF, ATTACK, BREAK, CONSTUPRATE, DEBAUCH, MAN-RAPE (male), OUTRAGE, PLOW, RAVAGE, RAVISH, SHORT-ARM HEIST, SKIN-HEIST, STATUTORY OFFENSE.

ass-backwards in reverse; in an awkward or jumbled fashion. *Cf.* BACK-ASSWARDS, BASSACKWARDS. [U.S., mid 1900s-pres.]

asseroonie the anus; the posteriors. [U.S. slang, mid 1900s]

ass-fuck to copulate anally, usually between males. *Cf.* BUTT-FUCK. [U.S., mid 1900s-pres.]

ass-hammer a motorcycle with reference to the jolts suffered while operating it. [U.S., mid 1900s-pres.]

ass-hole 1. the anus. [since the 1400s or before] **2.** bad; rotten. [U.S., 1900s] **3.** a contemptible person. [U.S. slang, early 1900s-pres.] **4.** a very good pal or buddy. *Cf.* ASS-HOLE FRIEND. [U.S., mid 1900s-pres.]

ass-hole friend (also **ass-hole buddy**) a good friend or buddy. [U.S., mid 1900s-pres.]

assignation a rendezvous for illicit romance or sex with a lover or prostitute. Literally, "an appointment." [since the late 1600s]

assignation house 1. a place to meet for an illicit romance; any "house" or hotel where such meetings take place. **2.** a brothel. *Cf.* HOUSE OF ASSIGNATION. [primarily euphemistic, 1800s-1900s]

ass-kisser (also **ass-licker**) a sycophant; an A.K. (sense 1). *Cf.* ASS-SUCKER. [U.S. slang, early 1900s-pres.]

ass-man 1. a sexually active man; one who is able to SCORE (*q.v.*) frequently. For synonyms see LECHER. [U.S., early 1900s-pres.] **2.** a man who is sexually aroused by shapely feminine buttocks; a man who is attracted to a particular woman because of her shapely buttocks. [U.S., mid 1900s-pres.]

ass over head head over heels, especially when falling. *Cf.* ARSEY-VERSEY, TOPSY-TURVY. [U.S., 1800s, Green]

ass-peddler 1. a pimp; a procurer. [U.S., 1900s] **2.** a prostitute. [U.S., 1900s]

ass-sucker a sycophant; a BUM-SUCKER (*q.v.*). *Cf.* ASS-KISSER, EGG-SUCKER. [U.S., mid 1900s-pres.]

assteriors the buttocks. A blend of ASS and POSTERIORS (both *q.v.*). [U.S., 1900s] See also CATASTROPHE.

ass up mess up; BUGGER UP or FUCK UP (both *q.v.*). [U.S., 1900s]

ass-wipe 1. toilet paper. **2.** a real jerk; a sycophant; someone who would wipe someone else's anus if asked to. *Cf.* BUM-SUCKER. [both senses, U.S., 1900s].

assy uppity, overbearing, or brash. [U.S., early 1900s-pres.]

Athanasian wench a sexually loose woman; one who grants sexual favors to whoever asks. For synonyms see LAY. From the Athanasian Creed, which begins with the words, "Whosoever desires." [British, late 1700s, Grose]

athenaeum the penis. For synonyms see YARD. [British, late 1800s-early 1900s]

athletic supporter an undergarment designed to support and contain the VIRILIA (*q.v.*). A euphemism for JOCK-STRAP (*q.v.*). [U.S., 1900s]

at-need "at the time of death." Euphemistic funeral trade jargon pertaining to plans or purchases which must be made at death in contrast to those made before death. [U.S., mid 1900s]

attached pertaining to a person who is romantically or legally linked to another person. *Cf.* LOOSE (sense 1), UNATTACHED. [U.S. colloquial, 1900s]

attack a truncation of "sexual attack," usually meaning "rape." *Cf.* ASSAULT. [U.S., 1900s]

Auld Hornie 1. Satan. [Scots, 1700s-pres., (Robert Burns)] **2.** the penis. Not usually capitalized in this sense. [Scots, 1800s-1900s]

au naturel* 1. naked; nude; raw. Occasionally (and erroneously) "in the au naturel." *Cf.* NATURAL, IN THE. **2.** undoctored or untreated, as with undiluted liquor. [both senses, French, 1900s]

aunt 1. a prostitute, especially an old prostitute. [since the early 1600s] **2.** the madam of a brothel; a procuress. [slang, 1900s] **3.** an aged sodomist. [U.S., 1900s] **4.** an aged fellator. *Cf.* AUNTIE. [U.S., 1900s, Goldin, O'Leary, and Lipsius] **5.** the woman's restroom, especially "the aunt." *Cf.* UNCLE (sense 1).[slang, 1900s]

Aunt Emma morphine. Based on the letter "M." *Cf.* MISS EMMA. [U.S. drug culture, mid 1900s]

Aunt Hazel heroin. *Cf.* H.[U.S. drug culture, mid 1900s-pres.]

auntie an elderly homosexual male. Also a homosexual male past his prime period of desirability. [U.S. homosexual use, 1900s]

Auntie Nelly the stomach or abdomen. Rhyming slang for "belly." [British, 1900s, *Dictionary of Rhyming Slang*]

Aunt Jane a black woman who is a traitor to her race; a black woman who adopts aspects of a Caucasian lifestyle. Based on UNCLE TOM (*q.v.*). [U.S., mid 1900s]

Aunt Tom a woman who does not cooperate with or who works against Women's Liberation movements. Based on UNCLE TOM (*q.v.*). [U.S., mid 1900s]

Aussie Wuzzie a dark-skinned person native to New Guinea. [Australian, 1900s]

awaken the libido to arouse sexually. [euphemistic]

awash intoxicated with alcohol. For synonyms see WOOFLED. [1900s]

away from one's desk a phrase sometimes meaning that an office worker has gone to the W.C. [U.S., mid 1900s-pres.]

awkward euphemistic for "pregnant," especially applicable in the later months of pregnancy. For synonyms see FRAGRANT. [colloquial, 1800s-1900s]

awry-eyed intoxicated with alcohol; cockeyed drunk. *Cf.* HOARY-EYED, ORIE-EYED. [U.S. slang, early 1900s]

Aztec two-step diarrhea, specifically that contracted in Mexico or South America. *Cf.* MONTEZUMA'S REVENGE, TOURISTAS. For synonyms see QUICKSTEP. [U.S., mid 1900s-pres.]

B

B. "Benzedrine" (trademark), an amphetamine. For synonyms see BENZ. [U.S. drug culture, mid 1900s-pres.]

babe a term of endearment for a woman. *Cf.* BABY (sense 2). [U.S. slang, early 1900s-pres.]

babe of love an illegitimate child; a bastard. [euphemistic, early 1700s]

baboon an oaf or a jerk. Especially in the expression "big baboon." [British and U.S., 1900s]

baby 1. marijuana. [U.S. drug culture, mid 1900s-pres.] **2.** a woman or a girlfriend. *Cf.* BABE. [U.S. slang and colloquial, early 1900s-pres.] **3.** a homosexual male. From sense 2. [U.S. underworld, early 1900s, Montelone] **4.** a prostitute's customer. [British, 1900s, *Dictionary of the Underworld*]

baby-bound pregnant. *Cf.* BOUND (sense 1). For synonyms see FRAGRANT. [U.S. slang, early 1900s]

baby-juice semen. For synonyms see METTLE. [recurrent nonce; attested as British slang, 1800s]

baby-maker 1. the penis. **2.** the female genitals. [both senses, slang, 1800s-1900s]

baby pillows the breasts. *Cf.* PILLOWY. [U.S. slang or colloquial, 1900s]

bachelor-mother an unwed mother. [U.S. slang, mid 1900s, Wentworth and Flexner]

bachelor's baby (also **bachelor's son**) an illegitimate child. *Cf.* SON OF A BACHELOR. [since the late 1700s]

bachelor's wife 1. a real or imagined "perfect wife." **2.** a prostitute. **3.** a mistress. For synonyms see LAY. [all senses, U.S., 1900s]

back a privy. A truncation of BACKHOUSE (*q.v.*). *Cf.* BACKY, REAR. [British, 1800s]

backasswards backwards; pertaining to something done very badly. From ASS-BACKWARDS (*q.v.*). *Cf.* BASSACK-

WARDS. [U.S. slang and colloquial 1900s]

backdoor 1. the anus in anal intercourse. *Cf.* BACK-DOOR WORK. **2.** the anus in general. [both senses, U.S. 1900s]

back-door trots (also **back-door trot**) diarrhea. Refers to the use of the back door to get to the privy or refers to the anus. See BACKDOOR (sense 2). The plural form is most prevalent in the U.S., analogous to other terms for diarrhea. For synonyms see QUICKSTEP. [British and U.S., 1800s-1900s]

back-door trumpet the anus considered as a musical instrument in the breaking of wind. *Cf.* ARS MUSICA. [British, mid 1800s, *Dictionary of Slang and Unconventional English*]

back-door work PEDERASTY (*q.v.*). *Cf.* BACK-DOOR (sense 1). [cant of slang, 1800s-1900s]

backed-up intoxicated with drugs. For synonyms see TALL. [U.S. drug culture, mid 1900s-pres.]

backgammon-player the INSERTOR (*q.v.*) in pederasty. Refers to entry from the back. This and the previous entry may also refer to a harlot who "plays" on her "back." [British, late 1700s]

backhouse a privy. *Cf.* BACK, BACKY. [U.S. colloquial, mid 1800s-1900s]

back in circulation 1. single after being divorced. **2.** available again after a broken engagement or other broken commitment. [U.S. slang, 1900s]

back-land the buttocks. *Cf.* BACKSIDE. [since the 1600s]

back-parts the posteriors; the buttocks. *Cf.* PARTS BELOW, UNDERPARTS. [U.S. euphemism, 1800s]

back-scuttle (also **back-scull**) **1.** PEDERASTY (*q.v.*). **2.** to commit pederasty **3.** to coit woman from the rear, presumably anally. *Cf.* SCUTTLE. [al senses, British, 1800s, *Dictionary of Slang and Unconventional English*]

backside the buttocks. In some parts of the world euphemistic, and in others extremely vulgar. [since the 1500s]

back-staircase a bustle. [slang, mid 1800s]

back-talk. 1. an impertinent remark; sauciness. [U.S., 1900s or before] **2.** flatulence; a release of intestinal gas. For synonyms see GURK. [U.S. jocular colloquial, 1900s]

back-up serial copulation of one female with a number of males. [Australian, mid 1900s, *Dictionary of Slang and Unconventional English*]

back-way the anus; the anus in anal copulation. *Cf.* BACKDOOR. [U.S., early 1900s]

backy a privy. *Cf.* BACK. [U.S. colloquial, 1900s and before]

bacon a country bumpkin; a rustic oaf. [from *Henry IV*, Part One (Shakespeare)]

bad blood 1. anger. **2.** syphilis. See BAD DISEASE. [British euphemism, early 1900s, *Dictionary of the Underworld*]

bad disease (also **foul disease**) syphilis. [British and U.S. euphemism, late 1800s-1900s]

bad disorder a veneral disease, probably syphilis. [U.S., 1800s, Green]

bad egg a rotten fellow. [British and U.S., mid 1800s-pres.]

badger a smelly prostitute; a low whore. For synonyms see HARLOT. [British slang, 1800s, Farmer and Henley]

bad nigger a Negro who refuses to accept the stereotypical role which U.S. society is alleged to have given him. For related subjects see NIGGER. [U.S. black use, mid 1900s-pres.]

bad shape, in 1. injured or debilitated in any manner. **2.** pregnant. From sense 1. [U.S. slang, 1900s] **3.** intoxicated with alcohol. From sense 1. [U.S. slang, 1900s]

bad shit 1. a rotten person, usually a male. *Cf.* SHIT (sense 9). [U.S. slang, 1900s] **2.** bad luck. Possibly from

"bad shot." *Cf.* TOUGH SHIT! [U.S., 1900s]

bad-time to be unfaithful to one's spouse or lover. [U.S. slang, mid 1900s-pres.]

bad trip 1. a bad experience with drugs. **2.** any bad experience. From sense 1. [U.S. drug culture and general slang, mid 1900s-pres.]

bag 1. an udder or a breast. See BAGS (sense 2). [colloquial, mid 1500s] **2.** a low and despicable person. A truncation of DOUCHE BAG (*q.v.*). [U.S. slang, 1900s] **3.** an old hag; any old woman. Usually "old bag." **4.** a prostitute, especially an old one. Probably from sense 3. *Cf.* BAGNIO. [British and U.S. slang and colloquial, late 1800s-pres.] **5.** the female genitals. [U.S. slang, mid 1900s] **6.** the scrotum. For synonyms see TOOL BAG. [colloquial and nonce, 1900s and certainly long before] **7.** a condom. *Cf.* BAGGIE, JO-BAG, JOY-BAG. [U.S., 1900s] **8.** a contraceptive diaphragm. [U.S., 1900s, Wentworth and Flexner] **9.** a sexual talent or preference. See WHAT'S YOUR BAG? **10.** a quantity or package of drugs. [U.S. drug culture, mid 1900s-pres.]

bag ass to depart in a hurry. *Cf.* BARREL ASS, CUT ASS, DRAG ASS, HAUL ASS, SHAG ASS. [U.S. slang, mid 1900s-pres.]

baggage 1. a flirtatious young woman. **2.** a prostitute; a woman of bad character. For synonyms see HARLOT. [both since the late 1600s, B.E.]

bagged 1. pregnant. [since the 1400s] **2.** intoxicated with alcohol. [U.S. slang, 1900s]

baggie a condom. From the trademarked name of a food packaging product. *Cf.* BAG (sense 7), SCUMBAG (sense 1). For synonyms see EEL-SKIN. [U.S. slang, 1900s]

bag lady a female narcotics pusher. *Cf.* BAG-MAN. [U.S. drug culture, mid 1900s-pres.]

bagman 1. a tramp. From the bundle with which he travels. [Australian,

1800s, Baker] **2.** a seller of marijuana or illicit drugs. From the bags or packages in which drugs are sold. *Cf.* BAG (sense 10), SWING MAN. **3.** any racketeer. [U.S. underworld, early 1900s-pres.]

bagnio a brothel. Originally a Turkish bath. *Cf.* STEWS, THE. [since the early 1600s]

bag of tricks the male genitals, especially the scrotum. *Cf.* PAWPAW TRICKS. [British, 1800s and nonce elsewhere]

bagpipe **1.** an act of PENILINGUS (*q.v.*). According to Grose, "a lascivious practice too indecent for explanation." **2.** to perform an act of PENILINGUS (*q.v.*). *Cf.* FLUTE, PICCOLO, SILENT FLUTE. [British, late 1700s] **3.** the penis. *Cf.* BAG (sense 6), PIPE (sense 1). [nonce]

bags **1.** trousers. *Cf.* HAM-BAGS, RICE-BAGS. [British and U.S., mid 1800s-1900s] **2.** the breasts. *Cf.* BAG (sense 1). [since the late 1500s]

bag-shanty a brothel. *Cf.* BAG (sense 4), BAGNIO. [British naval slang, 1900s]

bait **1.** a sexually attractive young woman; bed bait or JAIL BAIT (*q.v.*). [British and U.S., mid 1900s] **2.** an effeminate male or a masculine female who draws attention from homosexuals. For synonyms see FRIBBLE. [U.S., 1900s, Wentworth and Flexner]

baked intoxicated with drugs. *Cf.* FRIED (sense 2). [U.S. drug culture, mid 1900s-pres.]

baker a bitch; a bastard. An elaboration of Baker, which is the "phonetic" name for "B" in international signalling. *Cf.* S.O.B. [U.S. military, World War II]

balcony **1.** a protruding bosom. [Australian, early 1900s, *Dictionary of Slang and Unconventional English*] **2.** protruding buttocks. [U.S., 1900s]

balderdash **1.** adulterated wine; a jumbled mix of different types of alcoholic drink. [1600s-1800s] **2.** nonsense. From sense 1. [since the late 1600s]

bald-headed hermit the penis. This

"hermit" lives in a CAVE (sense 1), the vagina. *Cf.* HERMIT. [British, 1800s, Farmer and Henley]

bald-headed mouse the penis. From the "baldness" of the glans. [U.S., mid 1900s]

bale a pound or kilogram of marijuana. Literally, "a full bale of marijuana." [U.S. drug culture, mid 1900s-pres.]

ball **1.** a testicle. See BALLS. For synonyms see WHIRLYGIGS. **2.** to copulate. [both senses, British and U.S. slang, mid 1900s-pres.] **3.** to absorb narcotics through the mucous membranes of the genitals. [U.S. drug culture, mid 1900s-pres.]

ball and chain **1.** a wife or sweetheart. The woman who restrains a man. For synonyms see WARDEN. [British and U.S., 1900s] **2.** marriage. From sense 1. **3.** a tramp's catamite. From sense 1. [U.S. underworld, early 1900s, Montelone]

ball-bearing mousetrap a tomcat. A play on "ball-bearing." *Cf.* BALLS (sense 1). [mid 1900s]

ball-buster (also **ball-breaker, ball-wracker**) **1.** a difficult task. **2.** the person who assigns difficult tasks; a hard taskmaster. **3.** a sexually attractive woman. **4.** a castrating woman. [all senses, U.S. slang, mid 1900s-pres.]

ball-dozed intoxicated with liquor. A play on BULL-DOZED (*q.v.*). [Australian, mid 1900s, Baker]

ball-face a derogatory term for a Caucasian, used by Negroes. For synonyms see PECKERWOOD. [attested as U.S. (Salem, Mass.), 1810-1820, Farmer and Henley]

ballix a mess; a messed-up or balled-up situation. See BALL UP. *Cf.* BALLOCKS.

ballock (also **ballick, ballok, balluk, balok**) **1.** a testicle. See BALLOCKS. **2.** to coit a woman. See BALL (sense 2). [British slang, 1800s-1900s]

ballock-cod the scrotum. *Cf.* BALLOCKS, COD. [mid 1400s]

ballocker a lecher; a whoremonger. [British colloquial, 1800s]

ballock-naked stark naked with the genitals uncovered, said of both males and females. *Cf.* STARK-BALLOCK-NAKED. [British, 1900s or before]

ballocks (also **ballicks, balloks, balluks, ballux, bolaxe, bollix, bollocks, bolloks, bollox**) **1.** the testicles of a man or animal. For synonyms see WHIRLYGIGS. **2.** the scrotum and its contents. [senses 1 and 2 since *c.* 1000] **3.** a nickname for a whoremonger. [British, 1800s] **4.** an exclamation, "Ballocks!"; the same as BALLS (sense 4), an expression of surprise or disbelief. [primarily British and Australian with U.S. dialect use]

ballocky naked. *Cf.* BALLOCK-NAKED. [British, early 1900s, *Dictionary of Slang and Unconventional English*]

ball off to masturbate, said of a male. From BALL (sense 2). For synonyms see WASTE TIME. [primarily British, 1900s]

balloon 1. a condom. *Cf.* BAGGIE, SCUMBAG. [U.S. slang, 1900s] **2.** a bag or toy balloon used for carrying heroin or other drugs. [U.S. drug culture, mid 1900s-pres.]

balloon juice 1. soda water. [British slang, late 1800s, Ware] **2.** nonsense; the same as GAS (sense 2). For synonyms see ANIMAL. [U.S., since 1900]

balloon room a room where marijuana is smoked. From the elevated feeling experienced. [U.S. drug culture, mid 1900s-pres.]

balloons the breasts. [U.S. slang, 1900s]

balls 1. the testicles. For synonyms see WHIRLYGIGS. **2.** courage; virility. [both senses, U.S., 1900s or before] **3.** masculine behavior in a female. **4.** "nonsense" when used as an exclamation, "Balls!" *Cf.* BALLOCKS (sense 4). [senses 3 and 4 are U.S., 1900s] Disguises: COBBLER'S AWLS, COBBLER'S STALLS, COFFEE STALLS.

balls and bat the male genitals; the same as BAT AND BALLS (*q.v.*). *Cf.* STICK AND BANGERS. [U.S. euphemism, early 1900s-pres.]

Balls to you! a curse and a rude

exclamation. *Cf.* ORCHIDS TO YOU!, TESTICLES TO YOU! [British, 1800s-1900s]

balls-up (also **ball-up**) a mess. *Cf.* BALLIX, BALL UP. Ball-up is the U.S. form. [British slang, early 1900s-pres.]

ballsy (also **ballsey**) courageous. Derogatory or jocular when directed to women. *Cf.* BALLS (sense 2). [U.S. slang, mid 1900s-pres.]

ball up (also **balls up**) **1.** a man's underwear flap. Also **ball-lap.** [British dialects, *c.* 1600, Halliwell] **2.** to confuse; to mess up. **3.** a mess; a confused situation. Usually hyphenated in this sense. [senses 2 and 3 are primarily U.S., 1900s]

bally 1. BLOODY (*q.v.*). [British euphemism, early 1800s-1900s] **2.** exceedingly; very. Essentially the same as sense 1. [1900s]

ballyhack (also **ballywack**) perdition; hell. [U.S. slang, 1800s, Wentworth]

ballyhoo (also **bally hooey**) overstated and unwarranted praise or promotion; nonsense. Said to be named for "Ballyhooly," County Cork, Ireland. The "bally" is probably from BALLY (sense 1), and "hoo" is "whole." *Cf.* HOOEY (sense 1). [slang, late 1800s-pres.]

balmy 1. crazy; giddy and aloof. [colloquial, 1900s or before] **2.** intoxicated with alcohol. [U.S. slang, mid 1800s-pres.]

baloney (also **bologna, boloney**) **1.** a woman of loose morals. [U.S. underworld, early 1900s, Goldin, O'Leary, and Lipsius] **2.** nonsense. [senses 1 and 2 are U.S., mid 1900s-pres.] **3.** the penis. From its shape. *Cf.* LIVE SAUSAGE, SAUSAGE (sense 1). [U.S. slang, 1900s]

bam 1. a mixture of barbiturates and amphetamines. **2.** amphetamines. [both senses, U.S. drug culture, mid 1900s-pres.]

bambalacha marijuana. For synonyms see MARI. [U.S. drug culture, mid 1900s]

bamboo an opium pipe in expressions such as SUCK BAMBOO (*q.v.*). [U.S. drug culture, 1900s]

bamboozled intoxicated with alcohol. [U.S. slang and colloquial, mid 1800s-pres.]

banana 1. a sexually attractive mulatto or light black woman. From the yellow color. *Cf.* YELLOW (sense 1). [U.S. slang, mid 1900s] **2.** the penis in expressions such as "have one's banana peeled." [slang and nonce, 1800s-1900s]

band 1. a woman of easy morals; a prostitute. *Cf.* BELT (sense 3). [British and U.S., early 1900s] **2.** a brothel. [Australian, mid 1900s, Baker]

bandage a sanitary napkin; a PERINEAL PAD (*q.v.*). For synonyms see MANHOLE COVER. [widespread jocular colloquial; attested as British, 1800s, Farmer and Henley]

B. and B. "breast and buttock," pertaining to magazines featuring female nudity. *Cf.* T. AND A. [U.S. slang, mid 1900s]

B. and D. "bondage and discipline," a form of sadism and masochism. See BONDAGE, SADISM. [U.S. slang, mid 1900s-pres.]

band-house 1. a brothel. Also **band-box.** *Cf.* BAND. [British slang, 1900s] **2.** a prison. [U.S. underworld, early 1900s, Berrey and Van den Bark]

bandit a sadistic homosexual male. *Cf.* LEATHER (sense 2), WOLF (sense 3). [U.S. slang, mid 1900s-pres., Wentworth and Flexner]

bang 1. narcotics in general. [U.S. drug culture, mid 1900s-pres.] **2.** an injection of a narcotic; a puff of a marijuana cigarette. *Cf.* HIT (sense 2). [U.S. drug culture, early 1900s-pres.] **3.** to inject narcotics intravenously. [U.S. underworld and drug culture, early 1900s-pres.] **4.** "Damn!" [U.S. euphemism, early 1900s] **5.** a brothel. [Australian, early 1900s, Baker] **6.** to coit a woman; to copulate. For synonyms see OCCUPY. **7.** an act of human copulation. [senses 6 and 7 are British and U.S. slang, 1900s]

bang a reefer to smoke a marijuana cigarette. *Cf.* BANG (sense 2). [1900s]

bangers the testicles. See STICK AND BANGERS, WHIRLYGIGS.

bang room a room where drugs are used. *Cf.* BALLOON ROOM. [U.S. underworld, early 1900s]

bangster 1. a sexually loose woman; a prostitute. *Cf.* BANG (sense 7). [British, 1800s] **2.** one who injects drugs. Modeled on "gangsters." [U.S. underworld, early 1900s, Rose]

banji marijuana. Said to be a word from an African language. [U.S. drug culture, mid 1900s-pres.]

banjo a bedpan. From its shape. *Cf.* DUCK. [mid 1800s]

bank 1. a privy, the place where one makes a DEPOSIT (sense 2). For synonyms see AJAX. [U.S. slang, 1900s] **2.** the female genitals. *Cf.* DEPOSIT (sense 1). [British slang, 1800s]

banner the female pubic hair. For synonyms see DOWNSHIRE. [British slang or nonce, 1800s, Farmer and Henley]

baptized 1. drowned. [Australian, early 1800s] **2.** pertaining to adulterated liquor. [U.S. slang, early 1900s] **3.** saturated with alcohol; intoxicated with alcohol. [U.S. slang or nonce, mid 1900s]

barb a barbiturate tablet or capsule. Usually in the plural. [U.S. drug culture, mid 1900s-pres.] Synonyms and related terms: BLOCK-BUSTER, BLUNT, CANDY, CHRISTMAS TREE, COURAGE PILLS, DOUBLE-TROUBLE, DOWNER, FENDER-BENDER, GANGSTER PILLS, G.B., GOOF-BALL, GOOFER, GORILLA PILLS, GREEN DRAGON, HORS D'OEUVRES, IDIOT PILLS, KING KONG PILLS, MARSHMALLOW REDS, MEXICAN RED, PEANUT, PHENNIES, PINK LADY, PURPLE HEART, RED AND BLUE, SECONAL, SLEEPER, STUM, STUMBLER, THRILL PILLS, TUIE.

barbecue an attractive female; a woman who looks good enough to EAT (*q.v.*). *Cf.* GOOD-EATING, TABLE-GRADE. [U.S. slang, early 1900s-pres.]

barber's chair a common prostitute who is used by all customers. *Cf.* BICYCLE, FERRY. [early 1600s-1800s]

bare-assed 1. naked; completely nude

with the buttocks uncovered. **2.** immature; pertaining to a young male whose buttocks are not hairy. *Cf.* HAIRY-ASSED. [both senses, U.S. slang, 1900s]

bareback pertaining to an act of copulation performed without a condom. *Cf.* ROUGH-RIDING. [U.S. slang, 1900s, Wentworth and Flexner]

bare-naked naked. [U.S. colloquial, 1900s]

barepoles naked. "Poles" refers to the legs.

barf 1. to vomit. For synonyms see YORK. **2.** vomit. [both senses, U.S. colloquial, mid 1900s-pres.]

bar-fly a drunkard, especially one who lingers around bars. [U.S. colloquial, early 1900s-pres.]

barge-arse 1. markedly protruding buttocks. **2.** a nickname for a person with markedly protruding buttocks. [both senses, British, 1800s]

bark a derogatory term for an Irishman. For synonyms see HARP. [British, mid 1800s]

barely broth (also **barley juice, barley water**) beer. *Cf.* OIL OF BARLEY. [British and U.S. slang, late 1700s-pres.]

barley-corn beer or ale. See JOHN BARLEYCORN. [British dialect, 1800s or before]

barleycorn sprints diarrhea caused by drinking whisky. *Cf.* JOHN BARLEYCORN. [colloquial, 1900s and before]

barnacle 1. a prostitute. For synonyms see HARLOT. [U.S. underworld, early 1900s, Goldin, O'Leary, and Lipsius] **2.** a pickpocket. [cant, mid 1800s]

barnyard smutty; obscene. Refers to the dung found in barnyards. [U.S., 1900s or before]

barrack-hack a soldier's prostitute; a camp follower. [British, 1800s]

barrel 1. to drink to excess; to consume "barrels" of drink [U.S. slang, 1900s] **2.** the drug L.S.D. (*q.v.*). [U.S. drug culture, mid 1900s-pres.]

barrel ass to move or drive carelessly and rapidly. *Cf.* BAG ASS, DRAG ASS,

HAUL ASS, SHAG ASS. [U.S. slang or colloquial, 1900s]

barreled-up (also **barreled**) intoxicated with alcohol. *Cf.* BARREL (sense 1). [U.S. slang, 1900s]

barrel-fever 1. intoxication with alcohol. **2.** a HANGOVER (*q.v.*). **3.** the DELIRIUM TREMENS (*q.v.*). For synonyms see ORK-ORKS. **4.** a name for the cause of death when a lethal dose of alcohol has been ingested. [widespread, 1800s-1900s] .

barrel-house bum a beggar-drunkard. [U.S., mid 1900s]

barrel-house drunk heavily intoxicated with alcohol. [U.S. slang, early 1900s]

barren 1. sterile. [standard English] **2.** the vagina of an animal. [British colloquial dialect, 1800s or before, Halliwell]

baseballing the use of FREE BASE (*q.v.*), a form of pure cocaine. See BALL (sense 3). [U.S. drug culture, late 1970s-pres.]

base-begotten child a bastard; an illegitimate child. [U.S. colloquial, 1900s or before]

base-son a bastard. [British dialect, 1800s or before, Halliwell]

bash, on the involved in prostitution as a prostitute. [British military, 1900s, *Dictionary of Slang and Unconventional English*]

basher a lecher; a fornicator. [British, early 1900s, *Dictionary of Slang and Unconventional English*] See also CANDLE-BASHER.

Basimecu! (also **Bozzimacoo!**) "Kiss my ass!" [from the French *baise mon cul*, British since the 1600s]

basket 1. the stomach, as in BREAD-BASKET (*q.v.*). [U.S., 1900s] **2.** the female genitals. *Cf.* BOX (sense 2), PANNIER. [U.S. slang, 1900s, Montelone] **3.** the male genitals considered as a package; the bulging shape of the VIRILIA (*q.v.*) when contained in any garment constructed like an athletic supporter. [U.S. homosexual use, mid 1900s-pres.] **4.** the scrotum or the scrotum and its contents. [U.S. slang, 1900s]

basket days warm weather when clothing revealing the outline of the male genitals is likely to be worn. See BASKET (sense 3). [U.S. homosexual use, mid 1900s-pres., Farrell]

basket for days a catch phrase describing large male genitals. Based on MEAT FOR DAYS (*q.v.*). *Cf.* MENTULATE. [U.S. homosexual use, mid 1900s-pres.]

basket-making copulation. For synonyms see SMOCKAGE. [British, late 1700s, Grose]

bassackwards (also **basackwards, bassackards**) done the wrong way. Based on "ass backwards." *Cf.* ASSBACKWARDS, BACKASSWARDS. [U.S. colloquial and slang, early 1900s-pres.]

bastard 1. a child born of unlawful sexual intercourse; a child conceived in haste, *e.g.*, on a bed-roll or packsaddle, (French *bast*). [since the 1200s, *Oxford English Dictionary*] **2.** a despicable male or any male buddy. [U.S. slang, 1900s or before]

basted 1. intoxicated with alcohol. Refers to having liquid poured over oneself. For synonyms see WOOFLED. [U.S. slang, early 1900s-pres.] **2.** drug intoxicated. From sense **1.** *Cf.* BAKED, FRIED (sense 2). For synonyms see TALL. [U.S. drug culture, mid 1900s-pres.]

bastrich a curse and a nickname for a despised person. A blend of "bastard" and "bitch" modeled on "ostrich." [U.S., 1900s or before]

bat 1. a low prostitute; one who moves about at night. *Cf.* NIGHT-HAWK. [British and U.S., 1800s-pres.] **2.** any unattractive young woman. For synonyms see BUFFARILLA. [U.S. slang, 1900s] **3.** a drunken spree. [U.S. slang, mid 1800s-1900s] **4.** a drunkard. [U.S. slang, 1900s, Wentworth and Flexner] **5.** to masturbate. From "batchelor." For synonyms see WASTE TIME. [U.S. dialect (Boontling), late 1800s-early 1900s, Charles Adams] **6.** the penis,

especially the erect penis. [U.S. slang, early 1900s-pres.] **7.** in the plural, crazy.

bat and balls (also **balls and bat**) the VIRILIA (*q.v.*). [U.S. slang and nonce, 1900s]

batch (also **bach**) to live alone or in the company of one's own sex, originally said of males. From "bachelor." [late 1800s-pres.]

bath 1. a BATHROOM (*q.v.*) regardless of the presence or absence of bathing facilities. The essential piece of equipment in a bathroom is a water-flush toilet bowl. [U.S., 1900s or before] **2.** "hell" in "Go to Bath!" [British colloquial, 1800s]

bathroom a W.C., a small room set aside for elimination, bathing, and personal grooming. The primary function of the bathroom is to provide privacy. A bathroom in a public building is usually referred to as a restroom. The term bathroom is most often used in the home by the family members and is out of place in public. [colloquial]

bathroom basin (also **bathroom bowl**) **1.** the water-flush toilet bowl. **2.** the lavatory basin. [both senses, U.S. euphemisms, 1900s]

bathroom roll (also **bathroom tissue**) toilet paper. *Cf.* LAVATORY ROLL. [U.S. advertising euphemism, mid 1900s-pres.]

bathtub gin homemade gin. From prohibition times. [U.S., early 1900s]

batshit nonsense. A variation of BULLSHIT (*q.v.*). [U.S. slang, mid 1900s-pres.]

batted intoxicated with alcohol. For synonyms see WOOFLED. [U.S. slang, 1900s, Berrey and Van den Bark]

batter to coit a woman. *Cf.* CANE (sense 1). [British, 1900s, *Dictionary of Slang and Unconventional English*]

battered intoxicated with alcohol. [U.S. slang, mid 1800s-pres.]

battering-piece the penis, especially when erect. [British slang, 1800s, Farmer and Henley]

battle-axe a mean old lady; the stereotypical mother-in-law. *Cf.* WAR-HORSE. [U.S., early 1900s-pres.]

bauble (also **bawble**) **1.** the penis. [from *Romeo and Juliet* (Shakespeare)] **2.** a testicle. See BAUBLES.

baubles (also **bawbels, bobbles**) the testicles. *Cf.* BOBBLES. For synonyms see WHIRLYGIGS.

bauffe to belch. *Cf.* BARF. [British dialect, 1800s or before, Halliwell]

bawd (also **baud**) a male or female keeper of a brothel. Originally a procurer, later a MADAM (sense 3). [since the 1300s]

bawdry (also **baudy**) **1.** bad or obscene language. [British, 1800s, Halliwell] **2.** illegal copulation. [mid 1400s-1600s]

bawdy **1.** to make dirty; to defile. [obsolete, 1300s] **2.** lewd; obscene. [since the early 1500s]

bawdy basket **1.** a member of one of the orders of thieves in England in the 1500s. Usually women who sold obscene materials from innocent-looking cloth-covered baskets. [cant, mid 1500s] **2.** a prostitute. [cant, late 1500s]

bawdyhouse (also **bawd's house**) a brothel. [since the 1600s]

bayonet the penis. [British slang, 1800s, Farmer and Henley]

bazoo **1.** a jeer; a raspberry [U.S. slang, 1900s] **2.** the female genitals, especially the vagina. For synonyms see MONOSYLLABLE. [U.S. slang, mid 1900s-pres.] See also WAZOO.

bazooms (also **bazoom**) the human breasts. From BOSOM (*q.v.*). [U.S. slang, mid 1900s-pres.]

bazoongies (also **bazongas**) the human breasts, especially if large and shapely. For synonyms see BOSOM. [U.S. slang, mid 1900s-pres.]

B.B. **1.** a "bloody bastard." [British, 1900s] **2.** a "blue bomber," a ten-milligram tablet of Valium (trademark). [U.S. drug culture, mid 1900s-pres.]

B-B-brain an oaf; a person with a brain the size of shot. [U.S. slang, mid 1900s]

B.C. "birth control," usually in the form of conception control. [U.S., 1900s] Specific terms for birth control devices or methods: BIRTH CONTROL, COIL, COITUS INTERRUPTUS, CONTRACEPTION, DIAPHRAGM, FAMILY PLANNING, I.C.U.D., I.U.D., JELLY, LOOP, PILL, PUSSY BUTTERFLY, RHYTHM METHOD, RING, RUBBER, RUBBER RING, SANITARY SPONGE, SHOWER-CAP, TABLET, VATICAN ROULETTE. See EEL-SKIN for condom synonyms.

B./D. "bondage and discipline." Activities involve restraint and domination of an individual by another, producing sexual gratification in one or both. *Cf.* B. AND D. [U.S., mid 1900s-pres.]

B.D.T.s "back-door trots," diarrhea. [colloquial, 1800s-1900s]

bead-puller (also **bead-counter**) a derogatory term for a Roman Catholic. [colloquial, 1800s-1900s]

beak the penis. *Cf.* STROP ONE'S BEAK. [British slang, 1800s, Farmer and Henley]

beam the buttocks or hips, especially if wide. *Cf.* KEEL. [colloquial, 1800s-pres.]

beaming intoxicated with marijuana. For synonyms see TALL. [U.S. drug culture, mid 1900s-pres.]

bean **1.** a capsule or tablet of Benzedrine (trademark), an amphetamine. [U.S. drug culture, mid 1900s-pres.] **2.** as an exclamation, "Bean!" meaning "Damn!" [U.S., early 1900s] **3.** a derogatory term for a Mexican. See also BEANER. [U.S. slang, mid 1900s-pres.] **4.** the hymen. *Cf.* CHERRY (sense 1). [U.S. slang, early 1900s, Goldin, O'Leary, and Lipsius] Synonyms for sense **4:** BUG, CHERRY, CLAUSTRUM VIRGINALE, FLOWER, MAIDEN GEAR, MAIDENHEAD, MAID'S RING, ROSE, TAIL-FEATHERS, THAT, TOY, VIRGINAL MEMBRANE, VIRGINHEAD, VIRGIN-KNOT. **5.** the penis. *Cf.* BEAN-TOSSER. [British, 1900s or before] **6.** a PEYOTE BUTTON (*q.v.*). [U.S. drug culture, mid 1900s-pres.] **7.** in the plural, nonsense. See BEANS.

bean-eater 1. a Bostonian. From "Boston baked beans." **2.** a derogatory term for a Mexican, especially a poor Mexican. [both senses, U.S., 1900s and before]

beaner (also **bean**) a derogatory term for a Mexican or a Mexican-American. From BEAN-EATER (*q.v.*). [U.S. slang, 1900s]

beanhead an oaf. From the small size of the brain. [U.S. slang, early 1900s-pres.]

beans nothing; nonsense. As in the expression "That's not worth beans!" [U.S., mid 1800s-pres.]

bean-tosser the penis. *Cf.* BEAN (sense 5). [British slang, 1800s, Farmer and Henley]

bear 1. a difficult task. [U.S. slang, mid 1900s-pres.] **2.** an ugly woman. [U.S. slang, mid 1900s-pres.]

beard the female pubic hair. For synonyms see DOWNSHIRE. [since the 1600s if not before]

beard-jammer a whoremonger. [U.S. underworld, early 1900s, Irwin]

beard-splitter. 1. a whoremonger. *Cf.* WHISKER-SPLITTER. For synonyms see LECHER. [cant, late 1600s-1700s] **2.** the penis. [cant, 1800s or before]

bearskin the female public hair. *Cf.* TWAT-RUG. [British slang, 1800s, Farmer and Henley]

beast 1. a low prostitute. *Cf.* ANIMAL (sense 7). [U.S., early 1900s, Goldin, O'Leary, and Lipsius] **2.** an ugly woman. [U.S. slang, mid 1900s-pres.] **3.** a Caucasian. For synonyms see PECKERWOOD. [U.S. black use, 1900s] **4.** the drug L.S.D. (*q.v.*). [U.S. drug culture, mid 1900s-pres.]

beast with two backs a man and a woman copulating. [from *Othello* (Shakespeare)]

beat moll a streetwalker. [U.S. underworld, early 1900s]

beat off to masturbate, said of a male. For synonyms see WASTE TIME. [U.S. slang, mid 1900s-pres.]

beat the bishop to masturbate. Com-

pare the shape of the glans penis to a bishop's miter. *Cf.* BOX THE JESUIT AND GET COCKROACHES, POLICEMAN'S HELMET. [U.S. underworld, early 1900s, Goldin, O'Leary, and Lipsius]

beat the dummy to masturbate, said of a male. *Cf.* DUMMY (sense 3). [U.S. slang, 1900s]

beat the gun (also **jump the gun**) to copulate with one's intended spouse before marriage. [British and U.S. colloquial and nonce, 1900s or before]

beat the meat (also **beat one's meat**) to masturbate, said of a male. *Cf.* POUND THE MEAT. [U.S. slang, 1900s]

beat the pup to masturbate, said of a male. For synonyms see WASTE TIME. [U.S., early 1900s]

beat the shit out of to strike very hard; to beat some sense into someone. [U.S., 1900s]

beausom large and well-proportioned breasts. A blend of "beautiful" and "bosom." [U.S. slang, 1900s, Berrey and Van den Bark]

beauts large and well-proportioned breasts, as in the expression "two beauts." *Cf.* T.B. (sense 2). [U.S. slang, mid 1900s]

beauty parlor a brothel thought of as a parlor full of beauties who are prostitutes. [U.S. slang, early 1900s, Montelone]

beauty-spot 1. the female genitals. [British slang, 1800s, Farmer and Henley] **2.** a mole or a wart. [euphemistic, 1900s or before]

beaver 1. the female pubic region. From the fur of a beaver and a play on a nickname for a beaver, "flat tail." [U.S., early 1900s-pres.] **2.** the female genitals, specifically the vagina. [U.S. slang, early 1900s-pres.] **3.** any woman. From sense 2. [primarily citizens band radio slang; U.S., mid 1900s-pres.]

beaver base a brothel. *Cf.* BEAVER (sense 3). [U.S. citizens band radio slang, mid 1900s-pres.]

beaver den a woman's home; the place where a woman citizens band radio operator lives. [U.S. citizens band radio slang, mid 1900s-pres.]

beaver-flick a pornographic film featuring sexual activity with women. *Cf.* BEAVER. [U.S. slang, mid 1900s-pres.]

beaver hunt (also **beaver patrol**) keeping a lookout for women while traveling; watching for women drivers, especially those whose skirts are pulled up while they drive. [U.S. citizens band radio slang, mid 1900s-pres.]

beaver pose a picture of a woman, usually nude or partially nude, with her legs spread in a manner that will expose her genitals. See BEAVER (sense 1). [1900s]

beaver-shot a view, possibly a photograph of a woman's pubic area. *Cf.* BEAVER POSE. [U.S. slang, mid 1900s-pres.]

become a lady to begin the menses; to reach the MENARCHE (*q.v.*). [colloquial, 1900s or before]

become ill to vomit; to become sick. [U.S. euphemism]

bed 1. to take a woman to bed and copulate with her. *Cf.* CHAMBER (sense 1), COUCH. [since the 1500s] **2.** afterbirth. [1600s]

Bedad! a mild oath and an exclamation, "By God!" and "By Dad!" or "By Gad!" [British and U.S., early 1700s-1900s]

bed-bunny (also **bed-bug**) a woman easy to get into bed. *Cf.* CONY, CUDDLE-BUNNY. [U.S. slang, mid 1900s]

bed faggot (also **bed fagot**) a bedfellow, male or female. Sometimes refers to a prostitute. See FAGGOT (senses 1-5). [British; mid 1800s]

bed-fellow (also **bed-mate**) **1.** any person with whom one shares a bed. **2.** a concubine. [since the late 1400s]

bed-glass a chamber pot; the same as NIGHT-GLASS (*q.v.*). For synonyms see POT. [Caribbean (Jamaican) and elsewhere, Cassidy and Le Page]

bed-house a place where beds can be rented for copulation; a brothel. [British and U.S., late 1800s-1900s]

bedpan 1. a device for collecting wastes from bedridden patients. [1900s or before] **2.** a sexually easy woman. A reinterpretation of sense 1. See PAN (sense 2). [slang or nonce, 1900s]

bed-presser a whoremonger; a fornicator. [from *Henry IV*, Part One (Shakespeare)]

bed-rite copulation. For synonyms see SMOCKAGE. [1600s]

bed-time story coition. *Cf.* DO THE STORY WITH. [U.S. slang, 1900s]

bedworthy pertaining to a desirable woman or one who is sexually aroused for copulation. *Cf.* FUCKABLE, FUCKSOME, PUNCHABLE, ROMPWORTHY, SHAFTABLE. [British, early 1900s, *Dictionary of Slang and Unconventional English*]

Beecham's Pills the testicles. Rhyming slang for "testi-kills." From the name of a patent medicine. [British, 1800s, *Dictionary of Rhyming Slang*]

beef 1. the female genitals; women considered sexually; a prostitute. *Cf.* MEAT (sense 2). [since the 1600s, (Shakespeare)] **2.** the penis. *Cf.* MEAT (sense 4), MUTTON (sense 5). [slang and nonce, 1800s-1900s] **3.** any large and muscular male. [colloquial, mid 1800s-pres.] **4.** to coit a woman. [U.S. slang, mid 1900s-pres.] **5.** a popular and sexually attractive young woman. *Cf.* MUTTON (sense 4). [U.S. slang, mid 1900s-pres.]

beefcake 1. a display of the male physique, usually in photographs; a well-built or muscularly handsome male. Based on CHEESE CAKE (senses 1 and 2). *Cf.* BEEF (sense 3). **2.** a male on display in some degree of undress. [both senses, U.S., mid 1900s-pres.]

beef-head an oaf; a MEATHEAD (*q.v.*). For synonyms see OAF. [colloquial, 1700s-1900s]

beef-hearts beans. Because they cause intestinal gas. Rhyming slang for "farts," breakings of wind. See BREAK WIND. [British, 1800s]

beefsteak a prostitute who works for a pimp. *Cf.* BEEF (sense 1), based on "grubstake." [British, early 1900s,

Dictionary of Slang and Unconventional English]

beef-witted (also **beef-headed**) oafish, stupid, and bovine. *Cf.* BEEF-HEAD. [primarily British; late 1500s-1800s]

bee-hive the female genitals. *Cf.* HONEY, HONEY-POT. [British slang, 1800s, Farmer and Henley]

been at an Indian feast intoxicated with alcohol. [U.S., early 1700s, Ben Franklin]

been had 1. cheated. 2. deflowered. [both senses, U.S. slang and colloquial, 1900s]

been in the sun intoxicated with alcohol. For synonyms see WOOFLED. [late 1800s, Ware]

been in the sun too long crazy. For synonyms see DAFT. [colloquial, 1900s]

been playing tricks pregnant. *Cf.* BAG OF TRICKS, PAW-PAW TRICKS. [British slang, 1800s]

been there 1. experienced sexually, said of a woman. 2. experienced in general, said of either sex. [both senses, 1800s-pres.]

been to France intoxicated with alcohol. [U.S. slang, early 1700s, Ben Franklin]

beerified intoxicated with alcohol. For synonyms see WOOFLED. [U.S. slang, 1900s, Berrey and Van den Bark]

beer-jerker 1. a tippler; a drunkard. For synonyms see ALCHY. [U.S. slang, mid 1800s, Farmer and Henley] 2. a bartender. Based on "soda jerk" and "tear-jerker." [U.S. slang, 1900s, Berrey and Van den Bark]

beerslinger 1. a bartender. [U.S. slang, late 1800s] 2. a beer-drinker. [slang, late 1800s-1900s]

beer-swiper a drunkard. For synonyms see ALCHY. [Australian, Baker]

beery (also **beer, in**) intoxicated with alcohol. [since the mid 1800s]

beetle a loose girl; a sexually loose woman. *Cf.* BUG (sense 3). [U.S. slang, 1900s]

beetle-brain an oaf; a stupid person with a small brain. [U.S., 1900s]

beetle-head a dull oaf. *Cf.* BEETLE-BRAIN. [British and U.S. slang, early 1800s-1900s]

beeveedees men's underwear. See B.V.D. For synonyms see NETHER GARMENTS. [U.S., 1900s]

befuddle to intoxicate with alcohol. See FUDDLED. [U.S. slang and colloquial, 1900s and before]

beggar to BUGGER (sense 4) in the oath "I'll be beggared!" [British euphemism, 1800s, Farmer and Henley]

begonias the breasts. For synonyms see BOSOM. [U.S. euphemism, 1900s]

Begorra! (also **Begorry!**) "By God!" An oath and an exclamation. Also FAITH AND BEGORRA! [Anglo-Irish, British, and U.S., 1800s-1900s]

Begosh! an oath and an exclamation, "By God!" From "By gosh!" Also **Begosh and begolly!** [U.S. colloquial, late 1800s]

Begum! an oath and an exclamation, "By God!" From "By Gum!" [colloquial, 1800s]

behind the posteriors. The first syllable is usually accented. [colloquial since the 1700s or before]

behind-door work copulation, especially that among the household servants. [from *A Winter's Tale* (Shakespeare)]

behind the cork intoxicated with alcohol. Patterned on "behind the eight-ball." [U.S. slang, 1900s]

beige a mulatto. For synonyms see MAHOGANY. [U.S., 1900s or before]

Bejesus! (also **Begaises!, Bejabers!, Bejaises!, Bejazus!, Bejazuz!**) an oath and an exclamation. From "By Jesus!" Also in the expression "beat the Bejesus out of." [British and U.S., late 1800s-1900s]

belch 1. to bring up stomach gas. [since *c.* 1000] 2. an eructation; a burp; an upwards release of stomach gas. [since the late 1500s] Synonyms for both senses: BERP, BREAK WIND UP-

WARDS, BRING UP GAS, BURP, ERUCT, ERUCTATE, GROWL, GRUNT, MAKE A RUDE NOISE, REPROVE, RETURN, RIFT, RUCT. **3.** beer, especially inferior beer. For synonyms see SUDS. [since the late 1600s]

belch-guts a drunkard. For synonyms see ALCHY. [British and U.S. slang, 1800s]

Belgeek a Belgian. *Cf.* GEEK (sense 1). [from the French pronunciation *Belgique;* British and U.S., World War II]

bell-bastard the illegitimately-born child of an illegitimately-born mother. Possibly dub-bell (double) bastard (Farmer and Henley). [British, 1800s]

belle (also **bell**) **1.** an attractive young woman. [since the early 1600s] **2.** an attractive, effeminate homosexual male. [U.S. homosexual use, 1900s]

bell-end the glans penis. From its shape. *Cf.* BELL-ROPE, BELL-TOPPED, BLUNT-END. For synonyms see HEAD. [British, 1900s, *Dictionary of Slang and Unconventional English*]

bell-rope the penis. *Cf.* BELL-END. [U.S. slang, mid 1900s-pres.]

bell-topped pertaining to a penis with a large glans penis. [British slang, 1800s, Farmer and Henley]

belly 1. the abdomen or a large paunch. [since the 1500s] Synonyms: ABDOMEN, ALVUS, AUNTIE NELLY, BASKET, BAY WINDOW, BINNY, BREADBASKET, DEEP CHEST, ELLY-BAY, EPIGASTRIUM, GUT-BUCKET, GUTS, LITTLE MARY, MIDDLE, MIDSECTION, NED KELLY, SHITBAG, SHIT LOCKER, TABLE-MUSCLE, TUMMY, TUM-TUM, VENTER. **2.** a person's guts or intestines. [U.S., 1900s] **3.** the penis. *Cf.* LAP. [attested as U.S. (New York), early 1900s]

bellyache 1. a stomachache; the colic. [since the mid 1500s] **2.** to complain. [widespread colloquial, late 1800s]

belly-bound constipated. [since the mid 1600s]

belly-bristles the female pubic hair. *Cf.* BELLY-THICKET, BELLY-WHISKERS. [British slang, 1800s, Farmer and Henley]

belly-bumper a lecher; a whoremonger. [late 1600s]

belly-bumping coition. For synonyms see SMOCKAGE. [1600s, (Urquhart)]

belly-button the navel. [U.S. colloquial, 1800s-1900s]

belly-cork the navel. [colloquial, 1900s or before]

belly-dale (also **belly-dingle, belly-entrance**) the female genitals. [British slang, 1800s. Farmer and Henley]

belly-full pregnant, as in "have a belly-full." [colloquial, 1700s-1800s]

belly-naked completely nude. [1500s]

belly-piece (also **belly-lass**) a mistress or a concubine. [British, early 1600s]

belly-plea the plea of pregnancy by a female felon on trial. [cant, late 1700s-early 1800s]

belly-ride an act of copulation. [U.S. slang, 1900s or before, Read]

belly-thicket the female pubic hair. *Cf.* BELLY-BRISTLES, BELLY-WHISKERS. [British slang, 1800s, Farmer and Henley]

belly to belly copulating; in the act of copulation. [U.S., 1900s]

belly-up (also **bellied-up**) pregnant. [British and later, U.S. colloquial, 1600s-1900s]

belly-warmer an act of copulation. [British colloquial, 1800s, Farmer and Henley]

belly-wash 1. weak or inferior liquor or any liquor. [British and U.S. slang, 1800s-pres.] **2.** lemonade; any sweet, nonalcoholic or noncarbonated drink. [British and U.S. slang and colloquial, late 1800s-1900s]

belly-whiskers the female pubic hair. *Cf.* BELLY-BRISTLES, BELLY-THICKET. For synonyms see DOWNSHIRE. [British slang, 1800s, Farmer and Henley]

belongings trousers. For synonyms see GALLIGASKINS. [U.S. euphemism, 1800s, Farmer and Henley]

below the belt pertaining to a blow to the pubic area or groin. [euphemistic, 1900s]

belsh beer and ale. As if one were saying "belch" while under the influence of alcohol. *Cf.* BELCH (sense 3). For synonyms see SUDS. [British slang, 1600s, B.E.]

belswagger 1. a pimp. **2.** a whoremonger; a lecher. A truncation of "bellyswagger." [both senses, late 1500s]

belt 1. to coit, said of the male. [British, 1800s] **2.** an act of copulation. [British, 1900s or before, *Dictionary of Slang and Unconventional English*] **3.** a prostitute *Cf.* BELTER, ENDLESS BELT. [Australian, 1900s, Baker] **4.** a marijuana cigarette. **5.** the CHARGE (sense 1) from narcotics or from a marijuana cigarette. [senses 4 and 5 are U.S. drug culture, 1900s] **6.** a drink or shot of alcohol. [U.S. slang and colloquial, 1900s]

belted 1. intoxicated with alcohol. *Cf.* BELT (sense 6). For synonyms see WOOFLED. **2.** intoxicated with drugs or marijuana. *Cf.* BELT (sense 5). For synonyms see TALL. [both senses, U.S., 1900s]

belter a prostitute. *Cf.* ENDLESS BELT. [British dialect, 1800s or before, Halliwell]

belt the grape to drink heavily. Refers to the grapes from which wine is made. [U.S. slang, mid 1900s]

bemused intoxicated with alcohol. From a word meaning "confused." [slang, 1700s-1800s]

bend down for to position oneself for and submit to anal copulation. *Cf.* BEND ONE OVER. [since the 1800s]

bender 1. a drunken binge. [U.S. colloquial, early 1800s-pres.] **2.** a catamite. For synonyms see BRONCO. [U.S. underworld, early 1900s, Goldin, O'Leary, and Lipsius]

bend one over to position someone for pederasty; to dominate or humiliate someone, usually said of a male. *Cf.* BEND DOWN FOR. [U.S. underworld, early 1900s, Goldin, O'Leary, and Lipsius]

benny (also **bennie**) **1.** a Benzedrine (trademark) tablet or capsule. [U.S. slang and drug culture, early 1900s] **2.** a state of intoxication from Benzedrine (trademark); the same as BENNY JAG (*q.v.*). [U.S. slang, mid 1900s-pres.]

benny jag intoxication from Benzedrine (trademark). *Cf.* JAG (sense 5). [U.S. slang, mid 1900s]

bent 1. intoxicated with alcohol. Also **bent out of shape.** *Cf.* CURVED. [U.S., early 1800s-1900s] **2.** drug or marijuana intoxicated. From sense 1. [U.S. drug culture, mid 1900s-pres.] **3.** homosexual; pertaining to a homosexual male. The opposite of STRAIGHT (sense 2). Reinforced by the positioning for pederasty. *Cf.* BEND DOWN FOR, BENDER (sense 2). [U.S. slang, mid 1900s-pres.]

benz Benzedrine (trademark), an amphetamine. [U.S. drug culture, mid 1900s-pres.] Synonyms: BEAN, BENNY, BROTHER BEN, CO-PILOT BEN, HI-BALL, PEP PILL, WHITES.

berk (also **birk**) the female genitals. For synonyms see MONOSYLLABLE.

Berkeley Hunt (also **Berkeley, Sir Berkeley, Sir Berkeley Hunt**) **1.** the female genitals. Rhyming slang for "cunt." *Cf.* BERKSHIRE HUNT, BIRK, LADY BERKELEY. **2.** a fool or an oaf; a CUNT (sense 4). [both senses, British, 1800s-pres.]

berker a brothel. *Cf.* BERK. [British military slang, World War II]

berks (also **berkeleys, burks**) the human breasts. For synonyms see BOSOM. [said to be from a Gypsy word, *berk* or *burk*, (Farmer and Henley); British, 1800s]

Berkshire Hunt 1. the female genitals. Rhyming slang for "cunt." *Cf.* BERKELEY HUNT. **2.** a fool. *Cf.* CUNT FACE, JOE ERK, JOE HUNT. For synonyms see OAF. [both senses, British, 1800s, *Dictionary of Rhyming Slang*]

bernice (also **bernies, burnese**) cocaine. Sometimes capitalized. [U.S. underworld and drug culture, 1900s]

berp (also **burp**) an (upward) release of stomach gas; a belch. See BURP. [U.S. colloquial, 1900s or before]

berps (also **burps**) alcoholic liquor. *Cf.* BERP-WATER. [U.S. slang, 1900s]

berpwater beer, ale, and sometimes champagne; the same as BERPS (*q.v.*). Because it causes belching.

berries the testicles. *Cf.* JINGLE-BERRIES. For synonyms see WHIRLYGIGS. [U.S. slang, 1900s, Berrey and Van den Bark]

Bessie Smith nonsense. A reinterpretation of B.S., *i.e.*, BULLSHIT (both *q.v.*). [U.S. euphemism, mid 1900s-pres.]

best and plenty of it coition from the female point of view. *Cf.* IT (sense 3). [British slang, 1800s, Farmer and Henley]

best leg of three the penis. *Cf.* MIDDLE LEG, THIRD LEG. [British slang, 1800s]

best piece 1. one's girlfriend. **2.** one's wife. [both senses, U.S. slang, mid 1900s-pres.]

betray to seduce a woman. [euphemistic and old]

better half one's wife; the majority, more than one-half of the marital union. *Cf.* BITTER HALF. [colloquial since the late 1500s]

Betty a homosexual male. For synonyms see ETHEL. [U.S. slang, mid 1900s]

betwattled confused; stupefied by love. A play on "bemused" and "twat." *Cf.* TWAT (sense 1). [British, late 1700s, Grose]

between the sheets (also **between the sheet**) in the act of copulating. *Cf.* SHEETS. [from *Much Ado About Nothing* (Shakespeare)]

Beulahland (also **Beulah**) heaven or a peaceful resting place on the way to heaven. [Biblical (Isaiah); U.S. colloquial, 1900s and before]

bevvy (also **bevie**, **bevy**, **bivvy**) **1.** beer. From "beverage." **2.** to drink; to drink beer. [both senses, British and U.S. slang, 1900s]

bewitched intoxicated with alcohol. [U.S. slang, early 1700s-pres.]

Beyond, the (also **Great Beyond, the**) heaven; death; the afterlife. [U.S. euphemism, late 1800s-pres.]

bezzle (also **beezzle**) to drink greedily. [British dialect, early 1600s]

bezzler a tippler; a drunkard. *Cf.* BEZZLE. [late 1500s]

B.F. 1. a "blood fool." [British, 1900s] **2.** a "boyfriend." [U.S., 1900s]

B'Gawd! an oath and exclamation, "By God!" [U.S. colloquial (eye-dialect), early 1900s]

B-girl a "bar-girl" who solicits drinks from male customers. **2.** a semiprofessional prostitute who works in bars. **3.** a nickname for any sexually promiscuous woman. [all senses, U.S. slang, 1900s]

B.H. "bloody hell" in oaths and curses. [British, 1900s]

bhang 1. the leaves and stems of the marijuana plant; Indian hemp. Usually a liquid extract of marijuana, which is drunk. [since the mid 1500s] **2.** any commonly available marijuana. [U.S. drug culture, mid 1900s-pres.] See also BONG (sense 2).

bhang ganjah marijuana. *Cf.* GANJAH. [U.S. drug culture, mid 1900s-pres.]

bhong See BONG (sense 2).

bi a BISEXUAL (*q.v.*) person. Someone capable of homosexual or heterosexual acts. [U.S. slang, mid 1900s-pres.]

bibble to drink often or much; to tipple. [late 1500s, *Oxford English Dictionary*]

bibble-babble nonsense; idle talk. For synonyms see ANIMAL. [colloquial and nonce, late 1800s-pres.]

bibbler a tippler; a drunkard. *Cf.* BIBBLE. [mid 1500s]

Bible-pounder (also **Bible-banger, Bible-basher, Bible-puncher, Bible-thumper**) a clergyman; a chaplain. For synonyms see SKY-PILOT. [colloquial and slang, 1800s-1900s]

bicho the penis. [from Spanish; U.S. slang, mid 1900s-pres.]

bicycle a prostitute; something to RIDE (sense 2). *Cf.* BARBER'S CHAIR, FERRY.

[British slang, early 1900s, *Dictionary of Slang and Unconventional English*]

biddy 1. an Irish woman; an Irish maidservant. [since the 1800s] **2.** a young wench. [British, late 1700s, Grose]

bidet a basin which will support a woman's body in a sitting position so that the pubic area can be cleaned with the water. [from the French name for a small pony, 1700s-pres.]

bier a coffin or a stand for displaying a coffin. Occasionally used in error for "corpse." [since *c*. 1000, *Oxford English Dictionary*]

biffer a sexually loose woman. For synonyms see LAY. [attested as "rare," (Wentworth and Flexner), possibly nonce; U.S., 1900s]

biffy (also **bif**) **1.** a W.C. [British and U.S. slang, 1900s] **2.** intoxicated with alcohol. A variant of BUFFY (*q.v.*). [British slang, 1900s, *Dictionary of Slang and Unconventional English*]

big animal a euphemism for "bull." [U.S. rural colloquial, 1800s-1900s]

bigass big, important, or overly important. [U.S. slang, mid 1900s]

big bloke cocaine. Rhyming slang for "coke." [U.S. underworld and drug culture, early 1900s-pres.]

big brown eyes the breasts. The EYES (*q.v.*) are the nipples. For synonyms see BOSOM. [U.S. slang, early 1900s-pres.]

big-C. 1. cancer. [U.S., mid 1900s-pres.] **2.** cocaine. *Cf.* C. (sense 1). [U.S. drug culture, mid 1900s-pres.]

big chief MESCALINE (*q.v.*). [U.S. drug culture, 1900s]

big-D. 1. Dilaudid (trademark) tablets, an analgesic taken as a RECREATIONAL DRUG (*q.v.*). [U.S. drug culture, mid 1900s-pres.] **2.** the drug L.S.D. (*q.v.*). [U.S. drug culture, mid 1900s-pres.] **3.** damn. [euphemistic, 1800s-1900s]

big-H. heroin. *Cf.* BIG-C. (sense 2). [U.S. drug culture, mid 1900s-pres.]

big Harry heroin; the same as HARRY

(*q.v.*). A reinterpretation of BIG-H. (*q.v.*). [U.S. drug culture, mid 1900s-pres.]

big-headed 1. pertaining to a person with a hangover. [British and U.S., 1800s-pres.] **2.** vain; conceited. [U.S. colloquial, mid 1900s-pres.]

big hit 1. dung; an act of defecation. **2.** a wretched man. Rhyming slang for "shit." [both senses, Australian, 1900s, *Dictionary of Rhyming Slang*]

big-O. opium. *Cf.* BIG-C., BIG-H. [U.S. drug culture, mid 1900s-pres.]

big one a bowel movement (compared to urination). For synonyms see EASEMENT. [U.S. juvenile, 1900s]

big potty a bowel movement. *Cf.* BIG ONE. [U.S. juvenile, 1900s]

big shit 1. an exclamation of surprise or disbelief, "Big shit!" *Cf.* SHIT (sense 8). [U.S. slang, mid 1900s] **2.** a dysphemism for "big shot." [U.S. slang, mid 1900s]

big time copulation (compared to petting and kissing). For synonyms see SMOCKAGE. [U.S. slang, mid 1900s-pres.]

big-time operator a big shot; a lecher; a real HUSTLER (sense 5). [U.S. slang, mid 1900s-pres.]

big twenty 1. a twenty-dollar fee for a prostitute. **2.** a promiscuous female; a prostitute. *Cf.* GUINEA-HEN. [both senses, U.S. slang, mid 1900s-pres.]

big with child pregnant. Based on GREAT WITH CHILD (*q.v.*). For synonyms see FRAGRANT. [U.S. colloquial, 1900s]

bike a sexually loose woman. *Cf.* BICYCLE. [Australian, 1900s, Baker]

biled owl (also **boiled owl**) a drunkard. *Cf.* BOILED AS AN OWL, DRUNK AS A BOILED OWL. [U.S., late 1800s-1900s]

bilge 1. nonsense; the equivalent of BULLSHIT (*q.v.*). From "bilge water." **2.** to talk boastfully; to BULLSHIT (*q.v.*). [both senses, British and U.S. nautical, 1900s and before]

bim 1. a sexually loose girl. *Cf.* BIMBO (sense 1). For synonyms see LAY.

[U.S. slang, early 1900s-pres.] **2.** the posteriors. *Cf.* BOM, BUM (sense 1). [Scots, 1900s, *Dictionary of Slang and Unconventional English*]

bimbo 1. a young woman or a girl. [U.S. slang, 1900s] **2.** a sexually loose woman. [U.S. slang, early 1900s] **3.** the female genitals. Probably a variant of BUMBO (sense 1). [British, mid 1900s, *Dictionary of Slang and Unconventional English*] **4.** a woman considered sexually. [British and U.S., 1900s] **5.** a tramp's catamite. For synonyms see BRONCO. [Australian, mid 1900s, Wilkes]

bimmy a prostitute, especially a habitually drunken one. *Cf.* BIM (sense 1), BIMBO (sense 2). [U.S. underworld, early 1900s, Goldin, O'Leary, and Lipsius]

bimph toilet paper. *Cf.* BUMF. [British slang, 1800s]

bindle-boy a tramp's CATAMITE (*q.v.*); a young BINDLE-MAN (*q.v.*); a young hobo. For synonyms see BRONCO. [U.S. underworld, early 1900s, Goldin, O'Leary, and Lipsius]

bindle-man a tramp; a "bundle-man."

bindle-stiff 1. a hobo who carries a bundle or bedroll; the same as BLANKET-STIFF (*q.v.*). [U.S. slang, early 1900s] **2.** a drug addict. From sense 1. [U.S. underworld, 1900s]

binge a drunken spree. From a British dialect term meaning "soak." [slang, late 1800s-pres.]

binged intoxicated with alcohol; having been on a BINGE (*q.v.*). Rhymes with "cringed." [U.S. slang, early 1900s, Rose]

bingle 1. a drug-peddler. **2.** drugs; a large supply of drugs. [both senses, U.S. underworld, 1900s]

bingo brandy; any alcoholic drink. Possibly a (linguistic) blend of "brandy" and "stingo." [originally cant; since the 1600s]

bingo-boy a drunkard. For synonyms see ALCHY. [slang since the 1800s]

bingoed intoxicated with alcohol, having drunk too much BINGO (*q.v.*). [British and U.S., early 1900s]

bing-room a dope den; a place where drugs are consumed illicitly. *Cf.* BANG ROOM. [U.S. underworld, early 1900s, Irwin]

bingy the penis. One of many diminutives for the male member. [attested as Anglo-Irish juvenile (nursery), 1800s-1900s, *Dictionary of Slang and Unconventional English*]

binny (also **bingy**) the stomach; the belly. [Australian and U.S. juvenile colloquial, 1900s or before, Wentworth]

bint 1. a young woman or girlfriend. *Cf.* GIPPY BINT. **2.** a prostitute. [World War I] **3.** to girl; to seek a woman for sexual purposes. [all are from the Arabic word for "girl" or "daughter"; all senses, British and U.S., World War I]

bip-bam-thank-you-ma'am pertaining to a rapid and unemotional sexual encounter. *Cf.* WHAM-BAM-THANK-YOU-MA'AM. [U.S. slang, 1900s or before]

bird 1. a girl or woman. [in various senses, occasionally derogatory, since the 1300s] Synonyms: ANKLE, BABE, BABY, BACHELOR-GIRL, BAGGAGE, BAIT, BARBECUE, BEAVER, BEEF, BEETLE, BEST PIECE, BIDDY, BIM, BIMBO, BINT, BIRDEEN, BITCH, BIT OF JAM, BIT OF MUSLIN, BIT OF SKIN, BLINT, BOB MY PAL, BONNET, BRABUSTER, BRIDE, BROAD, BROAD BOD, BROOD, BRUSH, BUFF, BUNCH OF CALICO, BUTTERCUP, CABBAGE, CANARY, CHARLEY WHEELER, CHERRY, CHERRY PIE, CHICK, CHICK-A-BIDDY, CHICKEN, CHIPPY, COVER GIRL, CRACK, DELL, DISH, DOBASH, DOE, DOLL, FAIRY, FEMME, FILLY, FLAPPER, FLOOSEY, FOX, FRILL, FRISGIG, GAL, HUNK OF HEAVEN, MINI-SKIRT, MOUSE, MUFF, MUFFET, OCEAN PEARL, PIECE, SQUIRREL, SWEET YOUNG THING, TART, TIT, TITTER, TITTY, TOMATO, TWIRL, TWIST, TWIST AND TWIRL, WENCH. For terms for sexually loose women see LAY. **2.** the penis. A play on COCK (sense 3). [slang, 1800s-pres.] **3.** the female genitals. A play on COCK (sense 6). [U.S. slang, 1900s] **4.** the FINGER (*q.v.*); a particular obscene gesture made with the middle finger. *Cf.* FLIP THE BIRD. [U.S. slang, mid 1900s-pres.] **5.** a Bronx cheer. [U.S. slang, mid 1900s-pres.] **6.** a prostitute. [British slang, 1800s, Farmer and Henley] **7.** any odd person, as in "odd bird." [U.S. slang, 1900s]

birdcage 1. a bustle. See DRESS-IMPROVER. [British and U.S. slang, mid 1800s-1900s] **2.** a brothel. *Cf.* BIRD (sense 6). [U.S. underworld, early 1900s, Montelone]

birdie a homosexual male. From BIRD (sense 1, 6, or 7). [U.S. slang, early-mid 1900s, Rose]

birdie stuff any kind of powdered drug. For synonyms see COTICS. [U.S. drug culture, early 1900s, Berrey and Van den Bark]

birds and the bees the details of human sexual reproduction; sexual reproduction as explained to a child. [U.S., 1900s]

bird seed nonsense. An elaboration of B.S. *i.e.,* BULLSHIT (both *q.v.*). [U.S. slang, early 1900s, Weseen]

bird's-eggs the testicles. For synonyms see WHIRLYGIGS. [British slang, 1800s, Farmer and Henley]

bird's-nester a lecher; a whoremonger. [British, 1800s]

bird-taker a sodomite. [U.S. underworld, early 1900s, Montelone]

bird-turd 1. nonsense. Based on BULLSHIT (*q.v.*). *Cf.* COWSH, FROGSH. **2.** to BULLSHIT (*q.v.*); to talk nonsense. [both senses, U.S., 1900s]

bird-washing CUNNILINGUS (*q.v.*); mutual cunnilingus. *Cf.* BIRD (sense 3). [U.S. homosexual use, mid 1900s-pres., Farrell]

birdwood marijuana. For synonyms see MARI. [U.S. slang, mid 1900s-pres.]

birk an oaf; a dullard. Rhyming with "jerk." *Cf.* BERK, BERKELEY HUNT. [U.S. slang, mid 1900s-pres.]

birthday suit nakedness; one's bare skin. The term is from the name of a suit worn for the king's birthday cele-

bration (early 1700s). *Cf.* SUNDAY SUIT. [since the late 1700s]

birth-naked nude; naked as at birth. [colloquial, 1900s and before]

biscuit a sexually loose woman or a prostitute. *Cf.* BUN (sense 4), CAKE (sense 3). For synonyms see LAY. [U.S. slang, mid 1900s, Rose]

biscuit, in the 1. in the head. **2.** in the anus. *Cf.* BUN (sense 2). [both senses, U.S. slang, early 1900s]

bisexual 1. pertaining to a HERMAPHRODITE (*q.v.*). [medical] **2.** ambisexual. *Cf.* BI. **3.** a homosexual who is also capable of orthogenital intercourse. *Cf.* BI. [U.S. slang and colloquial, mid 1900s-pres.]

bish 1. a bishop. **2.** a ship's clergyman. [both senses, 1900s]

bishop 1. a large condom used as a package to carry other condoms. *Cf.* BALLOON. [British, late 1700s, Grose] **2.** a CHAMBER POT (*q.v.*). For synonyms see POT. [British slang, 1800s, Farmer and Henley] **3.** a bustle. [U.S. slang, mid 1800s]

bit 1. the female genitals. **2.** copulation. **3.** women considered sexually. [all senses, primarily British slang, 1800s-1900s, Farmer and Henley]

bitch 1. a female dog. No negative connotations. [since *c.* 1000, *Oxford English Dictionary*] Synonyms: BRACHE, DOGGESS, DOG'S LADY, DOG'S WIFE, LADY-DOG, PUPPY'S MAMMA, SHE-DOG. **2.** a derogatory term for a woman. The derogation comes from comparing a woman to a female dog in heat and suggesting that the woman acts out of carnal lust. Refers primarily to sexual appetite. [since the 1400s] **3.** a derogatory term for a male; a "dog." [British, 1500s-1700s] **4.** a blatant or BITCHY (*q.v.*) male homosexual. [U.S. homosexual use, mid 1900s-pres.] **5.** a derogatory term for any woman; a woman with vicious tendencies; any rude woman. Refers primarily to temperament. For synonyms see BUFFARILLA. [U.S. slang, 1900s] **6.** a prostitute. See BITCHERY. [colloquial, 1900s and before] **7.** the queen at cards and at chess. [U.S., 1900s] **8.** to womanize; to whore. [British slang, 1800s, Farmer and Henley] **9.** to complain. [U.S. slang, mid 1900s-pres.] **10.** one who complains or is in a BITCHY (*q.v.*) mood, either a male or a female. [U.S. slang, mid 1900s-pres.] **11.** a difficult thing or person. [U.S. slang, 1900s] **12.** a CATAMITE (*q.v.*). From sense 5. [U.S. underworld, early 1900s, Monte-lone] **13.** copulation. [British slang, 1800s, Farmer and Henley] **14.** to botch something up; to mess it up. [U.S., 1900s] **15.** a "bitch lamp," a can of grease with a wick. [U.S., early 1900s]

bitch's blind a wife or girlfriend who is a "cover" for the sexual activities of a homosexual male. *Cf.* BITCH (sense 4). [U.S. homosexual use, 1900s]

bitch session an informal gathering where people air their grievances. [U.S., mid 1900s-pres.]

bitchy 1. pertaining to a mood wherein one complains incessantly about anything. Although this applies to men or women, it is usually associated with women, especially when they are menstruating. **2.** sexy; in the manner of a dog in heat. [U.S. slang, 1900s] **3.** spiteful, hateful, and rude. [widespread, 1900s]

bite 1. the female genitals. [British, late 1600s] **2.** a rascal; a rogue. For synonyms see SNAKE-HORN. [British, late 1600s, B.E.] **3.** a fool; an oaf; a dupe. Perhaps like a fish which bites the bait. [Australian, early 1900s, Baker]

biter a woman who is so sexually aroused that her genitals are "ready to bite her a-se" (Grose). "A-se" is ARSE (*q.v.*). [British, late 1700s]

bite the dust to die. *Cf.* KISS THE DUST. [originally U.S. slang and colloquial, late 1800s-pres.]

bit for the finger a digital investigation of a woman's vagina. *Cf.* FINGER-FUCK, TIP THE MIDDLE FINGER. [British, 1800s, *Dictionary of Slang and Unconventional English*]

bit of black velvet copulation with a black woman. Also refers to an Australian aborigine woman. *Cf.* BLACK VELVET. [British military, late 1800s, *Dictionary of Slang and Unconventional English*]

bit of blink any alcoholic beverage. Rhyming slang for "drink." [British slang, late 1800s, Ware]

bit of brown pederasty. *Cf.* BROWN (sense 1), "anus." [British, 1800s, *Dictionary of Slang and Unconventional English*]

bit of cauliflower copulation. *Cf.* CAULIFLOWER. [British slang, 1800s]

bit of ebony a nickname for a Negro or a Negress. No sexual connotation. *Cf.* EBONY. [British slang, 1800s, Farmer and Henley]

bit of fish an act of copulation. *Cf.* FISH (sense 1). [British slang, 1800s]

bit of flat copulation. *Cf.* FLAT COCK. [British slang, 1800s, Farmer and Henley]

bit of front-door work copulation. [primarily British slang, 1800s]

bit of goods a woman considered sexually. For synonyms see TAIL.

bit of hair copulation. *Cf.* AFTER HAIR, HAIR. [British slang, 1800s, Farmer and Henley]

bit of hard (also **bit of stiff**) **1.** the erect penis. For synonyms see ERECTION. **2.** copulation from the female point of view. [both senses, British slang, 1800s]

bit of hard for a bit of soft copulation. The "hard" is the penis; the "soft" is the vagina. [British slang, 1800s, Farmer and Henley]

bit of jam 1. a sexually loose young woman, especially a wanton woman. [British slang, late 1800s, Ware] **2.** the female genitals. **3.** copulation. [both senses, British slang, 1800s, Farmer and Henley]

bit of meat 1. a prostitute. **2.** an act of copulation. *Cf.* MEAT (sense 2). [both senses, British slang, 1800s]

bit of mutton a prostitute. *Cf.* LACED-

MUTTON, MUTTON. [British slang, 1800s or before]

bit of nifty (also **nifty**) copulation. [British slang, 1800s-1900s, *Dictionary of Slang and Unconventional English*]

bit of pork the female genitals; an act of copulation. *Cf.* MEAT (sense 1), PORK (sense 1). [British slang, 1800s]

bit of rough copulation. [British slang, 1800s, Farmer and Henley]

bit of skin a sexually loose young woman; a woman considered sexually. [British slang, 1900s]

bit of snug 1. copulation from the female point of view. *Cf.* SNUG (sense 1). **2.** the penis. [both senses, British slang, 1800s, Farmer and Henley]

bit of snug for a bit of stiff 1. the vagina. For synonyms see PASSAGE. **2.** copulation from the female point of view. [both senses, British slang, 1800s, Farmer and Henley]

bit of the goose's-neck copulation from the female point of view. *Cf.* GOOSE'S-NECK. [British slang, 1800s, Farmer and Henley]

bit of the other coition. *Cf.* ANTIPODES, THE. [British slang, early 1900s, *Dictionary of Slang and Unconventional English*]

bit on, a intoxicated with alcohol. [British and U.S., 1800s-1900s]

bit on a fork 1. the female genitals. **2.** copulation, getting into the fork of the female's body. [both senses, British slang, 1800s]

bitter half one's wife. A play on BETTER HALF (*q.v.*). For synonyms see WARDEN. [U.S. slang, mid 1900s]

B.J. a BLOW-JOB (*q.v.*), an act of PENILINGUS (*q.v.*).

black 1. a person of the Negro race. Sometimes capitalized in this sense. The word-of-choice since the 1960s to refer to the American Negro. For synonyms see EBONY. **2.** pertaining to a Negro. Sometimes capitalized in this sense. [both since the early 1600s] **3.** opium. [See BLACK STUFF.]

blackamoor 1. a Negro. For synonyms see EBONY. [British, mid 1500s-1800s] **2.** a devil; the devil. [mid 1600s]

black and tan 1. a mulatto. **2.** pertaining to a mulatto. For synonyms see MAHOGANY. [U.S., 1800s-1900s]

black bean a Negro. Mildly derogatory. Possibly nonce. *Cf.* BEAN (sense 3). [U.S. slang, 1900s]

black beauties amphetamine capsules; Biphetamine (trademark), which comes in black or black-and-white capsules. From the name of a horse in children's fiction. For synonyms see AMP. [U.S. drug culture, mid 1900s-pres.]

black belt any area in the South where the Negro population is the most dense. *Cf.* LAND OF DARKNESS. [U.S., late 1800s-pres.]

black Bess the female genitals. [British slang, 1800s, Farmer and Henley]

blackbird 1. a Negro. Mildly derogatory and jocular. [slang, late 1800s-early 1900s] **2.** an amphetamine capsule. *Cf.* BLACK BEAUTIES, BLUEBIRD, REDBIRD, SPECKLED BIRD. [U.S. drug culture, mid 1900s-pres.]

black diamond a Negro of "good" (servile) traits. From a colloquial term for "coal." [U.S. slang, early 1900s]

black dog the delirium tremens. For synonyms see ORK-ORKS. [British and U.S. slang, 1800s-1900s]

black doll a black woman. [U.S. slang, early 1900s]

blacked ebony a mulatto. Possibly in error for BLEACHED EBONY (*q.v.*). *Cf.* EBONY. [U.S. slang, early 1900s]

black fay a Negro. Derogatory. *Cf.* FAY, OFAY. [U.S. dialect, 1900s or before]

blackguard 1. a low household servant. [British, early 1500s-1700s] **2.** a derogatory term for a man, especially one who behaves badly. [British and U.S., late 1700s-1900s]

black gungeon (also **gungeon**) a type of marijuana from Africa or Jamaica. From GANJAH (*q.v.*). [U.S. drug culture, mid 1900s-pres.]

black gunny a type of marijuana. From black GUNGEON (*q.v.*). Reinforced by "gunny" of a HEMP (*q.v.*) gunny sack. [U.S. drug culture, mid 1900s-pres.]

blackhead 1. a COMEDO (*q.v.*); a sebaceous gland clogged with dirt or secretions. For synonyms see BURBLE. [since the late 1800s] **2.** a derogatory term for a Negro. See NIGGERHEAD. [U.S. colloquial, 1900s]

black-hole the female genitals. A reinterpretation of the "black hole of Calcutta." [British slang, 1800s, Farmer and Henley]

black ivory African slaves considered as merchandise. [British and U.S., late 1800s]

black-jock (also **brown-jock, grey-jock**) the female genitals. The color refers to the color of the pubic hair. *Cf.* BLACK JOKE. [British slang, 1800s, Farmer and Henley]

black joke the female genitals. From a popular song of the times. [British slang, early 1800s]

Black-Man, the 1. the devil. **2.** a bugbear to frighten children. *Cf.* BLACKGENTLEMAN. [both senses, colloquial, 1500s-1900s]

black meat (also **dark meat**) **1.** a Negro contemplated as a sexual partner. Usually refers to a black woman. *Cf.* CHANGE ONE'S LUCK. **2.** a Negress prostitute. *Cf.* WHITE MEAT. [both senses, U.S. slang, 1900s]

black moat (also **black mo**) a type of marijuana. [U.S. drug culture, mid 1900s]

black mollies an amphetamine capsule. From the name of a popular tropical fish, *Mollienisia latipinna*. *Cf.* BLACK BEAUTIES. [U.S. drug culture, mid 1900s-pres.]

black oil an alcohol extract of hashish. For synonyms see OIL. [U.S. drug culture, mid 1900s-pres.]

blackout a nickname for a Negro. Not necessarily derogatory. *Cf.* BLACKIE, MIDNIGHT.

black pills opium. *Cf.* BLACK STUFF. For synonyms see OPE. [U.S. drug culture, 1900s]

black-pot a drunkard. Originally from the name for a beer mug. Rhyming slang for "sot." [British slang, 1500s-1800s]

black-ring the female genitals. *Cf.* RING (sense 1). [British slang, 1800s, Farmer and Henley]

Black Russian HASHISH (*q.v.*). For synonyms see HASH. [U.S. drug culture, mid 1900s-pres.]

black smoke (also **black silk**) opium. For synonyms see OPE. [1900s]

blacksnake the penis of a Negro. From the common name for a species of long, black snake. *Cf.* ROCK PYTHON. [slang and recurrent nonce, 1900s or before]

black spot an opium den. [U.S. slang, 1900s]

black stuff (also **black**) opium. [U.S. underworld, early to mid 1900s]

black velvet a female aborigine. *Cf.* BIT OF BLACK VELVET. [Australian slang, 1900s or before]

blade the penis. *Cf.* BRACMARD. [British, 1800s, Farmer and Henley]

blah (also **blah-blah-blah**) nonsense. For synonyms see ANIMAL. [U.S., early 1900s]

blamed (also **blame**) "damned." [British and U.S., early 1800s-pres.]

Blame it! Damn it! [colloquial, 1800s-1900s]

Blamenation! Damnation! [colloquial, 1800s-1900s]

blank "damn" in combinations. From the spelling "d-mn." *Cf.* DASH.

blankard a bastard. [Australian euphemism, mid 1900s, Baker]

blanked 1. damned. *Cf.* BLANK. [colloquial, 1800s-1900s] **2.** intoxicated with alcohol. [from French *vin blanc*; British and U.S., World Wars]

blanket drill 1. a night's sleep. No negative connotations. **2.** copulation. **3.** masturbation. [all senses, British with some U.S. use, early 1900s, *Dictionary of Slang and Unconventional English*]

blanket hornpipe copulation. For synonyms see SMOCKAGE. [British slang, early 1800s, *Lexicon Balatronicum*]

blankity-blank (also **blankety-blank, blankity**) a filler word for any type of swear word. From the blanks in words like f- -k, d- -n; used as a swear word in children's comics and in mixed company. [U.S. euphemism, late 1800s-1900s]

blanks heroin. [U.S. drug culture, mid 1900s-pres.]

Blarm me! an oath and an exclamation, "May God blind me!" *Cf.* BLIMEY! [British (Cockney), late 1800s]

blarney 1. flattery; nonsense. **2.** to flatter with nonsense. Based on "Blarney Castle," in County Cork, Ireland, and a type of Irish flattery associated with the Lord of Blarney. [both senses, British and U.S., late 1700s-pres.]

blast 1. an exclamation or a curse, "Damn!" Now a euphemism for BLOODY (*q.v.*). [colloquial, late 1600s-pres.] **2.** to smoke marijuana. *Cf.* BLASTED (sense 3). [U.S. drug culture, mid 1900s-pres.] **3.** to use any narcotic. [U.S. drug culture, mid 1900s-pres.] **4.** a release of intestinal gas. For synonyms see GURK. [U.S. slang, 1900s; much older as nonce]

blasted 1. damned; BLOODY (*q.v.*). *Cf.* BLAST (sense 1). [British and later, U.S., late 1600s-pres.] **2.** intoxicated with alcohol. [U.S. slang, early 1900s-pres.] **3.** intoxicated with drugs, especially marijuana. [U.S. drug culture, early 1900s-pres.]

blast party a session of marijuana smoking. *Cf.* BLAST (sense 2). [U.S. drug culture, mid 1900s-pres.]

blather (also **blether**) **1.** nonsense. **2.** to utter nonsense. [from Scots dialect; colloquial, late 1800s-1900s]

blatherskite (also **blatherskate, bletherskite**) a boaster; someone who speaks nonsense. Literally, "a dungtalker." *Cf.* BULLSHITTER, SKITE (sense

2). For synonyms see BULLER. [from Scots dialect; British and U.S. colloquial, late 1800s-pres.]

blazes "hell" in expressions such as "Go to blazes!" "Like blazes!" "What in blazes!" "What the blazes!" Refers to the flames of hell. [colloquial since the early 1800s]

bleached ebony a nickname for a mulatto. *Cf.* EBONY. See MAHOGANY for synonyms. [U.S. slang, 1900s, Berrey and Van den Bark]

bleary-eyed intoxicated with alcohol. [U.S. slang, early 1900s-pres.]

bleating bloody. A phonological disguise of BLEEDING (*q.v.*). [British, 1900s or before]

blech 1. a belch. **2.** to belch. A play on BELCH (*q.v.*). *Cf.* ERUCTATE. [both senses, U.S., mid 1900s-pres.]

bleeding damned; BLOODY (*q.v.*). *Cf.* BLEATING. [British with some U.S. use, late 1800s-pres.]

blemish 1. a derogatory nickname for the Belgian language, Flemish. Sometimes capitalized in this sense. A blend of "Belgian" and "Flemish." [U.S. slang, 1900s, Berrey and Van den Bark] **2.** a pimple. *Cf.* ACNE-TYPE SURFACE BLEMISH. For synonyms see BURBLE. [U.S. advertising euphemism, mid 1900s]

blessed DAMNED, BLASTED, or BLOODY (all *q.v.*). [British and U.S. euphemism, 1800s-pres.]

Bless my soul to hell! an exclamation. Euphemistic for "Damn it to hell!" [U.S. colloquial, 1900s]

blighted BLASTED, BLOODY, OR DAMNED (all *q.v.*). [British and U.S., early 1900s]

blighter a contemptible fellow; someone who causes a blight of unpleasantness. For synonyms see SNOKE-HORN. [British slang, late 1800s-pres.]

Blimey! a disguised oath or exclamation, "May God blind me!" *Cf.* BLARM ME! [originally Cockney; British, 1800s-pres.]

blimp 1. a fat prostitute; a sexually

loose woman. [U.S. underworld, early 1900s, Montelone] **2.** any fat person. [U.S. slang and colloquial, early 1900s-pres.]

blimped intoxicated with alcohol; gorged and swollen with drink. [U.S. slang, mid 1900s-pres.]

blind 1. intoxicated with alcohol. See BLIND DRUNK. [since the early 1600s] **2.** intoxicated with marijuana or other drugs. From sense 1. For synonyms see TALL. [U.S. drug culture, mid 1900s-pres.] **3.** uncircumcised. Because the EYE-HOLE (q.v.) is covered. [U.S. homosexual use, mid 1900s]

blind Bob, old the penis. Because it has only one eye, which does not see. Cf. BOB TAIL (sense 3). [British (Cockney), 1900s]

blind cheeks the posteriors. Cf. CHEEKS. [British, late 1600s, B.E.]

blind cupid the posteriors. For synonyms see DUFF. [British slang, early 1800s, Egan's Grose]

blind drunk deeply intoxicated with alcohol. Cf. BOOZEBLIND. [British and U.S., 1700s-pres.]

blinded intoxicated with alcohol. For synonyms see WOOFLED. [U.S. slang, 1900s]

blinders intoxicated with alcohol. [British slang, early 1900s]

blind-eye 1. the anus. Cf. ROUNDEYE (sense 2). [British, 1800s or before] **2.** the female genitals with reference to the vulva and the vagina. In expressions such as GET A SHOVE IN ONE'S BLIND-EYE (q.v.). Cf. LONG-EYE, SQUINT.

blind fart an inaudible but nevertheless potent release of intestinal gas. For synonyms see GURK. [British, 1800s, *Dictionary of Slang and Unconventional English*]

Blind me! an oath and an exclamation, "May God blind me!" Cf. BLARM ME!, BLIMEY! [British]

blindo 1. intoxicated with alcohol. [British and U.S., 1800s] **2.** a drunken spree. [British, 1800s, *Dictionary of Slang and Unconventional English*] **3.**

to die. Farmer and Henley show this as a verb. [British military, 1800s]

blind staggers intoxication with alcohol. [widespread slang, 1900s or before]

blind tiger strong or inferior alcoholic drink. [U.S. slang, 1900s]

blink (also **blinking**) damn; bloody. From BLANK (q.v.). [U.S., 1900s and before]

blint a sexually loose young woman; a prostitute. Cf. BINT. [U.S., 1900s, Berrey and Van den Bark]

blissom 1. in heat; lascivious. Especially in reference to a ewe. Also applied to humans. **2.** to behave as if in heat, especially as a ewe in heat. [both senses, mid 1600s] **3.** to copulate with a ewe, said of a ram. Cf. TUP. [since the early 1400s]

blister 1. any unpleasant or annoying person regardless of sex. [U.S. colloquial, mid 1800s-pres.] **2.** to damn; to curse. See BLISTERING. [British, early 1800s] **3.** a sexually perverted man. [U.S., 1900s and before] **4.** a prostitute. See BLISTERINE. [U.S. slang, 1900s] **5.** an unattractive young woman. [U.S. slang, mid 1900s]

blisterine (also **blister**) a prostitute. Possibly patterned on "Listerine," a trademarked brand of antiseptic. Cf. BLISTER (sense 4). [U.S. slang, 1900s]

blistering bloody; damned. See BLISTER (sense 2). [British and U.S., 1900s]

blithered intoxicated with alcohol. For synonyms see WOOFLED. [Australian, early 1900s, Baker]

blitzed 1. intoxicated with alcohol. [U.S. slang, mid 1900s-pres.] **2.** drug intoxicated. From sense 1. [U.S. drug culture, mid 1900s-pres.]

bloat 1. a drunkard. [British and U.S. slang, 1800s] **2.** a drowned corpse. For synonyms see CORPSE. [U.S., 1800s]

bloated 1. intoxicated with alcohol; overfilled with drink. [U.S. slang, early 1900s-pres.] **2.** bloody; damned. [British, early 1900s]

bloater a drunkard; the same as BLOAT (sense 1). [U.S., 1900s]

blob, be on to be sexually aroused, said of men. Possibly related to LOB (sense 2). *Cf.* BLOTTY, BE. For synonyms see HUMPY. [British, 1900s, *Dictionary of Slang and Unconventional English*]

block 1. an oaf; a blockhead. [early 1500s] **2.** to copulate with a woman. For synonyms see OCCUPY. [British and U.S. slang, 1800s-pres.]

blockbuster a Nembutal (trademark) capsule; amphetamines in general. From the nickname of a powerful bomb used in World War II. [U.S. drug culture, mid 1900s-pres.]

blocked 1. intoxicated with alcohol. [British and U.S., mid 1900s] **2.** intoxicated with drugs. From sense 1. [U.S. drug culture, mid 1900s-pres.]

blockhead a stupid oaf. *Cf.* BLOCK (sense 1). [since the mid 1500s]

blodgie a hoodlum; a punk. [Australian, 1900s]

bloke (also **bloak**) **1.** a mildly contemptuous term for a man, especially a stupid man. [British and some U.S. use, 1800s-pres.] **2.** a drunkard. *Cf.* BLOAT (sense 1). [U.S., 1900s] **3.** cocaine. Rhyming slang for "coke." From BIG BLOKE (*q.v.*). For synonyms see NOSE-CANDY. [U.S. drug culture, mid 1900s-pres.]

blomboll a drunkard. [British slang, 1800s, Farmer and Henley]

blond hashish. A truncation of BLOND HASHISH (*q.v.*). For synonyms see HASH. [U.S. drug culture, 1900s]

blond hashish (also **blond hash**) a mild form of hashish. *Cf.* HASHISH. [U.S. drug culture, 1900s]

blooch 1. to masturbate. For synonyms see WASTE TIME. **2.** a state of mental retardation erroneously attributed to excessive masturbation. [both senses, U.S. dialect (Boontling), late 1800s-early 1900s, Charles Adams]

blood 1. a fop; a dandy; a high-spirited male, as in "noble-blood" or "blueblood." [British, mid 1500s-1900s] **2.** a Negro; one's fellow black. From "blood brother." [U.S. black use, mid 1900s-pres.] **3.** catsup. A dysphemism. For similar terms see DOG'S VOMIT. [U.S., 1900s]

Blood!, My an oath and an exclamation, "Upon my bloody oath!" [Australian, 1900s, *Dictionary of Slang and Unconventional English*]

blood-box an ambulance. *Cf.* BONE-BOX. [U.S. slang, 1900s]

blood-bucket an ambulance; the same as BUCKET OF BLOOD (*q.v.*). [U.S. slang, 1900s]

blood disease syphilis. *Cf.* BAD DISEASE. [U.S. euphemism, early 1900s-pres.]

blood of a bitch a term of contempt meaning the blood descendent of a bitch. *Cf.* S.O.B. [U.S., 1900s or before, Wentworth]

Blood of Christ!, By the an oath and an exclamation. For synonyms see 'ZOUNDS! [1300s]

blood-tub an ambulance. *Cf.* BLOOD-BUCKET. [British military, 1900s]

blood-wagon an ambulance. [British military, early 1900s]

bloody damned; cursed. In the 1800s, the British equivalent of U.S. "fucking." The word was originally a very low-class "decoration" for almost any utterance. The immense impact of the word is attributable to its low-class origins rather than its "real" meaning. The utterance of such a rude lower-class term was itself the source of shock. See BLOOD (sense 1) for the most likely source. Before it became symbolic as a marker of the Cockney, the word had numerous uses. Many etymologies have been proposed to account for the intense power this word once had when uttered in polite society. It has been suggested that it is a corruption of "By our Lady!" [primarily Australian and British, 1800s-pres.] Synonyms and related terms: BALLY, BLANKITY, BLASTED, BLEEDING, BLIGHTED, BLISTERING, BLOATED, BLOOMING, BLUGGY, BLURRY, BLUSHING, CRIMSONEST

OF ADJECTIVES, GREAT AUSTRALIAN ADJECTIVE, HEMATOID, IM-BLOODY-POSSIBLE, N.B.G., N.B.L., PINK, PLURRY, Q.B.I., RUDDY, SANGUINARY.

bloody Mary 1. the menstrual period. From the name of an alcoholic mixed drink and Queen Mary 1 (Mary Tudor). [U.S. slang, 1900s] **2.** catsup. [U.S. slang, 1900s]

blooming bloody; damned. [used as an intensifier as early as the early 1700s; British and some U.S. use, late 1800s-pres.]

blot the posteriors; the anus. For synonyms see DUFF. [Australian, 1900s, Baker]

blotter 1. a drunkard. From the way a drunkard soaks up alcohol. [U.S., 1900s and before] **2.** the drug L.S.D. (*q.v.*). From the practice of ingesting bits of blotter saturated with L.S.D. [U.S. drug culture, mid 1900s-pres.]

blotto 1. intoxicated with alcohol; dead drunk. [British and U.S., early 1900s-pres.] **2.** any strong alcoholic beverage. For synonyms see BOOZE. [British military, early 1900s, *Dictionary of Slang and Unconventional English*]

blotty, be sexually aroused, said of men. *Cf.* BLOB, BE ON. For synonyms see HUMPY. [British, 1900s, *Dictionary of Slang and Unconventional English*]

blow 1. a prostitute, mistress, or concubine. [cant, late 1700s or before, Grose] **2.** a drunken spree. See also BLOW-OUT. [British and U.S., early 1800s-1900s] **3.** to perform penilingus. See BLOW-JOB. [U.S., early 1900s-pres.] **4.** to perform CUNNILINGUS (*q.v.*). [U.S., mid 1900s-pres.] **5.** cocaine. *Cf.* SUPERBLOW. [U.S. drug culture, mid 1900s-pres.] **6.** to SNORT (sense 2) drugs. [U.S. drug culture, mid 1900s-pres.] **7.** to smoke marijuana. [U.S. drug culture, mid 1900s-pres.]

blow a stick (also **blow gage, blow hay, blow jive, blow pot, blow tea**) to smoke marijuana. [U.S. drug culture, mid 1900s-pres.]

blow beets to vomit. *Cf.* BLOW LUNCH.

For synonyms see YORK. [U.S. slang, mid 1900s-pres.]

blow-boy 1. a man who plays the bugle. Not necessarily with negative connotations. [U.S., 1900s] **2.** a fellator. From sense 1. For synonyms see PICCOLO-PLAYER. [mid 1900s, *Dictionary of the Underworld*]

blowed damned. [British and U.S., early 1800s-1900s]

blowed-away 1. intoxicated with alcohol. For synonyms see WOOFLED. **2.** drug intoxicated. *Cf.* BLOW-AWAY. For synonyms see TALL. [both senses, U.S. slang, mid 1900s-pres.]

blow-hole a hole made in a men's bathroom partition allegedly for PENILINGUS (*q.v.*), but more likely to enable the male seated in a stall to observe the penis of a man who is standing at a urinal. From the term for a whale's nostril. See GLORY HOLE. [U.S. slang, mid 1900-pres.]

blow-job 1. an act of FELLATIO OR PENILINGUS (both *q.v.*). *Cf.* B.J., BLOW (sense 3). For synonyms see PENILINGUS. [U.S. slang, mid 1900s-pres.] **2.** an act of cunnilingus. Less common than sense 1. For synonyms see CUNNILINGUS. [U.S. slang, mid 1900s-pres.]

blow lunch (also **blow one's lunch**) to vomit. *Cf.* BLOW BEETS. [U.S. slang, mid 1900s-pres.]

blown-away 1. dead; killed. [U.S. colloquial, 1900s] **2.** deeply drug intoxicated. *Cf.* BLOWED-AWAY. [U.S. slang, mid 1900s-pres.]

blown-out intoxicated with drugs. *Cf.* BLOWN-AWAY. [U.S. drug culture, mid 1900s-pres.]

blown-up (also **blown**) intoxicated with alcohol. Refers to the pressure in one's head and to being bloated with drink. [U.S. slang, mid 1800s-pres.]

blow off 1. to ejaculate; to have an orgasm. [cant or slang, 1600s-1700s] **2.** to break wind; to release intestinal gas audibly. [British colloquial, 1900s] **3.** to masturbate. **4.** to goof off; to waste time; to procrastinate. **5.** a timewaster; a procrastinator. Usually hyphenated in this sense. **6.** to perform fellatio on someone. **7.** to cheat, deceive, or lie to someone. [senses 2-7, U.S. current slang]

blow one's roof to smoke marijuana. *Cf.* BLOW (sense 7). For synonyms see SMOKE. [U.S. drug culture, mid 1900s-pres.]

blow-out a drinking spree. From a colloquial term for a feast or a period of gluttony. [U.S., 1900s or before]

blow the coke (also **blow coke**) to SNORT (sense 2) or inhale cocaine. [U.S. underworld, 1900s]

blow the horn to release intestinal gas audibly. *Cf.* ARS MUSICA, TRUMP. [British slang, 1800s, Farmer and Henley]

blowtorch the penis. *Cf.* TORCH OF CUPID. Possibly in reference to PENILINGUS (*q.v.*). See BLOW (sense 3). [attested as U.S. underworld (tramps), early 1900s, Montelone]

blow up 1. to ejaculate. *Cf.* THROW UP (sense 3). [a vague reference occurring in *Pericles* and other plays (Shakespeare)] **2.** to become pregnant. In reference to a woman's swollen abdomen. [colloquial, 1900s]

blubbers the breasts. *Cf.* CHUBBIES, SPORT BLUBBER. [British and U.S. slang, late 1800s-1900s]

bludgeon the penis, especially the erect penis. *Cf.* WEAPON. For synonyms see ERECTION. [British slang, 1800s, Farmer and Henley]

bludgeoner (also **bludger**) a pimp; a whore's bully; later an idler or a con-man. *Cf.* BLUDGET. [Australian and British, mid 1800s-1900s]

bludget 1. a female thief who decoys a man, perhaps with offers of prostitution, and then robs him. [British, 1800s] **2.** a prostitute. From sense 1. [U.S., 1900s]

blue 1. lewd; obscene. *Cf.* PURPLE. [colloquial, 1800s-1900s] **2.** intoxicated with alcohol. *Cf.* BLUE DEVILS (sense 2). [U.S. and elsewhere, early 1800s-1900s] **3.** a Negro. [U.S., 1900s or before] **4.** the drug L.S.D. **5.** depressed. See BLUE DEVILS (sense 1). [colloquial, 1900s and before]

blue acid the drug L.S.D. [U.S. drug culture, mid 1900s-pres.]

blue angel an Amytal (trademark) capsule. Refers to jet planes flying in formation, *i.e.*, the Blue Angels. *Cf.* BLUEBIRD, BLUE HEAVEN. [U.S. drug culture, mid 1900s-pres.]

blue balls venereal disease, especially gonorrhea. *Cf.* HOT ROCKS, STONE-ACHE. [U.S. slang, mid 1900s]

bluebeard a lecher; a whoremonger. [British, 1800s]

Bluebeard's closet the female genitals; the vagina. This BEARD (*q.v.*) is the female pubic hair. [British slang, 1800s, Farmer and Henley]

bluebird an Amytal (trademark) capsule, a barbiturate. *Cf.* BLACKBIRD, REDBIRD. [U.S. drug culture, mid 1900s-pres.]

blue blazes 1. hell. From the blue flames of hell. A euphemism occurring in many oaths and exclamations. See BLAZES. [British and U.S. colloquial, 1800s-pres.] **2.** an alcoholic beverage. [British slang, late 1800s, Barrère and Leland]

blue bomber a (blue) ten-milligram tablet of Valium (trademark). Abbreviated as B.B. (sense 2). [U.S. drug culture, mid 1900s-pres.]

blue boy a venereal BUBO (*q.v.*). [British, 1800s]

blue cheer the drug L.S.D. (*q.v.*). From the trademarked brand name of a laundry detergent. *Cf.* BLUE (sense 4). [U.S. drug culture, mid 1900s-pres.]

bluecoat a policeman; any man in a blue uniform. For synonyms see FLATFOOT. [slang, mid 1600s-pres.]

blued (also **blewed**) intoxicated with alcohol. [British and U.S. slang, 1800s-1900s]

blue devils 1. very low spirits up to and including severe clinical depression. [colloquial, late 1700s-1800s] **2.** the DELIRIUM TREMENS (*q.v.*). Blue devils and red monkeys are typical hallucinations seen while having the delirium tremens. *Cf.* PINK ELEPHANTS. [slang since the early 1800s] **3.** capsules of Amytal (trademark), a barbiturate. *Cf.* RED DEVIL. [U.S. drug culture, mid 1900s-pres.]

blue-eyed intoxicated with alcohol. For synonyms see WOOFLED. [U.S. slang, mid 1800s, Wentworth and Flexner]

blue-eyed devil 1. a Caucasian. *Cf.* DEVIL (sense 3). [U.S. black use, mid 1900s-pres.] **2.** a person who is overtly kind and as innocent as a lamb, but is evil underneath. [U.S., 1900s]

blue fever venereal disease. *Cf.* BLUE BALLS. [British nautical, 1900s, Granville]

blue flag the drug L.S.D. (*q.v.*). *Cf.* BLUE (sense 4), ROYAL BLUE. [U.S. drug culture, mid 1900s-pres.]

blue gown a harlot; a sexually loose woman; a known whore. From the color of the uniform of an imprisoned prostitute. [British, early 1600s]

blue heaven 1. an Amytal (trademark) capsule. Usually in the plural. [U.S. drug culture, mid 1900s-pres.] **2.** the drug L.S.D. (*q.v.*). *Cf.* HEAVENLY BLUE. [U.S. drug culture, mid 1900s-pres.]

blue horrors (also **horrors**) the DELIRIUM TREMENS (*q.v.*). *Cf.* BLUE DEVILS (sense 2), HORRORS. [U.S. slang, mid 1800s]

blue Johnnies the DELIRIUM TREMENS (*q.v.*). [Australian, 1800s, Farmer and Henley]

blue mist the drug L.S.D. (*q.v.*). [U.S. drug culture, mid 1900s-pres.]

blueness indecency. *Cf.* BLUE (sense 1). [colloquial, 1800s-1900s]

blue ribbon (also **blue ribband**) gin; the same as BLUE TAPE (*q.v.*). *Cf.* BLUE RUIN. [British slang, 1800s]

blue ruin gin; inferior gin. *Cf.* LIGHT BLUE, RUIN. [British and U.S. slang, early 1800s-pres.]

blues 1. despondency; depression. *Cf.* BLUE (sense 5). **2.** the DELIRIUM TRE-

MENS (*q.v.*). A truncation of BLUE DEVILS (q.v.). [colloquial since the 1800s] **3.** Amytal (trademark) capsules. [U.S. drug culture, mid 1900s-pres.]

blue sage a marijuana cigarette. For synonyms see MEZZROLL. [drug culture, mid 1900s]

blueskin 1. a Negro. [U.S., early 1800s] **2.** the child of a black woman and a white man. [Caribbean, 1800s] **3.** the penis. [British slang, 1800s, Farmer and Henley]

blue star morning glory seeds used as a mild hallucinogenic. From the color name. For synonyms see SEEDS. [U.S. drug culture, mid 1900s-pres.]

blue stone inferior gin or whisky. "Blue stone" is an old term for "copper sulfate." [British slang, mid 1800s, Farmer and Henley]

blue tape gin. For synonyms see RUIN. [British and U.S. slang, 1700s-1900s]

bluff a female homosexual who assumes either the active or passive sexual role. A blend of "bitch" and "fluff." [U.S. homosexual use, mid 1900s, Stanley]

bluggy bloody. A euphemism of disguise for "bloody" in the sense "gory." [allegedly mock baby talk; U.S., late 1800s]

blunt 1. barbiturates in general. For synonyms see BARB. **2.** a capsule of Seconal (trademark), a barbiturate used as a recreational drug. [both senses, U.S. drug culture, mid 1900s-pres.]

blunt end the glans penis. *Cf.* BELL-END. [British military, 1900s, *Dictionary of Slang and Unconventional English*]

blushing bloody. [British euphemism, late 1800s-early 1900s]

B.M. a "bowel movement," an act of defecation.

B.N. a "bloody nuisance." [British slang, 1900s]

bo 1. Colombian marijuana. *Cf.* COLUMBIAN RED, LIMBO (sense 4), LUMBO. [U.S. drug culture, mid 1900s-pres.] **2.**

a tramp's catamite or "boy." Reinforced by "beau." For synonyms see BRONCO. [U.S. underworld, early 1900s, Weseen]

B.O. "body odor," a sweaty or other unpleasant body odor. [used euphemistically in advertising and U.S. slang, mid 1900s-pres.]

board to coit a woman. *Cf.* CLIMB, MOUNT. [in *Love's Labour's Lost* (Shakespeare)]

boat and oar a prostitute. Rhyming slang for "whore." *Cf.* BROKEN OAR. [U.S. slang, 1900s or before]

bob 1. gin. For synonyms see RUIN. [British, mid 1700s] **2.** to masturbate. [British slang, 1800s, Farmer and Henley] **3.** an oath and an exclamation, "Swelp me Bob!" [slang or colloquial, early 1800s-1900s]

bobbers the breasts. *Cf.* BLUBBERS. [attested as British slang, mid 1900s, *Dictionary of Slang and Unconventional English*]

bobbles the testicles. From a dialect word meaning "stones." *Cf.* BAUBLES. [British, 1800s, Barrère and Leland]

bo-bo bush marijuana. [U.S. underworld, mid 1900s]

bob squirt a worthless fellow. *Cf.* SQUIRT (sense 1). [British, 1800s]

bob tail 1. a lewd woman; a woman who masturbates herself. [British, late 1600s-1800s] **2.** an impotent man; a eunuch. As if his penis had been bobbed. [British, 1800s, *Lexicon Balatronicum*] **3.** the penis. *Cf.* CUTTY-GUN, SHORT-ARM, TAIL (sense 3). **4.** a worthless oaf; a jerk. [since the early 1600s]

bod 1. a body of any type, living or dead. [U.S., 1900s] **2.** an especially good male or female body. *Cf.* ANTI-BOD. [U.S. slang, mid 1900s-pres.]

bodewash buffalo chips; dried cattle dung used for fuel. Also some use as BULLSHIT (*q.v.*). For synonyms see COW-CHIPS. [from the French *bois-de-vache*, literally, "wood from the cow"]

bodikin (also **bodkin**) **1.** a mild oath

or exclamation, "By God's little body!" [late 1500s] **2.** a brothel. From "bawdy-ken," where "ken" is a cant term for "house." [cant, early 1800s, Jon Bee]

bodkin the penis. [British slang, 1800s, Farmer and Henley] See also BODIKIN.

Bodkins! (also **Ods bodkins!**) an oath and an exclamation, "By God's (little) body!"

body-naked naked. [U.S., 1800s, Wentworth]

body queen a male homosexual who is aroused by men with muscular bodies. See QUEEN for similar topics. [U.S. homosexual use, mid 1900s, Stanley]

body's captain, my a man's penis. From the notion that the male is totally controlled by his sexual urges. [British euphemism, 1800s, Farmer and Henley]

body-snatcher 1. a ghoul; a grave robber. *Cf.* RESURRECTIONIST. [since the early 1800s] **2.** an undertaker. [British and U.S. jocular euphemism, early 1800s-pres.] **3.** a kidnapper. [U.S. slang, 1900s] **4.** a stretcher-bearer. [British military, 1900s, Fraser and Gibbons]

body wax dung; human feces. [U.S., early 1900s]

boff 1. to obtain sexual relief through copulation. [U.S., 1900s] **2.** to vomit. A disguise of BARF (*q.v.*). For synonyms see YORK. [U.S., 1900s, Wentworth and Flexner] **3.** to masturbate, usually said of a male. [U.S., 1900s]

bog 1. a W.C.; a restroom. **2.** to retire to the W.C. **3.** to urinate or use the W.C.; to defile with excrement. [current colloquial use; some senses since the 1500s or 1600s]

Bogart to linger with a marijuana cigarette before passing it on to another person; to get more than one's share of marijuana smoke. From the proper name "Humphrey Bogart," who did this with a tobacco cigarette in a movie. [U.S. drug culture, mid 1900s-pres.]

bog-house (also **bog-shop**) a privy; an outhouse. [British, late 1600s-1800s]

bog-lander (also **bog-hopper, bog-trotter**) an Irishman. Derogatory. *Cf.* PATLANDER. Halliwell defines bog-trotter as "an Irish robber." [since the late 1600s, B.E.]

bog-shop a privy. For synonyms see AJAX. [British, 1600s-1800s]

bogstuff excrement; human excrement. [British, 1500s-1600s]

bogy (also **bogey**) **1.** the posteriors; the anus. Usually spelled "bogy" and pronounced "bog-y." [cant, late 1700s, Grose] **2.** a ghost or bugbear; the devil. Usually spelled "bogey." [British and U.S., early 1800s-pres.]

bohunk (also **bohak, bohawk, boho**) **1.** any low-class southern European; any immigrant laborer. A blend of "bohemian" and "Hungarian." **2.** any of the languages of low-class southern Europeans. **3.** any stupid or awkward person. [all senses, U.S. slang and colloquial, late 1800s-1900s] **4.** a Caucasian from the point of view of a Negro. See HONKY, HUNK (sense 3). For synonyms see PECKERWOOD.

boiled intoxicated with alcohol. *Cf.* PAR-BOILED. [slang, late 1800s-1900s]

boiled as an owl intoxicated with alcohol. *Cf.* BILED OWL, DRUNK AS A BOILED OWL, OWLED. [British and U.S., late 1800s-1900s]

boilmaker **1.** a virile male; a rough cave man. **2.** beer with a shot of whisky in it. **3.** a very hard punch or blow to the body. [all senses, U.S. slang, 1900s]

boiling drunk heavily intoxicated with alcohol. Based on "boiling mad." [U.S. slang, 1900s]

bollix up (also **bollix**) to foul something up; to ball something up. From BALLOCKS (*q.v.*), but not usually recognized as such. *Cf.* BALL-UP. [U.S. slang, mid 1900s] Synonyms: ASS UP, BALLIX, BALLS-UP, BALL-UP, BOLLIX UP, BUGGER, BUGGER UP, COCK UP, FRIG-UP, FUCK UP.

bolts and taps bolts and nuts. A euphemistic phrase avoiding NUTS (sense

1), "testicles." [U.S. dialect (Ozarks), Randolph and Wilson]

bom the posteriors; the anus. An obsolete form of BUM (sense 1). *Cf.* BIM (sense 2). [1300s]

bombed **1.** intoxicated with alcohol. [U.S. slang, early 1900s-pres.] **2.** drug intoxicated. From sense 1. [U.S. drug culture, mid 1900s-pres.]

bomber (also **bomb**) a thick marijuana cigarette. *Cf.* TORPEDO. [U.S. drug culture, mid 1900s-pres.]

bombo **1.** a cheap wine. [Australian slang, early 1900s] See also BUMBO (sense 3). **2.** the female genitals; the same as BIMBO (sense 3). see BUMBO (sense 1).

bombosity the posteriors. [U.S., early 1900s]

bondage a type of sexual activity wherein sexual pleasure is experienced when one is bound and made helpless. Considered to be a part of MASOCHISM (*q.v.*). See B. and D.

bone **1.** the FINGER (*q.v.*). **2.** the penis, especially the erect penis. *Cf.* HAMBONE, MARROW-BONE. **3.** a trombone. No negative connotations. **4.** a marijuana cigarette. [all senses, U.S. slang, colloquial, and nonce, 1900s and before]

bone-ache (also **bone-ague**) syphilis. *Cf.* BONE (sense 2). [late 1500s-1600s]

bone-bender (also **bone-breaker**) a nickname for a physician. For synonyms see DOC. [U.S., 1900s, Wentworth and Flexner]

bone-box **1.** a coffin. **2.** an ambulance. *Cf.* BLOOD-BOX. [both senses, U.S., 1900s] Synonyms: BLOOD-BOX, BLOOD-BUCKET, BLOOD-TUB, BLOOD-WAGON, BONE-BOX, BUCKET OF BLOOD, MEAT-WAGON.

boned intoxicated with alcohol. For synonyms see WOOFLED. [British, early 1900s, *Dictionary of Slang and Unconventional English*]

bone-on **1.** an erection in "have a bone-on." *Cf.* BONE (sense 2). For synonyms see ERECTION. **2.** lustful; to be sexually aroused. For synonyms see

HUMPY. [both senses, U.S. slang, 1900s and before]

bone-orchard a graveyard. *Cf.* BONE-YARD, MARBLE ORCHARD. [British and U.S. colloquial, 1900s]

boner 1. the erect penis. *Cf.* BONE (sense 2). **2.** a mistake; a silly or serious error. [both senses, U.S. slang, mid 1900s-pres.]

bones, on the pregnant. [British slang, 1800s, Farmer and Henley]

bonetop an oaf; a dullard. [U.S. slang, mid 1900s]

bone-yard a cemetary. *Cf.* BONE-ORCHARD, MARBLE ORCHARD. [U.S. colloquial, late 1800s-pres.]

bonfire the penis. *Cf.* BLOWTORCH. [British slang, 1800s, Farmer and Henley]

bong 1. dead. Possibly from an Australian aboriginal language. [attested as Australian Pidgin, 1800s, Barrère and Leland] **2.** a device used in smoking marijuana. Also **bhong.** [U.S. drug culture, 1900s]

bongoed (also **bongo, bongo'd**) intoxicated with alcohol. *Cf.* BINGOED. [U.S. slang, mid 1900s-pres.]

bonkers 1. insane; crazy. For synonyms see DAFT. [U.S. slang, 1900s] **2.** slightly intoxicated with alcohol. [British military, early 1900s, Granville]

bonnet a woman. *Cf.* SKIRT. [colloquial, late 1800s]

boo (also **bu**) **1.** marijuana. [U.S. drug culture, early 1900s] **2.** a derogatory nickname for a Negro. From JIGABOO (*q.v.*).

boob 1. a gullible oaf; a bumpkin. A truncation of BOOBY (sense 2). [U.S. slang, early 1900s-pres.] **2.** a breast. See BOOBIES, BOOBS.

booberkin a fat oaf; a bumpkin. The diminutive of BOOB (*q.v.*). [British, late 1600s, B.E.]

boobies (also **boobys**) the human breasts. See the much older form, BUBBIES. [U.S. slang and colloquial, 1900s]

boo-boo 1. a derogatory nickname for

a Negro. A reduplication of BOO (sense 2). [U.S. slang, 1900s] **2.** the posteriors. [British, 1800s, *Dictionary of Slang and Unconventional English*] **3.** feces; human feces. [primarily juvenile, U.S. colloquial, 1900s] **4.** a testicle. Usually in the plural. [U.S., 1900s, (Truman Capote)]

boobs the breasts. *Cf.* BOOBIES, BUBBIES. [U.S. slang and colloquial, mid 1900s-pres.]

Boobus americanus a typical (or stereotypical) foolish and gullible American citizen. [mock-Latin modeled on scientific binomial taxonomy; U.S. slang, early 1900s]

booby 1. to behave like a booby. [late 1500s] **2.** a country bumpkin; a jerk. *Cf.* BOOB (sense 1). [since the 1600s, B.E.] **3.** a breast. See BOOBIES.

booby hatch 1. a jail; any type of a lock-up. **2.** an insane asylum. Both are from the nautical name of a specific type of hatch on a ship. [both senses, U.S. slang, early 1900s-pres.]

boodie 1. a hobgoblin; a specter. [British (from Scots), 1700s] **2.** the buttocks. See BOODY (sense 1).

boody (also **bootie**) **1.** the buttocks. **2.** a young woman with particularly well-proportioned buttocks; women considered sexually. **3.** the female genitals, specifically the vagina. **4.** coition, especially in the expression "get some boody." Sense 1-4 are synonymous with ASS (*q.v.*). **5.** male coition *per anum*. From sense 4. [all senses, U.S. slang, mid 1900s-pres.]

boof stupid. Possibly from BUFFOON or *bouffe*. [British, 1800s or before]

boogie 1. syphilis. [U.S. slang, mid 1900s, Deak] **2.** a derogatory nickname for a Negro. Also **boog.** [U.S. slang, early 1900s] **3.** nasal mucus; a glob of nasal mucus. [U.S. colloquial, 1900s] Synonyms and related terms: BUBU, BUG-ABOO, BUGGER, CATARRH, PHLEGM, SNOB, SNOT, SNOTTER.

booly-dog copulation. For synonyms see SMOCKAGE. [U.S. slang, 1900s or before]

boom-boom a bowel movement. For synonyms see EASEMENT. [U.S. juvenile, 1900s]

boom the census to impregnate a woman. For synonyms see STORK. [British slang, 1900s, *Dictionary of Slang and Unconventional English*]

boon-dagger a virago; a masculine lesbian. *Cf.* BULL-DAGGER, BULLDIKER. [U.S. slang, mid 1900s-pres.]

boor an illiterate oaf or rustic; an uncouth man. For synonyms see OAF. [from Dutch Boer, "peasant"; since the early 1900s]

boosey cock (also **boosy cock**) a drunkard. [British, 1700s-1800s]

boot 1. an instrument of torture which encases the lower leg. Also **bootikins.** [Scots, late 1500s] **2.** to vomit. For synonyms see YORK. [U.S. slang, mid 1900s, *Current Slang*] **3.** a derogatory nickname for a Negro. A truncation of BOOTLIPS (*q.v.*). [U.S. slang, mid 1900s-pres.]

boot hill a cemetery. A frontier cemetery where gunfighters were buried. [U.S. colloquial, 1900s or before]

bootleg 1. to sell alcohol illegally during Prohibition. **2.** alcohol during Prohibition and after. Both are from a U.S. term used in the 1800s for a man who smuggled moonshine by concealing bottles in his boot tops. [both senses, U.S. slang, early 1900s]

boot-licker (also **boot-lick**) a sycophant. [colloquial, mid 1800s-pres.]

bootlips a derogatory nickname for a Negro. *Cf.* BOOT (sense 3). [U.S. colloquial, 1900s]

booze (also **boose, bowse, bowze**) **1.** to drink alcohol; to spree. [since the 1300s] **2.** alcohol; liquor. [since the 1300s; cant by the 1600s; widespread slang, 1800s-pres.] Synonyms, names of specific beverages, and related terms for sense 2: A-BOMB JUICE, ALCHY, AL COHOL, AL K. HALL, ALKI HALL, ANTI-FREEZE, APPLE-JACK, AQUA VITAE, ARDENT SPIRITS, BARLEY BROTH, BARLEY JUICE, BARLEY WATER, BATHTUB GIN, BELCH, BELLY-VENGEANCE, BELLY-WASH, BELSH, BERPS, BERPWATER, BEVVY, BITCHES' WINE, BIT OF BLINK, BIVVY, BLOTTO, BLUE BLAZER, BLUE BLAZES, BLUE PIG, BLUE RIBBON, BLUE RUIN, BLUE STONE, BLUE TAPE, BOB, BOILER-MAKER, BOMBO, BOOTLEG, BREAKY-LEG, BRIAN O'LINN, BUB, BUBBLE-WATER, BUBBLY, BUCKET OF SUDS, BUDGE, BUG JUICE, BUMBO, CACTUS JUICE, CANEBUCK, CAPER-JUICE, CATGUT, CAT'S WATER, CHAIN LIGHTNING, CHALK, CHAM, CHOC, CHOKE-DOG, CLAP OF THUNDER, COCK-ALE, COFFIN VARNISH, COLD COFFEE, COLORADO COOLAID, CONK-BUSTER, CORN, CORN-JUICE, CORN-MULE, COUGAR-MILK, CRAZY WATER, DIDDLE, DIDO, DOCTOR HALL, DONK, DRAIN, DRUDGE, DUTCH COURAGE, EMBALMING FLUID, EYEWASH, EYE-WATER, FAMILY DISTURBANCE, FAR AND NEAR, FINGER AND THUMB, FIREWATER, FIZZ, FLASH OF LIGHTNING, FOGRAM, FOX-HEAD, GARGLE, GAS, GATOR SWEAT, GAUGE, GAY AND FRISKY, GIDDY-WATER, GIGGLE-JUICE, GIGGLE-WATER, GOLDEN CREAM, GRAVE-DIGGER, GREEK FIRE, GROWLER, GUT-ROT, HARD LIQUOR, HARD STUFF, HIGH-LAND FRISKY, HOGWASH, HOOCH, JACK-A-DANDY, JACKY, JOHN BARLEYCORN, JOHN HALL, JOLLOP, JOY JUICE, JOY-WATER, JUICE, JUNGLE-JUICE, JUNIPER-JUICE, KILL-DEVIL, KILL-GRIEF, KINGDOM COME, KNOCK-ME-DOWN, KOOL-AID, LAGE, LAUGHING SOUP, LIGHTNING, LIGHT WET, LIQUID-FIRE, LIQUOR, LONDON MILK, LOTION, LUBE, LUSH, MAX, MEDICINE, MEXICAN MILK, MISERY, MOONSHINE, MOTHER'S MILK, MOUNTAIN-DEW, MUR, MYRRH, NANNY-GOAT SWEAT, NANTZ, NEAR BEER, NELSON'S BLOOD, NEVER-FEAR, NIG, NOSE PAINT, O-BE-JOYFUL, OIL OF BARLEY, OLD TOM, PAIN-KILLER, PALEFACE, PANTHER JUICE, PANTHER PISS, PANTHER PIZEN, PANTHER SWEAT, PHYSIC, PIG'S EAR!, PIG SWEAT, PINE-TOP, PISH, PISS, PISS-MAKER, PIZEN, PLINK, PLONK, PLUCK, PONG, PONGELOW, POP-SKULL, POTATO SOUP, PRAIRIE-DEW, PRUNE JUICE, PURGE, QUEER BEER, RAG-WATER, RED-EYE, RED NED, REEB, RIGHT-SORT, ROT-GUT, ROTTO, RUIN, SATIN, SAUCE, SCAMPER JUICE, SCOOCH, SCREECH, SHAM, SHAMPOO,

SHEEPWASH, SHICKER, SHINE, SILKEN TWINE, SILLY MILK, SILO DRIPPINGS, SISSY BEER, SKEE, SKIT, SKY, SKY BLUE, SLOSH, SNAKE, SNAKEBITE MEDICINE, SNAKE-JUICE, SNAKE MEDICINE, SNAKE-POISON, SPIRITS, SPIRITUS FRUMENTI, SQUAW PISS, STAGGER-JUICE, STAGGER-SOUP, STAGGER-WATER, STARK NAKED, STINGO, STINKI-BUS, STINKIOUS, STREAK OF LIGHTNING, STRIP-ME-NAKED, STRONG AND THIN, STRONG WATERS, STUMP-LIKKER, SUCK, SUDS, SUGAR-CANDY, SUPER SUDS, SWIG, SWILL, SWIPES, SWIZZLE, TANGLEFOOT, TANGLE-LEG, TAPE, TARANTULA-JUICE, TEA, THE DEMON RUM, THIMBLE AND THUMB, TICKLE-BRAIN, TIGER JUICE, TIGER MILK, TIGER PISS, TIGER SWEAT, TIPPLE, TITLEY, TITTERY, TOM THUMB, TONSIL BATH, TONSIL PAINT, TWANKAY, UN-SWEETENED, VARNISH-REMOVER, WANKS, WATER OF LIFE, WHISTLE-BELLY VEN-GEANCE, WHITE, WHITE COFFEE, WHITE LIGHTNING, WHITE LINE, WHITE MULE, WHITE PORT, WHITE SATIN, WHITE STUFF, WHITE TAPE, WHITE VELVET, WHITEWASH, WHITE WINE, WHOOPEE-WATER, WILD MARE'S MILK, WITCH-PISS, WHOOZLE-WATER, YARD OF SATIN.

boozeblind intoxicated with alcohol. *Cf.* BLIND DRUNK.

boozed (also **boozed-up, bowzed**) intoxicated with alcohol. [widespread slang, mid 1800s-pres.]

booze-fighter a drunkard; an alcohol-ic. [Australian and U.S. 1900s]

booze-freak a drunkard. [U.S. slang, mid 1900s-pres.]

boozefuddle liquor; alcohol. A play on "befuddle," meaning "confuse." [U.S. dialect, 1900s or before]

boozegob a drunkard. "Gob" is a cant word for "mouth." [U.S. slang, 1900s, Weseen]

booze-heister a drunkard. [U.S. slang, 1900s]

booze-hound a drunkard; a heavy drinker. [U.S. slang, early 1900s-pres.]

booze-hustler a bootlegger; a seller of illegal alcohol during Prohibition. [U.S. slang, early 1900s]

booze-king a drunkard. [Australian, 1900s, Baker]

boozer (also **bouser**) **1.** a drunkard. [since the 1500s or before] **2.** a tavern; a saloon. [British slang, late 1800s, Ware]

boozician a drunkard. For synonyms see ALCHY. [Australian, 1900s, Baker]

boozington a drunkard; the same as LUSHINGTON (*q.v.*). [Australian and British, 1800s-1900s]

boozle coition. For synonyms see SMOCKAGE. [mid 1900s, *Dictionary of Slang and Unconventional English*]

boozy (also **boosy, bousey, bousy, bowsy**) intoxicated with alcohol. [since the early 1500s]

bore 1. the female genitals, specifi-cally the vagina. *Cf.* CYLINDER, PISTON ROD. **2.** to copulate. [both senses, British slang, 1800s, Farmer and Henley]

bosh nonsense; idle talk. [from Turkish; colloquial, early 1800s-pres.]

boshy intoxicated with alcohol. From BOSKY (*q.v.*), pronounced as if one were intoxicated. [British underworld, early 1900s, *Dictionary of the Under-world*]

bosiasm the bosom; a woman's breasts. [U.S. slang, mid 1900s-pres.]

bosko absoluto intoxicated with alco-hol. *Cf.* BOSKY. [mock-Latin; British (Kipling)]

bosky almost drunk; nearly intoxi-cated with alcohol. From "bosk," a thicket. *Cf.* BOSHY. [slang since the early 1700s]

bosom 1. the breasts. Also **bosoms.** [U.S. euphemism, 1800s-1900s] Syn-onyms: APPLE DUMPLING SHOP, APPLES, APPURTENANCES, BABY PILLOWS, BABY'S PUBLIC HOUSE, BAGS, BALCONY, BAL-LOONS, BAZONGAS, BAZOOMS, BAZOON-GIES, BEAUSOM, BEAUTS, BEGONIAS, BERKS, BIG BROWN EYES, BLUBBERS, BOBBERS, BOOBIES, BOOBS, BOSIASM, BOSOMS, BOULDERS, BREASTWORKS, BREESTS, BRISTOL CITIES, BRISTOLS, BUB-BIES, BUBBLES, BUFFERS, BULBS, BUMP-ERS, BUMPS, BUST, BUTTER-BAGS, BUTTER-

BOXES, CABMAN'S RESTS, CANS, CAT AND KITTIES, CAT HEADS, CATS AND KITTIES, CHARLIES, CHARMS, CHE-CHEES, CHEST AND BEDDING, CHESTNUTS, CHUBBIES, COKER-NUTS, CREAM-JUGS, DAIRIES, DIDDIES, DINNERS, DROOPERS, DUGS, DUMPLINGS, DUMPLING-SHOP, EAST AND WEST, EYES, FEEDING-BOTTLES, FIGURE, FLIP-FLAPS, FORE-BUTTOCKS, FRIED EGGS, FRONT, GAZONGAS, GLOBES, GOONAS, GRAPEFRUITS, GROWTHS, HAND-WARMERS, HANGERS, HEADLIGHTS, HEMISPHERES, HOG JAWS, HONEYDEW MELONS, HOOTERS, JELLY-ON-SPRINGS, JERSEY CITIES, JUGS, KETTLEDRUMS, KNOCKERS, LEMONS, LEWIS AND WITTIES, LOLLOS, LOVE-BUBBLES, LOVE TIPS, LUNGS, MAE WEST, MAMMETS, MANCHESTER CITY, MANCHESTERS, MARACAS, MARSHMALLOWS, MEAT, MEAT-MARKET, MELONS, MILK-BOTTLES, MILK-SHOP, MILK-WALK, MILKYWAY, MOSOB, MOUNTAINS, MOUNT OF LILIES, MUFFINS, MURPHIES, NATURE'S FONTS, NICK-NACKS, NINNIES, NINNY-JUGS, NORGIES, NUBBIES, NUGGETS, ORANGES, OTHER PARTS, PAIR, PANTERS, PANTRY SHELVES, PAPS, PEACHES, PELLETS, PLAYGROUND, POONTS, PRIZE FAGGOTS, PUMPS, RACKS, SACKS, SNORBS, SUPERDROOPERS, SWINGERS, TEACUPS, THE PERSON, THOUSAND PITIES, THREEPENNY BITS, TONSILS, TOP, TOP BALLOCKS, TOP ONES, TORALOORALS, TOWN AND CITIES, TREASURE, TREY BITS, TWIN LOVELINESS, TWINS, UDDER, UPPER-DECK, UPPER-WORKS, VEILED TWINS, VOOS, WALLOPIES, WARTS, WATERMELONS. **2.** a woman's upper thorax; the bust. **3.** the center of one's feelings.

bosom chums 1. lice. For synonyms see WALKING DANDRUFF. [British and U.S., 1900s] **2.** rats. [U.S. slang, early 1900s, Rose]

bosom friend 1. a louse. Usually in the plural. *Cf.* BOSOM CHUMS. [British, 1700s] **2.** alcohol. [U.S. slang, 1900s]

bosom of the pants the posteriors. *Cf.* FORE-BUTTOCKS. [U.S. slang, mid 1900s]

boss pimp a powerful pimp with a large collection of prostitutes. [U.S. prostitute's argot, James]

Botheration! an oath and an exclamation, "Damnation!" [colloquial euphemism, early 1800s-1900s]

both sheets in the wind intoxicated with alcohol. *Cf.* THREE SHEETS IN THE WIND, TWO SHEETS TO THE WIND. [U.S. and elsewhere, 1900s and before]

bottle 1. prostitution, especially male prostitution. [U.S., 1900s] **2.** pederasty. **3.** to coit a woman anally. **4.** to coit and impregnate a woman. Senses 1-4 are related to BOTTLE AND GLASS (*q.v.*), "ass." [all senses above, British, 1900s, *Dictionary of Slang and Unconventional English*] **5.** an amphetamine tablet. [U.S. drug culture, mid 1900s-pres.]

bottle-ache 1. a hangover. See WINEACHE. [British and U.S., 1800s-1900s] **2.** the DELIRIUM TREMENS (*q.v.*). [British slang, 1800s, Farmer and Henley]

bottle and glass the anus; the posteriors. Rhyming slang for "ass." [slang, 1900s]

bottle-baby a drunkard. From the term for a baby who is bottle-fed or who is dependent on a bottle. [U.S. slang, 1900s]

bottled intoxicated with alcohol. For synonyms see WOOFLED. [British and U.S., 1900s]

bottle-fatigue a hangover. From the military term "battle-fatigue." [U.S. slang, mid 1900s]

bottle-head an oaf. [colloquial, mid 1600s-1800s]

bottle-man a drunkard. *Cf.* BOTTLE-BABY. For synonyms see ALCHY. [U.S. slang, mid 1900s]

bottle-merchant a CATAMITE (*q.v.*) prostitute, a male prostitute specializing in anal copulation as the receiver. *Cf.* BOTTLE (senses 1 and 2). For synonyms see BRONCO. [British, 1900s, *Dictionary of the Underworld*]

bottle-stopper a policeman. Rhyming slang for "copper." [U.S., mid 1900s]

bottle-sucker a drunkard. [British and U.S. slang, 1800s-early 1900s]

bottom 1. the buttocks. [British and U.S. colloquial euphemism since the 1700s] **2.** the female genitals; the female genital area including the PERINEUM (*q.v.*). [colloquial, 1900s or before]

bottomless-pit 1. the female genitals, specifically the vagina. *Cf.* DEAD-END STREET, HELL (sense 2). [British and later, U.S., early 1800s-pres.] **2.** hell. [usually attributed to a Biblical source (Revelations); British and U.S. euphemism]

bottoms a nickname for a catamite. For synonyms see BRONCO. [U.S. slang, mid 1900s-pres.]

bottom's up 1. copulation wherein the male enters the vagina from the rear. **2.** anal heterosexual copulation. From the drinking toast. [both senses, U.S. slang, 1900s]

boulders breasts, especially large or pendulous breasts. *Cf.* OVER-THE-SHOULDER-BOULDER-HOLDER. [U.S. slang, 1900s]

bounce to copulate with a woman; to coit a woman. [slang, late 1800s-1900s]

bouncing-powder cocaine. Because it makes you HIGH (sense 2). [nonce, early 1900s, *Dictionary of the Underworld*]

bouncy-bouncy copulation. *Cf.* BOUNCE. [U.S., 1900s, Wentworth and Flexner]

bound 1. pregnant. *Cf.* BABY-BOUND. Also in the sense of being firmly bound to the expected child and to its father. [1400s or before] **2.** constipated. [colloquial since the early 1500s]

bounder a vulgar cad; a man who behaves badly in the company of women. [colloquial, late 1800s-1900s]

bouquet of ass-holes something extremely contemptible; an excess of something extremely contemptible. [U.S. slang, 1900s]

bovine excrement 1. cattle dung. **2.** a jocular euphemism for BULLSHIT (*q.v.*). [both senses, U.S. slang, mid 1900s]

bovine excrescence the same as BOVINE EXCREMENT (*q.v.*).

bovril nonsense; BULLSHIT (*q.v.*). From the brand name of a beef extract. [Australian, early 1900s, Baker]

bow the penis. For playing the FIDDLE (sense 2), the vagina. *Cf.* FIDDLE-BOW. [slang, 1800s-1900s]

bowel movement 1. an act of defecation. For synonyms see EASEMENT. **2.** feces; human feces. Both are abbreviated "B.M." [both senses, U.S. euphemism, 1900s]

bowel off to have diarrhea. [U.S. dialect (Ozarks), Randolph and Wilson]

bowser 1. a MERKIN (*q.v.*). It is not known to which of the merkin senses this refers, probably a pudendal wig, *i.e.*, false female pubic hair. **2.** an ugly young woman. See BOWZER.

bow-sow narcotics. [Chinese or mock-Chinese; U.S. underworld, early 1900s, Berrey and Van den Bark]

bowzer 1. an ugly woman; a "real dog." From the traditional dog name. [U.S. slang, mid 1900s-pres.] **2.** a merkin. See BOWSER.

box 1. coffin. [U.S., 1800s and probably before] **2.** the female genitals, specifically the vagina. [widespread slang, 1900s] **3.** the male or female genitals. [U.S. homosexual use, mid 1900s] **4.** the male genitals, especially as made visible in revealing clothing. *Cf.* BASKET (sense 3). [U.S. homosexual use, mid 1900s, Farrell] **5.** to copulate with a woman. [U.S. slang, mid 1900s-pres.]

box, in the copulating; having the penis in the vagina. *Cf.* BOX (sense 2). [U.S. slang, mid 1900s]

boxed-up (also **boxed**) **1.** intoxicated with alcohol. [U.S. slang, mid 1900s, Wentworth and Flexner] **2.** drug intoxicated. From sense 1. [U.S. drug culture, mid 1900s-pres.]

boxer a catamite. For synonyms see BRONCO. [U.S. slang, mid 1900s-pres.]

box lunch CUNNILINGUS (*q.v.*). Based on the colloquial term for a picnic lunch. *Cf.* BOX (sense 2). [U.S. slang, mid 1900s-pres.]

box of glue a nickname for a Jewish man or woman. Rhyming slang for "Jew." Not necessarily derogatory. For synonyms see FIVE AND TWO. [U.S., 1900s, *Dictionary of Rhyming Slang*]

box the Jesuit and get cockroaches (also **box the Jesuit**) to masturbate, said of the male. *Cf.* FLOG THE BISHOP. For synonyms see WASTE TIME. [British, 1700s-1800s]

box-unseen the female genitals. *Cf.* BOX (sense 2). [vague references from *All's Well That Ends Well* (Shakespeare)]

boy 1. a derogatory term for a Negro male of any age. [U.S. 1800s-1900s] **2.** a catamite. [U.S. underworld, mid 1900s] **3.** heroin. *Cf.* GIRL (sense 9). [U.S. drug culture, mid 1900s-pres.] **4.** an effeminate male homosexual. Similar to sense 2. [U.S. slang, 1900s, Wentworth and Flexner] **5.** a masculine woman. *Cf.* TOM (sense 6). For synonyms see AMAZON. [U.S., 1900s, Berrey and Van den Bark]

boy-in-the-boat the clitoris. *Cf.* LITTLE MAN IN THE BOAT, TALK TO THE CANOE DRIVER. [British, 1800s, *Dictionary of Slang and Unconventional English*]

boy scout 1. a gentle and helpful person; a person who insists on helping even when help is needed. [U.S., 1900s] **2.** an effeminate male. For synonyms see FRIBBLE. [U.S. slang, early 1900s]

Bozzimacoo! "Kiss my ass!"; the same as BASIMECU! (*q.v.*). [from the French *baise mon cul;* British dialect, 1800s-1900s]

bra a brassiere. [U.S. colloquial, early 1900s-pres.] Synonyms: BRASSIERE, DOUBLE-BARRELLED CATAPULT, DOUBLE-BARRELLED SLING-SHOT, FLOPPER-STOPPER, FRONT-SUSPENSION, HAMMOCK FOR TWO, OVER-THE-SHOULDER-BOULDER-HOLDER, SOUNDPROOF BRA, TIT-BAG, TIT-HAMMOCK.

bra-burner a derogatory nickname for a militant female who supports

Women's Liberation movements. [U.S., 1960s]

bra-buster a shapely female; a woman with large or extremely large breasts. [U.S. slang, mid 1900s-pres.]

brace and bit a girl; woman considered sexually. Rhyming slang for TIT (sense 2). [U.S., 1900s, *Dictionary of Rhyming Slang*]

brache 1. a female dog; a bitch. [1300s] **2.** a wretched or cursed person. [early 1600s]

brack to make a vomiting sound; to vomit. [onomatopoetic]

bracmard the penis. One of a series of "sword" words for this organ. *Cf.* BLADE, CUTLASS, DAGGER, DIRK, LANCE, POINT. [from the French *braquemart*, a type of straight broadsword; British slang, 1800s, Farmer and Henley]

brakes the female pubic hair. "Brakes" refers to a thicket. [double entendre from *A Midsummer Night's Dream* (Shakespeare)]

brandle to masturbate. From a term meaning "shake." [early 1600s]

brass nail a prostitute. Rhyming slang for TAIL (sense 6). [British, early 1900s, *Dictionary of Rhyming Slang*]

brass nob a prostitute. Possibly rhyming slang for JOB (sense 2 or 3). [British, early 1900s, *Dictionary of the Underworld*]

brat 1. a derogatory name for a troublesome child. [since the early 1500s] **2.** a bastard. For synonyms see ACCIDENT. [since the 1500s] **3.** a young CATAMITE (*q.v.*). *Cf.* BOY (sense 2). [U.S. underworld, early 1900s, Goldin, O'Leary, and Lipsius]

brat-getting place the female genitals. For synonyms see MONOSYLLABLE. [British slang, 1800s, Farmer and Henley]

bravo a Mexican or Mexican American. Derogatory when used as a generic term. For synonyms see MEX. [U.S. slang, mid 1900s]

bread the female genitals. *Cf.* BUN (sense 3), JELLY-ROLE (sense 1), YEAST-

POWDER BISCUIT. [U.S. slang, 1900s, Wentworth and Flexner]

bread-basket the belly; the stomach. [since the mid 1700s]

bread-winner the female genitals, specifically the vagina. [British prostitute's slang, 1800s, Farmer and Henley]

break 1. to devirginate. [1600s] **2.** to break down a woman's resistance and coit her; to rape a woman. [U.S. slang, mid 1900s]

break a lance with to copulate with a woman. *Cf.* LANCE. [British slang, 1800s, *Dictionary of Slang and Unconventional English*]

break a leg 1. to get pregnant; to get seduced and pregnant. **2.** to copulate with a woman. [both senses, U.S. slang, late 1800s-early 1900s, Barrère and Leland]

break one's balls (also **bust one's nuts**) to suffer adversity or discomfort to accomplish something. *Cf.* BALL-BUSTER. [U.S. slang, mid 1900s-pres.]

break up 1. to separate; to divorce; to cease going steady. **2.** a separation; a divorce. Usually hyphenated when used as a noun. [U.S. colloquial, mid 1900s-pres.] Synonyms and related terms for both senses: DEWIFE, GREAT DIVIDE, HOLY DEADLOCK, MATCHRUPTCY, RENOVATE, SPLIT THE BLANKETS, SPLIT UP.

break wind originally to release wind upwards or release wind downwards. Now usually the latter. There is no single word for this subject for use in "polite speech," where the subject would almost never be mentioned. This most closely approaches a word-of-choice for this subject. For synonyms see GURK. [since the 1500s]

breast 1. one of the human mammary glands. Occurs in the singular or plural, and is virtually the only polite word for this gland which is used in the singular. For synonyms see BOSOM. **2.** a woman's chest or thorax, including the mammary glands; the place on a woman's body to which a baby is held. **3.** the chest or thorax of a man, used especially when referring to

love or tenderness. [all senses since *c.* 1000]

breast-work fondling, petting, or kissing the breasts. A reinterpretation of an old term for a defense wall or a parapet. [continuous nonce use]

breastworks the human breasts. [U.S. slang, mid 1900s-pres.]

breath strong enough to carry coal with intoxicated with alcohol. [British and U.S., late 1800s-1900s]

breech 1. a garment covering the genitals and buttocks. The garment has evolved into trousers, and the term is found now as "breeches" or "britches." [since *c.* 1000] **2.** the area covered by a BREECH (sense 1), primarily the buttocks. **3.** the rear of anything.

breech-cloth (also **breech-clout**) a garment which covers the buttocks (or at least the gluteal furrow) and the genitals. See BREECH (sense 1).

breeches (also **breech**) originally the equivalent of BREECH-CLOTH (*q.v.*); later, knee-breeches, trousers, and men's underwear. See BREECH (sense 1), BRITCHES. For synonyms see GALLI-GASKINS.

breeze a release of intestinal gas. For synonyms see GURK. [U.S. slang, 1900s]

breezy intoxicated with alcohol. Refers to the drinker's alcohol-laden breath. [U.S. slang, mid 1800s, Wentworth and Flexner]

Brian O'Linn gin; a glass of gin. Rhyming slang for "gin." [British slang, mid 1800s, Farmer and Henley]

brick 1. opium. [U.S. underworld, early 1900s] **2.** a pound or a kilogram of marijuana molded in the shape of a brick. *Cf.* KEY, KI [U.S. drug culture, mid 1900s-pres.]

brick gum (also **brick**) opium; gum opium. [U.S. underworld, early 1900s]

bridgey intoxicated with alcohol. [U.S. slang, early 1700s, Ben Franklin]

briefs 1. a type of pants (usually underwear or beach attire) with a low-cut waist and no legs. **2.** a euphemism for men's underpants. For synonyms see NETHER GARMENTS. [both senses, 1900s]

bright 1. a dandy; a fop. See BLOOD (sense 1). **2.** a mulatto. A truncation of BRIGHT MULATTO (*q.v.*). For synonyms see MAHOGANY. [U.S. slang, 1800s-1900s]

bright in the eye tipsy; intoxicated with alcohol. [British slang, late 1800s, Farmer and Henley]

bright mulatto an OCTOROON or a QUADROON. *Cf.* BRIGHT (sense 2). [U.S., 1900s, Berrey and Van den Bark]

Brighton Pier a homosexual male. Rhyming slang for "queer." For synonyms see EPICENE. [British slang, early 1900s, *Dictionary of Slang and Unconventional English*]

brim 1. a lewd woman; a furious woman; a BITCH (sense 2). See BRIMSTONE (sense 1). [British, early 1700s-1800s] **2.** a boar. [dialect, 1400s] **3.** for a sow to be in heat; to desire the BRIM (sense 2), the boar. [dialect, 1400s] **4.** the copulation of hogs. [dialect, 1400s] **5.** human copulation. From sense 4. [British, 1600s] **6.** a prostitute. From sense 3. [British, early 1700s]

brimming lustful. Originally pertaining to a sow which is ripe for a boar. *Cf.* BRIM, BULLING. Also extended to humans. [British and later U.S. use, 1900s]

brimstone 1. a lewd woman; a prostitute. [British, 1600s, B.E.] **2.** a virago; a spitfire. [British, 1700s, Farmer and Henley]

bring down by hand to abate an erection by masturbating to ejaculation, accomplished by oneself or someone else. The opposite of BRING UP BY HAND (*q.v.*). *Cf.* BRING OFF BY HAND, TAKE DOWN. [British slang, 1800s, Farmer and Henley]

bring off (also **bring someone off**) to cause ejaculation in oneself or another person. *Cf.* BRING OFF BY HAND. [colloquial or slang since the 1600s]

bring off by hand to cause orgasm in oneself or another person by masturbation. [British, 1800s]

bring on to arouse sexually; to TURN ON (sense 1). [colloquial since the 1500s]

bring out to introduce or initiate (someone) into homosexual activities; to cause someone to COME OUT OF THE CLOSET (*q.v.*). *Cf.* DAUGHTER, MOTHER (sense 3). [U.S. homosexual use, mid 1900s-pres., Stanley]

bring up 1. to vomit; to vomit something. **2.** to cough up something, as in "bring up blood." [both senses, U.S. colloquial, 1900s or before]

bring up by hand to produce an erection (one's own or someone else's) through manual stimulation. A play on the expression describing the careful nurturing of a living thing. *Cf.* BRING DOWN BY HAND. [British slang, 1800s, Farmer and Henley]

brisket 1. the chest; the BREAST (sense 2). **2.** fat gathered at the waistline; a SPARE TIRE (*q.v.*). [widespread slang, 1900s]

Bristol cities (also **Bristol city**) the human breasts. Rhyming slang for "titties," usually seen as BRISTOLS (*q.v.*). *Cf.* JERSEY CITIES, MANCHESTER CITY. For synonyms see BOSOM. [British slang, early 1900s-pres.]

Bristols the human breasts. From BRISTOL CITIES (*q.v.*). *Cf.* MANCHESTERS. [British slang, early 1900s-pres.]

britches trousers; breeches. For synonyms see GALLIGASKINS. [U.S. dialect and colloquial, 1800s-1900s]

broad 1. a mistress or a prostitute. [U.S. underworld use and general slang, early 1900s-pres.] **2.** any woman. Mildly derogatory. [U.S. slang, mid 1900s-pres.]

broad-jumper 1. a rapist. *Cf.* BROAD (sense 2), JUMP. [early 1900s] **2.** a thief who leaves (jumps out on) his woman; a jilter. [U.S. underworld, early 1900s]

Broadway broad 1. a prostitute. **2.** a young woman trying to break into the theater. [both senses, U.S. slang, mid 1900s]

broccoli marijuana. For synonyms see MARI. [U.S. drug culture, mid 1900s-pres.]

broiler an attractive female; a sexually tempting or seductive female. Based on the "heat" of passion and on a "broiler" chicken. From CHICK (sense 1). [U.S. slang, early 1900s, Berrey and Van den Bark]

broken her teacup to have been deflowered. See DEFLOWER. *Cf.* CRACK A JUDY'S TEACUP. [British euphemism, 1800s, Farmer and Henley]

broken-kneed (also **broken-legged**) pertaining to a woman who was seduced and made pregnant. Refers to a difficulty in remaining upright. *Cf.* BREAK A LEG, SPRAIN ONE'S ANKLE. [British, 1700s-1800s]

broken oar a prostitute. Rhyming slang for "whore." *Cf.* BOAT AND OAR. [British, 1900s, *Dictionary of Rhyming Slang*]

broken-rib a divorced woman. *Cf.* RIB, SPARE RIB.

broken-wrist a homosexual male; the same as LIMP-WRIST (*q.v.*). For synonyms see EPICENE. [U.S. slang, mid 1900s-pres.]

bronco (also **bronc, bronk**) a CATA-MITE (*q.v.*). [from a Spanish word for a "rough" horse; U.S. underworld, early 1900s, Montelone] Synonyms: AN-GELINA, AUNT, BALL AND CHAIN, BEND-ER, BIMBO, BINDLE-BOY, BITCH, BO, BOONG-MOLL, BOTTOMS, BOXER, BOY, BRAT, BROWN, BRUNSER, BUM-BOY, CATCH, CHERRY-PICKER, CHUFF, CINAEDUS, COMFORT FOR THE TROOPS, FAG, FAIRY, FRUIT, GAL-BOY, GANYMEDE, GASH, GAY-CAT, GAZOOK, GAZOONEY, GAZOONY, GINCH, GONSEL, HAT, HIDE, HUMP, INGLE, KID LAMB, KIFE, LAMB, LAY, LILYWHITE, LITTLE LADY, MALE VARLET, MASCULINE WHORE, MISS NANCY, MUSTARD-POT, NAN-BOY, NANCE, NEPHEW, NIGH ENOUGH, ONE OF THE BROWN FAMILY, ONE OF THOSE, PAINTED-WILLIE, PANSY, PASSIVE PARTICIPANT, PATHIC, PEDDLE-SNATCH, PEG BOY, PIECE OF SNATCH, PINK PANTS, POGER, POSSESH, POUFTER, PRESHEN, PRUSHUN, PUNCE, PUNK, PUNK KID, RECEIVER, RING-TAIL, RING-TAIL WIFE, ROAD KID, ROUNDEYE, SNATCH-PEDDLER, TRUG, TWIDGET, WIFE, WILLIE, YOUTHFUL VICTIM OF DEGENERATE.

brood 1. a good-looking young woman; a sexually attractive female. **2.** a young woman who is known to permit copula-tion without much fuss. [both senses, U.S. slang, mid 1900s-pres.]

broom 1. the female genitals. This term matches the male member, BROOM-HANDLE (*q.v.*). **2.** the female pubic hair. For synonyms see DOWNSHIRE. [both senses, British slang, 1800s, Farmer and Henley]

broom-handle (also **broomstick**) the penis. *Cf.* BROOM (sense 1). [harlot's use, (Farmer and Henley); British slang, 1800s]

brothel a house of prostitution; a place where prostitutes perform their services; a brothelhouse. Originally a good-for-nothing man (1300s), and then a prostitute (1400s). Now used in the "house" sense exclusively. Currently the U.S. polite word-of-choice for this topic. These synonyms refer to female brothels unless indicated otherwise: ACADEMY, ACCOMMODATION HOUSE, ASSIGNATION HOUSE, BAGNIO, BAG-SHANTY, BAND, BAND-BOX, BAND-HOUSE, BANG, BAT HOUSE, BAWD'S HOUSE, BAWDYHOUSE, BEAUTY PARLOR, BEAVER BASE, BED-HOUSE, BERKER, BIRDCAGE, BODIKIN, BORDEL, BORDELLO, BROTHEL-HOUSE, BULL-RING CAMP (male), BUTTON-HOLE FACTORY, CAB, CAB-JOINT, CAKE-SHOP, CALL-HOUSE, CAMP, CAN HOUSE, CASA, CAT-FLAT, CAT-HOUSE, CAVAULTING SCHOOL, CHAMBER OF COMMERCE, CHIPPY-HOUSE, CHIPPY-JOINT, CORINTH, COU-PLING-HOUSE, COW-BAG, CREEP-JOINT, CRIB, CRIB-HOUSE, DIRTY SPOT, DISOR-DERLY HOUSE, DIVE, DOSS, DOSS HOUSE, DRESSHOUSE, DRUM, FANCY HOUSE, FAST HOUSE, FISH-MARKET, FLASH-CASE, FLASH-CRIB, FLASH-DRUM, FLASH-HOUSE, FLASH-KEN, FLASH-PANNY, FLEA AND LOUSE, FLESH-FACTORY, FLESH-MARKET, FLESH-POT, FLESH-SHAMBLES, FORNIX, FRANZY HOUSE, FUCKERY, FUCK-HOUSE,

GARDEN-HOUSE, GAY HOUSE, GIRLERY, GIRL SHOP, GOAT-HOUSE, GOOSEBERRY-RANCH, GOOSING-RANCH, GOOSING-SLUM, GRINDING-HOUSE, HEIFER BARN, HEIFER DEN, H. OF I.F., HOOK-SHOP, HOT-HOLE, HOT-HOUSE, HOUSE IN THE SUBURBS, HOUSE OF ALL NATIONS, HOUSE OF ASSIGNATION, HOUSE OF CALL, HOUSE OF CIVIL RECEPTION, HOUSE OF ENJOYMENT, HOUSE OF ILL-DELIGHT, HOUSE OF ILL-FAME, HOUSE OF ILL-REPUTE, HOUSE OF JOY, HOUSE OF LEWDNESS, HOUSE OF PROFESSION, HOUSE OF RESORT, HOUSE OF SALE, HUMMUMS, ICE PALACE, JACKSIE, JAG-HOUSE (male), JOINT, JOY HOUSE, JUKE-HOUSE, KIP, KIP SHOP, KNOCKING-HOUSE, KNOCKING-JOINT, KNOCKING-SHOP, LADIES' COLLEGE, LEAPING-HOUSE, LEWD HOUSE, LOOSE-LOVE CENTER, LUPANAR, MEAT HOUSE, MOLL-SHOP, MOLLY-HOUSE (male), MONKEY-HOUSE, NANNY-HOUSE, NANNY-SHOP, NAUGHTY-HOUSE, NAUTCH-JOINT, NOTCHERY, NOTCH-HOUSE, NOTCH-JOINT, NUGGING-HOUSE, NUGGING-KEN, NUNNERY, OCCUPYING-HOUSE, ONERY-HOUSE, PARLOR HOUSE, PEG-HOUSE (male), PHEASANTRY, PUNCH-HOUSE, PUSHING SCHOOL, RED LAMP, RED LIGHT, RED-LIGHT HOUSE, RIB-JOINT, SCHOOL OF VENUS, SERAGLIETTO, SERAGLIO, SHANTY, SLAUGHTER-HOUSE, SMOONGY, SMUGGLING-KEN, SNOOZING-KEN, SPINTRY (male), SPORTER, SPORTING-HOUSE, SPORTING-TAVERN, STEW, TEMPLE OF VENUS, THE STEWS, TIMOTHY, TOUCH-CRIB, TRUGGLING-KEN, VAULTING-HOUSE, VAULTING-SCHOOL, VROW-CASE, WALK-UP, WARM SHOP, WARREN, WHOREHOUSE, WHORE-SHOP, WINDOW TAPPERY, WOP-SHOP.

brother 1. heroin. *Cf.* BOY (sense 3). [U.S. drug culture, mid 1900s-pres.] **2.** a black man. A term of address used by blacks. *Cf.* BLOOD (sense 2). [U.S. slang, mid 1900s-pres.]

brother Ben an amphetamine, Benzedrine. See CO-PILOT BEN. [U.S. drug culture, mid 1900s-pres.]

brown 1. the anus. A truncation of ''brown asshole'' or similar expression. [British and U.S., 1800s-1900s] **2.** to perform anal intercourse as a

receiver or an insertor. [U.S., 1900s or before] **3.** a CATAMITE (*q.v.*). [U.S. underworld, early 1900s, Goldin, O'Leary, and Lipsius] **4.** pertaining to the anus or to human feces. [U.S., 1900s] Senses 1-4 refer to the color of feces. **5.** a Mexican or a Puerto Rican. Derogatory. [U.S. slang, mid 1900s-pres.] **6.** heroin. *Cf.* BROWN SUGAR (sense 2). [U.S. drug culture, mid 1900s-pres.] **7.** a mulatto. Derogatory. [U.S., 1900s]

brown boy a male who obtains sexual gratification through COPROPHILIA (*q.v.*). See FECAL-FREAK, KITCHEN-CLEANER, POUND-CAKE QUEEN. [U.S. slang, mid 1900s-pres.]

brown bucket the rectum. *Cf.* BROWN (sense 1), BUCKET (sense 2). For synonyms see ANUS. [U.S. slang, 1900s]

brown dots the drug L.S.D. (*q.v.*). *Cf.* DOTS, MICRODOTS. [U.S. drug culture, mid 1900s-pres.]

browned 1. darned. A mild euphemism for ''damned.'' [U.S., 1900s or before] **2.** angered.

brown-eye (also **eye**) anal copulation; an act of anal copulation. Usually said of males. *Cf.* BROWN (sense 2). [U.S. slang, 1900s]

Brown family, the pederasts in general. *Cf.* ONE OF THE BROWN FAMILY. [U.S. slang, 1900s]

brown-hatter a pederast. *Cf.* BROWN (sense 2), BUD SALLOGH. [British naval slang, early 1900s, *Dictionary of Slang and Unconventional English*]

brown hole 1. to commit or permit anal sexual intercourse. [both homosexual and heterosexual use] **2.** anal copulation; pederasty. For synonyms see SODOMY. [both senses, U.S. slang, mid 1900s]

brownie 1. a good-natured goblin; a Scottish house spirit. Also **Browny. 2.** the anus. *Cf.* BROWN (sense 1). [U.S. slang, mid 1900s] **3.** a homosexual male who prefers anal coition. [U.S. homosexual use, mid 1900s-pres., Farrell] **4.** a chewy square of chocolate cake which has marijuana among its ingredients. *Cf.* ALICE B. TOKLAS. [U.S. drug culture, mid 1900s-pres.]

brownie king a pederast; the "active" partner; the INSERTOR (*q.v.*). The opposite of BROWNIE QUEEN (*q.v.*). *Cf.* ARSE KING, ASPRO. [U.S. homosexual use, mid 1900s, Farrell]

brownie queen a pederast; the "passive" partner; a RECEIVER (*q.v.*). *Cf.* BROWNIE KING. [U.S. homosexual use, mid 1900s, Farrell]

browning copulating anally. *Cf.* BROWN (sense 2). [U.S. homosexual use, 1900s]

brown-job ANILINGUS (*q.v.*). *Cf.* ANILINGISM, EAT POUND-CAKE, REAM, RIM, RIM-JOB, TONGUE-FUCK.

brown-nose 1. to curry favor; to be a sycophant. **2.** a sycophant. Both refer to the BROWN (sense 4) of feces. *Cf.* BROWN-TONGUE. [both senses, U.S. slang, 1900s]

brown polish a mulatto. For synonyms see MAHOGANY. [U.S. slang, 1900s]

brown rine heroin. Possibly rhyming, "heroine." [early 1900s, *Dictionary of the Underworld*]

browns amphetamines. Both Benzedrine (trademark) and Dexedrine (trademark) are sold in capsules which are half brown and half some other color. [U.S. drug culture, mid 1900s-pres.]

brown-skin baby a young black woman. [U.S. underworld, 1900s]

brown stuff opium. [U.S., 1900s]

brown sugar 1. a Negro, especially one's black boyfriend or girlfriend. [U.S. slang, 1900s] **2.** heroin. [U.S. drug culture, mid 1900s-pres.]

brown-tongue a sycophant. This term refers to ANILINGUS (*q.v.*). *Cf.* BROWN-NOSE. [British, 1900s, *Dictionary of Slang and Unconventional English*]

brown Windsor, the the anus. [Australian, early 1900s, Baker]

bruised intoxicated with alcohol. For synonyms see WOOFLED. [U.S. slang, mid 1800s-1900s]

brunser a CATAMITE (*q.v.*) who accompanies a tramp. For synonyms

see BRONCO. [U.S. underworld, early 1900s]

Brunswick the rectum; the anus. *Cf.* BROWN (sense 1). [U.S. slang, early 1900s, Berrey and Van den Bark]

brush 1. the female pubic hair. For synonyms see DOWNSHIRE. [widespread slang, mid 1800s-pres.] **2.** a woman considered sexually. [Australian and British, 1800s-1900s] **3.** coition. [British, mid 1800s, Barrère and Leland] **4.** to coit a female. [British and U.S. slang, mid 1800s-pres.]

brush-ape a hillbilly; a rural oaf. [U.S. slang, 1900s and before, Wentworth]

brute the bull. *Cf.* ANIMAL (sense 1). [U.S. dialect, 1900s or before]

B.S. 1. "bullshit," nonsense. [U.S. euphemism, 1900s] **2.** a "bad situation." A reinterpretation of the initials in sense 1. [U.S., 1900s]

bub 1. strong beer or any alcoholic beverage. [British, late 1600s, B.E.] **2.** a breast; a BUBBY (sense 1). Usually in the plural. For synonyms see BOSOM. [British slang, 1800s, Farmer and Henley]

bubber 1. a drunkard; a beer-drinker. *Cf.* BUB (sense 1). [British, late 1600s] **2.** an old woman with extremely large breasts or "bubs." [U.S., mid 1800s, Farmer and Henley]

bubbies the human breasts. See BOOBIES, BOOBS. [British and U.S. colloquial, 1800s-1900s]

bubbles the human breasts. From the roundness and from BUB (sense 2). *Cf.* LOVE-BUBBLES. [U.S. slang, 1900s]

bubble-water champagne. For synonyms see WHOOPEE-WATER. [U.S. slang, 1900s]

bubbly 1. rum, especially dark rum. [British military, 1900s, Fraser and Gibbons] **2.** champagne. [U.S. slang, mid 1900s]

bubby 1. a human breast. Usually in the plural. *Cf.* BOOB (sense 2). [widespread colloquial English since the late 1600s] **2.** intoxicated with alcohol. From BUB (sense 1). [British slang, 1600s]

bubo a swelling of a lymph node in the groin, as with syphilis or the bubonic plague. *Cf.* BLUE BOAR, BLUE BOY. [since the late 1300s] Synonyms: ADEN, BLUE BOY, CHANCRE, CHANK, DUMB WATCH, FRENCH PIG, GOOSE, HARD SORE, IRISH BUTTON, PEARL, PIMPLE, PINTLE-BLOSSOM, POULAIN, WART, WINCHESTER-GOOSE, WINCHESTER-PIGEON.

bucket 1. the female genitals. Despite the dates, probably from sense 2. [British slang, 1800s, Farmer and Henley] **2.** the anus or buttocks. *Cf.* BROWN BUCKET. [U.S. slang since the early 1900s or before] **3.** jail; prison. [U.S. underworld (tramps), mid 1900s-pres.]

bucket-broad a prostitute who permits or specializes in anal intercourse. From BUCKET (sense 2). [U.S. underworld, mid 1900s]

bucket of blood (also **blood-bucket**) an ambulance. [U.S. slang, mid 1900s]

bucket of suds a bucket or a mug of beer. *Cf.* SUDS. [U.S. slang, 1900s]

buck fitch a lecher; an old lecher. Possibly from "fitchew," the name of a polecat. [British slang or cant, 1600s, B.E.]

buckle my shoe (also **buckle**) a nickname for a Jewish man or woman. Rhyming slang for "Jew." Not necessarily derogatory. For synonyms see FIVE AND TWO. [British, 1900s, *Dictionary of Rhyming Slang*]

buck-naked completely naked. [U.S. dialect and colloquial, 1900s]

buck nigger a derogatory nickname for a black man. [U.S., early 1800s-pres.]

buckra (also **backra**) a white man; a white master. From a word for "white man" in various West African languages, *e.g.*, Efik *mbakara*, or Duala *bakara*. [widespread colloquial, 1700s-1900s]

buck's face a cuckold. Refers to horns. [British, late 1600s, B.E.]

buckskin a condom. For synonyms see EEL-SKIN. [U.S. slang, 1900s]

buck snort an audible release of

intestinal gas. For synonyms see GURK. [U.S. slang, mid 1900s]

bucksom lewd; wanton. *Cf.* BUXOM. [British, late 1600s, B.E.]

bud a virgin young woman. *Cf.* FLOWER (sense 2). [U.S. slang, 1900s, Montelone]

buddha stick a marijuana cigarette. *Cf.* THAI STICKS. For synonyms see MEZZROLL. [U.S. drug culture, mid 1900s-pres.]

budget the female genitals. From a term for a leather bottle. See LEATHER (sense 1). [British slang, 1800s, Farmer and Henley]

budgy intoxicated with alcohol. [British and U.S. slang, late 1800s-early 1900s]

bud sallogh a pederast; an INSERTER (*q.v.*). Literally, "a shitten prick," a penis fouled with feces (Grose). [Irish; British, late 1700s]

buff 1. the bare skin; nudity. [colloquial, mid 1600s-pres.] **2.** to strip naked. Primarily in "to buff it." [British, mid 1800s] **3.** an oaf; a jerk. [U.S., 1900s or before] **4.** a girl or woman. A truncation of BUFFALO (sense 2). [U.S. slang, 1900s] **5.** a movie containing nudity. From sense 1. [U.S. slang, mid 1900s-pres.]

buff, in the (also **buff, in**) naked; nude. *Cf.* BUFF (sense 1). [since the early 1600s]

buffalo 1. a black man. For synonyms see EBONY. [U.S. underworld and slang, early 1900s-pres.] **2.** a girl or woman, especially a fat girl or woman. [U.S. slang, 1900s] **3.** a husband, man, or any male. From sense 1. [U.S. slang, mid 1900s-pres.]

buffalo chips dried buffalo (or cattle) dung used as fuel. *Cf.* BODEWASH, PRAIRIE COAL, SURFACE FUEL. For synonyms see COW-CHIPS. [U.S. colloquial, mid 1800s-1900s]

buffarilla an ugly young woman. A blend of "buffalo" and "gorilla." *Cf.* BUFFALO (sense 2). [U.S. slang, mid 1900s] Synonyms: BAT, BEAR, BEAST, BITCH, BOWZER, BURNT CHEESE, COOL-

ER, DRACK, GRODDESS, HOG, MACKA-BROIN, MIVVY, PIG, PILL, PITCH, PORKER, SCAG, SCUZZ, SNAG, WITCH, ZELDA.

buff-bare naked; nude. *Cf.* buff (sense 1). [U.S., 1900s or before]

buffers the breasts. For synonyms see BOSOM. [British slang, 1800s-1900s, *Dictionary of Slang and Unconventional English*]

buffy intoxicated with alcohol. For synonyms see WOOFLED. [British and U.S. slang, mid 1800s-1900s]

bug 1. an insane person. **2.** a psychoanalyst. **3.** a prostitute. [all senses, U.S., 1900s, Wentworth and Flexner]

bugaboo 1. nasal mucus, especially dry mucus. [Caribbean (Jamaican), Cassidy and Le Page] **2.** a ghost. [colloquial since the early 1700s]

bug doctor psychiatrist or psychologist. *Cf.* BUG (sense 2). [U.S. slang, early 1900s]

bugger 1. a heretic. From "Bulgar." Sexual perversion of all types was ascribed to these early heretics. [1300s-1500s] **2.** someone who practices forms of sexual perversion; a sodomist. [since the mid 1500s] **3.** a PEDERAST (*q.v.*). [British and U.S., early 1700s-pres.] **4.** to perform PEDERASTY (*q.v.*) or other nonorthogenital sexual activities. [primarily British, since the early 1600s] **5.** a fellow or pal. No negative connotations. [British 1800s or before to the present] **6.** a small person or thing, especially in the expression "little bugger." **7.** as an oath, "Bugger!", a strong exclamation. The equivalent of U.S. "Oh, fuck!" [Australian and British, 1900s and before] **8.** a ghost. [U.S. dialect] **9.** to mess up. A truncation of BUGGER UP (*q.v.*). **10.** a bad situation or difficult task. *Cf.* BITCH (sense 11). [1900s]

Bugger off! a curse or an exclamation, "Get the hell out of here!" The equivalent of FUCK OFF (sense 4). [British, 1900s]

bugger up (also **bugger**) to mess something up. *Cf.* FUCK UP. [British and later U.S. via the World Wars]

buggery sodomy; sexual perversion. Usually includes at least anilingus, bestiality, cunnilingus, anal copulation, penilingus, and sometimes masturbation. For synonyms see SODOMY. [since the early 1300s]

Bugger you! a strong curse, the equivalent of "Fuck you!" [British, 1900s]

buggy a derogatory term for a Negro. See BOOGIE (sense 2).

bug juice 1. strong liquor; whisky. For synonyms see BOOZE. [U.S. slang, late 1800s-early 1900s] **2.** an opiate; a narcotic. For synonyms see COTICS. [U.S. slang, 1900s]

built like a brick shit-house 1. pertaining to a well-built woman. Referring to the curves of an unevenly laid brick wall. **2.** pertaining to a sturdily-built male. *Cf.* STACKED LIKE A BRICK SHIT-HOUSE. [both senses, U.S., 1900s]

bulbs the human breasts. From "electric light bulb." [U.S. slang, mid 1900s]

bull 1. for a cow to desire copulation with a bull. **2.** for a bull to copulate with a cow. It is sense 2 which caused speakers of American English to use euphemisms for "bull" such as GENTLEMAN COW (*q.v.*). [British and later U.S. colloquial and dialect, 1300s-pres.] Terms for the bull (animal) that are avoidances for these senses are: ANIMAL, BIG ANIMAL, BRUTE, BUTTERMILK COW, COW-BRUTE, COW'S SPOUSE, CRITTER, GENTLEMAN COW, GENTLEMAN OX, HE-COW, HE-THING, JONATHAN, MALE BEAST, MALE BRUTE, MALE COW, MAN-COW, OX, ROGER, SEED-OX, STOCK BEAST, STOCK BRUTE, STOCK COW, SURLY, TOP COW. **3.** nonsense. This sense was recorded without reference to "bull-shit" and appears to have developed independently from the coarser term, although it is now regarded as a truncation of BULLSHIT (*q.v.*). [the form may be from Medieval Latin meaning "bubble," *i.e.*, "as fleeting as a bubble," or perhaps cognate with

Icelandic *bull,* "nonsense," or a Middle English term for a joke or a jest; since the early 1600s] **4.** a lecher. *Cf.* TOWN BULL. [1600s-1700s] **5.** to cheat or lie; to BULLSHIT (sense 2). [British and U.S. slang, 1900s] **6.** a lesbian; a masculine lesbian. *Cf.* BULLDIKER. [U.S. slang mid 1900s-pres.] **7.** to copulate with a woman. From sense 2. [British and U.S. slang, late 1700s-pres.] **8.** an officer of the law. [originally and primarily underworld (tramps), U.S., 1900s or before]

bull ants (also **bull's aunts**) trousers; pants. Rhyming slang for "pants." *Cf.* INSECTS AND ANTS. [British and U.S., 1900s, *Dictionary of Rhyming Slang*]

bull bitch a masculine female or a virago. From the name for a female bulldog and from BULLDIKER (*q.v.*). [U.S. slang, mid 1900s]

bull-dagger a lesbian. See BULLDIKER. [U.S. slang, mid 1900s]

bulldiker (also **bulldike**) a masculine woman or a masculine lesbian. Usually considered quite derogatory. *Cf.* DIKE (sense 2). [U.S. slang, early 1900s-pres.]

bull-dozed intoxicated with alcohol. *Cf.* HALF-BULLED. From "dose of the bull," a beating with a strip of cowhide. [Australian, early 1800s-1900s]

bull-dust (also **bull-fodder**) **1.** nonsense. **2.** to talk nonsense; to deceive. Both are euphemisms for BULLSHIT (*q.v.*). [both senses, Australian, 1900s, Baker]

bulldyker (also **bulldyke**) a variant of BULLDIKER (*q.v.*).

buller 1. one who talks nonsense; a BULLSHITTER (*q.v.*). *Cf.* BULL (sense 5). Synonyms: BLOWHARD, BULL JOCKEY, BULLSHITTER, BULLSHIT ARTIST, BULLSHITTER, BULL SHOOTER, CRAPPER. **2.** a cow in heat. *Cf.* BULL (sense 1). [Australian, mid 1900s, Baker]

bullets 1. the testicles. **2.** semen. *Cf.* I.O.F.B., SHOOT (sense 1). [widespread recurrent nonce since at least the 1600s]

bull-feathers nonsense. A disguise of BULLSHIT (*q.v.*). *Cf.* HORSEFEATHERS. [U.S., 1900s]

bullfest a gathering for discussing matters very informally; a group discussion where much bullshit is thrown. Patterned on "songfest." [U.S. slang, mid 1900s]

bull-fodder nonsense; a euphemism for BULLSHIT (*q.v.*). *Cf.* BULL-DUST. [Australian, 1900s, Baker]

bull fuck 1. a thick gravy with chunks of meat. A dysphemism based on "bull semen." *Cf.* FUCK (sense 3). **2.** a custard. [attested as Canadian, early 1900s, *Dictionary of the Underworld*]

bull gravy a thick cream gravy. Probably means "bull semen." See BULL FUCK. [U.S. dialect, 1900s]

bullhead a stupid, stubborn oaf. [colloquial since the early 1600s]

bulling 1. pertaining to a cow which desires copulating with a bull. *Cf.* BULL (sense 1). **2.** boasting idly; lying. *Cf.* BULL (sense 5). [both senses, U.S., 1900s]

bullo nonsense; BULLSHIT (*q.v.*). [Australian, mid 1900s, Baker]

bullock's heart a release of intestinal gas. Rhyming slang for "fart." *Cf.* BEEF-HEARTS. [British, late 1800s, *Dictionary of Rhyming Slang*]

bull-ring camp a brothel offering virile males for male and female customers. [U.S. underworld, early 1900s, Goldin, O'Leary, and Lipsius]

bull-roar nonsense; BULLSHIT (*q.v.*). [slang, 1900s]

bull-scutter the dung of a bull. [British dialect, 1900s and before]

bull-seg (also **bull-stub**) a castrated bull; a bull stag. [British dialect, 1800s and before]

bull's eye the female genitals, specifically the vagina. [British slang, 1800s, Farmer and Henley]

bullsh (also **bulsh**) nonsense. A truncation of BULLSHIT (*q.v.*). [attested as Boontling, late 1800s-early 1900s; otherwise attested as Australian, World Wars]

bullshartist a boaster and talker of nonsense; a teller of tall tales. *Cf.*

BULLSH, BULLSHIT ARTIST. [Australian, 1900s, Baker]

bullshit 1. nonsense. **2.** to utter nonsense; to lie or deceive. Based on BULL (sense 5), of which it is an elaboration. [U.S. slang, 1900s] Disguises and synonyms for both senses: ALLIGATOR BULL, BATSHIT, BESSIE SMITH, BIRD SEED, BOVINE EXCREMENT, BOVINE EXCRESCENCE, BOVRIL, B.S., BULL, BULL-DUST, BULL-FEATHERS, BULL-FODDER, BULLO, BULL—ONEY, BULL—ROAR, BULLSH, BULLSHOT, BULLSKATE, BULL'S WOOL, BULSH, BURMA SHAVE, BUSHWAH, CORRAL DUST, COW-CONFETTI, COWSH, COWYARD CONFETTI, FROGSH, HOGWASH, HORSE, HORSE APPLE, HORSE FEATHERS, HORSERADISH, HORSESHIT, HORSH, TAURI EXCRETIO. See ANIMAL for other terms for nonsense.

bullshit artist a well-known teller of tall tales; a liar; a cheat. *Cf.* BULLSHARTIST. For synonyms see BULLER. [U.S. slang, mid 1900s]

bullshitter a liar; a teller of tale tales; a boaster. For synonyms see BULLER. [U.S. slang and colloquial, 1900s]

bullshot nonsense. A euphemism for BULLSHIT (*q.v.*). [U.S. slang, 1900s, Wentworth and Flexner]

bull's wool nonsense. A disguise of BULLSHIT (*q.v.*). [Australian, 1900s, Baker]

bully 1. a mean fellow. **2.** a cowardly fighter. **3.** a protector of prostitutes or a robber-accomplice of a prostitute. [since the 1600s or before]

bulsh nonsense. See BULLSH.

bum 1. the posteriors. [colloquial, late 1300s-pres.] **2.** a prostitute in the sense of TAIL (sense 6). **3.** the female genitals. *Cf.* ASS (sense 3), BUTT (sense 3). **4.** a hobo; an oaf. [early 1500s-pres.] **5.** a SPREE (sense 2). [U.S., 1900s and before] **6.** bad. The opposite of "rum," meaning "good." [British and U.S. slang and colloquial, 1900s]

bum-bags trousers. For synonyms see GALLIGASKINS. [British slang, mid 1800s]

bumblebee an amphetamine tablet or capsule. For synonyms see AMP. [U.S. drug culture, mid 1900s-pres.]

bumbo 1. the female genitals. *Cf.* BUM (sense 3). [attributed to various West African languages; British, 1700s] **2.** the buttocks. *Cf.* BUM (sense 1). [Caribbean (Jamaican), Cassidy and Le Page] **3.** a rum drink. [from Italian; British, mid 1700s]

bum-boozer a drunkard. *Cf.* ALKY BUM.

bum-boy a CATAMITE (*q.v.*). *Cf.* NANBOY. For synonyms see BRONCO.

bumf toilet paper. From BUM-FODDER (*q.v.*). For synonyms see T.P. [British, 1600s-1900s]

Bumfay! (also **Bum-lady!, Bumtroth!**) an oath and an exclamation, "By my fay!" or "By my faith!" For synonyms see 'ZOUNDS! [late 1500s]

bum fiddle 1. to copulate; to fiddle with a BUM (sense 3). [slang, mid 1500s] **2.** the posteriors; the anus considered as a musical instrument. *Cf.* ARS MUSICA. [British, 1600s] **3.** the female genitals. *Cf.* BUM (sense 3). [British slang, late 1600s]

bum-fiddler a fornicator. For synonyms see LECHER. [British, 1600s or before]

bumfluff nonsense. *Cf.* BUMF. [Australian, 1900s, Baker]

bum-fodder 1. toilet paper. [colloquial, mid 1600s-pres., (Urquhart)] **2.** obscene reading material; cheap, trashy reading material. From sense 1. [British slang, mid 1700s]

bummer 1. a bad drug experience. [U.S. drug culture, mid 1900s-pres.] **2.** any bad experience. From sense 1. [U.S. slang, mid 1900s-pres.] **3.** an idle loafer; a worthless BUM (sense 4). [British, 1800s] **4.** a sodomite; a person who participates in anal copulation. Usually said of a male. [slang, 1900s]

bummerkeh a sexually loose woman; a prostitute. For synonyms see HARLOT. [Yiddish]

bummy the posteriors. *Cf.* BUM (sense 1). [U.S. slang, early 1900s, Weseen]

bump 1. to coit and impregnate a woman. [U.S. slang, 1900s] **2.** a pimple. See BUMPS (sense 1). [U.S. colloquial, 1900s] **3.** a baby's bottom. [U.S. juvenile, 1900s]

bumpers the human breasts. [British and U.S. slang, mid 1900s]

bumpkin (also **bumkin**) a country oaf; a dull rustic. [since the late 1500s] Synonyms: BACON, CHAW-BACON, CHURL, CLOD-HOPPER, CLOWN, CLUMPERTON, CLUNCH, CLUNK, COUNTRY JAKE, DUNG-FORK. See OAF for similar terms.

bump off to kill someone. [U.S. underworld, early 1900s-pres.]

bumps 1. pimples. [U.S. colloquial, 1900s] **2.** breasts, especially if small or fledgling. [both senses, British and U.S. slang, 1900s]

bumps and grinds the stereotypical dance of a stripper, including the swindling and thrusting of the pelvis. [U.S. slang, early 1900s-pres.]

bumpsy (also **bumpsie**) intoxicated with alcohol. [British, early 1600s]

bum-shop 1. a brothel. **2.** the female genitals. Cf. BUM (sense 3). [both senses, British, 1900s]

bum-sucker a sycophant; a toady. Cf. EGG-SUCKER, KISS-ASS, SUCK-ASS. [British slang, mid 1800s-pres.]

bum-tickler the penis. [British slang, 1800s, Farmer and Henley]

bum wad toilet paper. Cf. BUMF. For synonyms see T.P. [slang, mid 1900s]

bun 1. the tail of a hare. No negative connotations. Cf. SCUT (sense 1). [early 1500s] **2.** a buttock. See BUNS (sense 1). Also used for the buttocks. **3.** the female genitals. See TOUCH BUN FOR LUCK. [British slang and cant, 1600s-1700s] **4.** a prostitute. From sense 3 or from TART (q.v.). [British slang, late 1800s, Barrère and Leland] **5.** a drunk; a buzz. Cf. HAVE A BUN ON. [U.S. slang, 1900s or before]

bunch-punch the legendary GANG-BANG (q.v.), serial copulation of one person by a number of males. See similar terms at GROUP SEX. [U.S. slang, mid 1900s-pres.]

bunchy a nickname for the buttocks.

For synonyms see DUFF. [Caribbean (Jamaican), Cassidy and Le Page]

buncombe (also **bunk, bunkum**) nonsense; idle talk meant to be so by design. Named for "Buncombe" County, North Carolina, and a filibuster performed by its representative in Congress. [U.S. colloquial, 1900s]

bundle 1. for a man and a woman to occupy the same bed fully dressed as a means of courting. The BUNDLING-BOARD (q.v.) was employed to prevent them from copulating, should that enter their minds. [found in Wales and the U.S., 1600s-1700s] **2.** a sexually desirable female. Halliwell defines this as "a low woman." Cf. PACKAGE. [U.S. slang, 1900s] **3.** a supply of illicit drugs. [U.S. drug culture, mid 1900s]

bundler a male sadist who practices BONDAGE (q.v.). Cf. SADIST. [British, early 1900s, Dictionary of the Underworld]

bundling-board a board placed between a man and woman (occupying the same bed) to prevent them from copulating. See BUNDLE (sense 1).

bung 1. the anus. [since the 1600s] **2.** intoxicated with alcohol. Cf. BUNGED. [British, early 1700s]

bungalow the female genitals, specifically the vagina. Based on "bung below." [U.S. slang, 1900s]

bunged intoxicated with alcohol. Cf. BUNG (sense 2). For synonyms see WOOFLED.

bung-eyed intoxicated with alcohol. [British, 1800s, Sinks of London Laid Open]

bung-fodder toilet paper. Cf. BUM-FODDER, BUNG (sense 1). [U.S. colloquial, 1800s-1900s]

bungfu intoxicated with alcohol. A truncation of "bungfull." [U.S. slang, 1900s or before]

bung hole 1. anal intercourse. Cf. BUNG (sense 1). **2.** to permit or perform anal sexual intercourse. **3.** the anus. [all senses, U.S., 1900s] **4.** the female genitals, specifically the vagina. [slang, 1800-pres.]

bunk nonsense. From BUNCOMBE (*q.v.*). [U.S., early 1900s]

bunker 1. a pederast; the INSERTOR (*q.v.*). [U.S. underworld, early 1900s, Irwin] **2.** to commit pederasty; to perform anal copulation. [U.S. slang, early 1900s]

bunker shy pertaining to a young male (presumably a prison inmate) who is afraid of being forced into SODOMY as a CATAMITE (both *q.v.*). [U.S. underworld, early 1900s, Irwin]

bunned intoxicated with alcohol. *Cf.* BUN (sense 5), HAVE A BUN ON. [U.S. slang and colloquial, 1900s or before]

bunny 1. the female genitals. *Cf.* CONY. [British, 1700s] **2.** a sexually loose woman. *Cf.* BED-BUNNY. [U.S. slang, mid 1900s-pres.] **3.** a male or female prostitute. [senses 2 and 3 are U.S., mid 1900s-pres.]

bunny-fuck very rapid sexual intercourse; an act of sexual intercourse involving very rapid thrusting by the male. [U.S. slang, mid 1900s-pres.]

buns 1. the posteriors. From the shape of the buttocks and the gluteal furrow. *Cf.* BUN (sense 2). [U.S. slang, mid 1900s-pres.] **2.** formed lumps of horse dung. From the shape. [U.S., 1900s]

Burbage! a mock oath and an exclamation, "Damn it!" For synonyms see 'ZOUNDS! [U.S. slang, mid 1900s]

burble a PIMPLE (sense 1) or a boil. [mid-1500s] Synonyms are related terms: ACNE, ACNE-TYPE SURFACE BLEMISH, ACNE VULGARIS, BLACKHEAD, BLAIN, BLEMISH, BLOB, BOIL, BUBUKLE, BULLA, BUMP, CARBUNCLE, COMEDO, FURUNCLE, GOOB, GUBERS, HICKIE, HICKY, JERK BUMPS, MACULATION, PIMGINNIT, ROSY-DROP, RUM-BLOSSOM, SPOTS, ZIT.

burese cocaine. [U.S. underworld and drug culture, 1900s]

burglar 1. a pederast; the INSERTOR (*q.v.*). *Cf.* BACK-DOOR WORK, USHER. [U.S. underworld, early 1900s] **2.** a Bulgarian. [military, Fraser and Gibbons]

burlap copulation. See BURLAP SISTER. [U.S. dialect (Boontling), late 1800s-early 1900s, Charles Adams]

burlap sister a prostitute. See BAG (sense 4). [U.S. slang, early 1900s]

Burma Shave a reinterpretation of "B.S.," BULLSHIT (*q.v.*). A euphemism of disguise. *Cf.* BESSIE SMITH, B.S. [U.S. slang, mid 1900s]

burn 1. to lust after someone. [since *c.* 1000, *Oxford English Dictionary*] **2.** to infect someone with a venereal disease, probably gonorrhea. [since the early 1500s] **3.** an exclamation or a curse, "Go to hell!" [U.S. colloquial, early 1900s]

burn bad powder to release extremely bad-smelling intestinal gas. *Cf.* BURNT CHEESE (sense 1). For synonyms see GURK. [British, 1900s]

burner a case of venereal disease, especially gonorrhea. *Cf.* BURN (sense 2), FLAME. [British slang, early 1800s, Egan's Grose.]

burnese (also **bernese**) cocaine. Sometimes capitalized. *Cf.* BERNICE, BURESE. [U.S. underworld, early 1900s]

burn one's poker to contract a venereal disease. *Cf.* BURN (sense 2). [British slang, 1800s, *Dictionary of Slang and Unconventional English*]

burnt (also **burned**) infected with a venereal disease. [since the late 1600s]

burnt cheese 1. a foul-smelling release of intestinal gas. *Cf.* BURN BAD POWDER, CHEEZER, CUT ONE'S FINGER, CUT THE CHEESE. **2.** an extremely ugly young woman. [U.S. slang, mid 1900s-pres.]

burn the grass to urinate outdoors on the grass, usually said of males. *Cf.* KILL A TREE. [Australian, 1900s, Baker]

burp (also **berp**) **1.** to eructate; to BELCH (sense 1). **2.** an eructation; a BELCH (sense 2). [U.S. colloquial since the early 1900s or before]

burrhead 1. a prison inmate, especially a black inmate. From the typical very short Negro haircut of the period. [U.S. underworld, early 1900s] **2.** a Negro. Derogatory. From the growth patterns of Negroid hair. [U.S. slang, 1900s]

burst a drinking SPREE (sense 2); a drunken BUST (sense 3). [widespread slang, 1800s]

burst at the broadside to release intestinal gas. For synonyms see GURK. [British, 1600s–1800s]

burster a drunkard. Cf. BURST. [British slang, 1800s, Farmer and Henley]

bury a quaker to defecate. Cf. QUAKER'S BURYING-GROUND. [originally Anglo-Irish, British slang, 1800s]

bury one's wick to copulate. [British slang, mid 1800s, Dictionary of Slang and Unconventional English]

bush 1. the female genitals. Refers to the pubic hair. Cf. HAIR. [U.S. slang, 1900s] **2.** pubic hair, especially female pubic hair. [U.S. slang, 1900s] **3.** a substantial patch of hair on a man's chest. Cf. MOSS ON THE BOSOM. **4.** an Afro-style hairdo; any head of hair. [U.S. slang, 1900s] **5.** a woman considered sexually. For synonyms see TAIL. **6.** marijuana. Cf. BO-BO BUSH, WEED (sense 1). [U.S. drug culture, early 1900s-pres.]

bush-beater the penis. Cf. BUSH (sense 2), BUSHWHACKER. [British slang, 1800s, Farmer and Henley]

bush colt a bastard; an illegitimate child. For synonyms see ACCIDENT. [U.S. colloquial, 1900s or before]

bush patrol 1. a session of necking and petting. **2.** a session of copulation. **3.** an imaginary search through college campus shrubbery to flush out the necking couples. See BUSH (sense 2). [all senses, U.S. slang, mid 1900s]

bush-scrubber a rural prostitute. Cf. BUSH (sense 2). [Australian, 1900s, Baker]

bushwah (also **booshwa, booshwah, boushwa, bushwa**) **1.** dried cattle or buffalo dung used as fuel. Cf. BODEWASH. [from the French bois-de-vache, "wood from the cow"; U.S. colloquial, 1900s and before] **2.** nonsense. A disguise of and avoidance for BULLSHIT (q.v.). [U.S. slang, 1900s]

bushwhacker 1. originally a rural feller of trees. By extension, an outlaw who resides in the bush and is not to be trusted; a guerrilla. In Australia, one who lives in the bush. In the U.S., a Civil War deserter. [1800s–1900s] **2.** the penis. Cf. BUSH (sense 1), TALLY-WHACKER. [British slang, 1800s, Farmer and Henley] **3.** a marijuana smoker. Cf. BUSH (sense 6). [U.S. drug culture, mid 1900s-pres.]

business girl a prostitute, especially one who is independent and not connected with a pimp or a brothel. Cf. WORKING GIRL. [British, early 1900s]

busk the penis. From the name of whalebone or wooden stiffeners for corsets. [British slang, 1800s]

buss 1. a kiss. **2.** to kiss. [both since the mid 1700s] Synonyms of both senses: MOUSE, MOUSLE, MOUTH, MOW, MUCKLE ON, MUZZLE, OSCULATION.

buss beggar 1. a low prostitute. [British, 1800s and before] **2.** a miserable old fumbler whom only beggar women will kiss. [British, late 1700s, Grose]

bust 1. a woman's bosom; the breasts; the general shape or outline of the breasts. Also in the plural meaning "breasts." [euphemistic since the early 1700s] **2.** as an oath and an exclamation, "Bust!" meaning "Damn!" **3.** a drunken spree. Cf. BURST. [British and U.S., mid 1800s-pres.] **4.** to ejaculate prematurely. [U.S. slang, mid 1900s-pres.] **5.** an arrest for shoplifting or drug possession. [U.S. slang and drug culture, mid 1900s-pres.] **6.** to arrest; to raid and arrest. [U.S. underworld and general slang, mid 1900s-pres.] **7.** a failure; a disastrous mess. [U.S. slang, mid 1900s-pres.]

bust a cap to take a narcotics capsule. Cf. CAP, CAP OUT. [U.S. drug culture, mid 1900s-pres.]

bust a gut 1. to strain oneself physically, perhaps sufficiently to produce a hernia. **2.** to strain oneself mentally. [both senses, U.S. slang, mid 1900s-pres.]

bust ass to make a valiant physical effort. Cf. BUST A GUT. [U.S. slang, mid 1900s-pres.]

buster a loud release of intestinal gas. *Cf.* TRUMP. [U.S. slang, mid 1900s-pres.]

bustle (also **bustler**) a pad, a roll of fabric, or a wire frame worn under the skirts and over the buttocks of a woman. It was worn to emphasize the smallness of the waist. [British and U.S., late 1700s-pres.] Synonyms: ARSE-COOLER, BACK-STAIRCASE, BIRDCAGE, BISHOP, CANARY CAGE, DRESS-IMPROVER, FALSE HEREAFTER, JOHNNY RUSSELL, LORD JOHN RUSSELL, RAT-TRAP, RUMP-ROLL, SCOTCH BUM, TOURNURE.

bust one's nuts 1. to ejaculate. *Cf.* BUST (sense 4), GET ONE'S NUTS CRACKED, POP A NUT. [U.S. slang, mid 1900s-pres.] **2.** the same as BREAK ONE'S BALLS (*q.v.*), to suffer adversity or discomfort to accomplish something.

butch 1. a masculine lesbian; a lesbian in the male role. For synonyms see LESBYTERIAN. **2.** a virile homosexual male. [both senses, U.S. homosexual use, mid 1900s-pres.] **3.** for a homosexual (male or female) to act more masculine than is customary. Found in the expression "butch it up." [U.S. homosexual use, mid 1900s-pres., Farrell] **4.** a physician. From "butcher." [U.S. nautical, Berrey and Van den Bark]

butcher's shop the female genitals. [British slang, 1800s, Farmer and Henley]

Butchski a derogatory nickname for a Czechoslovakian. [U.S., 1900s]

butt 1. the bottom or thicker end of anything. Sometimes taboo even in this sense. [since the mid 1400s] **2.** the posteriors. Originally impolite, but now used more freely. For synonyms see DUFF. [U.S. colloquial, 1800s–1900s] **3.** women considered sexually. *Cf.* ASS, FANNY, RUMP. [U.S. slang, 1900s] **4.** copulation. [U.S. slang, 1900s]

butter semen in compound words, BUTTERED-BUN, DUCK-BUTTER, MELTED-BUTTER (all *q.v.*). For synonyms see METTLE. [British slang, 1800s, Farmer and Henley]

butter-bags the human breasts. *Cf.* BUTTER-BOXES. [British slang, 1800s, Farmer and Henley]

butterball 1. a fat person. **2.** an oaf; a plump bumpkin. [both senses, U.S., 1900s or before]

butter-boat the female genitals. *Cf.* BUTTER. [British slang, 1800s, Farmer and Henley]

butterbox (also **butterbag**) a derogatory term for a Dutchman. [slang, 1600s–1900s] Synonyms: BUTTER-MOUTH, CABBAGEHEAD, CHEESE-EATER, FROGLANDER, NIC FROG, OFFAL-EATER.

butter-boxes the human breasts. *Cf.* BUTTER-BAGS. [British slang, 1800s, Farmer and Henley]

buttered bun 1. a woman's vagina containing semen from a recent ejaculation. Said of prostitutes who have repeated or serial coition. *Cf.* BUN (sense 3), WET DECK. **2.** a mistress; a prostitute. [both senses, British, 1600s–1800s]

butter flower marijuana. [U.S. drug culture, mid 1900s-pres.]

butterfly queen a homosexual male who prefers mutual FELLATIO (*q.v.*). For synonyms see QUEEN. [U.S. homosexual use, mid 1900s, Farrell]

butter-knife the penis. Refers to spreading the BUTTER on the BUN (both *q.v.*). [British, mid 1600s]

buttermilk semen. *Cf.* BUTTER, CREAM (sense 1), HOT MILK, MILK (sense 2). [British slang, 1800s, Farmer and Henley]

buttermilk cow a bull. BUTTERMILK (*q.v.*) is a jocular reference to semen. [U.S. jocular, early 1900s]

butter-queen (also **butter-whore**) a scolding woman; a shrew. [British, mid 1600s]

butt-fuck 1. anal copulation. **2.** to practice anal copulation. [both senses, U.S. slang, mid 1900s-pres.]

buttock 1. one of the prominences formed by the gluteal muscles. Usually in the plural. [since the 1300s] **2.** a common strumpet; a harlot. *Cf.* ASS (sense 3), BUTT (sense 3), FANNY (sense 1), RUMP (sense 2). [British, 1600s–1800s]

buttock-broker a madam or a pimp. Cf. FLESH-PEDDLER. [British slang, late 1600s, B.E.]

buttocks the posteriors. See BUTTOCK (sense 1).

buttock-stirring copulation. Cf. BUTTOCK (sense 2). [British slang, 1800s, Farmer and Henley]

button 1. the clitoris. [colloquial, 1800s–1900s] **2.** a baby's penis. [British, 1800s, Dictionary of Slang and Unconventional English] **3.** an opium pellet. [underworld, early 1900s, Dictionary of the Underworld] **4.** a PEYOTE BUTTON (q.v.). [U.S. drug culture, mid 1900s-pres.]

button-hole the female genitals. Cf. BUTTON (sense 1). [British slang, 1800s, Farmer and Henley]

button-hole factory a brothel. Cf. BUTTON (sense 1). [British slang, 1800s]

button-hole-worker 1. a whoremonger. **2.** the penis. [both senses, British, 1800s]

buttons 1. the testes of animals. **2.** the dung of a hare, sheep, or other animals with similar small, pellet-shaped feces. [British, mid 1700s] **3.** tips of the Peyote cactus. See PEYOTE BUTTON. [U.S. drug culture, mid 1900s-pres.]

butt-peddler 1. a pimp. **2.** a prostitute. Cf. ASS-PEDDLER. [both senses, U.S., early 1900s]

butt-wipe 1. toilet paper. For synonyms see T.P. **2.** a sycophant. Cf. ASS-WIPE. [both senses, U.S. slang, mid 1900s-pres.]

buxom 1. pertaining to a healthy, plump girl or woman. [since the late 1500s] **2.** pertaining to a large or full-breasted woman. [since the 1800s or before]

buy the farm (also **buy it**) to die. [U.S. slang, early 1900s-pres.]

buzz 1. an audible release of intestinal gas. For synonyms see GURK. [widespread recurrent nonce, 1900s and before] **2.** the mellowness of alcohol or drug intoxication in "to have a buzz on." **3.** a sexual thrill or feeling. [senses 2 and 3 are U.S. slang, 1900s]

buzzed (also **buzzed-up**) slightly intoxicated. Cf. BUZZ (sense 2). [U.S. slang, mid 1900s-pres.]

buzzer 1. a homosexual male. For synonyms see EPICENE. [U.S. homosexual use, mid 1900s] **2.** a pickpocket. [underworld, early 1900s or before]

buzzey intoxicated with alcohol. [U.S. slang, early 1700s, Ben Franklin]

buzz the brillo to copulate. "Brillo" is the trademarked brand name of a metallic wool scourer. Refers to the female pubic hair. [U.S. slang, mid 1900s, Current Slang]

B.V.D. men's underwear. From "Bradley, Voorhies, and Day," the manufacturers of underwear for men. Usually in the plural. Cf. BEEVEEDEES.

B.Y.O. "Bring your own" liquor. Pertaining to a party. [slang, mid 1900s-pres.]

B.Y.O.B. (also **B.Y.O.G.**) "Bring your own booze" or "bottle." Pertaining to a party. The Australian version is "Bring your own grog." [slang, mid 1900s-pres.]

C

C. 1. "cocaine." *Cf.* H., M. [U.S. underworld and drug culture, early 1900s-pres.] **2.** women considered as sexual objects. From "cunt." [U.S. slang, mid 1900s]

caballo heroin. *Cf.* HORSE. [from the Spanish word for "horse"; U.S. drug culture, mid 1900s-pres.]

cabbage-garden (also **cabbage-field, cabbage-patch**) the female genitals. [British and U.S., 1800s-1900s]

cabbagehead 1. an oaf or fool. [British and U.S. slang and colloquial, mid 1800s-1900s] **2.** a derogatory nickname for a German or a Dutchman. For synonyms see GERRY. [U.S., mid 1800s–1900s]

cabinet d'aisance* a W.C.; a restroom. For synonyms see W.C. [French]

cab-joint an establishment offering illegal goods or services (*e.g.*, alcohol or prostitution). Customers are supposedly referred to such places by taxicab drivers. [British and U.S., late 1800s-pres.]

cabman's rests the bosom; the human breasts. Rhyming slang for "breasts." [British slang, late 1800s, Farmer and Henley]

cab-moll a prostitute in a CAB-JOINT (*q.v.*). For synonyms see HARLOT. [British and U.S., 1800s]

caboose 1. the human posteriors. From the name of the car at the end of a railroad train. [U.S. colloquial and slang, 1900s or before] **2.** a nickname for the last male to copulate in a group sex act. See PULL A TRAIN. [U.S. slang, mid 1900s-pres.]

ca-ca (also **caca, ka-ka**) **1.** heroin; sometimes false or adulterated heroin. See SHIT (sense 5). [from Spanish via U.S. Mexican and Puerto Rican slang; U.S. drug culture and slang, mid 1900s-pres.] **2.** to defecate. [Caribbean (Jamaican), 1900s, Cassidy and Le Page] **3.** feces; dung. [slang, 1900s

and certainly much older] **4.** defecation. [slang, 1900s or before]

cacafuego literally, "shit-fire," a very difficult or devilish person. *Cf.* SPIT-FIRE (sense 1). [British, 1600s–1900s]

cack 1. dung; feces. **2.** to eliminate. [both since the early 1400s] **3.** to vomit. *Cf.* BARF, SHIT (sense 6). [U.S. colloquial, 1900s]

cackling fart a hen's egg. [British jocular slang or cant, late 1600s]

cactus the Peyote cactus, which is the source of mescaline, a hallucinogenic substance. *Cf.* MESCALINE, PEYOTE. [U.S. drug culture, mid 1900s-pres.]

cactus juice tequila. An alcoholic beverage associated, like the cactus, with Mexico. [U.S. slang, mid 1900s-pres.]

cadet a pimp or procurer. [U.S. underworld, early 1900s, Goldin, O'Leary, and Lipsius]

Cadillac 1. cocaine. *Cf.* C. (sense 1). **2.** the drug P.C.P. (*q.v.*). [both senses, U.S. drug culture, mid 1900s-pres.]

Caesaration! a mock oath and an exclamation; similar to GREAT CAESAR'S GHOST! (*q.v.*). For synonyms see 'ZOUNDS! [U.S. slang and colloquial, late 1800s-pres.]

café au lait* a mulatto; a person with some fraction of Negro heritage. For synonyms see MAHOGANY. [British slang, 1900s]

caged intoxicated with alcohol. [U.S. slang, 1900s]

cager (also **cadger**) a drunkard; someone who sponges drinks. [U.S. slang, 1900s]

cake 1. the female genitals. For synonyms see MONOSYLLABLE. [U.S. slang, 1900s] **2.** the buttocks of a woman, especially if well-formed. *Cf.* ASS (senses 2 and 3). [British and U.S. slang, mid 1900s] **3.** a sexually desirable woman. *Cf.* PIE, TART. [U.S. slang, 1900s] **4.** a prostitute. For synonyms see HARLOT. [Australian, early 1900s]

cake-eater an effeminate male; one who is quite comfortable at fussy tea parties. [U.S. slang, early 1900s]

calf-clingers trousers, especially tight-fitting trousers. For synonyms see GALLIGASKINS. [British slang, early 1800s]

calf-slobber (also **calf slobbers**) a dysphemism for "meringue." For related terms see DOG'S VOMIT. [U.S. slang, late 1800s–1900s]

calico a woman; women considered as sexual objects. [U.S. slang and colloquial, mid 1800s–1900s]

calico queen a fast woman of the saloons and honky-tonks. Cf. CALICO. [U.S., 1800s]

California cornflakes cocaine. Cf. JOY FLAKES. [U.S. slang, mid 1900s-pres.]

California sunshine the drug L.S.D. (q.v.). [U.S. drug culture, mid 1900s-pres.]

called to straw pertaining to a woman who has gone into LABOR (q.v.). Refers to a cow giving birth. [U.S. dialect, 1900s and before]

call-girl 1. a prostitute who makes appointments by telephone or a prostitute who can be called on (visited) for her services. **2.** any prostitute. Cf. C-GIRL. [both senses, U.S., early 1900s-pres.]

call-house (also **call-joint**) a brothel. Proposed origins include: a place where someone makes a call to find the telephone number of a prostitute, a brothel where prostitutes make appointments by telephone, and a brothel where you can call on prostitutes to do anything. Cf. HOUSE OF CALL. [U.S. slang, 1900s]

camp 1. a brothel. **2.** a residence or gathering place for male homosexuals. [both senses, U.S. slang or nonce, Montelone] **3.** pertaining to obvious and open or exaggerated male homosexual behavior. Also **campy.** [U.S. and British slang and underworld, early 1900s-pres.] **4.** to display one's homo-

sexual behavior openly or in an exaggerated manner. Cf. CAMP IT UP. [U.S. homosexual use, mid 1900s-pres.]

camp it up to overdo effeminacy. Refers to behavior in theatrical roles (Partridge) or in the public behavior of a homosexual. [British and U.S. slang, early 1900s-pres.]

campy the same as CAMP (sense 3).

can 1. a restroom or toilet. In addition to referring to the receptacle, "can" may have been reinforced by the "gan" or "ken" of "donegan" or "dunnaken." See DONIKER. [U.S. slang and colloquial, 1900s if not before] **2.** a jail; a prison. For synonyms see COW. [U.S. slang, 1900s] **3.** the female genitals. [British slang, 1800s] **4.** a breast. See CANS. **5.** the buttocks; the bottom. [U.S. slang and colloquial, 1900s or before] **6.** one ounce of marijuana. From a tobacco "can" (in which the plant was commonly transported) and from "Cannabis." [U.S. drug culture, mid 1900s]

Canadian black a type of marijuana said to be grown in Canada. [U.S. drug culture, mid 1900s-pres.]

canary 1. a young woman or girl, especially a female vocalist; a BIRD (sense 1) who sings. [U.S., 1900s and before] **2.** a Chinese. From the yellow color of a canary. For synonyms see JOHN CHINAMAN. [Australian, 1900s and before, Baker]

cancer-stick a dysphemism for "cigarette." Cf. COFFIN-NAIL. [U.S. slang, 1900s]

C. and H. a mixture of "cocaine and heroin." For synonyms see HOT AND COLD. [U.S. slang and drug culture, mid 1900s-pres.]

candle the penis. A mate to the CANDLESTICK (q.v.). See CANDLE-BASHER. [British slang, 1800s, Farmer and Henley]

candle-basher a spinster; a female masturbator. Cf. BASHER, CANDLE. [British, early 1900s or before, *Dictionary of Slang and Unconventional English*]

candlestick the female genitals. *Cf.* CANDLE. [British slang, 1800s, Farmer and Henley]

C. and M. a mixture of "cocaine and morphine." For similar terms see HOT AND COLD. [U.S. drug culture, mid 1900s-pres.]

candy 1. intoxicated with alcohol. For synonyms see WOOFLED. [British slang, early 1800s, Egan's Grose] **2.** any drug. Usually refers to hard drugs, specifically cocaine, hashish, L.S.D., and barbiturates. Originally only cocaine. *Cf.* CANDY MAN, NEEDLE-CANDY, NOSE-CANDY. [U.S. drug culture, early 1900s-pres.]

candy-ass a coward; a timid and helpless person. *Cf.* PUCKER-ASSED. [U.S. slang, mid 1900s-pres.]

candy man a seller of hard drugs. *Cf.* CANDY (sense 2) for examples. [U.S. drug culture, 1900s]

cane 1. to copulate with a woman in the sense "beat." [British slang, 1900s, *Dictionary of Slang and Unconventional English*] **2.** the penis in the expression VARNISH ONE'S CANE (*q.v.*). [British, 1800s]

canebuck strong, intoxicating liquor. [U.S. dialect (Southern), 1900s or before]

can house a brothel. See CAN (sense 3). [U.S., 1900s or before]

canister The female genitals. British slang for "hat," which is slang for the female sexual organ. See HAT, OLD. *Cf.* CAN (sense 3). [British slang, 1800s, Farmer and Henley]

cannabinol the drug P.C.P. (*q.v.*); the drug P.C.P. sold as T.H.C. (*q.v.*), the active ingredient in marijuana which is widely sought for its CHARGE (sense 1). [U.S. drug culture, mid 1900s-pres.]

Cannabis americana* American hemp; a common name for the American varieties of CANNABIS SATIVA (*q.v.*). For synonyms see MARI. [U.S., 1900s]

Cannabis indica* (also **Cannabis**) a common name for the Indian varieties

of CANNABIS SATIVA (*q.v.*). [U.S., 1900s]

Cannabis mexicana* Mexican hemp; a common name for the Mexican varieties of CANNABIS SATIVA (*q.v.*). [U.S., 1900s]

Cannabis sativa* (also **Cannabis**) the botanical name for marijuana. For synonyms see MARI. [1900s]

canned goods male or female virgins. With reference to their being "sealed" like a can. [U.S. underworld, 1900s, Goldin, O'Leary, and Lipsius]

cannibal a fellator, specifically a homosexual male. *Cf.* MANEATER (sense 1). For synonyms see PICCOLO-PLAYER. [U.S. underworld, 1900s]

cannon balls the testicles. *Cf.* BULLETS (sense 1). [British slang and nonce, late 1800s, Farmer and Henley]

canoe to neck, pet, and make love. [U.S., 1900s and before] See also TALK TO THE CANOE DRIVER.

canoodle to pet and fondle lovingly. *Cf.* FIRKYTOODLE. [U.S. slang and colloquial, mid 1800s-pres.]

can-paper toilet paper. For synonyms see T.P. [U.S. slang or colloquial, 1900s]

cans the breasts. Usually in the plural. For synonyms see BOSOM. [U.S., 1900s] See also CAN (sense 4).

cantrip 1. witchcraft; a charm or a spell. **2.** pertaining to any real or imagined magical act. [both senses, Scots and British, early 1700s]

can't see a hole in a ladder a catch phrase pertaining to a person who is heavily intoxicated. Occurs in numerous variants. [British and U.S. slang, 1800s–1900s]

Canuck 1. in Canada, a French Canadian. **2.** in the U.S., any Canadian. Professor James Sledd makes a very good case that this word is from Hawaiian *kanaka*, "man." See KANAKAS. [both recognized since the mid 1800s]

canvasback a harlot; a sexually loose woman; a woman who spends considerable time with her back on a canvas-covered floor, presumably copulating. A reinterpretation of the common name of a duck.

canyon yodeling CUNNILINGUS (q.v.). Cf. YODEL. [U.S. slang, 1900s]

cap to buy or use narcotics. Originally from "capsule," now refers to various forms of drugs. Cf. CAP OUT. [U.S. drug culture, mid 1900s-pres.]

Cape Horn the female genitals. The HORN (sense 3) is the penis. [British slang, 1800s, Farmer and Henley]

Cape of Good Hope the female genitals. For synonyms see MONOSYL-LABLE. [British slang, 1800s, Farmer and Henley]

caper-juice whisky. "Caper" refers here to a SPREE (sense 2). [U.S. slang, late 1800s]

capernoited intoxicated with alcohol. [from a Scots word meaning "muddle-headed"; U.S., 1800s]

capon 1. a castrated male bird. No negative connotations. [since the late 1500s] **2.** a eunuch. [since the 1600s] **3.** a homosexual male; a pederast; an effeminate male. [U.S. slang, mid 1900s]

capoop 1. to defecate. **2.** dung. Cf. POOP (senses 3 and 7). [both senses, U.S. dialect (Ozarks), 1900s or before, Randolph and Wilson]

cap out to pass out from the use of marijuana or drugs. Cf. CAP. [U.S. drug culture, mid 1900s-pres.]

capsize to castrate. [U.S. dialect and colloquial, 1900s or before]

captain is at home a catch phrase indicating that a woman is menstruating. Cf. ENTERTAINING THE GENERAL. [British colloquial, late 1700s–1800s]

Captain Standish the erect penis. Cf. BODY'S CAPTAIN, MY. [British slang, 1800s, Farmer and Henley]

cark the penis. From a British dialect term for "load" or possibly from a similar term meaning "stiff" (Halliwell). It seems to be but is not a dialect pronunciation of "cock." [attested as U.S. slang, mid 1900s]

carnal 1. pertaining to fleshly, as opposed to spiritual, matters. In particular, sexual matters or desires. [mid 1400s-pres.] **2.** to copulate. Cf. CARNALIZE. [mid 1600s; rare then and obsolete now]

carnal acquaintance copulation. An early euphemism. Cf. CARNAL KNOWL-EDGE, KNOWLEDGE.

carnal connection (also **carnal engagement**) sexual intercourse. A euphemism for "copulation." [1800s or before]

carnal copulation sexual intercourse. Now "copulation" alone carries the full meaning. [euphemistic, 1500s–1800s]

carnal enjoyment sexual pleasure; presumably a euphemism for "copulation."

carnal intercourse copulation, now usually "intercourse."

carnality 1. lechery, lust, and lewdness. **2.** copulation. [both since the early 1400s, *Oxford English Dictionary*]

carnalize 1. to arouse sexually; to awaken the libido. **2.** to copulate with a woman. For synonyms see OCCUPY. [both senses, early 1700s]

carnal knowledge copulation. As a legal term, this refers to even the slightest penetration of the vulva. Cf. CARNAL ACQUAINTANCE. [euphemistic, 1400s-pres.]

carnal parts the genitals of a male or female; the sexual parts. [early 1700s]

carnal stump the penis. Cf. MIDDLE STUMP. [written nonce; late 1600s]

carnal trap the female genitals, specifically the vagina. For synonyms see MONOSYLLABLE. [mid 1600s, (Urquhart)]

Carrie a reinterpretation of the initial "C" of "cocaine." From the proper name. Not always capitalized. Cf. C. [U.S. drug culture, mid 1900s-pres.]

carrion 1. a rotting carcass. [since the 1200s] **2.** anything putrid. **3.** dung. **4.** a prostitute. [British, 1800s or before] **5.** the human body, living or dead. [British, 1800s or before]

carrion-hunter an undertaker. [British slang, late 1700s, Grose]

carrot the penis, especially the penis of a child. [slang, nonce, or juvenile since the 1600s or before]

carrying a flag having a menstrual period. For synonyms see FLOODS. [U.S. slang, 1900s]

carrying something heavy intoxicated with alcohol, as if the drinker's difficulty in moving were due to carrying a heavy load. [U.S. slang, early 1900s]

carrying two red lights (also **carrying three red lights**) intoxicated with alcohol. Based on the signal for a ship out of control. Refers to the uncontrolled gait of a drunkard. [British and U.S., nautical and World War II]

carry-knave a harlot; a prostitute. [British slang or colloquial, early 1600s]

carry on 1. to have a loud and exciting time at a party. No negative connotations. **2.** to chatter endlessly. **3.** to have an illicit love or sexual affair. [all senses, U.S., 1900s or before]

carsey (also **carsi**) **1.** a house, den, or crib. *Cf.* CASA (sense 1). [cant, 1800s or before] **2.** a restroom, toilet, or JOHN (*q.v.*). Also **carzy, karzy.** *Cf.* CASA (sense 2). [possibly from the Hindi word *khazi;* primarily Cockney, British, late 1800s-pres.]

cartwheel an amphetamine tablet marked on one side with cross-scoring to make it easy to break. *Cf.* CROSS-ROAD, DOUBLE-CROSS. [U.S. drug culture, mid 1900s-pres.]

carving-knife one's own wife; anyone's wife. Rhyming slang for "wife." For synonyms see WARDEN. [British, 1900s, *Dictionary of Rhyming Slang*]

casa 1. a brothel, a HOUSE (*q.v.*). Also **case.** [British, 1600s] **2.** a toilet; a W.C. See CARSEY. [British slang or cant, 1800s or before]

cascade to vomit. [slang and colloquial, late 1700s-1900s]

case 1. the female genitals. See CAZE. *Cf.* BOX (sense 2), KEESTER (sense 3). [British, 1600s-1800s] **2.** a W.C.; a

toilet. Originally "house." *Cf.* CARSEY, CASA. [cant, 1600s]

case vrow a prostitute who works in a brothel, in contrast to one who works the streets. See CASE (sense 1). [from Dutch *vrow,* "woman" cant, late 1700s or before, Grose]

cash in one's chips (also **cash in one's checks**) to die. [British and U.S., late 1800s-pres.]

casket 1. a coffin. Recognized as an American euphemism in the late 1800s, now the word-of-choice for "coffin." [U.S., late 1800s-pres.] **2.** to place a corpse in a coffin. [U.S. funeral trade, 1900s]

cast 1. to vomit. Also **cast up.** *Cf.* THROW UP ONE'S ACCOUNTS. [British slang or cant, early 1600s] **2.** to bear young, as in "cast kittens." [late 1500s-1800s] **3.** to excrete; to cast dung. Said mostly of animals in avoidance of more direct terms. [British, early 1700s] **4.** drunk; very drunk. For synonyms see WOOFLED [British slang or colloquial, early 1900s]

casting-couch a legendary couch found in the offices of casting directors for use in seducing young women by offering them acting roles in theatrical productions. The legend has been extended to include homosexual favors. [U.S. slang, 1900s]

castor oil artist a medical doctor. For synonyms see DOC. [British and U.S. military]

castrate 1. to remove the testicles by cutting. Synonyms: ALTER, ARRANGE, CAPSIZE, CHANGE, DEHORN, DESEXUALIZE, DEVIRILIZE, DOCTOR, DOMESTICATE, FIX, GELD, GLIB, KNACKER, LIB, MAIM, MARK, MUTILATE, NUT, THROW, TRIM, UN-MAN, UNSEX, WORK ON. **2.** to remove the ovaries surgically. Rare if not obsolete. [both since the early 1600s] **3.** to expurgate a book. [since the early 1600s]

cast up one's accounts to vomit. See CAST (sense 1). From a phrase meaning "balance the books." For synonyms see YORK.

Cat "God" in oaths such as "Swelp me Cat!" [1700s or before]

cat 1. a prostitute. [British, early 1400s-pres.] **2.** intoxicated with alcohol. [U.S., early 1700s, Ben Franklin] **3.** a gossip; a shrewish woman. [late 1700s-pres.] **4.** a male; a buddy. [U.S. slang, 1900s] **5.** to seek women for sex; to chase women. From TOMCAT (sense 2). [U.S., 1900s or before] **6.** the female genitals. "Cat" is a nickname for a lady's MUFF (sense 1), which refers to the female genitals, and it is further reinforced by PUSSY (sense 1). [British and U.S., mid 1800s-pres.] **7.** to vomit. Cf. SHOOT THE CAT. For synonyms see YORK. [British and U.S. slang, 1800s-1900s] **8.** heroin. Cf. BOY (sense 3), BROTHER (sense 1). [U.S. drug culture, mid 1900s-pres.]

catamite 1. a young boy who serves as a passive pederast or RECEIVER (q.v.); a boy kept solely for sexual purposes. Cf. PATHIC, PEG BOY. [from the Latin name Catamitus; since the late 1500s] **2.** any male, regardless of age, who serves as a RECEIVER (q.v.) in pederasty.

cat and kitties (also **cats and kitties**) the breasts. Rhyming slang for "titties." For synonyms see BOSOM. [U.S., early 1900s, Dictionary of Rhyming Slang]

catastrophe the posteriors. From the "ass" in the second syllable. Sometimes pronounced "cat-ass-trophy." [nonce and slang since the late 1500s]

catch 1. in male homosexual intercourse, the male receiving the phallus and the semen. Cf. INSERTOR, PASSIVE PEDERAST, RECEIVER. [U.S. homosexual use, 1900s] **2.** to become pregnant Cf. KETCHED, TAKE (sense 2). [British and U.S. colloquial and dialect, 1800s-1900s] **3.** a matrimonially desirable male or female. [British and U.S., late 1500s-pres.]

catch an oyster coition from the point of view of the woman. OYSTER (sense 3) refers to semen. [British slang, 1800s, Farmer and Henley]

catch a packet to catch a venereal disease. The expression generally means to get into trouble, to be reprimanded, or to be disciplined. [British military, early 1900s]

catch-colt a colt whose paternity is unknown. Also used for a human bastard. Cf. WOODS-COLT. [U.S. dialect and colloquial, 1900s and before]

catch-'em-alive-O the female genitals. From a nickname for a type of sticky flypaper used in the mid 1800s. [British slang, mid 1800s, Farmer and Henley]

catch-fart a page or footboy who follows closely behind his master. [British, late 1600s-1700s]

caterpillar a drunkard; someone drunk enough to crawl. For synonyms see ALCHY. [Australian, early 1900s, Baker]

cat-flat a brothel. Cf. CAT (sense 1), CAT HOUSE. [U.S. underworld, early 1900s]

catgut inferior liquor; rot-gut. For synonyms see EMBALMING FLUID [U.S. slang, 1900s]

Cat-harn! a mild oath. Rhyming slang for DARN (q.v.). See CAT. [U.S. colloquial]

cat heads (also **cat's heads**) the breasts. From a popular species of very large apples. [British slang, early 1800s or before, Lexicon Balatronicum] See also CAT'S-HEAD-CUT-OPEN.

cat-house a brothel. [U.S. slang, mid 1900s-pres.]

cat-house cutie a prostitute. For synonyms see HARLOT. [U.S. slang, 1900s, Montelone]

cat's-head-cut-open the female genitals, especially the vulva. Refers to a cross section of a large apple. Cf. CUT CABBAGE, RED ONION. [British slang, early 1900s, Dictionary of Slang and Unconventional English] See also CAT HEADS.

cat-skin the female pubic hair. See CAT (sense 6). For synonyms see DOWNSHIRE. [British slang, 1800s, Farmer and Henley]

cat's meat the female genitals. For synonyms see MONOSYLLABLE. [British slang, 1800s, Farmer and Henley]

Cat's nouns! an oath of avoidance, "By God's wounds!" Sometimes interpreted as "By God's words!" [1700s]

catso (also **catzo**) **1.** the penis. [from Italian *catzo*; British, 1600s–1700s] **2.** a rogue; a "ne'er-do-well." Probably from sense 1. For synonyms see SNOKE-HORN. [British slang, early 1600s] **3.** an exclamation, the same as GADSO! and GODSO! (both *q.v.*). Usually capitalized in this sense.

catsood intoxicated with alcohol; drunk on four sous. [corruption of the French *quatre sous;* British military, 1900s, Fraser and Gibbons]

cattle 1. to coit. *Cf.* BULL (sense 2). **2.** prostitutes. [British, late 1600s, B.E.] **3.** women in general. [U.S. underworld, early 1900s]

cattle-truck an act of copulation; to coit. Rhyming slang for "fuck." [slang, 1900s, *Dictionary of Rhyming Slang*]

caught pregnant. *Cf.* CATCH (sense 2), KETCHED, TAKE (sense 2). [U.S. colloquial and dialect, 1900s or before]

caught in a snowstorm intoxicated with cocaine. See SNOW and the entries which follow it for additional expressions on the SNOW-CAINE (*q.v.*) theme. [U.S. slang, mid 1900s]

caught with one's pants down said of a person caught doing something which he ought not to be doing, or ought to be doing in private.

cauliflower the female genitals. *Cf.* CABBAGE and see the explanation at RED ONION. [British slang, 1800s or before]

caulk to copulate. With reference to forcing material between the planks of a ship's hull. A play on COCK (sense 4). [British, 1800s, Farmer and Henley]

cavaulting (also **cavolting**) copulation. From horses and horseback-riding. *Cf.* PRIG (sense 1), RIDE. [British, 1800s or before]

cave 1. the female genitals, specifically the vagina and especially if large.

2. women considered solely as sexual objects. *Cf.* CAVE OF HARMONY. For synonyms see TAIL. [both senses, U.S. slang, 1900s and earlier as nonce]

cave man a strong, virile man, especially one bearing much body hair or body hair in unusual places. [British and U.S., late 1800s-pres.]

cave of harmony the female genitals. *Cf.* CAVE. [1800s and probably much earlier]

caze (also **case, kaze**) the female genitals. *Cf.* CASE (sense 1), KAZE. [British, late 1800s, Farmer and Henley]

C.B. an abbreviation of COCK-BLOCK (*q.v.*), an attempt to interfere with another man's woman. Punning on the initials of citizens band radio. [U.S. slang, mid 1900s-pres.]

Cecil cocaine. *Cf.* C. (sense 1). From the proper name. Not always capitalized. [U.S. underworld, mid 1900s-pres.]

cee cocaine. *Cf.* C. (sense 1). [U.S. underworld, mid 1900s]

cellar the female genitals, specifically the vagina. *Cf.* BOTTOMLESS-PIT (sense 1). [British slang, 1800s, Farmer and Henley]

cellar-door the female genitals; probably also the hymen. For synonyms see MONOSYLLABLE. [British, 1800s, Farmer and Henley]

cemetery a place for the interment of the dead. Originally for Roman catacombs and later for the land surrounding a Christian church. [from Greek; in English since the 1300s] Synonyms: BONE-ORCHARD, BONE-YARD, BOOT HILL, CHURCHYARD, CITY OF THE DEAD, COLD STORAGE, DEAD CENTER, FINAL RESTING PLACE, GOD'S ACRE, GRAVEYARD, LAND-YARD, LAST HOME, MARBLE CITY, MARBLE ORCHARD, MEMORIAL PARK, NECROPOLIS, OSSUARY, PERMANENT REST CAMP, POLYANDRION, POLYANDRIUM, POTTER'S FIELD, REST CAMP, SAINT TERRA.

center of attraction the female genitals. *Cf.* POINT-OF-ATTRACTION. [U.S. slang, 1800s]

center of bliss the female genitals. [1800s or before]

central furrow the female genitals, especially the PUDENDAL CLEAVAGE (*q.v.*). [British, 1800s, Farmer and Henley]

central office the female genitals. [British, 1800s, Farmer and Henley]

cesspit a cesspool; the hole under an outhouse. [British and U.S., mid 1800s]

cesspool a pit or pool for receiving human wastes. [since the late 1700s]

C-girl a prostitute; a CALL-GIRL (*q.v.*). *Cf.* B-GIRL. [U.S. slang, 1900s]

C-habit a "cocaine-habit." *Cf.* C. (sense 1). [U.S. drug culture, 1900s]

chafer to copulate. From "chauver," meaning "rub." [British, 1800s, Farmer and Henley]

chaff nonsense; worthless talk or idle chatter. [usually thought of as Biblical (Matthew); colloquial since the 1600s or before]

chain lightning inferior whisky or other liquor. For synonyms see EMBALMING FLUID. [U.S. slang or colloquial, 1800s]

chair the electric chair. [U.S. underworld and stereotypical gangster talk, 1900s] Synonyms: DEATH CHAIR, FLAME CHAIR, HOT CHAIR, HOT SEAT, HOT SQUAT, JUICE CHAIR, OLD MONKEY, OLD SMOKY, OLD SPARKY, SMOKY SEAT.

chalk 1. liquor. The same as CHOC (*q.v.*). For synonyms see BOOZE. [U.S., early 1900s] **2.** amphetamines. From the color and texture of powdered chalk. For synonyms see AMP. [U.S. drug culture, mid 1900s-pres.]

chalker a Negro who acts like a Caucasian; a Negro who spends so much time with Caucasians that it's beginning to rub off on him like chalk. Essentially derogatory. *Cf.* OREO. [U.S. black use, mid 1900s-pres.]

cham (also **chammy**) champagne. [British slang, late 1800s]

chamber 1. to take a woman to the bedroom for sexual purposes. From "bedchamber." Literally, "to BED (sense 1) a woman." [early 1600s] **2.** a truncation of "chamber pot." From "bedchamber pot." [late 1500s-early 1900s]

chamber of commerce 1. a brothel. See SEXUAL COMMERCE. [U.S. underworld, Montelon] **2.** a chamber pot or toilet; a restroom. [U.S. slang and colloquial, 1800s-1900s]

chamber pot a vessel kept in bedrooms for the reception of urine during the night. This eliminated the necessity of transporting oneself to an outdoor privy. A truncation of "bedchamber pot." For synonyms see POT. [since the 1500s]

chamber work the sexual activities of a male; sexual work done in a bedchamber. For synonyms see SMOCKAGE. [early 1500s]

chancre (also **shanker**) **1.** formerly any ulcer or sore. **2.** recently a venereal sore, especially one associated with syphilis. *Cf.* CHANK (sense 1), SHANK (sense 2), SHANKER.

change to castrate an animal or, jocularly, a man. *Cf.* ALTER. [U.S. colloquial, 1800s-1900s]

chank (also **chanck**) **1.** a syphilitic chancre; a case of syphilis. *Cf.* SHANK (sense 2). [U.S., 1900s or before] **2.** a prostitute. See SHANK (sense 1).

channel 1. to inject drugs intravenously. **2.** a vein used as a place to inject drugs. [both senses, U.S. drug culture, 1900s]

chanticleer the penis. From a nickname for the rooster. See COCK (sense 1). [British jocular euphemism, 1800s]

chantie (also **chanty**) a CHAMBER POT (*q.v.*). [Scots, 1800s and before]

chapel of ease (also **chapel**) a privy; a W.C. From a term for a chapel of worship located on the outskirts of a parish. [British slang, mid 1800s]

charcoal a derogatory nickname for a Negro. From the blackness of charcoal. For synonyms see EBONY. [U.S., 1900s]

charcoal blossom (also **charcoal lily**) a black woman. Derogatory. For synonyms see RAVEN BEAUTY. [U.S. slang and colloquial, mid 1900s]

charcoal nigger a very dark Negro. Derogatory. [U.S., 1900s and before]

charge 1. a thrill or jolt produced by drugs. See JOLT (sense 2). [U.S. underworld, 1900s] **2.** marijuana. [U.S., 1900s] **3.** a burst of sexual excitement or an experience of sexual excitement. [U.S., mid 1900s-pres.] **4.** an erection of the penis. For synonyms see ERECTION. [U.S., 1900s]

charity dame (also **charity girl, charity moll**) a woman who is sexually accommodating but not a prostitute, who charges a fee. She gives it away. In wartime, a girl who yields charitably to servicemen. [widespread slang, 1900s]

Charles 1. cocaine, a euphemistic disguise based on the initial "C" of "cocaine." Not always capitalized. [U.S. drug culture, 1900s] **2.** a Caucasian. See CHARLIE.

Charley Coke 1. cocaine. **2.** a heavy user of cocaine. [both senses, U.S. underworld, mid 1900s]

Charley Frisky Scotch whisky; any whisky. Rhyming slang for "whisky." Cf. GAY AND FRISKY. [British slang, mid 1800s]

Charley Hunt (also **Charley**) the female genitals. Rhyming slang for CUNT (q.v.). Cf. BERKELEY HUNT. [British slang, late 1800s, Dictionary of Slang and Unconventional English]

Charley is dead a catch phrase which cautions a girl that her petticoat is showing. One is to incline one's head in respect to "Charley" and notice the visible undergarment. [British juvenile, mid 1900s, Dictionary of Catch Phrases]

Charley Wheeler a girl or a woman; one's girlfriend. Rhyming slang for "Sheila," a generic nickname for a young woman. [Australian, 1900s]

Charlie (also **Charles**) **1.** a male Caucasian from the point of view of a black man. Cf. MISTER CHARLIE. **2.** white society in general. [both senses, U.S. black slang, mid 1900s-pres.] **3.** cocaine. [U.S. drug culture, 1900s] **4.** a breast. See CHARLIES. **5.** a girl; a young woman. From sense 4 or from

rhyming slang "Charlie Wheeler," meaning "Sheila." [Australian slang, mid 1900s, Wilkes]

Charlie Ronce a pimp or a ponce. Rhyming slang for PONCE (q.v.). [British, 1800s, Dictionary of Rhyming Slang]

Charlies (also **Charleys**) **1.** the breasts. [British and U.S., late 1800s-pres.] **2.** the testicles. [British slang, 1900s, Dictionary of Slang and Unconventional English]

charras (also **charas, churrus**) marijuana, especially refined marijuana; resin from marijuana flowers. [from Hindi; U.S. drug culture, mid 1900s-pres.]

chaste 1. pertaining to a virgin and to virginity. **2.** pertaining to someone (now usually a woman) who has never voluntarily had sexual intercourse unlawfully. [since the 1200s, Oxford English Dictionary]

chastity sword a sword placed between a man and woman sleeping in the same bed to insure that they do not copulate.

chat the female genitals. Cf. PUSSY. [from the French chat, "cat"; British slang, 1800s, Farmer and Henley]

chatterbox (also **chatterpie**) an incessant talker. Often a talker of nonsense. For synonyms see BULLER. [since the 1700s]

chatts (also **chates, chats**) lice. For synonyms see WALKING DANDRUFF. [cant or slang, late 1600s, B.E.; attested as U.S. underworld, Weseen]

chatty untidy; slovenly; lousy, i.e., infested with lice or CHATTS (q.v.). [cant or slang, early 1800s-1900s]

chawmouth a derogatory term for an Irishman. [U.S., 1900s and before]

chaws copulation. For synonyms see SMOCKAGE. [British, mid 1800s]

cheap pertaining to a woman who lacks sexual control. For synonyms see LAY. [U.S. slang, 1900s]

cheap shanty Mick a derogatory term for an Irishman, especially a poor

Irishman. For synonyms see HARP. [U.S., 1900s]

cheater a condom. For synonyms see EEL-SKIN. [slang, mid 1900s]

cheaters 1. false breasts; FALSIES (q.v.). [U.S., mid 1900s] **2.** any padding to make the body more attractive by increasing the size of or improving the shape of the hips or buttocks. [U.S. slang, 1900s]

cheat on to be sexually unfaithful to someone. [U.S. colloquial, 1900s]

che-chees the breasts. Cf. CHICHI (sense 4). [U.S., 1900s]

check the ski rack to retire to urinate, usually said by a male. Based on WATER THE HORSES (q.v.). For synonyms see RETIRE. [probably nonce; U.S. slang, mid 1900s]

cheeks the posteriors; the buttocks. Cf. BLINDCHEEKS. [since the mid 1700s]

cheese 1. SMEGMA (sense 2). Cf. CROTCH-CHEESE. [British and U.S. slang, 1800s–1900s] **2.** an attractive young woman. From "cheese cake." [U.S., mid 1900s]

Cheese and Crust! (also **Cheese on Crackers!**) a euphemistic disguise of "Jesus Christ!" For synonyms see SWEET CHEESECAKE. [U.S. colloquial, late 1800s-early 1900s, Ware]

cheese cake 1. pictures of scantily-clad girls. Usually not totally nude and usually not shown in unusual sex acts or in the process of excreting. [U.S. slang, early 1900s-pres.] **2.** a scantily-clad young woman with the restrictions listed in sense 1. Occasionally a nickname for a cute young woman. Also used for a group of such women. [U.S. slang, early 1900s-pres.] **3.** photographs of virile men. From sense 1 and not common. Cf. BEEFCAKE. [U.S., mid 1900s-pres.]

cheese-eater 1. a derogatory nickname for a Dutchman. [Australian, Baker] **2.** a term of address directed at non-Catholics who call Catholics "fish-eaters." See FISH-EATER. [jocular and derogatory, 1800s–1900s]

cheese-head an oaf; a dullard. [U.S. slang, early 1900s]

cheezer a very bad-smelling breaking of wind. Cf. BURNT CHEESE, CUT THE CHEESE. For synonyms see GURK. [slang since the early 1800s, *Lexicon Balatronicum*]

chemozzle a row; a fight or riot; the same as SCHLEMOZZLE (q.v.).

cherry 1. the hymen. [widespread slang and colloquial, 1900s] **2.** a woman's nipple. Often in the plural. **3.** virginity. [widespread slang, 1900s] **4.** a virgin, male or female. [U.S., 1900s, Montelone] **5.** pertaining to a virgin or to virginity; virginal. [widespread slang, 1900s] **6.** a girl or young woman. [British and U.S. slang, mid 1800s–1900s]

cherry leb an alcohol extract of marijuana. [U.S. drug culture, mid 1900s-pres.]

cherrylets (also **cherrilets**) a woman's nipples. This may include other feminine charms such as the lips. Cf. CHERRY (sense 2). [late 1500s-1600s]

cherry-merry mildly intoxicated with alcohol; tipsy. For synonyms see WOOFLED. [slang since the early 1700s]

cherry orchard a girls' college dormitory; any gathering of young women. Cf. CHERRY (senses 1 and 6). [based on the name of a play by Anton Chekhov; U.S. slang, 1900s]

cherry-picker 1. a catamite. Possibly based on the image of someone bending over and picking up cherries. Cf. BEND DOWN FOR. [attested as British naval slang, 1900s, *Dictionary of Slang and Unconventional English*] **2.** a man who pursues young girls (virgins) for sexual purposes. [U.S. slang, 1900s]

cherry-pipe sexually aroused; ready for copulation. Rhyming slang for "ripe," pertaining to a sexually aroused woman. [British slang, late 1800s]

cherry top the drug L.S.D. (q.v.). [U.S. drug culture, mid 1900s-pres.]

cherubimical intoxicated with alcohol. [U.S. and elsewhere, early 1700s, Ben Franklin]

Cheskey a derogatory nickname for a Czechoslovakian. [U.S. slang, 1900s, or before]

chest and bedding the breasts. For synonyms see BOSOM. [British nautical slang, late 1700s, Grose]

chestnuts 1. the breasts, the nuts on the chest. **2.** the testicles. *Cf.* NUTS (sense 1). [both senses, U.S. slang, 1900s, Landy]

Chicago green a variety of marijuana. *Cf.* ILLINOIS GREEN. For synonyms see MARI. [U.S. drug culture, mid 1900s-pres.]

chichi 1. fancy or affected. [U.S. slang, mid 1900s] **2.** pertaining to anything which is sexually stimulating. **3.** pertaining to a homosexual male. *Cf.* KIKI. [U.S. slang, 1900s] **4.** a breast. See CHICHIS.

chichis the breasts. For synonyms see BOSOM. [U.S. slang, mid 1900s-pres.]

chick 1. any female. *Cf.* SLICK-CHICK. [U.S. slang, early 1900s-pres.] **2.** heroin. [U.S. drug culture, mid 1900s-pres.] **3.** a male prostitute for males. *Cf.* CHICKEN (senses 1 and 2). [mid 1900s, *Dictionary of Slang and Unconventional English*]

chicken 1. a homosexual teenage boy. [U.S. underworld and slang, early 1900s-pres.] **2.** a teenage boy considered as a sex object by male homosexuals. [U.S. homosexual use, mid 1900s-pres.] **3.** a coward. [U.S. slang, 1900s] **4.** a cute young woman or any female. *Cf.* CHICK (sense 1). [U.S. slang and colloquial, 1900s] **5.** the penis in expressions such as CHICKEN-CHOKER (*q.v.*). A play on COCK (sense 3).

chicken-breasted pertaining to a FLAT-CHESTED (*q.v.*) woman. [British slang, early 1800s, Egan's Grose]

chicken-choker a male masturbator. [well-known euphemism used on citizens band radio; U.S., mid 1900s-pres.]

chicken-grabbing pertaining to a despised man; masturbating. A euphemistic disguise. See CHICKEN (sense 5). [U.S. slang, 1900s]

chicken-hawk a male homosexual who is particularly attracted to teenage boys; the same as CHICKEN QUEEN (*q.v.*). [U.S. slang, mid 1900s-pres., Wentworth and Flexner]

chicken powder amphetamines. With the implication that a person is a coward to use amphetamines rather than stronger drugs. *Cf.* KIDSTUFF. [U.S. drug culture, mid 1900s-pres.]

chicken queen a homosexual male who is strongly attracted to adolescent males; the same as CHICKEN-HAWK (*q.v.*). *Cf.* CHICKEN (sense 2). See QUEEN for similar subjects. [U.S. slang and homosexual use, mid 1900s-pres.]

chicken-shit 1. any thing or person which is unpleasant. **2.** to boast and to lie; to BULLSHIT (sense 2). [both senses, U.S. slang, 1900s] **3.** anything that is small or worthless. [U.S. slang, mid 1900s-pres.] **4.** military decorations, especially the type which appears on the shoulders of the uniform. [U.S. military slang, World War II]

chickory (also **chickery**) intoxicated with alcohol. For synonyms see WOOFLED. [U.S. slang, early 1700s, Ben Franklin]

Chic Sale an outhouse. From the name of the author of a book about outhouses. For synonyms see AJAX. Not always capitalized. [U.S. slang, early 1900s-pres.]

chief, the the drug L.S.D. (*q.v.*). [U.S. drug culture, mid 1900s-pres.]

child-getter the penis. [British slang, 1800s, Farmer and Henley]

chili-chomper (also **chili, chili-belly, chili-eater**) A Mexican. Usually derogatory. [U.S. slang and colloquial in the Southwest, 1900s and before]

chimney the female genitals, specifically the vagina. In the expressions GET ONE'S CHIMNEY SWEPT OUT, MAKE THE CHIMNEY SMOKE (both *q.v.*). For synonyms see MONOSYLLABLE. [British slang, 1800s]

chimney sweep 1. a wencher; a whoremonger. *Cf.* CHIMNEY. [British slang, 1800s or before] **2.** a clergyman;

a preacher. From the blackness of his vestments. For synonyms see SKY-PILOT. [British, 1800s, Farmer and Henley]

Chinaman a derogatory term for a Chinese or a person of Chinese ancestry. Frequently used without malice, however. For synonyms see JOHN CHINAMAN. [since the mid 1800s]

Chinamang a derogatory nickname for a Chinese. From CHINAMAN (*q.v.*). [U.S. slang, 1900s, Berrey and Van den Bark]

China white heroin as compared to opium, which is black. [U.S. drug culture, mid 1900s-pres.]

Chinee a Chinese. A jocular and erroneous singular form of "Chinese." [U.S. slang and colloquial, late 1800s]

Chinese-fashion a sexual position supposedly used by the Chinese wherein the partners lie on their sides facing one another, or the male and female are crossed like an X. This, according to jokes and limericks, is because the PUDENDAL CLEAVAGE (*q.v.*) is horizontal. [British military, 1900s, *Dictionary of Slang and Unconventional English*]

Chinese red heroin. [U.S. drug culture, mid 1900s-pres.]

Chinese saxophone an opium pipe. For synonyms see GONGER. [attested, early 1900s, *Dictionary of the Underworld*]

Chinese tobacco opium. [U.S. underworld, 1900s or before]

Chinese white (also **China white**) very potent heroin. [U.S., 1900s]

chingus the penis. *Cf.* DINGUS. For synonyms see YARD. [U.S. slang, mid 1900s, Berrey and Van den Bark]

chink 1. the female genitals. *Cf.* CHINK-STOPPER. [British colloquial, 1800s, Farmer and Henley] **2.** a person of the Mongoloid race; an Oriental. Usually derogatory for a Chinese. Recently derogatory for a Vietnamese. [widespread slang, mid 1800s-pres.]

chinkerings the menses. For synonyms see FLOODS. [U.S. dialect, 1900s and before]

chink-stopper the penis. *Cf.* CHINK (sense 1). [British slang, 1800s, Farmer and Henley]

Chinky (also **chinky**) **1.** a derogatory nickname for a Chinese. For synonyms see JOHN CHINAMAN. [Australian and U.S., late 1800s] **2.** pertaining to a Chinese or any Oriental. Derogatory. [slang, late 1800s-pres.]

Chino a derogatory nickname for a Chinese. [U.S. slang, early 1900s]

chip to use drugs occasionally and not addictively. *Cf.* CHIPPER, CHIPPY (sense 3). [U.S. drug culture, mid 1900s-pres.]

chipper an occasional heroin user. *Cf.* CHIP. [U.S. drug culture, mid 1900s-pres.]

chippy (also **chippie**) **1.** a woman, especially a sexually loose woman. **2.** an amateur prostitute who works only occasionally. For synonyms see HARLOT. [both senses, slang, 1900s] **3.** a person who uses strong drugs only occasionally; the same as CHIPPER (*q.v.*). [U.S. drug culture, mid 1900s-pres.] **4.** mild narcotics. [U.S. slang, 1900s]

chippy around to be sexually promiscuous. *Cf.* CHIPPY (sense 2). [U.S. underworld and slang, mid 1900s-pres.]

chippy-chaser a male who chases sexually loose women and girls. For synonyms see lecher. [U.S. slang, 1900s]

chippy on to CHEAT ON (*q.v.*); to be sexually unfaithful to someone; to step out with a CHIPPY (sense 1), said of a male. [U.S. slang, 1900s]

chism (also **chissom, chissum**) **1.** to germinate; to sprout. [British dialect, mid 1700s–1900s] **2.** semen. See GISM, JISM. [U.S. dialect (Virginia), 1800s, Green]

chit 1. an obnoxious person; a worthless person. From a term for a child or a brat. Probably cognate with "kit" and "kitten." [colloquial, 1600s] **2.** a SHIT (sense 9); an obnoxious person; a deliberate disguise of "shit." [U.S. slang, mid 1900s]

chitterlings (also **chitlings**) **1.** the small intestines of animals used for food. [since the 1200s; now U.S.,

Southern dialect] 2. the human bowels. [U.S. jocular slang, 1900s]

chivalry copulation. For other examples of the "riding" theme see CAVAULTING, PRIG (sense 1), RIDE. [British, 1800s or before]

choc liquor; alcohol. *Cf.* CHALK. For synonyms see BOOZE. [U.S. slang, early 1900s]

chocha the female genitals. Farmer and Henley list **chocho**, *c.* 1900. [from Spanish; in U.S. slang, mid 1900s-pres.]

chocolate hashish. [U.S. drug culture, mid 1900s-pres.]

chocolate chips the drug L.S.D. (*q.v.*). [U.S. drug culture, mid 1900s-pres.]

chocolate drop a Negro. *Cf.* HOT CHOCOLATE, SWEET CHOCOLATE. [U.S. colloquial, 1900s or before]

chocolate highway the anus in anal intercourse. [U.S. slang, mid 1900s-pres.]

choke-dog bad food or drink; a wretched substance which would choke a dog; a strong variety of home-distilled liquor. [U.S. slang or dialect, early 1800s, Wentworth and Flexner]

choke the chicken to masturbate. *Cf.* CHICKEN (sense 5), CHICKEN-CHOKER. For synonyms see WASTE TIME. [U.S. slang, mid 1900s-pres.]

Cholly cocaine. A pronunciation variant of CHARLIE (sense 3). [U.S. drug culture, mid 1900s-pres.]

choo-choo (also **chuga-chuga**) a series of copulations performed by a number of males and one female. *Cf.* PULL A TRAIN. [U.S. slang, mid 1900s-pres.]

chopper the penis. See MARROW-BONE-AND-CLEAVER. [British, 1900s, *Dictionary of Slang and Unconventional English*]

chopping pertaining to a sexually forward young woman. [British slang, 1800s, Farmer and Henley]

chorus boy an effeminate young man. For synonyms see FRIBBLE. [U.S. slang, 1900s]

Chow-Chow a derogatory nickname for a Chinese. [Australian, mid 1800s-pres., Wilkes]

chowder-head (also **chowdar-head**) an oaf. [British and U.S. dialect and colloquial, early 1800s-pres.]

Christ-all-bleeding-mighty! an oath and an exclamation. [U.S., 1900s or before]

Christ-all-Jesus! an oath and an exclamation. [U.S. colloquial, 1900s]

Christ-almighty-wonder! 1. an oath and an exclamation. For synonyms see 'ZOUNDS! 2. an extraordinary person or thing. [colloquial, 1900s or before]

Christmas! (also **Holy Christmas!**) an oath and an exclamation. Usually a disguise for "Christ!"

Christmas tree 1. a Dexamyl (trademark) capsule, an amphetamine. [U.S. drug culture, mid 1900s-pres.] 2. a barbiturate that is packaged in a red and green capsule. Also Tuinal (trademark), which is orange and blue. For synonyms see BARB. [U.S. drug culture, mid 1900s-pres.]

Christ-on-a-crutch! an oath and an exclamation. For synonyms see 'ZOUNDS! [U.S., 1900s or before]

Christopher Columbus! an oath and disguised euphemism for "Christ!" [U.S. colloquial, 1900s or before]

Christ's foot!, By an old oath and an exclamation. [1300s, (Chaucer)]

chromo a prostitute. From CROW (sense 3). [Australian, 1900s, Baker]

chubbies large and well-proportioned breasts. *Cf.* BLUBBERS. For synonyms see BOSOM. [U.S. slang, mid 1900s-pres.]

chuck 1. to desire someone sexually. Possibly a back-formation on CHUCKED (sense 2). 2. to copulate with a woman. See STUFF (sense 1). For synonyms see OCCUPY. 3. a Caucasian or Caucasians in general. From the Negro point of view. From CHARLES (*q.v.*). For synonyms see PECKERWOOD. Sometimes capitalized in this sense. [U.S. black use, mid 1900s-pres.]

chuck a tread to coit a woman. [British slang, 1800s, Farmer and Henley]

chuck a turd to defecate. For synonyms see EASE ONESELF. [British slang, 1800s, Farmer and Henley]

chucked 1. intoxicated with alcohol. *Cf.* SCREWED (sense 1). [British slang, late 1800s] **2.** sexually aroused and therefore copulating very rapidly. Said by prostitutes of their more amorous customers. For synonyms see HUMPY. [British, 1800s, Farmer and Henley]

chuck up to vomit. *Cf.* THROW UP (sense 1); UPCHUCK [attested as Australian, 1800s–1900s, Brophy and Partridge]

chuff 1. a pelvic thrust in the act of copulation. **2.** a CATAMITE (*q.v.*). For synonyms see BRONCO. [British underworld, mid 1900s, *Dictionary of Slang and Unconventional English*] **3.** to masturbate. Also **chuffer**. [British slang, 1800s, Farmer and Henley] **4.** the posteriors or the anus. [Australian, Baker] **5.** a churl, oaf, or bumpkin. [British dialect, 1800s or before]

chuff box the female genitals, specifically the vagina. See CHUFF (sense 1).

chuff chums a pair of homosexual males. *Cf.* CHUFF (senses 2 and 4). [British 1900s, *Dictionary of Slang and Unconventional English*]

chuff-nut fecal matter clinging to anal or pubic hairs. From CHUFF (sense 4). *Cf.* DINGLEBERRY, FARTLEBERRY.

chuga-chuga See CHOO-CHOO.

chum 1. the female genitals. **2.** a man's own penis. **3.** a louse. See BOSOM CHUMS. [all senses, British slang, 1800s, Farmer and Henley]

chunder 1. to vomit. **2.** vomitus. For synonyms see YORK. [both senses, Australian, early 1900s-pres., Wilkes]

chunk copulation. Similar to PIECE (sense 5). [U.S. slang, early 1900s-pres.]

chunk of meat a woman considered as a sexual object. Occasionally said of a man. For synonyms see TAIL. [U.S. slang, 1900s]

churl 1. a male. No negative connotations. [from *c.* 800 to 1200, *Oxford English Dictionary*] **2.** an oaf; a bumpkin. [1200s–1800s]

churn the female genitals. Refers to the action of the churn-dasher. See BUTTER, which is the semen. [British slang, 1800s, Farmer and Henley]

churrus marijuana. See CHARRAS.

cinder bull (also **cinder dick**) a nickname for a railroad yard policeman or detective. See BULL (sense 8). [U.S. tramps, early 1900s]

circle the female genitals. For synonyms see MONOSYLLABLE. [euphemistic, 1600s–1700s]

circle-jerk (also **chain-jerk, ring-jerk**) real or imagined mutual masturbation in a circle. It may involve males and females or males alone. See GROUP SEX for similar subjects. [U.S. slang, mid 1900s-pres.]

circular protector a euphemism for "condom." For synonyms see EEL-SKIN. [British advertising, 1800s, Farmer and Henley]

circus love a real or imagined sexual orgy. See similar subjects at GROUP SEX. [U.S. slang, mid 1900s]

civet the female genitals. From "civet cat" and possibly the strong odor of the civet cat. *Cf.* CAT (sense 6). [British slang, 1800s, Farmer and Henley]

C.J. an abbreviation of "crystal joint," *i.e.*, P.C.P. (*q.v.*). P.C.P. is often consumed by smoking it with tobacco or other burnable vegetable substances. See JOINT (sense 2). [U.S. drug culture, mid 1900s-pres.]

C-jam cocaine. See JAM (sense 5). [U.S. drug culture, mid 1900s-pres.]

claff the female genitals. An obsolete form of CLEFT (*q.v.*). For synonyms see MONOSYLLABLE. [British dialect, 1800s, Farmer and Henley]

clam an oaf or blockhead; someone with a totally closed mind. [U.S. slang, late 1800s, (Samuel Clemens)]

clammux a worthless slattern. *Cf.* SLUMMOCKS. For synonyms see TROLLY-MOG. [British dialect, 1800s or before]

clangers the testicles. *Cf.* CLAPPERS. [British, 1900s or before]

clangers the testicles. *Cf.* CLAPPERS. [British, 1900s or before]

clanks the delirium tremens. *Cf.* TRIANGLES. [U.S. slang, early 1900s]

clap (also **clapp**) 1. venereal disease, usually gonorrhea but occasionally (in error) for syphilis. [since the late 1500s] 2. to infect with gonorrhea. [since the mid 1600s]

clap of thunder a glass of gin. *Cf.* LIGHTNING (sense 1). For synonyms see RUIN. [British slang, early 1800s]

clapped (also **clapt**) infected with gonorrhea. *Cf.* CLAP (sense 2).

clappers the testicles. Like the swinging clapper in a bell. *Cf.* CLANGERS. [probably written nonce; British, early 1900s, *Dictionary of Slang and Unconventional English*]

clapster a male who is infected with gonorrhea. [British slang, 1800s, Farmer and Henley]

clapt infected with gonorrhea; the same as CLAPPED (*q.v.*).

claptrap 1. nonsense; something introduced solely to get applause. [colloquial since the 1800s] 2. a sexually loose woman presumed to be infected with gonorrhea. A reinterpretation of sense 1.

clarabelle tetrahydrocannabinol, (T.H.C.), *i.e.*, synthetic marijuana, the "active ingredient" in marijuana. *Cf.* CLAY. [U.S. drug culture, mid 1900s-pres.]

claret blood. [jocular colloquial, early 1600s–1900s]

clart 1. to make dirty or to smear with any sticky substance. [1200s–1800s] 2. a slovenly person. In particular, a slatternly woman. 3. mud or filth. 4. nonsense; flattery or cheap talk. [senses 2–4 are British dialect, early 1800s–1900s] 5. feces. 6. to defecate. [senses 5 and 6 are U.S. dialect, 1900s or before]

clarty-paps a filthy, slatternly woman or wife. See CLART. [British colloquial dialect, 1800s or before, Halliwell]

clawed-off infected with venereal disease. [cant or slang, late 1600s, B.E.]

clay T.H.C. (*q.v.*), the active ingredient in marijuana. *Cf.* CLARABELLE. [U.S. drug culture, mid 1900s-pres.]

clay-brained stupid; with brains made of clay. [from *Henry IV*, Part One (Shakespeare)]

clear intoxicated with alcohol. [slang, late 1600s-pres.]

clear light the drug L.S.D. [U.S. drug culture, mid 1900s–pres.]

cleat the glans penis. From an old term for "wedge." *Cf.* WEDGE. [British slang or colloquial, 1800s, *Dictionary of Slang and Unconventional English*]

cleavage 1. the space between a woman's breasts, especially when the breasts are large, close together, and partially exposed. 2. a crease at the top of the buttocks; the upper part of the gluteal furrow. A jocular extension of sense 1. [both senses, U.S. colloquial, 1900s or before]

cleave a wanton or sexually loose woman; a woman who copulates readily. For synonyms see LAY. [British slang or cant, late 1700s, Grose]

cleaver a sexually loose woman; a CLEAVE (*q.v.*). For synonyms see LAY. [British slang, late 1700s, Grose]

cleft 1. pertaining to a nonvirgin female. [British slang or cant, late 1700s, Grose] 2. the female genitals. For synonyms see MONOSYLLABLE. [colloquial, 1800s, Farmer and Henley]

cleft of flesh the female genitals. *Cf.* CLOVEN SPOT. [British 1800s, Farmer and Henley]

click to get on well with a person or an idea, especially to experience mutual sexual attraction with a member of the opposite sex. [U.S., 1900s]

climax the end of any activity, specifically orgasm; the end of the sexual act. A euphemism and the polite word-of-choice for "orgasm." [U.S., 1900s]

climb to copulate with a woman; to mount and coit a woman. *Cf.* BOARD, MOUNT. [since the 1600s]

climb the golden staircase to die. For synonyms see DEPART. [U.S. colloquial, late 1800s–1900s]

clinch a passionate embrace. [U.S. slang, 1900s]

clinchpoop (also **clinchpoup**) a term of contempt for an oaf; a dunce. [colloquial, mid 1500s]

clings like shit to a shovel (also **sticks like shit to a shovel**) a catch phrase describing the adherence of a sticky substance or a clingy person. [colloquial since the 1800s]

clink a derogatory term for a Negro. From "coal clinker." For synonyms see EBONY. [attested as black use, U.S. slang, 1900s]

clinker fecal or seminal matter adhering to the anal or pubic hairs. *Cf.* CHUFF-NUT, DINGLEBERRY, FARTLEBERRY. [British slang, 1800s]

clinkerballs balls of dried dung in sheep's wool. *Cf.* CHUFF-NUT, CLINKER, DINGLEBERRY, FARTLEBERRY. [British dialect, 1800s or before]

clipped-dick a derogatory nickname for a Jewish man. Refers to circumcision. *Cf.* CUTCOCK. For synonyms see FIVE AND TWO. [U.S. slang, 1900s, Wentworth and Flexner]

clish-clash (also **clishmaclaver**) nonsense; idle talk. For synonyms see ANIMAL. [Scots, 1700s–early 1800s]

clit the clitoris. *Cf.* CLITTY. [U.S. slang, mid 1900s–pres.]

clitoris the erectile sensory organ which is part of the female genitals. [since the early 1600s] Synonyms: BOY-IN-THE-BOAT, BUTTON, CLIT, CLITTY, LITTLE MAN IN THE BOAT, MAN IN THE BOAT, MEMBRUM MULIEBRE, PENIS EQUIVALENT, PENIS FIMINEUS, PENIS MULIEBRIS, SLIT.

clitorize to stimulate a woman sexually by manipulating the clitoris; to perform sexual foreplay on a woman. For synonyms see FIRKYTOODLE. [British, 1800s, Farmer and Henley]

clitty the clitoris. A playful nickname similar to CLIT (*q.v.*). [U.S. slang, mid 1900s–pres.]

cloak-and-suiter a Jewish tailor or simply a derogatory term for a Jewish man. [U.S. slang, early 1900s, Weseen]

cloakroom 1. a place to hang or check coats. No negative connotations. [since the mid 1800s] **2.** a restroom. For synonyms see W.C. [originally a euphemism; British, late 1800s–pres.]

clobbered intoxicated with alcohol. For synonyms see WOOFLED. [U.S. slang, 1900s]

clock the female genitals. [British slang, 1800s, Farmer and Henley]

clock-weights the testicles. [British slang, 1800s, Farmer and Henley]

clod an oaf or simpleton. A truncation of CLOD-HOPPER (*q.v.*). [colloquial since the late 1500s]

clod-head (also **clod-pate, clod-pole, clod-poll**) an oaf; a dolt. [British and U.S., 1600s–pres.]

clod-hopper a bumpkin; a rustic plowman; an oaf who walks among clods of dirt. From the type of shoe worn by farmers. The term is now used for the shoe itself. [rural colloquial, late 1600s-pres.]

clodpolish stupid. From CLOD-POLL (*q.v.* at CLOD-HEAD). [U.S. colloquial, 1900s]

clod-skulled stupid; oafish. [British colloquial, 1700s]

clomps an oaf. [British dialect, 1800s or before]

close stool a covered CHAMBER POT (*q.v.*); a chamber pot concealed in a chest or other furniture. *Cf.* COMMODE, SIR HARRY, STOOL (sense 4). [British, early 1400s–1900s]

closet 1. a privy; a water closet. See CLOSET OF EASE, WATER CLOSET. [colloquial since the 1700s] **2.** the water tank of a modern toilet. [U.S., 1900s]

closet case 1. one who engages in homosexual activity but will not admit being a homosexual. *Cf.* CLOSET QUEEN. **2.** anyone who does anything in secret. [U.S. colloquial, mid 1900s–pres.]

closet-man a sanitary inspector; an inspector of privies. *Cf.* CLOSET. [Jamaican and elsewhere; 1900s and before, Cassidy and Le Page]

closet of decency a water closet; a privy. [British euphemism, 1800s or before]

closet of ease a privy; a W.C. [British, mid 1600s]

closet queen 1. a homosexual male who keeps his homosexuality a secret. *Cf.* CLOSET CASE. **2.** a LATENT HOMOSEXUAL (*q.v.*). For related subjects see QUEEN. [both are originally homosexual use and now are U.S. slang, 1900s]

closet queer the same as CLOSET QUEEN (*q.v.*) [U.S. slang, mid 1900s]

closet stool the toilet; the water-flush basin found in a bathroom. *Cf.* CLOSE STOOL. [U.S., 1900s]

clot (also **clot-head**) a fool; an oaf. [slang and colloquial, 1800s–1900s]

clothes prop the penis, especially when erect. For synonyms see ERECTION. [British slang, 1800s]

clout 1. a sanitary napkin; a PERINEAL PAD (*q.v.*). For synonyms see MANHOLE COVER. [British colloquial, 1800s, Farmer and Henley] **2.** a diaper. [U.S. dialect (Ozarks), Randolph and Wilson] **3.** a woman's underclothes. [British, 1800s, Farmer and Henley] See also BREECH-CLOUT at BREECH-CLOTH.

cloven (also **cleaved, cleft**) pertaining to a nonvirgin female. [British slang or cant, late 1700s, Grose]

cloven spot the female genitals. *Cf.* CLEFT OF FLESH. [British, 1800s, Farmer and Henley]

cloven tuft the female genitals. For synonyms see MONOSYLLABLE. [British, late 1600s–1800s]

clover-field the female pubic hair. [British, 1800s]

clowes (also **clows**) a rogue. For synonyms see SNOKE-HORN. [British slang or cant, late 1600s, B.E.]

clown 1. a bumpkin or rustic oaf. [1500s–1600s] **2.** any oaf or jerk. [U.S., 1900s and before]

club 1. the penis. For synonyms see YARD. [widespread recurrent nonce since

the 1600s or before] **2.** to coit a woman; to use the CLUB (sense 1) on a woman. For synonyms see OCCUPY. [British slang, 1800s, Farmer and Henley]

club sandwich a type of real or imaginary sexual intercourse for three. See CLUB (sense 1). See GROUP SEX for similar subjects. [U.S. slang, mid 1900s-pres.]

cluck (also **kluck**) **1.** a stupid oaf; a DUMB CLUCK (*q.v.*). [U.S. colloquial, 1900s] **2.** a very dark Negro. Derogatory. For synonyms see EBONY. [U.S. slang, Montelone]

cluckhead a stupid oaf. [U.S. colloquial, 1900s]

clucky 1. pregnant. Refers to a brooding hen. [Australian, early 1900s, Baker] **2.** stupid; oafish. *Cf.* DUMB CLUCK. [U.S. colloquial, 1900s]

clumperton a bumpkin or rustic. [British slang or colloquial, 1800s]

clunch a bumpkin or a boor. *Cf.* HOB-CLUNCH. [British colloquial, early 1600s]

clunk (also **clunks**) a stupid clod or lump; an oaf. *Cf.* CLUNCH. [U.S. slang, early 1900s-pres.]

clunkhead an oaf; a stupid dolt. [U.S., 1900s]

clyde a stupid person. From the proper name, sometimes capitalized. For synonyms see OAF. [U.S. slang, 1900s]

coach a hearse. [U.S. funeral trade, 1900s]

coachman on the box a venereal disease. Rhyming slang for POX (*q.v.*). In this case, syphilis or other venereal diseases. [British, 1900s, *Dictionary of Rhyming Slang*]

coals syphilis. *Cf.* WINTER COALS. For synonyms see SPECIFIC STOMACH. [British slang, 1800s, Farmer and Henley]

coal-shute (also **coal-chute**) a very dark Negro. Derogatory. For synonyms see EBONY. [U.S., early 1900s, Montelone]

coarse piece a vulgar woman. *Cf.* PIECE. [U.S., 1900s or before]

coast to experience the effects of marijuana or other drugs. [U.S. drug culture, mid 1900s-pres.]

coast-to-coasts amphetamine tablets or capsules. Referring to the use of amphetamines by cross-country truck drivers. *Cf.* L.A. TURN-ABOUTS. [U.S. slang and drug culture, mid 1900s-pres.]

cob 1. a male swan. [late 1500s] **2.** to GOOSE (sense 6) a person or to commit pederasty upon a person. **3.** a testicle. See COBS.

cobbler's awls (also **cobbler's**) the human testicles; nonsense. Possibly an elaboration of COBS (*q.v.*), "testicles." Rhyming slang for "balls." [British, 1900s]

cobbler's stalls the human testicles; nonsense. Possibly an elaboration of COBS (*q.v.*), "testicles." Rhyming slang for "balls." See ORCHESTRA STALLS. [British, 1900s, *Dictionary of Rhyming Slang*]

cobics heroin. *Cf.* COBY. [U.S. drug culture, mid 1900s-pres.]

cobs (also **cobbs**) the testicles. The colloquial term for any stone, pebble, or pit. [British colloquial, early 1800s]

coby morphine. Usually in the plural, "cobies." *Cf.* COBICS. [U.S. drug culture, mid 1900s-pres.]

cocainized under the influence of cocaine. [U.S., early 1900s]

Cock (also **Cocke, Cokis, Cox, Gock**) a disguise of "God" in expressions such as By Cock!, By Cock's body!, By Cock's bones!, By Cock's heart!, By Cock's mother!, By Cock's pain!, By Cock's passion! *Cf.* CORKS! [1300s]

cock 1. a male chicken. No negative connotations. [since the 800s, *Oxford English Dictionary*] **2.** a spout or tap, such as in a barrel. No negative connotations. [since the late 1400s] **3.** the penis. A nickname based on sense 2. Some etymologies suggest that the erectile cock's comb is a reinforcing factor. This is the most widespread nickname for the penis and is considered quite vulgar in some parts of the world. *Cf.* CHICKEN (sense 5), ROOSTER

(sense 1), ROOSTERED. [widespread English since the early 1700s] **4.** to copulate with a woman, from the male point of view. [numerous written attestations, since the 1800s] **5.** any male; the equivalent of "buddy" or "chum." Also in compounds such as "turkey-cock." [since the 1600s] **6.** the female genitals. In much of the Southern U.S. and Caribbean, "cock" refers to the female organs exclusively. Possibly related to COCKLES (*q.v.*). *Cf.* sense 2. [U.S. dialect and Negro usage, 1800s and before] **7.** women considered solely as sexual objects. From sense 6. **8.** to receive a man in copulation, said of a woman. [British, 1800s, Farmer and Henley] **9.** nonsense. A truncation of POPPYCOCK (*q.v.*).

cock-ale beer or ale, allegedly with an aphrodisiac quality. Also due to its diuretic qualities. [British, late 1600s]

cock-alley the female genitals. For synonyms see MONOSYLLABLE. [British slang or cant, late 1700s, Grose]

cockamamie pertaining to nonsense. Probably from "cockalane," meaning "nonsense" or "lies." [from the French *coq-à-l'âne*, *i.e.*, COCK AND BULL (*q.v.*)]

cock and bull a tedious and deceptive story or simply a lie. [colloquial since the early 1600s]

Cock-and-pie!, By an oath and an exclamation. [mid 1500s]

cockapert an impudent, arrogant male. [mid 1500s]

cock-bawd a pimp. [British slang or cant, late 1600s, B.E.]

cock-bite a castrating woman; an extremely hateful young woman or girl; a BITCH (sense 5). Refers to COCK (sense 3), the penis. [U.S. slang, mid 1900s-pres., Landy]

cock-block to interfere with a man's sexual activity with a woman. Abbreviated C.B. (*q.v.*). [U.S. black use, mid 1900s-pres.]

cock-brain an oaf; a birdbrain. [colloquial, mid 1500s]

cock-chafer 1. the treadmill. A reinterpretation of the colloquial name of a large and destructive, grayish beetle. [British, 1800s] **2.** the female genitals. With reference to the role of the vagina in copulation. [British slang, 1800s, Farmer and Henley] **3.** a female who excites a male sexually, but who refuses to copulate with him; a C.T. (sense 3). *Cf.* COCK-TEASER, PRICK-TEASER. [British slang, 1800s, *Dictionary of Slang and Unconventional English*]

cock-cheese SMEGMA (sense 2). *Cf.* CHEESE (sense 1), CROTCH-CHEESE. [British slang, 1800s–1900s]

cocked 1. intoxicated with alcohol. *Cf.* ROOSTERED. For synonyms see WOOFLED. [U.S. and elsewhere, early 1700s, Ben Franklin] **2.** having been copulated with (said of a woman), or having copulated (said of a man). [British, 1800s, Farmer and Henley]

cocked-up pregnant. From COCK (sense 4). For synonyms see STORKED. [British slang, 1800s, Farmer and Henley]

cock-fighter a whoremonger; a notorious copulator. For synonyms see LECHER. [British slang, 1700s–1800s]

cock-hall the female genitals. *Cf.* COCK-INN. [British slang, 1700s–1800s]

cock-happy pertaining to a girl or woman who desires to be copulated with. [U.S., 1900s]

cock-holder the female genitals. *Cf.* COCK (sense 3). [slang, 1800s–1900s]

cocking 1. copulation; the use of the COCK (sense 3), "penis." [British and U.S. colloquial and slang, 1800s–1900s] **2.** a euphemism for "fucking." *Cf.* COCK (sense 4).

cock-inn the female genitals. *Cf.* COCK-ALLEY. [British slang, 1700s–1800s]

cockish pertaining to a wanton woman or a lecherous man. [British colloquial, late 1500s–1800s]

cock-lane the female genitals. *Cf.* COCK-ALLEY. [British slang, late 1700s, Grose]

cockle burr an amphetamine tablet or capsule. [U.S. slang, mid 1900s–pres.]

cockles the labia minora. Possibly the origin of or an elaboration of COCK (sense 6). [British slang, 1700s]

cock-loft the female genitals. From the name of the place where chickens are kept. [British slang, 1700s–1800s]

cock of the game a lecher; a whoremonger. [British, 1800s or before]

cock-pimp the keeper of a prostitute; a pimp. [cant, late 1600s, B.E.]

cock-pipe a penis-shaped pipe for smoking marijuana. The smoke is sucked out of the "glans." [U.S. drug culture, mid 1900s–pres.]

cockpit the female genitals; the vagina. *Cf.* BOTTOMLESS-PIT. [recurrent nonce; British slang, 1700s–1800s]

cock-quean 1. a female cuckold, a woman whose husband copulates with other women. [British slang, 1800s or before, Barrère and Leland] **2.** a beggar or a con man. [British, 1800s or before, Halliwell]

cock's eggs 1. a name for imaginary or nonexistent items; the equivalent of "hen's teeth," which are nonexistent. [British colloquial, 1800s] **2.** rooster droppings. [British, 1900s, *Dictionary of Slang and Unconventional English*]

cockshire the female genitals. *Cf.* MEMBER FOR THE COCKSHIRE. [British slang, 1800s, Farmer and Henley]

cocksman (also **cockhound, cocksmith**) a notorious woman-chaser; a lecher. [U.S. slang, 1900s]

cock snooks a gesture similar to thumbing the nose. See ANNE'S FAN for a description.

cock-stand an erection of the penis. *Cf.* CUNT-STAND. [primarily British; colloquial, 1700s–1900s]

cocksucker (also **cock-sucker**) **1.** a male and sometimes a female who performs fellatio. *Cf.* CORK-SACKING. [widespread slang, 1800s-pres.] **2.** a toady; a sycophant. [U.S. slang, 1800s-pres.] **3.** a strong term of contempt used by one male to another. The equivalent of calling a man a homosexual. [U.S. slang, 1900s]

cocktail 1. a prostitute. For synonyms see HARLOT. [British slang, 1800s] **2.** a coward. For synonyms see YELLOW-DOG. [British slang or colloquial, 1800s] **3.** a cigarette which is a mixture of marijuana and tobacco. [U.S. drug culture, mid 1900s]

cocktails diarrhea. [Australian, 1900s, Baker]

cock-teaser (also **cock-tease**) a woman who leads a man on sexually but who refuses to permit copulation. *Cf.* COCK-CHAFER, C.T. (sense 3), PRICK-TEASER. [British and U.S., 1800s-1900s]

cock up 1. to beat; to beat up. **2.** a mess. Usually hyphenated in this sense. [both senses, British colloquial, 1900s, and both senses taboo in some parts of the world] **3.** copulated with; impregnated. For synonyms see OCCUPY. See also COCKED-UP.

cod 1. a husk, shell, or bag. No negative connotation [*c.* 1000, *Oxford English Dictionary*] **2.** the scrotum and the testicles; sometimes the VIRILIA (*q.v.*). [1300s] **3.** a fool; an oaf. [British slang, 1600s–1900s] **4.** a drunkard. [British slang, 1800s]

codger a mean and unpleasant old man; now just an old man. [British and U.S. colloquial, 1700s-pres.]

cod-hopper a harlot; a sexually loose woman. Patterned on "clod-hopper." See COD (sense 2).

codpiece 1. a baglike flap in the crotch of the trousers which covers or contains the male genitals. Popular in England in the 1400s. [mid 1400s-pres.] **2.** something similar to a CODPIECE (sense 1) worn about the breast by a woman. [1500s, *Oxford English Dictionary*] **3.** the penis or the VIRILIA (*q.v.*). [British, late 1700s and before]

cods the testicles. *Cf.* COBS. [since the 1800s or before]

Codsfish! an oath and an exclamation, "By God's flesh!" A play on "codfish."

cod's head an oaf; a blockhead. With reference to the intellect of a codfish. [mid 1500s–1800s]

cod's wallop (also **cod's wallops**)

nonsense; BALDERDASH (sense 2). [British, 1900s, *Dictionary of Slang and Unconventional English*]

coffee the drug L.S.D. (*q.v.*). [U.S. drug culture, mid 1900s-pres.]

coffee-grinder 1. a prostitute. With reference to her pelvic motions. **2.** a striptease dancer with reference to the BUMPS AND GRINDS (*q.v.*). [both senses, U.S. slang, 1900s, Wentworth and Flexner]

coffee house 1. a privy; an outhouse. For synonyms see AJAX. **2.** the vagina in the expression "make a coffee house of a woman's cunt," to "go in and out and spend nothing" (Grose). [both senses, British slang or cant, 1700s, Grose]

coffee-shop 1. a euphemism for "coffin." [British slang, 1800s, Barrère and Leland] **2.** a privy; a W.C.; the same as COFFEE HOUSE (sense 1). [both senses, British slang, 1800s]

coffee stalls the testicles. Rhyming slang for "balls." *Cf.* ORCHESTRA STALLS. [British, 1900s, *Dictionary of Rhyming Slang*]

coffin a burial case for a corpse. [since the early 1500s] Synonyms: BIER, BONE-BOX, BONE-HOUSE, BOX, BURIAL CASE, CASKET, CATAFALQUE, CHICAGO-OVER-COAT, COFFEE-SHOP, COLD-MEAT BOX, ETERNITY-BOX, FERETORY, MAN BOX, PAINTED-BOX, PINE-OVERCOAT, PLANTING CRATE, SARCOPHAGUS, SCOLD'S CURE, THREE PLANKS, WOODEN-COAT, WOODEN-KIMONA, WOODEN-OVERCOAT, WOODEN-SUIT, WOODEN-SURTOUT.

coffin-nail (also **coffin-tack**) a dysphemism for "cigarette." *Cf.* CANCER-STICK. [British and U.S., late 1800s-pres.]

coffin varnish any inferior alcoholic beverage, especially bad whisky. For synonyms see EMBALMING FLUID. [U.S. slang, 1900s]

cognacked intoxicated with alcohol. *Cf.* INCOG. [U.S. slang, early 1900s]

coguey intoxicated with alcohol. [from a Scots word for "cup"; British slang or colloquial, early 1800s, Jon Bee]

cohabit 1. originally to dwell together. [since the early 1500s] **2.** to live together as man and wife; to live together and copulate.

coil a nickname for an intrauterine contraceptive device. *Cf.* I.U.C.D., I.U.D. [U.S., mid 1900s-pres.]

coil up one's ropes to die. [British naval slang, Fraser and Gibbons]

coit 1. an act of copulation; copulation and impregnation; a sexual union of animals or of humans. Probably in use only as a scientific term. [from the Latin *coire*, late 1600s] **2.** to SCREW (sense 1); to PHALLICIZE (*q.v.*) a woman. Used here and elsewhere (*e.g.*, *Dictionary of Slang and Unconventional English*) as a euphemism for less polite terms for sexual intercourse from the male point of view. There is no "polite," single-syllable, transitive verb for the male act of penetration and thrusting in copulation.

coit dorsally 1. to perform male-female, orthogenital copulation with the male approaching the female from behind. **2.** to perform pederasty; to coit anally. [1900s or before]

coition (also **coitus**) **1.** the act of moving the penis inward past the opening formed by the vulva. This degree of penetration constitutes sufficient contact to support a charge of rape. In the narrowest definition, the act of penetration completes the act of coition. Usually, however, it is interpreted in the following sense. **2.** the act of penetrating (as in sense 1) with sufficient movement on the part of one or both parties to produce orgasm in one or both parties. See COIT.

coitu, in* "in the act of copulating"; during sexual intercourse; the same as ACTUS COITU, IN (*q.v.*). [Latin; English use by the 1300s, *Oxford English Dictionary*]

coitus the same as COITION (*q.v.*). For synonyms see SMOCKAGE. [from Latin]

coitus interruptus* COITION (sense 2) followed by the withdrawal of the penis before ejaculation; the same as

WITHDRAWAL (*q.v.*). This is considered to be an early form of birth control and is still practiced.

coitus per anum* a euphemism for PEDERASTY (*q.v.*) with the exception that there is no age implication as there is in pederasty. Also used in reference to anal penetration in women. [Latin]

coitus reservatus* a sexual practice where the male sustains phallic movements and delays ejaculation until the female has experienced orgasm.

cojones the testicles. The "j" is pronounced as an "h." For synonyms see WHIRLYGIGS. [from Spanish; U.S. slang, 1900s]

coke cocaine. [U.S. underworld and drug culture, early 1900s-pres.]

coked intoxicated with or under the effects of cocaine. [U.S. underworld, early 1900s]

coke-freak a frequent user of cocaine. *Cf.* SPEED-FREAK. [U.S., 1900s]

coke-head a heavy user of cocaine. For synonyms see USER. [U.S. drug culture, early 1900s-pres.]

coke-party a gathering where cocaine is consumed as the primary activity. From the nickname for a party where carbonated soft drinks are served. [U.S. drug culture, early 1900s-pres.]

coker-nuts the breasts, especially if well-developed. From the size and shape of the coconut. For synonyms see BOSOM. [British slang, late 1800s-early 1900s, Ware]

cokespoon a spoon used in sniffing cocaine; the same as SPOON (sense 7). [U.S. drug culture, early 1900s-pres.]

coke-stop (also **coke-break**) euphemistic for a stop at a restroom. From the Coca-Cola (trademark) advertisement for a "coke-break." *Cf.* NATURE STOP. [U.S. slang, 1900s]

cokey (also **cokie**) a heavy user of cocaine. [British and U.S. underworld and drug culture, early 1900s-pres.]

cold 1. sexually FRIGID (*q.v.*). [since the 1600s] **2.** dead. For synonyms see DONE FOR. [U.S. slang, 1900s or before]

cold biscuit a cold, unresponsive woman. *Cf.* BISCUIT, YEAST-POWDER BISCUIT. [U.S. slang, early 1900s-pres.]

cold coffee beer. For synonyms see SUDS. [British slang, late 1800s, Ware] See also COFFEE.

cold cook an undertaker; someone who works with COLD MEAT (*q.v.*). [British colloquial, 1700s–1900s]

cold cookshop an undertaker's place of business. [British colloquial, 1800s or before]

cold-fish 1. a cold or unresponsive woman. From FISH (sense 1). [U.S. slang, early 1900s-pres.] **2.** a wishy-washy jerk; a RUBBER SOCK or WET SOCK (both *q.v.*). [U.S. colloquial, mid 1900s-pres.]

cold meat a corpse. *Cf.* DEAD-MEAT. [British and U.S. colloquial, 1700s–1900s]

cold-meat box a coffin. *Cf.* COLD MEAT. [colloquial, early 1800s]

cold-meat cart a hearse, specifically a horsedrawn hearse. *Cf.* COACH. [British and U.S. colloquial, 1800s–1900s]

cold-meat party a funeral. [U.S. colloquial, 1800s–1900s]

cold-meat ticket a military identification disc; a "dog-tag" used to identify dead military personnel. [British and U.S. wartime slang, 1900s]

cold mud a grave. [U.S. slang, 1900s]

coldness a euphemism for "frigidity." *Cf.* COLD (sense 1). [colloquial, 1900s and before]

cold storage a grave; the cemetery; death. [U.S. slang, 1900s]

colfabias a W.C. [mock-Latin based on Irish; British slang, 1800s]

coli marijuana; Colombian marijuana. For synonyms see MARI. [U.S. drug culture, mid 1900s-pres.]

collar and cuff (also **collar**) an effeminate male; a homosexual male. Rhyming slang for PUFF (sense 2), a homosexual male. [British slang, early 1900s, *Dictionary of Slang and Unconventional English*]

Colleen Bawn an erection of the penis. Rhyming slang for "horn." [British, mid 1800s, *Dictionary of Rhyming Slang*]

collywobbles (also **gollywobbles**) **1.** a stomachache; an upset stomach; a rumbling, growling stomach. From the colloquial term "colly-wobble," meaning "uneven." *Cf.* MULLIGRUBS, WIFFLE-WOFFLES. [British and U.S., 1800s-pres.] Synonyms: GOLLYWOBBLES, GRIPES, MULLIGRUBS, WIFFLE-WOFFLES. **2.** the menses and the accompanying uterine cramps. [colloquial, 1800s-pres.]

Colombian gold See COLUMBIAN GOLD.

colonial puck an act of copulation; to coit. Rhyming slang for FUCK (*q.v.*). [U.S., 1900s, *Dictionary of Rhyming Slang*]

color, in intoxicated with alcohol. For synonyms see WOOFLED. [U.S. slang, mid 1900s-pres.]

color, of pertaining to a person who has dark skin as a racial characteristic. In expressions such as "man of color," "person of color," or "woman of color." [euphemistic and polite, 1900s and before]

Colorado coolaid (also **Colorado Kool-aid**) beer, especially Coor's Beer (trademark), a brand of beer brewed in Colorado. From the trademarked brand name of a flavored drink mix, "Kool-aid." [U.S. slang, mid 1900s-pres.]

colored 1. pertaining to a person of the Negroid race. For many years the most polite term and the word-of-choice. *Cf.* BLACK, NIGGER. **2.** pertaining to a person of mixed heritage and sometimes to all non-Caucasians.

colored folks (also **colored, colored folk, colored people**) the Negro people in the U.S., particularly those found in rural areas or those who behave docilely. Once considered polite and nonderogatory. [U.S. colloquial, 1700s–1900s]

Columbian gold (also **Colombian gold**) marijuana grown in Colombia. Based on ACAPULCO GOLD (*q.v.*). *Cf.* GOLD. Appears in a variety of spellings. [U.S. drug culture, mid 1900s-pres.]

Columbian red (also **bo, coli, Colombian red, Colombo, Columbian, Columbia red, Columbo, limbo, lumbo**) marijuana grown in Colombia. *Cf.* GOLD COLUMBIAN. Appears in a variety of spellings. [U.S. drug culture, mid 1900s-pres.]

columbine a prostitute. Probably a deliberate malapropism for "concubine." [British, 1800s]

comboozelated intoxicated with alcohol. From BOOZE (*q.v.*). [U.S. slang, mid 1900s]

come (also **cum**) **1.** in the male, to ejaculate during orgasm. **2.** in the female, to experience orgasm. [both senses, colloquial, 1800s-pres.] **3.** semen. From sense 1 [slang and colloquial, 1900s or before]

come about to copulate with a woman, said by women of men. For synonyms see OCCUPY. [British colloquial, 1800s or before]

come about a woman to coit a woman. [British colloquial, 1800s or before, Farmer and Henley]

come across to deliver sexually, usually said of a woman by a man, particularly if the woman has been holding out for a long time. [U.S. slang, 1900s]

come aloft 1. to coit a woman. [British slang, 1800s, Farmer and Henley] **2.** to get an erection. [both senses are nautical in origin, British, 1500s-1700s]

come around 1. to acquiesce to something, particularly copulation; to agree to copulate after a long time spent holding out. *Cf.* COME ACROSS. [U.S., 1900s] **2.** to begin the menses later than expected, relieving built-up fears of pregnancy. [U.S., 1900s] **3.** to enter into HEAT (*q.v.*), said of livestock. [U.S., 1900s]

come bad to contract a venereal disease. *Cf.* BAD DISEASE. [U.S. dialect (Ozarks), 1900s or before, Randolph and Wilson]

come-by-chance a bastard; an illegitimate child. For synonyms see ACCI-

DENT. [British and U.S. colloquial, late 1700s–1900s]

comedo a blackhead; a pimple. For synonyms see BURBLE. [since the mid 1800s]

come off to ejaculate; to have an orgasm, said of the male. [British and U.S., 1800s-pres.]

come-on a flirt; a male or female who initiates or encourages advances. [U.S. slang, 1900s]

come one's cocoa to ejaculate. For synonyms see MELT. [British slang, 1900s, *Dictionary of Slang and Unconventional English*]

come one's mutton (also **come one's turkey**) to masturbate, said of the male. *Cf.* GOOSE'S-NECK, MUTTON. [British slang, 1800s, *Dictionary of Slang and Unconventional English*]

come out of the closet (also **come out**) **1.** to begin to participate in homosexual social and sexual life. See CLOSET CASE. *Cf.* BRING OUT, GO OVER. [originally homosexual use, mid 1900s-pres.] **2.** to bring any practice or belief out into the open. [U.S. colloquial, mid 1900s-pres.]

comfortable pleasantly intoxicated with alcohol. For synonyms see WOOFLED. [U.S. colloquial, 1900s]

comfort for the troops a CATAMITE (*q.v.*). A jocular reinterpretation of a term for any type of comfort or treat for military personnel. [military slang, early 1900s]

comfort room a bathroom; the W.C. [attested in Newfoundland, 1900s]

comfort station a W.C.; a public restroom. [U.S. colloquial euphemism, 1900s]

coming pertaining to a person, usually a woman, who is obviously sexually willing and able to copulate. This is probably not directly related to COME (*q.v.*). *Cf.* COMING WOMAN. [British colloquial, mid 1700s, Grose]

coming fresh pregnant, usually said of livestock. [U.S. dialect (Ozarks), Randolph and Wilson]

comings semen or semen and natural vaginal lubrication. *Cf.* COME (sense 3), SPENDINGS. [British colloquial, 1800s–1900s, *Dictionary of Slang and Unconventional English*]

coming woman (also **coming wench**) a sexually willing woman. For synonyms see LAY. [British, 1600s–1700s]

COMMFU a "complete monumental military fuck-up." For synonyms see SNAFU. [U.S. military, early 1900s]

commode 1. a chamber pot built into a chair for comfort and disguise; a CLOSE STOOL (*q.v.*). [since the mid 1800s] **2.** a toilet; a water-flush toilet bowl. From sense 1. [U.S. dialect (Southern), 1900s and before]

commodity 1. the female genitals. *Cf.* WARE (sense 2). **2.** women considered solely as sexual objects and objects of sexual commerce, *i.e.*, prostitutes. [both senses, late 1500s–1800s]

common-jack a prostitute for military men. [British, 1800s, Farmer and Henley]

common sewer a low prostitute. With reference to her reception of just anyone's DIRTY WATER (*q.v.*). *Cf.* DRAIN, SCUPPER. [British slang, late 1800s]

company bull a policeman who works for a private firm. Primarily in reference to a railroad detective. See BULL (sense 8). [U.S. underworld (tramps), 1900s or before]

company girl a prostitute; a CALL-GIRL (*q.v.*). For synonyms see HARLOT. [U.S. slang, early 1900s, Deak]

con 1. a trickster or swindler. **2.** a homosexual male. See GONIF. [both senses, U.S., mid 1900s-pres.]

concern the male or female genitals. Often pluralized when referring to the male genitals. [British, mid 1800s]

concerned intoxicated with alcohol. For synonyms see WOOFLED. [British and U.S. colloquial, late 1800s-pres.]

conciliatrix a prostitute. For synonyms see HARLOT.

concomitant of desire presumably, an erection of the penis in the male. Also includes sexual response in the female. *Cf.* CONSTITUTIONALLY INCLINED TO GALLANTRY. [British euphemism, 1800s]

condom (also **cundum**) a sheath of various materials worn on the penis during copulation to prevent conception in the female and to prevent the contraction of venereal disease. Supposedly named after its inventor, a Colonel Cundum, (Grose). For synonyms see EEL-SKIN. [since the 1600s]

confinement the last month of a woman's pregnancy. *Cf.* CALLED TO STRAW.

conflummoxed intoxicated with alcohol. For synonyms see WOOFLED. [U.S. slang, 1900s or before]

confounded a euphemism for "damned." [colloquial, 1800s–1900s]

Confound you! a curse, "Damn you!" [since the 1300s]

Congo a member of the Congregationalist Church. [Australian, 1900s, Baker]

conjugate to copulate. Heard frequently as joking and double entendre. [since the late 1700s]

conjure it down to make an erect penis flaccid by causing an orgasm in the male. *Cf.* BRING DOWN BY HAND. [from *A Winter's Tale* (Shakespeare)]

conk-buster inferior liquor. The "conk" is the head. For synonyms see EMBALMING FLUID. [U.S., 1900s, Wentworth and Flexner]

connect to purchase drugs. See CONNECTION.

connection 1. a seller of drugs. **2.** established traffic in drugs, as in the "French connection." [both senses, U.S. drug culture and slang, early 1900s-pres.] **3.** copulation. See CARNAL CONNECTION.

consarned damned. [U.S. colloquial, 1800s-pres.]

Consarn ye! a curse, the equivalent of "Damn you!" [U.S. colloquial, 1800s]

conskite to defecate in fear. [mid 1600s, (Urquhart)]

conspute to spit, especially to spit in a show of contempt. For synonyms see SPIT. [early 1500s]

constitutionally inclined to gallantry sexually aroused or aroused with an erect penis. *Cf.* CONCOMITANT OF DESIRE, GALLANTRY. [British euphemism, 1800s]

constuprate to defile, ravish, or debauch a woman. *Cf.* MANUSTUPRATION. [from the Latin *stuprum,* "defilement"; mid 1500s]

consummation 1. the sealing of a marriage contract by copulation. [since the early 1500s] **2.** orgasm. *Cf.* CLIMAX.

contact lens the drug L.S.D. put into the mouth in the manner some people employ to "clean" contact lenses before inserting them into the eyes. [U.S. drug culture, mid 1900s-pres.]

continuations trousers; breeches. For synonyms see GALLIGASKINS. [British and U.S. slang, 1800s-early 1900s]

contrapunctum the female genitals, "the opposite of the point." "Point" here means "penis." *Cf.* ANTIPODES, THE; POINT. [based on Latin; British slang, 1800s, Farmer and Henley]

contrary sexual a sexual INVERT (*q.v.*), usually a homosexual male.

conundrum the female genitals. *Cf.* WHAT (sense 2). [written nonce, British, early 1600s]

convenience 1. a CHAMBER POT (*q.v.*). For synonyms see POT. [British euphemism, 1800s] **2.** a public restroom; a PUBLIC CONVENIENCE (*q.v.*). [British and U.S., 1900s]

convenient a mistress or a prostitute. For synonyms see HARLOT. [cant or slang, late 1600s, B.E.]

cony the female genitals. From the colloquial term for a rabbit. [British slang or cant, late 1500s-1700s]

Coo! an exclamation derived from COO LUMMY! (*q.v.*). [British dialect (Cockney), 1800s-1900s]

cooch 1. the female genitals. **2.** women considered sexually. [both senses, U.S. slang, 1900s]

cook 1. to prepare opium for smoking. [U.S. underworld, early 1900s or before] **2.** to be electrocuted in the electric chair; the same as FRY (*q.v.*). [U.S. slang, early 1900s]

cooked 1. intoxicated with alcohol. *Cf.* FRIED (sense 1). [U.S. slang, 1900s or before] **2.** intoxicated with marijuana. *Cf.* FRIED (sense 2). [U.S. drug culture, mid 1900s-pres.]

cookie 1. a black who adopts a white lifestyle. A derogatory term used by a Negro for a Negro. From OREO (*q.v.*), the trademarked brand name of a cookie. **2.** the female genitals. *Cf.* BUN (sense 3), CAKE (sense 1). [U.S. slang, 1900s] **3.** a place for smoking opium. *Cf.* COOK (sense 1). **4.** an opium addict. Also **cookee, cooky**. [senses 3 and 4 are U.S. underworld, early 1900s] **5.** cocaine. [U.S. underworld, early 1900s]

cool to cool the heat of passion. [since the 1600s or before]

cooler 1. an unattractive young woman who cools one's ardor in an anaphrodisiac manner. [U.S. slang, 1900s, Wentworth and Flexner] **2.** the buttocks. **3.** women considered as sexual objects; women used as a means of abating a man's sexual heat. [British slang or cant, 1600s-1800s]

coolie-do the female genitals. For synonyms see MONOSYLLABLE. [U.S. slang, mid 1900s]

coolie mud low-grade opium. See MUD (senses 2-4), which covers a wide variety of drugs. "Coolie" refers to "Chinese." See CHINA WHITE. [U.S. underworld, early 1900s]

cool out to copulate. For synonyms see OCCUPY. [U.S. slang, mid 1900s-pres.]

Coo lummy! an oath and an exclamation, "God love me!" *Cf.* COR LUMMIE! [Cockney, 1800s-1900s]

coon 1. a highly derogatory term for a Negro. For synonyms see EBONY. **2.** pertaining to a Negro or to black culture. Both are derogatory. [both senses, U.S. colloquial, mid 1800s-pres.]

coosie 1. a derogatory term for a

Chinese. Possibly related to sense 2. [U.S. military World War II, Wentworth and Flexner] **2.** the female genitals. [slang, mid 1900s]

coot 1. the female genitals. *Cf.* COOCH. For synonyms see MONOSYLLABLE. **2.** coition. [both senses, U.S. slang, mid 1900s-pres.] **3.** an oaf; a worthless fellow, especially in "old coot." [U.S. colloquial, 1800s–1900s] See also DRUNK AS A COOT.

cooties real or imagined lice. For synonyms see WALKING DANDRUFF. [U.S. slang, 1900s]

cooze (also **cooz, coosie, coozie**) **1.** women considered solely as sexual objects. **2.** the female genitals. *Cf.* COOCH, CUZZY. [Both senses, U.S. slang, mid 1900s-pres.]

coozey a sexual "pervert." Related to the previous entry. Possibly a CATAMITE (*q.v.*). [U.S. underworld, mid 1900s, Goldin, O'Leary, and Lipsius]

cop 1. to purchase marijuana. [U.S. drug culture and slang, mid 1900s-pres.] **2.** a policeman. For synonyms see FLATFOOT. [U.S. slang, 1900s or before]

cop a bean to deflower a virgin. *Cf.* BEAN (sense 4), "hymen." [U.S. slang, early 1900s, Goldin, O'Leary, and Lipsius]

cop a buzz to become intoxicated with marijuana. *Cf.* BUZZ (sense 2). [U.S. drug culture, mid 1900s-pres.]

cop a cherry to deflower a virgin. *Cf.* CHERRY (sense 1), "hymen." [U.S. slang, early 1900s-pres.]

cop a feel to touch or feel a woman's sexual parts either as if it were an accident or quite blatantly. Usually refers to touching the breasts. [U.S. slang, mid 1900s-pres.]

co-pilot Ben Benzedrine (trademark), an amphetamine. With reference to some long-distance trucker's dependence on amphetamines. See BROTHER BEN. [U.S. drug culture, mid 1900s-pres.]

co-pilots amphetamine tablets or capsules. From CO-PILOT BEN (*q.v.*). [U.S. slang and drug culture, mid 1900s-pres.]

cop it get pregnant. *Cf.* CATCH (sense 2), TAKE (sense 2). [Australian, early 1900s, *Dictionary of Slang and Unconventional English*]

copper-nose a drunkard. From the color of the nose. [British and U.S. colloquial, 1800s]

copperstick the penis. For synonyms see YARD. [British slang, 1800s, Farmer and Henley]

coprophilia 1. an abnormal interest in feces. **2.** a love of pornography or obscene literature. [both senses, from Greek *kopros*, "dung"]

cop the brewery to get drunk. [British slang, late 1800s, Ware]

coral branch the penis. See GARGANTUA'S PENIS [1600s–1800s]

corey the penis. [British dialect (Cockney), 1900s-pres.]

Corine cocaine. *Cf.* C. (sense 1). [U.S. drug culture, early 1900s-pres.]

Corks! "Gods!" A truncation of CORKSCREW! (*q.v.*). *Cf.* COCK. For synonyms see 'ZOUNDS!

cork-sacking a euphemistic disguise of "cock-sucking." An adjective derived from COCKSUCKER (*q.v.*). [U.S. slang, mid 1900s-pres.]

Corkscrew! "By God's Truth!", a disguised oath or an exclamation. [British, late 1800s, Ware]

corky (also **corkey**) intoxicated with alcohol. For synonyms see WOOFLED. [British slang, 1800s or before]

Cor lummie! (also **Cor lummy!**) an oath and an exclamation, "God love me!" *Cf.* COOLUMMY!, GORAMITY! [British, 1900s or before]

corn whisky distilled from corn or any home-distilled alcoholic liquor. *Cf.* MOONSHINE (sense 2). [U.S. slang, early 1900s or before to the present]

corned (also **corny**) intoxicated with any liquor or intoxicated with CORN (*q.v.*). *Cf.* PICKLED, PRESERVED, SALTED-DOWN. [British and U.S., 1700s-pres.]

corner the female genitals. *Cf.* CRANNY, NICHE-COCK. [1600s]

cornered intoxicated with alcohol; to be in a (drunken) predicament. Possibly from CORN (*q.v.*). [colloquial, 1800s–1900s]

corn hole 1. the anus. May relate to the use of corn cobs for anal cleansing. [U.S. slang, 1900s] **2.** to push a real or imagined object up someone's anus; to GOOSE (sense 6). [U.S. slang, 1900s] **3.** to perform anal intercourse upon a male; to commit pederasty. [U.S. slang, early 1900s-pres.] **4.** to perfrom anal intercourse upon a woman. [U.S. slang, mid 1900s-pres.]

corn-holer a pederast, the INSERTOR (*q.v.*). *Cf.* CORN HOLE (sense 3). [British and U.S. slang, 1900s]

corn-juice alcoholic liquor brewed from corn; any alcoholic liquor. For synonyms see MOONSHINE. [U.S. slang and colloquial, 1800s]

corn-mule whisky distilled from corn mash; any whisky. *Cf.* DONK (sense 1), WHITE MULE. [U.S. slang, 1900s]

cornucopia 1. cuckoldry. Based on the "horn of plenty." [British, 1600s] **2.** the female genitals. [British, 1800s, Farmer and Henley]

corpse 1. the deceased body of a person. [since the 1300s] Synonyms: BLOAT, CADAVER, CARRION, COLD MEAT, CORPUS, CROAKER, DEADER, DEAD MAN, DEAD-MEAT, DEAR DEPARTED, DECEDENT, DOCTOR'S MISTAKE, DUSTMAN, GONER, LANDOWNER, LATE-LAMENTED, LOVED ONE, MORGUE-AGE, PORK, REMAINS, SHOT, STIFF, STIFF ONE, STIFFY, THE DECEASED, THE DEPARTED, WORM-FOOD. **2.** to kill a person; to turn a person into a corpse. [British slang or cant, late 1800s, Farmer and Henley]

corpse-provider a physician. For synonyms see DOC. [British slang, early 1800s, Farmer and Henley]

corpse ticket a military identification disc, a dog-tag. *Cf.* COLD-MEAT TICKET. [U.S. military slang, World Wars]

corral a group of prostitutes who work for the same pimp; the same as STABLE (sense 2). [U.S. underworld, mid 1900s-pres.]

corral dust nonsense, lies, and exaggeration. A jocular play on BULLSHIT

(*q.v.*). *Cf.* BULL-DUST, HEIFER-DUST. [U.S., 1900s or before]

cotics a truncation of "narcotics." [U.S. slang, mid 1900s-pres.] *Cf.* BINGLE, BIRDIE STUFF, BOW-SOW, DRECK, DRY GROG, DUTCH COURAGE, DYNAMITE, MAHOSKA, MOJO, MOOCH, NEEDLE-CANDY, SCHLOCK, SCHMECK, SMECKER, SWEET STUFF.

cotquean 1. an effeminate male; a man who busies himself with women's affairs. **2.** a mean and scolding woman; a virago. [both senses, British colloquial, late 1500s]

Cotszooks! (also **Cotzooks!**) an oath and an exclamation, "By God's hooks!" (*i.e.*, "nails"). *Cf.* GADZOOKS! For synonyms see 'ZOUNDS! [British, early 1700s]

Cott (also **Cot**) a disguised form of "God." *Cf.* COCK. [early 1500s]

cottage of convenience (also **cottage**) a privy; an outhouse. See CONVENIENCE. For synonyms see AJAX. [British colloquial, late 1800s, Ware]

cotton the female pubic hair. For synonyms see DOWNSHIRE. [U.S. slang, mid 1900s-pres.]

cotton-picker 1. a derogatory nickname for a Negro. For synonyms see EBONY. [U.S., 1900s or before] **2.** a chum or buddy. **3.** a damn fool; son OF A BITCH (sense 2). **4.** a jocular reference to a real or imagined woman who has broken the string on her sanitary tampon. [senses 2-4 are U.S., 1900s]

cotton-picking a euphemism for "damned" or "damnable," especially in the expression "cotton-picking hands." [U.S. slang, 1900s]

couch to copulate; essentially "lie down with." *Cf.* BED (sense 1), CHAMBER (sense 1). [from *Othello* (Shakespeare)]

cougar-milk strong liquor or inferior liquor. For synonyms see EMBALMING FLUID. [U.S., 1900s or before]

council-houses trousers; pants. Rhyming slang for "trousers." [British slang, early 1900s, *Dictionary of Slang and Unconventional English*]

counter a prostitute's term for an act of intercourse that "counts" against a quota which she must fulfill. *Cf.* SCORE (sense 3). [attested as British underworld, early 1900s, *Dictionary of Slang and Unconventional English*]

counting-house a privy; an outhouse. For synonyms see AJAX. [British slang or cant, mid 1800s]

country, old 1. the Negro district of a town. From the black point of view. **2.** Africa. From the black point of view. [both senses, U.S. colloquial, 1900s or before]

country cousin the menses. One of a series of VISITORS (*q.v.*). For synonyms see FLOODS. [U.S. colloquial, 1900s or before]

country Jake a bumpkin or rustic oaf.[U.S., 1900s, Deak]

couple 1. to marry; to copulate in marriage. [since the 1300s] **2.** to copulate, especially in reference to animals. **3.** to cohabit; to live together as man and wife unmarried. [U.S. slang, 1800s-1900s]

coupler the female genitals, specifically the vagina. [British, 1800s, Farmer and Henley]

couple with to copulate with someone. [colloquial, 1800s-1900s]

courage pills drugs. Usually in reference to a specific narcotic, *i.e.*, heroin or a barbiturate. *Cf.* DUTCH COURAGE. [U.S. underworld and drug culture, early 1900s-pres.]

courses the menses. In the expression "her courses." [British and U.S. euphemism, 1800s-pres.]

courtesan (also **courtisane, curtezan**) a harlot; a mistress of the court. A euphemism for "prostitute." [since the mid 1500s]

cousin Betty an oaf; a half-wit. [British colloquial, mid 1800s]

cousin sis urine; an act of urination; to urinate. Rhyming slang for "piss." [British, 1900s, *Dictionary of Rhyming Slang*]

cover 1. to copulate, usually said of male quadrupeds. Literally, "to MOUNT (sense 1) and impregnate." [colloquial, early 1500s-1900s] **2.** a young woman. See SEAT COVER.

cover girl 1. a girl or woman attractive enough to appear on the cover of a magazine. [U.S., 1900s] **2.** a pretty young woman sitting in the front seat of an automobile. Used by the long-distance truckers to inform other drivers by radio that a young woman worth trying to look at is in their vicinity. [U.S. slang, mid 1900s-pres.]

cover the waterfront 1. to wear a perineal pad at the time of the menses. *Cf.* ALL'S NOT QUIET ON THE WATERFRONT. [jocular colloquial, 1900s] **2.** to work the dock districts. Said of a prostitute who frequents the waterfront soliciting sailors and dockworkers. [Australian, 1900s, Baker]

covess-dinge a Negress prostitute; out of context, simply a black woman. "Covess" is a cant word meaning "woman." DINGE (*q.v.*) is a term for a Negro. [attested as U.S. underworld, mid 1800s]

covey a collection of prostitutes. From "covey of quail." *Cf.* QUAIL. [cant or slang, 1600s-1700s]

cow 1. a rude term for a woman. [since the mid 1600s] **2.** a jail. From HOOSEGOW (sense 1). [U.S. underworld slang, 1800s and early 1900s] Synonyms: CALABOOSE, CAN, COLLEGE, COOP, HOOSEGOW, HOUSE OF CORRECTION, HOUSE OF DETENTION, LIMBO. **3.** an old prostitute. From sense 1. [British slang, 1800s, Farmer and Henley] **4.** cow dung. [euphemistic, 1900s or before]

cow-blakes (also **blakes**) dried cow dung used as fuel. For synonyms see COW-CHIPS. [British dialect, 1800s or before, Halliwell]

cowboy a homosexual male, specifically a masculine male homosexual. *Cf.* MIDNIGHT COWBOY, TRUCK-DRIVER. [U.S. slang, mid 1900s-pres.]

cow-brute a euphemism for "bull." [U.S., 1900s and before]

cow-chips cow dung dried for use as

fuel. Sometimes euphemistic for BULL-SHIT (*q.v.*). *Cf.* BODEWASH, BUFFALO CHIPS. [U.S. dialect and colloquial, 1800s-1900s] Synonyms: BLAKES, BODE-WASH, BOOSHWAH, BUFFALO CHIPS, CAS-INGS, COW-BLAKES, PRAIRIE COAL, PRAI-RIE FUEL, SCHARN, SHARN, SIT-STILL-NEST, SKARN, SURFACE FUEL. Additional variants are listed at DROPPINGS.

cow-clap (also **cow-cake, cow-flop, cow-pat**) cow dung. [British dialect, 1800s]

cow-clod cow dung. [U.S. dialect and colloquial, 1900s or before]

cow-cod a whip or a club made from a dried bull's penis. [attested as Jamaican, Cassidy and Le Page]

cow-confetti nonsense; a euphemism for BULLSHIT (*q.v.*). *Cf.* MEADOW-MAYONNAISE. [Australian, early 1900s, Baker]

cow-cunted pertaining to a woman whose genitals have been deformed by giving birth or by "debauchery" (Farmer and Henley). [British slang, 1800s]

cow-dab cow dung. [U.S. dialect (Virginia), 1800s, Green]

cow-kissing kissing with much movement of the tongues and lips. [U.S. slang, mid 1900s]

cow-pie a mass of cow dung. [U.S. colloquial, 1900s]

cow-pucky cow dung. [colloquial, 1900s or before]

cows and horses will get out a catch phrase uttered to signal a male that his fly is undone. [U.S., 1900s]

cowsh "cowshit"; nonsense; BULLSHIT (*q.v.*). Parallel to BULLSH (*q.v.*). *Cf.* FROGSH. [Australian, 1900s or before, Baker]

cow-shard (also **cow-plat, cow-sharn, cow-shern**) cow dung; a mass of cow dung. [British dialect and colloquial, late 1500s-1900s]

cowslip cow dung, especially fresh cow dung. From the flower name. [U.S. colloquial, 1900s, Berrey and Van den Bark]

cowson a term of contempt, "son of a

bitch." *Cf.* WHORESON. [British, 1900s, *Dictionary of Slang and Unconventional English*]

cow's spouse a euphemism for "bull." [British slang or colloquial, late 1700s, Grose]

cowyard confetti (also **farmyard confetti**) nonsense. A jocular euphemism for "bullshit." *Cf.* COW-CONFETTI, MEADOW-MAYONNAISE. [Australian, early 1900s, Baker]

Coxbones! an oath and an exclamation, "By God's bones!"

coxcomb (also **cockscomb**) a fool; a fop or dandy. [since the late 1500s]

COYOTE a prostitute's organization, "Call off Your Old Tired Ethics."

coyote the female genitals. *Cf.* CAT (sense 6), PUSSY (sense 1). [British slang, 1800s or before]

c- -r a disguise of COCKSUCKER (*q.v.*). [U.S.,1900s]

crab on the rocks a phrase describing an itching (possibly from lice) on the scrotum. ROCKS (*q.v.*) refers to the testicles. *Cf.* STONES (sense 2). [British, 1800s-1900s, *Dictionary of Slang and Unconventional English*]

crabs 1. body lice, specifically those found in the pubic hair. [British and U.S., since the 1800s] **2.** syphilis. For synonyms see SPECIFIC STOMACH. [U.S., 1900s]

crabwalk the perineum. An area presumably traveled by lice when going from the anal to the pubic areas. [U.S. slang, 1900s]

crack 1. the female genitals. A term describing the PUDENDAL CLEAVAGE (*q.v.*). [widespread recurrent nonce since the 1500s or before] **2.** coition. [U.S., 1900s] **3.** a prostitute. [since the late 1600s] **4.** the anus; the gluteal furrow. [widespread and very old; attested as U.S. colloquial and slang, 1900s or before] **5.** women considered as sexual objects. [U.S. slang, 1900s and before] **6.** any young woman or any girl. [U.S. slang, 1900s]

crack a Judy's teacup (also **crack a

pitcher) to DEFLOWER (*q.v.*) a girl. [British slang, 1800s-1900s]

cracked 1. crazy. For synonyms see DAFT. [since the early 1600s] **2.** intoxicated with alcohol. [U.S., early 1700s, Ben Franklin] **3.** deflowered. See DEFLOWER. [British and U.S. slang or colloquial, 1800s-1900s]

cracked in the ring deflowered. See DEFLOWER. *Cf.* RING (sense 1). [derived from "cracked within the ring" from *Hamlet* (Shakespeare)]

cracked pitcher (also **cracked piece**) a prostitute or a sportive, nonvirgin young woman. For synonyms see LAY. [British slang, early 1700s]

cracker 1. a Caucasian; a Southerner. A truncation of GEORGIA CRACKER (*q.v.*). For synonyms see PECKERWOOD. [U.S. black colloquial, 1800s-1900s] **2.** the anus of the buttocks. [British, late 1600s, B.E.]

crackers crazy; insane. [widespread slang, 1900s]

crackfart a boaster; someone whose words are just HOT AIR (*q.v.*). [British dialect, 1800s or before, Halliwell]

crack-hunter (also **crack-haunter**) the penis. A pun on "crack-marksman." [British slang, 1800s, Farmer and Henley]

crackish pertaining to a woman who is wanton or behaves like a prostitute. *Cf.* CRACK (sense 1). [British slang, late 1600s, B.E.]

crack it to copulate; to SCORE (*q.v.*). [Australian, mid 1900s-pres., Wilkes]

crack salesman 1. a pimp. **2.** a prostitute. *Cf.* CRACK (sense 2). [both senses, U.S. underworld, 1900s]

cracksman the penis. *Cf.* CRACK (sense 2). A reinterpretation of a cant term meaning "house-breaker." [British, mid 1800s, Farmer and Henley]

Cracky!, By (also **Crackity!, By**) an oath and an exclamation; a disguise of "Christ!" [British and U.S. colloquial, early 1800s-pres.]

craddon (also **cradden**) a coward or a CRAVEN (*q.v.*). For synonyms see YELLOW-DOG. [early 1500s]

cradle the female genitals. For synonyms see MONOSYLLABLE. [British slang, 1800s, Farmer and Henley]

cradle-custard a baby's feces, especially when soft. [U.S. colloquial, 1900s or before]

cradle-snatcher (also **cradle-robber, baby-snatcher**) a person who flirts with, has a romance with, or marries a very young person of the opposite sex. [U.S., 1900s or before]

cram to coit a woman; to intromit the penis. [British and U.S., 1800s-1900s]

Cram it! an exclamation equivalent to "Cram it up your ass!", said to a man or a woman; "Cram it up your vagina!", said to a woman. "It" refers to words, objects, or a situation. [U.S. slang, 1900s]

cramped intoxicated with alcohol. For synonyms see WOOFLED. [U.S., early 1700s, Ben Franklin]

cramps menstrual pains; uterine cramps associated with the menses. [U.S., 1900s or before]

cranberry eye an eye reddened from excessive drinking. [U.S. colloquial, late 1800s-1900s]

cranks amphetamine tablets or capsules. For synonyms see AMP. [U.S. drug culture, 1900s]

cranny the female pudendum. *Cf.* CORNER, NICHE-COCK. [widespread recurrent nonce, 1800s-1900s]

cranny-hunter the penis. *Cf.* CRACK-HUNTER. [British slang, 1800s]

crap 1. nonsense; lies. *Cf.* BULLSHIT, SHIT (sense 4). [British and U.S., 1800s-pres.] **2.** feces; dung. Lightly euphemistic for SHIT (sense 3). Occurs frequently in "take a crap." [U.S., 1900s] **3.** to defecate. [British and U.S., mid 1800s-pres.] **4.** heroin. Sometimes used for counterfeit heroin. *Cf.* CA-CA (sense 1), SHIT (sense 5). **5.** chaff; later junk or dregs; the dregs of beer or ale. [British and U.S. slang and colloquial, 1800s-pres.] **6.** the gallows. [cant, early 1800s, Vaux] **7.** to hang a man. [cant, 1800s] **8.** an exclamation somewhat milder than "Damn!" or

"Shit!" but still objectionable to some people. [U.S. colloquial, 1900s]

crap-house a privy; an outhouse. Somewhat milder than SHIT-HOUSE (*q.v.*). For synonyms see AJAX. [U.S. colloquial and slang, 1900s]

crap-list a euphemism for "shit-list." [U.S. colloquial, 1900s]

crapper 1. a toilet, privy, or restroom. [U.S. colloquial and slang since the early 1900s or before] **2.** a bragger; a teller of lies and nonsense. *Cf.* BULLSHITTER, SHITTER (sense 2). [U.S. slang, mid 1900s-pres.]

crappery a privy, outhouse, or restroom. [U.S. slang and colloquial, 1900s]

crapping-castle (also **crapping-casa, crapping-case, crapping-ken**) a privy; an outhouse. *Cf.* CARSEY. [cant and slang, 1800s]

craps diarrhea; euphemistic for the SHITS (*q.v.*). [U.S. slang, 1900s]

craven 1. pertaining to a person who gives up without a fight. [1200s] **2.** a coward. For synonyms see YELLOW-DOG. [late 1500s]

crawl 1. a sycophant; a toady. Also **crawler.** [British, 1800s or before, Farmer and Henley] **2.** to copulate with a woman. For synonyms see OCCUPY. [U.S. slang, 1900s] **3.** a male who coits or "crawls" a woman. [U.S. slang, early 1900s, Wentworth and Flexner] **4.** to grope and fondle a woman.

crazy 1. intoxicated with alcohol. [U.S. slang, 1900s] **2.** drug intoxicated. From sense 1. [U.S. drug culture, mid 1900s-pres.]

crazy water alcoholic beverages. For synonyms see BOOZE. [U.S. slang, 1900s]

cream 1. semen. *Cf.* HOT MILK. For synonyms see METTLE. [British and U.S. slang and colloquial, 1800s-pres.] **2.** to ejaculate semen. For synonyms see MELT. [U.S., 1900s and before] **3.** to coit a woman; to impregnate a woman. For synonyms see STORK. **4.** to beat the opposite team in a sporting event. No

negative connotations. [U.S. slang, mid 1900s-pres.] **5.** to kill someone. [U.S., 1900s]

creamed intoxicated with alcohol. From CREAM (sense 4). [U.S., mid 1900s-pres.]

creamed foreskins a dysphemism for creamed chipped beef. *Cf.* SHIT ON A SHINGLE. [U.S., mid 1900s, Berrey and Van den Bark]

cream-jug 1. the female genitals, specifically the vagina. The receiver for CREAM (sense 1). [British slang, 1800s, Farmer and Henley] **2.** a breast. See CREAM-JUGS.

cream-jugs the breasts. *Cf.* DAIRIES, JUGS, MILK-BOTTLES, NINNY-JUGS. [British slang, 1800s, Farmer and Henley]

cream one's jeans to ejaculate semen in one's trousers. A catch phrase describing the intensity of sexual excitement or any excitement sufficient to cause a male to ejaculate. [U.S. slang, 1900s]

cream puff 1. a woman. [U.S., 1900s] **2.** an effeminate male. For synonyms see FRIBBLE. [U.S. slang, early 1900s-pres.]

creamstick the penis. From CREAM (sense 1). [British slang, 1800s]

crease the female genitals, specifically the vulva. *Cf.* PUDENDAL CLEAVAGE. [U.S. colloquial, 1900s]

create fuck to display anger or annoyance; to create an angry scene or cause others annoyance. [U.S. and elsewhere, 1900s]

credentials the male genitals; the VIRILIA (*q.v.*). *Cf.* TESTIMONIALS. [British, late 1800s]

creep a jerk; an unpleasant or slimy oaf. For synonyms see SNOKE-HORN. [U.S. slang, early 1900s-pres.]

creeper marijuana of a slow-acting type. With reinforcement from "creeper" as a type of plant or weed. [U.S. drug culture, mid 1900s-pres.]

creepers lice. For synonyms see WALKING DANDRUFF. [British colloquial, 1800s, Farmer and Henley]

creeping crud 1. a variety of skin diseases. Refers to fungi which attack the feet, groin, or anus, or refers to any skin disorder. [U.S. military, World War II] **2.** any kind of nastiness made even worse by implying that it is ambulatory. [U.S. slang, mid 1900s]

Creeping Jesus! 1. an oath and an exclamation. [Australian, 1900s or before, Baker] **2.** one who simpers around sanctimoniously. In this sense, CREEPING-JESUS. [early 1800s-1900s]

creep-joint a brothel where one is robbed or otherwise badly treated. [U.S. underworld, early 1900s, Goldin, O'Leary, and Lipsius]

crevice the female genitals. *Cf.* CRACK, CRANNY, CREASE. [used as slang and as a polite avoidance]

crib (also **crib-house**) a brothel. *Cf.* FLASH-CRIB at FLASH-CASE. [Australian and U.S. underworld, 1800s-1900s]

Crickety!, By (also **Cricket!, By; Cricky!, By; Criky!, By**) an oath and an exclamation, "By Christ!" For synonyms see 'ZOUNDS! [U.S. colloquial, 1800s-1900s]

crime against nature 1. a euphemism for SODOMY (*q.v.*) as defined in various ways by the various states of the U.S. **2.** any nonorthogenital sexual activity. [both senses, euphemistic, 1800s-1900s]

crimen innominatum* "the offense which is not to be named," *i.e.*, SODOMY (*q.v.*). [Latin euphemism]

Crimeny sakes alive! an oath and an exclamation, "For Christ's sake!" For synonyms see 'ZOUNDS! [U.S. colloquial, 1800s-pres.]

criminal conversation (also **criminal correspondence**) a criminal act committed by a man when he seduces and copulates with another man's wife. The CUCKOLD (*q.v.*) is considered the damaged party, the seducer is the guilty and punishable person, and the wife is an adulteress. [law]

Criminey! (also **Crimany!, Criminy!**) an exclamation based on "Christ!" [British and U.S., 1600s-pres.]

Criminitly! an exclamation based on an oath. A partial disguise of "Christ!"

Crimp's sake!, For a euphemistic disguise of "For Christ's sake!" [U.S. euphemistic and colloquial]

crimson-chitterling the penis; the penis of Gargantua. See GARGANTUA'S PENIS for additional terms. [mid 1600s, (Urquhart)]

crimsonest of adjectives a pedantic euphemism for "bloody," a common and traditional adjective and exclamation in Australia. *Cf.* GREAT AUSTRALIAN ADJECTIVE.

crinkum-crankum the female genitals. [British slang or cant, 1700s-1800s]

crinkums (also **crincomes, crincum, crinkum**) venereal disease, probably syphilis. [British slang or cant, early 1600s, B.E.]

crinoline women in general; women considered sexually. For synonyms see TAIL. [British slang, mid 1800s, Farmer and Henley]

Cripes! a euphemism for "Christ!" Possibly pronounced with two syllables. [U.S. slang and colloquial, early 1800s-pres.]

crisp intoxicated with marijuana. *Cf.* FRIED (sense 2). [U.S. drug culture, mid 1900s-pres.]

crispy-critter 1. a person who is intoxicated with marijuana. *Cf.* CRISP, FRIED (sense 2). [U.S. drug culture, mid 1900s-pres.] **2.** a person (usually Vietnamese) who has been burned with napalm. Both are from the trademarked brand name of a breakfast cereal. [U.S., 1960s]

critter a euphemism for "bull." [U.S. dialect and colloquial, 1900s and before]

croak 1. a rumbling in the bowels. Also **croake.** [mid 1500s] **2.** to die. For synonyms see DEPART. [cant and slang, early 1800s-pres.] **3.** to murder someone; to hang a man. [British and U.S. underworld, 1800s-early 1900s]

croaked hanged; murdered. From the sputtering and gurgling of a hanged man. *Cf.* CROAK (sense 3). [cant, early 1800s, Egan's Grose]

croaker 1. a physician in various realms; any medical officer; an M.D.

known to write prescriptions for abused drugs; an M.D. known to treat criminals without reporting injuries caused by violence. [British and U.S., 1800s-1900s] **2.** a corpse, *i.e.*, the result of a croaking. See CROAK (sense 3). [British slang, 1800s, Farmer and Henley]

crock 1. a worthless person. Compared to a chipped or cracked vessel or to a chamber pot. [British and U.S., late 1800s-pres.] **2.** a CHAMBER POT (*q.v.*). For synonyms see POT. [British colloquial, 1900s or before] **3.** a drunkard. [U.S. and elsewhere, 1900s] **4.** nonsense. See CROCK OF SHIT.

crocked intoxicated with alcohol. For synonyms see WOOFLED. [U.S. slang, early 1900s-pres.]

crocko intoxicated with alcohol. A variant of CROCKED (*q.v.*). [U.S. slang, 1900s, Berrey and Van den Bark]

crock of shit a mass of lies; bragging or nonsense; bullshit. Common in its shortened form, CROCK (sense 4). [U.S. slang, mid 1900s-pres.]

crocus (also **croakus**) a physician or a quack doctor. From the flower name and from CROAKER (sense 1). [British and U.S. underworld, late 1700s-early 1900s]

cronk (also **krank, kronk**) **1.** ill. [slang and colloquial, 1800s-pres.] **2.** intoxicated with alcohol; sick with drink. [from German *krank*, "sick"; U.S. slang and colloquial, mid 1800s-pres.]

crook the penis. *Cf.* JOINT (sense 1).

cross 1. to bestride or mount a horse; to mount and copulate with a woman. **2.** to cheat or deceive. For both *cf.* BOARD, MOUNT, PRIG (sense 1), RIDE. [both senses, British, late 1700s-1800s]

cross-eyed intoxicated with alcohol. [U.S. slang, 1900s or before]

cross over to die; to have "crossed over" is to be dead. *Cf.* PASS OVER. [U.S. euphemism, 1900s or before]

crosspatch a grouchy, complaining, ill-tempered person. [colloquial, late 1600s-pres.]

crossroad an amphetamine tablet or capsule. For synonyms see AMP. With reference to the X scoring on the tablet. [U.S. drug culture, mid 1900s-pres.]

cross the great divide *Cf.* CROSS OVER. For synonyms see DEPART.

crotch 1. the area where the legs join the trunk of the body. **2.** the male or female genitals. [euphemistic, 1800s-1900s]

crotch-cheese 1. smegma. *Cf.* CHEESE, COCK-CHEESE, DUCK-BUTTER (sense 2). [U.S. slang, 1900s or before] **2.** a real or imagined nasty and smelly substance found in unclean pubic areas. [U.S. slang, 1900s]

crotch-pheasants lice. For synonyms see WALKING DANDRUFF. [U.S. slang, early 1900s]

crotch-rot a skin irritation or disease characterized by itching of the groin and scrotum. *Cf.* CREEPING CRUD, GALLOPING KNOB-ROT, JOCK-ITCH. [British and U.S. slang, 1900s]

croup the haunches of a quadruped; the buttocks of a man. *Cf.* CRUPPER. [since the late 1400s, *Oxford English Dictionary*]

crow 1. a Negro. From the blackness of a crow. Derogatory. **2.** a shipboard troublemaker, especially a drunkard. [British nautical, 1900s or before] **3.** a prostitute. Also **cro.** See CHROMO. [Australian slang, mid 1900s-pres., Wilkes]

crower a rooster. A euphemism for COCK (sense 1). See ROOSTER for similar avoidances. [U.S. colloquial and dialect, 1900s and before]

crown and feathers the female genitals. For synonyms see MONOSYLLABLE. [British slang, 1800s, Farmer and Henley]

crown jewels 1. gaudy jewels worn by male homosexuals in DRAG (*q.v.*). **2.** the male genitals. *Cf.* DIAMONDS, FAMILY JEWELS, ROCKS, STONES (sense 2). [both senses, homosexual use, mid 1900s-pres.]

crow-pee "dawn" in the expression "at crow-pee." This and SPARROW-FART (*q.v.*) are jocular plays and mock euphemisms based on "at cock-crow."

crud (also **crut**) **1.** an older British

dialect form of "curd" dating from the 1300s with no early negative connotations. **2.** any junk or worthless matter. *Cf.* CRAP (sense 5). **3.** fecal matter; CRAP (sense 2); a euphemism for SHIT (sense 3). [U.S. slang, 1900s] **4.** dried semen as might be found on clothing or bedclothes some time after ejaculation. [U.S. military, 1900s, Wentworth and Flexner] **5.** venereal disease, especially syphilis. *Cf.* SCRUD. [U.S. slang, mid 1900s-pres.] **6.** a repulsive male; a creep or jerk. [U.S. slang, mid 1900s-pres.] **7.** any skin disease. *Cf.* CREEPING CRUD. [U.S. slang and colloquial, 1900s]

cruise 1. to stalk the streets in search of a homosexual or heterosexual sex partner. **2.** to size up someone as a potential sexual partner; to try to establish eye contact with a potential sex partner. [both senses, primarily homosexual use, U.S., early 1900s-pres.]

cruiser 1. a prostitute in search of a customer. [British and U.S., 1800s-1900s] **2.** a homosexual male searching for a sex partner. [U.S. slang, 1900s]

crumb 1. a louse. The insect. See CRUMBS. **2.** a dirty and disliked person; someone suspected of being infected with lice due to a lack of personal cleanliness. [U.S. slang, 1900s]

crumbs 1. lice. One might remove them from clothing the same way one would remove crumbs of food. [British slang, 1800s or before] **2.** as an exclamation equivalent to "Christ!" [U.S. euphemism, 1900s or before]

crum bum (also **crumb bum**) a dull, stupid person. *Cf.* CRUMB (sense 2). [U.S. slang, 1900s]

crumped-out intoxicated with alcohol. For synonyms see WOOFLED. [U.S. slang, 1900s, Wentworth and Flexner]

crumpet 1. the female genitals. *Cf.* BISCUIT, BUN (sense 3). [British, early 1900s] **2.** copulation; women considered sexually. Reinforced by STRUMPET (*q.v.*). [British slang, 1800s-early 1900s, *Dictionary of Slang and Unconventional English*] **3.** the buttocks considered by a homosexual male for the purposes of pederasty. From sense 1.

crump-footed intoxicated with alcohol. From an old term meaning "club-footed." In reference to the drinker's staggering gait. [U.S. slang, early 1700s, Ben Franklin]

crupper 1. the haunches of a horse. [since the 1300s] **2.** the human posteriors. [colloquial since the 1500s]

crutch 1. a crock or a jar used as a chamber pot. [British dialect and colloquial, 1800s or before] **2.** a holder for a marijuana cigarette. *Cf.* ROACH CLIP. [U.S. drug culture, mid 1900s-pres.]

crying drunk intoxicated with alcohol and weeping. This is not a degree of drunkenness but a type of behavior peculiar to some drinkers. *Cf.* MAUDLIN DRUNK. [since the 1800s]

crying out loud!, For an oath and exclamation euphemistic for "For Christ's sake!" [U.S. colloquial, 1900s or before]

crystal 1. some form of amphetamine sulphate, *e.g.*, methedrine. [U.S. drug culture, mid 1900s-pres.] **2.** a toilet; a JOHN (sense 2). [U.S. slang, 1900s, Weseen] **3.** the drug P.C.P. See CRYSTAL JOINT.

crystal joint (also **crystal**) the drug P.C.P. (*q.v.*). JOINT (sense 2) refers to a marijuana cigarette. [U.S. drug culture, mid 1900s-pres.]

C-section a caesarean section.

C-stick a cigarette. From CANCER-STICK (*q.v.*).

C.T. 1. "colored-time." **2.** CUNT-TEASER (*q.v.*). **3.** COCK-TEASER (*q.v.*).

cube 1. a packet of morphine. [U.S. underworld and drug culture, early 1900s-pres.] **2.** the drug L.S.D. From the practice of ingesting it in a sugar cube. [U.S. drug culture, mid 1900s-pres.]

cubehead a frequent user of the drug L.S.D. *Cf.* CUBE (sense 2). [U.S. drug culture, mid 1900s-pres.]

cubes the testicles. For synonyms see WHIRLYGIGS. [U.S. slang, mid 1900s-pres.]

cuck 1. excrement. **2.** to excrete. *Cf.* CACK. For synonyms see EASE ONESELF. [both since the early 1400s] **3.** an obsolete abbreviation of CUCKOLD (*q.v.*). [British, early 1700s] See also KUCKY.

cucking-stool 1. a chamber pot; a CLOSE STOOL (*q.v.*). [1300s-1700s] **2.** a seat where social offenders were placed in order to receive public scorn. One account is that the seat used was a close stool to further humiliate the offender. Another is that the cucking-stool was used to dip offenders into excrement or CUCK (sense 1). *Cf.* DUCKING-STOOL. [1300s-1700s]

cuckle to commit adultery; to CUCKOLD (*q.v.*). [British and U.S. dialect, 1600s-1700s]

cuckold 1. a man whose wife has committed adultery. [since the 1200s] **2.** to make a man a cuckold by seducing his wife. [late 1500s-pres.] Synonyms for both senses: ACTAEON, BUCK'S FACE, CHEAT ON, CHIPPY ON, CORNUTO, CUCKOL, CUCKOO, GRAFT, GREEN-GOOSE, HALF-MOON, HODDY-POLL, HORN, HORN-GROWER, HORN-MERCHANT, RAMHEAD.

cuckold the parson for a man to copulate with his intended wife before marriage. [British slang, late 1700s, Grose]

cuckoo 1. a fool; a dull oaf. [colloquial, 1500s-pres.] **2.** a cuckold. A corruption of "cuckold." [from *Love's Labour's Lost* (Shakespeare)] **3.** the penis. For synonyms see YARD. [British juvenile, 1800s, Farmer and Henley]

cuckoo's nest the female genitals. A place for the CUCKOO (sense 3). [British slang, 1800s, Farmer and Henley]

cuckquean 1. a female CUCKOLD (*q.v.*). **2.** to cause a woman to be a female cuckold. [both senses, mid 1500s]

cuddle 1. to pet and fondle. **2.** to copulate. [both senses, British and U.S., 1800s-1900s]

cuddle-bunny a sexually loose woman. *Cf.* BED-BUNNY. For synonyms see LAY. [U.S. slang, 1900s]

Cud's (also **Cudsho, Cudso**) "God's" in oaths such as "By Cud's bobs!" and "By Cud's nigs!" [late 1500s]

cuerpo, in naked or not entirely or properly attired. For synonyms see STARKERS. [from Spanish; early 1600s]

Cuff a nickname for a Negro. Used as a term of direct address. Derogatory when used as a generic term. From CUFFEE (*q.v.*). [U.S. colloquial, 1800s-1900s]

Cuffee (also **Cuffy**) a Negro. From a common West African "day name," the Fanti name *Kofi*, "boy born on Friday." [colloquial, early 1700s-1900s]

cuffin (also **cuff, cuffen, cuffer**) a man; sometimes used for an oafish man. [British slang or cant, mid 1500s-1800s]

culbutizing exercise copulation. [from a French word meaning "drive back in confusion"; originally from Urquhart; British, 1800s, (Farmer)]

cull (also **cully**) **1.** a prostitute's customer; a thief's target; a dupe. Probably from CULLION (*q.v.*). [British slang or cant, early 1600s-1800s] **2.** in the plural, testicles. See CULLS.

cullion 1. in the plural, testicles. [1300s, *Oxford English Dictionary*] **2.** a low and mean fellow; a rascal. From sense 1. [1500s]

culls the testicles. A truncation of CULLION (sense 1). [colloquial, 1500s-1600s]

cully-shangy coition. See CULLS. For synonyms see SMOCKAGE. [British slang and cant, 1800s, Farmer and Henley]

culo the anus, rectum, or buttocks. [Spanish; U.S. slang, mid 1900s-pres.]

culturally deprived environment a slum; an environment which lacks a nurturing social structure and lacks a traditional set of cultural and educational goals. [U.S. euphemism, mid 1900s]

culty-gun the penis. Literally, "a short-gun." See GUN, PISTOL, SHORT-ARM. Similar to CUTTY-GUN (*q.v.*). [British slang, 1800s, Farmer and Henley]

culver-head a fool or an oaf; a thick-headed fool. The adjective "culver-headed" appeared in the 1500s. From "culver," meaning "dove." [British colloquial, late 1800s, Ware]

cum See COME.

cum freak a young woman interested only in copulating. *Cf.* COCK-HAPPY. [U.S. slang, mid 1900s]

cundum a condom made from the gut of a sheep. Used in the prevention of venereal disease. Said by Grose to have been invented by a Colonel Cundum. See CONDOM. This spelling is still extant. [British, 1700s or before, Grose]

cunnicle the female genitals, especially the vagina. Used as a diminutive form of CUNT (*q.v.*). From the standard meaning, "an underground passage." [British slang, 1800s or before, Farmer and Henley]

cunnikin the female genitals. A diminutive form of CUNT (*q.v.*). [British, 1800s, Farmer and Henley]

cunnilinguist (also **cunnilingist**) one who performs cunnilingus. [originally medical] Synonyms: DIVER, GROWL-BITER, LICK-TWAT, LINGUIST, MUFF-DIVER.

cunnilingus the act of tonguing a woman on the vulva and clitoris. [Latin, both the form and the meaning] Synonyms and related terms: BIRD-WASHING, BLOW, BLOW-JOB, BOX LUNCH, CANYON YODELING, DIVE A MUFF, EAT OUT, FRENCH TRICKS, FRENCH WAY, LARKING, LICKETY-SPLIT, MUFF-BARKING, PEARL-DIVING, SKULL-JOB, SNEEZE IN THE BASKET, SODOMY, SUCK, TALK TO THE CANOE DRIVER, TONGUE-FUCK.

cunnus* 1. the female genitals. Often cited as the antecedent of CUNT (*q.v.*). [the Latin word for the female genitals] **2.** a prostitute; an unchaste woman.

cunny (also **cunni**) **1.** from CONY (*q.v.*), "female genitals." Reinforced by Latin CUNNUS (*q.v.*). [colloquial, 1600s] **2.** a diminutive of "cunt." [British, 1700s]

cunny-burrow the female genitals, especially the vagina. From a term for a rabbit-burrow. See CONY, CUNNY. [British slang, 1700s]

cunny-catcher the penis. [British slang, 1700s] See also RABBIT-CATCHER.

cunny-haunted lewd and lecherous. For synonyms see HUMPY. [British slang, 1700s]

cunny-hunter a lecher; a whoremonger. Literally, "a rabbit-hunter." [British, 1600s]

cunny-skin the female pubic hair. From a word for "rabbit-skin." *Cf.* CAT-SKIN. [British slang, 1700s]

cunny-warren a brothel. From "coney-warren," a place for breeding rabbits. [British slang or cant, late 1700s, Grose]

cunt (also **c*nt, c**t, c***, ****, ----**) **1.** the female genitals, specifically the vagina. [said to be from Latin CUNNUS (*q.v.*)] **2.** women considered sexually. **3.** copulation. [in numerous spellings since the 1300s] The word was banned from print in much of the British Empire until the middle of this century, and it is the most elaborately avoided word in the English language. There are numerous diminutives: CUNNICLE, CUNNIKIN, CUNTKIN, CUNTLET, CUNNY. Avoidances are: INEFFABLE, MONOSYLLABLE, NAME-IT-NOT, NAMELESS. Disguises are: GRUMBLE AND GRUNT, SHARP AND BLUNT, SIR BERKELEY HUNT, TENUC, UNTCAY. See MONOSYLLABLE for additional synonyms. **4.** a rotten fellow; a low, slimy man. [colloquial, 1800s-pres.] **5.** to intromit the penis. [attested in a limerick, late 1800s] See also DECUNT.

cunt cap (also **cunt hat**) the military cap with two points. [since World War I]

cunt-curtain the female pubic hair. For synonyms see DOWNSHIRE. [British slang, 1800s, Farmer and Henley]

cunt face a derogatory nickname or a description of an ugly person. *Cf.* CUNT (sense 4), GASH (sense 4). [British slang, 1800s, *Dictionary of Slang and Unconventional English*]

cunt-hair the female pubic hair. [widespread nonce and U.S. slang, 1900s or before]

cunt-hat 1. a felt hat. Because it must be "felt" to be enjoyed. [British, early

1900s] **2.** the same as CUNT CAP (*q.v.*).

cunt-hooks (also ****** hooks**) the fingers. A rude play on "cant-hook," meaning "fingers." *Cf.* SHIT-HOOKS. [British slang or cant, late 1700s, Grose]

cunt-hound a lecher; a male who is a notorious whoremonger or woman-chaser. [U.S., mid 1900s]

cunting fucking. [British with some U.S. use, 1800s-1900s]

cunt-itch sexual arousal in the woman. *Cf.* COCK-HAPPY. [British slang, 1700s-1900s]

cunt-juice (also **juice**) natural vaginal lubrication; natural vaginal lubrication and ejaculated semen. For synonyms see FEMALE SPENDINGS. [since the 1800s or before]

cuntkin a diminutive of CUNT (*q.v.*). *Cf.* CUNT-LET. [British, 1700s]

cunt-lapper 1. a CUNNILINGUIST (*q.v.*). *Cf.* LAPPER. **2.** a LESBIAN (sense 2). For synonyms see LESBYTERIAN. **3.** any disliked person. *Cf.* COCKSUCKER. [all senses, slang, 1900s]

cuntlet a diminutive of CUNT (*q.v.*). A play on "cutlet," a portion of MEAT (sense 2). *Cf.* CUNTKIN. [British, 1700s]

cunt-rag a perineal pad. For synonyms see MANHOLE COVER. [slang or nonce, 1900s or before]

cunt-stand sexual arousal in the woman. Based on COCK-STAND (*q.v.*). [British slang, 1800s, Farmer and Henley]

cunt-struck 1. utterly fascinated with the sexual possibilities of a specific woman. **2.** sexually fascinated with all women. *Cf.* COCK-HAPPY. [both senses, British slang, 1700s-1900s]

cunt-teaser 1. a male who stimulates a woman sexually but refuses to copulate. **2.** a male who stimulates a woman but is unable to carry out the act because of impotence. **3.** a female who knowingly or unknowingly stimulates a lesbian sexually but will not participate in sexual relations. *Cf.* C.T. [all senses, U.S., 1900s]

cup-cake 1. an effeminate male, pos-

sibly a homosexual. [U.S. slang, 1900s, Weseen] **2.** a cute young woman. **3.** a dose of L.S.D. [U.S. drug culture, mid 1900s-pres.]

Cupid's arbor the female pubic hair. [British euphemism, 1800s or before]

Cupid's cave the female genitals, specifically the vagina. [British, 1800s or before]

Cupid's cloister the female genitals. For synonyms see MONOSYLLABLE. [British euphemism, late 1800s, (Farmer)]

Cupid's corner the female genitals. *Cf.* CORNER, CRANNY. [British, 1800s, Farmer and Henley]

Cupid's hotel the female genitals. *Cf.* COCK-INN. [British, 1800s]

Cupid's itch venereal disease. [U.S. euphemism, early 1900s-pres., Irwin]

Cupid's kettle drums the breasts. For synonyms see BOSOM. [British slang, early 1800s or before, *Lexicon Balatronicum*]

Cupid's scalding-house a brothel where one is likely to get a SCALDER (*q.v.*), a case of gonorrhea. [late 1500s]

Cupid's torch (also **torch of Cupid**) the penis. *Cf.* BLOWTORCH. [British, 1800s or before]

cups the breasts. Possibly from the cup-shaped supports of a brassiere. [U.S. slang, 1900s] See also TEACUPS.

cups, in one's intoxicated with alcohol. [since the late 1500s]

cup-shot intoxicated with alcohol. *Cf.* GRAPE-SHOT, POT-SHOT. [slang, 1600s-1900s]

cupshotten intoxicated with alcohol. An earlier form of CUP-SHOT (*q.v.*). [1300s-1500s]

curbstone sailor a streetwalking prostitute. One who cruises the curbs as opposed to a prostitute operating in a brothel. [British and U.S., 1800s-early 1900s]

cure for the horn copulation. *Cf.* HORN (sense 3), which is the erect penis. [British slang, 1800s, Farmer and Henley]

cure the horn 1. to coit a woman,

said of a man. **2.** to copulate with a man, said of a woman. [1800s or before]

curiosa a euphemism for PORNOGRAPHY (*q.v.*) or indecent publications. [1900s and before]

curlies the pubic hairs. From SHORT AND CURLY (*q.v.*). *Cf.* SHORT HAIRS. Sometimes euphemistically defined as "the shorter hairs at the back of the neck." For synonyms see PLUSH. [British, 1900s or before]

curl paper a euphemism for "toilet paper." From the name for a thin paper used in the curling of women's hair. For synonyms see T.P. [British colloquial, 1800s]

curse, the the menses. For synonyms see FLOODS. [British and U.S. colloquial, late 1800s-pres.]

curse of Eve the menses; the same as, or an elaboration of, "the curse." [since the 1800s or before]

curse rag a sanitary towel; a PERINEAL PAD (*q.v.*) for the menses. *Cf.* RAG. [British, early 1900s, *Dictionary of Slang and Unconventional English*]

Curse you! a curse. The equivalent of "Damn you!" [1900s and before]

curved intoxicated with alcohol; the same as BENT (sense 1). [U.S. slang, 1900s]

cush 1. copulation or some other form of sexual gratification. [U.S., 1900s] **2.** the female genitals. [British military, 1900s, *Dictionary of Slang and Unconventional English*]

cushion the female genitals. See the following entry. [British, 1800s, Farmer and Henley]

cushion for pushing 1. the female genitals. **2.** women considered as sexual objects, as in "just a cushion for pushin'." For synonyms see TAIL. [both senses, U.S. slang, mid 1900s-pres.]

cushion-thumper a clergyman; a Methodist preacher, (Halliwell). For synonyms see SKY-PILOT. [British dialect, 1800s or before]

cuss 1. to curse; to swear. A dialect pronunciation of "curse." [British and

U.S. colloquial, mid 1800s-pres.] **2.** a man, as in "old cuss." [U.S. colloquial, mid 1800s-pres.]

cuss-fired damned. An exclamation avoiding stronger terms such as HELL-FIRED (*q.v.*). [U.S. colloquial, 1900s]

custard a pimple. Usually in the plural. [Australian, early 1900s, Baker]

cut 1. to castrate. [colloquial since the mid 1400s] **2.** intoxicated with alcohol. *Cf.* DEEP CUT. [colloquial and slang since the late 1600s] **3.** the female genitals with reference to the PUDENDAL CLEAVAGE (*q.v.*). *Cf.* GASH (sense 1), WOUND. [since the 1700s] **4.** a prostitute. [British slang, 1700s] **5.** to adulterate drugs or alcoholic beverages. [U.S. underworld slang and drug culture, 1900s] **6.** to coit a woman. [U.S. slang, early 1900s-pres.] **7.** a testis. **8.** excrement. [slang or colloquial, 1900s or before]

cut and come again the female genitals. See CUT (sense 3). From a catch phrase indicating that there will be second helpings of meat. [British slang, 1800s, Farmer and Henley]

cut ass to depart in a hurry, as in "cut ass out of here." *Cf.* DRAG ASS, HAUL ASS, SHAG ASS. [U.S. slang, mid 1900s-pres.]

cut cabbage the female genitals, especially of a black woman. With reference to the visual image suggested by the cross section of a cabbage. [U.S. dialect (Boontling), late 1800s-early 1900s, Charles Adams]

cut-cock a derogatory term for a Jewish man. With reference to circumcision. *Cf.* CLIPPED-DICK. For synonyms see DOC. [U.S. slang, mid 1900s or before]

cutemup a surgeon or any physician. From "cut-them-up." For synonyms see DOC.

cut in the leg (also **cut in the back**) very drunk. As if the drinker were unable to stand up or walk due to an injury. *Cf.* CUT (sense 2). [British slang, late 1600s, B.E.]

cutlass the penis. Reinforced by CUT

(sense 6) and "lass," a girl. *Cf.* BLADE, BRACMARD. For synonyms see YARD. [British slang, 1800s, Farmer and Henley]

cut off the joint an act of copulation; some MEAT (sense 2), from the male point of view. *Cf.* CUT AND COME AGAIN. [British, 1900s]

cut one to release intestinal gas, perhaps loudly. *Cf.* LET ONE. [U.S. colloquial, 1900s]

cut one's finger (also **cut a finger**) to break wind. For synonyms see GURK. [British and U.S. euphemism, late 1800s-pres.]

cut one's leg to be drunk. [colloquial, 1600s-1900s]

cut out to be a gentleman circumcised. Adapted from the standard expression meaning "destined" to be a gentleman. [British, 1900s, *Dictionary of Slang and Unconventional English*]

cut puss an effeminate male. Refers to a castrated cat. *Cf.* CUT (sense 1). [Caribbean (Jamaican), Cassidy and LePage]

cuts the testicles. For synonyms see WHIRLYGIGS. [U.S. slang, 1900s]

cut the cheese (also **cut the mustard**) to break wind. With reference to the odor rather than the sound. *Cf.* BURNT CHEESE, CHEEZER. [U.S., 1900s]

cutty-gun the penis. Literally, SHORT-ARM (*q.v.*). Similar to CULTY-GUN (*q.v.*). [from the Scots term for a short tobacco pipe, 1800s]

cut-up well WELL-BUILT (*q.v.*); looking good naked; having a good body. *Cf.* STRIP WELL. [British slang, 1800s]

cuz 1. a defecation. For synonyms see EASEMENT. **2.** the W.C. [possibly from a Hebrew term for a refuse container; both senses, British, 1800s, *Dictionary of Slang and Unconventional English*]

cuzzy 1. copulation. **2.** the female genitals. *Cf.* COOZE. [both senses, U.S. slang, early 1900s-pres., Wentworth and Flexner]

cyclone a dose of the drug P.C.P. (*q.v.*). [U.S. drug culture, mid 1900s-pres.]

cylinder the vagina. *Cf.* PISTON ROD. [widespread recurrent nonce; attested as Australian, early 1900s, *Dictionary of Slang and Unconventional English*]

Cyprian 1. pertaining to a lewd person or object. **2.** a prostitute. For synonyms see HARLOT. [literary; late 1500s-pres.]

Cyprian lodge a brothel. [British, early 1800s, Egan's Grose]

Czezski a derogatory nickname for a Czechoslovakian. [U.S., 1900s]

D

D. "Dilaudid" (trademark), a pain-killer used as a RECREATIONAL DRUG (*q.v.*). *Cf.* BIG-D. (sense 1). [U.S. drug culture, mid 1900s-pres.]

d--- (also **D.**, **dee**) "damn." *Cf.* BIG-D. (sense 3). [since the late 1800s]

D.A. 1. "duck ass" or "duck's ass" as in "duck's ass haircut." [U.S. slang, mid 1900s] **2.** a "drug addict"; the same as A.D. (*q.v.*). [U.S. slang, mid 1900s] **3.** "domestic affliction," the menses. Usually in the plural. *Cf.* D.A.s, FLOODS. [British euphemism, late 1800s-1900s]

Dad 1. the devil. Also **Dad, old.** For synonyms see FIEND. **2.** "God" in oaths such as "By Dad!" *Cf.* DAG, DOD, DOG, DOL. Also "God" in avoidances for "Goddamn." [in various forms since the 1600s; most are attested as U.S.] Oaths with Dad are: By Dad!, Dad-bean it!, Dad-bing!, Dad-binged!, Dad-blame!, Dad-blamed!, Dad-blank!, Dad-blanked!, Dad-blast!, Dad-blasted!, Dad-boggle!, Dad-burn!, Dad-burned!, Dad-burn it!, Dad-dang!, Dad-dash!, Dad-dashed!, Dad-drat!, Dad-dratted!, Dad-fetch!, Dad-fetched!, Dad-gan!, Dad-gast!, Dad-gasted!, Dad-gern!, Dad-goned!, Dad-gorn!, Dad-gum!, Dad-gummed!, Dad-gun!, Dad-rot!, Dad-rum!, Dad-rummed!, Dad-seize!, Dad-shame!, Dad-shimed!, Dad-sizzle!, Dad-snatch!, Dad-snatched!, Dad-swamp!

daddy 1. a PEDERAST (*q.v.*). From the point of view of his CATAMITE (*q.v.*). *Cf.* ANGEL, AUNTIE. [U.S. underworld, mid 1900s, Goldin, O'Leary, and Lipsius] **2.** a woman's male lover. *Cf.* SUGAR-DADDY. [U.S. slang, 1900s]

daff an oaf; a simpleton. *Cf.* DAFT. [British, 1300s-1800s]

daffodil an effeminate male, possibly a homosexual male. *Cf.* DAISY, PANSY. For synonyms see FLOWER. [British, mid 1900s, *Dictionary of Slang and Unconventional English*]

daft stupid; insane; silly. [since the 1300s] Synonyms: BATS, BATTY, BEEN IN THE SUN TOO LONG, BONKERS, BRAIN-SICK, CRACKED, CRACKERS, HALF-CRACKED, LOONY, MESHUGA, NUTS, OFF ONE'S NUT, PSYCHO, SCREWY, SICK, TOUCHED.

Dag backslang for "God" in oaths such as "Dag bust it!", "Dag gone it!", and "Dag nab it!" *Cf.* DAD, DOG. [U.S. colloquial, 1800s-1900s]

dagga marijuana. [from South African English; U.S. drug culture, mid 1900s-pres.]

dagged intoxicated with alcohol. Literally, "dewy." [since the 1600s]

dagger the penis. See similar words at BRACMARD. [British slang, 1800s, Farmer and Henley]

daggle-tail a dirty slattern; a slut. "Dag" refers to clinging dirt. An early form of DRAGGLE-TAIL (*q.v.*). For synonyms see TROLLYMOG. [mid 1500s]

dago 1. a derogatory nickname for a Southern European male, usually an Italian. Used later for a Mexican or a Puerto Rican. [attributed to the U.S., 1800s-1900s] **2.** the Italian language; a professor or student of Italian. **3.** an inferior red wine. See DAGO RED. [all are from Diego; senses 2 and 3 since the 1800s]

dago red 1. cheap red wine from Spain. **2.** cheap dago red wine. *Cf.* RED NED. [slang, early 1900s]

dairies the breasts. *Cf.* CREAM-JUGS, MILK-BOTTLES. For synonyms see BOSOM. [British slang, 1700s-1800s]

dairy the breasts filled with milk. [British slang, early 1800s and before, *Lexicon Balatronicum*]

dairy arrangements the breasts; the same as DAIRY (*q.v.*).

daisy 1. a homosexual male. *Cf.* DAFFODIL, PANSY. For synonyms see FLOWER. [U.S. slang, mid 1900s-pres.] **2.** the female genitals. *Cf.* FLOWER (sense

2). [British slang, 1800s, Farmer and Henley] **3.** a chamber pot. [British use, late 1800s, *Dictionary of Slang and Unconventional English*]

daisy chain homosexual males engaged in simultaneous, mutual sexual activity. The usual image is a line of pederasts and catamites copulating anally. [U.S. slang, mid 1900s-pres.] See also FUGITIVE FROM A DAISY CHAIN GANG.

daisy-pushing dead; the same as PUSHING UP DAISIES (*q.v.*). For synonyms see DONE FOR.

Dal a disguise of "God" or sometimes "Damn." Dee DOL. [British dialect, 1800s or before]

dam 1. the female parent of a quadruped. **2.** a term of contempt for a woman. [both since the 1300s] **3.** damn. Usually a spelling error.

damaged intoxicated with alcohol. For synonyms see WOOFLED. [since the mid 1800s]

damaged goods a nonvirgin female. *Cf.* CRACKED PITCHER, UNDAMAGED GOODS. [U.S. slang, early 1900s]

damber-bush the female pubic hair. For synonyms see DOWNSHIRE. [British slang, 1800s, Farmer and Henley]

Damfino! "Damned if I know!" A contrived form usually seen as eye-dialect. [U.S. slang, early 1900s]

damfool (also **damn-fool, damphool, damphule**) **1.** a damned fool. **2.** damnably foolish. [both senses, colloquial since the 1800s]

Dammit! an oath and an exclamation. Usually spelled "Damn it!"

damn to damn, condemn, or curse. A few of the disguises for "damn" are: D., —, DANG, DEE, DEEN, DEMME, DEMN, DERN, DING. [since the 1300s] Synonyms and related terms: BANG, BEAN, BEDAMN, BIG-D., BLAME, BLANK, BLANKITY, BLANKITY-BLANK, BLAST, BLINK, BLISTER, BOTHER, BURN, BUST, CAESARATION!, CHIT, CONFOUND, CONSARN, CONTINENTAL, CONTINENTAL DAMN, CRAP, DAL, DAMN IT ALL!, DAMPEN, DANG, DARN, DASH, DAST, D.B., DEE, DEEN, DEMME!, DEMN, DERN, DIDDLY-SHIT, DING, DING-

BUST!, DING-DANG, DING-SWAGGLE, DISH, DOGGONE, DOUBLE-DAMN, DUM, DURN, GARN!, GERN!, TARN.

damnable cursed; damned; worthy of being damned. [since the 1300s]

damnation 1. condemnation; sentencing. [since the 1300s] **2.** the act of damning to hell; cursing someone or something. As an oath and an exclamation, "Damnation!" [since the mid 1700s] Similar terms: BLAMENATION!, BOTHERATION!, DANGNATION, DINGNATION, HANGNATION, MURDERATION, NATION!, TARNATION, THUNDERATION.

damned 1. all the evil souls being punished in hell. [since the early 1500s] **2.** cursed; condemned to hell; pertaining to any undesirable person or thing. *Cf.* DAMN, DEUCED, DINGED. [since the late 1500s] Synonyms: ALL-FIRED, BLAMED, BLANKED, BLARMED, BLASTED, BLEEDING, BLESSED, BLISTERING, BLOODY, BLOWED, BROWNED, CONFOUNDED, COTTON-PICKING, DANGED, DASHED, D . . . ED, DEE'D, DEEDEED, DEUCED, DEUCEDLY, DINGED, DING-GONED, DING-SWIZZLED, DOGGONED, DOOMED, DRATTED, DUMBED, ETERNAL, FRIGGING, GAST, GUMMED, HANGED, PLAGUE-GONED, QUALIFIED, SWIGGERED.

Damn it all! a curse and an exclamation, an elaboration of "Damn it!" [1900s and before]

damn sight an elaboration of "damn." [U.S. colloquial, mid 1900s]

Damn you! a curse, "Go to hell!" Other curses are: BALLS TO YOU!, BUGGER YOU!, CRAM IT!, CRUD YOU!, FORK YOU!, FUCK YOU!, FUJ, GARDENIA!, GO AND GET CUT!, GO AND GET FUCKED!, GO AND GET VERBED!, GOD ROT YOUR SOUL!, GO TO!, GO TO BATH!, GO TO HELEN B. HAPPY!, GO TO HELL!, G.T.H., GURU-YOU!, HOPE YOUR RABBIT DIES!, KISS MY ASS!, KISS MY TAIL!, ORCHIDS TO YOU!, RAM IT!, SCREW YOU!, SHOVE IT!, STICK IT!, TAKE YOUR HOOK!, TESTICLES TO YOU!, UP IT!, UPYA!, UP YOUR ASS!, UP YOUR BROWN!, UP YOURS!

Damn your eyes! a curse. [colloquial, 1800s or before]

damsel morphine. *Cf.* GIRL (sense 9). For synonyms see MORPH. [U.S., 1900s]

dance 1. to be hanged. [U.S. slang and sterotypical cowboy jargon, 1900s] **2.** to phallicize; to thrust in copulation. Said of the male. See DANCE THE BUTTOCK JIG.

dance the buttock jig to coit. From the action of the male in coition. [British, 1800s]

dance the goat's jig to copulate. For synonyms see OCCUPY. [British, 1800s]

dance the married man's cotillion to copulate. [British, 1800s, Farmer and Henley]

dance the matrimonial polka to copulate. [British, 1800s]

dance the mattress jig to copulate. [British, 1800s or before]

D. and D. 1. "drunk and disorderly." [since the late 1800s] **2.** "deaf and dumb." [1900s]

dandy an effeminate male; a homosexual male. *Cf.* FOP. [since the 1800s]

dandysette a female homosexual; a lesbian. [British, early 1800s]

dang 1. damn. A euphemism of disguise. *Cf.* DAD, DAG, GOL. [since the late 1700s] **2.** the penis. From DANGLE or DONG (both *q.v.*). [U.S. slang, mid 1900s-pres.]

dange broad a sexually attractive black woman. *Cf.* DINGE. [U.S. slang, mid 1900s]

danger-signal a menstrual cloth; a PERINEAL PAD (*q.v.*). *Cf.* RED FLAG. [British, 1800s, Farmer and Henley]

dangle 1. to be hanged. [since the late 1600s] **2.** to hover longingly about a woman without initiating anything. [British and U.S. colloquial, since the early 1700s] **3.** a nickname for an act of male exhibitionism. *Cf.* DANGLER (sense 2). [U.S., 1900s] **4.** the penis. [recurrent nonce]

dangle, on the pertaining to a flaccid penis. See DANGLE-PARADE, DANGLER (sense 2). [U.S. slang, mid 1900s, *Current Slang*]

dangle-parade group military inspection of the genitals for venereal disease. *Cf.* POULTRY-SHOW, PRICK-PARADE, SHORT-ARM INSPECTION, SMALL-ARM INSPECTION. [attested as New Zealand, 1900s, *Dictionary of Slang and Unconventional English*]

dangler 1. a seducer of women. From DANGLE (sense 2). In error for sense 2. [a misinterpretation by Matsell, 1800s] **2.** an exhibitionist of the penis. *Cf.* DANGLE (sense 3). [U.S. underworld, early 1900s]

danglers the testicles. For synonyms see WHIRLYGIGS. [British, 1800s, *Dictionary of Slang and Unconventional English*]

dangnation a euphemism for "damnation." [U.S., 1800s-1900s]

dangus a slattern. For synonyms see TROLLYMOG. [British dialect and colloquial, 1800s or before]

danna excrement; feces. *Cf.* DONIKER. [cant, 1700s-1800s]

danna-drag the cart used by the collector of NIGHT-SOIL. *Cf.* HONEY-BUCKET, HONEY-WAGON. [cant, 1800s or before, Vaux]

dant a prostitute; a sexually loose woman. For synonyms see LAY. [early 1500s]

dard the penis. Used in French by Rabelais with the same meaning. *Cf.* DART OF LOVE, LOVE-DART. [French for "dart"; British, 1600s]

dark cloud 1. an American Negro. **2.** an Australian aborigine. Mildly derogatory. [both senses, slang, 1900s or before]

dark cully a married man with a mistress whom he sees only at night. [cant, late 1700s, Grose]

Dark Gable a suave black man; a ladies' man. A play on "Clark Gable." [U.S., 1900s, Berrey and Van den Bark]

dark meat 1. a black woman considered solely as a sexual object. **2.** the genitals of a black woman. [both senses, U.S., 1900s]

darky (also **darkee, darkey, darkie**)

a Negro; an Australian aborigine; any person having very dark skin as a racial trait. [since the late 1700s]

darn (also **dern, durn**) a euphemism for "damn." [primarily U.S., late 1700s-pres.]

dart of love the penis. *Cf.* DARD, LOVE-DART. [British, 1800s or before, Farmer and Henley]

D.A.s the DOMESTIC AFFLICTIONS (*q.v.*), the menses. *Cf.* D.A. [British colloquial, 1800s-pres.]

dash a euphemism of avoidance for "damn." From the hyphens (dashes) in "d--n." In expressions such as "Dash it all!" and "So help me dash!" [primarily British colloquial since the early 1800s]

dashed damned. See DASH. [U.S. colloquial, 1900s]

dasher 1. a showy or dashing prostitute. [British slang, 1700s] **2.** a dashing young man; the same as BLOOD (sense 1). [British, late 1700s] **3.** a masturbator. See DOODLE-DASHER.

Dash it all! an oath and an exclamation, "Damn it all!" See DASH. [originally and primarily British colloquial, 1800s-1900s]

dast See GOL.

dastard 1. a coward. For synonyms see YELLOW-DOG. **2.** a dullard; a dolt. For synonyms see OAF. [both since the early 1400s]

date the anus. [Australian slang, 1900s or before] See also DOT.

daub of the brush 1. coition. **2.** pederasty. Referring to the actions of the INSERTOR (*q.v.*). From sense 1. [both senses, U.S. underworld, mid 1900s, Goldin, O'Leary, and Lipsius]

daughter a homosexual male introduced into homosexual society by another homosexual male who is called a MOTHER (sense 3). [U.S. homosexual use, mid 1900s, Stanley]

daughter of joy a prostitute. [U.S. euphemism, 1900s]

dawkin 1. a fool; a simpleton. Also

dawpate. [British dialect, mid 1500s-1800s] **2.** a slattern.

D.B. an abbreviation of "damn bad." [British, late 1800s, Ware]

dead intoxicated with marijuana. For synonyms see TALL. [U.S. drug culture, mid 1900s-pres.]

dead born stillborn; pertaining to a child born dead. [1300s, *Oxford English Dictionary*]

dead center a cemetery. From the expression meaning "right on center." [British, mid 1900s, *Dictionary of Slang and Unconventional English*]

dead drunk heavily intoxicated with alcohol. *Cf.* DEAD. [since the late 1500s]

dead-end street the female genitals. *Cf.* BOTTOMLESS-PIT. [Canadian and U.S., 1900s, *Dictionary of Slang and Unconventional English*]

deader a corpse. [British and U.S. slang, mid 1800s-1900s]

deadly nightshade a prostitute; a very low prostitute. From the plant name. For synonyms see HARLOT. [British slang, 1800s]

dead man empty liquor bottles. See DEAD SOLDIER (sense 2). [cant, late 1700s, Grose]

dead-meat a corpse. *Cf.* COLD MEAT. [colloquial, 1800s]

deads heavily intoxicated with alcohol; DEAD DRUNK (*q.v.*). See DEAD. [British Navy, early 1900s, *Dictionary of Slang and Unconventional English*]

dead soldier 1. a formed lump of excrement. *Cf.* TURD. **2.** an empty beer or liquor bottle. *Cf.* DEAD MAN. [U.S. slang, 1900s]

dead to the world 1. sleeping deeply. No negative connotations. **2.** intoxicated with alcohol. [both senses, U.S., late 1800s-pres.]

dead wagon a hearse. *Cf.* COACH. [U.S. slang, 1900s]

dealer a seller of narcotics or marijuana. *Cf.* BAGMAN, PUSHER. [U.S. drug culture, mid 1900s-pres.]

dear departed a deceased person. [U.S. euphemism, 1900s or before]

dearest bodily part the female genitals. For synonyms see MONOSYLLABLE. [from *Cymbeline* (Shakespeare)]

dearest member the penis. *Cf.* DEAREST BODILY PART. [ultimately Scots, 1700s, (Robert Burns)]

Dear Gussie! a mild oath and an exclamation. *Cf.* GUSSIE (sense 2). [U.S. colloquial, 1900s]

death's head the death's head mushroom, the AMANITA MUSCARIA (*q.v.*). [U.S. drug culture, mid 1900s-pres.]

decayed intoxicated with alcohol. For synonyms see WOOFLED. [U.S. slang, mid 1900s]

deceased, the a dead person. One of a number of euphemisms used for a corpse to avoid offending the mourners at a funeral. *Cf.* DEAR DEPARTED. [since the late 1400s]

decedent a deceased person; a corpse. *Cf.* DECEASED, THE. [since the late 1500s]

decent 1. chaste. The opposite of "indecent." [since the mid 1500s] **2.** dressed; clothed appropriately for the occasion.

deck a package of drugs, specifically a package of heroin. [U.S. underworld and drug culture, mid 1900s-pres.]

decks awash intoxicated with alcohol. [originally nautical; U.S. slang, early 1900s]

decunt to withdraw the penis from the vagina. *Cf.* CUNT (sense 5). [British use, late 1800s, (Farmer)]

d . . . ed (also **dee'd**) damned. A spelling disguise.

Dedigitate! a command to PULL YOUR FINGER OUT! (*q.v.*), *i.e.*, "Take your finger out of your anus!" The camouflaged version is "Take your finger out of your mouth!" [from World War II, British and U.S. slang]

deedeed damned. From "d--d." *Cf.* BIG-D. (sense 3). [U.S. euphemism, 1900s]

deed of kind copulation. *Cf.* ACT OF KIND. [British, 1800s or before]

deed of pleasure copulation. For synonyms see SMOCKAGE. [British, 1800s or before]

deen "damn" in "God deen you!" See GARDENIA!

deep cut heavily intoxicated with alcohol. *Cf.* CUT (sense 2). [colloquial, 1900s or before]

deep six 1. a grave. Referring to the customary six-foot depth of a grave. For synonyms see LAST ABODE. [U.S. colloquial, 1900s] **2.** to kill someone or bury someone or something; to throw something away. [U.S., mid 1900s-pres.]

defecate 1. to remove dregs or wastes. [obsolete; since the early 1500s] **2.** to void feces. [since the late 1700s]

defecation the elimination of fecal wastes. For synonyms see EASEMENT. [since the early 1800s]

deflower to terminate a woman's virginity; to rupture the HYMEN (sense 2). [since the 1300s] Synonyms: BREAK, COP A BEAN, COP A CHERRY, CRACK A JUDY'S TEACUP, CRACK A PITCHER, DEFLORATION, DEVIRGINATE, DEVIRGINIZE, DOCK, DOUBLE-EVENT, EASE, GET THROUGH, PERFORATE, PICK HER CHERRY, PLUCK, PUNCH, PUNCTURE, RANSACK, RUIN, SCUTTLE, TRIM, TRIM THE BUFF, VIOLATE.

defood to vomit. For synonyms see YORK. [U.S. slang, 1900s, Berrey and Van den Bark]

dehorn 1. to castrate. *Cf.* HORN (sense 3). [U.S. dialect (Ozarks), Randolph and Wilson] **2.** to copulate, especially after a long wait. *Cf.* HORN (sense 3). [U.S. slang, mid 1900s] **3.** as a noun "de-horn," a drunkard. [U.S. slang, mid 1900s-pres.]

deknackered castrated; emasculated. *Cf.* KNACKERS.

deleerit intoxicated with alcohol. For synonyms see WOOFLED. [U.S. colloquial, 1900s or before]

Delhi belly diarrhea, a malady suffered by tourists in India. *Cf.* MONTEZUMA'S REVENGE. [U.S. slang, 1900s]

delicate condition pregnancy. [U.S. euphemism, 1900s]

delicate taint venereal disease, especially GONORRHEA (*q.v.*). [British euphemism, early 1800s, Egan's Grose]

delicious jam semen. For synonyms see METTLE. [attributed to Walt Whitman by Farmer and Henley]

delirium tremens the ''trembling delirium.'' A neural disorder induced by the ingestion of excessive amounts of alcohol. [since the early 1800s]

delo-diam backslang for ''old maid.'' *Cf.* NAMO. [British and U.S., late 1800s-early 1900s, Ware]

delo-nammow (also **dillo-namo**) backslang for ''old woman.'' [costermonger's slang, British, mid 1800s]

demesnes a woman's genital area, her ''domain.'' [from French; in *Romeo and Juliet* (Shakespeare)]

demimondaine a COURTESAN (*q.v.*); a harlot. [mid 1800s-1900s]

demirep (also **demy rep**) a flighty woman; a woman of doubtful character. [since the early 1700s]

demis Demerol (trademark) tablets or capsules. [U.S. drug culture, mid 1900s-pres.]

demise death. [euphemistic and cultured; since the early 1700s] Synonyms and related terms: COLD STORAGE, EVERLASTING KNOCK, EXITUS, FINAL SLEEP, GREAT UNKNOWN, GREAT WHIPPER-IN, KINGDOM COME, KING OF TERRORS, KISS OFF, LAST MUSTER, LAST REWARD, LAST ROUNDUP, LEAD-POISONING, LIGHTS OUT, LONG LIB, OLD, OLD GRIM, OLD MR. GRIM, OLD, STONY LONESOME, QUIETUS, SWEET-BY-AND-BY, THE GRIM REAPER, THE OLD, UNDERSIDE.

Demme! (also **Dem!**) Damn! [British, mid 1700s]

demn damn. [since the 1700s]

demon a very low-grade deity; an evil spirit. [since the 1300s, *Oxford English Dictionary*] *Cf.* BASILISK, CACODEMON, DHOUL, DIABLOTIN, GNOME, GOBLIN, GOGMAGOG, HODGE-POKER, HUMGRUFFIN, LAMIA, NIGHT-HAG, NIGHTMARE, OGRE, PUCK, SPOORN, SUCCUBA, SUCCUBUS, TITIVIL, TROLL.

demon rum, the alcohol or liquor,

especially rum. [U.S., early 1900s] Synonyms and disguises: BUBBLY, BUMBO, FINGER AND THUMB, GOLDEN CREAM, KINGDOM COME, MUR, MYRRH, NELSON'S BLOOD, THIMBLE AND THUMB, TOM THUMB.

den the female genitals. From an old term for ''ravine.'' [vague innuendo from *King John* (Shakespeare)]

denatured alcohol alcohol which has been rendered unfit for human consumption, usually by the addition of methyl alcohol.

denims sturdy trousers made from denim, a type of fabric originally made in France. [U.S., 1900s]

depantsing in a group of adolescent males, the removal of the trousers of one of their number, especially in the presence of adolescent females. [U.S., 1900s]

depart to die. [since the early 1500s] Synonyms: ABIIT AD MAJORES, ABIIT AD PLURES, ANSWER THE FINAL SUMMONS, ANSWER THE LAST CALL, ANSWER THE LAST MUSTER, BE NO MORE, BITE THE DUST, BLINDO, BREATHE ONE'S LAST, BUY ONE'S LUNCH, BUY THE FARM, CASH IN ONE'S CHIPS, CLIMB THE GOLDEN STAIRCASE, COCK UP ONE'S TOES, COIL UP ONE'S ROPES, COME OVER, CROAK, CROSS OVER, CROSS THE GREAT DIVIDE, DEPART TO GOD, DROP OFF THE HOOKS, EXPIRE, FADE, GIVE UP THE GHOST, GO, GO ALOFT, GO FORTH, GO HOME, GO OFF, GO ON TO A BETTER WORLD, GO THE WAY OF ALL FLESH, GO TO MEET ONE'S MAKER, GO TO SLEEP, GO UP, GO WEST, HAND IN ONE'S CHIPS, HOP OFF, JOIN THE ANGELS, JOIN THE GREAT MAJORITY, KICK OFF, KICK THE BUCKET, KISS THE DUST, LAY DOWN THE KNIFE AND FORK, OFF, PASS AWAY, PASS IN ONE'S CHIPS, PASS IN ONE'S MARBLE, PASS ON, PASS OUT, PASS OVER, PERISH, PIP OFF, POP OFF, POP OFF THE HOOKS, PULL A CLUCK, RAISE THE WIND, SHUFFLE OFF THIS MORTAL COIL, SKIP OUT, SLING ONE'S HOOK, SLIP ONE'S BREATH, SLIP ONE'S CABLE, SLIP ONE'S WIND, SNUFF IT, SQUIFF IT, STEP INTO ONE'S LAST BUS, STEP OFF, STEP OUT, STICK ONE'S SPOON IN THE WALL, SUC-

CUMB, SUN ONE'S MOCCASINS, SWELT, TAKE AN EARTH BATH, TAKE THE LONG COUNT, TIP OVER, YIELD UP THE GHOST.

depart to God to die. [since the mid 1500s]

deposit 1. to ejaculate semen. See BANK (sense 2). For synonyms see MELT. **2.** an act of defecation; dung; feces. Cf. BANK (sense 1), MAKE A DEPOSIT. [U.S. slang, 1900s]

depraved sexually abnormal or perverted. Refers to persons performing nonorthogenital sexual acts or to the acts themselves.

dern (also **darn**) damn. Cf. DOD, DOL, GOL.

derrière the posteriors; the behind. Usually refers to a woman, except in "his cute little derrière" which is usually said by a woman. [from French; U.S. colloquial, 1900s]

desires of the flesh food, drink, and sex, usually the latter. [euphemistic and vague]

deuce, the (also **deuce, dewce**) the devil in expressions such as "What the deuce?", meaning "What the devil?" For synonyms see FIEND. [since the late 1600s]

deuced damned; pertaining to the devil. [since the late 1700s]

deucedly damned. [British, early 1800s]

develop to mature sexually; for the primary and secondary sexual characteristics to mature as part of human development. Cf. WELL-DEVELOPED.

deviant 1. a truncation of "deviant sexual behavior." **2.** occasionally used for DEVIATE (sense 2).

deviate 1. a person who is markedly different from normal. **2.** a sexual PERVERT (q.v.); a sodomite. [both senses, euphemistic, 1800s-1900s]

devil 1. Satan; the devil; the supreme being of evil. Usually seen capitalized in older writings. For synonyms see FIEND. [since c. 800, *Oxford English Dictionary*] **2.** any malevolent spirit, either a servant of the Prince of Devils or a minor deity. Usually conceived of

as male. **3.** a Caucasian. Cf. BLUE-EYED DEVIL. [U.S. black use, mid 1900s-pres.]

devil catcher a clergyman; any overly pious person. Other similar forms are: devil-chaser, devil-dodger, devil-driver. For synonyms see SKY-PILOT. [various British and U.S. uses since the 1700s]

devil's dung ASAFETIDA (q.v.), a plant resin with a strong smell. Used in folk medicine. Cf. RUMPITYFETIDA. [since the early 1600s]

devirginate 1. pertaining to a woman who has been deflowered. **2.** to deflower. [since the 1400s]

devirginize to DEFLOWER (q.v.). [U.S. slang or colloquial, mid 1900s]

dew marijuana. For synonyms see MARI. [U.S. drug culture, mid 1900s-pres.]

dewbaby a dark-skinned black man. Not necessarily derogatory. [U.S. black use, mid 1900s]

dewife to divorce one's wife. [U.S. slang, 1900s]

Dexedrine the trademarked brand name of dextroamphetamine sulphate, a central nervous system stimulant which can become addictive. Cf. DEXY.

dexo Dexedrine (trademark).

dexy (also **dexie**) DEXEDRINE (trademark) (q.v.). [U.S. drug culture, mid 1900s-pres.] Synonyms: DEXEDRINE, ORANGE, PEACH, PEP PILL, PURPLE HEART.

dhobie itch tinea, a skin irritation. Usually in the groin. "*Dhobi*" is Hindi for "laundry boy."

diamonds the testicles. From ROCKS (q.v.), a nickname for diamonds and for testicles. Cf. FAMILY JEWELS, STONES (sense 2). [U.S. slang, 1900s]

diaper 1. a menstrual cloth; a PERINEAL PAD (q.v.). [British and U.S. colloquial, 1800s] **2.** the cloth garment put on babies to clothe them and to catch their excrement. [primarily U.S. since the 1800s] Synonyms: BRITCHINGS, CLOUT, HIPPANY, NAPKIN, NAPPY.

diaphragm a contraceptive device. A circular device designed to cover the cervix and thereby prevent spermatozoa from reaching the uterus or fallopian tubes. A truncation of "diaphragm pessary." Cf. PESSARY.

diarrhea (also **diarrhoea**) **1.** thin, watery fecal material. **2.** the intestinal disorder associated with expelling watery fecal material. [from a Greek word with the same meaning; in English since the 1300s]

diarrhea of the mouth (also **diarrhea of the jawbone**) an imaginary condition involving constant talking or a constant stream of nonsense. [U.S. colloquial, 1900s]

dibble 1. the penis. From the shape of a gardening dibbler. For synonyms see YARD. [originally Scots, British, 1800s] **2.** to coit a woman. From sense 1. [British, 1800s, Farmer and Henley] **3.** the devil. [colloquial, 1800s-1900s]

dick 1. the penis. Rhyming slang for PRICK (sense 1). [British and U.S., 1800s-pres.] **2.** a dictionary. [British slang, 1800s] **3.** to cheat or deceive. See SCREW. **4.** to seduce and coit a woman. [senses 3 and 4 are U.S. (Boontling), late 1800s-early 1900s, Charles Adams] **5.** to coit a woman; to COCK (sense 4) a woman. [U.S. slang, mid 1900s-pres.]

dicked cheated, literally, "screwed." Cf. DICK (sense 3). [U.S. slang, mid 1900s-pres.]

dickens (also **dickings, dickins, dickons**) the devil; hell. Found now in expressions such as "What the dickens?" and "Get the dickens out of here!" [since the late 1500s]

dick-head (also **pecker-head**) a jerk or an oaf; a despised man. [U.S. slang, mid 1900s-pres.]

dickory dock the penis. Rhyming slang for "cock." Cf. ALMOND ROCK, COCK (sense 3). [British, 1900s, Dictionary of Rhyming Slang]

dick-sucker a FELLATOR (q.v.). Cf. COCK-SUCKER, DICKY-LICKER. [U.S. slang, 1900s]

dicky (also **dickey, dickie**) **1.** a thing; a gadget. [U.S. colloquial, 1900s, Berrey and Van den Bark] **2.** the penis. From

DICK (sense 1). [British and U.S. slang and colloquial, late 1800s-pres.]

dicky-diddle urine or to urinate. Rhyming slang for PIDDLE (q.v.). [British, 1900s, Dictionary of Rhyming Slang]

dicky-dido (also **dickey-dido**) **1.** an idiot. [British slang, 1800s] **2.** the female genitals. [attested as Canadian, 1900s, Dictionary of Slang and Unconventional English]

dicky-dunk copulation. Cf. DICKY (sense 2). [slang, 1900s]

dicky-licker 1. a fellator. **2.** a derogatory term for a homosexual male. Cf. COCKSUCKER, DICK-SUCKER. **3.** a derogatory nickname for any male. [all senses, U.S. slang, mid 1900s-pres.]

diddies (also **didds**) the breasts or nipples. The singular is "diddey" or "diddy." Cf. TIT, TITTY. [British, 1700s-1800s]

diddle 1. alcoholic drink, especially gin. [since the early 1700s] **2.** to copulate; to coit a woman. [British and U.S. colloquial, 1800s-1900s] **3.** to masturbate oneself or another, said of a male. [U.S., 1900s] **4.** to masturbate a woman vaginally with the finger. [1900s] **5.** to perform any sexual act, ORTHOGENITAL or NONORTHOGENITAL (both q.v.). **6.** any sexual act. [senses 5 and 6 are U.S., mid 1900s-pres.] **7.** to cheat; to deceive. [since the early 1800s] **8.** to dawdle; to waste time. **9.** the penis. [British, late 1800s, Farmer and Henley] **10.** the female genitals. [British, 1800s, Farmer and Henley]

diddler 1. a type of sexual offender who seeks sexual contacts with juveniles or teenagers; a person who practices hebephilia. Cf. CHICKEN-HAWK, CHICKEN QUEEN. [U.S. underworld, mid 1900s, Goldin, O'Leary, and Lipsius] **2.** someone who toys sexually with a woman.

diddleums the DELIRIUM TREMENS (q.v.). For synonyms see ORK-ORKS. [Australian, 1900s, Baker]

diddly-pout the female genitals. Cf. DIDDLE (sense 10), POUTER. [British slang, 1800s, Farmer and Henley]

diddly-shit 1. worthless. **2.** a damn. Something very trivial, as in "I don't give a diddly-shit" [both senses, U.S. slang, mid 1900s-pres.]

diddy a breast. See DIDDIES.

dido liquor; gin. [U.S. slang, early 1900s, Weseen] See also DICKY-DIDO.

die in a woman's lap to have an orgasm; to ejaculate, said of a male. See LAP. [based on a line in *Much Ado About Nothing* (Shakespeare)]

die in one's shoes (also **die in one's boots**) to be hanged. *Cf.* DIE WITH ONE'S BOOTS ON. [mid 1600s, (Urquhart)]

die in the furrow to copulate without ejaculating; to become impotent while copulating. The "furrow" is the pudendal furrow. [British slang, 1800s, Farmer and Henley]

diesel dyke a masculine lesbian; a BULLDIKER (*q.v.*). *Cf.* TRUCK-DRIVER (sense 1). For synonyms see LESBY-TERIAN. [U.S. slang, mid 1900s-pres.]

die with one's boots on 1. to be hanged. *Cf.* DIE IN ONE'S SHOES. **2.** to die while (still) active, not of old age or illness. [U.S. colloquial and stereotypical cowboy jargon, 1800s-1900s]

differential the posteriors; the rear end. Named for the rear axle gearbox of a vehicle. [U.S. slang, mid 1900s-pres.] See also GEAR.

digitate to masturbate, said of a woman. [British, 1800s]

dig oneself to scratch or rearrange one's genitals (through one's clothes) visibly, said of a male. [U.S. colloquial, mid 1900s]

Dig swigger it! a vague euphemism for "Goddamn it!" [U.S. colloquial]

dike (also **dyke**) **1.** a latrine; a privy. From an old dialect term for a hole, pit, or trench. [Australian slang, early 1900s-pres.] **2.** a lesbian or a virago. Also **dikey.** Possibly from the dialect term for "trench." *Cf.* BULLDIKER. [U.S. slang, early 1900s-pres.]

dil (also **dill**) a simpleton; an oaf. From DILLY (*q.v.*), "silly." *Cf.* DILDO (sense 4). [Australian and U.S., 1900s]

dilberry (also **dillberry**) fecal matter caught in the pubic or anal hair. *Cf.* DINGLEBERRY, FARTLEBERRY. [British and U.S. slang, 1800s-1900s]

dilberry-bush the female pubic hair. [British slang, 1800s, Farmer and Henley]

dilberry creek a privy. For synonyms see AJAX. [British, 1800s]

dilberry-maker the anus. [British slang, early 1800s, *Lexicon Balatronicum*]

dildo (also **dildoe**) **1.** to arouse a woman sexually by fondling her sexual parts. [British, 1600s-1700s] **2.** an artificial penis made of various substances. (*e.g.,* wax, leather, horn) and used by women to obtain sexual gratification. It can be fastened to the body of a female homosexual who then functions as a male. They have occasionally been equipped with ribs and other appendages to heighten their effectiveness. *Cf.* FRENCH-TICKLER. [since the 1600s] **3.** the penis. **4.** an oaf or jerk. *Cf.* DIL. [since the 1600s] **5.** an effeminate male. [U.S., 1900s or before]

dillies tablets of Dilaudid (trademark), a habit-forming painkiller similar to morphine. [U.S. drug culture, mid 1900s-pres.]

DILLIGAF an irresponsible person. "Do I look like I give a fuck?" Also **DILLIGAS,** "Do I look like I give a shit?" [U.S. slang, Vietnamese War, *Current Slang*]

dilly silly. See DIL. [Australian, early 1900s-pres.; Wilkes]

dillydonce a pimp; a ponce. Rhyming slang for "ponce." [U.S., *Dictionary of Rhyming Slang*]

dillypot (also **dillpot, dollypot**) an oaf; a fool; the female genitals. Rhyming slang for "twat." [Australian slang, 1900s, Baker]

dim bulb a dolt; an oaf. The opposite of a "bright light," a bright or smart person. [attested as Canadian, early 1900s, *Dictionary of Slang and Unconventional English*]

dime (also **dime's worth**) a ten-dollar

bag of drugs or marijuana. [U.S. drug culture, mid 1900s-pres.]

dimple the female genitals. For synonyms see MONOSYLLABLE. [British, 1800s]

ding 1. a euphemism of avoidance for "damn." *Cf.* GOL. [U.S. colloquial, early 1800s-pres.] **2.** a derogatory nickname for an Italian. A truncation of DINGBAT (sense 4). [Australian, 1900s, Baker] **3.** the penis. A variant of and a euphemism for DONG (*q.v.*). [possibly from German *Ding*, "thing"; U.S., mid 1900s or before] **4.** a beggar; an alcoholic tramp or beggar. A truncation of DINGBAT (sense 6). [U.S. underworld (tramps), mid 1900s-pres.]

ding, old the female genitals. *Cf.* DONG. [British, early 1800s, *Lexicon Balatronicum*]

ding-a-ling an oaf; an odd, giddy person who hears bells. [U.S. slang, mid 1900s-pres.]

dingbat 1. the penis. See also DINGBATS. [U.S. slang, 1900s] **2.** a gadget. [U.S. colloquial, 1900s] **3.** a Chinese. [Australian and British, 1900s] **4.** a derogatory nickname for an Italian. *Cf.* DING (sense 2). [slang, 1900s] **5.** an oaf. [U.S. slang, 1900s] **6.** an alcoholic tramp or beggar. [U.S. underworld (tramps), mid 1900s-pres.]

dingbats 1. the male genitals. See DINGBAT (sense 1). [U.S. slang and colloquial, early 1900s-pres.] **2.** the DELIRIUM TREMENS (*q.v.*). [Australian, 1900s]

Ding-busted!, I'll be an oath and an exclamation, "I'll be damned!" *Cf.* DAMNED. [U.S. colloquial, 1900s or before]

Ding bust it! an oath and an exclamation, "Damn it!" [U.S. colloquial, 1900s or before]

ding-dang a mild euphemism for "damn." *Cf.* DING-DONG IT! [U.S. colloquial, 1900s]

ding-dong 1. the penis. *Cf.* DING (sense 3), DONG [U.S. juvenile and colloquial, 1900s] **2.** a fool; an oaf. [U.S. slang, 1900s]

ding-dong bell hell. Rhyming slang. [British, 1900s, *Dictionary of Rhyming slang*]

Ding-dong it! (also **Ding-dang it!**) a mild oath or exclamation. [U.S. colloquial, 1900s or before]

dinge 1. a Negro. Derogatory. For synonyms see EBONY. [U.S. slang, mid 1800s-pres.] **2.** a male Negro homosexual. [U.S. homosexual use, mid 1900s-pres.] **3.** any non-Caucasian; a Vietnamese. [U.S. military (Vietnam), 1960s-1970s]

dinge alley the Negro district of a town. *Cf.* BLACK BELT, LAND OF DARKNESS. [U.S. slang, 1900s, Berrey and Van den Bark]

dingleberry 1. fecal matter clinging to anal hair. *Cf.* CHUFF-NUT, FARTLEBERRY. [U.S. slang, 1900s] **2.** an oaf; a person stupid enough to ingest dingleberries while performing ANILINGUS (*q.v.*). [U.S. slang, 1900s]

dingle-dangle the penis. *Cf.* DANGLE-PARADE. [since the late 1800s; probably older as a nonce word]

dingnation damnation. [U.S. colloquial, 1800s-1900s]

ding-swaggle (also **ding-swoggle**) damn. [U.S. colloquial, 1900s]

ding-swizzled damned. [U.S. colloquial, 1900s]

dingus 1. a thing or gadget. **2.** the penis. *Cf.* CHINGUS. [both senses, colloquial, 1800s-pres.]

dingy a derogatory nickname for a Negro. *Cf.* DINGE. [U.S., 1900s]

Dingy!, By a weak oath. Rhymes with "clingy." *Cf.* DING (sense 1). [1800s or before]

dink 1. an Oriental; a Chinese. Rhyming slang for CHINK (sense 2). Derogatory. [widespread slang, early 1900s] **2.** a derogatory nickname for a Negro. *Cf.* DINGE (sense 1). [U.S., 1900s] **3.** a dull oaf. [U.S., 1900s] **4.** a ladies' man. For synonyms see FOP. [U.S. slang, early 1900s, Montelone] **5.** the penis. [slang, mid 1900s]

dinkey a Negro child. *Cf.* DINK (sense 2).

dinky dow a marijuana cigarette. [mock-Chinese; U.S. drug culture, mid 1900s]

dinners the human breasts. [U.S. colloquial (Ozarks), Randolph and Wilson]

dino a nickname for a Mexican or Italian laborer. Mildly derogatory. [U.S., 1900s]

dip 1. a drunkard. [U.S. slang, mid 1900s-pres.] **2.** a drug addict. From sense 1. [U.S. slang, 1900s] **3.** a stupid, sloppy oaf. See DIPSHIT. [Australian and U.S., mid 1900s-pres.]

dip in the fudge pot anal coition. [U.S. homosexual use, mid 1900s, Farrell]

dip one's wick (also **dip the wick**) to coit a woman. Cf. WET ONE'S WICK, WICK. [slang, 1800s-1900s]

dipped mulatto; having some Negro heritage; having been dipped in tar. [U.S. colloquial, 1900s, Wentworth]

dips a drunkard. See DIP (sense 1). [early 1900s, *Dictionary of the Underworld*]

dipshit a stupid jerk; an oaf. A rude elaboration of DIP (sense 3). [U.S. slang, mid 1900s-pres.]

dipso (also **dypso**) a drunkard. From "dipsomaniac." [British and U.S. slang, mid 1900s-pres.]

dipstick 1. a jerk; a stupid oaf. Cf. DIPHEAD, DIPSHIT. **2.** the penis in "put lipstick on his dipstick." Refers to a woman performing penilingus. [both senses, U.S. slang, mid 1900s-pres.]

dirk the penis. Cf. BRACMARD. [from a Scots word for a type of dagger, 1700s-1800s]

dirt 1. dung, especially animal dung, as in "horse-dirt." Also in the plural, as in "mouse dirts." [since the 1300s] **2.** filth; obscenity; gossip. [U.S. colloquial, 1900s] **3.** a sadistic man who beats homosexual males after having sex with them.

dirt-chute (also **dirt-road, poop-chute**) the rectum. Cf. SEWER, SLOP-CHUTE. [U.S. slang, early 1900s]

dirty having illegal drugs on one's person or using illegal drugs habitually. The opposite of "clean," i.e., having no drugs on one's person. [U.S. drug culture, mid 1900s-pres.]

dirty dog 1. a vile rascal. Cf. DOG (sense 1). **2.** a lecher. Cf. DOG (sense 6). [British, late 1800s, *Dictionary of Slang and Unconventional English*]

dirty-drunk heavily intoxicated with alcohol. Cf. SLOPPY-DRUNK. [British colloquial, 1900s]

dirty-leg a sexually promiscuous girl or woman. Cf. LEG (sense 3).

dirty mouth to slander someone. [U.S. slang, mid 1900s-pres.]

dirty old man 1. an old man who displays a childish interest in excrement and sex, especially NONORTHOGENITAL (q.v.) sexual matters. Usually considered psychopathological. **2.** a male of any age showing an extremely high degree of interest in sexual matters. Abbreviated D.O.M. [both senses, U.S. slang, mid 1900s-pres.] **3.** an elderly homosexual male; an "old man" in the sense of DADDY (sense 1). Cf. AUNTIE. [U.S. slang or nonce, 1900s, Wentworth and Flexner]

dirty puzzle a slattern or a slut. [British since the 1600s]

dirty spot a brothel. [U.S. slang, 1900s, Berrey and Van den Bark]

dirty water semen in the expression GET THE DIRTY WATER OFF ONE'S CHEST (q.v.). The phrase itself is a common way of saying "make a clean breast of it." For synonyms see METTLE.

dirty word!, I'll be a a euphemistic mock oath or an exclamation, "I'll be damned!" Further euphemized as "I'll be a dirty bird!" [U.S. euphemism, 1900s, Berrey and Van den Bark]

discharge 1. to ejaculate semen. For synonyms see MELT. [since the 1600s or before] **2.** a bowel movement. For synonyms see EASEMENT. [U.S. euphemism, 1900s]

discouraged intoxicated with alcohol. [U.S. slang, 1900s]

discumfuddled intoxicated with alcohol. *Cf.* FUDDLED. [U.S. colloquial, 1900s]

disguised intoxicated with alcohol. For synonyms see WOOFLED. [since the early 1600s]

dish 1. damn; dash. [U.S. colloquial, 1900s] **2.** an attractive man or woman, said by a member of the opposite sex. Usually refers to a woman. [British and U.S., 1900s] **3.** to cheat or deceive. [U.S. dialect (Boontling), late 1800s-early 1900s, Charles Adams] **4.** to engage in gossip; to dish out gossip. [U.S. homosexual use, mid 1900s-pres.]

dish-clout a dirty slattern. For synonyms see TROLLYMOG. [British, late 1700s, Grose]

dishearten to abate or cancel a man's sexual arousal, possibly a play on "dis-harden." *Cf.* HARD. [euphemism from *Macbeth* (Shakespeare)]

dish queen a homosexual male who delights in spreading rumors and gossiping. See DISH (sense 4). [U.S. homosexual use, mid 1900s, Stanley]

dishy sexy. See DISH (sense 2).

dishybilly in a state of undress. Deliberately and comically illiterate. [from French *déshabillé;* U.S., 1900s]

disorderly 1. a prostitute. For synonyms see HARLOT. [British slang, 1800s, Farmer and Henley] **2.** intoxicated with alcohol. [U.S., 1900s]

disorderly house a brothel. [U.S. euphemism, 1900s]

dispatch one's cargo to defecate. *Cf.* DISCHARGE (sense 2). [British, early 1900s]

distillery stiff a drunken tramp; a hobo-drunkard. *Cf.* STIFF (sense 7). [U.S. slang, 1900s or before]

ditch weed marijuana; low-grade marijuana. [U.S. drug culture, mid 1900s-pres.]

dithered intoxicated with alcohol. From "dither," which means "shake" or "quiver." [Australian, early 1900s]

dithers the DELIRIUM TREMENS (*q.v.*). *Cf.* DITHERED. [U.S. slang, 1900s]

dive 1. a saloon; a low drinking estab-

lishment. **2.** a brothel. [both senses, U.S. slang, late 1800s-pres.] See also DO A DIVE IN THE DARK.

dive a muff to perform CUNNILINGUS (*q.v.*). See MUFF-DIVER. [U.S. slang, mid 1900s]

divel (also **divil**) the devil. A disguise. *Cf.* DARBLE. [dialect and colloquial]

diver 1. a male. **2.** the penis. *Cf.* DIVING SUIT. [both senses, widespread nonce use]

divine monosyllable the female genitals. An avoidance for "cunt." See MONOSYLLABLE. [British euphemism, 1800s, Farmer and Henley]

divine scar the female genitals. *Cf.* CUT, GASH, SLIT, WOUND. [British, late 1800s, (Farmer)]

diving suit a condom. *Cf.* RAINCOAT. For synonyms see EEL-SKIN. [mid 1900s]

dizzy as a goose (also **dizzy as a coot**) intoxicated with alcohol. [U.S. slang, early 1700s-pres., Ben Franklin]

do 1. to perform any sexual act. [in various uses both homosexual and heterosexual since the 1600s] **2.** to rob or cheat; to deceive. [British slang or cant, early 1800s, *Lexicon Balatronicum*]

D.O.A. 1. "dead on arrival," a notation indicating that a person was pronounced dead upon arrival at a hospital. [U.S., 1900s] **2.** the drug P.C.P. (*q.v.*), a strong and sometimes dangerous, illegal drug. From sense 1. [U.S. drug culture, mid 1900s-pres.]

do a bottom-wetter to copulate, said by a woman. [British slang, 1800s]

do a dive in the dark to coit a woman. *Cf.* DIVER. [British slang, 1800s]

do a flop to coit a woman. [British and U.S. slang, late 1800s-1900s]

do a grind to copulate. *Cf.* GRIND. [widespread slang, 1800s-pres.]

do a grouse to find and copulate with a woman. *Cf.* GROUSE. [British slang, late 1800s, Farmer and Henley]

do a job (also **do the job**) **1.** to defecate. [colloquial, 1800s-1900s] **2.** to coit and impregnate or just coit a woman. [British and U.S., 1900s] **3.** to perform the job of undertaker. [British euphemism, 1800s, Hotten]

do a kindness to to coit a woman. *Cf.* DO A RUDENESS TO. [British euphemism, early 1700s-1900s]

do and dare underpants; any underclothing. Rhyming slang for "underwear."

do an inside worry to copulate. [British, mid 1800s, Farmer and Henley]

do a number on to mistreat someone very badly; to put someone in a very bad situation. Literally, "to urinate or defecate on someone." *Cf.* NUMBER ONE, NUMBER TWO. [U.S. slang, mid 1900s-pres.]

do a push to coit a woman. [British slang, 1800s]

do a put to coit a woman; to intromit the penis. *Cf.* PUT (sense 3). [British, 1800s]

do a rudeness to to copulate with a woman. *Cf.* DO A KINDNESS TO, DO ILL TO.

do a shoot up the straight to coit a woman. From horseracing jargon. *Cf.* SHOOT (sense 1). [British slang, 1800s, Farmer and Henley]

do a spread to coit, from the female point of view. *Cf.* PUT DOWN (sense 1). [slang, 1800s-1900s]

do away with to kill. *Cf.* PUT AWAY (sense 5), PUT DOWN (sense 2).

do away with oneself to commit suicide. [euphemistic, 1900s and before]

do a woman's job for her to coit a woman; to stimulate a woman until she has an orgasm. [slang since the 1800s]

doc a physician. A truncation of "doctor." [colloquial, mid 1800s-pres.] The following synonyms usually refer to males unless indicated otherwise: BOLUS, BONE-BENDER, BONE-BREAKER, BONES, BUTCHER, CASTOR OIL ARTIST, CORPSE-PROVIDER, CROAKER, CROCUS, DOCTORINE (female), FEMME D. (female), FIXEMUP, FLESH-TAILOR, HEN MEDIC (female), MEDICINER, MEDICO, PILL-PUSHER, PINTLE-SMITH, PISS-PROPHET, PRICK-SMITH, QUACK, SAWBONES, SIPHOPHIL, SMALL-ARM INSPECTOR, STICK-CROAKER.

dock 1. to DEFLOWER (*q.v.*) a woman. **2.** to copulate with a woman. **3.** the posteriors. For synonyms see DUFF. [all senses, since the 1500s]

doctor to castrate or spay a pet. [euphemistic, 1900s]

Doctor Hall a personification of alcohol. *Cf.* AL K. HALL. For synonyms see BOOZE. [U.S. slang, 1900s]

Doctor Johnson the penis. From the statement "There is no one that Dr. Johnson was not prepared to stand up to (Partridge)." An elaboration of JOHN (sense 6). See JOHNSON. [British, late 1700s-1800s]

Doctor White cocaine. *Cf.* LADY WHITE, OLD; WHITE STUFF (sense 2). [U.S. underworld, early 1900s, Berrey and Van den Bark]

Dod God, especially in oaths. *Cf.* DAD, DAG, DOG. [British, late 1600s, *Oxford English Dictionary*] DOD oaths are: Dod-bing!, Dod-burn it!, Dod-dang it!, Dod-dern!, Dod-drot!, Dod-dum!, Dod-fetched!, Dod-gast!, Dod-gasted!, Dod-gum!, Dod-rabbit it!, Dod-retted!, Dod-rot!, Dod-rotted!, Dod-rottedest!, Dod-seize it!

dodo (also **dumb-dodo**) a stupid oaf. From the term for the awkward and extinct bird. [British and U.S. colloquial, 1800s-pres.]

do-do See DOO-DOO.

do drugs to take recreational drugs; to be addicted to drugs. [U.S. drug culture, mid 1900s-pres.]

dodunk a jerk or an oaf; a stupid person. [U.S. colloquial, 1800s-1900s]

do for 1. to kill. *Cf.* DONE FOR. [British, 1900s] **2.** to care for and nurture. [colloquial, 1800s-1900s]

do for trade to provide someone with some sexual activity. *Cf.* TRADE. [U.S. slang, mid 1900s]

dofunny (also **doofunny, dufunny**) **1.** a gadget. **2.** the penis. [both senses, U.S., early 1900s-pres.]

Dog God. *Cf.* DAD, DAG, DOD. One of the earliest instances of reverse spelling used as an avoidance. [in various forms since the mid 1500s]. See also DOGGONE.

dog 1. a rotten and low man. *Cf.* DIRTY DOG (sense 1). [since the 1300s, *Oxford English Dictionary*] **2.** to coit a woman. [British slang, 1800s] **3.** to coit a woman vaginally from the rear; to coit DOG-FASHION (*q.v.*). [British slang, 1800s]. **4.** any ugly or unpleasant woman; an old prostitute. [U.S. slang, mid 1900s-pres.] **5.** a derogatory nickname for a Caucasian. Probably the same as sense 1. [Negro use; U.S., mid 1900s-pres.] **6.** a lecher. *Cf.* DIRTY DOG (sense 2). [U.S. slang, mid 1900s-pres.]

dog, the old syphilis. [U.S. slang, mid 1900s, Goldin, O'Leary, and Lipsius]

Dog bite me! an oath and an exclamation, "May God bite me!" For synonyms see 'ZOUNDS! [British dialect, 1800s, Northall]

dog-bline-me! an oath and an exclamation, "May God blind me!" See GORBLIMEY! [wide-spread colloquial, 1800s-1900s]

dog days the days of a woman's menstrual period. Because a woman is supposedly "bitchy" at that time. For synonyms see FLOODS. [U.S. slang, mid 1900s, Wentworth and Flexner]

dog dirt dog feces. See DIRT (sense 1), PURE. [U.S. colloquial, 1900s]

dogess a female dog; a euphemism for BITCH (sense 1). Also a jocular euphemism for BITCH (sense 2). [British, mid 1700s]

dog-fashion (also **dog-style, dog-ways**) **1.** pertaining to copulation where the male enters the vagina from the rear. **2.** pertaining to anal copulation performed on a woman. [both senses, 1900s or before]

doggone a minced version of "Goddamn." *Cf.* DOG. [British and U.S. colloquial, mid 1800s-pres.]

doggoned damned. [since the 1800s]

dog nuisance dog feces, especially dog feces deposited in urban public places. [euphemistic, U.S., 1970s]

dog's lady a female dog. A euphemism for BITCH (*q.v.*). *Cf.* DOGESS. [British, 1800s or before]

dog's stone a species of orchid named for the testicular shape of its tubers. [late 1500s]

dog's vomit very poor-quality food. [Australian, mid 1900s, Baker] Similar terms: BLOOD, BULL FUCK, CALF-SLOBBER, CATSUP, CHATTER-BROTH, CHOKE-DOG, CREAMED FORESKINS, FISH'S EYES, FROG'S EYES, FROGSPAWN, GISM, GNAT'S PISS, HEMORRHAGE, HORSECOCK, SCANDAL-BROTH. See EMBALMING FLUID for alcohol dysphemisms.

dog's wife a BITCH (sense 1 or 2). *Cf.* DOGESS, DOG'S LADY. [British euphemism, 1800s]

Dog's wounds! a harsh oath and an exclamation, "By God's wounds!" *Cf.* DOG. [mid 1500s, *Oxford English Dictionary*]

Dog take! an oath and an exclamation, "God take me!" *Cf.* DOG. [U.S. colloquial, 1900s]

dohickies the male genitals. For synonyms see VIRILIA. [U.S. slang and colloquial, 1900s, Berrey and Van den Bark]

dohicky (also **dohickey, dohickie, dohickus, doohickey**) **1.** a gadget. **2.** the penis. [both senses, U.S. colloquial, 1900s]

do ill to to copulate with a female. *Cf.* DO A RUDENESS TO. [from Scots, 1800s or before]

do in to kill. *Cf.* DO FOR (sense 1). [British and U.S., 1900s]

do it to copulate. For synonyms see OCCUPY. [since the 1600s or before]

do-it-yourself to masturbate. [double entendre and recurrent nonce; U.S., mid 1900s-pres.]

dojigger (also **dojiggie, dojiggum, dojiggus, dojiggy, doojigger**) **1.** a gadget. [U.S. colloquial, 1900s] **2.** the penis. See DOJIGGERS. *Cf.* JIGGER (sense 1). [U.S. colloquial, 1900s]

dojiggers 1. the testicles. For synonyms see WHIRLYGIGS. **2.** the male genitals. [both senses, colloquial and slang, 1900s]

dojohnnie the penis. *Cf.* JOHNNY (sense 1). [U.S., 1900s]

dokus the posteriors. For synonyms see DUFF. [from the Yiddish TOKUS (*q.v.*); U.S. slang, mid 1900s, Wentworth and Flexner]

Dol God. In expressions such as "Dol dern!" and "Dol dum!"

doll 1. a person attractive to either sex. [U.S. slang, mid 1900s-pres.] **2.** any illicit drug in pill form. [from the novel *Valley of the Dolls*; U.S. drug culture, mid 1900s-pres.]

dolly 1. Dolophine (trademark), a brand of METHADONE (*q.v.*). [U.S. drug culture, mid 1900s-pres.] **2.** the penis in the sense of "plaything." [British and some U.S. use, 1800s-1900s]

dolly-man a derogatory nickname for a Jewish man. Named for the (Jewish) operator of a "dolly-shop," a rag, bone, and bottle shop. For synonyms see FIVE AND TWO. [British, 1800s-1900s]

dolly-mop a kept woman; a prostitute. *Cf.* DOLLY (sense 2). [primarily British, early 1800s-1900s]

dolly-mopper a whoremonger; a lecher; someone who keeps a DOLLY-MOP (*q.v.*). [British slang, 1800s]

D.O.M. 1. an abbreviation of 2,5-Dimethoxy-4-methylamphetamine; the same as S.T.P. (*q.v.*). Possibly a reinterpretation of *Deo optimo maximo*, "to God the highest," or *datur omnibus mori*, "it is allotted to all who die." [U.S. drug culture, mid 1900s-pres.] **2.** "dirty old man." [U.S. slang, mid 1900s]

domes the drug L.S.D. (*q.v.*). [U.S. drug culture, mid 1900s-pres.]

domestic afflictions the menses. *Cf.* D.A.s. For synonyms see FLOODS. [British euphemism, mid 1800s-pres.]

domino a dark-skinned Negro. From the color of the domino game pieces. For synonyms see EBONY. [U.S. slang, 1900s]

domus a W.C.; a toilet; an outhouse. Refers specifically to a privy. [from Latin *domus*, "house"; U.S. slang, 1900s or before]

donagher a W.C., privy, or restroom. See other forms at DONIKER. [U.S., early 1900s]

done for dead. *Cf.* DO FOR (sense 1). Synonyms: ASLEEP IN JESUS, AT REST, BACKED, BONG, COLD, DAISY-PUSHING, EASY, ELIMINATED, GONE, GONE FOR SIX, GONE TO GLORY, GONE TO MEET ONE'S MAKER, GONE TRUMPET-CLEANING, GONE UNDER, GRAVED, GRINNING AT THE DAISY ROOTS, JACKED IT, LAID-OUT, LATE, OUTED, OUT OF MESS, PUSHING UP DAISIES, PUT TO BED WITH A SHOVEL, RAN THE GOOD RACE, ROCKED TO SLEEP, SALTED, SCRAGGED, SENT TO THE SKIES, SHOULDERED, SMABBLED, SNABBLED, SNOTTERED, STONE DEAD, THREW SIXES, USED-UP, WAY OF ALL FLESH. See also the list at DEPART.

donegan a W.C.; a privy. See DONIKER. [U.S. slang and colloquial, early 1900s]

done-over 1. deflowered; copulated with. [British, 1700s] **2.** intoxicated with alcohol. [British colloquial, 1800s]

dong the penis. [U.S. colloquial and slang, mid 1900s-pres.]

donigan a W.C. or a privy. See DONIKER. [U.S., early 1900s]

doniker (also **donagher, donegan, donicker, donigan, donneker, donnekin, donnicker, dunagen, dunnaken, dunnakin, dunnekin, dunnykin**) a privy; a restroom; any room or place used for elimination. See DANNA. Based on "donnez," meaning "give" and "ken," meaning "house," both British canting words. [underworld, 1800s-early 1900s]

donjem marijuana. For synonyms see MARI. [U.S. drug culture, mid 1900s]

donk 1. beverage alcohol, especially home-brewed whisky. From "donkey." See WHITE MULE. [U.S. slang and colloquial, 1900s] **2.** an oaf; a fool. See DONKEY. [1900s]

donkey an oaf; a blockhead; an ASS

(*q.v.*). *CF*. MOKE (sense 3). [since the 1800s]

donkey-rigged pertaining to a man with a notably long penis. Named for the male donkey, which is so equipped. See MENTULATE. [British, 1800s, *Dictionary of Slang and Unconventional English*]

do-nothing a lazy person; a poorly performing male; a SLOW (*q.v.*) and unaggressive male. [U.S., 1900s]

Don't get any on you! a vague catch phrase of warning used between males. It is to be interpreted rather freely as: "Don't contract a venereal disease through your abundant sexual activity!" or "Don't dribble urine down your trouser-leg!" or "Don't get your semen on your body or clothing!" [U.S., mid 1900s]

don't-name-'ems trousers. For synonyms see GALLIGASKINS. [British, mid 1800s]

doob the penis. [there is an extremely remote possibility that this is related to Latin *dubius*, "moving alternately in two directions"; attested as Australian juvenile, 1900s, *Dictionary of Slang and Unconventional English*]

doobie (also **dubee, duby**) a marijuana cigarette. [U.S. drug culture, mid 1900s-pres.]

doodle 1. a silly oaf. Possibly from "noodle." [since the early 1600s] **2.** to cheat or deceive. See DIDDLE (sense 7). [British, 1800s] **3.** the penis, especially that of a child. Also **duddle**. See DOODLE-DASHER, WHERE UNCLE'S DOODLE GOES. [colloquial and nonce, 1700s-pres.] **4.** any gadget. [U.S. colloquial, 1900s]

doddle-case the female genitals. *Cf.* NEEDLE-CASE [British slang, 1800s, Farmer and Henley]

doodle-dasher a male masturbator. *Cf*. DASHER (sense 3). For synonyms see HUSKER. [British slang, 1800s]

doodle-sack the female genitals. Based on an old nickname for the bagpipes. [British slang, late 1700s, Grose]

doo-doo (also **do-do**) **1.** feces. For

synonyms see DUNG. **2.** to defecate. For synonyms see EASE ONESELF. [both senses, British and U.S. juvenile, 1800s-pres.]

doof (also **doofus**) an oaf; a fool. [U.S. slang, mid 1900s-pres., *Current Slang*]

dooflicker 1. a gadget. **2.** the penis. [U.S. slang, 1900s or before]

doogie (also **dogie, dojee, dojie, doojee, dooji, dujer, duji**) heroin. [U.S. drug culture, mid 1900s-pres.]

do one's office to copulate with a woman. *Cf*. DO A WOMAN'S JOB FOR HER. [euphemistic since the 1600s]

door-keeper a prostitute; a prostitute who occupies a doorway waiting for clients. For synonyms see HARLOT. [cant, 1600s, Dekker]

doozandazzy a gadget. [U.S. slang, early 1900s]

dope 1. all drugs and marijuana. It is said that this word originally referred to opium and is derived from the first syllable of that word. See DOPIUM. A more likely source is the intoxicating nature of early airplane varnish, *i.e.*, airplane "dope." [U.S. slang and colloquial, late 1800s-pres.] **2.** a jerk; an oaf. It is assumed that sense 2 is from sense 1. [attested as British dialect, 1800s, Halliwell; current U.S. slang]

dope fiend a drug addict or a drug user. [U.S. slang, early 1900s-pres.]

dopenik a drug addict. Patterned on "sputnik" and "beatnik." For synonyms see USER. [U.S. slang, mid 1900s]

doper a drug user, addict, or seller. *Cf*. PUSHER. [U.S. slang, mid 1900s-pres.]

dopestick a marijuana cigarette. [U.S. drug culture, 1900s]

dopey 1. a beggar's woman. **2.** the anus. [both senses, British, 1700s-1800s]

dopium opium. See DOPE (sense 1). Probably a blend of DOPE (*q.v.*) and "opium." [U.S. slang, early 1900s]

dork 1. the penis. **2.** an odd or eccentric person. [both senses, U.S. slang, mid 1900s-pres.]

dorky pertaining to a person, thing, or situation which is unpleasant, unfair, or strange. From DORK (sense 2). [U.S. slang, mid 1900s-pres.]

dormouse the female genitals. *Cf.* TYTMOSE. [British, 1800s, Farmer and Henley]

dose 1. an infection of venereal disease. [British and U.S. slang, mid 1800s-pres.] **2.** to infect with venereal disease. [U.S. slang, mid 1900s-pres.] **3.** a LOAD (sense 4) of liquor or a drink of liquor. *Cf.* MEDICINE. [slang since the 1800s]

dose of claps a case of gonorrhea. [U.S. slang, 1900s]

do some good for oneself to copulate, said of a male. *Cf.* SCORE (sense 1). [Australian euphemism, 1900s, Baker]

doss house (also **doss**) a low brothel. "Doss" is from "dorse." [since the late 1700s]

dot the anus. [Australian, 1900s, *Dictionary of Slang and Unconventional English*] See DOTS.

do the chores to copulate with a woman, especially in a perfunctory manner. Also euphemistic for "coition." *Cf.* DO A JOB (sense 2). [U.S., mid 1900s]

do the do to coit a woman. *Cf.* DO, DO IT. [U.S. slang, mid 1900s-pres.]

do the naughty 1. to practice prostitution. **2.** to copulate, said of a woman. *Cf.* NAUGHTY (sense 2). [both senses, British, mid 1800s]

do the story with to copulate with a woman. [colloquial, 1700s-pres.]

do the trick 1. to impregnate a woman. For synonyms see STORK. [British and later U.S., early 1800s-pres.] **2.** to copulate with a woman. [U.S. slang, 1900s]

dots the drug L.S.D. (*q.v.*). *Cf.* BROWN DOTS, MICRODOTS. [U.S. drug culture, mid 1900s-pres.]

double-assed (also **double-arsed**) having very large or very fat posteriors. [British and U.S. slang, 1800s-1900s]

double-barrelled pertaining to a pros-titute who permits both vaginal and anal copulation. *Cf.* FORE-AND-AFTER. [British slang, 1800s]

double-barrelled slingshot (also **double-barrelled catapult**) a brassiere. For synonyms see BRA. [the first entry is U.S. and the "also" is British; both senses, 1900s]

double-cross an amphetamine tablet, especially one with cross-scoring. *Cf.* CARTWHEEL, CROSSROAD. For synonyms see AMP. [U.S. drug culture, mid 1900s-pres.]

double-cunted pertaining to a woman with large genitals. *Cf.* COW-CUNTED. [British, 1800s, *Dictionary of Slang and Unconventional English*]

double-dugged large-breasted. *Cf.* TITS FOR DAYS. [British, 1800s]

double-event 1. the contraction of a case of gonorrhea and a case of syphilis at the same time. **2.** getting deflowered and impregnated in the same act of coition. [both senses, British slang, late 1800s, Farmer and Henley]

double-gaited bisexual or ambisexual. For synonyms see HALF AND HALF. [U.S. slang, early 1900s]

double juggs the posteriors. For synonyms see DUFF. [British, 1700s or before]

double one's milt to coit to a second ejaculation without an intermediate withdrawal. MILT (sense 2) is semen. [British, 1800s, Farmer and Henley]

double-ribbed pregnant. For synonyms see FRAGRANT. [colloquial, 1800s]

double-shung pertaining to a male with notably large genitals. Suspected of being a mis-copy for "double-hung" or "double-slung." *Cf.* WELL-HUNG [British, 1800s, *Dictionary of Slang and Unconventional English*]

double-sucker female genitals with very large *labia*. [British, late 1800s, Farmer and Henley]

double-trouble Tuinal (trademark), a barbiturate. [U.S. drug culture, mid 1900s-pres.]

douche 1. a shower bath. Rarely heard

in the U.S., its meaning having been supplanted by sense 2. **2.** a vaginal douche or the instrument used to administer one. [U.S., mid 1900s-pres.] **3.** an obnoxious person. *Cf.* BAG (sense 2), DOUCHE BAG. [U.S. slang, mid 1900s-pres.]

douche bag 1. a device used to administer a DOUCHE (sense 2) **2.** a contemptuous term for a person of either sex; the same as DOUCHE (sense 3). *Cf.* LOUSE-BAG, SCUMBAG (sense 2). [both senses, U.S. slang, mid 1900s-pres.]

dough-head (also **dough-face**) a dunce; an oaf. [U.S. slang and colloquial, 1900s]

do vum!, I a mild oath avoiding stronger terms, "I swear!" *Cf.* VUM, I. For synonyms see 'ZOUNDS!

down 1. to position a woman for copulation. [1800s-1900s] **2.** the female pubic hair. [British colloquial and nonce, 1800s] **3.** a barbiturate. See DOWNER. [U.S. drug culture, mid 1900s-pres.]

downer (also **down**) a depressant; a barbiturate. For synonyms see BARB. [U.S. drug culture, mid 1900s-pres.]

down-leg the penis. *Cf.* BEST LEG OF THREE. [British slang, 1800s, Farmer and Henley]

Downshire the female pubic hair. [British slang, 1800s, Farmer and Henley] See also MEMBER FOR THE COCKSHIRE. Synonyms: BANNER, BEARD, BEARSKIN, BELLY-BRISTLES, BELLY-THICKET, BELLY-WHISKERS, BOSKAGE OF VENUS, BROOM, BRUSH, BUSH, BUSHY PARK, CAT-SKIN, CLOVER-FIELD, COTTON, CUNT-HAIR, DAMBER-BUSH, DOWN, FEATHER, FLEECE, FLUFF, FOREST, FRONT-DOOR MAT, FUR, FURBELOW, FURZE-BUSH, GARDEN-HEDGE, GOOSEBERRY-BUSH, GREEN GROVE, GROVE OF EGLANTINE, LADY'S LOW TOUPEE, MERKIN, MOSS, MOTT-CARPET, MOTTE, MUSTARD AND CRESS, NATURE'S VEIL, NETHER EYEBROW, NETHER EYELASHES, PARSLEY, PUMPKIN-COVER, QUIM-BUSH, QUIM-WHISKERS, QUIM-WIG, RUG, SCUT, SHAVING-BRUSH, SHRUBBERY, SILENT BEARD, STUBBLE, SWEETBRIAR, TAIL-

FEATHERS, THATCH, TOUPEE, TUFTED-HONORS, TWAT-RUG, WHIN-BUSH. Many of the terms listed at MONOSYLLABLE also refer to the female pubic hair.

downy-bit the female genitals. For synonyms see MONOSYLLABLE. [British slang, early 1800s]

dowsetts the testicles. For synonyms see WHIRLYGIGS.

doxology-works a nickname for a church. The parson is the "head clerk of the doxology-works" (Farmer and Henley). [British slang, late 1800s]

doxy (also **doccy, doxey**) **1.** a beggar's mistress or woman; a female beggar. **2.** a common prostitute. **3.** any girl, girlfriend, or mistress. [all senses, since the early 1500s]

drab a sexually loose woman; a low prostitute. [colloquial, early 1500s-1800s]

D'rabbit! an oath and an exclamation, "God rabbit!" For synonyms see 'ZOUNDS! [British, late 1700s, *Provincial Glossary*]

drabble-tail a slattern; a DRAGGLE-TAIL (*q.v.*); a woman who has dirtied the hem of her skirt. [British and U.S. colloquial, 1800s]

drack a plain, dull woman; a female oaf. Possibly from "dracula" but more likely a variant of DRECK (*q.v.*). [Australian, mid 1900s]

drack sort an unattractive or unpleasant man or woman. *Cf.* DRACK, DRECK. [Australian, 1900s, Baker]

drag. 1. skirts or petticoats used by actors when playing female parts. A great favorite of British music hall audiences in the late 1800s. Refers to skirts which drag. [British, late 1800s] **2.** women's clothes and make-up on a man. Usually implies an imitation of feminine traits. Found in the phrase "in drag." Full drag refers to a complete costume rather than only a few feminine items as in HALF DRAG (*q.v.*). [primarily U.S., mid 1900s-pres.]

drag ass 1. to decamp; to get out in a hurry. *Cf.* CUT ASS, HAUL ASS. [U.S. slang, 1900s] **2.** pertaining to a person who is droopy and depressed. Usually hyphenated in this sense. [U.S. slang, 1900s]

drag-ball (also **drag-party**) a party for homosexual males who attend in drag. See DRAG. *Cf.* DRAG-PARTY. [U.S. homosexual use, mid 1900s]

draggle-tail 1. an untidy woman. **2.** a low, dirty slattern. For synonyms see TROLLYMOG. **3.** a filthy prostitute. *Cf.* DRABBLE-TAIL. [all senses, since the late 1500s]

dragon 1. a wanton woman; a prostitute, especially an old prostitute. [British, 1600s] **2.** a scold; a battle-axe; a WAR-HORSE (*q.v.*). **3.** the penis in the expression DRAIN THE DRAGON (*q.v.*).

drag-party the same as DRAG-BALL (*q.v.*). [U.S. slang, mid 1900s-pres.]

drag queen a female impersonator; a homosexual male who derives libidinal pleasure from dressing in women's clothing. See QUEEN for persons with similar tastes. [U.S. homosexual use, early 1900s-pres.]

drag show a performance by a female impersonator. See DRAG. [U.S. slang and homosexual use, mid 1900s-pres.]

drain 1. to urinate. *Cf.* DRAIN THE DRAGON. For synonyms see WHIZ. [U.S. slang and nonce, early 1900s-pres.] **2.** gin. For synonyms see RUIN. [British slang, early 1800s, *Lexicon Balatronicum*] **3.** the female genitals. Because they receive a lot of DIRTY WATER (*q.v.*), "semen." *Cf.* COMMON SEWER, SCUPPER.

drainist a drunkard who consumes a considerable amount of DRAIN (sense 2). [British slang, 1800s]

drain one's radiator (also **drain one's crankcase**) to urinate. For synonyms see WHIZ. [U.S., 1900s]

drain one's snake to urinate. See DRAIN (sense 1). [British slang, early 1900s]

drain the bilge to vomit. For synonyms see YORK. [Australian military, 1900s, Baker]

drain the crankcase to urinate. [U.S. slang, 1900s]

drain the dragon (also **water the dragon**) to urinate. *Cf.* DRAIN (sense 1). [Australian, 1900s or before]

drain the lizard to urinate. The LIZARD (*q.v.*) is the penis. [U.S. slang, mid 1900s]

drain the spuds to urinate. Based on a reason for leaving the room, *i.e.*, to remove the water from boiling potatoes. See STRAIN ONE'S TATERS. [Australian, 1900s]

drain the suds to urinate after drinking beer. *Cf.* SUDS.

Drat it! (also **Drat!**) an oath and an exclamation, "Damn it!" or "God rot it!" [colloquial, early 1800s-pres.]

drawers underpants for males or females. In their earliest form, long hose worn next to the skin. [since the mid 1500s]

draw him off (also **draw off**) to produce an ejaculation in the male. [British, 1800s]

draw his fireworks to produce ejaculation in the male. *Cf.* FIREWORKS. [British, 1800s]

draw off to urinate, usually said of the male. [British euphemism, 1900s, *Dictionary of Slang and Unconventional English*]

dreadnought a condom. From the name of a heavy overcoat and that of a man-of-war (ship). *Cf* FEARNOUGHT. It allays the fear of conception or infection. [British, 1900s, *Dictionary of Slang and Unconventional English*]

dream cocaine. Borrowed from a term for opium. See DREAMS [U.S. drug culture, mid 1900s-pres.]

dream beads opium pills or pellets. [U.S. drug culture, 1900s or before]

dream gum opium. For synonyms see OPE. [U.S. underworld, early 1900s or before]

dreams opium. *Cf.* DREAM. [U.S. underworld, 1900s or before]

dreamstick 1. a marijuana cigarette or any cigarette. [U.S. slang and drug culture, 1900s] **2.** opium. [U.S., 1900s or before] **3.** an opium pipe. For synonyms see GONGER. [U.S. underworld, 1900s or before]

dream wax opium. *Cf.* GREASE. [U.S. underworld, 1900s or before]

dreck dirt, trash, or feces; often a euphemism for SHIT (sense 4). *Cf.* DRACK. [from German via Yiddish; U.S. slang, 1900s]

drenched intoxicated with alcohol. [U.S. slang, 1900s]

dress for sale a prostitute. [U.S. slang, mid 1900s-pres.]

dress goods a woman; a woman considered sexually. See DRY GOODS. [U.S. slang, early 1900s]

dress-house a brothel. [slang, early 1800s-1900s]

dress-improver a bustle. [British, late 1800s, (Ware)]

dribbling dart of love the penis considered as one of Cupid's arrows. *Cf.* DART OF LOVE. [from *Measure for Measure* (Shakespeare)]

drink, in intoxicated with alcohol. *Cf.* LIQUOR, IN. [colloquial, late 1500s-1900s]

drinking intoxicated with alcohol. For synonyms see WOOFLED. [U.S. colloquial, 1900s]

drinkster a drunkard. For synonyms see ALCHY. [British slang, 1800s]

drinky intoxicated with alcohol. [British colloquial, 1800s or before]

drip 1. an oaf; a dunce; a disliked male; the same as JERK (sense 3). [1900s] **2.** nonsense. **3.** to utter nonsense. [senses 2 and 3 are British, 1900s, *Dictionary of Slang and Unconventional English*]

dripping for it pertaining to a woman who is sexually aroused. Refers to vaginal secretions. [British slang, early 1900s]

dripping-tight intoxicated with alcohol. For synonyms see WOOFLED. [British slang, early 1900s]

drive French horses to vomit. From the sounds made while vomiting. [in imitation of *hue donc*, the French equivalent of "giddy-up"; British euphemism, 1800s]

drive home to coit; to penetrate a woman [U.S. slang, mid 1900s-pres.]

drive into to coit; to intromit the penis. See DRIVE HOME. [British slang and colloquial, 1800s and nonce elsewhere]

droddum the posteriors; the BREECH (*q.v.*). For synonyms see GALLIGASKINS. [Scots dialect, late 1700s, (Robert Burns)]

droob (also **drube**) a dull person; an oaf. *Cf.* DOOB. [Australian, mid 1900s-pres., Wilkes]

droopers heavy and pendulous breasts. *Cf.* SUPERDROOPERS. [nonce use; U.S. slang, 1900s]

droopy-drawers 1. a sloppy woman; a slattern. *Cf.* DRAGGLE-TAIL. For synonyms see TROLLYMOG. **2.** a child whose pants are falling down. [both senses, U.S. colloquial, 1900s]

drop 1. give birth, said of livestock, especially sheep. [since the mid 1600s] **2.** to move into position for delivery, said of an unborn child. **3.** to have one's unborn child move into position for delivery, causing the abdomen to lower, said of an expectant mother. [senses 2 and 3 are U.S. colloquial, 1900s]

drop a ballock (also **drop a ball, drop a clanger, drop a goolie, drop one's balls**) to make a very serious error. *Cf.* BALLOCKS, CLANGERS, GOOLIES, which all mean "testicles." [British, early 1900s, *Dictionary of Slang and Unconventional English*]

drop a rose to release foul-smelling intestinal gas. Based on PLUCK A ROSE (*q.v.*), a euphemism for "retire to the garden privy." [U.S. slang, mid 1900s]

drop hairpins (also **drop one's beads**) to reveal one's homosexuality by dropping hints. [U.S. homosexual use, mid 1900s]

drop off the hooks to die. For synonyms see DEPART. [British euphemism, 1800s, Farmer and Henley]

drop one's beads (also **drop beads**) to reveal one's homosexuality by dropping hints; the same as DROP HAIRPINS (*q.v.*). [U.S. homosexual use, 1900s]

drop one's guts (also **blow one's guts out**) to release foul-smelling intestinal gas. [slang, early 1900s]

drop one's load. 1. to ejaculate *Cf.* LOAD (sense 1). **2.** to defecate. *Cf.* LOAD (sense 5). [both senses, colloquial or slang, 1900s or before]

drop one's wax to defecate. *Cf.* BODY WAX. [slang, 1800s-1900s]

dropping member the penis, especially if diseased or impotent. *Cf.* DOWN-LEG. For synonyms see YARD. [British euphemism, early 1800s, *Lexicon Balatronicum*]

droppings the dung of birds; the dung of animals; any dung or fecal material. [since the late 1500s] Various kinds of droppings are: BILLETING, BLAKES, BODEWASH, BOOSHWAH, BUFFALO CHIPS, BULL-SCUTTER, BUNS, BUTTONS, CASINGS, COCK'S EGGS, COW-BLAKES, COW DUNG, COW-PLAT, CROTILES, DAGLINGS, DOG DIRT, FEWMETS, FIANTS, FAUNTS, FUMETS, FUMISHINGS, GUANO, GUBBINS, HEN-DOWN, HORSE APPLE, MUTING, NEST, POOH, POOP, PRAIRIE COAL, PRAIRIE FUEL, PURE, SCHARN, SHARN, SIT-STILL-NEST, SKARN, SPRAINTS, SURFACE FUEL, TAN-TADLIN TART, TREDDLE, TROTTLES, WAGGYING, WERDROBE. See related terms at DUNG.

drossel (also **dratchell, drazel, drazel-drozzle, drazil, drosell, drossel, drozel**) a slut; a low slattern. [British colloquial, 1600s-1800s]

drozzle-tail a slovenly woman; the same as DRAGGLE-TAIL (*q.v.*). *Cf.* DROSSEL. [U.S. colloquial, 1900s, Wentworth]

drug 1. a medicinal compound. [since the 1300s, *Oxford English Dictionary*] **2.** a medicine or chemical substance used solely for its effect on the mind and body aside from any prescribed therapeutic purposes. See DOPE. **3.** all substances which can be used to produce a CHARGE (sense 1) or a HIGH (sense 3) including alcohol, amphetamines, barbiturates, cocaine, heroin, L.S.D.,

marijuana, P.C.P., and S.T.P. For other drug names see COTICS. [U.S. colloquial and drug culture, mid 1900s-pres.]

drug abuse the habitual use of, overuse of, or addiction to a drug. The meaning has been broadened to include tranquilizers and aspirin to demonstrate societal dependence on drugs in the U.S. [U.S., mid 1900s-pres.]

druggy (also **druggie**) a drug user or addict. [U.S. drug culture, mid 1900s-pres.]

drug habit 1. the frequent or habitual use of drugs. **2.** addiction to drugs. See HABIT. [both senses, U.S. colloquial and euphemism, mid 1900s-pres.]

drughead a heavy drug user; an addict. For synonyms see USER. [U.S. drug culture, mid 1900s-pres.]

drug-store cowboy an effeminate male; a ladies' man. For synonyms see FOP. [U.S. slang, 1900s]

drum 1. a virile black male. [U.S. slang, mid 1900s-pres.] **2.** a brothel. [Australian and possibly British use, 1900s, Wilkes]

drumstick the penis. [widespread recurrent nonce, British, 1800s]

drumstick cases trousers. The drumsticks are the leg. *Cf.* PAIR OF DRUMS. For synonyms see GALLIGASKINS. [British slang, 1800s]

drunk 1. pertaining to a person in a state of physical and mental impairment due to the ingestion of alcohol. See WOOFLED. [since the 1300s and before] **2.** a drinking spree. [since the 1800s or before] **3.** a drunkard. For synonyms see ALCHY. [colloquial, late 1800s-pres.] **4.** intoxication with drugs. [U.S. drug culture, mid 1900s-pres.] **5.** drunkenness as a crime; a criminal charge of "drunk," *i.e.*, "arrested for drunkenness." [U.S. underworld (tramps), 1900s]

drunk as a bastard extremely intoxicated with alcohol. For synonyms see WOOFLED. [colloquial and nonce, 1900s or before]

drunk as a besom very drunk; as drunk as a broom. From the fact that a broom cannot stand alone or from the motions of a broom sweeping. [British colloquial, early 1800s]

drunk as a boiled owl heavily intoxicated with alcohol. [British and U.S., late 1800s-1900s]

drunk as a brewer's fart intoxicated with alcohol; drunk and reeking with alcohol. [British, 1800s]

drunk as a broom heavily intoxicated with alcohol; the same as DRUNK AS A BESOM (*q.v.*). [British, 1800s]

drunk as a coot heavily intoxicated with alcohol. Patterned on "crazy as a coot." *Cf.* DIZZY AS A GOOSE. [U.S. slang, early 1900s]

drunk as a cunt heavily intoxicated with alcohol. Patterned on "black as a cunt." [British, *Dictionary of the Underworld*]

drunk as a fiddler intoxicated with alcohol; as drunk as a fiddler who is paid in drink. *Cf.* DRUNK AS A PIPER. [slang since the 1800s]

drunk as a fly intoxicated with alcohol. [British, 1800s]

drunk as a fowl intoxicated with alcohol. *Cf.* DRUNK AS A COOT. [Australian, early 1900s, Baker]

drunk as a lord (also **drunk as an earl**) intoxicated with alcohol. [since the late 1600s]

drunk as a mouse intoxicated with alcohol. From "drunk as a drowned mouse." *Cf.* DRUNK AS A RAT. [1300s-1500s]

drunk as a newt (also **tight as a newt**) heavily intoxicated with alcohol. As saturated as the amphibious newt. [British military, 1900s, *Dictionary of Slang and Unconventional English*]

drunk as an owl heavily intoxicated with alcohol. *Cf.* DRUNK AS A BOILED OWL. [widespread slang and colloquial, 1800s-1900s]

drunk as a piper (also **drunk as a tinker**) heavily intoxicated with alcohol. *Cf.* DRUNK AS A FIDDLER. [British slang, late 1700s]

drunk as a piss-ant intoxicated with alcohol; euphemistic for "drunk as piss." *Cf.* PIS-ANT. [Australian, early 1900s]

drunk as a rat heavily intoxicated with alcohol. Worse than being DRUNK AS A MOUSE (*q.v.*). From "drunk as a drowned rat." [mid 1500s]

drunk as a rolling fart (also **drunk as a brewer's fart**) intoxicated with alcohol. [British, mid 1800s]

drunk as a skunk intoxicated with alcohol. [U.S. colloquial, 1900s or before]

drunk as a tapster intoxicated with alcohol; as drunk as a bartender. [British, 1800s, Farmer and Henley]

drunk as a tick intoxicated with alcohol; as full of alcohol as a tick is full of blood. From TIGHT AS A TICK (*q.v.*). [U.S. colloquial, 1900s]

drunk as a top intoxicated with alcohol; wobbling like a top running down.

drunk as a wheelbarrow intoxicated with alcohol. [U.S. colloquial, 1900s]

drunk as Bacchus intoxicated with alcohol; extremely drunk. [British, 1800s, Farmer and Henley]

drunk as buggery extremely intoxicated with alcohol. [British, 1800s]

drunk as Chloe (also **drunk as Floey**) heavily intoxicated with alcohol. [widespread slang, 1800s-1900s]

drunk as David's sow (also **drunk as Davy's sow**) heavily intoxicated with alcohol. For synonyms see WOOFLED. [British, 1700s]

drunken horrors the delirium tremens. For synonyms see ORK-ORKS. [U.S. colloquial, 1900s]

drunky intoxicated with alcohol. [British, mid 1800s]

drunok intoxicated with alcohol. For synonyms see WOOFLED. [British, early 1900s, *Dictionary of Slang and Unconventional English*]

dry bob copulation without ejaculation, possibly due to impotence. *Cf.* DRY FUCK. [British slang, late 1700s, Grose]

dry fuck the motions of copulation

performed without removing the clothing. [U.S. slang, mid 1900s]

dry goods a woman; a woman considered sexually. [U.S. colloquial, 1900s] Synonyms and related terms: BIT OF MUSLIN, BUNCH OF CALICO, CALICO, CRINOLINE, HUNK OF SKIRT, LIFT-SKIRTS, LIGHT SKIRTS, LOOSE-BODIED GOWN, MINI-SKIRT, MUSLIN, PETTICOAT, PIECE OF STUFF, PLACKET, SKIRT, SMOCK, SMOCK-TOY.

dry grog narcotics; a nonalcoholic source of a HIGH (sense 3); "dry booze." [U.S. underworld, early 1900s]

dry high marijuana. A nonalcoholic source of a HIGH (sense 3). *Cf.* DRY GROG. [U.S. drug culture, mid 1900s-pres.]

dry hole a cold and unresponsive woman. From the name of an unproductive hole drilled for oil. *Cf.* HOLE (sense 6). [U.S. slang, early 1900s]

dry hump an act of coition without copulation; the same as DRY BOB (*q.v.*). [U.S. slang, mid 1900s-pres.]

dry run coition with a condom. [U.S. slang, 1900s, Wentworth and Flexner]

D.T. 1. the DELIRIUM TREMENS (*q.v.*). Usually D.T.s (*q.v.*). For synonyms see ORK-ORKS. [British, mid 1800s] **2.** a "dick-teaser"; the same as COCK-TEASER (*q.v.*). *Cf.* C.T. [U.S. slang, mid 1900s-pres.]

D-T-ist a drunkard. From D.T. (sense 1). [British slang, 1800s, Farmer and Henley]

D.T.s the DELIRIUM TREMENS (*q.v.*). [since the 1800s]

dubby a W.C. Based on the "dub" in double-u, "W." [British juvenile, 1900s, *Dictionary of Slang and Unconventional English*]

Duchess of Fife (also **Duchess**) one's own wife; anyone's wife. Rhyming slang for "wife." [British, 1800s, *Dictionary of Rhyming Slang*]

duck 1. a male urinal bedpan. [U.S. slang, 1900s] **2.** a young woman; a woman considered sexually. *Cf.* QUAIL. For synonyms see LAY. [U.S. slang, 1900s]

duck-butt a short person, especially someone with large posteriors. [U.S. slang, mid 1900s-pres.]

duck-butter 1. semen. *Cf.* BUTTER, MELTED-BUTTER. For synonyms see METTLE. [U.S. dialect (Ozarks), Randolph and Wilson] **2.** SMEGMA (sense 2). *Cf.* GNAT-BREAD. [U.S. colloquial, 1900s]

duckey an effeminate male. *Cf.* DUCK (sense 2). For synonyms see FRIBBLE. [U.S. slang, 1900s, Montelone]

duck-fucker the man in charge of poultry aboard ship. [British nautical, late 1700s, Grose]

ducking-stool a device used to punish scolding women and dishonest tradesmen; the same as CUCKING-STOOL (*q.v.*). A "machine" used to duck or dip offenders into water or excrement. [since the 1500s]

duck-plucker a rude nickname for a despised person. *Cf.* DUCK-FUCKER, for which this is a disguise.

duck's ass a style of hair known as the duck-tail. Popular in the 1940s and 1950s. *Cf.* D.A. [U.S. slang, mid 1900s]

ducy the penis. *Cf.* LUCY. [U.S. colloquial, 1900s]

dude 1. an affected male; a FOP (*q.v.*); a sissified male resident of a dude ranch. [U.S. slang, 1800s-pres.] **2.** any male buddy or chum. [U.S. slang, mid 1900s-pres.]

duff 1. the posteriors. *Cf.* JUFF. [U.S. slang, mid 1900s-pres.] Synonyms: AMPERSAND, ANATOMY, ASS, ASSTERIORS, BACK-LAND, BACK-PARTS, BACKSIDE, BALCONY, BEAM, BEHIND, BIM, BLIND CUPID, BLOT, BOGEY, BOGY, BOM, BOMBOSITY, BOO-BOO, BOODY, BOSOM OF THE PANTS, BOTTOM, BOTTY, BREECH, BUCKET, BUM, BUMBO, BUM FIDDLE, BUMMY, BUMP, BUNCHY, BUNS, BUTT, BUTTOCKS, CABOOSE, CAKE, CAMERA OBSCURA, CAN, CANETTA, CATASTROPHE, CHEEKS, CHUFF, CLUNES, COOLER, CORYBUNGUS, CROUP, CRUMPET, CRUPPER, CULO, DERRIÈRE, DIFFERENTIAL, DISH, DOCK, DOKUS, DOUBLE JUGGS, DRODDUM, DUMMOCK, DUSTER, FANNY, FIFE AND DRUM, FLANKEY, FLESHY PART OF THE THIGH, FRANCES, FUD, FUN,

FUNDAMENT, FUNDAMENTAL FEATURES, GLUTEAL REGION, GLUTEUS MAXIMUS, HAMS, HANGOVER, HAUNCH, HEINIE, HIND, HIND-END, HINDER-END, HINDER PARTS, HINDSIDE, HINTERLAND, HUNKERS, JACKSY-PARDY, JEER, JERE, JIBS, JUBILEE, JUFF, JUTLAND, KEEL, KEESTER, LABONZA, LATTER-END, LUDS, MOON, MOTTOB, NANCY, NATES, NOCKANDRO, OIL BAGS, PARTS BEHIND, PART THAT WENT OVER THE FENCE LAST, POD, PODEX, POOP, POSTERIORS, POSTERN, PRATS, PRESSED-HAM, PROMONTORIES, QUOIT, REAR, REAR-END, ROBY DOUGLAS, RUMBLE-SEAT, RUMDA-DUM, RUMP, RUMPUS, RUSTY-DUSTY, SADDLE-LEATHER, SCUT, SEAT, SESS, SITTER, SITTING-ROOM, SNATCH, SPREAD, STERN, SUNDAY FACE, TAIL, TOBY, TOCKS, TOKUS, TOUTE, TWAT, UNDERSIDE. **2.** a feminine lesbian. *Cf.* FLUFF (sense 4). [U.S. homosexual use, mid 1900s-pres.]

duffer a foolish oaf; a bumbler. [since the mid 1800s]

dugs nipples or teats. Vulgar or derrogatory when used for a woman's breasts. [since the early 1500s]

dull in the eye intoxicated with alcohol. [British, 1800s]

dum damn. A euphemism. *Cf.* DOD, GOL. [U.S. colloquial, 1900s]

dumbbell (also **dumbell**) an oaf; a stupid or unthinking person. [U.S. colloquial, early 1900s-pres.]

dumb bunny a stupid person; an oaf. [U.S. slang, mid 1900s-pres.]

dumb cluck a stupid oaf; a person as stupid as a chicken. *Cf.* CLUCK. [U.S. colloquial, early 1900s-pres.]

dumb Dora any stupid girl or woman. [U.S. slang, early 1900s-pres.]

dumb-dumb (also **dum-dum**) a stupid oaf; a dull, heavy LUMMOX (*q.v.*). [U.S. slang, mid 1900s-pres.]

dumbed damned. *Cf.* DUM [U.S. euphemism, late 1800s, Ware]

dumb-glutton the female genitals. Possibly rhyming slang for MUTTON (*q.v.*). *Cf.* FEED THE DUMB-GLUTTON. For synonyms see MONOSYLLABLE. [British slang or cant, late 1700s]

dumbo 1. a large and stupid oaf. **2.** a

derogatory nickname for a person with large ears. From the name of a fictitious elephant. [both senses, U.S. slang, mid 1900s-pres.]

dumb ox an oaf; a heavy dullard. [U.S. colloquial, 1900s]

dumbshit a stupid oaf. An elaboration of SHIT (sense 9). [U.S., mid 1900s-pres.]

dumbsocks 1. a derogatory nickname for a Scandinavian. **2.** an oaf. [both senses, U.S. slang, 1900s]

dumb-squint the female genitals, especially the vulva. *Cf.* LONG-EYE, SQUINT. [British slang, 1800s, Farmer and Henley]

dumb watch a venereal BUBO (*q.v.*) in the groin, causing a bulge in a man's trousers like a pocket watch. [British, late 1700s, Grose]

dummock the posteriors. For synonyms see DUFF. [British, 1800s]

dummy. 1. a stupid oaf. [since the late 1500s] **2.** the female genitals. Probably from "dumb-glutton." *Cf.* FEED THE DUMMY. For synonyms see MONOSYLLABLE. [British slang, 1800s] **3.** the penis. *Cf.* BEAT THE DUMMY. For synonyms see YARD. [U.S. slang, mid 1900s-pres.]

dummy dust the drug P.C.P. (*q.v.*). *Cf.* ANGEL DUST. [U.S. drug culture, mid 1900s-pres.]

dump 1. to defecate. **2.** an act of defecation. **3.** to vomit. [all senses, U.S. slang, mid 1900s-pres.]

dumplings the breasts. *Cf.* APPLE DUMPLING SHOP. [British slang, 1800s]

dumpling-shop the breasts. *Cf.* APPLE DUMPLING SHOP. For synonyms see BOSOM. [British slang, 1800s]

dump on to defecate on; literally, "to shit on." *Cf.* DUMP (sense 1). [U.S. slang, mid 1900s-pres.]

dum squizzled!, I'll be a mild oath or exclamation. [U.S. colloquial, 1900s]

dunce an oaf; a blockhead. From the proper name of the learned "John Duns Scotus," who died in the 1300s. [since the late 1500s]

dung any fecal matter, usually animal excreta. [since the 1200s] Synonyms and related terms: ALLEY APPLE, ALVINE DEJECTIONS, B.M., BODY WAX, BOG-STUFF, BOO-BOO, BOWEL MOVEMENT, BOWELS, CA-CA, CACK, CACKY, CARRION, CASINGS, CLART, COMPOST, COW, COW-CAKE, COW-CLAP, COW-CLOD, COW-DAB, COW-FLOP, COW-PAT, COW-PIE, COW-PUCKY, COW-SHARD, COW-SHARN, COW-SHERN, COWSLIP, CRADLE-CUSTARD, CRAP, CUT, DANNA, DEAD SOLDIER, DEJECTA, DEJECTIONS, DEJECTURE, DIRT, DOO-DOO, DOODY, DRECK, DROPPINGS, DUTY, EXCREMENTUM, FECAL MATTER, FECULENCE, GERRY, GONG, GUANO, HOCKEY, HORSE AND TRAP, HORSE DUMPLING, JANK, JOB, JOBBER, KA-KA, MANURE, MEADOW DRESSING, MERD, MERDA, MOLLOCK, MUCK, MUTE, NIGHT-SOIL, ORDURE, ORTS, PILGRIM'S SALVE, PONY AND TRAP, POO, POOH, POOP, POO-POO, QUAKER, RECREMENT, RECTAL EXCRETA, RESIDUUM, RICH DIRT, SCHARN, SCUMBER, SEWAGE, SHARN, SHIT, SIEGE, SIGN, SIRREVERENCE, SOFT AND NASTY, SOFT-STUFF, SOZZLE, SPRAINTS, STERCUS, STOOL, TAD, TANT-ADLIN, TART, TANTOBLIN TART, TAUNTY, TURD, WASTE, YACKUM.

dungarees trousers made of a sturdy fabric; trousers which will stand up under considerable wear. [from Hindi *dungri*, "coarse, cotton cloth"; U.S. colloquial since the mid 1800s]

dung heap 1. a pile of dung, especially in a barnyard; any pile of debris which contains fecal matter. [since the 1300s] **2.** a wretched, sloppy person. [since the 1500s]

dunnaken-drag (also **dunnick-drag**) a cart for hauling away night soil. *Cf.* DANNA-DRAG, HONEY-WAGON. [cant, early 1800s, Vaux]

dunny a privy; a W.C. From "dunny-kin." *Cf.* DONIKER. [Australian, late 1800s-pres. Wilkes]

dupe a sucker or a patsy; a person who can be used as an unknowing tool in a ploy; a victim of a con artist. [since the 1600s or before] Synonyms: ÂME, DAMNÉE, BUZZARD, COLL, FRUIT, GAY, GORK, PIGEON, SUCKER.

Durham nonsense. A truncation of

"Bull Durham." See BULL (sense 3). [U.S. slang, 1900s]

durn (also **dern**) an avoidance for "damn." *Cf.* GOL. [U.S. colloquial, late 1800s-pres.]

dust 1. cocaine. See HEAVEN DUST. **2.** a truncation of ANGEL DUST, which is P.C.P. (both *q.v.*). [both senses, U.S. drug culture, mid 1900s-pres.]

dust-bin the final resting place; a grave; the grave or death. From the British term for "wastebasket." [British, 1800s]

duster 1. the female genitals. [British slang, 1800s] **2.** the posteriors. *Cf.* RUSTY-DUSTY. [U.S. slang, mid 1900s-pres.] **3.** a cigarette combining tobacco and heroin. [U.S. drug culture, mid 1900s] **4.** a testicle. See DUSTERS.

dusters the testicles. For synonyms see WHIRLYGIGS. [British military, early 1900s, *Dictionary of Slang and Unconventional English*]

dustman a dead man; a corpse; a "man" who has passed "from dust to dust." A reinterpretation of "dustman." The British equivalent of U.S. "garbage man." *Cf.* DUST-BIN. [British, 1800s or before, Farmer and Henley]

dusty butt 1. an ugly prostitute. **2.** a short person; someone whose posteriors are low-slung enough to drag in the dust. [both senses, U.S. slang, 1900s]

Dutch, in pregnant and not married. *Cf.* TROUBLE, IN. [U.S., 1900s]

Dutch act (also **Dutch cure**) a cowardly act, namely suicide. For synonyms see SELF-DESTRUCTION. [U.S. slang, 1900s, Deak]

Dutch courage 1. alcoholic drink. *Cf.* POT-SURE, POT-VALIANT. [British and U.S., 1800s-1900s] **2.** narcotics. From sense 1. [U.S. underworld, early 1900s]

Dutcher (also **Dutchie**) a derogatory nickname for a German or a Dutchman. For synonyms see GERRY. [U.S. slang, 1900s]

Dutch-widow a prostitute. [slang, early 1600s-1800s]

duty (also **doody**) feces; usually human feces. [U.S. juvenile, 1900s]

dyke the female genitals. See comments at DIKE. [British slang, 1800s, Farmer and Henley] **2.** a virile lesbian; an obvious lesbian. *Cf.* BULLDIKER. For synonyms see LESBYTERIAN. [U.S. slang, 1900s]

dykey in the manner of a DYKE (*q.v.*).

Cf. BULLDIKER. [U.S. slang, mid 1900s-pres.]

Dyna a homosexual male. Possibly based on ''Dyna might.'' [U.S. slang, mid 1900s, *Current Slang*]

dynamite 1. strong, hard drugs, *i.e.*, heroin or opium. **2.** marijuana. **3.** cocaine. [all senses, U.S. drug culture, mid 1900s-pres.]

E

eager-beaver 1. a person who is very eager to obtain something; a person who is always on time or always early; someone who volunteers for everything. [U.S. colloquial, 1900s] **2.** a man or woman who is very eager for sexual activity. [U.S. slang, 1900s]

eagle-beak a derogatory nickname for a Jewish man or woman. *Cf.* HOOK-NOSE. For synonyms see FIVE AND TWO. [U.S. slang, early 1900s-pres.]

early door a prostitute. Rhyming slang for "whore." *Cf.* BROKEN OAR. [British, 1800s, *Dictionary of Rhyming Slang*]

early doors underpants; women's underpants. Rhyming slang for "drawers." [British, late 1800s]

earp (also **urp**) **1.** vomit. **2.** to vomit. *Cf.* BARF, RALPH, YORK. [both senses, U.S. slang and colloquial, 1900s]

earth-bath a grave. [colloquial, early 1800s-1900s]

ease 1. to copulate or ejaculate, said of a male. **2.** to coit a woman to orgasm. **3.** to DEFLOWER (*q.v.*) a woman. [all senses, British slang, mid 1800s, Farmer and Henley]

easement elimination, primarily defecation. Synonyms: BIG ONE, BIG POTTY, B.M., BOOM-BOOM, BOWEL MOVEMENT, DEJECTION, DISCHARGE, ELIMINATION, JOBBY, MAJOR NEED, MOTION, NATURE'S CALL, NUMBER TWO, PAUSE THAT REFRESHES, STOOL.

ease nature 1. to copulate, said of a man or a woman. [U.S. colloquial, 1900s] **2.** to defecate. [since the mid 1400s]

ease onself 1. to defecate or urinate. [euphemistic since the 1600s] Synonyms for defecate: ALVUM EXONERARE, BIG HIT, B.M., BURY A QUAKER, CA-CA, CAPOOP, CAST, CHUCK A TURD, CLART, CUCK, DEPOSIT, DISPATCH ONE'S CARGO, DO A JOB, DROP ONE'S LOAD, DROP ONE'S WAX, DROP TURDS, DUMP, EASE NATURE, EVACUATE THE BOWELS, FILL ONE'S PANTS, GEORGE, GO, GO TO THE BATHROOM, GRUNT, HOCKEY, IRISH SHAVE, JOB, MAKE A DEPOSIT, PERFORM THE WORK OF NATURE, PICK A DAISY, POOP, POO-POO, POST A LETTER, POTTY, QUAT, RELIEVE ONESELF, RUMP, SCUMBER, SHIT, SIEGE, SMELL THE PLACE UP, SOIL ONE'S LINENS, SQUAT, STOOL, TAKE A CRAP, TAKE A DUMP, TAKE A SHIT, UNFEED, VOID. **2.** to copulate or ejaculate. [British colloquial, 1700s]

easings dung; feces. *Cf.* EASEMENT. [colloquial, 1800s or before]

east and west the bosom; a human breast. Rhyming slang for "breast." [British slang, early 1900s]

easy lay a woman who can be persuaded to copulate easily. Later this also refers to a man. [U.S. slang, 1900s]

easy make (also **easy mark**, **easy meat**) **1.** an EASY LAY (*q.v.*), a woman who can be persuaded to copulate easily. Later this also refers to a man. **2.** a dupe; an easy target for deception. [both senses, British and U.S. slang, 1900s]

easy-rider 1. a man who lives off the earnings of a prostitute. [U.S. slang, mid 1900s-pres.] **2.** a young woman who copulates on the first date. *Cf.* RIDE. For synonyms see LAY. [U.S. slang, mid 1900s]

easy virtue a prostitute or an EASY MAKE (*q.v.*). From WOMAN OF EASY VIRTUE (*q.v.*). [British slang, late 1700s, Grose]

eat to perform any type of oral sexual intercourse, usually PENILINGUS or CUNNILINGUS, but also ANILINGUS (all *q.v.*). *Cf.* MUNCH. [U.S. slang, mid 1900s-pres.]

eating-stuff 1. a woman who looks delicious and desirable, *i.e.*, good enough to eat. **2.** a good-looking woman who inspires a male to perform CUNNILINGUS (*q.v.*). *Cf.* TABLE-GRADE. [U.S. slang, mid 1900s-pres.]

Eat it! a coarse remark; a curse. Literally, EAT SHIT! (sense 3) or "Eat me!", *i.e.*, "perform PENILINGUS (*q.v.*) on me." [U.S. slang, mid 1900s-pres.]

eat out 1. to perform PENILINGUS or CUNNILINGUS (both *q.v.*). From the expression meaning "to dine out at a restaurant." **2.** to berate or verbally chastise someone. [both senses, U.S. slang, mid 1900s-pres.]

eat pound-cake to perform ANILINGUS (*q.v.*). *Cf.* POUND-CAKE QUEEN. [U.S. slang, 1900s]

eat shit 1. to put up with a lot of abuse; to knuckle under. **2.** to swallow or believe BULLSHIT (*q.v.*). **3.** an epithet, "Eat shit!" [all senses, U.S. slang, mid 1900s-pres.]

ebony 1. a Negro man or woman. Synonyms and related terms: ACE OF SPADES, AFRAMERICAN, AFRO, AFRO-AMERICAN, ALLIGATOR BAIT, APE, BLACK, BLACKAMOOR, BLACK BEAN, BLACKBIRD, BLACK DIAMOND, BLACK FAY, BLACK-FELLOW, BLACKHEAD, BLACKIE, BLACK IVORY, BLACKOUT, BLOMAN, BLOOD, BLUE, BLUEGUM, BLUEGUM MOKE, BLUE-SKIN, BONEHEAD, BOO, BOO-BOO, BOOG, BOOGIE, BOOTLIPS, BOY, BROTHER, BROTHER IN BLACK, BROWNSKIN, BUCK, BUCK NIGGER, BUFFALO, BUGGY, BURRHEAD, BUTTERHEAD, CHARCOAL, CHARCOAL NIGGER, CHIMNEY CHOPS, CHOCOLATE DROP, CLINK, CLUCK, COLORED, COLORED FOLK, COON, CROW, CUFF, CUFFEE, CULLUD GEMMAN, DARK CLOUD, DARK GABLE, DARKY, DEWBABY, DINGE, DINGHE, DINGY, DINK, DOMINO, DRUM, EIGHT-BALL, EIGHT-ROCK, ETHIOPIAN, FIELD DARKY, FIELD NIGGER, FIELD SLAVE, FUZZY-WUZZY, GANGE, GAR, GEECHEE, GROID, HANDKER-CHIEF-HEAD, HARD-HEAD, HEADLIGHT TO A SNOWSTORM, HOME BOY, HOOFER, INK, INKFACE, INKY-DINK, INTERNATIONAL NIGGER, JACK, JAR-HEAD, JAY-BEE, JAZZBO, JIBAGOO, JIG, JIGA, JIGABOO, JIGGABOO, JIM CROW, JIT, JUBA, JUNGLE-BUNNY, KELTCH, KINK, KINKY-HEAD, KINKY-NOB, LILYWHITE, LOAD OF COAL, MAU-MAU, MEMBER, MIDNIGHT, MOKE, MOSE, MOSS, MOSSHEAD, MUNGO, NAP, NAPPY, NEGRO, NIG, NIGGRA, OREO, OXFORD, PICCANINNY (child), PICKANINNY (child), POSSUM, QUASHIE, RAISIN, RASTUS, REGGIN, SAMBO, SCHVARTZA, SCHWARZ, SCUTTLE, SEAL, SEEDY, SHADE, SHAD-MOUTH, SHADOW, SHINE, SHINY, SKILLET, SKUNK, SMIDGET, SMOKE, SMOKED-IRISHMAN, SMOKEY, SMUDGE, SMUT BUTT, SNOWBALL, SPADE, SPAGINZY, SPEAR-CHUCKER, SPILL, SPLIB, SPOOK, SQUASHO, STOVE-LID, SUEDE, SUPERSPADE, SWARTZY, SWEET CHOCOLATE, TAR BABY (child), TAR POT (child), TEAPOT, THICKLIPS, UNBLEACHED AMERICAN, UNCLE TOM, WILLIE, WOOLY-HEAD, ZIGABOO, ZIGGERBOO, ZULU. **2.** pertaining to a Negro. [both senses, colloquial, mid 1800s-1900s]

Ecod! an oath and an exclamation, "By God!" *Cf.* EGAD! [British, early 1700s]

edged intoxicated with alcohol. For synonyms see WOOFLED. [U.S. slang, early 1900s]

eel the penis. *Cf.* EEL-SKIN. [widespread nonce since the 1600s or before]

eel-skin a condom. *Cf.* FISH-SKIN. [U.S. slang, early 1900s, Wentworth and Flexner] Synonyms: AMERICAN LETTER, ARMOUR, BAG, BAGGIE, BALLOON, BISHOP, BUCKSKIN, CHEATER, CIRCULAR PROTECTOR, CONDOM, CUNDUM, DIVING SUIT, DREADNOUGHT, ENVELOPE, FEAR-NOUGHT, FISH-SKIN, F.L., FRENCH LETTER, FRENCH SAFE, FRENCHY, FROG, FROG-SKIN, GOSSY, ITALIAN LETTER, JO-BAG, JOHNNIE, JOY-BAG, LATEX, LETTER, LUBIE, MACHINE, MALE PESSARY, MALE SHEATH, ONE-PIECE OVERCOAT, PHALLIC THIMBLE, PORT SAID GARTER, PRO, PROPHO, PROPHYLACTIC, RAINCOAT, RUBBER, SAFE, SAFETY, SAFETY-SHEATH, SCUMBAG, SHEATH, SHOWER-CAP, SPANISH LETTER, SKIN, SPECIALTIES, SPITFIRE. See also EEL-SKINS.

eel-skinner the female genitals. *Cf.* EEL, "penis." [British slang, 1800s, Farmer and Henley]

eel-skins trousers; very tight trousers; any tight-fitting article of clothing. [British slang, early 1800s]

eer-quay pertaining to a homosexual

male and sometimes a female. Pig
Latin for QUEER (sense 3). [U.S., 1900s]

eff a respelling of F. (*q.v.*), an abbreviation of FUCK (*q.v.*). See EFFING. [Brit-
ish and U.S., 1900s]

effeminate male 1. a male who displays feminine characteristics. For synonyms see FRIBBLE. **2.** a euphemism for
"homosexual male." *Cf.* FOP (sense
2). This expression has been vague and
ambiguous for at least a century.

effeminatio PEDERASTY (*q.v.*). Refers
primarily to the "feminine" role played
by a CATAMITE or a RECEIVER (both
q.v.).

effing a disguise of F-ING (*q.v.*),
"fucking." [British and U.S., 1900s]

egg intoxicated with alcohol. For synonyms see WOOFLED. [Australian, 1900s,
Baker]

eggs the testicles. Refers both to the
shape and the fragility. [jocular and
nonce, 1900s and before]

egg-sucker a sycophant; a flatterer. A
euphemism for ASS-SUCKER (*q.v.*). [U.S.
colloquial, 1900s, or before]

Egypt a W.C.; a toilet. See GO TO
EGYPT. [U.S. slang and colloquial,
1900s]

eight-ball 1. a Negro. Derogatory.
From the color of the eight ball in
billiards. [U.S. slang, early 1900s, Rose]
2. a square; an unsophisticated Negro.
[U.S. black use, mid 1900s]

eight-rock a derogatory term for a
very dark Negro. See EIGHT-BALL. [U.S.
slang, mid 1900s, Deak]

elastic band (also **elastic**) used in
avoidance of RUBBER (*q.v.*) or "rubber
band." [1900s]

elbow-bender a drunkard. For synonyms see ALCHY. [U.S. slang, mid
1900s]

elbow-crooker a drunkard. [British
slang, 1800s, Farmer and Henley]

elder 1. an udder. **2.** a breast; a human
breast. By extension from sense 1.
Usually in the plural and usually derogatory when referring to human breasts.
[both since the late 1600s]

electric cure electrocution in the electric chair. [U.S. underworld, early 1900s,
Weseen]

electrified intoxicated with alcohol;
stunned with alcohol. [British slang,
1800s, Farmer and Henley]

elephant the drug P.C.P. (*q.v.*). A
truncation of ELEPHANT TRANQUILIZER
(*q.v.*). *Cf.* HOG (sense 3). [U.S. drug
culture, mid 1900s-pres.]

elephant and castle the anus; an oaf.
Rhyming slang for ASS-HOLE (*q.v.*). The
term is from the official crest of an
ivory trading firm (1800s), and later
the name of a pub. [British, 1800s,
Dictionary of Rhyming Slang]

elephant's trunk (also **elephants,
elephant's**) intoxicated with alcohol.
Rhyming slang for "drunk." [British
slang and some U.S. use, 1800s-1900s]

elephant tranquilizer the drug P.C.P.
(*q.v.*). Refers to the potency of the
drug. *Cf.* ELEPHANT, HORSE TRANQUIL-
IZER, PIG TRANQUILIZER. [U.S. drug culture, mid 1900s-pres.]

elevated mildly intoxicated with alcohol. [British and U.S. slang, 1800s-pres.]

elevation 1. drunkenness. **2.** a nickname for opium. [both senses, British
slang, 1800s, Farmer and Henley]

elevens!, By the an oath and an
exclamation, "By the eleven disciples!"

eliminated 1. killed; murdered. [U.S.
underworld, early 1900s-pres.] **2.** intoxicated with alcohol. *Cf.* WIPED-OUT.
[U.S. slang, mid 1900s-pres.]

elimination urination and defecation.
[since the 1800s]

elly-bay the stomach. Pig Latin for
"belly." [U.S. slang, early 1900s]

em an abbreviation of "morphine." A
spelling-out of M. (*q.v.*). *Cf.* AUNT
EMMA. [U.S. underworld, early 1900s,
Irwin]

embalmed intoxicated with alcohol.
[U.S. slang, 1900s]

embalming fluid inferior or strong
liquor; any alcoholic liquor. [U.S. slang,
early 1900s-pres.] Synonyms: BLUE PIG,
BLUE STONE, BUG JUICE, BUSTHEAD,

CAPER-JUICE, CATGUT, CHARLEY FRISKY, CHOKE-DOG, COFFIN VARNISH, CORN-MULE, DRUDGE, FAMILY DISTURBANCE, GAY AND FRISKY, GREEK FIRE, HIGHLAND FRISKY, JOHN BARLEYCORN, LIQUID-FIRE, MOUNTAIN-DEW, NANNY-GOAT SWEAT, NIGGER-GIN, PALEFACE, PINE-TOP, PISH, PIZEN, PRAIRIE-DEW, SCREECH, SKEE, SKY, SNAKE, SNAKEBITE MEDICINE, SNAKE-JUICE, SNAKE MEDICINE, SNAKE-POISON, TANGLE-LEG, TARANTULA-JUICE, TIGER SWEAT, WHITE LIGHTNING, WOOZLE-WATER.

embrace 1. to copulate. For synonyms see OCCUPY. [from *Much Ado About Nothing* (Shakespeare)] **2.** to clasp a female for copulation; to hold a woman while copulating, said of animals and extended to humans. [euphemistic since the 1800s or before]

emsel a nickname for "morphine." *Cf.* EM. For synonyms see MORPH. [U.S. drug culture, mid 1900s-pres.]

enceinte pregnant. For synonyms see FRAGRANT. [from French; in English since the 1800s]

enchilada-eater a derogatory nickname for a Mexican. For synonyms see MEX. [U.S. slang, mid 1900s]

end 1. the penis. [since the 1600s or before] **2.** the foreskin. **3.** the glans penis. *Cf.* BELL-END. For synonyms see HEAD. [senses 2 and 3 are colloquial, 1800s-1900s]

endless belt (also **belt**) a prostitute. *Cf.* BELTER. [Australian, early 1900s, Baker]

enemy the penis. For synonyms see YARD. [British slang, 1800s, Farmer and Henley]

engine the equipment used by an opium smoker. [U.S. underworld, early 1900s or before, Berrey and Van den Bark]

enjoy to coit a woman. See ENJOY A WOMAN. [from *The Rape of Lucrece* (Shakespeare)]

enjoy a woman to copulate with a woman. [euphemistic, 1800s if not long before]

enjoy a woman vigorously to copulate with strength and rapidity, said of the male.

enob backslang for "bone," the erect penis. See BONE (sense 2). [U.S., 1900s, Wentworth and Flexner]

ensign-bearer a drunkard. From his red face. [British slang, early 1800s]

entanglement an illicit love affair. For synonyms see AFFAIR. [U.S. euphemism, 1900s or before]

entertaining the general pertaining to a woman who is experiencing the menses. *Cf.* CAPTAIN IS AT HOME.

envelope a condom. From FRENCH LETTER (*q.v.*). For synonyms see EEL-SKIN. [British, 1800s, *Dictionary of Slang and Unconventional English*]

Epar! a mock exclamation. Backslang for "rape!" [U.S. slang, mid 1900s]

epicene 1. pertaining to nouns which fall into the same grammatical gender regardless of the biological sex of the named phenomenon in the real world. Found in Latin and Greek. In the English language, "common gender." **2.** of indeterminate or indeterminable sex. This includes (colloquially) homosexual, hermaphroditic, and effeminate. **3.** a homosexual male. Euphemistic. [all senses, since the 1600s] Synonyms and related terms for senses. 2 and 3: ACTIVE SODOMIST, AFGAY, AG-FAY, ANGEL, ANSY-PAY, ARSE-KING, ASPRO, AUNTIE, BABY, BADLING, BAG, BANDIT, BARDACHE, BELLE, BENT, BETTY, BIRDIE, BITCH, BOY, BRIGHTON PIER, BROKEN-WRIST, BROWN-HATTER, BROWNIE, BUTCH, BUTTERCUP, BUZZER, CAMP, CANNIBAL, CAPON, CHARLIE, CHICHI, CHICKEN, CHICKEN-HAWK, CLOSET QUEEN, CLOSET QUEER, CON, COWBOY, DAISY, DANDY, DAUGHTER, DINGE, DIRTY OLD MAN, DOLL, DYNA, EER-QUAY, EFFEMINATE MALE, ETHEL, FAG, FAGGART, FAGGOT, FAIRY, FARG, FART-CATCHER, FEMME, FEY, FLOWER, FLUTE, FLUTER, FLY BALL, FOOPER, FOUR-LETTER MAN, FOXY LADY, FREAK, FREEP, FRIT, FRUIT, FRUITCAKE, FRUITER, FRUIT-FLY, FRUIT-PLATE, FUGITIVE FROM A DAISY CHAIN GANG, FUNNY, GAY, GAY-BOY, GEAR, GEAR-BOX, GINGER BEER, GIRL,

GOBBLER, GONSEL, GREEN AND YELLOW FELLOW, HAIRBURGER, HAT, HESH, HE-SHE, HIM-HER, HIMMER, HOCK, HOMIE, HOMO, HOMOPHILE, HOMOSEXUAL, HORSE'S HOOF, INSERTEE, INSERTOR, INSPECTOR OF MANHOLES, INVERT, JERE, JOY-BOY, K., KING LEAR, KINKY, KISS-ER, KWEER, LACY, LARRO, LAVENDER, LAVENDER BOY, LEATHER, LIGHT-FOOTED, LIGHT ON HIS FEET, LILY, LIMP-WRIST, MAN'S MAN, MARY, MEAT HOUND, MID-NIGHT COWBOY, MINCE, MINTIE, MO, MOTHER, MOUSER, MUZZLE, NANCE, NANCY, NANCY HOMEY, NELLY, NEUTER GENDER, NICK-NACK, NIC NAC, NIGH ENOUGH, NIGHT-SNEAKERS, NOLA, NOT INTERESTED IN THE OPPOSITE SEX, ODD, ODDBALL, ONE OF THOSE, ORCHESTRA, OSCAR, OTHER SEX, PANSY, PATO, PER-VERT, PETER PANSY, PIXY, POOD, POOF, POOFTER, POUFFE, PUFF, PUNCE, PUNK, PURE SILK, PUSSY NELLIE, Q., QUAEDAM, QUEAN, QUEEN, QUEER, QUEERVERT, QUINCE, RENTER, RIMADONNA, SCREAM-ING FAIRY, SECKO, SHIM, SISSY, SISTER, SKIPPY, SPINTRY, SPURGE, SWEET, SWEET-IE, SWISH, THAT WAY, THING, THIRD SEX, THIRD-SEXER, THREE-DOLLAR BILL, THREE-LEGGED BEAVER, THREE-LETTER MAN, TICKLE-YOUR-FANCY, TRICK, TRUCK-DRIV-ER, TWANK, TWINK, UNDERCOVER MAN, URANIST, URNING, WEIRD, WILLIE, WONK.

equipment the male genitals. *Cf.* AP-PARATUS, GEAR, OUTFIT. [U.S. colloqui-al, 1900s]

erb marijuana. In error for "herb." *Cf.* HERB, YERBA. [U.S. drug culture, mid 1900s-pres.]

erection an erection of the penis. A truncation of PENILE ERECTION (*q.v.*). The word is seen in other senses in its verb form, but in the noun form it always refers to the penis. Synonyms and related expressions: BIT OF HARD, BIT OF SNUG, BIT OF STIFF, BONE, BONE-ON, BONER, CAPTAIN STANDISH, CHARGE, COCK-STAND, COLLEEN BAWN, CONCOM-ITANT OF DESIRE, CRACK A FAT, DISTEN-SION OF THE PHALLUS, ERECTIO PENIS, FIXED BAYONETS, FULL, HANG A HARD, HARD, HARD BIT, HARD-ON, HAVE A HARD-ON, HAVE A HARD-UP, HAVE IT ON, HAVE

THE HORN, HORN-COLIC, HORNIFICATION, IN ONE'S BEST CLOTHES, IN ONE'S SUN-DAY BEST, IRISH TOOTHACHE, JACK, LANCE IN REST, LOB, LOB-PRICK, MARQUESS OF LORN, MATUTINAL ERECTION, MORNING PRIDE, OLD HORNINGTON, OLD HORNY, ON THE STAND, PENILE ERECTION, PENIS IN ERECTUS, PISS-PROUD, PRIAPISM, PRICK, PRICK-PRIDE, PROD, PROUD, PROUD BELOW THE NAVEL, RAIL, RAMROD, REAMER, RISE IN ONE'S LEVIS, ROARING HORN, ROAR-ING JACK, ROCK PYTHON, ROOT, SPIKE, STABLE, STALK, STAND, STANDARD, STANDING-MEMBER, STANDING-WARE, STIFF, STIFF AND STOUT, STIFF-DEITY, STIFF ONE, STIFF PRICK, STIFFY, TEMPORARY PRIAPISM, THE OLD ADAM, TOOTHACHE, TUMESCENT, UP, VIRILE MEMBER, VIRILE REFLEX, WOOD.

erring sister a prostitute. For syn-onyms see HARLOT. [euphemistic, 1900s or before]

eruct 1. to belch. **2.** a belch. [both since the mid 1600s]

eructate to belch; to vomit forth. [early 1600s]

eternal damned. A play on "infer-nal." [jocular or illiterate; since the 1800s]

eternal God!, By the (also **Eternal!, By the**) an oath and an exclamation. "Eternal" does not mean "damned" here. For synonyms see 'ZOUNDS!

eternity-box a coffin. [British and U.S. colloquial, 1700s-1800s]

Ethel a derogatory nickname for an effeminate male or a homosexual male. [U.S. slang, mid 1900s] Similar names are: BETTY, DYNA, ETHEL, GUSSIE, JENNY, JENNY WILLOCKS, LIZZIE BOY, MARGERY, MARY, MARY ANN, MISS NANCY, NAN-BOY, NANCE, NANCY, NANCY DAWSON, NANCY HOMEY, NEL-LIE FAG, NELLY.

Ethiopian 1. a nickname for a Negro. **2.** pertaining to Negroes. Neither sense is necessarily derogatory. [both senses, U.S. colloquial and slang, 1800s-1900s]

Ethiopian opera a minstrel show. [U.S. slang, early 1900s or before]

Ethiopian paradise the highest balcony in a segregated theater. *Cf.* NIGGER-HEAVEN. [U.S. slang, early 1900s or before]

Ethiopian serenader a Negro minstrel. [U.S. slang, early 1900s or before]

eunuch a male whose testicles or penis and testicles have been removed or whose testicles never developed. [from Greek; in English since the early 1400s] Synonyms: ABEILARD, ANDROGYNE, BOB TAIL, CAPON, CASTRATO, GELDING, RASCAGLION, SPADO, THIRD SEX, WETHER.

evacuate the bladder to urinate. For synonyms see WHIZ. [medical]

evacuate the bowels to defecate. [medical]

eventration cutting open the abdomen and removing the bowels. The "drawing" in "drawing and quartering."

everhard pertaining to a very hard erection of the penis. [U.S. slang, mid 1900s-pres.]

everlasting knock death. [U.S. colloquial, late 1800s-1900s]

everlasting-staircase the treadmill as used for punishment in England. [British slang, mid 1800s]

everlasting wound the female genitals, specifically the PUDENDAL CLEAVAGE (*q.v.*). *Cf.* CUT (sense 3), GASH (sense 1), SLIT, WOUND. [British slang, 1800s, Farmer and Henley]

ever-loving a disguise of "motherloving," which is a disguise of "motherfucking." See MOTHER-FUCKER. [slang, 1900s]

everythingathon an orgy in which various types of sexual activity are performed. *Cf.* CIRCUS LOVE. See GROUP SEX for similar terms. [U.S. homosexual use, mid 1900s, Farrell]

Eve's custom-house the female genitals. Because that is where Adam made his first entry. [British slang, late 1700s, Grose]

evil eye a gaze which inflicts injury.

ewe-mutton an elderly prostitute, implying "old meat." *Cf.* MEAT (sense 2). [British slang, 1800s, Farmer and Henley]

exchange spits to kiss or to copulate. [British, 1800s-1900s]

excrement (also **excrements**) **1.** dung or urine. In the plural, usually refers to feces or to feces and urine. **2.** any of the substances lost or cast off from the body. Specifically: blackheads, breast milk, dandruff, earwax, feces, fingernails (when cut), hair (when cut or shed), menstrual effluvium, nasal mucus, phlegm, pus, saliva, scabs, semen, squamous cells (when shed), sweat, tears, urine, and vomitus. Blood and lymph are not usually considered excrements except as part of a scab.

excrementum cerebellum vincit* "bullshit baffles brains." [mock-Latin catch phrase; British military, 1900s, *Dictionary of Slang and Unconventional English*]

excuse me, the a toilet; a bathroom; a restroom. Rhyming slang for W.C. [British and U.S. slang and euphemism, 1900s]

excuse oneself leave the room to go to the W.C. with or without making a formal excuse for one's departure. [U.S. euphemism, 1900s]

execution the carrying out of a judicial order of punishment. Now usually in reference to the death penalty. Extended from the notion of executing a sentence of death to the actual killing of a person. [since the 1300s] Synonyms and related terms: BURYING ALIVE, DEMEMBRATION, DISEMBOWEL, DRAWN AND QUARTERED, DROWNING, ELECTRIC CURE, EMPALEMENT, EVENTRATION, EXCARNIFICATION, EXENTERATION, GANCH, LAPIDATION.

exercise the dog (also **walk the dog**) to accompany an urban dog when it goes out to eliminate. [1900s]

exhibitionism 1. any type of showing-off to get attention. No negative connotations. **2.** male exhibitionism; the exhibition of the male genitals. A pathological act arising from castration anxieties. A male exposes his genitals in public to prove that he is not castrated. The penis may be erect and masturbation may precede, accompany, or follow the act; total nudity is relatively rare.

exitus* death, especially death from disease. [medical]

expecting (also **expectant**) pregnant; expecting a child. For synonyms see FRAGRANT. [British and U.S. colloquial, late 1800s-pres.]

expectorate to spit. Often used euphemistically in avoidance of "spit."

expire to die; to breathe out one's last breath. For synonyms see DEPART. [since the mid 1400s]

explicit sex the detailed portrayal of homosexual and heterosexual sexual acts. [U.S., mid 1900s-pres.]

exposure of the person the intentional exposure of the naked body or the private parts of a person for shock or corrupt purposes.

express a secret vice to masturbate. For synonyms see WASTE TIME. [British euphemism, 1800s]

extract the urine from to TAKE THE PISS OUT OF SOMEONE (*q.v.*). [British military, early 1900s, *Dictionary of Slang and Unconventional English*]

extracurricular activities adultery. [British and U.S. colloquial, 1900s]

eye 1. the anus in reference to anal copulation. **2.** anal copulation, usually PEDERASTY (*q.v.*). [both senses, U.S. slang, mid 1900s-pres.] **3.** a breast. See BIG BROWN EYES, EYES.

eyeball palace a homosexual bar; any place where homosexual males can meet one another. *Cf.* EYE SHOP. [U.S. homosexual use, mid 1900s-pres.]

eye doctor a sodomite. *Cf.* EYE (sense 2). [U.S. underworld, early 1900s, Montelone]

eye-hole the external opening of the urethra. [British, 1800s, *Dictionary of Slang and Unconventional English*]

eye-opener 1. the penis. [British slang, 1800s, Farmer and Henley] **2.** a PEDERAST (*q.v.*). *Cf.* BROWN-EYE, EYE (sense 2). [U.S. slang, 1900s] **3.** a substance which gives a charge or a jolt, such as a drink of alcohol, an amphetamine tablet, or even a cold shower. [U.S. drug culture and general slang, mid 1900s-pres.]

eyes the breasts; the nipples. A reference to the nipples. An obvious avoidance in expressions such as "And she's got two beautiful, big brown—uh—eyes." See BIG BROWN EYES. [U.S. slang, 1900s]

eye shop to shop with the eyes, to seek a homosexual partner through prolonged eye contact. *Cf.* EYEBALL PALACE. [U.S. homosexual use, mid 1900s, Farrell]

eye that weeps most when best pleased the female genitals; the vagina. Refers to a woman's sexual secretions. For synonyms see MONOSYLLABLE. [British slang, 1800s, Farmer and Henley]

eyewash 1. nonsense. For synonyms see ANIMAL. **2.** alcohol. [both senses, U.S. slang, 1900s or before]

eye-water gin. For synonyms see RUIN. [British slang, 1800s, Egan's Grose]

Eyties a derogatory nickname for Italians. From "Eyetalians." [World War II]

F

F. an abbreviation or a disguise for FUCK or FUCKING (both *q.v.*). [colloquial, 1900s and before]

face a derogatory term for a Caucasian. A truncation of PALEFACE (*q.v.*). *Cf.* PALE. For synonyms see PECKERWOOD. [U.S., 1900s, Wentworth and Flexner]

faced intoxicated with alcohol. A truncation of SHIT-FACED (*q.v.*). [U.S. slang, mid 1900s-pres., *Current Slang*]

face queen a homosexual male who is attracted to men's faces. See QUEEN for similar terms. [U.S. homosexual use, mid 1900s, Farrell]

factotum the female genitals, "that which controls everything." *Cf.* REGULATOR. [British, 1800s, Farmer and Henley]

fade 1. a Caucasian. From the Negro point of view. Derogatory. *Cf.* PALE. For synonyms see PECKERWOOD. [U.S. colloquial, 1900s] **2.** a Negro who acts like a Caucasian. Derogatory. *Cf.* COOKIE (sense 1), OREO. [U.S., 1900s] **3.** to die. [U.S. euphemism]

faded boogie a black who has taken on (undesirable) Caucasian characteristics. Derogatory. *Cf.* BOOGIE (sense 2). [both Negro and Caucasian use; U.S., early 1900s]

fag 1. an effeminate male; a sissy. **2.** a homosexual male. [senses 1 and 2 are U.S. underworld and general slang, early 1900s-pres.] **3.** a CATAMITE (*q.v.*). Senses 1-3 are from FAGGOT (sense 6). [early 1900s-pres.] **4.** the penis. From FAGGOT (sense 1), *i.e.*, "a stick." [U.S. slang, 1900s, Berrey and Van den Bark] **5.** a pimp. An epithet referring to the effeminate attire of some pimps. [U.S., 1900s]

fag-bag a woman who consorts with a homosexual male. *Cf.* FAG-HAG. [U.S. slang, mid 1900s]

fag-factory a gathering place for male homosexuals. [U.S., early 1900s]

faggart a homosexual male; an obsessive practitioner of nonorthogenital sexual acts. For synonyms see EPICENE. [U.S., early 1900s]

faggot (also **faggit, fagot**) **1.** a term of contempt for a person. Literally, "a bag of sticks." [from French; 1300s] **2.** a strong term of contempt for a woman, especially an old or dissipated woman. [British, late 1500s-1800s] **3.** a prostitute. For synonyms see HARLOT. [British and U.S., 1800s-1900s]. **4.** to copulate with a woman. *Cf.* FAG (sense 4). [British slang, 1800s, Farmer and Henley] **5.** to womanize; to consort with sexually loose women. [British slang, 1800s] **6.** a male homosexual. Usually considered a strongly derogatory term. For synonyms see EPICENE. [U.S. slang, early 1900s-pres.] **7.** a derisive term of contempt for a nonhomosexual male. *Cf.* FAIRY (sense 4). [U.S., 1900s] **8.** an unattractive young woman. Possibly from sense 2. For synonyms see BUFFARILLA. [U.S. slang, mid 1900s, *Current Slang*]

faggoteer (also **faggotmaster**) a lecher; a whoremonger. From FAGGOT (sense 5). [British slang, 1800s, Farmer and Henley]

faggotry homosexuality (usually male); the world of homosexuals. *Cf.* FAGGOT (sense 6). [U.S. slang, mid 1900s]

faggoty effeminate; in the manner of an effeminate male homosexual. [U.S. slang, early 1900s, Goldin, O'Leary, and Lipsius]

fag-hag a heterosexual female who consorts with homosexual males for sex or for safety. *Cf.* FAG-BAG. [U.S. slang, mid 1900s-pres.]

fag-joint a meeting place for homosexual males. *Cf.* FAG-FACTORY. [U.S. slang, early 1900s-pres.]

fag-mag a magazine or other publication featuring male nudity for homosexual males. [U.S., mid 1900s-pres., Farrell]

fail in the furrow to become impotent while copulating. *Cf.* FALL IN THE FURROW. [British, 1800s]

fair play fornication; copulation where neither partner is married to anyone. *Cf.* FOUL PLAY. [British slang, 1800s, Farmer and Henley]

fair sex the female sex; women in general. [1900s and before]

fairy 1. a jaded and debauched old woman. [British, 1800s, Ware] **2.** an effeminate male. [U.S. colloquial, early 1900s-pres.] **3.** a male homosexual or any male practitioner of nonorthogenital sexual acts. For synonyms see EPICENE. [U.S. and elsewhere, early 1900s-pres.] **4.** a term of contempt for a nonhomosexual male; the same as FAGGOT (sense 7). [U.S., 1900s] **5.** a pretty young woman. [colloquial, 1900s or before]

fairy lady a lesbian in the passive role. [U.S. slang, mid 1900s]

fairy nice homosexual. From "very nice." [U.S. slang, mid 1900s-pres.]

faker a pimp; a PONCE (*q.v.*). [British slang, 1800s, Farmer and Henley]

fall to conceive; to become pregnant. *Cf.* CATCH (sense 2). [British colloquial, 1800s, Farmer and Henley]

fallen woman a prostitute. [U.S. euphemism, 1900s]

falling apart pregnant; getting ready to DROP (*q.v.*). *Cf.* FALL TO PIECES. [U.S. dialect (Ozarks), Randolph and Wilson]

falling-down drunk intoxicated with alcohol; drunk and stumbling. [colloquial, 1900s and before]

fall in the furrow to ejaculate, perhaps to ejaculate prematurely. *Cf.* DIE IN THE FURROW, FAIL IN THE FURROW. The furrow is the PUDENDAL CLEAVAGE (*q.v.*). [British slang, 1800s, Farmer and Henley]

fall off the roof to begin the menses. *Cf.* ROOF, OFF THE. [U.S. colloquial, early 1900s-pres.]

fall-out the public exposure of the breasts due to their shifting to the outside of a bikini top. From the frequently heard expression "nuclear fallout." *Cf.* HANGOVER (sense 2). [mid 1900s, *Dictionary of Slang and Unconventional English*]

fall to pieces to give birth. *Cf.* DROP, FALLING APART. [Australian, early 1900s, Baker]

false hereafter a bustle. [U.S. euphemism, 1800s]

false pregnancy a state including some of the symptoms of a pregnancy caused by the growth of a tumor or a mole. [medical]

falsies 1. false breasts; pads or forms which have the effect of making the breasts appear larger and more shapely. *Cf.* NIAGARA FALSIES. **2.** false buttocks or other body padding designed to make one's body more sexually attractive. [both senses, U.S. colloquial, early 1900s-pres.]

fam to feel or grope a woman. From the cant term for hand, "fam." [cant, 1700s-1800s]

familiars lice. In the sense of "intimate friends." *Cf.* BOSOM CHUMS. [British slang, 1800s, Farmer and Henley]

familiar-way pregnant. A jocular play on "family way." For synonyms see FRAGRANT. [British and U.S. colloquial, 1800s-1900s]

familiar with, to be to be sexually intimate with; to copulate with. [euphemistic, since the mid 1400s]

family disturbance whisky or other strong alcoholic drink. [U.S. slang, 1800s]

family jewels 1. the testicles. So named for their great value and their role in creating a family. *Cf.* DIAMONDS. [U.S. slang, 1900s] **2.** the male genitals. Less well-known than sense 1. [U.S. slang, 1900s]

family of love prostitutes in general; lewd women. A play on the name of a fanatical religious sect in England (mid 1500s). [cant, 1600s-1700s, B.E.]

family organ the penis. A euphemism of avoidance. *Cf.* FAMILY JEWELS. [U.S. colloquial, 1900s or before]

family way, in a pregnant. *Cf.* FAMILIAR-WAY. [widespread colloquial, 1800s-1900s]

fan 1. the female genitals. From FANNY (sense 1). [British slang, mid 1900s] **2.** to coit a woman; to cool a woman's ardor. [Caribbean (Jamaican), Cassidy and Le Page]

fancy-bit the female genitals. For synonyms see MONOSYLLABLE. [British slang, 1800s, Farmer and Henley]

fancy house a brothel. [British slang, 1800s, Farmer and Henley]

fancy-Joseph a prostitute's PIMP or PONCE (both *q.v.*). [British slang, 1800s, Farmer and Henley]

fancy man a PIMP or PONCE (both *q.v.*). Originally a term for a ladies' man. [British and U.S., early 1800s-1900s]

fancy piece a prostitute. For synonyms see HARLOT. [British slang, early 1800s, Egan's Grose]

fancy woman a prostitute or a mistress. [since the mid 1800s]

fancy-work the male genitals and pubic area. [British, 1800s]

fang-carpenter a dentist. [Australian, 1900s, Baker]

fang-faker a dentist. [British slang or cant, 1800s, Farmer and Henley]

fang-farrier a dentist; a dental surgeon. *Cf.* FANG-CARPENTER. [nautical, 1900s or before]

fanny 1. the female genitals. [British slang, mid 1800s-pres.] **2.** the posteriors. The meaning "posteriors" occurs only in a secondary sense as with ARSE, ASS, RUMP (all *q.v.*). [U.S. colloquial, early 1900s-pres.]

fanny-artful a nickname for the female genitals; an elaboration of FANNY (sense 1). For synonyms see MONOSYLLABLE. [British slang, 1800s]

fanny-fair the female genitals. [British slang, 1800s]

fanny rag a sanitary cloth or napkin; a perineal pad. For synonyms see MANHOLE COVER. [Australian, mid 1900s,

Dictionary of Slang and Unconventional English]

fap intoxicated with alcohol. For synonyms see WOOFLED. [from *Merry Wives of Windsor* (Shakespeare)]

farahead a drunkard or a person intoxicated in a particular instance; someone who is "far ahead" in his drinking. [U.S. slang, early 1900s, Weseen]

far and near beer; a glass of beer. Rhyming slang for "beer." For synonyms see SUDS. [British and U.S. slang, 1900s]

farg an effeminate male homosexual. A permutation of FAG (sense 2). *Cf.* FAGGART. [British, 1900s, *Dictionary of the Underworld*]

Farmer Giles hemorrhoids. Rhyming slang for "piles." [Australian, mid 1900s, *Dictionary of Slang and Unconventional English*]

fart 1. to release intestinal gas. [since the 1200s] **2.** an audible or inaudible release of intestinal gas; a breaking of wind. [since the 1300s] **3.** a term of contempt implying that the addressee is worthless. [since the 1500s]

fart about to waste time; to goof off; the same as FART AROUND (*q.v.*). [British, 1800s-1900s]

fart around to waste time; to goof off. *Cf.* FART ABOUT. [U.S. colloquial, 1900s]

fart-blossom an oaf; a stupid person; the equivalent of TURD (sense 2). [U.S. slang, mid 1900s]

fart-catcher 1. a footman; a servant who follows his master closely enough to be aware of his master's breaking of wind. *Cf.* CATCH-FART. [British, late 1700s, Grose] **2.** a PEDERAST (*q.v.*). From the position associated with coiting *per anum*. [written nonce; British, early 1900s, *Dictionary of Slang and Unconventional English*]

fart-Daniel the female genitals. For synonyms see MONOSYLLABLE. [British slang, 1800s, Farmer and Henley]

fart hole an oaf; a real jerk; the equivalent of ASS-HOLE (*q.v.*). [U.S. slang, mid 1900s-pres.]

fartick a small release of intestinal gas; "a little fart." *Cf.* FARTKIN. [British, 1800s or before]

farting-clapper the anus. Refers to crepitation. [British, 1800s]

farting-crackers breeches; trousers. For synonyms see GALLIGASKINS. [British slang or cant, late 1600s, B.E.]

farting-spell a very short period of time. Based on the amount of time it takes for released intestinal gas to dissipate or other similar analogies. *Cf.* PISSING-WHILE. [U.S. dialect, 1800s, Green]

fartkin a small FART (sense 1). *Cf.* FARTICK. [British slang, 1800s, Farmer and Henley]

fartleberry fecal matter clinging to the anal hairs. *Cf.* CHUFF-NUT, DINGLE-BERRY. [British, late 1700s, Grose]

fartlicker a low rascal; a sycophant. [British, 1700s or before]

fart off to goof off. See FART ABOUT, FART AROUND. [U.S. slang, mid 1900s]

fart-sucker a sycophant; the same as BUMSUCKER (*q.v.*). [British slang, 1800s, Farmer and Henley]

fast amoral; wanton; easily encouraged to participate in sexual activity. *Cf.* SLOW (sense 1). [since the 1700s]

fast-fuck 1. a rapid act of copulation or one done very vigorously. **2.** a person who participates in rapid copulation. [both senses, slang and nonce, 1800s-1900s]

fast house a brothel. [British and U.S., 1800s-early 1900s]

fast life prostitution. [U.S. euphemism, 1900s]

fast woman (also **fast-fanny**) a strumpet; a prostitute. *Cf.* FAST. [British and U.S., 1800s-pres.]

fat-assed (also **fat-arsed**) **1.** with very large or fat buttocks. **2.** a generally derisive term applied to anyone who is lazy or unpleasant. [both senses, British and U.S., 1800s-pres.]

fat cock female genitals with extremely large *labia minora*. From COCK (sense 6). *Cf.* COW-CUNTED, DOUBLE-SUCKER.

[British slang, 1800s, Farmer and Henley]

fat-head an oaf; one whose brain is composed of fat and is therefore useless. [since the mid 1800s]

father-confessor the penis. For synonyms see YARD. [British slang, 1800s, Farmer and Henley]

father-fucker a PEDERAST (*q.v.*); a contemptuous term of address; patterned on MOTHER-FUCKER (*q.v.*). [U.S. homosexual use, mid 1900s]

father-stuff the male seed in a figurative sense; semen. [not in general use; from "Song of Myself," *Leaves of Grass* (Walt Whitman)]

fat jay a fat joint; a fat marijuana cigarette. *Cf.* J. (sense 1). [U.S. drug culture, mid 1900s-pres.]

fatty 1. a derogatory nickname for a fat person. [British and U.S. since the 1800s or before] **2.** a thick marijuana cigarette. [U.S. drug culture, mid 1900s-pres.]

fatty cake a young woman with a plump, well-rounded figure. Patterned on "patty cake," a children's game.

fat-un (also **fat-one**) an extremely loud and bad-smelling breaking of wind; a ROUSER (*q.v.*). *Cf.* CHEEZER, WET ONE. [British slang, 1800s, Farmer and Henley]

faucett the female genitals. *Cf.* COCK (sense 6). [British slang, 1800s, Farmer and Henley]

faunlet (also **faunet**) an attractive, postadolescent male viewed as a potential sexual partner by a homosexual male; a CHICKEN (sense 2). The opposite of a nymphet or NYMPH (sense 2). [U.S. slang, mid 1900s, Wentworth and Flexner]

favor, the copulation thought of as a gift granted by the female to the male; the same as the ULTIMATE FAVOR (*q.v.*). [1800s-1900s]

fay 1. a derogatory nickname for a Caucasian from the point of view of a Negro. *Cf.* BLACK FAY, OFAY. For synonyms see PECKERWOOD. **2.** a Caucasian who seeks the association of blacks. [both senses, U.S., 1900s]

feague (also **feak**) a filthy, slatternly person of either sex. [mid 1600s]

feak 1. the anus. [British 1800s or before, *Lexicon Balatronicum*] **2.** a filthy man or woman; the same as FEAGUE (*q.v.*). Related to sense 1.

fearnought a condom. *Cf.* DREAD-NOUGHT. For synonyms see EEL-SKIN. [British, 1900s]

fears no man intoxicated with alcohol. *Cf.* DUTCH COURAGE. [U.S. slang, early 1700s, Ben Franklin]

feather the female pubic hair. Possibly related to COCK (sense 6). [British, 1700s]

feather-bed jig coition. *Cf.* DANCE THE MATTRESS JIG. For synonyms see SMOCK-AGE. [British slang, 1800s or before]

feather-bed soldier an expert whoremonger. For synonyms see LECHER. [British colloquial, 1800s or before]

featured intoxicated with alcohol. For synonyms see WOOFLED. [U.S., early 1900s]

fecal-freak a type of nonorthogenital sex practitioner who is sexually stimulated (possibly to orgasm) by fecal material. This may include the ingestion of fecal material. [U.S., 1900s]

fecks!, I' an oath, "In faith!" For synonyms see 'ZOUNDS!

fed-up and far from home a euphemism for "fucked-up and far from home."

feeding-bottles the breasts. From the British expression for "baby-bottle." *Cf.* CREAM-JUGS, DAIRIES. [British colloquial, 1800s, Farmer and Henley]

feed the dumb-glutton to copulate, from the point of view of the male. *Cf.* DUMB-GLUTTON. [British slang, 1800s, Farmer and Henley]

feed the dummy to copulate. The "dummy" here is the DUMB-GLUTTON (*q.v.*), "vagina." See DUMMY (sense 2). [British slang, 1800s, Farmer and Henley]

feel (also **feel-up**) to explore or stimu-

late the vagina, breasts, or virilia of another person. [since the 1700s]

feel fuzzy to be sexually aroused; a variant of FEEL HAIRY (*q.v.*). [U.S. slang, 1900s]

feel gay to feel sexually aroused. *Cf.* GAY (sense 1). [British, 1800s and before, Farmer and Henley]

feel hairy to be sexually aroused. *Cf.* FEEL FUZZY. For synonyms see HUMPY. [British and later, U.S. slang, mid 1800s-pres.]

feeling good intoxicated with alcohol. Recently, intoxicated with drugs or drugs and alcohol. [colloquial euphemism, mid 1800s-pres.]

feeling no pain intoxicated with alcohol, drugs, or both. [mid 1900s-pres.]

feeling poorly (also **feeling unwell**) experiencing the menses. An expression describing mild, nonspecific disorders. For synonyms see FLOODS.

feelthy pictures sexually tantalizing or pornographic pictures. The first word is in imitation of a non-English accent. Refers to the speech of peddlers of obscene pictures in seaports and occupied countries. [U.S. and British, 1900s]

feel-up (also **feel**) to caress sexually. [U.S. colloquial, 1900s]

feeze (also **feaze, feize, pheeze**) to copulate; to SCREW (sense 1). For synonyms see OCCUPY. [British, early 1600s-1800s]

felch (also **feltch**) to perform ANILINGUS (*q.v.*) on a male. [U.S. homosexual use, mid 1900s, Farrell]

felch queen (also **feltch queen**) **1.** one who obtains sexual gratification from coming into close contact with fecal matter. *Cf.* FECAL-FREAK. **2.** a homosexual male who specializes in performing ANILINGUS (*q.v.*). [both senses, U.S. homosexual use, mid 1900s]

fellate to perform PENILINGUS (*q.v.*). [nonce or a neologism; U.S., mid 1900s, (Humphreys)]

fellatio (also **fellation**) PENILINGUS (*q.v.*); the act of one person (a man or a woman) sucking, licking, kissing, or nibbling the penis of a man. The act may lead to orgasm, but the term is also used to refer to sexual stimulation of the male in preparation for other types of sexual activity. [from the Latin for "suck" in an obscene sense]

fellatrice 1. a MOUTH-WHORE (q.v.); a prostitute who performs FELLATIO (q.v.). **2.** a professional female CUNNILINGUIST (q.v.). [assumed to be in error; late 1800s, Farmer] **3.** a female performer of fellatio; a female RECEIVER (q.v.) in contexts other than in prostitution.

fellatrix 1. a male RECEIVER (q.v.) in fellatio. Cf. FELLATRICE. This is in the feminine form, but it appears in Stedmann in reference to a male. **2.** a female performer of FELLATIO (q.v.); the same as FELLATRICE (sense 3).

fellatrix of women a lesbian; a woman who performs CUNNILINGUS (q.v.). [late 1800s, (Farmer)]

fell of a hix a deliberate spoonerism of "hell of a fix." Cf. MELL OF A HESS. [U.S. colloquial and euphemistic, early 1900s, Weseen]

female pudendum (also **female pudend**) the female genitals. Usually "female *pudendum*." Literally, "that about which one ought to be modest or ashamed." PUDENDUM (q.v.) can be used by itself, and usually refers to the female parts. [Latin]

female spendings vaginal secretions or vaginal secretions and ejaculated semen. Cf. SPENDINGS. [British, 1800s, (Farmer and Henley)] Synonyms: CONCOMITANT OF DESIRE, CUNT-JUICE, GOOSE-GREASE, GRAVY, OIL OF GIBLETS, OIL OF HORN, SEXUAL DISCHARGE, SEXUAL SECRETION, VAGINA-JUICE.

female trouble (also **female disorder, female problem**) **1.** various physical and mental disabilities known to occur in women, *i.e.*, the menopause, severe menstrual cramps, etc. **2.** the menses. [both senses, U.S. euphemism, 1900s]

female verenda the female genitals; the female "parts of shame." Usually "female *verenda*." For synonyms see

MONOSYLLABLE. [Latin; euphemistic, 1800s, or before, Halliwell]

femme (also **fem**) **1.** any woman or girl. [from French; U.S. slang, early 1900s] **2.** a passive female homosexual. [U.S. slang, mid 1900s-pres.] **3.** a male homosexual in the passive role; a CATAMITE (q.v.) or the receiver in fellatio; an effeminate male homosexual. [U.S., 1900s]

femme D. a female medical doctor. Contrived rhyming slang for "M.D." [U.S. slang, mid 1900s]

femme fatale a vamp; a seductress. [from French; U.S., 1900s]

fen a prostitute. For synonyms see HARLOT. [cant, 1600s, B.E.]

fender-bender a barbiturate tablet or capsule, especially Seconal (trademark). From a slang term for a minor automobile collision. For synonyms see BARB. [U.S. drug culture, mid 1900s-pres.]

ferblet an effeminate or weak male. Cf. FRIBBLE. [1300s, Shipley]

ferret 1. to coit a woman. **2.** the penis in expressions such as HIDE THE FERRET (q.v.). Cf. MOLE. [both senses, British slang, 1800s, Farmer and Henley]

ferry a prostitute. Because she carries many men. [Australian and British, early 1900s]

fetch 1. the manifestation of the spirit of a person; a wraith. [since the 1700s] **2.** semen. Cf. FETCH METTLE. For synonyms see METTLE. [British and elsewhere, 1800s, *Dictionary of Slang and Unconventional English*]

fetch mettle to masturbate; to bring forth semen. Cf. FETCH (sense 2). [British, 1600s]

fettered intoxicated with alcohol. [U.S. slang, early 1700s, Ben Franklin] See also GOOD FETTLE, IN.

fettle to coit a woman. From a standard term meaning "scour." [British, 1800s, *Dictionary of Slang and Unconventional English*]

fey 1. a homosexual male. For synonyms see EPICENE. [U.S. slang, 1900s] **2.** a Caucasian. See FAY.

fice (also **foist, foyce, foyse, foyst, fyst**) a strong-smelling but inaudible breaking of wind. *Cf.* BLIND FART, FOYST. For synonyms see GURK. [British, late 1700s-1800s]

fiddle 1. to cheat or swindle. *Cf.* DIDDLE (sense 7). 2. the female genitals. The FIDDLE-BOW (*q.v.*) is the penis. *Cf.* BUM FIDDLE. (sense 3). [British, 1800s] 3. to play sexually. *Cf.* FIRKY-TOODLE. [British and U.S. since the 1800s] 4. to copulate. [British slang, 1800s]

fiddle-bow the penis, a bow for the FIDDLE (sense 2). *Cf.* BOW. For synonyms see YARD. [British slang, 1800s, Farmer and Henley]

fiddle-cup a drunkard. For synonyms see ALCHY. [British slang, 1800s, Farmer and Henley]

fiddled intoxicated with alcohol. [U.S. slang, 1900s, Weseen]

fiddlededee nonsense. For synonyms see ANIMAL. [since the late 1700s]

fiddle-faddle (also **fiddle-cum-faddle**) 1. to utter nonsense; to talk idly. [since the early 1600s] 2. nonsense. Also **fible-fable**. [since the 1600s]

fiddle-farting wasting time; messing around. Similar to MONKEY-FARTING (*q.v.*). A blend of "fiddling around" and "farting around." [U.S. slang, mid 1900s-pres.]

fiddlestick 1. the penis; the same as FIDDLE-BOW (*q.v.*). *Cf.* FIDDLE (sense 2). 2. in the plural, nonsense. [since the mid 1800s]

Fie! an oath and an exclamation. Also well-known in its extended forms, "Fie, fie, a pox on you!" or "Fie for shame!" Supposedly onomatopoetic for a sound of disgust made upon smelling a bad smell. [currently in jocular uses; since the 1200s, *Oxford English Dictionary*]

fie-for-shame the female genitals. A catch phrase reminding a girl (usually of school age) that her genitals should be covered. From the exclamation "Fie for shame!" [British, early 1800s, Farmer and Henley]

field colt, old a bastard. *Cf.* WOODS-COLT. [U.S. dialect, 1900s or before]

field nigger (also **field Negro**) 1. a farm slave. 2. a derogatory term for a Negro. *Cf.* HOUSE NIGGER. [both senses, U.S., 1800s-1900s]

field-whore a very low and common prostitute, one who will work anywhere. *Cf.* HEDGE-WHORE. [British, 1800s or before, Halliwell]

fiend 1. the devil. [since *c.* 1000, *Oxford English Dictionary*] Synonyms: APOLLYON, ARCH-FIEND, AULD HORNIE, AUTHOR OF EVIL, AVERNUS, BAD MAN, BEELZEBUB, BELIAL, BLACKGENTLEMAN, BLACK-SPY, BUGGAR-MAN, CLOOTS, DAR-BLE, DIABLO, DIABOLARCH, DIABOLUS, DIAVOLO, DIBBLE, DICKENS, DIVEL, DIVIL, D---L, FALLEN ANGEL, FATHER OF LIES, GENTLEMAN IN BLACK, GOODMAN, HIS SATANIC MAJESTY, HOBB, LORD HARRY, LUCIFER, MEPHISTOPHELES, MIFFY, NI-CHOLAS, NICKEY, OLD BENDY, OLD BILLY, OLD BLAZES, OLD BOOTS, OLD BOY, OLD CAIN, OLD CLOOTIE, OLD DAD, OLD DRIV-ER, OLD GENTLEMAN, OLD GOOSEBER-RY, OLD HARRY, OLD HORNY, OLD LAD, OLD NED, OLD NICK, OLD NICK BOGEY, OLD POGER, OLD POKER, OLD ROGER, OLD ROUND-FOOT, OLD RUFFIN, OLD SCRATCH, OLD SERPENT, OLD SPLIT-FOOT, OLD TOAST, PRINCE OF DARKNESS, QUEED, RAGAMUFFIN, RAGMAN, RUFFIAN, SAINT NICHOLAS, SAM HILL, SATAN, SCRATCH, SKIPPER, TANTARABOBS, THE BLACK-MAN, THE BLACK PRINCE, THE DARK ONE, THE DEUCE, THE EVIL ONE, THE NOSELESS ONE, THE OLD ONE, THE WICKED ONE, TITIVIL, TOAST, TOOT, WAR-LOCK. 2. a person who is obsessed with specific things or activities. [U.S., late 1800s-pres.]

fife and drum a hobo; a person of low character. Rhyming slang for BUM (*q.v.*). [British, 1900s, *Dictionary of Rhyming Slang*]

fifteen and two a Jewish man or woman. Rhyming slang for "Jew." Not necessarily derogatory. For synonyms see FIVE AND TWO. [British, mid 1900s, *Dictionary of Rhyming Slang*] fig　　　　　　　　141　　　　　　　finger-fuck

fig the female genitals. Possibly from the fig leaf theme, *i.e.*, that which the fig leaf covers. Also possibly ironic for something worthless, as in the expression "not worth a fig." [British slang, 1800s, Farmer and Henley]

fight one's turkey to masturbate. *Cf.* GOOSE'S-NECK. For synonyms see WASTE TIME. [British slang, 1800s, Farmer and Henley]

figure the breasts and buttocks of a woman, considered for their shapeliness and appeal. [since the 1800s]

figure-fancier a man who favors WELL-BUILT (*q.v.*) women. *Cf.* TIT-MAN. [British slang, 1800s, Farmer and Henley]

figure-maker a lecher; a whoremonger; a man who enlarges the figures of women by impregnating them. [British, late 1800s, Farmer and Henley]

file a young woman, especially a young harlot. [an early spelling of the French *fille*; in English by the 1300s, *Oxford English Dictionary*]

fill in to impregnate a woman; to fill a woman's womb. For synonyms see STORK. [colloquial and nonce; attested as Australian, 1900s, *Dictionary of Slang and Unconventional English*]

fill in for to serve a woman sexually as a substitute for her lover. Refers both to "substitution," as implied by the idiomatic interpretation, and "filling" a woman sexually. [colloquial and nonce]

fill one's pants 1. to defecate in one's pants out of fear or prolonged delay. **2.** to defecate in a diaper, said of a baby. [both senses, U.S., 1900s]

filly a girl, especially a wanton girl. *Cf.* FILE. [from the French *fille*; since the mid 1600s; U.S. stereotypical Western jargon, early 1900s]

filly-hunting chasing women for sexual purposes. [British slang, 1800s, Farmer and Henley]

filth 1. pus; corruption. **2.** obscenity. [both senses, since *c.* 1000, *Oxford English Dictionary*] **3.** a prostitute, especially an old prostitute. [1400s-1600s] **4.** dung; carrion. See DIRT (sense 1).

final resting place a cemetery; one's grave. *Cf.* LAST HOME. For synonyms see LAST ABODE.

find to give birth to. Usually said of animals, as in "the cat found her kittens." *Cf.* CAST (sense 2), DROP (sense 1). [U.S. dialect and colloquial, 1900s and before]

F-ing (also **effing**) a disguise of FUCKING (*q.v.*). [U.S. slang, mid 1900s-pres.]

F-ing around goofing off; FUCKING AROUND (*q.v.*). [U.S. slang, mid 1900s-pres.]

finger 1. to caress a woman sexually. For synonyms see FIRKYTOODLE. [1800s-1900s] **2.** to masturbate the vagina. *Cf.* FINGER-FUCK. [since the 1600s] **3.** to give someone the finger. [U.S. slang, mid 1900s-pres.] **4.** "the finger," a specific obscene gesture. See FINGER, THE. [U.S., mid 1900s-pres.]

finger, the a curse expressed as a gesture. The form of the gesture in its undisguised state consists of the middle finger pointed straight up with the remaining fingers clinched in a fist. Variations include some type of concealment or attenuation of the gesture or making it ambiguous by mixing it with other gestures. The verbalization of the curse is assumed to be "Fuck you!" or "Stick it up your ass!" The upright finger is assumed to symbolize the erect penis. *Cf.* BONE (sense 1). In the 1970s the "free speech movement" and the frequent use of this gesture by defiant children and youths has weakened its potence. The gesture was known in Ancient Rome. [1900s]

finger and thumb rum; a glass of gin. Rhyming slang for "rum." For synonyms see RUIN. [British, late 1800s-early 1900s]

finger artist a male or female homosexual who favors masturbating others. [U.S. homosexual use, mid 1900s]

fingerer one who plays with one's own or someone else's genitals. [British and some U.S. use, 1800s-1900s]

finger-fuck to masturbate a woman by inserting a finger into the vagina.

This may be done by a man, the woman, or another woman. *Cf.* FUCK-FINGER. [British and U.S., 1800s-1900s]

finger-job an act of sexual play possibly leading to orgasm. The finger is used to stimulate the vagina or anus. [U.S., mid 1900s-pres.]

finger wave the FINGER (*q.v.*). *Cf.* BIRD (sense 4), BONE, ONE-FINGER SALUTE. [U.S., mid 1900s-pres.]

fink 1. a guard hired to protect strikebreakers. **2.** a strikebreaker. **3.** a stool pigeon. **4.** to inform on illegal activity. **5.** any undesirable oaf or jerk. All are derived from sense 1. [all senses, U.S. slang, early 1900s-pres.]

finkydiddle sexual play; sexual foreplay. See FIRKYTOODLE. [British, 1900s, *Dictionary of Slang and Unconventional English*]

fire 1. sexual excitement. *Cf.* HEAT (sense 1). [since the 1400s] **2.** syphilis [British, 1900s, Farmer and Henley]

fire and damnation hell. An avoidance for "hellfire and damnation." [U.S. colloquial since the 1800s]

fire a shot to ejaculate. *Cf.* SHOT (sense 2). For synonyms see MELT. [British slang, 1800s, Farmer and Henley]

fire blanks 1. to coit to ejaculation but fail to impregnate. **2.** to ejaculate sterile semen. Occurs in joking about the seduction of a woman by a man who claims he is sterile. *Cf.* I.O.F.B. [U.S. slang, mid 1900s-pres.]

firebrand the penis. *Cf.* BLOWTORCH, TORCH OF CUPID. [British slang, 1800s, Farmer and Henley]

fired-up intoxicated with alcohol. For synonyms see WOOFLED. [since the mid 1800s]

fire escape a clergyman. Because his ministrations will save one from the fires of hell. For synonyms see SKY-PILOT. [British slang, 1800s, Farmer and Henley]

fire insurance agent a clergyman; the same as FIRE ESCAPE (*q.v.*). [U.S. slang, early 1900s, Weseen]

fire in the air 1. to have a premature ejaculation. **2.** to have any ejaculation outside the vagina, especially ejaculation from masturbation. *Cf.* SHOOT IN THE BUSH. [both senses, British slang, 1800s, Farmer and Henley]

firelock the female genitals. Named for an early rifle which required rubbing to produce sparks to ignite the primary. [British slang, 1800s, Farmer and Henley]

fire-plug a male infected with venereal disease, usually gonorrhea. Refers to the burning felt in the urethra. From the nickname for a fire hydrant. *Cf.* PLUG (sense 3), which refers to the penis. [British slang, early 1800s, John Bee]

fire queen a sadist who burns other people to arouse sexual pleasure. [U.S. slang, 1900s]

firewater alcohol. So named because it burns the throat like fire, or because it could be ignited if the proof were high enough. Said to be a word used by American Indians. Possibly an English translation of an American Indian word. For synonyms see BOOZE. [U.S. stereotypical American Indian jargon and U.S. slang, early 1800s-pres.]

fireworks an orgasm. *Cf.* DRAW HIS FIREWORKS. [slang and nonce, 1800s-pres.]

firk (also **ferk, furk**) to copulate. Currently a frequently-heard disguise of FUCK (*q.v.*). From a word meaning "beat." [since the 1600s]

firkin 1. a gadget, the FUCKING (*q.v.*) or "firking" thing. [British military, early 1900s, *Dictionary of Slang and Unconventional English*] **2.** "fucking." Also spelled "firking." [1900s]

firkytoodle 1. sexual play; sexual foreplay. **2.** to perform sexual play. *Cf.* FINKYDIDDLE. [both senses, British, 1700s-1800s] Synonyms and related terms for both senses: BRING ON, CANOE, CANOODLE, CARESS, CATERWAUL, CLITORIZE, CONTRECTATION, COP A FEEL, DALLY, DIDDLE, DILDO, FAM, FEEL, FEEL-UP, FIDDLE, FINGER, FINKYDIDDLE, FOREPLAY, FRISKING, FUDGE, FUMBLE, FUTZ AROUND, GET ONE'S HAND ON IT, GET OVER SOME-

ONE, GRABBLE, GRUBBLE, GUDDLE, HAN-
DLE, HORN, LING-GRAPPLING, LOVE UP,
MAKE LOVE, MEDDLE WITH, MESS ABOUT,
MIRD, MOUSE, MUGGING-UP, NECK, NETH-
ER-WORK, NUG, PADDLE, PAW, PET UP,
PITCH HONEY, PRACTICE IN THE MILKY-
WAY, RUMMAGE, SAMPLE, SEXAMINATION,
SEXUAL FOREPLAY, SPOON, SPRUNCH,
SPUNK UP, STROKE, THUMB, TICKLE, TIP
THE MIDDLE FINGER, TOUCH-UP, TOY.

first line morphine. For synonyms see
MORPH. [U.S. drug culture, mid 1900s-
pres.]

fish 1. a woman considered sexually;
probably the same as FLESH (sense 2).
[since the 1600s or before] **2.** a prostitute; an easy woman. [U.S. slang, mid
1900s] **3.** a heterosexual female. [U.S.
homosexual use, mid 1900s-pres.] **4.**
as an oath and an exclamation, "Fish!"
Probably "By God's flesh!" [British
dialects, 1800s or before] **5.** A Roman
Catholic. Derogatory. A truncation of
FISH-EATER (q.v.). [U.S. colloquial,
1900s or before] **6.** an oaf. [U.S. slang,
1900s or before] **7.** the female genitals.
Probably an extension of sense 4, i.e.,
the use of "fish" in avoidance for
"flesh." See FISH-MARKET. [British
slang, 1800s, Farmer and Henley] **8.**
the penis. [late 1800s-pres.]

fish and shrimp a pimp; a PONCE
(q.v.). Rhyming slang for "pimp."
[U.S., early 1900s, Montelone]

fish-eater a nickname for a Roman
Catholic. Derogatory. From the prac-
tice of eating fish rather than meat on
Fridays. Cf. MACKEREL-SNAPPER. [U.S.
slang, early 1900s-pres.] Synonyms:
BEAD-COUNTER, BEAD-PULLER, MICK,
PAPIST.

fishing rod the penis. From FISH (sense
7). For synonyms see YARD. [British
slang, 1800s, Dictionary of Slang and
Unconventional English]

fish-market a brothel; a low brothel
with bad-smelling whores. [British, mid
1800s]

fishmonger 1. a pimp or procurer. Cf.
FISH (sense 2). [since the 1500s] **2.** a
lecher; a whoremonger. [British, 1800s,
Farmer and Henley]

fish pond the female genitals. Cf. FISH
(sense 7), FISHING ROD. [U.S. slang,
mid 1900s]

fish-skin a condom. Cf. EEL-SKIN, FISH
(sense 8). [slang, 1900s]

fishwife the female wife or consort of
a homosexual male. Cf. FISH (sense 3).
Based on a term for an ill-tempered
woman. [U.S. slang, mid 1900s-pres.]

fishy about the gills intoxicated with
alcohol. Cf. GILLS, UP TO THE. [late
1800s-1900s, Ware]

fist-fuck 1. to masturbate, said of a
male. The opposite of FINGER-FUCK
(q.v.). Cf. FUCK ONE'S FIST. [British
slang, 1800s, Farmer and Henley] **2.** in
sadism, the insertion of a hand or
fingers into the rectum of a masochist.
[U.S., 1900s]

fist it to grasp a penis for masturbation
or as a guide for intromission, performed by a man or a woman. [British
slang, 1800s, Farmer and Henley]

fit ends to copulate. "End" refers to
the genitals, male or female. Cf. FIT
END TO END. [British slang, 1800s,
Farmer and Henley]

fit end to end to copulate. Cf. FIT
ENDS, MAKE ENDS MEET. [British slang,
1800s, Dictionary of Slang and Unconventional English]

five against one masturbation. The
"five" refers to the fingers. The "one"
is the phallus. [jocular nonce, 1900s or
before]

five and two (also **five, five by two**) a
Jewish man or woman. Rhyming slang
for "Jew." Not necessarily derogato-
ry. [British, early 1900s, Dictionary of
Rhyming Slang] Synonyms and related
terms: ABBIE, ABE, ABIE, BOX OF GLUE,
BUCKLE, BUCKLE MY SHOE, CHRIST-
KILLER, CLIPPED-DICK, CLOAK-AND-SUIT-
ER, DOLLY-MAN, EAGLE-BEAK, FIFTEEN
AND TWO, FIVE BY TWO, FOUR-BY-TWO,
FRONT-WHEEL SKID, GHETTO FOLKS, HEBE,
HEEB, HOOK-NOSE, IKE, IZZY, JEWBOY,
JEWEY, JEWIE, JEWY, KANGAROO, KIKE,
KODGER, KOSHER CUTIE (female), KO-
SHIATOR, MOCKY, MOTZY, MOUCHEY, NON-
SKID, PITCHY-MAN, PORK, PORKER, PORKY,

POT O' GLUE, QUARTER-TO-TWO, REFF, REFFO, REFUJEW, SARAH SOO, SAUCE-PAN LID, SHEENY, SHONKY, SHONNICKER, SMOUSE, TEAPOT, LID, TEN-TO-TWO, THREE-BY-TWO, WEDGE, WOODEN-SHOE, YEHUDA, YID, YIDDLE, YIT.

five-H. man "hell how he hates himself." A sarcastic accusation of vanity based on FOUR-LETTER MAN (q.v.). [U.S. slang, early 1900s, Weseen]

five-letter woman a BITCH. Based on FOUR-LETTER MAN (q.v.). [British, early 1900s, *Dictionary of Slang and Unconventional English*]

fives 1. an amphetamine capsule. From the strength as expressed in milligrams. See TENS. For synonyms see AMP. [U.S. drug culture, mid 1900s-pres.] **2.** a derogatory reference to Jews. See FIVE AND TWO.

fix 1. to castrate, said of animals or jocularly of a man. [U.S., 1900s or before] **2.** an injection or dose of a drug. [U.S. drug culture, early 1900s-pres.]

fix her plumbing to copulate with a woman. [euphemistic and double entendre; U.S., mid 1900s-pres.]

fix someone up 1. to get a date for someone. **2.** to secure a prostitute for someone. **3.** to copulate with a woman, said of a man. **4.** to impregnate a woman. For synonyms see STORK. [all senses, U.S., 1900s]

fixture a toilet. Often "bathroom fixture." [U.S. euphemism, 1900s]

fizgig (also **fisgig**) a wanton young woman; a flirt. [British, 1500s-1800s]

fizz champagne. For synonyms see WHOOPEE-WATER. [U.S. slang, mid 1900s]

fizzle to break wind inaudibly or nearly so. For synonyms see GURK. [colloquial, 1500s-1900s]

F.L. a "French letter," a condom. For synonyms see EEL-SKIN. [British, 1800s-1900s]

flag 1. a jade; a wanton woman. Implying that she is worthy only a few pence. From an old term for a coin worth fourpence. [early 1500s] **2.** a

menstrual cloth or perineal pad considered as a danger signal. A truncation of RED FLAG (q.v.). [British slang, 1800s] **3.** an effeminate male; a homosexual male. [U.S. underworld, early 1900s, Montelone] **4.** to signal a prostitute that her services are desired. [U.S. colloquial, 1900s]

flag-about a strumpet; a low woman. Cf. FLAG (sense 1). [British slang, 1800s, Farmer and Henley]

flagging an expression indicating that a woman is experiencing the menses. Cf. RED FLAG. [U.S., 1900s]

flag is up (also **flag is out**) an expression indicating that a woman is experiencing the menses. [British and U.S., mid 1800s-pres.]

flake 1. a dummy; an oaf. See FLEAK. [U.S. slang, mid 1900s-pres.] **2.** a male who practices FELLATIO (q.v.). [U.S. homosexual use, mid 1900s-pres.] **3.** cocaine. [U.S. drug culture, mid 1900s-pres.]

flakers intoxicated with alcohol. A truncation of HARRY FLAKERS (q.v.). [Australian, mid 1900s, *Dictionary of Slang and Unconventional English*]

flamdoodle nonsense; the same as FLAPDOODLE (sense 3). Cf. FLUMMADID-DLE. "Flam" means "deception." [U.S., late 1800s]

flame 1. lust; sexual passion. [since the 1300s] **2.** a venereal disease, probably gonorrhea. Cf. BURNER. [British slang, 1800s, Farmer and Henley] **3.** a girlfriend; a mistress. [U.S., early 1900s-pres.]

flaming queen a very obvious and exaggerated effeminate male homosexual. Cf. SCREAMING QUEEN. [U.S. homosexual use, mid 1900s-pres.]

flankey the posteriors. For synonyms see DUFF. [British, mid 1800s, Farmer and Henley]

flannel mouth 1. a derogatory nickname for an Irishman. **2.** any smooth talker. [both senses, U.S., 1900s]

flap 1. the female genitals. **2.** to coit a woman. [both senses, British slang, 1800s, Farmer and Henley] **3.** a sexually loose woman. *Cf.* FLAPPER. [U.S., mid 1900s, Goldin, O'Leary, and Lipsius]

flapdoodle 1. the penis. For synonyms see YARD. [1600s] **2.** the female genitals. *Cf.* FLAP (sense 1). [mid 1600s, (Urquhart)] **3.** nonsense. *Cf.* FLAMDOODLE, FLAP-SAUCE (sense 2). [British and U.S., early 1800s-1900s]

flap dragon 1. a venereal disease, probably gonorrhea. From a game where burning raisins are swallowed, and from FLAP (sense 1). [cant, 1600s, B.E.] **2.** a derogatory nickname for a German or a Dutchman. [early 1600s]

flapper 1. the penis. *Cf.* FLAPDOODLE (sense 1). [British slang, 1800s, Farmer and Henley] **2.** a young prostitute; an immoral teenage girl. [British, late 1800s] **3.** a lively, active young woman, cynical about society and sexually free. From sense 2. [U.S. colloquial, early 1900s]

flap-sauce 1. a glutton. [British, 1500s, *Oxford English Dictionary*] **2.** nonsense. *Cf.* FLAPDOODLE. [British slang, 1800s, Farmer and Henley]

flash 1. to vomit. From FLASH THE HASH (*q.v.*). For synonyms see YORK. [U.S. slang, mid 1900s] **2.** to exhibit the penis, especially if done fleetingly. [1900s] **3.** to exhibit any of the private parts of the body, *i.e.*, those which are usually covered. **4.** cant, the language or special vocabulary of thieves and prostitutes. [cant, 1700s-1800s] See also FLASH-CASE.

flash a bit to expose the genitals, said of a woman. [British slang or cant, 1800s or before]

flash-case (also **flash-crib, flash-drum, flash-house, flash-ken, flash-panny**) a brothel. [cant, late 1700s-1800s]

flasher a male exhibitionist. See FLASH (sense 2).

flash in the pan a fast act of coition without ejaculation. *Cf.* PAN. [British nonce, 1700s, *Dictionary of Slang and Unconventional English*]

flash in the pants 1. a burst of sexual arousal. **2.** a brief sexual infatuation. Both are based on "flash in the pan." [both senses, U.S. jocular, 1900s]

flash it to exhibit the genitals, usually said of men. *Cf.* FLASH A BIT. [slang since the early 1800s]

flash meat to expose the penis. One who does this is a "meat-flasher." *Cf.* FLASH (sense 2). [cant, 1700s]

flash-tail a harlot; a prostitute. [cant, mid 1800s]

flash the bubs to expose the breasts. [cant, late 1800s, Farmer and Henley]

flash the hash (also **flash hash**) to vomit. See FLASH (sense 1) for U.S. survival or reintroduction. [cant, 1700s, Grose]

flash the red flag to indicate that one is experiencing the menses, said of women. [British slang, 1800s]

flash the upright grin to expose the vulva. The "grin" is made with the *labia majora,* and the PUDENDAL CLEAVAGE (*q.v.*). *Cf.* UPRIGHT GRIN, WEARING A SMILE. [British slang, 1800s, Farmer and Henley]

flat 1. FLAT-CHESTED (*q.v.*); pertaining to a girl or woman with little or no breast development. **2.** the female genitals. See BIT OF FLAT, FLAT COCK. [slang, 1900s and before] **3.** the drug L.S.D. See FLATS. [U.S. drug culture, mid 1900s-pres.] **4.** an oaf; a blockhead. [British, 1800s or before]

flat-back to act as a prostitute. *Cf.* GRASSBACK. [U.S. slang, mid 1900s-pres.]

flatbacker a prostitute who offers only regular intercourse in the *Figura Veneris Prima.* This is viewed as an amateurish limitation in the profession. [U.S. slang, mid 1900s-pres.]

flat-chested pertaining to a woman with little or no breast development. Pertains to little girls and men as well. [U.S., 1900s]

flat cock the female genitals as compared to the male. *Cf.* COCK (sense 6), FLAT (sense 2). [British slang, 1700s-1800s] See also FAT COCK.

flat floosie a prostitute who operates from a room or a flat. *Cf.* FLOOSEY (sense 3), HOTEL HOTSY. [U.S., 1900s, Berrey and Van den Bark]

flatfoot a policeman. [U.S. slang and colloquial, 1900s] The following synonyms usually refer to men unless indicated otherwise: ARM OF THE LAW, BEAT-POUNDER, BLUEBOTTLE, BLUECOAT, BOBBY, BOTTLE-STOPPER, BULL, CINDER BULL, CINDER DICK, CONSTABLE, COP, COPESS (female), COPPER, ESCLOP, FLATHEAD, FRY, FRESH BULL, FROG, FUZZ, GENDARME, GIRLIE BEAR (female), GOLDIE LOCKS (female), GUMSHOE, HARNESS-BULL, JOHNNY LAW, LADY BEAR (female), LOBSTER, LONG ARM OF THE LAW, MAMA BEAR (female), MAMA SMOKEY (female), MORK, MULDOON, NAMESCLOP, OCCIFER, OFFICERETTE (female), OSSIFER, PADDY, PAVEMENT-POUNDER, PEELER, PERCENTAGE BULL, PIG, RAILROAD BULL, ROACH, SHAM, SHAMUS, SLOP, SMOKEY BEAVER (female), STICK MAN, STRING AND TOP, THE MAN, WOOLY BEAR (female).

flat-fuck 1. a sexual union of two lesbians rubbing their genitals together. *Cf.* FLAT COCK, PRINCETON RUB. **2.** to perform a FLAT-FUCK (sense 1). [both senses, British, 1800s, *Dictionary of Slang and Unconventional English*]

flatophile a "lover of flatulence"; someone who gets pleasure out of creating, hearing, or smelling flatulence; a person, fascinated by loud releases of intestinal gas. [contrived and jocular, early 1900s]

flats the drug L.S.D. (*q.v.*). *Cf.* BLOTTER (sense 2), CUBE (sense 2), PURPLE FLATS. [U.S. drug culture, mid 1900s-pres.]

flat tire 1. an impotent man; a worthless, powerless man. [early 1900s] **2.** a flaccid penis. [1900s] **3.** a fool; an oaf; a worthless man. *Cf.* RUBBER SOCK, WET SOCK. [U.S. slang, early 1900s]

flavour to be sexually aroused or nearly so, said of men or women in the expression "get the flavour." Possibly a euphemism for SALT (sense 1). For synonyms see HUMPY. [British slang, 1800s, Farmer and Henley]

flawed (also **flawd**) **1.** intoxicated with alcohol. [British, late 1600s-1800s] **2.** deflowered. See DEFLOWER. [British slang, 1800s, Farmer and Henley]

flay the fox (also **flay**) to vomit. Based on SHOOT THE CAT, WHIP THE CAT (both *q.v.*). [British slang, early 1800s, Egan's Grose]

fleak a derogatory term for a woman; a foolish or giddy woman. A dialect variant of "flake." See FLAKE (sense 1). [British colloquial or nonce, early 1600s]

flea powder heroin. [U.S. drug culture, mid 1900s-pres.]

fleas and ants trousers; pants. Rhyming slang for "pants." *Cf.* BULL ANTS. [U.S. slang, 1900s, Berrey and Van den Bark]

fleece the female pubic hair. [British slang, 1800s or before]

fleece-hunter (also **fleece-monger**) a whore-monger; a lecher; a man who is after female pubic hair. [British slang, 1800s, Farmer and Henley]

flesh 1. to copulate. For synonyms see OCCUPY. [late 1500s, Florio] **2.** the genitals, male or female. A synonym of MEAT (senses 1 and 4). See CARNAL (sense 1). [from *A Winter's Tale* (Shakespeare)] See also FISH.

flesh-broker a bawd; a procurress. [British, late 1600s, B.E.]

flesh-factory a brothel. [U.S., early 1900s-pres.]

flesh-fly (also **flesh-maggot**) a whore-monger; a pimp. [British, late 1700s-1800s]

flesh it to coit a woman. *Cf.* FLESH (sense 1). [1500s]

fleshly-idol the female genitals. For synonyms see MONOSYLLABLE. [British slang, 1800s, Farmer and Henley]

fleshly-part the female genitals. *Cf.* FLESH (sense 1). [British slang, 1800s, Farmer and Henley]

flesh-market a brothel. [British and U.S., 1800s-1900s]

flesh-monger 1. a procurer; a pimp; the male keeper of a brothel. **2.** to seek copulation. [both senses, 1600s]

flesh-peddler 1. a pimp. **2.** a prostitute. *Cf.* LOVE-PEDDLER. [both senses, U.S. slang, mid 1900s]

flesh-pot 1. a brothel. [Biblical (Exodus), "the flesh-pots of Egypt"] **2.** any district or establishment which caters to sexual desires and other physical needs. [colloquial since the 1500s] **3.** a harlot; a sexually loose woman. See SEXPOT.

flesh session a session of lovemaking and copulation. *Cf.* FLESH (sense 1). [U.S. slang, mid 1900s]

flesh-tailor a surgeon. For synonyms see DOC. [early 1600s]

fleshy part of the thigh the posteriors. [British and U.S. euphemism, late 1800s-pres.]

flibbertigibbet (also **flittertigibbet**) **1.** a scatterbrain; an oaf; a gossiper. [since the mid 1500s] **2.** a devil or a fiend. [from *King Lear* (Shakespeare)]

flicking fucking. A thin disguise of FRICKING (*q.v.*). [British and some U.S. use, 1900s]

flimp 1. to coit a woman. [British slang, mid 1800s, Farmer and Henley] **2.** to cheat or deceive. **3.** a pickpocket. [senses 2 and 3 are U.S. underworld, early 1800s-early 1900s]

fling 1. a penile thrust in the sexual act. [early 1500s] **2.** a love affair. [U.S., 1900s]

fling-dust (also **fling-stink**) a streetwalker; a slattern. *Cf.* GLUE NECK. [early 1600s-1800s]

fling up to vomit. For synonyms see YORK. [U.S. colloquial, early 1900s or before]

flip-flap 1. the penis. Rhymes with "watergap." See WATER-BOX, "genitals." *Cf.* FLAP-DOODLE. [mid 1600s, (Urquhart)] **2.** a flighty woman. Probably related to FLIP-FLAPS (*q.v.*). *Cf.* FLAPPER. [British slang, 1700s]

flip-flaps 1. the human breasts, especially bouncing and wobbling breasts. **2.** young women with jiggling and bouncing breasts. See FLOPPER-STOPPER. [both senses, Australian slang, early 1900s, *Dictionary of Slang and Unconventional English*]

flip-flop mutual oral sexual intercourse involving males or females in any combination of two. *Cf.* LOOP-DE-LOOP, SIXTY-NINE. [U.S. slang, mid 1900s-pres.]

flipper a wanton young woman; a young prostitute. See FLAPPER.

flipping an intensifier. A disguise of "fucking." *Cf.* FLICKING. [slang, early 1900s]

flip the bird to give someone the finger. See FINGER, THE. *Cf.* THROW A BIRD. [U.S. slang, mid 1900s-pres.]

flirt-gill a flirtatious or wanton woman. A truncation of "flirtgillian." *Cf.* GILL-FLIRT for additional forms. [from *Romeo and Juliet* (Shakespeare)]

flirtigiggs (also **flirtigig**) a flirtatious and wanton young woman. [British dialect and colloquial, late 1600s]

flit 1. an effeminate male homosexual. *Cf.* FRIT. [U.S. underworld and slang, early 1900s-pres.] **2.** pertaining to a homosexual male or to male homosexuality.

flitty homosexual; obviously effeminate. From FLIT (*q.v.*). See CAMP (sense 4). [U.S. slang, mid 1900s-pres.]

floater the penis. For synonyms see YARD. [British slang, 1800s, Farmer and Henley]

floating 1. intoxicated with alcohol. [U.S. slang, 1900s] **2.** drug intoxicated. [U.S. drug culture and slang, mid 1900s-pres.]

flog to masturbate. *Cf.* FLOG ONE'S DONKEY. [Australian, 1900s, *Dictionary of Slang and Unconventional English*]

flogging whipping to arouse sexual feelings; flagellation. [cant, 1600s, B.E.]

flog one's donkey (also **flog one's meat, flog one's sausage**) to masturbate. *Cf.* FLOG. [British slang, 1800s, *Dictionary of Slang and Unconventional English*]

flog the bishop to masturbate. The bishop's miter is compared here to the glans penis. *Cf.* BOX THE JESUIT AND GET COCKROACHES. [British, 1800s, *Dictionary of Slang and Unconventional English*] See also BISHOP.

flommax a slattern. For synonyms see TROLLYMOG. [British, 1800s]

flong one's dong to masturbate. Patterned on other rhyming expressions for this matter, *i.e.*, BEAT THE MEAT (*q.v.*). *Cf.* DONG. For synonyms see WASTE TIME. [U.S. slang, mid 1900s-pres.]

floods the menses. [U.S., 1900s] Synonyms and related terms: ALL'S NOT QUIET ON THE WATERFRONT, AT NUMBER ONE LONDON, BECOME A LADY, BLOODY MARY, CAPTAIN IS AT HOME, CARRYING A FLAG, CATAMENIA, CATAMENIAL DISCHARGE, CATAMENIAL STATE, CHINKERINGS, COLLYWOBBLES, COUNTRY COUSIN, COURSES, CURSE OF EVE, D.A.S, DOMESTIC AFFLICTIONS, DYSMENORRHEA, ENTERTAINING THE GENERAL, FEELING POORLY, FEELING UNWELL, FEMALE DISORDER, FIELD DAY, FLAGGING, FLAG IS OUT, FLAG IS UP, FLASH THE RED FLAG, FLOWERS, FLOWING, FLYING BAKER, FLY THE FLAG, FRIENDS TO STAY, GOT THE RAG ON, HAMMOCK IS SWINGING, HAVE IT ON, HAVE THE FLOWERS, HAVE THE GATE LOCKED AND THE KEY LOST, HIGH TIDE, HOLY WEEK, INDISPOSED, KNOCKED-UP, LITTLE FRIEND, LITTLE SISTER IS HERE, LITTLE VISITOR, LOSE, MENSES, MICKEY MOUSE IS KAPUT, MONTHLIES, MONTHLY CYCLE, MONTHLY FLOWERS, MONTHLY FLUX, MONTHLY TERMS, MONTHS, MOTHER-NATURE, NATURE, OFF THE ROOF, ON THE RAG, O.T.R., OUT OF ORDER, OUT OF THIS WORLD, PERIOD, RAGGING, RAGTIME, REALLY SLICK, RED FLAG, RED SAILS IN THE SUNSET, RED TUMMY-ACHE, RIDING THE COTTON BICYCLE, RIDING THE RAG, RIDING THE WHITE HORSE, ROADMAKING, ROAD UP FOR REPAIRS, ROSES, SICK, SO, STREET UP FOR REPAIRS, TAILFLOWERS, TERMS, THAT TIME, THAT WAY, THE CURSE, THE NUISANCE, THE THING, THOSE DAYS OF THE MONTH, THOSE DIFFICULT DAYS, TURNS, UNDER THE WEATHER, UNWELL, VAPORS, VISITOR, WOMAN'S HOME COMPANION.

flooey intoxicated with alcohol. For synonyms see WOFFLED. [U.S. slang, early 1900s] See also DRUNK AS FLOEY at DRUNK AS CHLOE.

floored intoxicated with alcohol; dead drunk, as if the drinker had been knocked out. [slang, 1800s-1900s]

floor fuck to copulate on the floor. [Australian, early 1900s, *Dictionary of Slang and Unconventional English*]

floosey (also **floosie, floosy, floozie, flossie, fluzie**) 1. a girl; a young woman; a woman. 2. a wanton woman; a sexually loose woman. For synonyms see LAY. 3. a prostitute. *Cf.* FLAT FLOOSIE. [all senses, U.S. slang, early 1900s-pres.]

flop a woman to place a woman, literally or figuratively, in a position to perform sexual intercourse. *Cf.* LAY DOWN, PUT DOWN (sense 1), SPREAD (sense 2). [British, 1800s, *Dictionary of Slang and Unconventional English*]

flop in to penetrate the vagina. [British colloquial, 1800s]

flop in the hay 1. to go to bed with a person for sexual activity. *Cf.* ROLL IN THE HAY, TOSS IN THE HAY. 2. a rapid act of sexual intercourse. [both senses, U.S. slang, early 1900s-pres.]

flopper-stopper a brassiere; a bra. [attested as Australian, 1900s]

flower 1. the hymen. Implied in DEFLOWER (*q.v.*). For synonyms see BEAN. 2. the female genitals. [British slang, 1800s, Farmer and Henley] See FLOWERS. 3. in the plural, the menses. 4. a homosexual male. *Cf.* PANSY. [U.S., 1900s] Synonyms for sense 4: ANSYPAY, BUTTERCUP, DAFFODIL, DAISY, LILY, PANSY.

flower-fancier a whoremonger; a keeper of whores. See FLOWER (sense 2). [British slang, 1800s, Farmer and Henley]

flower of chivalry the female genitals. *Cf.* FLOWER (sense 2). [British, 1800s, Farmer and Henley]

flowers the menses. *Cf.* ROSES (sense 1). For synonyms see FLOODS. [since the 1400s or 1500s]

flowers and frolics the testicles. Rhyming slang for BALLOCKS (*q.v.*). [British, 1900s, *Dictionary of Rhyming Slang*]

fluff 1. the female pubic hair. *Cf.* FLEECE. [widespread recurrent nonce since the 1800s] **2.** to release intestinal gas. For synonyms see GURK. [Australian, 1900s, Baker] **3.** a young woman. [U.S., early 1900s-pres.] **4.** a lesbian with feminine traits. [U.S. homosexual use, mid 1900s]

flummadiddle (also **flummydiddle**) nonsense. *Cf.* FLAMDOODLE. [U.S., 1800s-pres.]

flurgle (also **flergle**) to copulate. For synonyms see OCCUPY. [U.S. slang, mid 1900s]

flurt an insignificant person; a fool. *Cf.* GILL-FLIRT. [British dialect, 1800s]

flush intoxicated with alcohol; full of alcohol, as in "flush with the brim" of a vessel, or related to FLUSHED (*q.v.*) [British slang, 1800s]

flushed intoxicated with alcohol; reddened with alcohol. [British and U.S., early 1700s-1900s]

flusterated (also **flustrated**) intoxicated with alcohol. For synonyms see WOOFLED. [British and U.S. slang, 1800s-1900s]

flustrated intoxicated with alcohol. A jocular blend of "flustered" and "frustrated." [British colloquial, 1700s-1800s]

flute (also **one-holed flute, living flute, silent flute**) **1.** the penis. *Cf.* BAGPIPE, PICCOLO. [British slang, early 1700s or before] **2.** a homosexual male. Possibly a deliberate mispronunciation of FRUIT (sense 4). *Cf.* FLUTER, PICCOLO-PLAYER. [U.S., 1900s]

fluter the male homosexual receiver in fellation. *Cf.* PICCOLO-PLAYER. [U.S. underworld and slang, early 1900s-pres.]

fluxes diarrhea, especially bloody diarrhea; dysentery. [1900s or before]

fluzz dyke a passive lesbian; a feminine female homosexual. *Cf.* BULL-DIKER, FLUFF. For synonyms see LESBYTERIAN. [U.S. homosexual use, mid 1900s, Farrell]

fly 1. a policeman. [in various usages since the mid 1800s] **2.** a wanton woman; a prostitute. From FLY THE FLAG (sense 1). [British, late 1800s, Farmer and Henley] **3.** to take narcotics habitually.

4. to experience a HIGH (sense 3) from narcotics. [senses 3 and 4 are U.S. drug culture and slang, mid 1900s-pres.]

fly ball 1. a homosexual male. A play on the "fly" of men's trousers. **2.** an oddball or eccentric person. Both are based on the baseball term. [both senses, U.S. slang, 1900s, Wentworth and Flexner]

fly-blown 1. intoxicated with alcohol. For synonyms see WOOFLED. [British slang, 1800s] **2.** deflowered. See DEFLOWER. [British slang, 1800s, Farmer and Henley] **3.** tainted with a venereal disease. *Cf.* FLY (sense 2). [British and U.S., 1800s-1900s]

fly-by-night 1. a witch. [late 1700s, Grose] **2.** a prostitute. [British, early 1800s, *Lexicon Balatronicum*] **3.** the female genitals. [British, early 1800s, *Lexicon Balatronicum*] **4.** intoxicated with alcohol. Rhyming slang for TIGHT (*q.v.*) [British, *Dictionary of Rhyming Slang*]

flyer (also **flier**) to coit rapidly and briefly with a woman. [British slang, late 1700s, Grose]

flying a state of drug intoxication. *Cf.* FLY (sense 4). For synonyms see TALL. [U.S. drug culture, mid 1900s-pres.]

flying Baker to be experiencing the menses. Flying is a transitive verb here. The "Baker" signalling flag is red. *Cf.* FLY THE FLAG. [1900s]

flying-fuck 1. "nothing" in expressions such as GIVE A FLYING-FUCK and GO TAKE A FLYING-FUCK (both *q.v.*). [mid 1900s-pres.] **2.** an imaginary act of coition accomplished in the air, as in an airplane or at the end of a great leap made by the male.

flying handicap diarrhea. For synonyms see QUICKSTEP. [Australian, 1900s]

flying pasty human dung wrapped in paper and thrown about as an act of vandalism. [British slang, early 1800s, *Lexicon Balatronicum*]

flying saucers morning glory seeds as a source of a hallucinogenic alkaloid.

For synonyms see SEEDS. [U.S. drug culture, mid 1900s-pres.]

fly the flag 1. to walk the streets, said of prostitutes who are soliciting customers. [British slang, 1800s, Farmer and Henley] **2.** to experience the menses. *Cf.* FLAGGING, RED FLAG. [British and U.S., 1800s-1900s]

fly-trap the female genitals. [British slang, 1800s, Farmer and Henley]

F.O. 1. a ''fuck-off,'' a worthless do-nothing; a jerk. **2.** a masturbator. For synonyms see HUSKER. [both senses, U.S., 1900s]

foaming at the mouth about to ejaculate; extremely anxious to proceed with sexual activity. *Cf.* DRIPPING FOR IT, READY TO SPIT. [colloquial, 1900s]

fobus the female genitals. For synonyms see MONOSYLLABLE. [British, late 1800s, Farmer and Henley]

fodder toilet tissue. From BUM-FODDER (*q.v.*). [British slang, 1800s]

fogey an old, eccentric man; a man or woman who is considerably out of step with the times. [U.S. colloquial, 1900s and before]

fogged intoxicated with alcohol. [British and U.S. slang, 1800s-1900s]

foggy intoxicated with alcohol. For synonyms see WOOFLED. [British and U.S. slang, early 1800s-1900s]

fog-matic intoxicated with alcohol. [U.S., mid 1800s, Wentworth and Flexner]

fogram (also **fogrum**) **1.** a fussy old man; a stuffed shirt. [since the late 1700s, Grose] **2.** liquor; possibly the rum which causes one to be FOGGED (*q.v.*). [U.S. nautical, Berrey and Van den Bark]

foin to copulate; to thrust. From an old word meaning ''thrust with a pointed weapon.'' [late 1500s, Florio]

foist a breaking of wind. See FICE, FOYST.

folded intoxicated with alcohol; the same as BENT (sense 1). [U.S. slang, early 1900s, Weseen]

fondle 1. to caress sexually; to handle the breasts of a woman or the genitals

of a male or female of any age. [since the 1600s] **2.** to copulate. For synonyms see OCCUPY. [British, 1800s, Farmer and Henley]

fond of meat amorous in general; sexually active; lecherous. See MEAT (sense 2). [British slang, 1800s, Farmer and Henley]

fonkin a giddy little oaf. [colloquial or nonce, late 1500s, *Oxford English Dictionary*]

fool around 1. to tease. **2.** to engage in sexual activity short of copulation. **3.** to engage in an extramarital romance. [all senses, since the late 1800s]

foolish powder 1. any powdered narcotic. [U.S. underworld, early 1900s, Irwin] **2.** heroin. [U.S. underworld, early 1900s, Weseen]

fool-sticker the penis. For synonyms see YARD. [British slang, 1800s, Farmer and Henley]

fool-trap 1. a harlot. **2.** the female genitals. *Cf.* FLY-TRAP. [both senses, British slang, 1800s]

foop to engage in homosexual practices. Possibly backslang for POOF (*q.v.*). [U.S. slang, mid 1900s-pres., Underwood]

fooper a homosexual male. *Cf.* FOOP. [U.S. slang, mid 1900s-pres., Underwood]

foot 1. to copulate. See FOUTRE!, FUT! [from an innuendo in *Merry Wives of Windsor* (Shakespeare)] **2.** an oath and an exclamation, ''Foot!'' and ''My foot!'' [1600s]

footballs amphetamine tablets or capsules. From the shape of a brand of amphetamine tablets. For synonyms see AMP. [U.S. drug culture, mid 1900s-pres.]

footlicker a sycophant. For synonyms see ACQUIESCE-MAN. [from *The Tempest* (Shakespeare)]

foot queen a homosexual male who derives sexual pleasure from fondling or kissing someone else's feet. *Cf.* SHRIMP QUEEN, TOE QUEEN. [U.S. homosexual use, mid 1900s, Farrell]

foozlified intoxicated with alcohol. For synonyms see WOOFLED. [British slang, late 1800s, *Dictionary of Slang and Unconventional English*]

fop 1. a fool. [since the mid 1400s, *Oxford English Dictionary*] **2.** a male who is excessively concerned about dress and appearance; an effeminate dandy. [since the late 1600s] Synonyms for sense 2: ADONIS, BEAU, BLOOD, BRIGHT, COXCOMB, DANDIPRAT, DINK, JACK-A-DANDY, JEMMY, LARDY-TARDY TOFF, POPIN-JAY, PRINCOCK, STRUT-NOD-DY.

fop-doodle an insignificant man; a fool; an oaf. *Cf.* FOP (sense 1). [since the 1600s]

forbidden fruit 1. a young girl; a virgin. *Cf.* JAIL BAIT. [U.S. slang, 1900s] **2.** sex in general. Based upon the fruit of the tree of knowledge in the Garden of Eden.

forbidden fruit eater a lascivious man; a man who has known many women sexually. For synonyms see LECHER. [U.S. slang, early 1900s, Weseen]

fore and aft coition. Possibly rhyming slang for SHAFT (sense 2). See FORE-AND-AFTER. [British slang, 1800s, Farmer and Henley]

fore-and-after a prostitute offering both vaginal and anal copulation. Based on the nautical terms. *Cf.* DOUBLE-BARRELLED. [British slang, 1800s, Farmer and Henley] See also FORE AND AFT.

fore-buttocks the human breasts. An old term recognizing the similarity and possibly the similar attraction of the breasts and the posteriors. *Cf.* TOP BALLOCKS. [British, early 1700s]

forecaster the female genitals. See CAST (sense 2). For synonyms see MONO-SYLLABLE. [British slang, 1800s, Farmer and Henley]

forecastle the female genitals. Based on the nautical term and its pronunciation, "f'c'sle," *i.e.*, "fuck-sle." [British slang, 1800s]

fore-court the female genitals. [British slang, 1800s]

forefinger the penis. *Cf.* LITTLE FINGER, MIDDLE FINGER, THUMB OF LOVE. [from *All's Well That Ends Well* (Shakespeare)]

forehatch the female genitals. *Cf.* HATCHWAY. [British slang, 1800s, Farmer and Henley]

foreman the penis. *Cf.* FOREWOMAN. For synonyms see YARD. [British euphemism, mid 1600s]

foreplay sexual stimulation practiced by one or both parties, usually in preparation for copulation. A truncation of "sexual foreplay." For synonyms see FIRKYTOODLE.

foreskin skin which covers the glans penis or glans clitoridis. Usually refers to the male prepuce, a cylinder of loose epidermis which is an extension of the skin of the shaft of the penis. Synonyms: END, JEWISH NIGHTCAP, LACE CURTAINS, SHEATH, SNAPPER, WHICKER-BILL.

foreskin-hunter a prostitute. [British slang, 1800s, Farmer and Henley]

forest the female pubic hair. [implied as early as the 1500s and repeated nonce use; colloquial since the early 1700s or before]

forewoman the female genitals. *Cf.* FOREMAN. [British slang, 1800s]

forget-me-not an infection of gonor-rhea or syphilis. [early 1900s, *Dictionary of the Underworld*]

forget oneself 1. for a child to have a temporary lapse of toilet-training. [euphemistic, 1800s-1900s] **2.** to behave in an ungentlemanly or unladylike manner. This can cover anything from the most trivial breach of etiquette to impassioned and lustful advances. [euphemistic and occasionally jocular in the U.S.]

forgotten woman a prostitute. For synonyms see HARLOT. [U.S. euphemism, 1900s]

fork 1. to prepare a woman for copulation; to arouse a woman sexually and to arrange her physically for the sexual act. [British slang, 1800s, Farmer and Henley] **2.** a gibbet. [British, 1800s or before] **3.** a prostitute. For synonyms see HARLOT. [Australian, Baker]

fork and knife one's own wife; anyone's wife. Rhyming slang for "wife." [British, 1900s, *Dictionary of Rhyming Slang*]

Fork you! "Fuck you!" [euphemism of disguise; U.S., 1900s, Wentworth and Flexner]

fornicate 1. to copulate, said of an unmarried person copulating with anyone. [since the mid 1500s] **2.** to copulate, said (erroneously) of any illicit copulating. **3.** to tell lies; to invent tales. A jocular or ignorant error for "prevaricate." [British dialect, 1800s]

Fornicate the poodle! an oath and an exclamation; an elaboration of "Fuck a dog!" [British, 1900s, *Dictionary of Slang and Unconventional English*]

fornicating-engine (also **fornicating-member, fornicating-tool**) the penis. Based on "reciprocating engine." *Cf.* MACHINE (sense 1). [British slang, 1800s, Farmer and Henley]

fornicator the penis. [British slang, 1800s, Farmer and Henley]

fornix 1. a brothel, said to be named for the arches of public buildings in Rome where prostitution or solicitation took place. [from Latin] **2.** fornication.

Forsooth! an oath and an exclamation, "For His truth!" For synonyms see 'ZOUNDS! [since the late 800s, *Oxford English Dictionary*]

fort the female genitals. A truncation of FORTRESS (*q.v.*). [British, 1600s]

Fort Bushy the female genitals. [attested as Canadian, 1900s, *Dictionary of Slang and Unconventional English*]

fortress (also **fort**) the female genitals. [British slang, 1800s, Farmer and Henley]

forty-four a prostitute. Rhyming slang for WHORE (sense 1). [British, 1900s, *Dictionary of Rhyming Slang*]

forwards amphetamine tablets or capsules. *Cf.* PEP PILL. [U.S. drug culture, mid 1900s-pres.]

F.O.S. "full of shit," pertaining to a

person who is phony or who lies and boasts constantly. [U.S. slang, mid 1900s-pres.]

foul blow a blow struck to the groin or pubic area of a man. *Cf.* BELOW THE BELT. [1900s or before]

foul disease (also **foul disorder**) syphilis. *Cf.* BAD DISEASE. For synonyms see SPECIFIC STOMACH. [euphemistic, early 1700s, *New Canting Dictionary*]

foul mouth a person who uses obscene words habitually. [British and U.S., 1800s-1900s; earlier as an adjective, "foul-mouthed," in *Henry VI*, Part One (Shakespeare)]

foul play adultery. *Cf.* FAIR PLAY. [British slang, 1800s, Farmer and Henley]

fountain of life the female genitals. [British euphemism, 1800s, (Farmer)]

four-by-two a Jewish man or woman. Rhyming slang for "Jew." Not necessarily derogatory. For synonyms see FIVE AND TWO. [British, World War I, *Dictionary of Rhyming Slang*]

four-F. method a juvenile male view of a masculine or hypermasculine approach to women and sex, "find 'em, feel 'em, fuck 'em, and forget about 'em." Also occurs in other variations. [since the late 1800s]

four-letter man a man whose character can be described by any one of a series of four-letter words, *e.g.*, HOMO, DUMB, SHIT. From the term used to describe an athlete who has received four letters in team sports. *Cf.* FIVE-LETTER WOMAN, THREE-LETTER MAN. [British and U.S., 1900s]

four-letter word one of the traditional "dirty words" most of which are spelled with four letters. These are known worldwide: COCK, CUNT, FART, FUCK, PISS, SHIT, TURD. Less widely known are ARSE, QUIM, TWAT. *Cf.* ANGLO-SAXON.

four-sheets to the wind intoxicated with alcohol. *Cf.* BOTH SHEETS IN THE WIND, THREE SHEETS IN THE WIND, TWO SHEETS TO THE WIND. [slang, 1800s-pres.]

Foutre! an exclamation. Literally,

"Fuck!" [from Latin *futuere* via French *foutre;* in *Henry IV*, Part Two (Shakespeare)]

fox an extremely attractive female. [originally black use; U.S. slang, mid 1900s-pres.]

fox-drunk intoxicated with alcohol; drunk and crafty or stinking drunk. [1500s]

foxed intoxicated with alcohol. From the red color of the fox or the "stinking" in "stinking drunk." [British and U.S. colloquial, early 1600s-1900s]

fox-head homebrewed alcohol; moonshine. [U.S. dialect (Ozarks), Randolph and Wilson]

foxy (also **foxey**) **1.** stinking, especially stinking with perspiration odor. [British and U.S., 1800s-1900s] **2.** pertaining to a sexually desirable female. [U.S. slang, mid 1900s-pres.] **3.** intoxicated. From the reddish color of the skin from heavy drinking. *Cf.* FOX-DRUNK, FOXED. [U.S. colloquial, 1800s, Green]

foxy lady 1. a sexually attractive female. [U.S. slang, mid 1900s-pres.] **2.** a sexually attractive male homosexual. From sense 1. [U.S. homosexual use, mid 1900s-pres., Farrell]

foyst (also **fice, fust, fyst**) **1.** an inaudible release of intestinal gas. For synonyms see GURK. [mid 1600s-1700s] **2.** to copulate. For synonyms see OCCUPY. [mid 1600s, (Urquhart)]

fractured intoxicated with alcohol. For synonyms see WOOFLED. [U.S. slang, early 1900s-pres.]

fragrant pregnant. A jocular avoidance. [U.S. colloquial, 1900s] Synonyms and related terms: ABOUT TO FIND PUPS, APRON-UP, AWKWARD, BABY-BOUND, BAGGED, BEEN PLAYING TRICKS, BELLY-FULL, BELLY-UP, BIG WITH CHILD, BOUND, BROKEN-KNEED, BROKEN-LEGGED, CHILDING, CLUCKY, COCKED-UP, COMING, COMING FRESH, DELICATE CONDITION, DOUBLE-RIBBED, ENCEINTE, EXPECTING, FAMILIAR-WAY, FULL-IN-THE-BELLY, FULL OF HEIR, GONE, GONE TO SEED, GRAVID, GREAT WITH CHILD, HAVE A DUMPLING ON, HAVE A HUMP IN FRONT, HAVE A NINE-MONTHS DROPSY, HAVE ONE IN THE OVEN, HAVE ONE'S CARGO ABOARD, HIGH-BELLIED, HOW-CAME-YOU-SO?, IN A FAMILY WAY, IN A FIX, IN AN INTERESTING CONITION, IN BAD SHAPE, IN DUTCH, IN FOR IT, IN POD, IN THE PUDDING CLUB, IN TROUBLE, IN YOUNG, IRISH TOOTHACHE, I.T.A., JUMBLED-UP, KETCHED, KIDDED, KNAPPED, KNOCKED-UP, LADY IN WAITING, LAP-CLAP, LIVING IN SEDUCED CIRCUMSTANCES, LOADED, LOOKING PIGGY, LUMPY, LUSTY, ON THE BONES, ON THE HILL, ON THE WAY, OTHERWISE, PARTURIENT, P.G., PILLOWED, PIZENED, PODDY, POISONED, PREGGERS, PREGGY, PREGO, PUMPED, RUN TO SEED, SEWED-UP, SHORT-SKIRTED, SHOT IN THE GIBLETS, SHOT IN THE TAIL, SO, SPRINGING, STORKED, STORK-MAD, STUNG BY A SERPENT, SWALLOWED A WATER-MELON SEED, TEEMING, TOO BIG FOR HER CLOTHES, UP-AND-COMING, UP THE POLE, UP THE STICK, WEARING THE BUSTLE WRONG, WEDGED-UP, WELL-ALONG, WITH CHILD, WITH SQUIRREL, WITH YOUNG.

frail-job 1. a sexually promiscuous woman, especially if attractive. For synonyms see LAY. [U.S., mid 1900s] **2.** coition. [U.S. slang, 1900s, Wentworth and Flexner]

frail-sister (also **frail-one**) a prostitute. [U.S. euphemism, 1900s]

Frances the posteriors; an elaboration of FANNY (sense 2). For synonyms see DUFF. [U.S., mid 1900s]

frank racy; obscene; explicitly descriptive of sexual matters. Usually pertaining to films, books, or theatrical presentations. [British and U.S. euphemism, 1900s]

franzy house a brothel. [U.S. colloquial or dialect, 1900s or before, Wentworth]

frazzled intoxicated with alcohol. For synonyms see WOOFLED. [U.S. slang, late 1800s-pres.]

freak 1. a male homosexual or a practitioner of nonorthogenital sex acts. *Cf.* SEX FIEND. **2.** a nymphomaniac. [Both senses, U.S. slang, mid 1900s-pres.]

freaked-out (also **freaked**) under the influence of marijuana. For synonyms see TALL. [U.S. drug culture, mid 1900s-pres.]

freaking a disguise of "fucking." *Cf.* FLICKING. [U.S., mid 1900s-pres.]

freak off to copulate in an unconventional manner. *Cf.* FREAK (sense 1). [U.S. slang, mid 1900s-pres.]

freak trick a customer who demands that a prostitute be the object of VOYEURISM (*q.v.*) or sadism. *Cf.* FREAK OFF, TRICK. [U.S., mid 1900s-pres.]

free base cocaine separated from other chemical components. [U.S. drug culture, late 1970s-pres.]

free-for-all a promiscuous woman. For synonyms see LAY. [U.S. slang, mid 1900s-pres.]

free-fucking pertaining to a lewd man or woman, particularly to a woman who acts as an unpaid prostitute. [British and U.S., 1800s-1900s]

free-lance pertaining to a married woman who acts as a paid or unpaid prostitute. *Cf.* PRIVATEER. [British and U.S., 1800s-1900s]

free love 1. prostitution. [an old euphemism] **2.** promiscuous copulation at will without legal or moral constraint.

free ride a prostitute. [U.S. slang, 1900s or before]

free show a peek at a woman's breasts, thighs, or pelvic area allowed on purpose or by accidental circumstances. [U.S. colloquial, 1900s]

French (also **french**) **1.** deviant, sensuous, lewd, KINKY (*q.v.*), syphilitic, or illicit. [widespread in reference to syphilis, since the 1500s] **2.** to kiss sensuously using the tongue to explore the mouth of the partner. [slang, 1900s] **3.** FELLATIO (*q.v.*) or any type of oral sexual intercourse. [U.S. slang, mid 1900s-pres.] **4.** dirty words or swear words in English, as in PARDON MY FRENCH (*q.v.*). [U.S. colloquial, 1900s]

French abortion the swallowing or spitting out of semen after fellatio. "The oral disposition of the semen incidental to fellation" (Roback). See SNOWBALL (sense 4), SNOWBALL QUEEN.

French-crown syphilis. So named for baldness produced by advanced syphilis. Ultimately from the name of a French coin. For synonyms see SPECIFIC STOMACH.

French-disease syphilis. One of a very old series of nicknames for syphilis implying that syphilis is indigenous to a country other than England.

Frencher 1. a Frenchman. Not necessarily derogatory. [since the mid 1800s] **2.** a practitioner of FELLATIO (*q.v.*) or similar sexual acts. *Cf.* FRENCH (senses 1 and 3). [slang, 1900s or before]

French-fried intoxicated with marijuana. An elaboration of FRIED (sense 2). [U.S. slang, mid 1900s-pres.]

French-fried-fuck a contemptible bit of nothing; a damn. *Cf.* FLYING-FUCK.

French goods syphilis. For synonyms see SPECIFIC STOMACH.

French gout syphilis and occasionally (perhaps in error) gonorrhea. [since the 1600s, B.E.]

Frenchified infected with venereal disease. [British, 1600s-pres., B.E.]

French kiss 1. a kiss where the tongue is used. See FRENCH (sense 2). [British and U.S., 1900s] **2.** penilingus or cunnilingus. See FRENCH (sense 3). [U.S. slang, 1900s, Wentworth and Flexner]

French letter (also **American letter, Italian letter, Spanish letter**) a condom. See FRENCH (sense 1). Not necessarily capitalized. *Cf.* ENVELOPE, LETTER. For synonyms see EEL-SKIN. [British and U.S., 1800s-pres.]

French pig a syphilitic BUBO (*q.v.*). *Cf.* WINCHESTER-GOOSE. [British euphemism, late 1800s]

French pox syphilis and occasionally (perhaps in error) gonorrhea; the same as FRENCH-DISEASE (*q.v.*). [since the 1500s]

French prints (also **French postcards**) obscene pictures; the same as FEELTHY PICTURES (*q.v.*). See FRENCH (sense 1). [colloquial since the mid 1800s]

French safe a condom. *Cf.* FRENCH LETTER, SAFE. For synonyms see EELSKIN. [attested as Canadian, early 1900s, *Dictionary of Slang and Unconventional English*]

French-tickler a DILDO (sense 2) or a condom equipped with ridges or larger protuberances designed to increase vaginal stimulation. *Cf.* FRENCH (sense 1). [U.S. slang, mid 1900s-pres.]

French vice any NONORTHOGENITAL (*q.v.*) sexual practice. [British euphemism, 1800s, Farmer and Henley]

Frenchy 1. a Frenchman. Not necessarily derogatory. *Cf.* FRENCHER (sense 1). [British and U.S., 1800s-1900s] **2.** sexually attractive; sexy. *Cf.* FRENCH (sense 1). [U.S. slang, 1900s] **3.** a condom. See FRENCH LETTER [widespread slang, 1900s]

fresh 1. intoxicated with alcohol. For synonyms see WOOFLED. [British and U.S. slang and colloquial, early 1800s-pres.] **2.** sexually aggressive or FAST (*q.v.*). [U.S., 1900s] **3.** dung; recently excreted dung, especially cattle or dog dung. [U.S. euphemism, 1900s]

fresh bit a woman new to copulation, either a virgin or one to whom the coiter has not yet grown accustomed. [British slang, mid 1800s, Farmer and Henley]

fresh cow a man with a fresh case of gonorrhea. See MILK (sense 3), SURGE. [U.S. underworld, early 1900s, Irwin]

fresh greens the same as FRESH BIT (*q.v.*). See GREENS. [British slang, 1800s, Farmer and Henley]

fresh meat copulation; the same as FRESH BIT OR FRESH GREENS (both *q.v.*). For synonyms see SMOCKAGE. [British and U.S. colloquial, 1900s]

fribble 1. a silly oaf. **2.** an effeminate male; a homosexual male; possibly a transvestite. *Cf.* FERBLET. [both senses, British, 1600s-1700s] Synonyms and related terms for sense 2: BADLING, BOY SCOUT, BUN-DUSTER, BUTTERCUP, CAKE-EATER, CHORUS BOY, COCK-QUEAN, COLLAR, COLLAR AND CUFF, CREAM PUFF,

DAFFODIL, DILDO, DRUG-STORE COWBOY, DUCKEY, EFFEMINATE MALE, ETHEL, FAG, FAIRY, FLAG, FLIT, GENTLEMISS, GIRLIE, GUSSIE, HEN-HUSSY, JAISY, JENNY, JENNY WILLOCKS, JOEY, LAD-LASS, LISPER, LITHPER, LIZZIE BOY, MALKIN, MAMA-POULE, MARGERY, MARY ANN, MEA-COCKE, MILKSOP, MISS NANCY, MOLLY-CODDLE, MOLLY-MOP, NAMBY-PAMBY, NAN-BOY, NANCE, NANCY, NANCY DAWSON, NANCY HOMEY, NELLIE FAG, NICE NELLIE, NO BULLFIGHTER, ONE OF THE BOYS, PANSIFIED, PANSY, PANTY-WAIST, PAP-MOUTH, PEE-WILLIE, PERCY, PETAL, POOD, POOF, POOFTER, POWDER PUFF, PRETTY-BOY, PUSS-GENTLEMAN, PUSSY, QUEAN, QUEEN, QUEENIE, QUINCE, SHE-HE, SHE-MAN, SIS, SISSY-BRITCHES, SKIPPY, SOAPY, SOFTIE, SPURGE, THITHY, TINKLE-TINKLE, TONK, TWANK, TWIDDLE-POOP, TWIXTER, WEAK SISTER, WHOOPS BOY, WILLIE BOY, WOMAN. See similar terms at EPICENE.

fricatrix 1. a woman who masturbates herself. *Cf.* FUCK-FINGER. [from Latin *fricatrix*, which has the same meaning; British slang, 1800s, Farmer and Henley] **2.** a woman known to copulate frequently or well. For synonyms see LAY. Based on "frick." See FRICKING.

fricking a phonological disguise of FUCKING (*q.v.*). *Cf.* FRIGGING. [British and U.S., 1900s]

fried 1. intoxicated with alcohol. [U.S. slang, early 1900s-pres.] **2.** intoxicated with marijuana. *Cf.* CRISP, CRISPY-CRITTER, FRENCH-FRIED. [U.S. slang, mid 1900s-pres.]

fried to the gills intoxicated with alcohol, an elaboration of FRIED (sense 1). A mixture of FRIED (sense 1) and "up to the gills." [U.S. slang, mid 1900s]

frig 1. to masturbate oneself. From an old term originally meaning "rub" or "chafe," this sense has now replaced the original sense. [ultimately cognate with Latin *fricatus*, "rubbing"; since the 1500s] **2.** to waste time. See JACK OFF (sense 2). [British, 1700s-1800s] **3.** to copulate; a euphemism for FUCK (*q.v.*). [primarily U.S., 1900s]

frigging 1. masturbation. [since the 1500s] **2.** time-wasting; demanding too much time. Said of a person or a task. [British, 1700s] **3.** copulation. [U.S., 1900s, Berrey and Van den Bark] **4.** damned; "fucking." *Cf.* FREAKING. [U.S. slang, mid 1900s-pres.]

friggle to masturbate. From a term originally meaning "jerk" or "wiggle." [British slang, 1800s, Farmer and Henley]

frigid originally sexually disabled; a weak or impotent male or a sterile woman. Now used almost exclusively for an inorgasmic woman. [since the mid 1600s]

frigidity 1. impotence. See FRIGID. **2.** the condition of an inorgasmic woman. **3.** an abnormal disinterest in sex, usually said of a woman.

Frig it! a euphemism for "Fuck it!" [U.S. slang, mid 1900s]

frig oneself to masturbate oneself. [1500s-pres.]

frigster a male who masturbates himself. For synonyms see HUSKER. [British, 1800s or before]

frigstress a female who masturbates herself. [British, 1800s or before]

frig-up (also **frigg-up**) a mess; a muddle, slightly euphemistic for "fuck-up." [Australian and U.S., 1900s]

frillery (also **frillies**) women's underwear. For synonyms see NETHER GARMENTS. [British and U.S. slang, late 1800s-1900s, Farmer and Henley]

frills sexually aroused, primarily in the expression "in one's frills." *Cf.* FLAVOUR, SALT (sense 1). [British slang, 1800s, Farmer and Henley]

frip an oaf. Possibly a blend of "freak" and "drip." [U.S. slang, mid 1900s]

frisgig (also **frizgig**) a silly, giddy young woman. [British dialects and U.S. slang, 1800s-1900s]

frisking petting or groping. From the patting and pressing done by police searching for concealed weapons on arrested persons. For synonyms see FIRKYTOODLE. [U.S. slang, 1900s]

frisky playful; amorous. [British and U.S., 1900s and before]

frit a homosexual male. Possibly a blend of FRUIT and FLIT (both *q.v.*). For synonyms see EPICENE. [both senses, U.S. slang, mid 1900s, Wentworth and Flexner]

frog 1. a Frenchman; a Parisian. From the *fleur-de-lis*, the bogy site of Paris and frog's legs eaten for food. *Cf.* FROGGY, OG-FRAY. [since the 1700s] **2.** a policeman. Because he pounces on criminals. [British, 1800s-1900s] **3.** an adolescent male whose voice is changing. [U.S., 1900s] **4.** a condom. From FRENCHY (senses 1 and 3). For synonyms see EEL-SKIN. [attested as Australian, 1970s, Wilkes]

frog-eater a derogatory nickname for a Frenchman. See FROGGY. [British and U.S. slang, mid 1800s-1900s] Synonyms: FRENCHER, FRENCHY, FROG, FROGGY, OG-FRAY, PARLEYVOO.

froggy a Frenchman. From the eating of frog's legs. More jocular than derogatory. See FROG (sense 1). [British and U.S., 1900s]

froglander a derogatory nickname for a Dutchman. From the marshy (froggy) areas of Holland. [British, 1600s-1800s]

frog's eyes (also **fish's eyes, frog spawn**) tapioca. A dysphemism. For related terms see DOG'S VOMIT. [colloquial, 1900s]

frogsh nonsense. A jocular avoidance of BULLSHIT (*q.v.*), patterned on BULLSH, COWSH, HORSH (all *q.v.*). [Australian, military, 1900s, Baker]

frog-skin a condom. *Cf.* EEL-SKIN, FISH-SKIN. [Australian, early 1900s, Baker]

frolic 1. to be in heat; to be sexually aroused. [U.S. colloquial euphemism, 1900s or before] **2.** to play sexually. [colloquial, 1800s-1900s]

front-door mat the female pubic hair. [British slang, 1800s]

front-garden the female genitals. *Cf.* FORE-COURT. [British slang, 1800s]

front-parlor (also **parlor**) the female genitals. [British, early 1800s]

front-suspension a brassiere. From the term for the devices which support the front wheels of an automobile. For synonyms see BRA. [Australian, early 1900s, *Dictionary of Slang and Unconventional English*]

front-wheel skid a Jewish man or woman. Rhyming slang for YID (*q.v.*). Derogatory. For synonyms see FIVE AND TWO. [British, early 1900s, *Dictionary of Rhyming Slang*]

front-window the female genitals. [British slang, 1800s]

frosty 1. cold; sexually unresponsive; frigid. [from *Venus and Adonis* (Shakespeare)] **2.** a Caucasian. From "Frosty the Snowman." **3.** an OREO (*q.v.*), a black who prefers to act like a Caucasian. [senses 2 and 3 are U.S. black use, mid 1900s]

froze his mouth became intoxicated with alcohol. [U.S. slang, early 1700s, Ben Franklin]

frozen intoxicated with alcohol. [U.S. slang, early 1700s, Ben Franklin]

fruit 1. a woman of easy morals. This sense is related to "easy-picking," and it is the likely semantic ancestor of sense 3 via sense 2. [U.S. underworld, early 1900s, Goldin, O'Leary, and Lipsius] **2.** a dupe; an easy mark. *Cf.* sense 3. There are numerous terms which mean both "dupe" and "male homosexual." See GAY (sense 3). [U.S. underworld, early 1900s, Irwin] **3.** an effeminate male; a passive homosexual male. See sense 2 above. [U.S. underworld, mid 1900s, Goldin, O'Leary, and Lipsius] **4.** any male homosexual. A derogatory term used by homosexuals and others. This term and QUEER (*q.v.*) are among the most resented of all derogatory nicknames for homosexuals. They are also the most widespread. [U.S., early 1900s-pres.] **5.** any strange person. [U.S. colloquial, mid 1900s]

fruitcake 1. a homosexual male, an elaboration of FRUIT (sense 4). **2.** any jerk or oaf. From "nutty as a fruitcake." *Cf.* NUT (sense 1). [both senses, U.S. slang, mid 1900s-pres.]

fruiter a homosexual male. *Cf.* FRUIT (sense 4). For synonyms see EPICENE. [U.S. underworld, early 1900s]

fruit-fly 1. a homosexual male, an elaboration of FRUIT (*q.v.*). **2.** a heterosexual woman who associates with homosexual males for sex or for security. *Cf.* FAG-BAG, SCAG-HAG. Both are from the common name for drosophila, an insect. [both senses, U.S. slang, mid 1900s-pres.]

fruitful vine the female genitals; the womb. Because it "has flowers every month, and bears fruit in nine months" (*Lexicon Balatronicum*). [British, early 1800s]

fruiting living a sexually promiscuous life. See FRUIT, FRUITER. [attested as black use, mid 1900s, Major]

fruit-picker a male who has occasional homosexual experiences. *Cf.* FRUIT-FLY. [U.S. homosexual use, mid 1900s, Wentworth and Flexner]

fruit-plate a homosexual male. An elaboration of FRUIT (sense 4), perhaps a variant of DISH (*q.v.*). [U.S., 1900s]

fruit-stand a homosexual bar; a gathering place for homosexual males. [U.S., mid 1900s]

frump 1. an old woman with one or more of the following qualities: primness, wrinkles, slatternliness, gossipiness, grouchiness, or a holier-than-thou attitude. [British and U.S., 1800s-1900s] **2.** any ugly or unpleasant male or female. [colloquial, 1900s]

fry to die in the electric chair. [U.S. underworld, early 1900s]

fu marijuana. For synonyms see MARI. [U.S., mid 1900s]

F.U. 1. a "foul-up" or a "fuck-up." **2.** "to foul up" or "to fuck up." [both senses, British with some U.S. use, mid 1900s]

FUBAR "fucked-up beyond all recognition," pertaining to a horribly messed-up person or situation. For synonyms see SNAFU. [U.S. slang, mid 1900s] .

FUBB "fucked-up beyond belief," pertaining to an inconceivably confused person, object, or situation. For synonyms see SNAFU. [U.S. slang, mid 1900s]

FUBIS "fuck you buddy, I'm shipping (off or out)," pertaining to a particular type of antisocial attitude in the military. For synonyms see SNAFU. [U.S. slang, mid 1900s]

FUCK a contrived acronym for an imaginary etymology of FUCK (*q.v.*), "for unlawful carnal knowledge," or perhaps, "fornication under the consent of the king." [U.S., 1900s]

fuck (also **f*ck, f**k, f***, ****, f--k, f---**) **1.** to copulate. **2.** a copulation. [both since the early 1500s] **3.** semen. *Cf.* BULLFUCK. [since the 1500s] **4.** any sex act leading to orgasm. This includes all homosexual acts and other practices which are covered by the term SODOMY (*q.v.*). [mid 1900s-pres.] **5.** a woman considered as a sex object, as in the phrase "a good fuck." [British and U.S., 1900s] **6.** a man considered as a sex object, as in the phrase "a good fuck." [British and U.S., 1900s] **7.** vigor, especially sexual vigor in males. From sense 3. [British and some U.S. use, 1900s] **8.** to cheat, deceive, or ruin. *Cf.* FUCK UP. [U.S. slang, mid 1900s-pres.] **9.** to confuse. *Cf.* FUCK UP, MIND FUCK. [U.S. slang, mid 1900s-pres.] **10.** a damn, especially in expressions such as "don't give a fuck." [U.S., mid 1900s-pres.] **11.** as an expletive or exclamation, "Fuck!" Note: This term is popularly regarded as the worst of the "dirty words" and as the most reviled word in the English language. The most likely source is German *ficken*, "strike." A less likely source is Latin *pungo*, "to prick," but the origin of the word cannot be demonstrated conclusively. The word originally and primarily referred to the male aspects of copulation, and referred to the penetration, thrusting, and ejaculating of any male animal which copulates. It should be noted that most English words that refer exclusively to that act are not to be uttered in polite company. In the 1972 supplement of the *Oxford English Dictionary*, "fuck" is listed as an entry with its origin unknown. Numerous etymologies have been proposed: a truncation of "fecund"; an acronym for "fornication under the consent of the king"; an acronym for "for unlawful carnal knowledge"; an acronym for "for the use of carnal knowledge." It is possibly a disguise of FOUTRE (*q.v.*), which is from Latin *futuere* via French. Both FOOT and FUT (both *q.v.*) were used as disguises of *foutre,* and FUCK may have originally been a minced version of *foutre*. The word was probably in use by the 1400s and may have been Scots originally. The earliest attestations were in the North of England and dated from 1503. If the word were strongly tabooed, it may not have appeared in writing as early as it would have otherwise. Disguises are: ********, COLONIAL PUCK, F., F***, F---, F*CK, F**K, F--K, FRIAR TUCK, FRIG, FUDGE, FUG, FULKE, FURK, FUTZ, GOOSE AND DUCK, IM-FUCKING-POSSIBLE, IRRE-FUCK-ING-SPONSIBLE, JOE BUCK, LAME DUCK, MRS. DUCKETT!, MUCK, PUSH IN THE TRUCK, RUCK, RUSSIAN DUCK, TROLLEY AND TRUCK, UCK-FAY. See list at OCCUPY.

fuckable pertaining to a sexually desirable woman. *Cf.* APPROACHABLE, BEDWORTHY, PUNCHABLE, ROMPWORTHY, SHAFTABLE. [British and U.S. slang, 1800s-1900s]

Fuck a duck! (also **Fuck a dog!**) an exclamation. *Cf.* DUCK-FUCKER, FORNICATE THE POODLE! [U.S. slang, mid 1900s-pres.]

fuckathon an extended period of paired or group homosexual activity usually involving FELLATIO and PEDERASTY (both *q.v.*). *Cf.* EVERYTHINGATHON. [U.S. slang, mid 1900s-pres.]

fuck buttock to coit anally. *Cf.* ASS-FUCK, BUTT-FUCK, GUT-BUTCHER. Possibly also meant PEDERAST (*q.v.*). [British colloquial, 1800s, Farmer and Henley]

fucked-out (also **fucked**) **1.** worn-out as from excessive copulating. **2.** worndown as from continual abuse. [both senses, British and U.S., 1900s and before]

fucked-up (also **fucked**) **1.** temporarily confused or seriously mentally disturbed. **2.** in trouble; malfunctioning. **3.** intoxicated with drugs. For synonyms see TALL. [all senses, U.S. slang, mid 1900s-pres.]

fucker 1. a male lover. [British and U.S. colloquial, 1800s or before] **2.** a chum or buddy. [British and U.S. slang, 1800s-1900s] **3.** the penis. For synonyms see YARD. [recurrent nonce use] See also GUT-BUTCHER. **4.** a rude nickname, usually for a male.

fuck-film a pornographic film which features explicit scenes of various types of copulation. *Cf.* SKIN-FLICK. [U.S. slang, mid 1900s-pres.]

fuck-finger a female masturbator. *Cf.* FINGER-FUCK, FRICATRIX. [British slang, 1800s, Farmer and Henley]

fuck-fist a male masturbator. A term of contempt. *Cf.* FIST-FUCK. For synonyms see HUSKER. [British slang, 1800s, Farmer and Henley]

fuck-freak a woman, especially a prostitute, who is obsessed with copulation. [U.S. slang, mid 1900s-pres.]

fuck-head an oaf or jerk. [U.S. slang, mid 1900s-pres.]

fuck-hole the female genitals, especially the vagina. [British and U.S. colloquial and nonce]

fucking 1. copulation. For synonyms see SMOCKAGE. **2.** an intensifier; the U.S. equivalent of "bloody." Also **fuckin'.**

fucking around goofing off; playing and not attending to duty. [U.S. slang, mid 1900s-pres.]

fucking machine a legendary machine (most often seen in limericks) which provides a variety of sexual services tirelessly. [since the 1800s]

fucking-rubber a condom. An elaboration of RUBBER (*q.v.*), which might otherwise be construed as a rubberband or an eraser. For synonyms see EEL-SKIN. [U.S., mid 1900s-pres.]

fuckish 1. sexually aroused. See FUCKABLE. **2.** pertaining to a sexually loose woman. [both senses, British slang, 1800s, Farmer and Henley]

Fuck it all! (also **Fuck all!**, **Fuck 'em all! Fuck it!**) a rude exclamation, "Damn it!" or "Damn it all!" [British and U.S. 1800s-1900s]

fuckle to copulate. For synonyms see OCCUPY. [British slang, 1800s, Farmer and Henley]

fuck like a rattlesnake to PHALLICIZE (*q.v.*) vigorously; to coit as vigorously as a rattlesnake shakes its tail. [Partridge suggests that it is of U.S. origin; attested as Australian, late 1800s, *Dictionary of Slang and Unconventional English*]

Fuck me gently! (also **Fuck me pink!**) **1.** an exclamation, "I'll be damned!" [British and U.S., 1900s] **2.** "Destroy me or cheat me in a genteel manner!"; "Screw me politely!" [U.S. slang, mid 1900s-pres.]

fuck off 1. to masturbate. **2.** to waste time; to GOOF OFF (*q.v.*). **3.** a person who wastes time; a goof-off. Usually hyphenated in this sense. **4.** "Get out!" or "Buzz off!" [all senses, U.S. slang, mid 1900s-pres.]

fuck one's fist to masturbate, said of a male. *Cf.* FIST-FUCK. [British slang, 1800s, Farmer and Henley]

fuck over 1. to work over; to beat up; to use physical violence to teach someone a lesson. **2.** to cheat or deceive someone. *Cf.* FUCK (sense 8). [both senses, U.S. slang, mid 1900s-pres.]

fuck-shit a term of contempt for a despised person. [U.S., 1900s]

fucksome pertaining to a sexually desirable woman. Punning on BUXOM (*q.v.*). *Cf.* FUCKABLE. [British slang, 1800s, Farmer and Henley]

fuck someone's mind to badger and confuse someone into behavior or a particular manner of thinking; to fuck someone up. *Cf.* FUCK (sense 9), FUCK UP. [U.S. slang, mid 1900s-pres.]

fuckster a lecher or a whoremonger; a man noted for his sexual prowess or interest in women. For synonyms see LECHER. [British, 1800s]

fuckstress 1. a prostitute. **2.** a woman who is known to be sexually willing and satisfying. *Cf.* FUCK (sense 5). For synonyms see LAY. [both senses, British slang, 1800s, Farmer and Henley]

fuck up 1. to ruin; to mess up; to confuse. *Cf.* BUGGER UP. **2.** a mess; a confusion. Usually hyphenated in this sense. [both senses, U.S. slang, 1900s]

Fuck you! a very strong curse. Stronger than "Damn you!" Occasionally "Fuck you, Charlie!" or something similar. [U.S., 1900s] See also FUBIS.

fuddle 1. a drink of alcohol. [British, 1600s-1800s] **2.** to confuse with drink. **3.** a drunken bout; a spree. *Cf.* BEFUDDLE. [senses 2 and 3 are slang, 1800s-1900s]

fuddle-cap a drunkard. See FIDDLE-CUP. For synonyms see ALCHY. [British, 1600s-1700s, Dekker, *New Canting Dictionary*]

fuddled intoxicated with alcohol. [colloquial, 1600s-1900s]

fudge 1. nonsense. For synonyms see ANIMAL. [British and U.S. colloquial, 1700s-1900s] **2.** to masturbate someone to orgasm. From the colloquial sense "cheat." [U.S. slang, 1900s, Wentworth and Flexner] **3.** a phonological disguise of "fuck"; an exclamation, "Fudge!" [U.S. slang, mid 1900s-pres.]

fug a phonological disguise of "fuck." *Cf.* FUDGE (sense 3). [U.S., mid 1900s-pres.]

fugitive from a daisy chain gang a homosexual male. Based on the expression "fugitive from a chain gang." *Cf.* DAISY CHAIN. [U.S. jocular, 1900s]

fugle (also **fugel**) to copulate. From a word meaning to cheat or trick. *Cf.* FUCKLE, FUG, HONEY-FUGGLE. [British slang, early 1700s]

fugo the anus; the rectum. [a play on a form of this Latin word meaning "to discharge, to let fly"; British, 1700s or before]

FUJ "Fuck you Jack!" The "you" becomes "U." An expression proclaiming one's self-centeredness. See FUBIS. [British military, early 1900s]

full 1. intoxicated with alcohol. [widespread colloquial, 1700s-pres.] **2.** erect, said of the penis. [British slang, 1800s, Farmer and Henley]

full as a--the basis of a series of terms for "drunk" most of which are from the 1800s or before: full as a boot, full as a bull, full as a fiddle, full as a goat, full as a goog, full as a lord, full as a tick. *Cf.* DRUNK AS A LORD, TIGHT AS A TICK.

full-flavored 1. really rotten; obscene. *Cf.* FLAVOUR. **2.** pertaining to a very bad-smelling release of intestinal gas. *Cf.* CHEEZER.

full-fledged sexually aroused, usually pertaining to a female. For synonyms see HUMPY. [British slang, 1800s, Farmer and Henley]

full hand a case of gonorrhea and syphilis together. *Cf.* FULL HOUSE. [Australian, 1900s]

full house all of the venereal diseases at once. [U.S., early 1900s, Goldin, O'Leary, and Lipsius]

full-in-the-belly pregnant. *Cf.* BELLYFULL. For synonyms see FRAGRANT. [British colloquial, 1800s]

full of fuck 1. virile and full of masculine vigor. *Cf.* FUCK (sense 7). **2.** sexually aroused; full of desire or full of semen. *Cf.* FUCK (sense 3). For synonyms see HUMPY. [both senses, slang, 1900s]

full of gism the same as FULL OF FUCK (*q.v.*). [U.S. slang, 1900s]

full of heir pregnant. A pun based on the homonyms "air" (as in "full of hot air") and "heir." [U.S. jocular slang, 1900s]

full of it deceitful; full of nonsense. An avoidance for FULL OF SHIT (*q.v.*). [British and U.S., 1900s]

full of piss and vinegar (also **full of vim and vinegar**) energetic and vigorous. [U.S. colloquial, 1900s]

full of shit (also **full of bull, full of crap**) deceitful; full of nonsense and lies. [U.S. slang, 1900s]

full-on sexually excited and desirous of copulation, the same as TURNED-ON (sense 2). *Cf.* FLAVOUR, FULL-FLEDGED, ON, SALT (sense 1).

full to the bung intoxicated with alcohol. *Cf.* BUNGEY. For synonyms see WOOFLED. [primarily British, 1800s-1900s]

full to the guards intoxicated with alcohol. [British, 1900s, *Dictionary of Slang and Unconventional English*]

FUMTU "fucked-up more than usual," pertaining to a state considerably more messed up than usual. For synonyms see SNAFU. [British and U.S., mid 1900s]

fun the anus or the posteriors. From FUNDAMENT (*q.v.*). [British, 1600s-1800s, B.E.] See also FON.

fun and frolics the testicles. Rhyming slang for "ballocks." For synonyms see WHIRLYGIGS. [British, 1800s, *Dictionary of Rhyming Slang*]

fun and games sexual play or intercourse. *Cf.* PLAY AROUND [U.S. slang, mid 1900s-pres.]

fundament the anus or the posteriors. [since the 1200s, *Oxford English Dictionary*]

fundamental features the posteriors. From the standard expression referring to "important factors," and the term FUNDAMENT (*q.v.*). [British jocular and euphemistic, early 1800s, Farmer and Henley]

funeral a ceremony or rites concerned with the burial or commemoration of a dead person. Synonyms: COLD-MEAT PARTY, MEMORIAL SERVICE, OBSEQUIES, PLANTING.

funny 1. intoxicated with alcohol. [colloquial since the 1700s] **2.** effeminate; homosexual. A vague euphemism for QUEER (sense 3). [U.S. slang, mid 1900s-pres.]

funny bit the female genitals. [British slang, 1800s]

funny stuff marijuana. For synonyms see MARI. [U.S. drug culture, mid 1900s-pres.]

fur 1. the female pubic hair. For synonyms see DOWNSHIRE. [British and U.S. colloquial, 1800s-1900s] **2.** the female genitals; women considered sexually. [U.S. slang, 1900s]

furbelow the female pubic hair. A reinterpretation of the name of a fur edge on a dress or petticoat. [British, 1600s]

furburger the female genitals and pubic hair. *Cf.* HAIRBURGER (sense 1). [U.S. slang, mid 1900s-pres.]

Fut! an oath, possibly a disguise of "Fuck!" Related to FUTTER (*q.v.*).

futter to copulate. For synonyms see OCCUPY. [literary euphemism; British, late 1800s, Farmer and Henley]

futuere* to copulate. See FOOT, FOUTRE!., FUTTER. [Latin]

future the scrotum and its contents; the testicles. That which a man needs to father his descendants. Also, when said of a boy, that upon which one's future sex life depends. *Cf.* FAMILY JEWELS. [U.S., mid 1900s-pres.]

futz 1. to coit. [U.S., 1800s-1900s] **2.** the female genitals. [U.S., 1900s] **3.** to cheat or deceive. From sense 1. See PHUTZ. A disguise of FUCK (sense 8). [U.S., mid 1900s-pres.]

futz around 1. to play sexually. **2.** to GOOF OFF (*q.v.*); to FUCK OFF (*q.v.*). [both senses, U.S. slang, 1900s]

futzed-up a disguise of FUCKED-UP (*q.v.*). [U.S., 1900s]

fuzzle to make someone or oneself

drunk. *Cf.* FUDDLE. [British, early 1600s, *Oxford English Dictionary*]

fuzzled intoxicated with alcohol. *Cf.* FUDDLED. [since the early 1700s]

fuzzy intoxicated with alcohol. For synonyms see WOOFLED. [British and U.S. slang, late 1700s-pres.]

fuzzy-wuzzy 1. an indigenous African. Refers to the Negroid hair type. Derogatory. [British, late 1800s, (Kipling)] **2.** a person indigenous to New Guinea. From sense 1. [Australian slang, World War II, Wilkes]

G

gab room a women's restroom. [U.S. slang, mid 1900s]

Gad "God" in expressions such as "Gads me!" and "Gads my life!" meaning "God save me!" and "God save my life!" Also an oath and an exclamation, "Gad!" [early 1600s-pres.]

gadget 1. a thing or tool. Many of the following synonyms have also been used to mean "penis" and, in the plural, "testicles" or VIRILIA (*q.v.*). Synonyms for "gadget": DEEDEE, DICKY, DIDDENWHACKER, DIDDLEDYFLOP, DIDDLEHEIMER, DINGBAT, DINGLE, DINGUS, DINKUS, DINKY, DOBAUBLE, DOBOB, DOBOBBIS, DOBOBBLE, DOBOBBUS, DO-BOBBY, DODAD, DODADDY, DODINGLE, DODINKUS, DOFLICKETY, DOFLOPPY, DO-FUNNY, DOGADGET, DOHICKEY, DOHICKIE, DOHICKUS, DOHICKY, DOJIGGER, DOJIGGIE, DOJIGGUM, DOJIGGUS, DOLOLLY, DO-MAGGUS, DOMAJIG, DOMAJIGGER, DOO-DAD, DOODLE, DOOFLICKER, DOOFUNNY, DOOHICKEY, DOOJIGGER, DOOMAJIG, DOOSENWHACKER, DOOWHISTLE, DOO-WILLIE, DOOZANDAZZY, DOWHACKER, DOWHOPPER, DUDENWHACKER, DUFUNNY, FAKUS, FANDANGLE, FIRKIN, FOLDEROL, FRIGAMAJIG, FUMADIDDLE, GAZINKUS, GAZUNKUS, GEEGAW, GEWGAW, GIG-AMAREE, GILGUY, GILHOOLEY, GIMCRACK, GIMIX, GINGAMBOB, GINKUS, GIZMO, GOOFUS, HICKEY, HICKIE, HICKUS, HICKY, HINKUS, HOOFEN-POOFER, HOOTMALIE, HOOTNANNY, JIGALORUM, JIGGAMY, JIG-GER, JIGGIE, JIGGUM JIGGUMBOB, JIGGUS, JIGGY, JINGUMBOB, JOBBER, JOBBY, KAJODY, KNACK, MAJIG, RIGAMAJIG, THINGABOB, THINGABOBBLE, THINGA-BOBBUS, THINGABOBBY, THINGAMABOB, THINGAMADING, THINGAMADOODLE, THINGAMAJIG, THINGAMAJIGGER, THING-AMAJINGIE, THINGAMAJOHN, THING-AMAREE, THINGDOODLE, THINGMAJIGGUS, THINGUMABOB, THINGUMBOB, THINGUM-MIE, THINGUMTIBOB, THINKUMTHINKUM, THUMADOODLE, UNIT, WHACKER, WHAM-DITTY, WHANGDOODLE, WHANGYDOODLE, WHATCHAMACALLEM, WHATCHAMACALL-IT, WHATCHAMADAD, WHATCHAMADAD-DY, WHATCHAMADIDDLE, WHATCHAMA-DINGLE, WHATCHAMADOODLE, WHATCH-AMAGADGET, WHATCHAMAHICKEY, WHAT-CHAMAJIGGER, WHATSIS, WHATSIT, WHAT-ZIT, WHAZZIT, WHINGDING, WHOSERMY-BOB, WHOSERMYJIG, WIDGET, WING-DING, WINGDOODLE. **2.** the penis. For synonyms see YARD. [both senses, U.S. slang and colloquial, mid 1900s-pres.]

Gad's bud! an oath and an exclamation, "By God's blood!" *i.e.*, "By God's offspring!" For synonyms see 'ZOUNDS! [British, 1700s or before]

Gadso! (also **Catso!, Godso!**) **1.** an oath based on "God" or GAD (*q.v.*). **2.** an exclamation, literally, "Penis!" [from Italian *cazzo*, "penis"; both senses, British, 1700s]

Gadzooks! an oath and an exclamation, "By God's hooks!" *Cf.* COTSZOOKS! [British, 1600s]

gagger 1. a rustic old man; an old bumpkin. Also **old gaffer**. A telescoping of "grandfather." [since the late 1500s] **2.** to coit a woman. [British slang, 1800s, Farmer and Henley]

gag 1. to retch, especially to retch noisily. **2.** to choke on food or foreign matter in the throat. **3.** to attempt to make oneself vomit by placing an ojbect such as a finger far back in the throat. [all senses, U.S. colloquial, 1900s or before]

gaged (also **gauged**) intoxicated with alcohol. For synonyms see WOOFLED. [U.S. slang, early 1900s]

Gainesville green a variety of marijuana named for "Gainesville," Florida. [U.S. drug culture, mid 1900s-pres.]

gal. 1. a prostitute. **2.** a girl, especially a girlfriend. [British and U.S. colloquial, 1800s-1900s]

gal-boy 1. a masculine woman. [U.S. slang, late 1900s, Farmer and Henley] **2.** a CATAMITE or a FELLATOR (both *q.v.*). [U.S. underworld, mid 1900s, Goldwin, O'Leary, and Lipsius]

gallantry copulation; the world of male-female relations; male-female sexual relations and the male sexual pursuit of women. [British, 1600s-1700s]

galligaskins (also **galigaskins**) **1.** a type of hose or breeches. One etymology is that this is from "galley gaskins," *i.e.*, the type of trousers worn in a ship's galley. The exact origin of the word is unknown. *Cf.* GASKINS. [in other spellings, 1500s; in this spelling since the 1800s] **2.** trousers. [British and U.S. colloquial, 1800s-1900s] Synonyms usually refer to men's trousers unless indicated otherwise: ARSE-RUG, ARTICLES, BAG, BELONGINGS, BLOOMERS (female), BREECH, BREECHES, BREEKS, BRITCHES, BROGUES, BULL ANTS, BULL'S AUNTS, BUM-BAGS, BUM-CURTAIN, CALF-CLINGERS, CONTINUATIONS, COUNCIL-HOUSES, DENIMS, DON'T-NAME-'EMS, DRUMSTICK CASES, DUNGAREES, EEL-SKINS, FARTING-CRACKERS, FLEAS AND ANTS, GALLYSLOPES, GAM-CASES, GAS-KINS, HAM-CASES, HAMS, HOLY-FALLS, INDESCRIBABLES, INDISPENSABLES, IN-EXPLICABLES, INEXPRESSIBLES, INNOMIN-ABLES, INSECTS AND ANTS, IRREPRESSI-BLES, JEANS, JOLLY ROWSERS, KICK, KICK-CLOY, KICKS, KICKSIES, KICKSTERS, KNICK-ER-BOCKERS, LEG-BAGS, LEG-COVERS, LEVIS, LIMB-SHROUDERS, MARY-WALKERS, MUSTN'T-MENTION-'EMS, NETHER GARMENTS, NEVER-MENTION-'EMS, PAIR OF DRUMS, PANTALOONS, PANTS, PLUS FOURS, RAMMIES, RANK AND RICHES, RESWORT, RICE-BAGS, RIPS, RIPSEY ROUSERS, ROUND-ME-HOUSES, ROUND-MES, ROUNDS, ROUND-THE-HOUSES, SACKS, SCRATCHES, SIN-HIDERS, SIT-DOWN-UPONS, SIT-UPONS, SKILTS, SONG AND DANCE, SRES-WORT, STOVE-PIPES, STRIDERS, STRIDES, STROSSERS, THINGUMBOBS, TROLLY-WAGS, TROLLY-WOGS, TROU, TROUSERLOONS, TROUSIES, TRUCKS, UNCLES AND AUNTS, UNHINTABLES, UN-MENTIONABLES, UNSPEAKABLES, UN-UTTERABLES, UNWHISPERABLES.

gallimaufrey (also **galimaufry**) **1.** a mistress. [from *Merry Wives of Wind-*

sor (Shakespeare)] **2.** the female genitals. Both are from a term meaning "hodgepodge." [British, Farmer and Henley]

galloot (also **galoot**) an oaf, especially an oafish soldier. [widespread slang, 1800s-pres.]

galloping knob-rot a phallic itch, an itching in the male genital area. *Cf.* KNOB. [British military, mid 1900s, *Dictionary of Slang and Unconventional English*]

gallop one's antelope to masturbate, said of males. From "hand-gallop" in horsemanship, an easy gallop. [British, 1800s-1900s]

gallop one's maggot to masturbate, said of males. From "hand-gallop" in horsemanship, an easy gallop. [British slang, 1800s, *Dictionary of Slang and Unconventional English*]

gallows a framework from which a man could be hanged by the neck until dead. Synonyms: BOUGH, CHATES, CRAP, DEADLY NEVERGREEN, FORKS, FURCA, GIBBET, GOVERNMENT-SIGNPOST, HORSE FOALED OF AN ACORN, LEAFLESS TREE, MARE WITH THREE LEGS, MORNING DROP, NUBBING-CHEAT, PICTURE-FRAME, SCRAG-GING-POST, SHERIFF'S PICTURE FRAME, SQUEEZER, STALK, STIFFLER, SWING, THE THREE TREES, THREE-LEGGED MARE, THREE-LEGGED STOOL, TOPPING CHEAT, TREE, TRIPLE-TREE, TURNING TREE, TWO-LEGGED TREE, WOODEN HORSE, WOODEN-LEGGED MARE.

gamahuchery (also **gamaroosh**, **gamaruche**) PENILINGISM (*q.v.*). [based on French, *gamahucher;* British, late 1800s, (Farmer)]

gam-cases trousers; breeches. *Cf.* HAM-CASES. For synonyms see GALLIGASKINS. [British slang, 1800s, Farmer and Henley]

game 1. a women; prostitutes in general; any woman considered solely as a sexual object. For synonyms see TAIL. [British slang or cant, 1600s-1900s] **2.** pertaining to someone who is willing to copulate. *Cf.* SPORT, TRADE. [U.S. colloquial, 1900s]

game-cock a whoremonger. Based on

a term used for wildfowl. *Cf.* COCK (senses 3 and 5), GAME (sense 1). For synonyms see LECHER. [British, 1800s]

gamester a prostitute; any lewd woman. *Cf.* SPORT. [from *All's Well That Ends Well* (Shakespeare)]

gang-bang 1. a real or fantasized sexual activity where one person is coited by a group of males serially; group rape. [both heterosexual and homosexual use, mid 1900s] **2.** an activity similar to sense 1 where promiscuous copulation takes place within a group. This is the original model for a series of similar rhyming pairs. See GROUP SEX for a list. [U.S. slang, mid 1900s-pres.]

gange a derogatory nickname for a Negro. *Cf.* DANGE BROAD. [U.S. slang, 1900s, Wentworth and Flexner]

gang-shag (also **gang-shay**) group copulation; the same as GANG-BANG (*q.v.*), but usually heterosexual only.

gangster 1. a hoodlum; a thug. [U.S., early 1900s-pres.] **2.** marijuana. **3.** a marijuana cigarette. [senses 2 and 3 are U.S. underworld, mid 1900s]

gangster pills barbiturate tablets or capsules. *Cf.* GANGSTER (senses 2 and 3). For synonyms see BARB. [U.S. drug culture, mid 1900s-pres.]

ganjah (also **ganja, gunja**) a potent variety of marijuana; a Jamaican term for marijuana. [from Handi; in English since 1800]

ganymede a PEDERAST or a SODOMITE (both *q.v.*). Sometimes capitalized. Ganymede was the cupbearer to Zeus. [from Greek via Latin and French; in English since the late 1500s]

gap (also **gape**) **1.** the female genitals. See PUDENDAL CLEAVAGE. [recurrent nonce; attested as early 1700s] **2.** the space between the breasts. [slang, 1900s]

gaper the female genitals. For synonyms see MONOSYLLABLE. [British slang, 1800s, Farmer and Henley]

gap-stopper 1. a whoremonger. For synonyms see LECHER. [British, late 1700s, Grose] **2.** the penis. [British slang, 1800s, Farmer and Henley]

gar a derogatory nickname for a Negro. Based on NIGGAR (*q.v.*). [U.S. slang and colloquial, 1900s]

Gar!, By an oath and an exclamation, "By God!" For synonyms see 'ZOUNDS! [since the late 1500s]

garbage can an old prostitute. *Cf.* COMMON SEWER, DRAIN, SCUPPER. [U.S. slang, early 1900s, Irwin]

garbage mouth a user of obscene language. [U.S. slang, mid 1900s] Synonyms and related terms: BLACK MOUTH, BUCKET MOUTH, CUD-CASTER, FOUL MOUTH, FOUL-TONGUED, POTTY MOUTH, SEWERMOUTH, TOILET MOUTH.

garden the female genitals. Where one sows SEED (sense 1). [translation of Latin *hortus;* British slang and euphemism, 1500s-1800s]

garden-engine the penis. The name of a water pump used for watering gardens. See GARDEN, GREENS. [British slang, 1800s, Farmer and Henley]

gardener the penis. [British slang, 1800s, Farmer and Henley]

garden-gate the *Labia Minora;* [British slang, 1800s, Farmer and Henley]

garden-gout venereal disease contracted in a Covent Garden brothel. [British slang, early 1700s]

garden-hedge the female pubic hair. *Cf.* GARDEN. [British slang, 1800s, Farmer and Henley]

garden-house 1. a brothel. [British, 1600s] **2.** a privy. For synonyms see AJAX. [U.S. colloquial, 1800s]

Gardenia! a curse, "God deen (damn) you!" [the flower name appeared in the mid 1700s and this euphemistic disguise soon thereafter]

garden of Eden the female genitals. *Cf.* GARDEN. [British slang, 1800s, Farmer and Henley]

garderobe 1. a wardrobe; a locked closet. No negative connotations. [1300s-1500s] **2.** a privy built within a large residence or a castle. Some which were built in castles extended outward from the castle walls and opened from great heights into a moat below.

[1500s-1600s] **3.** any privy. [British, 1800s]

Gardy loo! a maid's cry (said to be Scots) warning persons in the street that the contents of chamber pots were being dumped out of a window. See LOO. [from French *gardez l'eau*, "Watch out for the water," or from "Guard yourself (ye) below (loo)"; British, 1700s]

Gargantua's penis There are a large number of terms for Gargantua's member found in the English translations (Motteux, Urquhart) of Rabelais. Some of these were in use before the translations appeared and are listed separately in this dictionary. Some of them recur frequently in the older slang dictionaries: borer, branch of coral, bungpeg, bunguetee, busherusher, coney-borowferret, coral branch, corking-pin, crimson-chitterling, Cyprian scepter, dandilollie, dangling hangers, darling faucet, dresser, faucetin, futilletie, gallant wimble, garden, horny pipe, jewel for the ladies, jolly kyle, lever, linkie pinkie, little dille, little piercer, lusty andouille, membretoon, placket-racket, pouting stick, pretty boarer, pretty pillicock, pretty rogue, private hardware, pusher, quickset imp, quillety, ramrod, ruddy sausage, spikebit, staff of love, stop-gap, stopple, swagdangle, trunnion.

gargle 1. to drink alcohol. **2.** alcoholic drink; a drink of alcohol. [both senses, U.S. slang, 1900s]

Garn it! (also **Garn!**) an oath based on "Gol darn it!" [U.S. colloquial, 1900s or before]

gas 1. intestinal gas. For synonyms see GURK. [colloquial, 1800s-1900s] **2.** nonsense. *Cf.* BALLOON JUICE. **3.** to talk nonsense. [senses 2 and 3 are British and U.S. colloquial, mid 1800s-pres.] **4.** liquor. For synonyms see BOOZE. [U.S., 1900s, Berrey and Van den Bark]

gash 1. the female genitals. *Cf.* SLIT. [widespread recurrent nonce and slang, 1700s-pres.] **2.** a sexually loose woman; women considered sexually. From sense 1. [widespread slang, 1900s or before] **3.** a CATAMITE (*q.v.*). From sense 2. For synonyms see BRONCO. **4.** an ugly male. From sense 1.

gash-bucket a refuse bucket; a bucket used as a urinal.

gash-hound a whoremonger; possibly also a PEDERAST (*q.v.*). *Cf.* GASH (sense 1). [U.S. slang, 1900s]

gaskins a type of wide hose; breeches. Later, a term for trousers. Related to GALLIGASKINS (*q.v.*). [since the 1600s]

gasp and grunt the female genitals. Rhyming slang for CUNT (*q.v.*). [British, 1900s, *Dictionary of Rhyming Slang*]

gate the female genitals, specifically the Vulva. *Cf.* GARDEN-GATE, JANUA VITAE. [1800s and before]

gate-of-horn (also **gate-of-life, gate-of-plenty**) the female genitals. See HORN (sense 3), "penis." *Cf.* JANUA VITAE. [British, 1800s, Farmer and Henley]

gator sweat homebrewed whisky, especially that which is aged in earthen mounds. From the manner in which an alligator incubates its eggs, and patterned on PANTHER SWEAT (*q.v.*). [U.S. colloquial (Southern), 1900s or before]

gaubshite a filthy and slovenly man; the same word as GOBSHITE (*q.v.*). "Shite" is an old form of SHIT (*q.v.*). [British dialect, 1800s]

gaucho to MOON (sense 1); to expose the buttocks, usually in the window of a car as an insult to someone. *Cf.* HANG A B.A., PRESSED-HAM. [U.S. slang, mid 1900s, *Current Slang*]

gauge (also **gage**) **1.** a CHAMBER POT (*q.v.*). For synonyms see POT. [British, 1700s] **2.** cheap whisky; inferior whisky which might have come out of a chamber pot. For synonyms see EMBALMING FLUID. [U.S. slang, 1900s] **3.** marijuana. [U.S. drug culture, mid 1900s-pres.]

gauge-butt (also **gage-butt**) a marijuana cigarette. [U.S. slang, mid 1900s]

gay 1. sexually loose; dissipated. Originally pertaining only to a woman. [clearly implied in the 1300s, (Chaucer); occurs in *Othello* (Shakespeare); used for a male, mid 1700s, (Farmer and Henley); British slang and colloquial, early 1800s-1900s] **2.** intoxicated with alcohol. Refers primarily to one's uplifted spirits. [slang and nonce, 1800s-early 1900s] **3.** the dupe of a prostitute or of a con man. *Cf.* FRUIT (sense 2). **4.** pertaining to a homosexual, usually thought of as a male as in sense 5. Also used currently for a lesbian. [U.S. underworld and then slang, early 1900s-pres.; now widely-known U.S. slang] **5.** a young, unattached, highly visible, and highly social homosexual male. The term preferred by homosexual males. [U.S. slang and later widespread, mid 1900s-pres.]

gay and frisky Scotch whisky; any whisky. Rhyming slang for "whisky."

gay as pink ink pertaining to an obvious homosexual person, usually a male. [U.S. homosexual use, mid 1900s-pres.]

gay bar a bar that caters to and serves as a meeting place for homosexual males. [U.S. slang and colloquial, mid 1900s-pres.]

gay-boy a homosexual male, *Cf.* NAN-BOY. [Australian, early 1900s, *Dictionary of Slang and Unconventional English*]

gay-cat a young tramp; most likley a CATAMITE (*q.v.*). *Cf.* ANGELINA [U.S. underworld, early 1900s, Goldin, O'Leary, and Lipsius]

gay deceivers false breasts. No relation to GAY (*q.v.*). *Cf.* CHEATERS, FALSIES. [U.S. slang, mid 1900s]

gay dog a philanderer; a lecher. Ultimately from GAY (sense 1). [U.S. colloquial, 1900s]

gay-girl (also **gay-bit, gay-piece, gay-woman**) a prostitute. See GAY (sense 1). For synonyms see HARLOT. [British slang, early 1800s, Farmer and Henley]

gay house a brothel. [British and U.S. slang, 1800s-1900s]

gaying instrument the penis. *Cf.* GAY (sense 1). [British slang, early 1800s, *Lexicon Balatronicum*]

gay in the groin (also **gay in the arse, gay in the legs**) pertaining to a sexually loose woman. [British slang, 1800s, Farmer and Henley]

gay it to copulate, said of either sex. [British slang, 1800s, Farmer and Henley]

Gay Lib a political movement (patterned on the Women's Liberation movements) which advocates the establishment and guaranteeing of specific rights for homosexuals. A truncation of "Gay Liberation." [U.S., mid 1900s-pres.]

gay life an immoral life; a life of prostitution, said of women. [British, 1800s]

gay-man a whoremonger; a man who seeks GAY (sense 1) women. [British slang, 1800s, Farmer and Henley]

gay wench a prostitute; a sexually loose woman. *Cf.* GAY-GIRL. [U.S. slang, early 1900s]

gay-woman a prostitute. For synonyms see HARLOT. [British and U.S. slang, late 1800s-early 1900s]

gazongas the breasts; extremely well-shaped breasts. For synonyms see BOSOM. [U.S. slang, 1900s]

gazook 1. a clumsy oaf. [U.S. slang, early 1900s] **2.** a CATAMITE (*q.v.*). For synonyms see BRONCO. [U.S. underworld, mid 1900s]

gazoony (also **gazooney**) a PEDERAST or a CATAMITE (both *q.v.*); a hobo's catamite. [U.S. underworld, early 1900s, Rose]

G.B. 1. a mixture of cocaine and heroin. **2.** a mixture of amphetamines and barbiturates. **3.** barbiturates. All are from GOOF-BALL (*q.v.*). [all senses, U.S. drug culture, mid 1900s-pres.]

G.D. an abbreviation of GODDAMN! (*q.v.*). *Cf.* GEE-DEE, GOSHDARN, GOSH DING!, INDEGODDAM-PENDENT. [U.S. colloquial, 1900s]

gear 1. the male genitals. *Cf.* APPARATUS, KIT, LOT. [colloquial and nonce, 1600s-1900s] **2.** the female genitals. [1500s, Florio] **3.** to coit a woman. [British slang, 1800s, Farmer and

Henley] **4.** a homosexual male. Rhyming slang for QUEER (*q.v.*). Also **gearbox.** [British, early 1900s, *Dictionary of Rhyming Slang;* U.S. attestation, 1970s]

Gee! either "Jesus!" or "God!" Usually considered as a very mild exclamation, the origins of this word are known to few of its users. [U.S. colloquial and slang, 1900s or before]

Gee and Jay!, By an oath and an exclamation, "By God and Jesus!"

geech 1. to copulate with a woman; to masturbate a woman. [U.S. dialect (Boontling), late 1800s-early 1900s, Charles Adams] **2.** an unattractive person. [U.S. slang, mid 1900s, *Current Slang*]

gee-dee "Goddamned." See G.D. [U.S. colloquial, 1900s]

geed-up intoxicated with alcohol. *Cf.* GEEZED-UP. [U.S. slang, mid 1900s]

Gee-hollikens! a disguised oath used as an exclamation. See GEE-WHOLLIKER!

geek (also **geke**) **1.** a disliked person. **2.** a drunkard. **3.** a sexual degenerate or a homosexual male; a practitioner of nonorthogenital sexual acts. [all senses, U.S. slang, early 1900s]

Geekus crow! a disguise of "Jesus Christ!" For synonyms see 'ZOUNDS! [U.S. colloquial, 1900s]

gee stick an opium pipe. See GONG. [based on Chinese or mock-Chinese; U.S. slang, 1900s or before]

Gee-whillicats! (also **Gee-whilligins!**) a disguised oath used as an exclamation. See GEE-WHOLLIKER!

Gee-whillikers! (also **Gee-whillikens!**) an oath and an exclamation, "Jesus!" See GEE-WHOLLIKER! [British and U.S. colloquial, late 1800s-pres.]

Gee-whiskers! a disguised oath used as an exclamation. See GEE-WHOLLIKER!

Gee-whittakers! a disguised oath used as an exclamation. See GEE-WHOLLIKER!

Gee-whizzard! an oath and an exclamation.

Gee-wholliker! an oath and an exclamation. For synonyms see 'ZOUNDS.

Geez! a partial disguise of "Jesus!" [U.S. colloquial, 1900s]

geezed-up (also **geezed**) **1.** intoxicated with alcohol. For synonyms see WOOFLED. **2.** drug intoxicated. For synonyms see TALL. [both senses, U.S. slang, early 1900s-pres.]

geezer 1. a strange old man. [British and U.S. colloquial, late 1800s-pres.] **2.** a drink of alcohol; strong alcoholic drink. **3.** a shot of narcotics. [senses 2 and 3 are U.S. slang, early-mid 1900s]

geld 1. to castrate a male animal; to spay a female animal. Now primarily to castrate. [since the 1300s] **2.** to expurgate a book. [since the late 1500s, *Oxford English Dictionary*]

gelding 1. a castrated animal, especially a horse. **2.** a eunuch. [both since the 1300s]

Gemmenie! an exclamation and a disguised oath, "Jesus!" [colloquial, 1600s-1900s]

gender 1. to procreate; to impregnate. [1300s] **2.** to copulate. [British, 1400s-1800s] **3.** a euphemism for "biological sex," *i.e.,* male and female. Used primarily for grammatical gender (not sex) *i.e.,* masculine, feminine, and neuter.

generating place the female genitals. [British slang, 1800s, Farmer and Henley]

generation tool the penis. *Cf.* TOOL (sense 1). [British slang, 1800s, Farmer and Henley]

generous 1. intoxicated with alcohol. [U.S. slang, early 1700s, Ben Franklin] **2.** sexually willing.

genitalia the genitals, male and female. [based on Latin; medical since the late 1800s]

genital primacy a state wherein genital coition with another person dominates the libido of an individual. In contrast to narcissism, sadism, or masturbation. Considered by most societies as NORMAL (*q.v.*) for the adult when the coition is performed with a person of the opposite sex. *Cf.* ORTHOGENITAL. Also euphemistic for or in avoidance of "sexual normalcy."

genitals the male and female genitals. The term refers to the organs of reproduction, both internal and external, but is often used solely for the visible, external genitals of the male or female. Synonyms: APPARATUS UROGENITALIS, AREA, BOX, CARNAL PARTS, CONCERN, CROTCH, DODADS, EDEA, FLESH, GADGETS, GENITALIA, LOINS, LOVE-FLESH, NAKEDNESS, NATURA, NATURALIA, NATURAL PARTS, NATURAL PLACES, NATURALS, NATURE, ORGAN OF GENERATION, PARTS, PARTS BELOW, PLACE, PRIVATE PARTS, PRIVATE PROPERTY, PRIVATES, RHUBARB, SECRETS, SECRET WORKS, THE PERSON, UNDERPARTS, VITALS, WARE, WATER-BOX, WATER-COURSE, WATER-ENGINE, WATER-GAP, WATER-WORKS, WORKS.

genital zone the external genitals and the area surrounding them in either sex. *Cf.* AREA, PARTS, PLACE (sense 2).

gentleman cow a bull; a euphemism of avoidance for "bull." [U.S. rural colloquial, 1900s or before]

gentleman of the back door a PEDERAST (*q.v.*). *Cf.* BACK-DOOR WORK, USHER. [British, 1700s, Grose]

gentleman ox a euphemism for "bull." [U.S. rural colloquial, 1900s or before]

gentleman's companion a louse. *Cf.* BOSOM CHUMS. For synonyms see WALKING DANDRUFF. [British slang, late 1700s, Grose]

gentleman's complaint gonorrhea. [1900s or before]

gentleman's pleasure-garden the female pubic area. [British slang, 1800s, Farmer and Henley]

gentlemen's pleasure-garden padlock a menstrual cloth; a sanitary napkin. *Cf.* GARDEN. [British slang, 1800s, Farmer and Henley]

gentlemen's room the men's restroom. [U.S. colloquial, mid 1900s-pres.]

gentlemen's walk the men's restroom. *Cf.* LADIES' WALK. [U.S. colloquial, late 1800s]

gentlemiss an effeminate male. For

synonyms see FRIBBLE. [U.S. slang, early 1900s, Weseen]

gent's room, the (also **gent's, the**) the men's restroom. [British and U.S: colloquial, 1900s]

geography the female genitals. Because it is something to be explored. [British jocular slang, early 1900s, *Dictionary of Slang and Unconventional English*]

george 1. to seduce and copulate. [U.S. slang, mid 1900s, Dahlskog] **2.** a bowel movement. For synonyms see EASEMENT. [British, 1900s, *Dictionary of Slang and Unconventional English*]

Georgia cracker (also **cracker**) a Caucasian from Georgia. Derogatory in some usage. For synonyms see PECKERWOOD. [U.S. slang, 1900s]

Gern! an oath and an exclamation, "Darn!" or "Damn!" See DAD. [U.S. colloquial, 1900s, Wentworth]

gerry 1. excrement. For synonyms see DUNG. [cant, 1500s, Harman] **2.** a German, especially a German soldier. Often capitalized in this sense. Usually considered derogatory. Said to be from JERRY (sense 1), a chamber pot. More likely the diminutive of "ger" from "German." [World War II] Synonyms: BUCKET-HEAD, CABBAGEHEAD, DUTCHER, DUTCHIE, DUTCHMAN, GOON, HUN, JERRY, LIMBURGER.

get 1. offspring. The result of begetting. For synonyms see TAIL-FRUIT. [British, early 1800s, *Lexicon Balatronicum*] **2.** a bastard. **3.** to receive the male sexually, said of a woman. [British slang, 1800s, Farmer and Henley] **4.** a divorce. [from Hebrew via Yiddish; U.S., 1900s]

get a bellyful of marrow-pudding to coit. From the point of view of a woman. [British slang, 1800s, Farmer and Henley]

get about her to effect intromission; to penetrate a woman. [British colloquial, late 1800s]

get a crumpet to coit. *Cf.* CRUMPET (senses 1 and 2). [British, mid 1900s, *Dictionary of the Underworld*]

Get any? a question addressed to one male by another after a date with a young woman, "Did you score?" or "Did you copulate?" *Cf.* GETTING ANY? [U.S. slang, mid 1900s-pres.]

get a pair of balls against one's butt to copulate. From the female point of view. [British slang, 1800s, Farmer and Henley]

get a rise 1. to get someone to respond, either to laugh or to become angry. **2.** to cause an erection in the male. The ambiguity of senses 1 and 2 is the source of much jest. [frequent double entendre; British and U.S., 1800s-1900s]

get a shove in one's blind-eye to coit, from the woman's point of view. *Cf.* BLIND-EYE (sense 2). [British slang, 1800s, Farmer and Henley]

get blown to receive an act of FELLATIO (*q.v.*). Occasionally used in reference to CUNNILINGUS (*q.v.*). See BLOW (senses 3 and 4). [U.S. slang, mid 1900s-pres.]

get caught to get pregnant. *Cf.* CATCH (sense 2). [U.S. slang, early 1900s]

get cockroaches (also **eat cockroaches**) to masturbate. A truncation of BOX THE JESUIT AND GET COCKROACHES (*q.v.*). [British slang, 1800s, Farmer and Henley]

get down to perform CUNNILINGUS (*q.v.*). See GO DOWN. [U.S. slang, mid 1900s-pres.]

get down to it (also **get down to business**) to copulate. [British and U.S. slang, 1900s]

get fixed-up 1. to copulate; to receive a man. **2.** to seek a woman for sexual purposes. [both senses, U.S. colloquial, 1900s]

get hilt and hair to copulate, said of a woman. [British slang, 1800s, Farmer and Henley]

get home 1. to penetrate and coit a woman. **2.** to coit a woman to orgasm. [British and some U.S. use, 1900s]

get hulled between wind and water to copulate with a man; to be coited by a man. Said of a woman. From a nautical expression describing the taking of a cannon ball in the vulnerable part of a ship's hull, that which is exposed to deterioration by both the wind and water. Refers here to the anus (wind) and the urethra (water). *Cf.* TAINT (sense 2). [British slang, 1800s, Farmer and Henley]

get hunk to commit PEDERASTY (*q.v.*). [U.S. underworld, mid 1900s, Goldin, O'Leary, and Lipsius]

get into to penetrate a woman. [very old colloquial and slang]

get it off to obtain sexual relief, preferably through coition, usually said of the male. Refers to ejaculation. *Cf.* GET THE DIRTY WATER OFF ONE'S CHEST. [U.S. slang, 1900s]

get it on 1. to become excited about anything. **2.** to become sexually excited. **3.** to get an erection. **4.** to copulate. [all senses, U.S. slang, mid 1900s-pres.]

get it up to get an erection. [U.S. slang, mid 1900s-pres.]

get Jack in the orchard to penetrate a woman. *Cf.* ORCHARD. [British slang, 1800s, Farmer and Henley]

get layed to have sexual intercourse, said originally of the female, now of both sexes. [U.S. slang, 1900s or before]

get off 1. to ejaculate. *Cf.* GET IT OFF. For synonyms see OCCUPY. [U.S. slang, mid 1900s-pres.] **2.** to become intoxicated with marijuana or other drugs. [U.S. drug culture, mid 1900s-pres.]

get off the nut to ejaculate. *Cf.* GET ONE'S NUTS OFF. For synonyms see MELT. [U.S. slang, mid 1900s]

get one's ashes hauled to copulate. *Cf.* HAUL ONE'S ASHES. [U.S. slang, 1900s]

get one's ass in gear to get oneself in order. [U.S. slang, mid 1900s-pres.]

get one's chimney swept out to be copulated with; to copulate. From the point of view of a woman. *Cf.* CHIMNEY. [British slang, 1800s, Farmer and Henley]

get one's cookies off to ejaculate.

For synonyms see MELT. [U.S. slang, mid 1900s-pres.]

get one's greens to copulate. *Cf.* GREENS. [British slang, 1800s, Farmer and Henley].

get one's hair cut to copulate. [British slang, late 1800s, Farmer and Henley]

get one's hand on it to manage to fondle a woman's genitals. [British, mid 1800s, *Dictionary of Slang and Unconventional English*].

get one's leather stretched to copulate. From the point of view of a woman. *Cf.* LEATHER (sense 2). [British slang, 1800s, Farmer and Henley]

get one's leg across to copulate with a woman; to master a woman. *Cf.* BOARD, MOUNT. [British and U.S., 1800s-1900s]

get one's leg lifted to get copulated with, from a woman's point of view. [British slang, 1800s, Farmer and Henley]

get one's nuts cracked to achieve copulation, said of a man. [U.S. slang, mid 1900s-pres.]

get one's nuts off (also **get one's rocks off**) to ejaculate. [U.S. slang, mid 1900s-pres.]

get one's oats from someone to copulate with someone. *Cf.* SOW ONE'S WILD OATS. [Australian, mid 1900s, Baker]

get one's oil changed to copulate, said of a male. *Cf.* MAN OIL, OIL OF MAN. For synonyms see OCCUPY. [U.S. slang, mid 1900s]

get one's rocks off to ejaculate; the same as GET ONE'S NUTS OFF (*q.v.*).

get on top of to copulate. *Cf.* MOUNT. [British and U.S., late 1800s-1900s]

get outside of (also **get outside of it**) to receive a man sexually, said of a woman. [British slang, 1800s, Farmer and Henley]

get over the garter to feel a woman's genitals; to manage to grope one's way

above the garter line. [British slang, 1800s, *Dictionary of Slang and Unconventional English*]

get some action to get some sex; to copulate. *Cf.* ACTION. [U.S. slang, mid 1900s-pres.]

get some ass (also **get some tail**) to achieve copulation; to SCORE (*q.v.*). *Cf.* ASS (sense 3). [U.S. slang, mid 1900s-pres.]

get some cold cock to copulate. For synonyms see MELT. [U.S. slang, mid 1900s-pres.]

get some cunt to achieve coition. [U.S. slang, mid 1900s-pres.]

get some roundeye to perform PEDERASTY or ANILINGUS (both *q.v.*). *Cf.* ROUNDEYE. [U.S. slang, mid 1900s-pres.]

get the dirty water off one's chest to ejaculate. [British, 1900s, *Dictionary of Slang and Unconventional English*]

Get the lead out of your ass! (also **Get the lead out!**) a command to hurry. [U.S. slang, mid 1900s-pres.]

get there 1. to get drunk. [British slang, 1800s, *Dictionary of Slang and Unconventional English*] **2.** to copulate; to SCORE (*q.v.*). [British and U.S. slang, 1900s]

get the upshoot to receive the ejaculation of a man, said of a woman. [from *Love's Labour's Lost* (Shakespeare)]

get through 1. to DEFLOWER (*q.v.*) **2.** to copulate with a woman. [both senses, British colloquial, 1800s-1900s]

Getting any? a friendly greeting question asked of one male by another. Literally, "Are you getting any sexual activity, especially sexual intercourse?" See GET ANY? [primarily Australian and U.S.; slang and colloquial, early 1900s-pres.]

getting off using drugs or alcohol. A truncation of "getting off on a high." See HIGH. [U.S. drug culture and slang, mid 1900s-pres.]

getting up coiting or impregnating a woman. *Cf.* GET INTO. [from *The Merchant of Venice* (Shakespeare)]

get up the pole to copulate, said of a woman. *Cf.* POLE, UP THE. [since the 1600s]

get with child to impregnate a woman. For synonyms see STORK [from *Measure for Measure* (Shakespeare)]

gewgaw 1. a jew's-harp. There is a possibility that this was pronounced "jew jaw." *Cf.* JAW HARP. [from Scots dialect; since the early 1500s] 2. a gadget; a bauble; a bit of nothing. From sense 1. [U.S. colloquial, 1900s]

G.F. a "girlfriend." *Cf.* B.F. (sense 2). [U.S. slang, 1900s]

G.F.U. "general fuck-up," a person who is a lazy good-for-nothing or a troublemaker; a confused situation. [World War II]

gherkin the penis in JERK ONE'S GHERKIN (*q.v.*). From the name of a small cucumber used in pickling. *Cf.* PUMP ONE'S PICKLE. [U.S. slang, 1900s]

Ghin a derogatory nickname for an Italian. From GUINEA (*q.v.*). *Cf.* GINNEY, GUIN. [U.S. slang, 1900s, Berrey and Van den Bark]

giblets 1. intestines of various sorts. [since the 1400s] 2. the male and female genitals in JOIN GIBLETS (*q.v.*). *Cf.* JUMBLE-GIBLETS, TROUBLE-GIBLETS. [British slang, mid 1700s, Grose] 3. the male genitals. The testicles in OIL OF GIBLETS (*q.v.*), "semen."

G.I. cocktail a "gastrointestinal cocktail," a dose of purgative salts. [U.S., World War II]

gifted pertaining to a homosexual male. A euphemism referring to the real or imagined high degree of creativity of male homosexuals in general. [U.S. slang and colloquial, 1900s]

gig (also **gigg, gigge**) 1. a wanton young woman; a mistress. [1300s (Chaucer) to the 1800s] 2. the female genitals. [British and later U.S., late 1600s-1900s] 3. to cheat or deceive. [U.S. slang, mid 1900s] 4. a fool; an oaf. [Australian, 1900s] 5. the rectum or anus. [U.S. juvenile, 1900s, Wentworth and Flexner]

giggle-smoke (also **giggles-smoke**) marijuana. For synonyms see MARI. [U.S. drug culture, mid 1900s-pres.]

giggle-stick the penis. Rhyming slang for "prick." For synonyms see YARD. [U.S., 1900s, *Dictionary of Rhyming Slang*]

giggle-water (also **giggle-juice**) alcoholic drink, especially champagne. *Cf.* BUBBLE-WATER, JOY-WATER, LAUGHING SOUP. [U.S. slang, early 1900s-pres.]

giggle-weed marijuana. *Cf.* GIGGLE-SMOKE [U.S. drug culture, mid 1900s-pres.]

giggling-pin the penis. *Cf.* GIGGLE-STICK. [British, 1900s, *Dictionary of Slang and Unconventional English*]

gigolo 1. a PONCE (*q.v.*) a man living on the earnings of a prostitute. 2. a paid professional male escort; a man paid to serve a woman sexually. [from French]

gill 1. a wench; a young girl. See GILL-FLIRT. [mid 1600s] 2. a fellow. [cant, early 1800s or before, Vaux]

gill-flirt (also **gilflurt, gill-flurt, jill-flirt, jill-flurt**) a wanton or silly girl or woman. [colloquial, early 1600s-1900s]

gills, up to the (also **gills, to the**) intoxicated with alcohol. The expression is frequently combined with other terms to indicate a high degree of intoxication. [U.S. colloquial, 1900s or before]

gin 1. a device for torturing; the rack. From "engine." [1200s, *Oxford English Dictionary*] 2. fetters. From sense 1. [mid 1600s] 3. a black prostitute. From "aborigine." [Australian and U.S. slang, early 1900s] 4. cocaine. For synonyms see NOSE-CANDY. [U.S. drug culture, mid 1900s-pres.] See also GHIN, GINNEY.

ginch 1. a girl; a sexually loose woman. 2. a prostitute. 3. a CATAMITE (*q.v.*). 4. copulation. 5. women considered sexually. [all senses, U.S. slang, early 1900s-pres.]

gin disposal unit a gin drunkard. [British, jocular and nonce]

gingambob (also **gingumbob**) 1. a gadget; a bauble. [since the 1600s] 2. a testicle. See GINGAMBOBS.

gingambobs (also **gingumbobs**) the testicles. For synonyms see WHIRLYGIGS. [British, 1700s-1800s]

Ginger!, By an oath and an exclamation, "By God!" [U.S. colloquial, mid 1800s]

ginger beer 1. an engineer. Rhyming slang. No negative connotations. **2.** a homosexual male. Rhyming slang for QUEER (*q.v.*). [both senses, British, 1900s, *Dictionary of Rhyming Slang*]

gingered-up intoxicated with alcohol; stimulated or enervated as from ginger. [colloquial, 1900s and before]

gingo a derogatory nickname for an Italian. [U.S. slang, mid 1900s, Deak]

ginicomtwig to coit a woman. Probably a telescoped phrase. [late 1500s, Florio]

gin-jockey (also **gin-burglar, gin-shepherd**) a white man who maintains an aboriginal concubine. See GIN (sense 3). [Australian, 1900s, Wilkes]

Ginney (also **Ghin**) a derogatory nickname for an Italian. From GUINEA (*q.v.*). Cf. GINGO. (U.S. slang, early 1900s]

Gippy bint (also **Gyppy bint**) an Egyptian girl or woman. Usually considered derogatory. Cf. BINT. [British, World War I, Fraser and Gibbons]

girl 1. a prostitute; a harlot. [late 1700s-pres.] **2.** to wench; to WOMANIZE (*q.v.*); to pursue women for sexual purposes. [1700s-1900s] **3.** a mistress; a concubine. [since the 1800s] **4.** a servant girl. [British and U.S. colloquial, 1800s and before] **5.** to flirt and court a young woman; to date women. [1900s] **6.** a woman or a girl. Found quite objectionable by the members of some of the Women's Liberation movements. Otherwise in wide usage for females of all ages. [U.S. colloquial, early 1900s-pres.] **7.** a homosexual male. [U.S. homosexual use and slang, mid 1900s-pres.] **8.** a male whore. See SHE (sense 2). [British, early 1900s, *Dictionary of Slang and Unconventional English*] **9.** cocaine. Cf. HER. [U.S. drug culture, mid 1900s-pres.]

girl at ease a prostitute. Refers to the "ease" with which she agrees to copulate. For synonyms see HARLOT. [U.S. slang, early 1900s, Montelone]

girl-bird a bird or fowl of the female sex. Used in avoidance of "female bird." [U.S. colloquial euphemism, 1900s]

girlery a brothel. [British slang, late 1800s, Farmer and Henley]

girlometer the penis. Cf. MANOMETER, YARD MEASURE. [British slang, 1800s, Farmer and Henley]

girl shop a brothel. [slang, 1800s-1900s]

girl street 1. women considered sexually. **2.** the female genitals. [both senses, British slang, 1800s, Farmer and Henley]

girl-trap a woman-chaser; a lecher. Cf. MANTRAP. [British slang, 1800s, Farmer and Henley]

G.I.'s "gastrointestinal" troubles; diarrhea. See G.I. (sense 1). [U.S. slang since the mid 1900s or before]

G.I. shits diarrhea. Cf. G.I., G.I.'s. [U.S. military, World War II]

gism (also **chism, jism**) **1.** any syrupy type of food. **2.** gravy. See BULL FUCK (sense 1). [U.S. colloquial, 1900s] **3.** semen. For synonyms see METTLE. **4.** physical strength and vigor; male vigor and potency. [senses 3 and 4 are colloquial and slang, 1900s or before]

give to copulate anally. The opposite of TAKE (sense 3). From the point of view of the INSERTOR (*q.v.*). [U.S. underworld, mid 1900s, Goldin, O'Leary, and Lipsius]

give a dose to infect with a venereal disease. Cf. DOSE (sense 2). [U.S. underworld, 1900s]

give a flying-fuck to care not at all, as in "I don't give a flying-fuck." [U.S. slang, mid 1900s-pres.]

give a hole to hide it in to grant copulation, said of a woman. [British slang, 1800s, Farmer and Henley]

give and take girl a prostitute who gives sexual favors and takes money. [U.S. jocular euphemism, early 1900s, Montelone]

give a shit to care. Usually in the negative, "don't give a shit," a stronger version of "don't give a damn." [U.S. colloquial, 1900s]

give a woman a shot to coit, specifically to ejaculate while copulating. *Cf.* SHOOT (sense 1). [British slang, 1800s]

give hard for soft to coit, said of a man. See HARD. [British slang, 1800s, Farmer and Henley]

give head 1. to copulate with a woman; to INTROMIT (*q.v.*). **2.** to perform FELLATIO (*q.v.*). *Cf.* HEAD-JOB, SERVE HEAD. [both senses, U.S. slang, mid 1900s-pres.]

give her a frigging (also **give her a hosing, give her a screwing**) to copulate with a woman. For synonyms see OCCUPY. [U.S. slang, 1900s]

give her a past to copulate with a woman; to give a woman memories or a reputation. [U.S. slang and colloquial, early 1900s-pres.]

give her the business to coit a woman. [U.S. slang, 1900s]

give juice for jelly to copulate with a woman. The "juice" is the semen; the "jelly" is the vagina. See JELLY (sense 2), JUICE (sense 1). [British slang, 1800s, Farmer and Henley]

give mutton for beef to copulate; to permit copulation. Said of a woman. See BEEF, MUTTON. [British slang, 1800s, Farmer and Henley]

give nature a fillip to SPREE (*q.v.*); to debauch with drink and women. [British, late 1600s, B.E.]

give one a stab to coit a woman. [U.S. slang, mid 1900s, Goldin, O'Leary, and Lipsius]

give one's gravy to ejaculate. *Cf.* GRAVY (sense 1). For synonyms see MELT. [British slang, 1800s, Farmer and Henley]

give one the works to copulate with a woman roughly; to rape a woman. [U.S. slang, mid 1900s, Goldin, O'Leary, and Lipsius]

give standing-room for one to permit copulation, said of a woman. *Cf.* STAND. [British slang, 1800s, Farmer and Henley]

give the Chinaman a music lesson to retire to urinate. "Chinaman" refers to the vitreous china toilet bowl. "Music" refers to TINKLE (*q.v.*). [U.S. slang, mid 1900s, Deak]

give the old man his supper to provide copulation for one's husband or lover, said of a woman. [British, 1800s]

give way to permit coition, said of a woman. [British slang, 1800s, Farmer and Henley]

gixie (also **gixy**) **1.** a mincing and affected woman. [late 1500s, Florio] **2.** a strumpet; a wanton woman. [1600s]

glad intoxicated with alcohol. *Cf.* GAY (sense 2), MERRY (sense 2). [U.S. slang, early 1700s, Ben Franklin]

glad-stuff hard drugs, *i.e.*, cocaine, morphine, opium. *Cf.* BLACK STUFF, WHITE STUFF. [early 1900s, *Dictionary of the Underworld*]

glands 1. the testicles. For synonyms see WHIRLYGIGS. **2.** the breasts. For synonyms see BOSOM. [both senses, U.S. euphemisms, 1900s]

glassy-eyed 1. intoxicated with alcohol. [U.S. slang, early 1900s-pres.] **2.** sexually aroused or sexually spent. [U.S., 1900s]

globes the breasts. *Cf.* BUBBLES, HEMISPHERES. [British and U.S. slang, mid 1800s-pres.]

globular intoxicated with alcohol. [U.S. slang, early 1700s, Ben Franklin]

glorious intoxicated with alcohol; gloriously drunk. For synonyms see WOOFLED [Scots, late 1700s, (Robert Burns)]

glory hole 1. any drawer, niche, locker, cubbyhole, or pigeon-hole for the storage of odds and ends. [British and U.S. colloquial, 1800s-1900s] **2.** a church; a Salvation Army meeting hall. [British and U.S. slang and colloquial, late 1800s-1900s] **3.** a dugout. [British military, World Wars] **4.** a hole in a stall partition in a men's public restroom.

Said to be used for fellatio, with the INSERTOR (*q.v.*) standing on one side of the partition and the RECEIVER (*q.v.*) on the other side. Observation (by Humphreys) has shown it to be used primarily for spying on the penis of a man urinating or for signalling to a potential sex partner. *Cf.* TEAROOM. [U.S. slang and homosexual use, mid 1900s-pres.]

glory seeds morning glory seeds used as a drug. For synonyms see SEEDS. [U.S. drug culture, mid 1900s-pres.]

glow worm a drunkard who is LIT-UP (*q.v.*). [U.S. slang, 1900s, Berrey and Van den Bark]

glue 1. gonorrhea. From the secretion. [British, 1800s] **2.** semen. [British, late 1800s, (Farmer), and nonce] **3.** nasty sweat. See GLUE NECK.

glued 1. infected with gonorrhea. [British slang, 1900s or before] **2.** intoxicated with alcohol. From the immobility experienced in heavy intoxication. [U.S. slang, 1900s, Wentworth and Flexner]

glue neck a filthy prostitute. Refers to a nasty, unwashed neck. *Cf.* SARDINE. [U.S. underworld, early 1900s, Irwin]

glutton a man or woman with a large sexual appetite. A specialized use of the standard sense. *Cf.* DUMB-GLUTTON.

gnat-bread SMEGMA (sense 2). *Cf.* DUCK-BUTTER (sense 2). [U.S. colloquial, 1900s or before]

gnat's piss weak tea; any weak or inferior drink including alcoholic drinks. [slang, 1800s-1900s]

go 1. to die. For synonyms see DEPART. [since the 1600s] **2.** to coit a woman. Particularly in reference to an energetic act of copulation. *Cf.* GOER. [British, 1800s, Farmer and Henley] **3.** to urinate. For synonyms see WHIZ. [U.S. colloquial euphemism, 1900s or before] **4.** to defecate. [1900s or before]

go and catch a horse to depart to urinate; to urinate. [Australian, 1900s, Baker]

Go and get cut! a curse, "Go to hell!" [Australian, early 1900s, Baker]

Go and get fucked! "Get the hell out of here! [slang, 1800s-1900s].

Go and get verbed! a timid euphemism for GO AND GET FUCKED! (*q.v.*).

go and look at the crops (also **go look at the crops**) to retire to urinate. [colloquial, 1800s-pres.]

goat 1. a lecher; a lascivious man. [since the late 1500s] **2.** to act lecherously, said of a man. [British slang, 1800s, Farmer and Henley] **3.** body odor, especially underarm odor. *Cf.* FOXY (sense 1). [U.S. colloquial and slang, 1900s]

goat-drunk intoxicated with alcohol and lustful. *Cf.* TIGHT AS A GOAT. [since the early 1600s]

goat-house a brothel. *Cf.* GOAT (senses 1 and 2). [British, 1800s or before]

goatish 1. lecherous; sexually aroused. *Cf.* RAMMISH. [since the late 1500s] **2.** pertaining to a person with strong underarm odor or to the odor itself. *Cf.* GOAT (sense 3). [colloquial, 1900s or before]

goat-milker 1. a prostitute. *Cf.* MILK. **2.** the female genitals. [both senses, British slang, 1800s, Farmer and Henley]

goat's jig (also **goat's gigg**) copulation. For synonyms see SMOCKAGE. [British slang, late 1700s, Grose]

gob 1. to spit. **2.** spittle. Both are from cant "gob," the "mouth." [both since the mid 1700s]

go ballocking to go womanizing or copulating. *Cf.* BALLOCK (sense 2). [British slang, 1800s, Farmer and Henley]

gobble to commit FELLATIO (*q.v.*). *Cf.* GOBBLER, MUNCH. [British and U.S., 1800s-1900s]

gobbledygook nonsense; officialese or government jargon; gibberish. For synonyms see ANIMAL. [U.S. colloquial, 1900s]

gobble-prick a wanton and lewd woman. Possibly a reference to fellation. [British slang, late 1700s, Grose]

gobbler (also **gobler**) a FELLATOR (*q.v.*). *Cf.* MOUSER (sense 2), NIBBLER. For synonyms see PICCOLO-PLAYER. [U.S. slang, 1900s or before]

go bed-pressing to go coiting. [British slang, 1800s, Farmer and Henley]

go-between 1. a pimp or a BAWD (*q.v.*). [in *Merry Wives of Windsor* (Shakespeare); 1600s-pres.] **2.** a prostitute. The male "goes between" her legs. [British slang, 1800s, Farmer and Henley]

go bird's-nesting to go coiting. *Cf.* NEST (sense 3). [British slang, 1800s, Farmer and Henley]

gobshite a fool; the same word as GAUBSHITE (*q.v.*). Possibly ."shit-mouth." See GOB. [British, 1900s, *Dictionary of Slang and Unconventional English*]

go bum-faking to go coiting; to go womanizing. [cant, 1800s or before, Farmer and Henley]

go bum-fighting (also **go bum-faking**) to go coiting. [British slang, 1800s, Farmer and Henley]

go bum-tickling to go coiting. *Cf.* BUM TICKLER. [British, 1800s or before]

go bum-working to go coiting. *Cf.* WORK (sense 1). [British, 1800s or before]

go buttocking to go coiting. *Cf.* BUTTOCK (sense 2). [British, 1800s or before]

Gock "God" in oaths; the same as COCK (*q.v.*). [1600s]

go cock-fighting to go coiting. *Cf.* COCK (senses 1 and 6). [British slang, 1800s, Farmer and Henley]

go cunny-catching to go womanizing. "Cunny-" or "cony-" catching is rabbit-hunting. *Cf.* CUNNY. [British slang, 1800s, Farmer and Henley]

God 1. the Supreme Being. [since the early 800s, *Oxford English Dictionary*] **2.** also used as a profane oath meaning "By God!" There are numerous avoidances and disguises for the name of God. Many examples are found among the oaths listed at 'ZOUNDS! *Cf.* ADONAI, ADS, CAT, COCK, COCKE, COD, COK, COKIS, COX, CUD'S, DAL, DOD, DOL, ELOHIM, GAD, GED!, GEE!, GOCK, GOD!,

GODFREY!, GOG, GOL, GOLLY, GOM, GOSH!, GOSSE, GREAT DISPATCHER IN THE SKY, GUD, GUM, GUN, HORN SPOON, JEHOVAH, JHVH, LA, LUD!, MY LAND!, 'OD, 'ODDS, 'ODS, 'S, THE ALMIGHTY, THE BIG GUY, THE CREATOR, THE DEITY, THE DIVINITY, THE LORD, THE SUPREME BEING, YAHWEH.

Godamercy! an oath based on "May God have mercy!" [1400s-1900s]

Godamighty! a partially disguised exclamation, "God almighty!" [U.S. colloquial, 1900s]

God bless him! 1. an oath and an exclamation occurring in many forms. [widespread and very old] **2.** a disguise of "God damn him!" [colloquial, 1900s]

God blind me! (also **Godblimey!, God bline me!**) an oath based on "May God blind me!" *Cf.* GORBLIMEY!

God-botherer a clergyman. For synonyms see SKY-PILOT. [British military, early 1900s, *Dictionary of Slang and Unconventional English*]

God burn! a disguise of "Goddamn!" *Cf.* DAD-BURN! at DAD. [U.S. colloquial, 1900s]

Goddamn (also **goddamn**) a very strong variety of "damn." Also an oath and an exclamation, "Goddamn!" Although considered profanity if not blasphemy until the mid 1900s when "Fuck!" and "Shit!" "went public," Goddamn was the strongest curse ever heard in mixed middle-class company. This form is from the adjective "God-damned" or from "God damn it!" Abbreviated G.D. (*q.v.*).

God damn me! an oath and an exclamation based on "May God damn me!" [since the early 1600s]

Godfrey!, By a disguised oath and an exclamation, "By God!" [U.S. colloquial, 1900s]

Godfrey dorman! a contrived disguise of "Goddamn!" [U.S. colloquial, 1900s]

Godfrey mighty! a contrived disguise of "God almighty!" For synonyms see 'ZOUNDS! [U.S. colloquial, 1900s]

go doodling to go coiting. *Cf.* DOO-

DLE (sense 3). [British slang, 1800s, Farmer and Henley]

go down 1. For a woman to submit to copulation. **2.** for a man or woman to copulate. Extended from sense 1. *Cf.* GET DOWN. [both senses, U.S. slang, mid 1900s-pres.]

go down on 1. to perform PENILINGUS (*q.v.*) on a man or CUNNILINGUS (*q.v.*) on a woman. [both homosexual and heterosexual use, U.S., mid 1900s-pres.] **2.** for a man or woman to perform any NONORTHOGENITAL (*q.v.*) sexual act. **3.** to commit sodomy. Possibly referring to PEDERASTY (*q.v.*) exclusively. Also **get down on.** [U.S. slang, mid 1900s-pres.]

go drabbing to go coiting; to associate with a DRAB (*q.v.*). [British, 1600s-1800s]

God rot your soul! a curse, "May God rot your soul!" See DRAT IT!

God's bodkin! (also **God's bodikin!**) an oath and an exclamation, "By God's (little) body!" For synonyms see 'ZOUNDS!

God's corpus!, By an oath and an exclamation, "By God's body!"

God's diggers!, By an oath and an exclamation, "By God's fingernails!" [mid 1600s]

God's dignity!, By an oath and an exclamation.

God's hooks! an oath and an exclamation, "By God's hooks!" The "hooks" are either the fingernails or the nails of the Crucifixion. See ADZOOKS!

God's medicine morphine. For synonyms see MORPH. [U.S., 1900s or before]

Godso! an oath and an exclamation.

God's pittikins!, By an oath and an exclamation, "By God's (little) pity!" [1600s]

God's santy!, By an oath and an exclamation, "By God's sanctity!" [1500s]

Godsworbet! a disguise of "God forbid!" [mid 1600s]

go fishing to go coiting. *Cf.* FISH. [British, 1800s or before]

go flashing it to go coiting. [British slang, 1800s or before]

go flat to lose an erection. *Cf.* FLAT TIRE. [U.S. colloquial, 1900s]

go for the drag off to SCORE (*q.v.*); to succeed in copulating a woman. [Australian, 1900s, Baker]

Gog a disguise of "God." [1300s-1600s]

Gog!, By a partially disguised oath and an exclamation, "By God!" [1300s]

go goosing to go coiting. *Cf.* GOOSE (sense 3). [British slang, 1800s, Farmer and Henley]

Gog's wouns!, By an oath and an exclamation, "By God's wounds!" See GOG.

go home to die. [British and U.S. colloquial, late 1800s-1900s]

go in unto to copulate. [Biblical euphemism; since the 1600s]

go jottling to go coiting. *Cf.* JOTTLE. [British slang, 1800s, Farmer and Henley]

Gol "God" in oaths. Oaths with "Gol" are: By Goldam!, Gol blank it!, Gol blink it!, Gol burn it!, Goldang!, Goldarn!, Goldast!, Goldern!, Golding!, Goldinged!, Gol ding it!, Gol durn it!, Golhorn!

gold any high-powered (and expensive) variety of marijuana. The name comes from the color and the quality. *Cf.* ACAPULCO GOLD, GOLD COLUMBIAN. [U.S. drug culture, mid 1900s-pres.]

gold Columbian a nickname for marijuana from Colombia. *Cf.* COLUMBIAN RED. Appears in a variety of spellings. For synonyms see MARI. [U.S. drug culture, mid 1900s-pres.]

gold-digger a woman who courts a man solely for his money; a man who courts a woman solely for her money. [U.S. slang, early 1900s-pres.]

gold dust 1. cocaine. *Cf.* POWDERED DIAMOND. For synonyms see NOSE-CANDY. [U.S. underworld and later drug culture, early 1900s-pres.] **2.** heroin.

Extended from sense 1. [U.S. drug culture, mid 1900s-pres.]

golden cream a type of rum. *Cf.* LONDON MILK. [British slang, late 1800s, Ware]

golden leaf marijuana, especially a high grade of marijuana. *Cf.* ACAPULCO GOLD, GOLD. [U.S. drug culture, mid 1900s-pres.]

golden shower boy in male homosexuality, a sexual perversion wherein sexual gratification is obtained from being urinated on or from other close contacts with urine; the same as GOLDEN SHOWER QUEEN (*q.v.*). [U.S. homosexual use, mid 1900s-pres.]

golden shower queen (also **shower queen**) a homosexual male who obtains sexual gratification from being urinated on. See QUEEN for similar nicknames. [U.S. homosexual use, mid 1900s-pres.]

goldfinch's nest the female genitals. *Cf.* MAGPIE'S NEST. [British, early 1800s]

go leather-stretching to go coiting. [British, 1800s or before, Farmer and Henley]

go like a belt-fed motor (also **go like a rat up a rhododendron**) to copulate with great vigor. *Cf.* FUCK LIKE A RATTLESNAKE. [Australian, 1900s]

gollumpus a large, clumsy oaf or lout. [British slang, late 1700s, Grose]

golly (also **golli**) a "native," especially one of dark skin-color; a Negro. The source of or an elaboration of WOGS (*q.v.*), "golliwogs." [British slang, 1900s]

golly!, By a disguised oath and an exclamation, "By God!" [since the 1700s]

go loco to smoke a marijuana cigarette. From an expression meaning "go crazy." *Cf.* LOCO-WEED. [U.S. underworld, early 1900s, Berrey and Van den Bark]

go look at the crops an excuse to retire to urinate. See GO AND LOOK AT THE CROPS. [U.S. colloquial, 1900s]

goma opium; crude opium. *Cf.* GUM.

For synonyms see OPE. [U.S. underworld or drug culture, 1900s]

gone 1. pregnant. For synonyms see FRAGRANT. [British and U.S. colloquial, 1800s] **2.** dead. [euphemistic and nonce] **3.** intoxicated with alcohol; dead drunk. [U.S. slang and colloquial, mid 1900s-pres.]

gone for six dead. From the game of cricket and "six-feet under" in the burial of the dead. *Cf.* DEEP SIX.

goner a dead person or one who is nearly dead.

gone to glory dead. For synonyms see DONE FOR. [U.S. colloquial, 1900s or before]

gone trumpet-cleaning dead. [British military, World Wars, Fraser and Gibbons]

gone under 1. dead; dead and buried. See PUT DOWN. [euphemistic, mid 1800s-1900s] **2.** having succumbed to the effects of alcohol, drugs, or anesthetic. [U.S., 1900s]

gong 1. a privy. For synonyms see AJAX. **2.** dung in a privy. *Cf.* GONG HOUSE. [senses 1 and 2 since *c.* 1000, *Oxford English Dictionary*] **3.** opium. For senses 3-6, see SHIT (sense 5) and GONG (sense 2). [U.S. underworld, 1900s-pres.] **4.** an opium pipe. For synonyms see GONGER. [U.S. underworld, early 1900s, Irwin] **5.** an opium addict. [U.S. underworld, early 1900s, Irwin] **6.** to smoke opium. For synonyms see SMOKE. [U.S. underworld, early 1900s]

gonga 1. the anus. Possibly "gonger." See GONG (sense 2). [British, 1900s, *Dictionary of Slang and Unconventional English*] **2.** marijuana. *Cf.* GANJAH. [U.S. underworld, mid 1900s, Goldin, O'Leary, and Lipsius]

gong-beater an opium-smoker. [U.S. underworld and drug culture, early 1900s-pres.]

gonger 1. opium. **2.** an opium pipe. [both senses, U.S. underworld, 1900s or before] Synonyms: BAMBOO, CHINESE SAXOPHONE, GEE-STICK, GONG, GONGOLA,

HOP-STICK, JOY-STICK, LOG, SAXOPHONE, STEM, WATER-PIPE.

gonger, on the to be smoking opium; addicted to opium. *Cf.* GONGER. [U.S. underworld, early 1900s]

gong-farmer (also **gong-fermor**) an emptier of cesspools. *Cf.* JAKES-FARMER. [British, late 1500s-1800s]

gong house (also **gong**) a privy. *Cf.* GONG (sense 1). For synonyms see AJAX.

gong-kicker 1. an opium smoker. **2.** a marijuana smoker. From sense 1. [U.S. underworld and drug culture, mid 1900s]

gongola an opium pipe. [U.S. slang, 1900s, Berrey and Van den Bark]

gonif (also **ganef, ganev, ganov, gonef, goniff, gonnoff, gonof, gonoph, gonov**) **1.** a thief; a pickpocket. [from Yiddish; British and U.S. underworld and slang, mid 1800s-pres.] **2.** a SODOMITE (*q.v.*). [U.S. slang, 1900s]

Gonnows! an exclamation, "God knows!" [British, 1800s, Ware]

gonorrhea a venereal disease. Greek for "flow of semen." The mucous discharge is not semen, but the more accurate term blennorrhea never replaced this term. [from Greek; since the mid 1500s] Synonyms: BLENNORRHEA, BUBE, BURNER, CLAP, DELICATE TAINT, DOSE OF CLAPS, G.C., GENTLEMAN'S COMPLAINT, GLEET, GLIM, GLUE, GONOBLENNORRHEA, HAT AND CAP, HORSE AND TRAP, LULU, NEISSERIAN INFECTION, OLD JOE, PISS PINS AND NEEDLES, PISS PURE CREAM, STRAIN, TEAR, V.D.G.

gonsel (also **gonsil, gonzel, guncel, gunsel, gunsil, guntzel, gunzel**) **1.** a tramp's CATAMITE (*q.v.*). **2.** any catamite. **3.** any young boy. *Cf.* PUNK. [senses 1-3 are U.S. underworld, early 1900s] **4.** any homosexual male. **5.** any slob or jerk. [senses 4 and 5 are U.S. slang, mid 1900s-pres.; all senses, from the German word for "gosling," via Yiddish]

gonus an oaf; a dunce. [U.S., 1900s or before]

goob a pimple. A truncation of GOOBER (sense 2). *Cf.* GUBERS. For synonyms see BURBLE. See also GOO.

goober 1. the penis. "Goober" is a name for the peanut. Possibly a play on PEE and NUT (both *q.v.*). For synonyms see YARD. **2.** a pimple. See GUBERS.

goober-grabber 1. a pea-picker; a person who picks peanuts. No negative connotations. **2.** a lascivious woman. *Cf.* FIST IT. For synonyms see LAY. [both senses, U.S. dialect (Ozarks), Randolph and Wilson]

Good Christmas! (also **Holy Christmas!**) a disguise of "Jesus Christ!" or "Good Christ!" For synonyms see 'ZOUNDS! [colloquial, 1900s]

good-eating pertaining to an attractive woman who looks good enough to eat. *Cf.* BARBECUE, EATING-STUFF, TABLE-GRADE. [Australian, 1900s, Baker]

good fettle, in (also **fine fettle, in**) intoxicated with alcohol. For synonyms see WOOFLED. [British and later, U.S. colloquial, 1800s-pres.]

Good Godfrey Daniel! a euphemistic blend of "Good God!" and "Goddamn!" [U.S. colloquial, 1900s]

good lay 1. a passionate and satisfying man or woman. Originally said of a woman. **2.** a sexually easy woman; an easy target for sex. For synonyms see LAY. **3.** a satisfying act of copulation. [all senses, U.S. slang, early 1900s-pres.]

goodman-turd a contemptible fellow. The equivalent of "Mister Turd." [late 1500s, Florio]

goodness!, My an oath and an exclamation; an avoidance for "My God!" Mild and completely acceptable.

Goodness gracious! (also **Good gracious!**) an oath and an exclamation. Mild and completely acceptable. [colloquial]

goods heroin. [U.S. drug culture, 1900s]

good shit anything good; a dysphemism for "good luck." [U.S. colloquial, 1900s or before]

goody morphine. [U.S. drug culture, mid 1900s-pres.]

Goody goody Goddamn! an elaboration of GODDAMN! (*q.v.*). [U.S. slang, mid 1900s]

Goody goody gumdrop! a mock oath and an exclamation. Possibly based on GOODY GOODY GODDAMN! (*q.v.*). [U.S. slang, mid 1900s]

goof (also **goofer, goofus**) **1.** an oaf; a ridiculous jerk. [U.S. slang and colloquial, 1900s] **2.** marijuana. [U.S. underworld, mid 1900s, Goldin, O'Leary, and Lipsius]

goof-ball 1. marijuana. [U.S. slang, mid 1900s-pres.] **2.** a portion of narcotics, especially barbiturates in various forms. See G.B. [U.S. drug culture, mid 1900s-pres.] **3.** a jerk; an oaf. [U.S. slang, mid 1900s-pres.]

goof-butt (also **goofy-butt**) a marijuana cigarette. For synonyms see MEZZROLL. [U.S. drug culture, mid 1900s-pres.]

goofed-up 1. intoxicated with drugs. **2.** mentally confused; disoriented. [both senses, U.S. drug culture and slang, mid 1900s-pres.]

goofer 1. a jerk; the same as GOOF (sense 1). [U.S. slang, mid 1900s] **2.** a drug user. [U.S. drug culture, mid 1900s-pres.] **3.** a barbiturate capsule or tablet; the same as GOOF (sense 2). For synonyms see BARB. [U.S. drug culture, mid 1900s-pres.]

go off 1. to die. For synonyms see DEPART. [colloquial, 1600s] **2.** to ejaculate. For synonyms see MELT. **3.** to have an orgasm. [both senses, colloquial, 1800s-pres.]

go off half-cocked (also **go off at half-cock**) to ejaculate prematurely. A semantic play based on the misfiring of a gun. *Cf.* COCK (sense 3), GO OFF (sense 2). [British and U.S. slang and colloquial, mid 1800s-pres.]

goof off 1. to waste time; to play aimlessly when there is work to be done. **2.** a person who plays aimlessly. Usually hyphenated. [both senses, U.S. colloquial, mid 1900s-pres.]

gook 1. a prostitute, especially a low prostitute. For synonyms see HARLOT. [British and U.S., late 1800s-1900s] **2.**

a tramp. **3.** a fool. **4.** any slimy thing or person. **5.** an Oriental; in recent times, a Vietnamese. [senses 2 through 5 are U.S. slang, 1900s]

goolies the testicles. From the dialect term "gooly," meaning "stone." [British, Australian, and elsewhere, 1800s-1900s]

goon 1. an ugly or despised man; a hooligan. For synonyms see SNOKEHORN. [U.S. slang, early 1900s-pres.] **2.** the drug P.C.P. (*q.v.*). [U.S. drug culture, mid 1900s-pres.]

goonas the human breasts. For synonyms see BOSOM. [U.S. slang, mid 1900s, Berrey and Van den Bark]

go on the piss to go on a heavy drinking spree. For synonyms see PLAY CAMELS. [British, early 1900s, *Dictionary of Slang and Unconventional English*]

go on to a better world to die. *Cf.* LEAVE THIS WORLD. [euphemistic, 1900s or before]

goop (also **goup**) a clod; an oaf. *Cf.* GOOF. [U.S. slang and colloquial, 1900s]

goopus a stupid GOOF (sense 1). (sense 2), GOOP. [U.S. slang, mid 1900s-pres.]

goose 1. a prostitute. **2.** copulation; sexual release; women considered sexually. **3.** to GIRL (sense 2); to womanize. [all senses, British slang, 1800s] **4.** a syphilitic chancre. A truncation of WINCHESTER-GOOSE (*q.v.*). [British and U.S. slang, 1800s-1900s] **5.** a silly oaf; a silly goose. [since the 1500s] **6.** to poke something, perhaps a finger, in someone's anus. [U.S. slang, mid 1900s-pres.] **7.** to make something or someone give a sudden start, *e.g.*, to stamp down on the accelerator of a car. No negative connotations. [U.S. slang and colloquial, mid 1900s-pres.] **8.** PEDERASTY (*q.v.*); perhaps to perform pederasty. [U.S. underworld, early 1900s, Montelone] **9.** a derogatory nickname for a Jewish man. Possibly from GONSEL (*q.v.*). [U.S. underworld, early 1900s, Montelone]

goose and duck an act of copulation; to coit a woman. Rhyming slang for "fuck." [U.S., late 1800s, *Dictionary of Rhyming Slang*]

gooseberries the testicles. *Cf.* JINGLE-BERRIES. [British slang, mid 1800s, Farmer and Henley]

gooseberry 1. a fool; an oaf. [British slang, 1800s, Farmer and Henley] **2.** a testicle. See GOOSEBERRIES.

gooseberry-bush the female pubic hair. [British slang, 1800s, Farmer and Henley]

gooseberry-grinder the anus; the posteriors. See DINGLEBERRY. [British slang, late 1700s, Grose]

gooseberry-pudding a wanton woman; a slatternly woman. [British and U.S. slang, mid 1800s-early 1900s]

gooseberry-ranch a brothel. *Cf.* GOOSING-RANCH. [U.S. underworld, early 1900s, Irwin]

gooser 1. the penis. *Cf.* GOOSE (sense 2). For synonyms see YARD. [British slang, 1800s, Farmer and Henley] **2.** a PEDERAST (*q.v.*). *Cf.* GOOSE (sense 8). ·

goose's-neck the penis. From the image of the skinned neck of a fowl. *Cf.* BIT OF THE GOOSE'S-NECK. [British slang, late 1800s, Farmer and Henley]

goosey 1. unusually sensitive in the anal region. **2.** very cautious. **3.** liable to be startled. [all senses, U.S. slang and colloquial, mid 1900s-pres.]

goosing-ranch a brothel. *Cf.* GOOSE, GOOSEBERRY-RANCH. [U.S. slang, mid 1900s]

goosing-slum a brothel. [British and U.S., 1800s-early 1900s]

go over to become a homosexual. Similar to "going over to the enemy." *Cf.* COME OUT OF THE CLOSET. [Australian, early 1900s, Baker]

Goramity! (also **Goramighty!**) a disguise of "God almighty!" [British, 1800s]

Gorblimey! (also **Gawblimey!**, **Gorblimy!**) a disguise of "God blind me!" [British dialect (Cockney), late 1800s-1900s]

Gordelpus! an oath and an exclamation, "God help us!" [British dialect (Cockney), 1800s-1900s]

gorey-eyed intoxicated with alcohol. *Cf.* ORIE-EYED. [U.S. slang, early 1900s, Weseen]

goric a truncation of "paregoric," a tincture of opium. [U.S. drug culture, mid 1900s-pres.]

gorilla pills barbiturate tablets or capsules; the same as KING KONG PILLS (*q.v.*). For synonyms see BARB. [U.S. drug culture, mid 1900s-pres.]

gorilla pimp a brutal and cruel pimp. [U.S. slang, mid 1900s-pres.]

gork a fool; a dupe. *Cf.* DORK (sense 2). For synonyms see OAF. [U.S. slang, mid 1900s]

go rump-splitting to go coiting. See RUMP-SPLITTER.

go see if the horse has kicked off his blanket an excuse given to explain leaving the room to urinate. A vague combining of WATER THE HORSES (*q.v.*) and "leave the room to see if the baby has kicked off his covers." *Cf.* PONY. [Australian, 1900s]

gosh!, By (also **Gosh!**) a disguise of "By God!" The origin is rarely known to its many users. For synonyms see ZOUNDS! [since the mid 1700s]

Gosh-all-lightning! a contrived mock oath and an exclamation. [U.S. colloquial, 1900s]

Gosh almighty! (also **Goshamighty!**) a disguise of "God almighty!" [U.S. colloquial, 1900s]

Goshdang!, By a disguise of "By God!" [U.S. colloquial, 1800s-1900s]

goshdarn "Goddamn." *Cf.* DARN; GOSH!, BY. [U.S. colloquial, 1900s or before]

Gosh ding! a mild disguise of "God-damn!" [U.S. colloquial, 1800s-1900s, Ware]

Goshwalader! (also **Gosh wallader!**) a mild, mock oath. [U.S., 1900s]

gospel-shooter (also **gospel-cove, gospel-grinder, gospel-postilion, gospel-pusher, gospel-shark, gospel-sharp, gospel-whanger**) a clergyman; a preacher, especially an evangelical preacher. For synonyms see SKY-PILOT. [in the various senses, 1800s-1900s]

gospel-shop (also **gospel-mill**) a church. [colloquial, late 1800s-1900s]

gossy a condom. For synonyms see EEL-SKIN.

go star-gazing on one's back to copulate, from a woman's point of view. [British slang, 1800s, Farmer and Henley]

go straight to give up homosexual activities. From an expression describing criminal reform. [U.S. slang, mid 1900s-pres.]

got a brass eye intoxicated with alcohol. [U.S. slang, early 1700s, Ben Franklin]

Go take a flying-fuck! "Get out!" "Go jump in the lake!" "Go take a long walk on a short pier!" From "flying-leap." See FLYING-FUCK. [U.S. slang, 1900s]

go the limit to permit or achieve copulation. Cf. ALL THE WAY; LIMIT, THE. [British and U.S. slang, early 1900s]

go through a woman to coit a woman. [British slang, late 1800s, Farmer and Henley]

Go to! an avoidance for "Go to hell!" [colloquial, 1800s-1900s]

Go to Bath! a curse, "Go to hell!" [British colloquial, 1800s]

go to bed with to have sexual intercourse with someone. Cf. SLEEP WITH. [colloquial and euphemistic, early 1600s-pres.]

go to Egypt to depart to urinate; to urinate. For synonyms see WHIZ. [U.S. colloquial, early 1900s]

Go to Helen B. Happy! a contrived disguise of "Go to hell!" [U.S. colloquial, early 1900s]

go to it to copulate. Implying rapid movement. Cf. GO (sense 2), IT (sense 5). [colloquial since the 1600s]

go to meet one's maker to die. Seen often in the past tense. [U.S. euphemism, 1900s or before]

go to one's reward to die and go to heaven or hell. [U.S. colloquial, 1900s or before]

go to sleep to die. Cf. PUT TO SLEEP.

[U.S. colloquial euphemism, 1900s and before]

go to the bathroom 1. to leave present company and retire to the bathroom. For synonyms see RETIRE. **2.** to eliminate wastes in the bathroom; to urinate or defecate. [both senses, U.S. colloquial, 1900s] **3.** to eliminate wastes, said of animals. [primarily juvenile euphemism, 1900s]

go to town to do anything very rapidly or very well. Used in this sense for copulation. Cf. GO TO IT. [U.S. slang, early 1900s-pres.]

go to work with to copulate with a woman. Cf. WORK (sense 1). [since the 1600s]

got the gout intoxicated with alcohol. [U.S. slang, early 1700s, Ben Franklin]

got the rag on experiencing the menses. Occurs in a variety of additional forms. Cf. RAG, ON THE. For synonyms see FLOODS. [colloquial, late 1800s-pres.]

go up 1. to die, especially by hanging. [U.S. euphemism, mid 1800s, Farmer and Henley] **2.** to become HIGH (sense 2) on narcotics. [U.S. drug culture, mid 1900s-pres.]

goup an oaf. See GOOP.

go up a ladder to bed (also **go up the ladder to rest**) to be hanged. [British, late 1700s, Grose]

go vaulting to go coiting. Cf. VAULTING-SCHOOL. [British slang, 1800s, Farmer and Henley]

government inspected meat a soldier considered sexually by a homosexual male. Cf. SEAFOOD. [U.S. homosexual use, mid 1900s]

gow (also **ghow**) 1. opium. [U.S. underworld, 1900s or before, Irwin] **2.** drugs of any type, including marijuana. From sense 1. [U.S. underworld and drug culture, early-mid 1900s]

gowed-up intoxicated with drugs. From GOW (q.v.). For synonyms see TALL. [U.S. underworld and slang, early 1900s, Weseen]

go wenching to go coiting; to go out after a harlot. [British and U.S. slang, 1800s-1900s]

go west to die. [British and U.S., World War I]

gow-head an opium addict. From GOW (sense 1). [U.S. underworld, early 1900s]

go womanizing to go coiting. [British slang, 1800s, Farmer and Henley]

gowster 1. an opium addict. [U.S. underworld, early 1900s or before] **2.** a marijuana smoker. Extended from sense 1. [U.S. drug culture, mid 1900s]

goy (also **goi**) a mildly derogatory nickname for a non-Jew. [from Hebrew via Yiddish; slang, early 1900s-pres.]

grabble to feel, fondle, or grope a woman. Cf. GRUBBLE. [early 1700s]

Grabs!, By (also **Grab!, By**) an oath and an exclamation. A disguise of ''By God!'' [U.S. colloquial, 1900s]

gracious!, By a disguise of ''By God!'' or ''By gracious God!'' [U.S. colloquial, 1900s or before]

graduate 1. a sexually loose woman; a female expert in sexual performance. [British slang, 1800s, Farmer and Henley] **2.** a person experienced in life. In the expression ''graduate of the School of Hard Knocks.'' [U.S. slang, mid 1900s]

grant the favor to permit coition, said of a woman. [British, early 1700s]

grapefruits the human breasts. For synonyms see BOSOM. [U.S. slang and colloquial, 1900s]

grape-monger a wine tippler; a WINO (q.v.). [cant or slang, 1600s, Dekker]

grape-shot intoxicated with wine. From the term ''small shot.'' Cf. CUP-SHOT. [British and U.S. slang, late 1800s-1900s, Farmer and Henley]

grass 1. marijuana. For synonyms see MARI. [U.S. drug culture, mid 1900s-pres.] **2.** straight hair; Caucasian hair. [U.S. black use, mid 1900s]

grassback a promiscuous young woman, one who spends quite a bit of time on her back. Cf. FLAT-BACK, GREEN GOWN. For synonyms see LAY. [U.S. slang, mid 1900s]

grass colt a bastard. See WOODS-COLT (sense 2). For synonyms see ACCIDENT.

grasshead a marijuana smoker. [U.S. drug culture, mid 1900s]

grasshopper a marijuana smoker. From the common name of the insect and from GRASS (sense 1). [U.S. slang, mid 1900s-pres.]

grass weed marijuana. Cf. GRASS, WEED. [U.S. drug culture, mid 1900s]

gravel-grinder a drunkard. [British slang, mid 1800s, Farmer and Henley]

gravelled intoxicated with alcohol. [British slang, 1800s, Farmer and Henley]

graveyard a cemetery. [since the early 1800s]

gravy 1. the sexual secretions of the male and female; sexual SPENDINGS (q.v.). Cf. BULL FUCK, BULL GRAVY. [British slang, late 1700s] **2.** a mixture of blood and heroin in a syringe used to inject heroin. [U.S. drug culture, mid 1900s-pres.]

gravy!, By an oath and an exclamation; a mild disguise of ''By God!'' [U.S. colloquial, 1800s]

gravy-giver (also **gravy-maker**) **1.** the penis. **2.** the female genitals, specifically the vagina. See GRAVY (sense 1). [both senses, British slang, 1800s, Farmer and Henley]

gray a nickname for a Caucasian. Cf. PALE. [U.S. black use, mid 1900s-pres.]

grease opium. Cf. DREAM WAX. [U.S. underworld, 1900s or before]

greaseball a person, usually a male, of Latin descent; anyone with thick, black, oily hair; a derogatory term for a Mexican. [U.S. slang, early 1900s-pres.]

greased intoxicated with alcohol. From OILED and WELL-OILED (both q.v.). [U.S. slang, early 1900s]

grease gut a derogatory nickname for a Mexican or a Mexican American. [U.S. slang, mid 1900s]

greaser 1. the same as GREASEBALL (q.v.), a Mexican. Cf. OILER (sense 2). [U.S. slang and colloquial, 1800s-1900s] **2.** a sycophant. In the sense ''slimy.''

Also **grease-boy.** [British and U.S., late 1800s-1900s]

grease the wheel to copulate. [British euphemism, 1800s]

Grease us twice! a mild disguised oath. A rhyming play on "Jesus Christ!" [U.S. colloquial, 1900s or before]

great Australian adjective a euphemistic name for "bloody" as used in Australia by Australians. *Cf.* CRIMSONEST OF ADJECTIVES. [attributed to H.L. Mencken]

Great Beyond, the heaven; the afterlife; the GREAT UNKNOWN (*q.v.*). [colloquial, 1900s and before]

Great Caesar's Ghost! a mock oath or an exclamation. *Cf.* CAESARATION! [U.S., mid 1900s and before]

Great Dispatcher in the Sky "God." A jocular expression used by truckers on citizens band radio. [U.S., mid 1900s-pres.]

Great Father!, By the a euphemism of avoidance for "By God!" [U.S. colloquial, 1900s or before]

Great guns! an oath and an exclamation. A euphemism for "Great God!" [British and U.S. colloquial, late 1800s-1900s]

Great Horn Spoon!, By the a contrived disguise of "By God!" [U.S. colloquial, mid 1800s-1900s]

Great Jehovah!, By the an oath and an exclamation; a variant of "By God!"

Great Scott! (also **Great Scot!**) an oath and an exclamation. "Great Scotland Yard" is a British elaboration of this oath. [U.S. colloquial, late 1800s-pres.]

Great snakes! a mock oath and an exclamation. For synonyms see 'ZOUNDS! [U.S. colloquial, 1900s or before]

great tobacco opium. [early 1900s, *Dictionary of the Underworld*]

Great Unknown death; heaven; the afterlife. [U.S. colloquial, 1900s or before]

great with child pregnant; the same as BIG WITH CHILD (*q.v.*). For synonyms see FRAGRANT.

greefo (also **greafa, greapha, greefa, grefa, griefo, griffa, griffo, grifo**) marijuana or a marijuana cigarette. [U.S. underworld and later drug culture, early 1900s-pres.]

Greek 1. a derogatory nickname for an Irishman. [British and U.S. slang, early 1800s-1900s] **2.** anal copulation, heterosexual and homosexual. *Cf.* GREEK WAY. **3.** to coit anally. [senses 2 and 3 are U.S., mid 1900s-pres.]

Greek fire inferior whisky; ROT-GUT (*q.v.*). A reinterpretation of the name of a combustible compound used by the Byzantine Greeks to set fire to enemy holdings. For synonyms see EMBALMING FLUID. [British slang, late 1800s]

Greek love PEDERASTY (*q.v.*). Refers to the practice of pederasty among the ancient Greeks and their gods. [U.S. euphemism, 1900s]

Greek way anal copulation. *Cf.* ITALIAN MANNER. [U.S. slang, mid 1900s-pres.]

green a variety of marijuana. A truncation of CHICAGO GREEN, ILLINOIS GREEN, JERSEY GREEN, VERMONT GREEN (all *q.v.*).

green and yellow fellow a homosexual male. For synonyms see EPICENE. [U.S. slang, mid 1900s]

green-ass pertaining to a "green" or inexperienced person, usually a male. *Cf.* GREENHORN. [U.S. slang, mid 1900s, Wentworth and Flexner]

green dragon 1. an amphetamine capsule or tablet. **2.** a barbiturate capsule or tablet. For synonyms see BARB. [both senses, U.S. drug culture, mid 1900s-pres.]

green-goods a prostitute new to her trade. [British slang, 1800s, Farmer and Henley]

green gown to tumble a girl in the grass, staining her dress. The details vary according to the times: kissing (B.E.), coiting (Farmer and Henley), pinching the pins out of the girl's frock (Pierce Egan), and, again, kissing (*Webster's New International Dictionary*, Second Edition). *Cf.* GRASSBACK. [mid 1600s-1900s]

green-grocery the female genitals. *Cf.* GARDEN, GREENS. For synonyms see MONOSYLLABLE. [British slang, 1800s, Farmer and Henley]

green grove the male or female pubic hair. Usually in reference to the female. *Cf.* GREENS. [British slang, 1800s, Farmer and Henley]

greenhorn 1. an oaf; a newcomer, said to be so named after the green, mossy fuzz growing on the new horns of deer in the spring. [since the mid 1700s] **2.** a male virgin; an undebauched young man. The HORN (sense 3) is the penis. [cant or slang, late 1700s-1800s]

greenie an amphetamine capsule. For synonyms see AMP. [U.S. drug culture, mid 1900s-pres.]

green queen a homosexual male who is known to prefer sexual experiences in the woods or "bushes." See QUEEN for similar subjects. [U.S. homosexual use, mid 1900s, Farrell]

greens sexual activity; sexual release. *Cf.* AFTER ONE'S GREENS. [British slang and euphemism, 1800s]

green snow the drug P.C.P. (*q.v.*). SNOW (sense 2) is cocaine. [U.S. drug culture, mid 1900s-pres.]

griffin 1. a mulatto. Also **griff, griffane, griffe, griffo, griffon, griffone.** For synonyms see MAHOGANY. [since the early 1700s] **2.** a forbidding woman. [British, 1800s] **3.** a GREENHORN (*q.v.*). [British, mid 1800s]

grind 1. to coit a woman. Recently, to have sex with anyone. [British and later U.S., late 1500s-pres.] **2.** the movements of the male during copulation. *Cf.* MILL. [British and U.S. use, mid 1900s-pres.] **3.** an act of coition. [British, early 1800s-pres.] **4.** a sex partner; someone who will provide a GRIND (sense 3). [slang and colloquial, 1800s-1900s] **5.** to arouse a woman sexually. For synonyms see FIRKY-TOODLE. **6.** to masturbate. [senses 5 and 6 are British, 1900s, *Dictionary of Slang and Unconventional English*]

grind, on the 1. pertaining to a person who is sexually active. **2.** pertaining to a prostitute [slang, 1800s-1900s]

grinding-house a brothel. [British slang, 1800s, Farmer and Henley]

grinding-tool the penis. For synonyms see YARD [British slang, 1800s]

grind one's tool to coit a woman. *Cf.* GRIND (sense 1). [British slang, 1800s, Farmer and Henley]

grindstone the female genitals. *Cf.* GRINDING-TOOL, HONE, TOOL (sense 1). [British slang, 1800s, Farmer and Henley]

grinning at the daisy roots dead. A variant of PUSHING UP DAISIES (*q.v.*). [British colloquial, late 1800s, Ware]

grip to masturbate. *Cf.* FIST IT, TAKE ONESELF IN HAND. For synonyms see WASTE TIME. [U.S. slang, mid 1900s-pres.]

gristle the penis. For synonyms see YARD. [British slang, mid 1800s, Farmer and Henley]

gritch 1. to complain. A blend of "gripe" and "bitch." [U.S. slang, mid 1900s] **2.** a complainer. [U.S. slang, mid 1900s]

grod (also **groddess**) a sloppy man or woman. **Groddess** is the feminine form. The terms are patterned on "god" and goddess." *Cf.* GROTTY. [U.S. slang, mid 1900s]

grog alcohol; booze. From the nickname for Admiral Vernon ("old Grog"), who diluted the ship's rum with water to discourage or delay his sailor's intoxication. The admiral's nickname is from the grogram coat which he wore. [slang since the early 1700s]

grogged intoxicated with alcohol. [slang, mid 1800s-pres.]

groggery 1. intoxicated with alcohol. From GROGGY (*q.v.*). [dialect and colloquial, 1800s or before] **2.** a public bar; a tavern. Also **grogmill.** [British and some U.S. use, mid 1800s-1900s]

groggified intoxicated with alcohol. From GROG (*q.v.*). [British slang, early 1800s]

groggy intoxicated with alcohol. For

synonyms see WOOFLED. [since the 1700s]

groghound a drunkard. For synonyms see ALCHY. [U.S. slang, 1900s]

groin 1. the seat of lust. [euphemistic since the early 1600s] **2.** the male genital area; the testicles. Euphemistic when referring to being struck in the groin. Also for the female pubic area. [U.S. euphemism, mid 1900s-pres.]

gronk dirt which collects between the toes. *Cf.* CROTCH-CHEESE, TOE-JAM. Also for any junk or dirt. [U.S. slang, mid 1900s-pres.]

grope 1. to feel a woman; to rudely grasp a woman's private parts, the genitals or the breasts. **2** any sexual foreplay. [both senses, primarily British since the 1300s; sense 1 is current U.S. slang] **3.** a verbal feeler from a homosexual male to a prospective sex partner; a visual groping. *Cf.* EYE SHOP. [U.S. homosexual use, mid 1900s-pres.]

gross crude; vulgar; obscene. [since the early 1500s]

grotto the female genitals. *Cf.* CAVE OF HARMONY. [British slang, 1800s, Farmer and Henley]

grotty grotesque; highly undesirable. Attributed to the Beatles. *Cf.* GROD. [British and U.S., mid 1900s]

ground sweat burial in a grave; a grave. To "take a ground sweat" is to be buried. [colloquial and slang, 1600s-pres.]

group-grope a group of people engaged in sexual activities. See GROUP SEX for other similar terms. [U.S. slang, mid 1900s-pres.]

groupie a girl who follows a band and makes herself sexually available to the players. [U.S. slang, mid 1900s-pres.]

group rape the serial rape of a male or female. See GANG-BANG.

group sex a general term covering sexual activities involving more than

two persons. Specific activities are: BACK-UP, BUNCH-PUNCH, CHAIN-JERK, CHOO-CHOO, CHUGA-CHUGA, CIRCLE-JERK, CIRCUS LOVE, CLUB SANDWICH, DAISY CHAIN, EVERYTHINGATHON, FUCKATHON, GANG-BANG, GANG-SHAG, GANG-SHAY, GROUP-GROPE, MAZOLA PARTY, MUTUAL MASTURBATION, ORGY, PETTING-PARTY, PULL A TRAIN, PULL-PARTY, RING-JERK, ROUND-POUND, SPINTRIA, SUCKATHON, SWING PARTY, TEAM-CREAM, THREE-WAY, WESSON PARTY.

grouse 1. a woman; women considered sexually. *Cf.* QUAIL. [U.S. slang, 1900s] **2.** to neck; to pet and kiss. [U.S. slang, mid 1900s-pres.] **3.** to complain constantly. [slang, 1900s or before]

growl 1. the female genitals. [British, 1800s, *Dictionary of Slang and Unconventional English*] **2.** to belch. [U.S. euphemism, 1900s]

growler 1. a toilet. [U.S. slang, mid 1900s-pres.] **2.** beer. *Cf.* GROWL (sense 2). [U.S. slang, 1900s]

growths the human breasts. For synonyms see BOSOM. [vague euphemism and jocular avoidance; U.S., 1900s]

grubble to feel; to GROPE (sense 1). *Cf.* GRABBLE. [British, late 1600s]

grumble and grunt the female genitals. Rhyming slang for CUNT (*q.v.*). *Cf.* GASP AND GRUNT, GROWL (sense 1). [British, 1900s, *Dictionary of Rhyming Slang*]

grunge 1. any nasty substance. *Cf.* CRAP, GRONK, GUNGY. [U.S. slang, mid 1900s-pres.] **2.** an ugly or nasty person. [U.S. slang, mid 1900s-pres.]

grunt 1. to belch. **2.** to defecate. [euphemistic juvenile, 1900s or before] **3.** an act of defecation. [all senses, U.S. slang or colloquial, 1900s]

gubers acne; facial pimples. From a Southern dialect term meaning "peanut." The pustule and the peanut both grow "underground." *Cf.* GOOB, GOOBER. For synonyms see BURBLE. [U.S. slang, mid 1900s-pres.]

guddle to GROPE (*q.v.*); to do sexual foreplay. For synonyms see FIRKY-

TOODLE. [from a Scots word meaning "groping for fish"; British, early 1800s, Farmer and Henley]

guffin an awkward, clumsy oaf. [British and U.S. dialect and colloquial, mid 1800s-1900s]

guffoon an oaf. [from Irish use; British, 1800s, Ware]

gug an extremely unpleasant person. [U.S. slang, mid 1900s, *Current Slang*]

Guin a derogatory nickname for an Italian. From "Guinea." *Cf.* GHIN, GINNEY. [U.S. slang, 1900s or before]

Guinea (also **Guinee**) an Italian immigrant. Usually considered derogatory. See GUIN. [U.S. slang, late 1800s-1900s]

Guinea!, By an oath and an exclamation; a disguise of "By God!" [U.S. colloquial, 1900s]

guinea-hen a courtesan; a prostitute. Either in reference to her fee (one guinea) or to the bird image of women. See QUAIL. *Cf.* BIG TWENTY (sense 2). [British, 1600s]

gulf a public restroom. [U.S. slang, early 1900s, Montelone]

gull 1. a simpleton; an oaf. [late 1500s-1900s] **2.** a prostitute, one who frequents the coastal areas. A play on "gal" or "girl." *Cf.* QUAIL. [U.S. slang, 1900s]

gull-finch a fool; a simpleton. [British, early 1600s]

gullion 1. a contemptible and mean wretch. For synonyms see SNOKE-HORN. [British dialect, 1800s or before] **2.** a stomachache. [U.S. colloquial, 1900s or before] **3.** a drunkard. [British, early 1800s]

gully-hole (also **gully**) the female genitals. From a once-current term for "gullet." *Cf.* DEN. [British slang, 1800s, Farmer and Henley]

gum 1. opium. *Cf.* BRICK GUM, LEAF GUM. [U.S. underworld, 1900s or before] **2.** God. Usually capitalized in this sense. See DAD, DOD.

Gum!, By an oath and an exclamation, "By Gum!" [British and U.S. colloquial, early 1800s-pres.]

guma semen. *Cf.* GLUE (sense 2). For synonyms see METTLE. [U.S. colloquial, late 1800s, Green]

Gum godfrey! an oath and an exclamation, the equivalent of "By God!"

gummed damned, as in "Dad-gummed!" *Cf.* DAD. [British and U.S. colloquial, late 1800s-pres.]

gump an oaf; a dolt. [British and U.S. colloquial, early 1800s-1900s]

gumpuncher (also **gumdigger**) a dentist. From the gums (ginguvae) and the Australian gum tree. [Australian, 1900s, Baker]

gumshoe (also **gumfoot, gumheel**) a policeman or a detective known for wearing silent, gum-rubber soles. [U.S. slang, early 1900s-pres.]

gun the penis. *Cf.* CUTTY-GUN, PISTOL, SHORT-ARM. [slang and colloquial, mid 1900s and nonce long before] See also GREAT GUNS!

gun, in the intoxicated with alcohol. Because one is almost SHOT (sense 1). [British, 1600s B.E.]

gungeon marijuana. See BLACK GUNGEON.

gungy (also **grungy**) messy, ugly, smelly, old, or ragged. See GRUNGE. [U.S. slang, mid 1900s-pres.]

gunk 1. any nasty, messy stuff. [U.S. colloquial, mid 1900s-pres.] **2.** glue sniffed as a recreational drug. From sense 1. [U.S. drug culture, mid 1900s-pres.]

gunny marijuana; HEMP (*q.v.*). From GUNGEON (*q.v.*) and the "gunny" of a hemp gunny-sack. [U.S. slang, mid 1900s-pres.]

gunzel-butt a strange-looking person. Possibly a nickname for a CATAMITE (*q.v.*). *Cf.* GONSEL (senses 2 and 5), GOOSE (sense 5). [U.S. slang, mid 1900s, *Current Slang*]

gurk 1. to release intestinal gas audibly. **2.** an audible release of intestinal gas. [both senses, Australian, early 1900s, Baker] Synonyms and related terms for both senses: BACK-TALK, BEEF-HEARTS, BLAST, BLIND FART, BLOW OFF,

BLOW THE HORN, BORBORYGMUS, BREAK WIND, BREAK WIND BACKWARDS, BREAK WIND DOWNWARDS, BREEZE, BUCK SNORT, BULLOCK'S HEART, BURN BAD POWDER, BURNT CHEESE, BURST AT THE BROADSIDE, BUSTER, BUZZ, CARMINATE, CHEEZER, CREPITATE, CREPITATION, CREPITUS, CUT ONE, DROP A ROSE, DROP ONE'S GUTS, FART, FARTICK, FARTKIN, FAT-UN, FICE, FIZZLE, FLATULENCE, FLATUS, FLUFF, FOIST, FOYST, HINDER-BLAST, HONK, INTESTINAL WINDINESS, LAY A FART, LET ONE, MAKE A NOISE, MAKE A RUDE NOISE, MAKE WIND, PASS AIR, PASS GAS, PASS WIND, POCKET-THUNDER, POOP, POOT, P.U., PUFF, PUMP, RAISE WIND, RASPBERRY TART, RASPER, ROUSER, RUMP, SCAPE, SCOTCH WARMING-PAN, SHOOT RABBITS, SNEEZE, STINKER, TAIL-SHOT, TALK GERMAN, THROUGH-COUGH, TOM TART, TRUMP, VENT, WET ONE, WHIFFER, WINDER.

gurry (also **gurr**) diarrhea. [British colloquial and dialect, early 1500s-1800s]

Guru-you! a disguised curse, "Screw you!" or "Fuck you!" [U.S. slang, mid 1900s-pres.]

gusset the female genitals; a woman, especially a woman considered sexually. [British, 1600s]

gusseteer a whoremonger; a lecher. *Cf.* GUSSET. For synonyms see LECHER. [British, 1800s or before, Farmer and Henley]

gut bucket 1. a CHAMBER POT (*q.v.*), especially one used in a prison cell. [U.S. underworld, early 1900s, Montelone] **2.** a toilet. For synonyms see W.C. [U.S. slang and colloquial, early 1900s] **3.** the stomach. [U.S. slang and colloquial, 1900s]

gut-butcher (also **gut-fucker, gut-monger, gut-reamer, gut-scraper, gut-sticker, gut-stretcher, gut-stuffer, gut-vexer**) a PEDERAST (*q.v.*); the INSERTOR (*q.v.*). [British and U.S., 1800s-1900s]

gut-rot inferior liquor; ROT-GUT (*q.v.*). For synonyms see EMBALMING FLUID. [British slang, 1900s]

guts 1. courage; masculine valor. **2.** the belly; the intestines. [both senses, British and U.S. slang and colloquial, 1900s]

gut-stick the penis. For synonyms see YARD. [British slang, 1800s, Farmer and Henley]

gutter the female genitals. *Cf.* COMMON SEWER, DRAIN, SCUPPER. [British slang, 1800s, Farmer and Henley]

gutter slut a low prostitute; a common whore. For synonyms see HARLOT. [U.S., early 1900s]

guttersnipe 1. a GUTTER SLUT (*q.v.*). [widespread colloquial, 1800s-pres.] **2.** a prostitute. [British 1800s, Farmer and Henley]

guttle a drunkard. From the standard word meaning "to make a glutton of oneself." [British slang, 1800s, Farmer and Henley]

guzunder a CHAMBER POT (*q.v.*). A jocular term based on "goes under" the bed. For synonyms see POT. [Australian slang, early 1900s, *Dictionary of Slang and Unconventional English*]

guzzle 1. to drink alcohol in great quantities. For synonyms see PLAY CAMELS. [since the 1500s] **2.** a. drinking SPREE (sense 3). [since the early 1800s]

guzzled intoxicated with alcohol. *Cf.* GUZZLE. [U.S. slang or colloquial, 1900s]

guzzle-guts a drunkard. For synonyms see ALCHY. [British slang, 1700s-1800s]

guzzler a drunkard. [since the late 1700s]

gyppy tummy diarrhea; an upset stomach. For synonyms see QUICKSTEP. [U.S. slang or colloquial, mid 1900s-pres.]

gyve marijuana. For synonyms see MARI.

H

H. 1. "heroin." [U.S. underworld and drug culture, early 1900s-pres.] **2.** "hell." [euphemistic, 1900s and before]

habit the habit of using drugs. Occasionally euphemistic for "addiction." *Cf.* DRUG HABIT. [U.S. underworld and drug culture, mid 1900s-pres.]

hack 1. a prostitute. From HACKNEY (*q.v.*). [British slang, early 1700s] **2.** to vomit; to spit up. Related to "hacking cough." *Cf.* HAWK UP. Onomatopoetic. [U.S., mid 1900s-pres.]

hackney a prostitute. From a term used for a horse or MOUNT (*q.v.*) for rent. For synonyms see HARLOT. [slang, 1500s-1600s]

Hades 1. hell. [from the Classical Greek name for the underground home of the dead; colloquial and euphemistic] **2.** Pluto, the god of the dead in Classical mythology. [both in English since the late 1500s]

hag a witch; an extremely ugly girl or woman. [since the early 1500s]

haggage a slattern. Possibly a blend of "hag" and "baggage." For synonyms see TROLLYMOG. [British dialect, 1700s]

hail-fellow-all-wet a jocular reference to a drunkard. Based on "hail-fellow-well-met," where "hail" means "healthy." [U.S., mid 1900s]

hair 1. women considered sexually. From the female pubic hair. *Cf.* AFTER HAIR, BIT OF HAIR. **2.** copulation. [both senses, British slang, 1800s] **3.** virile strength and courage. *Cf.* HAIRY-ASSED. [U.S. slang, mid 1900s-pres.]

hairburger 1. the female genitals with reference to CUNNILINGUS (*q.v.*). *Cf.* FURBURGER. [U.S. slang, mid 1900s-pres.] **2.** a homosexual male hairdresser. From sense 1. [U.S. homosexual use, mid 1900s-pres.]

hair-court 1. the female genitals. **2.** copulation. *Cf.* FORE-COURT. [both senses, British slang, 1800s, Farmer and Henley]

hair-divider the penis. *Cf.* BEARD-SPLITTER. For synonyms see YARD. [British slang, early 1800s]

hair-monger a whoremonger; a lecher. *Cf.* HAIR (sense 2). [British slang, 1800s, Farmer and Henley]

hair-pie the female genitals; the female pubic hair. *Cf.* HAIRBURGER. [U.S. slang, mid 1900s-pres.]

hair-splitter the penis. *Cf.* HAIR-DIVIDER. [British slang, early 1800s]

hairy 1. sexually aroused. [said of women, British, mid 1800s; said of men, U.S., mid 1900s-pres.] **2.** covered with hair; crinatory. **3.** virile; masculine. See HAIRY-ASSED. [U.S. slang, mid 1900s-pres.] **4.** difficult; frightening; exciting. [U.S. slang, mid 1900s] See also FEEL HAIRY.

hairy-assed pertaining to a mature, virile, and hairy male. *Cf.* BARE-ASSED (sense 2). [slang, mid 1900s-pres.]

hairy wheel 1. the male genitals. For synonyms see VIRILIA. [British slang, late 1800s, *Dictionary of Slang and Unconventional English*] **2.** the female genitals. [Australian, 1800s, *Dictionary of Slang and Unconventional English*]

half and half 1. half drunk. *Cf.* ARF AN ARF. [British and U.S., early 1700s-pres.] **2.** BISEXUAL (*q.v.*). [U.S. slang, mid 1900s-pres.] Synonyms and related terms for sense 2: A.C.-D.C., AMBIDEXTROUS, AMBISEXTROUS, AMBISEXUAL, AMBOSEXUAL, AMPHIGENOUS INVERSION, BI, BISEXUAL, BISEXUOUS, DOUBLE-GAITED, INTERSEX, KIKI, SWITCH-HITTER. **3.** an act of fellatio followed by sexual intercourse. [U.S. slang, mid 1900s-pres.]

half-assed worthless; stupid; ill-planned; trivial. [U.S. slang, mid 1900s-pres.]

half-blind intoxicated with alcohol. *Cf.* BLIND DRUNK. [U.S. colloquial, mid 1900s-pres.]

half-breed (also **breed**) a derogatory nickname for a person of mixed ancestry. Typically one-half American Indian, Negro, or Spanish and one-half Caucasian. [since the late 1700s]

half-bulled intoxicated with alcohol; mildly BULL-DOZED (*q.v.*), "drunk." [Australian, 1900s, Baker]

half-canned lightly intoxicated with alcohol.

half-cocked intoxicated with alcohol. For synonyms see WOOFLED. [widespread, late 1800s-pres.]

half-cut intoxicated with alcohol. *Cf.* CUT (sense 2). [widespread slang, mid 1800s-pres.]

half drag the state of a homosexual male partly dressed like a woman. Something less than full drag. See DRAG. [U.S. homosexual use, mid 1900s, Farrell]

half-gone half drunk; mildly intoxicated with alcohol. [British and U.S. slang, 1800s-1900s]

half-hard (also **half-mast**) **1.** pertaining to a semierect penis. See LOB (sense 2), LOB-COCK (sense 2). [widespread nonce, 1900s or before] **2.** stupid. See LOB (sense 1), LOB-COCK (sense 1). [British, 1900s, *Dictionary of Slang and Unconventional English*]

half in the bag intoxicated with alcohol. [U.S. slang, mid 1900s-pres.]

half-lit intoxicated with alcohol. *Cf.* LIT (sense 1). [U.S. slang, mid 1900s-pres.]

half-moon 1. the female genitals. [British, early 1600s] **2.** a CUCKOLD (*q.v.*). [British, mid 1600s]

half-pint a small person; an ineffectual person, especially a slightly-built male. Sometimes used as an affectionate term for a small child. [U.S. slang, mid 1900s-pres.]

half-pissed intoxicated with alcohol; partially intoxicated with alcohol. *Cf.* PISSED. [British and U.S. slang, early 1900s-pres.]

half-rats partially intoxicated with alcohol. *Cf.* RATS, THE. [British slang, late 1800s, Ware]

half-rinsed partially intoxicated with alcohol. [slang, early 1900s-pres.]

half-screwed partially intoxicated with alcohol. *Cf.* SCREWED (sense 1). [British and U.S. slang, early 1800s-1900s]

half-seas-over partially intoxicated with alcohol. Like a ship which is washed over by low waves or a ship which is half-way to its destination. [in the mid 1500s, the midpoint of any act; this sense since the 1600s]

half-shaved intoxicated with alcohol. *Cf.* SHAVED. [colloquial and slang, 1800s or before]

half-shot intoxicated with alcohol. *Cf.* SHOT (sense 1). [British and U.S. slang, 1900s or before]

half-under mildly intoxicated with alcohol; partially under the influence of alcohol. [U.S. slang, early 1900s-pres.]

half up the pole intoxicated with alcohol. *Cf.* POLE, UP THE.

Halifax a euphemism for "hell." [primarily British, colloquial since the 1600s]

hall a disguise of "alcohol." *Cf.* AL K. HALL. [U.S. slang, 1900s or before]

hallelujah-peddler a clergyman; an evangelist. For synonyms see SKY-PILOT. [U.S. slang, early 1900s, Irwin]

halo a nickname for the AREOLA (*q.v.*). [U.S. slang, mid 1900s, Montelone]

ham-bags women's underpants; trousers. *Cf.* BAGS, HAM-CASES. [British colloquial, 1800s]

hambone the penis. *Cf.* BONE (sense 2). [U.S. slang, 1900s and nonce]

ham-cases (also **hams**) BREECHES (*q.v.*); trousers. *Cf.* GAM-CASES. For synonyms see GALLIGASKINS. [British, late 1700s, Grose]

hammer 1. a woman; a girl. *Cf.* NAIL (sense 1), POUND. [originally black use; U.S. slang, mid 1900s-pres.] **2.** the penis. [Australian and Canadian attestations, 1900s]

hammered intoxicated with alcohol. [U.S. slang, mid 1900s-pres.]

hammerhead an oaf; a dullard. *Cf.* MALLET-HEAD. [since the early 1500s]

hammock for two a brassiere. For synonyms see BRA. [U.S. jocular slang, 1900s]

hammock is swinging a catch phrase indicating that a woman is experiencing the menses. The hammock refers to a SANITARY NAPKIN (*q.v.*) attached to a sanitary napkin belt. [U.S., 1900s or before]

Hampton Wick (also **Hampton**) the penis. Rhyming slang for "prick."

[British, 1800s-1900s, *Dictionary of Rhyming Slang*]

hams 1. the buttocks. *Cf.* PRESSED-HAM. [colloquial, early 1700s-pres.] 2. breeches; trousers. See HAM-CASES. [cant, early 1700s]

hanced intoxicated with alcohol. From an earlier sense meaning "elevated." [British euphemism, 1600s-1700s]

H. and C. a mixture of "heroin and cocaine." A reinterpretation of the abbreviation for "hot and cold." [U.S. drug culture, mid 1900s-pres.]

hand-job the masturbation of oneself or of another person. Modeled on BLOW-JOB (*q.v.*). See JOB (sense 2) for similar "jobs." [U.S. slang, mid 1900s-pres.]

handkerchief-head an UNCLE TOM (*q.v.*). Refers to the wearing of a cloth on the head to protect a hairdo. *Cf.* RAG-HEAD. [U.S. black use, mid 1900s-pres.]

handle 1. to pet; to fondle. [U.S. slang, 1900s and nonce] 2. to masturbate. [British and U.S. colloquial euphemism, 1800s-1900s] 3. to copulate. In the sense "manage." 4. the penis. 5. a breast. Usually in the plural. [senses 3-5, U.S. slang, 1900s]

handle for the broom the vagina. For synonyms see PASSAGE. [British slang, 1800s, Farmer and Henley]

handstaff the penis. [British slang or colloquial, mid 1800s, Farmer and Henley]

hand-warmers the breasts. [Australian and U.S., early 1900s-pres.]

handy-dandy (also **handie-dandie**) copulation. [since the late 1400s]

hang a B.A. to hang a "bare ass"; to MOON (sense 1), to expose the buttocks for shock or insult. *Cf.* GAUCHO, MOON (sense 1), PRESSED-HAM. [U.S. slang, mid 1900s]

hangedest the damnedest. [U.S. colloquial, 1900s or before]

hanging Johnny the penis, espcially when flaccid or diseased. *Cf.* JOHNNY (sense 1). [British slang, 1800s, Farmer and Henley]

Hang it! an oath and an exclamation, "May God hang it!" Now used mostly as a euphemism for "Dammit!" [U.S. colloquial, 1800s-1900s]

hangover 1. an unpleasant period of recovery from heavy alcohol intoxication. [1900s] Synonyms and related terms: BOTTLE-FATIGUE, CRAPULA, LONG STALE DRUNK, SNOZZLE-WOBBLES, WINE-ACHE, WOOFITS. 2. large buttocks which hang over the chair. 3. a large belly which hangs over the belt. See also FALL-OUT Both are from sense 1. [senses 2 and 3 are U.S. slang and colloquial, 1900s]

hanky-panky 1. trickery; deceit. [since the early 1800s] 2. sexual play; illicit sexual activity; adultery. [British and U.S. slang and colloquial, 1900s]

happy mildly intoxicated with alcohol. *Cf.* GLAD, MERRY (sense 2). [since the 1700s]

happy dust (also **happy powder, happy stuff**) any of the powdered narcotics, specifically morphine or cocaine. [U.S. underworld and drug culture, early 1900s-pres.]

happy hunting-grounds 1. the female genitals. [British slang, 1800s, Farmer and Henley] 2. the North American Indian "heaven." [U.S., 1800s-pres., (Washington Irving)]

happy returns vomit; vomitus. *Cf.* RETURN. Also in the catch phrase "many happy returns," said when someone belches. [slang, 1800s-1900s]

happy valley the female genitals. *Cf.* DEN. [British, 1900s, *Dictionary of Slang and Unconventional English*]

hard 1. erect; pertaining to the erectness of the penis. [since the 1600s and most certainly before] 2. lightly intoxicated with alcohol. For synonyms see WOOF-LED. [British dialect, 1800s or before]

hard-ass a person who has been seasoned or made tough by the ways of the world. A stronger version of "hard-nosed." [U.S. slang, mid 1900s-pres.]

hard bit 1. the erect penis. For synonyms see ERECTION. 2. copulation from the woman's point of view. [both senses, British slang, 1800s, Farmer and Henley]

hard-core 1. pornographic. This is considered by some to relate to depictions of erect penes. 2. pertaining to anything extreme. From sense 1. *Cf.* SOFT-CORE. [U.S. slang, mid 1900s-pres.]

hard mack a cruel pimp; the same as GORILLA PIMP (*q.v.*). *Cf.* MACK (sense 1).[U.S., 1900s]

hard-on 1. pertaining to an erect penis. [British, 1800s, Farmer and Henley] **2.** an erect penis. [British and U.S. colloquial, late 1800s-pres]

hard sore a syphilitic chancre as opposed to a SOFT SORE (*q.v.*), which is not from a venereal disease.

hard stuff 1. hard liquor. [British and U.S; slang and colloquial, 1800s–1900s] **2.** strong and addictive drugs, specifically heroin and morphine. For synonyms see COTICS. [U.S. drug culture, mid 1900s-pres.]

hard-up 1. intoxicated with alcohol [since the late 1800s] **2.** very much in need of sexual release. [widespread colloquial; U.S., 1900s] **3.** pertaining to an erect penis. [U.S. slang, 1900s]

hard word a sexual proposition. In the expression PUT THE HARD WORD ON HER (*q.v.*). [attested as Australian and U.S. slang, 1900s]

hardy intoxicated with alcohol. [U.S. slang, early 1700s, Ben Franklin]

harebrain (also **hairbrain**) **1.** an oaf; a fool. **2.** stupid and heedless. Also **harebrained.** Brewer lists ''air-brained'' [both senses, since the mid 1500s]

harlot 1. a rascal; a knave; a fornicator. [1200s, *Oxford English Dictionary*] **2.** a prostitute. Now with some notion of youth and excitement. [since the early 1400s] Synonyms for sense 2 refer to women unless indicated otherwise: ACADEMICIAN, ALLEY CAT, ANIMAL, ANONYMA, ARTICHOKE, ARTICLE, ASS-PEDDLER, ATHANASIAN WENCH, AUNT, BACHELOR'S WIFE, BADGER, BAG, BAGGAGE, BANGSTER, BARBER'S CHAIR, BARNACLE, BARRACK-HACK, BARREN-JOEY, BAT, BAWDY BASKET, BEAST, BEAT MOLL, BED-FAGGOT, BEEFSTEAK, BELT, BELTER, BICYCLE, BIMMY, BINT, BIRD, BISCUIT, BITCH, BIT OF MEAT, BIT OF MUSLIN, BIT OF MUTTON, BIT OF STUFF, BLACK MEAT, BLIMP, BLINT, BLISTER, BLISTERINE, BLOSS, BLOSY, BLOUSER, BLOUZA-LINDA, BLOUZE, BLOW, BLOWER, BLOWSE, BLOWZY, BLUDGET, BOAT AND OAR, BOB TAIL, BONA ROBA, BOONG-MOLL, BRASS NAIL, BRASS NOB, BRIM, BRIMSTONE, BROAD, BROADWAY BROAD, BROKEN OAR, BROWN BESS, BUCKET-BROAD, BUG, BULKER, BUM, BUN, BUNNY, BUNTER, BURICK, BURLAP SISTER, BUSH-SCRUBBER, BUSINESS GIRL, BUSS BEGGAR, BUTTOCK, BUTT-PEDDLER, CAB-MOLL, CAKE, CALLET, CALL-GIRL, CANNON WOMAN, CANVASBACK, CARRION, CARRY-KNAVE, CASE VROW, CAT, CAT-HOUSE CUTIE, CATTLE, C-GIRL, CHARLIE, CHICK (male), CHIPPY, CHROMO, CLAPTRAP, COCKATRICE, COCK-EYED JENNY, COCK-TAIL, COFFEE-GRINDER, COLUMBINE, COMMON-JACK, COMMON SEWER, COMPANY GIRL, CONCILIATRIX, CONVENIENT, COURTESAN, COVENT GARDEN NUN, COVESS-DINGE, COW, CRACK, CRACKED PITCHER, CRACK SALESMAN, CRO, CROSHA-BELLE, CROW, CRUISER, DANT, DASHER, DAUGHTER, DEADLY NIGHTSHADE, DEAD-MEAT, DEAD-PICKER, DEMIMONDAINE, DEMIREP, DIRTY PUZZLE, DOG, DOOR-KEEPER, DOXY, DRAB, DRAGON, DRESS FOR SALE, DUSTY BUTT, DUTCH-WIDOW, EARLY DOOR, EASY VIRTUE, ENDLESS BELT, ENTERTAINER, ERRING SISTER, EWE-MUTTON, FAGGOT, FALLEN WOMAN, FANCY PIECE, FANCY WOMAN, FAST-FANNY, FAST WOMAN, FEN, FERRY, FILLE DE JOIE, FILTH, FIRESHIP, FISH, FLAG-ABOUT, FLAPPER, FLASH-TAIL, FLAT-BACK, FLATBACKER, FLAT FLOOSIE, FLAX-WENCH, FLEABAG, FLESH-PEDDLER, FLESH-POT, FLING-DUST, FLIPPER, FLOOSEY, FLUZIE, FLY, FLY-BY-NIGHT, FORE-AND-AFTER, FORESKIN-HUNTER, FORGOTTEN WOMAN, FORK, FORTY-FOUR, FRAIL, FRAIL-ONE, FRAIL-SISTER, FREAK TRICK, FREE RIDE, FROW, FUCK-FREAK, GAL, GAME, GAMESTER, GARBAGE CAN, GAY-BIT, GAY-GIRL, GAY-PIECE, GAY-WOMAN, GIGSY, GIN, GINCH, GIRL, GIRL AT EASE, GIVE AND TAKE GIRL, GLUE NECK, GOAT-MILKER, GO-BETWEEN, GOOH, GOOK, GOOSE, GREEN-GOODS, GREEN-GOOSE, GRISETTE, GUINEA-HEN, GULL, GUTTER SLUT, GUTTERSNIPE, HACK, HACKNEY, HALF-AND-HALFER, HARPIE, HAT, HAT RACK, HAY, HAY-BAG, HIDE, HIGHWAY HOOKER, HIP-FLIPPER, HIP-PEDDLER, HO, HOBBY-HORSE, HOLER, HOOK, HOOKER, HOP-PICKER, HOT BEEF, HOTEL HOTSY, HOT MEAT, HOT MUTTON, HOT ROCKS, HOUSEKEEPER, HUMP, HUNT-ABOUT, HURRY-WHORE, HUSTLER, HUSTLER (male), HYPE, IMPURE, INCOGNITA, IRON (male), IRON

HOOF (male), JACK WHORE, JADE, JAGA-BAT, JANE SHORE, JERKER, JILT, JOY-GIRL, JOY SISTER, JUANITA, JUDY; KID-LEATHER, KIFE, KITTOCK, KNOCK-'EM-DOWN, LACED-MUTTON, LADY, LADY OF EXPANSIVE SEN-SIBILITY, LADY OF LEISURE, LADY OF PLEASURE, LADY OF THE EVENING, LAY, LEASE-PIECE, LEWD WOMAN, LIFT-SKIRTS, LIONESS, LITTLE BIT, LIVESTOCK, LOON, LOOSE-BODIED GOWN, LOOSE FISH, LOOSE-LOVE LADY, LOST LADY, LOVE-PEDDLER, LOW-HEEL, LOWIE, LUSHER, MAB, MADAM RAN, MADAM VAN, MADGE, MAGGIE, MALLEE ROOT, MARK, MASSEUSE, MAT, MATTRESS, MAUD (male), MAUKS, MED-LAR, MERETRICE, MERETRIX, MERMAID, MERRY LEGS, MINX, MISS, MIXER, MOB, MODEL, MOONLIGHTER, MORSEL, MORT, MORT WOP-APACE, MOTH, NAFFGUR, NAFKEH, NAG, NANNY, NAUTCH-BROAD, NECESSARY, NEEDLE-WOMAN, NESTCOCK, NESTLE-COCK, NIGH ENOUGH (male), NIGHTBIRD, NIGHT-HAWK, NIGHT-HUNTER, NIGHTINGALE, NIGHT-JOBBER, NIGHT-PIECE, NIGHT-SHADE, NIGHT-WALKER, NIT, NOCKSTRESS, NOCTURNAL, NOCTURNE, NOFFGUR, NOTCH-BROAD, NOTCH-GIRL, NUN, NYMPH DU PAVE, NYMPH OF DARK-NESS, NYMPH OF THE PAVEMENT, OCCU-PANT, OLD RIP, OLD TIMER, OMNIBUS, OUTLAW, OVERNIGHT-BAG, OWL, PACK, PAGAN, PAINTED-CAT, PAINTED-LADY, PAINTED-WOMAN, PALLIASSE, PAPHIAN, PARTRIDGE, PASTRY, PAVEMENT-POUNDER, PAVEMENT PRINCESS, PEDDLE-SNATCH, PERFECT LADY, PHEASANT, PICKER-UP, PIECE, PIECE OF TRADE, PIG, PINCH-PRICK, PINNACE, PINTLE-FANCIER, PINTLE-MER-CHANT, PINTLE-MONGER, PINTLE-TWISTER, PIPER'S WIFE, PLEASURE LADY, PLOVER, POKER-BREAKER, POKER-CLIMBER, POLE-CAT, PONCESS, PRINCESS OF THE PAVE-MENT, PRIVATEER, PRO, PROFESSIONAL, PROSS, PROSSO, PROSSY, PROSTITUTE, PROSTY, PUBLIC LEDGER, PUG, PUG-NASTY, PUNCHABLE NUN, PUNK, PURE, PURITAN, PURSE-FINDER, PUT, PUTA, PUTAIN, PUT-TOCK, PYNNAGE, QUAEDAM, QUAIL, QUAN-DONG, QUIFF, RABBIT-PIE, RAGS, RANNEL, RASPBERRY TART, RATTLESNAKE, RE-CEIVER GENERAL, RED LIGHT, RED-LIGHTER, RED-LIGHT SISTER, REP, RIBALD, ROACH, ROAD, ROMP, RORY O'MORE, RUMPER, SAILOR'S BAIT, SAILOR'S DELIGHT, SALES LADY, SAMPLE OF SIN, SARDINE, SCAR-LET SISTER, SCARLET WOMAN, SCOLO-PENDRIA, SCREW, SCROUSHER, SCRUB, SCRUDGE, SCUFFER, SCUPPER, SHAD, SHAKE, SHANK, SHE SAILS, SHINGLER, SHOREDITCH-FURY, SHRIMP, SINGLE-WOMAN, SINNER, SIN-SISTER, SISTER OF MERCY, SIX-TO-FOUR, SKIRT, SKRUNT, SLOOP OF WAR, SNATCH-PEDDLER, SOILED-DOVE, SOSS-BRANGLE, SPEEDY SISTER, SPINSTER, SPLIT-ARSE MECHANIC, SPOFF-SKINS, SPORTING-GIRL, SPORTSWOMAN, SQUAW, STALE, STALLION, STEM SIREN, STEW, STIFF-QUEAN, STRAM, STREET SISTER, STREET-WALKER, STRUM, STRUM-PET, SUBURBAN, SUBURB-SINNER, SWALLOW-COCK, TAIL, TAIL-PEDDLER, TARRY ROPE, TART, TENDERLOIN MADAM, THOROUGHBRED, THRILL DAME, TIGER, TIT, TOBY, TOFFER, TOLL-HOLE, TOMATO, TOTTIE, TRADER, TRAFFIC, TRAT, TREADLE, TREBLE-CLEFT, TREDDLE, TRICK, TRICK BABE, TRICKING-BROAD, TRICKSTER, TRIED VIRGIN, TRIP, TROLLOPS, TROOPER, TRUG, TRUGMOLDY, TRUGMULLION, TRULL, TUMBLE, TWEAK, TWEAT, TWIDGET, TWIG-GER, TWO-BIT HUSTLER, TWO-BY-FOUR, TWOFER, UNFORTUNATES, UNFORTUNATE WOMAN, VENT-RENTER, VENTURER, VICE-SISTER, VIRTUE AFTER, WAPPING-DELL, WAPPING-MORT, WARM MEMBER, WASP, WEED MONKEY, WHEAT BELT, WHISKER, WHITE-APRON, WHORE, WHORE-BITCH, WINDOW-GIRL, WINDOW-TAPPER, WOMAN, WOMAN ABOUT TOWN, WOMAN OF ACCOM-MODATING MORALS, WOMAN OF A CERTAIN CLASS, WOMAN OF LOOSE MORALS, WOMAN OF PLEASURE, WOMAN OF THE TOWN, WOP, WORKING GIRL, WREN, ZOOK.

harp a derogatory nickname for an Irishman. [U.S. slang, early 1900s, Irwin] Synonyms: BARK, BOG-HOPPER, BOG-LANDER, BOG-TROTTER, BOILED DIN-NER, CHAW, CHAW-MOUTH, CHEAP SHANTY MICK, FLANNEL MOUTH, MICK, MICKY, MIKE, NARROWBACK, PADDY, PAT, PAT-LANDER, POOKA, SALT-WATER TURKEY, SHAM, SHAMROCK, SHANTY IRISH, SPUD, TERRIER, TURF-CUTTER.

harpie 1. a prostitute. From the "Harpy" of Classical mythology, a nasty creature with the head of a woman on the body of a bird. **2.** a shrewish virago. [U.S. slang, mid 1900s-pres.]

Harry heroin. *Cf.* BIG HARRY [U.S. drug culture, mid 1900s-pres.]

Harry Flakers (also **flakers**) intoxicated with alcohol. [Australian, mid 1900s, *Dictionary of Slang and Unconventional English*]

Harry Starkers naked; nude. A personification of nudity. Related to STARK NAKED (*q.v.*) and possibly HAIRY (sense 2). *Cf.* STARKERS. [British, mid 1900s, *Dictionary of Slang and Unconventional English*]

has marijuana. From HASH (sense 3). [U.S. drug culture, mid 1900s-pres.]

hash 1. vomit; vomitus in FLASH THE HASH (*q.v.*) *Cf.* FLASH (sense 1). **2.** to vomit. [attested as U.S., 1800s, Farmer and Henley] **3.** HASHISH (*q.v.*). Synonyms: BLACK RUSSIAN, BLOND, BLOND HASH, CANDY, CHOCOLATE, KIF, QUARTER MOON, SHISHI, SOLES. **4.** any drugs, including marijuana. [senses 3 and 4 are U.S. drug culture, mid 1900s-pres.]

hash head a user of HASHISH (*q.v.*) or marijuana. [U.S. drug culture, mid 1900s-pres.]

hashish (also **hasheesh**) the leaves and flowers of Indian hemp, both raw and in processed form. The term is used in the U.S. for a very strong preparation. [from an Arabic word which is roughly translated as HAY (*q.v.*); in English since the late 1500s.]

hash oil an alcohol extract of CANNABIS SATIVA (*q.v.*). For synonyms see OIL. [U.S. drug culture, mid 1900s-pres.]

hat 1. an old prostitute; a prostitute of long-standing [from Scots; British, early 1800s, Farmer and Henley] **2.** a sexually loose woman. Because, like a hat, she is frequently felt. See HAT, OLD. [British and U.S. slang, early 1800s-mid 1900s] **3.** a homosexual male, especially a CATAMITE (*q.v.*). From sense 2. [U.S., mid 1900s, Goldin, O'Leary, and Lipsius]

hat, old the female genitals. From HAT (sense 2) and because it is frequently felt. [British slang, mid 1700s-1800s]

hat and cap gonorrhea. Rhyming slang for "clap." [U.S., early 1900s, *Dictionary of Rhyming Slang*]

hatch 1. to be brought to bed for childbirth; to be CALLED TO STRAW (*q.v.*). [British slang or colloquial, 1800s

or before] **2.** to give birth. [British and U.S. colloquial, 1800s-pres.]

hatchway the female genitals. *Cf.* FOREHATCH. [British, 1800s]

haul ass (also **haul tail**) to get out in a hurry. *Cf.* BAG ASS, CUT ASS, DRAG ASS, SHAG ASS. [U.S., World Wars and general slang, early 1900s-pres.]

haul-devil a clergyman. For synonyms see SKY-PILOT. [British, 1800s, Farmer and Henley]

haul one's ashes to copulate. See GET ONE'S ASHES HAULED. [attested as Canadian, 1800s, *Dictionary of Slang and Unconventional English*]

have 1. to cheat or deceive a person. **2.** to copulate with a woman. [both since the 1600s or before]

have a bar on (also **have a bar**) to have an erection of the penis. *Cf.* HARD-ON, RAIL. [British slang, 1900s, *Dictionary of Slang and Unconventional English*]

have a beat on to have an erection of the penis. [British slang, 1900s, *Dictionary of Slang and Unconventional English*]

have a bit to copulate, said of males. [British slang, 1800s]

have a bit of bum to copulate, said of the male. See BUM (sense 3), "female genitals." [British, 1800s-1900s]

have a bit of bum-dancing to copulate, said of the male in reference to the male motions of copulation. *Cf.* DANCE THE BUTTOCK JIG. [British slang, 1800s, Farmer and Henley]

have a bit of curly greens to copulate, said of the male. [British, 1800s, Farmer and Henley]

have a bit of fish to coit, said of the male. See FISH (sense 1). [British, 1800s, Farmer and Henley]

have a bit of giblet pie to copulate, said of the male. *Cf.* JOIN GIBLETS. [British, 1800s, Farmer and Henley]

have a bit of rough to copulate, said of the male. *Cf.* ROUGH-AND-TUMBLE [British slang, 1800s, Farmer and Henley]

have a bit of skirt to copulate, said of the male. *Cf.* SKIRT. [British slang, 1800s]

have a bit of summer-cabbage to copulate. [British slang, 1800s, Farmer and Henley]

have a bit of the creamstick to copulate, said of the female. *Cf.* CREAMSTICK, which is the penis. [British slang, 1800s, Farmer and Henley]

have a blow-through to copulate, said of a woman. [British slang, 1800s]

have a brick in one's hat to be drunk. Refers to the swollen feeling in one's head. [British and U.S. slang, 1800s-1900s]

have a brush with the cue to copulate, said of the female. The "cue" here is the penis. [British slang, late 1700s, Grose]

have a bun in the oven (also **have one in the oven**) to be pregnant. [British and U.S. colloquial, 1800s-1900s]

have a bun on to be drunk. *Cf.* BUN (sense 5). [U.S. slang and colloquial, 1900s or before]

have a dumpling on to be pregnant. [British colloquial, late 1800s, Ware]

have a flutter to copulate; to DEFLOWER (*q.v.*). [British slang, 1800s, Farmer and Henley]

have a game in the cock-loft to copulate. The cock-loft is the residence of the COCK (senses 1 and 3). [British slang, 1800s, Farmer and Henley]

have a glow on to be mildly intoxicated with alcohol. *Cf.* LIT. [U.S. slang, mid 1900s-pres.]

have a hard-on to have an erection of the penis. See HARD-ON. *Cf.* HAVE A BAR ON. [slang and colloquial, 1900s]

have a hard-up to have an erection of the penis. [British slang and colloquial, 1800s, *Dictionary of Slang and Unconventional English*]

have a hump in the front to be pregnant. [euphemistic and vague; colloquial, 1800s-pres.]

have a jag on to be intoxicated with alcohol. *Cf.* JAG (sense 1). [U.S. slang, late 1800s-pres.]

have a load on to be drunk. *Cf.* LOAD (sense 4). [British and U.S., 1800s-1900s]

have a man by the balls to have rendered a man powerless. Nearly always in a figurative sense. *Cf.* HAVE A MAN BY THE SHORT HAIRS. [U.S. slang, 1900s]

have a man by the short hairs to have a man in a compromising situation; to have rendered a man power-less to defend himself; the same as HAVE A MAN BY THE BALLS (*q.v.*). Refers to the pubic hairs, but "short hairs" is also euphemistically defined as "the short hairs at the nape of the neck." [British and U.S. slang, late 1800s-1900s]

have a nine-months dropsy to be pregnant. [British slang, 1800s, Farmer and Henley]

have a package on to be intoxicated with alcohol. *Cf.* HAVE A JAG ON, HAVE A LOAD ON. [U.S. slang, 1900s]

have a rusty-rifle to have a venereal disease. *Cf.* LONG-ARM INSPECTION, SHORT-ARM INSPECTION. [British military, early 1900s, *Dictionary of Slang and Unconventional English*]

have a skate on to be drunk. From one's difficulty in walking. [1900s or before]

have a slant on to be intoxicated with alcohol. Based on the expressions "have an angle" or "have a new slant on" and the unsteadiness of a drunkard. [U.S. slang, early 1900s]

have a snoot full to be intoxicated with alcohol. Refers to an elephant's trunk filled with liquid. See ELEPHANT'S TRUNK. [U.S. slang and colloquial, 1900s]

have a turkey on one's back to be intoxicated with alcohol. [U.S. slang, 1800s]

have a turn on one's back (also **take a turn on one's back**) to copulate, said of a woman. [British slang, 1800s, Farmer and Henley]

have a wipe at the place to copulate. *Cf.* PLACE (sense 2). [British slang, 1800s, Farmer and Henley]

have connection to copulate. *Cf.* CONNECTION. [British euphemism, 1800s]

have fifty-up to copulate with a woman. [British slang, 1900s, *Dictionary of Slang and Unconventional English*]

have a gin on the rocks to copulate. "Gin" is an "aborigine." See GIN (sense 3), presumably an aboriginal prostitute or concubine. [Australian, 1900s]

have given pussy a taste of cream to have been deflowered; to have been copulated with, said of a woman. See

DEFLOWER. *Cf.* PUSSY(sense 1). CREAM (sense 1) is semen. [British slang, 1800s, Farmer and Henley]

have ink in one's pen to be sexually potent. *Cf.* HAVE LEAD IN ONE'S PENCIL. [jocular and euphemistic colloquial, 1900s]

have it off to coit; to ejaculate. *Cf.* GET IT OFF. [British slang and colloquial, 1900s]

have it on 1. to be experiencing the menses; to have a SANITARY NAPKIN (*q.v.*) on. [British colloquial, 1800s, Farmer and Henley] **2.** to have an erection. [U.S. slang, mid 1900s-pres.]

have lead in one's pencil 1. to be potent, virile, and vigorous. **2.** to be in a state of sexual need. **3.** to have an erection. *Cf.* HAVE INK IN ONE'S PEN. [all senses, colloquial, 1900s]

have live sausage for supper to copulate, said of a woman. *Cf.* LIVE SAUSAGE. [British slang, 1800s, Farmer and Henley]

have no more ink in the pen to be sexually exhausted from ejaculation; to be impotent from advanced age. *Cf.* HAVE INK IN ONE'S PEN, HAVE LEAD IN ONE'S PENCIL. For synonyms see IMPUDENT. [colloquial, 1900s and possibly long before]

have one in the oven (also **have one in the box**) to be pregnant; to be pregnant with yet another child. *Cf.* HAVE A BUN IN THE OVEN. [colloquial, 1800s-1900s]

have one's ass in a sling 1. to have suffered unjustly at the hands of another. **2.** to be in an unfortunate predicament. **3.** to complain constantly; to be bitchy. [all senses, U.S. slang, mid 1900s-pres.]

have one's back teeth awash (also **have one's back teeth afloat**) **1.** to be heavily intoxicated with alcohol. [British and U.S., 1900s] **2.** to have a very full bladder. [U.S. colloquial, 1900s]

have one's cargo aboard to be pregnant. [British slang, 1800s]

have one's cut to copulate; to coit a

woman; to have one's share of sexual gratification. *Cf.* CUT. [British, 1800s, *Dictionary of Slang and Unconventional English*]

have one's grandmother in (also **have one's auntie in, have one's friend in**) to experience the menses. [British colloquial, 1800s]

have one's oats to copulate; to sow wild oats. See WILD OATS (sense 1). [British colloquial, late 1800s-1900s]

have one's will of a woman to coit a woman. [euphemistic, 1800s-1900s]

have sex to copulate. See SEX (sense 4), "copulation." [U.S. euphemism, mid 1900s-pres.]

have snakes in one's boots to have the DELIRIUM TREMENS (*q.v.*). *Cf.* SNAKES. [U.S. slang or colloquial, 1800s]

have the flowers to experience the menses. Refers vaguely to the redness of roses and thus to blood. *Cf.* FLOWERS [British euphemism, 1500s-1800s]

have the gate locked and the key lost a catch phrase indicating that one is experiencing the menses. [British colloquial, 1800s, Farmer and Henley]

have the horn to be sexually aroused; to have an erection. *Cf.* HORNY (sense 3). [British slang and colloquial, 1700s-1800s]

have the hots for someone to have strong sexual desire for a specific person. *Cf.* HOT FOR SOMEONE. [U.S. slang, 1900s]

have the rag on to be experiencing the menses. *Cf.* RAG, ON THE. [U.S. colloquial, 1900s]

Hawaiian marijuana. Presumably a Hawaiian variety. *Cf.* KAUI, MAUI. [U.S. drug culture, mid 1900s-pres.]

hawk, the the drug L.S.D. (*q.v.*). *Cf.* CHIEF, THE. [U.S. drug culture, mid 1900s-pres.]

hawk it to solicit, said of a prostitute. [British, 1800s]

hawk up (also **hawk**) to spit; to cough up and spit phlegm. [U.S. colloquial, 1900s and before]

hay marijuana. *Cf.* HASHISH, INDIAN HAY, STRAW. [translation of the Arabic word "hashish"; U.S. underworld and drug culture, mid 1900s-pres.]

hay-bag a low prostitute whom one lies on like a mattress. [British, mid 1800s]

hay-burner a marijuana smoker. From a nickname for a horse. [U.S. drug culture, mid 1900s-pres.]

hay-butt a marijuana cigarette. *Cf.* GOOF-BUTT. [U.S. underworld and drug culture, mid 1900s]

hay-eater a derogatory nickname for a Caucasian. [some Negro use]

hay-head a marijuana user. *Cf.* HOP-HEAD. [U.S. drug culture, mid 1900s-pres.]

haze the drug L.S.D. (*q.v.*). See PUR-PLE HAZE. [U.S. drug culture, mid 1900s-pres.]

hazy intoxicated with alcohol. Confused with drink. [British and U.S. slang and colloquial, early 1800s-pres.]

head 1. the HYMEN (*q.v.*). A truncation of MAIDENHEAD (*q.v.*). For synonyms see BEAN. **2.** the toilet on a ship. [colloquial, 1800s-pres.] **3.** any toilet or bathroom. For synonyms see W.C. [U.S. slang, early 1900s-pres.] **4.** the end of the penis, especially the erect penis. [U.S. slang and colloquial, 1900s and nonce long before] Synonyms for sense 4: BELL-END, BLUNT END, CLEAT, END, KNOB, NUT, POINT, POLICEMAN'S HELMET, RED-END. **5.** a drug addict or a drug user. *Cf.* ACID-HEAD, A-HEAD, COKE-HEAD, CUBEHEAD, DRUGHEAD, GOW-HEAD, HOP-HEAD, METH-HEAD, PILL-HEAD, PIN-HEAD. [U.S. drug culture, early 1900s-pres.] See also GIVE HEAD.

head-cheese smegma. A reinterpretation of the name for a specific food-stuff. *Cf.* CROTCH-CHEESE. [U.S. slang, mid 1900s]

headfucker 1. a disorienting or disruptive person, situation, or object. [U.S. slang, mid 1900s-pres.] **2.** a powerful and disorienting drug. *Cf.* MIND FUCK. [U.S. slang and drug culture, mid 1900s-pres.]

headhunter a lecher; a hunter of maid-enheads, [recurrent nonce; attested as U.S. slang, mid 1900s-pres.]

head-job an act of PENILINGUS (*q.v.*); the same as BLOW-JOB (*q.v.*). See HEAD (sense 4). [U.S. slang, mid 1900s-pres.]

headlight 1. a mulatto; a light Negro who stands out in a crowd. For synonyms see MAHOGANY. [U.S. slang and colloquial, early 1900s] **2.** a breast. See HEADLIGHTS.

headlights the human breasts. From their position and prominence. [Australian and U.S., early 1900s-pres.]

headlight to a snowstorm (also **headlight in a snowstorm**) a very dark Negro. Based on the sharp contrast between dark skin and white snow. For synonyms see EBONY. [U.S. colloquial, 1900s or before]

head queen a homosexual male who seeks partners for PENILINGUS (*q.v.*) in public restrooms. See QUEEN for similar topics. *Cf.* HEAD (senses 3 and 4). [U.S. homosexual use, mid 1900s, Farrell]

head-shop a place where devices used in marijuana smoking and the taking of other drugs are sold. [U.S. culture, mid 1900s-pres.]

heart 1. the glans penis. Suggested by its shape or from HARD (*q.v.*). [U.S. slang, mid 1900s, Wentworth and Flexner] **2.** a Benzedrine (trademark) tablet, especially a tablet in the shape of a heart. Also used for other amphetamines. [U.S. drug culture, mid 1900s-pres.]

heart and dart a release of intestinal gas. Rhyming slang for "fart." [British slang, 1800s, Farmer and Henley]

hearten to arouse a man sexually. Playing on "harden." *Cf.* DISHEARTEN. [1600s]

hearty intoxicated with alcohol. For synonyms see WOOFLED. [British, 1800s]

heat, in sexually aroused, said properly of female mammals. Said jocularly of women and even of men. [U.S. colloquial and slang, 1900s and before]

heat, on sexually aroused. The British equivalent of "in heat." See HEAT, IN.

heave to vomit. See HEAVES. For synonyms see YORK. [colloquial, early 1900s-pres.]

heaven 1. the afterlife for good people. The opposite of hell. [since *c.* 1000, *Oxford English Dictionary*] Synonyms: ABRAHAM'S BOSOM, BEULAH, BEULAHLAND, BY-AND-BY, CITY OF GOD, ELYSIUM, GREAT UNKNOWN, HAPPY HUNTING-GROUNDS, HAPPYLAND, KINGDOM COME, NEW JERUSALEM, PARADISE, THE GREAT BEYOND. **2.** the female genitals; the same as PARADISE (sense 3). [British, 1800s, Farmer and Henley]

heaven dust cocaine. *Cf.* ANGEL DUST. [U.S. underworld and drug culture, early 1900s-pres.]

heavenly blue 1. the drug L.S.D. (*q.v.*). *Cf.* BLUE HEAVEN (sense 2). **2.** a color variety of morning glory seeds used as a hallucinogenic agent. For synonyms see SEEDS. [both senses, U.S. drug culture, mid 1900s-pres.]

heaven-reacher a clergyman. [U.S. slang, early 1900s, Irwin]

Heavens to Betsy! a mild exclamation. [U.S. colloquial, 1900s and before]

heaver the breast or bosom. *Cf.* PANTERS. [cant, 1600s, B.E.]

heaves a bout of retching or vomiting. *Cf.* HEAVE. [colloquial, 1900s or before]

heave up Jonah to vomit from one's depths; to HEAVE (*q.v.*). Referring to the (Biblical) vomiting up of Jonah by the great fish. [U.S. colloquial, 1800s or before]

heavies hard or "heavy" drugs; potent or illegal drugs. For synonyms see COTICS. [U.S. drug culture, mid 1900s]

heavy-footed pregnant. For synonyms see FRAGRANT. [U.S. colloquial, 1900s or before]

heavy joint marijuana with the drug P.C.P. added to it. See HEAVIES. [U.S. drug culture, mid 1900s-pres.]

heavy-necking kissing and caressing sexually. Involving anything up to copulation. For synonyms see FIRKYTOODLE. [U.S. slang and colloquial, 1900s]

heavy-petting the same as HEAVY-NECKING (*q.v.*). [U.S. slang and colloquial, 1900s]

hebe (also **heeb**) **1.** the early growth of pubic hair in puberty. From the name of the Greek goddess of youth and spring. Pronounced as two syllables. [since the 1600s] **2.** a derogatory nickname for a Jewish man or woman. A truncation of "Hebrew." For synonyms see FIVE AND TWO. [U.S. slang, 1900s]

Hebrew an avoidance for "Jew." Often derogatory. *Cf.* HEBE (sense 2). [U.S. colloquial, 1900s or before]

Hec!, By (also **Heck!, By**) a truncation of "By Hecate!" Hecate is the Greek goddess of the sun, moon, and hell. [U.S. colloquial, 1900s and before]

heck a euphemism for "hell" based on "Hecate," the Greek goddess of Hades. [U.S. colloquial, mid 1800s-pres.]

Heckelorum! an exclamation based on HECK (*q.v.*). [mock-Latin; U.S. colloquial or slang, mid 1900s, Berrey and Van den Bark]

he-cow a euphemism for "bull." [U.S. rural colloquial, 1900s and before]

hedge-bit a prostitute who works out-of-doors in a hedge row. [cant or slang, 1800s or before]

hedge-born illegitimate. Perhaps born of a HEDGE-WHORE (*q.v.*).

hedge-docked deflowered in the open air. See DEFLOWER. [British slang, 1800s or before]

hedge on the dyke the female pubic hair. See DIKE. For synonyms see DOWNSHIRE. [British slang, 1800s, Farmer and Henley]

hedge-whore a prostitute who works in the open air or in the nearest thicket. *Cf.* HEDGE-BIT. [British, 1500s-1700s]

H.E. double L. "hell." [U.S. colloquial euphemism, 1900s]

H.E. double toothpicks a jocular avoidance for "hell." [U.S. colloquial euphemism, 1900s]

Heeb a derogatory nickname for a Jewish man or woman. See HEBE (sense 2). From "Hebrew." For synonyms see FIVE AND TWO.

Heebess a derogatory nickname for a

Jewish woman. Patterned on "Jewess." *Cf.* HEBE (sense 2). [U.S. slang, 1900s, Berrey and Van den Bark]

heeby-jeebies (also **heebie-jeebies**) **1.** fright; nerves. [U.S. slang, 1900s] **2.** the DELIRIUM TREMENS (*q.v.*). [U.S. slang, early 1900s, Weseen]

heeled intoxicated with alcohol. [U.S. slang, 1900s]

heesh HASHISH (*q.v.*). A telescoping of "hashish" or "hasheesh." [U.S. underworld, early 1900s]

he-haw a homosexual male. [U.S. slang, mid 1900s-pres.]

heifer 1. a sexually loose woman; a harlot. [from *Henry IV*, Part Two (Shakespeare)] **2.** a girl or woman; a young COW (sense 1). [British and U.S. slang or colloquial, 1800s-pres.]

heifer barn (also **heifer den**) a brothel. [U.S. slang, early 1900s]

heifer-dust nonsense. An avoidance for BULLSHIT (*q.v.*); a variant of BULL-DUST (*q.v.*). [Australian and U.S., 1900s]

heinie 1. a German, especially a German soldier. Derogatory. From the proper name "Heinrich." [U.S. World Wars] **2.** the posteriors. From "hind(end)." [primarily juvenile; U.S. colloquial, 1900s]

Helen Maria an avoidance of "hell." *Cf.* GO TO HELEN B. HAPPY! [U.S. colloquial, 1900s]

hell 1. originally the abode of the dead; later the abode of the dead who were wicked in life; HADES (*q.v.*). [since the 800s, *Oxford English Dictionary*] **2.** an oath or curse. Synonyms and related terms for senses 1 and 2: ABYSS, ALL GET-OUT, AVERN, AVERNUS, BALLYHACK, BALLYWACK, BARATHRUM, B.H., BICKLEBARNEY, BLAZES, BLUE BLAZES, BOTTOMLESS-PIT, CAIN, DING-DONG BELL, FIRE AND DAMNATION, GEHENNA, H., HADES, HAIL COLUMBIA! HOT PLACE, INFERNAL REGIONS, INFERNO, JERICHO, KINGDOM COME, L., LOWER REGIONS, NETHER REGIONS, NETHERWORLD, PERDITION, PIT, SAM HILL, SHEOL, SMACK, THE OTHER PLACE, TOPHET, TUNKET, UNDERWORLD, VERY UNCOMFORTABLE PLACE, YOU-KNOW-WHERE. **3.** the female genitals. *Cf.* BOTTOMLESS-PIT, HEAVEN (sense 2). [British slang, 1800s]

hell!, The an exclamation expressing disbelief. [widespread colloquial, 1900s or before]

hell around to play aimlessly; to waste time or GOOF OFF (*q.v.*). [U.S. slang, mid 1900s-pres.]

hell-bender a drunken spree. See BENDER (sense 1). [U.S. slang, 1900s]

hell bent recklessly determined. [U.S. slang, mid 1900s]

hell-broth inferior whisky; bad liquor. *Cf.* FIREWATER.

hellcat 1. a wild, devil-may-care person. **2.** a witch. **3.** a furious or high-spirited girl or woman. [these and similar senses since the early 1600s]

hell dust any of the powdered narcotics. *Cf.* ANGEL DUST, HEAVEN DUST. [British, 1900s, *Dictionary of the Underworld*]

Hellfire and damnation! a fairly strong oath. *Cf.* HELL'S FIRE! [colloquial since the 1700s]

hell-fired all-out; enthusiastic. [since the mid 1700s]

hell-hole any terrible or hot place. [U.S. colloquial, 1900s or before]

hell-hound 1. the hound of hell. The watchdog of hell. ["Cerberus" from Classical mythology; since the 800s, *Oxford English Dictionary*] **2.** a fiendish person; a hellish person. [since the early 1400s, *Oxford English Dictionary*]

Hell's bells! an oath or an exclamation. [widespread colloquial, 1800s-1900s]

Hell's bells and buckets of blood! a mild oath, an elaboration of HELL'S BELLS (*q.v.*).

Hell's fire! an oath and an exclamation, "By hell's fire!" *Cf.* HELLFIRE AND DAMNATION! [U.S. colloquial, 1800s]

helluva (also **heluva**) a respelling (eye-dialect) of "hell of a." A partial avoidance. *Cf.* MELL OF A HESS. [British and U.S. colloquial, 1900s and before]

hell you say!, The (also **Like hell you say!**) an exclamation of disbelief. [U.S. colloquial, 1900s or before]

helpless intoxicated with alcohol. For

synonyms see WOOFLED. [British and U.S. coloquial, mid 1800s-pres.]

hemispheres the breasts. *Cf.* GLOBES. For synonyms see BOSOM. [British and U.S., 1800s-1900s]

hemp marijuana. *Cf.* GUNNY, ROPE. [U.S. slang, mid 1900s-pres.]

hempen fever a jocular term for the "illness" which causes death in an instance of hanging. [British, late 1700s, Grose]

hempy (also **hempie**) a rogue suitable for the gallows. [British, early 1800s]

hen-down fowl feces. *Cf.* COCK'S EGGS (sense 2). For synonyms see DROPPINGS. [U.S. euphemism, 1900s]

hen-hussy an effeminate male. For synonyms see FRIBBLE. [U.S. slang, mid 1900s]

Henry heroin *Cf.* H. [U.S. drug culture, mid 1900s-pres.]

her cocaine. *Cf.* GIRL (sense 9). [U.S. drug culture, mid 1900s-pres.]

herb (also **herbs**) marijuana. *Cf.* ERB, YERBA. [U.S. drug culture, mid 1900s-pres.]

hermaphrodite 1. one who has both male and female sex organs. From Greek mythology, Hermaphroditos, the son of Hermes and Aphrodite. A blend of the two sexes in one person. [since the 1400s] Synonyms and related terms: AMBOSEXOUS, ANDROGYNE, BISEXUAL, EPICENE, GYNANDROUS, JENNY WILLOCKS, JOHN-AND-JOAN, MOFF, MORPHADITE, MORPHODITE, PANATROPE, SCRAT, WILL-GILL, WILL-JILL. **2.** a person with the psychological characteristics of the opposite sex, an effeminate male or a virago. [since the late 1500s] **3.** a CATAMITE (*q.v.*); any homosexual male. In this sense, a euphemism for "homosexual." [since the early 1700s]

hermit the penis. *Cf.* BALD-HEADED HERMIT. For synonyms see YARD. [British slang, 1800s, Farmer and Henley]

hero heroin. A truncation of HEROIN (*q.v.*). *Cf.* H. [U.S. drug culture, mid 1900s-pres.]

heroin a semisynthetic derivative of morphine. A highly addictive opiate.

[from the name "Hero" of Classical mythology; discovered and named in 1898] Synonyms: A-BOMB, ANTIFREEZE, AUNT HAZEL, BIG-H., BIG-HARRY, BLANKS, BOY, BROTHER, BROWN, BROWN RINE, BROWN SUGAR, CABALLO, CA-CA, CHINA WHITE, CHINESE RED, CHINESE WHITE, CHIVA, COBICS, COURAGE PILLS, CRAP, DECK, DOGIE, DOJEE, DOJIE, DOOGIE, DOOJEE, DOOJI, DOPE, DUJER, DUJI, DYNAMITE, FLEA POWDER, FOOLISH POWDER, GOLD DUST, GOODS, H., HARD STUFF, HARRY, HENRY, HERO, HIM, HORSE, JOY POWDER, JUNK, KA-KA, MEXICAN MUD, NOSE-CANDY, NOSE POWDER, POISON, SALT, SCAG, SCAR, SCAT, SCHMACK, SCHMECK, SCHMECKEN, SCHMEE, SHIT, SHMECK, SMACK, SMECK, STUFF, TECATA, THING, WHITE, WHITE LADY, WHITE STUFF, WITCH HAZEL, YEN-SHEE.

herring a female virgin. *Cf.* FISH (sense 1). [U.S. slang, mid 1900s, Monteleon]

herring-choker a derogatory nickname for a Scandinavian. [U.S. slang, 1900s]

her time 1. the time for a woman to give birth. **2.** a woman's menstrual period. Also **her times.** For synonyms see FLOODS. [both senses, U.S. colloquial, 1900s or before]

hesh a HE-SHE (*q.v.*); an effeminate male or a homosexual male. *Cf.* SHIM. [U.S. slang, mid 1900s, Berrey and Van den Bark]

he-she a homosexual male. *Cf.* LAD-LASS. For synonyms see EPICENE. [U.S. slang, mid 1900s-pres.]

he-thing a bull. [U.S. colloquial or jocular colloquial, 1900s or before]

het-up 1. intoxicated with alcohol, "heated-up." **2.** angry; "heated-up." **3.** sexually aroused. [all senses, U.S. dialect or colloquial, 1900s or before]

hi-ball a dose of amphetamines. Named for the mixed drink. *Cf.* AMP. [U.S. drug culture, mid 1900s-pres.]

hiccius-doccius (also **hicksius-doxius, hictius-doctius**) intoxicated with alcohol. [from an expression used by jugglers, based on Latin *hic est doctus,* "this is a learned man"; British, 1600s-1700s]

hicklebarney hell. [British dialect (Northumberland), 1800s or before, Halliwell]

hickoryhead an oaf. Implying that the oaf's head is very hard. [U.S. colloquial, 1900s or before]

hicksam a fool. [U.S., early 1800s, Matsell]

hicksius doxius intoxicated with alcohol. See HICCIUS DOCCIUS.

hicky (also **hickey, hickie**) **1.** mildly intoxicated with alcohol. Probably from HICCIUS DOCCIUS (q.v.). See HOCKEY (sense 1). [slang, 1700s-1900s] **2.** a pimple. For synonyms see BURBLE. [U.S. colloquial, early 1900s-pres.] **3.** a gadget. Cf. DOHICKY. [U.S. colloquial, mid 1900s-pres.] **4.** the penis, especially that of a child. Cf. PIMPLE. (sense 4). [U.S. slang or colloquial, 1900s] **5.** a red mark left on the body from kissing, biting, or sucking the skin. Cf. MONKEY-BITE. [U.S. slang or colloquial, mid 1900s-pres.]

hide 1. a prostitute; prostitutes or copulation with prostitutes. See SKIN (sense 4). **2.** a CATAMITE (q.v.); catamites. [both senses, U.S. underworld, mid 1900s] **3.** any young woman. Cf. LEATHER (sense 1), SKIN (sense 4). [U.S. slang, mid 1900s-pres.]

hide the ferret to copulate. Cf. FERRET. [Australian slang, 1900s]

hide the sausage to copulate. Cf. LIVE SAUSAGE. For synonyms see OCCUPY. [Australian slang, 1900s]

high 1. intoxicated with alcohol. Cf. ALTITUDES, IN ONE'S. [since the early 1600s] **2.** intoxicated with drugs. [U.S. underworld and slang, early 1900s-pres.] **3.** a charge or kick from intoxicating drugs; any charge, kick, or elevated sense of well-being. [originally drug culture; U.S. slang, mid 1900s-pres.]

high as a kite intoxicated with alcohol. Rhyming slang for TIGHT (q.v.). An elaboration of HIGH (sense 3). [British and U.S. slang, 1800s-1900s]

high-bellied pregnant. For synonyms see FRAGRANT. [British colloquial or slang, 1800s, Farmer and Henley]

high-brow 1. an intellectual; someone with cultured tastes. **2.** pertaining to a cultured person or to cultured tastes. [both senses, U.S. colloquial, early 1900s-pres.]

high-brown a mulatto. Cf. HIGH-YELLOW, LIGHT BROWN. For synonyms see MAHOGANY. [U.S. colloquial, early 1900s]

higher Malthusianism PEDERASTY (q.v.); SODOMY (q.v.). Cf. KEEP THE CENSUS DOWN, MALTHUSIAN THEORY. Based on the name "Thomas R. Malthus," who wrote on population control. [jocular and euphemistic, British slang, 1800s, Farmer and Henley]

higher than a kite intoxicated with alcohol. See HIGH AS A KITE. For synonyms see WOOFLED. [U.S. colloquial, mid 1900s-pres.]

highflyer a lewd prostitute; a fashionable harlot. [British, 1600s, B.E.]

high-kilted obscene; smutty. A jocular reference to the image of a Scotsman with a kilt worn high enough to expose his VIRILIA (q.v.). [British slang, 1800s, Farmer and Henley]

highland frisky Scotch whisky. Rhyming slang for "whisky." [British, late 1800s, *Dictionary of Rhyming Slang*]

highly-sexed (also **oversexed**) having a need for frequent or highly varied sexual activity.

high-pooped with large and protruding buttocks. Cf. POOP (sense 1). [British, early 1800s, Farmer and Henley]

high tide the menses. For synonyms see FLOODS. [U.S. slang, mid 1900s]

highty-tighty a wanton girl or woman. [British, 1600s, B.E.]

highway hooker a prostitute who uses citizens band radio to set up customers at truck stops. [U.S. slang, mid 1900s-pres.]

high-yellow (also **high-yaller, high-yella**) a mulatto. Cf. HIGH-BROWN. [U.S. colloquial and slang, early 1900s-pres.]

hijack to commit PEDERASTY (q.v.) upon a boy forcibly. [U.S. slang, 1900s]

hikes a derogatory nickname for an Italian. For synonyms see SKY. [U.S., 1900s]

hilding 1. a jaded slut. [late 1500s] **2.** a good-for-nothing; a worthless oaf. [1600s-1800s]

hill, on the pregnant. The hill is the bulging abdomen. [U.S. slang, mid 1900s]

him heroin. *Cf.* BOY (sense 3). [U.S. drug culture, mid 1900s-pres.]

him-her a homosexual male. See HESH, SHIM. For synonyms see EPICENE. [U.S. slang, mid 1900s]

himmer a homosexual male. From "him" and "her." *Cf.* HESH, HIM-HER, SHIM. [U.S. slang, mid 1900s]

hind 1. an oaf; a dolt. [late 1500s] **2.** the posteriors. *Cf.* HIND-END. For synonyms see DUFF. [U.S. colloquial, 1900s]

hind-end the posteriors. [U.S. colloquial, 1900s and before]

hinder-blast a loud release of intestinal gas. For synonyms see GURK. [slang, mid 1500s]

hinder-end the posteriors. *Cf.* HIND-END. [British, 1800s]

hinder-entrance the posteriors; the anus. [British, 1800s, Farmer and Henley]

hinder parts the posteriors. *Cf.* DOUBLE-ASSED. [euphemistic, 1600s-1800s]

hinterland the posteriors; the breech. [since the 1800s or before]

hip-layer an opium smoker. *Cf.* LAY THE HIP (sense 2). [U.S., 1900s or before]

hipped intoxicated with alcohol. [U.S. slang, early 1900s]

hip-peddler (also **hip-flipper**) a prostitute. *Cf.* ASS-PEDDLER (sense 2). [U.S. underworld, mid 1900s]

his shoe pinches him "he is drunk." Given as an explanation for a drinker's uneasy gait. [U.S. slang, early 1700s, Ben Franklin]

hit 1. to coit a woman. *Cf.* SCORE (sense 1). [since the 1500s] **2.** a dose of a drug; a puff of a marijuana cigarette. [U.S. drug culture, mid 1900s-pres.]

hit and miss 1. a kiss. Rhyming slang. [U.S. slang, 1900s] **2.** urine; an act of urination; to urinate. Rhyming slang for "piss."

hitched married. [U.S. colloquial, mid 1800s-pres.]

hit it off to copulate. From an idiom meaning "get along well." [U.S. slang, mid 1900s]

hit on the tail to coit a woman. *Cf.* HIT (sense 1). [slang or nonce, early 1500s]

hittery pertaining to a cow suffering from diarrhea. Possibly an avoidance for some form of SHIT (*q.v.*). *Cf.* SKIT (sense 1) and SKITTER, which are ultimately cognate with SHIT (*q.v.*). [British dialect, 1800s, Dartnell]

hit the flute (also **hit the pipe**) to smoke opium. [U.S. underworld, 1800s-early 1900s]

hit the gonger (also **hit the gow**) to smoke opium. *Cf.* GONGER. [U.S. underworld, early 1900s or before]

hive the female genitals. *Cf.* HONEY. [British slang, mid 1800s, Farmer and Henley]

hive it 1. to coit a woman. **2.** to ejaculate. [both senses, British slang, 1800s, Farmer and Henley]

H.M.C. a mixture of heroin, morphine, and cocaine. *Cf.* H. AND C. [U.S. underworld, early 1900s]

ho 1. any girl or woman; a girlfriend. **2.** a prostitute; a sexual outlet for males. Both are from WHORE (*q.v.*). For synonyms see HARLOT. [both senses, U.S. black use, 1900s]

hoary-eyed intoxicated with alcohol. *Cf.* AWRY-EYED, ORIE-EYED. [U.S. slang, early 1900s]

hobby-horse a wanton woman; a prostitute. From the rocking motions in copulation and from PRIG or RIDE (both *q.v.*). [British, 1500s-1800s]

hob-clunch a bumpkin; an oaf. *Cf.* CLINCH-POOP, CLUNCH. [colloquial, late 1500s]

hock a PEDERAST (*q.v.*). Rhyming slang for "cock." Possibly related to HOCKEY (sense 2). [Australian, 1900s, Baker]

hocker a gob of phlegm. *Cf.* HAWK UP. [U.S. slang, mid 1900s]

hockey 1. intoxicated with alcohol; drunk on hock, "stale beer." [British slang, late 1700s, Grose] **2.** dung; feces. **3.** to defecate. Also **hocky, hookey, hooky.** [U.S. colloquial and dialect, 1900s or before] **4.** semen. For synonyms see METTLE. [U.S. slang, mid 1900s-pres.]

hocus 1. morphine. [U.S. drug culture, mid 1900s-pres.] **2.** intoxicated with alcohol. See HOCUS-POCUS.

hocus pocus (also **hocus**) **1.** intoxicated with alcohol. *Cf.* HICCIUS-DOCCIUS. [British slang, early 1700s-1800s] **2.** drugged liquor. [British slang or cant, early 1800s, Jon Bee]

hoe-handle the penis. [U.S. dialect (Ozarks), Randolph and Wilson, 1900s or before]

H. of I.F. a "house of ill-fame," a brothel.

hog 1. to coit a woman. [British slang, 1800s, Farmer and Henley] **2.** an ugly, overweight young woman. For synonyms see BUFFARILLA. [U.S. slang, mid 1900s-pres.] **3.** the drug P.C.P. (*q.v.*). *Cf.* ELEPHANT. [U.S. drug culture, mid 1900s-pres.]

hog eye the female genitals. [U.S. slang, mid 1900s]

hog jaws the human breasts. From the rounded sag of hog jowls. [U.S. slang, 1900s]

hogwash (also **pigwash**) **1.** swill and garbage to be fed to pigs; something worthless. **2.** nonsense. No negative connotations. [U.S. colloquial, 1900s or before] **3.** BULLSHIT (*q.v.*). A euphemism for "hog shit." [all senses above, U.S. slang and colloquial, 1900s and before] **4.** alcoholic beverages, diluted with water. *Cf.* SHEEPWASH. [British and U.S. use, 1800s-1900s]

hokum nonsense. For synonyms see ANIMAL. [U.S. slang and colloquial, 1900s or before]

hokus (also **hocus**) narcotics. [U.S. underworld, early 1900s]

hole 1. the anus. [since the 1300s] **2.** the vagina. For synonyms see PASSAGE. [since the 1500s] **3.** to coit; to penetrate the vulva. **4.** copulation. **5.** ejaculation. **6.** women considered sexually.

[sense 3-6 are British and U.S. slang and colloquial, 1800s-1900s]

hole of content the female genitals; the vagina. [late 1500s, Florio]

hole of holes the female genitals. Patterned on HOLY OF HOLIES (*q.v.*). [British slang, 1800s, Farmer and Henley]

holer 1. a prostitute. **2.** a whoremonger. [both senses, British, 1700s and before]

hole to hide it in the female genitals, specifically the vagina. [British slang, 1800s, Farmer and Henley]

holing whoring; chasing after sexually loose women. [British slang, 1800s, Farmer and Henley]

Holland the anus; the anal area. From "hole land." *Cf.* LOWLANDS. [from *Henry IV*, Part Two (Shakespeare)?]

holy bedlock an extralegal sexual union of a man and a woman. Based on "holy wedlock." [U.S. slang, mid 1900s, Monteleone]

Holy cats! a mild oath and an exclamation. Based on "Holy God!" [U.S. colloquial, 1900s or before]

Holy cow! a mock oath and an exclamation, an avoidance for Holy Christ! [U.S. colloquial, 1900s or before]

holy deadlock a marriage wherein the battles between the man and wife are hopelessly stagnated. Based on "holy wedlock." *Cf.* HOLY BEDLOCK. [U.S. slang, early 1900s]

Holy dog crap! a crude mock oath and an exclamation. Euphemistic for "Holy dog shit!" *Cf.* DOG. [U.S. colloquial, 1900s]

holy-falls breeches with a flap in front. For synonyms see GALLIGASKINS. [British dialect, 1800s, Northall]

Holy fuck! (also **Holy shit!**) a crude mock oath and an exclamation. [U.S. slang and colloquial, mid 1900s-pres.]

Holy Gee! an oath and an exclamation avoiding "Holy Jesus!" [U.S. colloquial, 1900s or before]

Holy Gumdrops! an oath and an exclamation, an avoidance of Holy God! [U.S. colloquial, 1900s]

Holy Jerusalem! an oath and an exclamation. [U.S. colloquial, 1900s]

holy-Joe a chaplain; any pious person. [British and U.S. slang and colloquial, 1800s-pres.]

Holy jumping mother of Jesus! (also **Holy jumping Jesus!, Holy jumping mother of Moses!**) a contrived oath or an exclamation. [colloquial, 1800s-1900s]

Holy Kerist! an emphatic elaboration of Holy Christ! [U.S. colloquial, 1900s]

Holy mackerel! a mock oath and an exclamation. [from the U.S. radio show *Amos and Andy*, mid 1900s]

Holy Moly! a mock oath and an exclamation. The characteristic exclamation of Captain Marvel, a comic-book character. [U.S. slang and colloquial, mid 1900s]

Holy Moses! an oath and an exclamation. "Moses" is often used as an avoidance for "Christ" or "God." [U.S. colloquial, 1900s]

Holy of Holies 1. the female genitals. [British slang, 1800s, Farmer and Henley] **2.** a toilet. Refers to the opening in the seat of a privy. [U.S. colloquial, 1900s or before]

holy poker the penis. *Cf.* POKER. [British slang, 1800s, Farmer and Henley]

Holy smokes! (also **Holy smoke!**) a mild and jocular oath and an exclamation. Perpetuated in the old joke "The church burned down, Holy smoke!" [since the 1800s]

Holy snooks! an oath and an exclamation. Possibly based on "Holy saints!" [U.S. colloquial, 1800s-1900s]

Holy socks! a mild mock oath and exclamation. [U.S. colloquial, 1900s]

Holy Swiss Cheese! a mock oath and an exclamation based ultimately on "Holy Jesus!" *Cf.* CHEESE AND CRUST! [U.S. colloquial, 1900s or before]

Holy Toledo! an oath and an exclamation. [from "Toledo," Spain, 1900s or before]

holy week a woman's menstrual period. Comparing sexual abstention during the menses to sexual abstention practiced during religious observances. From the name of the last week in Lent. [British and U.S. slang and colloquial, 1800s-pres.]

home 1. to have or cause an orgasm. **2.** to impregnate a female. *Cf.* SCORE. [both senses, British slang, 1800s, Farmer and Henley]

homebrewed semen. From the term used for homemade liquor. [British slang, 1800s, Farmer and Henley]

homegrown 1. marijuana grown privately or secretly at one's residence. **2.** domestic marijuana as opposed to that smuggled from abroad. [both senses, U.S. drug culture, mid 1900s-pres.]

home-sucker a derogatory term used by cattlemen for homesteaders or farmers who turned grazing land into farmland. A play on "home-seeker." [Western jargon, Ramon Adams]

home sweet home the female genitals. *Cf.* HOME. For synonyms see MONO-SYLLABLE. [British slang, 1800s, Farmer and Henley]

homie a homosexual male; a HOMO (q.v.). [U.S. slang, mid 1900s, Montelone]

homo a truncation of "homosexual." Usually used for a male homosexual. Sometimes used for a LESBIAN (q.v.). [slang, early 1900s-pres.]

homo boobus an oaf; a BOOB (sense 1). [mock-Latin; U.S. slang, 1900s]

homosexual 1. pertaining to a person whose libidinal object is a person of the same sex or persons of the same sex. See EPICENE and LESBYTERIAN. **2.** pertaining to anything which reflects the proclivities described in sense 1. **3.** a homosexual person, usually a male.

hone the female genitals. *Cf.* GRIND-STONE, WHETING-CORNE. [British, early 1700s]

Honest to God! 1. an oath and an exclamation. [U.S. colloquial, 1900s or before] **2.** genuine. Usually written "honest-to-God." [U.S. colloquial, 1900s]

honest-to-goodness (also **honest-to-Gotham**) **1.** pertaining to something which is unique or genuine. **2.** an avoidance for HONEST-TO-GOD! (*q.v.*).

honey semen. *Cf.* HIVE, WHITE HONEY. [colloquial and slang since the 1800s or before]

honey-bucket 1. any mobile tank or container used to carry away the contents of privies or latrines. **2.** the receptacle in a latrine. **3.** a wagon to carry manure used as fertilizer. *Cf.* DANNADRAG, HONEY-WAGON. [all senses, slang since the 1800s]

honey-bucket hop a quick trip to the W.C. [U.S. slang, 1900s]

honeydew melons the human breasts. *Cf.* MELONS, ORANGES, WATERMELONS. For synonyms see BOSOM. [U.S. slang, 1900s]

honey-dipper a man who cleans septic tanks or privies; a sewer worker. [British and U.S. colloquial, 1900s]

honey-fuggle (also **honey-fackle, honey-fogle, honey-foogle, honey-fugle**) **1.** to cheat, cajole, or seduce. Related to a British dialect term, "cony-foggle." **2.** deception; subterfuge. [both senses, U.S. colloquial and slang, 1800s-1900s]

honey-house a toilet; a privy. *Cf.* HONEY-BUCKET. [U.S. colloquial, 1900s or before]

honey man 1. a. lover; a pimp. *Cf.* HONEY. **2.** a term of endearment for a man, used by a woman. [both senses, U.S. colloquial, early 1900s-pres.]

honeymoon the first month after marriage. [since the mid 1500s]

honey oil an alcohol extract of CANNABIS SATIVA (*q.v.*). For synonyms see OIL. [U.S. drug culture, mid 1900s-pres.]

honey-pot the female genitals. [British, early 1700s]

honey-pot cleaver the penis. For synonyms see YARD. [U.S. slang, mid 1900s-pres.]

honey-star a mistress or concubine. [British, early 1900s, *Dictionary of Slang and Unconventional English*]

honey-wagon the same as HONEY-BUCKET (*q.v.*). [U.S. slang, mid 1900s-pres.]

Hong Kong dog a form of dysentery. [British and U.S. wartime, 1900s]

honk 1. to vomit. Onomatopoetic. *Cf.* BARF, EARP, RALPH, YORK. [British, early 1900s, *Dictionary of Slang and Unconventional English*] **2.** to blow one's nose loudly. [U.S., 1900s] **3.** to release intestinal gas loudly. [slang, 1900s or before]

honked (also **honkers**) intoxicated with alcohol. *Cf.* TOOT (senses 1 and 2). [British, mid 1900s, *Dictionary of Slang and Unconventional English*]

honky (also **honkey, honkie, hunk, hunky**) a derogatory term for a Caucasian. [U.S. black use, mid 1900s-pres.]

honor (also **honour**) female chastity; virginity. [since the 1600s]

hooch 1. alcohol; homebrewed alcohol. See HOOTCH. [slang, 1900s or before] **2.** marijuana. From sense 1. [U.S. drug culture, mid 1900s-pres.]

hooched-up (also **hooched**) intoxicated with alcohol. [U.S. slang, mid 1900s-pres.]

hooch-hound a drunkard. For synonyms see ALCHY. [U.S. slang, mid 1900s]

hooey 1. nonsense. [U.S. slang and colloquial, 1900s] **2.** dung. From sense 1 and BULLSHIT (*q.v.*). [U.S., 1900s]

hook 1. a prostitute. A truncation of HOOKER (sense 2). [U.S. slang, 1900s] **2.** narcotics. [U.S. underworld and drug culture, 1900s]

hook alley an area in a city where prostitution is known to be available. [U.S. slang, 1900s]

hooker 1. one of the nails used in the Crucifixion of Christ. Also a fingernail of Christ. **2.** a prostitute. This hooker is a "fisher, angler, or hooker of men" (Farmer and Henley). Hookers were thieves who used a pole with a hook on the end to snare goods through open windows. For synonyms see HARLOT. [ultimately from the cant of the 1500s; by the 1800s, "hooker" meant any thief; U.S. underworld and slang, 1800s-pres.]

hook-nose a derogatory nickname for a Jewish man or woman. For synonyms see FIVE AND TWO. [U.S. slang, 1900s]

hook-shop a brothel. A play on "hock shop." [U.S. underworld and slang, 1800s-pres.]

hoon a procurer; a pimp. [Australian slang, 1900s]

hoop the female genitals. [British slang, 1800s, Farmer and Henley]

hoople a Caucasian. For synonyms see PECKERWOOD. [U.S. slang, mid 1900s]

hoosegow 1. a prison; a jail. For synonyms see COW. [U.S. colloquial, mid 1800s-pres.] **2.** a public restroom. [U.S., early 1900s, Weseen]

hootch (also **hooch**) any alcoholic beverage. Cf. HOOCH, SCOOCH. For synonyms see BOOZE. [U.S. slang and colloquial, 1800s-pres.]

hootchee (also **hootchie, hotchie**) **1.** a whoremonger. [U.S. underworld, early 1900s] **2.** the penis. [U.S. slang, mid 1900s-pres.]

hootcher a drunkard. Cf. HOOTCH. [U.S. slang, mid 1900s-pres.]

hooted intoxicated with alcohol. Cf. HONKED. [U.S. slang, 1900s]

hooters the human breasts. [U.S. slang, mid 1900s-pres.]

Hooverism an act of FELLATIO (q.v.). From the brand name of a vacuum cleaner. [U.S., mid 1900s-pres.]

hop opium; any drug or narcotics, including marijuana. [U.S. underworld, early 1900s]

hop-head (also **hop-fiend, hop-hog, hop-merchant**) an opium addict or seller. Cf. HAY-HEAD. [U.S. underworld and slang, late 1800s-early 1900s]

hop-joint an opium den. [U.S. underworld, early 1900s or before]

hop on to coit a woman. Cf. BOARD, MOUNT. [British and U.S. slang, 1900s]

hopped 1. intoxicated with narcotics. Originally intoxicated with opium. Now with any drug, including marijuana. Also **hopped-up.** [U.S. underworld and

drug culture, early 1900s-pres.] **2.** intoxicated with alcohol, especially with beer. From sense 1 and the hops in beer.

hopper 1. a drug addict; originally an opium addict. Cf. HOP-HEAD. [U.S. drug culture, 1900s or before] **2.** a toilet; the water-flush basin. [British and U.S. colloquial, 1800s-1900s]

hopper-arsed (also **cushion-rumped**) pertaining to a person with large, protruding buttocks. [British and U.S. colloquial, 1800s-1900s]

hopper-hipped pertaining to a person with a wide frame and large buttocks. [British, 1600s]

hop-picker a prostitute. For synonyms see HARLOT. [British, 1800s]

hoppie a dope addict. Cf. HOP-HEAD. [U.S. slang, mid 1900s or before]

hops (also **hop**) opium or any narcotics. [U.S. underworld, early 1900s]

hopster an opium addict. [U.S. underworld, early 1900s or before]

hop-stick 1. an opium pipe. [U.S. underworld, early 1900s or before] **2.** a marijuana cigarette. From sense 1. [U.S. drug culture, mid 1900s-pres.]

hop-stiff a drug addict. Cf. HOP-HEAD. For synonyms see JUNKER. [U.S. underworld, 1900s or before]

horizontal intoxicated with alcohol. [slang, 1900s]

horn 1. to become sexually aroused, said of the male or female. **2.** to CUCKOLD (q.v.) someone's spouse; to bedeck someone's spouse, usually the husband, with horns. **3.** the penis, especially the erect penis. [all senses, since the 1400s] **4.** to sniff drugs. [U.S. drug culture, mid 1900s-pres.] **5.** damn in "Gol-horn." See GOL.

horn-colic 1. a normal erection. [British slang or colloquial, late 1700s, Grose] **2.** a persistent erection possibly with pain in the testicles. See PRIAPISM (sense 1). [U.S. dialect (Ozarks), Randolph and Wilson]

horner a user of cocaine. Cf. HORN (sense 4). [U.S. drug culture, mid 1900s-pres.]

hornification an erection of the penis; the erecting of a penis. [British, 1800s or before, Farmer and Henley]

hornify 1. to CUCKOLD (*q.v.*). **2.** to cause a penile erection. [both senses, British, 1800s or before]

horniness lust; sexual arousal, particularly after a period of abstinence. *Cf.* HORNY (sense 1). [U.S. slang, 1900s]

horning sexually aroused; having an erection of the penis. [colloquial and slang since the 1800s or before]

Hornington, old the penis, especially the erect penis. *Cf.* MISS HORNER. [British slang, 1800s, Farmer and Henley]

horn-mad 1. with an erect penis. **2.** extremely lecherous. **3.** enraged at being cockolded. See CUCKOLD. [possibly apocryphal, since the 1500s]

horn of plenty a husband. From HORN (sense 3) and the notion of a husband as a provider. [U.S. slang, 1900s]

horny 1. sexually aroused especially after a long period of abstinence. For synonyms see HUMPY. **2.** pertaining to a person with a lecherous nature. **3.** with an erect penis. [all senses, slang and colloquial, 1800s-pres.] **4.** virile and capable of copulation, said of a male. *Cf.* HAIRY. [U.S. slang, 1900s]

horrors the DELIRIUM TREMENS (*q.v.*). *Cf.* BLUE HORRORS. For synonyms see ORK-ORKS. [British and U.S. slang and colloquial, mid 1800s]

hors d'oeuvres Seconal (trademark) capsules. For synonyms see SEC. [U.S. drug culture, mid 1900s-pres.]

horse 1. to MOUNT (*q.v.*) and coit a woman. [British slang, early 1600s-1800s] **2.** as an exclamation, "Horse!" A euphemism for "Horseshit!" A variation of "bullshit." [U.S. slang, mid 1900s] **3.** heroin. A reinterpretation of "H." for heroin. See CABALLO. [U.S. drug culture, mid 1900s-pres.]

horse and trap 1. a case of gonorrhea. Rhyming slang for CLAP (*q.v.*). [British slang, late 1800s] **2.** dung; to defecate. Rhyming slang for CRAP (*q.v.*). [British slang, 1900s]

horse apple 1. a formed lump of horse dung. Also **horse dumpling.** *Cf.* ALLEY APPLE, ROAD APPLE. [U.S. slang, mid 1900s] **2.** nonsense; BULLSHIT (*q.v.*). *Cf.* horse (sense 2).

horseback intoxicated with alcohol. For synonyms see WOOFLED. [U.S. slang, early 1900s, Weseen]

horsecock 1. an observation balloon. [U.S., World War I, Lighter] **2.** a sausage. From its phallic shape. *Cf.* LIVE SAUSAGE. [U.S. slang, mid 1900s-pres.]

horse collar the female genitals. A visual image based on the resemblance of a horse collar to the *labia majora*. [British slang, 1800s, Farmer and Henley]

horsed under the influence of heroin. From HORSE (sense 3). [U.S. drug culture, mid 1900s-pres.]

horsefeathers nonsense; a mild form of "horseshit." [U.S. slang and colloquial, early 1900s-pres.]

horsemanship copulation, from the male point of view. *Cf.* HORSE (sense 1), PRIG (sense 1), RIDE. [from *Henry V* (Shakespeare)]

horseradish nonsense; a disguise of "horseshit." [U.S. colloquial, 1900s or before]

horse's ass an idiot; a fool. [U.S. colloquial, 1900s]

horseshit nonsense; an exclamation of disbelief, a variation of BULLSHIT (*q.v.*). [U.S. slang, 1900s]

horse-shoe the female genitals. *Cf.* HORSE COLLAR. [British, 1800s or before, Farmer and Henley]

horse's hoof a homosexual male. Rhyming slang for POOF (*q.v.*). For synonyms see EPICENE. [British, early 1900s, *Dictionary of Slang and Unconventional English*]

horse tranquilizer the drug P.C.P. (*q.v.*); the same as ELEPHANT TRANQUILIZER (*q.v.*). [U.S. drug culture, mid 1900s-pres.]

horsh nonsense; a disguise of "horseshit," which is a variant of BULLSHIT (*q.v.*). A blend of "horse" and "shit." [U.S. slang, 1900s]

hose 1. the penis. **2.** to coit a woman; to PHALLICIZE (*q.v.*). **3.** copulation. **4.** to cheat or deceive. [all senses, U.S. slang, early 1900s-pres.]

hosing 1. copulation; an act of copulation from the male point of view. **2.** a cheating; a deception. *Cf.* SCREW (sense 6). [both senses, U.S. slang, 1900s]

hot 1. sexually aroused; lustful; in heat. *Cf.* ARD. For synonyms see HUMPY. [since the 1500s] **2.** infected with a venereal disease. [colloquial, 1800s-1900s] **3.** intoxicated with alcohol. [U.S. colloquial, 1800s-1900s]

hot air 1. nonsense. **2.** gas from the intestines. *Cf.* GAS (sense 1). [both senses, colloquial, early 1900s-pres.]

hot and bothered lustful; HORNY (*q.v.*). See HOT (sense 1). [U.S. slang and colloquial, 1900s or before]

hot and cold heroin and cocaine. *Cf.* H. AND C. [U.S. drug culture, mid 1900s-pres.] See the following for other drug mixtures: BAM, C. AND H., C. AND M., G.B., H.M.C., M AND C., PEACE PILL, POT-LIQUOR, SET, SPANSULA, SPEEDBALL, WHIZ-BANG.

hot as a red wagon intoxicated with alcohol. [U.S. slang, mid 1900s]

hot chocolate a sexually attractive black woman. *Cf.* CHOCOLATE DROP. [U.S. slang, mid 1900s]

hot cock nonsense. For synonyms see ANIMAL. [Australian, mid 1900s, Baker]

hotel the female genitals. *Cf.* COCK-INN, CUPID'S HOTEL. [British slang, 1800s, Farmer and Henley]

hotel hotsy a prostitute. Patterned on FLAT FLOOSIE (*q.v.*). Named for her place of business. [U.S. slang, early 1900s]

hot flash 1. a sudden spell of sweating, dilation of the blood vessels in the skin of the head and chest area, and a suffocating feeling. Experienced by women during the menopause. Usually in the plural. [medical] **2.** a sudden spasm of sexual passion or arousal. A jocular play on or a misunderstanding

of sense 1. [U.S. colloquial, mid 1900s-pres.]

hot for someone sexually aroused for someone. For synonyms see HUMPY. [U.S. slang, mid 1900s-pres.]

hot-house a brothel. *Cf.* STEW (sense 1). [from *Measure for Measure* (Shakespeare)]

hot in the biscuit sexually stimulated; ready to copulate. *Cf.* BISCUIT, BUN. [U.S. underworld, early 1900s, Goldin, O'Leary, and Lipsius]

hot lay 1. a sexually loose woman. **2.** a passionate act of copulation. [both senses, U.S. slang, early 1900s, Montelone]

hot meat (also **hot beef, hot mutton**) **1.** a prostitute. **2.** the female genitals. From MEAT (sense 1). [slang since the 1800s] **3.** an expanse of exposed female flesh. [U.S. slang, mid 1900s]

hot member a lascivious man or woman. See HOT NUMBER. MEMBER (sense 1) may have phallic references. [British and U.S., 1800s-1900s]

hot milk semen. *Cf.* CREAM (sense 1). For synonyms see METTLE. [British slang, 1800s, Farmer and Henley]

hot number a passionate and accessible woman. Possibly refers to her telephone number. From the merchandizing term for an item in great demand. [U.S. slang, mid 1900s-pres.]

hot nuts 1. a nickname for a lascivious man. [U.S. slang, early 1900s-pres.] **2.** testalgia. See HOT ROCKS (sense 2).

hot pants 1. HORNINESS (*q.v.*); sexual arousal. *Cf.* ITCHY PANTS. **2.** lust. **3.** the same as HOT NUTS (*q.v.*); a lecher. **4.** a sexually desirable girl or woman. [all senses, U.S. slang, early 1900s-pres.]

hot rocks 1. a prostitute. [U.S. slang, mid 1900s] **2.** testalgia, pain in the testicles. [U.S. slang and colloquial, mid 1900s-pres.]

hot-rod 1. the penis. **2.** to masturbate. [both senses, U.S. slang, mid 1900s-pres.]

hot roll with cream copulation. HOT (sense 1) is "lustful," ROLL (*q.v.*) is "copulation," and CREAM (sense 1) is "semen." *Cf.* BANANAS AND CREAM. [British, 1800s, *Dictionary of Slang and Unconventional English*]

hots, the sexual desire with a special person as its target. *Cf.* HEAT, IN; HEAT, ON. [U.S. slang, mid 1900s-pres.]

hot shit an arrogant male; a man who thinks he is very important. In expressions such as "he really thinks he's hot shit." [U.S. slang, mid 1900s-pres.]

hot-stick a marijuana cigarette. *Cf.* HOP-STICK, STICK OF TEA. For synonyms see MEZZROLL. [U.S. drug culture, mid 1900s]

hot stuff 1. a sexually attractive and obliging girl or woman. **2.** the same as HOT SHIT (*q.v.*); an arrogant male. [both senses, U.S. slang, 1900s]

hotter than hell very, very hot. Refers to the weather, touchy situations, or passion. [colloquial, 1900s or before]

hot tomato a passionate girl or woman. For synonyms see LAY. [U.S. slang, mid 1900s-pres.]

hot-tongue 1. to kiss passionately and sensually using the tongue. [U.S. slang, early 1900s-pres.] **2.** a sexually aroused woman. A possible reference to PENILINGUS (*q.v.*). [U.S. slang, early 1900s-pres.]

house a brothel. [British and U.S., 1800s-1900s] Most of the following brothels retain female prostitutes. Those supplying males for sodomy are so indicated: ACCOMMODATION HOUSE, ASSIGNATION HOUSE, BAND-HOUSE, BAT HOUSE, BAWD'S HOUSE, BAWDYHOUSE, BEDHOUSE, BROTHEL-HOUSE, CALL-HOUSE, CAN HOUSE, CAT-HOUSE, CHIPPY-HOUSE, COUPLING-HOUSE, CRIB-HOUSE, DISORDERLY HOUSE, DOSS HOUSE, DRESS-HOUSE, FANCY HOUSE, FAST HOUSE, FLASH-HOUSE, FRANZY HOUSE, GARDEN-HOUSE, GAY HOUSE, GOAT-HOUSE, GRINDING-HOUSE, HOT-HOUSE, HOUSE IN THE SUBURBS, HOUSE OF ALL NATIONS, HOUSE OF ASSIGNATION, HOUSE OF CALL, HOUSE OF CIVIL RECEPTION, HOUSE OF ENJOYMENT, HOUSE OF ILL-DELIGHT, HOUSE OF ILL-FAME, HOUSE OF ILL-REPUTE, HOUSE OF JOY, HOUSE OF LEWDNESS, HOUSE OF PROFESSION, HOUSE OF RESORT, HOUSE OF SALE, JAG-HOUSE (male), JOY HOUSE, JUKE-HOUSE, KNOCKING-HOUSE, LEAPING-HOUSE, LEWD HOUSE, MEAT HOUSE, MOLLY-HOUSE (male), MONKEY-HOUSE, NANNY-HOUSE, NAUGHTY-HOUSE, NOTCH-HOUSE, NUGGING-HOUSE, OCCUPYING-HOUSE, ONERY-HOUSE, PARLOR HOUSE, PEG-HOUSE (male), PUNCH-HOUSE, RED-LIGHT HOUSE, SLAUGHTER-HOUSE, SPORT-ING-HOUSE, VAULTING-HOUSE, WHORE-HOUSE. See a full list at BROTHEL.

housebreak to train a pet to control its bladder and bowels while indoors; jocular for human toilet-training.

house in the suburbs a brothel. *Cf.* SUBURB. [British slang, 1800s]

housekeeper 1. a MADAM (sense 3); the keeper of a brothel-house. **2.** a prostitute. See LIGHT HOUSEWIFE. [both senses, U.S. slang and colloquial, early 1900s-pres.]

house-mother a MADAM (sense 3). A jocular play on the term used for a woman who supervises the living quarters of college girls. [U.S. slang, mid 1900s, Goldin, O'Leary, and Lipsius]

house nigger (also **house Negro**) **1.** a domestic slave. *Cf.* FIELD NIGGER. [U.S., 1700s-1900s] **2.** a Negro manipulated by Caucasians. A highly derogatory term. [U.S., mid 1900s-pres.]

house of all nations a brothel employing prostitutes of many races and nationalities. [U.S. underworld, mid 1900s, Goldin, O'Leary, and Lipsius]

house of assignation a brothel. See ASSIGNATION HOUSE.

house of call a brothel; the same as CALL-HOUSE (*q.v.*). [U.S. underworld and colloquial, 1900s]

house of civil reception a brothel. [British, late 1700s, Grose]

house of ill-delight a brothel. [U.S. colloquial, early 1900s]

house of ill-fame a brothel. One of the most common and most polite of the "house" euphemisms. [U.S. colloquial, 1900s and before]

house of ill-repute a brothel. [U.S. colloquial, 1900s and before]

house of lewdness a brothel. [U.S. colloquial, 1900s and before]

House of Lords a men's urinal. [British, 1900s]

house of office a privy. *Cf.* OFFICE, PRIVATE OFFICE. For synonyms see AJAX. [British, 1500s-1800s]

house of profession (also **house of resort**) a brothel. [from *Measure for Measure* (Shakespeare)]

house of sale a brothel. [from *Hamlet* (Shakespeare)]

house of security the female genitals, especially the vagina. [U.S. slang, 1900s]

house under the hill the female genitals. The "hill" is the mons veneris. [British slang, 1800s, Farmer and Henley]

housewife the female genitals. [British slang, 1800s, Farmer and Henley]

How-came-you-so? 1. intoxicated with alcohol. [British and U.S. colloquial, early 1800s-1900s] 2. pregnant. [U.S. colloquial, 1900s or before]

huddle to hug or embrace a woman; possibly to coit a woman. [British, 1700s]

huffle to coit a woman. [British, 1800s or before]

hug 1. to embrace a woman; possibly to coit a woman. [since the 1600s] 2. to garrot a person. [British, mid 1800s]

hugsome cuddlesome; sexually attractive, said of a woman. [British, 1800s, Farmer and Henley]

humbug 1. anything false or deceptive. 2. nonsense. [both senses since the 1700s]

hum-job a type of oral sexual intercourse where sensation is created by placing a part of the body in the mouth and humming. Usually performed on the male genitals. [U.S. slang, mid 1900s-pres.]

hump 1. to carry a person or a load on one's back. No negative connotations. [attested as Australian, mid 1800s-pres.] 2. any difficulty; a problem. No negative connotations. 3. to thrust the pelvis in the manner of a male copulating; to copulate from the male point of view. From the repeated arching or "hump-

ing" of the back. [since the mid 1700s] 4. to copulate, said of either a man or a woman. [since the 1700s] 5. copulation; an act of copulation. For synonyms see SMOCKAGE. [U.S. slang, mid 1900s-pres.] 6. a prostitute; a sexually loose woman; women considered sexually. [U.S. slang, mid 1900s-pres.] 7. a CATAMITE (*q.v.*). For synonyms see BRONCO. [U.S. underworld, mid 1900s, Goldin, O'Leary, and Lipsius] 8. to cheat; to SCREW (sense 6). [U.S. underworld, mid 1900s, Goldin, O'Leary, and Lipsius]

humpery copulation. [U.S. slang or nonce, mid 1900s-pres.]

humpy sexually desirable; sexually aroused. [U.S. slang, mid 1900s-pres.] Synonyms and related terms: ACCENSUS LIBIDINE, AFFY, AMATIVE, AMOROUS, APPETENT, BE BLOTTY, BE MUSTARD, BE ON BLOB, BONE-ON, BRIMMING, BULLING, CAGEY, CHUCKED, COCK-HAPPY, COCKISH, CONCUPISCENT, CONSTITUTIONALLY INCLINED TO GALLANTRY, DRIPPING FOR IT (female), FEEL FUZZY, FEEL GAY, FEEL HAIRY, FLAVOUR, FRISKY, FUCKISH, FULL OF FUCK, FULL OF GISM, FULL-ON, GAMY, HAIRY, HAVE AN ITCH IN THE BELLY, HET-UP, HORNING, HORN-MAD, HORNY, HOT, HOT AND BOTHERED, HOT-ASSED (female), HOT-BLOODED, HOT IN THE BISCUIT, HUNKY, IN SEASON, IN THE MOOD, ITCHY PANTS, JUICY, LICKERISH, LIQUOROUS, LUST-PROUD, MANISH, MARIS APPENTENS (female), MASHED, METTLED, ON, ONCOMING, ON FOR ONE'S GREENS, PEAS IN THE POT, PRIME, PROUD, PROUD BELOW THE NAVEL, PRUNEY, PRURIENT, PURSE-PROUD, RAMMISH, RAMMY, RAMSTUDIOUS, RANDY, RANTING, RED-COMB, ROLLICKY, ROOTY, RUSTY, RUTTISH, SALT, SEXED-UP, TICKLE, TOUCHABLE, TUMBLING-RIPE, TURNED-ON, WET (female), WHISK-TELT.

Hun a derogatory nickname for a German or a German soldier. [slang, late 1800s and World Wars]

hung 1. pertaining to a male with large to very large genitals; pertaining to an older male from the point of view of a younger, immature male. A truncation of WELL-HUNG (*q.v.*). [widespread colloquial, 1600s-pres.] 2. a physically

WELL-ENDOWED (*q.v.*) male or female. In the male, either a well-built body or large genitals or both. In the female, a well-built body and large, well-proportioned breasts. A reinterpretation of or a misunderstanding of sense. [U.S. slang, mid 1900s] **3.** a truncation of "hungover." A mischievous reintepretation of sense. [U.S. slang, mid 1900s]

hung like a bull pertaining to a male with very large genitals. *Cf.* HUNG (sense 1), WELL-HUNG. [U.S. homosexual use, mid 1900s]

hung like a chicken pertaining to a male with small genitals, possibly having the genitals of an adolescent boy; having virtually no VIRILIA (*q.v.*) at all. See CHICKEN (sense 2).

hunk 1. a sexually attractive male or female. [U.S. slang and colloquial, 1900s] **2.** an act of copulation. [U.S. slang, mid 1900s] **3.** a Caucasian. A truncation of HUNKIE or BOHUNK (both *q.v.*). See HONKY. [U.S. slang, mid 1900s] **4.** a large man; a "hunk of man," not necessarily in a sexual sense. [U.S. colloquial, mid 1900s-pres.]

hunkers the buttocks. For synonyms see DUFF. [U.S. colloquial, 1900s or before]

hunkie 1. a derogatory nickname for a Hungarian. [U.S. slang, 1900s] **2.** a Caucasian. See HONKY.

hunk of meat 1. a sexually attractive adult person. **2.** the penis. [both senses, U.S. slang, mid 1900s-pres.]

hunk of tail (also **hunk of ass, hunk of butt, hunk of skirt**) copulation; a woman considered sexually. *Cf.* HUNK (sense 2). [U.S. slang, 1900s]

hunky 1. sexually aroused; the same as HORNY (*q.v.*). [U.S. slang, mid 1900s-pres.] **2.** a derogatory nickname for a Hungarian. Also **hunkie**. [U.S. slang and colloquial, 1900s] **3.** an oaf; a dolt. From sense 2. See HONKY. [U.S. slang, early 1900s] **4.** a Caucasian. See HONKY. From sense 2.

hurry-whore a streetwalking prostitute. [British, early 1600s]

husker a masturbator. In reference to the action of husking corn. [U.S. dialect (Boontling), late 1800s-early 1900s,

Charles Adams] The following synonyms usually refer to males unless noted otherwise: CANDLE-BASHER (female), CHICKEN-CHOKER, DIDDLER, DOODLE-DASHER, FRIGSTER, FRIGSTRESS (female), FUCK-FINGER (female), FUCK-FIST, JACKER, JAG-OFF, JERK, JERK-OFF, MILKER, MILKMAN, MILK-WOMAN (female), ONANIST, PUSH-PUDDING, WHANKER.

hustle 1. to copulate. [U.S. slang, early 1800s-1900s] **2.** to work as a prostitute. [U.S. underworld, early 1900s-pres.] **3.** to gamble as a profession. [U.S. slang, 1900s] **4.** to steal. [U.S. slang, early 1900s-pres.] **5.** to sell drugs. [U.S. slang and drug culture, mid 1900s-pres.]

hustler 1. a female prostitute. For synonyms see HARLOT. [U.S. slang, early 1900s-pres.] **2.** a homosexual male prostitute. [U.S. slang, mid 1900s-pres.] **3.** a pimp. [U.S. slang, mid 1900s-pres.] **4.** any thief or con man. [U.S. underworld and slang, 1900s] **5.** a sexually successful male. One who can SCORE (*q.v.*) easily. [U.S. slang, mid 1900s-pres.]

hymen 1. when capitalized, Hymen, the Greek god of marriage, the son of Aphrodite and Bacchus. [from Greek; in English by the late 1500s] **2.** a membrane which blocks or partially blocks the external orifice of the vagina. For synonyms see BEAN. [since the 1600s]

hymie copulation in "hunk of hymie." From HYMEN (*q.v.*). [U.S. underworld (tramps), early 1900s, Goldin, O'Leary, and Lipsius]

hyp a dose of a strong drug. From "hypodermic syringe." [U.S. underworld, early 1900s]

hype 1. a drug addict, especially a heroin addict. [U.S. underworld and drug culture, 1900s] **2.** under the influence of narcotics. From HYP (*q.v.*) or "hyperactive."

hyped under the influence of narcotics. From HYP (*q.v.*) or "hyperactive." [U.S. drug culture, mid 1900s-pres.]

hypogastric-cranny the female genitals. Literally, "the gap or cranny in the lower region of the abdomen." [1600s, (Urquhart)]

I

iceberg 1. a cold and unresponsive woman; a frigid woman. *Cf.* ICE WAGON. [U.S., 1900s] **2.** any unemotional person. [colloquial, 1900s or before]

iceberg slim 1. a pimp. **2.** a person who exploits others, *i.e.*, a cold, heartless person. [both senses, U.S. slang, 1900s]

ice-boxed 1. sexually rejected by a woman. [U.S. slang, 1900s] **2.** pertaining to a man who cannot copulate because his sexual partner is menstruating. Also a play on BOX (sense 2), "vagina." [U.S. slang, 1900s]

ice-cream opium. For synonyms see OPE. [U.S. drug culture, early 1900s-pres.]

ice-cream man an opium dealer. [U.S. drug culture, early 1900s-pres.]

ice palace a high-class brothel. Refers to mirrors and cut glass. [U.S. underworld and colloquial, early 1900s or before]

ice wagon a frigid woman. *Cf.* ICEBERG (sense 1). [U.S. slang, early 1900s, Montelone]

idiot pills barbiturate tablets or capsules. For synonyms see BARB. [U.S. drug culture, mid 1900s-pres.]

If you can't use it, abuse it! a citizens band radio sign-off expression meaning "If you can't copulate, masturbate!" [U.S. slang, mid 1900s-pres.]

Igad! "By God!" For synonyms see 'ZOUNDS! [late 1600s]

Ike (also **Ikey, Ikey Mo, Ikie**) **1.** a nickname for a Jewish male. Derogatory when used generically. From the proper name "Isaac." "Ikey Mo" is from "Isaac Moses." For synonyms see FIVE AND TWO. [British and U.S., mid 1800s-1900s] **2.** to cheat. Derogatory. [British and U.S., 1900s or before]

Illegitimis non carborundum!* "Don't let the bastards wear you down!" [mock-Latin catch phrase; originally military slang, early 1900s-pres.]

Illinois green a type of marijuana. *Cf.* CHICAGO GREEN. For synonyms see MARI. [U.S. drug culture, mid 1900s-pres.]

ill-piece an unattractive male homosexual. [U.S. homosexual use, mid 1900s, Stanley]

illuminated intoxicated with alcohol. An elaboration of LIT (*q.v.*). [U.S. slang, 1900s or before]

IMBARS BIDBIB "I may be a rotten sod, but I don't believe in bullshit." *Cf.* DILLIGAF for length and complexity. [British, early 1900s, *Dictionary of Slang and Unconventional English*]

IMFU an immense military blunder, an "imperial military fuck-up." For synonyms see SNAFU. [World War II]

impudent impotent. An error, jocular or otherwise. [British, early 1600s] Synonyms and related terms: ANANDRIOUS, ANAPHRODISIA, APANDRY, ASTYSIA, ASYNODIA, IMPOTENT, IMPOTENTIA, IMPOTENTIA COEUNDI, IMPOTENTIA ERIGENDI, IMPROCREANT, NO MONEY IN HIS PURSE, ORGIASTIC IMPOTENCE.

impure a prostitute. *Cf.* PURE. [British, late 1700s or early 1800s]

incident a bastard. *Cf.* ACCIDENT (sense 1). [U.S. colloquial, 1900s]

in-cog intoxicated with alcohol. From "incognito." [British slang, early 1800s, Jon Bee]

indescribables trousers. For synonyms see GALLIGASKINS. [British, early 1800s, (Dickens)]

India the female genitals. For synonyms see MONOSYLLABLE. [British, early 1600s]

Indian hay Indian marijuana; *Cannabis indica*. [U.S. drug culture, 1900s]

Indian hemp marijuana; one of the common names for *Cannabis indica*. *Cf.* INDIAN HAY. For synonyms see MARI. [U.S. underworld and drug culture, early 1900s-pres.]

Indian oil an alcohol extract of *Cannabis sativa*. For synonyms see OIL. [U.S. drug culture, mid 1900s-pres.]

indispensables trousers. [British, early 1800s]

indisposed 1. ill. **2.** having the menses. For synonyms see FLOODS. [both senses, colloquial euphemisms, 1900s or before]

indoor plumbing a bathroom or W.C. as opposed to a privy. *Cf.* OUTDOOR PLUMBING. [U.S. colloquial, early 1900s-pres.]

indorse 1. to commit PEDERASTY (*q.v.*); to commit sadistic acts. Literally "to be behind" someone. Synonyms: COMMIT PEDERASTY, CORN HOLE, GET HUNK, HAVE A BIT OF NAVY CAKE, INGLE, NAVIGATE THE WINDWARD PASSAGE, RIDE THE DECK, SHOOT IN THE TAIL, SNAG, SOD. **2.** to masturbate. Possibly a misunderstanding of sense 1. For synonyms see WASTE TIME. [both senses, British, late 1700s]

indorser 1. a SODOMITE (*q.v.*). [British, late 1700s, Grose] **2.** a sadist; one who flogs the back of another. *Cf.* INDORSE (sense 1). [U.S. underworld, early 1900s, Montelone]

ineffable 1. the female genitals, specifically the vagina. Literally, "the inexpressible." *Cf.* NAME-IT-NOT, NAMELESS. [British, 1800s] **2.** in the plural, trousers. For synonyms see GALLIGASKINS. [British, mid 1800s]

inexplicables trousers; breeches. [British and U.S., early 1800s]

inexpressibles trousers; breeches. [British and U.S., late 1700s-1800s]

ingle 1. a CATAMITE (*q.v.*). For synonyms see BRONCO. [since the late 1500s] **2.** to commit PEDERASTY (*q.v.*). [late 1500s]

ingle-nook the female genitals. *Cf.* NOOKER, NOOKY. [British slang, 1800s, Farmer and Henley]

ingler a PEDERAST (*q.v.*). See INGLE. [late 1500s, Florio]

injun (also **injin**) an American Indian. Not necessarily derogatory. [U.S. dialect and stereotypical cowboy jargon, 1800s-pres.]

ink a derogatory term for a Negro. *Cf.* INKY-DINK. For synonyms see EBONY. [U.S., early 1900s]

inked intoxicated with alcohol. *Cf.* INKY. [Australian, late 1800s-pres.]

inkface a derogatory term for a Negro. *Cf.* PALEFACE (sense 1). [U.S. slang, early 1900s or before]

inky intoxicated. *Cf.* INKED. [World War I, Fraser and Gibbons]

inky-dink a derogatory term for a very dark Negro. *Cf.* DINK (sense 2). INKFACE. [U.S. slang, 1900s, Wentworth and Flexner]

inkypoo intoxicated with alcohol. *Cf.* INKY. [Australian, Baker]

innominables trousers. [British, early 1800s]

insects and ants trousers; pants. Rhyming slang for "pants." *Cf.* BULL ANTS. [British slang, 1900s or before]

insertee a male, usually homosexual, who receives the penis of another male in his mouth (see FELLATIO) or anus (see PEDERASTY). Generally either of these acts is referred to as "passive" owing to its similarity to the female reception of the penis. In the act of fellatio, the oral "action" is performed by the insertee. A more exact term is RECEIVER (*q.v.*). The opposite is INSERTOR (*q.v.*). *Cf.* CATCH (sense 1), TAKE (sense 3). [U.S., 1900s, (Humphreys)]

insertor a male, usually homosexual, who places his penis into the mouth or anus of a male sexual partner. *Cf.* INSERTEE.

inspector of manholes a PEDERAST (*q.v.*). The "manhole" is the anus. [British slang, early 1900s, *Dictionary of Slang and Unconventional English*]

inspired intoxicated with alcohol. For synonyms see WOOFLED. [British, 1800s, Farmer and Henley]

instant Zen the drug L.S.D. (*q.v.*), [U.S. drug culture, mid 1900s-pres.]

instrument the penis. *Cf.* GAYING IN-

STRUMENT, TOOL (sense 1). [British and U.S. euphemism, early 1600s-1900s]

intercourse 1. copulation. Originally "communication and commerce" (late 1400s). A truncation of SEXUAL INTERCOURSE (*q.v.*). [since the late 1700s] **2.** to copulate. A contrived transitive and intransitive verb used as euphemistic jargon and avoidance, *e.g.*, "Intercoursing makes me tired" or "Intercourse you!" [U.S., mid 1900s-pres.]

interesting condition, in an (also **interesting situation, in an**) pregnant. [colloquial, mid 1700s-1900s]

into, be 1. to be copulating with a woman. *Cf.* GET INTO. [British and U.S., 1800s-pres.] **2.** to be interested in or involved in something. No negative connotations. [U.S. general slang, mid 1900s-pres.]

intoxed intoxicated with marijuana. For synonyms see TALL. [U.S. drug culture, mid 1900s-pres.]

introduce Charley to intromit the penis. [British slang, 1900s, *Dictionary of Slang and Unconventional English*]

intromit to insert the penis into the vagina.

intromittent organ the penis or any male copulatory organ which is inserted into the female for reproductive purposes. *Cf.* PENIS.

invert a male or female homosexual. See EPICENE and LESBYTERIAN.

I.O.F.B. "I only fire blanks," a catch phrase attributed to a sterile man or a man trying desperately to persuade a woman to copulate.

Irish button a syphilitic BUBO (*q.v.*). Possibly in error for IRISH MUTTON (*q.v.*). *Cf.* WINCHESTER-GOOSE.

Irish fortune the female genitals in a specialized sense. Farmer and Henley define it as "cunt and pattens," *i.e.*, the female genitals and a pair of crude country clogs. This and the following "Irish" entries are examples of the derogations directed toward the Irish. [British, 1800s]

Irish kiss a slap in the face. [U.S. slang, 1900s and before]

Irish mutton syphilis. *Cf.* MUTTON. [U.S., early 1900s, Montelone]

Irish root the penis. For synonyms see YARD. [British colloquial, early 1800s]

Irish shave to defecate. [U.S. colloquial, early 1900s, Montelone]

Irish toothache 1. an erection. [British colloquial, 1800s] **2.** a pregnancy. [British, late 1800s, Ware]

Irish whist copulation where "the jack takes the ace." An elaboration of the name of the card game "whist." *Cf.* ACE (sense 2), JACK (sense 1). [British slang, 1800s, Farmer and Henley]

ironhead a stupid oaf. [1900s or before]

iron hoof (also **iron**) a homosexual male; a male prostitute. Rhyming slang for POOF (*q.v.*). [British slang, 1900s, *Dictionary of Slang and Unconventional English*]

irre-fucking-sponsible extremely irresponsible. *Cf.* ABSO-FUCKING-LUTELY, IM-FUCKING-POSSIBLE.

irrepressibles trousers. For synonyms see GALLIGASKINS. [British, 1800s]

irrigated intoxicated with alcohol. [U.S. slang, mid 1800s-1900s]

irrumation (also **irrumatio**) PENILINGUS (*q.v.*). [from Latin *irrumo*, "give suck"; euphemistic]

ishkimmisk intoxicated with alcohol. *Cf.* SKIMISHED. [British, 1800s]

it 1. a CHAMBER POT (*q.v.*). [British, 1800s, Farmer and Henley] **2.** the female genitals. [very old euphemism] **3.** the penis. [very old euphemism] **4.** sex appeal; the ability to sexually stimulate persons of the opposite sex, *i.e.*, turn them on. [U.S., 1900s] **5.** copulation. [widespread avoidance; very old euphemism]

it, in for pregnant. For synonyms see FRAGRANT. [British and U.S. slang, 1900s]

I.T.A. IRISH TOOTHACHE (sense 2), a pregnancy. [British, late 1800s, Ware]

Italian manner anal copulation. *Cf.*
GREEK WAY. [1900s or before]

Italian perfume garlic. [U.S. slang,
early 1900s, Montelone]

itch sexual desire. [since the late 1600s]

itcher the female genitals, specifically
the vagina. *Cf.* ITCHING JENNY. [British
slang, 1800s, Farmer and Henley]

itching jenny the female genitals,
specifically the vagina. *Cf.* ITCHER.
[British slang, 1800s, Farmer and
Henley]

itchy pants sexual arousal in expressions such as ''have itchy pants.'' *Cf.*
HOT PANTS (sense 1). [U.S. slang, mid
1900s]

Ite (also **Eytie, Itey**) a derogatory term
for an Italian. [British and U.S., early
1900s-pres.]

it-shay dung; a curse; an oaf or a fool.
Pig Latin for ''shit.'' [U.S., 1900s]

It's snowing down South! a catch
phrase said to a woman whose slip is
showing. *Cf.* CHARLEY IS DEAD. [U.S.
slang, 1900s]

I.U.C.D. an ''intrauterine contraceptive
device.'' See I.U.D.

I.U.D. a euphemistic abbreviation of
''intrauterine device.'' An object which,
when inserted into the uterus, prevents
the development of a fetus. A specific
birth control device. [U.S., mid
1900s-pres.]

ivory-carpenter a dentist. [British
slang, 1800s, Farmer and Henley] Syn-
onyms: FANG-CARPENTER, FANG-FAKER,
FANG-FARRIER, GUMDIGGER, GUM-
PUNCHER, SNAG-CATCHER, SNAG-FENCER,
TOOTH-CARPENTER, TOOTH-DOCTOR.

ivory gate the female genitals. [British,
1800s, Farmer and Henley]

ivy-covered cottage (also **ivy cottage**) an outdoor privy. For synonyms
see AJAX. [British and U.S. colloquial,
1800s-1900s]

Izzy a nickname for a Jewish man.
From the proper name ''Isaac.'' De-
rogatory when used as a generic term.
[U.S., early 1900s, Montelone]

J

J. 1. a marijuana cigarette. From JOINT. (sense 2). [U.S. drug culture, mid 1900s-pres.] **2.** a fool; an oaf. From JAY (sense 1). [British, 1800s]

JAAFU "joint Anglo-American fuck-up," a confused situation caused by American and British military personnel. For synonyms see SNAFU. [World War II]

jaboff 1. an injection of drugs. **2.** the CHARGE (sense 1) or thrill obtained from an injection of drugs. [both senses, U.S. underworld, early to mid 1900s, Weseen]

JACFU "joint American-Chinese fuck-up," a confused situation caused by American military personnel. For synonyms see SNAFU. [World War II]

jack 1. the penis, especially when erect. [British, 1800s] **2.** to copulate. [British slang, 1800s, Farmer and Henley] **3.** a derogatory term for a black man. Possibly from "jackass." See MOKE. [U.S., 1900s] **4.** a prostitute's customer. *Cf.* JOHN.

jack around to waste time, act childish, or be ineffective, usually said of males. A blend of JACK OFF and PLAY AROUND (both *q.v.*). [U.S. slang and colloquial, mid 1900s-pres.]

jackass 1. an ass; a donkey. Because of "ass," this word is often avoided in the U.S. **2.** a dolt; an oaf. [both senses, British and U.S. colloquial, 1800s-pres.]

jacked it dead; died. For synonyms see DONE FOR. [British slang, late 1800s, Ware]

jacker 1. a male who masturbates frequently. **2.** a derogatory term for a male. *Cf.* JACKOFF. [U.S. dialect (Boontling), late 1800s-early 1900s, Charles Adams]

jack-in-the-box 1. an unborn child in the womb. [British colloquial, 1800s, Farmer and Henley] **2.** the penis. The BOX (sense 2) is the vagina. [British slang, 1800s, Farmer and Henley] **3.**

syphilis. Rhyming slang for "pox." [British, late 1800s]

jack nasty-face the female genitals. [British, early 1800s]

jack off 1. to masturbate oneself or another, said of males. From "ejaculate" or JACK (sense 1). *Cf.* JAG OFF. **2.** to waste time; to goof off. **3.** a jerk or incompetent oaf. Usually hyphenated in this sense. *Cf.* JACKER. [all senses, U.S. slang, 1900s and before]

Jack-sauce an impudent fellow; a little oaf. [British, 1600s-1700s]

jack shit 1. a worthless good-for-nothing. Occasionally capitalized in this sense. **2.** nonsense. **3.** any worthless bit of nothing; a damn; a farthing, as in the phrase "not worth jack shit."

jacksie 1. a brothel. [Australian, 1900s, Baker] **2.** the anus; the same as JAXY (sense 1). See JACKSY-PARDY.

Jack Sprat a dwarf or a very small man. Survives in the children's rhyme "Jack Sprat could eat no fat." [since the 1600s]

Jack Straw's Castle the female genitals. From the pubic hair and from the name of a children's game of the period. [British, 1800s, Farmer and Henley]

jacksy-pardy (also **Jacksie, jacksy-pardo**) the anus or buttocks. [British, mid 1800s]

jack whore a large, masculine prostitute. [British slang, late 1700s]

jacky (also **jackey**) **1.** gin. For synonyms see RUIN. [British slang, late 1700s] **2.** a male Australian aborigine. Sometimes capitalized. *Cf.* MARY (sense 5), the female counterpart of Jacky. [Australian, 1900s or before, Baker]

Jacob 1. a fool; an oaf. [cant and later slang, late 1700s] **2.** the penis. *Cf.* JACOB'S LADDER. [British colloquial, 1800s, Farmer and Henley]

Jacob's ladder the female genitals. From the Bible (Genesis). In a dream

Jacob saw angels ascending and descending this ladder. *Cf.* JACOB (sense 2). For synonyms see MONOSYLLABLE. [Biblical; British colloquial, late 1800s, Farmer and Henley]

Jacque's 1. a privy. See JAKES for more recent forms. [early 1500s] **2.** the penis. See JAQUES.

jade a rough and contemptible girl or woman; a MINX (*q.v.*). [since the mid 1500s]

jaded jenny (also **cock-eyed jenny**) a prostitute. *Cf.* ITCHING JENNY. For synonyms see HARLOT. [U.S. slang, 1900s, Berrey and Van den Bark]

jag 1. a drinking spree in the expression "have a jag on." [late 1600s-pres.] **2.** a drunkard. For synonyms see ALCHY. [U.S., late 1700s-early 1900s] **3.** a load, specifically a load of liquor; a stomach full of beverage alcohol. See HAVE A JAG ON. [colloquial, 1800s-1900s] **4.** to be a male prostitute to other males. *Cf.* JAG-HOUSE. [U.S. slang and homosexual use, mid 1900s-pres.] **5.** drug intoxication. From sense 3. [U.S. drug culture, early 1900s-pres.]

jag, on intoxicated with alcohol. *Cf.* HAVE A JAG ON. [since the late 1600s]

jagabat a prostitute. *Cf.* BAT (sense 1). [Caribbean (Trinidad), 1900s or before]

jagged intoxicated with alcohol. *Cf.* HAVE A JAG ON, JAG (sense 1). For synonyms see WOOFLED. [U.S. slang, early 1700s-pres.]

jag-house a brothel offering male prostitutes for males. *Cf.* JAG (sense 4). [U.S. slang, mid 1900s-pres.]

jag off 1. to masturbate. *Cf.* JACK OFF. See JAG (sense 4). **2.** an incompetent time-waster; a jack-off. Usually hyphenated when written as a noun. [U.S., mid 1900s-pres.]

jail bait a sexually attractive or flirtatious girl who has not reached the age of consent. *Cf.* BAIT, SAN QUENTIN JAIL-BAIT. [U.S. slang, 1900s]

jaisy an effeminate male; a homosexual male. *Cf.* DAISY (sense 1). [British slang, 1900s]

jake 1. a toilet or W.C., usually for men. From JAKES (*q.v.*). [U.S. colloquial, 1900s or before] **2.** an oaf; a bumpkin. Also **country jake.** [U.S. slang, 1900s]

jake-house a privy or W.C. See JAKES [U.S. colloquial, 1900s or before]

jakes (also **Jacks, jacques, jake, jake's**) a privy; an outhouse. [British and U.S. colloquial, early 1500s-pres.]

jakes-farmer (also **jakes-barreller, jakes-man, jakes-raker**) a man whose calling is to empty the cesspits of privies. *Cf.* GONG-FARMER, NIGHTMAN, TOM TURDMAN. [late 1500s-1600s]

jam 1. the female genitals. For synonyms see MONOSYLLABLE. [British and U.S. slang, 1800s-1900s] **2.** semen. *Cf.* JELLY (sense 3). [British slang, 1800s, Farmer and Henley] **3.** a pretty young woman. Not necessarily with any sexual connotation. [British slang, mid 1800s, Ware] **4.** pertaining to a nonhomosexual or straight person. [U.S. homosexual use, mid 1900s] **5.** cocaine. [U.S. drug culture, mid 1900s-pres.]

jambled intoxicated with alcohol. For synonyms see WOOFLED. [U.S. slang, early 1700s, Ben Franklin]

jam-pot the female genitals. [British, 1800s]

jam-tart one's girlfriend or lover; a mistress. *Cf.* JAM (sense 1), TART. [British, 1800s]

Jane a women's restroom; the same as RUTH (*q.v.*). *Cf.* JOHN (sense 1). [U.S. slang, 1900s]

Jane Shore a prostitute. Rhyming slang for "whore." [British, 1800s-1900s, *Dictionary of Rhyming Slang*]

JANFU "joint army-navy-fuck-up," a colossal military blunder with contributions from the Army and the Navy. For synonyms see SNAFU. [U.S. slang, World War II, mid 1900s]

jang the penis. A spelling variant of YANG (*q.v.*). For synonyms see YARD. [U.S. slang, mid 1900s-pres.]

jank excrement; human excrement. [For synonyms see DUNG. [British dialect, 1800s or before, Northall]

jankhole a CESSPIT (*q.v.*); a privy. *Cf.* JANK. [British dialect, 1800s]

janney to copulate. Possibly from railroad jargon meaning "to couple." [U.S., 1900s, Wentworth and Flexner]

janua vitae* the "gates of life," the female genitals. Partly jocular and mockpedantic. For synonyms see MONOSYLLABLE.

JAP "Jewish-American prince" or "Jewish-American princess," usually the latter. A derogatory term for a young Jewish person who acts haughty and spoiled. [U.S. slang, mid 1900s-pres.]

Jap 1. a Japanese. Derogatory but lessening in impact. [U.S. and British slang, mid 1800s-pres.] Synonyms and related terms: JAP, JEEP, JERKANESE, LITTLE YELLOW BASTARDS, NIP, SKIBBY, TOJO. 2. pertaining to the Japanese people or Japanese things. Derogatory. 3. a Negro. Rare and possibly in error. Most likely derogatory. [U.S., early 1900s, Goldin, O'Leary, and Lipsius]

jape 1. to copulate with a woman; to have sexual intercourse. For synonyms see OCCUPY. [since the 1300s] 2. an act of copulation. 3. to cheat or deceive. [slang, 1900s or before]

Japland Japan. From JAP (sense 1). [U.S. slang, 1900s]

Jaques 1. the penis. [French for the "John" of JOHN THOMAS (*q.v.*); British, 1800s-1900s] 2. a privy. See JACQUE'S, JAKES.

jargonelle the penis. [from a French name for a type of pear; see POPERINE PEAR; British, 1800s, Farmer and Henley]

jar-head 1. a fool or an oaf. [U.S. slang, 1900s or before] 2. a mule. No negative connotations. *Cf.* MOKE (sense 1). 3. a derogatory term for a Negro. *Cf.* MOKE (sense 2). [both senses, U.S. Southern colloquial, 1900s and before]

jasper 1. any male fellow or chum. [stereotypical Western jargon for "stranger"; U.S., 1900s or before] 2. a lesbian. [U.S. slang, mid 1900s-pres.]

jawharp (also **jaws harp**) an avoidance for "jew's-harp." *Cf.* JUICE HARP. [U.S. colloquial, 1900s] Synonyms: JEW'S-HARP, JEW'S TRUMP, JUICE HARP.

jaxy (also **joxy**) 1. the anus. 2. the female genitals. See JACKSY-PARDY. [both senses, British slang, 1900s]

jay 1. an oaf or a rascal; a frivolous person. See POPINJAY. For synonyms see OAF. [since the late 1500s] 2. marijuana or a marijuana cigarette. A respelling of the "J" of JOINT (sense 2). [U.S. drug culture, mid 1900s-pres.]

jaybee a respelling of J.B. (*q.v.*), "jet black," a Negro. Derogatory. For synonyms see EBONY. [colloquial, 1900s]

jazz 1. an act of copulation or copulation in general. 2. to coit a woman. 3. women considered solely as sexual objects. 4. the female genitals. 5. semen. See JIZZ. [all senses, U.S. underworld and later slang; always related to the Negro in America and often etymologized as having an African origin; the first written attestations were in the early 1900s]

jazz baby a woman of easy sexual morals. *Cf.* JAZZ. [U.S. slang, 1900s]

jazz-bo a black man, particularly if up-to-date and stylish. Not necessarily derogatory. [U.S. slang, early 1900s]

jazzed-up (also **jazzed**) intoxicated with alcohol. For synonyms see WOOFLED. [U.S. slang, early 1900s]

jazz it to copulate. *Cf.* JAZZ. [U.S. slang, early 1900s]

jazz oneself to masturbate. See JAZZ. [U.S. slang, 1900s]

jazz up to impregnate a woman. [U.S. slang, early 1900s]

J.B. a Negro. From "jet black." Derogatory. See JAYBEE.

jean queen 1. a homosexual male who is particularly attracted to males in denim jeans. 2. a homosexual male who habitually wears denim jeans. See QUEEN for similar terms. [both senses, U.S. homosexual use, mid 1900s]

jeans at half-mast (also **pants at half-mast**) a catch phrase implying that someone has been caught serving as a

CATAMITE (*q.v.*). Extended to mean "caught in the act," an elaboration of CAUGHT WITH ONE'S PANTS DOWN (*q.v.*). Based on "flag at half-mast." [U.S. underworld slang, early 1900s, Goldin, O'Leary, and Lipsius]

Jee! an oath and an exclamation for "Jesus!" Usually spelled GEE! (*q.v.*). [U.S., late 1800s-pres.]

jeep a Japanese. A distortion of JAP (*q.v.*), possibly from the military "jeep" automobile. [Australian, 1900s, Baker]

Jeepers! (also **Jeepers Creepers!**) an avoidance for "Jesus!" [U.S., 1900s and before]

Jee-whiskers! a mild oath or exclamation; the same as GEE-WHISKERS! (*q.v.*). See GEE-WHOLLIKER! [attested as New Zealand, early 1900s, *Dictionary of Slang and Unconventional English*]

Jeez! (also **Geeze!, Jees!, Jeeze!, Jese!**) a disguise of "Jesus!" Usually used without knowledge of its source. [U.S. slang and colloquial, 1900s or before]

jeff a Caucasian. Not necessarily derogatory. For synonyms see PECKERWOOD. [U.S. Negro use, mid 1900s-pres.]

Jefferson airplane a device used to hold the stub of a marijuana cigarette. *Cf.* ROACH CLIP. [U.S. drug culture, mid 1900s-pres.]

Jehoshaphat! (also **Jehoshaphat!, By; Jehosophat!**) an oath and an exclamation, possibly avoiding "Jesus!" *Cf.* JUMPING JEHOSHAPHAT! The entry is given in its correct spelling. The colloquial pronunciation is closer to "jee-ho-suh-fat," or even "jee-ho-suh-fant." [from the name of the Biblical King of Judah; 1900s and before]

jelly 1. an attractive, buxom girl. *Cf.* JAM (sense 3), JELLY-ON-SPRINGS. [British slang, early 1800s] **2.** the female genitals. *Cf.* JAM (sense 1), JAM-POT, JELLY-ROLL (sense 1). [U.S. slang, 1900s] **3.** semen. *Cf.* JAM (sense 2). For synonyms see METTLE. [since the early 1600s] **4.** a type of vaginal contraceptive; a vaginal contraceptive jelly. [U.S., mid 1900s-pres.]

jelly baby an amphetamine tablet or capsule. Usually in the plural. See JELLY BEAN. For synonyms see AMP. [U.S. drug culture, mid 1900s]

jelly bag 1. the female genitals. A container for JELLY (sense 3), "semen." *Cf.* JAM-POT. [British, 1600s] **2.** the scrotum. See JELLY (sense 3). From the name of the cloth bag through which jelly is strained. [British, 1800s or before, Farmer and Henley]

jelly bean an amphetamine tablet or capsule. Usually in the plural. [U.S. drug culture, mid 1900s]

jelly belly a coward. For synonyms see YELLOW-DOG. [widespread slang and colloquial, 1900s]

jelly-on-springs a catch phrase describing large, bouncing or quivering female breasts or buttocks. [U.S. slang, 1900s]

jelly-roll 1. the female genitals. **2.** a sexual lover. **3.** a soiled sanitary napkin. [all senses, U.S. slang, 1900s]

Jemima 1. a CHAMBER POT (*q.v.*). [British, 1800s, Farmer and Henley] **2.** sometimes used as an oath, "Jemima!" A euphemistic disguise of "Jesus!" [U.S., 1900s]

jemmison (also **jemsom**) the penis. [U.S. dialect (Ozarks), Randolph and Wilson]

Jenny Hills the testicles. Rhyming slang for "testicles" when pronounced "test-i-kills." [British, 1900s or before, *Dictionary of Rhyming Slang*]

Jenny Willocks 1. an effeminate male; a man overly concerned with women's affairs. [British and U.S., 1900s or before] **2.** a HERMAPHRODITE (*q.v.*). Possibly a homosexual male. [British, early 1900s]

jere (also **jeer**) **1.** the buttocks. For synonyms see DUFF. **2.** excrement. For synonyms see DUNG. [both senses, British since the 1600s or before] **3.** a homosexual male. Possibly rhyming slang for QUEER (*q.v.*). See GEAR (sense 4). For synonyms see EPICENE. [British, 1900s or before, *Dictionary of Rhyming Slang*]

Jericho hell or some similar remote place as in "Go to Jericho!" [colloquial since the mid 1600s]

jerk 1. to masturbate. [British, 1800s] **2.** a masturbator. From JERK OFF (sense 2). For synonyms see HUSKER. [U.S. slang, 1800s-pres.] **3.** an oaf or incompetent fool. The connection with sense 1 is rarely recognized. [U.S. slang, 1800s-pres.] **4.** to act like a jerk in expressions such as "jerk around." [U.S., 1900s] **5.** to coit a woman. [U.S. slang, mid 1900s-pres.]

jerk bumps pimples; acne. From a jocular myth that adolescent masturbation leads to acne. Cf. JERK OFF. For synonyms see BURBLE. [colloquial and slang, 1900s]

jerker 1. a CHAMBER POT (q.v.). [British, late 1800s] **2.** a prostitute. [British, late 1800s, Farmer and Henley] **3.** a drunkard; a tippler. [British slang, early 1800s] **4.** a male masturbator. See JERK.

jerk off 1. to masturbate oneself or another. See JERK (sense 1). [British and U.S., 1800s-pres.] **2.** a chronic masturbator; an incompetent do-nothing. Usually hyphenated in this sense. [U.S. and British slang, 1900s and before] **3.** a jerk or oaf; a contemptuous term of address. Usually hyphenated in this sense. Cf. JACK OFF. [U.S. and British, 1900s or before]

jerk one's gherkin (also **jerk one's gerkin**) to masturbate. Often in the form "jerkin' his gherkin." The gherkin is a type of cucumber which is made into pickles. Cf. PUMP ONE'S PICKLE. [U.S. slang, 1900s]

jerk one's mutton to masturbate. See MUTTON, which means "sexual gratification" here. For synonyms see WASTE TIME. [British slang, 1800s, Dictionary of Slang and Unconventional English]

jerks the DELIRIUM TREMENS (q.v.). Cf. JUMPS. [British and U.S., early 1800s-1900s]

jerk the cat to vomit. Cf. CAT (sense 7), SHOOT THE CAT, WHIP THE CAT. For synonyms see YORK. [British slang, early 1600s to 1900s]

jerky games masturbation. [British, 1800s]

jeroboam (also **joram**) a CHAMBER POT (q.v.). From the standard term for a large bowl or other vessel. [from the name of an early king of Palestine; British slang, early 1800s]

Jerps!, By an exclamation, possibly a disguise for "By Jesus!" [U.S., 1900s or before]

jerry 1. a CHAMBER POT (q.v.). From JEROBOAM (q.v.). [British and U.S. slang, early 1800s] **2.** a German soldier or airplane. Often capitalized. Usually considered derogatory. Cf. GERRY. From the pot-shaped German helmet, see JERRY (sense 1), or a respelling of "ger" from "German." [U.S. military, World War II]

Jerry Riddle urine; to urinate; an act of urination. Rhyming slang for PIDDLE (q.v.). Cf. JIMMY RIDDLE. [British slang, 1800s-1900s]

Jersey cities the human breasts. Rhyming slang for "titties." Based on BRISTOL CITIES (q.v.). For synonyms see BOSOM. [U.S., early 1900s, Dictionary of Rhyming Slang]

Jersey green a particular type of marijuana. For synonyms see MARI. [U.S. drug culture, mid 1900s-pres.]

jesuit 1. a term for a sodomite or a practitioner of disapproved sexual practices. **2.** the penis in BOX THE JESUIT AND GET COCKROACHES (q.v.). [both senses, British slang and colloquial, early 1600s-1800s]

Jesus H. Christ! (also **Jesus X. Christ!**) a profane oath and an exclamation. For synonyms see SWEET CHEESECAKE. [U.S. colloquial, 1800s-1900s]

Jesus-screamer (also **Jesus-shouter**) **1.** a Christian, especially if evangelical or Pentecostal. **2.** a clergyman; a missionary. For synonyms see SKY-PILOT. [both senses, U.S., 1900s and before]

jet one's juice to ejaculate. Cf. JUICE (sense 1), "semen." For synonyms see

MELT. [British slang, 1800s, Farmer and Henley]

Jewboy a derogatory nickname and term of address for a Jewish male of any age. For synonyms see FIVE AND TWO. [British and U.S. slang and colloquial, mid 1800s-pres.]

Jew butter goose grease; chicken fat. Usually considered to be derogatory. [U.S. slang, late 1800s-1900s]

Jew chum 1. "new chum," a new-comer to Australia. Specifically a Jew-ish newcomer. Rhyming slang. [Australian, 1900s, Baker] **2.** a tramp. Rhyming slang for "bum." Usually considered to be derogatory. From sense 1. [1900s]

jewel the hymen; virginity; the female genitals. Cf. FAMILY JEWELS (sense 2). Essentially the same as JEWELRY (sense 1).

jewel case a CHAMBER POT (q.v.). For synonyms see POT. [British, early 1900s, *Dictionary of the Underworld*]

jewelry 1. the female genitals. Cf. JEWELS. **2.** the male genitals. Cf. FAM-ILY JEWELS. [both senses, U.S. slang, 1900s]

jewels the testicles. A truncation of FAMILY JEWELS (q.v.). Cf. DIAMONDS. For synonyms see WHIRLYGIGS. [U.S. slang, early 1900s-pres.]

Jewess a Jewish woman or girl. Usu-ally derogatory. [since the 1300s]

Jew flag (also **Jewish flag**) the dollar bill or U.S. currency of other denomi-nations. Usually considered to be de-rogatory. [U.S. slang, 1900s]

Jew food ham, bacon, or pork of any kind. Intended as jocular and ironic. Usually considered derogatory. [slang, 1900s]

Jewie (also **Jewey, Jewy**) a deroga-tory term for a Jewish man. A highly derogatory term of direct address. For synonyms see FIVE AND TWO. [colloqui-al, 1800s-1900s]

Jewish nightcap the foreskin of the penis. [slang, 1900s]

Jew Nersey "New Jersey" with ref-erence to the Jewish population. Usu-ally considered derogatory. Cf. JEW YORK. [U.S. slang, 1900s]

jew's-harp a small musical instrument held between the teeth and plucked. Thought to be more recent than JEW'S TRUMP (q.v.). Cf. JAW HARP, JUICE HARP.

Jew's trump a JEW'S-HARP (q.v.). [the anglicized spelling of the French *jeu tromp;* attested as British dialect, late 1500s, Halliwell]

Jew York "New York," with refer-ence to the Jewish population. Usually considered to be derogatory. Cf. JEW NERSEY. [U.S. slang, 1900s]

Jezebel 1. a shrewish woman. [mid 1500s] **2.** the penis. [British slang, 1800s, Farmer and Henley]

jibagoo a nickname of ridicule for a Negro. A jocular distortion of JIGABOO (q.v.).

jibs 1. the lips or jaw, and therefore talk or chatter. [U.S. dialect, 1900s and before] **2.** the buttocks. With refer-ence to their projection. [U.S. black use, 1900s]

jick-head a drunkard. For synonyms see ALCHY. [U.S. black use, 1900s]

jig 1. a Negro. Derogatory; possibly from "jigger," which is rhyming slang for NIGGER (sense 1). For synonyms see EBONY. [U.S., 1900s or before] **2.** cop-ulation or an act of copulation. See JIG-A-JIG. Cf. DANCE THE BUTTOCK JIG. [British slang, early 1800s, *Lexicon Balatronicum*] **3.** the female genitals. From JIGGER (sense 2). For synonyms see MONOSYLLABLE. [British and U.S., 1800s-1900s] **4.** the penis. [colloquial, 1800s-1900s] **5.** a cheater or swindler. [British, 1800s, *Dictionary of Slang and Unconventional English*]

jiga a Negro. Rhyming with "niga." From NIGGER (sense 1). Derogatory. [colloquial, 1900s or before]

jigaboo (also **jiggaboo**) a Negro. De-rogatory and belittling. Cf. BOO, JIBAGOO, JIG (sense 1), JIGA, ZIGABOO. [U.S. slang, late 1800s-pres.]

jigger 1. the penis. [British and U.S., 1800s-pres.] **2.** the female genitals.

[British colloquial, 1800s, Farmer and Henley] **3.** a gadget.

jiggered 1. intoxicated with alcohol. [U.S. slang, early 1900s] **2.** damned. See the following entry. [U.S. colloquial, 1800s-1900s]

jiggered!, I'll be an oath of avoidance, "I'll be damned!" For synonyms see 'ZOUNDS! [since the early 1800s]

jiggery-pokery humbuggery; trickery; nonsense. [British and U.S., 1800s]

jiggle 1. to copulate, said of a man or a woman. **2.** to coit a woman. From the standard meaning (U.S. and British), "rock or move with a jerky motion." [British slang, mid 1800s]

jiggling-bone the penis, especially when erect. *Cf.* JIGGLE (sense 2). For synonyms see YARD. [British slang, 1800s, Farmer and Henley]

jiggumbob 1. a gadget. [since early 1600s] **2.** the female genitals. For synonyms see MONOSYLLABLE. [British slang, late 1600s] **3.** a testis. See JIGGUMBOBS.

jiggumbobs testicles. For synonyms see WHIRLYGIGS. [British slang, late 1700s, Grose]

jill-flurt (also **gill-flirt, gill-flurt**) **1.** a wretched and wanton slut. [British and U.S. dialect, 1800s-1900s] **2.** to surgically enlarge the birth canal of a woman, resulting in the accidental puncturing of the vaginal wall and the adjacent rectum. **3.** a woman who crepitates vaginally due to a rupture of the vaginal wall and rectum as in sense 2. Sense 3 may be apocryphal. [U.S. dialect, 1900s or before]

jilliver (also **gillyflower**) a silly, giddy young woman; a termagant. [British colloquial and dialect, late 1700s, Nodal and Milner]

jilt 1. a prostitute who lures a man, accepts his money for her services, and then disappears without performing them. [cant, late 1600s, B.E.] **2.** a woman who casts off her lover or betrothed. Now said also of a man. [since the late 1600s] **3.** any prostitute or slattern. [British dialect, 1800s and before] **4.**

to break one's engagement. [slang, 1900s]

jim 1. a urinal. *Cf.* JAKES, JOHN (sense 1). **2.** to urinate. For synonyms see WHIZ. [both senses, U.S. dialect, 1900s and before]

Jim Crow 1. a derogatory nickname for a Negro. *Cf.* BLACKBIRD (sense 1). For synonyms see EBONY. [known in England, early 1700s] **2.** a personification of discrimination against Negroes. **3.** pertaining to a system of forced segregation. [all senses, from the name of a minstrel song of the early 1800s; U.S. slang and colloquial, 1800s-pres.]

Jiminitly! a mild oath or exclamation; a disguise of "Jesus!" [U.S. colloquial, 1900s or before]

Jiminy! a mild oath or exclamation. Also in expressions such as "Jumping Jiminy!"

Jiminy Crickets! an oath and an exclamation, a disguise of "Jesus Christ!" [U.S., 1900s and before]

jimjams (also **jams**) **1.** the jitters; extreme anxiety or nervousness. **2.** the DELIRIUM TREMENS (*q.v.*). [both senses, British and U.S. slang, 1800s-1900s]

jimmies the DELIRIUM TREMENS (*q.v.*); the shakes. For synonyms see ORK-ORKS. [U.S. slang, 1900s]

Jimmy Britts (also **the Jimmys**) diarrhea. Rhyming for the SHITS (*q.v.*). [Australian, 1900s]

Jimmy Riddle urine; to urinate; an act of urination. Rhyming slang for PIDDLE (*q.v.*). See JERRY RIDDLE (*q.v.*). [British slang, 1800s]

jim-swiggered!, I'll be a common oath or exclamation, "I'll be damned!" essentially the same as "I'll be jig-swiggered!" [U.S. colloquial, 1900s and before]

jing-jang 1. the penis. *Cf.* JANG. **2.** the female genitals. **3.** coition or an act of coition. *Cf.* YING-YANG. [all senses, U.S. slang, 1900s]

jingle 1. a drunken spree. **2.** a state of mellowness from drinking [both senses, U.S., late 1800s-1900s]

jingle-berries the testicles. *Cf.* BERRIES, GOOSEBERRIES. For synonyms see WHIRLYGIGS. [U.S. dialect (Ozarks), Randolph and Wilson]

jingled intoxicated with alcohol. *Cf.* WHOOPS and JINGLES. For synonyms see WOOFLED. [from World War I; British and U.S. slang, 1900s]

Jingo!, By an oath and an exclamation, "By God!" [possibly from the Basque word for God, "Jinko" or "Jenco," reinforced by the proper name "Jingo," which served as the basis of "jingoism" in Britain, late 1800s; British, late 1600s-pres.]

jinker a male who copulates frequently, fast, or notably well. For synonyms see LECHER. [slang, early 1700s]

Jinks!, By (also **Jinks!**) a mild oath or exclamation. Related to JINGO!, BY (*q.v.*). [U.S. slang and colloquial, 1800s]

jism (also **chism, gism, jizz**) 1. semen. For synonyms see METTLE. 2. manly vigor and energy; the same as GISM (sense 4). See also the dialect form CHISM. [both senses, slang, 1900s or before]

jit a derogatory term for a Negro. For synonyms see EBONY. [U.S. slang, 1900s]

jive (also **gyve**) 1. copulation. For synonyms see SMOCKAGE. [U.S. slang, early 1900s-pres.] 2. marijuana. For synonyms see MARI. [U.S. drug culture, early 1900s-pres.] 3. to copulate; to coit a woman. Originally black use. [U.S. slang, mid 1900s-pres.] 4. to cheat or deceive. 5. nonsense; idle boasting. [both senses, U.S. slang, mid 1900s-pres.]

jive-stick (also **gyve-stick**) a marijuana cigarette. [U.S. drug culture, 1900s]

jizz 1. semen. 2. manly vigor. *Cf.* JISM, METTLE, SPUNK. [both senses, primarily U.S. slang, mid 1900s-pres.]

job 1. a drunkard. [Australian, Baker] 2. a truncation of BLOW-JOB (*q.v.*), "penilingus." [U.S. slang, 1900s] There are a number of other sexual "jobs": BROWN-JOB, FRAIL-JOB, HAND-JOB, HEAD-JOB, HUM-JOB, KNOB-JOB, PIPE-JOB, PISTON-JOB, RAM-JOB, RIM-JOB, SEX-JOB, SKULL-JOB. 3. to coit a woman. *Cf.* DO A WOMAN'S JOB FOR HER, WORK. [slang, early 1500s] 4. a BOWEL MOVEMENT (sense 1). *Cf.* DO A JOB (sense 1), JOBBY. For synonyms see EASEMENT. [U.S. colloquial euphemism, 1900s or before] 5. excrement; feces. [U.S. colloquial and slang, 1900s] 6. a gadget. See JOBBER.

job, on the in the act of copulating. *Cf.* DO A JOB. [widespread colloquial, 1900s]

jo-bag a condom. *Cf.* JOY-BAG. For synonyms see EEL-SKIN. [military, World Wars]

jobbing copulation; coiting a woman. *Cf.* JOB, WORK. [British, 1700s and before]

jobby a bowel movement. [mostly juvenile; U.S. colloquial, 1900s or before]

jock 1. to copulate with a woman. This is from "jockey," meaning "ride a horse." Also related to "jock," meaning "jolt" in British dialects. [British slang, late 1600s, B.E.] 2. the penis. From JOCKUM (sense 1). [since the late 1700s and before] 3. the female genitals. From sense 1. [British slang, late 1700s] 4. an athletic supporter. Literally, "a strap for the penis." A truncation of JOCK-STRAP (*q.v.*). [U.S. colloquial, 1900s] 5. a male athlete, especially if large and stupid. [U.S. slang, 1900s] 6. a female athlete or sports enthusiast. From sense 5. [U.S., mid 1900s-pres.] 7. a Scots soldier or any Scotsman. [World War II and before] 8. to cheat or deceive. [British slang, mid 1700s] 9. a nickname for a bull. Capitalized in this sense. [from Scots colloquial, 1800s or before]

jocker (also **jockey**) a PEDERAST (*q.v.*) tramp who lives off the begging of his CATAMITE (*q.v.*). [U.S. underworld, early 1900s]

jockey a PEDERAST (*q.v.*); the same as JOCKER (*q.v.*). See also GIN-JOCKEY.

jockey-and-boxer a PEDERAST and his CATAMITE (both *q.v.*). [U.S. slang, mid 1900s-pres.]

jock-itch an itching of the male genitals or of the groin. Associated with the area supported by a JOCK-STRAP (*q.v.*). *Cf.* CREEPING CRUD, CROTCH-ROT, GALLOPING KNOB-ROT. [U.S. colloquial, mid 1900s-pres.]

Jocks!, By (also **Jockum!, By**) an oath and an exclamation. [U.S., 1900s or before]

jock-strap (also **jockey-strap**) an athletic supporter for the male genitals. *Cf.* JOCK (sense 4). [U.S. colloquial, 1900s]

jockum (also **jockam, jocum**) **1.** the penis. See JOCK (sense 2). [cant, mid 1500s] **2.** to coit a woman. See JOCK (sense 1). For synonyms see OCCUPY. [British, 1700s]

jockum-gage a CHAMBER POT (*q.v.*). Literally, MEMBER MUG (*q.v.*). See JOCKUM (sense 1). "Gage" is a vessel. [cant, 1600s, B.E.]

jocky (also **jockey, jockie**) the penis. A diminutive of JOCKUM (sense 1). For synonyms see YARD. [cant, late 1600s] See also JOCKER.

joe (also **Joe**) **1.** a W.C.; a urinal. [U.S. slang, 1900s or before] **2.** to urinate or defecate. [U.S. slang, 1900s and before]

Joe, old 1. syphilis. For synonyms see SPECIFIC STOMACH. [U.S. slang, early 1900s] **2.** any venereal disease. [U.S. slang, mid 1900s-pres.]

Joe Beeswax!, By an exclamation; a mock oath. [U.S. slang, 1900s or before]

Joe Blakes the DELIRIUM TREMENS (*q.v.*). Rhyming slang for SHAKES (sense 2). [Australian, 1900s]

Joe Buck an act of copulation; to coit a woman. Rhyming slang for FUCK (*q.v.*). [Australian, early 1900s]

Joe Erk an oaf; a jerk; a wretched man. Rhyming both on JERK and BERK (both *q.v.*). The equivalent of JOE CUNT (*q.v.*). [from the World Wars]

Joe Hunt an oaf; a jerk; a wretched man. Rhyming slang for "cunt." [British, 1900s, *Dictionary of Rhyming Slang*]

Joe Ronce a pimp; a PONCE (*q.v.*). Rhyming slang for "ponce." [British slang, early 1900s]

Joe-trots diarrhea. *Cf.* JOE (sense 1). [U.S., 1900s or before]

Joe-wad toilet paper. *Cf.* JOE. For synonyms see T.P. [U.S., 1900s or before]

joey 1. a HERMAPHRODITE (*q.v.*); possibly a homosexual male. **2.** a SODOMITE (*q.v.*). Refers to a pederast or a practitioner of other homosexual activities. **3.** an effeminate male. Related to "joey," the juvenile kangaroo. [all senses, Australian, 1900s, Baker] **4.** the menses. [British slang, 1900s, *Dictionary of Slang and Unconventional English*]

jog to coit a woman. From the standard sense "move up and down in a heavy, steady motion." [British slang or colloquial, early 1600s]

John (also **john**) **1.** a privy; an outhouse. *Cf.* JAKES, JIM, JOE. For synonyms see AJAX. [since the 1600s] **2.** a toilet; a restroom. For synonyms see W.C. [U.S. colloquial, 1900s] **3.** a nickname for a prostitute's customer. Used by both male and female prostitutes. [U.S. slang and underworld, mid 1900s-pres.] **4.** a woman's lover or steady boyfriend. [U.S. slang, mid 1900s-pres.] **5.** a Chinese. *Cf.* JOHN CHINAMAN. [Australian, 1900s or before] **6.** the penis. A truncation of JOHN THOMAS (*q.v.*). [slang, 1900s] **7.** an older male homosexual who supports a young one. *Cf.* SUGAR-DADDY. [U.S. slang, 1900s]

John-and-Joan 1. a HERMAPHRODITE (*q.v.*). [British, 1800s or before, Farmer and Henley] **2.** a homosexual male. This sense is probably the more accurate of the two. See HERMAPHRODITE. [British colloquial, 1700s-1800s]

John Barleycorn (also **Sir John Barleycorn**) whisky; a personification of whisky and the evils of drink. Originally ale or beer made from barley. [colloquial, late 1700s-pres.]

John Chinaman (also **John**) the Chinese people; a Chinese. [widespread colloquial, 1800s-1900s] Synonyms: CANARY, CHINAMAN, CHINAMANG, CHINEE, CHINK, CHINKY, CHINO, CHOW, COOSIE, DINGBAT, DINK, GOOK, JOHN, JOHNNIE, MUSTARD, PADDY, PIGTAIL, PONG, RICEBELLY, RICEMAN, SLOPIE, YELLOW-BELLY, YELLOW BOY.

John Hall alcohol; liquor. *Cf.* ALCOHOL. [U.S. slang, 1900s]

Johnnie Ronce a pimp; a PONCE (*q.v.*). Rhyming slang for "ponce"; the same as JOE RONCE (*q.v.*). [British, 1900s, *Dictionary of Rhyming Slang*]

Johnny (also **Johnnie, johnnie, johnny**) **1.** a personification of the penis; the diminutive of JOHN (sense 6). Based on JOHN THOMAS (*q.v.*). [British and U.S. slang, 1800s] **2.** a Chinese. *Cf.* JOHN CHINAMAN. [Australian, early 1900s, Baker] **3.** a toilet; a restroom; the W.C. *Cf.* JOHN (sense 1). [1900s] **4.** a condom. [British military, 1900s]

Johnny bum euphemistic and jocular for "jackass." See BUM (sense 1). [British slang, late 1700s, Grose]

Johnson the penis; a personification of the penis. *Cf.* DOCTOR JOHNSON, JOHN (sense 6). [attested as British slang, 1800s, *Dictionary of Slang and Unconventional English*; U.S. black use, mid 1900s] See also JOHNSON GRASS.

Johnson Grass (also **Johnson**) marijuana. From a common name for a type of sorghum and also from the release from inhibitions that marijuana provides. *Cf.* JOHNSON. [U.S. drug culture, mid 1900s-pres.]

John Thomas 1. a general nickname for a flunky; a servant. [British slang and colloquial, mid 1800s] **2.** the penis; a personification of the penis. Implies that the penis is the servant of men. [British colloquial, early 1800s-pres.]

John Willie the penis; a personification of the penis. *Cf.* JOHN (sense 6), LITTLE WILLIE. [British colloquial, early 1900s]

join giblets 1. for man and woman to unite in marriage. [British, late 1600s]

2. to copulate; to copulate casually. [British slang or cant, 1700s, Grose]

joint 1. the penis. For synonyms see YARD. [U.S. slang and underworld, early 1900s-pres.] **2.** a marijuana cigarette. *Cf.* J. (sense 1). [U.S. drug culture, mid 1900s-pres.] **3.** an opium den. Also any establishment where vice is available. [U.S. slang, late 1800s to early 1900s] See also CRYSTAL JOINT.

join the great majority (also **join the ever-increasing majority**) to die. [since the late 1800s]

jollies sexual pleasure; sexual excitement. [U.S. slang, 1900s]

jolly bean an amphetamine tablet or capsule. A play on JELLY BEAN (*q.v.*). [U.S. drug culture, mid 1900s-pres.]

jolly rowsers trousers; pants. Rhyming slang for "trousers." [U.S., 1900s]

jolt 1. to coit a woman. From a term meaning "move up and down in a jerky manner." [British slang, 1800s, Farmer and Henley] **2.** the kick or charge from an electric shock or a drink of whisky. **3.** the CHARGE (sense 1) or effects of marijuana or other narcotics. [U.S. slang, 1900s]

Jones 1. the penis; a personification of the penis. *Cf.* JOHN (sense 6), JOHNSON. [originally U.S. black use, 1900s] **2.** a drug habit. See SCAG JONES.

joss-house an opium den. Based on a pidgin term for a Chinese temple or "God house." [early 1900s]

jottle 1. to copulate. **2.** an act of copulation. [both senses, British, 1800s, Farmer and Henley]

jounce to copulate, from the male point of view. From the meaning "shake by bumping." [British slang or colloquial, 1800s]

Jove!, By an oath and an exclamation, "By God!" [since the late 1500s or before]

joy-bag a condom; the same as JO-BAG (*q.v.*). For synonyms see EEL-SKIN. [British military, mid 1900s, *Dictionary of Slang and Unconventional English*]

joy-boy 1. a sexually overactive male.

[U.S. slang, 1900s] **2.** a homosexual male. [British and U.S. slang, 1900s] **3.** a male drug addict. [U.S. drug culture, 1900s]

joy flakes a powdered narcotic; cocaine or morphine. *Cf.* CALIFORNIA CORNFLAKES. [U.S. underworld, early 1900s]

joy house a brothel. [U.S. slang or colloquial, early 1900s]

joy juice 1. alcohol; liquor. **2.** a liquid substance used for stimulant or narcotic purposes. [both senses, U.S. slang, 1900s]

joy knob the penis, especially the glans penis. *Cf.* GALLOPING KNOB-ROT. [U.S. slang, 1900s, Wentworth and Flexner]

joy-pop a hypodermic injection of narcotics. [U.S. underworld, 1900s]

joy-popper an occasional user of narcotics. *Cf.* CHIPPY (sense 3), JOY-RIDER. [U.S. underworld, mid 1900s]

joy powder one or more of the narcotics used in powder form, *i.e.*, cocaine, heroin, morphine. Originally used for "morphine." [U.S. underworld and later, drug culture, early 1900s-pres.]

joy prong the penis. *Cf.* PRONG. [British and U.S. slang, early 1900s]

joy-ride 1. copulation. *Cf.* RIDE. [U.S. slang, 1900s] **2.** a CHARGE (sense 1) or intoxication from the use of drugs. [1900s] **3.** an execution; a death-ride; a kidnap-murder. [U.S. underworld slang, 1900s]

joy-rider an occasional user of drugs. *Cf.* CHIPPY, JOY-POPPER. [U.S. underworld, early 1900s]

joy sister (also **joy-girl**) a prostitute. [U.S. slang, 1900s]

joy smoke marijuana or a marijuana cigarette. [U.S. slang, mid 1900s-pres.]

joy-stick 1. the penis. [British and U.S. since the 1800s] **2.** a pipe for smoking opium. [U.S. underworld, 1900s] **3.** a marijuana cigarette. [U.S. drug culture, mid 1900s-pres.]

joy-water alcohol; liquor. *Cf.* GIGGLE-WATER. [U.S. slang, early 1900s]

joy-weed marijuana. For synonyms see MARI. [U.S. underworld and drug culture, 1900s]

J-smoke marijuana or a marijuana cigarette, *Cf.* J., JOINT (sense 2). [U.S. drug culture, mid 1900s-pres.]

J.T. JOHN THOMAS (*q.v.*), the penis. [British slang and colloquial, early 1900s-pres.]

juane a truncation of "marijuana." Either marijuana or a marijuana cigarette. [U.S. slang, early 1900s, Wentworth and Flexner]

Juanita 1. marijuana. [U.S. drug culture, 1900s] **2.** a prostitute. [U.S. underworld, 1900s, Goldin, O'Leary, and Lipsius]

Juanita weed marijuana. *Cf.* JUANITA (sense 1). [U.S. drug culture, mid 1900s-pres.]

Juckies!, By a mild oath or exclamation. [U.S. slang and colloquial, 1900s and before]

Judas!, By an oath and an exclamation. For synonyms see 'ZOUNDS! [U.S. slang and colloquial, 1800s]

Judas Priest! an oath and an exclamation, the equivalent of "Jesus Christ!" [U.S. colloquial, mid 1800s-pres.]

Judy (also **Jude**) **1.** a prostitute. [British, early 1800s] **2.** any girl or woman. *Cf.* CRACK A JUDY'S TEACUP. [U.S. slang, 1900s] **3.** a fool; an oaf. [British slang, early 1800s-1900s]

juff the posteriors; the buttocks. *Cf.* DUFF. [British slang, 1800s]

jug 1. a term of contempt for a man or a woman. [British, late 1800s] **2.** a mistress or sexual lover. [slang, mid 1500s] **3.** a CHAMBER POT (*q.v.*). *Cf.* CROCK (sense 2). [U.S. colloquial, 1900s or before] **4.** an amphetamine tablet or capsule. [U.S. drug culture, mid 1900s-pres.] **5.** a breast. See JUGS.

jug-bitten intoxicated with alcohol. For synonyms see WOOFLED. [British slang, early 1600s]

jugged-up (also **jugged**) intoxicated with alcohol. [U.S. slang, 1900s]

juggins a fool or an oaf. [British slang, late 1800s]

jugs the breasts. *Cf.* CREAM-JUGS, NINNY-JUGS. For synonyms see BOSOM. [U.S. and elsewhere, early 1900s-pres.]

jug-steamed intoxicated with alcohol. [U.S. slang, mid 1800s]

juice 1. semen. *Cf.* JET ONE'S JUICE. For synonyms see METTLE. [widespread nonce use; attested as British slang, 1800s, Farmer and Henley] **2.** vitality; male vigor. *Cf.* METTLE (sense 1). SPUNK (sense 1). [U.S. colloquial, mid 1900s-pres.] **3.** any alcoholic drink. For synonyms see BOOZE. [U.S. colloquial, early 1900s-pres.] **4.** to drink alcoholic beverages. Usually implying drinking to excess. [U.S. slang, mid 1900s-pres.] **5.** to sexually arouse a woman to the point of producing vaginal lubrication. [attested as U.S. slang, 1900s] See also JUICY (sense 1), which is considerably older.

juiced-up (also **juiced**) **1.** drunk; intoxicated with alcohol. *Cf.* JUICE (sense 3). [U.S. slang, 1900s] **2.** electrocuted. Usually in the electric chair. [U.S., early to mid 1900s] **3.** sexually aroused, said of a woman. *Cf.* JUICE (sense 5).

juice harp a JEW'S-HARP (*q.v.*). *Cf.* JEW'S TRUMP. [U.S. colloquial, 1900s and before]

juicehead a drunkard; a heavy drinker. *Cf.* JUICE (sense 3). [U.S. slang, mid 1900s-pres.]

juicy 1. pertaining to a woman who is sexually aroused. Refers to vaginal lubrication. *Cf.* JUICE (sense 5), SLICK-CHICK (sense 2). [Slang and colloquial since the late 1600s] **2.** intoxicated with alcohol. *Cf.* JUICE (sense 3), [colloquial since the early 1700s] **3.** pertaining to something which is bawdy or lewd. [British and some U.S. use, late 1800s-1900s]

juju a marijuana cigarette. [U.S. underworld and slang, early 1900s]

juke (also **juk**) **1.** to coit a woman. **2.** coition in general or an act of coition. [attested in various parts of the Caribbean and the Southern U.S.]

juke-house a brothel. [originally black use; U.S., early 1900s]

jumble to copulate. For synonyms see OCCUPY. [late 1500s-1700s]

jumbled-up pregnant. For synonyms see FRAGRANT. [British slang, 1800s or before]

jumble-giblets an act of copulation; copulation in general. *Cf.* JOIN GIBLETS. [British slang, 1800s]

jumbler a man or a woman who copulates notably frequently, fast, or well. For synonyms see LECHER. [British, early 1600s]

jumm to coit a woman. Possibly from JUMBLE (*q.v.*). [mid 1600s, (Urquhart)]

jump to copulate, usually said of a man, especially in reference to vigorous copulation. Possibly with an element of brutality. See MOTHER-JUMPER at MOTHER-GRABBER. [from *A Winter's Tale* (Shakespeare); currently a U.S. euphemism]

Jumping Jehoshaphat! an oath and an exclamation, sometimes "Jumping Jehoshaphant!" [U.S. slang, 1800s-pres.]

Jumping jew's-harps! a mock oath and an exclamation. [U.S. jocular colloquial, 1900s or before]

Jumping Moses! an oath and an exclamation. [U.S. and British, late 1800s, Ware]

jumps the DELIRIUM TREMENS (*q.v.*). *Cf.* JERKS. [colloquial, late 1800s-pres.]

jungle-bunny a derogatory name for a Negro. [U.S. slang, mid 1900s-pres.]

jungled drunk; intoxicated with alcohol from too much JUNGLE-JUICE (*q.v.*). [U.S. slang, early 1900s]

jungle-juice 1. African rum. [British, early 1900s] **2.** any homebrewed beverage with an alcoholic content achieved by fortifying, fermentation, or distillation. [Australian and U.S. military, World War II]

juniper-juice hard liquor, specifically gin. From the juniper berry flavoring of gin. [U.S. slang, 1900s]

junk, on the on drugs; pertaining to a regular drug user. [U.S. underworld and drug culture, mid 1900s]

junker 1. a seller of narcotics, particu-

larly of heroin. [U.S., early 1900s-pres.]
2. a drug addict or heavy user; the same
as JUNKY (*q.v.*). [U.S. underworld and
drug culture, early 1900s-pres.] Terms
for various types of addicts: ACID-
DROPPER, ACID-FREAK, ACID-HEAD, A.D.,
A-HEAD, BINDLE-STIFF, COKE-FREAK,
COKE-HEAD, COKEY, COKOMO, CUBEHEAD,
DOPE FIEND, DOPENIK, DOPER, DRUGGY,
DRUGHEAD, GONG, GOW-HEAD, GOWSTER,
HOP-FIEND, HOP-HEAD, HOP-HOG, HOPPER,
HOPPIE, HOPSTER, HOP-STIFF, HORNER, JOY-
BOY, JUNK-HOG, JUNK-HOUND, JUNKY,
KOKOMO, LOBBY-GOW, MORFIEND, NEE-
DLE-MAN, SCHMECKER, SMOKEY, SNOW-
BIRD, SPEED-FREAK, SPOOK, TECATO,
TWITCHER, USER.

junk-hog a drug addict or heavy user.
[U.S. slang, mid 1900s]

junk-hound a drug addict or heavy
user. [U.S. slang, 1900s, Weseen]

junk-peddler a dope peddler. [U.S.
underworld, early 1900s-pres.]

junky (also **junkie**) a drug addict.
[U.S. slang and drug culture, mid
1900s-pres.]

Jupiter!, By a disguise of "By God!"
[U.S. dialect and colloquial, mid
1800s-pres.]

jupper to coit a woman. A disguise
for "up her," *i.e.*, coit her. [Austra-
lian, early 1900s, *Dictionary of Slang
and Unconventional English*]

jutland the posteriors; the buttocks.
From their projection; based on a name
for Denmark. [British, 1800s or
before]

K

K. a homosexual male; "kweer," *i.e.*, QUEER (*q.v.*). [1900s, *Dictionary of the Underworld*]

kaif marijuana. *Cf.* KEEF. [U.S. drug culture, mid 1900s-pres.]

ka-ka 1. a defecation. **2.** feces; dung. [1900s and probably long before] **3.** heroin or counterfeit heroin, literally, SHIT (sense 5); the same as CA-CA (sense 1). [U.S. drug culture, mid 1900s-pres.]

kanakas the testicles. A play on KNACK-ERS (*q.v.*) and a nickname given to Melanesians brought to Australia to work on the plantations. [from the Hawaiian word *kanaka,* "man"; Australian, 1900s or before, *Dictionary of Slang and Unconventional English*]

kangaroo 1. a Jewish man or woman. Rhyming slang. Not necessarily derogatory. For synonyms see FIVE AND TWO. [1900s, *Dictionary of Rhyming Slang*] **2.** a nickname for an Australian. [since the late 1800s]

Kate a harlot; a prostitute, a nickname for a loose woman. [U.S. slang and underworld, 1900s]

Kaui a variety of marijuana. From the name of one of the Hawaiian Islands. *Cf.* HAWAIIAN, MAUI. [U.S. drug culture, mid 1900s-pres.]

kaze (also **caze**) the female genitals. [British, late 1800s]

keck to cough or choke; to retch or vomit noisily; to make retching sounds to show disgust. For synonyms see YORK. [onomatopoetic, since the early 1600s]

keef (also **kaif, kef, kief, kif, kiff**) **1.** marijuana or the pleasure derived from smoking it. **2.** HASHISH (*q.v.*) and mixtures of marijuana and tobacco. [both senses are from an Arabic word meaning "pleasure"; in English since the early 1800s; U.S. underworld and drug culture, early 1900s-pres.]

keek 1. to take a peep; to spy on someone. [British, late 1700s] **2.** a

peeping Tom; a VOYEUR (*q.v.*). [U.S. slang, 1900s]

keel the posteriors. *Cf.* BEAM. For synonyms see DUFF. [from Scots dialect, since the 1800s]

keep the census down 1. to abort a fetus. **2.** to masturbate. *Cf.* HIGHER MALTHUSIANISM, SIMPLE INFANTICIDE. [both senses, British, 1800s, Farmer and Henley]

Keep your pecker up! "Keep your chin up!" "Pecker" here refers to "mouth." This expression is misunderstood in the U.S., where "pecker" means "penis." [British colloquial, early 1800s-pres.]

keester (also **keister, keyster, kiester, kister**) **1.** a valise; a chest or box. **2.** the posteriors or the anus. [U.S. underworld and slang, mid 1900s] **3.** the female genitals. *Cf.* BOX (sense 2). [U.S. underworld, early 1900s]

keifer the female genitals. For synonyms see MONOSYLLABLE. [British slang, 1800s, Farmer and Henley]

kelks the testicles. From a word meaning "fish roe." [British dialect, 1800s, Rye]

keltch (also **kelt**) **1.** a Caucasian. A derogatory term used by Negroes. [U.S., early 1900s] **2.** a very light mulatto. Derogatory. [U.S., mid 1900s]

Ke-rist! an intensified oath and an exclamation, "Christ!" [U.S., 1900s]

kerterver-cartzo venereal disease, especially syphilis. [attested, mid 1800s, Hotten]

ketched pregnant. "Eye-dialect" for the illiterate form "catched." *Cf.* CAUGHT. For synonyms see FRAGRANT. [U.S. dialect, 1800s-1900s]

kettle the female genitals. *Cf.* PAN, POT (sense 1). [British, early 1700s]

kettledrums the breasts. [British slang, late 1700s, Grose]

key 1. the penis. Because "it lets the

man in and the maid out'' (Farmer and Henley). [British slang, late 1700s] **2.** a kilogram of marijuana. *Cf.* KI. [U.S. drug culture, mid 1900s-pres.]

keyed 1. intoxicated with alcohol. The same as KEYED-UP (sense 2). [U.S. slang, 1900s] **2.** intoxicated with marijuana or with other drugs. *Cf.* KEY (sense 2). [U.S. drug culture, mid 1900s-pres.]

keyed to the roof heavily intoxicated with alcohol. See KEYED (sense 1). [U.S. slang, 1900s]

keyed-up 1. extremely nervous and distraught. **2.** intoxicated with alcohol. *Cf.* KEYED (sense 1). [both senses, U.S. slang, 1900s]

keyhole the female genitals, especially the vagina. *Cf.* KEY (sense 1). [British slang, 1800s or before, Farmer and Henley]

keystone of love the female genitals. For synonyms see MONOSYLLABLE. [British, 1800s, Farmer and Henley]

Khyber Pass (also **Khyber**) the anus; the posteriors. Rhyming slang for ''ass.'' *Cf.* KYBO. [early 1900s, *Dictionary of Rhyming Slang*]

ki a kilogram of marijuana. *Cf.* KEY. [U.S. drug culture, mid 1900s-pres.]

kick 1. trousers. See KICKS. **2.** a CHARGE (sense 1) from drugs or alcohol; a thrill of any type. [both senses, slang, 1900s]

kick-cloy a pair of breeches. [mid 1800s, Matsell]

kick in the ass 1. shocking or disappointing news. **2.** an unwarranted punishment or letdown. [both senses, U.S. colloquial, mid 1900s-pres.]

kick off to die. For synonyms see DEPART. [Australian and U.S., mid 1900s-pres.]

kick party a party where L.S.D. or some other drug is used. [U.S. drug culture, mid 1900s-pres.]

kicks (also **kick**) trousers. For synonyms see GALLIGASKINS. [cant and slang since the late 1600s]

kicksies (also **kickseys**) trousers; breeches. *Cf.* KICKS. [cant, early 1800s,

Vaux; attested as U.S., Berrey and Van den Bark]

kicksters trousers; breeches. *Cf.* KICKS. [British, early 1800s]

kick-stick marijuana; a mariguana cigarette. [U.S. drug culture, mid 1900s-pres.]

kick the bucket to die. [cant and slang since the 1700s, Grose]

kick the clouds to be hanged. [cant and slang, early 1800s, *Lexicon Balatronicum*]

kick the gong (also **kick the gong around**) to smoke opium or marijuana. [U.S. underworld and drug culture, mid 1900s-pres.]

kid lamb a tramp's catamite. *Cf.* LAMB (sense 1). [U.S. underworld, early 1900s]

kid-leather young prostitutes in general. *Cf.* LEATHER (sense 1). [British slang, 1800s, Farmer and Henley]

kidney-scraper (also **kidney-wiper**) the erect penis. *Cf.* LUNG-DISTURBER. For synonyms see ERECTION. [British slang, 1900s, *Dictionary of Slang and Unconventional English*]

kid-simple having a lust for young boys; pertaining to a PEDERAST (*q.v.*). *Cf.* PUSSY-SIMPLE. [U.S. underworld, early 1900s, Irwin]

kid-stretcher a lecher; a user of young prostitutes. *Cf.* KID-LEATHER. [British slang, 1800s, Farmer and Henley]

kidstuff marijuana. A mild drug for beginners. *Cf.* SCHOOL BOY. [U.S. underworld, mid 1900s, Deak]

kiester stab PEDERASTY (*q.v.*). *Cf.* KEESTER (sense 2). [U.S. slang, 1900s]

kiester stash the rectum as a place for concealing illegal drugs. *Cf.* KEESTER (sense 2). [U.S. underworld and drug culture, mid 1900s-pres.]

kife 1. a prostitute. **2.** a CATAMITE (*q.v.*). **3.** a fellator. [all senses, U.S. underworld, early 1900s]

kike 1. a highly derogatory term for an uncouth Jewish merchant. **2.** a highly derogatory term for any Jewish man or woman. From Yiddish *kikel*, the ''circle'' which was used by illiterate Jewish immigrants in place of a cross (X) as a signature. For synonyms see FIVE AND TWO. [both senses, U.S. slang, early 1900s-pres.]

kiki BISEXUAL (*q.v.*). *Cf.* CHICHI (sense 3). [U.S. homosexual use, mid 1900s-pres.]

kill a snake to urinate; a possible reason for leaving the room to urinate. For synonyms see WHIZ. [Australian, early 1900s, Baker]

kill a tree to urinate against a tree, said of males. *Cf.* BURN THE GRASS. [U.S., 1900s]

killer a marijuana cigarette. For synonyms see MEZZROLL. [U.S. drug culture, mid 1900s]

killer-weed 1. the drug P.C.P. (*q.v.*). **2.** a mixture of marijuana and P.C.P. (*q.v.*). *Cf.* WEED. [both senses, U.S. drug culture, mid 1900s-pres.]

kill-grief any strong alcoholic drink. [British, early 1700s]

kill one's dog to be drunk. [U.S., early 1700s, Ben Franklin]

kindness coition, primarily in the expression DO A KINDNESS TO (*q.v.*). [euphemism, early 1700s]

king!, By a mild oath or a mock oath. See KING OATH!, MY. [U.S. colloquial, 1900s or before]

kingdom come 1. the next life, either heaven or hell. From "God's kingdom come on earth." [colloquial, 1700s-pres.] **2.** rum. Rhyming slang. [British, 1900s]

King Kong pills barbiturate tablets or capsules. For synonyms see BARB. [U.S. drug culture, mid 1900s-pres.]

King Lear a male homosexual. Rhyming slang for "queer." [British, early 1900s]

king-member the penis. For synonyms see YARD. [British slang, 1800s, Farmer and Henley]

king oath!, My a euphemism of disguise of "My fucking oath!" [Australian, early 1900s, Baker]

king of clubs a lecher, a whoremonger. The CLUB (sense 1) is the penis.

From playing cards. [British slang, 1800s, Farmer and Henley]

king's elevator a disguise of the ROYAL SHAFT (*q.v.*). [U.S., mid 1900s]

king 1. a derogatory term for a Negro. *Cf.* KINKYHEAD. [U.S. colloquial, 1900s] **2.** a person with deviant or nonorthogenital sexual desires. **3.** a deviant or nonorthogenital sexual practice. [U.S. slang, mid 1900s-pres.]

kinky 1. pertaining to a weird or crooked person. [British and U.S., late 1800s-pres.] **2.** pertaining to a male or female homosexual. [British and U.S., 1900s] **3.** pertaining to deviant or nonorthogenital sexual acts. *Cf.* KINKYSEX, TWISTY. [U.S. slang, mid 1900s-pres.]

kinky-head (also **kinky-nob**) a derogatory term for a Negro. *Cf.* KINK (sense 1). [U.S. colloquial, 1900s or before]

kinky-sex NONORTHOGENITAL (*q.v.*). sex acts. See GROUP SEX. [U.S. slang, mid 1900s]

kip a brothel. From the cant word for "sleep." [cant and slang, mid 1700s-1900s]

kippy-dope a woman considered solely as a sexual object. [U.S. military, World War I, Lighter]

kip shop a brothel. *Cf.* KIP.

kiss 1. to copulate. **2.** copulation. [both senses, British euphemisms, early 1700s]

kiss-ass 1. to curry favor; to act the sycophant. **2.** flattery; nonsense. **3.** a sycophant. *Cf.* SUCK-ASS. [all senses, U.S. slang, mid 1900s-pres.]

kisser a homosexual male. [U.S. slang, mid 1900s-pres.]

kiss Mary to smoke marijuana. [U.S. drug culture, mid 1900s-pres.]

Kiss my ass! a curse; also an oath and an exclamation. *Cf.* BASIMECU! [colloquial, 1900s or before]

Kiss my tail! a euphemism for KISS MY ASS! (*q.v.*).

kiss off 1. to perform PENILINGUS (*q.v.*). [U.S. underworld, early 1900s,

Montelone] **2.** to kill. **3.** death. Usually hyphenated in this sense. [senses 2 and 3 are U.S. underworld, 1900s]

kiss the dust to die; the same as BITE THE DUST (*q.v.*). [British, 1800s]

kiss the fish to smoke hashish. [U.S. drug culture, mid 1900s-pres., Landy]

kit the male genitals. *Cf.* APPARATUS, GEAR.

kitchen the female genitals. For synonyms see MONOSYLLABLE. [British slang, 1800s, Farmer and Henley]

kitchen-cleaner one who performs ANILINGUS (*q.v.*). [U.S. homosexual use, mid 1900s, Farrell]

kitty the female genitals. Named for FUR (sense 1), the pubic hair. *Cf.* CAT (sense 6), PUSSY (sense 1). [British slang, 1800s, Farmer and Henley]

K.J. CRYSTAL (krystal) JOINT (*q.v.*); the drug P.C.P. (*q.v.*). [U.S. drug culture, mid 1900s-pres.]

klutz (also **klotz**) an oaf; a clod or a bungler. [from German *Klotz*, "blockhead," via Yiddish; U.S. slang, mid 1900s-pres.]

knacker 1. to castrate. [British colloquial and slang, mid 1800s] **2.** a testis. See KNACKERS.

knackers (also **nackers**) the testicles. For synonyms see WHIRLYGIGS. [British colloquial and slang, 1800s-pres.]

knapped 1. pregnant. [British, early 1800s, Egan's Grose] **2.** intoxicated with alcohol. See KNAPT.

knapt (also **knapped**) intoxicated with alcohol. For synonyms see WOOFLED. [U.S. slang and colloquial, early 1700s, Ben Franklin]

knave 1. a male child; any little boy. [*c.* 1000] **2.** a rascally servant or simply a rascal; now used in jest for any rascal. [since the 1200s]

knee deep in shit (also **knee deep**) the state one is in when the lies and boasting have accumulated considerably. *Cf.* OXOMETER. [U.S. slang, mid 1900s]

kneeling at the altar pertaining to

the position of a receiving PEDERAST (*q.v.*) during the act of pederasty. [U.S. underworld, early 1900s, Irwin]

knee-trembler an act of copulation accomplished standing up. [British slang, 1800s, Farmer and Henley]

knee-walking drunk intoxicated with alcohol; so drunk as to have to walk on one's knees. [U.S. regional or nonce, 1900s]

knick-knack 1. a gadget. **2.** the female genitals. **3.** the penis. **4.** a testicle. Usually in the plural. [all senses, British and U.S., 1800s-pres.]

knob (also **nob**) **1.** the penis. **2.** the glans penis. *Cf.* KNOB-JOB. [colloquial since the 1800s or before] **3.** to masturbate. [U.S. slang, mid 1900s-pres.]

knob-job an act of PENILINGUS (*q.v.*). See JOB for related subjects. [U.S. slang, mid 1900s-pres.]

knock 1. the penis. See KNOCKER (sense 1). [British, 1700s or before] **2.** an act of copulation. [since the mid 1500s] **3.** to copulate. *Cf.* KNOCK UP. [cant and slang, 1700s-1900s] **4.** a sexually easy young woman. [slang, 1900s]

knock down a prick to bring an end to an erection; to cause a man to have an orgasm. *Cf.* BRING DOWN BY HAND. [British slang, 1800s, Farmer and Henley]

knocked-out 1. intoxicated with alcohol. For synonyms see WOOFLED. [U.S. slang, early 1900s-pres.] **2.** drug intoxicated. For synonyms see TALL. [U.S. drug culture, mid 1900s-pres.]

knocked-up 1. experiencing the menses. **2.** pregnant. **3.** intoxicated with alcohol. [all senses, U.S., 1900s]

knock-'em-down a prostitute. [British slang, 1800s, Farmer and Henley]

knocker 1. the penis. **2.** a lecher; a man who copulates frequently. [since *c.* 1500] **3.** a breast or a testis. See KNOCKERS. **4.** an important or self-important male; a showoff. Pronounced "k'nocker." [Yiddish; U.S., 1900s]

knockers 1. breasts, especially well-shaped breasts. [British and U.S., 1900s] **2.** the testicles. *Cf.* KNACKERS. [British and U.S. slang and colloquial, 1900s or before]

knocking copulation. For synonyms see SMOCKAGE. [since the 1500s]

knocking-house (also **knocking-joint, knocking-shop**) a brothel. [British slang, 1800s and before]

knocking-jacket a nightgown. [written nonce; early 1700s]

knocking-shop a brothel. Because one gains entrance by means of a secret knock (Barrère and Leland), or from KNOCKING (*q.v.*) meaning "copulation." See WINDOW TAPPERY.

knock it off to copulate. A reinterpretation of an expression meaning "Shut-up!" or "Stop it!" [U.S. slang, 1900s]

knock-me-down any extremely strong liquor. [British, early 1800s; attested as U.S., mid 1800s, Matsell]

knock over 1. to kill. [British and U.S. underworld, 1900s] **2.** to rob; to commit a planned crime of robbery. [U.S. underworld, 1900s]

knock the shit out of someone to beat someone. *Cf.* TAKE THE PISS OUT OF SOMEONE. [British and U.S. colloquial, 1800s-pres.]

knock up to make pregnant; in British English, "wake someone up by knocking." For synonyms see STORK. [U.S. slang and colloquial, 1900s]

knot the posterior ridge of the glans penis. [British slang or colloquial, 1800s, *Dictionary of Slang and Unconventional English*] See also VIRGIN-KNOT.

know to have sexual intercourse with someone; to have CARNAL KNOWLEDGE (*q.v.*) of a woman. [since the 1200s]

knowledge copulation. A truncation of CARNAL KNOWLEDGE (*q.v.*). *Cf.* CARNAL ACQUAINTANCE. [since the 1400s]

kokomo a cocaine user. From COKE (*q.v.*) and the name of a city in Indiana. [U.S. underworld and drug culture, early 1900s-pres.]

kook an odd person; a weirdo. [U.S. slang, mid 1900s-pres.]

kraut (also **krauthead**) a derogatory term for a German, especially a German soldier during wartime. For synonyms see GERRY. [U.S. slang, early 1900s-pres.]

kucky (also **cucky**) dirty, said of children and animals. See CUCK.

Ku Kluxer a derogatory term for a Caucasian, specifically a member of the Ku Klux Klan.

kweer a homosexual male. A respelling of "queer." *Cf.* K. For synonyms see EPICENE.

KYBO 1. "keep your bowels open," a catch phrase meaning "keep healthy." [U.S. slang, mid 1900s-pres.] **2.** a privy. For synonyms see AJAX. [1900s]

L

L. "hell." [U.S., 1900s]

labonza the posteriors. For synonyms see DUFF. [U.S. slang, mid 1900s]

labor the period in childbearing when the uterus contracts at regular intervals, beginning the process of expelling the baby.

labor leather to copulate with a woman. Cf. LEATHER (sense 1). [1500s]

labourer of nature the penis. [1600s, (Urquhart)]

labour-lea to copulate. Cf. LEA-RIGS. [Scots, 1800s or before]

lace curtains 1. whiskers, especially false whiskers used in the theater. No negative connotations. [U.S. slang, 1900s, Berrey and Van den Bark] **2.** the foreskin of the uncircumcised penis. [U.S. homosexual use, 1900s]

laced-mutton 1. a prostitute. For synonyms see HARLOT. **2.** any woman. [both senses, British, since the late 1500s]

ladder the female genitals, specifically the vagina. Cf. JACOB'S LADDER. [British slang, 1800s, Farmer and Henley]

ladies' the ladies' room; the ladies' restroom. [colloquial, 1900s or before]

ladies' college a brothel. A play on "seminary," i.e., "semen-ary." Cf. SEMINARY. [British slang, 1800s, Farmer and Henley]

ladies' delight the penis. Cf. LADIES' LOLLIPOP. [British, 1800s]

ladies' fever any venereal disease. [British jocular euphemism, mid 1800s]

ladies' lollipop (also **ladies' lollipop**) the penis. [British jocular euphemism, 1800s]

ladies' man 1. a man well-known and well-liked by women; a suave woman-chaser. **2.** a man, not necessarily effeminate, who spends a great deal of time with women. [both senses, colloquial, 1900s or before]

ladies' room a women's restroom; a W.C. [U.S., 1900s and before]

ladies' tailor a lecher; a whoremonger. Cf. TRIM. [British, 1800s]

ladies' tailoring copulation. See TRIM. [British, early 1800s]

ladies' treasure the penis. For synonyms see YARD. [British, 1800s]

ladies' walk a women's restroom; a W.C. Cf. GENTLEMEN'S WALK. [U.S., 1800s]

lad-lass an effeminate male, possibly a male homosexual. Cf. HE-SHE. [British dialect, 1900s or before]

lady 1. a high-class prostitute. [U.S. colloquial, 1900s] **2.** cocaine. Cf. GIRL (sense 9). [U.S. drug culture, mid 1900s-pres.]

lady, old (also **woman, old**) **1.** the female genitals. Cf. MAN, OLD (sense 1). [British, 1800s, Farmer and Henley] **2.** one's wife, girlfriend, or mother. [U.S. colloquial, 1900s]

Lady Berkeley the female genitals. From BERKELEY HUNT (q.v.) which is rhyming slang for CUNT (q.v.). [British slang, 1800s, Farmer and Henley]

lady-bird 1. a nice, ladylike, kept mistress. **2.** a lewd or wanton woman. For synonyms see LAY. [both since the 1600s]

lady-dog a rude and shrewish woman; a bitchy woman. Cf. SHE-DOG. [euphemistic or jocular, mid 1800s-1900s]

lady-feast sexual intercourse, especially when indulged in gluttonously. [British, mid 1600s]

lady-flower the female genitals; women considered sexually as the female counterpart of "the hairy wild-bee," the male. [from "Spontaneous Me," *Leaves of Grass* (Walt Whitman)]

lady in waiting a pregnant woman. [British and U.S. colloquial and nonce, 1900s or before]

Lady Jane the female genitals. For

synonyms see MONOSYLLABLE. [British, mid 1800s, Farmer and Henley]

lady-lover a female homosexual; a female lover of ladies. For synonyms see LESBYTERIAN. [U.S. underworld and slang, early 1900s-pres.]

lady of expansive sensibility a prostitute. Refers in part to SPREAD (sense 1), *i.e.*, spreading the legs. [British, early 1800s]

lady of leisure a prostitute. For synonyms see HARLOT. [U.S. underworld, early 1900s]

lady of pleasure a prostitute; a mistress or female lover. [euphemistic, mid 1600s-pres.]

lady of the evening a prostitute, a streetwalker. [U.S. euphemism, 1900s]

lady's low toupee the female pubic hair. *Cf.* LOWER-WIG, MERKIN. [British slang, early 1700s]

Lady Snow cocaine. *Cf.* LADY WHITE, OLD; WHITE LADY.

lady-star the female genitals. [British written nonce, late 1500s]

lady-ware 1. the male genitals, in particular, the penis. [late 1500s] **2.** the female genitals. [British, mid 1600s] See also WARE.

Lady White, old any powdered narcotic. *Cf.* LADY SNOW, WHITE LADY. [U.S. underworld, early 1900s]

lag 1. to water down or adulterate wine or spirits. **2.** to urinate. For synonyms see WHIZ. Both are from a word meaning "water" or "make wet." [both senses, 1500s-1800s]

lage 1. to drink. [cant, mid 1500s, Harman] **2.** weak liquor. *Cf.* LAG (sense 1), TIGER PISS. [British colloquial, 1600s]

lagging-gage a CHAMBER POT (*q.v.*). *Cf.* LAG (sense 2). [British colloquial or cant, 1800s or before]

laid having copulated; having been copulated with; the same as LAYED (sense 1). Originally said of women, now said of both men and women.

laid-out 1. dead; pertaining to a corpse arranged for a wake. **2.** intoxicated with alcohol. [U.S., early 1900s-pres.]

3. marijuana intoxicated. From sense 2. [U.S. drug culture, mid 1900s-pres.]

laid to the bone intoxicated with alcohol. For synonyms see WOOFLED. [U.S. colloquial, mid 1900s-pres.]

lally-gag (also **lolly-gag**) **1.** to flirt, court, or make love. [U.S. colloquial, mid 1800s-pres.] **2.** to be idle; to waste time out of ineptitude or malicious design. [U.S. colloquial, 1900s] **3.** to copulate. An extension of sense 1, possibly an overexaggeration. [U.S. colloquial, 1900s]

lamb 1. a CATAMITE (*q.v.*), especially a much abused and passive one. *Cf.* CHICKEN (sense 1), KID LAMB. For synonyms see BRONCO. [U.S. underworld, early 1900s and homosexual use, mid 1900s-pres.] **2.** a simpleton; an oaf. [British, mid 1600s]

lamb fries lamb's testicles eaten as food. *Cf.* MOUNTAIN OYSTERS. [U.S., 1900s and before]

lamp habit the habit of smoking opium; opium addiction. *Cf.* COOK (sense 1). [U.S. underworld, early 1900s]

lamp of life the penis. For synonyms see YARD. [British euphemism, 1800s]

lamp of love the female genitals. *Cf.* LIGHT THE LAMP. [British euphemism, 1800s]

lance the penis. *Cf.* BREAK A LANCE WITH. See BRACMARD for similar terms. [widespread nonce use since the 1600s or before]

lance in rest the erect penis. From the image of a long-shafted weapon held ready for attack in a comfortable or self-supporting position. For synonyms see ERECTION. [British, 1800s]

lance of love the penis, especially the erect penis. [British, 1800s or before]

Land!, My a mild oath and an exclamation. Probably euphemistic for "My Lord!" but few of its users are aware of that possibility. [U.S. colloquial, 1900s and before]

land of darkness the Negro district of town. *Cf.* DINGE ALLEY. [U.S., 1900s]

Land of Goshen! an oath and an exclamation. [1800s]

landowner a dead person; someone who "owns" and occupies a grave. [British and U.S. colloquial, 1800s-1900s]

Land sakes! a euphemism of avoidance for "Lord sakes!" See LAND!, MY. For synonyms see 'ZOUNDS!

langolee the penis. [possibly Irish or Scots; possibly related to an old dialect form "langele" or "langol," meaning "bind together." British, 1800s, Farmer and Henley]

lant 1. a stale urine, specifically stale urine collected for use as a cleaning agent. **2.** to urinate. [both senses, colloquial since *c.* 1000]

lap the female genitals. For synonyms see MONOSYLLABLE. [euphemism from *Much Ado About Nothing* (Shakespeare)]

lap-clap 1. copulation. **2.** conception; a pregnancy. [both senses, British, early 1700s or before]

lap-full 1. a lover or a husband. *Cf.* LAP. **2.** an unborn child. [both senses, British, 1800s, Farmer and Henley]

lapland 1. the female genitals. *Cf.* LAP, LOW-COUNTRIES, LOWLANDS. [British slang, early 1800s, Farmer and Henley] **2.** women in general; women considered sexually. [British, 1800s]

lapper 1. a heavy drinker, a drunkard. [British colloquial, mid 1800s] **2.** one who performs oral sexual intercourse, primarily PENILINGUS and CUNNILINGUS (both *q.v.*). [U.S. underworld, early 1900s, Montelone]

lappy intoxicated with alcohol. For synonyms see WOOFLED. [cant, colloquial, and dialect, 1700s-1800s]

lard to copulate. Refers to inserting fat into meat in preparation for roasting. Reinforced by the sense "fatten," *i.e.*, "make pregnant." [British, 1800s or before, Farmer and Henley]

lard ball a very fat person. [U.S. colloquial, early 1900s]

lardhead an oaf; a FAT-HEAD (*q.v.*). [colloquial, 1900s]

lark to masturbate; to practice PENILINGUS (*q.v.*). See comments at LARKING. [British, 1800s or before]

larker a frolicking rascal. [U.S. dialect, 1900s or before, Wentworth]

larking possibly FELLATIO but could also be CUNNILINGUS (both *q.v.*). Farmer and Henley define it as IRRUMATION (*q.v.*), which means "suck." Partridge suggests cunnilingus. Grose's euphemistic definition is "a lascivious practice that will not bear explanation." From a verb "lark," meaning to trap or catch larks. [British, late 1700s]

larro a homosexual male. Backslang for "oral" with reference to FELLATIO (*q.v.*). For synonyms see EPICENE. [U.S. slang, mid 1900s-pres.]

larydoodle the penis. For synonyms see YARD. [British colloquial, 1800s or before, Halliwell]

last abode the grave; death. [U.S., 1900s] Synonyms: CHURCH HOLE, COLD MUD, COLD STORAGE, DEEP SIX, DUST-BIN, EARTH-BATH, FINAL RESTING PLACE, GROUND SWEAT, PIT-HOLE.

last home the grave; death; a cemetery. *Cf.* FINAL RESTING PLACE. [U.S. euphemism, 1900s or before]

last muster death in expressions such as "go to the last muster." *Cf.* ANSWER THE FINAL SUMMONS, LAST ROUNDUP. [U.S. euphemism, 1900s]

last resort the W.C. *Cf.* PLACE OF RESORT. [U.S. jocular euphemism, 1900s]

last reward death. [U.S. euphemism, early 1900s-pres.]

last roundup death. [stereotypical Western jargon, U.S., 1900s]

lat the "latrine"; a privy or a W.C., often "the lats." [British military, mid 1900s, Brophy and Partridge]

late dead, as in "the late Mr. Jones." [since the 1400s]

latent homosexual a male who does not know or will not recognize that he is a homosexual. *Cf.* TENDENCIES.

LATER "Ladies' After Thoughts on Equal Rights," an organization opposed to some of the goals of the women's rights movements. A play on NOW, the "National Organization for Women." [U.S., 1970s]

latex a euphemism for a latex condom. For synonyms see EEL-SKIN. [U.S., 1900s]

lather sexual secretions; semen, natural vaginal lubricants, or both. [British, 1800s, Farmer and Henley]

lathered intoxicated with liquor. From an old term meaning "beaten." For synonyms see WOOFLED. [U.S. slang, early 1900s or before]

lather-maker the female genitals with reference to natural vaginal lubrication and semen. A paraphrase of "shaving brush." [British, 1800s]

latrine lips someone (usually a citizens band radio operator) who habitually uses obscene language. Cf. SEWER-MOUTH. [U.S. slang, mid 1900s-pres.]

latrine rumor any rumor, especially one which is alleged to spread at the latrine. [World War II]

latrine wireless the exchange of gossip at a latrine; a latrine "grapevine," the source of a LATRINE RUMOR (q.v.). [British, World War II]

latrinogram (also **latrino**) a LATRINE RUMOR (q.v.). [British and U.S., World War II]

latter-end the posteriors; the same as HINDER-END (q.v.). For synonyms see DUFF. [British colloquial, 1800s]

L.A. turnabouts amphetamine tablets with reference to their use by long-distance truckers. Cf. COASTS-TO-COASTS. [U.S. drug culture, mid 1900s-pres.]

laughing soup alcoholic liquor. Cf. GIGGLE-WATER. For synonyms see BOOZE. [U.S., 1900s, Wentworth and Flexner]

laundry queen a black woman. For synonyms see RAVEN BEAUTY. [U.S. slang, early 1900s]

lav a W.C. A truncation of "lavatory," which is an old euphemism for "bathroom." Cf. LAVO, LAVY. [U.S., 1900s]

lavatory 1. a sink; a wash basin. [since the 1300s] **2.** the bathroom itself. [from Latin *lavatorium*, "place to wash"; since the 1900s]

lavatory roll a roll of toilet paper. Cf.

BATHROOM ROLL. For synonyms see T.P. [British and U.S. euphemism, 1900s]

lavender boy a homosexual male. For synonyms see EPICENE. [U.S. underworld, early 1900s]

lavo a W.C.; a lavatory. Cf. LAV, LAVY. [Australian slang, early 1900s]

lavy (also **lavvy**) a W.C.; a lavatory. Cf. LAV, LAVO. [British colloquial, 1900s]

Lawdy sakes alive! (also **Lawdy sakes!**) the same as LORD SAKES ALIVE! (q.v.). For synonyms see 'ZOUNDS! [U.S. colloquial, 1900s and before]

lawful jam a wife. Cf. JAM (sense 1). [British slang, late 1800s, Farmer and Henley]

Lawks! (also **Lawk!**) an oath and an exclamation, a disguised euphemism for "Lord." [since the early 1700s]

Law's sakes! an oath and an exclamation, "For the Lord's sake!" For synonyms see 'ZOUNDS! [colloquial, 1900s and before]

Lawsy's sakes! an oath and an exclamation, "For the Lord's sake!" [U.S., 1900s or before]

lax (also **lask**) diarrhea; loose bowels. Also an adjective in "lax bowels." [colloquial and dialect, early 1500s-1900s]

lay 1. a job; a deal. A basic cant term for any enterprise (usually illegal) which brings a monetary return. [cant, late 1700s, Grose] **2.** copulation. [U.S. colloquial, since the early 1900s or before] **3.** a woman considered solely as a sexual object. [U.S. colloquial, 1900s] Synonyms and related terms for sense 3: ADULTERA, ADULTRESS, ALLEY CAT, AMORET, AMOROSA, ASS, ATHANASIAN WENCH, BALL-BUSTER, BALONEY, BAND, BANGSTER, BED-BUNNY, BEETLE, BED-BUG, BELLY-LASS, B-GIRL, BIFFER, BIG TWENTY, BIKE, BIMBO, BITER, BIT OF JAM, BLIMP, BLUE GOWN, BOB TAIL, BOMB-SHELL, BROOD, BUMMERKEH, BUNDLE, BUNNY, CAKE, CALICO QUEEN, CHARITY DAME, CHARITY GIRL, CHARITY STUFF, CHIPPY, CLAPTRAP, CLEAVE, CLEAVER, COMING WENCH, COMING WOMAN, CUDDLE-BUNNY,

DANGEROUS CURVES, DEAD EASY, DEB-GENERATE, DIRTY-LEG, DRESS GOODS, EASY, EASY LAY, EASY MAKE, EASY MARK, EASY MEAT, EASY-RIDER, EASY VIRTUE, FAD-CATTLE, FIZGIG, FLAP, FLAPPER, FLIRT-GILL, FLIRTIGIGGS, FLOOSEY, FLY, FORNICATRESS, FRANION, FREE-FOR-ALL, GASH, GAY, GAY IN THE GROIN, GIG, GIGLER, GIGLETTING, GIGLOT, GIGSY, GILL, GILL-FLURT, GIXIE, GLUTZ, GOBBLE-PRICK, GOOBER-GRABBER, GOOD GIRL, GOOD LAY, GOOSEBERRY-PUDDING, GRADUATE, GRASS-BACK, GRIND, GROUPIE, HAIRY BIT, HAT, HIGHFLYER, HO, HOBBY, HOBBY-HORSE, HOGMINNY, HORNS-TO-SELL, HOT-BOT, HOT LAY, HOT MEMBER, HOT NUMBER, HOT PANTS, HOT SKETCH, HOT STUFF, HOT TAMALE, HOT TOMATO, HOT-TONGUE, HUMMER, HUMP, HUNK, HUSSY, JAY, JAZZ BABY, KNOCK, LADY-BIRD, LETCHING-PIECE, LIBERTINE, LIGHT FRIGATE, LIGHT HOUSEWIFE, LIGHT O' LOVE, LIGHT SKIRTS, LIGHT WOMAN, LOOSE, LOOSE-KIRTLE, LOOSE WOMAN, LOW RENT, MADAMOI-ZOOK, MERRY-BIT, MISS HORNER, MUT-TON, NESTLE-COCK, NIT, NYSOT, OPEN-ARSE, PARNEL, PEACH, PICK-UP, PIE, PIECE OF ASS, PIECE OF SNATCH, PIECE OF STRAY, PIECE OF TAIL, PIG, PIG-MEAT, PLAYGIRL, PLAYTHING, PLEASER, POKE, POLL, PUSH-OVER, PUTA, QUAIL, QUEAN, QUIFF, RIG-MUTTON, ROUNDHEEL, RUTTER, SCATE, SCUPPER, SEX-JOB, SEXPOT, SHAGSTRESS, SHORT-HEELED WENCH, SHORT-HEELS, SHTUP, SLACK, SLEEPING-PARTNER, SLEEZ, SLOTTED-JOB, SMOCK-TOY, SNAKE, SNATCH, SOFT-JAW, SOFT LEG, SOFT ROLL, SPLIT, SPLIT-TAIL, STIFF, STROLLOP, SUB, SUBURB-SINNER, TABLE-GRADE, TAINT, TIB, TICKLE-TAIL, TICKLE-TOBY, TIT, TOMRIG, TOWN PUNCH, TRAMP, TRASH, TROT, TUBE, WAG-TAIL, WALK-UP FUCK, WANTON, WARM BIT, WARMING-PAN, WILLING-TIT, YES-GIRL. **4.** to copulate with a woman, possibly by force. [U.S. colloquial, 1900s] **5.** to copulate with a man, said of a woman. [U.S. slang, mid 1900s-pres.] **6.** a prostitute. [U.S. colloquial, 1900s] **7.** a CATAMITE (*q.v.*). From senses 3 and 6. For synonyms see BRONCO. [U.S. underworld, early 1900s] **8.** anal copulation; PEDERASTY (*q.v.*).

From sense 2. [U.S. underworld, early 1900s, Goldin, O'Leary, and Lipsius]

lay down 1. to position a woman for copulation. *Cf.* SPREAD (sense 2). [since the late 1500s] **2.** to permit copulation, said of women, as in "lay down for a man."

lay down the knife and fork to die. As if one were finished with a meal. *Cf.* STICK ONE'S SPOON IN THE WALL. [British jocular euphemism, 1800s, Barrère and Leland]

layed 1. having been copulated with. From LAY (senses 3 and 4). Also **laid.** [U.S. colloquial, 1900s] **2.** intoxicated with marijuana. From LAY (sense 4); *i.e.*, SCREWED (*q.v.*). *Cf.* LAID-OUT (sense 3). [U.S. drug culture, mid 1900s-pres.]

lay off with to copulate with. The "off" may refer to ejaculation. [Australian, 1900s]

lay out to coit a woman. *Cf.* LAY DOWN, SPREAD (sense 2). [British, 1800s]

lay some pipe to coit a woman. From the act of placing a length of pipe in a trench. *Cf.* PIPE (sense 1). [U.S. slang, mid 1900s-pres.]

lay the hip 1. to copulate. [U.S. slang, early 1900s] **2.** to smoke opium, *i.e.*, to "lie on the hip." *Cf.* HIP-LAYER. [U.S., early 1900s or before]

lay the leg to coit a woman. *Cf.* LIFT ONE'S LEG. [U.S. colloquial, early 1900s]

leading article the female genitals. *Cf.* WARE (sense 2). [British, 1800s, Farmer and Henley]

lead-poisoning death from being shot with a lead bullet. [stereotypical underworld and cowboy jargon; U.S., 1900s or before]

leaf, the cocaine. For synonyms see NOSE-CANDY. [U.S. drug culture, mid 1900s-pres.]

leaf gum narcotics. *Cf.* GUM. [U.S. underworld, early 1900s]

leak 1. the female genitals. [probably written nonce; British slang, early 1700s] **2.** urination; an act of urination. **3.** to urinate. For synonyms see WHIZ. [both colloquial since the 1500s]

leakery (also **leak-house**) a privy or a latrine; a male urinal. [Australian, 1900s]

leap to copulate. Also nominalized in terms such as LEAPING-HOUSE (*q.v.*). *Cf.* JUMP. [slang since the 1500s]

leaping intoxicated with alcohol. For synonyms see WOOFLED. [U.S. slang, early 1900s]

leaping-house a brothel. *Cf.* LEAP. [from *Henry IV*, Part One (Shakespeare)]

lea-rigs the female genitals. *Cf.* LABOUR-LEA. [Scots, 1800s]

leary (also **leery**) intoxicated with alcohol. [U.S. slang, late 1800s-early 1900s]

lease-piece a prostitute. [U.S. nonce, mid 1900s]

leather 1. the female genitals, specifically the vagina. "Leather" here is synonymous with SKIN (sense 4). [early 1500s] **2.** a homosexual male, especially one who is cruel and sexually sadistic. *Cf.* SADISM. [U.S. slang, mid 1900s-pres.] **3.** pertaining to any sadistic, virile male, homosexual or not. Senses 2 and 3 refer to virile males wearing leather jackets. [U.S. slang, 1900s]

leather-brained stupid. [U.S. colloquial, 1900s]

leather-dresser a lecher; a man who copulates frequently. *Cf.* LEATHER (sense 1). [British slang, 1800s, Farmer and Henley]

leather-head 1. an oaf. Possibly referring to the wearing of a leather cap or to baldness. [colloquial since the late 1600s] **2.** a policeman. Because he "leathers" (beats with a leather strap) people's heads. [U.S., late 1800s, Thornton]

leather lane the female genitals, specifically the vagina. A reinterpretation of a London street name. For synonyms see MONOSYLLABLE. [British, early 1800s or before]

leather queen an aggressive and possibly sadistic male homosexual who wears leather clothing. *Cf.* LEATHER (sense 2). [U.S. homosexual use, mid 1900s-pres.]

leather-stretcher the penis. *Cf.* LEATHER (sense 1), STRETCH LEATHER. For synonyms see YARD. [British, 1800s or before]

leave the room to retire to the W.C.; to depart to the restroom. [U.S. euphemism, 1900s]

leave this world to die. *Cf.* GO ON TO A BETTER WORLD. [euphemistic, 1900s or before]

leaving-shop the female genitals, a place where one's SPENDINGS (*q.v.*) are left. From an old term for "pawn shop." [British slang, mid 1800s]

lech (also **letch**) **1.** a sexual urge; a sexual thought or fantasy. [British and U.S., 1700s-pres.] **2.** to pursue or enjoy sexual matters, especially illicit sex. [from French *lecher*; British and U.S., early 1900s-pres.] **3.** a lewd man; a lecher. [U.S. colloquial, early 1900s-pres.] **4.** to ogle or stare at a woman; to study a woman sexually. [slang, 1900s]

lecher (also **leacher, letcher**) **1.** a lewd man; a habitual fornicator. [since the 1100s, *Oxford English Dictionary*] Synonyms and related terms: ADULTER-ER, ALLEY CAT, AMORIST, AMOROSO, AN-IMAL, ASS-MAN, AVOWTERER, BALLOCKER, BALLOCKS, BASHER, BED-PRESSER, BELLY-BUMPER, BIRD'S-NESTER, BLUEBEARD, BUCK FITCH, BULL, BUM-FIDDLER, BUST-MAKER, CARNALITE, CASANOVA, CHIM-NEY SWEEP, CHIPPY-CHASER, COCK-FIGHT-ER, COCK-HOUND, COCK OF THE GAME, COCKSMAN, COCKSMITH, CORINTHIAN, DIRTY DOG, DIVER, DOG, DOLLY-MOPPER, D.O.M., DON JUAN, DUNDERING RAKE, EAGER-BEAVER, FAGGOTEER, FAGGOT-MASTER, FAGGOTMONGER, FEATHER-BED SOLDIER, FIGURE-MAKER, FISHMONGER, FLEECE-HUNTER, FLEECE-MONGER, FLESH-FLY, FLESH-MAGGOT, FLESH-MONGER, FLOWER-FANCIER, FORBIDDEN FRUIT EATER, FOX-HUNTER, FRANION, FUCKSTER, GAME-COCK, GAP-STOPPER, GASH-HOUND, GAY DOG, GAY-MAN, GETTER, GIN-BURGLAR, GIN-SHEPHERD, GIRL-TRAP, GOAT, GOER, GROUSER, GULLY-RAKER, GUSSETEER, HAIR-MONGER, HEADHUNTER, HIGH PRIEST OF PAPHOS, HOLER, HOOTCHEE, HORSE-MAN, HOT MEMBER, HOT NUTS, HOT PANTS,

JINKER, JUMBLER, KID-STRETCHER, KING OF CLUBS, KNOCKER, LADIES' TAILOR, LEACHER, LEATHER-DRESSER, LEG-LIFTER, LIBERTINE, LOTHARIO, LOVER, LUSTY-GUTS, LUSTY-LAWRENCE, MAKE-OUT ARTIST, MAKER, MEAT HOUND, MEAT-MONGER, MILLER, MINK, MOLL-HUNTER, MOLROWER, MORMON, MOUSE-HUNT, MR. HORNER, MUTTON-COVE, MUTTONER, MUTTON-MONGER, NUGGING-COVE, PARISH-BULL, PARISH-PRIG, PARISH-STALLION, PEACH-ORCHARD BOAR, PELTER, PERFORMER, PHILANDERER, PINCH-BOTTOM, PINCH-BUTTOCK, PINCH-CUNT, POOPSTER, PRIGGER, PUNKER, QUAIL-HUNTER, QUIMSTICKER, RANGER, RATTLE-CAP, RATTLER, RIBALD, RIDER, ROOSTER, ROUNDER, RUMPER, RUMP-SPLITTER, RUTTER, SCORTATOR, SERVANT, SEXPERT, SEXUAL ATHLETE, SHAG, SHARP-SHOOTER, SHIFTER, SKIN-DOG, SKIRT-FOIST, SMELL-SMOCK, SMOCK-SQUIRE, SMOCKSTER, SON OF VENUS, SPORT, SPORTSMAN, SQUIRE OF THE BODY, STALLION, STOAT, STRINGER, STUD, SWINGER, SWIVER, TAD, THRUMSTER, TOMCAT, TOUGH CAT, TOWN BULL, TOWN RAKE, TOWN STALLION, TUG-MUTTON, TUMMY-TICKLER, TWAT-FAKER, TWEAK, TWIGGER, WARM MEMBER, WENCHER, WHISKER-SPLITTER, WHORE-HOPPER, WHORE-HOUND, WHOREMASTER, WOLF, WOMAN-CHASER, WOMANIZER, WOODMAN, YENTZER. **2.** to copulate. For synonyms see OCCUPY. [late 1500s]

leery intoxicated with alcohol. See LEARY. For synonyms see WOOFLED.

left-handed 1. crooked, phony, or counterfeit. **2.** homosexual. [both senses, U.S. colloquial, mid 1900s-pres.]

left-handed wife a concubine; the equivalent of a common-law wife. [mid 1600s-1900s]

left-hand son a male bastard. [U.S. underworld, early 1900s]

left the minority died. A play on JOIN THE GREAT MAJORITY (q.v.). [British, late 1800s, Ware]

leg 1. copulation in expressions such as "get some leg." [U.S. slang, mid 1900s-pres.] **2.** a young woman; women considered sexually. [U.S. colloquial, mid 1900s-pres.] **3.** a promiscuous

woman; a prostitute. A truncation of DIRTY-LEG (q.v.). [U.S. slang, mid 1900s-pres.]

leg-bags trousers. Cf. BAGS (sense 1), HAM-BAGS, RICE-BAGS. For synonyms see GALLIGASKINS. [British colloquial, mid 1800s]

leg-business 1. copulation. **2.** prostitution. [both senses, British, 1800s, Farmer and Henley]

leg-covers trousers. [colloquial since the late 1800s]

leg-lifter a lecher; a male fornicator. Cf. LIFT ONE'S LEG. [British slang, 1700s-1800s]

leg-man a man strongly attracted to women with beautiful legs; a man sexually stimulated by women's legs. From the nickname for a man who does message-carrying and expediting, i.e., "leg-work." Cf. ASS-MAN, TIT-MAN. [U.S. colloquial, mid 1900s-pres.]

lem-kee opium. For synonyms see OPE. [Chinese or mock-Chinese; U.S. underworld, early 1900s or before]

lemon 1. a light-skinned Negro; a mulatto. Not necessarily derogatory. Cf. HIGH-YELLOW. For synonyms see MAHOGANY. [U.S. slang, 1900s] **2.** a dud; any thing or person that malfunctions habitually. [U.S. colloquial, 1900s] **3.** a breast. See LEMONS. **4.** adulterated or counterfeit narcotics. From sense 2. [U.S. drug culture, 1900s]

lemons the human breasts; small breasts. Cf. ORANGES. For synonyms see BOSOM. [U.S. slang, 1900s]

lericompoop 1. a buffoon; an oaf. Cf. LIRRIPOOP. [British colloquial, 1500s-1700s] **2.** to coit. Also **lerripup.** See POOP (sense 2). [British slang, 1800s or before]

les a truncation of LESBIAN (senses 2 and 3). [British and U.S., early 1900s-pres.]

lesbian 1. pliant and accommodating. No negative connotations, but often misunderstood during the 1600s-1700s when the word was used in this sense. [now obsolete] **2.** a woman who is emotionally or sexually and emotionally devoted to members of her own sex; a female homosexual. **3.** pertaining to a female homosexual. [both since the late 1800s]

lesbine lesbian. A deliberate and contrived mispronunciation of "lesbian." [U.S. slang, mid 1900s, Wentworth and Flexner]

lesbo a lesbian. For synonyms see LESBYTERIAN. [Australian and U.S., early 1900s]

Lesbos the Greek island (also called Mytilene) for which lesbianism is named.

lesbyterian a jocular nickname for a lesbian. Based on "Presbyterian." *Cf.* LESBO. [U.S. homosexual use, mid 1900s, Farrell] Synonyms: AMY-JOHN, BLUFF, BOON-DAGGER, BULL, BULL-DAGGER, BULLDIKE, BULLDIKER, BULLDYKE, BULLDYKER, BUTCH, DIESEL DYKE, DIKE, DUFF, DYKE, DYKEY, FAIRY, FAIRY LADY, FEM, FEMME, FLUFF, FLUZZ DYKE, FUTUTRIX, GAL-BOY, JASPER, LADY-LOVER, LES, LESBINE, LESBO, LESLIE, LEZ, LEZO, LOVER UNDER THE LAP, MAN, MARGE, MARY, MASON, MINTIE, NELLY, QUEEN, RUFFLE, SAPPHIC LOVE, SCREAMING QUEEN, SCREWBALL, SERGEANT, SUCKER, THIRD-SEXER, TOOTSIE, TOP SERGEANT, WOLF.

leslie a lesbian. [Australian, early 1900s]

let a fart to release intestinal gas, usually audibly. For synonyms see GURK.

letching-piece a sexually loose woman; a woman considered sexually. For synonyms see LAY. [British slang, 1900s, *Dictionary of Slang and Unconventional English*]

letch-water semen or natural vaginal lubrication, especially as an indication of sexual arousal. [British, 1700s]

let fly 1. to urinate. For synonyms see WHIZ. **2.** to spit. **3.** to break wind. [all senses, U.S. colloquial or slang, 1900s]

let fly a fart to release intestinal gas. [originally "let flee a fart" in "The Miller's Tale" (Chaucer); colloquial since the 1300s]

let go 1. to ejaculate. For synonyms see MELT. [British, 1800s] **2.** to fire; to

terminate the employment of someone. [U.S. colloquial, 1900s or before]

let nature take its course 1. to begin petting and progress all the way to coition. [colloquial, 1900s or before] **2.** to permit sexual attraction to accomplish some appropriate task such as breeding animals or restoring harmony to a marriage. [U.S. euphemism, 1900s or before]

let one to release intestinal gas. The "one" is euphemistic for FART (sense 2). For synonyms see GURK. [U.S. colloquial, mid 1900s-pres.]

letter a condom. A truncation of FRENCH LETTER (*q.v.*). *Cf.* ENVELOPE, POST A LETTER. [British, 1800s]

leukorrhea (also **leucorrhea**) **1.** a regular or occasional whitish or yellowish discharge from the vagina. Sometimes associated with ovulation. *Cf.* WHITES (sense 3). **2.** an increase in normal leukorrhea volume, and changes in consistency, odor, and bacterial content. This is usually indicative of disease in the pelvic region. [colloquial and medical]

Levy and Frank (also **Levy**) to masturbate; an act of masturbation. Rhyming slang for WANK (*q.v.*). For synonyms see WASTE TIME. [British, late 1800s, *Dictionary of Slang and Unconventional English*]

lewd obscene; lascivious. Originally meant "rude." [since the 1300s] Synonyms and related terms: AFTER ONE'S GREENS, ANATOMICAL, APPROACHABLE, BESTIAL, BUCKSOM, CLINICAL, COMING, CRACKISH, DISSOLUTE, EROGENOUS, FAST, FESCENNINE, FILTHY, FOND OF MEAT, FREE-FUCKING, FRENCH, FRUITING, FULL-FLAVORED, GAY, GOATISH, LASCIVIOUS, LENOCINANT, LIBIDINOUS, LICENTIOUS, LIGHT, LIGHT-HEELED, LOOSE, LOOSE IN THE HILT, LOOSE IN THE RUMP, LOOSE-LEGGED, MERRY, PAPHIAN, PERVE, PERVY, PLAYSOME, RADGY, RIBALD, RIG, RIGGISH, RUMP-PROUD, SPICY, SPORTFUL, SPORTIVE, SULTRY, TENTIGINOUS, THICK, TORRID, UNCHASTE, UP-LIFTING, VESTAL, WANTON, WELL-BRED, X-RATED. See also HUMPY.

lewd house a dwelling, not necessarily a brothel, where illicit copulation takes place.

lewd infusion 1. semen. For synonyms see METTLE. [British euphemism, 1800s] **2.** coition; the process of impregnating with semen. [euphemistic, early 1900s]

lewdness 1. prostitution. **2.** fornication. [both senses, euphemistic]

lewdster a lewd and wanton person. [late 1500s-1800s]

lewd woman a sexually loose woman; a prostitute. [U.S. euphemism, 1900s or before]

lez (also **les**) a lesbian. [U.S. slang, mid 1900s-pres.]

lezo a lesbian. Cf. LESBO. [Australian slang, early 1900s]

lib 1. to castrate. [British dialect, 1300s-1700s] **2.** to sleep. No negative connotations. [cant, late 1600s-1800s] **3.** to copulate. For synonyms see OCCUPY. [British, late 1600s and possibly a century earlier]

library any privy or W.C., in reference to the reading one might do while seated there. [U.S. colloquial euphemism, 1900s or before]

lick-box a SODOMITE, presumably a fellator. Cf. BOX (sense 4). [U.S. underworld, early 1900s]

lickerish lewd; lustful; the same as LIQUOROUS (q.v.). Reinforced by "lecherous." [since the 1600s or before]

lickety-split CUNNILINGUS (q.v.). "Split" refers to the PUDENDAL CLEAVAGE (q.v.), a jocular reapplication of the adverb describing speed in running. [U.S. slang, mid 1900s-pres.]

lick-spigot 1. a MOUTH-WHORE (q.v.). The spigot is the penis. [British slang, 1700s] **2.** a drunkard who would lick the spigot of a cask to get the alcohol. [British colloquial, 1800s]

lick-twat a CUNNILINGUIST (q.v.), presumably a male. [mid 1600s]

lick-wimble a heavy drinker; a drunkard who would lick the stopper in a cask (cf. WIMBLE) to get at the alcohol. Cf. LICK-SPIGOT (sense 2).

lid one ounce of marijuana. Cf. O.Z., TIN. [U.S. drug culture, mid 1900s-pres.]

lidpoppers amphetamine tablets or capsules. Refers to eyelids. For synonyms see AMP. [U.S. drug culture, mid 1900s-pres.]

lie down 1. to be brought to bed for childbirth. [euphemistic, late 1500s-1700s] **2.** to smoke opium. Cf. LAY THE HIP (sense 2). For synonyms see SMOKE. [U.S. underworld, early 1900s]

lie with to sleep with; to copulate with. [since the 1300s]

life-preserver the penis. From the name of a flotation device. [British, 1800s, Farmer and Henley]

lift a leg on a woman to copulate with a woman. Cf. LEG-LIFTER. [Scots, late 1700s, (Robert Burns)]

lift his leg (also **heave one's leg, lift one's gam**) to urinate. Referring to the manner in which a male dog urinates. [U.S. euphemism, 1900s or before]

lift one's leg to copulate. Cf. LAY THE LEG, LEG-LIFTER, PLAY AT LIFT-LEG. [British euphemistic colloquial, 1700s]

lift-skirts a prostitute. For synonyms see HARLOT. [British, 1800s]

lift up to get an erection. [colloquial and euphemistic, 1900s and before]

light 1. lewd; wanton. [numerous written attestations since the 1300s] **2.** intoxicated with alcohol. [U.S., early 1700s, Ben Franklin]

light blue gin. Cf. BLUE RUIN. [British, 1800s-1900s]

light-brown a mulatto. Cf. HIGH-BROWN. For synonyms see MAHOGANY. [U.S. colloquial, early 1900s]

light bulb a pregnant woman. Describes a woman's shape in late pregnancy. [U.S. slang, mid 1900s]

light-footed pertaining to a homosexual male. Cf. LIGHT (sense 1), LIGHT ON HIS FEET. [U.S. slang, 1900s]

light frigate a woman of loose morals. "Light" means wanton. Cf. LIGHT (sense 1). [British slang, late 1600s, B.E.]

light-heeled wanton; pertaining to a

sexually loose woman. *Cf.* LIGHT (sense 1), ROUND-HEEL. [since the early 1600s]

light housekeeping the activities of a male and a female living together unmarried. *Cf.* LIGHT (sense 1). [U.S. slang, mid 1900s-pres.]

light housewife a lewd woman; a prostitute. *Cf.* LIGHT (sense 1). [British slang or cant, late 1600s, B.E.]

lightning 1. gin. *Cf.* CLAP OF THUNDER. For synonyms see RUIN. [British slang, 1700s-1800s] **2.** inferior whisky. *Cf.* WHITE LIGHTNING. [British and U.S., late 1700s-pres.] **3.** amphetamines. For synonyms see AMP. [U.S. drug culture, mid 1900s-pres.]

light o' love 1. a wanton woman. *Cf.* LIGHT (sense 1). [late 1500s] **2.** a harmless term of endearment for a girlfriend. [colloquial, 1900s or before]

light on his feet pertaining to an effeminate male. *Cf.* LIGHT (sense 1), LIGHT-FOOTED, possibly referring to a male dancer. [U.S. slang, mid 1900s-pres.]

lights a fool; an oaf. [British colloquial, mid 1800s]

light skirts a wanton woman. Named for the ease with which her skirts come up. [colloquial, late 1500s]

lights out death. [U.S. underworld, early 1900s]

light the lamp to have sexual intercourse, said of a woman. *Cf.* LAMP OF LOVE. [British euphemism, 1800s]

light troops lice. For synonyms see WALKING DANDRUFF. [British slang, early 1800s]

light up have an orgasm. [British euphemism, mid 1900s]

light wet gin. For synonyms see RUIN. [British slang, early 1800s]

light woman a lewd woman. *Cf.* LIGHT FRIGATE. For synonyms see LAY. [cant or colloquial, late 1600s, B.E.]

like to be fond of someone; to feel the beginnings of love for someone. Occasionally euphemistic for "to desire sexually." [since the 1500s or before]

like a bat out of hell extremely fast. [U.S. colloquial, early 1900s-pres.]

Like fuck! an exclamation; a disbelieving reply. [British and U.S., 1900s]

Like fun! a disguise of LIKE FUCK! (*q.v.*). [U.S. colloquial, mid 1900s-pres.]

Like hell! a disbelieving reply or exclamation, "The hell you say!" [U.S. colloquial, 1900s]

likkered-up intoxicated with alcohol. See LIQUORED-UP.

lilly a Seconal (trademark) tablet. From the manufacturer's name, "Eli Lilly and Company." *Cf.* ABBOT (sense 2). For synonyms see SEC. [U.S. drug culture, mid 1900s-pres.]

lily an effeminate male or a homosexual male. See PANSY. [U.S. slang, mid 1900s-pres.]

lily-liver a coward. For synonyms see YELLOW-DOG. [since the early 1600s]

lilywhite 1. a Negro. For synonyms see EBONY. [British slang, 1600s-1800s] **2.** a chimney sweep. [British slang, late 1600s] **3.** a derogatory term for a Caucasian (used by a Negro); a WASP (*q.v.*). [U.S. colloquial, 1900s or before] **4.** a CATAMITE (*q.v.*). *Cf.* LILY. For synonyms see BRONCO. [British slang, 1800s]

limb a leg. A term of avoidance for the word "leg," whether human or of furniture. [British and U.S., early 1700s-1800s]

limber intoxicated with alcohol. For synonyms see WOOFLED. [U.S., early 1700s, Ben Franklin]

limbo 1. the female genitals. [British slang, 1800s, Farmer and Henley] **2.** a prison; a place or period of confinement. [since the 1500s] **3.** a region at the border of hell for those damned only technically. [from Latin *limbus*, "border"; since the 1300s; U.S. colloquial, 1900s or before] **4.** Colombian marijuana. See LUMBO.

limb-shrouders trousers. *Cf.* LIMB. For synonyms see GALLIGASKINS. [late 1800s]

limburger a derogatory term for a German. From the name of a strong cheese. [slang, World War II, Berrey and Van den Bark]

lime (also **line**) to impregnate a bitch (dog). Cf. LINE. [mid 1500s and obsolete]

limejuicer a jocular and mildly derogatory nickname for a British sailor. [Australian and U.S. since the late 1800s]

limey a truncation of LIMEJUICER (q.v.). [colloquial, 1900s or before]

limit, the coition. Can also refer to any or all sexual activity except coition. Cf. ALL THE WAY. [U.S. colloquial, 1900s]

limp intoxicated with alcohol. Cf. LIMBER. [U.S. colloquial, 1900s]

limp-wrist an effeminate male or a homosexual male; the same as BROKEN-WRIST (q.v.). [U.S. slang, mid 1900s-pres.]

line 1. to copulate, said of dogs. [since the 1300s] **2.** to impregnate a bitch (dog), said of a male dog. Possibly cognate with "loin." [since the 1300s] **3.** to copulate, said of humans. From sense 2. [1600s] **4.** a young girl or woman. [Australian, mid 1900s] **5.** a dose of powdered cocaine "lined up" on a mirror, ready to be sniffed or snorted. [U.S. drug culture, mid 1900s-pres.]

lined intoxicated with alcohol; lined with a coating of alcohol. [U.S. slang, early 1900s]

linen underwear. For synonyms see NETHER GARMENTS. [since the 1800s or before]

lingerie women's underwear. [French; U.S., 1900s]

ling-grappling 1. groping or feeling a woman. **2.** copulating with a woman. [both senses, British slang, 1800s, Farmer and Henley]

linguist a CUNNILINGUIST (q.v.). [slang, mid 1900s-pres.]

lion drunk intoxicated with alcohol. Cf. ROARING-DRUNK. [slang, late 1500s]

lioness a harlot; a prostitute. For synonyms see HARLOT. [slang, late 1500s]

lip 1. to kiss intimately. Cf. MOUTH (sense 1). [from Othello (Shakespeare)] **2.** a lawyer. [U.S. slang, early 1900s]

lip-clap 1. a kiss. **2.** to kiss. Cf. LAP-CLAP. [both senses, late 1500s]

Lipton's a poor grade of marijuana. From "Lipton's Tea" (trademark). [U.S. drug culture, mid 1900s]

liquefied intoxicated with alcohol. For synonyms see WOOFLED. [U.S. slang, early 1900s-pres.]

liquidate to kill. [U.S. slang, 1900s]

liquid-fire bad whisky. For synonyms see EMBALMING FLUID. [colloquial, late 1800s-pres.]

liquor 1. any fluid. No negative connotations. [1200s] **2.** alcoholic drink. For synonyms see BOOZE. [since c. 1300, Oxford English Dictionary] **3.** to drink liquor, especially to drink to excess. For synonyms see PLAY CAMELS. [since the early 1800s]

liquor, in intoxicated with alcohol. Cf. DRINK, IN. [since the early 1700s]

liquored-up (also **likkered-up, liquored**) intoxicated with alcohol. [since the mid 1600s]

liquorish intoxicated with alcohol. For synonyms see WOOFLED. [U.S. slang, 1900s]

liquor one's boots 1. to CUCKOLD (q.v.) someone. [British, early 1700s] **2.** to drink a lot before a journey. [British slang, late 1700s, Grose]

liquorous (also **lykerous**) lecherous; lustful; the same as LICKERISH (q.v.). [mid 1600s-1800s]

liquor plug a drunkard. For synonyms see ALCHY. [U.S. slang, early 1900s, Montelone]

lirripoop a silly oaf; a silly, pedantic person. Cf. LERICOMPOOP. [British, early 1600s]

lisper an effeminate male. Cf. LITHPER. For synonyms see FRIBBLE. [U.S. slang, 1900s]

lists of love copulation. Refers to jousting. [from the expression "in the very lists of love" in Venus and Adonis (Shakespeare)]

Lit a derogatory nickname for a Lithuanian. Also the abbreviation of "Litas," a former monetary unit of Lithuania. Cf. LITVAK. [U.S. slang, 1900s]

lit 1. intoxicated with alcohol. [U.S. colloquial, 1900s] **2.** intoxicated with marijuana or other drugs. *Cf.* LIT TO THE GUARDS, LIT-UP. [U.S. slang and drug culture, early 1900s-pres.]

lithper an effeminate male, possibly a homosexual. A lisping pronunciation of LISPER (*q.v.*). [U.S. slang, 1900s]

little bit copulation. For synonyms see SMOCKAGE. [U.S. colloquial, mid 1900s-pres.]

little bit of keg copulation. [British slang, 1800s]

little boy's room the men's W.C. *Cf.* LITTLE GIRL'S ROOM. [U.S., early 1900s-pres.]

little brother the penis. *Cf.* LITTLE SISTER. [British euphemism, 1800s]

little brown men Japanese military personnel. [Australian wartime, Baker]

Little Davy the penis; a personification of the penis. [British, 1800s, Farmer and Henley]

little finger the penis. *Cf.* FOREFINGER, MIDDLE FINGER, POTATO FINGER, THUMB OF LOVE. [originally Biblical (I Kings); since the 1600s]

little friend the menses. For synonyms see FLOODS. [British euphemism, early 1900s-pres.]

little girl's room a women's W.C. *Cf.* LITTLE BOY'S ROOM. [U.S. colloquial, early 1900s-pres.]

little house (also **littlest house**) a privy; an outhouse. *Cf.* PETTY-HOUSE, SMALLEST ROOM. For synonyms see AJAX. [widespread colloquial, early 1700s-pres.]

little lady a CATEMITE, a RECEIVER (both *q.v.*). For synonyms see BRONCO. [U.S. underworld, early 1900s]

little man in the boat 1. the clitoris. *Cf.* BOY-IN-THE-BOAT. [British and U.S., 1800s-1900s] **2.** the naval. [British, 1800s-1900s, *Dictionary of Slang and Unconventional English*]

little Mary 1. the female genitals, especially the vagina. [U.S. slang, 1900s] **2.** the stomach. [euphemism, early 1900s, (J.M. Barrie)]

little sister the female genitals. *Cf.* LITTLE BROTHER. [British euphemism, 1800s]

little sister is here a catch phrase indicating that the menses have begun. [euphemistic, 1900s or before]

little visitor the menses. For synonyms see FLOODS. [colloquial, 1900s and before]

little Willie the penis; a personification of the penis. [British, 1900s]

little yellow bastards (also **little yellow men**) a derogatory term for the Japanese; Orientals in general. [military slang, World War II]

lit to the guards (also **lit to the gills**) intoxicated with alcohol. *Cf.* LIT. [U.S. slang, early 1900s-pres.]

lit-up (also **lit**) **1.** intoxicated with alcohol, especially in expressions such as "lit up like a Christmas tree." [U.S. colloquial, early 1900s-pres.] **2.** drug intoxicated; intoxicated with marijuana. [U.S. drug culture, mid 1900s-pres.]

Litvak (also **Litvac**) a Lithuanian or a Lithuanian Jew. Not necessarily derogatory. *Cf.* LIT. [U.S. slang, 1900s]

live rabbit the penis, especially the erect penis. [British slang, 1800s, Farmer and Henley]

live sausage the penis. *Cf.* LIVE RABBIT. [mid 1600s, (Urquhart)]

livestock prostitutes. [U.S. underworld, early 1900s]

living fountain the female genitals. For synonyms see MONOSYLLABLE. [British euphemism, mid 1600s]

Liza a nickname for a young black woman. Derogatory when used as a generic term. [U.S., 1900s and before]

lizard the penis. *Cf.* STROKE THE LIZARD. [U.S. slang, mid 1900s-pres.]

lizzie a lesbian. For synonyms see LESBYTERIAN. [slang, 1900s]

Lizzie boy (also **Lizzie**) an effeminate male. *Cf.* NAN-BOY. For synonyms see FRIBBLE. [U.S.,1900s]

load 1. semen. For synonyms see METTLE. [late 1500s-pres]. **2.** the weight of a man's body during copulation. **3.** a venereal disease. [slang and euphemistic, 1800s] **4.** sufficient alcohol in the bloodstream to produce intoxication. *Cf.* HAVE A LOAD ON, JAG. [colloquial or slang since the mid 1700s] **5.** the feces; the fullness of feces in the bowels. *Cf.* DROP ONE'S LOAD (sense 2). For synonyms see DUNG.

loaded 1. intoxicated with alcohol. [U.S. and British colloquial, 1800s-pres.] **2.** drug-intoxicated with marijuana or heroin. [U.S. underworld, colloquial and drug culture, early 1900s-pres.] **3.** pregnant. *Cf.* LOAD (sense 1). [colloquial, 1800s-1900s]

loaded for bear 1. intoxicated with alcohol. [U.S. colloquial, 1800s-1900s] **2.** very angry. [U.S. colloquial, 1900s]

loaded to the gills (also **loaded to the barrel, loaded to the guards**) intoxicated with alcohol. [U.S. colloquial, 1900s]

loaded to the gunwales (also **loaded to the gunnels**) intoxicated with alcohol. [U.S. nautical, late 1800s]

loaded to the plimsoll mark intoxicated with alcohol; holding as much as possible. The plimsoll mark or line indicates the limit of legal submergence of a British merchant vessel. From the proper name "Samuel Plimsoll." [colloquial, 1900s]

load of coal a derogatory term for a group of Negroes. [U.S. slang, 1900s]

lob 1. a clumsy fellow; an unwieldy, lumpish oaf. [since the early 1500s] **2.** a partial erection of the penis. [British colloquial, 1700s] **3.** a W.C., usually "the lob." Possibly from "lobby" or from "lob," a cant term for a cash box. See MAKE A DEPOSIT. [British slang, 1900s, *Dictionary of Slang and Unconventional English*] **4.** the penis, especially the erect penis. Originated independently of sense 2. [U.S. slang, mid 1900s-pres.]

lobberheaded stupid. *Cf.* LOB (sense 1). [U.S. colloquial, 1900s or before]

lobbus (also **loppus**) a LUMMOX (*q.v.*); an oaf. [1900s or before]

lobby-gow an opium smoker and ad-

dict. *Cf.* GOW. [U.S. underworld, early 1900s]

lob-cock (also **lob**) **1.** a dull oaf; a stupid LUMP (*q.v.*). *Cf.* LOB (sense 1). [colloquial or cant, mid 1500s] **2.** a large, flaccid or semierect penis; the same as LOB (sense 2). *Cf.* LOB-PRICK. From COCK (sense 3). [British colloquial, 1700s, Grose] **3.** a large woodpecker. From COCK (sense 1), no negative connotations. [U.S. colloquial, 1800s]

lob in to insert the penis. [British colloquial, 1900s]

loblolly (also **loplolly**) a fool; an oaf. *Cf.* LOB (sense 1), LOBBUS. For synonyms see OAF. [British colloquial, early 1600s]

lobo an ugly young woman. From the scientific name for the timber wolf, *Canis lupus*. For synonyms see BUFFARILLA. [U.S., 1900s]

lob-prick a partial erection or an insufficient erection. *Cf.* LOB-COCK (sense 2). [British, late 1800s, (Farmer)]

lobscouse an oaf. Originally the name of a type of nautical stew and the nickname for a person who ate it. [since the early 1700s]

Lob's Pound 1. a prison; a place or period of confinement. *Cf.* LOB-COCK (sense 1). [late 1500s] **2.** the female genitals, especially the vagina, considered as a "prison" for a LOB-COCK (sense 2). [British slang, early 1600s]

lobster 1. an oaf. *Cf.* LOB-COCK (sense 1). [U.S. slang, 1900s] **2.** the penis. An elaboration of "lob." *Cf.* LOB (sense 2). [British, Farmer and Henley] **3.** a soldier or policeman; any man wearing a red uniform. [slang, mid 1600s-1800s]

lobster-pot the female genitals, specifically the vagina, viewed as a receiver for the LOBSTER (sense 2). [British slang, 1800s, Farmer and Henley]

lobster tails 1. lice. **2.** venereal disease. [both senses, U.S. slang, 1900s]

lock the female genitals. The counterpart of KEY (sense 1), "penis." [1600s-1700s]

locker the female genitals; the vagina. [slang, 1900s or before]

locker-room butyl nitrate sold as a room deodorant stick, the vapors of which are inhaled producing the same effect as amyl nitrite. The term is also used for other drugs. [U.S. drug culture, mid 1900s-pres.]

locoweed marijuana or a marijuana cigarette. From the common name of a plant which grows in the Southwest U.S. grazing lands and is said to drive cattle mad or "loco." *Cf.* GO LOCO. [U.S. slang, early 1900s-pres.]

locus a W.C. *Cf.* PLACE (sense 1). [from the Latin word for "place"; U.S. slang, 1900s]

Lod-a-massy! an imprecation, "Lord have mercy!" or "Lord of mercy." [U.S. colloquial, 1900s and before]

log 1. an opium pipe. [U.S. underworld, early 1900s] **2.** the erect penis. *Cf.* POLE (sense 1), RAIL. For synonyms see ERECTION. [widespread jocular nonce]

logged intoxicated with alcohol; the same as WATER-LOGGED (*q.v.*). [colloquial, 1900s]

loggerhead an oaf; a blockhead; a person with an overly large head. Also the colloquial name of a species of snapping turtle. [British, late 1500s-1800s]

loin 1. the region of the body extending from the pelvis to the false ribs. Usually in reference to cuts of meat. No negative connotations. **2.** the poetic "seat of generative power"; the genitals. Occasionally confused with "groin" as an anatomical location. [since the early 1500s]

loins the "seat of generative power"; the male or female genitals. See LOIN (sense 2). [since the 1500s]

lollos well-proportioned breasts. From the proper name "Gina Lollobrigida" or from "lollopalooza." *Cf.* LULUS (*q.v.*). [British slang, mid 1900s]

lollypop (also **lollipop**) the penis. *Cf.* LADIES' LOLLIPOP. For synonyms see YARD. [British slang, 1800s, Farmer and Henley]

London milk gin. *Cf.* GOLDEN CREAM.

For synonyms see RUIN. [British slang, late 1800s, Barrère and Leland]

long-arm inspection an inspection of the erect penis. Based on SHORT-ARM INSPECTION (*q.v.*). [U.S., 1900s]

long-eye the female genitals. From the configuration of the PUDENDAL CLEAVAGE (*q.v.*). *Cf.* BLIND-EYE (sense 2), SQUINT. [British slang, mid 1800s]

long John the penis. *Cf.* JOHNSON, JOHN THOMAS. [U.S. slang, 1900s]

long knife a Caucasian from the point of view of a Negro. [U.S. slang, 1900s]

long Tom the penis. *Cf.* LONG JOHN, MISTER TOM. [British colloquial, late 1800s]

loo a W.C. There are a number of suggested etymologies. Possibly from French *l'eau*, "water"; possibly from GARDY LOO! (*q.v.*); possibly from the numeral "100." The *Lexicon Balatronicum* has an entry "loo," which is "For the good of the loo; for the benefit of the company or community." The word is most likely from "lieu," the "place." *Cf.* LOCUS, PLACE (sense 1). [British colloquial, early 1900s-pres.; recently a part of U.S. vocabulary]

looking piggy pregnant. For synonyms see FRAGRANT. [U.S. dialect (Ozarks), Randolph and Wilson]

look pricks to OGLE (*q.v.*) and appear to be inviting coition; to make a sexual proposition with the eyes. [British slang, 1800s, Farmer and Henley]

loop 1. a fool; an oaf. [Australian, early 1900s, Baker] **2.** an I.U.C.D. (*q.v.*). [U.S., mid 1900s-pres.]

loo paper toilet paper. For synonyms see T.P. [British colloquial, 1900s]

loop-de-loop mutual oral-genital copulation. *Cf.* FLIP-FLOP, SIXTY-NINE. [U.S. slang, mid 1900s]

looped intoxicated with alcohol. From the expression "thrown for a loop." [U.S. slang, early 1900s-pres.]

loop-legged intoxicated with alcohol. For synonyms see WOOFLED. [U.S. slang, 1900s]

loose 1. wanton; lewd; sexually loose and legally unattached. *Cf.* LIGHT (sense 1). [since the late 1400s] **2.** pertaining to laxness in the bowels. See LAX. [since the early 1500s]

loose-bodied gown a prostitute. A harlot. *Cf.* LIGHT SKIRTS. [early 1600s]

loose-coat game copulation. See LOOSE-BODIED GOWN. [mid 1600s, (Urquhart)]

loose-ended 1. wanton, said of women. Also **loose-bodied.** [late 1600s] **2.** LAX (*q.v.*) in the bowels; having diarrhea. [colloquial, 1800s or before]

loose fish a prostitute; better known as an expression for a common ne'er-do-well. *Cf.* FISH (sense 2). [British slang, early 1800s, Farmer and Henley]

loose in the hilt (also **loose in the haft**) **1.** intoxicated with alcohol. [U.S. slang, early 1700s, Ben Franklin] **2.** wanton. [British slang, 1800s, Farmer and Henley] **3.** having diarrhea. [British, 1800s, Farmer and Henley]

loose in the rump wanton, said of woman. *Cf.* LOOSE-ENDED (sense 1). [British, 1800s]

loose-kirtle a wanton woman; a prostitute. A "kirtle" is a woman's gown. *Cf.* LIGHT SKIRTS, LOOSE-BODIED GOWN. [British slang, 1800s or before]

loose-legged wanton; sexually promiscuous. For synonyms see LEWD. [late 1500s]

loose-love center a brothel. [U.S. slang, 1900s]

loose-love lady a prostitute. [U.S. slang, early 1900s]

loose woman a sexually indiscreet female. *Cf.* LOOSE (sense 1). [U.S. colloquial, 1900s]

lop-lollard (also **loplolly**) a lazy fellow. See LOBLOLLY. [British dialect, 1800s, Holland]

Lord love a duck! a mock oath and an exclamation. [colloquial, 1900s]

Lord of heaven!, By the an oath and an exclamation. For synonyms see 'ZOUNDS! [colloquial, 1900s and before]

Lord sakes alive! an oath and an exclamation. [since the mid 1800s]

Lordy me! (also **Lordy!**) a mild oath or exclamation. [colloquial, 1800s-pres.]

lorg a stupid person; an oaf. [U.S. slang, early 1900s]

Lorgamighty! "Lord God Almighty!" [U.S. colloquial, 1900s]

Lors! a mild oath or exclamation. "Lord!" [since the mid 1800s]

lose to menstruate; to "lose" the menstrual flux. [U.S. colloquial, 1900s or before]

lose a meal to vomit. For synonyms see YORK. [Australian euphemism, early 1900s, Baker]

lose one's cookies to vomit. [U.S. slang, mid 1900s-pres.]

lost lady a prostitute. For synonyms see HARLOT. [U.S. colloquial, 1900s]

lost the key a catch phrase uttered upon smelling a fecal odor or intestinal gas. A truncation of "lost the key to the restroom." [U.S. slang or colloquial, 1900s]

lot the male genitals, in expressions such as "my lot" and "his lot." *Cf.* GEAR, KIT. [British, 1800s]

louse a thoroughly disliked male. [U.S. colloquial, 1900s] See also WALKING DANDRUFF.

louse-bag a contemptuous term for a disliked male. As if he were infested with lice. *Cf.* DOUCHE BAG. [British slang, 1900s or before]

love 1. sex; copulation. **2.** to copulate with. [both senses, euphemistic, since the 1500s or before]

love-apples the testicles. From the colloquial term for an eggplant or a tomato. *Cf.* APPLES (sense 2). [British, 1800s, Farmer and Henley]

love-begotten child a bastard. For synonyms see ACCIDENT. [colloquial euphemism, 1800s]

love-brat a bastard. [British slang, 1800s]

love-bubbles the breasts, especially well-formed breasts. *Cf.* BUBBLES. For synonyms see BOSOM. [British, 1900s,

Dictionary of Slang and Unconventional English]

love chamber the vagina. For synonyms see PASSAGE. [written nonce; U.S. slang, mid 1900s-pres.]

love-child a bastard. [colloquial euphemism, early 1800s]

love-dart (also **dart of love**) the penis. *Cf.* DARD. [British euphemism, 1800s, Farmer and Henley]

love for sale prostitution. [U.S., 1900s]

love-handles fat on the sides of a man or woman held onto during copulation. [U.S. slang, mid 1900s-pres.]

love-juice semen; male or female sexual secretions. [euphemistic nonce, 1800s-pres.]

love-lane the female genitals. For synonyms see MONOSYLLABLE. [British, 1800s, Farmer and Henley]

love-life sexual activity; the quality of one's sexual activity; one's SEX LIFE (*q.v.*). [euphemistic, 1900s]

love-liquor semen. For synonyms see METTLE. [British euphemism, 1800s, Farmer and Henley]

love magic a love charm; an aphrodisiac.

love-nuts pain in the testicles due to sexual excitement. *Cf.* HOT ROCKS (sense 2), STONE-ACHE. [U.S. slang, 1900s]

love object the libidinal object; the object (or its substitute) which is the intended object of one's love.

love of Mike!, For the (also **love of Pete!, For the**) an oath and an exclamation. Refers to St. Michael (or St. Peter). [U.S. colloquial, 1900s]

love of mud!, For the a mock oath and an exclamation. [U.S. colloquial, 1900s]

love-pad the mons veneris; the vagina. [U.S. slang, 1900s]

love-peddler a prostitute. *Cf.* ASS-PEDDLER, FLESH-PEDDLER. [U.S., early 1900s]

love-pot a drunkard who loves pots of drink. [British, 1800s or before]

lover **1.** a regular and exclusive sexual lover, heterosexual or homosexual. [since

the 1500s or before] **2.** a man found guilty of sexual offenses against a woman. [U.S. underworld slang, early 1900s, Goldin, O'Leary, and Lipsius]

lover's nuts pain in the testicles due to sexual excitement; the same as LOVE-NUTS (*q.v.*).

lover under the lap a lesbian. For synonyms see LESBYTERIAN. [Australian, 1900s]

love tips the breasts; the nipples. [U.S. slang, mid 1900s-pres.]

love up to fondle and arouse sexually. *Cf.* RUB UP. For synonyms see FIRKY-TOODLE. [colloquial, mid 1900s]

love weed marijuana. From its alleged aphrodisiac qualities. See JOHNSON GRASS. [U.S. drug culture, mid 1900s-pres.]

low-countries the female genitals. *Cf.* LAPLAND, LOWLANDS. [British, 1700s]

low-downer a poor Caucasian. *Cf.* POOR WHITE TRASH. [U.S. colloquial, 1900s]

lower regions hell. [British and U.S. euphemism, late 1800s-pres.]

lower-wig the female pubic hair. *Cf.* LADY'S LOW TOUPEE, MERKIN (sense 2). For synonyms see DOWNSHIRE. [British slang, 1800s, Farmer and Henley]

lowlands the female genitals. *Cf.* LOW-COUNTRIES, NETHERLANDS. [British euphemism, 1700s]

low rent an easy girl; a sexually loose woman. [U.S. slang, 1900s, *Current Slang*]

L.S.D. **1.** "lysergic acid diethylamide," a hallucinogenic drug. Not sold as an ethical drug. For synonyms see ACID. [U.S. drug culture, mid 1900s-pres.] **2.** an abbreviation of "Lake Shore Drive" in Chicago, Illinois. From sense 1. No negative connotations. [U.S., mid 1900s-pres.] **3.** the standard abbreviation of "pounds, shillings, and pence." No negative connotations. **4.** "long, skinny Davy," a nickname for a lanky boy. No negative connotations. [senses 3 and 4 are British, late 1800s-early 1900s]

lubber (also **lubber-head, lubby**) a hulking oaf. [British, 1300s-1800s]

lube alcohol, especially beer. From "lubricant." [Australian, mid 1900s, Baker]

lubie a lubricated condom. For synonyms see EEL-SKIN. [U.S. slang, mid 1900s-pres.]

lubricate 1. to copulate. From the male point of view. [British, 1700s] **2.** to drink liquor to excess. For synonyms see PLAY CAMELS. [British and U.S., late 1800s-pres.]

lubricated intoxicated with alcohol. [U.S. slang and colloquial, 1900s]

lucky-bag the female genitals, specifically the vagina. From the colloquial term for a grab-bag. *Cf.* BAG (sense 5). [British slang, 1800s]

Lucy the penis. *Cf.* DUCY. [U.S. dialect, 1900s or before] See also SWEET LUCY.

Lucy in the sky with diamonds a code name for the drug L.S.D. (*q.v.*). Initials of the name of a rock song. *Cf.* SWEET LUCY. [U.S. drug culture, mid 1900s-pres.]

Lud! an exclamation, "Lord!" [since the early 1700s] See also LUDS.

lude methaqualone, usually Quaalude (trademark), a tranquilizer. [U.S. drug culture, mid 1900s-pres.]

luggage the male genitals, the VIRILIA (*q.v.*). *Cf.* BASKET (sense 3). [British colloquial, 1800s, Farmer and Henley]

lug-loaf an oaf; a blockhead. [British, early 1600s]

lug-pot a drunkard. Rhyming slang for "sot." For synonyms see ALCHY. [British colloquial, 1800s]

lulu 1. a serious or fresh case of gonorrhea. [U.S. underworld, early 1900s, Goldin, O'Leary, and Lipsius] **2.** a W.C. From LOO (*q.v.*). [British, early 1900s, *Dictionary of Slang and Unconventional English*] **3.** a breast. See LULUS.

lulus 1. the human breasts. See LOLLOS. **2.** two or more of anything good. No negative connotations. [both senses, U.S. slang, 1900s]

lumber stems and other hard chunks found in marijuana. [U.S. drug culture, mid 1900s-pres.]

lumbo (also **limbo**) Colombian marijuana. *Cf.* COLUMBIAN RED. For synonyms see MARI. [U.S. drug culture, mid 1900s-pres.]

lummox (also **lommix, lummux**) a heavy, awkward oaf. *Cf.* DUMB OX [British and U.S., 1800s-pres.]

lump an oaf; a stupid clod of a man. *Cf.* LOB (sense 1). [since the late 1500s]

lumpus an oaf. For synonyms see OAF. [U.S. colloquial, 1900s]

lumpy 1. intoxicated with alcohol. **2.** pregnant. For synonyms see FRAGRANT. [both colloquial since the 1800s]

lung-disturber the penis; the erect penis. [British, 1800s]

lungs the breasts. *Cf.* TONSILS. For synonyms see BOSOM. [U.S. jocular euphemism, 1900s]

lunker (also **lunk**) an oaf. [U.S. colloquial, 1900s]

lunkhead an oaf. For synonyms see OAF. [U.S. colloquial, late 1800s-pres.]

lurkies diarrhea. For synonyms see QUICK-STEP. [U.S. colloquial, 1900s]

lurn the scrotum. [possibly Scots dialect; British use, 1900s]

lush 1. beer or other drink. [British and U.S. since the late 1700s] **2.** a drunkard. [slang and colloquial since the 1800s] **3.** to drink frequently or heavily. For synonyms see PLAY CAMELS. [U.S. slang, 1900s]

lushed-up (also **lushed**) **1.** intoxicated with alcohol. For synonyms see WOOFLED. [U.S. colloquial, 1900s or before] **2.** intoxicated with narcotics. From sense 1. For synonyms see TALL. [U.S. drug culture, mid 1900s-pres.]

lusher 1. a prostitute. [U.S. underworld, early 1900s] **2.** a drunkard who "tanks up" quickly. [slang, 1900s]

lushing man a drunkard. [British, 1800s]

lushington a drunkard. [British slang, 1800s or before]

lush merchant a drunkard. [Australian, 1800s]

lushy (also **lushey, lushie**) **1.** intoxicated with alcohol. **2.** a drunkard. [both senses, British and U.S., 1800s-1900s]

lust strong sexual cravings. [since c. 1000, *Oxford English Dictionary*] Synonyms and related terms: AMATIVENESS, ARD, ARDOR, ARDOUR, BONE-ON, B.U., BURN, CARNALITY, CONCUPISCENCE, DESIRES OF THE FLESH, GOONA-GOONA, HORNINESS, HOT PANTS, ITCH, NASTIES, NATURE, PRIDE, THE HOTS, THE OLD ADAM. See also HUMPY.

lusty 1. pregnant. [U.S. dialect, 1800s] **2.** full-bodied, as in "lusty baby boy." No negative connotations. [since the 1700s]

lusty-guts a notorious copulator; a good wencher. For synonyms see LECHER. [slang, late 1500s]

lusty-Lawrence a lecher; a whoremonger; a LUSTY-GUTS (*q.v.*). [British, early 1600s]

M

M. 1. "morphine." For synonyms see MORPH. [U.S. underworld, early 1900s-pres.] **2.** "marijuana." [both senses, U.S. drug culture, mid 1900s-pres.]

mac a pimp. A truncation of MACKEREL (sense 1). [British and U.S. underworld, late 1800s-pres.]

macaroni 1. an affected fop; a dandy. [British, 1700s] **2.** nonsense. [Australian, 1900s, Baker] **3.** a derogatory nickname for an Italian soldier. [British slang, 1900s] **4.** a ladies' man; a PONCE (q.v.) or a pimp. Cf. MAC. [U.S. slang, mid 1900s-pres.]

macaroon an oaf; a buffoon; a fop. Possibly rhyming slang for "buffoon." [British, early 1600s]

MacGimp a pimp; a PONCE (q.v.). Rhyming slang for "pimp." Cf. McGIMPER. [U.S. slang, early 1900s]

mach marijuana. [U.S. drug culture, mid 1900s-pres.]

machine 1. the penis. Cf. FORNICATING-ENGINE. For synonyms see YARD. **2.** the female genitals. For synonyms see MONOSYLLABLE. **3.** a condom. For synonyms see EEL-SKIN. [all senses, British slang, 1800s]

mack (also **mac**) **1.** a pimp; a PONCE (q.v.). A truncation of MACKEREL (sense 1). [British and U.S., late 1800s-early 1900s] **2.** an Irishman. Derogatory. For synonyms see HARP. [1500s]

mackerel (also **mac, mack**) **1.** a pimp; a PONCE (q.v.). See MACGIMP. **2.** a BAWD (q.v.). [both since the early 1400s]

mackerel-snapper a derogatory nickname for a Roman Catholic. Cf. FISH-EATER. [U.S. slang, 1900s, Wentworth and Flexner]

macking pimping for a living. Cf. MACKEREL. [U.S. slang, mid 1900s-pres.]

mack man a pimp; the same as MACKEREL (sense 1). [U.S. slang, mid 1900s-pres.]

madam 1. a kept woman; a mistress or a concubine. [British, early 1600s]

2. a wench; a hussy. [British, early 1700s] **3.** the female keeper of a brothel. Cf. ABBESS. [since the 1700s] Synonyms: ABBESS, AUNT, BAWD, CASE-KEEPER, COVENT GARDEN ABBESS, FLESH-BROKER, HOUSEKEEPER, HOUSE-MOTHER, LADY ABBESS, MOTHER, PROVINCIAL, TENDERLOIN MADAM.

madamoizook a sexually loose French girl. Cf. ZOOK. [U.S. slang, World War I]

Madam Van (also **Madam Ran**) a prostitute. [B.E. has "Van" and Grose has "Ran," probably in error; cant, 1600s]

maddikin the female genitals. For synonyms see MONOSYLLABLE. [British, 1800s]

madge 1. the female genitals. A truncation of Magdalene. [from a Scots word for "woman"; British, late 1700s, Grose] **2.** a prostitute. [U.S. dialect (Boontling), late 1800s-early 1900s, Charles Adams]

Mae West the bosom; a breast. Rhyming slang for "breast." [1900s]

mag a magazine. See FAG-MAG, STAG-MAG. Cf. B. AND B., NUDIE, SKIN-MAG, STAG-MAG.

Maggie Moores underpants. Rhyming slang for "drawers." [Australian, early 1900s, Baker]

maggoty intoxicated with alcohol. From an old term meaning "bad-tempered" or "whimsical." [colloquial, 1900s or before]

magic mushroom a species of mushroom containing the hallucinogenic agent psilocybin. [U.S. drug culture, mid 1900s-pres.]

magic wand the penis, especially the erect penis. Cf. TWANGER, WAND. [colloquial and nonce, 1900s or before]

magnet the female genitals, that which draws the male. Possibly a play on "magnetic pole." [British, 1700s]

magpie's nest the female genitals.

Cf. GOLDFINCH'S NEST. [British, early 1700s]

mahogany a mulatto. [U.S., early 1900s] Synonyms: BEIGE, BIRD'S-EYE MAPLE, BLACK AND TAN, BLACKED EBONY, BLEACHED EBONY, BRIGHT MULATTO, BROWN, BROWN GIRL, BROWN MAN, BROWN POLISH, BROWN-SKIN, CAFÉ AU LAIT, CASTE, GRIFANE, GRIFFE, GRIFFIN, GRIFFO, GRIFFONE, GRIFIN, GRIFON, HIGH-BROWN, HIGH-YELLOW, LEMON, LIGHT-BROWN, MUSTARD-YELLOW, PINKY, SEPE, SEPIA, SEPIAN, TAN, TAWNYMOOR, YELLER, YELLOW, YELLOW-BLACK, YELLOW GIRL, YOLA.

mahoska narcotics. *Cf.* MOHASKY, MOSHKY. [U.S. underworld, mid 1900s]

maiden 1. a young woman. Sometimes euphemistic for "virgin." **2.** a nickname for the Scottish guillotine. [early 1500s] **3.** a truncation of iron maiden.

maiden gear 1. virginity. **2.** the hymen. For synonyms see BEAN. [both senses, British, early 1700s]

maidenhead 1. virginity. **2.** the hymen. [both since the 1300s] **3.** newness. [1500s; impolite by the 1600s]

maim to castrate. *Cf.* CUT (sense 1). [euphemistic]

main to inject narcotics directly into a vein; to MAINLINE (*q.v.*). [U.S. drug culture, 1900s]

main avenue the female genitals, specifically the vagina. [British slang, 1800s, Farmer and Henley]

mainline (also **main**) to inject narcotics directly into a vein. [U.S. drug culture, mid 1900s-pres.]

mainliner a drug addict; someone who injects drugs intravenously. [U.S. slang, mid 1900s-pres.]

main queen 1. a homosexual male who takes the female role; a RECEIVER (*q.v.*). [U.S. slang, mid 1900s] **2.** one's steady girlfriend. [U.S. slang, mid 1900s]

main squeeze 1. one's boss; the head man. No negative connotations. [U.S. colloquial, 1900s] **2.** a steady girlfriend. [originally black use; U.S., mid 1900s-pres.]

main vein the female genitals. For synonyms see MONOSYLLABLE. [British slang, 1900s, *Dictionary of Slang and Unconventional English*]

major need defecation (contrasted to urination). *Cf.* BIG ONE, BIG POTTY. [colloquial euphemism, 1900s or before]

make 1. the copulation of wolves. [late 1600s, B.E.] **2.** copulation. **3.** a sexually loose woman. **4.** to urinate. *Cf.* MAKE WATER. For synonyms see WHIZ. **5.** to seduce; to seduce and copulate. See MAKE IT. [senses 2-5 are U.S., mid 1900s-pres.]

make, on the 1. pertaining to the actions of a sexually promiscuous person. **2.** pertaining to a sexually receptive woman. **3.** pertaining to a person trying to convince someone to copulate. **4.** self-employed as a prostitute. [all senses, U.S. slang, early 1900s-pres.]

make a branch to urinate. Refers to a branch of a stream. *Cf.* MAKE (sense 4). [U.S. dialect (Ozarks), Randolph and Wilson]

make a deposit 1. to defecate. **2.** to urinate. See BANK (sense 1). *Cf.* DEPOSIT (sense 2). [both senses, U.S. colloquial, 1900s]

make a noise 1. to release intestinal gas audibly. [euphemistic avoidance since the 1800s] **2.** to boast; to give forth hot air. Based on sense 1. [U.S. slang, 1900s]

make a pass at to make a sexual advance toward someone. This may include many activities from flirtation to fondling. [U.S. slang and colloquial, 1900s]

make a rude noise 1. to release intestinal gas audibly. For synonyms see GURK. **2.** to belch. [both senses since the 1800s]

make a sale to vomit. For synonyms see YORK. [widespread colloquial, 1900s]

make ends meet (also **make both ends meet**) to copulate. *Cf.* FIT END TO END. [since the 1800s or before]

make faces to conceive children. [British, 1800s or before]

make feet for children's shoes to copulate. For synonyms see OCCUPY. [British, 1800s]

make it to coit, said of a man or a woman or both. [frequent source of double entendre; U.S. slang and colloquial, mid 1900s-pres.]

make love 1. to caress and kiss. **2.** to copulate. A euphemism for "human copulation." [both since the 1600s]

make Ms and Ws to be drunk; to walk in a zig-zag fashion. *Cf.* ZIG-ZAG. [British slang, 1800s, Farmer and Henley]

make one's love come down 1. to cause an orgasm. **2.** to copulate. **3.** to cause one to become sexually aroused. [all senses, U.S. black use and slang, mid 1900s-pres.]

make out 1. to kiss and caress. **2.** to copulate. [both senses, U.S. slang, mid 1900s-pres.]

make-out artist a seducer; a lecher. See MAKE OUT. [U.S. slang, mid 1900s-pres.]

make the chimney smoke to cause a woman to have an orgasm. *Cf.* CHIMNEY, SMOKE (sense 1). [British slang, 1800s]

make water (also **make**) to urinate. For synonyms see WHIZ. [colloquial since the 1300s]

make wind to break wind; to release intestinal gas. Parallel to MAKE WATER (*q.v.*). [U.S. slang, 1900s]

mala de Franzos* the "French-disease," syphilis. *Cf.* FRENCH-DISEASE.

malady of France syphilis. *Cf.* FRENCH-DISEASE. For synonyms see SPECIFIC STOMACH. [from *Henry IV*, Part One (Shakespeare)]

malarky (also **malarkey**) nonsense; flattery. [traditionally attributed to the Irish; U.S. colloquial, 1900s]

male a euphemism for a bull, boar, or stallion. [U.S. colloquial, 1900s or before]

male brute (also **male beast**) a euphemism for a bull or a stallion. [U.S. rural colloquial, 1900s or before]

male cow (also **he-cow**) a bull. [U.S. rural colloquial, 1900s or before]

male genital organ the penis; in the plural, the VIRILIA (*q.v.*). A polite avoidance.

male member the penis. A translation of MEMBRUM VIRILE (*q.v.*).

male-mules the human testicles. For synonyms see WHIRLYGIGS. [British, 1600s]

male pessary a condom. In this usage, "pessary" seems to be generic for a birth control device. [1900s or before]

male prostitute 1. a male, presumably a homosexual male, who provides sexual services to other males. [1800s-1900s] **2.** a male who provides sexual services to women. [1900s or before]

male pudendum the penis. Literally, "that about which a male ought to be modest." Usually seen as "male *pudendum.*" Patterned on the female PUDENDUM (*q.v.*). [U.S., mid 1900s]

male sheath a condom. For synonyms see EEL-SKIN. *Cf.* SHEATH (sense 3). [Euphemistic, 1900s or before]

male varlet a CATAMITE (*q.v.*). Probably rhyming for "male harlot." [from *Troilus and Cressida* (Shakespeare)]

malkin (also **mawkin**) **1.** a female specter or a female ghost. [1200s, *Oxford English Dictionary*] **2.** an effeminate male. For synonyms see FRIBBLE. [1400s] **3.** a slattern; a woman of low character. A diminutive of "Mary." See MOLL. [since the late 1500s] **4.** the female genitals. See PUSSY (sense 1). "Malkin" is a nickname for a cat. [since the 1500s]

mallee root a harlot; a prostitute. Possibly rhyming slang for "prostitute," *i.e.,* "pros-ti-toot." From "Mallee," the name of a species of eucalyptus grown in Australia. *Cf.* ROOT (sense 2), ROOTLE. [Australian, 1900s, Baker]

mallet-head an oaf. Similar to HAMMERHEAD (*q.v.*). For synonyms see OAF. [U.S. colloquial, mid 1900s]

malted intoxicated with alcohol. Refers to the malt in beer. *Cf.* HOPPED (sense 2). [U.S. slang, mid 1900s]

Malthusian Theory (also **Malthusian Doctrine**) the notion that population increases geometrically and the food supply increases arithmetically. Sometimes cited as an argument for birth control. *Cf.* HIGHER MALTHUSIANISM. From the name "Thomas R. Malthus," 1766-1834.

malt-worm (also **malt-bug, malt-horse**) a beer-drinker. A derogatory nickname for a drunkard. *Cf.* MALTED. [mid 1500s]

man 1. to coit a woman. [since the 1600s or before] **2.** a lesbian in the masculine role. [U.S. slang, mid 1900s-pres.] See also MAN, THE.

man, old 1. the penis. *Cf.* LADY, OLD (sense 1). [British colloquial, 1800s] **2.** a male; one's husband, boyfriend, or father. [British and U.S. colloquial, 1800s-pres.]

man, the 1. a working boss; the Caucasian male to whom a Negro slave or convict is subservient. [U.S. Negro colloquial, 1900s and before] **2.** a personification of white society, especially racially repressive white society. [U.S. black use, mid 1900s-pres.] **3.** a policeman, either Negro, Caucasian, or otherwise. [U.S. black use, mid 1900s-pres.]

man-balls the testicles. For synonyms see WHIRLYGIGS. [from "I Sing of the Body Electric," *Leaves of Grass* (Walt Whitman)] See also MAN-ROOT.

man box a coffin. [colloquial, 1800s-1900s]

Manchester city a breast. Rhyming slang for TITTY (sense 1.) Often seen in the plural. *Cf.* BRISTOL CITIES, JERSEY CITIES. [British, 1800s-1900s, *Dictionary of Rhyming Slang*]

Manchesters the human breasts. A truncation of "Manchester cities," which is rhyming slang for "titties." See MANCHESTER CITY. *Cf.* BRISTOLS. The words "man" and "chest" provided the basis for sexual imagery. [British slang, 1800s]

man-cow a euphemism for "bull." *Cf.* MALE COW. [Caribbean (Jamaican), 1800s-1900s, Cassidy and Le Page]

M. and C. a mixture of "morphine" and "cocaine." *Cf.* H. AND C. [U.S. underworld, early 1900s]

mandrake METHAQUALONE (*q.v.*). [U.S. drug culture, mid 1900-pres.]

maneater 1. a FELLATOR or FELLATRIX. [euphemistic double entrendre] **2.** a woman determined to get a husband. [U.S. slang, 1900s]

mangle the female genitals. Possibly from the street cry "Has your mother sold her mangle?" [this is either nonce or a rude reinterpretation of a nontaboo expression; British, 1800s, Farmer and Henley]

manhole 1. the female genitals. *Cf.* MANHOLE COVER, MANTRAP. [colloquial and nonce, 1800s-1900s] **2.** a man's anus in INSPECTOR OF MANHOLES (*q.v.*).

manhole cover a sanitary napkin; a menstrual cloth. [widespread slang, 1900s] Synonyms: AMMUNITION, BANDAGE, CLOUT, CUNT-RAG, DANGER-SIGNAL, DIAPER, FANNY RAG, FLAG, GENTLEMAN'S PLEASURE-GARDEN PADLOCK, GRANNY-RAG, MENSTRUAL CLOTH, MONTHLY RAG, NAPKIN, PAD, PERINEAL PAD, PERIODICITY RAG, PLEASURE-GARDEN PADLOCK, RAG, RED FLAG, RED RAG, SANITARY, SANITARY NAPKIN, SANITARY TOWEL, SHOE, S.T., WINDOW-BLIND, WINDOW-CURTAIN.

manhood 1. the period in the life of a human male after he reaches puberty or the age of majority. **2.** the male genitals; the penis. [euphemistic, 1900s]

man in the boat the clitoris. The "boat" refers to the shape of the *labia minora* and *labia majora*. See BOY-IN-THE-BOAT, LITTLE-MAN-IN-THE-BOAT.

manliness the male genitals. *Cf.* MODESTY (sense 2). [colloquial, 1900s or before]

man of the cloth a parson; a clergyman of any type. [since the 1600s]

man oil semen. Probably from "sperm whale oil," which was called "sperm oil" or "sperm." *Cf.* OIL OF MAN. [U.S. slang, 1900s]

manometer the female genitals, especially the vagina; the vagina considered as a device for measuring manliness as evidenced by penile size. A play on the name of an instrument used to measure air pressure. *Cf.* YARD MEASURE. [slang and nonce, 1900s]

man-rape homosexual rape; an act of PEDERASTY (*q.v.*) committed on a male by force.

man-root the penis. *Cf.* MAN-BALLS. [from "I Sing of the Body Electric," *Leaves of Grass* (Walt Whitman)]

man's man 1. a virile male. [U.S. colloquial, 1900s] 2. a homosexual male. For synonyms see EPICENE. [U.S. slang, 1900s]

mantan black a Negro who acts like a Caucasian; an OREO (*q.v.*). From the trademarked brand name of a suntanning agent, "Mantan." Derogatory. [U.S. black use, mid 1900s]

man Thomas, my (also **man Thomas**) the penis. From JOHN THOMAS (*q.v.*). [British colloquial, 1600s-pres.]

mantrap 1. the female genitals. *Cf.* MANHOLE. [British, 1700s] 2. a woman seeking a husband; a widow; the same as MANEATER (sense 2). [since the 1700s]

manual exercises masturbation. *Cf.* FIVE AGAINST ONE. [military slang, 1900s]

maracas the breasts. From the name of a pair of rounded gourd-rattles used in Latin America. [U.S. slang, early 1900s-pres.]

marble See PASS IN ONE'S MARBLES.

marble-arch the female genitals. For synonyms see MONOSYLLABLE. [British, mid 1800s, Farmer and Henley]

marble dome a stupid person. [U.S. slang, mid 1900s]

marble orchard (also **Marble City**) a cemetery. From the numerous monuments in a cemetery. *Cf.* BONE-ORCHARD. [U.S. slang and colloquial, early 1900s-pres.]

marble palace a W.C.; a toilet, especially a marble-finished public restroom. [U.S. slang, 1900s]

marbles 1. syphilis; syphilitic buboes. As if the infected person had a pocket full of marbles. [late 1500s] 2. the testicles. [British and U.S. colloquial and nonce since the 1800s or before]

Marge a passive lesbian; the same as MARGERY (*q.v.*). [U.S. homosexual use and slang, mid 1900s-pres.]

Margery an effeminate male; possibly a homosexual male. *Cf.* MARGE. [British slang, 1800s, Ware]

mari marijuana; a marijuana cigarette. *Cf.* MARY (sense 4). [U.S. underworld and drug culture, 1900s] Synonyms and related terms: A-BOMB, ACAPULCO GOLD, AFRICAN BLACK, ASHES, BABY, BAMBALACHA, BAMMY, BANJI, BHANG, BHANG GANJAH, BIRDWOOD, BLACK GUNGEON, BLACK GUNNY, BLACK MO, BLACK MOAT, BO, BO-BO BUSH, BOO, BRICK, BROCCOLI, BUSH, BUTTER FLOWER, CANADIAN BLACK, CANNABIS INDICA, CANNABIS SATIVA, CHARAS, CHARGE, CHICAGO GREEN, CHURRUS, COLI, COLUMBIAN, COLUMBIAN RED, COLUMBIA RED, CREEPER, DAGGA, DEW, DITCH WEED, DOGIE, DONJEM, DOPE, DRY HIGH, ERB, FAGGOT, FU, FUNNY STUFF, GAINESVILLE GREEN, GANGSTER, GANJA, GAUGE, GIGGLE-SMOKE, GIGGLE-WEED, GOLD, GOLD COLUMBIAN, GOLDEN LEAF, GONGA, GOOF, GOOF-BALL, GOOF-BUTT, GRASS, GRASS WEED, GREAFA, GREAPHA, GREEFA, GREEFO, GREEN, GREFA, GRIEFO, GRIFFA, GRIFFO, GRIFO, GUNGEON, GUNNY, GYVE, HAS, HAWAIIAN, HAY, HEMP, HERB, HOMEGROWN, HOOCH, HOP, ILLINOIS GREEN, INDIAN HAY, INDIAN HEMP, JERSEY, GREEN, JIVE, JOHNSON GRASS, JOY-WEED, JUANE, JUANITA, JUANITA WEED, KAIF, KAUI, KEEF, KICK-STICK, KID-STUFF, KIF, LIPTON'S, LOCOWEED, LOVE WEED, LUMBO, M., MACH, MAGGIE, MARIGUANA, MARIJUANA, MARJIE, MARY, MARY AND JOHNNIE, MARY ANN, MARY JANE, MARY WARNER, MARY WEAVER, MAUI, MEGG, MERRY, MEXICAN BROWN, MEXICAN GREEN, MEXICAN RED, MEZZ, M.J., MOHASKY, MOOCAH, MOOTAH, MOSHKY, MOTA, MU, MUGGLE, MUSTA, MUTAH, MUTHA, NICKEL, PANAMA GOLD, PANAMA RED, PANATELA, POD, POT, POTIGUAYA, PUNK, RAGWEED, RAINY-DAY WOMAN, RAMA, REAPER, RED, RED-

DIRT MARIJUANA, REEFER, REEFER WEED, RIGHTEOUS BUSH, ROUGH STUFF, SALT-AND PEPPER, SATIVA, SHISHI, SHIT, SIN-SEMILLA, SKINNY, SMOKE, SNOP, SPLAY, SPLIFF, SPLIM, STINK-WEED, STRAW, STUFF, STUM, SUPERPOT, SWEET LUCY, SWEET LUNCH, T., TEA, TEXAS TEA, THAI STICKS, THIRTEEN, TIN, TRIPWEED, VERMONT GREEN, VIPER'S WEED, VONCE, WACKY TABBACKY, WACKY WEED, WEED, WEED TEA, WHEAT, YERBA, YESCA, ZACATECAS PURPLE.

mariguana marijuana. For synonyms see MARI. [U.S., 1900s]

marijuana CANNABIS SATIVA (*q.v.*). [Mexican Spanish for *Cannabis sativa;* the U.S. word-of-choice for this substance]

marjie marijuana. For synonyms see MARI. [Australian, mid 1900s]

mark 1. a streetwalking prostitute. [U.S. slang, 1800s] **2.** to geld a lamb. [Australian and U.S. colloquial, 1900s or before] **3.** a dupe; a target for theft or the confidence racket. [underworld, 1900s or before]

market-dame a strumpet; a prostitute. [British, early 1700s]

mark of the beast the female genitals. [British, early 1700s]

Marquess of Lorn the erect penis. Rhyming slang for "horn." *Cf.* HORN (sense 3). [British, 1900s, *Dictionary of Rhyming Slang*]

marriage 1. a stable and sexually exclusive union of male and female; the legally recognized union of a man and a woman. [since the 1200s] Synonyms: BALL AND CHAIN, CONJUGACY, PLUNGE, THE BIG STEP, THE JUMP, THE NOOSE, UNION. **2.** a stable and sexually exclusive relationship of two homosexual males or two homosexual females. Not recognized in law. [attested as U.S. homosexual use, early 1900s-pres.]

married but not churched pertaining to a common-law union. [in various forms, 1800s-1900s]

married to Mary Fist accustomed to masturbation rather than coition. [U.S.

prison use, mid 1900s, Goldin, O'Leary, and Lipsius]

marrow semen. See MARROW-BONE. For synonyms see METTLE. [from *All's Well That Ends Well* (Shakespeare)]

marrow-bone the penis. *Cf.* MARROW. [British slang, 1800s, Farmer and Henley]

marrow-bone-and-cleaver the penis. *Cf.* HONEY-POT CLEAVER. [British slang, 1800s, Farmer and Henley]

marrow-pudding the penis. *Cf.* MARROW, PUDDING (sense 1). [British slang, 1800s]

Marshall Field a reinterpretation of "M.F.," "mother-fucker." From the name of a Chicago department store. [U.S. black use, mid 1900s]

marshmallow 1. a weak person; a useless male. [U.S. colloquial, mid 1900s] **2.** a derogatory nickname for a Caucasian. [U.S. black use, mid 1900s-pres.] See also MARSHMALLOWS.

marshmallow reds barbiturates, specifically red capsules of Seconal (trademark). [U.S. drug culture, mid 1900s-pres.]

marshmallows 1. the breasts. **2.** the testicles. [both senses, U.S. slang, mid 1900s-pres.]

martext a clergyman who misinterprets the Scriptures or other readings. *Cf.* PUZZLE-TEXT. [from the name "Sir Oliver Martext," a vicar in *As You Like It* (Shakespeare)]

Mary 1. any woman. **2.** a lesbian. **3.** a homosexual male; a RECEIVER (*q.v.*). **4.** marijuana. Not normally capitalized. *Cf.* MARI. [all senses, U.S. slang, 1900s] **5.** a generic term for "woman" or a nickname for any Australian aborigine woman. Common in the pidgin languages of the Pacific. [Australian and New Zealand, early 1800s-1900s]

Mary and Johnnie CANNABIS SATIVA (*q.v.*). Rhyming slang for "marijuana." [U.S. slang, 1900s]

Mary Ann 1. a homosexual male; a CATAMITE (*q.v.*). [British and U.S. slang, late 1800s-1900s] **2.** marijuana; a marijuana cigarette. [U.S. drug culture, mid 1900s-pres.]

Mary Jane 1. the female genitals. *Cf.* LITTLE MARY (sense 1). [British slang, 1800s, Farmer and Henley] **2.** marijuana. [U.S. drug culture, mid 1900s-pres.]

Mary Warner marijuana; a marijuana cigarette. [U.S. drug culture, mid 1900s-pres.]

Mary Weaver marijuana. [U.S. drug culture, mid 1900s-pres.]

masculine whore a CATAMITE (*q.v.*); a homosexual male; a RECEIVER (*q.v.*). [from *Troilus and Cressida* (Shakespeare)]

mash 1. a crush; a love affair. **2.** a lover. **3.** to flirt sexually; to make a pass at. [all senses, U.S. slang, 1900s]

mashed love-struck; amorous. [British, late 1800s]

masher a male flirt; a philanderer. [U.S. slang and colloquial, 1900s]

mashing courting; flirting. [since the late 1800s]

masochism the enjoyment of one's own pain; the heightening of one's sexual pleasure through being mistreated and abused by another person. Considered to be abnormal. From the name "Leopold von Sacher-Masoch," an Austrian novelist and historian, 1836-1895.

mason 1. a PEDERAST (*q.v.*); the INSERTOR (*q.v.*). **2.** a lesbian assuming a masculine role. Both refer to the sexual partner who does the "laying." See LAY. From the laying of bricks. [both senses, U.S., mid 1900s]

mass!, By the an oath and an exclamation. [British, 1700s]

Master John Thursday the penis, a personification of the penis. [1600s, (Urquhart)]

master member the penis. [British, 1800s, Farmer and Henley]

master of ceremonies the penis. The "ceremonies" are acts of copulation. [British slang, 1800s, Farmer and Henley]

masterpiece the penis. [British slang and jocular nonce, 1800s]

mastok intoxicated with alcohol. For synonyms see WOOFLED. [Australian, 1900s, Baker]

masturbate 1. to fondle the genitals (male or female) to induce sexual pleasure. Done by oneself or another person of either sex. **2.** to simulate the motions of copulation by hand until orgasm is achieved. Most euphemistic terms refer to male masturbation. See WASTE TIME. [from a Latin word with the same meaning; in English since the 1700s]

mat (also **mattress**) **1.** a woman. [U.S. colloquial, 1900s or before] **2.** a prostitute. [U.S. underworld, mid 1900s]

match 1. the female genitals. *Cf.* ANTIPODES, THE. **2.** the penis. *Cf.* MATE (sense 2). [both senses, U.S. dialect (Boontling), late 1800s-early 1900s, Charles Adams]

matchruptcy a divorce. A blend of "match" and "bankruptcy." [U.S. slang, 1900s]

mate 1. to copulate; to marry. [since the 1600s] **2.** the male or female genitals. *Cf.* MATCH. [U.S. dialect (Boontling), late 1800s-early 1900s, Charles Adams]

matrimonial peacemaker the penis. [British colloquial, late 1700s, Grose]

matrix 1. the uterus. [1500s] **2.** the female genitals. A euphemistic extension of sense 1. [both senses, Latin]

matutinal erection a morning erection. *Cf.* MORNING PRIDE.

Maud a male prostitute. [British, mid 1900s, *Dictionary of Slang and Unconventional English*]

maudlin drunk (also **mawdin drunk**) intoxicated with alcohol and crying. Ultimately based on "Mary Magdalene," who is often portrayed weeping for her sins. [British and U.S. colloquial, 1600s-pres.]

Maui (also **Maui wowie**) a variety of marijuana supposedly grown on the Hawaiian island of Maui. *Cf.* HAWAIIAN, KAUI. [U.S. drug culture, mid 1900s-pres.]

mauks (also **maux, mawk, mawkes, mawks**) **1.** a prostitute; a woman who sells sexual acts. **2.** a slattern; a slovenly-dressed woman. [both senses, British, 1600s-1700s]

maul to grope or feel a woman; to handle a woman excessively. [U.S. colloquial, 1900s]

mauled (also **mauld**) intoxicated with alcohol. [British colloquial, 1600s-pres.]

mau-mau a derogatory nickname for a Negro. Directed especially at militant blacks. [U.S. slang, mid 1900s]

mawbrish intoxicated with alcohol. For synonyms see WOOFLED. [British dialect, 1800s or before, Rye]

maw-wallop a disgusting substance. From a term for badly cooked or disgusting food. "Maw" (from the 700s) means "stomach." [British colloquial, 1700s]

max gin. From "maximum." For synonyms see RUIN. [British slang, early 1800s, *Lexicon Balatronicum*]

may a W.C.; a toilet. [U.S. slang, early 1900s]

May God blind me! an oath and an exclamation. *Cf.* GORBLIMEY!

mayhem 1. the maiming of a man. [since the late 1400s] **2.** euphemistic for "castration."

May I go to hell! as oath and an exclamation. For synonyms see 'ZOUNDS!

Mazola party a form of sexual activity where the participants cover their bodies with liquid cooking oil and perform various sexual activities; the same as WESSON PARTY (*q.v.*). From the trademarked brand name of a cooking oil.

McGimper a pimp. See MACGIMP.

M.D. 1. a physician; a doctor of medicine. **2.** a person who is mentally defective. An ironic reinterpretation of sense 1.

M.D.A. "methylenedioxyamphetamine," a recreational drug derived from nutmeg. Elaborated as "mellow drug of America." [U.S. drug culture, 1960s-pres.]

meacocke (also **meacock**) a sissy; an effeminate male. For synonyms see FRIBBLE. [1500s-1600s]

meadow dressing nonsense; a euphemism for BULLSHIT (*q.v.*). From a term for animal manure used to fertilize the soil of a field. [slang and colloquial, early 1900s]

meadow-mayonnaise nonsense; a euphemism for BULLSHIT (*q.v.*). *Cf.* COW-CONFETTI. [Australian slang, early 1900s]

mealer a drinker who imbibes only at meals. *Cf.* AFTER DINNER MAN. [British slang, 1800s, Farmer and Henley]

meaningful relationship a love affair; an affair of the heart, including sex. In contrast to either a purely sexual experience or a sexless friendship. [U.S., mid 1900s-pres.]

means of weakness and debility sexual debauchery. A vague euphemism (or perhaps a dysphemism) for "masturbation." [from *As You Like It* (Shakespeare)]

mean white poor Caucasians. *Cf.* POOR WHITE TRASH. Probably from "menial whites." Also an Anglo-Indian term for poor Englishmen. [U.S. Negro colloquial, early 1800s]

measles syphilis. *Cf.* PIMPLE (sense 2). For synonyms see SPECIFIC STOMACH. [U.S. slang and euphemism, early 1900s]

meat 1. the female genitals. For synonyms see MONOSYLLABLE. [since the 1500s] **2.** women considered as sexual objects. For synonyms see TAIL. [since the 1500s] **3.** the human breasts. [British and U.S. slang and nonce, 1800s-1900s] **4.** the penis. *Cf.* BEEF (sense 2). [British and U.S. slang and colloquial, 1800s-pres.] **5.** a strong but stupid male. *Cf.* BEEF (sense 3). [U.S. slang, 1900s] **6.** males considered as sexual objects by homosexual males. *Cf.* GOVERNMENT INSPECTED MEAT. [U.S. homosexual use, 1900s]

meat and drink a drunken spree including sexual adventures. [British slang, 1800s, Farmer and Henley]

meatball a stupid oaf. [U.S. slang, early 1900s-pres.]

meat-flasher an exhibitionist, a man who exposes his penis to public view. [British slang, 1800s, Farmer and Henley]

meat for days (also **meat for the poor**) pertaining to a male with large genitals; pertaining to large male genitals. *Cf.* BASKET FOR DAYS. [U.S. homosexual use, mid 1900s]

meat-grinder (also **meat-cooker**) **1.** the female genitals, specifically the vagina. **2.** a woman considered as a sexual object. For synonyms see TAIL. Refers to MEAT (sense 4). [U.S. slang or nonce]

meathead as oaf; the same as BEEF-HEAD (*q.v.*). [U.S. colloquial, mid 1900s-pres.]

meat hound 1. a whoremonger. *Cf.* MEAT (sense 2). **2.** a homosexual male. *Cf.* MEAT (sense 4), the penis. [both senses, U.S. slang, mid 1900s]

meat house a brothel. [British slang, 1800s, Farmer and Henley]

meat-market 1. a group of prostitutes; the location of a group of prostitutes. **2.** the human breasts. *Cf.* MEAT (sense 3). **3.** the female genitals. *Cf.* MEAT (sense 1). [senses 2 and 3 are slang, 1800s-1900s] **4.** an area used by homosexuals to make contacts. [U.S. homosexual use, mid 1900s, Stanley] **5.** a body-building gymnasium. [U.S. slang, mid 1900s]

meat-monger 1. a whoremaster. **2.** a male who is a brothel keeper. [both senses, primarily British slang, 1800s, Farmer and Henley]

meat-rack 1. an area where male homosexuals gather to seek partners. [U.S. homosexual use and general slang, mid 1900s] **2.** a body-building gymnasium. [U.S. slang, mid 1900s]

meat-wagon an ambulance. *Cf.* BLOOD-WAGON. [British and U.S. slang, World War II]

meaty obscene; with significant sexual content. [British and U.S., 1900s]

meddle to coit a woman; to copulate with a person of the opposite sex. *Cf.* MELL. [U.S. slang and colloquial, 1900s]

meddle with to be intimate with a woman; to coit a woman; to fondle a woman. Possibly to copulate with someone. *Cf.* MEDDLE. [since the 1600s]

medicine 1. copulation. In the expression "take one's medicine." [British, 1800s, Farmer and Henley] **2.** alcoholic liquor. *Cf.* SNAKEBITE MEDICINE. [British and U.S. colloquial, 1800s-pres.] **3.** methadone, a synthetic opiate used in the treatment of heroin and morphine addiction. [U.S. drug culture, mid 1900s-pres.]

medlar 1. the female genitals. [from *Measure for Measure* (Shakespeare)] **2.** the anus; the anal and pubic area. Possibly a misunderstanding of sense 1. **3.** a stinking fellow. All are from the name of the fruit of the medlar tree. [1800s]

megg marijuana. See MARGE, MARGERY. [U.S. drug culture, 1900s]

mell to coit a woman. A derivative of the word MEDDLE (*q.v.*). For synonyms see OCCUPY. [1300s-1900s]

mell of a hess a deliberate spoonerism for "hell of a mess." *Cf.* FELL OF A HIX. [U.S. slang and colloquial, mid 1900s]

mellow 1. intoxicated with alcohol. [since the 1600s] **2.** peaceful and relaxed due to the use of drugs. From sense 1. [U.S. drug culture, mid 1900s-pres.]

mellow-yellow 1. the skin of a banana dried for smoking. [U.S. drug culture, mid 1900s] **2.** the drug L.S.D. (*q.v.*). [U.S. drug culture, mid 1900s-pres.]

melonhead (also **melon**) an oaf. [Australian and U.S. slang, 1900s]

melons the human breasts. *Cf.* HONEYDEW MELONS, WATERMELONS. [U.S. slang and colloquial, 1900s]

melt to ejaculate. [euphemistic, early 1600s] Synonyms and related terms: BLOW UP, BUST, BUST ONE'S NUTS, COME, COME OFF, COME ONE'S COCOA, CREAM, DIE IN A WOMAN'S LAP, DISCHARGE, DOUBLE ONE'S MILT, DROP ONE'S LOAD, EASE, EASE ONESELF, EFFECT EMISSION, EJACULATE, EMISSIO, EMISSION, EMISSIO

SEMINIS, EMIT, FIRE A SHOT, FIRE IN THE AIR, GET IT OFF, GET OFF, GET OFF THE NUT, GET ONE'S COOKIES OFF, GET ONE'S NUTS OFF, GET ONE'S ROCK OFF, GET THE BUTTON OFF, GET THE DIRTY WATER OFF ONE'S CHEST, GIVE ONE'S GRAVY, GO, GO OFF, HIVE IT, HOLE, JET ONE'S JUICE, LET GO, MILK, NUMBER THREE, PISS ONE'S TALLOW, POP A NUT, POP ONE'S NUTS, SEMINAL EMISSION, SEMINIS EMISSIO, SEXUAL REFLEX, SHOOT, SHOOT OFF, SHOOT ONE'S MILT, SHOOT ONE'S ROE, SHOOT ONE'S WAD, SHOOT WHITE, SPEND, SPERMATIZE, SPEW, SPUNK, SQUEEZE UP, SQUIRT, THROW UP, UPSHOOT.

melted intoxicated with alcohol. [U.S. slang, early 1900s]

melted-butter semen. *Cf.* BUTTER, DUCK-BUTTER. [British, 1700s]

melting-pot the female genitals. *Cf.* MELT. [British slang, 1800s, Farmer and Henley]

member 1. the penis. A truncation of MALE MEMBER (*q.v.*). [since the 1300s] **2.** a fellow Negro. [U.S. black use, mid 1900s]

member for the cockshire the penis. *Cf.* PRIVY MEMBER, UNRULY MEMBER. [British, 1800s, Farmer and Henley]

member mug a chamber pot. [British jocular euphemism. 1600s-1700s]

membrum* the penis. Literally, "member." [truncation of *membrum virile;* Latin]

membrum muliebre* the clitoris, the "female member." *Cf.* MALE PUDENDUM. [Latin]

memorial park a cemetery; a commercial cemetery (not a churchyard) whose proprietors take great pride in design, landscaping, and maintenance. [U.S. euphemism, 1900s]

menarche the onset of the menses in the tenth to the seventeenth year of life. [medical]

menses 1. the PERIOD (*q.v.*) in which a woman experiences the monthly menstrual cycle. For synonyms see FLOODS. **2.** the material (blood and other cells) discharged during a menstrual period.

men's john a men's restroom. [U.S. colloquial, 1900s]

men's room a men's restroom. The U.S. word-of-choice for a public toilet for men. [U.S. colloquial, 1900s]

menstrual cloth the clean and absorbent cloth or rags used to absorb the menstrual flux. A sanitary napkin. Also used in reference to commercially produced pads. [colloquial, 1800s-1900s]

mental a deranged person; a mentally-deficient person. [British and U.S., early 1900s]

mentulate (also **mentulated**) pertaining to a man with an abnormally large penis. *Cf.* BASKET FOR DAYS, DONKEY-RIGGED, DOUBLE-SHUNG, HUNG, HUNG LIKE A BULL, MEGALOPENIS, MIRACLE-MEAT, TIMBERED, TONS OF BASKET, TONS OF MEAT, WELL-BUILT, WELL-ENDOWED, WELL-FAVORED BY NATURE, WELL-HUNG, WELT. [since the 1700s]

merd dung. Literally, "shit." Widely used in French and used by some speakers of English. Considerably less offensive than "shit." [ultimately from Latin *merda;* English use, 1900s or before]

meretrice (also **meretrix**) a prostitute. [from Italian; since the mid 1500s]

merkin 1. the female genitals. [British, mid 1600s] **2.** the female pubic hair. *Cf.* LOWER-WIG. [since the mid 1600s] **3.** false female pubic hair. [British, late 1700s-1800s]

mermaid a prostitute. For synonyms see HARLOT. [late 1500s]

merry 1. wanton; without sexual control. *Cf.* GAY (sense 1). For synonyms see LEWD. [British, 1600s] **2.** intoxicated with alcohol. [British and U.S., early 1700s-pres.] **3.** marijuana. *Cf.* MARY (sense 4). [U.S. underworld and drug culture, mid 1900s]

merry-begotten child a bastard. See MERRY (sense 1). For synonyms see ACCIDENT. [British colloquial, late 1700s-1800s]

merry-bit a sexually compliant woman. *Cf.* GAY (sense 1). [British slang, 1800s, Farmer and Henley]

merry bout an act of copulation. For

synonyms see SMOCKAGE. [British, 1700s]

merry legs a prostitute. [British slang, 1800s, Farmer and Henley]

merrymaker the penis. *Cf.* GAYING INSTRUMENT. [British slang, 1800s, Farmer and Henley]

mesc a MESCAL BUTTON (*q.v.*), containing mescaline. Synonyms: BEAN, BIG CHIEF, BUTTON, CACTUS, MESCAL, MESCAL BUTTON, MESCALINE, MOON, PEYOTE, PEYOTE BUTTON, PUMPKIN SEED.

mescal MESCALINE (*q.v.*) or a MESCAL BUTTON (*q.v.*). [U.S. drug culture, mid 1900s-pres.]

mescal button the emergent tip of the peyote cactus, which contains MESCALINE (*q.v.*). See PEYOTE BUTTON. [U.S. drug culture, mid 1900s-pres.]

mescaline the name of the hallucinogenic chemical compound 3,4,5-trimethoxyphenylethylamine. [U.S. underworld and drug culture, mid 1900s-pres.]

mess 1. to play around sexually; to MESS AROUND (*q.v.*). Usually said of a married person. [British and U.S. colloquial, 1900s] **2.** an oaf; a hopelessly stupid person; a mentally confused person. [U.S. slang and colloquial, early 1900s-pres.]

mess about to play sexually. *Cf.* MESS (sense 1). [British colloquial, late 1800s-pres.]

mess around to play with sexually; to copulate; to flirt. Said especially of a married person. *Cf.* MESS (sense 1). [U.S. slang and colloquial, 1900s]

meth Methedrine (trademark), an amphetamine, specifically methamphetamine. [U.S. drug culture, mid 1900s-pres.]

methadone a synthetic opiate which acts as a central nervous system depressant. Used in heroin addiction therapy. It blocks addictive craving for heroin. [U.S. drug culture, mid 1900s-pres.]

methaqualone a central nervous system depressant. [U.S. drug culture, mid 1900s-pres.]

meth-head (also **meth-freak**) a habitual user of Methedrine (trademark). [U.S. drug culture, mid 1900s-pres.]

meth monster a habitual user of Methedrine (trademark). [U.S. drug culture, mid 1900s]

Metho a nickname for a Methodist. [Australian slang, 1900s, Baker]

mettle 1. vigor; masculine vigor; virility. No negative connotations. [since the late 1500s] **2.** semen. *Cf.* FETCH METTLE, SPUNK. [British, 1600s-pres.] Synonyms and related terms for sense 2: BABY-JUICE, BULLETS, BULL GRAVY, BUTTER, BUTTERMILK, CHISM, CHISSOM, COME, COMINGS, CREAM, CRUD, DELICIOUS JAM, DUCK-BUTTER, EFFUSION, FATHER-STUFF, FETCH, FUCK, GISM, GLUE, GRAVY, GUMA, HOCKEY, HOMEBREWED, HONEY, HOT MILK, JAM, JAZZ, JELLY, JISM, JUICE, LETCH-WATER, LEWD INFUSION, LIQUOR SEMINALE, LOAD, LOVE-JUICE, LOVE-LIQUOR, MAN OIL, MARROW, MELTED-BUTTER, METTLE OF GENERATION, MILK, MILT, NATURE, OIL, OIL OF MAN, OINTMENT, OYSTER, PRICK-JUICE, PUDDING, SCUM, SEED, SEMEN, SEMEN VIRILE, SEMINAL FILAMENT, SEMINAL FLUID, SEXUAL DISCHARGE, SLIME, SNOWBALL, SOAP, SPEND, SPENDINGS, SPERM, SPERMA, SPERMATIC JUICE, SPEW, SPIRIT, SPUME, SPUNK, STARCH, STUFF, TAIL-JUICE, TAIL-WATER, TALLOW, TREAD, TREASURE, VICTORIA MONK, WHITE-BLOW, WHITE HONEY.

mettled sexually aroused, presumably in reference to the male. *Cf.* METTLE (sense 2). [British, 1800s, Farmer and Henley]

mettle of generation semen. For synonyms see METTLE. [British, early 1600s]

Mex 1. a Mexican. Usually considered derogatory. **2.** pertaining to Mexican things or persons. Derogatory. [both senses, U.S. slang, early 1900s-pres.] Synonyms for sense 1: BEAN, BEAN-EATER, BEANER, BRACERO, BRAVO, BROWN, CHICANO, CHILI, CHILI-CHOMPER, CHILI-EATER, DINO, ENCHILADA-EATER, GREASE-BALL, GREASE GUT, GREASER, HOMBRE, MEX, MEXICAN, MEXICANO,

MEXIE, MICK, NEVER-SWEAT, OILER, PAISANO, PEON, PEPPER, PEPPER-BELLY, SHUCK, SPIC, SPIG, SUN-GRINNER, TACO, TACO-BENDER, TAMALE (female), WET-BACK.

Mexican 1. anything inferior or cheap. Derogatory. *Cf.* MEXICAN BEER, MEXICAN MUD. [U.S. slang, 1900s] **2.** a variety of marijuana grown in Mexico. [U.S. drug culture, mid 1900s-pres.]

Mexican beer water. A dysphemism. See MEXICAN (sense 1). [U.S. slang, mid 1900s-pres.]

Mexican brown marijuana; a variety of marijuana grown in Mexico. [U.S. drug culture, mid 1900s-pres.]

Mexican green a variety of marijuana grown in Mexico. [U.S. drug culture, mid 1900s-pres.]

Mexican milk tequila, a Mexican alcoholic beverage. [U.S. slang, mid 1900s-pres.]

Mexican mud heroin. *Cf.* MUD (sense 3). [U.S. drug culture, mid 1900s-pres.]

Mexicano a citizen of Mexico. For synonyms see MEX. [U.S. slang and colloquial, 1900s]

Mexican red 1. a variety or grade of marijuana associated with Mexico. *Cf.* MEXICAN (sense 2). **2.** a homemade barbiturate capsule. See RED (sense 1). *Cf.* MEXICAN (sense 2). [U.S. drug culture, mid 1900s]

Mexie a derogatory term for a Mexican citizen. [U.S. colloquial, 1900s]

mezz (also **mighty mess**) marijuana or a marijuana cigarette. [U.S. underworld and drug culture, mid 1900-pres.]

mezzroll a fat marijuana cigarette. [U.S. drug culture, mid 1900s-pres.] Synonyms: ACE, BELT, BLUE SAGE, BOMB, BOMBER, BONE, BUDDHA STICK, BURNIE, COCKTAIL, DOOBIE, DOPE-STICK, DRAG, DREAMSTICK, DUBEE, DYNAMITE, FAT JAY, FATTY, GANGSTER, GAUGE-BUTT, GOOF-BUTT, GOOFY-BUTT, GOW, HAY-BUTT, HOP-STICK, HOT-STICK, J., JAY, JIVE STICK, JOINT, JOLT, JOY SMOKE, JOY-STICK, J-SMOKE, JUANE, JUJU, LOCOWEED, MARY WARNER, MEZZ, MIG, MIGGIES, MUGGLE, NAIL, NUMBER, PIN, REEF, REEFER, ROACH,

ROCKET, ROOT, ROPE, SAUSAGE, SEED, SKOOFER, SMOKE, SNIPE, SPLIFF, STENCIL, STICK, STICK OF TEA, STOGIE, THUMB, THUNDER-COOKIE, TORPEDO, TWIST, WEED.

M.F. a "mother-fucker." [U.S. slang, mid 1900s-pres.] Synonyms and disguises: MARSHALL FIELD, M.F., MOTHER, MOTHER-DANGLER, MOTHER-FUCKER, MOTHER-GRABBER, MOTHER-HUMPER, MOTHER-JUMPER, MOTHER-LOVER, MOTHER-RUCKER, MOTHER-UGLY, MUH-FUH.

M.F.U. a "military fuck-up." Also occurs as an extreme variety of F.U. (*q.v.*), a "monstrous fuck-up." For synonyms see SNAFU. [British military, early 1900s]

mick (also **mickey, micky, mike**) **1.** an Irishman; an Irish immigrant. Derogatory. For synonyms see HARP. [British and U.S. colloquial and slang, 1800s-pres.] **2.** a derogatory term for a Mexican citizen. Probably from sense 1. [U.S., 1900s or before] **3.** a Roman Catholic. From sense 1. Usually considered derogatory. [U.S. colloquial, early 1900s] **4.** an oaf; any immigrant or laborer. [U.S. slang, mid 1900s] **5.** something worthless; an easy college course. From "Mickey Mouse." [U.S. slang, mid 1900s-pres.]

Mick, old ill; vomiting. Rhyming slang for "sick." [British, 1800s]

mickey 1. the penis. Rhyming slang for DICKY (sense 2). [British, 1800s] **2.** a derogatory term for an Irishman. See MICK (sense 1).

Mickey Bliss (also **Bliss**) urine; an act of urination; to urinate. Rhyming slang for "piss." *Cf.* MIKE BLISS. [British slang, 1900s]

Mickey Finished intoxicated with alcohol. A play on MICKEY FINN (*q.v.*). [U.S. slang, mid 1900s]

Mickey Finn 1. a drug, usually chloral hydrate, added to an alcoholic drink for the purpose of rendering the drinker unconscious. **2.** a drink containing chloral hydrate. [both senses, U.S. slang, mid 1900s-pres.]

Mickey Mouse 1. the female genitals. *Cf.* MOUSE (sense 2). [U.S., mid

1900s] **2.** pertaining to any useless or worthless thing. [U.S. slang, mid 1900s-pres.] **3.** a derogatory nickname for a Caucasian. [U.S. black use, mid 1900s]

Mickey Mouse is kaput a catch phrase indicating that a woman is experiencing the menses. *Cf.* MICKEY MOUSE (sense 1). For synonyms see FLOODS.

Mickey Mouse mattress a sanitary napkin; a perineal pad. *Cf.* MICKEY MOUSE (sense 1). [U.S. slang, mid 1900s]

Micky 1. ill. From the rhyming slang for "sick." *Cf.* MICK, OLD. [British slang, late 1800s, Ware] **2.** a derogatory term for an Irishman. See MICK (sense 1).

microdots the drug L.S.D. (*q.v.*). *Cf.* DOTS, PURPLE MICRODOTS. [U.S. drug culture, mid 1900s-pres.]

middle finger the penis. *Cf.* FOREFINGER, LITTLE FINGER, THUMB OF LOVE. [British slang, 1800s]

middle-gate the female genitals. For synonyms see MONOSYLLABLE. [British, late 1600s]

middle kingdom the female genitals. From the name of a period in ancient Egyptian history. [British slang, 1800s]

middle leg the penis. *Cf.* BEST LEG OF THREE. [colloquial since the 1800s or before]

middle stump the penis. *Cf.* CARNAL STUMP. [British slang, 1900s, *Dictionary of Slang and Unconventional English*]

midlands the female genitals. *Cf.* LOWLANDS. [British slang, 1800s, Farmer and Henley]

midnight a very dark Negro. Derogatory when used generically. From the blackness of midnight. [U.S., early 1900s-pres.]

midnight cowboy a homosexual male. *Cf.* COWBOY. Also the title of a movie. [U.S., mid 1900s-pres.]

midnight oil opium. The expression "burning the midnight oil" refers to staying up late at night working. [U.S. underworld, 1900s or before]

mig 1. urine or liquid manure; water running off a dung-heap. Cow-mig comes from a heap of cow dung. [*c.* 1000] **2.** a marijuana cigarette. A linguistic blend of "marijuana" and "cigarette." [U.S. underworld, mid 1900s] See also MUGGLES.

miggies marijuana cigarettes. From MIG (sense 2). There is a remote possibility that this is a miscopy.

mike an Irishman. Derogatory when used generically. *Cf.* MICK (sense 1). For synonyms see HARP. [slang and colloquial, 1800s-1900s]

Mike Bliss (also **Mick Bliss**) urine; piss; the same as MICKEY BLISS (*q.v.*). [British, 1900s]

milk 1. to masturbate a male to ejaculation. [colloquial and slang, 1600s-pres.] **2.** semen. *Cf.* CREAM (sense 1). HOT MILK. [widespread slang and nonce since the 1600s] **3.** to manipulate the penis in such a way that a whitish fluid will be expressed if its owner is infected with gonorrhea. Done by prostitutes. *Cf.* FRESH COW. See also LONDON MILK.

milk-bottles the human breasts. *Cf.* CREAM JUGS, DAIRIES, FEEDING-BOTTLES. For synonyms see BOSOM. [widespread slang; attested as Australian and U.S. slang and colloquial, 1900s]

milker 1. the female genitals. [British, 1800s or before] **2.** a male masturbator. *Cf.* MILK (sense 1). For synonyms see HUSKER. [slang, 1800s]

milking-pail the female genitals. *Cf.* MILK (sense 2). [British, 1800s]

milk-jug the female genitals. *Cf.* MILK (sense 2). [British, 1700s]

milkman 1. a male masturbator. *Cf.* MILKER (sense 2), MILK-WOMAN. For synonyms see HUSKER. **2.** the penis. [both senses, British slang, 1800s, Farmer and Henley]

milk-pan the female genitals. *Cf.* PAN (sense 2). [British, 1800s]

milk-shop the human breasts. *Cf.* DAIRIES. [British, 1800s or before]

milksop a coward; an effeminate male. [since the 1300s]

milk-walk the human breasts. *Cf.* DAIRIES. [British, 1800s]

milk-woman 1. a wet nurse. [widespread colloquial; attested as Scots, 1800s or before] **2.** a woman who masturbates men. *Cf.* MILKMAN. [British slang, 1800s, Farmer and Henley]

milky-way the human breasts. [slang, early 1600s-pres.]

mill the female genitals. *Cf.* GRIND. [British slang, early 1700s]

milled intoxicated with alcohol. For synonyms see WOOFLED. [British colloquial, 1800s or before, Halliwell]

miller a lecher; a whoremonger. See GRIND, MILL. [British slang, 1700s]

milliner's shop the female genitals. See HAT (sense 2). For synonyms see MONOSYLLABLE. [British slang, 1800s, Farmer and Henley]

milt 1. the testes or seminal fluid of fish. [standard English] **2.** human semen. From sense 1. [British, 1800s, Farmer and Henley]

milt-market (also **milt-shop**) the female genitals. *Cf.* MILT (sense 2). [British slang, 1800s]

mince 1. a homosexual male. **2.** to walk or move in an effeminate manner. [both senses, U.S., mid 1900s-pres.]

mind fuck to pressure someone to do something that the person would not otherwise do; to confuse or bewilder someone intentionally. [U.S. slang, mid 1900s-pres.]

mind in the mud (also **mind in the gutter**) **1.** pertaining to a person who thinks vulgar thoughts. **2.** pertaining to a person who sees immediately the obscene senses of deliberate or accidental double entendre. [both senses, U.S. slang and colloquial, 1900s]

mine-of-pleasure the female genitals. For synonyms see MONOSYLLABLE. [late 1700s, (Robert Burns)]

mingle bloods to copulate and procreate; to join family lines. [from *A Winter's Tale* (Shakespeare)]

mingo a CHAMBER POT (*q.v.*). [from the Latin for "make water"; U.S. colloquial, 1800s]

minibennies amphetamines. For synonyms see AMP. [U.S. drug culture, mid 1900s-pres.]

mini-skirt a young woman; a girl. *Cf.* CALICO. [U.S. slang, mid 1900s-pres.]

mink 1. Refers to his frequent copulation. [U.S. slang and nonce, 1900s, Wentworth and Flexner] **2.** one's girlfriend. [U.S. slang, mid 1900s]

minks a flirtatious young woman. See MINX. [late 1600s, B.E.]

minor a W.C.; a privy. *Cf.* SMALLEST ROOM. [British, late 1700s, Grose]

mintie 1. a homosexual male, especially an effeminate male. Also **minty.** **2.** pertaining to a homosexual male. **3.** a masculine lesbian. [all senses, U.S. homosexual use and general slang, mid 1900s-pres.]

minx (also **minks**) **1.** a forward woman or girl; a hussy or a harlot. **2.** a prostitute; a whore. [both since the late 1500s]

miracle-meat a large penis; a penis which is essentially as large in the flaccid stage as it is in the erect stage. *Cf.* MENTULATE. [U.S. homosexual use, mid 1900s]

miraculous intoxicated with alcohol. [from Scots colloquial; British, 1900s]

miraculous-cairn the female genitals. "Cairn" refers to a mound. [British, 1800s, Farmer and Henley]

mird to play sexually; the same as MEDDLE (*q.v.*). [From Scots colloquial; since the early 1600s]

mischief you say!, The euphemistic for "The hell you say!" [U.S. colloquial, 1900s or before]

misery gin. *Cf.* BLUE RUIN. [British slang, 1800s, Farmer and Henley]

miss 1. a high-class prostitute. [British, early 1700s, *New Canting Dictionary*] **2.** to fail to have the menses at or soon after the expected time; to miss a period. [U.S. colloquial, mid 1900s-pres.]

Miss Brown the female genitals. For

synonyms see MONOSYLLABLE. [British slang, 1700s-1800s]

Miss Emma morphine. Emma is the name of the letter "M" used in signaling. [U.S. underworld, early 1900s-pres.]

Miss Horner 1. the female genitals. *Cf.* HORNINGTON, OLD. [British slang, 1800s, Farmer and Henley] **2.** a sexually loose woman. *Cf.* MR. HORNER.

missionary 1. a euphemism for "pimp." [U.S. underworld, 1900s] **2.** a drug peddler. [U.S. slang, mid 1900s-pres.]

missionary position a position for copulation wherein the man is above the woman, who receives him between her legs; the *figura veneris prima.* Implies that "natives" to whom missionaries minister in underdeveloped lands copulate in "primitive" ways, *i.e.,* dorsally.

Miss Laycock the female genitals. A play on COCK (sense 3), the penis. [British slang, 1700s, Grose]

Miss Nancy 1. a prim person of either sex. [British and U.S. colloquial, 1800s] **2.** an effeminate male. [British and U.S. slang, late 1800s] **3.** a CATAMITE (*q.v.*). From sense 2.

mist the drug P.C.P. (*q.v.*). [U.S. drug culture, mid 1900s-pres.] See also BLUE MIST.

Mist alcrity! a deliberate spoonerism for "Christ almighty!" *Cf.* MYST ALL CRIKEY! For synonyms see SWEET CHEESE-CAKE. [U.S. colloquial, 1900s or before]

Mister Charlie a nickname for a Caucasian. *Cf.* CHARLIE. [U.S. black use, mid 1900s]

Mister Tom the penis; a personification of the penis. *Cf.* LONG TOM. [U.S. black use, mid 1900s]

mistress a woman who is the lover of a married man; an upper-class kept woman; any concubine supported by a male lover. [since the 1500s]

mitten queen a homosexual male who derives special satisfaction from masturbating others. [U.S. homosexual use, mid 1900s-pres.]

mix one's peanut butter to commit pederasty. [U.S. slang, mid 1900s]

mizzled intoxicated with alcohol. For synonyms see WOOFLED. [colloquial, 1900s or before]

M.J. "Mary Jane," marijuana. [U.S. drug culture, mid 1900s-pres.]

mo a homosexual male. From "homo." *Cf.* MOLA. [U.S. slang, mid 1900s-pres.]

mob a strumpet; a prostitute. [British, mid 1600s]

mocky (also **mockie**) a derogatory term for a Jewish man. For synonyms see FIVE AND TWO. [U.S. slang, 1900s]

model (also **entertainer**) a euphemism for "prostitute." [British and U.S. colloquial, 1900s]

modesty 1. the state of conforming to a culture's traditions regarding which parts of the body may not be exposed in public. Pertaining particularly to women. [since the 1500s] **2.** the female genitals, especially in expressions such as "her modesty." *Cf.* MANLINESS. [translation of the Latin *pudendum*]

modicum 1. a woman. **2.** the female genitals. [both senses, British since the 1600s]

modiewart (also **mowdiwort**) the penis. [from a Scots word for "mole"]

modigger the penis [U.S. slang, mid 1900s]

moff a HERMAPHRODITE (*q.v.*). *Cf.* MORPHODITE. [British slang, 1900s, *Dictionary of Slang and Unconventional English*]

mohasky 1. marijuana. **2.** intoxicated with marijuana. *Cf.* MAHOSKA, MOSHKY. [both senses, U.S. drug culture, mid 1900s-pres.]

moist around the edges intoxicated with alcohol. For synonyms see WOOFLED. [colloquial or slang, 1900s]

moist 'un a drunkard. For synonyms see ALCHY. [British and U.S. slang, 1800s-1900s]

mojo narcotics, especially cocaine and morphine. [U.S. underworld and drug culture, mid 1900s-pres.]

moke 1. a donkey; a beast of burden.

No negative connotations. [British and U.S. colloquial, 1800s] **2.** a Negro; a Negro slave. Usually considered derogatory. Possibly from "mocha." For synonyms see EBONY. [British and U.S. colloquial, 1800s] **3.** a dolt; a dullard. [British and U.S. colloquial and slang, 1800s-1900s]

mokus 1. alcoholic drink; booze. **2.** intoxicated with alcohol. [both senses, U.S. slang, 1900s]

mola a homosexual male. *Cf.* MO, NOLA. For synonyms see EPICENE. [U.S. slang, mid 1900s-pres.]

mole the penis. Refers to the burrowing habits of the mole. See MOWDIWORT. [British, 1800s]

mole-catcher the female genitals; the "mate" of the MOLE (*q.v.*). [British slang, 1800s, Farmer and Henley]

molehills the human breasts, occasionally implying small breasts. Molehills are the opposite of MOUNTAINS (*q.v.*). [U.S. slang and nonce, 1900s]

molest to harm sexually; to rape. [U.S., mid 1900s-pres.]

moll 1. a girl. **2.** a thief's accomplice. **3.** a prostitute. **4.** one's girlfriend. "Moll" is a nickname for "Mary." See MALKIN. [in various senses since the 1600s]

moll-hunter a woman-chaser; a lecher. [British slang, late 1800s, Ware]

mollock (also **mullock**) dung. [British colloquial, 1800s, Axon] See also MULLOCKS.

moll-shop a brothel. [British slang, early 1900s]

molly (also **molley, mollie**) **1.** a harlot. *Cf.* MOLL. [slang since the early 1700s or before] **2.** an effeminate male; a MILKSOP (*q.v.*); a CATAMITE (*q.v.*). [British and U.S. underworld, 1800s-early 1900s] **3.** to commit an act of PEDERASTY (*q.v.*).

mollycoddle 1. to pamper. **2.** an effeminate male; a male who has been mollycoddled; anyone who has been mollycoddled. [both senses, colloquial, 1800s-1900s]

molly-head a simple oaf. [U.S. colloquial, 1900s]

molly-house a male brothel; a place where catamites may be hired. *Cf.* CATAMITE, MOLLY (sense 2). [British, 1700s]

molly-mop an effeminate male. *Cf.* DOLLY-MOP. [British, early 1800s, *Dictionary of Slang and Unconventional English*]

molly's-hole the female genitals. For synonyms see MONOSYLLABLE. [British slang, 1800s, Farmer and Henley]

momzer (also **mamzer**) **1.** an illegitimate child; a BASTARD (sense 1). For synonyms see ACCIDENT. **2.** a wretched and despised person; a BASTARD (sense 2). [Hebrew; attested in Latin as *manzer;* appears in English in the late 1500s; most of the current U.S. use is from Yiddish]

money the female genitals, a euphemism used with little girls. Patterned on the warning given to children when they are going shopping, *i.e.,* "Don't show your money!" [British, late 1700s, Grose]

money-box (also **money-maker, money-spinner**) the female genitals; the same as TILL (*q.v.*). See MONEY. [slang, 1800s or before, Farmer and Henley]

monger See GUT-BUTCHER, MUTTON-MONGER, WHOREMONGER.

mongrel 1. a bastard. **2.** pertaining to a bastard. [both since the late 1400s]

monkey 1. the female genitals. [slang and colloquial, 1800s-1900s] **2.** a derogatory nickname for a Caucasian. Possibly related to sense 1 or to APE (*q.v.*). [U.S. black use, mid 1900s]

monkey-bite a kiss that leaves a blotch or mark. *Cf.* HICKY (sense 5). [U.S. slang and colloquial, 1900s]

monkey-farting goofing off; wasting time. A blend of "monkeying around" and "farting around." See FIDDLE-FARTING. [British, 1900s]

monkey-house a brothel. *Cf.* MONKEY (sense 1). [U.S. underworld, mid 1900s]

monkey-Jesus an ugly person. *Cf.* CREEPING JESUS! [attested as Caribbean (Jamaican), Cassidy and Le Page]

monkey-tricks the taking of sexual liberties; fondling a woman's MONKEY (sense 1). A specialized use of the colloquial expression referring to any kind of mischief. *Cf.* PAW-PAW TRICKS. [British slang, late 1800s]

mono a truncation of "mononucleosis," an infectious disease of the lymphoid tissue. [U.S. colloquial, mid 1900s-pres.]

monocular-eyeglass the anus. *Cf.* EYE (sense 1). [British slang, 1800s, Farmer and Henley]

monosyllable the female genitals. From the monosyllabic word CUNT (*q.v.*). [British; early 1800s-1900s] Synonyms: A.B.C., ACE, ACE OF SPADES, ADAMS OWN, AFFAIR, AFFAIRS, ALCOVE, ALMANACH, ALTAR OF HYMEN, ALTAR OF LOVE, APHRODISIACAL TENNIS COURT, ASS, BABY-MAKER, BAG, BANK, BAZOO, BEAUTY-SPOT, BEAVER, BEE-HIVE, BELLY-DALE, BELLY-DINGLE, BELLY-ENTRANCE, BERKELEY, BERKELEY HUNT, BERKSHIRE HUNT, BILE, BIMBO, BIRD, BIT, BITE, BIT OF JAM, BIT ON A FORK, BLACK BESS, BLACK-HOLE, BLACK-JOCK, BLACK JOKE, BLACK-RING, BLUEBEARD'S CLOSET, BOB-AND-HIT, BOMBO, BOODY, BORE, BOTTOMLESS-PIT, BOX, BOX-UNSEEN, BRAT-GETTING PLACE, BREACH, BREAD, BREADWINNER, BROOM, BROWN-JOCK, BROWN MADAM, BROWN MISS, BUCKINGER'S BOOT, BUDGET, BULL'S EYE, BUMDO, BUM FIDDLE, BUM-SHOP, BUN, BUNGALOW, BUNNY, BUSH, BUSHY PARK, BUSINESS, BUTCHER'S SHOP, BUTTER-BOAT, BUTTONHOLE, C., CABBAGE, CABBAGE-FIELD, CABBAGE-GARDEN, CABBAGE-PATCH, CAKE, CAN, CANDLESTICK, CAPE HORN, CAPE OF GOOD HOPE, CARNAL TRAP, CASE, CAT, CATCH-'EM-ALIVE-O, CAT'S-HEAD-CUT-OPEN, CAT'S-MEAT, CAULIFLOWER, CAVE, CAVE OF HARMONY, CAZE, CELLAR, CELLAR-DOOR, CENTER OF ATTRACTION, CENTER OF BLISS, CENTRAL FURROW, CENTRAL OFFICE, CERTIFICATE OF BIRTH, CHARLEY, CHARLEY HUNT, CHAT, CHIMNEY, CHINK, CHOCHA, CHUFF BOX, CHUM, CHURN, CIRCLE, CIVET, CLAFF, CLEFT, CLEFT OF FLESH, CLOCK, CLOVEN SPOT, CLOVEN TUFT, COCK, COCK-ALLEY, COCK-HALL, COCK-HOLDER, COCK-INN, COCK-LANE, COCK-LOFT, COCKPIT, COCK-SHIRE, COCKSHY, COFFEE HOUSE, COFFEE-SHOP, COGIE, COMMODITY, CONCERN, CONTRAPUNCTUM, CONUNDRUM, CONY, COOCH, COOKIE, COLLIE-DO, COOSIE, COOT, COOZE, COOZIE, CORNER, CORNUCOPIA, COUPLER, COYOTE, CRACK, CRADLE, CRANNY, CREAM-JUG, CREASE, CREVICE, CRINKUM-CRANKUM, CROTCH, CROWN AND FEATHERS, CRUMPET, CUCKOO'S NEST, CUNNICLE, CUNNIKIN, DAISY, DEAD-END STREET, DEAREST BODILY PART, DEN, DICKY-DIDO, DIDDLE, DIDDLY-POUT, DILBERRY-BUSH, DIMPLE, DIVINE MONOSYLLABLE, DIVINE SCAR, DOODLE-CASE, DOODLE-SACK, DORMOUSE, DOWNY-BIT, DRAIN, DUMB-GLUTTON, DUMB-SQUINT, DUSTER, DYKE, ELL-SKINNER, EVERLASTING WOUND, EVE'S CUSTOM-HOUSE, EYE THAT WEEPS MOST WHEN BEST PLEASED, FACTOTUM, FAN, FANCY-BIT, FANNY, FANNY-ARTFUL, FANNY-FAIR, FART-DANIEL, FAUCET, FEMALE PUDEND, FEMALE PUDENDUM, FEMALE VERENDA, FIDDLE, FIE-FOR-SHAME, FIG, FIRELOCK, FIREPLACE, FISH, FISH-POND, FLAP, FLAP-DOODLE, FLAT COCK, FLESHLY-IDOL, FLESHLY-PART, FLITTER, FLOWER, FLOWER OF CHIVALRY, FLUSEY, FLY-BY-NIGHT, FLY-CAGE, FLY-CATCHER, FLY-TRAP, FOBUS, FOOL-TRAP, FORECASTER, FORECASTLE, FORE-COURT, FOREHATCH, FORE-ROOM, FORE-WOMAN, FORNICATOR'S HALL, FORT, FORT BUSHY, FORTRESS, FOUNTAIN OF LIFE, FOUNTAIN OF LOVE, FREE-FISHERY, FRONT-ATTIC, FRONT-DOOR, FRONT-GARDEN, FRONT-GUT, FRONT-PARLOR, FRONT-WINDOW, FRUITFUL VINE, FUCK-HOLE, FUNNIMENT, FUNNY BIT, FUR, FURROW, FUTY, FUTZ, GALLIMAUFREY, GAP, GAPE, GAPER, GARDEN OF EDEN, GASH, GASP AND GRUNT, GATE, GATE-OF-HORN, GATE-OF-LIFE, GATE-OF-PLENTY, GEAR, GENERATING PLACE, GENTLEMAN'S PLEASURE-GARDEN, GEOGRAPHY, GIG, GIGI, GIMCRACK, GIRL STREET, GOAT-MILKER, GOLDFINCH'S NEST, GRAVY-GIVER, GRAVY-MAKER, GREEN-GROCERY, GREEN MEADOW, GREY-JOCK, GRIND-

STONE, GROTTO, GROVE OF EGLANTINE, GROWL, GRUMBLE AND GRUNT, GRUMMET, GULLY, GULLY-HOLE, GUT-ENTRANCE, GUTTER, GYMNASIUM, GYVEL, HAIRBURGER, HAIR-COURT, HAIR-PIE, HAIRYFORDSHIRE, HAIRY ORACLE, HAIRY-RING, HALF-MOON, HANDLE FOR THE BROOM, HAPPY HUNTING-GROUNDS, HAPPY VALLEY, HARBOUR, HARBOUR OF HOPE, HAT, HATCHWAY, HEY-NONNY-NONNY, HIVE, HOG EYE, HOGSTYE OF VENUS, HOLE, HOLE OF CONTENT, HOLE OF HOLES, HOLLOWAY, HOLY OF HOLIES, HOME SWEET HOME, HONE, HONEY-POT, HOOP, HORSE COLLAR, HORSESHOE, HORTUS, HOT BEEF, HOT-BOX, HOTEL, HOT MEAT, HOT MUTTON, HOUSE OF SECURITY, HOUSE UNDER THE HILL, HOUSEWIFE, HYPOGASTRIC-CRANNY, INDIA, INEFFABLE, INGLE-NOOK, INSTRUMENT, INTERCRURAL TRENCH, IRISH FORTUNE, IT, ITCHER, ITCHING JENNY, IVORY GATE, JACK NASTY-FACE, JACK STRAW'S CASTLE, JACOB'S LADDER, JAM, JAM-POT, JAXY, JAZZ, JELLY, JELLY BAG, JELLY-ROLL, JEWEL, JEWELRY, JIG, JIGGER, JIGGUMBOB, JING-JANG, JOCK, JOE HUNT, KAM, KAZE, KEESTER, KEIFER, KENNEL, KETTLE, KEYHOLE, KEYSTONE OF LOVE, KITCHEN KITTY, KNICK-KNACK, LADDER, LADY BERKELEY, LADY-FLOWER, LADY JANE, LADY-STAR, LAMP OF LOVE, LAP, LAPLAND, LATHER-MAKER, LEADING ARTICLE, LEAK, LEA-RIGS, LEATHER, LIMBO, LITTLE MARY, LITTLE SISTER, LIVING FOUNTAIN, LOB'S POUND, LOBSTER-POT, LOCK, LOCKER, LONG-EYE, LOVE CHAMBER, LOVE-LANE, LOVE-PAD, LOVE'S CHANNEL, LOVE'S FOUNTAIN, LOVE'S HARBOUR, LOVE'S PARADISE, LOVE'S PAVILION, LOW-COUNTRIES, LOWER-WIG, LOWLANDS, LUCKY-BAG, LUTE, MACHINE, MADDIKIN, MADGE, MAGNET, MAGPIE'S NEST, MAIN AVENUE, MAIN VEIN, MALKIN, MANGLE, MANHOLE, MANTRAP, MARBLE-ARCH, MARK OF THE BEAST, MARY JANE, MASTERPIECE, MATCH, MATE, MATRIX, MAWKIN, MEAT, MEAT-COOKER, MEAT-GRINDER, MEAT-MARKET, MEDLAR, MELTING-POT, MERKIN, MICKEY MOUSE, MIDDLE-GATE, MIDDLE KINGDOM, MIDLANDS, MILKER, MILKING-PAIL, MILK-JUG, MILK-PAN, MILL, MILLNER'S SHOP, MILT-MARKET, MILT-SHOP, MINE-OF-PLEASURE,

MIRACULOUS-CAIRN, MISS BROWN, MISS HORNER, MISS LAYCOCK, MODESTY, MODICUM, MOLLY'S-HOLE, MONEY, MONEY-BOX, MONKEY, MONS MEG, MOOSEY, MORTAR, MOSS-ROSE, MOSSY-CELL, MOTHER OF ALL SAINTS, MOTHER OF ALL SOULS, MOUNT PLEASANT, MOUSE, MOUSER, MOUSE-TRAP, MOUTH-THANKLESS, MOUTH-THAT-CANNOT-BITE, MOUTH THAT SAYS NO WORDS ABOUT IT, MUFF, MULIEBRIA, MUMBLE-PEG, MUSHROOM, MUSTARD-POT, MUTTON, NAF, NAGGIE, NAME-IT-NOT, NAME-LESS, NATURA, NATUR-ALIA, NATURE, NATURE'S TUFTED-TREASURE, NAUGHTY, NAUTCH, NEEDLE-BOOK, NEEDLE-CASE, NEST, NEST OF SPICERY, NETHER END, NETHER-EYE, NETHERLANDS, NETHER LIPS, NICHE, NICHE-COCK, NICK, NICK-IN-THE-NOTCH, NICK-NACK, NOCK-ANDRO, NONE-SUCH, NONNY-NONNY, NOOKER, NOOKY, NOTCH, NOVELTY, NUMBER NIP, NURSERY, OAT-BIN, O.B.H., OLD DING, OLD HAT, OLD LADY, OLD MOSSYFACE, OLD THING, OLD WIFE, OLD WOMAN, OMNIBUS, OPEN C., ORACLE, ORANGE, ORCHARD, ORGAN-GRINDER, ORIFICE, ORNAMENT, OVEN, OYSTER, OYSTER-CATCHER, PALACE OF PLEASURE, PAN, PANCAKE, PANNIER, PARADISE, PARENTHESIS, PARLOR, PARSLEY-BED, PARTS OF SHAME, PATCH, PECULIAR RIVER, PEN, PENWIPER, PERIWINKLE, PFOTZE, PHOENIX-NEST, PIGEON-HOLE, PILLICOCK-HILL, PIN-CASE, PINCUSHION, PINTLECASE, PIPE-CLEANER, PIPKIN, PISSER, PIT, PITCHER, PIT-HOLE, PLACKET, PLACKET-BOX, PLACKET-HOLE, PLAYGROUND, PLAY-THING, PLEASURE-BOAT, PLUM-TREE, P-MAKER, POCKET-BOOK, POINT-OF-ATTRACTION, POKE-HOLE, POONOO, POONTANG, POOR MAN'S BLESSING, PORTAL OF VENUS, PORT-HOLE, POSTERN, POT, POUTER, POX-BOX, PRANNY, PRATS, PREMISES, PRETTY, PRICK-HOLDER, PRICK-POCKET, PRICK-PURSE, PRICK-SCOURER, PRICK-SKINNER, PRINCOCK, PRIVATE PARTS, PRIVATE PLACE, PRIVATES, PRIVY-HOLE, PUDDLE, PUDEND, PUDENDA, PUDENDA MULIEBRIS, PUDENDUM, PUDENDUM FEMINUM, PULPIT, PUMP, PUMP-DALE, PUMPKIN, PUNCE, PUNSE, PURSE, PUSS, PUSSY, QUAINT, QUARRY, QUAVER-CASE, QUEEN-OF-HOLES, QUEM, QUID, QUIFF, QUIM, QUIM-MY, QUIMSBY, QUIMSY, QUIN, QUIVER,

QUONIAM, RASP, RATTLE-BALLOCKS, RECEIPT-OF-CUSTOM, RECEIVING-SET, RED ONION, REGULATOR, REST-AND-BE-THANKFUL, RING, RINGERANGEROO, ROAD, ROAD TO HEAVEN, ROASTING-JACK, ROB-THE-RUFFIAN, ROOSTER, ROSE, ROUGH-AND-TUMBLE, ROUGH MALKIN, RUFUS, RUMP, SADDLE, SALLY-PORT, SALT-CELLAR, SAMPLER, SATCHEL, SCABBARD, SCUT, SCUTTLE, SEAR, SECRET PARTS, SEED-LAND, SEED PLOT, SEMINARY, SEX, SHADY SPRING, SHAFT, SHAKE-BAG, SHAPE, SHEATH, SHELL, Sir Berkeley Hunt, SKIN-COAT, SKIN-THE-PIZZLE, SLIPPER, SLIT, SLOT, SLUICE, SMOCK, SMOCK-ALLEY, SNATCH-BLATCH, SNATCH-BOX, SNIPPET, SOCKET, SOLUTION-OF-CONTINUITY, South Pole, SPENDER, SPERM-SUCKER, SPEW-ALLEY, SPITFIRE, SPLIT-APRICOT, SPORTS-MAN'S GAP, SPORTSMAN'S HOLE, SPOT, SQUARE PUSH, SQUINT, SQUIRREL, STAR, STREAM'S TOWN, STUFF, SUCK-AND-SWALLOW, SUGAR-BASIN, SUGAR DOUGH-NUT, SUPPER, SWEET-SCENTED HOLE, TAIL, TAIL-BOX, TAIL-GAP, TAIL-GATE, TAIL-HOLE, TAIL-TRIMMER, TARGET, TEAZLE, TEMPLE OF LOW MEN, TEMPLE OF Venus, TENCH, THAT, THATCH, THATCHED HOUSE UNDER THE HILL, THE ANTIPODES, THE NEVER OUT, THING, THINGAMY, THING-UMBOB, THINGUMMY, TICKLE-Thomas, TICKLE-TOBY, TILL, TIRLY-WHIRLY, TIT, TIT-MOUSE, TIVVY, TOBY, TOKEN, TOLL-HOLE, TOMBOY, TOOL-CHEST, TOUCH-HOLE, TOY, TOY-SHOP, TRAP, TREASURE, TRENCH, TRINKET, TUNNEL, TU QUOQUE, TWAT, TWATCHEL, TWIM, TWITCHER, TWITCHET, TWITTLE, TYTMOSE, UNDER-DIMPLE, UNDERS, UNDERTAKER, UPRIGHT GRIN, UPRIGHT WINK, VACUUM, VALVE, VENERABLE MONOSYLLABLE, VENT, VENUS'S-CELL, Venus's HONYPOT, VIRGIN-TREASURE, VULVA, WARE, WASTE-PIPE, WATER-BOX, WATER-MILL, WHAT, WHELK, WHERE UNCLE'S DOODLE GOES, WHETING-CORNE, WHIM-WHAM, WOMAN-HOOD, WORKS, WORKSHOP, WOUND, YARD MEASURE, YEAST-POWDER BISCUIT, YONI, YOU-KNOW-WHAT, YUM-YUM.

Montezuma's revenge diarrhea. Originated by tourists in Mexico afflicted with diarrhea. *Cf.* AZTEC TWO-STEP.

For synonyms see QUICK-STEP. [U.S. slang, mid 1900s-pres.]

monthlies the menses. For synonyms see FLOODS. [British and U.S. colloquial, late 1800s-pres.]

monthly flowers the menses. See FLOWERS. [colloquial euphemism, 1800s-1900s]

monthly rag a menstrual cloth. For synonyms see MANHOLE COVER. [U.S. colloquial, 1900s]

monthly terms the menses. [since the early 1600s]

months the menses. *Cf.* MONTHLIES. [since the early 1600s]

moocah marijuana. *Cf.* MOOTAH. [U.S. underworld and drug culture, early 1900s-pres.]

mooch narcotics in general. For synonyms see COTICS. [U.S. underworld, mid 1900s]

moon 1. to show one's nude posteriors through a window (usually of an automobile) at someone. *Cf.* HANG A B.A. Derived from, or the source of, sense 4. [U.S. slang, mid 1900s] **2.** alcohol; whisky. A truncation of MOONSHINE (*q.v.*). [U.S. colloquial, mid 1900s] **3.** MESCALINE (*q.v.*). [U.S. drug culture, mid 1900s-pres.] **4.** the buttocks. [slang, mid 1900s]

mooner 1. a drunkard. [British, 1800s, Farmer and Henley] **2.** an idler; one who seems to be staring at the moon. [colloquial, 1900s and before]

mooney intoxicated with alcohol. See MOONY. [1800s]

moon-eyed intoxicated with alcohol. [U.S., early 1700s-pres.]

moonhead an oaf; a fool. [U.S. colloquial, early 1900s]

moonlighter a prostitute. *Cf.* NOCTURNE. For synonyms see HARLOT. [British slang, mid 1800s, Farmer and Henley]

moonshine 1. nonsense; humbug. [since the late 1500s] **2.** homemade whisky; cheap or inferior alcohol; any alcohol. [cant and colloquial, late 1700s-pres.] Synonyms: A-BOMB JUICE, CORN, CORN-

UICE, CORN-MULE, MOUNTAIN-DEW, STUMP-LIKKER, WHITE MULE.

moony (also **mooney**) intoxicated with alcohol. [British and U.S. slang, 1800s-1900s]

noose 1. a derogatory nickname for a woman. [U.S. slang, mid 1900s-pres.] **2.** a big man; an overweight girl; anything big. [U.S. slang, mid 1900s-pres.]

noosey the female genitals. [U.S. dialect (Ozarks), Randolph and Wilson]

mootah (also **mooter, mootie, mota, mu, muta, mutah, mutha**) marijuana or a marijuana cigarette. Cf. MOOCAH. U.S. underworld and drug culture, early 1900s-pres.]

mop 1. a fool; an oaf. [since the 1300s] **2.** a drunkard who soaks up alcohol. [British slang, 1800s]

mope an oaf or a dolt. [since the early 1600s]

moppy intoxicated with alcohol. [British and U.S. slang, 1800s-1900s]

mops and brooms (also **all mops and brooms**) intoxicated with alcohol. [slang, 1800s-1900s]

more in one's belly than ever came through one's mouth pregnant. Found in numerous forms, typically, "There's more in her belly than ever went through her mouth." [colloquial, 1800s-pres.]

mores manners; fashion. Standards of behavior outside of legal restrictions. In most current use, refers to societal notions of sexual control, especially those which seem out-moded or prudishly restrictive. [from Latin *mos*, "custom, manner"]

morf 1. a hermaphrodite. Cf. MOFF, MORPHODITE. [U.S. slang, early 1900s] **2.** morphine. Also **morfo, morph, morpho.** Cf. MORPHIE. [U.S. drug culture, mid 1900s-pres.]

morfiend a morphine addict. A blend of "morphine" and "fiend." [U.S. slang, mid 1900s]

morning pride a morning erection. See PRIDE OF THE MORNING. A reinterpretation of the name of a quiet morning rain shower. Cf. MATUTINAL EREC-TION. [British, 1800s, *Dictionary of Slang and Unconventional English*]

Morocco, in naked; nude. From Morocco leather, a fine, soft leather. For synonyms see STARKERS. [British, mid 1800s]

morph morphine. See MORF. Synonyms: AUNT EMMA, COBY, CUBE, DOPE, EM, EMSEL, FIRST LINE, GLAD STUFF, GOD'S MEDICINE, GOODY, HAPPY DUST, HAPPY POWDER, HAPPY STUFF, HARD STUFF, HOCUS, M., MISS EMMA, MORF, MORPHIA, MORPHIE, MUD, NUMBER THIRTEEN, RED CROSS, SISTER, STUFF, UNKIE, WHITE MERCHANDISE, WHITE NURSE, WHITE STUFF.

morphie (also **morphy**) morphine. See MORF. [U.S. drug culture, 1900s]

morphodite (also **morphydite**) **1.** a sexual pervert; a homosexual male; a hermaphrodite (sense 3). [U.S. underworld, mid 1900s] **2.** a HERMAPHRODITE (sense 1). [U.S. dialect and colloquial, 1900s or before]

morsel a prostitute; a sexually attractive woman; a harlot or a tart. See TABLE-GRADE. [early 1500s]

mort 1. a girl or woman. [cant, mid 1600s, Harman] **2.** a sexually loose woman; any girl or woman. [British and U.S. underworld with some slang use, 1700s-1900s] **3.** death. **4.** a corpse. [senses 3 and 4 are British dialect, 1800s or before]

mortal intoxicated with alcohol; dead drunk. Cf. MORTALLIOUS. [British slang, early 1800s]

mortallious intoxicated with alcohol; dead drunk. An elaboration of MORTAL (*q.v.*). [British slang, 1800s]

mortar the female genitals. The mate of the PESTLE (sense 1). The penis. [British slang, 1800s, Farmer and Henley]

mort wop-apace an experienced prostitute. Cf. MORT (sense 2). [cant, 1600s-1700s]

Mose a nickname for a black man. Also a proper name derived from Moses. Derogatory when used as a generic term. [U.S. colloquial, 1900s and before]

moshky a user of marijuana. *Cf.* MAHOSKA, MOHASKY. [U.S. drug culture, mid 1900s-pres.]

mosob backslang for "bosom." [U.S. slang, 1900s]

moss 1. the female pubic hair. For synonyms see DOWNSHIRE. [British slang, 1800s, Farmer and Henley] **2.** a derogatory nickname for a Negro. From the texture of Negroid hair. *Cf.* MOSS-HEAD. See also MOSE. [U.S., mid 1900s]

mossback an out-of-date person; an old-fashioned person; a stuffed shirt. From the nickname for a turtle or an alligator which has been submerged so long that moss or algae is growing on its back. [U.S. colloquial, 1900s or before]

mosshead a derogatory nickname for a Negro. From the texture of the hair. *Cf.* MOSS (sense 2). [U.S., mid 1900s]

moss on the bosom hair growing on a man's chest. [U.S. slang, 1900s]

moss-rose the female genitals. See MOSS (sense 1), ROSE (sense 1). [British slang, 1800s, Farmer and Henley]

mossy hairy; crinatory. Pertaining to the human body. [British and U.S. slang and colloquial, 1800s-1900s]

mossy-cell the female genitals. *Cf.* MOSS (sense 1). [British slang, 1800s, Farmer and Henley]

mossyface, old (also **mossyface**) the female genitals. *Cf.* MOSS (sense 1). [British slang, 1800s or before, Farmer and Henley]

mota marijuana. See MOOTAH. [U.S. drug culture, mid 1900s]

moth a prostitute; a prostitute who prowls in the night. She seeks out men in the way that a moth seeks out a light. [British and U.S., late 1800s-1900s]

mother 1. a madam. [British slang and cant, 1600s-1700s] **2.** a truncation of MOTHER-FUCKER (*q.v.*). The truncation is in such wide use that its original negative connotation is unknown to many people. [U.S. slang and colloquial, mid 1900s-pres.] **3.** the "leader" of a group of homosexual males. The "sponsor" of a young homosexual in homosexual society. *Cf.* DAUGHTER. [U.S. homosexual use, mid 1900s-pres.] **4.** any homosexual male. *Cf.* FATHER-FUCKER. [U.S. homosexual use, mid 1900s-pres.]

mother-dangler euphemistic for MOTHER-FUCKER (*q.v.*). For synonyms see M.F. [U.S. slang, 1900s]

motherdear Methedrine (trademark), an amphetamine. For synonyms see AMP. [U.S. drug culture, mid 1900s, *Current Slang*]

mother-fucker (also **mother**) **1.** any despicable person or thing. **2.** a superb person or thing. **3.** a male buddy or chum. A term used between males. *Cf.* FATHER-FUCKER. [all senses, originally U.S. slang, mid 1900s-pres.]

mother-grabber (also **mother-humper, mother-jumper**) a euphemism for MOTHER-FUCKER (*q.v.*). For synonyms see M.F. [U.S. slang, mid 1900s]

mother-lover a euphemism for MOTHER-FUCKER (*q.v.*). [U.S. slang, 1900s]

mother-midnight 1. a midwife. **2.** a madam; a prostitute. *Cf.* MOONLIGHTER. [both senses, British, 1600s, B.E.]

mother-naked naked as at birth. Also Scots **modyr-nakyd**. For synonyms see STARKERS. [colloquial since the 1800s or long before]

mother-nature 1. the urge to eliminate bodily wastes; the biological nature of an organism requiring the elimination of body wastes. **2.** the menses. Also in expressions such as "mother-nature called." For synonyms see FLOODS. **3.** the sexual urge; sexuality. [all senses, colloquial euphemisms, 1900s or before]

mother of all saints (also **mother of all souls, mother of St. Patrick**) the female genitals. [British slang or colloquial, early 1800s]

mother-rucker a euphemism of disguise of MOTHER-FUCKER (*q.v.*). RUCK (*q.v.*) is a common way of disguising the graffito "fuck." For synonyms see M.F. [U.S. slang, mid 1900s]

mother's milk gin. *Cf.* LONDON MILK.

For synonyms see RUIN. [British slang, early 1800s]

mother-ugly 1. a MOTHER-FUCKER *(q.v.)*. **2.** extremely ugly. [both senses, U.S. slang, mid 1900s]

mott-carpet the female pubic hair. [British, 1800s, Farmer and Henley]

motter a user of marijuana. *Cf.* MOOTAH. [U.S. slang, mid 1900s-pres.]

motting copulating; wenching. *Cf.* MOTTE. [British slang, 1800s]

mottob backslang for "bottom." For synonyms see DUFF. [British, 1800s]

motzy a derogatory nickname for a Jewish man or woman. For synonyms see FIVE AND TWO. [U.S. slang, 1900s or before]

mouchey a derogatory nickname for a Jewish man. [British colloquial and slang, mid 1800s]

mount 1. to move into position to coit a woman; to copulate with a woman. *Cf.* BOARD, CLIMB, SCALE. [since the late 1500s; in *Venus and Adonis* (Shakespeare)] **2.** an act of moving into position to copulate with a woman. In "do a mount." [British, mid 1800s, Farmer and Henley] **3.** a wife; a woman. A woman viewed as a horse for mounting and riding, *i.e.,* coiting. [British slang, 1800s, Farmer and Henley]

mount a corporal and four to masturbate, said of the male. The "corporal" is the thumb and the "four" are the fingers. [British slang, late 1700s, Grose]

mountain-dew 1. a nickname for Scotch whisky. [British and Scots, 1800s] **2.** illicitly brewed whisky; moonshine. *Cf.* PRAIRIE-DEW. [U.S., 1800s-1900s]

mountain oysters the testicles of a bull, hog, or ram, roasted or fried. *Cf.* LAMB FRIES. [U.S. dialect and colloquial, 1900s and before]

mountains the human breasts. *Cf.* MOLEHILLS. [U.S. colloquial and nonce, 1900s]

mount of lilies the human breasts. For synonyms see BOSOM. [euphemism, late 1600s]

mouse 1. the penis. Considered as a borrowing creature. [British slang, 1800s, Farmer and Henley] **2.** the female genitals. The reference is to the soft fur of a mouse. *Cf.* TIT-MOUSE. [British slang, 1800s, Farmer and Henley] **3.** a girl or a woman. Possibly from sense 2. **4.** to kiss and pet. From MOUTH (sense 1). [senses 3 and 4 are slang, 1900s if not long before]

mouse-foot!, By the a mock oath and an exclamation. For synonyms see 'Zounds! [mid 1500s]

mouse-hunt a lecher; one who hunts for MOUSE (sense 2). [from *Romeo and Juliet* (Shakespeare)]

mouser 1. the female genitals. Paraphrased from PUSSY (sense 1). [British slang, 1800s, Farmer and Henley] **2.** a homosexual male; the RECEIVER *(q.v.)*. From his nibbling of the penis in the way that a mouse nibbles at cheese, or from "mouther," a MOUTH-WHORE *(q.v.)*. *Cf.* GOBBLER, NIBBLER. [U.S. underworld, early 1900s, Irwin]

mouse-trap the female genitals. See MOUSE (sense 1). [British slang, mid 1800s, Farmer and Henley]

mousle to nibble and tongue a woman's mouth; to MOUTH (sense 1) a woman. *Cf.* MOUSE (sense 4). [1600s-1700s]

mouth 1. to kiss passionately, perhaps with the tongue. [since the 1600s] **2.** a lawyer. See MOUTHPIECE. [U.S. underworld, early 1900s]

mouthpiece (also **mouth**) a criminal lawyer spokesman. For synonyms see SNOLLY-GOSTER. [British and U.S. underworld, late 1800s-pres.]

mouth-thankless the female genitals, especially the vagina. [Scots euphemism, 1400s-1500s]

mouth-that-cannot-bite the female genitals. [British euphemism, early 1700s]

mouth that says no words about it the female genitals. [British, 1700s]

mouth-whore a prostitute who performs FELLATIO *(q.v.)*, either male or female. [British, 1800s, (Farmer)]

movie queen a vain homosexual male. See QUEEN for similar subjects. [U.S. homosexual use, mid 1900s]

movies diarrhea. From the urgency that makes one move fast. Cf. RUNS, TROTS. [U.S. slang and colloquial, mid 1900s]

mow (also **mowe**) **1.** copulation; an act of copulation. [originally Scots, late 1500s-1800s] **2.** to kiss. Probably from "mow," an old dialect term (Scots) for "mouth." Cf. MOUSE (sense 4). [attested as U.S. slang, Weseen via Matsell]

mowdiwort (also **mowdiewark, mo-diewart**) the penis. The Scots word for "mole." See MOLE, MOUSE. From the burrowing habits of the rodent. [Scots, 1700s, (Robert Burns)]

Mr. Horner a lecher; a whoremonger. Cf. MISS HORNER. [British slang, 1800s, Farmer and Henley]

Mrs. Duckett! "Fuck it!" Rhyming slang. [British, 1900s, *Dictionary of Rhyming Slang*]

Mrs. Jones's place (also **Mrs. Jones, widow Jones**) a W.C.; a toilet. [slang and colloquial, 1800s-1900s]

Mrs. Murphy a W.C.; a bathroom. [U.S. colloquial, 1900s or before]

mu marijuana. See MOOCAH, MOOTAH. [U.S. underworld and drug culture, mid 1900s]

muck 1. anything nasty, *i.e.*, dirt, mud, sweat, feces. [since the 1200s] **2.** a disguise of FUCK (*q.v.*). [British, 1900s and before]

muck about 1. to mess around with a woman; to fondle a woman vaginally. [British slang, late 1800s] **2.** to fuck about; to mess up; to create confusion. [British colloquial, 1900s or before]

muck-heap a filthy, slovenly man or woman. [British slang, 1800s, Farmer and Henley]

muckibus intoxicated with alcohol. [probably written nonce; British slang, mid 1700s]

muck-rag a handkerchief. Cf. MUCK-SWEAT. [British colloquial, 1900s]

muck-scutcheon a filthy person. [British, 1800s, Farmer and Henley]

muck-spout a foul-mouthed person. [British and U.S. slang, late 1800s-1900s]

muck-suckle a filthy, slatternly woman. [British, 1800s, Farmer and Henley]

muck-sweat a very nasty, sweaty state. [British colloquial with some U.S. use, 1800s-pres.]

muck up a disguise of FUCK UP (*q.v.*). [U.S. slang, mid 1900s]

muck-wash a nasty, sweaty state. Cf. MUCK-SWEAT. [British colloquial, 1800s]

muckworm a selfish wretch; a miser. From the name of a worm which lives in dung. [colloquial, 1500s-1600s]

mud 1. an oaf. [British colloquial, 1700s-1800s] **2.** opium; raw opium. Cf. COOLIE MUD. [underworld, early 1900s and before] **3.** heroin. From sense 1. See MEXICAN MUD. **4.** morphine. [senses 3 and 4 are U.S. drug culture, mid 1900s or before]

muddle to copulate. Cf. MEDDLE. [originally Scots; British, 1800s]

muddled-up (also **muddled**) intoxicated with alcohol. For synonyms see WOOF-LED. [slang and colloquial, late 1600s-pres.]

muddlehead (also **mud-head**) an oaf; a fool. [British and U.S. colloquial, early 1800s-1900s]

mudger a coward; a milksop. For synonyms see YELLOW-DOG. [British, early 1800s, Farmer and Henley]

mudlark 1. a person of any age who made a living by gathering bits of coal, wood, rope, and nails from the mudflats of the River Thames (London) at low tide. [British, 1800s] **2.** an urchin of very low character. [British and U.S. colloquial, late 1800s-1900s]

muff 1. the female genitals. From the name of a hand-warming muff. In the bawdy verse: "Lost, lost and can't be found; a lady's thing with hair all 'round" (Farmer and Henley). [slang, 1600s-pres.] **2.** a prostitute. For synonyms see harlot. [U.S. colloquial, mid 1900s] **3.** any girl or woman. [U.S. slang, early 1900s] **4.** women considered sexually. From a nickname for a cat. For synonyms see TAIL. [British and U.S., 1900s] **5.** an oaf; a fool. [cant, early 1800s, Vaux]

muff-barking CUNNILINGUS (*q.v.*). [U.S. slang, 1900s]

muff-diver (also **diver**) a CUNNILIN-GUIST (*q.v.*). *Cf.* DIVE A MUFF, DIVER, PEARL-DIVING, SKIN-DIVER. [British and U.S. slang, 1900s]

muffet a young woman; a girl. From "Little Miss Muffet." An elaboration of MUFF (sense 3) reinforced by "Little Miss Muffet." [U.S. slang, mid 1900s-pres.]

muffins the human breasts, especially if small. [U.S. slang, 1900s]

mug 1. a fool; an oaf; a bumpkin. [British and U.S. colloquial, mid 1800s-1900s] **2.** to copulate. [U.S. slang, 1900s] **3.** to attack and rob. [U.S. colloquial, mid 1900s-pres.]

mugg blotts (also **mug blotto**) intoxicated with alcohol. *Cf.* BLOTTO. [U.S. slang, early 1900s]

mugged up (also **mugged**) intoxicated with alcohol. From a drinking mug. *Cf.* CUP-SHOT. [U.S. slang, mid 1900s]

mugget a false vulva with a pubic wig worn by male homosexual prostitutes in DRAG (*q.v.*). [slang, 1900s]

mugging-up making love; petting; caressing. [U.S. slang, mid 1900s]

muggins (also **juggins**) a fool; an oaf. [British colloquial, late 1800s]

muggle-head a user of marijuana. [U.S. underworld and drug culture, mid 1900s-pres.]

muggles (also **muggle**) **1.** marijuana **2.** a marijuana cigarette. [both senses, U.S. underworld, drug culture, early 1900s-pres.]

muggy intoxicated with alcohol. For synonyms see WOOFLED. [British and U.S. slang, mid 1800s-1900s]

muh-fuh a phonological disguise of MOTHER-FUCKER (*q.v.*). *Cf.* M.F. [primarily black use; U.S. slang, mid 1900s-pres.]

mule 1. an impotent male. [slang or colloquial, 1800s-1900s] **2.** a Caucasian male. *Cf.* MOKE. [U.S. slang, early 1900s, Irwin] See also WHITE MULE.

mull an oaf; a simpleton. [British colloquial, 1800s]

mulled-up (also **mulled**) intoxicated with alcohol. [U.S. slang, mid 1900s]

mullet-head a stupid oaf. [U.S. colloquial, 1900s or before]

mulligrubs (also **molligrunt**) **1.** complaining or bellyaching. **2.** the colic. [both senses, 1500s-1900s]

mullocks a slattern; a slovenly person. *Cf.* MOLLOCK. [British colloquial, late 1800s]

mumble-peg the female genitals. For synonyms see MONOSYLLABLE. [British slang, 1800s, Farmer and Henley]

mumbo-jumbo nonsense; jargon. In imitation of what a stereotypical African witch doctor is alleged to say. [colloquial, 1800s-pres.]

mump to copulate. *Cf.* HUMP. Related to a slang term meaning "cheat" or "deceive." [British slang, 1800s, Farmer and Henley]

munch to perform PENILINGUS (*q.v.*). *Cf.* EAT, GOBBLE, NIBBLE. [U.S. slang, mid 1900s-pres.]

muncher-boy (also **muncher**) a fellator; the RECEIVER (*q.v.*). *Cf.* GOBBLER. For synonyms see PICCOLO-PLAYER.

munch the bearded clam to perform CUNNILINGUS (*q.v.*). See BEARD, MUNCH. [slang, 1900s or before]

mur backslang for "rum." [British, 1800s, Farmer and Henley]

murphies the human breasts. From a nickname for "Irish potatoes." *Cf.* SWEET POTATOES. [U.S. slang, 1900s]

muscle moll a masculine woman; a virago. Based on "gun moll." [U.S. underworld, early 1900s]

muscle of love the penis. [U.S. slang, mid 1900s-pres.]

mush 1. nonsense. [U.S. colloquial, 1900s or before] **2.** romance; lovemaking; kissing. [U.S. colloquial, mid 1900s]

mushhead an oaf; a fool. [U.S. colloquial, mid 1900s]

mushroom 1. the female genitals. For

synonyms see MONOSYLLABLE. [British slang, 1800s, Farmer and Henley] **2.** a mushroom containing the hallucinogenic compound psilocybin; the same as MAGIC MUSHROOM (q.v.). [U.S. drug culture, mid 1900s-pres.]

mushroom-picker a derogatory nickname for a Czechoslovakian. [U.S. slang, 1900s]

musical fruit any variety of beans. Because they produce flatulence. Cf. ARS MUSICA, WHISTLE-BERRIES. [U.S. slang and colloquial, 1900s]

muslin woman considered sexually. For synonyms see TAIL. [British, late 1800s]

muss to coit a woman. Cf. MESS (sense 1). For synonyms see OCCUPY. [British slang, 1800s, Farmer and Henley]

musta marijuana. Cf. MOOTAH. For synonyms see MARI. [U.S., 1900s]

mustard, be to be sexually attractive; to be as HOT (sense 1) as mustard. [British slang, early 1900s, Dictionary of Slang and Unconventional English]

mustard and cress the female pubic hair. See MUSTARD-POT. [British slang, 1800s, Farmer and Henley]

mustard-pot 1. the female genitals, "hot like (English) mustard." [British slang, 1800s, Farmer and Henley] **2.** a CATAMITE (q.v.) in a prison. From sense 1. [attested as U.S., mid 1900s]

mustard-yellow a mulatto. Cf. HIGH-YELLOW. For synonyms see MAHOGANY. [U.S. slang, early 1900s]

mustn't-mention-'ems trousers. For synonyms see GALLIGASKINS. [British jocular slang, mid 1800s]

mute 1. liquid bird dung; the dung of hawks; the same as muting. Sometimes for any kind of dung. [colloquial, 1500s] **2.** a person hired to mourn at funerals. [British, 1700s-1800s]

mutha 1. marijuana. See MOOTAH. **2.** "mother"; the same as MOTHER-FUCKER (q.v.).

mutt 1. an oaf; a dullard. From MUTTONHEAD (q.v.). For synonyms see OAF. **2.** a worthless or hybrid dog. [both senses, U.S. slang and colloquial, 1900s]

mutton 1. a sexually loose woman. For synonyms see LAY. [numerous written attestations; British, 1500s-1800s] **2.** the female genitals. **3.** copulation. **4.** women considered sexually. Cf. LACED-MUTTON. [senses 2-4 are British, 1600s] **5.** sexual pleasures. See GREENS. Cf. JERK ONE'S MUTTON, where mutton is either sense 5 or the penis.

mutton, in her in the act of copulation with a woman. [British slang, 1800s, Farmer and Henley]

mutton-cove a whoremonger; a lecher; the same as MUTTON-MONGER (sense 1). [British slang, 1800s, Farmer and Henley]

mutton-dagger the penis. Cf. PORK-SWORD. For synonyms see YARD. [British slang, 1900s, Dictionary of the Underworld]

muttoner a whoremonger; a lecher. [British slang, 1800s]

muttonhead an oaf; a dullard. [British and U.S. colloquial, late 1700s-pres.]

mutton-monger 1. a whoremonger; a lecher. [1500s-1900s] **2.** a pimp, an occasional interpretation. See WHORE-MASTER, which has the same vagueness.

muzzle to kiss and pet. Cf. MOUSLE. [colloquial or slang since the late 1600s]

muzzy intoxicated with alcohol. [British and U.S. colloquial, early 1700s-pres.]

my man Thomas the penis. See JOHN THOMAS; MAN THOMAS, MY.

myrrh rum. A respelling of "mur," which is backslang for "rum." [U.S. slang, 1900s, Wentworth and Flexner]

myrtle copulation. Named for the relationship of the myrtle shrub to the worship of Venus. Cf. NURTLE. [Australian, 1900s, Baker]

Myst all Crikey! (also **Myst all Critey!, Myst all Kritey!**) a disguise of "Christ almighty!" Cf. MIST ALCRITY! For synonyms see 'ZOUNDS! [Australian, early 1900s, Baker]

My stars alive! (also **My stars!**) a mild oath and an exclamation. [U.S. colloquial, 1900s]

N

NABU a "nonadjustable balls-up," an irreconcilable mess. For synonyms see SNAFU. [British military, early 1900s]

nads the testicles. A truncation of "gonads." See NARDS. [slang]

naffgur (also **noffgur**) a prostitute. Possibly backslang, probably from NAFKEH (*q.v.*). [British slang, late 1800s]

nafkeh (also **nafka**) a prostitute. For synonyms see HARLOT. [Aramaic via Yiddish; 1900s or before]

nag 1. a prostitute. [late 1500s] **2.** the penis. *Cf.* STABLE-MY-NAGGIE. For synonyms see YARD. [British slang, late 1600s-1900s] **3.** a testicle. See NAGS.

naggie the female genitals. *Cf.* NAG (senses 1 and 2), STABLE-MY-NAGGIE. [Brtish slang, 1800s, Farmer and Henley]

nags the testicles. Possibly from KNACKERS (*q.v.*). For synonyms see WHIRLY-GIGS. [British slang, 1800s]

nail 1. to copulate with a woman. *Cf.* HAMMER. [U.S. slang, mid 1900s-pres.] **2.** a cigarette. See COFFIN-NAIL. **3.** a "male." Rhyming slang. *Cf.* HAMMER (sense 2). [U.S. black use, mid 1900s-pres.] **4.** a marijuana cigarette. From sense 2. [U.S. drug culture, mid 1900s-pres.]

nail, off the intoxicated with alcohol. For synonyms see WOOFLED. [colloquial, early 1800s-1900s]

nails and by blood!, By an oath and an exclamation. Refers to the nails of the Crucifixion.

nails two bellies together to copulate. A translation of the Scots *nail twa wames tegither*. [1600s]

naked 1. totally nude; no clothing and no covering over the genitals or breasts. For synonyms see STARKERS. **2.** unclothed, but with the genitals covered. **3.** lacking a shirt, said of the male. In various senses, depending on the sensitivities of the speaker, the audience, and the times. [since before 1000]

naked as my nail nude; as unclothed as a fingernail. [early 1600s]

naked buff nude; totally naked. *Cf.* BUFF (sense 1). For synonyms see STARKERS. [U.S. colloquial, 1900s or before]

nakedness the genitals, male or female. [euphemistic, early 1600s]

namby-pamby an overly nice person; an effeminate and weak male. [since the 1700s]

name-it-not the female genitals. An avoidance for CUNT (*q.v.*). *Cf.* INEFFABLE, NAMELESS. [British slang, 1800s, Farmer and Henley]

nameless the female genitals. A jocular avoidance for CUNT (*q.v.*). From a bawdy song. For synonyms see MONOSYLLABLE. [British, 1600s]

namo (also **nammow**) backslang for "woman." *Cf.* DELO-DIAM. [British, late 1800s]

Nan-boy (also **Nancy-boy**) **1.** an effeminate male. For synonyms see FRIBBLE. [British, late 1600s] **2.** a CATAMITE (*q.v.*). For synonyms see BRONCO. [British slang, 1800s or before]

Nance 1. an effeminate male. **2.** a PEDERAST (*q.v.*). [both senses, U.S. slang and colloquial, 1900s or before]

Nancy (also **Nancy-boy**) **1.** a homosexual male, the same as NANCE (*q.v.*). [British and U.S., 1800s-1900s] **2.** the posteriors; the BREECH (sense 2). [British slang, early 1800s]

Nancy Dawson an effeminate male; a homosexual male. Based on the name of a legendary prostitute. [British, late 1800s]

Nancy homey an effeminate male; a homosexual male. [British, 1800s, *Dictionary of Slang and Unconventional English*]

nanny a prostitute. See AUNT (sense 1). *Cf.* NANNY-HOUSE. [British, 1700s or before]

nanny-goat sweat whisky, especially

home-brewed or inferior whisky; moonshine. *Cf.* PANTHER SWEAT. [U.S. slang, mid 1900s]

nanny-house (also **nanny-shop**) a brothel. [British, 1700s-1800s]

nap 1. an infection of a venereal disease. **2.** to infect with a venereal disease. [both senses, British, late 1600s, B.E.] **3.** a derogatory nickname for a Negro. From the texture of the hair. *Cf.* NAPS. [U.S., 1900s, Wentworth and Flexner]

napkin 1. a diaper for a baby. [British colloquial, 1900s and before] **2.** a sanitary napkin; a menstrual pad; a perineal pad. For synonyms see MANHOLE COVER. [U.S. euphemism, 1900s]

nappy 1. intoxicated with alcohol. [from an old Scots term for "ale"; British and U.S., 1800s-1900s] **2.** a diaper. A truncation of "napkin." [British colloquial, 1900s] **3.** a derogatory nickname for a Negro. [U.S. slang, mid 1900s]

naps kinky hair; Negroid hair. [U.S. black use, 1900s]

nards the testicles. A phonological disguise of NERTS or NUTS (both *q.v.*). [U.S. slang, mid 1900s-pres., *Current Slang*]

nark 1. any police spy. [widespread slang, mid 1800s] **2.** a narcotics agent. [1900s] **3.** any unpleasant person; an oaf or jerk. For synonyms see SNOKEHORN. [World War II, Fraser and Gibbons]

narrowback a derogatory term for an Irishman. For synonyms see HARP. [U.S. slang, mid 1900s]

nase (also **nace, naze, nazy**) intoxicated with alcohol. For synonyms see WOOFLED. [cant, early 1500s-1700s]

nasties sexual desire or arousal. *Cf.* NASTY. [U.S., 1900s]

nasty oriented toward sex or sex and excrement; smutty. See NAUGHTY. [since the early 1600s]

natural 1. legitimate; born within a particular marriage. As opposed to an adopted child or a child from another union. [early 1400s] **2.** illegitimate;

born of a mistress or concubine. [late 1500s] **3.** an idiot. [early 1500s] **4.** a mistress. [British, late 1600s, B.E.] **5.** heterosexual; ORTHOGENITAL (*q.v.*). Refers to types of sexual copulation. See NORMAL.

natural, in the naked; nude. *Cf.* au naturel.

natural-child a bastard. *Cf.* NATURAL (sense 2). [since the 1600s]

natural member the penis. *Cf.* MEMBER. [1600s, (Urquhart)]

natural parts (also **natural places**) the genitals, male or female. [mid 1500s]

naturals the genitals, male or female. From NATURAL PARTS (*q.v.*). For synonyms see GENITALS [mid 1600s]

nature 1. the menses. *Cf.* MOTHER-NATURE (sense 2). [since the 1300s] **2.** semen. [euphemism, 1500s] **3.** the genitals, male or female. **4.** the female genitals, especially of a horse. **5.** the libido; male sexual potency. *Cf.* PIONEER OF NATURE. [senses 3-5 since the 1500s]

nature's call the feeling of a need to eliminate wastes; defecation or urination. *Cf.* MOTHER-NATURE (sense 1). [U.S. colloquial, 1900s]

nature's duty copulation. [British, 1700s or earlier]

nature's fonts the breasts. For synonyms see BOSOM. [British euphemism, late 1800s]

nature's garb nakedness. *Cf.* ADAM AND EVE'S TOGS. [British, 1800s, Farmer and Henley]

nature spot a birthmark, mole, or wart. *Cf.* BEAUTY SPOT (sense 2). [euphemistic]

nature's scythe the penis. For synonyms see YARD. [British, late 1700s]

nature stop a stop (in highway travel) to urinate. *Cf.* COKE-STOP, MOTHER-NATURE (sense 1). [U.S. colloquial, mid 1900s-pres.]

nature's tufted-treasure the female genitals. For synonyms see MONOSYLLABLE. [British, early 1800s]

nature's veil the female pubic hair.

Cf. NATURE (sense 3). For synonyms see DOWNSHIRE.

naughty 1. obscene; smutty. [since the mid 1500s] **2.** copulation. [Australian and elsewhere, 1800s-pres.]

naughty-dream an erotic dream, probably a wet dream. [British, 1600s]

naughty-house a brothel. [from *Measure for Measure* (Shakespeare)]

naughty-man a whoremonger. For synonyms see LECHER. [British, 1600s]

naughty pack a sexually loose woman; a prostitute. Also a general term of contempt for either sex. [1500s-1600s]

nautch-broad a prostitute. See NOTCH-BROAD for derivation. [U.S., early 1900s, Goldin, O'Leary, and Lipsius]

nautch-joint a brothel. See NOTCH-HOUSE for derivation. [U.S. slang, 1900s]

naval engagement copulation. From "naval engagement," a battle at sea. *Cf.* JOIN PAUNCHES. [widespread nonce use; attested as Canadian, 1900s, *Dictionary of Slang and Unconventional English*]

navigate the windward passage to copulate anally. The anus is the WINDWARD PASSAGE (*q.v.*).

nazy (also **nazie**) intoxicated with alcohol. *Cf.* NASE. [cant, mid 1500s-1900s]

nazy-cove a drunkard. For synonyms see ALCHY. [cant, 1600s, B.E.]

nazy-nab a drunkard, probably a drunken (fellow) thief. [cant, 1600s]

N.B.G. "no bloody good," used to avoid saying "bloody." An elaboration of N.G., "no good." [British and elsewhere, military, early 1900s, Fraser and Gibbons]

N.B.L. "not bloody likely," an avoidance for "bloody." [British colloquial, 1900s]

Neapolitan disease (also **Neapolitan, Neapolitan**) syphilis. [euphemistic, early 1600s]

Neapolitan favor (also **Neapolitan consolation**) syphilis. "Favor" is possibly "fever." For synonyms see SPECIFIC STOMACH. [British, 1700s-1800s]

near beer beer with low alcohol content; beer with less than .5 percent alcohol content. *Cf.* QUEER BEER, SISSY BEER, SQUAW PISS. [U.S. Prohibition times to the present]

neathie-set female underwear. For synonyms see NETHER-GARMENTS. [British slang, early 1900s]

nebbies Nembutal (trademark) capsules, barbiturate capsules. *Cf.* NEMBIES. [U.S. drug culture, mid 1900s-pres.]

Nebuchadnezzar the penis. *Cf.* TAKE NEBUCHADNEZZAR OUT TO GRASS. [British slang, 1800s, Farmer and Henley]

necessaries the VIRILIA (*q.v.*), primarily the testicles. For synonyms see WHIRLYGIGS. [based on *necessariae partes,* Latin for "the necessary parts"; British, early 1900s]

necessarium a privy; a NECESSARY HOUSE (*q.v.*). For synonyms see AJAX. [Latin]

necessary 1. a prostitute; a female companion to be used sexually. For synonyms see HARLOT. [British slang, 1800s, Farmer and Henley] **2.** a privy. A truncation of NECESSARY HOUSE (*q.v.*).

necessary chamber a privy; a W.C. [British, 1600s or before]

necessary house (also **necessary**) a privy. For synonyms see AJAX. [colloquial, early 1600s-1900s]

necessary vault a privy. A variation of NECESSARY HOUSE (*q.v.*). [British, early 1600s]

neck 1. a woman's bosom. [euphemistic and vague; from *Hamlet* (Shakespeare)] **2.** to hang. For synonyms see NUB. [cant or slang, 1700s] **3.** to kiss and pet. [U.S. colloquial, early 1900s-pres.]

necked naked. A regional pronunciation indicated by the spelling. For synonyms see STARKERS. [U.S. rural colloquial, 1900s and before]

needle the penis. *Cf.* PIN (sense 1), PRICK (sense 1). [British, 1600s]

needle, on the injecting drugs habitually. Pertaining to a drug addict. [U.S. slang, mid 1900s]

needle-book the female genitals. A holder for the NEEDLE (*q.v.*). [British slang, 1800s, Farmer and Henley]

needle-candy a narcotic which is injected. In contrast to narcotics which are sniffed. See NOSE-CANDY. *Cf.* CANDY. [U.S. drug culture, mid 1900s]

needle-case the female genitals. A holder for the NEEDLE (*q.v.*). [British slang, 1800s]

needle-man a narcotics addict who uses injected drugs. *Cf.* ARTILLERY MAN. [underworld, 1900s]

needle-woman a prostitute. *Cf.* NEEDLE. [British, mid 1800s]

Negro drunk heavily intoxicated with alcohol. Derogatory. [U.S., early 1800s, Thornton]

Negro-head 1. a loaf of brown or black bread. [attested as British, late 1700s, Grose] **2.** a plug of black tobacco. [British, early 1800s] **3.** the same as NIGGERHEAD (*q.v.*).

Negro-news the Negro grapevine, a rapid way of spreading news among blacks. [U.S. colloquial, 1800s]

Negro-nosed pertaining to a person with a broad or flat nose. [attested as late 1600s, B.E.]

Nellie fag an effeminate male homosexual. For synonyms see EPICENE. [U.S. slang, mid 1900s-pres.]

Nell's bells! euphemistic for HELL'S BELLS! (*q.v.*). [U.S. colloquial, 1900s or before]

Nelly 1. a lesbian. [U.S. slang, mid 1900s-pres., Underwood] **2.** a homosexual male. [slang, mid 1900s-pres.] **3.** effeminate; pertaining to an effeminate male.

Nelson's blood rum; navy rum. Lord Nelson's body was returned to England preserved in rum. [British, 1800s-1900s]

nembies (also **nimbies**) Nembutal (trademark) capsules; barbiturates. *Cf.* NEBBIES. [U.S. drug culture, mid 1900s-pres.]

nemish a Nembutal (trademark) capsule. [U.S. drug culture, mid 1900s-pres.]

nemmies (also **nems**) Nembutal (trademark) capsules; the same as NEMBIES (*q.v.*). [U.S. drug culture, mid 1900s-pres.] Synonyms: ABBOT, BLOCKBUSTER, NEBBIES, NEMISH, NEMS, NIMBIES, YELLOW, YELLOW ANGEL, YELLOW BULLETS, YELLOW-JACKET.

nephew 1. the illegitimate son of a clergyman. *Cf.* NIECE. [British, mid 1800s] **2.** a CATAMITE or FELLATOR kept by an older homosexual male. *Cf.* AUNT, AUNTIE. [U.S. underworld, early 1900s, Goldin, O'Leary, and Lipsius]

nerd (also **nurd**) an oaf; an undesirable male. For synonyms see OAF. [U.S. slang and colloquial, mid 1900s-pres.]

nerts (also **gnerts, nurts**) **1.** the testicles. A phonological disguise of NUTS (sense 1). *Cf.* NARDS. [U.S., 1900s] **2.** an exclamation of disbelief, "Nerts!" A phonological disguise of NUTS (sense 2). [British and U.S., 1900s]

nervous-cane the penis. *Cf.* VARNISH ONE'S CANE. [mid 1600s, (Urquhart)]

nest 1. to defecate. **2.** a mass of dung. [both senses, British, late 1600s] **3.** the female genitals. [British, late 1700s]

nestlecock (also **nescock, nestcock**) a prostitute; a wanton woman. *Cf.* QUAIL. [British, mid 1600s]

nest of spicery the female genitals and the female pubic hair. [from *Richard III* (Shakespeare)]

nether end the female genitals. For synonyms see MONOSYLLABLE. [British, early 1700s]

nether-eye the female genitals or the anus. [1300s, "The Miller's Tale," *The Canterbury Tales* (Chaucer)]

nether eyebrow (also **nether eyelashes, nether whiskers**) the female pubic hair. [British slang, 1800s]

nether garments 1. underwear. Synonyms: BRIEFS, DRAWERS, FRILLERY, INSIDE CLOTHES, SKIVVIES, SMALLCLOTHES, SMALLS, SMALL SNOW, SNOW, STEP-INS, SUB-TROUSERS, UNDERCLOTHING, UNDERGARMENTS, UNDERS, UNDERWARDROBE, UNDIES, UNHINTABLES, UNMENTIONABLES, UNWHISPERABLES, U-TROU, U-WEAR, WHEREABOUTS, WHITE SEWING, WHITE

WORK, WOOLENS, WOOLIES. **2.** trouser. [both senses, euphemistic, 1800s-1900s]

Netherlands 1. the male genitals. **2.** the female genitals. *Cf.* LOW-COUNTRIES, LOWLANDS. [both senses, British, 1800s, Farmer and Henley]

nether-limbs the legs. *Cf.* LIMB. [classic euphemism of the 1800s]

nether lips the female genitals. Refers to the *labia majora*. [British, 1800s, Farmer and Henley]

nether-work fondling a woman or copulating with a woman. For synonyms see FIRKYTOODLE. [British slang, 1800s, Farmer and Henley]

neuter gender pertaining to a homosexual male and presumably a lesbian. [U.S. colloquial, 1900s]

never-mention-'ems trousers. For synonyms see GALLIGASKINS. [British jocular euphemism, 1800s]

never out, the the female genitals, *i.e.*, that which is never exhausted. [British slang, 1800s, Farmer and Henley]

never-sweat 1. a man who is lazy or is a poor performer on the job. [U.S. colloquial, 1900s or before] **2.** a derogatory nickname for a Mexican. From sense 1. [U.S., 1900s or before]

Newgate hornpipe a hanging. Hangings in the London area were done at Newgate prison. The "hornpipe" is a type of dance. [British, 1800s]

newt a stupid person; an oaf. Named for the amphibian. [U.S. slang, early 1900s]

Niagara Falls the testicles. Rhyming slang for "balls." For synonyms see WHIRLYGIGS. [British, 1900s, *Dictionary of Rhyming Slang*]

niagara falsies false breasts; the same as FALSIES (*q.v.*). Niagara Falls is the stereotypical location for a honeymoon. This implies that an improved bust will help a woman land a husband or at least attract male attention. [U.S. slang, 1900s]

nibble 1. to steal, cheat, or deceive. [cant, 1600s-1800s] **2.** to copulate. **3.** copulation. [both senses, British slang, 1800s, Farmer and Henley]

nibbler a RECEIVER (*q.v.*). *Cf.* GOBBLER, MOUSER, MUNCHER-BOY. For synonyms see PICCOLO-PLAYER. [U.S. underworld, early 1900s, Goldin, O'Leary, and Lipsius]

nice Nellie 1. a prudish man or woman. *Cf.* NICE-NELLYISM. [U.S. colloquial, 1900s and before] **2.** an effeminate male, probably a homosexual male. *Cf.* NELLY (sense 2). [U.S. slang, early 1900s]

nice-Nellyism any euphemism; a euphemism. [U.S. colloquial, 1900s and before]

nic frog a derogatory term for a Dutchman. [U.S. slang]

niche-cock (also **niche**) the female genitals. *Cf.* ALCOVE, CRANNY. [British slang, 1800s or before, Farmer and Henley]

nick 1. the female genitals. *Cf.* PUDENDAL CLEAVAGE. [British, early 1700s] **2.** to copulate with a woman. [British, 1700s] **3.** the devil. Usually capitalized. [colloquial, 1800s-1900s]

nickel (also **nickel bag**) five dollars worth of marijuana. *Cf.* DIME. [U.S. drug culture, mid 1900s-pres.]

nick-in-the-notch the female genitals. *Cf.* NICK (sense 1). [British slang, 1800s, Farmer and Henley]

nick-nack 1. the female genitals. [British colloquial, 1700s] **2.** a homosexual male. See NIC NAC. **3.** a testicle. See NICK-NACKS. *Cf.* KNACKERS. [British, 1700s]

nick-nacks 1. the male genitals; the human testicles; the same as BAUBLES (*q.v.*). [colloquial, 1700s or before] **2.** the human breasts. [slang, 1900s and probably long before]

nickumpoop (also **nincompoop**) a fool; an oaf. [British, 1600s, B.E.]

nic nac a homosexual male. See NICK-NACK (sense 2). For synonyms see EPICENE.

nidge to copulate with a woman. From a term meaning "shake." [British, 1800s]

niece the illegitimate daughter of a

clergyman. *Cf.* NEPHEW. [British, mid 1800s]

nifty copulation. See BIT OF NIFTY.

nig 1. to coit a woman. A truncation of NIGGLE (sense 1). [British slang, 1700s] **2.** a Negro. A truncation of NIGGER (*q.v.*). Derogatory. [U.S., mid 1800s-pres.] **3.** backslang for "gin." For synonyms see RUIN. [British, 1800s]

niggar a derogatory term of address for a Negro. A spelling variant of NIGGER (*q.v.*). *Cf.* GAR. For synonyms see EBONY. [1700s-1800s]

nigger (also **niger, niggar, niggur**) **1.** a derogatory term for a Negro. For synonyms see EBONY. Currently one of the most contemptible terms for a Negro. See also BAD NIGGER, BUCK NIGGER, CHARCOAL NIGGER, FIELD NIGGER, HOUSE NIGGER, INTERNATIONAL NIGGER, NIGGAR, NIGGER-BRAND, NIGGERDOM, NIGGER-DRIVER, NIGGER-FISHING, NIGGER-GAL, NIGGER-GIN, NIGGERHEAD, NIGGER-HEAVEN, NIGGER-HEEL, NIGGER-JOCKY, NIGGER-LIPPING, NIGGER-LOVER, NIGGER-LUCK, NIGGER-NIGHT, NIGGER-POT, NIGGER-RICH, NIGGER-SHOOTER, NIGGERS-IN-A-SNOWSTORM, NIGGER'S KNACKERS, NIGGER-SHOOTER, NIGGER-SPECIAL, NIGGER-SPIT, NIGGER-STEAK, NIGGER-TIP, NIGGER-TOE, NIGGERTOWN, NIGGER-WOOL, NIGGERY, SHOWCASE NIGGER, WHITE NIGGER. **2.** a fellow black, a chum or an intimate friend. [used among blacks; from Latin *niger*, "black, sable, dark, dusky," via the romance languages; in various spellings since the late 1500s]

niggerdom (also **Negrodom**) the life and culture of the American Negro. Derogatory. [U.S., mid 1800s-1900s]

nigger-driver a hard taskmaster. One who drives blacks or one who is powerful and brutal. Derogatory. [U.S. colloquial, mid 1800s-early 1900s]

nigger-fishing fishing from the bank of a river or pond. Derogatory. [U.S. colloquial, 1900s or before]

nigger-gin bad gin or bad liquor in general. Derogatory. [U.S. colloquial, 1900s]

niggerhead 1. a black boulder or dark coral-head partially submerged in the water. Derogatory. [widespread colloquial, mid 1800s-early 1900s] **2.** a prune. Derogatory. [U.S. slang, early 1900s, Goldin, O'Leary, and Lipsius] **3.** a plug of black tobacco; the same as NEGRO-HEAD (sense 2). At one time, a brand name of chewing tobacco. Derogatory. [U.S., 1800s-1900s]

nigger-heaven 1. the upper balcony in a movie theater. Derogatory. *Cf.* ETHIOPIAN PARADISE. [attested as U.S. (Boston), late 1800s, Thornton] **2.** the roof of a freight train. Derogatory. [U.S., 1900s]

nigger-heel a Brazil nut; the same as NIGGER-TOE (*q.v.*), which is more common. Derogatory. [U.S. colloquial, 1900s or before]

nigger-lipping to wet the end of a cigarette with the lips. Derogatory. [U.S. colloquial, 1900s]

nigger-lover a derogatory term for a Caucasian who associates with Negroes or who takes up civil rights causes. [U.S. since the early 1800s]

nigger-luck amazingly good luck. Derogatory. [U.S. colloquial, mid 1800s-pres.]

nigger-pot homebrewed whisky. Derogatory. [U.S. dialect (Southern), 1900s]

nigger-rich having barely enough money to live on. Derogatory. [U.S. colloquial, 1900s]

nigger-shooter a slingshot. Derogatory. [U.S., 1800-1900s]

niggers-in-a-snowstorm stewed prunes and rice. *Cf.* HEADLIGHT TO A SNOWSTORM. More jocular than derogatory. [British, 1800s-early 1900s]

niggers' knackers prunes. From their shape and color; the "knackers" are the testes, derogatory. [British military, early 1900s, *Dictionary of Slang and Unconventional English*]

Niggers-noggers! an oath and an exclamation. This is not connected with NIGGER (*q.v.*). [early 1600s]

nigger-special a watermelon. From the stereotypical image of a Negro happily eating a slice of watermelon. The watermelon image is now considered derogatory. [U.S., 1900s]

nigger-spit lumps in cane sugar. Based in part on the legendary practice of slaves spitefully spitting in the master's soups or stew. [colloquial since the 1800s]

nigger-steak a slice of liver. Because liver was considered an inferior cut of meat and because of the color. Derogatory. [U.S. slang, 1900s]

nigger-toe 1. a Brazil nut. *Cf.* NIGGER-HEEL. Derogatory. [U.S. colloquial, 1800s-1900s] **2.** a small potato. Derogatory. [U.S. colloquial, mid 1900s]

niggertown the Negro district of a town. Derogatory. *Cf.* BLACK BELT, LAND OF DARKNESS. [U.S. colloquial, 1900s]

nigger up to outfit in a gaudy or outlandish manner. Refers to personal dress, cars, etc. [U.S. colloquial or slang, 1900s and before]

nigger-wench a black woman. Derogatory. [U.S. colloquial, 1900s or before]

nigger-wool a Negro's hair; kinky hair. Derogatory. [U.S. colloquial, 1900s]

niggle (also **nig, nygle**) **1.** to coit a woman. *Cf.* TWIGLE. [since the mid 1500s, Harman] **2.** to cheat or deceive. [since the early 1600s] **3.** to twitch or fidget from sexual interest or arousal, said of girls or young women. [British, early 1700s]

niggra (also **nigra**) a Negro. The Southern pronunciation of "Negro" or "nigger." This word is particularly offensive to some blacks. [U.S., 1800s-pres.]

nigh enough (also **nigh enuff**) a homosexual male; a male prostitute. Rhyming slang for PUFF (sense 2). [British, early 1900s, *Dictionary of Rhyming Slang*]

night-glass a CHAMBER POT (*q.v.*); the same as BED-GLASS (*q.v.*). *Cf.* VASE DU NUIT. [Caribbean (Jamaican), Cassidy and Le Page]

night-hag a witch; a female demon who rides at night. [mid 1600s]

night-hawk (also **night-hunter**) a thief or prostitute; a streetwalker. [Australian, early 1900s, Baker]

nightingale (also **nightbird**) a prostitute. *Cf.* NIGHT-HAWK, OWL. [British slang, 1800s or before, Farmer and Henley]

nightman the man who collects the SLOPS (*q.v.*); the man who empties the privy. *Cf.* GONG-FARMER, JAKES-FARMER. [colloquial, 1600s-1700s] Synonyms: DONEGAN-WORKER, GOLD-FINDER, GOLDIGGER, GONG-FARMER, HONEY-DIPPER, JAKES-BARRELLER, JAKES-FARMER, JAKES-MAN, JAKES-RAKER, SHIT-SHARK, TOM TURDMAN, TURD-WALLOPER.

nightmare 1. a female demon who flies in the night and settles on people in their sleep, making them think they have been smothered. *Cf.* NIGHT-HAG. [*c.* 1300] **2.** a terrible and frightening dream. From sense 1.

night-physic copulation. [euphemistic; early 1600s]

night-piece (also **night-jobber**) a prostitute. [slang, 1800s]

night-shade a prostitute. For synonyms see HARLOT. [British, early 1600s]

night-walker a thief or prostitute who works at night. *Cf.* STREETWALKER. [colloquial, 1600s-1800s]

night-work copulation. *Cf.* NIGHT-PHYSIC. [1500s]

nigmenog (also **nimenog**) a silly fellow; a fool. See NIG-NOG. [colloquial, 1600s-1700s]

nig-nog 1. a fool; an oaf. [British, 1800s] **2.** a Negro. Based on NEGRO or NIGGER (both *q.v.*). Derogatory. For synonyms see EBONY. [British, 1900s or before]

nigrified in the manner of a Negro, said of a Caucasian. A disparaging term used by Caucasians in reference to Caucasians. [U.S. colloquial, 1800s, Green]

nikin a fool; a simpleton. For synonyms see OAF. [colloquial, 1600s]

nimbies amphetamines, specifically Nembutal (trademark) capsules. See NEMBIES. [U.S. drug culture, mid 1900s-pres.]

nimble-hipped active and agile in copulation [slang or nonce, 1800s-1900s]

nimrod the penis. Named for the son of Cush, the great-grandson of Noah who was known to be a great hunter. [British slang, 1800s, Farmer and Henley]

nimshi a fool. For synonyms see OAF. [U.S. slang, late 1800s-early 1900s]

nincompoop (also **nickumpoop**, **ninkompoop**) a fool; an oaf; a jerk. [since the late 1600s]

ning-nong an oaf; the same as NONG (q.v.). Cf. DING-DONG (sense 2). [Australian, early 1900s]

ninnies the human breasts. See NINNY, NINNY-JUGS. For synonyms see BOSOM. [U.S. slang and colloquial, 1900s]

ninny 1. a fool; an oaf; a simpleton. [since the late 1500s] 2. a breast. See NINNIES. Cf. NINNY-JUGS, TITTY (sense 1). [U.S., 1900s] 3. human breast milk. Cf. TITTY (sense 2). [U.S. colloquial, 1900s and before]

ninny-jugs the breasts. Cf. CREAM-JUGS. [U.S. slang, 1900s]

nip 1. a derogatory nickname for a Japanese. [from "Nippon," the Japanese name for Japan; widespread slang, 1900s] 2. a nipple. See NIPS. 3. a small drink of whisky or other liquor. [1900s and before]

nipples the protuberances on the foremost part of the human breasts of the female or the undeveloped breasts of the male. Most euphemistic references are to the female nipples. Synonyms (singular and plural): CHERRY, CHERRY-LETS, DUBS, NIPS, PAP-HEAD, PAPILLA MAMMAE, TEAT, THELIUM, TIT.

nippy the penis, especially a child's penis, a nickname for the penis. [British slang, 1800s, Farmer and Henley]

nips the nipples. A truncation. [U.S. slang, mid 1900s-pres.]

nit 1. a sexually loose woman; a prosti-tute. [Scots colloquial, Farmer and Henley] 2. a truncation of NITWIT (q.v.); an oaf; a fool. [widespread colloquial, 1900s or before]

nitwit an oaf; a fool. Cf. NIT. [U.S. colloquial, 1900s or before]

nizy (also **nizzie**) a fool; an oaf. [British, late 1600s-1800s]

no bull-fighter an effeminate male; a sissy, primarily in the expression "he's no bull-fighter." For synonyms see FRIBBLE. [U.S., early 1900s]

nock a truncation of NOCKANDRO (q.v.). See also KNOCK.

nockandro (also **nock**) 1. the posteriors; the anus. [colloquial, 1500s-1900s] 2. female genitals. [late 1500s-1600s] 3. to coit a woman. Cf. KNOCK. [British, late 1500s-1700s]

nocks narcotics. Possibly a pronunciation variant. For synonyms see COTICS. [U.S. slang, 1900s]

nockstress a prostitute. Cf. NOCK. [British slang, 1800s, Farmer and Henley]

nocky boy (also **nocky**) a dull oaf; a fool. [colloquial, 1600s-1700s]

nocturne a prostitute. [British slang, 1800s or before]

nodcock an oaf. See NODGECOCK. [colloquial, 1700s or before]

noddipol an oaf; the same as NODDY-POLE (q.v.) under NODDY-HEAD. [colloquial, 1500s]

noddy an oaf; a simpleton. [numerous written attestations; colloquial, 1500s-1900s]

noddy-head (also **noddy-pate, noddy-peak, noddy-pole, noddy-poll**) an oaf; a simpleton. [colloquial, 1500-1700s]

noddy-headed intoxicated with alcohol. [British slang, 1800s or before]

nodge to copulate. For synonyms see OCCUPY. [Scots, 1800s or before, Farmer and Henley]

nodgecock (also **nodcock**) a simpleton; an oaf. [mid 1500s]

noffgur a prostitute. See NAFFGUR. Probably from NAFKEH (q.v.). [British slang, 1800s]

nola a homosexual male. *Cf.* MOLA. [U.S. slang, early 1900s]

no money in his purse impotent. For synonyms see IMPUDENT. [British slang, 1800s, Farmer and Henley]

no more, be to die. [euphemistic and colloquial, 1900s and before]

nonesuch (also **nonsuch**) the female genitals. Something unrivaled and unequaled. [British slang, late 1700s, Grose]

nong (also **nong-nong**) an oaf; a dolt. [Australian, mid 1900s, Baker]

nonny-nonny (also **hey nonny-nonny**) **1.** the female genitals. **2.** an oaf; a blockhead. **3.** a general term of avoidance; a word used to replace any word which is considered impolite or indelicate. [all senses, British slang, 1800s, Farmer and Henley]

nonorthogenital any sexual activity other than that between males and females which, if permitted to reach completion, will result in vaginal copulation and orgasm on the part of one or both parties. Used in avoidance of "normal" or "natural."

non-skid a Jewish man or woman. Rhyming slang for YID (*q.v.*), essentially derogatory. For synonyms see FIVE AND TWO. [British, 1900s, *Dictionary of Rhyming Slang*]

nooker copulation; the same as NOOKY (*q.v.*). For synonyms see SMOCKAGE. [U.S. slang, mid 1900s, *Current Slang*]

nooky (also **nooker, nookie**) **1.** the female genitals, specifically the vagina. **2.** copulation. **3.** women considered solely as sexual objects; the equivalent of PUSSY (sense 3). [all senses, U.S. slang, early 1900s-pres.]

nooney the penis. From "noodle." For synonyms see YARD. [attested as U.S. homosexual use, mid 1900s, Farrell]

noose, the marriage. *Cf.* BALL AND CHAIN. [U.S. slang, 1900s]

norgies (also **norgs, norks, norkers**) the breasts. From an Australian brand name for butter, "Norco," which pictures a cow's udder on the wrapper. *Cf.*

BUTTER-BAGS. [Australian, mid 1900s, *Dictionary of Slang and Unconventional English*]

normal in terms of behavior, conforming to societally-determined patterns or goals of average or usual behavior. In sexual behavior, conforming to societally-determined patterns or goals of naturalness or propriety. *Cf.* NATURAL (sense 5), ORTHOGENITAL.

NORMAL the "National Organization for the Reform of Marijuana Laws." [U.S. since the late 1960s]

Norski a nickname for a Swede. [U.S., 1900s]

north pole the anus. Rhyming slang for "hole." [British, late 1800s]

nose 1. the penis. [nonce; from *Antony and Cleopatra* (Shakespeare)] **2.** the clitoris. [colloquial and nonce] **3.** cocaine. A truncation of NOSE-CANDY (*q.v.*). [U.S. drug culture, 1900s] **4.** heroin. See NOSE HABIT. [U.S. drug culture, 1900s]

nose, on the smelly or stinking. [Australian colloquial, 1900s]

nose-candy cocaine. [U.S. underworld and drug culture, early 1900s-pres.] Synonyms: ANGEL, ANGIE, BERNICE, BIG BLOKE, BIG-C., BLOKE, BLOW, BOUNCING-POWDER, BURESE, C., CADILLAC, CALIFORNIA CORNFLAKES, CANDY, CARRIE, CECIL, CEE, CHARLES, CHARLEY COKE, CHARLIE, CHOLLY, C-JAM, COCA, COCAINE, COOKIE, CORINE, DOCTOR WHITE, DREAM, DUST, DYNAMITE, FLAKE, GIN, GIRL, GLAD STUFF, GOLD DUST, HAPPY DUST, HAPPY POWDER, HAPPY STUFF, HER, JAM, JOY FLAKES, JOY POWDER, LADY, LADY SNOW, NOSE, NOSE POWDER, NUMBER THREE, PARADISE, POWDERED DIAMOND, REINDEER DUST, SCHOOL BOY, SNORT, SNOW, SNOWBALL, SNOWBIRD, SNOW-CAINE, SNOW STUFF, STARDUST, SUPERBLOW, THE LEAF, TOOT, WHITE, WHITE CROSS, WHITE DRUGS, WHITE GIRL, WHITE MOSQUITOES, WHITE STUFF, WINGS.

nose habit drug addiction or use; the practice or habit of sniffing drugs. *Cf.* NOSE (sense 4). [U.S. drug culture, mid 1900s, *Current Slang*]

nose-hole a nostril. [colloquial since the early 1500s]

nose-painting lechery; whoremongering. See NOSE (sense 1), the penis. [vague innuendo from *Macbeth* (Shakespeare)]

nose-picker a bumpkin; a lout; a rude and uncouth male. [U.S. slang, mid 1900s-pres.]

nose powder powdered narcotics. Primarily cocaine, but also morphine and heroin. *Cf.* NOSE (senses 3 and 4). From "face powder." [U.S. drug culture, mid 1900s-pres.]

nose rag a handkerchief. *Cf.* SNOT-RAG. [colloquial since the early 1800s]

nose-wipe a handkerchief. Milder than NOSE RAG or SNOT-RAG (both *q.v.*). [colloquial since the 1800s]

No shit! an exclamatory assurance of truthfulness, "I'm not bullshitting you!" [U.S. slang, mid 1900s-pres.]

notch (also **nautch**) the female genitals. *Cf.* NOCKANDRO (sense 2). [since the 1700s if not earlier]

notch-broad (also **nautch-broad**) a prostitute. Punning on or at least reinforced by "nautch," an East Indian dancing exhibition, and "nautch-girl," a performer in such an exhibition. [U.S. underworld, mid 1900s]

notchery (also **notcherie**) a brothel. [U.S. slang, early 1900s-pres.]

notch-girl a prostitute; the same as NOTCH-BROAD (*q.v.*). For synonyms see HARLOT. [U.S. slang, 1900s]

notch-house (also **notch-joint**) a brothel. Punning on "nautch." See NOTCH-BROAD. [U.S. slang, early 1900s-pres.]

nub 1. to hang by the neck until dead. "Nub" is a cant word for "neck." [cant, late 1600s] Synonyms and related terms: CARNIFICATE, CLIMB THE STALK, DANCE UPON NOTHING, DANGLE, DIE IN ONE'S SHOES, GO UP A LADDER TO BED, IN DEADLY SUSPENSE, JERK TO JESUS, KICK THE CLOUDS, LEAP FROM THE LEAFLESS, NECK, PATIBULATE, SCRAG, SHAKE A CLOTH IN THE WIND, STRETCH, TOP, TOTTER, TRINE, TUCK, TWIST. **2.** copulation. [British, 1700s-1800s] **3.** an ugly

young woman. For synonyms see BUFFARILLA. [U.S., mid 1900s-pres.]

nubbies the breasts. [Australian, 1900s or before, Baker]

nubbing-cheat (also **nubbing-chit**) **1.** the gallows. [cant, 1600s, B.E.] **2.** copulation. [British, 1700s] See also NUGGING.

nubbing-cove the hangman. [cant, late 1600s, B.E.]

nubile fit for marriage, said of the female. [from Latin *nubilis;* English since the mid 1600s]

nuddy naked; nude. For synonyms see STARKERS. [Australian, mid 1900s]

nude completely without clothing. Somewhat more refined than NAKED (sense 1). Associated with "legitimate" nudity in painting and sculpture. Some connotations of "nakedness in public" as opposed to private, domestic nakedness as when one is bathing or dressing. [since the late 1800s]

nudie 1. a female nude entertainer or a nude woman pictured in a magazine. **2.** a magazine or a film which features nudity. [both senses, U.S. slang, mid 1900s-pres.]

nudism 1. the cult of living in a state of nudity. Usually refers to social nudism, *i.e.,* nudity in the company of other people. **2.** the obsessive desire to remove one's clothing. *Cf.* STREAK (sense 3).

nudity nakedness. See NUDE, NUDISM.

nug 1. to fondle a woman. **2.** to coit a woman. *Cf.* NIG (sense 1), NIGGLE (sense 1). [British colloquial, 1600s-1800s]

nuggets 1. amphetamine capsules. For synonyms see AMP. [U.S. drug culture, mid 1900s-pres.] **2.** the testicles. Also **nuggies, nugs.** [U.S. colloquial and nonce] **3.** the breasts. [U.S. slang, 1900s]

nugging copulation. This word appears to have been confused at various times with NUB (*q.v.*). The earliest attestations mention only "hanging." A "nugging-cove" is a hangman; a "nugging-house" or "nugging-ken" is a courthouse. Later "nugging-cove" means "fornicator" and the other two forms refer to a brothel. [British, 1700s]

nuisance, the the menses. For synonyms see FLOODS. [colloquial and nonce]

number 1. a girl; a sexually attractive girl, especially a "cute little number." [U.S. slang, 1900s] **2.** a marijuana cigarette. For synonyms see MEZZROLL. [U.S. drug culture, mid 1900s-pres.] See also DO A NUMBER ON.

number eight heroin. From "H," which is the eighth letter of the alphabet. [U.S. drug culture, mid 1900s]

number nip the female genitals. For synonyms see MONOSYLLABLE. [British slang, 1800s, Farmer and Henley]

number one to urinate. Spoken or indicated with finger signals. [colloquial and juvenile, 1800s-pres.]

Number One London, at experiencing the menses. For synonyms see FLOODS. [British slang, 1800s, Farmer and Henley]

number thirteen morphine. From "M," which is the thirteenth letter of the alphabet. [U.S. drug culture, mid 1900s]

number three 1. an ejaculation of semen. An extension of NUMBER ONE and NUMBER TWO (both *q.v.*). [British, 1900s, *Dictionary of Slang and Unconventional English*] **2.** cocaine. From "C," which is the third letter of the alphabet. [U.S. drug culture, mid 1900s]

number two a bowel movement. Can be either spoken or indicated with finger signals. *Cf.* NUMBER ONE. [colloquial and juvenile, 1800s-pres.]

numbhead a stupid oaf. [U.S. colloquial, 1900s or before]

numbskull (also **numscul, numskull**) a blockhead. For synonyms see OAF. [since the 1600s]

numps (also **nump**) a dolt or an oaf. [British, 1600s-1800s]

nurd (also **nerd**) an oaf; a jerk. [U.S. slang and colloquial, mid 1900s-pres.]

nursery the female genitals. For synonyms see MONOSYLLABLE. [British, 1800s, Farmer and Henley]

nurtle copulation. *Cf.* MYRTLE. [Australian slang, mid 1900s, Baker]

nurts (also **nerts**) nonsense. A phonological disguise of NUTS (sense 2). See NERTS (sense 2). [U.S. slang, early 1900s-pres.]

nut 1. an odd or strange person; an insane person. [U.S. colloquial, 1900s] **2.** to copulate; the same as BALL (sense 2). [U.S. slang, mid 1900s-pres.] **3.** the glans penis. [from Latin *glans*, meaning "acorn"] **4.** to castrate. *Cf.* KNACKER (sense 1). [U.S. underworld, mid 1900s, Goldin, O'Leary, and Lipsius] **5.** a testicle. See NUTS (sense 1).

nut, off one's 1. crazy. [colloquial, late 1800s-pres.] **2.** intoxicated with alcohol. From sense 1. [British, late 1800s, Farmer and Henley]

nut-cracker 1. the pillory. [cant or slang, 1600s, B.E.] **2.** an ugly young woman; an aggressive and castrating woman. [U.S. slang, 1900s]

nuthouse (also **nut factory, nut-foundry, nut-hatch**) an insane asylum. [U.S. colloquial, early 1900s-pres.]

nutmegs the testicles. Probably from the size and shape of the nutmeg. For synonyms see WHIRLYGIGS. [British, 1600s]

nuts 1. the testicles. See NUTMEGS. [since the 1700s] **2.** as an exclamation, "Nuts!" Slightly euphemistic for BALLS! (sense 4) and considered taboo in some quarters. [U.S. colloquial, 1900s] **3.** confused about; crazy about, as in "nuts about someone." [U.S. colloquial, 1900s]

nuttery an insane asylum. From the literal meaning, "a place for storing nuts." [U.S. slang, mid 1900s, Goldin, O'Leary, and Lipsius] Synonyms: BOOBY HATCH, BUGHOUSE, FUNNY FARM, LOONY BIN, NUT-FOUNDRY, NUTHATCH, NUTHOUSE, NUTTERY.

N.W.A.B. "necks with anybody." An initialism describing someone who will kiss and pet indiscriminately. [U.S., 1900s]

nymph 1. delightful, nubile females

with supernatural qualities. In Greek mythology, they cavorted with satyrs. **2.** any sensuous and sexy young woman. [U.S. colloquial, 1900s]

nymph du pave* a prostitute; a streetwalker. [based on French; U.S. slang, 1900s or before, Berrey and Van den Bark]

nymphet a diminutive of NYMPH (sense 2).

nympho a woman with an insatiable sex drive. A truncation of nymphomaniac. [colloquial and slang, early 1900s-pres.]

nymph of darkness a prostitute. For synonyms see HARLOT. [British colloquial, 1800s]

nymph of the pavement (also **nymph of the pave**) a prostitute. *Cf.* PRINCESS OF THE PAVEMENT. [since the mid 1800s]

O

O. "opium." *Cf.* C. (sense 1), M. For synonyms see OPE. [U.S. underworld, early 1900s or before]

oaf (also **auf, aufe, auph, oaph, ouph**) originally the child of an elf. Now the term embraces all of the negative characteristics of "dullard," "fool," "bumpkin," and "lummox." Such terms almost always refer to males. [since the early 1600s] Synonyms: ACE, ADDLE-BRAIN, ADDLE-HEAD, ADDLE-PATE, ANIMAL, AP-SAY, ARSWORM, ASS, BABOON, BAKE-HEAD, BALATRON, BALLOONHEAD, BANANA-HEAD, BAWCOCK, BEANHEAD, BEEF-HEAD, BEETLE-BRAIN, BEETLE-HEAD, BEN, BESOM-HEAD, B.F., BIRDBRAIN, BIRK, BITE, BLOB, BLOCK, BLOCK-HEAD, BLOKE, BLUBBERBRAIN, BLUBBERHEAD, BLUNDERBUSS, BLUNDERHEAD, BOEOTIAN, BOHUNK, BONEHEAD, BONETOP, BOOB, BOOBERKIN, BOOBUS AMERICANUS, BOOBY, BOOFHEAD, BOOR, BOSTHOON, BOTTLE-HEAD, BOZO, BUBBLE, BUBBLE-HEAD, BUFFLE, BUFFLE-HEAD, BUFFOON, BUGGER, BULLET-HEAD, BULLFINCH, BUM, BUMKIN, BUN-HEAD, BUTTER BACK, BUTTERBALL, BUTTERHEAD, CABBAGEHEAD, CAKEY, CALF, CALF-LOLLY, CALF'S HEAD, CHAW-BACON, CHEESE-HEAD, CHICKEN-HEAD, CHOWDER-HEAD, CHUCKLE-HEAD, CHUFF, CHUMP, CHUMP-HEAD, CHURL, CLABBER-HEAD, CLAM, CLINCH-POOP, CLOD, CLOD-HEAD, CLOD-HOPPER, CLOD-PATE, CLOD-POLE, CLOMPS, CLOT, CLOT-HEAD, CLOWN, CLUCK, CLUCKHEAD, CLUMPERTON, CLUNCH, CLUNK, CLUNKHEAD, CLYDE, COCKSCOMB, COD, COD'S HEAD, COKES, CONGEON, COOT, COUNTRY JAKE, COUSIN BETTY, CRACKBRAIN, CRUMB BUM, CUCK-OO, CUDDEN, CULVER-HEAD, DASTARD, DAWKIN, DAWPATE, DEADHEAD, DEAD-NECK, DICK-HEAD, DICKY-DIDO, DIDDLE-HEAD, DIL, DILLYPOT, DIM BULB, DIM-WIT, DING-A-LING, DINGBAT, DING-DONG, DINK, DIPHEAD, DIPSHIT, DIPSTICK, DIZZARD, DOBBY, DODDYPATE, DODDY-POLL, DODO, DODUNK, DOLDRUM, DOLT, DOLTHEAD, DONK, DONKEY, DOODLE, DOOF, DOPE, DOR, DORBEL, DORF, DORK, DOTARD, DOUGH-FACE, DOUGH-HEAD, DOWCOCK, DRIP, DROMEDARY, DROOB, DROUD, DRUMBLE, DUB, DUFFER, DULLARD, DULL-HEAD, DULL PICKLE, DULLY, DUMBARD, DUMB BUNNY, DUMB CLUCK, DUMB-DUMB, DUMBELL, DUMB-HEAD, DUMBKOPF, DUMBO, DUMB OX, DUMBSKI, DUMBSOCKS, DUM-DUM, DUMMEL, DUMMY, DUNCE, DUNDERHEAD, DUNDERPATE, DUNDERWHELP, FART-BLOSSOM, FART HOLE, FAT-HEAD, FEATHER-BRAIN, FEATHERHEAD, FEEB, FINK, FISH, FLAKE, FLAPDOODLE, FLAT, FLATHEAD, FLAT TIRE, FLEGMATIC FELLOW, FOGAY, FOLT, FOLTHEAD, FON, FONKIN, FOO-FOO, FOP, FOP-DOODLE, FRIP, FUCK-HEAD, FUCK-PIG, GAAPUS, GABEY, GALLOOT, GANDER-HEAD, GANEY, GAUM, GAWBY, GAW-GAW, GAWK, GAWNEY, GAZIZZEY, GAZOB, GAZOOK, GECK, GEEK, GIDDYHEAD, GIG, GILLY, GILLY-GAUPUS, GIM-CRACK, GIMP, GINK, GLEEP, GLOIK, GLOM, GNATBRAIN, GOBSHITE, GOLLUMPUS, GOMERAL, GOMUS, GONES, GONEY, GONIF, GONUS, GOOBRAIN, GOOBY, GOOF, GOOF-BALL, GOOFUS, GOOG, GOOK, GOON, GOOP, GOOPUS, GOOSE, GOOSEBERRY, GOOSECAP, GOOSEY-GANDER, GOUP, GOURD, GOWK, GREENHEAD, GROBIAN, GROUTNOLL, GROWTNOLL, GUFFIN, GUFFOON, GULL, GULL-FINCH, GULPIN, GUMMY, GUMP, GUMSUCKER, HAIRBRAIN, HAMMERHEAD, HANKTELO, HARDHEAD, HAREBRAIN, HAWBUCK, HAYSEED, HERKIMER JERKIMER, HICK, HICKJOP, HICKORYHEAD, HICKSAM, HILLBILLY, HIND, HOBALL, HOBB, HOBBIL, HOBBY, HOBCLUNCH, HOB-GOBLIN, HODDY-NODDY, HODDY-PEAK, HODDY-POLL, HODGE, HOMO BOOBUS, HOMOSAP, HONYOCK, HORSE'S ASS, HOTTENTOT, HUGMER, HULLOCK, HULVER-HEAD, HUNKY, IDIOT, IGNATZ, IGNORAMUS, IMBECILE, INNOCENT, INSIPID, IRON-HEAD, IVORY DOME, J., JABBERNOL, JACK ADAMS, JACKASS, JACK OFF, JACK-SAUCE, JACOB, JAKE, JAR-HEAD, JAY, JERK, JERK OFF, JOBBERNOLL, JOE CUNT, JOE ERK, JOLTERHEAD, JOLTHEAD, JOSH, JOSHER, JOSKIN, JUGGINS, JUGHEAD, KLOTZ, KLUCK,

KNOBHEAD, KNOCKSOFTLY, KNOTHEAD, KNUCKLEHEAD, LACK-BRAIN, LACKWIT, LALDRUM, LAMB, LAMEBRAIN, LARDHEAD, LEADEN-PATE, LEAD-HEAD, LEATHER-HEAD, LERICOMPOOP, LIGHTS, LIRRIPOOP, LOB, LOBBUS, LOBCOCK, LOBLOLLY, LOB-SCOUSE, LOBSTER, LOGGERHEAD, LOOBY, LOOGAN, LOON, LOPLOLLY, LOPPUS, LORG, LOUT, LOW-BROW, LUBBER, LUBBER-HEAD, LUBBY, LUG, LUG-LOAF, LUMMAKIN, LUMMOX, LUMP, LUMPKIN, LUMPUS, LUNK, LUNKER, LUNKHEAD, LURDAN, LUSK, LUSKARD, MACAROON, MALLET-HEAD, MARBLE DOME, MEAT, MEATBALL, MEAT-HEAD, MELON, MELONHEAD, MESS, MO-BARD, MOKE, MOME, MOONCALF, MOON-LING, MOONRAKER, MOP, MOPE, MOP STICK, MOREPORK, MORON, MUD, MUD-DLEHEAD, MUD-HEAD, MUFF, MUFFIN, MUG, MUGGINS, MULL, MULLET-HEAD, MUSCLE-HEAD, MUSHHEAD, MUT-HEAD, MUTT, MUTTONHEAD, NARK, NAZOLD, NE-ANDERTHAL, NEDDY, NED-FOOL, NERD, NEWT, NIAS, NICKNINNY, NICKUMPOOP, NIDDICOCK, NIDDIPOL, NIDIOT, NIGME-NOG, NIG-NOG, NIKIN, NIMSHI, NIN-COMPOOP, NIGG-NOGG, NINNY, NINNY-HAMMER, NIT, NITWIT, NIZY, NIZZIE, NOBBY, NOCKY, NOCKY BOY, NODCOCK, NODDIPOL, NODY, NODDY-PATE, NODDY-PEAK, NODDY-POLE, NODDY-POLL, NODGE-COCK NOGGERHEAD, NOG-HEAD, NOGMAN, NOKES, NOLE, NOLL, NOLT, NONG, NOO-DLE, NOODLEHEAD, NOSE-PICKER, NUMB-HEAD, NUMBSKULL, NUMPS, NUMSKULL, NUNNY-FUDGY, NUPSON, NURD, NUT, NYAS, OOFUS, OOLFOO, PALOOKA, PEA-GOOSE, PEAHEAD, PESTLE-HEAD, PIGHEAD, PIGSCONCE, PINHEAD, PISHER, PLAT, PLUMP-PATE, POON, POOP, POOPHEAD, POTATO-HEAD, POTHEAD, PRICK, PROW, PUDDINGHEAD, PUMPKINHEAD, PUNKIN-HEAD, PUT, PUTTYHEAD, PUTZ, QUEER, QUEER-CULL, QUINCE, QUOIT, RALPH, RALPH SPOONER, RATTLEHEAD, REDNECK, REJECT, REUBEN, ROCKHEAD, ROLY-POLY, RUBE, RUM-DUM, RUSTIC, SAMMY, SAMMY-SOFT, SAP, SAP-HEAD, SAPSKULL, SATE-POLL, SAUSAGE, SAWDUST-BRAINED, SAWDUST-HEAD, SAWNY, SCATTERBRAIN, SCHLEMIEL, SCHLUB, SCHLUMP, SCHMEKEL, SCHMENDRICH, SCHMENDRICK, SCHMOE, SCHMUCK, SCHNOOK, SHALLOW-PATE, SHANNY, SHATTERBRAIN, SHEEP'S-HEAD, SHIT FACE, SHIT-HEAD, SHITTERBRAIN, SHLUB, SHMENDRICK, SHMO, SHMUCK, SHNOOK, SHOHIZA, SHOON SHUTTLE-BRAIN, SHUTTLE-HEAD, SHUTTLE-WIT, SIDE SIM, SIMKIN, SIMON, SIMP, SINGLE-TON, SKITTER-BRAIN, SKRIMSHANKER, SKYTE, SLANGAM, SLANGRILL, SLOUCH, SLUBBERDEGULLION, SOAP, SOD, SOFT-HEAD, SONKY, SOP, SOT, SOUSECROWN, SOZZLE, SPARE PRICK, SPASTIC, SPAZ, SPLODGER, SPOON, SPOONY, SPOOPS, STICK, STOCK, STOOP, STOOPNAGEL, STOT, STUB, STUMBLE-BUM, STUMP, STUPE, STUPEHEAD, SUB, SUMPH, SWAD, TACK-HEAD, THICK, TIMDOODLE, TOM CONEY, TOM DOODLE, TOM-FARTHING, TOMMY, TOMMY NODDY, TOM NODDY, TOM TOWLY, TONK, TONY, TOOT, TOOTLE-DUMPATTICK, TRUNK, TUCK, TURKEY, TWIMBLE, TWINK, TWIRP, TWIT, TWO-FOOT RULE, ULLAGE, UM-BAY, UMP-CHAY, UNDERWIT, WAFFLES, WAG, WAG-WIT, WANK, WANTWIT, WARB, WEENIE, WET, WET-GOOSE, WETHER-HEAD, WET SOCK, WHIMP, WIDGEON, WIMP, WISEACRE, WISE GUY, WHITLING, WONK, WOODCOCK, WOODENHEAD, WOODEN SPOON, YACK, YAHOO, YAP, YAWNEY, YOB, YOCK, YOKEL, YOLD, YO-YO, YUCKEL, YULD, ZAMMY ZANY, ZERK, ZERO, ZHLUB, ZIB, ZOMBIE, ZONE, ZONK, ZONKO, ZOTY, ZOUCH.

oat-bin the female genitals. See HAVE ONE'S OATS, SOW ONE'S WILD OATS. [U.S. slang, early 1900s]

oath!, My an oath and an exclamation. [attested as Australian, 1800s, Baker]

o-be-joyful alcoholic beverages, rum in particular. For synonyms see BOOZE. [British and U.S., early 1800s-1900s]

obese fat; very fat, in reference to a human or an animal body. [since the mid 1600s]

obfuscated intoxicated with alcohol, "obscured" with alcohol. [British and U.S., mid 1800s]

O.B.H. the female genitals; "old Berkeley Hunt," which is rhyming slang for CUNT (*q.v.*). *Cf.* BERKELEY HUNT.

oblige 1. to yield to copulation; to oblige someone sexually. Said of a woman. *Cf.* ACCOMMODATE. **2.** to coit a woman, especially if it is to please her. [both senses, colloquial and nonce]

obli-goddamn-ation an emphatic form of "obligation" based on "goddamn" and "obligation."

obscene lewd; pertaining to a thing, person, or word representing sexual or excremental matters. Synonyms and related terms: BARNYARD, BAWDY, BLUE, FILTHY, HARD-CORE, HIGH-KILTED, INDECENT, MEATY, NASTY, OFF-COLOR, PAWPAW, PORNY, QUISI, RAUNCHY, RUDE, SMUTTY, SPICY, UNPARLIAMENTARY. See also LEWD.

occupant 1. a prostitute, a woman who is occupied by a man. *Cf.* OCCUPY. A resident of an OCCUPYING-HOUSE (*q.v.*). [late 1500s] **2.** a brothel. [British, 1700s or before, Farmer and Henley]

occupy to coit a woman; to take sexual possession of a woman. This word was avoided in polite company during the period [1400s-1600s] when it was used in this sense. The following synonyms and related terms refer to males or both males and females except as indicated. Both transitive and intransitive senses are included: ACCOMMODATE, ADAM AND EVE IT, ADAMIZE, BALL, BALLOCK, BANG, BATTER, BEEF, BE FAMILIAR WITH, BE IN A WOMAN'S BEEF, BELT, BLOCK, BLOW OFF ON THE GROUNSILLS, BLOW OFF THE LOOSE CORNS, BOARD, BOIL BANGERS, BORE, BOTTLE, BOUNCE, BOX, BREAK A LANCE WITH, BREAK A LEG, BRUSH, BULL, BUM-BASTE, BUMBLE, BUNNY-FUCK, BURDEN, BURY ONE'S WICK, BUZZ THE BRILLO, CANE, CANOE, CARESS, CARNALIZE, CATTLE, CAULK, CAVAULT, CHAFER, CHANGE ONE'S LUCK, CHARGE, CHUCK, CHUCK A TREAD, CLIMB, CLUB, COCK, COCK UP, COHABIT, COIT, COME ABOUT, COME ABOUT A WOMAN, COME ACROSS, COME ALOFT, COME OVER, COMPRESS, CONJUGATE, CONSUMMATE, COOL OUT, CORRESPOND, COUCH, COUPLE, COUPLE WITH, COVER, CRACK IT, CRAM, CRAWL, CREAM, CROSS, CUDDLE, DANCE THE BUTTOCK JIG, DANCE THE GOAT'S JIG, DANCE THE MARRIED MAN'S CATILLION, DANCE THE MARRIED MAN'S JIG, DANCE THE MATRIMONIAL POLKA, DANCE THE MATTRESS JIG, DEHORN, DIBBLE, DICK, DIDDLE, DIP ONE'S WICK, DO, DO A BIT, DO A BOTTOM-WETTER, DO A DIVE IN THE DARK, DO A FLOP, DO A GRIND, DO A GROUSE, DO A KINDNESS TO, DO AN INSIDE WORRY, DO A PUSH, DO A PUT, DO A RUDENESS TO, DO A SHOOT UP THE STRAIGHT, DO A SLIDE UP THE BOARD, DO A SPREAD, DO A WOMAN'S JOB FOR HER, DOCK, DOG, DO ILL TO, DO IT, DO ONE'S OFFICE, DO OVER, DORSE WITH, DO SOME GOOD FOR ONESELF, DO THE CHORES, DO THE DO, DO THE NAUGHTY (female), DO THE STORY WITH, DO THE TRICK, DRIVE HOME, DRIVE INTO, DRY RUN, EASE, EASE NATURE, EFFECT INTROMISSION, EMBRACE, ENJOY, ENJOY A WOMAN, EXCHANGE SPITS, FAGGOT, FAN, FEED THE DUMB-GLUTTON, FEED THE DUMMY, FEEZE, FERRET, FETTLE, FIDDLE, FIRK, FIT ENDS, FIT END TO END, FIX HER PLUMBING, FIX SOMEONE UP, FLAP, FLESH, FLESH IT, FLIMP, FLOP IN THE HAY, FLURGLE, FOIN, FONDLE, FOOT, FORAMINATE, FOREGATHER, FORNICATE, FOYST, FRIG, FUCK, FUCKLE, FUGLE, FULKE, FUMBLE, FUTUERE, FUTUO, FUTY, FUTZ, GAFFER, GAY IT, GEAR, GENDER, GEORGE, GET A BELLY FULL OF MARROW-PUDDING (female), GET ABOUT HER, GET A CRUMPET, GET AMONG IT, GET A PAIR OF BALLS AGAINST ONE'S BUTT (female), GET A SHOVE IN ONE'S BLIND-EYE (female), GET DOWN TO IT, GET FIXED-UP, GET HILT AND HAIR (female), GET HOME, GET HULLED BETWEEN WIND AND WATER (female), GET IN, GET INTO, GET INTO HER, GET INTO HER PANTS, GET IT ON, GET JACK IN THE ORCHARD, GET LAYED, GET OFF THE GUN, GET ONE'S ASHES HAULED, GET ONE'S CHIMNEY SWEPT OUT (female), GET ONE'S END IN, GET ONE'S END WET, GET ONE'S GREENS, GET ONE'S HAIR CUT, GET ONE'S LEATHER STRETCHED (female), GET ONE'S LEG ACROSS, GET ONE'S LEG LIFTED (female), GET ONE'S NUTS CRACKED, GET ONE'S OATS FROM SOMEONE, GET ONE'S OIL CHANGED, GET ON TOP OF, GET OUTSIDE IT (female), GET OUTSIDE OF (female), GET OVER SOMEONE, GET SOME, GET SOME ACTION, GET

SOME ASS, GET SOME COLD COCK, GET SOME CUNT, GET THERE, GET THE UPSHOT (female), GET THROUGH, GET UP THE POLE (female), GINICOMTWIG, GIRL, GIVE A HOLE TO HID IT IN (female), GIVE A WOMAN A SHOT, GIVE HARD FOR SOFT, GIVE HEAD, GIVE HER A FRIGGING, GIVE HER A HOSING, GIVE HER A PAST, GIVE HER A SCREWING, GIVE HER THE BUSINESS, GIVE IT TO SOMEONE, GIVE JUICE FOR JELLY, GIVE MUTTON FOR BEEF (female), GIVE NATURE A FILLIP, GIVE ONE A STAB, GIVE ONESELF (female), GIVE ONE THE WORKS, GIVE STANDING-ROOM FOR ONE (female), GO, GO BALLOCKING, GO BED-PRESSING, GO BIRD'S-NESTING, GO BUM-FAKING, GO BUM-TICKLING, GO BUM-WORKING, GO BUSH-RANGING, GO BUTTOCKING, GO COCK-FIGHTING, GO CUNNY-CATCHING, GO DOODLING, GO DOWN (female), GO DRABBING, GO FISHING, GO FLASHING IT, GO FOR THE DRAG OFF, GO GOOSING, GO IN UNTO, GO JOTTLING, GO LEATHER-STRETCHING, GO LIKE A BELT-FED MOTOR, GO LIKE A RAT UP A DRAIN PIPE, GO LIKE A RAT UP A RHODODENDRON, GOOSE, GO RUMPING, GO RUMPSPLITTING, GO STAR-GAZING ON ONE'S BACK (female), GO THE LIMIT, GO THROUGH A WOMAN, GO TO BED WITH, GO TO IT, GO TO TOWN, GO TO WORK WITH, GO TWAT-FAKING, GO VAULTING, GO WENCHING, GO WITH, GO WOMANIZING, GRANT THE FAVOR (female), GREASE, GREASE THE WHEEL, GRIND, GRIND ONE'S TOOL, HANDLE, HAUL ONE'S ASHES, HAVE, HAVE A BIT, HAVE A BIT OF BUM, HAVE A BIT OF BUM-DANCING, HAVE A BIT OF COCK, HAVE A BIT OF CUNT, HAVE A BIT OF CURLY GREENS, HAVE A BIT OF FISH, HAVE A BIT OF GIBLET PIE, HAVE A BIT OF GUTSTICK (female), HAVE A BIT OF MEAT, HAVE A BIT OF MUTTON, HAVE A BIT OF PORK, HAVE A BIT OF ROUGH, HAVE A BIT OF SKIRT, HAVE A BIT OF SPLIT-MUTTON, HAVE A BIT OF STUFF, HAVE A BIT OF SUGAR-STICK (female), HAVE A BIT OF SUMMER-CABBAGE, HAVE A BIT OF THE CREAMSTICK (female), HAVE A BLOWTHROUGH, HAVE A BRUSH WITH THE CUE, HAVE A BUN IN THE OVEN, HAVE A FLUTTER, HAVE A FUCK, HAVE A GAME IN THE COCK-LOFT, HAVE A LEAP UP THE LADDER, HAVE A NORTHWEST COCKTAIL, HAVE A POKE, HAVE A RIDE, HAVE A TURN ON ONE'S BACK (female), HAVE A WIPE AT THE PLACE, HAVE CONNECTION, HAVE FIFTY-UP, HAVE GIN ON THE ROCKS, HAVE GIVEN PUSSY A TASTE OF CREAM (female), HAVE HOT PUDDING FOR SUPPER (female), HAVE IT OFF, HAVE IT UP, HAVE LIVE SAUSAGE FOR SUPPER, (female), HAVE ONE'S CUT, HAVE ONE'S OATS, HAVE ONE'S WILL OF A WOMAN, HIDE THE FERRET, HIDE THE SALAMI, HIDE THE SAUSAGE, HIT, HIT IT OFF, HIT ON THE TAIL, HIVE IT, HOG, HOIST, HOME, HONEY-FUCK, HOOPER'S HIDE, HOP ON, HORIZONTALIZE, HORSE, HOSE, HUDDLE, HUFFLE, HUMP, HUSBAND, HUSTLE, IMPALE, INFEMURATE, INTERCOURSE, INTRODUCE CHARLEY, INVADE, JACK, JANNEY, JAPE, JAZZ, JAZZ IT, JERK, JIGGLE, JIG-JIG, JINK, JOB, JOCK, JOCKUM, JOG, JOIN GIBLETS, JOIN PAUNCHES, JOLT, JOTTLE, JOUNCE, JUKE, JUMBLE, JUMM, JUMP, KISS, KNOCK, KNOCK IT OFF, KNOW, LABOR LEATHER, LABOUR-LEA, LALLY-GAG, LARD, LAY, LAY OFF WITH, LAY OUT, LAY SOME PIPE, LAY THE HIP, LAY THE LEG, LEAP, LERICOMPOOP, LIB, LIBERATE, LIE FEET UP-PERMOST (female), LIE ON, LIE UNDER (female), LIE WITH, LIFT A LEG ON A WOMAN, LIFT ONE'S LEG, LIGHT THE LAMP (female), LINE, LOB IN, LOOK AT THE CEILING OVER A MAN'S SHOULDER (female), LOSE THE MATCH AND POCKET THE STAKE (female), LOVE, LUBRICATE, MAKE, MAKE ENDS MEET, MAKE FEET FOR CHILDREN'S SHOES, MAKE HER GRUNT, MAKE IT, MAKE LOVE, MAKE ONE'S LOVE COME DOWN, MAKE THE CHIMNEY SMOKE, MAKE THE SCENE, MAN, MATE, MEDDLE, MESS AROUND, MINGLE BLOODS, MINGLE LIMBS, MIX ONE'S PEANUT BUTTER, MOUNT, MUDDLE, MUG, MUMP, MUSS, NAIL, NAIL TWO BELLIES TOGETHER, NAUGHTY, NIBBLE, NICK, NIDGE, NIG, NIGGLE, NOCKANDRO, NODGE, NUG, NUT, NYGLE, OBLIGE, OFF, OPEN UP TO (female), PALLIARDIZE, PASH ON, PEEL ONE'S BEST END, PEG, PERFORM, PESTLE, PHALLICIZE, PHEESE, PIN, PIZZLE, PLANK, PLANT, PLANT A MAN, PLANT THE OATS, PLAY, PLAY AT ALL-FOURS, PLAY AT COCK-IN-COVER, PLAY AT COUPLE-YOUR-NAVELS, PLAY AT

IN-AND-OUT, PLAY AT ITCH-BUTTOCK, PLAY AT LEVEL-COIL, PLAY AT LIFT-LEG, PLAY AT PICKLE-ME-TICKLE-ME, PLAY AT PULLY-HAULLY, PLAY AT THE FIRST-GAME-EVER-PLAYED, PLAY AT TOPS-AND-BOTTOMS, PLAY AT TOP-SAWYER, PLAY CARS AND GARAGES, PLAY DOCTOR, PLAY HOSPITAL, PLAY ONE'S ACE (female), PLAY THE GOAT, PLAY THE ORGAN, PLAY TIDDLYWINKS, PLEASE, PLEASURE, PLOUGH, PLOW, PLOWTER, PLUCK, PLUG, PLOOK, POCKET THE RED, POKE, POLE, POOP, POP, POP IT IN, PORK, POSSESS, POSSESS CARNALLY, POST A LETTER, POUND, PRANG, PRAY, WITH THE KNEES UPWARD (female), PRIAPIZE, PRIG, PROD, PRONG, PUMP, PUNCH, PUSH, PUSH ON, PUSH-PIN, PUT, PUT FOUR QUARTERS ON THE SPIT, PUT IT IN, PUT IT TO HER, PUT THE BLOCKS TO, PUT THE BOOTS TO, PUT THE DEVIL INTO HELL, QUALIFY, QUIFF, QUIM, RABBIT, RAKE, RAKE OUT, RAM, RASP, RASP AWAY, RIDE, RIDE BELOW THE CRUPPER, RIFLE, RIP OFF, ROCK, ROD, ROGER, ROLLER SKATE, ROOT, ROOTLE, ROUST, ROUT, RUB BACONS, RUB UP, RUDDER, RUMBUSTICATE, RUMMAGE, RUMP, RUMPLE, SACRIFICE TO VENUS, SALT, SARD, SAW OFF A CHUNK, SCALE, SCORE, SCOUR, SCREW, SCROUPERIZE, SCUTTLE, SCUTZ AROUND, SEASON, SEE, SEE A MAN, SERVE, SERVICE, SEW UP, SHACK UP WITH SOMEONE, SHAFT, SHAG, SHAKE, SHAKE A SKIN-COAT, SHAKE A TART, SHARE THE SEXUAL EMBRACE, SHARGE, SHEG, SHOOT BETWEEN WIND AND WATER, SHOOT IN THE TAIL, SHOOT ONE'S WAD, SHOVE, SHTUP, SIN, SINK IN, SINK THE SOLDIER, SKLOOK, SLEEP WITH, SLIP HER A LENGTH, SLIP INTO, SLIP IT ABOUT, SMOCK, SMOCK-SERVICE, SMOKE, SNABBLE, SNAG, SNIB, SNUG, SOLACE, SPIT, SPLICE, SPLIT, SPOIL, SPOON, SPOT, STAB, STAB A WOMAN IN THE THIGH, STABLE-MY-NAGGIE, STAIN, STAND THE PUSH, STAND UP, STICK, STITCH, STRAIN, STRAP, STRETCH LEATHER, STRIKE, STRIP ONE'S TARSE IN, STROKE, STROP ONE'S BEAK, STRUM, SUBAGITATE, SUCCEED AMOROUSLY, SUCK THE SUGAR STICK, SUPPLE BOTH ENDS OF IT, SWING, SWINGE, SWITCH, SWITCHEL, SWIVE, TAIL, TAKE A TURN IN THE STUBBLE, TAKE A TURN ON SHOOTER'S HILL, TAKE IN AND DO FOR, TAKE IN BEEF, TAKE IN CREAM, TAKE NEBUCHADNEZZAR OUT TO GRASS, TAKE THE STARCH OUT OF (female), TASTE, TEAR OFF A PIECE, TETHER ONE'S NAG, THREAD, THREAD THE NEEDLE, THROW A LEG OVER, THROW ONE A HUMP, THRUM, THUMB, THUMP, TICKLE, TICK-TACK, TIE THE TRUE LOVER'S KNOT, TIFF, TIP, TIP THE LONG ONE, TO BE INTIMATE, TOM, TONYGLE, TOP, TOUCH, TOUZE, TRIM, TRIM THE BUFF, TROT OUT ONE'S PUSSY (female), TROUNCE, TUMBLE, TUMP, TURN UP, TWIDDLE, TWIGLE, TWIST, UP, USE, VARNISH ONE'S CANE, VAULT, WAG ONE'S BUM, WANK, WAP, WET A BOTTOM (female), WET ONE'S WICK, WHACK IT UP, WHAT MOTHER DID BEFORE ME, WHEEL, WHITEWASH, WIND UP THE CLOCK, WOMANIZE, WORK, WORK OUT, WORK THE DUMB ORACLE, WORK THE HAIRY ORACLE, WRIGGLE NAVELS, YARD, YENTZ, YIELD ONE'S FAVORS, ZIG-ZAG.

occupying-house a brothel; a bawdy-house. [late 1500s]

ocksecrotia intoxicated with alcohol; the same as OXYCROCIUM (*q.v.*). [cant, 1700s, Halliwell]

O Crimes! a disguise of "O Christ!" [British colloquial, 1800s, Hotten]

O.D. 1. an "overdose" of drugs. **2.** to take an overdose of drugs; to be hospitalized because of an overdose of drugs. [both senses, U.S. drug culture, mid 1900s-pres.]

oddball 1. a homosexual male. **2.** any eccentric person. [both senses, British and U.S. slang, mid 1900s-pres.]

oddish intoxicated with alcohol. For synonyms see WOOFLED. [British slang, 1800s]

'Odds bob! (also **'Odds bobs!**) an oath and an exclamation, "By God's blood!" or "By God's babe!" For synonyms see 'ZOUNDS! [mid 1700s]

Odds bones! an oath and an exclamation. "By God's bones!" For synonyms see 'ZOUNDS! [British, late 1800s]

'Odds fish! an oath and an exclamation, "By God's flesh!" [late 1600s]

'Odds wucks and tar! a meaningless

oath and exclamation. [British, late 1700s]

'Od rot it! a disguise of "God rot it!" [British colloquial, 1800s, Hotten]

'Odsbodikins! an oath and an exclamation, "By God's (little) bodies!" This is an oath sworn on the Communion wafers, thus the plural. [British, 1800s]

'Odsflesh! (also **'Ods fish!**) an oath and an exclamation, "By God's flesh!" For synonyms see 'ZOUNDS! [British, early 1700s]

ofay (also **fay, o-fay, old-fay, ole-fay, oofay**) 1. a derogatory term for a Caucasian. For synonyms see PECKERWOOD. [U.S. Negro use, early 1900s-pres.] 2. a Negro who acts like a Caucasian. Derogatory. Cf. OREA. Both are from "foe" or "oaf" in a form of backslang or of Pig Latin. [both senses, U.S. Negro use, [early 1900s-pres.]

off 1. to die. [British, World War II] 2. to kill. [U.S. slang, mid 1900s] 3. to coit a woman. Cf. BRING OFF. See also JERK OFF.

off-color 1. out of health; looking ill. [British and U.S. colloquial, 1800s-1900s] 2. slightly obscene or indecent. [U.S. colloquial, mid 1900s-pres.]

offend to smell bad; to offend someone with perspiration odor or with bad breath. [U.S. advertising, mid 1900s]

off-girl an illegitimate girl. [U.S. dialect (Southern), 1900s or before]

office a privy; a W.C. Cf. HOUSE OF OFFICE. [British and U.S. colloquial, early 1700s-1800s]

og-fray a Frenchman. Pig Latin for "frog." Cf. FROG (sense 1). [U.S. slang, 1900s]

ogle to stare at a woman; to catch the eye of a woman; to stare at a woman lustfully. [since the late 1600s]

oil 1. semen. See MAN OIL. For synonyms see METTLE. 2. an alcohol extract of hashish or CANNABIS SATIVA (q.v.). Cf. RED OIL. [U.S. drug culture, mid 1900s-pres.] Synonyms: AFGANI, BLACK OIL, CHERRY LEB, HASH OIL, HONEY OIL, INDIAN OIL, RED OIL, SMASH, SON OF ONE, THE ONE.

oil bags the buttocks. For synonyms see DUFF. [U.S. slang, mid 1900s, *Current Slang*]

oiled intoxicated with alcohol. Cf. WELL-OILED. [primarily U.S. slang, early 1700s-pres., Ben Franklin]

oiler 1. a drunkard who is frequently OILED (q.v.). For synonyms see ALCHY. [slang, 1900s] 2. a derogatory nickname for a Mexican. Cf. GREASER (sense 1). For synonyms see MEX. [U.S. slang, 1900s] 3. a smoker of hashish oil. [U.S. drug culture, mid 1900s-pres.]

oil of barley (also **oyle of barley**) beer. Cf. BARLEY BROTH. [British, 1600s]

oil of giblets (also **oil of horn**) a woman's vaginal secretions; natural vaginal lubricant. For synonyms see FEMALE SPENDINGS. [British slang, 1800s, Farmer and Henley]

oil of horn the same as OIL OF GIBLETS (q.v.). Cf. HORN (sense 3), the penis. [British slang, 1800s, Farmer and Henley]

oil of man semen. A play on "sperm oil" or "sperm whale oil." Cf. MAN OIL. Possibly a play on the "Isle of Man." For synonyms see METTLE. [British slang, 1800s, Farmer and Henley]

oil of tongue nonsense; flattery. [British, 1800s]

on 1. sexually aroused. Cf. TURNED ON (sense 2). For synonyms see HUMPY. 2. intoxicated with alcohol. [both senses, British, 1800s or before]

onanism 1. the practice of COITUS INTERRUPTUS (q.v.). From the name "Onan," the son of Judah (Genesis). 2. used incorrectly for "masturbation." Sometimes seen in the French spelling *onamisme*. A frequent euphemism for "masturbation." [1800s-1900s]

onanist a masturbator; one who practices ONANISM (sense 2). For synonyms see HUSKER. [some medical use; euphemistic]

One, The an alcohol extract of CANNABIS SATIVA (q.v.). A "brand name" for this illicitly manufactured product. Cf. SON OF ONE. [U.S. drug culture, mid 1900s]

one, the old the devil; Satan. For synonyms see FIEND. [since c. 1000]

one-eyed milkman the penis. *Cf.* MILK, MILKMAN (sense 2). For synonyms see YARD. [British, 1900s, *Dictionary of Slang and Unconventional English*]

one-eyed worm the penis. For synonyms see YARD. [U.S. nonce, mid 1900s]

one-finger exercise digital stimulation of the genitals of a woman. From "five-finger (piano) exercise." *Cf.* DIGITATE.

one-finger salute an obscene gesture; the FINGER (*q.v.*). [U.S. slang, mid 1900s-pres.]

one in the bush is worth two in the hand "an act of copulation is worth two acts of masturbation." The bush refers to the female genitals and the pubic hair. [Australian, 1900s, *Dictionary of Slang and Unconventional English*]

one-night stand a short-term sexual relationship, either homosexual or heterosexual. Originally in reference to men, with a veiled reference to a standing penis. Now also said of women. From the expression referring to a performance which runs only one night.

one-o'clock a catch phrase signalling a male that his trousers are unbuttoned or unzipped. [U.S. colloquial, 1900s]

one-o'clock at the waterworks a catch phrase signalling a male that his trousers are unbuttoned or unzipped; the same as ONE-O'CLOCK (*q.v.*). See WATERWORKS. [Australian, 1900s]

one of the boys an effeminate male. For synonyms see FRIBBLE. [U.S. colloquial, 1900s]

one of the Brown family a CATA-MITE (*q.v.*). Refers to PEDERASTY (*q.v.*). *Cf.* BROWN (sense 3). For synonyms see BRONCO. [U.S. slang and underworld, mid 1900s]

one of the faithful a drunkard; a man always seen at the same tavern or bar. *Cf.* RELIGIOUS. [since the early 1600s]

one of those a homosexual male. For synonyms see EPICENE. [British and U.S. slang and colloquial, 1900s]

one-over-eight intoxicated with alcohol. For synonyms see WOOFLED. [slang or colloquial, 1900s or before]

one-piece overcoat a condom. *Cf.* RAINCOAT. For synonyms see EEL-SKIN. [British, mid 1900s, *Dictionary of Slang and Unconventional English*]

onery-house a brothel. [U.S. colloquial, 1900s]

one's best clothes, in with an erect penis. *Cf.* ONE'S SUNDAY BEST, IN. [British slang, 1800s, Farmer and Henley]

one's ear, on 1. angry. **2.** broke; bankrupt. [both senses, U.S. slang, 1900s] **3.** intoxicated with alcohol. [all senses, euphemistic for "on one's ass"; sense 3 is slang, early 1900s-pres.]

one's ease, at intoxicated with alcohol. For synonyms see WOOFLED. [colloquial, 1900s]

one's flag is out one is intoxicated with alcohol. [British slang, 1800s, Farmer and Henley]

one's greens, on for sexually aroused. *Cf.* GREENS. For synonyms see HUMPY. [British slang, 1800s, Farmer and Henley]

one-shot a woman who agrees to a ONE-NIGHT STAND (*q.v.*). *Cf.* SHOT (sense 2). [U.S. slang, 1900s]

one's Sunday best, in with an erect penis. For synonyms see ERECTION. [British slang, 1800s, Farmer and Henley]

one-way street a heterosexual person who will not participate in homosexual activities. [U.S. slang, mid 1900s-pres.]

one with t'other copulation. For synonyms see SMOCKAGE. [British, 1600s]

oofay a derogatory term for a Caucasian; the same as OFAY (*q.v.*). For synonyms see PECKERWOOD.

oofus a stupid oaf. [U.S. slang, mid 1900s]

oogley pertaining to a sexually attractive woman. *Cf.* OGLE. [U.S. slang, mid 1900s, Wentworth and Flexner]

ope (also **op**) "opium." [U.S. underworld and slang, early 1900s or before]

Synonyms: BIG-O., BLACK PILLS, BLACK SILK, BLACK SMOKE, BLACK STUFF, BRICK, BRICK GUM, BROWN STUFF, BUTTON, CHINESE TOBACCO, COOLIE MUD DOPIUM, DREAM BEADS, DREAM GUM, DREAMS, DREAMSTICK, DREAM WAX, ELEVATION, GLAD STUFF, GOMA, GONG, GONGER, GOW, GREASE, GREAT TOBACCO, GUM, HOP, HOPS, JUNK, LEM-KEE, MIDNIGHT OIL, MUD, O., PEN YEN, PINYON, POPPY TRAIN, SHELL OF HOP, SKAMAS, TAR, YAM-YAM, YEN-CHEE, YEN-SHEE.

open and notorious adultery the crime of an unmarried man and woman living together with the public's knowledge. [law]

open-arse a lewd woman; a woman ready to copulate at any time. For synonyms see LAY. [British, late 1600s, B.E.]

open C. the female genitals. The "C" is for "cunt." [British slang, 1800s, Farmer and Henley]

opium den (also **opium joint**) a place to purchase and consume opium. [U.S. underworld, mid 1800s-early 1900s]

opposite sex 1. a male from the point of view of a female. **2.** a female from the point of view of a male.

oracle the female genitals. [British slang, 1800s or before, Farmer and Henley]

oral intercourse a truncation of "genital-oral sexual intercourse." See ANILINGUS, CUNNILINGUS, PENILINGUS.

orange 1. the female genitals. For synonyms see MONOSYLLABLE. [British, 1700s] **2.** a Dexedrine (trademark) tablet, an amphetamine. From the color of the tablet. [U.S. drug culture, mid 1900s-pres.] **3.** a breast. See ORANGES.

orange mushrooms the drug L.S.D. (q.v.). [U.S. drug culture, mid 1900s-pres.]

oranges the human breasts. Cf. GRAPE-FRUITS, MELONS. [U.S. slang, 1900s]

orange sunshine the drug L.S.D. (q.v.). Cf. YELLOW SUNSHINE. [U.S. drug culture, mid 1900s-pres.]

orange wedges the drug L.S.D. (q.v.). [U.S. drug culture, mid 1900s-pres.]

orchard the female genitals. In the expression GET JACK IN THE ORCHARD (q.v.). [British slang, 1800s, Farmer and Henley]

orchestra a homosexual male who will perform anything sexual with any object or body part. [U.S. homosexual use, mid 1900s]

orchestra stalls (also **orchestras**) the testicles. Rhyming slang for "balls." [British, 1800s, Dictionary of Rhyming Slang]

Orchids to you! a curse, "Balls to you!" [British, early 1900s]

oreo a Negro who thinks and acts like a Caucasian; a derogatory nickname for a Negro who is black on the outside and white on the inside. From the trademarked brand name of a cookie. [U.S. slang, mid 1900s-pres.] See also AFRO-SAXON, AUNT JANE, CHALKER, COOKIE, FADE, FADED BOOGIE, FROSTY.

organ the penis. Cf. FAMILY ORGAN. [colloquial, 1900s]

organ-grinder 1. a derogatory nickname for an Italian. [slang and colloquial, 1900s] **2.** the female genitals, specifically the vagina. **3.** a prostitute; a sexually loose woman.

organism a contrived euphemism for ORGASM (q.v.). [widespread, recurrent, jocular nonce; attested as U.S., 1900s]

organized intoxicated with alcohol. For synonyms see WOOFLED. [U.S. slang and colloquial, early 1900s]

organ music (also **organ recital**) **1.** growling or gurgling in the stomach or intestines. [U.S. colloquial, 1900s or before] **2.** the audible release of intestinal gas. [U.S. colloquial, 1900s]

orgasm 1. a climax; the sexual climax. [since the early 1800s] **2.** to reach a sexual climax; to have an orgasm. A convenient and polite avoidance for COME (senses 1 and 2). [attested as U.S. technical jargon; not in general use]

orgy a sustained period of lewd activity. Usually refers to sexual activity and especially to GROUP SEX (q.v.) activity. [since the early 1700s]

orie-eyed intoxicated with alcohol. *Cf.* GOREY-EYED, HOARY-EYED. [U.S. colloquial, early 1900s]

orifice the female genitals. There are a number of other orifices in the human body, but this one is associated with this euphemism more than others. For synonyms see MONOSYLLABLE. [colloquial and slang, 1800s-pres.]

ork-orks the DELIRIUM TREMENS (*q.v.*). [U.S. colloquial, early 1900s] Synonyms: ABSTINENCE DELIRIUM, ALCOHOL DEMENTIA, ALCOHOLIC SEIZURE, ALCOHOLISMUS ACUTUS, BARREL-FEVER, BLACK DOG, BLUE DEVILS, BLUE HORRORS, BLUE JOHNNIES, BLUES, BOTTLEACHE, CLANKS, DELIRIUM TREMENS, DIDDLEUMS, DINGBATS, DITHERS, DRUNKEN HORRORS, D.T.s, DYSPEPSIA, ELEPHANTS, ENOMANIA, GALLON DISTEMPER, HAVE SNAKES IN ONE'S BOOTS, HORRORS, JERKS, JIMJAMS, JIMMIES, JOE BLAKES, JUMPS, MANIA A POTU, PINK-SPIDERS, QUART-MANIA, SCREAMING-MEANIES, SCREAMING-MEEMIES, SHAKES, SNAKES, THE RAMS, THE RATS, TREMENS, TRIANGLES, UGLIES, WHOOPS AND JINGLES, WOOLIES.

orks the testicles. A truncation of "orchestras" or ORCHESTRA STALLS (*q.v.*), "balls." [British slang, early 1900s, *Dictionary of Slang and Unconventional English*]

ornament the female genitals. For synonyms see MONOSYLLABLE. [British slang, 1800s, Farmer and Henley]

orthogenital pertaining to sexual copulation. Describing acts of copulation optimally suitable for procreation, *i.e.*, acts leading directly to an ejaculation of semen in the vagina. The term is used in avoidance of "normal" or "biologically normal."

orts 1. any leavings, droppings, or crumbs. [early 1400s] **2.** mouse droppings. **3.** fish innards. [senses 2 and 3 are colloquial, 1800s-1900s]

oscar 1. a homosexual male. Often capitalized in this sense. For synonyms see EPICENE. **2.** to commit PEDERASTY (*q.v.*). From the proper name "Oscar Wilde." [British, 1800s]

oscarize to act as a PEDERAST (*q.v.*). See OSCAR.

ossified intoxicated with alcohol; turned into bone by alcohol. *Cf.* PETRIFIED. [U.S. slang, early 1900s]

other parts the human breasts. *Cf.* PRIVATE PARTS. For synonyms see BOSOM. [British, mid 1600s]

other sex 1. the same as OPPOSITE SEX (*q.v.*). **2.** homosexual. *Cf.* THIRD SEX (sense 1). [both senses, colloquial, 1800s-1900s]

otherwise pregnant. For synonyms see FRAGRANT. [U.S. dialect (Ozarks), 1900s or before, Randolph and Wilson]

O.T.R. expecting the menses; "on the rag." See RAG, ON THE. [U.S. slang, 1900s]

out 1. intoxicated with alcohol; unconscious from alcohol. [British and U.S. colloquial, 1700s-1900s] **2.** drug intoxication. [U.S. drug culture, mid 1900s-pres.] **3.** homosexual; out of the closet; pertaining to a person who practices homosexual acts and is a recognized member of the homosexual community. *Cf.* COME OUT OF THE CLOSET. [U.S. homosexual use, mid 1900s-pres.]

out-child a bastard; an illegitimate child. [Caribbean (Jamaican), Cassidy and Le Page]

outdoor plumbing a privy; an outhouse, in contrast to indoor plumbing. [U.S. colloquial, 1900s]

outed (also **offed**) dead; killed. *Cf.* OFF (sense 1). British and U.S. slang, World War 1]

outfit the male genitals. *Cf.* APPARATUS, EQUIPMENT, GEAR, KIT. [euphemistic]

outlaw a prostitute who works independently from a pimp.

out of order experiencing the menses. From a common expression describing anything which will not work. *Cf.* STREET UP FOR REPAIRS. [U.S. slang, 1900s]

out of this world experiencing the menses. For synonyms see FLOODS. [U.S. slang, 1900s]

out on the roof intoxicated with alcohol. [U.S. slang or nonce, mid 1900s]

outside chile (also **outside child**) a bastard; an illegitimate child; the same as OUTSIDE (sense 1). [attested as Caribbean (Trinidad)]

out to it intoxicated with alcohol. *Cf.* OUT (sense 1). [Australian, 1800s-1900s]

oven the female genitals. For synonyms see MONOSYLLABLE. [British, 1700s]

overboard intoxicated with alcohol. For synonyms see WOOFLED. [U.S. slang, 1900s]

overcome intoxicated with alcohol. For synonyms see WOOFLED. [British and U.S. slang, 1800s-1900s]

overnight-bag a prostitute. Punning on the name of a small valise. *Cf.* BAG (sense 4). [U.S. slang, early 1900s]

overseas intoxicated with alcohol. *Cf.* HALF-SEAS-OVER. [British, early 1900s, *Dictionary of Slang and Unconventional English*]

overseen intoxicated with alcohol. For synonyms see WOOFLED. [late 1400s-1600s]

overshot intoxicated with alcohol. *Cf.* CUP-SHOT, GRAPE-SHOT, POT-SHOT. [since the early 1600s]

oversparred intoxicated with alcohol. For synonyms see WOOFLED. [British, late 1800s]

overtaken intoxicated with alcohol. [slang, 1500s-1600s]

over the bay intoxicated with alcohol. *Cf.* OVERSEAS. [U.S. slang and colloquial, early 1800s-1900s]

over the mark intoxicated with alcohol. See LOADED TO THE PLIMSOLL MARK, of which this is a paraphrase. [British slang, early 1800s]

over-the-shoulder-boulder-holder a brassiere. *Cf.* BOULDERS. For synonyms see BRA. [U.S. jocular slang, mid 1900s-pres.]

owl a prostitute who walks the streets at night. *Cf.* NIGHTINGALE. [slang, 1800s]

owled intoxicated with alcohol. See DRUNK AS A BOILED OWL. For synonyms see WOOFLED. [U.S. slang, early 1900s]

owly-eyed (also **owl-eyed**) intoxicated with alcohol. *Cf.* ORIE-EYED. [U.S. slang and colloquial, early 1900s]

owsley the drug L.S.D. (*q.v.*). [U.S. drug culture, mid 1900s-pres.]

ox a bull. [U.S. rural colloquial, 1900s or before]

oxford a Negro who is as dark as black shoe leather. Derogatory. For synonyms see EBONY. [U.S. black use, mid 1900s]

oxometer an imaginary device used to measure the accumulated depth of BULLSHIT (*q.v.*). [British, World War II]

oxter (also **oxtar**) the human armpit. [British colloquial, 1800s and before]

oxycrocium intoxicated with alcohol. Possibly from "oxycroceum," a plaster containing saffron and vinegar. *Cf.* OCKSECROTIA. [U.S. slang, early 1700s, Ben Franklin]

oyster 1. a gob of phlegm. [since the late 1700s, Grose] Senses 1-3 are from the slimy nature of the oyster. 2. the female genitals. [British, 1800s, Farmer and Henley] 3. semen; an ejaculation of semen. [British, 1800s, Farmer and Henley] 4. a testicle used for food. See MOUNTAIN OYSTERS.

oyster-catcher the female genitals, specifically the vagina. *Cf.* OYSTER (sense 3). [British slang, 1800s, Farmer and Henley]

O.Z. one ounce of marijuana. Occasionally used for other drugs. *Cf.* LID, TIN, Z. From "oz.," the abbreviation of "ounce." [U.S. drug culture, mid 1900s-pres.]

ozone, in the intoxicated with marijuana. For synonyms see TALL. [U.S. drug culture, mid 1900s-pres.]

P

P. urine; to urinate; an act of urination. From PISS (*q.v.*).

pack 1. a prostitute; a harlot or tart. See NAUGHTY PACK. *Cf.* BAG (sense 4). [British, 1600s-1800s] **2.** to drink to excess. For synonyms see PLAY CAMELS. [U.S. slang, 1800s]

package a cute girl; a sexually attractive woman. *Cf.* BUNDLE (sense 2). [U.S. colloquial and slang, 1900s]

packaged intoxicated with alcohol. *Cf.* BOXED-UP. [U.S. slang and colloquial, late 1800s-1900s]

pad a sanitary napkin; a perineal pad. For synonyms see MANHOLE COVER. [U.S. colloquial, 1900s]

paddle to fondle a woman sexually. *Cf.* TALK TO THE CANOE DRIVER. [from *Hamlet* (Shakespeare)]

paddy 1. a nickname for an Irishman. Also *Patty*. Usually capitalized in this sense. Derogatory when used as a generic term. [since the late 1700s] **2.** a Chinese. From "rice paddy." For synonyms see JOHN CHINAMAN. [Australian colloquial, Baker] **3.** a policeman; an Irish policeman. [U.S., 1900s] **4.** a derogatory nickname for a Caucasian. *Cf.* PADDY BOY. [U.S. black use, 1900s] **5.** any lazy or worthless person. [U.S. slang, mid 1900s-pres.]

paddy boy (also **patty boy**) a nickname for a Caucasian. Based on PADDY (sense 1), a nickname for an Irishman. [U.S. black use, mid 1900s-pres.]

padre a clergyman; a priest, monk, or chaplain. For synonyms see SKY-PILOT. [from Latin *pater* via Spanish, Portuguese, and Italian; since the early 1800s]

paid intoxicated with alcohol. Possibly a reference to getting drunk on payday. [British, 1800s or before]

pain a bother; a bothersome person. From PAIN IN THE ASS or PAIN IN THE NECK (both *q.v.*). [U.S. colloquial, 1900s]

pain in the ass (also **pain in the derrière, pain in the rear**) **1.** an obnoxious person. *Cf.* PAIN. **2.** a difficult or unpleasant task or subject. *Cf.* PAIN. [both senses, U.S. colloquial, 1900s]

pain in the neck a bothersome person or thing. Euphemistic for PAIN IN THE ASS (*q.v.*). [U.S. colloquial, 1900s]

painkiller any alcoholic drink. *Cf.* MEDICINE (sense 2). SNAKEBITE MEDICINE. For synonyms see BOOZE. [U.S. colloquial and slang, 1900s]

painted-box a coffin. [probably nonce; U.S., late 1800s]

painted-cat a prostitute; a frontier harlot. *Cf.* CAT (sense 1). [U.S. colloquial, 1900s or before]

painted-lady (also **painted-woman**) a prostitute. "Paint" refers to heavy face make-up. [U.S. colloquial, 1900s or before]

painted-Willie a CATAMITE (*q.v.*). For synonyms see BRONCO.

paint the town red to go on a drinking spree; to celebrate wildly. [U.S. slang and colloquial, 1900s]

pair the breasts, especially large and shapely breasts. [U.S. colloquial, mid 1900s-pres.]

pair of drums trousers. An elaboration of DRUMSTICK CASES (*q.v.*). For synonyms see GALLIGASKINS. [British slang, mid 1800s]

pale a nickname for a Caucasian. From PALEFACE (sense 1). *Cf.* FACE. [U.S. black use, 1900s]

paleface 1. a nickname for a Caucasian. *Cf.* FACE, PALE. [U.S. colloquial, 1800s-pres.] **2.** a stereotypical American Indian name for a Caucasian. [widely-known in the U.S., mid 1900s; from the writings of James Fenimore Cooper; U.S. colloquial and slang, early 1800s-pres.] **3.** whisky. [U.S. slang, 1900s or before]

palimony alimony paid to a common-law wife or to a live-in girlfriend. [U.S. slang, 1970s-1980s]

palooka (also **paluka**) an oaf; an unskilled prizefighter; the name of a comic-strip prizefighter, "Joe Palooka." [U.S. slang, 1900s]

pan 1. a woman's body. **2.** the female genitals. *Cf.* KETTLE, MILK-PAN, POT (sense 1). [both senses, U.S. slang and colloquial, 1900s]

Panama gold (also **Panama**) a variety of marijuana said to be grown in Panama. [U.S. drug culture, mid 1900s-pres.]

Panama red (also **Panamanian red**) a potent variety of marijuana supposedly grown in Panama. [U.S. drug culture, mid 1900s]

panatela (also **panatella**) a potent type of marijuana. From the cigar name. [U.S. drug culture, mid 1900s]

pancake the female genitals. From "flat as a pancake." See FLAT COCK. *Cf.* PAN. [British slang, 1800s, Farmer and Henley]

pannier the female genitals; the womb. *Cf.* BASKET (sense 2). [British, early 1600s]

pansified effeminate; homosexual. *Cf.* PANSY. [U.S., 1900s]

pansy 1. a weakling; an effeminate male. For synonyms see FRIBBLE. **2.** a homosexual male, especially a RECEIVER (*q.v.*). For synonyms see EPICENE. [both senses, U.S. slang, early 1900s-pres.]

pansy-ball a dance attended by homosexual males. [U.S. slang, mid 1900s]

pansyland (also **pansy path**) a gathering place for homosexual males. [U.S. slang, mid 1900s]

pansy up to doll oneself up, said of a male. Not necessarily a homosexual male. *Cf.* PIMP UP, QUEER UP. [British, 1900s, *Dictionary of the Underworld*]

pantaloons a type of trousers. For synonyms see GALLIGASKINS. [from the Italian "Pantalone," a comic character; in English since the late 1600s]

panters the breasts. *Cf.* HEAVER. For

synonyms see BOSOM. [British slang, 1800s, Farmer and Henley]

panther juice any alcoholic beverage. [U.S. slang and colloquial, 1900s or before]

panther piss (also **panther's piss**) an inferior grade of alcohol; any strong alcoholic drink. *Cf.* COUGAR-MILK. [Australian and U.S. slang, 1900s]

panther pizen strong or inferior alcohol. *Cf.* PIZEN. For synonyms see EMBALMING FLUID. [U.S. slang, 1900s]

panther sweat any alcoholic drink. *Cf.* NANNY-GOAT SWEAT, PIG SWEAT. [U.S. slang, early 1900s]

panties (also **panteys**) women's or children's underpants. [colloquial, 1800s-pres.]

pantry shelves the human breasts. *Cf.* BALCONY (sense 1). [British, late 1800s]

pants 1. trousers; pantaloons. [U.S. colloquial, early 1800s-pres.] **2.** any human male. A jocular nickname. [U.S. slang, early 1900s-pres.]

pants rabbits lice. *Cf.* SEAM-SQUIRREL. For synonyms see WALKING DANDRUFF. [U.S. slang, early 1900s]

panty-stretcher a well-built young lady. [U.S. slang, mid 1900s-pres.]

pantywaist a timid or effeminate boy or man; a sissy. *Cf.* SISSY-BRITCHES. [U.S. slang and colloquial, 1900s]

pap 1. a lecher; a whoremonger. A truncation of "pappy." [U.S. slang or nonce, mid 1900s, Montelone] **2.** any soft food intended for infants. [U.S. colloquial, 1900s] **3.** nonsense; worthless talk. For synonyms see ANIMAL. [U.S. colloquial, 1900s] **4.** a breast. See PAPS.

paper acid the drug L.S.D. (*q.v.*). *Cf.* BLOTTER (sense 2). [U.S. drug culture, mid 1900s-pres.]

Paphian 1. a prostitute. For synonyms see HARLOT. [literary euphemism] **2.** pertaining to objects, persons, or acts which are lewd and illicit. [both are from Paphos, a Greek city in Cyprus with a famous temple of Aphrodite, where wantonness abounded; both senses, since the mid 1600s]

paps the breasts. [from Latin *papilla mammae;* since the 1300s]

paradise 1. heaven; the afterlife in which good behavior is rewarded. [since c. 1000] **2.** the Garden of Eden. [since c. 1100] **3.** the female genitals. *Cf.* ABRAHAM'S BOSOM, IN. [British euphemism, early 1600s] **4.** cocaine. *Cf.* HEAVEN DUST. For synonyms see NOSE-CANDY. [U.S. drug culture, 1900s]

parakeet a derogatory nickname for a Puerto Rican. [U.S. slang, mid 1900s]

parboiled intoxicated with alcohol. *Cf.* BOILED. [U.S. slang, early 1900s]

Pardee! "By God!" [from the French *par Dieu;* 1300s]

pardon my French (also **excuse my French**) a catch phrase signifying "Please excuse my use of swear words or taboo words." [British and U.S. colloquial, 1900s]

pardon my hard-on a catch phrase used simply to be rude or in reference to a sexually stimulating situation, person, or object. Refers to an erection at an inappropriate time or place. *Cf.* RISE IN ONE'S LEVIS. [U.S. slang, 1900s]

parenthesis the female genitals. From the image of the vulva suggested by (). [British euphemism, late 1800s, Farmer and Henley]

parish-bull (also **parish-prig**) **1.** a parson; a local clergyman. For synonyms see SKY-PILOT. [British slang, 1800s, Farmer and Henley] **2.** a lecher; a notorious local whoremonger. Also **parish-stallion.** *Cf.* TOWN BULL. [British slang, 1800s, Farmer and Henley]

park 1. a woman's body considered as a source of pleasure for men. **2.** to park one's car in a secluded spot for the purpose of kissing and petting. **3.** to participate in kissing and petting in a parked car. [senses 2 and 3 are U.S. slang and colloquial, mid 1900s-pres.]

parleyvoo a nickname for a Frenchman. *Cf.* FROG (sense 1). [from French *parlez-vous;* British and U.S. slang, 1800s-pres.]

parlor house a brothel. [U.S. slang and colloquial, 1900s]

parnel (also **panel, pernel, pernele**) a priest's mistress; a sexually loose woman; a prostitute. [British, 1300s-1700s]

parsley 1. pubic hair, especially female pubic hair. For synonyms see PLUSH. [British; 1700s-1800s] **2.** nonsense; a worthless and extraneous bit of nothing. [colloquial, 1900s]

parsley-bed a woman's genitals. The womb, especially in make-believe stories about where babies come from. [British, early 1700s-1800s]

parson's pox nonspecific urethritis, an inflammation of the male urethra not associated with venereal disease. [Australian, Baker]

partlet a woman. From the common nickname for a hen. [1300s-1800s]

partridge a prostitute; a harlot or a tart. From a bawdy song. *Cf.* QUAIL. [British, late 1600s, Farmer and Henley]

parts the genitals of a man or a woman. A truncation of "private parts." *Cf.* AREA, PARTS (sense 2). [U.S. colloquial, 1900s and before]

parts behind the posteriors. For synonyms see DUFF. [British, 1800s, Farmer and Henley]

parts below the genitals of a man or a woman. *Cf.* UNDERPARTS. [euphemistic, 1600s]

parts of shame the female genitals. *Cf.* FEMALE PUDENDUM. [British slang, 1800s or before]

part that went over the fence last 1. the rump of an animal (whether or not the animal jumps over fences). **2.** the human posteriors. [both senses, U.S. colloquial, 1900s or before]

party 1. drinking; sexual play. Used in expressions to refer to certain kinds of activity carried on in groups or in pairs. *Cf.* PETTING-PARTY, WESSON PARTY. [U.S. slang, 1900s] **2.** to drink; to smoke marijuana. Occasionally, the term may include additional illicit activities. [U.S. euphemistic slang, mid 1900s-pres.]

pash on (also **pash**) to be in a state of sexual arousal. Patterned on HARD-ON (q.v.) and "passion." [U.S. slang, mid 1900s]

pashy-petter a sexually obliging and passionate girl or woman. [U.S. slang, mid 1900s]

passage the vagina. [colloquial euphemism, 1900s and before] See also WINDWARD PASSAGE. Synonyms: LITTLE MARY, NOOKER, NOOKY, PEE HOLE, SNAPPER, STINK-POT, VENUS' GLOVE. See MONOSYLLABLE for related terms.

pass air (also **pass wind**) to release intestinal gas; euphemistic for PASS GAS (q.v.). For synonyms see GURK. [U.S. colloquial, 1900s]

pass a stone 1. to experience the painful movement of a gallstone. **2.** to eliminate a kidney stone during a painful urination.

pass a stool to defecate. For synonyms see EASE ONESELF. [colloquial, 1900s and before]

pass away to die. Cf. PASS ON. [colloquial, 1900s and before]

pass gas to release intestinal gas; to break wind. Cf. PASS AIR. For synonyms see GURK. [U.S. colloquial, 1900s]

pass in one's chips (also **pass in one's checks**) to die; to leave the game and turn in one's playing pieces. [U.S. colloquial, 1800s-pres.]

pass in one's marble to die. [Australian colloquial, 1900s, Wilkes]

passion flower a sexually passionate woman. From the name of the flower. [U.S. colloquial, mid 1900s]

passion pit a drive-in movie where a considerable amount of "necking" is supposed to take place. Also for any location where necking takes place. [U.S. slang, mid 1900s]

passive participant 1. the INSERTOR in FELLATIO; the RECEIVER in PEDERASTY (all q.v.). **2.** in male homosexuality, the partner who is dominated: the receiver in fellatio and pederasty. **3.** in female homosexuality, the more femi-

nine or "passive" party in homosexual acts.

passive pederast a CATAMITE (q.v.); a RECEIVER (q.v.). Cf. ACTIVE SODOMIST. [U.S., 1900s]

pass on to die. Cf. PASS AWAY. [U.S. colloquial, 1900s]

pass out 1. to faint. [colloquial, 1900s or before] **2.** to die. [British, World War I, Fraser and Gibbons] **3.** to lose consciousness due to intoxication with alcohol or drugs. An extension of sense 1. [U.S. slang, mid 1900s-pres.]

pass over to die. Cf. CROSS OVER, PASS ON. For synonyms see DEPART. [colloquial, 1900s or before]

pass urine to urinate; to excrete urine. For synonyms see WHIZ. [technical and medical]

pass water to urinate; to excrete urine.

pass wind to release intestinal gas. Cf. PASS AIR, PASS GAS. For synonyms see GURK. [U.S. colloquial, 1900s]

pasted 1. intoxicated with alcohol. **2.** intoxicated with drugs. [both senses, U.S. slang, mid 1900s-pres.]

pastry women, especially sexually loose women; tarts. Cf. CAKE (sense 3), PIE, TART. For synonyms see TAIL. [colloquial, 1800s]

pasty (also **pastie**) a small covering for the nipple in striptease artistry. [U.S. colloquial, mid 1900s-pres.]

Pat 1. a nickname for an Irishman. Derogatory when used as a generic term. [British and U.S., 1800s-pres.] **2.** a Chinese. From PADDY (sense 2). For synonyms see JOHN CHINAMAN. [Australian, 1900s, Baker]

Pat and Mick the penis. Rhyming slang for "prick." [British, 1800s, Dictionary of Rhyming Slang]

patch the female genitals. For synonyms see MONOSYLLABLE. [British slang, 1800s, Farmer and Henley]

Patess a contrived nickname for an Irishwoman. From PAT (sense 1).

path, the the path to the garden privy; the privy itself. [U.S. colloquial, 1900s or before]

pathic a CATAMITE (*q.v.*). For synonyms see BRONCO. [since the early 1600s]

Patlander an Irishman. Derogatory. *Cf.* BOGLANDER. For synonyms see HARP. [British slang, early 1800s, Jon Bee]

pato a homosexual male. For synonyms see EPICENE. [from Spanish; U.S. slang, mid 1900s-pres.]

patrol, old prostitution. [U.S. slang and colloquial, early 1900s]

pause that refreshes a rest break including an opportunity to use the restroom. From an advertising slogan for Coca-Cola (trademark). [U.S. slang and nonce, mid 1900s-pres.]

pavement-pounder 1. a policeman. **2.** a prostitute. [both senses, U.S. slang, mid 1900s]

pavement princess a prostitute. [U.S. slang, mid 1900s-pres.]

paw to fondle; to caress a woman against her will. *Cf.* GROPE, MAUL. [U.S. slang and colloquial, mid 1900s-pres.]

paw-paw naughty; obscene. For synonyms see LEWD. [British slang, 1800s, Farmer and Henley]

paw-paw tricks masturbation in expressions such as "play paw-paw tricks." This is a special application of a general term for "naughty tricks." [British slang, 1800s]

pay a visit to retire to the W.C. For synonyms see RETIRE. [U.S. colloquial, 1900s]

P.C.P. "phencyclidine," an animal tranquilizer and anesthetic used as a hallucinogenic drug. [U.S. drug culture, mid 1900s-pres.] Synonyms: ANGEL DUST, ANGEL HAIR, ANIMAL TRANQUILIZER, CADILLAC, CANNABINOL, C.J., CRYSTAL JOINT, D.O.A., DUMMY DUST, DUST, ELEPHANT, ELEPHANT TRANQUILIZER, GOON, GREEN SNOW, HOG, HORSE TRANQUILIZER, KILLER-WEED, K.J., MIST, PEACE PILL, PHENCYCLIDINE, PIG TRANQUILIZER, ROCKET-FUEL, SCUFFLE, SHEETS, SNORTS, SOMA, SUPERGRASS, SUPERWEED, SURFER, SYNTHETIC MARIJUANA, WEED.

P'd off PISSED-OFF (*q.v.*); extremely angry. [U.S. euphemism, mid 1900s-pres.]

peacemaker the penis. *Cf.* MATRIMONIAL PEACEMAKER. For synonyms see YARD. [British slang, late 1700s, Grose]

peace pill 1. a mixture of L.S.D. (*q.v.*) and Methedrine (trademark). **2.** the drug P.C.P. (*q.v.*). *Cf.* PEP PILL. [both senses, U.S. drug culture, mid 1900s-pres.]

peach a promiscuous woman. For synonyms see LAY. [U.S. slang, 1900s] See also PEACHES.

peaches 1. the breasts. *Cf.* ORANGES. [U.S. slang, mid 1900s] **2.** amphetamine tablets, especially peach-colored tablets or capsules. [U.S. drug culture, mid 1900s-pres.]

peanut a barbiturate tablet. For synonyms see BARB. [U.S. drug culture, mid 1900s-pres.]

pearl (also **pearly**) **1.** a syphilitic sore. [U.S. slang, mid 1900s] **2.** an amyl nitrite ampule. *Cf.* POPPER, SNAPPER (sense 5). [U.S. drug culture, mid 1900s-pres.]

pearl-diving CUNNILINGUS (*q.v.*). *Cf.* MUFF-DIVER. [U.S. slang, mid 1900s]

pearly gate 1. morning glory seeds. From the color variety name. **2.** the drug L.S.D. (*q.v.*). [both senses, U.S. drug culture, mid 1900s-pres.]

pearly whites morning glory seeds used as a hallucinogenic agent. From the color variety name. [U.S. drug culture, mid 1900s]

peas in the pot sexually aroused. Rhyming slang for "hot." [British slang, late 1800s]

pebbles the testicles. *Cf.* GOOLIES, ROCKS, STONES. For synonyms see WHIRLYGIGS. [British slang, 1800s, Farmer and Henley]

peck a derogatory nickname for a Caucasian. From PECKERWOOD (*q.v.*). [U.S. Southern Negro use, 1900s or before]

pecker 1. the "chin" in the British expression KEEP YOUR PECKER UP! (*q.v.*). No negative connotations in this sense.

[British slang and colloquial, 1800s-pres.]
2. the penis. For synonyms see YARD.
[primarily U.S. slang and colloquial,
1800s-pres.]

peckerwood (also **peckawood**) a de-
rogatory nickname for a Caucasian.
From the common name of a species
of woodpecker. The term may be an
elaboration of PECKER (sense 2). [from
Southern Negro dialect; U.S. black use
and slang, early 1900s-pres.] Synonyms:
BALL-FACE, BEAST, BLUE-EYED DEVIL,
BRIGHT SKIN, BUCKRA, CHARLES, CHAR-
LIE, CHUCK, CRACKER, DAP, DEVIL, DOG,
FACE, FADE, FAY, FROSTY, GEORGIA
CRACKER, GRAY, GRAY BOY, GREY BOY,
HAY-EATER, HINKTY, HONKY, HOOPLE,
HUNKY, JEFF, KELTCH, KU KLUXER, LILY-
WHITE, LONG KNIFE, MARSHMALLOW,
MEAN WHITE, MISTER CHARLIE, MON-
KEY, MULE, OFAY, OOFAY, PADDY, PADDY
BOY, PALE, PALEFACE, PECK, PEEK A
WOODS, PINK, PINKY, REDNECK, RIDGE-
RUNNER, ROUNDEYE, SHITKICKER, SILK,
SNAKE, THE MAN, WHITE MEAT, WHITE
PADDY, WHITEY.

peckish intoxicated with alcohol. [Brit-
ish slang, 1800s, Farmer and Henley]

peculiar river the female genitals.
This "peculiar" means "private." See
GUDDLE. [British, 1600s, from "grop-
ing for trouts in a peculiar river" in
Measure for Measure (Shakespeare)]

pederast 1. a man who performs anal
copulation upon boys. **2.** a man who
performs anal copulation upon males of
any age. Synonyms and related terms:
ACTIVE SODOMIST, ANGEL, ANGELINA,
ARSE-KING, BARDACHE, BIRDIE, BACK-
GAMMONER, BACKGAMMON-PLAYER, BIRD-
TAKER, BROWN-HATTER, BROWNIE, BROWN-
IE KING, BUD SALLOGH, BUG, BUGGAH,
BUGGER, BUNKER, BURGLAR, CAPON,
CINAEDUS, CORN-HOLDER, CORVETTE,
DADDY, EYE DOCTOR, EYE-OPENER, FATHER-
FUCKER, GENTLEMAN OF THE BACK DOOR,
GOOSER, GUT-BUTCHER, GUT-FUCKER,
GUT-MONGER, GUT-REAMER, GUT-SCRAPER,
GUT-STICKER, GUT-STRETCHER, GUT-STUF-
FER, GUT-VEXER, INDORSER, INGLER,
INSERTEE, INSERTOR, INSPECTOR OF MAN-
HOLES, JESUIT, JOCKER, JOCKEY, JOEY,

LICK-BOX, LIMP-WRIST, MASON, PRUSSIAN,
PUFF, REAMER, RING-SNATCHER, SHEEP-
HERDER, SHIT-HUNTER, SHIT-STIRRER, SOD,
SODOMIST, SODOMITE, STERN-CHASER,
STIR-SHIT, STUFFER, TURK, UNCLE, UN-
NATURAL DEBAUCHEE, USHER, VERT,
WOLF.

pederasty (also **paederasty**) **1.** anal
copulation where the INSERTOR (*q.v.*) is
an adult male and the RECEIVER (*q.v.*)
is an adolescent or preadolescent boy.
[since the 1300s] **2.** anal copulation
involving males of any age. Extended
from sense 1. Synonyms and related
terms: ASS-FUCK, BACK-DOOR WORK,
BACK-SCUTTLE, BIT OF BROWN, BOODY,
BOTTLE, BROWN-EYE, BROWN HOLE,
BROWNING, BUCKLEBURY, BUGGERY,
BUNG HOLE, BUTT-FUCK, COITUS IN ANO,
COITUS PER ANUM, CONCUBITUS CUM PER-
SONA EJUSDEM SEXUS, DAUB OF THE
BRUSH, DIP IN THE FUDGE POT, GREEK,
GREEK LOVE, GREEK WAY, HIGHER MAL-
THUSIANISM, ITALIAN MANNER, KIESTER
STAB, KNEELING AT THE ALTAR, LAY,
PAEDICATIO, PEDICATION, PIG-STICKING,
RAM-JOB, SHIP'S, SHIT-FUCK, SODOMY,
UNMENTIONABLE VICE, UNNATURAL CON-
NECTION, UNNATURAL OFFENSE, UNNAT-
URAL PURPOSES, UNNATURAL SEXUAL IN-
TERCOURSE, UNNATURAL VICE.

pee 1. urine. **2.** to urinate. [both senses,
widespread colloquial, 1800s-pres.]

pee'd off extremely angry. A variety
of "pissed-off." *Cf.* P'D OFF. [U.S.
slang and colloquial, 1900s]

pee-eyed intoxicated with alcohol. From
the P.I. of PISSED (*q.v.*). For synonyms
see WOOFLED.

pee hole the vagina. A childlike misunderstanding. [U.S. slang, mid 1900s-
pres.]

peek a woods an elaboration of and
confusion for "peckawood." See
PECKERWOOD.

peek-freak a voyeur. *Cf.* PEER-QUEER,
WATCH-QUEEN. [U.S. homosexual use,
mid 1900s-pres.]

peel to strip one's clothing off, perhaps as a striptease artist. [since the
late 1700s]

peeled naked. For synonyms see STARK-ERS. [since the early 1800s]

peeler a policeman. For synonyms see FLATFOOT.

peel one's best end (also **peel one's end**) to coit; to copulate. Refers to the retraction of the foreskin of an uncircumcised male. [British slang, 1800s, Farmer and Henley]

peenie the penis, especially that of a child. *Cf.* WEENIE. [U.S. slang, 1900s]

pee-pee (also **pee**) **1.** urine. **2.** to urinate. Both are from the initial letter of "piss." The reduplicated form is usually considered to be juvenile. [both since the late 1700s]

peep show 1. sights of a sexual nature, *i.e.*, nude women or couples copulating, as seen through a hole in a wall, originally in carnivals. **2.** any act featuring women in revealing clothing or in some state of nudity. **3.** any brief and even accidental display of otherwise concealed female flesh such as thighs and breasts. [all senses, U.S. slang and colloquial in various senses since the late 1800s]

peer-queer a homosexual male who derives special pleasure from watching others participate in sexual acts. See QUEEN for similar subjects. *Cf.* PEEK-FREAK, VOYEUR, WATCH-QUEEN. [U.S. homosexual use, mid 1900s]

pee-wee 1. the penis, especially that of a child. *Cf.* PEENIE. [primarily British juvenile] **2.** the female genitals. **3.** to urinate. *Cf.* WEE-WEE. [all senses, British and U.S. use, 1800s-1900s]

pee-Willie 1. an insignificant person, somewhat euphemistic for PISS-WILLY (*q.v.*). **2.** an effeminate male. For synonyms see FRIBBLE. [British, early 1900s]

peg boy a CATAMITE (*q.v.*). Probably from PEG (*q.v.*). See PEGO. One etymology states that this was a catamite who belonged to a sailor who kept the boy sitting on a large peg to dilate his anus for PEDERASTY (*q.v.*). For synonyms see BRONCO. [U.S., 1900s]

pegger a drunkard. For synonyms see ALCHY. [British slang, 1800s]

peg-house 1. a brothel catering to men who prefer catamites. See CATA-MITE. **2.** a prison where much PEDER-ASTY (*q.v.*) takes place. [both senses, U.S. underworld, mid 1900s]

pego the penis. [possibly from the Greek word for "fountain," reinforced by "peg" as in TENT-PEG (*q.v.*); British, early 1700s]

pelican a woman. *Cf.* QUAIL. [never common; U.S. slang, mid 1900s, Berrey and Van den Bark]

pellets 1. the human breasts, especially if very small. [U.S. slang or colloquial, 1900s] **2.** rabbit, deer, or goat dung. [colloquial and euphemistic, 1900s or before]

pelter a whoremonger; a lecher. This is from SKIN (sense 4) and LEATHER (sense 1), *i.e.*, "woman-flesh." See LEATHER-DRESSER. [British slang, 1800s, Farmer and Henley]

pen 1. the penis. One of the etymologically correct nicknames for this organ. [from Latin *peniculus*, an "artist's brush"; British, 1500s and widespread nonce] See also PIN (sense 1). **2.** the female genitals, primarily of sows. [British, 1800s or before] **3.** a state "penitentiary."

pencil 1. the penis. *Cf.* PEN (sense 1). [from Latin *peniculus*, an "artist's brush"; British and U.S. slang, 1800s-1900s] **2.** a small penis. [U.S. homosexual use, mid 1900s]

pencil and tassel the male genitals, especially those of a little boy. [British and U.S. slang, 1900s]

penile erection an erection of the penis, usually truncated to ERECTION (*q.v.*).

penile size the size of the male organ. The following are related to or are synonymous with penile size: BASKET FOR DAYS, DONKEY-RIGGED, DOUBLE-SHUNG, HUNG, HUNG LIKE A BULL, MEGAL-OPENIS, MENTULATE, MICROCAULIA, MI-CROGENITALISM, MICROPENIS, MICRO-PHALLUS, MIRACLE-MEAT, TIMBERED, TONS OF BASKET, TONS OF MEAT, WELL-BUILT, WELL-ENDOWED, WELL-FAVORED BY NATURE, WELL-HUNG, WELT.

penilingism (also **penilingus**) the use of the tongue or lips to stimulate the penis of a male; the same as FELLATIO (q.v.).

penilingus the use of the tongue or lips to stimulate the penis of a male; the same as FELLATIO (q.v.). See also BAG-PIPE, B.J., BLOW, BLOW-JOB, FELLATIO, FRENCH TRICKS, FRENCH WAY, GOBBLE, HEAD-JOB, HOOVERISM, IRRUMATION, JOB, KNOB-JOB, MUNCH, ORAL SERVICE, PIPE-JOB, PISTON-JOB, SERVE HEAD, SIXTY-NINE, SMOKE, SODOMY, SUCK, SUCK OFF, SUCK THE SUGAR-STICK, SUCKY-FUCKY, TITTY-OGGY, TONGUE-FUCK.

penis the male sexual and urinary organ. [from Latin *peniculus,* "artist's brush"] See list at YARD.

pen yen (also **pinyon**) opium. For synonyms see OPE. [Chinese or mock-Chinese; U.S. underworld, 1900s or before]

peon 1. a derogatory nickname for a Mexican. For synonyms see MEX. [from the Spanish word for "peasant"] **2.** a nickname for any insignificant person. [U.S. slang, mid 1900s-pres.]

pepper a derogatory nickname for a Mexican. Refers to spicy Mexican food. Cf. PEPPER-BELLY. [U.S. slang, mid 1900s]

pepper-belly (also **chili-belly, pepper-gut**) a derogatory nickname for a Mexican. For synonyms see MEX. [U.S. slang, 1900s]

peppered-off (also **peppered**) infected with a venereal disease. Probably refers to the stinging of gonorrhea. Cf. PEPPER-PROOF. [British, late 1600s, B.E.]

pepper-proof free from venereal disease or resistant to venereal disease. [British, late 1600s, B.E.]

pep pill an amphetamine tablet or capsule. Cf. PEACE PILL. [U.S. drug culture and slang, mid 1900s-pres.]

pepst intoxicated with alcohol. For synonyms see WOOFLED. [slang, late 1500s]

per a prescription for drugs. [U.S. slang and drug culture, 1900s]

Perce the penis. See PERCY (sense 1). For synonyms see YARD.

perch the penis. Possibly the erect penis as a perch for a bird. [U.S. homosexual use, mid 1900s, Farrell]

percolate to sweat. [U.S. slang, mid 1900s]

Percy (also **Perce**) **1.** the penis; a personification of the penis. Cf. POINT PERCY AT THE PORCELAIN. **2.** an effeminate male; a nickname for an effeminate male. [both senses, British and U.S. colloquial, 1900s]

perfect lady a prostitute. [ironic and euphemistic; late 1800s-1900s]

perforate 1. to DEFLOWER (q.v.) a woman. **2.** to coit a woman. [both senses, British, 1800s, Farmer and Henley]

perform 1. to copulate. See DO (sense 1). [British colloquial, 1800s, Farmer and Henley] **2.** to swear grandly and colorfully. [Australian, 1900s, Baker] **3.** to perform PENILINGUS or CUNNILINGUS (both q.v.). [primarily homosexual use, U.S., mid 1900s-pres.] **4.** to coit a woman. [U.S. euphemistic and colloquial, mid 1900s-pres.] See also PERFORM ON.

performer a male who is notorious for copulating frequently or well; a whoremonger; a lecher. [slang, 1800s-1900s]

perform on to deceive; to carry out a plan to cheat someone. [British slang or cant, 1800s, Hotten]

perform the work of nature to eliminate wastes. Cf. MOTHER-NATURE (sense 1). [colloquial, 1900s or before]

perineal pad a menstrual pad; a sanitary napkin; a commercially manufactured pad of absorbent material designed to absorb the menstrual effluvium. For synonyms see MANHOLE COVER.

perineum the region of the human body located between the anus and the scrotum in the male or the anus and the vulva in the female. Cf. TAINT (sense 2). [since the early 1600s]

period (also **periods**) the menses; a truncation of menstrual period. [since the early 1800s]

periodicity rag a menstrual cloth. [British slang, 1800s, Farmer and Henley]

perish 1. to die. [since the 1200s] **2.** to kill. [U.S. slang, 1900s]

perisher a drunken SPREE (sense 2), a "killer" of a drunken spree. See synonyms at SPREE. [Australian, 1900s, Baker]

periwinkle the female genitals. [British slang, 1800s, Farmer and Henley]

perk to vomit. Based on the image of a percolating coffee pot. [Australian, early 1900s, Baker]

perked intoxicated with alcohol. [British, World War 1, Fraser and Gibbons]

permanent rest camp a cemetery. [U.S. slang and colloquial, 1900s or before]

person, the the genitals; the breasts. Occasionally refers to any part of the body which is not normally exposed in public. *Cf.* EXPOSURE OF THE PERSON.

persuade to venery to seduce a woman; to persuade a woman to copulate. [British use, late 1800s, (Farmer)]

pert girl a hussy; a minx. Currently an alert and active girl or woman. [colloquial, 1800s-1900s]

pertish intoxicated with alcohol. [British slang, mid 1700s, *Dictionary of Slang and Unconventional English*]

perve (also **perv**) **1.** a sexual pervert. A truncation of "pervert," usually in reference to a homosexual male. [slang, early 1900s-pres.] **2.** to be perverted; to behave in a perverted manner. **3.** erotic; sexually arousing. **4.** to OGLE (*q.v.*) at a woman. [senses 2-4 are Australian, 1900s]

perve on, to to stare lustfully at a woman. *Cf.* OGLE, PERVE (sense 4). [Australian, 1900s, Baker]

pervert 1. a person who practices any nonorthogenital sexual act. **2.** a person whose libido is directed at any thing, cause, or person other than a member of the opposite sex. **3.** a homosexual male. Usually considered a rude epithet. [U.S. colloquial and slang, 1900s]

perverted a euphemism for "buggered" in expressions such as "I'll be perverted!" See BUGGER. [British, early 1900s, *Dictionary of Slang and Unconventional English*]

perve show a striptease show. *Cf.* PERVE (sense 3). [Australian, 1900s]

pervy 1. erotic. *Cf.* PERVE (sense 3). **2.** the anus. Probably related in some way to PEDERASTY (*q.v.*). [U.S. underworld (tramps), early 1900s]

pessary a vaginal support or suppository. The term is sometimes used for a contraceptive suppository or diaphragm. The term has been replaced in the U.S. by tampon. [since the 1400s] See also MALE PESSARY.

pestle 1. the penis; the mate of the MORTAR (*q.v.*). For synonyms see YARD. **2.** to coit a woman. Implies pelvic thrusting, as with the pestle into the mortar. For synonyms see OCCUPY. [both senses, British slang, 1800s, Farmer and Henley]

pet to kiss and caress; to fondle the breasts and genitals of a woman. [U.S. colloquial, early 1900s-pres.]

petal an effeminate male. *Cf.* FLOWER (sense 4). For synonyms see FRIBBLE. [British military, World War II]

peter the penis. Occasionally capitalized. *Cf.* SAINT PETER. [primarily U.S., 1800s-pres.]

peter out to give out; to wear out. As a nonce term, to lose an erection; to become impotent in the act of copulating. Based on PETER (*q.v.*). [U.S. colloquial nonce, 1900s or before]

peter pansy a homosexual male; one who practices FELLATIO (*q.v.*). See PETER. [U.S. slang, mid 1900s]

petrified intoxicated with alcohol. For synonyms see WOOFLED. [U.S. slang, early 1900s]

petticoat a woman, especially one considered as a sex object. [slang and colloquial since the 1600s]

petticoat-merchant 1. a pimp. **2.** a prostitute. **3.** a lecher. [all senses, British, 1600s-1800s]

petting-party a session of kissing, caressing, and fondling involving one or more couples. [U.S. slang, mid 1900s]

petty-house privy; an outhouse. *Cf.* LITTLE HOUSE, SMALLEST ROOM. For synonyms see AJAX. [British colloquial, 1800s]

pet up to arouse by petting and fondling. *Cf.* PET, RUB UP. [U.S. slang, mid 1900s]

peyote the tip of the Peyote cactus, which contains MESCALINE (*q.v.*). [U.S. drug culture, mid 1900s-pres.]

peyote button the tip of the Peyote cactus, which contains MESCALINE (*q.v.*), a hallucinogenic substance. Sometimes the tips are dried to be transported or sold, and look like shriveled buttons. [U.S. drug culture, mid 1900s-pres.]

pfotze (also **pfotz**) the female genitals. [British slang, mid 1700s]

P.G. 1. "pregnant." For synonyms see FRAGRANT. [U.S. colloquial euphemism, 1900s] **2.** "paregoric." *Cf.* PROCTOR AND GAMBLE. [U.S. drug culture, mid 1900s-pres.]

phallicize to coit a woman; to move the erect penis in and out of the vagina. [British slang, 1800s, Farmer and Henley]

phallic thimble a condom. A jocular play on PHALLIC SYMBOL (*q.v.*). For synonyms see EEL-SKIN. [British, early 1900s, *Dictionary of Slang and Unconventional English*]

phazed (also **phased**) intoxicated with marijuana. For synonyms see TALL. [U.S. drug culture, mid 1900s-pres.]

pheasant a prostitute; a wanton woman. *Cf.* QUAIL. [British slang, 1600s]

pheasantry a brothel. [British, 1800s or before]

phedinkus nonsense. For synonyms see ANIMAL. [U.S. slang, mid 1900s-pres.]

phencyclidine an animal tranquilizer and anesthetic used as a hallucinogenic drug. Popularly known as P.C.P. [U.S., mid 1900s-pres.]

phennies capsules of phenobarbital. *Cf.* BENNY. [U.S. drug culture, mid 1900s-pres.]

phooey (also **fooey**) nonsense. *Cf.* HOOEY (sense 1). [U.S., 1900s]

phutz (also **futz**) to rob, swindle, or cheat. *Cf.* FUTZED-UP. [U.S. slang, mid 1900s]

Phyllis "syphilis." From the feminine name. For synonyms see SPECIFIC STOMACH. [British, 1900s]

physic 1. copulation. *Cf.* NIGHT-PHYSIC. For synonyms see SMOCKAGE. [since the early 1600s] **2.** a laxative; a purgative. [since the early 1600s] **3.** any strong alcoholic drink. From sense 2. For synonyms see BOOZE. [British slang, 1800s, Farmer and Henley]

P.I. a pimp. From "pimp." For synonyms see PIMP. [U.S. underworld, mid 1900s]

piano a CHAMBER POT (*q.v.*). From "pee-ano." Related semantically to TINKLE (*q.v.*). For synonyms see POT. [British slang, 1900s, *Dictionary of Slang and Unconventional English*]

piccolo the penis, especially when used in FELLATIO (*q.v.*). *Cf.* BAGPIPE, FLUTE, SILENT FLUTE. [U.S. slang, 1900s]

piccolo-player a man or woman who performs PENILINGUS (*q.v.*). *Cf.* FLUTER. [U.S. slang, 1900s] The following synonyms refer to males unless indicated otherwise: BLOW-BOY, CANNIBAL, CATCH, COCKSUCKER, C--R, DICK-SUCKER, DICKY-LICKER, FLAKE, LAPPER, LICK-SPIGOT, MOUTH-WHORE, MUNCHER-BOY, NEPHEW, NIBBLER, PANSY, PIECE OF SNATCH, PINK PANTS, PUNK, QUEEN, RECEIVER, SKIN-DIVER, SMOKER (female), SPIGOT-SUCKER, STAND, SUCKSTER, SUCK-STRESS (female).

pick a daisy to retire to urinate or defecate. For synonyms see RETIRE. [British colloquial euphemism, 1900s]

pickaninny (also **picaninny**, **piccaninny**) a Negro child; the child of an Australian aborigine. [ultimately from

Portuguese *piquenino;* since the mid 1600s]

pick fruit to seek out homosexual males for sexual purposes or to rob them. From FRUIT (sense 4). See FRUIT-PICKER. [U.S. underworld, mid 1900s, Goldin, O'Leary, and Lipsius]

pick her cherry to DEFLOWER (*q.v.*) a woman. *Cf.* CHERRY (sense 1). [U.S. slang, mid 1900s-pres.]

pickle, in infected with a venereal disease. [cant, 1600s, B.E.]

pickled intoxicated with alcohol. *Cf.* CORNED, PRESERVED, SALTED-DOWN. [slang and colloquial, 1900s or before]

picklock the penis. *Cf.* KEY (sense 1). For synonyms see YARD. [British slang, 1800s, Farmer and Henley]

pick up 1. to seek out and find a sexually loose woman. **2.** a sexually loose and available man or woman. Usually hyphenated in this sense. [widespread slang, 1800s-pres.]

picnic 1. anything which is obtained easily. **2.** easily obtained sex or petting. **3.** a sexually available girl or woman. [all senses, U.S. slang and colloquial, 1900s]

piddle 1. urine. **2.** to urinate. For synonyms see WHIZ. [colloquial and slang, late 1700s-pres.] **3.** to waste time. A euphemism for PISS (sense 5). [colloquial, 1900s and before]

piddle potty a CHAMBER POT (*q.v.*). For synonyms see POT. [U.S. colloquial, 1900s or before]

pie a woman considered sexually. From the expression "as easy as pie," also reinforced by "nice piece of pie," which is euphemistic for "nice piece of ass." *Cf.* CAKE, TART. For synonyms see TAIL. [U.S. slang, mid 1900s-pres.]

piece 1. any person. [1200s] **2.** a girl or a woman. *Cf.* ARTICLE (sense 1). [British and U.S. colloquial, 1300s-pres.] **3.** a harlot. [slang and colloquial, 1800s-pres.] **4.** a woman considered sexually. See the entries beginning with PIECE OF– –. [slang, late 1800s-1900s] **5.** an orgasm; an act of copulation. Extended from sense 4. [U.S. slang, mid

1900s-pres.] **6.** An ounce of heroin. [U.S. drug culture, mid 1900s-pres.]

piece of ass 1. a woman considered as a sexual object. **2.** an act of copulation. [both senses, U.S. slang, mid 1900s-pres.]

piece of calico (also **bunch of calico**) **1.** a woman. **2.** a woman considered as a sexual object. For synonyms see TAIL. [both senses, U.S. slang and colloquial, mid 1800s-1900s]

piece of dark meat a black woman considered sexually. From the term referring to the dark meat of a domestic chicken. *Cf.* DARK MEAT, WHITE MEAT. [U.S. slang, early 1900s-pres.]

piece of Eve's flesh 1. a woman considered as a sexual object. **2.** an act of copulation. [both senses, U.S. slang, mid 1900s, Montelone]

piece of mutton 1. a woman. **2.** a woman considered as a sexual object. *Cf.* MUTTON. [both senses, British slang, 1600s]

piece of nice a nice young woman; a proper young woman. [British military, World War II]

piece of shit 1. a piece of junk. **2.** a lie; a deceptive story. **3.** a bad performance; a task done badly. **4.** a piece of bad luck. *Cf.* PILE OF SHIT. [all senses, U.S. slang, mid 1900s-pres.]

piece of snatch 1. a sexually loose woman; a woman who is known to copulate. *Cf.* SNATCH (sense 3). **2.** a homosexual male, especially a RECEIVER (*q.v.*). [both senses, U.S. underworld and slang, mid 1900s]

piece of stray a sexually loose woman. For synonyms see LAY. [colloquial and slang, 1900s]

piece of stuff a woman considered as a sexual object. *Cf.* STUFF (sense 3). For synonyms see TAIL. [since the 1700s]

piece of tail 1. a woman considered as a sexual object. For synonyms see TAIL. **2.** an act of copulation. *Cf.* TAIL. For synonyms see SMOCKAGE. [both senses, U.S. slang, mid 1900s-pres.]

piece of trade a prostitute. *Cf.* TRADE (sense 1). [U.S. slang, mid 1900s]

pie-eyed (also **pye-eyed**) intoxicated with alcohol. For synonyms see WOOF-LED. [U.S. slang, late 1800s-pres.]

piffed 1. dead; killed. Also **pifted.** For synonyms see DONE FOR. [U.S., 1900s] **2.** intoxicated with alcohol. [U.S. slang and colloquial, early 1900s-pres.]

piffle 1. nonsense. **2.** to utter nonsense. [both senses, British and U.S. colloquial, late 1800s-pres.] **3.** A mild exclamation, "Oh piffle!" [U.S. colloquial, early 1900s-pres.]

piffled intoxicated with alcohol. For synonyms see WOOFLED. [U.S. slang and colloquial, early 1900s-pres.]

pifflicated (also **pifficated**) intoxicated with alcohol. [U.S. colloquial and slang, early 1900s-pres.]

pig 1. an officer, a police officer or a military officer. For synonyms see FLAT-FOOT. [originally cant; widespread slang, early 1800s-pres.; U.S. underworld or revolutionary use, mid 1900s-pres.] **2.** a prostitute. [U.S. underworld, mid 1900s, Goldin, O'Leary, and Lipsius] **3.** an ugly young woman, especially if fat or dirty. For synonyms see BUFF-ARILLA. [U.S. slang, mid 1900s-pres.] **4.** a promiscuous girl or woman; one who will WALLOW (q.v.) readily. [U.S. slang, mid 1900s-pres.] **5.** any dirty or slovenly person. [U.S. colloquial, 1900s or before]

pigeon 1. a dupe; a sucker. [since the 1500s] **2.** a woman; a cute girl; a gentle woman. [U.S. colloquial, 1900s]

pigeon-eyed (also **pidgeon-eyed**) intoxicated with alcohol. [U.S. slang, early 1700s, Ben Franklin]

pigeon-hole the female genitals. From PIGEON (sense 2). For synonyms see MONOSYLLABLE. [slang and nonce, 1800s-pres.]

pigeon-pair twins of the opposite sex. [British, 1800s, Farmer and Henley]

pig-meat a sexually loose woman; a prostitute. Cf. PIG (sense 2). For synonyms see LAY. [originally black use; U.S. slang, mid 1900s-pres.]

Pig's ass! (also **Pig's arse!**) an excla-

mation. For synonyms see 'ZOUNDS! [widespread slang, 1900s]

Pig's ear! 1. an exclamation, a euphemism for PIG'S ASS! (q.v.). **2.** beer; a glass of beer. Rhyming slang. For synonyms see SUDS. [British slang, 1800s-early 1900s]

pig's knockers pig's testicles. Cf. KNACKERS, KNOCKERS (sense 2). [U.S. rural colloquial, 1900s or before]

pig-sticking PEDERASTY (q.v.). Cf. PORK-SWORD. [attested as Canadian, early 1900s, Dictionary of Slang and Unconventional English]

pig sweat 1. beer. **2.** any inferior alcoholic beverage. Cf. NANNY-GOAT SWEAT, PANTHER SWEAT. [both senses, U.S. slang, 1900s, Wentworth and Flexner]

pigtail a Chinese. From the braided pigtail worn by some Chinese. Usually considered derogatory. For synonyms see JOHN CHINAMAN. [British and U.S., late 1800s-1900s]

pig tranquilizer the drug P.C.P. (q.v.). Cf. ELEPHANT TRANQUILIZER, HOG, HORSE TRANQUILIZER. [U.S. drug culture, mid 1900s-pres.]

pike the penis, especially the erect penis. [widespread nonce; from *Much Ado About Nothing* (Shakespeare)]

piker 1. a petty thief. [1300s] **2.** a coward; a quitter. **3.** a cheapskate. [both senses, U.S. slang and colloquial, early 1900s-pres.]

pikestaff the penis. For synonyms see YARD. [the standard meaning since the 1300s; this sense, British nonce, 1700s]

pile to copulate. For synonyms see OCCUPY. [U.S. black use, mid 1900s-pres.]

pile-driver the penis, especially the erect penis. Cf. SCREWDRIVER. [colloquial and nonce, 1800s-pres.]

pile-driving copulation. Cf. PILE. For synonyms see SMOCKAGE. [colloquial, 1800s-1900s]

pile of shit 1. junk; anything worthless. **2.** a worthless person. **3.** nonsense; lies; a deceptive story. Cf. PIECE

OF SHIT. [all senses, U.S. slang, mid 1900s-pres.]

pilfered intoxicated with alcohol. For synonyms see WOOFLED. [U.S., 1900s]

pilgrim's salve human feces. For synonyms see DUNG. [British, 1600s–1700s]

pilgrim's staff the penis. [British, 1700s]

pill 1. a pill or pellet of opium. [U.S. underworld, early 1900s or before] **2.** an obnoxious person; a PAIN IN THE NECK (*q.v.*). [U.S. colloquial, mid 1900s-pres.] **3.** a birth control pill, "the pill." [U.S. colloquial, mid 1900s-pres.]

pill-head someone who takes drugs illicitly in tablet or capsule form. [U.S. drug culture, mid 1900s-pres.]

pillicock (also **pillock**) the penis, especially the erect penis. *Cf.* COCK (sense 3). [1500s, Florio]

pillicock-hill the female genitals. Refers to the *mons veneris*. *Cf.* PILLICOCK. [from *King Lear* (Shakespeare)]

pillowed pregnant. As if a woman were wearing a pillow over her abdomen. For synonyms see FRAGRANT. [U.S. slang, mid 1900s]

pillow-mate a female bed-partner. [slang and colloquial, 1800s-1900s]

pillowy large-breasted. From the softness of a pillow and "billowy." *Cf.* BABY PILLOWS. [euphemistic, 1900s, *Dictionary of Slang and Unconventional English*]

pill-pusher (also **pill-roller**) **1.** a physician. [U.S. slang and colloquial, early 1900s-pres.] **2.** a doctor who is known to be willing to supply narcotics illegally. [U.S. drug culture, mid 1900s-pres.]

pimp 1. a man who secures customers for one or more prostitutes. **2.** a man who lives off the earnings of one or more prostitutes. *Cf.* PONCE (*q.v.*). [both since the 1600s] **3.** to secure customers for one or more prostitutes. **4.** to live off the earnings of one or more prostitutes. [both since the 1600s] Synonyms: ALPHONSE, APPLE-SQUIRE, APRON-SQUIRE, ASS-PEDDLER, BELSWAGGER, BLUDGEONER, BOSS PIMP, BROTHER OF THE GUS-

SET, BUTTOCK-BROKER, BUTT-PEDDLER, CADET, COCK-BAWD, COCK-PIMP, CRACK SALESMAN, EASTMAN, ECNOP, FAG, FAKER, FANCY MAN, FISH AND SHRIMP, FISHMONGER, FLESH-BROKER, FLESH-PEDDLER, GAGGER, GO-BETWEEN, GORILLA, GORILLA PIMP, HONEY MAN, HOON, HUSTLER, ICEBERG SLIM, JACK-GAGGER, JOE RONCE, JOHNNIE RONCE, MAC MACGIMP, MACK, MACKEREL, MACK MAN, MCGIMPER, MISSIONARY, PANDER, PANDERER, PEEEYE, PETTICOAT-MERCHANT, P.I., PIMPLE, PONCE, PROCURER, PROSSER, RONI, RUFFIAN, RUNNER, RUSTLER, SILVER SPOON, SKIRT-MAN, SOUTENEUR, SPORTING-GIRL'S MANAGER, STABLE-BOSS, SUGAR PIMP, TOUTE, WELFARE PIMP, WHISKIN. **5.** a male prostitute for homosexual males. From senses 1 and 2. [U.S., mid 1900s]

pimple 1. a swelling on the skin. From an accumulation of material in a sebaceous gland. For synonyms see BURBLE. **2.** syphilis; a syphilitic pimple or rash. **3.** a PIMP (*q.v.*) or procurer. A dysphemism for "pimp." [U.S. slang, early 1900s, Montelone] **4.** a baby's penis. [British slang or colloquial, 1800s, *Dictionary of Slang and Unconventional English*]

pimple and blotch Scotch whisky. Rhyming slang for "Scotch." [British slang, 1900s, *Dictionary of Slang and Unconventional English*]

pimp on to inform on. [Australian, early 1900s, Baker]

pimp someone over to deceive or dupe someone; to do someone a bad turn. [U.S. slang, mid 1900s-pres.]

pimp steak a frankfurter. [primarily black use; U.S. slang, mid 1900s or before, Major]

pimp stick a cigarette. [U.S. underworld and World War I, early 1900s]

pimp talk the speech used by pimps and procurers. [U.S. slang and black use, mid 1900s-pres.]

pimp up to doll up; to fix oneself up like a fancy-dressed pimp. A dysphemism based on "primp up." See PANSY UP, QUEER UP.

pimp walk the slow, strutting style of

walk associated with a successful pimp. [U.S. slang and black use, mid 1900s-pres.]

pin 1. the penis. [colloquial and nonce, early 1600s-pres.] **2.** to copulate with a woman; to use a PIN (sense 1) on a woman. [British, 1900s or before] **3.** a thin marijuana cigarette. Also **pinner.** [U.S. drug culture, mid 1900s-pres.]

pin artist an abortionist; a "criminal abortionist." [U.S. underworld, early 1900s, Irwin]

pin-buttock a bony rump; very thin posteriors. [from *All's Well That Ends Well* (Shakespeare)]

pin-case the female genitals, especially the vagina. *Cf.* NEEDLE-CASE, PIN (sense 1), from a colloquial term for "pin-cushion." [British, 1600s]

pinch-bottom (also **pinch-buttock, pinch-cunt**) a lecher; a whoremaster. [British slang, 1800s, Farmer and Henley]

pinch-fart (also **pinch-gut**) a stingy person, a man so stingy that he tries to retain intestinal gas. [British colloquial, 1600s to the 1800s]

pinch-prick 1. a prostitute. **2.** a wife who demands copulation; a wife who insists on receiving all of her husband's sexual attention. [both senses, British slang, 1800s, Farmer and Henley]

pin-cushion the female genitals. *Cf.* PIN-CASE. [British euphemism, 1600s]

pine-overcoat a pine coffin. [U.S. colloquial, mid 1800s-1900s]

pinga the penis. [attested as Spanish slang, late 1800s, Farmer and Henley; U.S. slang, mid 1900s-pres.]

pinhead 1. an oaf; a fool. Someone with a very small head and a very small brain. [since the 1800s] **2.** someone who takes illicit narcotics by hypodermic injection. See HEAD (sense 5). [U.S. underworld and drug culture, mid 1900s]

pink 1. a disguise of "bloody." [British, early 1900s] **2.** a Caucasian. Derogatory. [U.S. black use, early 1900s] **3.** a Seconal (trademark) tablet. [U.S. drug culture, mid 1900s-pres.] **4.** the

drug L.S.D. (*q.v.*). See PINK SWIRL. [U.S. drug culture, mid 1900s-pres.]

pink, in the 1. really happy; in good fortune. [U.S. slang and colloquial, early 1900s-pres.] **2.** intoxicated with alcohol. *Cf.* MELLOW (sense 1). [U.S. slang, early 1900s]

pink-chaser a black man who seeks out white women. *Cf.* PINK (sense 2). [U.S. underworld, mid 1900s, Goldin, O'Leary, and Lipsius]

pinked mildly intoxicated with alcohol. *Cf* PINK, IN THE. For synonyms see WOOFLED. [U.S. slang, 1900s]

pink elephants the DELIRIUM TREMENS (*q.v.*), especially in the expression "see pink elephants." Visions of BLUE DEVILS (sense 2), red spiders, and red monkeys are typical of the hallucinations experienced while having the D.T.s (*q.v.*). For synonyms see ORKORKS. [U.S. slang and colloquial, mid 1900s-pres.]

pink lady a Seconal (trademark) capsule. *Cf.* PINK (sense 3). For synonyms see SEC. [U.S. drug culture, mid 1900s-pres.]

pinko 1. intoxicated with alcohol. [Australian slang, early 1900s] **2.** a communist. [U.S. slang, mid 1900s]

pink pants a CATAMITE (*q.v.*); an effeminate male homosexual. For synonyms see BRONCO. [U.S. underworld, mid 1900s, Goldin, O'Leary, and Lipsius]

pink-spiders the DELIRIUM TREMENS (*q.v.*). [slang, late 1800s-1900s]

pink swirl (also **pink**) the drug L.S.D. (*q.v.*). [U.S. drug culture, mid 1900s-pres.]

pinky (also **pinkie**) **1.** a mulatto. For synonyms see MAHOGANY. [U.S. colloquial and slang, 1900s or before] **2.** a Caucasian. *Cf.* PINK (sense 2).

pintle the penis of an animal or of a human. *Cf.* PINTLE-CASE. [since the 1100s]

pintle-bit (also **pintle-maid**) a concubine; a mistress. [British slang, 1800s, Farmer and Henley]

pintle-blossom a syphilitic chancre. For synonyms see BUBO. [British slang, 1800s or before, Farmer and Henley]

pintle-case the female genitals. A mate for the PINTLE (q.v.). Cf. NEEDLE-CASE. [British slang, 1800s, Farmer and Henley]

pintle-fancier (also **pintle-ranger**, **pintle-twister**) a prostitute. For synonyms see HARLOT. [British slang, 1800s or before]

pintle-fever a venereal disease. [British slang, 1800s or before]

pintle-monger (also **pintle-merchant**) a prostitute. [British slang, 1800s or before]

pintle-smith a physician who treats venereal diseases. This probably does not refer to circumcision. [British slang, late 1700s, Grose]

pint pot 1. a beer merchant. [colloquial, late 1500s] **2.** a drunkard. Rhyming slang for SOT (sense 2). [British, 1900s, *Dictionary of Rhyming Slang*]

pin-up girl 1. a girl or woman who appears partially clothed on posters and calendars. **2.** a girl or woman who is appealing enough to appear on posters and calendars. [both senses, U.S. slang and colloquial, mid 1900s]

pioneer of nature the penis. See GARGANTUA'S PENIS. [mid 1600s, (Urquhart)]

pip, the syphilis. For synonyms see SPECIFIC STOMACH. [late 1500s-1600s]

pipe 1. the penis. Cf. WATER-PIPE (sense 2). [colloquial and nonce since the 1600s] **2.** the female genitals. Comparing the vagina to the inside of a pipe. Cf. WATER-PIPE. [British slang, 1800s, Farmer and Henley] **3.** the urethra of the male or female. [slang and colloquial, 1800s-1900s] **4.** a user of marijuana. From WATER-PIPE (sense 1). [U.S. drug culture, mid 1900s-pres.]

pipe-cleaner 1. the vagina. For synonyms see PASSAGE. **2.** a woman considered as a sexual object. The PIPE (sense 1) is the penis. [both senses, slang, 1900s or before]

pipe-hitter 1. an opium smoker. [U.S.

underworld, mid 1900s or before] **2.** a marijuana smoker. Cf. PIPE (sense 4). [U.S. drug culture, mid 1900s-pres.]

pipe-job an act of FELLATIO (q.v.). Usually a request made of a prostitute. Cf. BLOW-JOB, PIPE (sense 1). [U.S. slang, mid 1900s-pres.]

pipkin the female genitals. A "pipkin" is a small vessel. Cf. CRACK A JUDY'S TEACUP. For synonyms see MONOSYLLABLE. [British, early 1700s]

pipped-up (also **pipped**) intoxicated with alcohol. For synonyms see WOOFLED. [British and U.S. slang, early 1900s]

pis-ant (also **ant-mire**, **pis-mire**, **pissannat**, **piss-ant**, **pissmote**) an ant. [U.S. colloquial, 1800s-1900s]

pish whisky. "Piss" as spoken by an inebriated person. See PISS (sense 4). [British military, World War I, Fraser and Gibbons]

pisher a young inexperienced male; a GREENHORN (q.v.); a nobody. Literally, "a pisser," a bed-wetter. [Yiddish from German *pissen*, "urinate"]

piss 1. urine. **2.** to urinate. In some parts of the English-speaking world this term can be used in polite conversation without giving offense. [onomatopoetic, from Vulgar Latin; both since the 1200s] Disguises: COUSIN SIS, MICKEY BLISS, MIKE BLISS, RATTLE AND HISS, SNAKE'S HISS, THAT AND THIS. **3.** an exclamation, "Piss!" **4.** any weak beer or alcoholic drink. Cf. PANTHER PISS, PISS-MAKER, SQUAW PISS, TIGER PISS, WITCH-PISS. [slang, 1900s] **5.** to waste time.

piss and vinegar energy; vigor. [U.S. colloquial, 1900s or before]

piss and wind nonsense; lies and deceit. Apparently in avoidance of BULLSHIT (q.v.). [early 1900s, *Dictionary of Slang and Unconventional English*]

pissant around to waste time; to goof off, a way to express "piss around" by using the non-taboo term PIS-ANT (q.v.). [Australian, mid 1900s, Baker]

piss blood to work very hard. [slang

and colloquial, 1800s-1900s; other senses since the 1600s]

piss-bowl a CHAMBER POT (*q.v.*). For synonyms see POT. [mid 1500s]

piss-can a toilet or a chamber pot. *Cf.* CAN (sense 1). [U.S. colloquial, 1900s or before]

piss-cutter a very excellent thing, person, or situation. Someone who can do the impossible. *Cf.* PISS-WHIZ. [U.S. slang, 1900s]

pissed 1. intoxicated with alcohol. *Cf.* PISSED-UP. For synonyms see WOOFLED. [British and U.S. slang, early 1900s-pres.] **2.** very angry. A truncation of PISSED-OFF (*q.v.*). [U.S. slang, 1900s]

pissed-off (also **pissed**) very angry. *Cf.* P'D OFF. [U.S. slang, mid 1900s-pres.]

pissed-up (also **pissed**) intoxicated with alcohol. [British slang, wartime]

pissed up to the eyebrows intoxicated with alcohol. An elaboration of PISSED (sense 1). [British military, early 1900s, *Dictionary of Slang and Unconventional English*]

piss-elegant quite elegant; pretentious. *Cf.* PISS-POOR. [U.S. slang, mid 1900s-pres.]

pisser 1. the penis. For synonyms see YARD. **2.** the female genitals. For synonyms see MONOSYLLABLE. [both senses, colloquial and nonce, 1800s-pres.] **3.** any difficult task or situation; a task which is likely to make you angry or PISSED (sense 2). **4.** a urinal. [British and U.S. colloquial and nonce, 1800s-pres.] **5.** a really superb party or spree. *Cf.* PISS-ELEGANT. [U.S. slang, mid 1900s-pres.]

piss-factory a tavern. Refers to the diuretic properties of beer. [British and U.S. slang, 1800s-1900s]

piss freak one who derives sexual pleasure from urine. [U.S. slang, mid 1900s-pres.]

piss hard-on a morning erection; a urinary erection. *Cf.* PISS-PROUD. [colloquial, 1900s or before]

piss-head 1. an oaf; a foolish jerk.

[U.S. slang, 1900s] **2.** a heavy drinker; a drunkard. *Cf.* PISSED (sense 1). [slang, 1900s]

pisshouse 1. a police station. **2.** a W.C.; a privy. *Cf.* PISSER (sense 4). [both senses, U.S. slang, mid 1900s]

pissing minimal; worthless; brief. [since the 1500s]

pissing-drunk heavily intoxicated with alcohol. For synonyms see WOOFLED. [British slang, 1800s or before]

pissing-while a minimal amount of time; the amount of time it takes to urinate; the amount of time it takes a drink of fluid to be assimilated and expelled as urine. *Cf.* FARTING-SPELL, PISSING. [colloquial, early 1500s]

piss-maker 1. a heavy drinker. [since the 1700s] **2.** alcoholic drink; beer. [U.S. slang, 1900s]

piss off 1. to depart in a hurry. Also used as an order meaning "beat it!" *Cf.* DRAG ASS. [British slang, 1900s or before] **2.** to make someone very angry. Also **piss someone off.** [U.S. slang, mid 1900s-pres.]

piss pins and needles to have gonorrhea. From the pain experienced in urinating. Usually said of males. [British slang, late 1700s, Grose]

pisspiration a dysphemism for "sweat." [U.S. jocular colloquial and nonce, early 1900s]

piss-poor really terrible; low-quality or ineffectual. *Cf.* PISS-ELEGANT. [British and U.S. slang, early 1900s-pres.]

piss-pot 1. a CHAMBER POT (*q.v.*). [colloquial, 1400s to the 1900s] **2.** a physician; an early urologist. A medical man who diagnosed diseases by studying urine. [1500s] **3.** a rotten rascal; a real stinker. For synonyms see SNOKE-HORN. [British slang, 1800s and nonce elsewhere]

piss-proud pertaining to a morning erection. *Cf.* PISS HARD-ON. [British, early 1800s or before, *Lexicon Balatronicum*]

piss-quick 1. an alcoholic drink of gin and hot water. [British slang or colloquial, early 1800s, Jon Bee] **2.** a nickname for a diruretic or a substance with diuretic properties. [colloquial, 1900s and before]

piss-up a drinking spree; a BENDER (*q.v.*). [British slang, 1900s]

piss-whiz very excellent. *Cf.* PISS-CUTTER. [U.S. slang, early 1900s]

piss-Willy an insignificant person. *Cf.* PEE- WILLIE. [U.S. colloquial, 1900s or before]

pissy-arsed intoxicated with alcohol; a tendency to become intoxicated with alcohol. [British slang, 1900s, *Dictionary of Slang and Unconventional English*]

pistol the penis. See GUN. [from *Henry IV*, Part Two (Shakespeare)]

piston-job an act of PENILINGUS (*q.v.*).

piston rod (also **piston**) the penis. *Cf.* CYLINDER. For synonyms see YARD. [slang and nonce, 1900s]

pit 1. the female genitals. *Cf.* BOTTOMLESS-PIT. [British slang, late 1600s] **2.** hell, especially as "the pit." [U.S. colloquial, 1900s and before]

pitch 1. the INSERTOR in PEDERASTY or PENILINGUS (all *q.v.*). The opposite of CATCH (sense 1). [U.S. slang, mid 1900s-pres.] **2.** a fat or ugly young woman; an undesirable woman. A blend of "pig" and "bitch," also possibly a disguise of BITCH (sense 2). [U.S. college slang, mid 1900s-pres., Underwood]

pitcher the female genitals. A remarkable pitcher which holds CREAM (sense 1) with its mouth downward. For synonyms see MONOSYLLABLE. [British slang, late 1600s-1800s]

pitcher-bawd a madam; a woman who serves up harlots or liquor. [British, 1600s, B.E.]

pitcher-man a drunkard. For synonyms see ALCHY. [British, early 1700s]

pit-hole 1. a grave. For synonyms see LAST ABODE. [British, early 1600s] **2.** the female genitals. See PIT (sense 1). [British, 1800s, Farmer and Henley]

pits, the 1. the armpits. **2.** anything really bad. [both senses, U.S. slang, mid 1900s-pres.]

pit stop 1. a pause to urinate. From the name of the refueling stop in automobile racing. [U.S. slang, mid 1900s-pres.] **2.** an underarm deodorant. Because it stops armpit odor. [U.S. slang and nonce, mid 1900s-pres.] **3.** a departure to the toilet. Based on sense 1. For synonyms see RETIRE.

pitty-tink the color pink. From "titty-pink," a deliberate spoonerism. [U.S. slang, mid 1900s]

pixilated intoxicated with alcohol; silly from alcohol. From a term meaning "daffy." [U.S. slang, mid 1800s]

pixy 1. a kind of fairy, elf, or brownie. [colloquial, 1800s or before] **2.** a homosexual male. An avoidance for FAIRY (sense 2). Also **pix.** [U.S. underworld and slang, mid 1900s]

pizen whisky. A dialect form of the word "poison." *Cf.* PANTHER PIZEN. [U.S. slang and colloquial, late 1800s-1900s]

pizened (also **poisoned**) pregnant. *Cf.* STUNG BY A SERPENT. [U.S. dialect (Ozarks), Randolph and Wilson]

pizzle (also **peezel, pissel, pizell**) **1.** the penis of an animal, especially that of a bull. [since the 1500s] **2.** the penis. For synonyms see YARD. [since the 1600s] **3.** to coit a woman; to copulate. For synonyms see OCCUPY. [British colloquial, 1600s-1800s]

place 1. a privy. *Cf.* LOCUS. For synonyms see AJAX. [euphemistic, 1800s-1900s] **2.** the male or female genitals or pubic areas. *Cf.* AREA, PARTS. [euphemistic and nonce, 1700s-pres.]

place of convenience a privy; an outhouse. For synonyms see AJAX. [British colloquial, 1800s]

place of resort (also **place of easement**) any place where one may excrete privately; a W.C. or a privy. Could also refer to any secluded nook. [British euphemism, 1800s or before]

place where you cough the bathroom; a W.C. Because when you are there, you cough to warn an approaching person of your presence. This practice includes sneezing, whistling, shuffling, and clearing the throat. [attested as British, early 1900s, *Dictionary of Slang and Unconventional English*]

placket 1. the female genitals. [numerous written attestations; British euphemism, late 1500s-1600s] **2.** a woman considered sexually; women considered sexually. [British, 1600s] Both are from the term for a skirt or petticoat or for the slit at the waist of a petticoat which aids in getting in and out of it.

placket-box the female genitals. For synonyms see MONOSYLLABLE. [British use, late 1800s, (Farmer)]

placket-hole the female genitals. [British slang, 1800s or before]

placket-racket the penis, the mate of the PLACKET (sense 1). [mid 1600s, (Urquhart)]

placket-stung infected with a venereal disease. [British, 1600s]

plague a venereal disease. See POX (sense 1). [U.S. slang, mid 1900s, and nonce]

plague-goned a disguise of DOGGONED (q.v.). [U.S. colloquial, early 1900s, Berrey and Van den Bark]

plague on you!, A (also **pox on you!, A**) a curse. [since the 1600s or before]

plant a man 1. to bury a man. [U.S. colloquial, 1900s or before. **2.** to coit a woman. [British, 1800s and before, Farmer and Henley]

plant the oats to coit a woman. Cf. HAVE ONE'S OATS, OAT-BIN, SOW ONE'S WILD OATS. "Oats" refers to semen. [U.S. colloquial and euphemistic, early 1900s]

plastered intoxicated with alcohol. Cf. STUCCOED. [British and U.S. slang, early 1900s-pres.]

play to copulate. For synonyms see OCCUPY. [euphemistic since the late 1300s]

play around 1. to court or copulate with a number of members of the opposite sex. **2.** to have extramarital sexual intercourse. **3.** to tease and trifle with members of the opposite sex. [all senses, U.S. colloquial, mid 1900s-pres.]

play at all-fours to copulate. [British slang, 1800s, Farmer and Henley]

play at cock-in-cover to copulate. Cf. COCK (sense 3), the penis. [British slang, 1800s, Farmer and Henley]

play at couple-your-navels to copulate. [British slang, 1800s, Farmer and Henley]

play at in-and-out (also **play at in-and-in**) to copulate. [British euphemism, early 1600s]

play at itch-buttock to copulate. "Itch-buttock" was a party game played in England in the 1500s-1700s. It was also called "level-coil" and "rise up good fellow." The term was extended to any exciting or wild activity. [British, late 1500s-1700s]

play at lift-leg to copulate. Cf. LIFT ONE'S LEG. [British, 1700s]

play at pickle-me-tickle-me to copulate. [mid 1600s, (Urquhart)]

play at pully-haully to tease and flirt with women; to coit a woman. [British, late 1700s, Grose]

play at stink-finger to fondle a woman's vagina. Cf. FINGER-FUCK. [British slang, 1800s, Farmer and Henley]

play at the first-game-ever-played to copulate. [British slang, 1800s, Farmer and Henley]

play at tops-and-bottoms to copulate. [British slang, 1800s, Farmer and Henley]

play at top-sawyer to copulate. For synonyms see OCCUPY. [British slang, 1800s, Farmer and Henley]

play away to be unfaithful to one's spouse. [British colloquial, 1900s]

play camels to get drunk; to see how much drink one can store up; to guzzle beverage alcohol. [British slang, late 1800s, Ware] Synonyms: BARREL, BEEZZLE, BELT THE GRAPE, BEVVY, BIBBLE,

COP THE BREWERY, CRAPULATE DE-BAUCH, GUZZLE, SPREE, TIPPLE.

play cars and trucks to coit. Rhyming slang for "fucks." Refers to driving in and out. [Australian slang, 1900s] See also PUSH IN THE TRUCK.

play doctor 1. children's satisfying their sexual curiosity by pretending they are examining each other medically. **2.** adult sex-play. From sense 1. [euphemistic, 1900s]

playground 1. the female genitals. [British slang, 1800s, Farmer and Henley] **2.** the human breasts. [U.S. slang, 1900s]

play hospital to copulate Cf. PLAY DOCTOR (sense 2). [Australian, 1900s]

play house 1. to copulate; to play at being man and wife. [U.S. colloquial, early 1900s-pres.] **2.** for an unmarried man and woman to live together. [U.S. colloquial, mid 1900s-pres.]

play off to masturbate. For synonyms see WASTE TIME. [British, 1800s or before, Farmer and Henley]

play one's ace to coit; said of a woman. Cf. ACE (sense 2). [British slang, 1800s, Farmer and Henley]

play the organ to copulate. Cf. FAMILY ORGAN, ORGAN. [colloquial and jocular, 1900s or before]

plaything 1. the penis. Cf. BAUBLE (sense 1), TOY (sense 4), TRIFLE (sense 3). [British and U.S. colloquial, 1800s-pres.] **2.** the female genitals. Cf. TOY (sense 2). [British and U.S. colloquial, 1800s-pres.] **3.** a sexually easy woman. For synonyms see LAY. [U.S. slang, early 1900s-pres.]

play tiddlywinks to copulate. [British slang, 1900s, Dictionary of Slang and Unconventional English]

pleasantly plastered intoxicated with alcohol. Cf. PLASTERED, STUCCOED. [U.S. slang, early 1900s pres.]

please to coit a woman; to coit a woman to orgasm. [euphemistic, early 1600s-1900s]

pleaser a sexually easy woman; a

woman who knows how to please a man sexually. Presumably this can also apply to a male who can please a woman. [U.S. slang, mid 1900s-pres.]

pleasure 1. copulation; copulation to orgasm. **2.** to coit a woman. Cf. ART OF PLEASURE, DEED OF PLEASURE. [both since the 1500s]

pleasure-boat (also **pleasure-garden, pleasure-ground, pleasure-palace**) the female genitals. Cf. BOY-IN-THE-BOAT, TALK TO THE CANOE DRIVER. Also a reference to the rocking motions of copulation. [British, 1600s (or before) to the 1800s]

pleasure-garden padlock a menstrual cloth. Cf. GARDEN, the female genitals. [British slang, 1600s-1700s]

pleasure lady a prostitute; a harlot. [British colloquial, early 1600s, Halliwell]

plenipo the penis. A truncation and standard abbreviation of "plenipotentiary," a "fully-empowered ambassador." [British slang, late 1700s]

plink a cheap and inferior local wine. Based on PLONK (sense 1). [Australian, 1900s, Baker]

ploll-cat a prostitute. Possibly a typographical error for POLECAT (q.v.). [attested by Farmer and Henley and Halliwell]

plonk 1. a cheap grade of alcohol or hard liquor. Also **plunk.** [originally Australian; from the French vin blanc; slang, World War II] **2.** a bore; a jerk. [U.S. slang, mid 1900s]

plonk-dot a wine-drinker; a WINO (q.v.). DOT (q.v.) is the anus. [Australian, 1900s]

plonked intoxicated with alcohol, done in by PLONK (sense 1). [U.S. slang, mid 1900s]

plonko a drunkard. Cf. PLONK (sense 1). [Australian, early 1900s]

plootered intoxicated with alcohol. For synonyms see WOOFLED. [British and U.S. slang, 1900s]

ploughed intoxicated with alcohol. *Cf.* PLOWED (sense 1).

plover a prostitute; a sexually loose woman. From the name of a bird. *Cf.* QUAIL. [British, early 1600s]

plow (also **plough**) **1.** to coit a woman. [since the early 1600s] **2.** to rape a woman. **3.** to have sexual intercourse, said of males and females in any combination. [senses 2 and 3 are U.S. underworld, mid 1900s, Goldin, O'-Leary, and Lipsius]

plowed (also **ploughed**) **1.** intoxicated with alcohol. [British and U.S. slang and colloquial, 1800s-pres.] **2.** having been copulated with. *Cf.* PLOW (sense 3).

pluck 1. to coit; to deflower; to pluck a girl's FLOWER (sense 2). [British euphemism, 1600s] **2.** to coit. A disguise of "fuck." Also **plook.** See SKLOOK. [U.S., mid 1900s or before] **3.** cheap wine. Possibly related to PLONK (*q.v.*). [U.S. slang, mid 1900s-pres.]

pluck a rose to retire to a garden privy or to a W.C. *Cf.* DROP A ROSE. [colloquial since the 1700s]

plug 1. to coit a woman. [slang since the 1700s] **2.** a tampon. [U.S. colloquial or slang, mid 1900s] **3.** the penis. [widespread nonce and slang]

plug-tail the penis. For synonyms see YARD. [British, 1700s-1900s, Grose]

plumbing a toilet; the bathroom plumbing. *Cf.* INDOOR PLUMBING, OUTDOOR PLUMBING. [U.S. colloquial, 1900s or before] See also FIX HER PLUMBING.

plump-pate a FAT-HEAD (*q.v.*); an oaf; a blockhead. [British colloquial, 1800s or before]

plums the human testicles. From their shape. [U.S., 1900s]

plum-tree the female genitals. Especially in the expression "have at the plum-tree." [euphemism, mid 1500s]

plum-tree shaker the penis. For synonyms see YARD. [British, 1600s or before]

plurry bloody. For synonyms see BLOODY. [from the aboriginal pronun-

ciation of "bloody"; Australian, 1800s, *Dictionary of Slang and Unconventional English*]

plush the pubic hair. *Cf.* FUR (sense 1). [British slang, 1800s, Farmer and Henley] Synonyms: BRAKES, BUSH, FUD, PUBES, SCRUBBING-BRUSH, SHORT AND CURLY, SPORRAN, TUFT. See also DOWNSHIRE.

P-maker the male or female genitals. Euphemistic for PISS-MAKER (*q.v.*). For synonyms see GENITALS. [British slang, 1800s, Farmer and Henley] See also PISS-MAKER.

P.M.T. "premenstrual tension." [U.S. euphemism, 1900s]

P.O. 1. a "piss-off," an oaf or a jerk. **2.** to make someone very angry or PISSED-OFF (*q.v.*). [both senses, U.S. slang, mid 1900s]

po (also **poh**) a CHAMBER POT (*q.v.*); a potty. [British slang and U.S. nonce, 1800s-1900s]

po buckra a "poor buckra," a poor Caucasian; the same as POOR WHITE TRASH (*q.v.*). See BUCKRA. [U.S. Negro colloquial, 1900s or before]

pockes syphilis. An early spelling of POX (*q.v.*). [1500s or before]

pocket-book the female genitals. *Cf.* MONEY. [U.S. black use, 1900s]

pocket-pool (also **pocket-billiards**) the act of a male playing with his genitals through his trouser pockets. *Cf.* STICK AND BANGERS. [U.S. slang, mid 1900s]

pocket the red to coit a woman; to penetrate a woman. From billiards. [British slang, 1800s, *Dictionary of Slang and Unconventional English*]

pocket-thunder an audible breaking of wind. *Cf.* THUNDER-BOX. [British slang, 1800s, Farmer and Henley]

pod 1. marijuana or a marijuana cigarette. *Cf.* POT. [U.S. drug culture, mid 1900s-pres.] **2.** the posteriors; the anus.

pod, in pregnant. For synonyms see FRAGRANT. [British, late 1800s]

poddy 1. pregnant. *Cf.* POD, IN. [British, 1800s] **2.** intoxicated with alcohol. *Cf.* POTTED (sense 1). [British and U.S. slang, late 1800s-1900s]

poet's corner a toilet; a W.C. [U.S. slang, early 1900s]

poger a CATAMITE (*q.v.*). Possibly connected with some sense of ROGER (*q.v.*). For synonyms see BRONCO. [U.S. underworld, mid 1900s, Goldin, O'Leary, and Lipsius]

poggled (also **puggled**) crazy; intoxicated with alcohol. [British, Fraser and Gibbons]

pogy (also **pogey**) intoxicated with alcohol; mildly drunk. [British and U.S. colloquial, 1800s-1900s]

point the penis, especially the glans penis. *Cf.* LANCE. [colloquial and nonce since the 1600s or before]

pointer the penis. For synonyms see YARD. [British slang, 1800s, Farmer and Henley]

point-of-attraction the female genitals. *Cf.* CENTER OF ATTRACTION. For synonyms see MONOSYLLABLE. [British, late 1700s]

point of possession, on the just before intromission of the penis. [British use, late 1800s, (Farmer)]

point Percy at the porcelain to urinate. PERCY (*q.v.*) is the penis. *Cf.* TRAIN TERRENCE ON THE TERRACOTTA. For synonyms see WHIZ. [contrived jocular euphemism; Australian, 1900s or before]

points the nipples; the breasts; conical and pointed breasts. Heard in the ambiguous catch phrase "Well, she has her points." [U.S. colloquial and slang, 1900s]

poison 1. alcohol considered seriously as a poison, *i.e.*, as a harmful substance rather than as a source of pleasure. [since the 1300s] **2.** any alcoholic drink, as in "name your poison," an invitation to request a drink. *Cf.* PIZEN. For synonyms see BOOZE. [U.S. colloquial, 1900s] **3.** heroin. [U.S. drug culture, mid 1900s-pres.]

poisoned (also **pizened, poyson'd**) pregnant; the same as PIZENED (*q.v.*).

Cf. STUNG BY A SERPENT. For synonyms see FRAGRANT. [late 1600s-pres., B.E.]

poke 1. to copulate with a woman. Also **poge, pogh, pogue**. [colloquial since the early 1700s or before] **2.** copulation; an act of copulation. [British and U.S., 1800s-1900s] **3.** a sexually loose woman; a mistress; a concubine. [slang, 1800s-1900s] **4.** a lazy person. From "slow-poke." [U.S. colloquial, 1800s-1900s] **5.** the scrotum. In the dialect sense "sack." [attested as dialect (Ozarks), Randolph and Wilson] **6.** a puff of a marijuana cigarette; the same as TOKE (sense 2). [U.S. drug culture, mid 1900s-pres.]

poke-hole the female genitals. For synonyms see MONOSYLLABLE. [British slang, 1800s, Farmer and Henley]

poker the penis, especially the erect penis. *Cf.* RED-HOT POKER. [slang and nonce since the 1700s]

poker-breaker (also **poker-climber**) **1.** a prostitute. **2.** a wife. For synonyms see WARDEN. [both senses, British slang, 1800s, Farmer and Henley]

polack a derogatory nickname for a Polish man or woman. From the nonderogatory Polish word for a Polish male. [since the 1600s]

pole 1. the penis, especially the erect penis. [widespread recurrent nonce; British and U.S. slang and colloquial, 1800s-1900s and certainly long before] **2.** to coit a woman. [British and U.S. slang and colloquial, 1800s-pres.]

pole, up the 1. pregnant. Also **stick, up the.** The "pole" is a vague reference to the penis. *Cf.* GET UP THE POLE. [widespread slang, 1900s] **2.** intoxicated with alcohol. *Cf.* HALF UP THE POLE. [slang, late 1800s-1900s]

polecat a prostitute. *Cf.* POLE (sense 1), the penis. [from *Merry Wives of Windsor* (Shakespeare)]

pole-work copulation. *Cf.* POLE (sense 1). [British slang, 1800s, Farmer and Henley]

policeman's helmet the *glans penis*. From the shape. *Cf.* BEAT THE BISHOP. For synonyms see HEAD. [British, 1900s,

Dictionary of Slang and Unconventional English]

polished-up (also **polished**) intoxicated with alcohol. For synonyms see WOOF-LED. [U.S. slang, early 1900s]

poll-axe the penis. [from *Love's Labour's Lost* (Shakespeare)]

polled-up living with a mistress or concubine. *Cf.* SHACKED-UP. [British slang, late 1800s]

pollute 1. to masturbate. 2. to defile or DEFLOWER. (*q.v.*) a woman. [since the 1600s or before]

polluted 1. intoxicated with alcohol. [U.S. slang, early 1900s-pres.] 2. intoxicated with drugs or marijuana. [U.S. drug culture and slang, mid 1900s-pres.]

pollution masturbation. [since the 1500s]

ponce 1. a pimp; a solicitor for a prostitute. 2. to solicit for a prostitute. [both senses, British and U.S., 1800s-1900s] 3. any man supported by a woman. From sense 1. [colloquial, 1800s] 4. a young and vigorous lover of an older woman. [U.S. underworld, early 1900s, Irwin]

ponce on to live on the earnings of a prostitute. [British, 1800s]

poncess a prostitute who supports a man with her earnings. [Australian and British, 1800s]

pondsnipe the penis. For synonyms see YARD. [British slang, 1800s, Farmer and Henley]

pong 1. a Chinese. For synonyms see JOHN CHINAMAN. [Australian and U.S. slang, early 1900s] 2. a nasty smell from cheese or people. [Australian, 1900s] 3. beer. See PONGELO. For synonyms see SUDS. [British slang, 1800s, Farmer and Henley]

pongelo (also **pong, pongelorum, pongelow**) ale, beer, or any liquor. [Anglo-Indian (Ware); British and U.S. slang, late 1800s-1900s]

pony the penis. *Cf.* NAGS. [from Scots; British, late 1700s]

pony and trap dung; to defecate; junk. Rhyming slang for CRAP (*q.v.*).

British, 1900s, *Dictionary of Rhyming Slang*]

poo 1. dung; feces. For synonyms see DUNG. [1900s and probably long before] 2. nonsense. *Cf.* PHOOEY. See also POO-POO.

pood an effeminate male; a homosexual male. *Cf.* POOF. [Australian slang, early 1900s, Baker]

poof (also **pouf, pouffe, puff**) an effeminate male; a homosexual male. *Cf.* FOOP, POOFTER. [Australian and British, early 1900s-pres.]

poof-rorting the robbing or mugging of homosexual males. *Cf.* POOF, POOFTER-RORTER. [attested as British, early 1900s, *Dictionary of Slang and Unconventional English*]

poofter 1. a homosexual male. 2. a pimp for a male prostitute. [both senses, Australian and British, 1900s or before]

poofter-rorter a male procurer for homosexual male prostitutes. *Cf.* POOF-RORTING. [Australian slang, mid 1900s, Baker]

poonoo the female genitals. *Cf.* POONTANG. For synonyms see MONOSYL-LABLE. [Caribbean (Jamaica), Cassidy and Le Page]

poontang 1. copulation with a black woman. 2. a black woman considered as a source of sexual gratification; the genitals of a black woman. [both senses, U.S. slang and colloquial, late 1800s-pres.] 3. an act of copulation, either heterosexual or homosexual. [all are from French *putain*, "prostitute"; U.S. slang, 1900s]

poontanger the penis. From POONTANG (sense 3). [attested as Canadian, 1900s, *Dictionary of Slang and Unconventional English*]

poonts the human breasts. Probably from "points." [British slang, 1800s, Farmer and Henley]

poop 1. the posteriors. For synonyms see DUFF. 2. to coit a woman. [both senses, British, 1600s] 3. to defecate. [colloquial, 1600s-pres.] 4. to release intestinal gas. For synonyms see GURK. [slang and colloquial, early 1700s-pres.]

5. a stupid oaf; a dullard. *Cf.* POOPHEAD.
6. to infect with a venereal disease.
[used in the past tense in *Pericles*
(Shakespeare)] **7.** feces; human feces.
[U.S. juvenile and colloquial, 1900s]

poophead an oaf; a simpleton. [U.S.
slang and colloquial, mid 1900s]

poopied intoxicated with alcohol. See
SHIT-FACED. For synonyms see WOOFLED.
[U.S. slang, mid 1900s, *Current Slang*]

poo-poo (also **poo, pooh**) **1.** to defecate. **2.** feces; an act of defecation.
[both senses, U.S. juvenile and colloquial, 1900s] **3.** to deride an idea.
[U.S. colloquial, 1900s or before]

poopster (also **pooper**) a lecher; a
whoremonger. *Cf.* POOP (sense 2). [Brit-
ish slang, 1800s, Farmer and Henley]

poorlander a poor Caucasian; POOR
WHITE TRASH (*q.v.*). [U.S. colloquial,
1900s or before]

poor man's blessing the female genitals; copulation. [British slang, 1800s,
Farmer and Henley]

poor white trash (also **po white
trash, white trash**) Caucasians of very
low status; a Southern white who ranks
below slaves. [U.S. colloquial, early
1800s-pres.]

poot 1. an audible release of intestinal
gas. **2.** to release intestinal gas audibly.
Cf. POOP (sense 4). [both senses, rural
colloquial, 1800s]

pop to coit a woman. *Cf.* POP IT IN.
[U.S. slang, mid 1900s-pres.]

pop a nut (also **pop one's nuts**) to
ejaculate. *Cf.* GET ONE'S NUTS CRACKED.
For synonyms see MELT. [U.S. slang,
mid 1900s-pres.]

poper a papist. A derogatory nickname for a Roman Catholic, based on
"pope." [appeared as nonce in the
1500s; U.S. use, 1900s]

poperine pear the penis; the penis
and the scrotum. From the shape of this
fruit. [in early editions of *Romeo and
Juliet* (Shakespeare)]

popinjay a gaudy fop; a jabbering
fool. From the name of a gaudily-colored
parrot. [since the 1500s]

pop it in to coit a woman; to penetrate
a woman. *Cf.* POP. [colloquial and nonce,
1800s-1900s]

pop off 1. to die. See POP OFF THE
HOOKS. [slang and colloquial, mid
1700s-pres.] **2.** to kill someone. [U.S.
slang, early 1900s]

pop off the hooks to die. For synonyms see DEPART. [British, 1800s]

popper an ampule of amyl nitrite. *Cf.*
PEARL (sense 2). POPSIE, SNAPPER (sense
5). [U.S. drug culture, mid 1900s-pres.]

poppycock nonsense. For synonyms
see ANIMAL. [U.S. colloquial, mid
1800s-pres.]

poppy-pill opium; a ball of opium.
For synonyms see OPE. [British colloquial or cant, 1800s or before, Halliwell]

poppy train opium. [U.S. slang, early
1900s or before]

popsie an ampule of amyl nitrite. *Cf.*
PEARL (sense 2). POPPER, SNAPPER
(sense 5). [U.S. drug culture, mid
1900s-pres.]

pop-skull inferior liquor; a bad batch
of MOONSHINE (sense 2). *Cf.* ROT-GUT.
For synonyms see EMBALMING FLUID.
[U.S. colloquial, 1900s]

pork 1. a woman considered as a
sexual object. *Cf.* MUTTON (sense 4).
[British slang, 1700s] **2.** the penis. *Cf.*
PORK-SWORD. [British slang, 1800s,
Farmer and Henley] **3.** to coit a woman.
[attested as British slang, 1800s, Farmer
and Henley; U.S. slang, mid 1900s-pres.]
4. a derogatory nickname for a Jewish
man or woman. *Cf.* PORKY. [U.S. slang,
mid 1900s] **5.** a corpse. U.S. slang,
1900s]

porker 1. a derogatory nickname for a
Jewish man or woman. *Cf.* PORK (sense
4), PORKY. [slang since the 1700s] **2.**
an ugly young woman, especially a fat,
ugly young woman. *Cf.* HOG (sense 2),
PIG (sense 3). For synonyms see
BUFFARILLA. [U.S. slang, mid 1900s]

pork-sword the penis. *Cf.* MUTTON-
DAGGER, PIG-STICKING, PORK (sense 2).
[British, 1900s, *Dictionary of the
Underworld*]

porky a derogatory nickname for a Jewish man or woman. *Cf.* PORKER (sense 1). [British slang, late 1800s, Ware]

porn a truncation of PORNOGRAPHY (*q.v.*). [from Greek *porne*, "prostitute"; slang and colloquial, mid 1900s-pres.]

pornography 1. a written discussion of prostitutes. [etymologically correct and obsolete; mid 1800s] **2.** obscene or lewd writing or art. [from Greek *porne*, "prostitute"; since the mid 1800s]

porny bawdy; smutty or obscene. [U.S. use patterned on "corny"; British and U.S. slang and nonce, 1900s]

portal of Venus the vagina. [literary euphemism; U.S., mid 1900s]

port-hole 1. the female genitals, especially the vagina. [slang, 1600s-pres.] **2.** the anus. [British and U.S. slang, 1800s-pres.]

Port Said garter a condom. For synonyms see EEL-SKIN. [British Army, World War II]

Portugoose 1. a jocular and derogatory nickname for a Portuguese. **2.** an imaginary and jocular singular form of "Portuguese." [U.S. slang, 1900s]

Portuguese pump masturbation; an act of masturbation. *Cf.* PUMP (sense 3). [British nautical slang, late 1800s, Ware]

position a truncation of "sexual position." Frequently heard as double entendre. See BREAD AND BUTTER, CHINESE-FASHION, COIT DORSALLY, COITION A POSTERIORI, COITUS À LA VACHE, DOG-FASHION, DOG-STYLE, DOG-WAYS, DRAGON UPON SAINT GEORGE, FIGURA VENERIS PRIMA, MATRIMONIAL, MISSIONARY POSITION, PENDULA VENUS.

poski a derogatory nickname for a Pole or a person of Polish descent. [U.S. slang, 1900s]

possess carnally to copulate with a member of the opposite sex. [euphemistic, 1600s-pres.]

possum a Negro or a Negress. Derogatory; similar to COON. [U.S. slang and colloquial, 1900s or before]

post 1. the penis. *Cf.* STERN-POST. [colloquial and nonce] **2.** copulation; an act of copulation. Probably related to sense 1. *Cf.* POLE (senses 1 and 2). [British slang, 1800s, Farmer and Henley] **3.** an autopsy, a post-mortem examination. [U.S. medical slang, 1900s]

post a letter 1. to copulate. For synonyms see OCCUPY. [British slang, 1800s] **2.** to retire to defecate. For synonyms see RETIRE. [primarily British use, late 1800s-pres.]

posteriors the buttocks; the rump. Used in avoidance of more specific terms. From a term referring to the past, lateness, or the back of anything. For synonyms see DUFF. [since the late 1500s]

postern 1. the female genitals. For synonyms see MONOSYLLABLE. **2.** the posteriors; the anus. [both senses, British, 1700s]

pot 1. the female genitals, a pot for MEAT (sense 4). [British slang, 1800s] **2.** a urinal; a CHAMBER POT (*q.v.*); later, a water-flush toilet bowl. A truncation of "chamber pot." [colloquial, 1600s-pres.] Synonyms: ALTAR, ARTICLE, BED-GLASS, BISHOP, CHAMBER OF COMMERCE, CHAMBER POT, CHAMBER UTENSIL, CHAMBER VESSEL, CHANTIE, CHARMBER, CLOSE STOOL, COMMODE, CONVENIENCE, CROCK, DAISY, GASH-BUCKET, GAUGE, GUT-BUCKET, GUZUNDER, IT, JEMIMA, JERKER, JEROBOAM, JERRY, JEWEL CASE, JOCK-UM-GAGE, JORDAN, JUG, LAGGING-GAGE, LOOKING-GLASS, MASTER-CAN, MEMBER MUG, MINGO, NIGHT-GLASS, NIGHT-STOOL. **3.** a drunkard; a sot, a truncation of POTHEAD (*q.v.*). [U.S. slang, mid 1900s-pres.] **4.** marijuana. [from a Mexican Indian term, *potaguaya*; U.S. drug culture and slang, mid 1900s-pres.]

potato-finger 1. the penis. From the name for a medical condition wherein a finger is elongated and thickened. *Cf.* FOREFINGER. [from *Troilus and Cressida* (Shakespeare)] **2.** a DILDO (sense 2).

potato-head a dunce; an oaf. [U.S. slang, mid 1900s-pres.]

pot-fury 1. a drunkard. Also **pot-**

knight. 2. intoxication with alcohol. [both senses, late 1500s]

pothead 1. an oaf. [since the early 1500s] **2.** a drunkard. *Cf.* POT (sense 3). [U.S. slang, 1900s] **3.** a user of marijuana. *Cf.* POT (sense 4). [U.S. drug culture, mid 1900s-pres.]

potiguaya marijuana. *Cf.* POT (sense 4). [from a Mexican Indian name, U.S. use, mid 1900s]

pot-liquor (also **pot-likker**) a brew of marijuana or marijuana and tea. From the U.S. colloquial term for juices from a cooking pot. [U.S. drug culture, mid 1900s-pres.]

pot o' glue a Jewish man or woman. Rhyming slang for ''Jew.'' Not necessarily derogatory. [U.S., 1900s, *Dictionary of Rhyming Slang*]

pot-shot intoxicated with alcohol. A reinterpretation of a term for a shot taken at game with the goal of providing something for the cooking pot. See POTTED. *Cf.* CUP-SHOT, GRAPE-SHOT. [British slang, 1800s, Farmer and Henley]

pot-sure courageous due to the alcohol one has consumed. *Cf.* DUTCH COURAGE, POT-VALIANT. [British, 1600s]

potsville the state of being intoxicated with marijuana; the use of marijuana. *Cf.* POT (sense 4). [U.S. drug culture, mid 1900s-pres.]

potted 1. intoxicated with alcohol; having been POT-SHOT (*q.v.*). *Cf.* POT-HEAD (sense 2). [U.S. slang, early 1900s-pres.] **2.** intoxicated with drugs; intoxicated with marijuana. Reinforced by POT (sense 4). For synonyms see TALL. [U.S. slang and drug culture, 1900s]

potty 1. a CHAMBER POT (*q.v.*); a W.C.; a water-flush toilet bowl. *Cf.* POT (sense 2). [U.S. juvenile and colloquial, 1900s] **2.** to urinate or defecate; to use the POTTY (sense 1). [U.S. juvenile, 1900s]

potty mouth a person who uses obscene or profane language in all or most social settings; the same as TOILET MOUTH (*q.v.*). [U.S. slang, mid 1900s-pres.]

potulent intoxicated with alcohol. For synonyms see WOOFLED. [since the mid 1600s]

pot-valiant (also **pot-sure**) intoxicated with alcohol and brave because of it. *Cf.* DUTCH COURAGE, POT-SURE. [slang and colloquial, early 1600s-pres.]

poultry women in general; women considered as sexual objects. *Cf.* QUAIL. [British, 1600s]

poultry-show a group inspection of penes for venereal disease. Poultry refers to COCK (sense 3), the penis. *Cf.* DANGLE-PARADE, SHORT-ARM INSPECTION, SMALL-ARM INSPECTION, TOOL-CHECK. [British military, 1900s]

pound to coit a woman. *Cf.* HAMMER. [U.S. slang, late 1800s-pres.]

pound-cake queen a male, usually described as homosexual, who derives special sexual pleasure from being defecated on. See QUEEN for similar subjects. [U.S. homosexual use, mid 1900s, Farrell]

pounders the testicles. For synonyms see WHIRLYGIGS. [British slang, late 1600s]

pound off to masturbate. *Cf.* BEAT OFF, JACK OFF, JAG OFF, JERK OFF. [U.S. slang, mid 1900s-pres.]

Pound salt up your ass! a curse; an order to go to hell. [U.S. slang, mid 1900s]

pound-text a parson; a fiery preacher. [British, 1800s, Farmer and Henley]

pound the meat to masturbate. *Cf.* BEAT THE MEAT, POUND OFF. For synonyms see WASTE TIME. [U.S. slang, mid 1900s-pres.]

pouter the female genitals. From the standard term meaning ''poke'' or ''stir.'' [British, early 1800s]

powdered diamond cocaine. *Cf.* GOLD DUST (sense 1). For synonyms see NOSE-CANDY. [U.S. drug culture, mid 1900s-pres.]

powdered-up (also **powdered**) intoxicated with alcohol. [U.S. underworld, early 1900s, Irwin]

powder one's nose (also **powder**

one's face) to retire to the W.C. Usually said by women or jocularly by men. [British and U.S. slang and colloquial, early 1900s-pres.]

powder puff 1. a silly girl or woman. **2.** an effeminate male. *Cf.* POOF. For synonyms see FRIBBLE. [both senses, U.S. slang, early 1900s]

pox (also **pockes**) **1.** syphilis, occasionally for "smallpox." *Cf.* PLAGUE. [since the early 1500s] **2.** to infect someone with syphilis. [British, 1600s] **3.** as an oath and an exclamation, "Pox!" Also in the curse, "A pox on you!" [British, 1600s-1900s]

poxbox a woman presumed to be infected with syphilis; the vagina of a woman presumed to be infected with syphilis. See BOX (sense 2).

poxology a study of syphilis. A play on "doxology." [British, 1700s]

P.P. "petticoat peeper." A warning from one girl to another that there is someone gazing up her skirts. *Cf.* S.S. [contrived euphemism]

P.R. 1. a "Puerto Rican." [U.S. slang, mid 1900s] **2.** "Panama red," a high grade of marijuana grown in Panama. For synonyms see MARI. [U.S. drug culture, mid 1900s-pres.]

prack the male genitals, especially the scrotum. Possibly from PRICK (*q.v.*). [U.S. dialect (Boontling), late 1800s-early 1900s, Charles Adams]

practice in the milky-way to fondle a woman's breasts. *Cf.* MILKY-WAY. [British, early 1600s]

prairie coal hunks of dried cow dung used as fuel for a fire. *Cf.* BUFFALO CHIPS, PRAIRIE FUEL. For synonyms see COW-CHIPS. [U.S. colloquial, 1900s or before]

prairie-dew whisky; homebrewed whisky. Patterned on MOUNTAIN-DEW (*q.v.*). [U.S. slang, mid 1800s]

prairie fuel hunks of dried cattle dung used for fuel. *Cf.* PRAIRIE COAL. [U.S. colloquial, 1900s or before]

prang to coit a woman. *Cf.* PRACK. [British slang, 1900s]

pranny (also **prannie**) **1.** the female genitals. *Cf.* FANNY (sense 1). **2.** a term of contempt between males. From sense 1. *Cf.* CUNT FACE. [British slang, 1800s-1900s]

pratfall a fall on the buttocks, especially an exaggerated fall on the buttocks on stage. [U.S. slang and colloquial, early 1900s-pres.]

prats (also **prat, pratts**) **1.** the buttocks. For synonyms see DUFF. [since the 1500s] **2.** to strike or beat on the buttocks. [1500s] **3.** the female genitals. *Cf.* ASS (sense 3). For synonyms see MONOSYLLABLE. [British slang, 1800s, Farmer and Henley]

prattle (also **prittle-prattle**) **1.** gossip. **2.** to gossip. [both since the mid 1500s]

pray with the knees upwards to copulate, said of a woman. [British slang, late 1700s, Grose]

preeze to urinate. For synonyms see WHIZ. [British colloquial dialect, 1800s, Farmer and Henley] See also FEEZE.

preggers pregnant. For synonyms see FRAGRANT. [originally British collegiate; slang, 1900s]

preggy pregnant. [British slang, early 1900s, *Dictionary of Slang and Unconventional English*]

pregnant roller skate a Volkswagen automobile. [U.S. slang, mid 1900s-pres.]

premises the female genitals. *Cf.* OCCUPY. [British slang, 1800s, Farmer and Henley]

Presbo (also **Pressie**) a Presbyterian. [Australian, 1900s]

preserved intoxicated with alcohol. *Cf.* CORNED, PICKLED, SALTED-DOWN. For synonyms see WOOFLED. [U.S. slang, early 1900s-pres.]

preshen a CATAMITE (*q.v.*); a tramp's catamite. See PRUSHUN.

pressed-ham the buttocks in the act of "mooning." See MOON. [U.S. slang, mid 1900s]

Pressie (also **Presbo**) a Presbyterian. [Australian, 1900s]

pretty the female genitals. For synonyms see MONOSYLLABLE. [British, 1800s or before]

pretty-boy an effeminate male. Probably refers to a CATAMITE (*q.v.*). [Australian, 1900s, Baker]

priapism 1. a continuous and painful erection of the penis due not to desire but to disease. [since the late 1500s] **2.** prurient or licentious display or behavior. [British, mid 1700s] **3.** literary English for an erection of the penis. Occasionally a general term for the penis. *Cf.* YARD. [1700s-1800s]

priapus (also **priap**) **1.** the penis. For synonyms see YARD. [since the 1600s] **2.** a DILDO (*q.v.*). **3.** a stallion. [in English by the 1600s; all are from "Priapus," which is the Latin version of Greek *Priapos*]

price of greens (also **price of meat**) the cost of a prostitute. [British slang, 1800s, Farmer and Henley]

prick 1. the penis; the erect penis. [since the 1500s or before] **2.** an oaf; an offensive male. [U.S. slang, mid 1900s-pres.] **3.** a hard taskmaster. [U.S. slang, early 1900s]

prick-chinking copulating. [British slang, 1600s]

prick-juice semen. *Cf.* CUNT-JUICE. [slang, 1900s or before]

prickle the penis. For synonyms see YARD. [slang, early 1600s]

prick-parade a group inspection for venereal disease in the military. *Cf.* POULTRY-SHOW. [British military, early 1900s, *Dictionary of Slang and Unconventional English*]

prick-pocket 1. the vagina. For synonyms see PASSAGE. **2.** a woman considered sexually. A play on "pick-pocket."

prick-pride an erection. For synonyms see ERECTION. [British, 1500s-1800s]

prick-skinner the female genitals. *Cf.* EEL-SKINNER. [British slang, 1600s]

prick-smith a military medical officer. From his treatment of venereal disease or from his giving hypodermic injections. *Cf.* PINTLE-SMITH. [British, early 1900s, *Dictionary of Slang and Unconventional English*]

prick-teaser a woman who leads a man on sexually but who refuses to copulate; a COCK-TEASER (*q.v.*). *Cf.* P.T. [U.S. slang, mid 1900s-pres.]

pride 1. sexual arousal; sexual appetite. [1400s-1500s] **2.** the ovary of an animal, especially a sow. See PRIDES. [British and U.S. rural colloquial, 1800s-1900s]

pride, in in heat; sexually aroused. [British colloquial, 1600s-1800s]

pride and joy one's penis. From the term for one's newborn baby or spouse. *Cf.* PRIDE (sense 1).

pride of the morning a morning erection. A reinterpretation of the Irish term for a morning shower of rain. *Cf.* MORNING PRIDE. [British, 1800s, *Dictionary of Slang and Unconventional English*]

prides 1. the male genitals. **2.** the genitals, male or female; the reproductive system of either sex. [both senses, British and U.S. rural colloquial, 1800s-1900s]

prig 1. to coit a woman. From the term meaning "ride," or a slang term meaning "steal," or a cognate of PRICK (*q.v.*). [British slang, 1600s-1800s] **2.** a prude. [since the late 1600s]

prigger a lecher; a whoremonger. [British slang, early 1800s, Jon Bee]

primed intoxicated with alcohol. For synonyms see WOOFLED. [British and U.S. slang, 1800s-pres.]

princess of the pavement a prostitute. *Cf.* NYMPH DU PAVE. For synonyms see HARLOT. [Australian, 1900s, Baker]

Princeton rub male homosexual hugging and petting to orgasm. *Cf.* FLAT-FUCK, TUMMY-FUCK.

princock (also **primcock, princox, princycock**) **1.** the female genitals. **2.** the penis. [both senses, British slang or cant, 1500s-1800s] **3.** a fop; a coxcomb. [1500s]

privateer an independent prostitute.

See FREE-LANCE. [British slang, 1800s, *Dictionary of Slang and Unconventional English*]

private office a privy; a W.C. *Cf.* HOUSE OF OFFICE. [U.S. slang, mid 1900s]

private parts the genitals of a man or of a woman. *Cf.* PRIVATES. For synonyms see GENITALS. [U.S. colloquial, 1900s]

private place the female genitals. For synonyms see MONOSYLLABLE. [euphemistic]

privates the genitals of a male or a female. [since the 1500s]

privities the male genitals. [British and U.S. euphemism, 1800s-1900s]

privy an outhouse. Cognate with "private." [ultimately from Latin *privatus*, "apart" or "secret"; since the 1300s]

privy-hole the female genitals, specifically the vagina, a "private hole." [British, 1800s, Farmer and Henley]

privy member the penis; a "private member." *Cf.* MEMBER FOR THE COCKSHIRE, UNRULY MEMBER. [euphemistic since the 1600s]

prize bull prize-winning nonsense. A partial disguise of the "bull" of BULLSHIT (*q.v.*). For synonyms see ANIMAL. [U.S. slang, mid 1900s-pres.]

prize faggots well-developed breasts. From the slang term for a type of oat dumpling sold in the streets. [British, late 1800s, Ware]

pro 1. a prostitute. From "professional." For synonyms see HARLOT. [U.S. slang, early 1900s-pres.] **2.** a prophylactic condom. [U.S. slang, mid 1900s-pres.]

pro-choice an avoidance of "proabortion." [U.S., mid 1900s-pres.]

Procter and Gamble a disguise of "paregoric." The name of a U.S. firm used as a reinterpretation of the initialism P.G. (*q.v.*), from "paregoric." [U.S. drug culture, mid 1900s-pres.]

procurer 1. a PIMP (sense 1). **2.** a man who obtains women or girls to serve as prostitutes. The feminine form is "procuress." [both since the 1600s]

prod 1. the penis, especially the erect penis. **2.** to copulate. [both senses, British and U.S. slang, 1800s-pres.]

Proddo (also **Prod**) a Protestant. [Australian, 1900s] Related terms: BAPPO, BIBLE-BELTER, BLUESKIN, CONGO, DIPPER, HOLY-ROLLER, JESUS-SCREAMER, METHO, PLUNGER, PRESBO, PRESSIE.

profane 1. to utter or write irreverence to God, holy matters, or things. [since the 1300s] **2.** pertaining to that which is not consecrated. [since the 1400s] **3.** obscene; smutty. [U.S. colloquial, 1900s]

promontories the posteriors. For synonyms see DUFF. [British, 1700s]

prone to venery lewd; wanton; easily persuaded to copulate. [British use, 1800s, Farmer and Henley]

prong 1. the penis. *Cf.* JOY PRONG. For synonyms see YARD. [slang, mid 1900s-pres.] **2.** to coit a woman. [slang, mid 1900s]

pro-pack a "prophylactic package," a kit for the prevention of venereal disease. It contains condoms and cleansing aids. [U.S. slang, World War II]

propho a "prophylactic condom." *Cf.* PRO (sense 2). [U.S., World War I and general slang, early 1900s-pres.]

pross a prostitute. *Cf.* PROSSY. [slang, 1800s-pres.]

prosser a pimp; a PONCE (*q.v.*). [British slang, late 1800s]

prosso a prostitute. For synonyms see HARLOT. [Australian, 1900s]

prossy (also **prossie**) a prostitute. For synonyms see HARLOT. [underworld, early 1900s]

prostitute 1. a woman who sells her sexual services. For synonyms see HARLOT. [since the 1500s] **2.** a catamite; a male prostitute who sells his sexual services in PEDERASTY (*q.v.*). [since the 1600s] **3.** to sell oneself cheaply; to do something which is beneath one.

prostitution the occupation or profession of selling sexual acts; indiscriminate sexual intercourse exchanged for money. Usually thought of as feminine but the term applies to both men and women. Synonyms: BITCHERY, BORDEL, BOTTLE, BUTTOCK BANQUETTING, FAST LIFE, LOVE-FOR-SALE, MRS. WARREN'S PROFESSION, OLD PATROL, PALLIARDY, PUTAGE, SACKING, SOCIAL E., SOCIAL EVIL, STREET OF SHAME, SUBURB TRADE, TAIL-TRADING, THE TRADE, VICE, WHORE-DOM.

prosty (also **prostie**) a prostitute. For synonyms see HARLOT. [U.S. slang, mid 1900s-pres.]

proud desirous of copulation; sexually excited; with swollen genitals. Often said of animals, especially of a bitch in heat. See PRIDES. [colloquial since the late 1500s]

proud below the navel sexually aroused. Refers to the swelling of the genitals. [British, early 1600s]

proud cut to partially castrate a horse in a way that his sex drive is not totally destroyed. Cf. CUT (sense 1). [U.S. rural colloquial (West Texas), 1900s]

proud-flesh swollen flesh around a wound or a sore. Occasionally used in double entendre for "genital tumescence." [U.S. colloquial, 1800s-1900s]

provincial 1. a MADAM (q.v.); a pro-curess. See PROCURER. [British, early 1600s] **2.** in the manner of a rural oaf. [since the mid 1700s] **3.** a rural oaf; a country bumpkin. [euphemistic, 1800s-1900s]

prune 1. to expurgate; to cut out offending material. **2.** to castrate. [U.S. jocular colloquial, 1900s or before]

pruned intoxicated with alcohol; in-capacitated by PRUNE JUICE (q.v.). Perhaps based on CUT (sense 2). For synonyms see WOOFLED. [U.S. slang, mid 1900s-pres.]

prune juice strong alcoholic liquor. With reference to gastric disturbances. For synonyms see EMBALMING FLUID. [British slang, early 1900s, *Dictionary of Slang and Unconventional English*]

pruney sexually aroused and desirous of copulation. For synonyms see HUMPY. [U.S. dialect (Ozarks), 1900s, Randolph and Wilson]

prushun (also **preshen**) a CATAMITE (q.v.); a tramp's catamite. From PRUS-SIAN (q.v.). [U.S. underworld (tramps), 1900s or before]

Prussian an active PEDERAST (q.v.); the INSERTOR (q.v.). Cf. PRUSHUN. Prob-ably from "Prussian Blue," a term of endearment (like "true blue") in the mid 1800s. [U.S., 1900s]

pscrew a derogatory nickname for a Pole. [U.S. slang, mid 1900s, Pedersen]

P.T. a PRICK-TEASER (q.v.); a woman who leads a man on sexually but who refuses to copulate. [U.S. slang, mid 1900s-pres.]

P.U. 1. an exclamation uttered upon sensing a bad odor. **2.** a release of intestinal gas. [both senses, U.S. slang or colloquial, 1900s]

public comfort station a W.C.; a restroom. For synonyms see W.C. [U.S. colloquial euphemism, mid 1900s]

public convenience a public W.C.; a restroom.

public ledger a prostitute. Because she is open to all parties. For synonyms see HARLOT. [British, early 1800s, *Lex-icon Balatronicum*]

Puck 1. an evil demon. Not usually capitalized in this sense. [since *c.* 1000] **2.** the devil. [since the 1300s] **3.** a mischievous sprite. [a character in *A Midsummer Night's Dream;* since the 1600s (Shakespeare)]

pucker-assed cowardly. Cf. CANDY-ASS. [U.S. slang, mid 1900s]

puck-fist a braggart. See BULLER for synonyms. From the common name of the puff-ball fungus. [late 1500s-1600s]

pud 1. the penis. Rhymes with "wood." Cf. PULL ONE'S PUDDING. [U.S. slang, 1900s] **2.** a jerk; a PRICK (sense 2). For synonyms see OAF. [U.S. slang, 1900s]

pudding 1. the penis. Probably from PUDENDUM (q.v.). Cf. PULL ONE'S PUD-DING. For synonyms see YARD. [since the 1600s] **2.** copulation. For synonyms see SMOCKAGE. [British, 1600s-1700s] **3.** semen. For synonyms see METTLE. [British, late 1600s] **4.** innards; guts;

stuffing. Sometimes in the plural. [British colloquial, 1700s and before]

pudding club, in the pregnant. [British colloquial, 1800s]

puddinghead (also **puddenhead**) an oaf. Comparing the head to a pudding bag filled with scrambled meat byproducts. [British and U.S. colloquial, 1800s-1900s]

puddle the female genitals. For synonyms see MONOSYLLABLE. [British slang, 1800s, Farmer and Henley]

pudendal cleavage the fissure or gap between the *labia majora*. Cf. CENTRAL FURROW, INTERCRURAL TRENCH, PUDENDAL FURROW.

pudendum* the genitals. Usually the female genitals but occasionally the penis. (See MALE PUDENDUM.) Occasionally in the plural, *i.e.*, *pudenda*, referring to the "things about which one should be modest." [from Latin; since the late 1300s] See MONOSYLLABLE.

puff 1. to release intestinal gas. Cf. POOP (sense 4). [colloquial and nonce, 1800s-1900s] **2.** a fop; an effeminate male; a homosexual male. A variant of POOF (*q.v.*). [British slang, 1800s-1900s]

pug a prostitute. Cf. PUGNASTY. [1500s-1600s]

puggled intoxicated with alcohol; crazy drunk. Cf. POGGLED.

puggy-drunk intoxicated with alcohol. Cf. POGY. [British slang, 1800s]

pugnasty a nasty slut; a dirty prostitute. From a nickname for a monkey. Cf. PUG. [British, 1600s, B.E.]

pug-ugly 1. pertaining to a very ugly person. **2.** a very ugly person. [both senses, U.S. slang and colloquial, 1900s]

puke 1. to vomit. **2.** vomit. [both since the 1600s] **3.** an obnoxious person; a real pest. [British and U.S. slang, early 1800s-pres.]

pukes nausea; vomiting.

pukish nauseated. [colloquial since the 1500s]

pull about 1. to take liberties with a woman; to play sexually with a woman.

2. to masturbate. [both senses, British, 1800s, Farmer and Henley]

pull a cluck to die. For synonyms see DEPART. [British, late 1800s, *Dictionary of Slang and Unconventional English*]

pull a rabbit to perform an abortion. [U.S. underworld, mid 1900s, Goldin, O'Leary, and Lipsius]

pull a train for a woman to have sexual intercourse with a succession of males. See GROUP SEX for similar topics. [U.S. slang, mid 1900s-pres.]

pull a trick to perform an act of FELLATIO or PEDERASTY (both *q.v.*). Cf. TRICK (sense 1). [U.S. slang, mid 1900s, Goldin, O'Leary, and Lipsius]

pull bacon to thumb the nose; to do an ANNE'S FAN (*q.v.*). [mid 1800s-1900s]

pull oneself off to masturbate. Cf. PLAY OFF. For synonyms see WASTE TIME. [slang, 1900s or before]

pull one's pud to masturbate. Cf. PUD (sense 1), the penis. [U.S. slang, mid 1900s-pres.]

pull one's pudding to masturbate. Cf. PUDDING (sense 1). [slang, 1900s]

pull one's wire to masturbate. Cf. WIRE. For synonyms see WASTE TIME. [British and some U.S. use, 1800s-1900s]

pull-ons women's underpants of the type that pull on and need no tying. [British and U.S. colloquial, 1900s]

pull-over a man who is easy to convince to copulate. The jocular opposite of PUSH-OVER (*q.v.*). [U.S. slang, mid 1900s]

Pull your finger out! a command to "hurry up!" "Pull your finger out of your ass-hole so that you can run!" Cf. DEDIGITATE! [British and U.S. military and general slang, 1900s]

pulpit the female genitals. For synonyms see MONOSYLLABLE. [British, mid 1600s]

pulpit-cuffer a Bible-pounding preacher. [British colloquial, 1800s, Halliwell]

pulse 1. a woman's sexual parts in "feel her pulse." [British, mid 1600s] **2.** the penis. For synonyms see YARD.

[slang, 1800s-1900s, *Dictionary of Slang and Unconventional English*]

pumblechook an oaf; a "human ass." [British and U.S., late 1800s, Ware]

pump 1. the female genitals. *Cf.* PUMP-DALE, PUMPKIN. For synonyms see MONOSYLLABLE. [British, 1600s] **2.** to vomit. *Cf.* PUMP SHIP (sense 2). For synonyms see YORK. [British slang, 1800s] **3.** to masturbate. See PUMP ONE-SELF OFF. [primarily British, 1800s] **4.** to coit a woman. *Cf.* PUMPED. [colloquial or slang, 1800s-pres.] **5.** a breaking of wind. For synonyms see GURK. [British slang, 1800s, Farmer and Henely] **6.** the penis. See PUMP-HANDLE. **7.** to urinate. *Cf.* PUMP SHIP (sense 1). [British and U.S. slang, 1800s-pres.] **8.** a breast. See PUMPS.

pump-dale (also **pump**) the female genitals. [British slang, early 1700s]

pumped pregnant. *Cf.* PUMP (sense 4). For synonyms see FRAGRANT. [U.S. slang, mid 1900s-pres.]

pump-handle (also **pump**) the penis. *Cf.* PUMP (sense 1). [British, early 1700s]

pumpkin the female genitals. A "little pump." [U.S. slang, 1800s, Farmer and Henley]

pumpkin-cover the female pubic hair. [U.S. slang, 1800s, Farmer and Henley]

pumpkinhead an oaf. [British and U.S. slang and colloquial, early 1800s]

pumpkin seed a tablet of MESCALINE (*q.v.*). [U.S. drug culture, mid 1900s-pres.]

pump oneself off to masturbate. [British and some U.S. use, 1800s-1900s]

pump one's pickle to masturbate. Based on JERK ONE'S GHERKIN (*q.v.*). [attested as Canadian, 1900s, *Dictionary of Slang and Unconventional English*]

pump one's python to masturbate. *Cf.* PUMP (sense 3), PYTHON. For synonyms see WASTE TIME. [U.S. slang, mid 1900s-pres.]

pumps the human breasts. For synonyms see BOSOM. [U.S. slang, early 1900s]

pump ship 1. to urinate. For synonyms see WHIZ. [originally nautical, 1700s-pres.] **2.** to vomit. For synonyms see YORK. [since the 1700s]

punce 1. an effeminate male; a homosexual male; a CATAMITE (*q.v.*). [Australian slang, 1900s, Baker] **2.** the female genitals. *Cf.* PUNSE. [Australian and British slang, 1900s]

punch 1. to coit and DEFLOWER (*q.v.*) a woman. [since the 1800s or before] **2.** to copulate. [U.S. slang, mid 1900s-pres.] **3.** women considered as sexual objects. From senses 1 and 2. [slang since the 1700s]

punchable pertaining to a woman who desires copulation. *Cf.* BEDWORTHY, FUCKABLE, FUCKSOME, ROMPWORTHY, SHAFTABLE. [since the 1700s, Grose]

punchable nun a prostitute. For synonyms see HARLOT. [British slang, 1900s, *Dictionary of Slang and Unconventional English*]

puncture 1. to DEFLOWER (*q.v.*). [British, 1800s, Farmer and Henley] **2.** to coit a woman. [widespread nonce, since the 1800s or before]

pungey intoxicated with alcohol. *Cf.* SPONGE (senses 1 and 2). [U.S. slang, early 1700s, Ben Franklin]

punk 1. a prostitute; a sexually loose woman. Also **punck, puncke, punque.** [British, late 1500s-1700s] **2.** to procure customers for a prostitute. [British, 1600s] **3.** a CATAMITE (*q.v.*). For synonyms see BRONCO. [U.S. underworld and slang, early 1900s] **4.** a homosexual male. [U.S. slang, mid 1900s-pres.] **5.** a woman who performs PENILINGUS (*q.v.*). [U.S. underworld, mid 1900s, Goldin, O'Leary, and Lipsius] **6.** any male; a chum; a young fellow. [U.S. slang and colloquial, mid 1900s-pres.] **7.** a weak person; a useless jerk, usually a male. [U.S. slang, mid 1900s-pres.] **8.** inferior marijuana. [U.S. drug culture, mid 1900s-pres.]

punker a whoremonger. From PUNK (sense 1). For synonyms see LECHER. [British slang, 1600s-1700s]

punkin-head an oaf or dolt. From

PUMPKIN-HEAD (*q.v.*). [U.S. rural colloquial, 1800s-1900s]

punk kid 1. a CATAMITE (*q.v.*). *Cf.* PUNK (sense 3). [U.S. slang, mid 1900s] **2.** any adolescent male. [U.S. slang, mid 1900s-pres.]

punk pills any tranquilizer taken illicitly. [U.S. drug culture, mid 1900s-pres.]

pup 1. the penis, especially in the expression BEAT THE PUP (*q.v.*). [attested as U.S., mid 1900s, Goldin, O'Leary, and Lipsius] **2.** an oaf; a dummy. [U.S. slang, mid 1900s, Goldin, O'Leary, and Lipsius]

pup, in pregnant, as with dogs. [British colloquial, mid 1800s, *Dictionary of Slang and Unconventional English*]

puppy's mamma a euphemism for BITCH (*q.v.*). [since the early 1800s]

pure 1. a mistress; a prostitute. *Cf.* IMPURE. [British, late 1600s] **2.** dog dung. A substance used by tanners to "purify" certain grades of leather. This term is for the dog dung gathered for sale to tanners for its alkaline properties. Usually in the plural. [British, 1800s]

pure silk pertaining to a homosexual male. [U.S. slang, mid 1900s-pres.] See also SILK.

purge 1. to remove undesirable substances from the body. **2.** to give an enema. [both since the 1400s] **3.** beer. [British slang, 1800s] **4.** to expurgate. **5.** to vomit. For synonyms see YORK. [senses 4 and 5 are U.S. colloquial, 1900s]

purple pornographic; grossly pornographic. Even more extreme than BLUE (sense 1). [U.S. slang, mid 1900s]

purple flats (also **purple**) the drug L.S.D. (*q.v.*). *Cf.* FLATS. [U.S. drug culture, mid 1900s-pres.]

purple haze (also **haze**) the drug L.S.D. (*q.v.*). [U.S.drug culture, mid 1900s-pres.]

purple heart a Dexedrine (trademark) tablet. A reinterpretation of the name of a U.S. military decoration. [U.S. drug culture, 1900s]

purple microdots the drug L.S.D. (*q.v.*). *Cf.* MICRODOTS. [U.S. drug culture, mid 1900s-pres.]

push 1. to copulate. *Cf.* DO A PUSH, STAND THE PUSH. [slang and colloquial, 1600s-1900s] **2.** to sell narcotics. [U.S. underworld and drug culture, 1900s]

pushed intoxicated with alcohol. For synonyms see WOOFLED. [British slang, 1800s, Farmer and Henley]

pusher a seller of narcotics and heroin. *Cf.* DEALER. [U.S. drug culture, mid 1900s-pres.] Synonyms: BAG LADY, BAGMAN, BINGLE, BROKER, CANDY MAN, DEALER, ICE-CREAM MAN, JUNK-PEDDLER, SWING MAN, TEN-TWO THOUSAND, TRAFFIKER.

pushing up daisies dead and buried. *Cf.* DAISY-PUSHING. [British and U.S. wartime and general slang, 1900s]

push in the bush is worth two in the hand a catch phrase signifying that "one act of coition is worth two acts of masturbation." [British, 1900s, *Dictionary of Slang and Unconventional English*]

push in the truck an act of copulation; to coit a woman. Rhyming slang for "fuck." [British, early 1900s, *Dictionary of Rhyming Slang*]

push on to copulate with; to coit. Said of a male. *Cf.* PUSH (sense 1). [colloquial, 1700s-1900s]

push-over a woman who yields easily to sexual propositions. *Cf.* PULL-OVER. [U.S. slang and colloquial, early 1900s-pres.]

push-pin to coit. For synonyms see OCCUPY. [British slang, 1600s]

push-pudding a bachelor; a masturbator. *Cf.* PUDDING (sense 1). [British slang, 1900s, *Dictionary of Slang and Unconventional English*]

puss 1. a cat; a nickname for a cat. No negative connotations. [since the early 1500s] **2.** a woman; a nickname for a woman. [since the late 1500s] **3.** the female genitals. *Cf.* PUSSY (sense 1). [colloquial, 1600s-pres.] **4.** a hare. [British colloquial, 1600s] **5.** copulation. *Cf.* PUSSY (sense 4). [U.S. slang mid 1900s-pres.] **6.** an effeminate male. *Cf.* CUT PUSS, PUSSYCAT. [U.S. slang, 1900s] **7.** a face; an ugly face. [U.S. slang and colloquial, mid 1900s-pres.]

pussy 1. the female genitals. *Cf.* PUSS (sense 3). [slang and colloquial, 1800s-pres.] **2.** an effeminate male. *Cf.* CUT PUSS. For synonyms see FRIBBLE. [U.S. slang, early 1900s-pres.] **3.** women considered sexually. For synonyms see TAIL. [U.S. slang, mid 1900s-pres.] **4.** copulation. [U.S. slang, mid 1900s]

pussy-bumping meaning uncertain. Most likely some type of lesbian sexual activity. Definitions include CUNNILINGISM, SODOMY, and LESBIANISM (all *q.v.*). See FLAT-FUCK. [U.S. slang mid 1900s-pres.]

pussy butterfly a birth control device; an I.U.D. (*q.v.*) of a specific design. [U.S. colloquial, mid 1900s-pres.]

pussycat 1. a girl, one's girlfriend. **2.** a timid male. [both senses, U.S. slang and colloquial, 1900s]

pussyfart (also **cunt-fart**) a sometimes audible release of air trapped in the vagina by the penis at the time of penetration.

pussy Nellie a homosexual male. *Cf.* LIZZIE BOY. [British naval slang, early 1900s, *Dictionary of Slang and Unconventional English*]

pussy posse the police prostitution squad; the vice squad. [U.S. slang, mid 1900s-pres.]

pussy-simple crazy or obsessed with copulation, said of a man. *Cf.* KID-SIMPLE, TWITCHET-STRUCK. [U.S. dialect (Ozarks), 1900s or before, Randolph and Wilson]

pussy-struck totally obsessed with the sexual possibilities of one woman or of all women. A milder and more recent version of CUNT-STRUCK (*q.v.*). *Cf.* PUSSY-SIMPLE. [1900s]

pussy-whipped henpecked; dominated by a demanding wife. Based on "horse-whipped." [U.S. slang, mid 1900s]

put 1. a dunce; an oaf. [British colloquial, 1600s-1700s] **2.** a prostitute. [based on French *putain* "prostitute";

British, 1700s] **3.** an act of copulation in DO A PUT (*q.v.*). Also **put-in.** [British, 1800s] **4.** to permit sexual intercourse, said of a woman. [U.S. slang, 1900s] **5.** to vomit. [U.S. colloquial euphemism, 1900s]

put, to be 1. to be copulated with. *Cf.* PUT (sense 4). **2.** to act as the RECEIVER in PEDERASTY or FELLATIO (all *q.v.*). [U.S. underworld, early-mid 1900s, Goldin, O'Leary, and Lipsius]

put and take copulation. For synonyms see SMOCKAGE. [British slang and nonce elsewhere, 1900s]

put away 1. locked up in jail, prison or a mental institution. **2.** killed. **3.** dead and buried. **4.** to lock someone up in jail, prison, or a mental institution. [senses 1-4 are U.S. colloquial, 1900s] **5.** to kill someone. [U.S. slang and colloquial, 1900s or before]

put balls on something to make something more masculine or powerful; to give something authority and strength. [U.S. slang, mid 1900s-pres.]

put birdie to vomit. For synonyms see YORK. [U.S. slang, early 1900s]

put down 1. to position a woman for copulation, possibly with force. *Cf.* LAY DOWN, SPREAD. [since the 1600s] **2.** to kill; to PUT AWAY (sense 5). [British colloquial, 1900s] **3.** to insult; to belittle. **4.** an insult. [senses 3 and 4, U.S. slang, mid 1900s-pres.]

put it to her to coit a woman. For synonyms see OCCUPY. [U.S. slang, 1900s]

put lipstick on his dipstick to perform FELLATIO (*q.v.*) on a man, said of a woman. *Cf.* DIPSTICK (sense 2). [U.S. slang, mid 1900s, *Current Slang*]

put out 1. to kill. From the extinguishing of a candle or a fire. [British, late 1800s, Ware]. **2.** to permit kissing and caressing readily, usually said of a cooperative date. [U.S. slang, mid 1900s-pres.]

put the blocks to to coit a woman. *Cf.* BLOCK (sense 2) [U.S. slang, mid 1900s-pres.]

put the boots to to coit a woman; to

RIDE (sense 2) a woman. [U.S. slang, early 1900s or before, Irwin]

put the eye on someone to flirt with a member of the opposite sex. [U.S. slang and colloquial, 1900s]

put the hard word on her to proposition a woman; to attempt to persuade a woman to copulate. [Australian and U.S. slang, 1900s]

put the make on (also **put the move on**) to flirt with a woman; to proposition a woman or a man. [U.S. slang, mid 1900s-pres.]

put to bed with a shovel 1. buried. [British and U.S. colloquial, 1800s-1900s] **2.** intoxicated with alcohol. For synonyms see WOOFLED. [U.S. slang, 1900s]

puttock 1. a prostitute; a common whore. **2.** a greedy person; a glutton. [both senses, British, 1500s-1600s]

put to sleep to kill something or someone, often used for killing a pet. *Cf.* GO TO SLEEP. [U.S. euphemism, 1900s]

puttyhead a fool; an oaf. [U.S. slang and colloquial, 1800s-pres.]

putz 1. a fool; an oaf. **2.** the penis. More rude than SCHMUCK (sense 1). [from Yiddish; both senses, U.S. slang, mid 1900s-pres.]

puzzle-text a parson; a clergyman or a preacher who tries to puzzle out the meaning of a text. *Cf.* MARTEXT. For synonyms see SKY-PILOT. [British slang or colloquial, early 1800s, *Lexicon Balatronicum*]

pye-eyed intoxicated with alcohol. See PIE-EYED.

python the penis in PUMP ONE'S PYTHON, ROCK PYTHON, SYPHON THE PYTHON (all *q.v.*). For synonyms see YARD.

Q

Q. an abbreviation of "queer," a male homosexual. For synonyms see EPICENE. [British slang, early 1900s, *Dictionary of Slang and Unconventional English*]

quack 1. a fraudulent physician; a seller of patent medicines; a derogatory term for any physician. [since the late 1600s] **2.** a methaqualone tablet. [U.S. drug culture, mid 1900s-pres.]

quad a methaqualone tablet. [U.S. drug culture, mid 1900s-pres.]

quail 1. a prostitute. For synonyms see HARLOT. [since the early 1600s] **2.** a spinster. No negative connotations. Also an early term for "co-ed." [U.S. underworld, 1800s-1900s] **3.** any sexually loose woman. [U.S. slang, 1900s] **4.** any girl or woman. [U.S. slang, 1900s] Synonyms: BIDDY, BIRD, CANARY, CHICK, DUCK, GOOSE, GROUSE, GUINEA-HEN, GULL, LOON, NESTLECOCK, PARTRIDGE, PELICAN, PHEASANT, PIGEON, PLOVER, POULTRY, WREN.

quail-hunter a woman-chaser; a whoremonger. *Cf.* QUAIL (sense 1). [U.S. slang, 1900s]

quaint (also **quaynte, queinte, queynte**) the female genitals. For synonyms see MONOSYLLABLE. [1300s, (Chaucer)]

quaker a lump of excrement. In the expression BURY A QUAKER (*q.v.*). [British slang, 1800s]

quaker's burying-ground a cesspit; a privy. [British, 1800s, Farmer and Henley]

qualified damned; bloody. [British euphemism, late 1800s]

qualify to succeed in copulating. *Cf.* SCORE. [British slang, 1800s, Farmer and Henley]

quarter moon HASHISH (*q.v.*). For synonyms see HASH. [U.S. drug culture, mid 1900s-pres.]

quarter pot a drunkard. Rhyming slang for "sot." [slang and underground, 1900s]

quarter-to-two a Jewish man or woman. Rhyming slang. Usually considered derogatory. For synonyms see FIVE AND TWO. [British, 1900s, *Dictionary of Rhyming Slang*]

quart-mania the DELIRIUM TREMENS (*q.v.*). For synonyms see ORK-ORKS. [British slang, 1800s]

quas the plural of "qua." A truncation of "methaqualone," specifically Quaalude (trademark), a tranquilizer. [U.S. drug culture, mid 1900s-pres.]

quean 1. a sexually loose woman; a prostitute. [since *c.* 1000] **2.** an effeminate male. *Cf.* COTQUEAN (sense 1). For synonyms see FRIBBLE. **3.** a homosexual male. [both senses, Australian, 1800s-1900s]

queanie pertaining to effeminacy or softness in males. [Australian, early 1900s]

queen 1. an effeminate male, not necessarily a homosexual male. *Cf.* QUEENIE. [U.S. slang, early 1900s] **2.** an effeminate male homosexual, especially one who prefers virile men. **3.** a type of male homosexual with specific preferences as to types of lovers and NONORTHOGENITAL (*q.v.*) behavior or other matters. There are numerous terms for queens, many of them are of a jocular nature. A few of the following list refer to personality traits rather than sexual appetite. *Cf.* BODY QUEEN, BROWNIE QUEEN, BUTTERFLY QUEEN, CHICKEN QUEEN, CLOSET QUEEN, DINGE QUEEN, DISH QUEEN, DRAG QUEEN, FACE QUEEN, FELCH QUEEN, FIRE QUEEN, FLAMING QUEEN, FOOT QUEEN, GOLDEN SHOWER QUEEN, GREEN QUEEN, HEAD QUEEN, JEAN QUEEN, MAIN QUEEN, MITTEN QUEEN, MOVIE QUEEN, POUND-CAKE QUEEN, SHOWER QUEEN, SHRIMP QUEEN, SIZE QUEEN, SNOWBALL QUEEN, SUCK QUEEN, TEAROOM QUEEN, TOE QUEEN, VIRGIN QUEEN, WATCHQUEEN. **4.** any homosexual male. [U.S. slang, 1900s] **5.** a fellator; a male who performs FELLATIO

(*q.v.*). [U.S. underworld, early 1900s]
6. a lovely young woman. No negative connotations. [colloquial since the 1700s or before] **7.** a beautiful lesbian. [U.S., 1900s]

queenie 1. an effeminate male. For synonyms see FRIBBLE. **2.** a charming and attractive young woman. *Cf.* QUEEN. [both senses, U.S., 1900s]

queening courting women or girls; flirting. [U.S. slang, early 1900s, Weseen]

queer (also **queere, quire**) **1.** pertaining to a thing or a person which is odd, naughty, eccentric, counterfeit, or worthless. [originally cant; since the 1600s] **2.** to spoil; to make bad or worthless, as in "queer the deal" [originally cant; since the late 1700s] **3.** pertaining to a male or female homosexual. [U.S., 1900s] **4.** a homosexual male. Usually considered to be a highly derogatory term. [U.S. underworld and general slang, early 1900s-pres.] **5.** a female homosexual; a lesbian. For synonyms see LESBYTERIAN. [U.S. slang, mid 1900s-pres.] **6.** intoxicated with alcohol. From sense 1. **7.** a fool. [underworld slang and colloquial, 1900s]

queer beer beer with low alcohol content, *e.g.*, three-two beer (3.2 percent alcoholic content). Rhyming with NEAR BEER (*q.v.*). *Cf.* SISSY BEER, SQUAW PISS. [U.S. slang, mid 1900s-pres.]

queered intoxicated with alcohol. *Cf.* QUEER (sense 6). For synonyms see WOOFLED. [British slang, early 1800s]

queer for to have a noticeably strong and obsessive desire for something. See the various senses of QUEER. [U.S. slang, mid 1900s-pres.]

queer queen a masculine woman; a lesbian. [U.S. slang, early 1900s]

queer up to primp, said of a man, not necessarily an effeminate man. [Australian, 1900s, Baker]

queervert a homosexual male. A blend of QUEER and PERVERT (both *q.v.*). [U.S. slang, early 1900s]

quickening-peg the penis. "Quicken" in the sense "bring life to." [mid 1600s, (Urquhart)]

quick-shits diarrhea; dysentery. *Cf.* SHITS, THE. [British military, early 1900s]

quickstep diarrhea. From the name of a dance step. [U.S. colloquial, early 1900s] Synonyms: AZTEC TWO-STEP, BACK-DOOR TROTS, BARLEY-CORN SPRINTS, B.D.T.S, BOWEL OFF, COCKTAILS, CRAPS, DDELHI BELLY, FLUXES, FLYING HANDICAP, GASTROINTESTINAL TROUBLES, G.I.S, G.I. SHITS, GURR, GYPPY TUMMY, JIMMY BRITTS, JOE-TROTS, LASK, LAX, LOOSE, LOOSE-ENDED, LOOSE IN THE HILT, LOOSENESS IN THE BELLY, LOOSENESS IN THE BOWELS, LURKIES, MONTEZUMA'S REVENGE, MOVIES, PURGE, QUICK-SHITS, RUNNING-BELLY, RUN OFF, RUNS, SCATE, SCATTERS, SCOOTS, SCOURS, SCREAMING SHITS, SHITS, SHITTERS, SHOOT, SHORTS, SKIT, SKITTER, SQUIRTS, SUMMER COMPLAINT, THREE-PENNY BITS, TOURISTAS, TREY-BITS, TROTS, WILD SQUIRT, WOG GUT.

quicky (also **quickie**) a very brief copulation. *Cf.* FLYER. [U.S. slang, mid 1900s-pres.]

quid the female genitals. *Cf.* QUIM. [British, 1800s]

quiff 1. the female genitals. *Cf.* QUIM. [slang, 1700s-1900s] **2.** women considered solely as sexual objects. **3.** a sexually loose woman; a slut. For synonyms see LAY. [slang, early 1900s-pres.] **4.** a cheap and low prostitute. [slang, 1900s or before] **5.** to copulate. [British slang or cant, 1700s]

quiffing copulating or chasing after women for sexual purposes. *Cf.* QUIFF. [British, late 1700s, Grose]

quim (also **quem, queme, quimsbox, quimsby, quimsy, quin, quint**) **1.** the female genitals. **2.** copulation. **3.** to copulate. [originally British, 1600s-pres.]

quim-bush the female pubic hair. For synonyms see DOWNSHIRE. [British slang, 1800s]

quiming copulating or chasing after women for sexual purposes. *Cf.* QUIFFING. [British, 1800s]

quimsby (also **quimmy**) the female genitals. See QUIM. [British, 1800s or before]

quim-stake the penis. For synonyms see YARD. [British, 1800s or before]

quim-sticker a lecher; a whoremonger. [British, 1800s or before]

quim-sticking copulating. In expressions such as "go quim-sticking." *Cf.* QUIM. [British, 1800s or before]

quimsy 1. the female genitals. **2.** copulation. Both are in expressions such as "bit of quimsy." *Cf.* QUIM. [both British, 1800s or before]

quim-wedge the penis. For synonyms see YARD. [British, 1800s]

quim-wig (also **quim-whiskers**) the female pubic hair. *Cf.* QUIM-BUSH. [British, 1800s]

quin the female genitals. See QUIM. [British, 1800s or before]

quince 1. an effeminate male. **2.** an oaf. **3.** a homosexual male. [all senses, Australian, early 1900s, Baker]

quisby drunk. From a mid 1800s term meaning "out of whack." [British slang, 1800s, Farmer and Henley]

quoob a misfit; an oaf. Possibly a blend of "queer" and "boob." [U.S. slang, 1900s]

R

rabbit 1. a coward; someone who is as timid as a rabbit. For synonyms see YELLOW-DOG. [U.S. slang, early 1900s-pres.] **2.** to coit a woman. *Cf.* LIVE RABBIT, SKIN THE LIVER RABBIT (sense 1). [British, 1900s, *Dictionary of Slang and Unconventional English*]

rabbit-catcher a nickname for a midwife. *Cf.* CUNNY-CATCHER. [British slang, late 1700s, Grose]

rabbit-pie 1. a prostitute. **2.** women considered sexually. [both senses, British slang, 1800s]

racked (also **racked-up**) **1.** intoxicated with alcohol. For synonyms see WOOFLED. [U.S. slang, 1900s] **2.** intoxicated with marijuana. For synonyms see TALL. [U.S. drug culture, mid 1900s-pres.]

rack off to urinate. For synonyms see WHIZ. [British, 1800s]

racks the human breasts. From "racks of meat" or "meat racks." For synonyms see BOSOM. [U.S. slang, 1900s]

racy spicy or sexy. *Cf.* FRANK, SUGGESTIVE. [U.S., 1900s]

rag a sanitary napkin; a PERINEAL PAD (*q.v.*). *Cf.* RIDING THE RAG. For synonyms see MANHOLE COVER. [U.S. colloquial, 1900s] See also RAGS.

rag, on the 1. menstruating. Abbreviated as O.T.R. (*q.v.*). [U.S. colloquial, mid 1900s-pres.] **2.** acting bitchy. From sense 1. Not limited to women. [U.S. slang, mid 1900s-pres.]

rag doll a slovenly woman. For synonyms see TROLLYMOG. [British and U.S. slang, mid 1800s-1900s]

ragged intoxicated with alcohol. For synonyms see WOOFLED. [U.S. slang, early 1700s-pres.]

ragged-arse unpleasant or disreputable. [British, 1800s, Farmer and Henley]

ragging having the menstrual period. From RAG, ON THE (*q.v.*). [U.S. slang, mid 1900s-pres.]

rag-head a nickname for anyone who wears a turban. *Cf.* HANDKERCHIEF-HEAD. [U.S. slang, early 1900s-pres.]

rags a cheap prostitute; any low and disreputable person. [U.S. slang and colloquial, 1900s]

ragtime the menses. From the name of a popular music style in the early 1900s. For synonyms see FLOODS. [U.S. slang, mid 1900s-pres.]

ragweed a low grade of marijuana. From the common name of a weed. *Cf.* WEED (sense 1).

rahl, the (also **ral**) syphilis. For synonyms see SPECIFIC STOMACH. [U.S.,mid 1900s]

rail an erection of the penis. For synonyms see ERECTION. [slang, mid 1900s-pres.]

rainbow 1. a nickname for a bow-legged person. [colloquial, 1900s] **2.** a Tuinal (trademark) capsule. [U.S. drug culture, mid 1900s-pres.] **3.** to have coition with a person of another race. From the mixture of colors in the rainbow. [U.S. slang, mid 1900s-pres.]

raincoat a condom. *Cf.* DIVING SUIT, ONE-PIECE OVERCOAT. For synonyms see EEL-SKIN. [U.S. slang, mid 1900s]

rainy-day woman marijuana; a marijuana cigarette. [U.S. drug culture, mid 1900s-pres.]

raise Cain to create a disturbance; to RAISE HELL (*q.v.*). [U.S. colloquial euphemism, mid 1800s-pres.]

raise hail a disguise of RAISE HELL (*q.v.*).

raise hell to create a disturbance, argument, or conflict. [U.S. and elsewhere, 1900s and before]

ralph 1. a fool; an oaf. See RALPH SPOONER. [colloquial since the 1700s] **2.** to vomit. *Cf.* BARF, EARP, YORK. [U.S. slang, mid 1900s-pres.]

Ralph Spooner a fool; an oaf. See SPOON (sense 1), SPOONY, WOODEN SPOON. [late 1600s, B.E.]

ram 1. an act of copulation. [colloquial and nonce, 1600s-pres.] **2.** to copulate with a female, from the male point of view. [colloquial since the 1800s or before] **3.** to perform PEDER-ASTY (*q.v.*). *Cf.* RAM-JOB. **4.** the penis, especially the erect penis. [colloquial, 1900s or before]

rama marijuana. [from the Spanish word for "branch"; U.S. drug culture, mid 1900s-pres.]

ram-bam a rapid and harsh act of copulation. From "Ram-bam, thank you ma'am." [U.S. slang, mid 1900s]

ramhead a CUCKOLD (*q.v.*). From the horns of cuckoldry. [British, early 1600s-1700s]

Ram it! a derisive exclamation, "Ram it up your ass!"; the same as SHOVE IT! (*q.v.*). [U.S. slang, mid 1900s]

ram-job an act of anal intercourse. *Cf.* RAM (sense 3). [U.S. slang, mid 1900s-pres.]

rammer the penis, especially the erect penis. *Cf.* RAM (sense 4). [colloquial and nonce, 1800s or before]

rammies trousers. For synonyms see GALLIGASKINS. [Australian, early 1900s]

rammish 1. stinking like a goat. [1300s, (Chaucer)] **2.** lustful; desirous of copulation. *Cf.* GOATISH. [colloquial, 1600s]

rammy lustful. For synonyms see HUMPY. [British colloquial, 1600s]

ramp a wanton woman or a whore. See ROMP. [1500s-1600s]

ramping mad 1. intoxicated with alcohol; drunk and angry. [British, mid 1800s] **2.** very angry. [U.S. slang, 1900s, Berrey and Van den Bark]

ramrod the penis, especially the erect penis. *Cf.* RAMMER. [colloquial and nonce, 1600s-pres.]

rams, the the DELIRIUM TREMENS (*q.v.*). For synonyms see ORK-ORKS. [U.S. slang, 1800s] See also RATS, THE.

ramstudious lustful. [U.S. colloquial, 1900s, Berrey and Van den Bark]

randy 1. coarse, rude, and violent. [colloquial, 1600s] **2.** lewd, salacious, and lustful; later sexy-looking. [colloquial, 1700s-pres.]

rantan, on the (also **randan, on the**) **1.** intoxicated with alcohol. **2.** on a drinking spree. [both senses, British, mid 1600s-1800s]

ran the good race died. [U.S. colloquial, 1900s or before]

ranting sexually aroused and lustful. *Cf.* RANDY. [British, 1800s or before]

rape fluid perfume. [U.S. slang, 1900s]

rare 1. to inhale powdered narcotics, *e.g.*, cocaine. [U.S. drug culture, mid 1900s-pres.]. **2.** a drink of an alcoholic beverage. [U.S., 1900s, Berrey and Van den Bark]

rascal 1. a person of the lowest imaginable class. [since the 1300s] **2.** a rogue. [since the 1600s] **3.** a man with no genitals; a eunuch. [British, 1700s-1800s]

rasp 1. the female genitals. For synonyms see MONOSYLLABLE. **2.** to coit a woman; to copulate. **3.** coition as in the expression "do a rasp." [all senses, British slang, 1800s, Farmer and Henley]

rasp away to copulate, from the male point of view. *Cf.* RASP. [Australian, early 1900s, *Dictionary of Slang and Unconventional English*]

raspberry tart 1. a release of intestinal gas. Rhyming slang for FART (*q.v.*). For synonyms see GURK. **2.** the heart. Rhyming slang. [both senses, British, 1800s]

rasper a loud release of intestinal gas. For synonyms see GURK. [British slang, 1900s, *Dictionary of Slang and Unconventional English*]

rat 1. a drunken man or woman arrested in the night by the authorities. [British, 1600s, B.E.] **2.** an extremely detestable person, usually a male. [U.S. slang, 1900s or before]

rat-fink an extremely unpleasant person, usually a male; a detestable variety of FINK (*q.v.*). [U.S. slang, mid 1900s-pres.]

Rat-fuck! an expletive and exclamation, somewhat milder than "Fuck!" Based on RAT-FINK (*q.v.*). [U.S. slang, mid 1900s-pres.]

Rats! an exclamation of despair or disapproval. [colloquial since the late 1800s]

rats, the the DELIRIUM TREMENS (*q.v.*). *Cf.* RAMS, THE. For synonyms see ORK-ORKS. [colloquial, 1800s-1900s]

rattle and hiss urine; to urinate; a urination. Rhyming slang for PISS (*q.v.*). [U.S., 1900s, *Dictionary of Rhyming Slang*]

rattle-ballocks the female genitals. [British, 1800s or before, Farmer and Henley]

rattle beads to express aggravation. *Cf.* DROP ONE'S BEADS. [U.S. homosexual use, 1900s, Stanley]

rattlebones a nickname for a very skinny person. [U.S. slang, 1900s, Montelone]

rattlebrain an oaf; a silly, stupid person. [since the early 1700s]

rattle-cap a whoremonger. For synonyms see LECHER. [British slang, 1800s, Farmer and Henley]

rattled heavily intoxicated with alcohol; distraught; with one's senses impaired. *Cf.* RADDLED. [colloquial, 1800s-pres.]

rattlehead an oaf; a scatterbrain whose brain has dried and is rattling about in his head. [British, mid 1600s]

rattler a man who copulates athletically. See FUCK LIKE A RATTLESNAKE. [British slang, 1900s, *Dictionary of Slang and Unconventional English*]

rattlesnake a prostitute. Because of the way she shakes her tail. *Cf.* FUCK LIKE A RATTLESNAKE. [Australian, Baker]

rat-trap a bustle. From the shape of the frame. [British slang, 1800s, Farmer and Henley]

raunchy (also **ronchie**) **1.** dirty, sloppy, and bad-smelling. **2.** racy, obscene, or off-color. **3.** intoxicated with alcohol. [all senses, U.S. slang, mid 1900s-pres.]

raven beauty a beautiful black woman. From the blackness of a raven and a play on "raving beauty." [U.S. slang, early 1900s] Synonyms: BANANA,

BIT OF EBONY, BLACK DOLL, BLACK MEAT, BLACK VELVET, BROWN-SKIN BABY, BROWN SUGAR, CHARCOAL BLOSSOM, CHARCOAL LILY, COVESS-DINGE, CULLUD GAL, DANGE BROAD, DARK MEAT, FEM-MOKE, HOT CHOCOLATE, LAUNDRY QUEEN, LIZA, MULATTO MEAT, NIGGER-GAL, NIGGER-WENCH, PIECE OF DARK MEAT, REDBONE, SAPPHIRE, SEAL, SHADY LADY.

raw, in the nude; naked. For synonyms see STARKERS. [U.S. and elsewhere, 1900s]

raw meat 1. the penis. *Cf.* MEAT (sense 4). For synonyms see YARD. [colloquial and nonce, 1700s-pres.] **2.** a naked person, usually a naked woman. [British and U.S. slang, 1800s-1900s]

R.D. a "red devil," a capsule of Seconal (trademark). For synonyms see SEC. [U.S. drug culture, mid 1900s-pres.]

ready to spit on the verge of ejaculating, said of the male when highly sexually aroused. *Cf.* DRIPPING FOR IT. [British slang, 1900s, *Dictionary of Slang and Unconventional English*]

ream 1. to stick something up someone's rectum. *Cf.* GOOSE (sense 6). **2.** to commit ANILINGUS (*q.v.*). **3.** anilingus. *Cf.* REAM-JOB, RIM. **4.** to commit PEDERASTY (*q.v.*). **5.** to cheat. *Cf.* SCREW (sense 6). [all senses, U.S. slang, 1900s]

reamer 1. the penis, especially the erect penis. **2.** a PEDERAST (*q.v.*). [both sense, U.S. underworld, early 1900s]

ream-job ANILINGUS (*q.v.*). See REAM (sense 3).

reaper marijuana. From REEFER (*q.v.*). [U.S., mid 1900s, *Current Slang*]

rear 1. a privy; an outhouse; the same as BACK (*q.v.*). For synonyms see AJAX. [British colloquial, late 1800s-1900s] **2.** the posteriors. For synonyms see DUFF. [U.S. colloquial, 1900s]

receiver 1. a catamite; a male who receives anally the phallus of the INSERTOR (*q.v.*). **2.** a male who receives the phallus of another male in his mouth in order to perform FELLATIO (*q.v.*). *Cf.* CATCH (sense 1), TAKE (sense 3). The term is more exact than "passive." See PASSIVE PARTICIPANT. [U.S., mid 1900s, (Humphreys)]

receiving-set 1. the female genitals. **2.** a toilet or chamber pot. Both are from a term for a radio receiver. [U.S., 1900s, Berrey and Van den Bark]

recreational drug a drug taken (virtually always illicitly or illegally) to produce thrills or stupor. The term is used euphemistically and contrasts with the therapeutic uses of a drug. [U.S., mid 1900s-pres.]

red 1. a Seconal (trademark) capsule. A truncation of RED DEVIL (*q.v.*). [U.S. drug culture, mid 1900s-pres.] **2.** red wine; cheap red wine. [slang, 1900s] **3.** a communist. [U.S., mid 1900s] **4.** marijuana. A truncation of PANAMA RED (*q.v.*). [U.S. drug culture, mid 1900s-pres.]

red and blue a Tuinal (trademark) capsule. [U.S. drug culture, mid 1900s-pres.]

red-assed very angry. From "red-faced." [U.S. slang, mid 1900s-pres.]

redbird a Seconal (trademark) capsule. *Cf.* BLACKBIRD, BLUEBIRD. [U.S. drug culture, mid 1900s-pres.]

red-cap the penis; the *glans penis*. [British, early 1900s, *Dictionary of Slang and Unconventional English*]

red cross morphine. From its common use in wartime. *Cf.* WHITE CROSS. [U.S., early 1900s or before]

red devil a capsule of Seconal (trademark), a barbiturate. *Cf.* BLACKBIRD, BLUEBIRD. [U.S. drug culture, mid 1900s-pres.]

red-dirt marijuana marijuana which grows freely in the wild. [U.S. drug culture, mid 1900s-pres.]

red-end the *glans penis*. *Cf.* RED-CAP. [British, 1900s, *Dictionary of Slang and Unconventional English*]

red-eye 1. inferior whisky. Because it causes one's eyes to redden. For synonyms see EMBALMING FLUID. **2.** any strong alcoholic beverage. *Cf.* POPSKULL, ROT-GUT. [both senses, U.S. colloquial, 1800s-pres.]

red flag 1. a sanitary napkin; a PERINEAL PAD (*q.v.*). *Cf.* DANGER-SIGNAL. **2.** the menses. *Cf.* FLAGGING. [both senses, 1800s-1900s]

red-handed in the act of copulating. The "red" is a play on the heat of passion and RED-END (*q.v.*). From an expression referring to taking someone by surprise and, in the minds of some, the redness of the erect penis.

red-hot poker the penis, especially the erect penis. *Cf.* POKER. [colloquial and nonce, 1800s-pres.]

red-jacket a capsule of Seconal (trademark). *Cf.* YELLOW-JACKET. [U.S. drug culture, mid 1900s-pres.]

red lamp a brothel. *Cf.* RED LIGHT (sense 2). [British, early 1900s, *Dictionary of Slang and Unconventional English*]

red light 1. a prostitute. **2.** a brothel. **3.** pertaining to brothels or to prostitution. [all senses, U.S. slang, early 1900s-pres.]

red-light district an area where prostitution is available; the "low" part of town. [U.S. colloquial, 1900s]

red-lighter a prostitute. *Cf.* RED LIGHT (sense 1). [U.S. slang, 1900s]

red-light house a brothel. [U.S., mid 1900s]

red-light sister a prostitute. For synonyms see HARLOT. [U.S. slang, early 1900s]

red-neck 1. a Southern Caucasian, particularly one who is poor and hates blacks. [U.S. colloquial, mid 1900s-pres.] **2.** any white person. A derogatory reference. For synonyms see PECKERWOOD. [U.S., mid 1900s-pres.]

red oil an alcohol extract of CANNIBIS SATIVA (*q.v.*). For synonyms see OIL. [U.S. drug culture, mid 1900s-pres.]

red onion the female genitals. Refers to the visual image of an onion halved on its axis compared to the configuration of the female genitals when a woman's legs are spread. *Cf.* CAT'S-HEAD-CUT-OPEN, CUT CABBAGE. [U.S., 1900s]

red rag a sanitary napkin; a perineal pad. For synonyms see MANHOLE COVER. [British slang, late 1800s, Farmer and Henley]

reds amphetamine capsules. For synonyms see AMP. [U.S. drug culture, mid 1900s-pres.]

red sails in the sunset the menses. For synonyms see FLOODS. [jocular euphemism, 1900s]

redskin a North American Indian. Sometimes derogatory. [colloquial since the late 1600s] Synonyms: BOW AND ARROW, BREED, BUCK, INJUN, UNCLE TOMMYHAWK, VANISHING AMERICAN.

red tummy-ache the menses. For synonyms see FLOODS. [U.S., 1900s]

reeb backslang for "beer." For synonyms see SUDS. [British and U.S. slang, 1800s-1900s]

reefer 1. marijuana or a marijuana cigarette. [U.S., early 1900s-pres.] **2.** a marijuana smoker. See GREEFO. [U.S. drug culture, early 1900s-pres.]

reefer man a seller of marijuana. [U.S. slang, mid 1900s-pres.]

reefer weed marijuana or a marijuana cigarette. Cf. WEED (sense 1). [U.S. drug culture, mid 1900s-pres.]

reeking intoxicated with alcohol; stinking drunk. For synonyms see WOOFLED. [U.S. slang, 1900s]

reeling ripe (also **reeling**) intoxicated with alcohol. [British and U.S., 1800s-1900s]

reely intoxicated with alcohol. Cf. REELING RIPE. [British slang, early 1900s, Dictionary of Slang and Unconventional English]

reggin backslang for "nigger." A recent instance of U.S. backslang. [attested in black use and not in derogatory use; U.S., current but not widely known]

regular 1. pertaining to regular bowel movements. **2.** pertaining to regular menstrual periods. [both senses, U.S. colloquial, 1900s]

regulator the female genitals. Because men's sexual lives are thereby regulated. [British, 1800s or before]

reindeer dust a powdered narcotic, specifically cocaine. Cf. SNOW (sense 2). [underworld, mid 1900s, Dictionary of the Underworld]

reject an oaf; a worthless person. Implying that a person could not pass physical or mental inspection. [U.S. colloquial, 1900s]

relations 1. copulation. A truncation of "sexual relations." For synonyms see SMOCKAGE. [U.S. euphemism, 1900s] **2.** relatives; one's kin. [British, 1900s]

relationship 1. any interpersonal intereaction or involvement between persons, objects, or situations. No negative connotations. **2.** a euphemism for "affair" or any sexual relationship. Cf. MEANINGFUL RELATIONSHIP. [U.S., mid 1900s-pres.]

released deflowered; divested of virginity, said of males and females. See DEFLOWER. [euphemistic, 1900s]

relief station a W.C.; a privy. [U.S. euphemism, early 1900s-pres.]

relieve oneself 1. to defecate. **2.** to urinate. [both senses, widespread euphemism, 1800s-1900s] **3.** to ejaculate; to achieve sexual satisfaction, said of the male. For synonyms see MELT. [British, 1800s, Farmer and Henley]

religious intoxicated with alcohol. Cf. ONE OF THE FAITHFUL. [U.S. slang, early 1700s, Ben Franklin]

relish copulation. For synonyms see SMOCKAGE. [British, 1800s, Lexicon Balatronicum]

remedy-critch a CHAMBER POT (q.v.). Cf. CRUTCH (sense 1). [British colloquial, 1700s-1900s]

rent (also **renter**) a homosexual male who charges for his services rather than provide them free. Cf. TRADE. [British, late 1800s-1900s, Dictionary of Slang and Unconventional English]

rep a prostitute. From "reputation." Cf. DEMI-REP. [British, late 1700s, Grose]

respond 1. to respond sexually, usually said of women. **2.** to respond sexually with an erection, said of men. [both senses, colloquial, 1800s-1900s]

rest, at 1. intoxicated with alcohol. [British and U.S. euphemism, 1800s-1900s] **2.** dead. [U.S. euphemism, 1900s]

rest-and-be-thankful the female genitals. [British slang, 1800s, Farmer and Henley]

restroom a W.C. found in a public building. Bathing facilities are rarely included. The word-of-choice for a public bathroom. [U.S., 1900s]

resurrection-cove a body-stealer; a RESURRECTIONIST (*q.v.*). [cant, 1800s or before, Vaux]

resurrection doctor a doctor who buys corpses which are stolen from graves or has people murdered and delivered to him. [British, 1800s]

resurrectionist (also **resurrection man**) a body-stealer. [British, late 1700s]

reswort trousers. Backslang for "trouser." For synonyms see GALLIGASKINS. [British, 1800s]

retch 1. to make an effort to vomit. **2.** to vomit loudly and with great muscular exertion. [both senses, colloquial since the 1800s]

retchsome nauseating. [U.S. dialect, 1900s or before, Wentworth]

retire to depart from the immediate premises to urinate. [euphemistic since the 1800s] Synonyms and related terms: ANSWER NATURE'S CALL, BOG, BURN THE GRASS, CHECK THE SKI RACK, COKE-STOP, DRAIN THE SPUDS, FIND A HAVEN OF REST, GIVE THE CHINAMAN A MUSIC LESSON, GO AND CATCH A HORSE, GO AND LOOK AT THE CROPS, GO AND SEE IF THE HORSE HAS KICKED OFF HIS BLANKET, GO TO EGYPT, PAY A VISIT, PLUCK A ROSE, POST A LETTER, POWDER ONE'S NOSE, SEE A MAN ABOUT A DOG, SEE A MAN ABOUT A HORSE, SEE JOHNNY, SEE MRS. MURPHY, VISIT THE SAND-BOX, WASH, WASH ONE'S HANDS, WASH UP.

retiring room a restroom, bathroom, or W.C. [U.S. euphemism, 1900s or before]

return a BELCH (*q.v.*). In the expression "many happy returns," said in mock-congratulation when someone belches. [colloquial, 1800s-1900s]

revenant the ghost of a dead person returning from the dead to haunt the living. [since the mid 1800s] Related terms: APPARITION, BANSHEE, BARGHEST, BOGEY, BOGGARD, BOGY, BOODIE, BOOGER MAN, BUGBEAR, BUGGER, BULL-BEAR, BULL-BEGGAR, DIBBUK, DUPPY, DYBBUK, EMPUSA, EPHIALTES, EVILS, FANTASM, FEAR-BABE, FEARIN', FETCH, GHOUL, HANTS, IMP, INCUBUS, JINNI, SPECTER, SPOOK, WILL O' THE WISP, WRAITH.

R.F. 1. a ROYAL FUCKING (*q.v.*). **2.** a RAT-FINK (*q.v.*). **3.** RAT-FUCK! (*q.v.*). [all senses, U.S. slang, mid 1900s-pres.]

Rhea sisters (also **rhea brothers, rheas, rhea twins**) a jocular term for leucorrhea, gonorrhea, diarrhea, and pyorrhea.

rhubarb the male or female genitals. *Cf.* GREENS. For synonyms see GENITALS. [British and U.S. dialect, 1800s-1900s]

rhythm method a method of birth control. The prevention of conception by avoiding coitus during a time period which includes ovulation. *Cf.* SAFE PERIOD, VATICAN ROULETTE. [colloquial, 1900s]

rhythms amphetamines or amphetamine capsules. For synonyms see AMP. [U.S. drug culture, mid 1900s-pres.]

rib a girl, woman, or wife. Based on "Adam's rib." [colloquial and slang, 1700s-pres.]

ribald (also **ribaud, ribold**) **1.** a harlot. **2.** a PONCE (*q.v.*); a pimp. **3.** a whoremonger. [all senses, British, 1300s] **4.** wanton; lascivious; spicy. [since the 1500s]

rib-joint a brothel. Based on a slang term for a restaurant which serves spareribs. *Cf.* RIB. [U.S. slang, early 1900s]

rib-roast a scolding from one's wife; a roasting from one's RIB (*q.*). [since the late 1500s]

rice-bags trousers. For synonyms see GALLIGASKINS. [British slang, late 1800s]

rice-belly a derogatory nickname for a Chinese or other Oriental person. For synonyms see JOHN CHINAMAN. [slang, 1900s]

riceman a derogatory term for a Chinese or other Oriental person. [U.S., 1900s]

Richard the Third 1. a bird, Rhyming slang, See BIRD for possible references. **2.** dung. Rhyming slang for TURD (q.v.). [British, early 1900s, *Dictionary of Rhyming Slang*]

rich dirt manure used as fertilizer. *Cf.* NIGHT-SOIL. [U.S. dialect and colloquial]

ride 1. an act of coition. Refers to the motions of coition. **2.** to copulate, said of a man or a woman. *Cf.* PRIG (sense 1). [colloquial since the 1500s or before]

ride below the crupper to copulate with a woman. For synonyms see OCCUPY. [colloquial, 1600s]

rider a sexually aroused male; one who is ready to RIDE (sense 2); a lecher or a whoremonger. [British, 1700s]

ride the deck to commit sodomy. The "deck" is the back of the RECEIVER (q.v.). [U.S. slang, early 1900s]

ridgerunner a derogatory term for a Caucasian. [U.S. colloquial, 1900s or before]

riding the cotton bicycle the menses. See RIDING THE RAG. [1900s]

riding the rag 1. having one's menstrual period. For synonyms see FLOODS. [U.S., 1900s] **2.** a catch phrase explaining why someone is in a bad humor; the same as RAG, ON THE (sense 2). Said of women and men. [U.S. slang, 1900s]

riding the white horse having one's menstrual period. "White" refers here to the PERINEAL PAD (q.v.). [U.S. slang, 1900s]

rifle 1. to coit. **2.** to caress sexually; to grope. Both are from the term meaning "plunder." **3.** the penis. See HAVE A RUSTY-RIFLE for phallic images [all senses, British, 1600s]

rifle-man a lecher; a whoremonger. *Cf.* RIFLE (sense 3). [British, 1800s]

rift (also **reft**) **1.** a belch; a burp. [colloquial and dialect since the 1400s]

2. to break wind. This is probably meant to include belching and flatulence. [British and U.S. colloquial, 1800s-pres.] **3.** to release intestinal gas. [U.S. dialect, 1900s or before]

righteous bush marijuana. *Cf.* BUSH (sense 6). [U.S. slang, mid 1900s-pres.]

rigid 1. intoxicated with alcohol. **2.** very angry; stiff with rage. [both senses, U.S. slang, mid 1900s]

rig-mutton a wanton or licentious person, usually said of a woman. [British, 1600s]

rileyed intoxicated with alcohol. For synonyms see WOOFLED. [U.S. slang, early 1900s]

rim 1. ANILINGUS (q.v.); the same as REAM (sense 3). **2.** to commit ANILINGUS (q.v.). [both senses, U.S. slang, 1900s] **3.** to reach ejaculation through masturbation. [U.S. slang, mid 1900s, Dahlskog] **4.** to coit a woman anally. [British slang, 1900s, *Dictionary of Slang and Unconventional English*]**5.** pertaining to a female who is ready and eager for copulation. Reminiscent of BRIM (sense 3). [U.S. dialect (Ozarks), 1900s or before, Randolph and Wilson]

rimadonna a homosexual male who prefers to perform or receive ANILINGUS (q.v.). A jocular play on "prima donna." [U.S. homosexual use, mid 1900s, Farrell]

rim-job an act of ANILINGUS (q.v.). See REAM-JOB.

ring 1. the female genitals, specifically the vagina. *Cf.* CIRCLE, HOOP. [slang, late 1500s] **2.** the anus. [slang, 1800s-pres.] **3.** a contraceptive diaphragm. [U.S. slang, 1900s]

ring-tail 1. a derogatory nickname for an Italian. [U.S., 1900s] **2.** a derogatory nickname for a Japanese. [World War II] **3.** a coward. [Australian slang, 1900s, Baker] **4.** a CATAMITE (q.v.). [U.S. underworld, early 1900s]

ring-tailed polecat, I'll be a a jocular oath or an exclamation of surprise. [stereotypical cowboy jargon; U.S., 1900s or before]

ring-tail wife a CATAMITE (q.v.). *Cf.*

RING (sense 2). RING-TAIL (sense 4). [U.S. underworld, early 1900s]

rip, old 1. a jaded old man. **2.** an aged prostitute. *Cf.* GASH (sense 2), REP, SLIT. [both senses, British and U.S., late 1800s-1900s]

ripe intoxicated with alcohol. For synonyms see WOOFLED. [colloquial and slang, 1800s-1900s]

ripped 1. intoxicated with alcohol. For synonyms see WOOFLED. **2.** drug intoxicated. *Cf.* TORE-UP. For synonyms see TALL. [both senses, U.S. slang, mid 1900s]

rise to get an erection of the penis. *Cf.* GET A RISE. [since the 1600s]

rise in one's levi's an erection, especially in the expression "I'm wise to the rise in your levi's." [U.S., mid 1900s]

rise to the occasion to get an erection. [nonce and double entendre; British and U.S. colloquial, 1900s]

rites of love copulation. For synonyms see SMOCKAGE. [euphemistic, 1600s]

roach 1. a cockroach. A truncation of "cockroach." [U.S., 1800s-1900s] **2.** a low prostitute. Based on "cockroach." [U.S., 1900s] **3.** the stub of a marijuana cigarette. The stub is highly valued because it contains accumulated deposits of T.H.C. (*q.v.*), the active ingredient in marijuana. See ROACH CLIP. [U.S. drug culture, mid 1900s-pres.] **4.** a girl, especially an unattractive girl. From the insect name. For synonyms see BUFFARILLA. [U.S. slang, 1900s] **5.** a policeman. [U.S. underworld, early-mid 1900s, Weseen]

roach clip a holder for smoking the butt of a marijuana cigarette. *Cf.* ROACH (sense 3). [U.S. drug culture, mid 1900s-pres.] See also JEFFERSON AIRPLANE.

road apple a formed lump of horse excrement; the same as ALLEY APPLE and HORSE APPLE (both *q.v.*). [U.S. colloquial, 1900s]

road kid a CATAMITE (*q.v.*); a tramp's catamite. [U.S. underworld, early 1900s]

road-making the menses. *Cf.* ROAD

UP FOR REPAIRS. [British colloquial, 1800s]

road up for repairs the menses; the same as STREET UP FOR REPAIRS (*q.v.*). [British colloquial, 1800s, Farmer and Henley]

roaring-drunk (also **roaring**) heavily intoxicated with alcohol. *Cf.* LION DRUNK. [U.S. slang, 1900s]

roaring horn a very hard erection. For synonyms see ERECTION. [Australian, 1800s, *Dictionary of Slang and Unconventional English*]

rock to coit a woman. From the motions of coition. [U.S. slang, mid 1900s]

rocked to sleep dead. Refers to rocking in the bosom of Abraham. See ABRAHAM'S BOSOM. [U.S. euphemism, late 1800s, Ware]

rocket a marijuana cigarette. Because it sends one on a HIGH (sense 3). *Cf.* ROCKET-FUEL, SKYROCKET. [U.S. underworld and drug culture, 1900s]

rocket-fuel phencyclidine, the drug P.C.P. (*q.v.*), *Cf.* ROCKET, SKYROCKET. [U.S. drug culture, mid 1900s-pres.]

rockhead an oaf; someone who has rocks in the head. A very hardheaded person. [U.S. colloquial, mid 1900s]

rock out to pass out from the use of marijuana or other drugs. *Cf.* CAP OUT, STONED (sense 2). [U.S. drug culture, mid 1900s-pres.]

rock python the erect penis. From the common name of a snake. *Cf.* SYPHON THE PYTHON. [British slang, mid 1900s-pres.]

rocks the testicles. *Cf.* GOOLIES, PEBBLES, STONES (sense 2). For synonyms see WHIRLYGIGS. [slang and colloquial, 1900s or before]

rocky intoxicated with alcohol. Related to instability and "rocking." [U.S. slang, early 1700s, Ben Franklin]

rod 1. to coit a woman. [colloquial, 1800s-1900s] **2.** the penis, especially the erect penis. [British and U.S., 1800s-1900s] **3.** a gun. [U.S. underworld and stereotypical gangster jargon, early 1900s-pres.]

roger 1. the penis. For synonyms see YARD. [British, mid 1600s-1800s] 2. the nickname for a bull and occasionally for a ram. [rural colloquial, 1700s-1800s] 3. to copulate with a cow, said of a bull. 4. to coit a woman. From sense 3. [British, 1700s-1900s; various senses are attested in U.S. dialects, 1800s-1900s] 5. to rape a woman. [U.S. dialect, 1900s, Wentworth]

roll copulation; coition as enjoyed by the male. See JELLY-ROLL (sense 1). [U.S. slang, early 1900s-pres.]

roller a prostitute who specializes in robbing (rolling) drunks. [U.S., 1900s]

roller skate to coit. [U.S. slang, mid 1900s, Current Slang]

rollies the testicles. A truncation of TOMMY ROLLOCKS (q.v.). Also from the "rolling" of a ball. [British, early 1900s, Dictionary of Slang and Unconventional English]

rolling-drunk (also **rulling-drunk**) intoxicated with alcohol. [colloquial and slang, 1900s and before]

rolling-pin the penis. From the shape. See ROLL. [colloquial and nonce, 1800s-pres.]

roll in the hay (also **toss in the hay**) copulation; a spontaneous or secret act of copulation performed in a barn or a haystack; any spontaneous or casual act of copulation. Cf. ROLL. [U.S. slang, early 1900s-pres.]

rollocks the testicles. From TOMMY ROLLOCKS (q.v.). Cf. ROLLIES. [British, 1900s]

romp (also **ramp**) 1. a wild-living, vulgar woman or girl. [mid 1400s] 2. a whore or a sexually loose woman. [mid 1500s-1800s] 3. a tomboy. [British and U.S. colloquial, late 1600s-1800s] 4. an act of copulation, as in the expression "a romp in the hay." [British and U.S., 1900s or before]

rompworthy sexually desirable and possibly sexually aroused. Usually refers to a woman. Cf. BEDWORTHY, FUCKSOME, PUNCHABLE. [British, early 1900s, Dictionary of Slang and Unconventional English]

roof, off the experiencing the menses. Cf. FALL OFF THE ROOF. [U.S. slang, mid 1900s-pres.]

rooster 1. the penis. A jocular and euphemistic avoidance of COCK (sense 3). [U.S., 1800s] 2. to cock a gun. An avoidance of "cock." [U.S. jocular euphemism, 1900s] 3. a lascivious man. Refers to a rooster and his harem of hens. For synonyms see LECHER. [U.S. colloquial, 1900s or before] 4. the female genitals. In avoidance of "cock." See COCK (sense 6). [British slang, 1800s, Farmer and Henley]

roostered intoxicated with alcohol. See COCKED (sense 1). [U.S. euphemism of avoidance, 1900s or before]

root 1. the penis. [since the 1600s] 2. to coit a woman. Also **root around**. From sense 1. Cf. ROOTLE. [colloquial, 1900s] 3. a marijuana cigarette. [U.S. drug culture, mid 1900s-pres.] 4. amphetamines or an amphetamine tablet or capsule. [U.S. drug culture, mid 1900s-pres.]

rootle 1. to coit. From a term meaning "grub" or "poke about." 2. copulation. Cf. ROOT (sense 2). [both senses, British slang, 1800s]

rooty sexually aroused. Cf. ROOT (sense 2). [U.S. slang, mid 1900s-pres.]

rope marijuana or a marijuana cigarette. Refers to a "hemp" rope. Cf. GUNNY, HEMP. [U.S. drug culture, mid 1900s-pres.]

rorty 1. sexually aroused; in the mood for love. [British, late 1800s, Dictionary of Slang and Unconventional English] 2. intoxicated with alcohol and quite noisy about it; wildly frivolous. [British, 1900s, Dictionary of Slang and Unconventional English]

Rory O'More a prostitute. Rhyming slang for "whore." [British slang, 1800s]

rose 1. the female genitals. 2. the maidenhead; the hymen. Cf. BUD. [both senses, British, 1800s, or before] See also ROSES.

roses 1. the menses. Cf. FLOWERS. [British euphemism, 1800s] 2. amphetamines; amphetamine tablets or capsules. For synonyms see AMP. [U.S. drug culture, mid 1900s-pres.]

rosy intoxicated with alcohol; reddened from drink. [U.S. slang, late 1800s-mid 1900s]

rosy about the gills intoxicated with alcohol. See GILLS, UP TO THE. [U.S. slang, early 1900s]

rosy-drop acne; pimples; acne vulgaris. [since the early 1800s, *Oxford English Dictionary*]

rot 1. nonsense. See TOMMY-ROT. [slang and colloquial, mid 1800s-pres.] **2.** inferior liquor. A truncation of ROT-GUT (*q.v.*). For synonyms see EMBALMING FLUID. See also DAD, DOD.

rot-gut weak beer; inferior liquor; strong homebrewed liquor. *Cf.* GUT-ROT, POP-SKULL. [colloquial and slang since the late 1500s] Synonyms: CONK-BUSTER, GNAT'S PISS, GREEK FIRE, PAINT-REMOVER, POP-SKULL, SNEAKY PETE, VARNISH-REMOVER, WILD MARE'S MILK.

rotten intoxicated with alcohol. [widespread slang, 1800s-pres.]

rottenlogging necking and petting. Based on SPARK and SPUNK UP (both *q.v.*), refers to an attempt to "start a fire" in tinder, *i.e.*, rotten wood. In this case, the fire is one of passion. [U.S. slang, early 1900s]

rough-riding copulation without a condom. From the male point of view. *Cf.* BAREBACK. [British slang, 1900s, *Dictionary of Slang and Unconventional English*]

rough stuff marijuana containing an excess of roots, stems, and seeds. *Cf.* LUMBER. [U.S. drug culture, mid 1900s-pres.]

rough trade a cruel and physically abusive male homosexual partner. He may beat or rob after sexual relations. *Cf.* LEATHER (sense 2), SISSY-BEATER. [U.S. homosexual use, mid 1900s-pres.]

rounder a whoremonger; a lecher. [British slang, 1800s, Farmer and Henley]

roundeye 1. a CATAMITE (*q.v.*). For synonyms see BRONCO. [U.S. under-world, early 1900s-pres., Goldin, O'Leary, and Lipsius] **2.** the anus. *Cf.* BLIND-EYE (sense 1). [U.S. slang, mid 1900s-pres.] **3.** a Caucasian. From the point of view of an Oriental. [U.S. slang, mid 1900s]

roundheel 1. (also **roundheels**) a woman who permits sexual intercourse without much fuss; a pushover. Her heels are round and she just falls over. **2.** a prizefighter who is knocked out easily. [both senses, U.S. slang, early 1900s-pres.]

round house a women's restroom. Based on the name of a device for changing the direction of a locomotive engine. [U.S. slang, early 1900s, Montelone]

round-mouth the anus. [British slang, early 1800s, *Lexicon Balatronicum*]

round-pound a type of mutual masturbation; the same as CIRCLE-JERK (*q.v.*). [U.S. slang, mid 1900s]

rounds trousers; pants. From rhyming slang, "round-the-houses." [slang, 1800s]

round-the-houses (also **round-me-houses, round-my-houses**) trousers; pants. Rhyming slang for "trousers." [British slang, mid 1800s]

rouser a very loud release of intestinal gas. *Cf.* TRUMP. For synonyms see GURK. [slang since the early 1700s]

roust 1. to coit a woman. **2.** coition. [both senses, British, late 1500s]

rout to copulate with a woman. *Cf.* ROOT (sense 2). From the standard sense "carve" or "scoop out." [U.S. slang, mid 1900s-pres.]

royal blue the drug L.S.D. (*q.v.*). [U.S. drug culture, mid 1900s-pres.]

royal fucking extremely bad treatment. Abbreviated as "R.F." [U.S. slang, mid 1900s-pres.]

royal shaft (also **royal screw**) an extreme putdown, disappointment, or affront. The shaft is one which is figuratively run up one's anus. See SHAFT (sense 4). [U.S. slang, 1900s]

rub to masturbate. See RUB-OFF, RUB UP. [since the 1500s]

rubber a condom. For synonyms see EEL-SKIN. [U.S.colloquial, mid 1900s-pres.]

rubber knackers an unpleasant or detested man. *Cf.* KNACKERS. [British, 1900s]

rubber ring a contraceptive diaphragm. *Cf.* RING (sense 3). [U.S., 1900s]

rubber sock a timid person; a jerk. *Cf.* WET SOCK. [U.S. slang, early 1900s-pres.]

rub-off 1. copulation. [British, 1600s] **2.** masturbation. [British and elsewhere, 1800s, Farmer and Henley]

rub out to kill. [U.S. stereotypical gangster talk, 1900s]

rub up (also **rub-off**) **1.** to masturbate. **2.** masturbation. Usually hyphenated in this sense. [both senses, British colloquial, 1600s-1900s] **3.** to coit a woman. [late 1500s] **4.** to stimulate sexually. *Cf.* LOVE UP, PET UP, TOUCH-UP. For synonyms see FIRKYTOODLE. [since the 1600s]

ruck a disguise of "fuck." Seen primarily as a camouflage of the graffito "fuck." See MOTHER-RUCKER.

rudder 1. the penis. **2.** to copulate. [both senses, British, early 1600s-1700s]

ruddy a disguise of "bloody." [British and U.S., late 1800s-1900s]

rude indecent; vulgar. [current U.S. slang]

rudeness See DO A RUDENESS TO.

ruffian 1. the devil. Also **old Ruffian.** See RUFFIN, OLD. For synonyms see FIEND. [colloquial since the 1400s] **2.** the penis. *Cf.* ROB-THE-RUFFIAN. [British slang, 1800s, Farmer and Henley] **3.** to pimp. [British slang, 1800s]

Ruffin, old (also **ruffian**) the devil. From RUFFIAN (*q.v.*). [cant and later, colloquial, mid 1400s-1800s]

ruffle the "passive" partner in a lesbian sexual relationship. *Cf.* FLUFF (sense 4). [U.S. homosexual use, mid 1900s, Stanley]

rufus the female genitals. [British slang, 1800s, Farmer and Henley]

rug 1. a wig of any type. No negative

connotations. **2.** the female pubic hair. *Cf.* MERKIN, TWAT-RUG. For synonyms see DOWNSHIRE. [both senses, U.S. colloquial and slang, 1900s or before]

ruin 1. to DEFLOWER (*q.v.*) a woman; to ruin a woman's reputation. [euphemistic, 1700s-1900s] **2.** gin. From BLUE RUIN (*q.v.*). [British and U.S. slang, 1800s-1900s] Synonyms for sense 2: BATHTUB GIN, BLUE RIBBON, BLUE RUIN, BLUE STONE, BLUE TAPE, BOB, BRIAN O'LINN, CAT'S WATER, CLAP OF THUNDER, DIDDLE, DRAIN, EYE-WATER, FLASH OF LIGHTNING, JACKY, LIGHTNING, LIGHT WET, LONDON MILK, MAX, MISERY, MOTHER'S MILK, NIG, OLD TOM, RIGHT-SORT, SATIN, SKY BLUE, STARK NAKED, STINKIOUS, STREAK OF LIGHTNING, STRIP-ME-NAKED, STRONG AND THIN, TANGLE-LEG, TAPE, TITTERY, TWANKAY, UNSWEETENED, WATER OF LIFE, WHITE, WHITE PORT, WHITE SATIN, WHITE TAPE, WHITE VELVET, WHITE WINE, YARD OF SATIN.

rule-of-three 1. the VIRILIA (*q.v.*), *i.e.*, one penis and two testicles. [British, early 1700s] **2.** copulation. For synonyms see SMOCKAGE. [British slang, 1800s, Farmer and Henley]

rum-bag a drunkard. For synonyms see ALCHY. [U.S., mid 1900s]

rumble-seat the posteriors. May include a reference to the audible breaking of wind. [U.S., 1900s]

rum-blossom (also **rum-bud**) a pimple on the nose caused by the excessive drinking of alcohol. [colloquial, 1800s-1900s]

rum-dumb (also **rum-dum**) **1.** a chronic drunkard. **2.** an oaf, sober or drunk. **3.** intoxicated with alcohol. [all senses, U.S., early 1900s-pres.]

rummed-up (also **rummed**) intoxicated with alcohol. [U.S. slang, early 1900s]

rummy a drunkard. For synonyms see ALCHY. [U.S. colloquial, mid 1800s-pres.]

rump 1. the hindquarters; the buttocks; the posteriors. [since the mid 1400s] **2.** the female genitals. [primarily British, since the mid 1600s] **3.** to coit a woman. [British slang, 1800s, Farmer and Henley] **4.** to copulate with a woman (vaginally) from the rear. [British, 1800s] **5.** to flog someone on the buttocks. [British, cant or colloquial early 1800s] **6.** to defecate on someone. **7.** to break wind at someone. [senses 6 and 7 are British slang, 1800s, Farmer and Henley]

rump-cleft the fissure between the buttocks. [British, 1900s]

rumper 1. a prostitute. **2.** a whoremonger. [both senses, British slang, 1800s]

rumpityfetida ASAFETIDA (*q.v.*). A jocular avoidance of "ass" in "asafetida." [nonce or highly localized; U.S., 1900s]

rumpot a drunkard. [U.S. slang, 1900s]

rump-proud wanton and lascivious, said of a woman. *Cf.* RUMP (sense 2). [Shipley]

rump-roll a bustle. [Shipley]

rump-splitter 1. the penis, especially the erect penis. [British slang, mid 1600s] **2.** a whoremonger. For synonyms see LECHER. [1600s (Urquhart)]

rumpus the posteriors. An elaboration of RUMP (sense 1). [U.S., mid 1900s]

rump-work copulation. For synonyms see SMOCKAGE. [British slang, 1800s, Farmer and Henley]

rum-sucker a drunkard. [U.S., mid 1800s]

runner a pimp; a smuggler; a bootlegger. [U.S., early 1900s]

running-belly diarrhea; dysentery. For synonyms see QUICKSTEP. [Caribbean]

running-off at the mouth talking too much. *Cf.* DIARRHEA OF THE MOUTH. [U.S. colloquial, 1900s]

run off 1. to have diarrhea. **2.** the effluvium of diarrhea. Usually hyphenated in this sense. [both senses, U.S. colloquial, 1900s or before] **3.** a urination; a stop at the W.C. Usually hyphenated in this sense. [British, early 1900s, *Dictionary of Slang and Unconventional English*]

run one's tail to work as a prostitute. [British slang, 1800s, Farmer and Henley]

runs diarrhea. *Cf.* MOVIES, SCOOTS, TROTS. For synonyms see QUICKSTEP. [colloquial, 1800s-1900s]

run to seed (also **gone to seed**) pregnant. See SEED (sense 1). For synonyms see FRAGRANT. [British jocular slang, 1800s]

Russian duck to coit a woman; an act of copulation. Rhyming slang for "fuck." [British, early 1900s, *Dictionary of Rhyming Slang*]

rusty-dusty the posteriors. For synonyms see DUFF. [U.S. slang, mid 1900s]

rut (also **rutt**) **1.** the copulation of deer. [since the 1400s] **2.** human copulation. [British, 1600s, B.E.]

Ruth a women's restroom. *Cf.* JANE, JOHN (sense 1). [U.S. slang and colloquial, early-mid 1900s]

rutter 1. a sexually aroused man or woman. [late 1500s-1600s] **2.** a lecher.

S

SABU "self-adjusting balls-up," a military blunder. *Cf.* BALLS-UP. For synonyms see SNAFU. [British military slang, 1900s]

sacking prostitution. *Cf.* BAG (sense 4), BURLAP SISTER. [slang, 1500s]

sacks 1. trousers. *Cf.* BAGS (sense 1). For synonyms see GALLIGASKINS. **2.** the human breasts. [U.S. slang, 1900s and nonce elsewhere]

saddie-maisie (also **sadie-masie**) a practitioner of sadism and masochism. *Cf.* S. AND M. [U.S. slang, mid 1900s-pres.]

saddle 1. the female genitals. For synonyms see MONOSYLLABLE. **2.** women considered sexually. See MOUNT (sense 1), RIDE. [both senses, British, early 1600s-1700s]

sadism a condition characterized by a strong desire to humiliate or physically harm a person as part of one's sexual passion. From the name "Marquis de Sade," 1740-1814, (Count Donatien Alphonse François de Sade).

safe a condom. *Cf.* SAFETY. For synonyms see EEL-SKIN. [British and U.S. colloquial, late 1800s-pres.]

safe period the time of the month where conception is least likely to take place because of the nature of the menstrual cycle. An important concept in the RHYTHM METHOD (*q.v.*) of birth control.

safety a condom *Cf.* SAFE. For synonyms see EEL-SKIN. [U.S. slang, mid 1900s]

safety-sheath a condom. *Cf.* MALE SHEATH. [British and U.S., 1900s]

sailor's bait a prostitute; any girl or woman. [U.S. slang, early 1900s]

sailor's delight a prostitute. [U.S. slang, mid 1900s]

sainted aunt!, By my a mock oath and an exclamation. For synonyms see 'ZOUNDS! [colloquial, 1900s or before]

Saint Peter the penis. *Cf.* PETER. [British slang, 1800s, Farmer and Henley]

sales lady a prostitute. For synonyms see HARLOT. [U.S. underworld, early 1900s]

sally-port the female genitals. [vague literary euphemism; British, mid 1600s]

salt 1. sexually aroused; lewd and lecherous. Said of bitches in heat, *i.e.,* "salt bitch," and extended to humans. *Cf.* FLAVOUR. [British, 1500s–1800s] **2.** copulation. **3.** to copulate. [senses 2 and 3 are 1600s] **4.** intoxicated with alcohol. A truncation of SALT JUNK (*q.v.*), "drunk." [British, late 1800s, Ware] **5.** powdered heroin. [U.S. drug culture, mid 1900s-pres.]

salt and pepper an inferior grade of marijuana. [U.S. drug culture, early 1900s]

saltcellar the female genitals. See SALT (sense 2). For synonyms see MONOSYLLABLE.

salted-down (also **salted**) **1.** intoxicated with alcohol. See SALT (sense 4). *Cf.* CORNED, PICKLED. [slang since the 1800s] **2.** dead. [U.S. slang, 1900s or before]

salt junk (also **salt**) intoxicated with alcohol. Rhyming slang for "drunk." *Cf.* SALT (sense 4). [British slang, late 1800s, Ware]

salt-water Negro 'a Negro born in Africa; an African who has crossed the ocean. [1900s and before]

salt-water turkey a derogatory nickname for an Irishman who has crossed the ocean. [U.S. slang, 1900s] See also TURKEY (sense 2).

Sambo 1. a derogatory nickname for a black man. [British and U.S. use, 1700s-1900s] **2.** a Negro who humbly accepts the stereotypical subservient role. *Cf.* OREO. [U.S. black use, mid 1900s-pres.]

SAMFU a "self-adjusting military fuck-up,'' a military mess which will straighten itself out in time. For synonyms see SNAFU. [British, World War II]

Sam Hill hell; the devil; hell personified. Ware suggests that this is a disguise of ''sóme hell,'' but the term is usually found in the sentence, ''What in the Sam Hill!'' [U.S. colloquial, early 1800s-pres.]

Sammy-Soft (also **Sammy**) a fool; an oaf. [British, 1800s and before]

sample 1. to fondle a woman sexually. **2.** to coit a virgin or to experience copulation with a particular woman for the first time. *Cf.* TASTE. [both senses, colloquial and nonce, 1800s-pres.]

sample of sin a prostitute. For synonyms see HARLOT. [British euphemism, mid 1700s]

sampler the female genitals. [British slang, 1800s, Farmer and Henley]

sand-box 1. a box prepared in such a way that most cats can be trained to use it for elimination. **2.** a W.C. A jocular extension of sense 1. [both senses, colloquial, 1900s]

S. and M. 1. sadism and masochism. **2.** any type of nonorthogenital sexual activity. **3.** any practitioner of nonorthogenital sexual activity. Senses 2 and 3 are an extension of or a misunderstanding of sense 1. [all senses, U.S. slang, mid 1900s-pres.]

sanitary 1. perineal pad. For synonyms see MANHOLE COVER. **2.** pertaining to feminine hygiene; concerning the menses. [both senses, British with some U.S. use, 1800s-1900s]

sanitary napkin a PERINEAL PAD (*q.v.*); the U.S. word-of-choice for an absorbent menstrual pad. [U.S. colloquial, 1900s]

sanitary sponge a contraceptive device. *Cf.* SANITARY (sense 1). [U.S. colloquial, 1900s]

sanitary towel a PERINEAL PAD (*q.v.*), or its equivalent. [somewhat vague and euphemistic in the U.S.; colloquial, 1800s-1900s]

San Quentin jail-bait a girl under the legal age for copulation even with consent. [U.S. slang, mid 1900s-pres.]

San Quentin quail an underage girl; a girl under the legal age for copulation even with consent. *Cf.* QUAIL. [U.S. slang, mid 1900s-pres.]

Santa Marta gold Colombian marijuana. [U.S. drug culture, mid 1900s-pres.]

sap a jerk; an oaf. [British and later, U.S. slang and colloquial, early 1800s-pres.]

SAPFU a military blunder ''surpassing all previous fuck-ups''; the greatest military blunder to date. For synonyms see SNAFU. [U.S. military, World War II]

sap happy intoxicated with alcohol. ''Sap'' refers to alcohol. Patterned on ''slap happy.'' [U.S. slang, mid 1900s]

sapphism lesbianism. [from the name of a Greek poetess, ''Sappho,'' born on the island of Lesbos; literary and euphemistic since the late 1800s]

Sarah Soo a Jewish man or woman. Rhyming slang for ''Jew.'' Not necessarily derogatory. [British slang, early 1900s, *Dictionary of Slang and Unconventional English*]

sard to copulate. For synonyms see OCCUPY. [since *c.* 900, *Oxford English Dictionary*]

sardine a prostitute; a low, smelly prostitute. Possibly a play on SARD (*q.v.*). [U.S. slang, early 1900s]

satchel the female genitals. *Cf.* TWATCHEL. [U.S. dialect (Ozarks), 1900s or before, Randolph and Wilson]

satchel-crazy obsessed with the sexual prospects of a specific woman or of all women. Possibly from TWATCHEL (*q.v.*). See SATCHEL.

satin gin. *Cf.* WHITE SATIN, YARD OF SATIN. For synonyms see RUIN. [colloquial, 1800s]

sativa marijuana. See CANNABIS SATIVA. For synonyms see MARI. [U.S. drug culture, mid 1900s-pres.]

sauce 1. a venereal disease. Probably refers to the secretions associated with gonorrhea. [British, late 1600s] **2.** alcohol; booze. [U.S. slang, early 1900s-pres.]

sauce, on the 1. drinking regularly; drinking in the manner of an alcoholic. **2.** intoxicated with alcohol. [both senses, U.S. slang, mid 1900s-pres.]

sauced intoxicated with alcohol. For synonyms see WOOFLED. [U.S. slang, early 1900s-pres.]

sauce-pan lid a derogatory nickname for a Jewish man or woman, *i.e.*, a "yid." For synonyms see FIVE AND TWO. [British, 1800s, *Dictionary of Rhyming Slang*]

sausage 1. the penis; the erect penis. *Cf.* LIVE SAUSAGE. [widespread recurrent nonce, since the mid 1600s or before] **2.** a derogatory nickname for a German or a German soldier. [U.S. slang, World War II] **3.** a stupid person; an oaf. [U.S. slang, mid 1900s-pres.] **4.** a marijuana cigarette, especially a fat one. [U.S. drug culture, mid 1900s-pres.]

sausage-grinder 1. the vagina. **2.** a prostitute. For synonyms see HARLOT. **3.** women considered sexually. See SAUSAGE (sense 1). For synonyms see TAIL.

sausage roll a person of Polish nationality or descent. Not necessarily derogatory. Rhyming slang for "Pole." [British, 1900s, *Dictionary of Rhyming Slang*]

sawbones a surgeon. For synonyms see DOC. [British and U.S. slang, 1800s-pres.]

sawdust-brained stupid; blockheaded. [U.S. slang, early 1900s]

sawdust-head an oaf; a blockhead; someone whose brains are more useless than sawdust. [U.S. colloquial, 1900s or before]

sawed intoxicated with alcohol. For synonyms see WOOFLED. [U.S. slang, 1900s or before]

saw off a chunk (also **saw off a piece**) to copulate; to coit a woman. *Cf.* CHUNK, PIECE (sense 5). [attested as Canadian, early 1900s, *Dictionary of*

Slang and Unconventional English; U.S. slang, early 1900s-pres.]

saxophone an opium pipe. For synonyms see GONGER. [U.S. underworld, early 1900s or before]

say to urinate. For synonyms see WHIZ. [British dialect, 1800s, Northall]

S.B.D. "silent but deadly." Refers to an inaudible release of intestinal gas which has a very potent odor. [U.S. slang, mid 1900s]

scab 1. a wretch; a mean and worthless scoundrel. [since the late 1500s] **2.** a strikebreaker. [since the early 1800s]

scadger a mean and wretched fellow. *Cf.* CODGER. [British, 1800s]

scag (also **skag**) **1.** an ugly young woman. For synonyms see BUFFARILLA. [U.S. slang, early 1900s-pres.] **2.** heroin. From sense 1. *Cf.* GIRL (sense 9). [U.S. drug culture, mid 1900s-pres.]

scag-hag a heterosexual woman who associates with homosexual males. *Cf.* FAG-BAG, FRUIT-FLY. [U.S. homosexual use, mid 1900s, Stanley]

scag Jones a herion addiction. [U.S. drug culture, mid 1900s]

scalded infected with venereal disease. Synonyms: CLAPPED, CLAWED-OFF, FRENCHIFIED, GLUED, HOT, IN PICKLE, PEPPERED, PEPPERED-OFF, PLACKET-STUNG, SUNBURNT, SWINGED-OFF, UPHOLSTERED.

scalder a venereal disease, especially gonorrhea. [British slang, early 1800s, *Lexicon Balatronicum*]

scale to mount and coit a woman. *Cf.* BOARD, CLIMB, MOUNT. [British euphemism, early 1600s]

scammered intoxicated with alcohol. [colloquial and slang, 1800s-1900s]

scamper juice low-quality alcohol which is likely to send one scampering to the W.C. *Cf.* BARLEYCORN SPRINTS. [U.S. slang, early 1900s]

Scandihoovian (also **Scandihuvian**) a derogatory nickname for a Scandinavian. [U.S. slang, early 1900s-pres.]

scank an ugly young woman; a scraggly and underdeveloped young woman. [U.S. slang, mid 1900s-pres.]

scanties women's underwear, especially underpants. A blend of "scant" and "panties." [U.S. slang and colloquial, early 1900s-pres.]

scanty trousers underpants. For synonyms see NETHER GARMENTS.

scape 1. fornication; a breach of chastity. [from *A Winter's Tale* (Shakespeare)] **2.** a release of intestinal gas. For synonyms see GURK. [colloquial, 1500s-1600s]

scar heroin. *Cf.* SCAG (sense 2). [U.S. drug culture, mid 1900s-pres.] See also DIVINE SCAR.

scared shitless (also **scared spitless**) very frightened; extremely worried; frightened enough to defecate. *Cf.* SHIT-SCARED. [slang, mid 1900-pres.]

scarf a joint to swallow a marijuana cigarette to avoid detection and arrest. See SCOFF. [U.S. drug culture, mid 1900s-pres.]

scarlet sister a prostitute. For synonyms see HARLOT. [U.S. euphemism, early 1900s]

scarlet woman 1. a prostitute. [euphemistic and colloquial] **2.** Rome, *i.e.*, the Roman Catholic Church. Capitalized in this sense.

scat heroin. *Cf.* SCAG (sense 2). [U.S. drug culture, mid 1900s-pres.]

scate 1. "a light-heels," presumably a sexually loose woman. From the common name for the ray, RAIA BATIS. [1800s, Farmer and Henley] **2.** to be loose in the bowels. **3.** a term of contempt. [senses 2 and 3 are British colloquial and dialect, and are cognate with SHIT (sense 9); 1600s-1800s]

scatters diarrhea, especially in animals. Possibly cognate with "shit." [rural colloquial, 1900s or before]

scavenger 1. an emptier of privies. *Cf.* TOM TURDMAN. [U.S. colloquial, 1900s or before] **2.** a garbageman; a collector of refuse. [U.S. colloquial euphemism, mid 1900s-pres.]

sceptre the penis. In the phrase "Cyprian sceptre." *Cf.* WAND. [widespread recurrent nonce, mid 1600s-1900s]

scharn cow dung. For synonyms see DROPPINGS.

schicker (also **shikker**) **1.** a drunkard. *Cf.* SHICKER. **2.** intoxicated with alcohol. See SHICKER. [from Hebrew *shikor*, via Yiddish]

schlange (also **schlang**) the penis. *Cf.* SCHLONG. [from the German word for "snake" via Yiddish; U.S. slang, mid 1900s-pres.]

schlemiel (also **schlemiehl, schlemihl, shlemiel**) an awkward, bumbling booby; a gullible dupe. [Yiddish; since the early 1800s]

schlemozzle a riot; a quarrel. The same word as CHEMOZZLE (*q.v.*). [Yiddish; slang or cant, late 1800s-pres.]

schlent (also **schlenter**) a con man; an imposter. [Yiddish; slang, 1900s]

schlimazl (also **schlimazel, shlimazl**) a person who always has bad luck; someone for whom everything goes wrong. *Cf.* SCHLEMOZZLE. [Yiddish]

schlock narcotics. For synonyms see COTICS. [from a Yiddish word for "junk"; U.S. underworld, mid 1900s]

schlong the penis. See SCHLANGE. [from the German word for "snake" via Yiddish; U.S. slang, 1900s]

schlub (also **shlub**) an oaf. [from Yiddish; U.S. slang, mid 1900s-pres.] See also ZHLUB.

schlump (also **schloomp**) an oaf; a dullard. [Yiddish; U.S. slang, mid 1900s-pres.]

schmack heroin. See SCHMECK. [U.S. underworld and drug culture, early 1900s-pres.]

schmeck (also **schmack, schmee, shmeck, smeck**) **1.** heroin. **2.** any narcotics. [ultimately from the German word for "taste" via Yiddish; both senses, U.S. underworld and drug culture, early 1900s-pres.]

schmecken narcotics, especially heroin; the plural of SCHMECK (*q.v.*). [ultimately from the German word for "taste" via Yiddish; U.S. underworld, 1900s]

schmecker (also **smecker**) **1.** a narcotic; a drug. See SCHMECK. [U.S. underworld and drug culture, mid 1900s] **2.** a heroin addict; someone who takes SCHMECK (*q.v.*). [U.S. drug culture, mid 1900s-pres.]

schmee (also **shmee**) heroin. See SCHMECK. [U.S. drug culture, mid 1900s-pres.]

schmekel 1. the diminutive of SCHMUCK (*q.v.*), "penis." **2.** an oaf. [U.S. drug culture, mid 1900s-pres.]

schmendrich (also **shmendrick**) **1.** an oaf; a dummy; an immature male; a nonvirile male. **2.** the penis. "Used derisively by women" (Rosten). [both senses are Yiddish; both senses, U.S. slang, 1900s]

schmock 1. the penis. **2.** a fool; an oaf. Both are the same as SCHMUCK (*q.v.*).

schmoe (also **schmo, shmo**) an oaf. A euphemism for SCHMUCK (sense 2). [from Yiddish; U.S. slang, mid 1900s-pres.]

schmuck (also **shmuck**) **1.** the penis. **2.** an oaf; a jerk; a dullard. [if this form comes from German *Schmuck,* "jewel" or "ornament," via Yiddish, it does so without obeying the usual German and Yiddish sound correspondences; both senses, U.S. slang, mid 1900s-pres.]

schnook (also **schnuck, shnook**) a dope; a sap; an oaf. [U.S. slang, mid 1900s-pres.]

schnorrer a beggar; a worthless fellow. [from Yiddish; since the late 1800s]

schnozzler a user of cocaine. One who uses the "schnozz" or the nose. [from Yiddish; 1900s]

school boy 1. codeine as found in cough syrups. Considered as a "starter" drug. *Cf.* KID-STUFF. [U.S. drug culture, mid 1900s] **2.** cocaine or a user of cocaine. [attested as mid 1900s-pres., Landy]

schtoonk a rotten fellow; a real stinker. [from Yiddish; U.S. slang, mid 1900s-pres.]

schwanz (also **shvance, shvontz**) the penis. [ultimately from the German

word for "tail"; also German slang for "penis"; U.S. slang, 1900s]

schween the penis. Possibly a blend of SCHMUCK and WEENIE (both *q.v.*). [U.S., mid 1900s]

scoff (also **scarf, scorf**) to commit an oral sex act. See SCARF A JOINT. [from a cant word meaning "eat" or "drink"; U.S. slang, mid 1900s]

scooch rum; any hard liquor. *Cf.* HOOTCH. [British military, early 1900s]

scooped intoxicated with alcohol. For synonyms see WOOFLED. [U.S. slang, mid 1900s, Berrey and Van den Bark]

scoots diarrhea. *Cf.* MOVIES, RUNS, TROTS. [U.S. slang, mid 1900s-pres.]

scorched 1. intoxicated with alcohol. [U.S. slang, mid 1900s-pres.] **2.** drug intoxicated. *Cf.* FRIED (sense 2). [U.S. drug culture, mid 1900s-pres.]

score 1. to achieve coition, said of a male. Said especially among males who are interested in keeping track of the number of copulations they have performed. [U.S. slang, mid 1900s-pres.] **2.** an act of copulation. For synonyms see SMOCKAGE. [U.S. slang, mid 1900s-pres.] **3.** a client of a male or female prostitute. *Cf.* TRICK (sense 4). See COUNTER. [U.S. slang and underworld, mid 1900s-pres.] **4.** to make a connection and purchase illegal narcotics. [U.S. drug culture, mid 1900s-pres.]

Scotch mist intoxicated with alcohol. Rhyming slang for "pissed." [British, early 1900s, *Dictionary of Rhyming Slang*]

Scotch warming-pan 1. a female bed companion; a chambermaid. [British, 1700s, Grose] **2.** a release of intestinal gas. For synonyms see GURK. [British, 1800s, Farmer and Henley]

scours diarrhea. From a verb meaning "purge" (1300s). [British and U.S. slang and colloquial, early 1900s]

scrag 1. to hang a person. [cant, mid 1700s if not much earlier] **2.** an ugly young woman. *Cf.* SCAG (sense 1). [U.S. slang, mid 1900s] **3.** a professor in college; any general collegiate bother. [U.S. slang, early 1900s, Berrey and Van den Bark] **4.** to kill. Probably from sense 1. [U.S. slang, mid 1900s-pres. and probably much older] Synonyms for sense 4: BUMP OFF, CREAM, CROAK, DO AWAY WITH, DO FOR, HUSH, JUGULATE, KNOCK OVER, LIQUIDATE, OFF, PERISH, PUT AWAY, PUT DOWN, PUT ONE OUT OF ONE'S MISERY, PUT OUT, PUT OUT OF THE WAY, PUT TO SLEEP, RUB OUT, TAKE FOR A RIDE, WASTE, WIPE OFF, WIPE OUT, ZAP.

scramble-brained stupid. [U.S. slang, mid 1900s]

scrambled intoxicated with alcohol. For synonyms see WOOFLED. [U.S. slang, mid 1900s]

scrape horns to coit after a long period of abstinence. *Cf.* HORN (sense 3). [U.S. slang, mid 1900s]

scraper See GUT-BUTCHER, KIDNEY-SCRAPER.

scratched intoxicated with alcohol. [since the early 1600s]

scratches trousers. For synonyms see GALLIGASKINS. [underworld (tramps), 1900s, *Dictionary of the Underworld*]

scraunched (also **scranched, scronched**) intoxicated with alcohol. [U. S. slang, mid 1900s]

screaming fairy a very obvious homosexual male. [U.S. slang, mid 1900s-pres.]

screaming-meemies (also **screaming-meanies**) the DELIRIUM TREMENS (*q.v.*). From a term for nonspecific nervous upset. [U.S. slang, early 1900s]

screaming queen 1. an obvious homosexual. See SCREAMING FAIRY. [U.S. slang, 1900s] **2.** a lesbian. For synonyms see LESBYTERIAN. [attested as U.S. college slang, Underwood]

screaming shits diarrhea. [originally military; British and U.S. slang, 1900s]

screw 1. to coit a woman. **2.** copulation. **3.** a prostitute. [senses 1-3 since the 1700s] **4.** a woman considered sexually. [British and U.S. slang, 1800s-1900s] **5.** to permit copulation; to actively copulate with a male, said of a woman. [U.S. slang, mid 1900s-

pres.] **6.** to cheat; to deceive. [U.S. slang, mid 1900s-pres.] **7.** to mess up. *Cf.* SCREW UP.

screw around to waste time. From SCREW (sense 7), but not strongly taboo. [U.S. slang, mid 1900s-pres.]

screwdriver the penis. *Cf.* PILE-DRIVER, TOOL (sense 1). [U.S. slang and nonce, 1900s]

screwed 1. intoxicated with alcohol. Also **screwed tight.** [British and U.S. slang, early 1800s-pres.] **2.** copulated with. **3.** cheated; deceived. [senses 2 and 3 are slang, 1900s] **4.** confused; messed-up. Also **screwed-up.** [U.S. colloquial, mid 1900s-pres.]

screwed, blued, and tattooed 1. cheated very badly. [U.S. slang, 1900s] **2.** heavily intoxicated with alcohol. [U.S. slang, mid 1900s]

screw off 1. to mess around; to goof off. *Cf.* SCREW AROUND. **2.** to masturbate. A milder version of FUCK OFF (sense 1). [both senses, U.S. slang, mid 1900s-pres.]

screw up (also **screw**) **1.** to mess up. **2.** a mess; utter confusion. Usually hyphenated. [both senses, slang, 1900s]

screwy 1. crazy. **2.** intoxicated with alcohol. From sense 1. [both senses, slang, early 1800s-pres.]

scrubbers 1. an unpleasant person. **2.** a petty person; a worthless person. Usually in the singular. [Australian and U.S. slang, 1900s]

scrud a venereal disease. *Cf.* CRUD (sense 5). [U.S. slang, 1900s, Wentworth and Flexner]

scuffer a prostitute. Possibly from the noisy way some prostitutes walk to get attention. [U.S. slang, mid 1900s-pres.]

scuffle 1. to identify and PICK UP (sense 1) someone for sexual purposes. [U.S. slang, mid 1900s] **2.** the drug P.C.P. (*q.v.*). [U.S. drug culture, mid 1900s-pres.]

scum semen. *Cf.* SCUMBAG. For synonyms see METTLE. [U.S. slang, mid 1900s-pres.]

scumbag 1. a condom. *Cf.* SCUM.

[U.S. slang, mid 1900s-pres.] **2.** a thoroughly disgusting person. *Cf.* DOUCHE BAG. [U.S. slang, mid 1900s-pres.]

scumber (also **scummer**) **1.** to defecate, originally said of a dog or a fox. [1400s-1600s] **2.** excrement. For synonyms see DUNG. [1600s and before]

scupper 1. a sexually loose woman. **2.** a prostitute. From the term for the opening used to drain a ship's deck. *Cf.* COMMON SEWER, DRAIN. [both senses, U.S. slang, 1900s, Wentworth and Flexner]

scut 1. the tail of an animal, especially that of a rabbit or a deer. No negative connotations. *Cf.* BUN. [rural colloquial, 1500s-1900s] **2.** the posteriors. From sense 1. **3.** the female genitals. [late 1500s-1700s] **4.** the female pubic hair. [1500s] **5.** a contemptible person. [U.S. slang, mid 1900s]

scuttle 1. the female genitals. Literally, "trap door." [British slang, 1800s, Farmer and Henley] **2.** to coit. *Cf.* BACK-SCUTTLE. [U.S. slang, mid 1900s] **3.** to DEFLOWER (*q.v.*) a woman. [British slang, 1800s, Farmer and Henley] **4.** a derogatory nickname for a Negro. From the blackness of a coal scuttle. [U.S. slang, early 1900s or before]

scutz a young male interested in girls for copulation only. See SCUZZ. [U.S. slang, mid 1900s-pres.]

scutz around to coit; to be sexually promiscuous. [U.S. slang, mid 1900s-pres.]

scuzz (also **scuz**) a scraggly or ugly person. [U.S. slang, mid 1900s-pres.]

seafood a sailor considered as a sexual object by a homosexual male. *Cf.* GOVERNMENT INSPECTED MEAT, MEAT, SHORE DINNER. [U.S. underworld and homosexual use, mid 1900s-pres.]

sea gull (also **gull**) a girl or a woman who follows the naval fleet or who follows a particular sailor. This includes sailors' wives. "Gull" is a play on "gal." [U.S. naval slang, World War II]

seal 1. a male or female Negro. Derogatory. For synonyms see EBONY. [U.S. slang, early 1900s] **2.** to impregnate a woman. For synonyms see STORK. [British slang, 1800s] **3.** a testicle. See SEALS.

seals the testicles. See WATCH-AND-SEALS. [British slang, 1800s, Farmer and Henley]

seam-squirrel a louse. *Cf.* PANTS RABBITS. For synonyms see WALKING DANDRUFF. [British and U.S. military, World Wars]

seat the posteriors. In British English, also "seats." [British and U.S., 1900s]

seat cover an attractive female driver. [U.S. citizens band radio slang, mid 1900s-pres.]

seat of easement a CLOSE STOOL (*q.v.*); a chamber pot contained in a case. [British, euphemism, early 1700s]

sec Seconal (trademark). Synonyms: PINK, R.D., RED, REDBIRD, RED DEVIL, RED-JACKET, SECCY, SECONAL, SEGGY.

seccy (also **sec**) Seconal (trademark), a barbiturate. [U.S. drug culture, mid 1900s-pres.]

secko a male sexual PERVERT (*q.v.*). *Cf.* SEXO. [Australian, mid 1900s-pres., Wilkes]

Seconal a barbiturate, Seconal sodium (trademark).

secret parts the female genitals. *Cf.* PRIVATE PARTS. [vague reference from *Hamlet* (Shakespeare)]

secrets the male or female genitals. *Cf.* PRIVATES. [British and U.S. colloquial since the 1800s or before]

secret services copulation in secret, especially with a partner kept for this purpose. [British euphemism. 1700s-1800s]

secret vice masturbation. *Cf.* SOLITARY SIN. [euphemistic, 1800s]

secret works the male or female genitals. For synonyms see GENITALS. [U.S. slang, mid 1900s]

see 1. to coit. Euphemistic for the act of copulation. [British slang, 1800s, Farmer and Henley] **2.** to consort with someone; to date someone; to copulate with someone. [U.S. colloquial, 1900s]

see a man 1. to have a drink of an alcoholic beverage. [British colloquial, late 1800s, Ware] **2.** to copulate.

see a man about a dog (also **see a man about a horse**) to depart to urinate. [U.S. colloquial, 1900s]

See anything? a catch phrase meaning "Has your menstrual period begun?" [British and U.S. use, 1800s-1900s]

seed 1. the semen or the spermatozoa in the semen. For synonyms see METTLE. [since the 1200s] **2.** a testis. See SEEDS. **3.** a marijuana cigarette. [U.S. drug culture, mid 1900s-pres.]

seed-horse a stallion. *Cf.* STABLE-HORSE, STONE-HORSE. [U.S. rural colloquial, 1900s or before]

see double to be intoxicated with alcohol. For synonyms see WOOFLED. [British and later U.S. slang, early 1600s-pres.]

seed-ox a bull. *Cf.* SEED-HORSE. [U.S. rural colloquial, 1900s or before]

seeds 1. the testicles. *Cf.* SEED (sense 2). [U.S. slang, mid 1900s] **2.** morning glory seeds. [U.S. drug culture, mid 1900s-pres.] See BLUE STAR, FLYING SAUCERS, GLORY SEEDS, PEARLY GATE, PEARLY WHITES, SUMMER SKIES.

seedy a Negro. Derogatory. [not widespread; U.S. slang or colloquial, 1800s]

seeing snakes 1. having the DELIRIUM TREMENS (*q.v.*). [British and U.S. slang, 1800s-1900s] **2.** intoxicated with alcohol. *Cf.* SNAKES. [U.S. slang, early 1900s-pres.]

seeing-things drunk heavily intoxicated with alcohol; drunk and hallucinating. [U.S. colloquial or mock-colloquial, 1900s]

see Johnny to retire to go to the toilet; to visit the JOHN (sense 2). For synonyms see RETIRE. [U.S. colloquial, mid 1900s]

see Mrs. Murphy to retire to urinate. MRS. MURPHY (*q.v.*) is the bathroom. [U.S. slang and colloquial, mid 1900s-pres.]

see Mrs. Murray to retire to the W.C. [Australian, 1900s, Baker]

see oneself off to commit suicide; to DO AWAY WITH ONESELF (*q.v.*). [colloquial, 1900s or before]

see pink elephants 1. to be heavily intoxicated with alcohol. **2.** to have the DELIRIUM TREMENS (*q.v.*). *Cf.* SEEING SNAKES. [both senses, U.S. slang and colloquial, 1900s]

see two moons to be drunk. [U.S. slang, early 1700s, Ben Franklin]

seg 1. a bull castrated after it is full-grown [British colloquial, 1600s] **2.** any castrated animal. [British colloquial, 1800s, Rye]

segged castrated. [British, 1800s-1900s]

seggy a Seconal (trademark) capsule, a barbiturate. *Cf.* SECCY. [U.S. drug culture, mid 1900s-pres.]

seldom see underwear; men's underpants. Rhyming slang for B.V.D. (*q.v.*). Usually in the plural. For synonyms see NETHER GARMENTS. [U.S., 1900s, *Dictionary of Rhyming Slang*]

self-abuse masturbation. [euphemism; since the early 1700s]

self-destruction suicide. [euphemistic since the late 1500s] Synonyms and related terms; DO AWAY WITH ONESELF, DUTCH ACT, DUTCH CURE, FELO-DE-SE, HARA-KIRI, SEE ONESELF OFF, SELF-VIOLENCE.

sell one's bacon (also **sell one's flesh, sell one's hip**) to be a prostitute. From the MEAT (sense 2) theme. [U.S. slang, mid 1900s]

sell out to vomit; the same as MAKE A SALE (*q.v.*). For synonyms see YORK. [Australian slang, early 1900s, Baker]

S'elp me God! an oath and an exclamation, "So help me God!" [since the 1300s]

S'elp me greens! a mock oath and an exclamation. Essentially taking an oath on one's sexuality. See GREENS. [British slang, 1800s, Farmer and Henley]

seminary the female genitals. A play on "semen-ary." *Cf.* LADIES' COLLEGE.

[British slang, 1800s, Farmer and Henley]

sensitive plant the penis. From a limerick. [British, 1800s]

sensitive-truncheon the penis. A sensitive club, shaft, or cudgel. [British slang, 1800s, Farmer and Henley]

sent 1. intoxicated with alcohol. **2.** drug intoxicated. From sense 1. [both senses, U.S. slang, early 1900s-pres.]

sent to the skies dead; killed. For synonyms see DONE FOR. [British, late 1800s, Ware]

sepe (also **sepian**) a mulatto. *Cf.* SEPIA. For synonyms see MAHOGANY.

sepia (also **sepian**) a mulatto. [U.S. slang or colloquial, 1900s or before]

sepia sin-spot a nightspot; a nightclub, a joint, or a dive in Harlem. [U.S. slang, early 1900s]

septic-stick a formed rod of excrement. [U.S. jocular slang, mid 1900s]

sergeant a lesbian; a masculine lesbian. For synonyms see LESBYTERIAN. [U.S. slang, mid 1900s]

serve to copulate and impregnate. Originally said of a stallion and later of a man. [since the late 1500s]

served-up intoxicated with alcohol. *Cf.* BOILED, FRIED (sense 1). [U.S. slang, early 1900s]

serve head to perform PENILINGUS (*q.v.*). *Cf.* GIVE HEAD. [U.S. homosexual use, mid 1900s-pres.]

service 1. to coit a female, usually said of an animal. **2.** an act of copulation intended to impregnate. [British and U.S. colloquial, 1800s-1900s] **3.** a truncation of "funeral service." [U.S., 1900s]

sess the posteriors. Possibly related to CESSPOOL. (*q.v.*). [U.S. slang, mid 1900s, *Current Slang*]

set a dose of drugs consisting of two Seconal (trademark) capsules and one amphetamine capsule. [U.S. drug culture, mid 1900s-pres.]

settlement-in-tail copulation. For synonyms see SMOCKAGE. [British slang, 1800s, Farmer and Henley]

sewed-up 1. intoxicated with alcohol. *Cf.* STITCHED. [colloquial and slang, early 1800s-pres.] **2.** pregnant. *Cf.* SEW UP. [British slang, 1800s, Farmer and Henley]

sewer the anus. *Cf.* DIRT-CHUTE. [U.S. slang, mid 1900s]

sewermouth one who uses vile language constantly. *Cf.* LATRINE LIPS. [U.S. slang, mid 1900s-pres.]

sew up to coit and impregnate a woman. [British slang, 1800s, Farmer and Henley]

sex 1. the quality or character of maleness or femaleness. [since the 1300s] **2.** the female genitals. [British slang, 1800s, Farmer and Henley] **3.** the pleasure associated with the stimulation of the genitals. **4.** copulation. [colloquial, 1900s]

sexed-up 1. sexually aroused. For synonyms see HUMPY. [U.S. slang and colloquial, mid 1900s-pres.] **2.** made sexier; made SPICY (*q.v.*) as in a sexed-up movie or song. [U.S. slang, mid 1900s-pres.]

sex experience a vague term used to cover a range of activities from the most minor sexual feeling all the way to copulation. Usually euphemistic for "copulation." [U.S., 1900s]

sex fiend 1. a maniacal, sexual criminal. **2.** a male who is overly sexually aggressive. [both senses, U.S. slang and colloquial, 1900s] **3.** an exaggeration of sense 2 applied to persons of either sex in a jocular fashion. [U.S., 1900s]

sex glands the testicles or the ovaries. [U.S. euphemism, 1900s or before]

sex-job 1. a sexually promiscuous woman; a sexually desirable woman. **2.** an act of copulation; any sex act. For synonyms see JOB. [both senses, U.S. slang, mid 1900s-pres.]

sex life one's sexual activity; the source and nature of one's sexual gratification. *Cf.* LOVE-LIFE. [U.S. colloquial, mid 1900s-pres.]

sexo a sexually perverted male. *Cf.* SECKO. [Australian slang, 1900s]

sex object 1. the object (person or thing) to which one is sexually attracted. Societies tend to encourage persons to enjoy attraction to a sex object which is human, not one's parent, and not oneself. **2.** a person considered as a thing good for no other purpose than sexual gratification. Primarily in reference to a woman. The expression and the concept frequently condemned by some of the Women's Liberation movements in the mid 1960s and 1970s.

sexpot a sexually attractive woman; a very sexy woman who labors to be nothing but a SEX OBJECT (*q.v.*). [U.S. slang, mid 1900s-pres.]

sex ring 1. organized prostitution. **2.** organized group sex activity. [both senses, U.S. slang, mid 1900s-pres.]

sex something up 1. to add sex to something; to put sexual scenes into a movie or a novel. See SEXED-UP. **2.** to JAZZ (*q.v.*) something up; to give it some cleverness or sparkle. [both senses, U.S. slang and colloquial, mid 1900s-pres.]

sexual athlete a male accomplished in sexual matters; a male who excels in the duration of or rapidity of his copulation. [U.S., 1900s]

sexual commerce copulation; essentially the same as SEXUAL INTERCOURSE (*q.v.*). *Cf.* CHAMBER OF COMMERCE. [euphemistic, 1800s-1900s]

sexual deviation a form (or forms) of sexual behavior which differs markedly from those considered NORMAL. (*q.v.*) for a society. In the U.S. this includes PENILINGISM, CUNNILINGISM, ANILINGISM, SADISM, MASOCHISM, EXHIBITIONISM, PEDERASTY, PEDOPHILIA, and ZOORASTY (all *q.v.*).

sexual discharge 1. semen. **2.** natural vaginal lubrication. [both senses, late 1800s-1900s]

sexual intercourse 1. penetration followed by pelvic movement which usually leads to orgasm in one or both partners. The U.S. word-of-choice for coition. **2.** PEDERASTY (*q.v.*). **3.** any type of sexual act which involves two

or more people and which leads to orgasm for at least one of them.

sexual preference one's ''choice'' of sexual activity. A euphemism constructed to escape the (negative) connotations of terms such as ''homosexual,'' ''sexual deviation,'' and ''sexual perversion.'' At present, it is somewhat vague as to what preferences are included other than homosexuality. [U.S. euphemism, mid 1900s-pres.]

sexy pertaining to persons or objects which are sexually stimulating or basically of a sexual nature. [colloquial, 1900s]

shack 1. a really worthless man; a tramp or a vagabond. Also **shackaback**. [since the early 1700s] **2.** a privy. For synonyms see AJAX. [U.S. slang, early 1900s or before] **3.** a mistress; a resident concubine. [U.S. slang, mid 1900s]

shacked-up 1. living with a woman or a concubine, said of a man. **2.** living together unmarried, said of a man and a woman. [both senses, U.S. slang, mid 1900s-pres.]

shacker a tramp; a low tramp. From SHACK (sense 1). [early 1900s or before]

shack-job a mistress or concubine; the same as SHACK (sense 3). [U.S. slang, mid 1900s]

shack man a man who keeps a mistress or concubine, said of soldiers in World War II.

shack rat a soldier who takes a resident concubine. A rhyme based on ''pack rat.'' [U.S. slang, World War II]

shack up with someone 1. to set up housekeeping with a person of the opposite sex to whom one is not married. *Cf.* SHACK (sense 3). [U.S. slang, mid 1900s-pres.] **2.** to conulate in a temporary relationship, said of heterosexual and homosexual couples. See ONE-NIGHT STAND. [U.S. slang, mid 1900s-pres.]

shad a prostitute. *Cf.* FISH (sense 2). [U.S. slang, 1800s, Farmer and Henley]

shade 1. a derogatory nickname for a Negro. [U.S. slang, 1800s-1900s] **2.** a ghost. [since the early 1800s]

shad-mouth a derogatory nickname for a Negro. [U.S. slang, early 1900s, Wentworth and Flexner]

shadow a derogatory nickname for a Negro. For synonyms see EBONY. [U.S. slang, 1900s or before]

shady lady 1. a black woman; a Negress prostitute. [U.S. slang, mid 1900s] **2.** a woman of questionable character, sexually or in her business dealings. [U.S. slang, mid 1900s-pres.]

shaft 1. the penis, especially the erect penis. Anatomically, the body of the penis as opposed to the *glans*. [U.S. slang, 1900s] **2.** to copulate with a woman. For synonyms see TAIL. [1900s] **3.** women considered sexually. [U.S. slang, mid 1900s-pres.] **4.** an imaginary pole which is thrust up someone's anus. **5.** to thrust (in one's imagination) a pole up someone's anus; essentially, to stop a person short; to punish or treat very badly. *Cf.* ROYAL SHAFT. [senses 4 and 5 are U.S. slang, mid 1900s-pres.]

shaftable pertaining to a woman who is so SEXY (*q.v.*) that she immediately makes a man think of copulation. Also pertaining to a woman known to permit copulation readily. *Cf.* PUNCHABLE. From SHAFT (senses 2 and 3).

shag 1. to wiggle; to shake; to toss about. Also the name for a U.S. dance. No negative connotations. [since the 1300s] **2.** a low rascal; the same as SHACK (sense 1). [British, early 1600s] **3.** to copulate; to coit a woman. **4.** copulation [both senses, British and U.S. slang, 1800s-pres.] **5.** a lecher. [1900s and before] **6.** to masturbate. [British slang, 1800s, Farmer and Henley] See also GANG-SHAG.

shag ass to depart in a hurry. *Cf.* CUT ASS, DRAG ASS, HAUL ASS. [U.S. slang, mid 1900s-pres.]

shag-bag (also **shag-rag**) a low, shabby fellow. See SHACK (sense 1). [slang, 1500s-1600s]

shaggy dog a sexually aroused dog; a dog in heat. [U.S. dialect (Ozarks), Randolph and Wilson]

shag-nasty an unpopular man; a villain. *Cf.* SHAG (sense 2). [British and U.S. slang or colloquial, 1900s]

shagstress a sexually loose woman; a FUCKSTRESS (*q.v.*). For synonyms see LAY. [late 1800s, Farmer]

shake 1. to coit a woman. *Cf.* ROCK. [British, 1600s] **2.** a prostitute. **3.** copulation. **4.** to masturbate. [senses 2-4 are British with some U.S. use, 1800s-1900s] See also SHAKES.

shake a cloth in the wind 1. to hang in chains. [British slang, late 1700s, Grose] **2.** to be intoxicated and shaking. See SHAKES. For synonyms see WOOFLED. [possibly nautical in origin; slang, mid 1800s-pres.]

shake a skin-coat to coit a female. *Cf.* SHAKE (sense 1), SKIN-COAT (sense 1). [mid 1600s, (Urquhart)]

shake a sock to urinate. *Cf.* WRING ONE'S SOCK OUT. For synonyms see WHIZ. [U.S. slang, mid 1900s]

shake hands with wife's best friend (also **shake hand's with one's best friend**) to urinate. The "friend" is the penis. [slang, World War II]

shaker a drunkard, especially one with the DELIRIUM TREMENS (*q.v.*). [U.S. slang, 1900s]

shakes 1. a nervous condition; nerves jangled from fear. **2.** the DELIRIUM TREMENS (*q.v.*). [both senses, U.S. slang, mid 1800s-pres.]

shake the dew off the lily (also **shake the lily**) to urinate. *Cf.* WRING THE DEW OFF THE BRANCH. [U.S. slang, early 1900s-pres.]

shake up to masturbate. *Cf.* SHAKE (sense 4). [British slang, 1800s, Farmer and Henley]

shaking of the sheets copulation. For synonyms see SMOCKAGE. [British, 1600s]

shallows, on the naked; half-naked. [slang or cant, early 1800s, Matsell]

sham 1. champagne. [slang, 1800s] **2.** an Irishman. More jocular than derogatory. From SHAMROCK (*q.v.*). For synonyms see HARP. [U.S. slang, 1900s or before] **3.** a policeman. From sense 1 or from SHAMUS (*q.v.*). For synonyms see FLATFOOT. [U.S. slang, early 1900s]

shampoo champagne. From the bubbles. *Cf.* SHAM. [U.S. slang, 1900s]

shamrock a nickname for an Irishman. *Cf.* SHAM (sense 2). [U.S. slang; 1900s or before]

shamus (also **sham, shammus**) a policeman. [from Yiddish; U.S. slang, early 1900s-pres.]

shank 1. a prostitute. See LEG (sense 3). [U.S. slang, mid 1900s-pres.] **2.** a venereal CHANCRE (sense 2).

shanker (also **chancre**) a BUBO (*q.v.*); a venereal CHANCRE (sense 2). [since the 1600s]

shanty a brothel. [slang, 1800s-pres.]

shanty Irish (also **lace-curtain Irish**) poor Irishmen; a derogatory nickname for an Irishman or for the Irish in general. [U.S. slang, 1900s]

share the sexual embrace to copulate. [euphemistic, 1800s]

shark a lawyer. For synonyms see SNOLLYGOSTER. [cant and slang since the 1800s]

shat a past tense of SHIT (*q.v.*). Also somewhat euphemistic for ''shit.'' [dialect and slang, 1800s-1900s]

shat-off angered; PISSED-OFF (*q.v.*). [Australian slang, mid 1900s, *Dictionary of Slang and Unconventional English*]

shatterbrain (also **shatterpate, shitterbrain**) a scatterbrain; an oaf; a giddy person. Possibly cognate with ''shit.'' See SCATTERS. [British 1600s-1700s]

shaved intoxicated with alcohol. *Cf.* HALF-SHAVED. For synonyms see WOOFLED. [late 1500s-pres.]

shaver a small child, usually a male child. [U.S. colloquial, early 1900s-pres.]

shave-tail an immature male; a GREENHORN (*q.v.*); a male yet to grow masculine body hair. *Cf.* BARE-ASSED, HAIRY-ASSED. [U.S. slang and colloquial, late 1800s-pres.]

she 1. the penis. [nonce, 1900s] **2.** the pronoun ''he'' in homosexual use.

sheath 1. the vagina. [since the 1800s

or before] **2.** the foreskin of the penis. [British slang, 1800s. Farmer and Henley] **3.** a condom. *Cf.* MALE SHEATH, SAFETY-SHEATH. For synonyms see EEL-SKIN. [originally medical]

Sheba a sexually attractive and exotic woman. From the ''Queen of Sheba.'' *Cf.* SHEILA. [slang, 1900s]

she-devil 1. a female devil. See DEVIL. **2.** a vile and evil woman. A SPITFIRE (sense 1).

she-dog 1. a bitch; a female dog. *Cf.* LADY-DOG. [colloquial, 1800s if not long before] **2.** to complain. [U.S. slang and colloquial, 1900s or before]

sheeny (also **sheen, sheenie, sheney**) a derogatory nickname for a Jewish man or woman. Considered to be a strongly derisive epithet. For synonyms see FIVE AND TWO. [slang, early 1800s-pres.]

sheeny-destroyer pork. A reference to the Jews' avoidance of pork. *Cf.* SHEENY. [U.S. slang, early 1900s]

sheep buck an avoidance for ''ram.'' *Cf.* RAM (sense 1). [U.S. rural colloquial, 1900s or before]

sheep-herder a PEDERAST (*q.v.*); a man who works sheep from behind. See LAMB (sense 1), which means CATAMITE (*q.v.*). *Cf.* KID LAMB, USHER. [U.S. slang, mid 1900s]

sheepwash inferior alcohol. *Cf.* HOGWASH (sense 4). For synonyms see EMBALMING FLUID. [Australian, 1900s, Baker]

sheet a jocular disguise of SHIT (*q.v.*). *Cf.* SHOOT (sense 3). [U.S. slang, mid 1900s]

sheets 1. bedsheets symbolizing human copulation. Always in a phrase such as SHAKING OF THE SHEETS (*q.v.*), ''lawful sheets,'' and ''nuptial sheets.'' [used frequently by Shakespeare; British, 1600s-1700s] **2.** the drug P.C.P. (*q.v.*). [U.S. drug culture, mid 1900s-pres.] See also TWO SHEETS TO THE WIND.

sheg 1. to annoy someone **2.** to seduce and coit a woman. Both senses, from SHAG (*q.v.*).

she-he an effeminate male; a homosexual male. See SHIM. *Cf.* HERMAPH-RODITE (sense 3). [U.S. slang, mid 1900s, Berrey and Van den Bark]

sheik a suave, sexually attractive male; the Rudolph Valentino type of man. [U.S. slang, early 1900s]

Sheila a young woman; a woman considered sexually. *Cf.* SHEBA. [primarily Australian slang, early 1800s-pres.]

shellacked 1. beaten; severely damaged. **2.** intoxicated with alcohol. *Cf.* VARNISHED. [both senses, U.S. slang, early 1900s-pres.]

shell of hop a container of opium. *Cf.* HOP. [U.S. underworld, early 1900s, *Dictionary of the Underworld*]

shemale a hateful woman; a BITCH (sense 5). [British and U.S. slang, late 1800s-early 1900s]

she-man an effeminate male; possibly a homosexual male. [U.S. slang, mid 1900s, Berrey and Van den Bark]

shicer (also **shice**) **1.** a rotten cheat; a contemptible male. Cognate with SHIT (*q.v.*). **2.** intoxicated with alcohol. See SHICKER. For synonyms see WOOFLED. [both senses, British slang, 1800s]

shick 1. intoxicated with alcohol. See SHICKED, SHICKER, SHICKERED. **2.** a drunkard. [both senses are from Yiddish; Australian slang, 1900s]

shicked (also **shick, shickery**) intoxicated with alcohol. [Australian and U.S. slang, mid 1800s-pres.]

shicker (also **shikker**) **1.** liquor; booze. **2.** intoxicated with alcohol. Also **on the shicker. 3.** a drunkard. [all are Yiddish; since the late 1800s]

shickered intoxicated with alcohol. *Cf.* SHICK (sense 1). [U.S. slang, early 1900s-pres.]

shifter 1. a worthless man; a shiftless man. [colloquial since the 1600s] **2.** a lecher; a man who specializes in SHIFT-WORK (*q.v.*), "copulation." [British slang, 1500s-1800s] **3.** a drunkard. [slang, 1800s]

shift-work (also **shift-service**) copulation; fornication. *Cf.* SMOCK-SERVICE. [British slang, 1800s, Farmer and Henley]

shim a homosexual male; a she-him. *Cf.* HESH, HE-SHE. [U.S. slang, mid 1900s-pres.]

shimmy a dance with pelvic movements simulating copulation. [U.S. slang, early 1900s-pres.]

shine 1. a truncation of MOONSHINE (*q.v.*), homebrewed or inferior liquor. [U.S. slang, early 1900s] **2.** a derogatory nickname for a Negro. *Cf.* SHINY (sense 1). [U.S. slang, early 1900s-pres.]

shined intoxicated with alcohol; done in by MOONSHINE (*q.v.*), *i.e.*, "moonshined." [U.S. slang, early 1900s]

shiny 1. a derogatory nickname for a Negro. *Cf.* SHINE (sense 2). [U.S. slang or colloquial, late 1800s-1900s] **2.** lightly intoxicated with alcohol. Also **shinny.** *Cf.* SHINED. [British and U.S. colloquial, 1800s-1900s]

ship's sodomy. From a generic term for commodities from a ship's store. [British naval slang, 1900s, *Dictionary of Slang and Unconventional English*]

shipwrecked intoxicated with alcohol. For synonyms see WOOFLED. [British slang, late 1800s, Ware]

shishi marijuana; hashish. From "hashishi." [U.S. drug culture, mid 1900s-pres.] See also CHICHI.

shit (also **sh**,s***,s--t**) **1.** diarrhea in cattle. *Cf.* SCATTERS. [*c.* 1000] **2.** to defecate. For synonyms see EASE ONE-SELF. [since the 1300s or before] **3.** fecal excrement. [since the 1500s] **4.** any unwanted junk; nonsense; rubbish. [U.S. slang, mid 1900s-pres.] **5.** heroin; marijuana; illicit drugs. *Cf.* GONG (sense 3). [U.S. drug culture, mid 1900s-pres.] **6.** to vomit. For synonyms see YORK. [British slang, late 1800s, *Dictionary of Slang and Unconventional English*] **7.** to lie. A truncation of BULLSHIT (*q.v.*). [U.S. slang, mid 1900s-pres.] **8.** as an exclamation, "Shit!" **9.** a rotten man; a hateful rascal. Disguises for the word SHIT: BIT HIT, IT-SHAY, SHEET, SHOOT, SKITE, SUGAR, TOM-TIT.

shit, in the in trouble; in a real sticky

mess. [British and later U.S. slang, 1800s-1900s]

shit a brick 1. to defecate an extremely hard stool as after a period of constipation. [British and U.S., 1800s-1900s] **2.** to do something that is recognized to be impossible, especially to show amazement, as in the expression "I could have shit a brick!" [U.S. slang, mid 1900s-pres.]

shit-ass 1. a contemptible person, usually a male. [U.S. slang, mid 1900s-pres.] **2.** pertaining to an undesirable person or matter. [U.S. slang, mid 1900s-pres.]

shit-ass luck very bad luck. [British and U.S. slang, 1900s]

shit-bag the abdomen; the belly; in the plural, the intestines. [slang or colloquial, 1800s-1900s]

shitcan 1. a trash or garbage can. **2.** to gossip about a person; to inform on a person. An elaboration of SHIT (sense 7). [both senses, U.S. slang, mid 1900s-pres.]

shit creek a bad place or a rotten situation; the stream named in the expression "Up shit creek without a paddle." [U.S. slang, mid 1900s-pres.]

shit face an oaf; a fool. Cf. CUNT FACE. [U.S. slang, mid 1900s-pres.]

shit-faced intoxicated with alcohol. Cf. POOPIED. [U.S. slang, mid 1900s-pres.]

shit-fire a bully; a mean rascal; based on SPITFIRE (sense 1); the same as CACAFUEGO (q.v.). [British slang, 1800s, Farmer and Henley]

shit for the birds nonsense. An elaboration of the expression "for the birds." [U.S. slang, mid 1900s]

shit-fuck 1. to copulate anally. **2.** an act of anal copulation. [both senses, 1900s or before]

shit-head a stupid jerk. For synonyms see OAF. [widespread slang and colloquial, 1900s]

shit-hole 1. the anus. **2.** a privy; a latrine. [both senses, British slang, 1800s, Farmer and Henley]

shit-hooks the fingers. Cf. CUNT-HOOKS.

shit-house a privy. For synonyms see AJAX. [slang and colloquial, late 1700s-pres.]

shit-house poet 1. someone who writes on the walls of outhouses or public restrooms. **2.** any very bad poet. From sense 1. [1900s or before]

shit on a shingle a meal of creamed chipped beef on toast. Cf. S.O.S. [U.S. military, World War II]

Shit on it! a rude exclamation; an exclamation of extreme disgust. [U.S. slang, mid 1900s-pres.]

shit on wheels a male who thinks he is the best that there is; a HOT SHIT (q.v.). [U.S. slang, mid 1900s]

Shit or get off the pot! a command for someone to act affirmatively and immediately accomplish the assigned task or give up and let someone else do it. Subject to elaborate euphemism, "If one does not intend to wash up, one should not monopolize the ablution facilities." [slang and colloquial, 1900s or before]

shit out of luck luckless; having only bad luck. Cf. S.O.L. [slang, mid 1900s-pres.]

shit-pot a deceitful and worthless person. [slang, 1800s, Farmer and Henley]

shits, the (also **shits**) diarrhea. For synonyms see QUICKSTEP. [U.S. colloquial, mid 1900s-pres.]

shit-sack a really rotten rascal. [British slang, late 1700s, Grose]

shit-scared terribly frightened; frightened enough to defecate in one's pants. Cf. SCARED SHITLESS. [British and U.S. slang, 1900s]

shit-shark the man who empties the CESSPIT (q.v.); a cleaner of privies. Cf. HONEY-DIPPER, TOM TURDMAN. [British slang, 1800s, Farmer and Henley]

shit-stick 1. a worthless oaf; a real jerk. **2.** a stick or cylinder of fecal material; the same as SEPTIC-STICK (q.v.). [both senses, U.S. slang, mid 1900s-pres.]

shitter 1. a toilet; a W.C. Cf. CRAPPER

(sense 1). **2.** a BULLSHITTER (*q.v.*); a liar or a braggart. *Cf.* CRAPPER (sense 2). For synonyms see BULLER. [both senses, U.S. slang, mid 1900s-pres.]

shitterbrain a scatterbrain. [British slang, 1800s, Farmer and Henley]

shitters diarrhea. *Cf.* SCATTERS. [1800s]

shitty lousy; really bad. [U.S. slang, mid 1900s-pres.]

shit-word a dirty word; a term of abuse. [since the 1200s]

Shiver my timbers! a mild, mock oath and an exclamation. [U.S. slang, 1900s or before]

shlemiel See SCHLEMIEL.

shlimazl a chronically unlucky person. *Cf.* SCHLEMOZZLE, SCHLIMAZL. [Yiddish]

shlub an oaf; a jerk. See SCHLUB. [from Yiddish; U.S. slang, 1900s]

shmeck heroin. See SCHMECK.

shmendrick an oaf. See SCHMENDRICH.

shmo an oaf. See SCHMOE.

shmuck **1.** a jerk. **2.** the penis. See SCHMUCK (sense 1). [both senses are Yiddish]

shnook an oaf. See SCHNOOK.

shoe a sanitary napkin; a PERINEAL PAD (*q.v.*). [Australian euphemism, mid 1900s, *Dictionary of Slang and Unconventional English*]

shoe-horn to CUCKOLD (*q.v.*). *Cf.* HORN (sense 2). [British, mid 1600s]

shonky (also **shonk, shonkey**) a trader or a peddler; a derogatory term for a Jewish merchant. *Cf.* SHONNICKER. For synonyms see FIVE AND TWO. [British and later U.S. slang, 1800s-1900s]

shonnicker (also **shon, shonnacker, shonniker**) a derogatory nickname for a Jewish man. [U.S. slang, mid 1900s]

shoon a fool; a bumpkin; a lout. Possibly based on an obsolete past tense of "shine." [cant, 1800s]

shoot **1.** to ejaculate. *Cf.* SHOOT OFF, SHOOT WHITE. For synonyms see MELT. [colloquial and slang, since the 1800s or before] **2.** to have a wet dream. [since the late 1800s] **3.** a euphemism

for SHIT! (sense 8). [British and U.S. slang, 1900s or before] **4.** to have diarrhea.

shoot a bishop to have a wet dream. The bishop's miter resembles the glans penis. *Cf.* POLICEMAN'S HELMET. [British slang, 1800s, Farmer and Henley]

shoot a lion to retire to urinate. A reason given for going outdoors to urinate, said by males. Possibly a play on "line" as a line or stream of urine. [British, 1800s]

shoot between wind and water 1. to coit a woman. **2.** to infect with a venereal disease. Both are from a nautical expression describing a weak zone in the hull of a ship. [both senses, British slang, 1700s or before]

shoot ducks to empty chamber pots. [U.S. slang, early 1900s or before, Weseen]

shooter's hill the female genitals; the *mons veneris*. *Cf.* SHOOT (sense 1), "ejaculate." [British slang, 1800s, Farmer and Henley]

shooting submarines defecating. As if one were bombing imaginary submarines in the toilet bowl. [mostly juvenile use; U.S., mid 1900s]

shoot in the bush to ejaculate prematurely. *Cf.* FIRE IN THE AIR. [British slang, 1700s]

shoot in the tail 1. to coit a woman. **2.** to commit PEDERASTY (*q.v.*). [both senses, British slang, 1800s, Farmer and Henley]

shoot off to ejaculate. *Cf.* SHOOT (sense 1). [U.S. slang, mid 1900s-pres.]

shoot one's cookies (also **shoot one's breakfast, shoot one's dinner, shoot one's lunch, shoot one's supper**) to vomit. For synonyms see YORK. [U.S. slang, early 1900s-pres.]

shoot one's milt to ejaculate. For synonyms see MELT. [British slang, 1800s, Farmer and Henley]

shoot one's roe to ejaculate. "Soft roe" is fish sperm. [British slang, 1800s, Farmer and Henley]

shoot one's wad 1. to ejaculate. **2.** to

copulate. [both senses, U.S. slang, mid 1900s-pres.]

shoot over the stubble to ejaculate prematurely. *Cf.* SHOOT IN THE BUSH. [British slang, 1800s, Farmer and Henley]

shoot rabbits to release intestinal gas. For synonyms see GURK. [colloquial euphemism, 1900s]

shoot the bull (also **shoot the crap, shoot the shit**) to chat and gossip. [U.S. slang, early 1900s-pres.]

shoot the cat to vomit. *Cf.* CAT, JERK THE CAT, WHIP THE CAT. [British and U.S. slang, early 1800s-1900s]

shoot the works to vomit. For synonyms see YORK. [U.S. slang, early 1900s]

shoot white to ejaculate. *Cf.* SHOOT (sense 1). [British slang, late 1800s, *Dictionary of Slang and Unconventional English*]

shop-door (also **barn-door**) the trouser fly. [colloquial, late 1800s-1900s]

shore dinner a homosexual male viewed by a sailor who would like to EAT (*q.v.*) him; a sailor whom a homosexual male would like to fellate on shore. *Cf.* SEAFOOD.

short 1. a SHORT SNORT (*q.v.*) of a drug, usually cocaine. **2.** to sniff or snort heroin or cocaine. *Cf.* SNORT (sense 2). [both senses, U.S. drug culture, mid 1900s-pres.]

short and curly the pubic hair. *Cf.* CURLIES, SHORT HAIRS.

short-arm the penis. *Cf.* CUTTY-GUN, GUN, PISTOL, SHORT-ARM INSPECTION. [U.S. military, World War II and general slang, mid 1900s-pres.]

short-arm drill a penile inspection for venereal disease. Probably also used to mean "copulation." See SHORT-ARM PRACTICE. [U.S. slang, mid 1900s]

short-arm heist rape. [U.S. underworld, mid 1900s, Goldin, O'Leary, and Lipsius]

short-arm inspection a penile inspection for venereal disease. *Cf.*

DANGLE-PARADE. [British and U.S. slang, World Wars]

short-arm practice copulation. Based on an expression for target practice with a pistol. *Cf.* SHORT-ARM. [U.S. military slang, mid 1900s]

short hairs the pubic hairs. Euphemistically defined as "the short hairs at the nape of the neck." *Cf.* SHORT AND CURLY. [British and U.S. slang, 1900s]

short out of luck a euphemism for SHIT OUT OF LUCK (*q.v.*). *Cf.* S.O.L. [U.S., 1900s]

short-skirted pregnant. The swelling makes skirts appear to be shorter. *Cf.* APRON-UP. For synonyms see FRAGRANT. [British slang, 1800s, Farmer and Henley]

short snort a dose of a drug taken by inhalation. Usually cocaine. [U.S. drug culture, 1900s]

shot 1. intoxicated with alcohol. [slang, late 1800s-pres.] **2.** an ejaculation of semen. [colloquial and slang, 1800s-pres.] **3.** a corpse. [British slang, 1800s, Farmer and Henley]

shot-away intoxicated with alcohol. For synonyms see WOOFLED. [British slang, 1800s]

shot for shot mutual PENILINGUS (*q.v.*). See SHOT (sense 2). [U.S. underworld, mid 1900s, Goldin, O'Leary, and Lipsius]

shot full of holes heavily intoxicated with alcohol. An elaboration of SHOT (sense 1). [widespread slang, 1900s or before]

shot in the giblets (also **shot in the tail**) pregnant. See GIBLETS (sense 2), SHOT (sense 2), TAIL (sense 1). [British slang, 1800s, Farmer and Henley]

shot in the neck intoxicated with alcohol. [U.S. slang, 1800s-1900s]

shot tower a toilet. For synonyms see W.C. [U.S. slang, early 1900s]

shot 'twixt wind and water infected with a venereal disease. See SHOOT BETWEEN WIND AND WATER. [British, 1600s]

shot-up 1. intoxicated with alcohol. **2.**

intoxicated with narcotics. [both senses, U.S., mid 1900s-pres.]

shouse a privy. A blend of "shit" and "house." [Australian slang, mid 1900s-pres.]

shove 1. an act of copulation. **2.** to copulate; the same as PUSH (sense 1). [slang since the 1600s]

Shove it! a curse, "Shove it up your ass!" [widespread slang, mid 1900s-pres.]

shovel the shit to lie or boast excessively; to bring on loads of BULLSHIT (*q.v.*). [U.S. slang, early 1900s-pres.]

show 1. the appearance of blood at the onset of the menses. [British and U.S. colloquial, 1800s-1900s] **2.** a small mass of blood-tinged mucus indicating the onset of labor. [colloquial, 1500s and before]

show-and-tell pants very tightly fitting men's pants which reveal the outlines of the genitals. *Cf.* BASKET DAYS. [U.S. slang, mid 1900s]

showcase nigger a token Negro employee. [U.S. slang, mid 1900s]

show drink (also **show one's drink**) to be or act intoxicated with alcohol. [U.S. slang, 1900s]

shower-cap 1. a condom. For synonyms see EEL-SKIN. **2.** a birth control diaphragm. For synonyms see B.C. [both senses, U.S. slang, mid 1900s-pres.]

shrew 1. a wicked rascal; a vexatious person of either sex. [1300s-1400s] **2.** the devil; Satan. For synonyms see FIEND. [1300s, (Chaucer)] **3.** a scolding woman; a virago; a hellcat of a woman. [since the 1500s]

shrimp queen a male who derives special pleasure from fondling or kissing someone's feet. "Shrimp" refers to the shape of the toes, the odor of unclean feet, or both. *Cf.* FOOT QUEEN, TOE QUEEN. See QUEEN for similar subjects. [U.S. homosexual use, mid 1900s]

shrink a psychoanalyst or psychotherapist. [U.S. slang and colloquial, 1900s] Synonyms: ANALYST, BUG, BUG DOC-

TOR, COUCH-DOCTOR, COUCH-JOB, DOME-DOCTOR, HEAD-SHRINKER, NUTPICK.

shrubbery the pubic hair, especially the female pubic hair. [slang or colloquial, 1800s-1900s]

shtup 1. to coit; to fornicate; to copulate. Literally, "push." **2.** copulation. **3.** a sexually easy woman. *Cf.* FUCK-STRESS. [all senses, from Yiddish; U.S. slang, mid 1900s-pres.]

shuck 1. a derogatory nickname for a Mexican. [U.S. slang, mid 1900s] **2.** a euphemism for BULLSHIT (*q.v.*). See SHUCKS! [U.S. slang, mid 1900s-pres.]

Shucks! (also **Aw shucks!**) a mild exclamation; possibly a euphemism for "Shit!" This has become a stereotypical expression used by a shy, awkward rustic. [U.S. colloquial, mid 1800s-pres.]

shuffle off this mortal coil (also **shuffle off**) to die. [U.S. colloquial, early 1900s-pres.]

shuttle-brain (also **shuttle-head, shuttle-wit**) an oaf; a dullard. [colloquial, 1500s and before]

shuttle-butt a female with extremely large posteriors. A play on "scuttle-butt." [U.S. slang, mid 1900s-pres., Underwood]

shvance the penis. See SCHWANZ.

shy-cock a coward. From COCK (sense 3 or 5). [British slang, late 1700s, Grose]

sick 1. having the menses. *Cf.* UNWELL. For synonyms see FLOODS. **2.** to vomit. *Cf.* SICK UP. [U.S. colloquial, 1900s] **3.** mentally ill; pertaining to a delight in horror, sexual perversions, or the plight of the physically handicapped. [U.S. slang and colloquial, mid 1900s-pres.]

sick up (also **sick**) to vomit. For synonyms see YORK. [U.S. colloquial, 1900s and before]

side dish a mistress, in the sense of "something extra." *Cf.* DISH (sense 2). [U.S. slang, mid 1900s]

side-slip a bastard; an illegitimate child. For synonyms see ACCIDENT. [British colloquial, late 1800s]

side-wind a bastard; an illegitimate

child. [British slang or colloquial, early 1800s or before]

side-wipe a bastard; an illegitimate child. [U.S. colloquial, 1800s]

siege 1. a privy. For synonyms see AJAX. [1400s] **2.** to defecate. [mid 1400s] **3.** dung; feces. [mid 1500s] **4.** the anus. [mid 1500s] All are from an obsolete sense of "siege," meaning "seat." *Cf.* STOOL.

siff (also **siph, syph**) syphilis. For synonyms see SPECIFIC STOMACH. [U.S. slang, mid 1900s-pres.]

sigma phi (also **sigma**) syphilis. [British slang, early 1900s, *Dictionary of Slang and Unconventional English*]

silent beard the female pubic hair. For synonyms see DOWNSHIRE. [British, 1700s or before]

silent flute the penis with a reference to FELLATIO (*q.v.*). *Cf.* FLUTE, PICCOLO, SKIN FLUTE, all of which mean "penis." [British slang, late 1700s, Grose]

silk a Caucasian. For synonyms see PECKERWOOD. [U.S. black use, mid 1900s-pres.]

silk broad a Caucasian woman. [U.S. black use, mid 1900s-pres.]

silken twine wine. Rhyming slang for "wine." [U.S. slang, mid 1900s, Berrey and Van den Bark]

silly milk any alcoholic drink. *Cf.* LONDON MILK. [U.S. slang, early 1900s, Rose]

silo drippings real or imaginary alcohol obtained by tapping the base of a silo containing fermenting corn. [U.S. rural colloquial]

simon a simpleton; a simple simon. Sometimes capitalized. [colloquial, 1800s-1900s]

Simon Legree a strict taskmaster; a "slave driver." From a character in *Uncle Tom's Cabin*, by Harriet Beecher Stowe. [U.S. colloquial, mid 1800s-pres.]

simp an oaf; a simpleton. [U.S. slang, early 1900s-pres.]

simple infanticide masturbation. *Cf.*

HIGHER MALTHUSIANISM. [British slang, 1800s, Farmer and Henley]

sin-bin (also **cock-wagon**) a van, especially one fitted with bedding as a place for necking and copulation. [U.S. slang, mid 1900s]

sin-hiders trousers. Because they conceal the private parts. [British, early 1900s, *Dictionary of the Underworld*]

sin-hound a chaplain; a parson. For synonyms see SKY-PILOT. [U.S. slang, early 1900s]

sink in to coit a woman; to penetrate a woman. [colloquial and nonce, since the 1600s or before]

sink the soldier to coit a woman. [British slang, 1900s, *Dictionary of Slang and Unconventional English*]

sinner 1. anyone who commits a SIN (sense 2). [since the 1300s, *Oxford English Dictionary*] **2.** a prostitute. For synonyms see HARLOT. [British, early 1600s]

sinsemilla marijuana; seedless marijuana. [U.S. drug culture, mid 1900s-pres.]

sin-sister a prostitute. For synonyms see HARLOT. [U.S. slang, early 1900s]

siph syphilis. *Cf.* SIFF. [U.S. slang, mid 1900s-pres.]

Sir Berkeley Hunt the female genitals. Rhyming slang for "cunt." An elaboration of BERKELEY HUNT (*q.v.*). [British slang, 1800s]

Sir Harry a chamber pot; a covered chamber pot. *Cf.* CLOSE STOOL. [British slang or colloquial, 1800s]

Sir Martin Wagstaff the erect penis personified. *Cf.* STAFF. For synonyms see ERECTION. [mid 1600s, (Urquhart)]

sirrah (also **sirah**) a contemptuous or jesting form of address to one's inferior. [British, 1500s-1800s]

sirreverence 1. a request for a pardon for an offensive statement. From "save reverence," similar to PARDON MY FRENCH (*q.v.*). [British, 1300s-1800s] **2.** a lump of excrement. [colloquial, 1500s]

Sir Walter Scott 1. a CHAMBER POT

(*q.v.*). Rhyming slang for "pot." [British slang with some U.S. use, 1800s] **2.** a vessel of beer. Rhyming slang for "pot." [British slang, 1800s, Farmer and Henley]

sis 1. a nickname for one's sister. No negative connotations. [U.S. colloquial, 1900s] **2.** a weak or effeminate boy; a cry baby. [U.S. slang and colloquial, 1900s] **3.** a homosexual male. For synonyms see EPICENE. [U.S. slang, mid 1900s-pres.] **4.** urine. Rhyming slang for "piss." [U.S. juvenile, 1900s]

sissified effeminate or homosexual. [British and U.S., 1900s]

sissy 1. a coward. **2.** a weak or effeminate boy. **3.** a homosexual male. [all since the late 1800s]

sissy-beater a sadistic male who derives special pleasure from beating up homosexual males. *Cf.* LEATHER (sense 2), ROUGH TRADE. [U.S. homosexual use, mid 1900s-pres., Farrell]

sissy beer beer with very low alcohol content. *Cf.* NEAR BEER, SQUAW PISS. [U.S. slang, early 1900s]

sissy-britches an effeminate male; a SISSY (sense 2). For synonyms see FRIBBLE. [U.S. slang or colloquial, 1900s]

sister 1. a prostitute. *Cf.* SIN-SISTER. [British, early 1600s] **2.** among homosexual males, one's pal or fellow. See SHE (sense 2). [U.S. homosexual use, mid 1900s-pres.] **3.** a black woman. [U.S. black use, mid 1900s-pres.] **4.** a supporter of women's movements; from the viewpoint of women's movements, any woman. [U.S. slang, mid 1900s-pres.] **5.** morphine. *Cf.* BROTHER (sense 1). For synonyms see MORPH. [U.S. drug culture, mid 1900s-pres.]

sisterhood prostitution. [British slang, early 1800s, Farmer and Henley]

sister-in-law a euphemistic name given to a prostitute by her pimp. [U.S. underworld, mid 1900s, Goldin, O'Leary, and Lipsius]

sister of mercy a prostitute. For synonyms see HARLOT. [U.S. slang, mid 1900s]

sitter the posteriors. For synonyms see DUFF. [U.S. colloquial euphemism, 1900s]

sitting-room the posteriors. From the term for a parlor or a living room. [British and U.S. slang and nonce, 1800s-1900s]

sit-upons 1. the posteriors. **2.** trousers. [both senses, British colloquial, 1800s] **3.** cushions for sitting. Usually in the singular. No negative connotations. [U.S. slang or colloquial, 1900s]

sit up with a sick friend a reason given for a spouse's absence from home. Assumed to be an excuse for a debauch of some type. [British and U.S. colloquial, mid 1800s-pres.]

siwash 1. a nickname (usually derogatory) for an American Indian. For synonyms see REDSKIN. [U.S. slang or colloquial, 1900s or before] **2.** any unclean or rude person. [U.S. underworld, early 1900s]

six-by-four toilet paper. From the size of the sheets in inches. [British military, late 1800s-early 1900s, *Dictionary of Slang and Unconventional English*]

six-pack to pass time or accompany some other act while consuming approximately six beers. Can also refer to the similar consumption of other alcoholic drinks.

six-to-four a prostitute. Rhyming slang for "whore." [British slang, 1900s]

sixty-nine (also **soixanteneuf, 69**) mutual PENILINGUS or CUNNILINGUS (both *q.v.*); simultaneous penilingus and cunnilingus. Used for both heterosexual and homosexual acts. *Cf.* FLIP-FLOP, LOOP-DE-LOOP. From the interlocking image of the numerals, 69. [U.S. slang, mid 1900s-pres.]

sixty-three a nonorthogenital sex act; a "sexual variant" (Montelone). Similar to SIXTY-NINE (*q.v.*), but the exact nature of the act cannot be determined. Possibly in error for SIXTY-NINE (*q.v.*). [attested as U.S. underworld, mid 1900s, Montelone]

size queen a homosexual male who is

particularly attracted to men with large penes, or to the penes themselves. Possibly from "queen size," a bed and mattress size designation. See QUEEN for similar topics. [U.S. homosexual use, mid 1900s-pres.]

sizzle to be electrocuted; to die in the electric chair. [U.S. underworld slang, mid 1900s] See also DAD.

skag an ugly and unpleasant young woman. For synonyms see BUFFARILLA. See SCAG (sense 1).

skalawag (also **skallywag**) a rascal; a little devil. [U.S. colloquial, 1900s]

skamas opium. For synonyms see OPE. [U.S. underworld, early 1900s or before]

skat a formed mass of feces. A word used when a word like "turd" is required but forbidden. Also in compounds like "bear-skat" and "dog-skat." [from the Greek combining form *skatos*, "dung"; U.S., 1900s]

skee whisky. From "whiskee." See SKY (sense 3). [U.S. slang, early 1900s]

skibby 1. a derogatory nickname for a Japanese, a Chinese, or any Oriental. [U.S. slang, early 1900s-pres.] **2.** an Oriental concubine or mistress. [U.S. underworld and slang, early 1900s]

skillet a derogatory nickname for a Negro. From a black iron skillet. [U.S. slang, 1900s or before]

skimished intoxicated with alcohol. From ISHKIMMISK (*q.v.*). For synonyms see WOOFLED.

skin 1. the prepuce of the penis. A truncation of "foreskin." [British, 1800s] **2.** to remove one's clothing; to strip. [British and U.S. colloquial, mid 1800s-pres.] **3.** a condom. *Cf.* EEL-SKIN, FROG-SKIN. [U.S. slang, mid 1900s-pres.] **4.** sexually attractive women; women considered sexually, as in "some skin." **5.** an act of copulation. [senses 4 and 5 are U.S. slang, 1900s]

skin a goat to vomit. Partly from the odor of vomitus. [U.S. colloquial, 1900s]

skin-coat 1. the female genitals, in the expression SHAKE A SKIN-COAT (*q.v.*). [1600s, (Urquhart)] **2.** one's skin;

the epidermis. [U.S. colloquial, 1900s or before]

skin-diver 1. a male copulating; the penis. [U.S. slang, mid 1900s-pres.] **2.** a fellator or fellatrix. *Cf.* MUFF-DIVER. [U.S. slang, mid 1900s-pres.]

skin-dog a lecher. See CUNT-HOUND. *Cf.* SKIN (sense 4). [attested as Canadian slang, mid 1900s, *Dictionary of Slang and Unconventional English*]

skin-flick a movie focusing on nudity or sex; a movie with nude scenes; a pornographic film or an X-rated film. [U.S. slang, mid 1900s-pres.]

skin flute the penis; the erect penis in reference to FELLATIO (*q.v.*). *Cf.* FLUTE, PICCOLO. [U.S. slang, mid 1900s]

skin-heist a rape. From SKIN (sense 5). *Cf.* SHORT-ARM HEIST. [U.S. underworld slang, mid 1900s, Goldin, O'Leary, and Lipsius]

skin-house a movie theatre featuring films of nude women or pornographic films. [U.S. slang, mid 1900s-pres.]

skin-mag (also **skin-magazine**) a magazine featuring male or female nudes. [U.S. slang, mid 1900s-pres.]

skinny 1. a girl or a woman. [Australian slang, early 1900s, Baker] **2.** marijuana. [U.S. drug culture, mid 1900s-pres.]

skinny-dip 1. to swim in the nude. **2.** a nude swim. [both senses, U.S. colloquial, mid 1900s-pres.]

skin-popping shooting drugs; injecting narcotics. [U.S. drug culture and slang, mid 1900s-pres.]

skin the live rabbit 1. to retract the prepuce of the uncircumcised male, presumably in copulation. See LIVE RABBIT. *Cf.* PEEL ONE'S BEST END. [British slang, 1800s, Farmer and Henley] **2.** to undress; to undress someone; to take the clothing off of a child. No negative connotations. [U.S. slang, 1900s]

skin-the-pizzle the female genitals, specifically the vagina. The PIZZLE (sense 2) is the penis. [British slang, 1800s, Farmer and Henley]

skip out to die. [British slang and colloquial, early 1900s]

skippy 1. an Oriental prostitute. From SKIBBY (sense 2). [U.S. slang, 1900s] **2.** a homosexual male. [U.S. black use, 1900s, Major]

skirt 1. a woman; women considered sexually; a sexually loose woman. **2.** a prostitute. [both since the 1500s]

skirt-foist a lecher, a lifter of skirts. [British, mid 1600s]

skirt-man 1. a pimp; a seller of skirts. See SKIRT (sense 2). [U.S. underworld, early 1900s] **2.** a man who prefers women in skirts rather than in trousers. [U.S. slang, mid 1900s-pres.]

skirt-patrol the search for a woman for romantic or sexual purposes. [military and later general slang, 1900s]

skit 1. diarrhea, especially that in animals. Cognate with SHIT (q.v.). Cf. SCATTERS. [British rural colloquial, 1400s-1800s] **2.** beer. From the gastrointestinal problems resulting from drinking bad beer. For synonyms see SUDS. [British military, early 1900s, Fraser and Gibbons]

skite 1. an early form of SHIT (q.v.). [mid 1400s] **2.** a braggart; a disgusting or unpleasant person. Cognate with SHIT (q.v.), but not as restricted in its use. Cf. BLATHERSKITE. [British colloquial, early 1800s]

skitterbrain a giddy person; an oaf. Probably cognate with SHIT (q.v.). [British, 1800s or before]

skivvies underwear; men's underwear, especially long underwear. [U.S. slang, mid 1900s-pres.]

sklook (also **plook**) to copulate. For synonyms see OCCUPY. [U.S. slang, early 1900s]

skoofer (also **skoofus, skrufer, skrufus**) a marijuana cigarette. Cf. SKAMAS. [U.S. drug culture, mid 1900s-pres.]

skull-job an act of CUNNILINGUS (q.v.). Cf. HEAD-JOB. [U.S. slang, mid 1900s-pres.]

skunk 1. a mean and hateful person. [U.S. slang and colloquial, early 1800s-pres.] **2.** an ugly and unpleasant young woman. [U.S. slang, mid

1900s-pres.] **3.** a derogatory nickname for a Negro. From the black fur of the skunk. [U.S. slang, early 1900s]

skuttywuck an attractive young woman; a sexy girl. Cf. SCUT (sense 3). [U.S. slang, mid 1900s, Berrey and Van den Bark]

sky 1. an unpleasant person; one's enemy. Possibly from SKITE (q.v.). [British slang, mid 1800s, Hotten] **2.** a derogatory nickname for an Italian. [Australian, early 1900s, Baker] Synonyms for sense 2: DINGBAT, DINO, EYTIES, EYTO, GHIN, GINGO, GINNEY, GINZO, GREASER, GUIN, GUINEA, GUINIE, GUINNEE, HIKES, ITE, ORGAN-GRINDER, RING-TAIL, SPAGHETTI, SPAGHETTI-BENDER, SPIC, WALLIYO, WOP, ZOOL. **3.** whisky. From "whisky." Cf. SKEE. [widespread slang, 1900s]

sky-pilot a preacher; a chaplain; an evangelist or a missionary. [British and U.S. slang, late 1800s-pres.] Synonyms: AMEN SNORTER, BIBLE-BANGER, BIBLE-BASHER, BIBLE-POUNDER, BIBLE-PUNCHER, BIBLE-THUMPER, BISH, BLACK COAT, CHIMNEY SWEEP, CHRISTER, CUSHION-THUMPER, DEVIL-CATCHER, DEVIL-CHASER, DEVIL-DODGER, DEVIL-DRIVER, DEVIL-PITCHER, DEVIL-SCOLDER, DEVIL-TEASER, DIVINE, DOMINIE, FIRE ESCAPE, FIRE INSURANCE AGENT, GLUEPOT, GOD-BOTHERER, GOSPEL-COVE, GOSPEL-GRINDER, GOSPEL-POSTILION, GOSPEL-PUSHER, GOSPEL-SHARK, GOSPEL-SHARP, GOSPEL-SHOOTER, GOSPEL-WHANGER, HAUL-DEVIL, HEAD CLERK OF THE DOXOLOGY-WORKS, HOLY-JOE!, JESUS-SCREAMER, JESUS-SHOUTER, MAN-IN-BLACK, MAN OF THE CLOTH, PADRE, PARISH-BULL, PARISH-PRIG, PARSON, POUND-TEXT, PULPIT-CUFFER, PUZZLE-TEXT, SALVATION-RANCHER, SIN-HOUND, SKY-RIDER, SKY-SCOUT, SNUB-DEVIL, SOUL-AVIATOR, SOUL-DOCTOR, SOUL-DRIVER, SPIRITUAL FLESH-BROKER, TICKLE-TEXT.

skyrocket an amphetamine tablet or capsule. Cf. ROCKET, ROCKET-FUEL. For synonyms see AMP. [U.S. drug culture, mid 1900s-pres.]

slack 1. to urinate. [British slang, 1800s, Farmer and Henley] **2.** a slovenly man or woman; a sexually loose woman. [Caribbean (Jamaican). Cassidy and Le Page]

slacks trousers. For synonyms see GAL-LIGASKINS. [U.S. colloquial, 1900s]

slant a derogatory nickname for any Oriental. From the shape of the Oriental eyes. *Cf.* SRANT. [U.S. slang, mid 1900s-pres.]

slant-eye (also **slant-eyes**) a derogatory nickname for an Oriental. [U.S. underworld and slang, early 1900s-pres.]

slap artist a sadist; a man who achieves erection (or orgasm) while beating or slapping a woman. [early 1900s, *Dictionary of the Underworld*]

slash 1. to urinate. *Cf.* SPLASH. For synonyms see WHIZ. **2.** urination; an act of urination. [both senses, British slang, 1900s, *Dictionary of Slang and Unconventional English*]

slashers the testicles. For synonyms see WHIRLYGIGS. [British slang, mid 1900s, *Dictionary of Slang and Unconventional English*]

slattern a carelessly dressed and sloppy woman; a dirty or sloppy housekeeper. Occasionally there is some reference to low manners or other negative characteristics. [since the early 1600s]

slaughter-house a brothel. *Cf.* CUT (sense 3), MEAT (sense 2). [British slang, 1900s, *Dictionary of Slang and Unconventional English*]

sleep around to be sexually promiscuous. [somewhat euphemistic; U.S. slang, mid 1900s-pres.]

sleeper a barbiturate or nonbarbiturate capsule or tablet. [U.S. slang and drug culture, mid 1900s-pres.]

sleep with to copulate with someone; to copulate with someone illicitly. This may or may not involve a period of time as long as a night and may or may not involve sleep. *Cf.* GO TO BED WITH. [U.S. colloquial euphemism, mid 1900s-pres.]

sleez a slut; a woman of very low character. From the adjective "sleazy." [U.S. slang, mid 1900s, *Current Slang*]

sleighride a cocaine party; the act of taking cocaine and being under its influence. From the SNOW (sense 2) theme. [U.S. drug culture, early 1900s-pres.]

slewed (also **slewy, slued**) intoxicated with alcohol. From a nautical term applied to a ship changing her tack. [British and U.S. slang, early 1800s-pres.]

slewther to penetrate a woman sexually with the finger. *Cf.* FINGER-FUCK. [British slang, 1800s, Farmer and Henley]

slick-chick 1. an attractive and cute young woman. [U.S. slang, mid 1900s-pres.] **2.** a sexually aroused woman. [U.S. slang, mid 1900s-pres.]

slightly-tightly mildly intoxicated with alcohol. For synonyms see WOOFLED. [British slang, late 1800s-early 1900s, Ware]

slim-dilly a girl or woman. [Australian, 1900s, Baker]

slime 1. semen. For synonyms see METTLE. [British slang, 1800s, *Dictionary of Slang and Unconventional English*] **2.** a worthless person; a low and wretched person. [U.S. slang, mid 1900s-pres.] **3.** pornography; low entertainment; degrading matters.

slimy, old the penis. For synonyms see YARD. [British, 1800s, Farmer and Henley]

sling a cat to vomit. *Cf.* CAT (sense 7), JERK THE CAT, WHIP THE CAT. [British and U.S. slang, 1800s-1900s]

sling a snot (also **sling**) to blow one's nose without a handkerchief. [British and U.S. slang and colloquial, mid 1800s-1900s]

sling one's hook to die. From an idiom meaning "depart." [British slang, mid 1800s]

sling one's jelly (also **sling one's juice**) to masturbate. *Cf.* JELLY (sense 3), JUICE (sense 1). [British slang, 1800s, Farmer and Henley]

sling the crap (also **sling the bull**) to tell tall tales or to lie; to BULLSHIT (*q.v.*). [U.S. slang, mid 1900s-pres.]

slip her a length to copulate with a woman. The "length" is the penis. [widespread slang, 1800s-1900s]

slip into to coit; to penetrate a woman. [British and U.S. colloquial, 1900s and before]

slit the female genitals; the clitoris (possibly in error); the PUDENDAL CLEAVAGE (*q.v.*). *Cf.* GASH (sense 1). [widespread recurrent nonce; slang since the mid 1600s]

slithery copulation. For synonyms see SMOCKAGE. [British slang, 1900s, *Dictionary of Slang and Unconventional English*]

slobber nonsense. From the term for a drivel of saliva running out of the mouth. [U.S. colloquial, 1900s or before]

slobberation a kiss; a messy kiss; kissing in general. A "slobbering celebration." [slang, early 1900s]

slommacky slovenly; sloppy. [U.S. colloquial, 1900s or before]

slommocks a slattern. [British dialect, 1800s, Northall]

sloop of war a prostitute. Rhyming slang for "whore," possibly from "frigate," *i.e.*, FRIG IT! (*q.v.*). [slang, 1800s]

slop-chute the anus. *Cf.* DIRT-CHUTE. [U.S. slang, mid 1900s]

slopdozzle a careless person; a sloppy person. [U.S. colloquial, 1900s or before]

slope (also **slopie**) an Oriental. A derogatory nickname. From the shape of the Oriental eyes. *Cf.* SLANT. [U.S. military and general slang, mid 1900s-pres.]

slop jar a CHAMBER POT (*q.v.*). [U.S. colloquial, 1900s or before]

slopped-over (also **slopped, slopped-up**) intoxicated with alcohol. For synonyms see WOOFLED. [U.S. slang and colloquial, early 1900s]

slopped to the ears intoxicated with alcohol. [U.S. slang, mid 1900s, Deak]

sloppy-drunk (also **sloppy**) intoxicated with alcohol. *Cf.* DIRTY-DRUNK. [U.S. slang, late 1800s-1900s]

sloppy seconds an act of copulation wherein the vagina of the woman still contains the spendings of a previous copulation. *Cf.* BUTTERED BUN. [U.S. slang, mid 1900s]

sloppy sex casual sex; nonorthogenital sex. [U.S. slang, mid 1900s-pres.]

slops 1. wide breeches. [British colloquial, early 1600s] **2.** any liquid household refuse, the contents of a chamber pot. *Cf.* SLOP JAR. [colloquial, early 1800s-1900s]

slosh alcohol; a drink of alcohol. [British and U.S. slang, late 1800s-1900s]

sloshed intoxicated with alcohol. For synonyms see WOOFLED. [U.S. slang since the early 1900s or before]

sloshed to the ears intoxicated with alcohol. [U.S. slang, mid 1900s]

slot the female genitals; the PUDENDAL CLEAVAGE (*q.v.*). [widespread recurrent nonce; slang, 1800s-1900s]

slotted-job a woman. From SLOT (*q.v.*). [British slang, early 1900s]

slouch an oaf; a lazy, worthless dullard. [U.S. colloquial, 1900s]

sloughed intoxicated with alcohol. See SLEWED. [U.S. slang and colloquial, mid 1900s]

sloven 1. a person of low repute; a mean rascal. [since the 1400s] **2.** a slatternly woman. [since the 1800s or before]

slow 1. slow to become sexually interested or aroused. *Cf.* FAST. [British and U.S. colloquial, 1800s-pres.] **2.** stupid. [colloquial since the 1800s]

slubberdegullion (also **slabberdegullion, slobberdegullion**) a heavy, stupid, oafish fellow. [colloquial, 1600s-1700s]

sludge 1. solid fecal waste in sewage. [since the late 1800s] **2.** nonsense. An avoidance for BULLSHIT (*q.v.*). *Cf.* BILGE (sense 1). [U.S. slang, 1900s]

slug 1. a globule of mucus from the nose. [U.S. slang or colloquial, 1900s] **2.** the penis. [Australian military slang, early 1900s, Baker]

slugged intoxicated with alcohol. For synonyms see WOOFLED. [U.S. slang, mid 1900s-pres.]

slum-bum a low thief; a beggar. [U.S. underworld, mid 1900s, Goldin, O'Leary, and Lipsius]

slummocks (also **slamakin, slamikin, slamkin, slammakin, slammerkin, slammock, slammockin, slommakin, slommockin, slummackin, slummick, slummock**) a slut; a sloppy and slatternly woman. [colloquial, 1700s-1900s]

slurks a drunkard. For synonyms see ALCHY.

slurrup a slattern. For synonyms see TROLLYMOG. [colloquial, 1900s]

slushed-up (also **slushed**) intoxicated with alcohol. [U.S. slang, mid 1900s]

slusher (also **slush**) a drunkard. [colloquial, 1800s-1900s]

slut 1. a nasty slattern; a sexually loose woman. [since the mid 1400s] **2.** to work as a servant. [British and U.S. colloquial, early 1800s] **3.** a bitch; a female dog; a rude woman. [British, mid 1800s] **4.** a promiscuous homosexual male. From sense 1. [U.S. homosexual use, mid 1900s-pres., Farrell]

S.M. SADISM and MASOCHISM (both *q.v.*); a "sado-masochist." [U.S. slang, mid 1900s-pres.]

smack 1. a kiss, especially a noisy one. [U.S. slang, early 1900s-pres.] **2.** heroin. *Cf.* SHMECK. [U.S. drug culture, 1900s]

small-arm the penis. A reinterpretation of the expression meaning "small gun" or "pistol." See SMALL-ARM INSPECTION. [military, early 1900s]

small-arm inspection visual inspection of the male genitals for signs of venereal disease or for lice. *Cf.* DANGLE-PARADE, POULTRY-SHOW, SHORT-ARM INSPECTION. [military, early 1900s]

smallclothes (also **inside clothes**) men's or women's underwear. *Cf.* SMALLS. For synonyms see NETHER GARMENTS. [British and U.S. colloquial, 1800s-1900s]

smallest room the W.C.; the bathroom. *Cf.* LITTLE HOUSE. [U.S. slang or colloquial, mid 1900s-pres.]

smalls underwear; underpants. From

SMALLCLOTHES (*q.v.*). For synonyms see NETHER GARMENTS. [British slang, 1900s]

smarmy in the manner of a sycophant. [widespread slang, 1900s]

smart aleck an impudent person; a disrespectful boy or girl. Usually refers to an adolescent boy. [U.S. colloquial, late 1800s-pres.]

smart-ass (also **smart-arse**) a smart aleck; a know-it-all. [widespread slang, mid 1900s-pres.]

smarty-pants 1. a smart aleck. [U.S. colloquial, 1900s] **2.** a young male who is beginning to feel strong sexual desire. [U.S. slang, mid 1900s]

smash an alcohol extract of CANNABIS SATIVA (*q.v.*). Probably related to SMASHED (sense 2). [U.S. drug culture, mid 1900s-pres.]

smashed 1. intoxicated with alcohol. [British and U.S. slang, mid 1900s-pres.] **2.** drug intoxicated. [U.S. drug culture, mid 1900s-pres.]

smashing kissing; petting. *Cf.* MASH. [U.S. slang, mid 1900s]

smeared 1. intoxicated with alcohol. [U.S. slang, mid 1900s-pres.] **2.** drug intoxicated. [U.S. drug culture, mid 1900s-pres.]

smeck heroin. See SCHMECK. [U.S. underworld and drug culture, early 1900s-pres.]

smecker any drug except marijuana. *Cf.* SCHMECKER. [U.S. underworld, mid 1900s]

smegma 1. a soap or detergent substitute. No negative connotations. [British, 1600s-1800s] **2.** a thick, cheesy, or soapy substance which collects beneath the foreskin and around the clitoris. [since the early 1800s] Synonyms for sense 2: CHEESE, COCK-CHEESE, CROTCH-CHEESE, DUCK-BUTTER, GNAT-BREAD, HEAD-CHEESE.

Smell me! a rude curse or exclamation; a command to smell one's pubic or anal area. [U.S., mid 1900s]

smell-smock 1. a woman-chaser; a lecher. *Cf.* SMOCK. [slang, late 1500s] **2.** the penis. [mid 1600s, (Urquhart)]

smell the place up (also **stink the place up**) to defecate; to use the BATHROOM (*q.v.*) for defecation. [U.S. slang, mid 1900s-pres.]

smidget a derogatory nickname for a Negro. [U.S. dialect (Southern), 1900s or before]

smig a mistress. [underworld, early 1900s, *Dictionary of the Underworld*]

smock 1. a woman; women considered sexually; the same as SKIRT (*q.v.*). [around the 1600s] **2.** to make womanish. [early 1600s] **3.** to coit a woman. **4.** to chase women; to act as a lecher. **5.** the female genitals. [senses 3-5 are British, 1700s-1800s]

smockage chasing women; copulating with women; copulation. [British slang, early 1600s] Synonyms and related terms: ACTION, ACT OF ANDROGYNATION, ACT OF DARKNESS, ACT OF GENERATION, ACT OF KIND, ACT OF LOVE, ACT OF PLEASURE, ACT OF SHAME, ACT OF SPORT, ALL THE WAY, AMOROUS CONGRESS, AMOROUS RITES, APHRODISIA, BANANAS AND CREAM, BANG, BASKET-MAKING, BATE-UP, BAWDY BANQUET, BED-RITE, BED-TIME STORY, BEDWARD BIT, BEE IS IN THE HIVE, BEHIND-DOOR WORK, BELLY-BUMPING, BELLY-RIDE, BELLY TO BELLY, BELLY-WARMER, BELT, BEST AND PLENTY OF IT, BIT TIME, BITCH, BIT OF BLACK VELVET, BIT OF FISH, BIT OF FLAT, BIT OF FRONT DOOR WORK, BIT OF FUN, BIT OF HAIR, BIT OF HARD, BIT OF HARD FOR A BIT OF SOFT, BIT OF JAM, BIT OF MEAT, BIT OF NIFTY, BIT OF QUIMSY, BIT OF ROUGH, BIT OF SNUG, BIT OF SNUG FOR A BIT OF STIFF, BIT OF THE GOOSE'S-NECK, BIT OF THE OTHER, BIT ON A FORK, BLANKET DRILL, BLANKET HORNPIPE, BOODY, BOOLY-DOG, BOOZLE, BOTTOM-WETTER, BOUNCY-BOUNCY, BRIM, BRUSH, BURLAP, BUSH PATROL, BUSINESS, BUTT, BUTTOCK-BALL, BUTTOCK-STIRRING, CARNAL ACQUAINTANCE, CARNAL CONNECTION, CARNAL COPULATION, CARNAL ENGAGEMENT, CARNAL INTERCOURSE, CARNAL KNOWLEDGE, CAULIFLOWER, CAVAULTING, CHAWS, CHIVALRY, CHUNK, COCKING, COITION, COITURE, CONCUBITUS, CONJUGAL ACT, CONJUGAL EMBRACE, CONJUGAL RELATIONS, CONJUGAL RITES, CONJUGALS, CONNECTION, CONNUBIAL RITES, CONSUMMATION, CONVERSATION, COOT, COPULATION, CRACK, CRUMPET, CULBUTIZING EXERCISE, CULLY-SHANGY, DAUB OF THE BRUSH, DEED OF KIND, DEED OF PLEASURE, DICKY-DUNK, DIRTY WORK AT THE CROSSROADS, FEATHER-BED JIG, FEDERATING, FLESH SESSION, FLOP, FORE AND AFT, FORNICATION, FOUR-LEGGED FROLIC, FRAIL-JOB, FRIGGING, FRISK, FRUIT THAT MADE MEN WISE, FUCK, FUCKING, FUN AND GAMES, FUTTER, GALLANTRY, GINCH, GOAT'S JIG, GREENS, GROUND RATIONS, GRUMBLE AND GRUNT, GRUMMET, HAIR, HAIR-COURT, HANDY-DANDY, HANKY-PANKY, HOGMAGUNDY, HOLE, HORIZONTAL EXERCISE, HORIZONTAL REFRESHMENT, HORSEMANSHIP, HOSE, HOSING, HOT LAY, HOT ROLL WITH CREAM, HUMP, HUMPERY, HUNK, HUNK OF ASS, HUNK OF BUTT, HUNK OF HYMIE, HUNK OF SKIRT, HUNK OF TAIL, HYMENEAL-SWEETS, HYMIE, IMPROPER INTERCOURSE, IMPROPERLY INTIMATE, IN ACTUS COITU, IN COITU, INTERCOURSE, IRISH WHIST, IT, JAPE, JAZZ, JIG, JIG-A-GIG, JIG-A-JIG, JING-JANG, JIVE, JOBBING, JOCKUM-CLOY, JOY-RIDE, JUMBLE-GIBLETS, KINDNESS, KISS, KNOCK, KNOCKING, KNOWLEDGE, LADIES' TAILORING, LADY-FEAST, LAP-CLAP, LAST COMPLIMENT, LAY, LEG-BUSINESS, LEWD INFUSION, LING-GRAPPLING, LISTS OF LOVE, LITTLE BIT, LITTLE BIT OF KEG, LOOSE-COAT GAME, LOVE-LIFE, MAKE, MARITAL DUTY, MEDICINE, MERRY BOUT, MOTTING, MOW, MUTTON, MYRTLE, NATTUM, NATURE'S DUTY, NAUGHTY, NAVEL ENGAGEMENT, NETHER-WORK, NIFTY, NIGHT-PHYSIC, NIGHT-WORK, NOOKY, NOSE-PAINTING, NUB, NUBBING, NUBBING-CHEAT, NUGGING, NUPTIAL RITES, NURTLE, ONE WITH T'OTHER, ON THE JOB, PAREUNIA, PASSION, PHYSIC, PIECE, PIECE OF ASS, PIECE OF EVE'S FLESH, PIECE OF TAIL, PILE-DRIVING, POKE, POLE-WORK, POON-TANG, POOP-NODDY, POST, POSTCONNUBIAL, PRANKS, PRICK-CHINKING, PROD, PUDDING, PULLY-HAWLY, PUSS, PUSSY, PUT AND TAKE, QUIFFING, QUIM, QUIMING, QUIM-STICKING, RAM, RANTUM-

SCANTUM, RELATIONS, RELISH, REM-IN-RE, RITES OF LOVE, RITES OF VENUS, ROLL, ROLL IN THE HAY, ROMP, ROOTLE, ROUST, RUB-BELLY, RUB-OFF, RULE-OF-THREE, RUMBLE, RUMP-WORK, RUT, RUT-TING, SALT, SCORE, SCREW, SECRET SER-VICES, SETTLEMENT-IN-TAIL, SEX, SEX ACT, SEX-JOB, SEXUAL COMMERCE, SEX-UAL CONGRESS, SEXUAL CONJUNCTION, SEXUAL CONNECTION, SEXUAL EMBRACE, SEXUAL INTERCOURSE, SEXUAL INTIMA-CY, SEXUAL RELATIONS, SEXUAL UNION, SHAG, SHAKE, SHAKING OF THE SHEETS, SHEETS, SHIFT-SERVICE, SHIFT-WORK, SHINES, SHORT-ARM PRACTICE, SHOVE, SHTUP, SLITHERY, SMOCKAGE, SNIBBET, SNIPPET, SOME, SOUL ROLL, SPORT, SPORT OF VENUS, SQUEEZE AND A SQUIRT, STUFF, SUBAGITATION, TAIL, TAIL-TICK-LING, TAIL-TWITCHING, TAIL-WAGGING, TAIL-WORK, THE ACT, THE FAVOR, THE LIMIT, THE ULTIMATE FAVOR, TOPS-AND-BOTTOMS, TOSS IN THE HAY, TRADING, TRAFFIC, TRIM, TRIP UP THE RHINE, TROMBONING, TUP, TURN, TWAT-RAKING, TWATTING, TWO-HANDED PUT, UGLY, UH-HUH, UPTAILS-ALL, UP TO ONE'S BALLS, USE OF THE SEX, VENEREAL ACT, VENERY, VENUS, VENUS'S HONEYPOT, WET-'UN, WHAT EVE DID WITH ADAM, WORKS.

smockster 1. a madam or a pimp. [British, early 1600s] **2.** a whoremonger; a lecher. [British slang, 1600s-1700s]

smoke 1. to coit a woman. *Cf.* CHIMNEY, MAKE THE CHIMNEY SMOKE. [British slang, 1800s] **2.** a derogatory nickname for a Negro. For synonyms see EBONY. [U.S. slang, early 1900s] **3.** to perform an act of PENILINGUS (*q.v.*). [British and U.S. slang, 1900s] **4.** to smoke marijuana; to smoke any drugs. [U.S. drug culture and slang, mid 1900s-pres.] Various types of drug smoking: BANG A REEFER (marijuana), BEAT THE GONG (opium), BLAST (marijuana), BLOW A STICK (marijuana), BLOW GAGE (marijuana), BLOW HAY (marijuana), BLOW JIVE (marijuana), BLOW ONE'S ROOF (marijuana), BLOW POT (marijuana), BLOW TEA (marijuana), GO LOCO (marijuana), HIT THE FLUTE (opium), HIT THE

GONGER (opium), HIT THE GOW (opium), HIT THE PIPE (opium), KICK THE GONG (opium), KISS MARY (marijuana), KISS THE FISH (hashish), LIE DOWN (opium), SUCK BAMBOO (opium), SUCK THE BAMBOO (opium), TOKE (marijuana), TORCH UP (marijuana). **5.** marijuana; a marijuana cigarette. [U.S. drug culture, mid 1900s-pres.]

smoked intoxicated with alcohol. *Cf.* CORNED, SALTED-DOWN. [U.S. slang or colloquial, 1800s, Wentworth and Flexner]

smoked-Irishman a derogatory nickname for a Negro. "Smoked" like a smoke- or soot-blackened piece of glass. *Cf.* SMOKE (sense 2). [U.S. underworld, mid 1900s, Goldin, O'Leary, and Lipsius]

smokehouse a privy; an outhouse. For synonyms see AJAX. [U.S., mid 1900s]

smoker 1. a CHAMBER POT (*q.v.*). Due to the steam from hot urine in cold weather (Partridge). [British slang, 1800s, Farmer and Henley] **2.** someone who is known to perform PENILINGUS (*q.v.*). *Cf.* SMOKE (sense 3). [British and U.S. slang, 1900s] **3.** someone who smokes marijuana or other drugs. Various types of smokers: BOWLER (opium), BUSHWHACKER (marijuana), GONG-BEATER (opium), GONG-KICKER (opium), GOWSTER (opium), GRASSHEAD (marijuana), GRASSHOPPER (marijuana), GRIEFER (marijuana), HASH HEAD (hashish), HAY-BURNER (marijuana), HAY-HEAD, HIP-LAYER (opium), MOTTER (marijuana), MUGGLE-HEAD (marijuana), OILER (hashish oil), PIPE-HITTER (marijuana), PIPE-HITTER (opium), POTHEAD (marijuana), REEFER (marijuana), REEFING MAN (marijuana), SNAKE (marijuana), TEA-BLOWER (marijuana), TEA-HEAD (marijuana), TEAHOUND (marijuana), TEA-MAN (marijuana), VIPER (marijuana), WEEDHEAD (marijuana).

smokeshell a CHAMBER POT (*q.v.*). *Cf.* SMOKER (sense 1). [British slang, 1800s, Farmer and Henley]

Smoley hoke! a deliberate spoonerism for "Holy Smoke!" [not widely-known; 1900s]

smooch (also **smoodge, smooge, smouch, smouge**) **1.** to kiss; to kiss and pet. [widespread colloquial, 1800s-pres.] **2.** a kiss. Also **smoucher.** [colloquial, 1800s-pres.] **3.** to act like a sycophant. *Cf.* ASS-KISSER. [Australian, 1900s, Baker] See also SMOUSE.

smoongy a brothel. [U.S. military, World War I, Lighter]

smooth as a baby's bottom (also **soft as a baby's bottom**) pertaining to something which is very smooth or soft. [colloquial, 1900s]

smouse (also **smouch, smous, smoutch**) a derogatory nickname for a Jewish man. [British colloquial or slang, early 1700s-1800s] See also SMOOCH.

smudge a derogatory nickname for a Negro. From the blackness of a "smudge pot." *Cf.* DINGE. [U.S. slang, 1900s]

smuggle to caress. *Cf.* SNUGGLE. [British, late 1600s]

smuggling-ken a brothel. [cant, 1700s]

smut 1. to make something obscene. **2.** obscene language. **3.** an obscene story; pornography in general. [all since the 1600s]

smut-butt a derogatory nickname for a Negro. "Smut" is from the name of a fungous plant disease which reduces a plant to a black powdery mass. [attested as U.S. college slang, Underwood]

smuthound 1. a man who revels in obscenity and pornography. [U.S. slang, mid 1900s-pres.] **2.** a censor; someone who is hunting for SMUT (sense 3). [U.S. slang, mid 1900s]

smut-peddler one who sells pornography. [U.S. slang, mid 1900s]

smuts obscene pictures. [U.S. underworld, early 1900s, Irwin]

smut-slut a low slut; a sexually loose woman. [U.S. slang, mid 1900s]

smutty obscene; bawdy. See SMUT. [since the 1600s]

SNAFU (also **snafu**) **1.** "situation normal, all fucked-up" or "situation normal, all fouled-up." [originally mili-tary use; U.S. slang, mid 1900s-pres.] **2.** to mess up; to make a blunder; to ruin something. The original meaning is unknown to many users of this acronym. Frequently appears in lower case in this sense. [U.S. slang, mid 1900s-pres.] Similar forms: COMMFU, FUBAR, FUBB, FUMTU, G.F.U., IMFU, JAAFU, JACFU, JANFU, M.F.U., NABU, SABU, SAMFU, SAPFU SNEFU, SNRAFU, SUSFU, TABU, TAFUBAR, TARFU, TAS-FUIRA, T.C.C.FU.

snag 1. to copulate; to rape. [U.S. slang, 1900s] **2.** to commit PEDERASTY (*q.v.*). [U.S. underworld, early 1900s] **3.** an ugly girl or woman. *Cf.* SCAG (sense 1). [U.S. slang, mid 1900s]

snag-fencer (also **snag-catcher**) a nick-name for a dentist. [British slang, 1800s or before]

snake 1. the penis. *Cf.* BLACKSNAKE, ROCK PYTHON, SNAKE IN THE GRASS. [widespread recurrent nonce] **2.** inferior whisky. A truncation of SNAKEBITE MEDICINE (*q.v.*). For synonyms see EMBALMING FLUID. [U.S. slang, early 1900s] **3.** a girl, especially an ugly girl or a promiscuous girl. [U.S. slang, mid 1900s] **4.** a derogatory nickname for a Caucasian. [U.S. black use, mid 1900s] **5.** a marijuana smoker. [U.S. underworld, mid 1900s or before, Goldin, O'Leary, and Lipsius]

snakebite medicine (also **snake medicine**) whisky; any strong alcoholic drink; the same as MEDICINE (sense 2), SNAKE (sense 2). [U.S. colloquial, 1900s or before]

snake in the grass 1. a sneaky and despised person; a lurking danger. [colloquial since the 1600s] **2.** the penis and the pubic hair. A reinterpretation of sense 1. [recurrent nonce]

snake-juice inferior alcohol; bad whis-ky; alcohol as potent as snake's venom. *Cf.* SNAKEBITE MEDICINE. [Australian, 1900s or before]

snake-poison inferior alcohol; bad whisky; the same as SNAKE-JUICE (*q.v.*). [U.S. slang or colloquial, late 1800s]

snakes the DELIRIUM TREMENS (q.v.). *Cf.* SEEING SNAKES. [U.S. slang or colloquial, late 1800s-mid 1900s]

snake's hiss urine; to urinate; an act of urination. Rhyming slang for "piss." [Australian, 1900s, *Dictionary of Rhyming Slang*]

snap one's cookies to vomit; to regurgitate. *Cf.* TOSS ONE'S COOKIES. [U.S. slang, mid 1900s-pres.]

snapped (also **schnapped**) intoxicated with alcohol. [U.S. slang, mid 1800s-1900s]

snapped-up intoxicated with narcotics. For synonyms see TALL. [U.S. drug culture, mid 1900s]

snapper 1. the penis. [British slang, 1800s, Farmer and Henley] **2.** the foreskin of the penis. [U.S. slang, mid 1900s-pres.] **3.** the vagina. [U.S. slang, mid 1900s-pres.] **4.** a very attractive girl; a very sexy girl. Probably from sense 2. [U.S. slang, mid 1900s-pres.] **5.** an ampule of amyl nitrite. A vasodilator sold in ampules which are crushed to release amyl nitrite vapor. *Cf.* PEARL (sense 2). POPPER. [U.S. drug culture, mid 1900s-pres.]

snap the rubber (also **snap the whip**) to masturbate. [U.S. underworld, mid 1900s, Goldin, O'Leary, and Lipsius]

snatch 1. a very rapid act of copulation. [British, early 1600s] **2.** the female genitals. [British and U.S. slang, 1900s] **3.** women considered sexually; women of loose sexual control. *Cf.* PIECE OF SNATCH (sense 1). [U.S. slang, mid 1900s-pres.] **4.** the posteriors. **5.** catamites. See CATAMITE. From senses 2 and 4. [senses 4 and 5 are U.S. underworld, mid 1900s, Goldin, O'Leary, and Lipsius] See also DAD.

snatch-box the female genitals, a play on "matchbox." *Cf.* BOX (sense 2), SNATCH (sense 2). [British slang, 1900s or before]

snatch-peddler (also **peddle-snatch**) **1.** a prostitute, either male or female. **2.** a CATAMITE (q.v.). For synonyms see BRONCO. [both senses, U.S. underworld, mid 1900s, Goldin, O'Leary, and Lipsius]

sneak out on to be sexually unfaithful to one's mate or spouse. [U.S. colloquial, 1900s or before]

sneaky Pete homebrewed liquor; moonshine. [U.S., early 1900s or before]

sneeze a release of intestinal gas, especially if forceful. *Cf.* THROUGH-COUGH. For synonyms see GURK. [U.S. euphemism, 1900s]

sneeze in the basket an act of CUNNILINGUS (q.v.). [U.S. slang, 1900s]

SNEFU "situation normal, everything fucked-up," describing a situation where everything is as confused as usual. A variation of SNAFU (q.v.). [nonce or synthetic military slang]

snide a wretched man; a hateful fellow. [U.S. slang or colloquial, 1900s]

sniff 1. to inhale or sniff cocaine. *Cf.* SNORT (sense 2). **2.** a dose of cocaine. **3.** drugs in general; a dose of drugs. [all senses, U.S. drug culture, mid 1900s-pres.]

sniffer (also **snifter**) a cocaine user. [U.S. underworld and drug culture, early 1900s-pres.]

snipe 1. a term of contempt. [British, early 1600s] **2.** the end of a marijuana cigarette. [U.S. drug culture, mid 1900s-pres.]

snippet 1. a bit. No negative connotations. [since the mid 1600s] **2.** the female genitals. **3.** copulation. *Cf.* BIT (sense 2). [senses 2 and 3 are British, 1900s or before]

snirp an insignificant person. [British slang and colloquial, 1800s, Northall]

snob nasal mucus. See SNOT (sense 1). For synonyms see BOOGIE. [British colloquial, 1800s]

snockered intoxicated with alcohol. From a term for "sock" or "knock." [U.S. slang, mid 1900s-pres.]

snog to neck; to kiss and caress. For synonyms see FIRKYTOODLE. [British slang, 1900s]

snoggle (also **snoogle**) to cuddle; to

snuggle; to kiss and caress. *Cf.* SNOG. [U.S. slang, mid 1900s]

snoke-horn a sneak; a devious rascal. "Snoke" is from "sneak." [mid 1400s] Synonyms: ANIMAL, ANTI-BOD, APE, ASS-HOLE, ASS-WIPE, BAD EGG, BEZONIAN, BITE, BLACKGUARD, BLIGHTER, BLODGIE, BLOOD OF A BITCH, BOB SQUIRT, BOB TAIL, BRIGAND, BUCKEEN, BULLY, CAD, CAITIFF, CATSO, CHIT, CLAPPER-DUDGEON, CLOWES, COCKAPERT, COCK-SUCKER, COISTRELL, COKIN, CONGEON, COVE, COWSON, CREEP, CRUMB, DAM-BER, DASTARD, DOUCHE, DOUCHE BAG, DROOP, FAT-ASSED, FOUR-LETTER MAN, GEECH, GEEK, GOODMAN TURD, GROD, GRUBBER, GRUNGE, GUG, GULLION, GUNZEL-BUTT, GUTTER PUP, HARLOT, HASKARD, HEANLING, HEMPIE, HOOD, HOODLUM, HOOLIGAN, ICK, JACK NASTY, JACK SHIT, LADRONE, LARRIKIN, LOON, LOUSE, LOUSE-BAG, LOWLIFE, LURCHER, LURKER, MISCREANT, MOMZER, MUCK-SPOUT, MUDSNOOT, NITHING, PAIN IN THE ASS, PALTRY FELLOW, PICAROON, PILL, PRICK, PUKE, PUP, QUEERE-COVE, RAFF, RAMPALLIAN, RAT, RAT-FINK, RIFF-RAFF, ROGER, ROGUE, ROPE-RIPE, SCAB, SCADGER, SCHTOONK, SCUBBADO, SCUT, SCUTZ, SHAB, SHABAROON, SHAG-BAG, SHAG-NASTY, SHAKE-BAG, SHICER, SHIT-ASS, SHITE-POKE, SHIT-FIRE, SHIT-POT, SHIT-SACK, SHIT-STICK, SIWASH, SKAL-AWAG, SKUNK, SLAM-TRASH, SLOBFOOT, SLUGGARD, SLUM-BUM, SLYBOOTS, SNAKE IN THE GRASS, SNARGE, SNIDE, SON-OF-A-BEE, SON-OF-A-BISCUIT-EATER, SON OF A FEMALE CANINE, SON OF A SEA COOK, SON OF A SOW, SON OF A WHORE, SONUVABITCH, STINKARD, STINKER, STITCHEL, TATTERDEMALION, THUG, TITIVIL, TROLL, TROLLY-BAGS, VARLET, VILLAIN, WARLOCK, WART, WEINER, WEI-SENHEIMER, WHANG, WORM, YAZZIHAMP-ER, YELLOW-DOG, ZARF.

snolly-goster a devious lawyer; a shyster. [U.S. slang and colloquial, mid 1800s-1900s] Synonyms: AMBULANCE-CHASER, LIP, MOUTH, MOUTHPIECE, PHILADELPHIA LAWYER, SHARK, SHYSTER.

snooted intoxicated with alcohol. See HAVE A SNOOTFUL.

snop marijuana. For synonyms see MARI. [U.S. drug culture, mid 1900s-pres.]

snorbs the breasts. For synonyms see BOSOM. [U.S. slang, mid 1900s, *Current Slang*]

snort 1. a drink; a swig of alcohol. [U.S. slang and colloquial, 1900s or before] **2.** to sniff cocaine or other drugs. [U.S. drug culture, mid 1900s-pres.] **3.** cocaine. "Some snort" is a portion of cocaine. From sense 2. [U.S. drug culture, mid 1900s-pres.] **4.** powdered drugs including P.C.P. [U.S. drug culture, mid 1900s-pres.]

snorts the drug P.C.P. (*q.v.*). From SNORT (sense 4). [U.S. drug culture, mid 1900s-pres.]

snot 1. nasal mucus. [since the 1400s] **2.** to blow the nose or wipe mucus from the nose. [since the 1500s; no longer in polite use] **3.** a term of contempt for a person. [since the early 1600s]

snot-box the nose. [British with some U.S. use, 1800s-1900s]

snot-rag a handkerchief. [widespread slang and colloquial, 1800s-1900s]

snots 1. gobs of nasal mucus. [U.S. colloquial, 1900s] **2.** oysters. [U.S. slang and colloquial, 1900s]

snotted intoxicated with alcohol. For synonyms see WOOFLED. [U.S. slang, early 1900s]

snotter 1. nasal mucus. Also **snoter-gob**. [British, late 1600s] **2.** a handkerchief; a handkerchief soiled with mucus. [British slang, early 1800s]

snotty (also **snottie**) **1.** nasty; fouled with mucus. [since the 1500s] **2.** bitchy; pertaining to fresh or rude behavior. [colloquial, 1900s]

snow 1. underwear; linen hanging on washlines drying. [cant (tramps), early 1800s, *Lexican Balatronicum*] **2.** cocaine; any powdered drug. [U.S. underworld and drug culture, early 1900s-pres.]

snowball 1. a single glob of semen. [British slang or nonce, late 1600s; attested as U.S. homosexual use, Farrell] **2.** a nickname for a Negro. Usually for a Negro with white hair. [British and U.S. slang and colloquial, 1700s-1900s] **3.** cocaine; any powdered narcotic. *Cf.* SNOW (sense 2). [U.S. underworld and drug culture, early 1900s] **4.** an oral exchange of semen between two homosexual males immediately after completing mutual PENILINGUS (*q.v.*). This is probably also used as a verb. *Cf.* FRENCH ABORTION. [attested as U.S. homosexual use, mid 1900s-pres., Farrell]

snowball queen a homosexual male who practices snowballing. See SNOWBALL (sense 4) for details and see QUEEN for similar subjects.

snow-bank a place for consuming cocaine. *Cf.* SNOW (sense 2). [U.S. underworld and drug culture, mid 1900s]

snowbird 1. a cocaine user. **2.** a heroin addict or an illicit user of any powdered drug. **3.** cocaine. [all senses, U.S. underworld and drug culture, early 1900s-pres.]

snow-caine cocaine. SNOW (sense 2) and "cocaine." [U.S. underworld slang and drug culture, mid 1900s-pres.]

snow-drifter 1. a cocaine user. **2.** a cocaine seller. See SNOW (sense 2). Both are from "snowdrift." [both senses, U.S. underworld, early 1900s]

snowed-under (also **snowed-in,** **snowed up**) **1.** under the influence of cocaine. **2.** under the influence of any narcotic. Both are from the standard expression meaning "buried." [both senses, U.S. underworld, early 1900s]

snow-flower a female user of cocaine. *Cf.* SNOW (sense 2). [possibly nonce; attested as early 1900s, *Dictionary of the Underworld*]

snow job 1. an act of deception. **2.** to deceive someone with lies and distortion. [both senses, U.S. slang, mid 1900s-pres.]

snowmobiling taking cocaine or other drugs. [U.S. drug culture and slang, mid 1900s]

snow-storm 1. a large amount of cocaine or other powdered drugs. **2.** a

party where abundant cocaine is available. *Cf.* CAUGHT IN A SNOWSTORM. [both senses, U.S. underworld and drug culture, mid 1900s-pres.]

snow-stuff cocaine. *Cf.* WHITE STUFF. [U.S. drug culture, mid 1900s-pres.]

snozzled intoxicated with alcohol. For synonyms see WOOFLED. [U.S. slang and colloquial, early 1900s]

snozzle-wobbles a hangover. *Cf.* SNOZZLED. [U.S. slang, mid 1900s, Berrey and Van den Bark]

SNRAFU "situation normal, really all fucked-up." a variant of SNAFU (*q.v.*). [nonce or synthetic military slang]

snubbed intoxicated with alcohol. For synonyms see WOOFLED. [U.S. slang, Wentworth and Flexner]

snuff it to die. Refers to snuffing out a candle. [British slang, early 1900s]

snuffy intoxicated with alcohol. For synonyms see WOOFLED. [British and U.S. slang, early 1800s-1900s]

snug 1. to coit; to copulate with a woman. *Cf.* BIT OF SNUG. [British slang, 1800s, Farmer and Henley] **2.** intoxicated with alcohol. [British and U.S. slang, 1800s-1900s]

snuggle to cuddle and kiss. *Cf.* SMUGGLE. [U.S. colloquial, 1900s]

so 1. intoxicated with alcohol. Also **so-so.** *Cf.* HOW-CAME-YOU-SO? (sense 1). [British euphemism, early 1800s] **2.** menstruating. Also **so-so.** [British colloquial euphemism, 1800s, Farmer and Henley] **3.** pregnant. *Cf.* HOW-CAME-YOU-SO? (sense 2). [British, 1800s] **4.** homosexual. [euphemistic slang, late 1800s-1900s]

soak 1. a drinking bout. **2.** a drunkard. **3.** to drink to intoxication. [senses 1-3 since the 1800s or before] **4.** to linger in coition after ejaculation. [British slang and nonce elsewhere, 1800s-1900s, *Dictionary of Slang and Unconventional English*]

soaked intoxicated with alcohol. [U.S. slang and colloquial, early 1700s-pres.]

soaker a heavy drinker; a drunkard. [British slang, 1700s or before]

soap 1. semen. For synonyms see METTLE. [British slang, 1800s, Farmer and Henley] **2.** a simpleton; a fool. For synonyms see OAF. [Australian slang, mid 1900s, Baker] **3.** a methaqualone tablet. Also **sope.** *Cf.* SUPER-SOAPER. [U.S. drug culture, mid 1900s-pres.]

soapy-eyed intoxicated with alcohol. [U.S. slang, early 1900s]

S.O.B. 1. "son of a bitch," a highly despised person. Synonyms: BLOOD OF A BITCH, COW-SON, DASTARD, SON-OF-A-BEE, SON-OF-A-BISCUIT-EATER, SON OF A FEMALE CANINE, SON OF A SEA COOK, SON OF A SOW, SON OF A WHORE, SONUVABITCH. [widespread slang, 1900s] **2.** "silly old bugger"; "silly old blighter." **3.** "shit or bust." [senses 2 and 3 are British slang, 1900s]

social disease venereal disease; syphilis or gonorrhea or both. [U.S. colloquial, 1900s] Synonyms: BAD BLOOD, BAD DISEASE, BAD DISORDER, BLOOD DISEASE, BLUE BALLS, BLUE BOAR, BLUE FEVER, BONE-AGUE, BURNER, CLAP, COVENT GARDEN AGUE, CRINKUMS, CRUD, DELICATE DISEASE, DELICATE TAINT, DOSE, DOUBLE-EVENT, FLAME, FLAP DRAGON, FORGET-ME-NOT, FULL HAND, FULL HOUSE, GARDEN-GOUT, GENITO-URINARY DISEASE, GOOSE, GOUT, GRINCUMS, KERTERVER-CARTZO, LOAD, LOBSTER TAILS, NAP, NOLI-ME-TANGERE, PINTLE-FEVER, PLAGUE, PREVENTABLE DISEASE, RHEA SISTERS, SAUCE, SCALDER, SCRUD, SEXUAL DISEASE, STICK, TOKEN, VENEREAL, VENEREAL DISEASE, VENUS'S CURSE, VICE DISEASE. Terms for "syphilis" are at SPECIFIC STOMACH.

social E. a "social evil," prostitution. [British, late 1800s or early 1900s]

social evil prostitution. See SOCIAL E. [euphemistic, 1800s-1900s]

Sock it to me! 1. a catch phrase meaning essentially, "Come on, let me have it!" Referring to bad news. [U.S. slang and colloquial, 1900s] **2.** "Copulate with me!" *Cf.* WHIP IT TO ME! [U.S. slang, mid 1900s-pres.]

sod 1. a SODOMITE (*q.v.*). [British and U.S., 1800s-1900s] **2.** to commit sod-

omy; to commit PEDERASTY (*q.v.*). A truncation of "sodomy." [British slang, 1900s] **3.** a derogatory term of address. Based on sense 1 or perhaps sense 4. Sometimes used in fun. [British, 1800s-1900s] **4.** a drunkard. From SOT (sense 2) or "sodden." [U.S. slang, early 1900s-pres.]

sodden bum a drunkard; a soggy and worthless wretch. [U.S. slang, mid 1900s-pres.]

Sod off! "Beat it!" "Stop bothering me!" A slight disguise of BUGGER OFF! (*q.v.*). [British slang, 1900s]

sodomite (also **sodomist**) a PEDERAST (*q.v.*); a man who habitually commits NONORTHOGENITAL (*q.v.*) sexual acts. From the ancient city of Sodom. [since the late 1700s] Synonyms: BARDACHE, BIRDIE, BIRD-TAKER, BROWN-HATTER, BROWNIE, BROWNIE KING, BUD SALLOGH, BUG, BUGGAH, BUGGER, BUM-FUCKER, BUNKER, BURGLAR, CAPON, CORN-HOLER, CORVETTE, DADDY, EYE DOCTOR, EYE-OPENER, GENTLEMAN OF THE BACK DOOR, GOOSER, GUT-BUTCHER, GUT-FUCKER, GUT-MONGER, GUT-REAMER, GUT-SCRAPER, GUT-STICKER, GUT-STRETCHER, GUT-STUFFER, GUT-VEXER, INDORSER, INGLER, INSERTEE, INSERTOR, INSPECTOR OF MAN-HOLES, JESUIT, JOCKER, JOCKEY, JOEY, LICK-BOX, LIMP-WRIST, MASON, PRUSSIAN, PUFF, REAMER, RING-SNATCHER, SHEEP-HERDER, SHIT-HUNTER, SHIT-STIRRER, SOD, SODOMITE, STERN-CHASER, STIR-SHIT, STUFFER, TURK, UNCLE, UNNATURAL DEBAUCHEE, USHER, VERT, WOLF.

sodomy 1. NONORTHOGENITAL (*q.v.*) sexual acts, especially those between males. [since the 1200s, *Oxford English Dictionary*] **2.** anal copulation between males; pederasty. [1800s-1900s] **3.** sexual perversions; nonorthogenital sexual acts proscribed by law. Whether or not the following acts are sodomy depends on the wording of the various state (U.S.) sodomy laws and the legal precedents set in the past: pederasty or any anal copulation, bestiality, fellation, cunnilingus, lesbian acts, mutual masturbation, anilingus, exhibitionism, and taking indecent liberties with a minor. Related terms for all senses: ASS-FUCK, BACK-DOOR WORK, BACK-SCULL, BACK-SCUTTLE, BIT OF BROWN, BOODY, BOTTLE, BROWN-EYE, BROWN HOLE, BROWNING, BUCKLEBURY, BUGGERY, BUNG HOLE, BUTT-FUCK, COITUS IN ANO, COITUS PER ANUM, CONCUBITUS CUM PERSONA EJUSDEM SEXUS, CRIME AGAINST NATURE, CRIMEN INNOMINATUM, DAUB OF THE BRUSH, DIP IN THE FUDGE POT, GREEK, GREEK LOVE, GREEK WAY, HIGHER MALTHUSIANISM, ITALIAN MANNER, KIESTER STAB, KNEELING AT THE ALTAR, LAY, NAMELESS CRIME, PAEDICATIO, PEDICATION, PIG-STICKING, RAMJOB, SEXUAL ANOMALY, SEXUAL PERVERSION, SHIP'S, SHIT-FUCK, UNMENTIONABLE VICE, UNNATURAL CONNECTION, UNNATURAL OFFENSE, UNNATURAL PURPOSES, UNNATURAL SEXUAL INTERCOURSE, UNNATURAL VICE.

soft and nasty pertaining to a bad situation; a nasty situation. This refers directly to dung. *Cf.* SHIT, IN THE; SOFT-STUFF. [British slang, 1900s]

soft-core 1. pornography where sexual acts are simulated. *Cf.* HARD-CORE. Softness is often understood to refer to the state of the penis in such portrayals. [U.S. slang and colloquial, mid 1900s-pres.] **2.** pertaining to anything mild compared to something extreme. [U.S. slang, mid 1900s-pres.]

soft-jaw a woman of loose sexual control; a woman who says "yes" easily. [U.S. slang, mid 1900s, Montelone]

soft leg a girl or a woman. *Cf.* LEG. [U.S. slang, mid 1900s]

soft roll a sexually easy young woman. From a term used for a pastry. Also a play on "roll," meaning "copulate." *Cf.* CAKE (sense 3), ROLL, TART. [slang, mid 1900s]

soft sore (also **soft venereal sore**) a nonsyphilitic sore on the genitals. The opposite of a hard syphilitic sore. *Cf.* HARD SORE. [medical]

soft-stuff nonsense; a euphemism for "bullshit." *Cf.* SOFT AND NASTY. [U.S. slang, mid 1900s]

soggy intoxicated with alcohol. For synonyms see WOOFLED. [U.S. slang, mid 1900s-pres.]

So help me! (also **So 'elp me!**) an oath and an exclamation. A truncation of "So help me God!" [British and U.S. colloquial, 1800s-pres.]

So help me God! a fairly strong oath and an exclamation; a real oath used in a court of law. For synonyms see 'ZOUNDS!

soiled-dove a prostitute of a high class; a FALLEN WOMAN (*q.v.*). [British and U.S. slang, 1800s-1900s]

soil one's linens 1. to dirty one's underpants with fecal matter or urine accidentally or in fright. See WET ONE'S PANTS. **2.** to do something nasty; to blunder badly. [both senses, British with some U.S. use, 1900s or before]

S.O.L. "shit out of luck." Euphemized as "short of luck" or "soldier out of luck." A reinterpretation of "Sol.," an abbreviation of "soldier." [military, World War I]

soldier's home, old the W.C. A DEAD SOLDIER (sense 1) is "dung." [U.S. colloquial, 1900s]

soles HASHISH (*q.v.*). For synonyms see HASH. [U.S. drug culture, mid 1900s-pres.]

solitary sin masturbation. *Cf.* SECRET VICE. A dysphemism of avoidance.

soma the drug P.C.P. (*q.v.*). From the name of an intoxicating drink. [U.S. drug culture, mid 1900s-pres.]

son 1. a truncation of SON OF A BITCH (*q.v.*). [U.S., 1900s] **2.** a term of contempt for a male. A truncation of "son of a bitch" and a play on the term of endearment for a young male. Usually pronounced derisively. [both senses, U.S., mid 1900s]

song and dance 1. trousers; pants. Rhyming slang for "pants." **2.** a homosexual male. Rhyming slang for NANCE (*q.v.*). [both senses, British, 1900s] **3.** nonsense. [U.S. slang, 1900s]

son of a bachelor a bastard; an illegitimate child. *Cf.* BACHELOR'S BABY. [since the 1600s]

son-of-a-bee a SON OF A BITCH (*q.v.*). The "bee" is "B" from "bitch." [U.S. euphemism, 1900s]

son-of-a-biscuit-eater an avoidance for SON OF A BITCH (*q.v.*). [U.S. colloquial, 1900s]

son of a bitch 1. a bastard; an illegitimate child. **2.** a rotten fellow; a contemptible male. [both senses, since the mid 1700s] **3.** a very difficult task. [U.S. slang, mid 1900s-pres.] **4.** an exclamation, "Son of a bitch!" A truncation of "I'll be a son of a bitch!" [U.S. slang, mid 1900s-pres.]

son of a female canine "son of a bitch!" A contrived avoidance. *Cf.* PUPPY'S MAMMA. [U.S., mid 1900s]

son of a gun 1. a soldier's bastard. This literal interpretation is no longer extant. [attested as British, early 1800s, Jon Bee] **2.** a pal; a fellow; a chum. A mild avoidance for SON OF A BITCH (*q.v.*). [British and U.S. slang and colloquial, early 1800s-pres.] **3.** an oath from "I'll be a son of a gun!" [U.S. colloquial, 1900s]

son of a sea cook a bastard; a contrived avoidance for SON OF A BITCH (*q.v.*). [British and U.S. slang and colloquial, 1800s-1900s]

son of one an alcohol extract of CANNABIS SATIVA (*q.v.*); the same as The One. See ONE, THE. [U.S. drug culture, mid 1900s-pres.]

sonuvabitch a phonetic respelling of SON OF A BITCH (*q.v.*). Seen often in print, especially direct quotes. [U.S. slang and colloquial, mid 1900s-pres.]

sop 1. a fool; a weak-minded simpleton. From MILKSOP (*q.v.*). [British colloquial, early 1600s-1800s] **2.** a drunkard. [U.S. slang, mid 1900s-pres.]

S.O.S. the best-known interpretation is "shit on a shingle," creamed chipped beef on toast. An initialism for "same old shit," euphemized as "same old slumgullion" or "same old stew." *Cf.* CREAMED FORESKINS. [U.S. military and general slang, early 1900s-pres.]

soshed intoxicated with alcohol. For synonyms see WOOFLED. [U.S. slang, early 1900s]

S.O.T. a "son of temperance"; a drunkard. [U.S. ironic slang, mid 1900s]

sot 1. an oaf; a dolt. [*c.* 1000, *Oxford English Dictionary*] **2.** a drunkard. [slang and colloquial since the late 1500s]

soul roll passionate and loving copulation. *Cf.* ROLL, SOFT ROLL. [primarily black use; U.S. slang, mid 1900s-pres.]

soundproof bra a padded brassiere. *Cf.* FALSIES. [U.S. slang, mid 1900s-pres.]

soused (also **soust**) heavily intoxicated with alcohol; the same as PICKLED (*q.v.*). For synonyms see WOOFLED. [slang since the 1600s]

sow-drunk intoxicated with alcohol. *Cf.* DRUNK AS DAVID'S SOW. [British colloquial, mid 1800s or before]

sow one's wild oats 1. to get youthful play out of one's system, said of the male. [British and later U.S. colloquial, 1600s-pres., B.E.] **2.** to lose one's virginity; to copulate in an unrestrained manner. Said of a male. There is a notion that such behavior will result in more mature and more faithful males. The oats here are the SEED (sense 1), "semen." [U.S. colloquial, 1900s or before]

sozzle 1. excrement. Also **sorzle**. For synonyms see DUNG. [British dialect, 1800s, Rye] **2.** to mix into a confused mess; to confuse. [British dialect] **3.** a slattern; a very sloppy woman. For synonyms see TROLLYMOG. [U.S. colloquial, mid 1800s] **4.** an oaf; a blockhead. [British, 1800s, Farmer and Henley] **5.** to drink to excess. [since the 1800s]

sozzled intoxicated with alcohol. For synonyms see WOOFLED. [British and U.S. slang, late 1800s-pres.]

sozzly intoxicated with alcohol. [U.S. slang, mid 1900s]

space cadet 1. a person who is always silly or giddy. **2.** a person who is always high on drugs. [both senses, U.S. slang, mid 1900s-pres.]

spaced-out 1. silly; giddy. **2.** intoxicated with drugs. [both senses, U.S. slang and drug culture, mid 1900s-pres.]

spade 1. to castrate; to desex. [early 1600s-pres.] 2. a eunuch. 3. a derogatory nickname for a Negro. From the black color of the spade in playing cards. Not connected with senses 1 or 2. [British and U.S. slang, early 1900s-pres.]

spaghetti a derogatory nickname for an Italian. [British and U.S. slang, 1900s]

spaghetti-bender a derogatory nickname for an Italian. [U.S. slang, 1900s]

spaginzy a derogatory nickname for a Negro. For synonyms see EBONY. [U.S. slang, mid 1900s]

Spanish athlete a boaster. Because he "throws the bull." For synonyms see BULLER. [U.S. slang, mid 1900s-pres.]

Spanisher a nickname for a Spaniard. Possibly in ignorance or jest. [U.S., 1900s]

Spanish-gout (also **Spanish-needle**) syphilis. [colloquial since the 1600s]

Spanish-pox syphilis. For synonyms see SPECIFIC STOMACH. [British, 1800s]

spanners a sexually attractive woman or girl. Because a spanner (a wrench) is used to tighten "nuts," the testes. [Australian, mid 1900s, *Dictionary of Slang and Unconventional English*]

spare part a useless man; an uneeded man on a work crew. See SPARE PRICK (*q.v.*), for which this is a euphemism. [British and U.S. wartime, 1900s]

spare prick a totally useless man; a lazy or incompetent man on a work crew. From the expression "as useless as a spare prick." See PRICK. [British and U.S. slang, early 1900s-pres.]

spare rib (also **sperrib**) a married man's mistress. Ware defines this as "wife." A reinterpretation of the term for lean cuts of pork ribs. *Cf.* RIB. [slang and nonce, U.S. and elsewhere, 1900s] Synonyms and related terms: BACHELOR'S WIFE, BELLY-LASS, BELLY-PIECE, BLOWEN, BROAD, CONVENIENT, DOLLY-MOP, FAIR LADY, FANCY WOMAN, FLAME, GALLIMAUFREY, GIRL, HONEYSTAR, INAMORATA, JAM-TART, JOMER, JUG, KEPT WOMAN, LADY-BIRD, LEVERET, LIE-A-SIDE, LIGBY, LINDA-BRIDES, LORETTE, LOTEBY, LYERBY, MADAM, MISTRESS, NATURAL, PECULIAR, PELLEX, PIECE OF STRAY, PINTLE-BIT, PINTLE-MAID, POKE, SIDE DISH, SLEEPING-DICTIONARY, SMIG, SMOCK-SERVANT, TACKLE, WIFE.

spare tire a thick waist; a roll of fat around one's waist. [U.S. colloquial, 1900s]

spark to court; to kiss and utter terms of endearment. See SPUNK UP. *Cf.* FIRKYTOODLE. [U.S. colloquial, late 1700s-pres.]

sparkle plenty an amphetamine tablet. From the name of a character in *Dick Tracy*, a comic strip by Chester Gould. [U.S. drug culture, mid 1900s-pres.]

sparrow-fart 1. daybreak; a play on "cockcrow." *Cf.* CROW-PEE. [British, 1800s] 2. **a worthless pipsqueak; an oaf.** *Cf.* FART (sense 3). [1900s, (James Joyce)]

sparrow's cough a euphemism for SPARROW-FART (*q.v.*).

spastic 1. a jerk; a giddy person; a term of general approbation. 2. pertaining to a blunderer; pertaining to a completely uncoordinated person. Both are references to the physically handicapped. [both senses, U.S. slang, mid 1900s-pres.]

spaz 1. a SPASTIC (sense 1); a jerk; a totally uncoordinated person. 2. a fit; an attack; a strong reaction to a bad or a funny situation. [both senses, U.S. slang, mid 1900s-pres.]

S.P.C.H. the "Society for the Prevention of Cruelty to Homosexuals." A jocular term for an imaginary society patterned on "S.P.C.A.," the "Society for the Prevention of Cruelty to Animals." [U.S. slang, mid 1900s-pres.]

spear-chucker a jocular and derogatory nickname for a Negro. Refers to a spear-throwing African. [U.S. slang, mid 1900s-pres.]

specialities condoms. A euphemism

used in publicly available printed matter. For synonyms see EEL-SKIN. [British, 1800s, Farmer and Henley]

specific stomach syphilis. [vague euphemism; U.S., 1900s] Synonyms and related terms: BAD BLOOD, BAD DISEASE, BAND-IN-THE-BOX, BANG AND BIFF, BLOOD DISEASE, BONE-ACHE, BOOGIE, CLAP, COACHMAN ON THE BOX, COALS, DELICATE DISEASE, DELICATE TAINT, ENVIABLE DISEASE, FIRE, FOUL DISEASE, FOUL DISORDER, FRENCH-CROWN, FRENCH-DISEASE, FRENCH GOODS, FRENCH GOUT, FRENCH POX, GOODYEAR, IRISH MUTTON, JACK-IN-THE-BOX, LADIES' FEVER, LUES VENEREA, MALA DE FRANZOS, MALADY OF FRANCE, MARBLES, MEASLES, MESOSYPHILIS, MORBUS GALLICUS, MORBUS HISPANICUS, MORBUS INDICUS, MORBUS NEOPOLITANUS, NEAPOLITAN, NEAPOLITAN CONSOLATION, NEAPOLITAN DISEASE, NEAPOLITAN FAVOR, NEOPOLITAN BONE-ACHE, NOLI-ME-TANGERE, OLD JOE, PHYLLIS, PIMPLE, PISS OUT OF A DOZEN HOLES, POCKES, POX, SCABBADO, SECONDARY, SYPHILIS, SECRET DISEASE, SIFF, SIGMA PHI, SPANISH-GOUT, SPANISH-NEEDLE, SPANISH-POX, SPECIFIC ULCER, SYPH, SYPHO, THE OLD DOG, THE PIP, THE RAHL, V.D.S., WINTER COALS.

specific ulcer syphilis. [U.S., 1900s]

speckled bird an amphetamine capsule. *Cf.* BLACKBIRD. [U.S. drug culture, mid 1900s-pres.]

speed amphetamines; Methedrine (trademark). For synonyms see METH. [U.S. drug culture, mid 1900s-pres.]

speedball a mixture of drugs injected with a syringe. May be heroin and cocaine, cocaine and morphine, or heroin and amphetamines. [underworld and drug culture, early 1900s-pres.]

speed-freak 1. a person who swallows or injects amphetamines. 2. a drug addict or user. [both senses, U.S. drug culture, mid 1900s-pres.]

speedy sister a prostitute. See FAST. [U.S. underworld, mid 1900s, Montelone]

spend 1. to ejaculate semen; to have an orgasm. [British, 1600s-1800s] 2.

semen; sexual spendings. [slang, 1800s-1900s]

spender the female genitals. That which causes the male to SPEND (*q.v.*). [British slang, 1800s or before]

spendings semen which has been ejaculated. *Cf.* COMINGS. [British, late 1500s-1800s]

spew (also **spue**) 1. to ejaculate. [British, 1600s] 2. to vomit. [British and U.S. slang and colloquial, late 1600s-pres.] 3. a dysphemism for "stew." For synonyms see DOG'S VOMIT. [British juvenile, 1900s, (Opie and Opie)] 4. semen; ejaculated semen. [slang or nonce, 1800s-1900s]

spic (also **spick, spik**) 1. an Italian. Derogatory. For synonyms see SKY. Also said to be from "no spica di English." [U.S. slang, early 1900s] 2. any Hispanic; a Latin American, a Mexican, a Spaniard, or a Portuguese. Derogatory. From sense 1. [U.S. slang, mid 1900s-pres.] 3. the Spanish language, especially as taught in college. Derogatory. [U.S. slang, mid 1900s-pres.]

spice 1. sexual attractiveness. 2. sexual content in literature or the performing arts. [both senses, British and U.S. colloquial, 1900s]

spice-island 1. the anus. 2. a privy. [both senses, British slang or colloquial, early 1800s, *Lexicon Balatronicum*]

spicy sexy; smutty; slightly sexually oriented. [slang since the early 1800s]

spifflicated (also **spiflicated**) intoxicated with alcohol; confused with drink. From a verb meaning "dumbfound." [slang, late 1700s-1900s]

spifflo intoxicated with alcohol. From SPIFFLICATED (*q.v.*). [U.S. slang, mid 1900s, Berrey and Van den Bark]

spig a derogatory nickname for a Mexican. See SPIC (sense 2). For synonyms see MEX. [U.S. slang, mid 1900s]

spike 1. an erection of the penis. For synonyms see ERECTION. [widespread recurrent nonce; attested as British slang, 1800s, Farmer and Henley] 2. to copulate. *Cf.* SPIT (sense 1). [British slang, 1800s]

spike-faggot the penis. FAGGOT (sense 3) is a prostitute. [British slang, 1800s, Farmer and Henley]

spill a derogatory term for a Negro or a Puerto Rican or a racial mixture of the two. [U.S. slang, mid 1900s-pres.]

spinster a prostitute; a harlot. A jocular and specialized reinterpretation of the standard meaning. From the spinning or beating of hemp as practiced by prostitutes in prison. [British slang or cant, 1600s]

spirit semen. An elaboration of "vital principle." *Cf.* METTLE, SPUNK. [vague and euphemistic, 1600s]

spiritual flesh-broker a parson; a clergyman. [colloquial, 1900s or before]

spit 1. to coit a woman; to penetrate a woman sexually. [British slang, 1800s, Farmer and Henley] 2. spittle. Synonyms for both senses: CONSPUTE, EXPECTORATE, GOB, LET FLY, SALIVA. 3. the penis. 4. to ejaculate semen. [slang, 1900s]

spitfire 1. a hot-tempered person; a spirited woman. [since the late 1600s] 2. the female genitals. Possibly infected with a venereal disease. [British slang, 1800s, Farmer and Henley] 3. a condom. [British naval slang, mid 1900s, *Dictionary of Slang and Unconventional English*]

spit-kit a cuspidor; a spittoon. [U.S. slang, early 1900s]

spit-swapping kissing; lingual kissing. [U.S. slang, early 1900s-pres.]

splash 1. to urinate, said of the male; to make a splash by urinating. *Cf.* SLASH, TINKLE. [slang, 1900s] 2. amphetamines. [U.S. drug culture, mid 1900s-pres.]

splib a derogatory nickname for a Negro. For synonyms see EBONY. [U.S. slang, mid 1900s-pres.]

spliff marijuana or a marijuana cigarette, especially a large cigarette. Often refers to Jamaican marijuana. [U.S. drug culture, mid 1900s-pres.]

splim marijuana. For synonyms see MARI. [U.S. drug culture, mid 1900s-pres.]

split 1. to coit a woman; to penetrate a woman. [British slang, 1700s] 2. a woman. See SPLIT-TAIL. [U.S. slang, mid 1900s]

split-apricot the female genitals. From the image of a cross section of an apricot with the pit removed. [British slang, 1800s, Farmer and Henley]

split beaver 1. the image of a woman's genitals when a woman sits with her legs spread. A real or imagined view. *Cf.* BEAVER (sense 1). 2. a stripper. [both senses, U.S. slang, mid 1900s-pres.]

Split my windpipe! an oath and an exclamation, "May God split my windpipe!" For synonyms see 'ZOUNDS!

split-rump the penis. *Cf.* RUMP-SPLITTER. [mid 1600s, (Urquhart)]

split-stuff women viewed as sexual objects. [Australian slang, early 1900s, Baker]

split-tail a woman; a crude term for a young woman or a girl. [U.S. slang, mid 1900s-pres.]

spoil a woman's shape (also **ruin a woman's shape**) to get a woman pregnant. For synonyms see STORK. [colloquial, 1600s-1900s]

sponge (also **spunge**) 1. a drunkard, one who soaks up drink. [slang and colloquial since the late 1500s] 2. to drink heavily at someone else's expense. [British, late 1600s, B.E.] 3. to beg or borrow from people constantly. 4. someone who begs and borrows constantly. (senses 3 and 4 are U.S. colloquial, 1900s or before] 5. the penis. [British slang, 1800s, Farmer and Henley]

spook 1. a ghost. [British and U.S. slang and colloquial, 1800s-pres.] 2. a derogatory nickname for a Negro. [U.S. Caucasian use, 1900s] 3. a derogatory nickname for a Caucasian. [U.S. Negro use, 1900s]

spookerican a person who is a racial mixture of Negro and Puerto Rican.

[U.S. slang, mid 1900s, Wentworth and Flexner]

spoon 1. an oaf; a simpleton. [slang since the late 1700s] **2.** to pet or neck; to SPARK (*q.v.*). [U.S. colloquial, early 1800s-pres.] **3.** to perform sexual foreplay. Possibly the same as sense **2.** [British slang, 1800s, Farmer and Henley] **4.** to copulate. **5.** a spoonful or approximately two grams of heroin. **6.** a spoon used for heating drugs which are to be injected. **7.** a spoon used for sniffing cocaine. [senses 5-7 are U.S. drug culture, mid 1900s-pres.] **8.** to lie together (and possibly copulate) like two spoons stacked bowl-in-bowl. [U.S., late 1800s, Farmer and Henley] **9.** a tonguing technique used in CUNNILINGUS (*q.v.*). Possibly related to sense 8. [U.S. slang, mid 1900s-pres.]

spoony (also **spooney**) **1.** a fool; a simpleton. [slang, late 1700s-1800s] **2.** an effeminate male. [British slang, 1800s]

spoony drunk intoxicated and melancholy. For synonyms see WOOFLED. [slang, 1800s]

spoops an oaf; a simpleton. For synonyms see OAF. [U.S. slang, mid 1800s]

sport 1. copulation. [since the late 1500s] **2.** a lecher. **3.** any male buddy, as in "old sport," said between males.

sport blubber to expose the breasts. *Cf.* BLUBBERS. [British slang, 1800s]

sporter a brothel; a SPORTING HOUSE (*q.v.*). [attested as Caribbean (Jamaican), Cassidy and Le Page]

sporting-girl a prostitute. For synonyms see HARLOT. [U.S. or colloquial, 1900s or before]

sporting-girl's manager a pimp. [U.S. underworld, mid 1900s]

sporting-house a brothel. [U.S. or colloquial, 1900s or before]

spotting a blood-tinged secretion from the vagina indicating the onset of the menses. [medical and colloquial]

spout the penis. [widespread recurrent nonce; colloquial and slang, 1800s-pres.]

sprain one's ankle to become pregnant; to have an ACCIDENT (sense 2). [colloquial since the late 1700s]

spraints (also **sprainting**) the droppings of otters. [colloquial, 1400s-1800s]

spread 1. to spread one's legs for copulation, said of a woman. [colloquial, late 1600s-pres.] **2.** to position or lay out a woman for copulation, said of a man. *Cf.* FLOP A WOMAN, LAY DOWN, PUT DOWN (sense 1). [British, 1600s] **3.** the posteriors. [U.S. slang, mid 1900s]

spread beaver 1. a glance at a woman's genitals; a photograph showing a woman's genitals. Also **spread shot**. See SPLIT BEAVER (sense 1). [U.S. slang, mid 1900s-pres.] **2.** pertaining to the posture of a woman sitting with her legs spread. [U.S. slang, mid 1900s-pres.]

spree 1. to drink to excess in the company of others; to DEBAUCH. **2.** a wild, drunken time; an orgy of drink. [both senses, British and U.S. slang and colloquial, early 1800s-pres.] Synonyms for sense 2: BAT, BENDER, BINGE, BLINDO, BLOW, BUM, BUN, BUST, COMUS, DEBAUCH, FUDDLE, GUZZLE, JAG, MEAT AND DRINK, PAINT THE TOWN RED, PERISHER, PISS-UP, SOAK, TEAR, TOOT, TOPE, TWIST, WHING-DING.

spreeing drinking; consorting with women. [U.S. colloquial, 1800s-1900s]

spring chicken a young and naive person, especially a young girl. [U.S. slang and colloquial, mid 1900s-pres.]

springing pregnant. Said of cows and then extended to women. [U.S. rural colloquial, 1900s or before]

sprout wings to die; to become an angel. [U.S., 1900s]

sprunch to engage in sexual play; possibly to copulate. [U.S. dialect (Ozarks), 1900s or before, Randolph and Wilson]

sprung 1. intoxicated with alcohol. [British and U.S. slang or colloquial, early 1800s-1900s] **2.** pregnant, as in "sprung out of shape." [U.S. dialect (Ozarks), 1900s or before, Randolph and Wilson]

spunk 1. METTLE (*q.v.*); SPIRIT (*q.v.*); vigor. [late 1700s-pres.] **2.** semen. [British, 1800s, Farmer and Henley] **3.** to ejaculate. From sense 2. [British, 1900s, *Dictionary of Slang and Unconventional English*]

spunk-bound pertaining to a man without vigor. *Cf.* SPUNK (sense 1). [British colloquial, 1800s, *Dictionary of Slang and Unconventional English*]

spunk-holders the testicles. *Cf.* SPUNK (sense 2). For synonyms see WHIRLY-GIGS. [British, 1800s, Farmer and Henley]

spunk up to fondle a woman sexually; to attempt to arouse a woman sexually. "Spunk" refers here to tinder or other stuff from which a fire can be built. [U.S. colloquial, mid 1800s] See also ROTTENLOGGING.

square 1. a strait-laced person; someone who probably does not smoke, drink, use drugs, or appreciate hard rock music. **2.** pertaining to a prude. [both senses, U.S. slang and colloquial, mid 1900s-pres.]

squarehead 1. a derogatory nickname for a Scandinavian or a German. [slang since the 1800s] **2.** any European. [Australian slang, 1900s, Baker]

square skirt a faithful and trustworthy woman. See SQUARE. [U.S. underworld, mid 1900s, Goldin, O'Leary, and Lipsius]

squatter's rites defecation; a jocular play on "squatter's rights." [U.S., mid 1900s-pres.]

squatter's writes writing done on the wall of a public restroom; graffiti produced while a person is seated and eliminating. A jocular play on "squatter's rights." [U.S., mid 1900s-pres.]

squaw 1. any woman or girl; one's wife. **2.** a prostitute; an ugly prostitute. [both senses, U.S. slang, mid 1900s]

squaw piss beer with a low alcohol content. *Cf.* NEAR BEER, SISSY BEER, TIGER PISS. For synonyms see SUDS. [U.S. slang, mid 1900s]

squeeze and a squirt copulation from the point of view of the male. [British slang, 1800s, Farmer and Henley]

squeeze-'em-close copulation; the sexual embrace. [British slang, 1800s, Farmer and Henley]

squeeze the lemon 1. to urinate, said of the male. [slang, 1800s-1900s] **2.** to masturbate, said of the male. [U.S. slang, mid 1900s-pres.]

squiffed intoxicated with alcohol. [British and U.S. slang, late 1800s-pres.]

squiffy 1. intoxicated with alcohol. [British and U.S. slang, late 1800s-pres.] **2.** stupid. [Australian, 1900s, Baker] **3.** sick; nauseated. [Australian and U.S. slang or colloquial, 1900s]

squill 1. a diuretic drug. **2.** an expectorant drug. Both are from the name of a plant. [since the 1500s]

squint the female genitals. From the PUDENDAL CLEAVAGE (*q.v.*). *Cf.* DUMB-SQUINT, LONG-EYE. [British slang, 1800s, Farmer and Henley]

squint-eyes a derogatory nickname for an Oriental; the same as SLANT-EYE (*q.v.*). [U.S., 1900s]

squirrel 1. the female genitals. **2.** the female pubic hair. Both senses are from FUR (*q.v.*). **3.** women in general; women considered as sexual objects. See BUNNY (sense 2), CONY. **4.** a psychoanalyst; a psychotherapist. Because each patient is a NUT (sense 1). [all senses, U.S. slang, mid 1900s-pres.]

squirt 1. a small person; a young child, especially a young boy. *Cf.* BOB SQUIRT. [U.S. colloquial, 1900s] **2.** to urinate. [U.S. slang and nonce, 1900s or before] **3.** to ejaculate semen. [widespread recurrent nonce; colloquial, 1900s and before]

squirts diarrhea. [in various forms since the 1500s]

srant a jocular and derogatory nickname for an Oriental. A corruption of SLANT (*q.v.*). [U.S. slang, mid 1900s]

sres-wort backslang for "trousers." For synonyms see GALLIGASKINS. [British, 1800s]

S.S. 1. the "screaming shits," diarrhea. [British with some U.S. use, mid 1900s] **2.** a warning that one has one's "shimmy showing," said by one (little) girl to another concerning a visible slip. *Cf.* P.P. [U.S. jocular and contrived, 1900s]

stable 1. an erection of the penis. [cognate with Latin *stabilis*, "firm, durable"; euphemistic word play in *A Winter's Tale* and *Much Ado About Nothing* (Shakespeare) **2.** a pimp's collection of prostitutes. *Cf.* CORRAL. [U.S. underworld and slang, early 1900s-pres.]

stable-boss 1. the manager of a brothel. **2.** a pimp. [both senses, U.S. underworld, early 1900s]

stable-dog the caretaker of a brothel. [U.S. underworld, mid 1900s, Montelone]

stable-horse a euphemism for STALLION (sense 1). *Cf.* SEED-HORSE, STONE-HORSE. [U.S. colloquial, 1900s or before]

stable-my-naggie (also **stable**) copulation. *Cf.* NAGGIE. For synonyms see SMOCKAGE. [British slang, 1800s, Farmer and Henley]

stacked pertaining to a woman with a sexually attractive body. Also used to describe a muscular male. [U.S. slang, mid 1900s-pres.]

stacked like a brick shit-house 1. pertaining to a woman with a sexually attractive body. One with many curves as might be found in the walls of a homemade brick privy. An elaboration of STACKED (*q.v.*). *Cf.* BUILT LIKE A BRICK SHIT-HOUSE. **2.** pertaining to a strong and muscular male. [U.S. colloquial, mid 1900s]

staff the penis. For synonyms see YARD. [widespread recurrent nonce; slang and colloquial, 1600s-pres.]

staff of life the penis. [widespread recurrent nonce; since the 1800s or before]

stag 1. pertaining to gatherings which are for men only. **2.** pertaining to a man who attends a gathering for couples without a female companion. [both senses, U.S. slang, mid 1900s-pres.]

staggerish intoxicated with alcohol. For synonyms see WOOFLED. [slang, 1900s]

stagger-juice strong alcoholic beverage. [Australian and U.S. slang, 1900s]

stagger-water (also **stagger-soup**) alcoholic liquor. [British and U.S. slang, mid 1900s]

stag-mag a magazine featuring nude women. *Cf.* FAG-MAG, STAG. [U.S. slang, mid 1900s]

stag movie 1. a privately shown movie for groups of men. Usually pornographic, SOFT-CORE or HARD-CORE (both *q.v.*). [U.S., early 1900s-pres.] **2.** any pornographic film. [U.S. slang, mid 1900s-pres.]

stake the penis. For synonyms see YARD. [recurrent nonce; since the 1600s or before]

stale 1. a very low prostitute. [late 1500s-1600s] **2.** urine. **3.** to urinate. Now said only of quadrupeds. [British rural colloquial, 1400s-1800s]

stale drunk intoxicated with alcohol; an intoxication lingering from the night before. [colloquial, 1800s]

stall a private compartment in a public restroom. [U.S., mid 1900s-pres.]

stallion 1. a male horse used for breeding purposes. *Cf.* STONE-HORSE. [since the 1300s] **2.** a lascivious man; a whoremonger; a man who copulates notoriously frequently or well. [since the early 1600s] **3.** a prostitute's customer. This may be the same as sense 2. [attested as British slang, 1800s, Barrère and Leland] **4.** a man kept by a woman for sexual purposes. [British cant, late 1700s, Grose] **5.** a beautiful and sexually attractive black woman. For synonyms see RAVEN BEAUTY. [U.S. black use, mid 1900s-pres.] **6.** the penis. [U.S. black use, 1900s]

stand 1. to erect the penis. [1500s-1600s] **2.** an erection of the penis. [colloquial, 1500s-1800s] **3.** a MOUTH-WHORE (*q.v.*). For synonyms see PICCOLO-PLAYER. [British slang, 1800s, Farmer and Henley]

stand, on the pertaining to the erect penis. [British colloquial, 1800s, Farmer and Henley]

standard an erection of the penis, the erect penis. [from *Love's Labour's Lost* (Shakespeare)]

standing erect; pertaining to the erect penis. [colloquial since the late 1500s]

standing too long in the sun intoxicated with alcohol. *Cf.* SUN, IN THE. [British colloquial, 1800s]

starch 1. semen in the expression TAKE THE STARCH OUT OF (*q.v.*). *Cf.* SPUNK. [British slang, 1800s] **2.** vigor; SPIRIT (*q.v.*); SPUNK (*q.v.*). [U.S. colloquial, mid 1900s-pres.] **3.** an adulterated drug. [U.S. drug culture, mid 1900s]

stardust cocaine. *Cf.* ANGEL DUST, HEAVEN DUST. [U.S. drug culture, mid 1900s-pres.]

stark-ballock-naked naked. *Cf.* BALLOCK-NAKED. [British, 1900s or before]

stark-ballux naked. A truncation of STARK-BALLOCK-NAKED (*q.v.*). [attested as Australian, late 1800s, *Dictionary of Slang and Unconventional English*]

starkers naked. [originally British; slang, early 1900s-pres.] Synonyms and related terms: ABRAM, ADAMATICAL, ALL FACE, AU NATUREL, BALLOCK-NAKED, BALLOCKY, BARE-ASSED, BARE-NAKED, BAREPOLES, BELLY-NAKED, BIRTH-NAKED, BLEAT, BLETE, BODY-NAKED, BUCK-NAKED, BUFF-BARE, FRONTAL NUDITY, HARRY STARKERS, IN CUERPO, IN MOROCCO, IN PURIS NATURALIBUS, IN STAG, IN THE ALTOGETHER, IN THE BUFF, IN THE NATURAL, IN THE RAW, MOTHER-NAKED, NAKED, NAKED AS MY NAIL, NAKED BUFF, NECKED, NUDDY, NUDE, ON THE SHALLOWS, PEELED, SKUDDY, STARBOLIC NAKED, STAR-BOLLOCK-NAKED, STARK-BALLOCK-NAKED, STARK-BALLUX, STARK NAKED, STARKO, STAR-NAKED, START-BONE-NAKED, START-BORN-NAKED, START-MOTHER-NAKED, START NAKED, STATE OF NATURE, SUNDAY SUIT, UNCLAD, UNCLOTHED, WEARING A SMILE, WHOLLY NAKED.

stark naked 1. nude; naked with the genitals uncovered. *Cf.* HARRY STARKERS. [since the early 1500s] **2.** gin. Because of its clearness. For synonyms see RUIN. [British slang and colloquial, early 1800s]

start-born-naked (also **start-bone-naked, start-mother-naked**) naked. [U.S. colloquial, 1800s]

stash a supply of marijuana or drugs; a cache of drugs. *Cf.* KIESTER STASH. [U.S. drug culture, mid 1900s-pres.]

state house a toilet; a privy. For synonyms see AJAX. [U.S. slang, early 1900s]

stay to maintain an erection for the completion of an act of copulation. [U.S. slang, mid 1900s-pres.]

steady-lapper a drunkard; a tippler. [Australian, 1900s]

steamed-up (also **steamed**) **1.** angry. [U.S. slang and colloquial, 1900s] **2.** intoxicated with alcohol. [U.S. slang, early 1900s] **3.** drug intoxicated. [U.S. underworld, early 1900s]

steeped intoxicated with alcohol. For synonyms see WOOFLED. [U.S. slang, early 1900s]

stem 1. an opium pipe. [U.S. underworld, early 1900s] **2.** the penis.

stemmer the penis. For synonyms see YARD. [U.S. slang, mid 1900s-pres.]

stem siren a prostitute. *Cf.* STEM (sense 2). [U.S. slang, mid 1900s, Montelone]

stencil a long, thin marijuana cigarette. [U.S. drug culture, mid 1900s-pres.]

step-ant a euphemism of avoidance for "piss-ant." See PIS-ANT. [U.S. dialect (Ozarks), 1900s or before, Randolph and Wilson]

step-ins women's underpants. [U.S. colloquial, 1900s]

step into one's last bus to die. For synonyms see DEPART. [British, 1800s]

step out on someone to be sexually unfaithful to someone. [U.S. colloquial, 1900s]

stepping-high intoxicated with drugs. *Cf.* HIGH (sense 2). For synonyms see TALL. [U.S. underworld, mid 1900s]

stern the posteriors. For synonyms see DUFF. [since the early 1600s]

stern-chaser a PEDERAST (*q.v.*); a SODOMITE (*q.v.*). [British slang, 1800s, Farmer and Henley]

stern-post the penis. *Cf.* POST (sense 1). [British slang, 1800s or before, Farmer and Henley]

stew 1. a brothel or an area of brothels; the same as the STEWS (*q.v.*). [since the 1300s] **2.** a prostitute. From sense 1. [British slang, 1600s-1800s] **3.** intoxicated with alcohol. *Cf.* STEWED. [U.S. slang, mid 1900s, Deak] **4.** a drunkard; a STEWIE (*q.v.*). [U.S. slang, early 1900s-pres.]

stew bum a drunken tramp; any drunkard. [U.S. underworld and slang, early 1900s-pres.]

stewed intoxicated with alcohol; very drunk. *Cf.* STEW (sense 3). For synonyms see WOOFLED. [slang, early 1700s pres., Ben Franklin]

stewie (also **stewy**) a drunkard, especially a low drunkard or a WINO (*q.v.*). [U.S. slang, mid 1900s-pres.]

stews, the a brothel or a street of brothels. From a nickname for a public bathhouse which grew to be associated with prostitution. *Cf.* BAGNIO. Halliwell defines "stews" as "strumpet." [since the 1300s]

stick 1. a venereal disease. [British, late 1800s, Farmer and Henley] **2.** an oaf; a dullard. [British colloquial, early 1800s-1900s] **3.** the penis. [widespread recurrent nonce; attested as U.S. slang, mid 1900s] **4.** to coit a woman. [widespread recurrent nonce; attested as British, 1800s, Farmer and Henley] **5.** a marijuana cigarette. For synonyms see MEZZROLL. [U.S. drug culture, mid 1900s-pres.]

stick, up the pregnant; the same as POLE, UP THE (sense 1). *Cf.* STICK (sense 3). [British slang, early 1900s]

stick and bangers the penis and testicles; the male genitals. From billiard jargon. *Cf.* POCKET-POOL. [British slang, late 1800s-early 1900s, Ware]

stick-croaker a physician specializing in venereal disease. *Cf.* STICK (senses 1 and 3). [U.S. underworld, mid 1900s, Goldin, O'Leary, and Lipsius]

Stick it! a curse. A variant of SHOVE IT! (*q.v.*). [British and U.S. colloquial, 1800s-1900s]

stick man a policeman. From the billy club he carries. For synonyms see FLAT-FOOT. [U.S. slang, mid 1900s]

stick of tea a marijuana cigarette. *Cf.* HOT-STICK, STICK (sense 5). [U.S. drug culture, mid 1900s-pres.]

stick one's spoon in the wall to die. *Cf.* LAY DOWN THE KNIFE AND FORK. [British slang, 1800s, Farmer and Henley]

sticks 1. a person's legs. No negative connotations. **2.** a woman's legs. Either very shapely legs or skinny and ugly legs. [U.S. slang, 1900s, Goldin, O'Leary, and Lipsius] **3.** a truncation of THAI STICKS (*q.v.*).

stiff 1. an erection of the penis. **2.** pertaining to the erectness of the penis. [both senses, colloquial since the early 1700s] **3.** intoxicated with alcohol. [U.S. slang, early 1700s-pres.] **4.** pertaining to a sexually loose person. [British slang, 1800s, Farmer and Henley] **5.** a drunkard. [U.S. slang, 1900s and before] **6.** a corpse. [widespread slang, late 1800s-pres.] **7.** a tramp; a hobo. [U.S. underworld and slang, 1900s] **8.** any male. [U.S. slang, mid 1900s-pres.]

stick and stout the erect penis. For synonyms see ERECTION. [mid 1600s, (Urquhart)]

stiffed intoxicated with alcohol. *Cf.* STIFF (sense 3). [U.S. slang, mid 1900s-pres.]

stiffeners pornography; materials used by males to cause erections; inspiration for sexual fantasies during masturbation. [U.S. slang, mid 1900s-pres.]

stiffo heavily intoxicated with alcohol. [U.S. slang, mid 1900s]

stiff one 1. an erection of the penis. [colloquial and nonce since the 1800s] **2.** a corpse. *Cf.* STIFF (sense 6). [U.S. slang, 1900s and before]

stiff prick 1. an erection of the penis. [widespread colloquial] **2.** a strict boss; a hard taskmaster. [U.S. slang, mid 1900s]

stiffy 1. an erection or partial erection.

Cf. STIFF (sense 1). [slang, 1800s-1900s] **2.** a corpse. *Cf.* STIFF (sense 6).

stimble to urinate. For synonyms see WHIZ. [British rural colloquial, 1800s]

sting the penis. *Cf.* STUNG BY A SERPENT. [British and elsewhere, 1800s, *Dictionary of Slang and Unconventional English*]

stinker 1. a rotten person; a SKUNK (sense 1). [since the 1600s] **2.** a small child; an infant. A jocular term for a baby with soiled diapers. [U.S. colloquial, 1900s] **3.** a release of intestinal gas. [U.S. slang, mid 1900s-pres.]

stinkibus inferior liquor; adulterated liquor. For synonyms see EMBALMING FLUID. [mock-Latin; British jocular slang, early 1700s]

stinko 1. smelling very badly. [U.S. slang, 1900s] **2.** intoxicated with alcohol. [widespread slang, early 1900s-pres.]

stink-pot 1. the vagina. *Cf.* PLAY AT STINK-FINGER. For synonyms see PASSAGE. [U.S. slang, mid 1900s] **2.** a juvenile term of contempt. [U.S., mid 1900s] **3.** a jocular nickname for a smelly baby. [U.S. colloquial, 1900s]

stink-weed marijuana. [U.S. underworld and drug culture, mid 1900s-pres.]

stir-shit a PEDERAST (*q.v.*); the INSERTOR (*q.v.*). *Cf.* BUTTOCK-STIRRING. [British slang, 1800s, Farmer and Henley]

stitch to coit a woman. See SEW UP. [British slang, 1800s, Farmer and Henley]

stitched intoxicated with alcohol. *Cf.* SEWED-UP (sense 1). [slang, early 1700s-1900s]

stogie a large, fat marijuana cigarette. From the slang term for a large cigar. [U.S. drug culture, mid 1900s]

stolled intoxicated with alcohol. Possibly from an earlier form of "stolen." [British slang, 1800s, Farmer and Henley]

stone-ache pain in the testicles. *Cf.* BLUE BALLS, HOT ROCKS. [U.S. dialect (Ozarks), 1900s or before, Randolph and Wilson]

stone blind heavily intoxicated with alcohol. From a term meaning "completely blind." [U.S. slang, mid 1900s]

stoned 1. intoxicated with alcohol. [U.S. slang, mid 1900s-pres.] **2.** intoxicated with drugs or marijuana. [U.S. drug culture, mid 1900s-pres.]

stone fox an attractive woman; a very sexy girl. [U.S. slang, mid 1900s-pres.]

stone-horse a stallion; a male horse kept for breeding purposes. *Cf.* SEED-HORSE, STABLE-HORSE. [colloquial, 1600s-1700s]

stones 1. kidney stones; gall stones. [since *c.* 1000] **2.** the testicles. *Cf.* GOOLIES, PEBBLES, ROCKS. For synonyms see WHIRLYGIGS. [since the 1100s]

stony blind intoxicated with alcohol; the same as STONE BLIND (*q.v.*). [British slang]

stool 1. an act of defecation. **2.** to defecate. [both since the early 1500s] **3.** feces; a mass of dung. [medical] **4.** the toilet; the water-flush toilet bowl.

stool of ease 1. a privy. **2.** a CHAMBER POT (*q.v.*); an enclosed chamber pot. [both senses, early 1500s]

stool of office a close stool; an enclosed CHAMBER POT (*q.v.*). [British, 1700s or before]

stoopnagel an oaf; a dullard. [U.S. slang and colloquial, mid 1900s-pres.]

stop-gap one's last child; one's final child. From "stopgap," a "temporary measure." *Cf.* GAP (sense 1). [British slang, early 1900s]

stork 1. to give birth. **2.** the process of giving birth. [both senses, U.S. slang, mid 1900s, Berrey and Van den Bark] **3.** to impregnate. From senses 1 and 2. [U.S. slang, mid 1900s-pres.] Synonyms for sense 3: BEGET, BOOM THE CENSUS, BUMP, COCK UP, DO A JOB, DO THE TRICK, DOUBLE-EVENT, FECUNDATE, FILL IN, FIX SOMEONE UP, GET WITH CHILD, GRAVIDATE, IMPREGNATE, INGRAVIDATE, INSEMINATE, JAZZ UP, KNOCK UP, PROGENERATE, RING THE BELL, SEAL, SEMINATION, SEW UP, SIRE, SPERMATIZE, SPOIL A WOMAN'S SHAPE, TIE UP.

storked pregnant. *Cf.* STORK (sense

3). For synonyms see FRAGRANT. [U.S. slang, early 1900s]

stork-mad 1. pregnant. **2.** eager to become pregnant; wanting to have a child. Said of women. [both senses, U.S. slang, mid 1900s, Berrey and Van den Bark]

stormy dick the penis. Rhyming slang for "prick." [U.S., 1900s, *Dictionary of Rhyming Slang*]

stozzled intoxicated with alcohol. *Cf.* SOZZLED. [U.S. slang, 1800s]

S.T.P. a stimulant and pseudo-hallucinogenic drug; the chemical compound 2,5-Dimethoxy-4-methylamphetamine. Also called D.O.M. (*q.v.*). From the trademarked name of a motor-oil additive reinterpreted as "serenity, tranquility, and peace." [U.S. drug culture, mid 1900s-pres.]

strain 1. offspring; children. No negative connotations. [1100s] **2.** to copulate. The *Oxford English Dictionary* defines this as "embrace tightly." [1300s, (Chaucer)] **3.** to apply force in an attempt to defecate; to strain at the stool. [since the mid 1600s] **4.** gonorrhea. The particular "strain" or species of microbes. [British euphemism, 1900s, *Dictionary of the Underworld*]

strain one's taters to urinate; an excuse to leave the room (to urinate) as if one were going to drain the water from boiled potatoes. *Cf.* DRAIN THE SPUDS. For synonyms see RETIRE. [British slang, late 1800s]

stram a prostitute; a strumpet. [British slang, 1800s, Farmer and Henley]

strap 1. to coit a woman; to copulate with a whore. [slang, colloquial, or nonce since the 1600s] **2.** the penis. *Cf.* YANK ONE'S STRAP. [U.S. slang, mid 1900s-pres.]

straw marijuana. *Cf.* HAY. [U.S. drug culture, mid 1900s-pres.]

strawberry fields the drug L.S.D. (*q.v.*). From the Beatles' song "Strawberry Fields Forever." [U.S. drug culture, mid 1900s-pres.]

streak 1. for a person to leave in a great hurry; to move very rapidly. No

negative connotations. [colloquial since the 1600s] **2.** to run around; to run around wildly. [attested as U.S. slang, 1970, *Current Slang*] **3.** to run about in public places totally nude. [U.S., late 1973-pres.] **4.** a wild party; a wild and exciting time. From sense 3. [U.S. slang, current]

streel a slattern; a slovenly woman. For synonyms see TROLLYMOG. [U.S. colloquial, 1800s-1900s]

street of sin (also **street of shame**) prostitution; the world of prostitutes. [U.S. euphemism, mid 1900s]

street pimp a pimp who works the streets with his prostitutes in order to be present when finances are arranged. [U.S. underworld, mid 1900s-pres.]

street sister a prostitute. [U.S. slang, mid 1900s]

street up for repairs the menses. See ROAD UP FOR REPAIRS. [British slang, 1800s, Farmer and Henley]

streetwalker a prostitute who solicits customers in the streets. [British and U.S. colloquial, 1800s-pres.]

stretcher a large penis. *Cf.* LEATHER-STRETCHER. [possibly written nonce; attested as British, mid 1700s]

stretch leather to coit a woman. [mid 1600s (Urquhart)]

stretch the rubber to be unfaithful to one's wife or mistress. *Cf.* SNAP THE RUBBER. [U.S. underworld, mid 1900s, Goldin, O'Leary, and Lipsius]

'Strewth! an oath and an exclamation, "By God's Truth!" For synonyms see 'ZOUNDS! (British, late 1800s]

strides (also **striders**) trousers. [widespread slang, late 1800s-1900s]

strike to coit a woman. For synonyms see OCCUPY. [British, 1600s]

Strike me dumb! (also **Strike me dead!**) an oath and an exclamation, "May God strike me dumb!" [colloquial, 1600s-1700s]

Strike me handsome! a mock oath and an exclamation, "May God strike me handsome!" [colloquial, 1900s]

stringer a whoremonger; a lecher. [British, early 1600s]

string of ponies a collection of prostitutes. Based on STABLE (sense 2) and horseracing jargon. [slang, 1900s]

striped intoxicated with alcohol. [U.S. slang, mid 1900s, Wentworth and Flexner]

strip well to look good unclothed or partially clothed; to have a sexually attractive body. Cf. CUT-UP WELL. [U.S., 1900s]

stroke 1. to coit a woman. [slang, late 1700s-pres.] **2.** to fondle; to caress a woman. For synonyms see FIRKYTOODLE. [British colloquial, 1800s and nonce elsewhere] **3.** to praise or compliment a person. [U.S. colloquial, mid 1900s-pres.]

stroke the lizard to masturbate. Cf. LIZARD. [U.S. slang, mid 1900s-pres.]

strollop 1. a woman of loose sexual morals; a TROLLOPS or a STRUMPET (both q.v.). [British and U.S. rural colloquial, 1900s or before] **2.** to wander about. From "stroll." [U.S. Southern colloquial, 1900s]

stromp a masculine woman; a woman exhibiting lesbian behavior. [U.S. dialect or colloquial, 1900s, Wentworth]

strong and thin gin; a glass of gin. Rhyming slang for "gin." For synonyms see RUIN. [U.S. slang, early 1900s]

strong waters alcoholic spirits. For synonyms see BOOZE. [colloquial, 1800s-1900s]

strop one's beak to coit a woman. Cf. BEAK. [British slang, 1800s, Farmer and Henley]

strossers a type of tight trousers. For synonyms see GALLIGASKINS. [1500s-1600s]

strull a female tramp; a tramp's woman. Cf. STROLLOP, TRULL. [U.S. dialect or colloquial, 1900s or before, Wentworth]

strum 1. a prostitute. A truncation of STRUMPET (q.v.). [cant or slang, late 1600s-1800s] **2.** to coit a woman; to copulate. [British slang or cant, late 1700s, Grose]

strumpet 1. a prostitute. [since the 1300s] **2.** to practice prostitution. [late 1500s]

strung-out 1. intoxicated with drugs. See LINE (sense 5). **2.** addicted to drugs. [both senses, U.S. drug culture, mid 1900s-pres.]

strut-fart a person, usually a male, who struts around looking very important. Cf. FART (sense 3). [U.S. colloquial, 1900s]

stub a fool; an oaf. [British and later, U.S. colloquial, early 1600s-early 1900s]

stubbed intoxicated with alcohol. For synonyms see WOOFLED. [U.S. slang, early 1700s, Ben Franklin]

stubble the female pubic hair. Cf. TAKE A TURN IN THE STUBBLE. [British, 1700s]

stuccoed intoxicated with alcohol. A play on PLASTERED (q.v.). [U.S. slang, early 1900s]

stud 1. a male horse used for breeding purposes. [U.S. colloquial, 1800s-1900s] **2.** a human male emphasizing one or more of the following characteristics: virility, stylishness, sex appeal, sexual success with women. [U.S. slang and colloquial, early 1900s-pres.]

studhammer a male who is very busy with women; a sexually successful male. [U.S. slang, mid 1900s]

stuff 1. to coit a woman; to penetrate a woman. **2.** semen. [senses 1 and 2 are colloquial 1600s-1900s] **3.** women considered as sexual objects. Also stuff in the sense "cloth." See DRESS GOODS, DRY GOODS. Cf. SPLIT-STUFF. [British and U.S. slang and colloquial, late 1800s-pres.] **4.** copulation; an act of copulation. **5.** the female genitals. [senses 4 and 5 are U.S. slang, mid 1900s-pres.] **6.** the penis; the VIRILIA (q.v.). [U.S. slang and colloquial, mid 1900s-pres.] **7.** marijuana. [U.S. drug culture, mid 1900s-pres.] **8.** heroin. Cf. WHITE STUFF. [U.S. underworld and drug culture, mid 1900s-pres.] **9.** morphine, Demerol (trademark), or other hard drugs. [U.S. underworld and slang, early 1900s-pres.]

stuffer a SODOMITE (*q.v.*); a PEDERAST (*q.v.*); the INSERTOR (*q.v.*). See the entries under GUT-BUTCHER. *Cf.* STUFF (sense 4). [U.S. slang, mid 1900s, Montelone]

stum 1. marijuana. **2.** a sleeping pill; a barbiturate tablet or capsule. Because it makes a person stumble. *Cf.* STUMBLER. [both senses, U.S. drug culture, mid 1900s-pres.]

stumble-bum 1. a tramp or hobo, possibly an alcoholic tramp. **2.** any oaf or dullard. [both senses, U.S. underworld and slang, mid 1900s-pres.]

stumbler a barbiturate capsule or tablet, usually Seconal (trademark). *Cf.* STUM (sense 2). For synonyms see BARB. [U.S. drug culture, mid 1900s-pres.]

stump 1. the penis. *Cf.* CARNAL STUMP. [British, 1600s] **2.** an oaf; a fool. [British slang, 1800s, Farmer and Henley]

stump-likker homebrewed whisky; moonshine. [U.S. slang, mid 1900s]

stung intoxicated with alcohol. [Australian slang, early 1900s-pres.]

stung by a serpent pregnant. *Cf.* PIZENED, POISONED, STING. [slang, 1800s or before]

stunned intoxicated with alcohol. For synonyms see WOOFLED. [widespread slang and colloquial, early 1900s-pres.]

stupehead an oaf; a blockhead. [U.S. colloquial, 1900s]

stupid 1. a blockhead; an oaf. From the literal meaning. [since the 1800s] Synonyms: AIR-BRAINED, ASS-BRAINED, BARMYBRAINED, BEEF-HEADED, BEEF-WITTED, BESOM-HEADED, BIRD-BRAINED, BLOCKHEADED, BLOCKY, BLUBBER-BRAINED, BLUBBER-HEADED, BLUNDER-HEADED, BONEHEADED, BOOF, BOTTLE-HEADED, BUFFLE-BRAINED, BUFFLE-HEADED, BULLET-HEADED, BULLHEAD, BUTT-HEADED, CLAY-BRAINED, CLOD-POLISH, CLOD-SKULLED, CLOUTER-HEADED, COCK-BRAIN, COCK-BRAINED, CULVER-HEADED, EMPTY-SKULLED, FEATHER-BRAINED, FEATHERHEADED, FUCK-BRAINED, HALF-HARD, HAMMER-HEADED, HARE-BRAINED, IDLEHEADED, LEATHER-BRAINED, LOBBER-HEADED, LOGGER-HEADED, MAGGOT-BRAINED, RUM-DUMB, SCRAMBLE-BRAINED, SHIT-BRAINED, SLOW, SQUIFFY, THICK, TIMBER-HEADED. **2.** heavily intoxicated with alcohol. [widespread slang, 1800s-1900s]

sub 1. an oaf; a person with subnormal intelligence. [U.S. slang, early 1900s] **2.** to be sexually promiscuous; to GO DOWN (*q.v.*) easily. **3.** a sexually promiscuous man or woman. Senses 2 and 3 from a truncation of "submarine." [both senses, U.S. slang, mid 1900s]

submarine a bedpan. *Cf.* DUCK (sense 1). [U.S. slang, mid 1900s, Berrey and Van den Bark]

sub-trousers underpants. *Cf.* U-TROU. [late 1800s]

suburb pertaining to moral disorder and sexually loose living. Refers to the vice once prevalent in areas adjacent to the City of London. [colloquial, late 1500s]

suburban a prostitute; a sexually loose woman. [1500s-1600s]

succeed amorously to achieve coition, from the male point of view. *Cf.* ACHIEVE, QUALIFY, SCORE. [British use, 1800s]

suck 1. strong alcoholic beverages. [British slang, 1600s-1700s] **2.** a sycophant. *Cf.* BUM-SUCKER, EGG-SUCKER, SUCK-ASS. [British and U.S. slang, 1900s] **3.** to toady; to act the sycophant. [U.S. slang, early 1900s-pres.] **4.** special influence with a person; "pull" with a person or an organization. [U.S. slang, mid 1900s] **5.** to perform PENILINGUS or CUNNILINGUS (both *q.v.*). *Cf.* SUCK OFF. [British and U.S. slang, 1800s-1900s] **6.** an act of penilingus. [U.S. slang, 1900s and before]

suck-and-swallow the female genitals, specifically the vagina. *Cf.* SWALLOW-COCK. [British slang, 1800s, Farmer and Henley]

suck-ass a sycophant. *Cf.* KISS-ASS. [U.S. slang, mid 1900s-pres.]

suckathon group sex where the principal activity is oral sex. See similar subjects at GROUP SEX. [U.S., mid 1900s-pres.]

suck bamboo (also **suck the bamboo**) to smoke opium. For synonyms see SMOKE. [U.S. underworld, early 1900s or before]

suck-bottle (also **suck-spigot**) a drunkard. [colloquial, mid 1600s]

sucked intoxicated with alcohol. For synonyms see WOOFLED. [British slang, 1800s, *Sinks of London Laid Open*]

sucker 1. the penis. *Cf.* LADIES' LOLLIPOP. [British slang, 1700s-1800s] **2.** a baby. [British slang, early 1800s, Jon Bee] **3.** a woman or a prostitute who performs penilingus; a COCKSUCKER (sense 1). *Cf.* MOUTH-WHORE. [British and later U.S. slang, 1800s-1900s] **4.** a dupe; a gullible person.

suck off to perform CUNNILINGUS or PENILINGUS (both *q.v.*). [British and U.S. slang, 1800s-pres.]

suck queen a homosexual male who prefers PENILINGUS (*q.v.*). See QUEEN for similar subjects. [(U.S. homosexual use, mid 1900s, Farrell]

sucks!, It a rude exclamation, "It is extremely bad." [U.S. slang, mid 1900s-pres.]

suckster a male performer of PENILINGUS (*q.v.*). *Cf.* SUCKSTRESS. [British slang, 1800s, Farmer and Henley]

suckstress a female performer of PENILINGUS (*q.v.*). *Cf.* SUCKSTER. [British slang, 1800s, Farmer and Henley]

suck the bamboo to smoke opium. See SUCK BAMBOO.

suck the sugar-stick to copulate, said of a woman. Perhaps to perform PENILINGUS (*q.v.*). *Cf.* SUGAR-STICK. [British slang, 1800s, Farmer and Henley]

sucky (also **suckey**) intoxicated with alcohol. For synonyms see WOOFLED. [British slang, 1600s-1700s]

sucky-fucky 1. an act of PENILINGUS (*q.v.*) followed by orthogenital copulation. **2.** an act of PENILINGUS (*q.v.*). [both senses, U.S. slang, mid 1900s-pres.]

suction influence; "pull"; the same as SUCK (sense 4). [U.S. slang, mid 1900s]

sudds, in the (also **suds, in the**) intoxicated with alcohol; intoxicated with beer or ale. [U.S. slang, early 1700s, Ben Franklin]

suds beer. [British and U.S. slang, 1900s] Synonyms: BARLEY BROTH, BARLEY JUICE, BARLEY WATER, BELCH, BELSH, BERPS, BEVVY, BUB, BUCKET OF SUDS, COCK-ALE, COLD COFFEE, COLORADO COOLAID, FAR AND NEAR, GROWLER, KOOL-AID, LUBE, LUSH, NEAR BEER, NEVER-FEAR, OIL OF BARLEY, PIG SWEAT, PISS, PONG, PONGELOW, PURGE, QUEER BEER, REEB, SISSY BEER, SKIT, SQUAW PISS, SUPER SUDS, SWIPES, TANGLE-LEG, WITCH-PISS.

suede a derogatory nickname for a Negro. [U.S. slang, mid 1900s-pres.]

suey bowl a Chinese opium den. From "chop suey." [U.S. slang, early 1900s]

Suffering cats! (also **Suffering catfish!**) a mock oath and an exclamation. For synonyms see 'ZOUNDS!

Suffering sassafrass! a mock oath based on "Suffering saints!" [U.S. colloquial, 1900s]

Suffering seaserpents! a mock oath based on "Suffering saints!" [U.S. colloquial, 1900s]

Suffering seaweeds! a mock oath derived from SUFFERING SEASERPENTS! (*q.v.*). [U.S. colloquial, 1900s]

Suffering snakes! (also **Great snakes!**, **Holy suffering snakes!**) a mock oath based on "Suffering saints!" For synonyms see 'ZOUNDS! [U.S. colloquial, 1900s]

sugar 1. shit. Partridge suggests this is a blend of SHIT and BUGGER (both *q.v.*). [British and U.S. slang, 1900s] **2.** heroin. [U.S. drug culture, mid 1900s-pres.] **3.** the drug L.S.D. (*q.v.*). From the use of sugar cubes in its ingestion. [U.S. drug culture, mid 1900s-pres.]

sugar-basin the female genitals, specifically the vagina. The mate for the SUGAR-STICK (*q.v.*). [British slang, 1800s, Farmer and Henley]

sugar-daddy 1. an older man who

keeps a young girl. [U.S. slang, early 1900s-pres.] **2.** an elderly homosexual male who keeps a younger homosexual male. [U.S. homosexual use, mid 1900s-pres.]

sugar doughnut the female genitals; the vagina. [U.S. slang, mid 1900s-pres.]

sugar lump (also **sugar**) the drug L.S.D. (q.v.). [U.S. drug culture, mid 1900s-pres.]

sugar pimp a suave, sweet-talking pimp. [U.S. underworld, mid 1900s-pres.]

sugar-stick the penis, especially the erect penis. [British slang, early 1800s]

suggestive obscene; possibly obscene. Cf. ADULT, FRANK. [vague and euphemistic; U.S. colloquial, 1900s]

summer complaint diarrhea, especially that experienced in the summer. For synonyms see QUICKSTEP. [colloquial, mid 1800s-pres.]

summer skies morning glory seeds used as a hallucinogenic agent. From the color variety name. For synonyms see SEEDS. [U.S. drug culture, mid 1900s-pres.]

sun, in the intoxicated with alcohol. Cf. STANDING TOO LONG IN THE SUN. [slang, 1800s-1900s]

Sunday face the posteriors; the naked posteriors. [British and U.S. colloquial, mid 1800s-1900s]

Sunday suit nakedness. Cf. BIRTHDAY SUIT; ONE'S SUNDAY BEST, IN. [U.S. slang, mid 1900s-pres.]

sun in the eyes intoxication with alcohol. [British and U.S. slang or colloquial, 1800s-1900s]

sun one's moccasins 1. to be thrown from a horse. [U.S. colloquial, mid 1900s, Berrey and Van den Bark] **2.** to die. For synonyms see DEPART. [U.S. colloquial, 1900s]

sunshine the drug L.S.D. (q.v.). Cf. ORANGE SUNSHINE, YELLOW SUNSHINE. [U.S. drug culture, mid 1900s-pres.]

superblow cocaine. Cf. BLOW (sense 5). [U.S. drug culture, mid 1900s-pres.]

supercharged 1. intoxicated with al-

cohol. [British and U.S. slang, 1900s] **2.** intoxicated with drugs. Cf. CHARGE (sense 1). [U.S. drug culture, mid 1900s-pres.]

superdroopers large breasts; pendulous breasts. Cf. DROOPERS. [U.S. slang, mid 1900s-pres.]

supergrass (also **superweed**) the drug P.C.P. (q.v.). Sometimes sold deceptively as T.H.C. (q.v.), the active ingredient in marijuana. Cf. GRASS (sense 1), WEED (sense 1). [U.S. drug culture, mid 1900s-pres.]

superjock 1. an excellent athlete. **2.** a very virile and well-built man regardless of athletic ability. [both sense, U.S. slang, mid 1900s-pres.]

superpot marijuana mixed with other drugs. [U.S. drug culture, mid 1900s-pres.]

superskirt a sexually attractive woman. Cf. SKIRT. For synonyms see DRY GOODS. [U.S. slang, mid 1900s-pres.]

super-soaper methaqualone. Cf. SOAP (sense 3). [U.S. drug culture, mid 1900s-pres.]

superspade a black man overly self-conscious of his race. Derogatory. A stereotypical SPADE (sense 3). [U.S. black use, mid 1900s]

super suds beer; Coor's (trademark) beer. Cf. SUDS. [U.S. slang, mid 1900s-pres.]

supper the female genitals. From the expression GIVE THE OLD MAN HIS SUPPER (q.v.). [British, 1800s]

supple both ends of it to copulate; to bring an end to an erection by causing an ejaculation. [from Scots; British slang, late 1700s-1800s, (Robert Burns)]

surface fuel dried cattle dung used for fuel. Cf. BODEWASH, BUFFALO CHIPS, PRAIRIE COAL. [U.S. euphemism, early 1900s]

surfer the drug P.C.P. (q.v.). [U.S. drug culture, mid 1900s-pres.]

surge a venereal discharge due to gonorrhea.

surly a nickname and an avoidance for "bull." [U.S. colloquial, early 1900s]

SUSFU "situation unchanged, still fucked-up," pertaining to a situation which is perpetually messed-up. [U.S. slang, mid 1900s]

swabler a dirty fellow. Possibly related to "swabber," a common laborer. [attested as 1800s, Matsell]

swab someone's tonsils to neck; to kiss deeply with the tongue. Named after the medical treatment. [U.S. slang, early 1900s-pres.]

swacked intoxicated with alcohol. For synonyms see WOOFLED. [U.S. slang, early 1900s]

SWAK "sealed with a kiss." *Cf.* SWANK. *[originally military; widespread slang, 1900s]*

swallow-cock a prostitute. *Cf.* SUCK-AND-SWALLOW. [British slang, 1800s, Farmer and Henley]

swallowed a watermelon seed pregnant. For synonyms see FRAGRANT. [U.S. colloquial, 1900s]

swamped (also **swampt**) intoxicated with alcohol. [slang since the early 1700s]

SWANK "sealed with a nice kiss." *Cf.* SWAK. *[British military, Fraser and Gibbons]*

swap spit (also **swap spits**) **1.** to kiss deeply using the tongue. [U.S. slang, 1900s] **2.** to perform mutual PENILINGUS (*q.v.*). [U.S. underworld, mid 1900s, Goldin, O'Leary, and Lipsius]

swarf a fainting spell; a swoon. [mid 1400s]

swash-bucket a slattern; an assemblage of human garbage. Also possibly a prostitute. [British colloquial, 1700s-1800s]

swattled intoxicated with alcohol. [British and U.S. slang, 1800s-1900s]

swazzled intoxicated with alcohol. A spelling variant of SWOZZLED (*q.v.*). [U.S. slang, 1900s]

sweaty-toe cheese inferior, soft cheese. *Cf.* CROTCH-CHEESE. [British slang, 1800s]

sweet 1. intoxicated with alcohol. *Cf.* HAPPY. [Caribbean (Jamaican), Cassidy

and Le Page] **2.** pertaining to a homosexual male; pertaining to male homosexuality. *Cf.* SWEETIE. [U.S. slang, mid 1900s-pres.] **3.** an amphetamine tablet or capsule. Usually in the plural. [U.S. drug culture, mid 1900s-pres.]

sweetbriar the female pubic hair. For synonyms see DOWNSHIRE. [British slang, 1800s, Farmer and Henley]

sweet-by-and-by heaven; death; the afterlife. [U.S. colloquial, 1900s or before]

sweet cheesecake a jocular disguise of "Sweet Jesus." [U.S. colloquial, 1900s] Synonyms and oaths: CHEESE AND CRUST!, CHRISTMAS!, CHRISTOPHER COLUMBUS!, CRIPES!, CRIPUS!, GEEKUS CROW!, GEEZ!, GEMMENIE!, GREASE US TWICE!, J.C. JEANSRICE!, JEE!, JEEPERS!, JERUSALEM SLIM, JIMINY!, LAMB, LAMB OF GOD, MESSIAH, SON OF RIGHTEOUSNESS, THE ANOINTED, THE ANOINTED ONE, THE DIVINITY, THE LORD, THE NAZARENE, THE REDEEMER, THE SAVIOUR, X., XPC, XS.

sweet chocolate a sexually attractive black woman. *Cf.* CHOCOLATE DROP, HOP CHOCOLATE. [U.S. slang, mid 1900s]

sweetie a homosexual male. *Cf.* SWEET (sense 2). For synonyms see EPICENE. [U.S. slang, mid 1900s-pres.]

sweet Lucy marijuana. *Cf.* LUCY IN THE SKY WITH DIAMONDS. [U.S. slang, mid 1900s-pres.]

sweet lunch marijuana. For synonyms see MARI. [U.S. drug culture, mid 1900s-pres.]

sweet-meat 1. the penis. *Cf.* MEAT (sense 4). [British slang, 1800s, Farmer and Henley] **2.** a young girl kept as a mistress. [British slang, 1800s, Farmer and Henley] **3.** any young girl or woman. [U.S. slang, mid 1900s-pres.]

sweet potatoes the human breasts. *Cf.* MURPHIES. [U.S. slang, 1900s]

sweet stuff any powdered narcotic. *Cf.* WHITE STUFF (sense 3). [U.S. underworld, mid 1900s]

sweet young thing a young girl; an innocent girl. [U.S. colloquial, mid 1900s-pres.]

swell-head 1. a conceited fellow; a person with an exaggerated sense of self-importance. [since the late 1800s] **2.** a drunkard. From the swollen feeling in one's head after drinking excessively. [slang, 1800s-1900s]

Swensker a nickname for a Swede. [U.S. colloquial, 1900s]

swig 1. to drink. [British, 1600s] **2.** a drink, especially a drink of an alcoholic beverage. Also **swiggle**. [since the 1600s or before]

swigged intoxicated with alcohol. *Cf.* SWIG. [British colloquial, 1800s]

swiggered damned. *Cf.* JIG-SWIG-GERED!, I'LL BE. [U.S. colloquial, 1900s or before]

swiggled intoxicated with alcohol. From the colloquial term "swiggle," meaning "drink." [British and U.S. colloquial, 1800s-pres.]

swill 1. to drink heavily. [since the early 1500s] **2.** alcoholic beverages. From a colloquial term for "hog-wash." [since the early 1600s]

swilled-up (also **swilled**) intoxicated with alcohol. [British and U.S. slang, 1800s-1900s]

swillocks a drunkard. *Cf.* SWILL. For synonyms see ALCHY.

swine-drunk heavily intoxicated with alcohol. *Cf.* SOW-DRUNK. [colloquial, late 1500s-1900s]

swing 1. to copulate. [colloquial, early 1500s-1600s] **2.** to hang; to be hanged. [colloquial since the early 1500s] **3.** the gallows. [British colloquial, 1700s or before] **4.** to neck and pet. [U.S. slang, early 1900s, Weseen] **5.** to engage in homosexual activities. [U.S., mid 1900s] **6.** to be involved in sexual fads, group sex, or the swapping of sexual partners. [U.S. slang, mid 1900s-pres.]

swing both ways to be bisexual; to practice homosexual and heterosexual sexual activities indiscriminately. [U.S. slang, mid 1900s-pres.]

swinge (also **swynge**) to copulate; the same as SWING (sense 1).

swinger 1. a person who participates in swinging. See SWING (sense 6). **2.** a youthful, socially active, and knowledgeable person. Not necessarily with sexual connotations. [both senses, U.S. slang, mid 1900s-pres.] **3.** a person who uses all forms of drugs. [U.S. drug culture, mid 1900s-pres.]

swingers 1. the testicles. For synonyms see WHIRLYGIGS. [colloquial and nonce, 1800s-pres.] **2.** breasts; breasts which jiggle and bounce when a woman is walking. For synonyms see BOSOM. [widespread colloquial and nonce, 1900s]

swing man a drug dealer. *Cf.* BAG-MAN. [U.S. drug culture, mid 1900s-pres.]

swing party a group sex party. See GROUP SEX for similar terms. From SWING (sense 6). [U.S. slang, mid 1900s-pres.]

swinny intoxicated with alcohol. For synonyms see WOOFLED. [British slang, 1800s, Farmer and Henley]

swipe the penis. [U.S. black use, 1900s, Dillard]

swiper a heavy drinker; a drunkard. [colloquial, early 1800s]

swipes inferior beer; beer weak in alcoholic content. [slang, mid 1800s-1900s]

swippington a drunkard. *Cf.* LUSHING-TON, THIRSTINGTON. [Australian slang, early 1900s]

swipy intoxicated with alcohol. See SWIPES. [British slang, mid 1800s]

swish 1. absent without leave. Onomatopoetic for the sound of a rapid departure. *Cf.* A.W.O.L. [Australian military, early 1900s, Baker] **2.** a homosexual male. [U.S. slang, mid 1900s] **3.** pertaining to a homosexual or effeminate male; pertaining to homosexuality. *Cf.* SWISHY. [U.S. slang, mid 1900s-pres.] **4.** to walk in an effeminate manner; to flaunt homosexual or effeminate characteristics. [U.S. slang, mid 1900s]

swishy effeminate; homosexual. [U.S. slang, mid 1900s]

switchel copulation. See SWITCH. [British, 1700s]

switch-hitter a bisexual person. From the baseball term. [U.S. slang, mid 1900s-pres.]

swive (also **swhyve, swyfe**) to coit a woman; to copulate. [1300s or before (Chaucer)]

swivelly intoxicated with alcohol. From the oscillations of a swivel. [British and U.S. slang, 1800s-1900s]

swiver 1. a lecher; a whoremonger. *Cf.* SWIVE. [mid 1400s] **2.** the penis. [slang or nonce, mid 1900s]

swizzle 1. to drink; to drink alcohol. [British slang, mid 1800s] **2.** alcohol; beer or ale, or a mixture of the two. [British and U.S. slang, mid 1800s-pres.]

swizzled intoxicated with alcohol. *Cf.* SWIZZLE. [British and U.S. slang, mid 1800s-pres.]

swizzle-guts a drunkard. For synonyms see ALCHY. [British and U.S. slang, 1800s-1900s]

swobsy large and fat. [British colloquial dialect, 1900s and before]

Swoggle my eyes! an oath and an exclamation, "May God swoggle my eyes!" *Cf.* HORNSWOGGLE. [U.S. nautical, 1900s or before]

sword the penis. *Cf.* BRACMARD, CUT-LASS, DIRK, PORK-SWORD. [widespread recurrent nonce]

'Swounds! (also **'Sowns!, 'Swonds!, 'Swones!, 'Swounds!, 'Swouns!**) an oath and an exclamation. "By God's wounds!" See 'ZOUNDS! [colloquial, late 1500s]

swow!, I "I declare!" [U.S. colloquial, mid 1800s]

swozzled intoxicated with alcohol. *Cf.* SWAZZLED. [U.S. slang, mid 1900s, Wentworth and Flexner]

synthetic grass synthetic marijuana, the chemical compound T.H.C. (*q.v.*). *Cf.* GRASS (sense 1). [U.S. drug culture, mid 1900s-pres.]

synthetic marijuana the drug P.C.P. or T.H.C. (both *q.v.*). [U.S. drug culture, mid 1900s-pres.]

syph 1. syphilis. For synonyms see SPECIFIC STOMACH. **2.** a person infected with syphilis. [U.S. slang and colloquial, 1900s]

syphon off to urinate. *Cf.* DRAW OFF. For synonyms see WHIZ. [U.S. slang, mid 1900s, Berrey and Van den Bark]

syphon the python to urinate. *Cf.* ROCK PYTHON. [Australian slang, 1900s]

T

T. 1. an abbreviation of TEA (sense 3), "marijuana." [U.S. drug culture, mid 1900s-pres.] **2.** Tuinal (trademark), a barbiturate. *Cf.* TOOIE, TUIE. [U.S. drug culture, mid 1900s-pres.]

table-grade pertaining to a sexually attractive female who looks good enough to eat. Refers to CUNNILINGUS (*q.v.*). *Cf.* BARBECUE, EATING-STUFF, GOOD-EATING.

tablet a contraceptive tablet, *i.e.*, the PILL (sense 3). [U.S. euphemism, mid 1900s-pres.]

TABU "typical army balls-up"; "typical army box-up," a typical army mess. Reinforced by "taboo." See SNAFU for similar expressions. [British military, World War II]

tackle 1. a mistress. [British, 1600s] **2.** the male genitals; the VIRILIA (*q.v.*). *Cf.* GEAR (sense 1), TAIL-TACKLE. [British, 1700s]

tacky intoxicated with alcohol; sticky with the moisture of alcohol. [U.S., 1900s or before]

taco (also **taco-bender**) a derogatory term for a Mexican or a Mexican American. Patterned on SPAGHETTI (*q.v.*). [U.S. slang, mid 1900s-pres.]

TAFUBAR "things are fucked-up beyond all recognition," said of an extremely bad situation. See SNAFU for similar expressions. [military, World War II]

tail 1. the female genitals. **2.** the posteriors; the buttocks; occasionally, the anus. [euphemistic and widespread] **3.** the penis. [senses 1-3 since the 1300s] **4.** to coit a woman. [since the 1700s] **5.** copulation. [U.S., early 1900s-pres.] **6.** a prostitute. [British and U.S., early 1800s-pres., *Lexicon Balatronicum*] **7.** women considered solely as sexual objects. [U.S. slang, 1900s or before] Synonyms for sense 7: ARTICLE, ASS, BIT OF GOODS, BIT OF ROUGH, BRUSH, BUSH, BUTT, C., CALI-CO, CATTLE, CAVE, CHUNK OF MEAT, COCK, COOLER, COOT, COVER GIRL, CRUMPET, FISH, FUCK, GASH, GIRL, GIRL STREET, GOOSE, GROUSE, GUSSET, HAIR, HAT, HOLE, JAZZ, KIPPY-DOPE, MAKE, MEAT, MUFF, NOOKY, PIECE, PIECE OF EVE'S FLESH, PIECE OF MUTTON, PIECE OF STUFF, PIECE OF TAIL, PLACKET, PORK, PUNCH, PUSSY, RABBIT-PIE, SAD-DLE, SCREW, SHAFT, SKIRT, SNATCH, SPLIT, SPLIT-ARSE MECHANIC, SPLIT-MUT-TON, SPLIT-STUFF, SPLIT-TAIL, STUFF, TIT, TRIM, WHISKER, WOMAN-FLESH.

tail-box the female genitals, specifically the vagina. *Cf.* BOX (sense 2). [U.S. slang, 1900s]

tail-fruit children; offspring. [British, 1800s] Synonyms: BODILY ISSUE, EN-CUMBRANCE, GET, INCREASE, ISSUE, OFF-SPRING, PATTER OF TINY FEET, TEAPOT LID, URCHIN.

tail-peddler a prostitute. For synonyms see HARLOT. [U.S. underworld, 1900s]

tail-pipe the penis. [slang and nonce, 1800s-pres.]

tail-shot an audible release of intestinal gas. For synonyms see GURK. [British, 1600s]

tail-tackle the penis or the VIRILIA (*q.v.*). *Cf.* GEAR (sense 1), TACKLE (sense 2). [U.S. slang, 1800s, Farmer and Henley]

tail-tickling copulation. *Cf.* TICKLE-TAIL. [British slang, 1800s, Farmer and Henley]

tail-water 1. semen. **2.** urine; the same as TAIL-JUICE (*q.v.*).

tail-work copulation. [British slang, 1800s or before]

taint 1. a very dirty slattern. [British, 1800s or before] **2.** the PERINEUM (*q.v.*) of a woman. Properly spelled " 'tain't" because the perineum " 'tain't cunt and 'tain't ass." [U.S. slang, mid 1900s]

take 1. to allow a man to intromit his penis. [British, late 1600s, Farmer and Henley] **2.** to become pregnant, usually said of animals. *Cf.* CATCH (sense 2), KETCHED. [British and U.S. colloquial, 1800s-1900s] **3.** to receive the penis into the mouth or anus, said of a CATAMITE or fellator. From sense 2. *Cf.* CATCH (sense 1), RECEIVER. [slang, 1900s or before]

take a crap to defecate. Somewhat milder than TAKE A SHIT (*q.v.*), for which it is euphemistic. *Cf.* CRAP. [U.S. colloquial, 1900s]

take a dump to defecate. See DUMP (sense 2). For synonyms see EASE ONE-SELF.]U.S. slang, 1900s]

take a leak to urinate. For synonyms see WHIZ. [U.S. colloquial, 1900s]

take an earth bath to die and be buried. [U.S., 1900s or before]

take a shard to become intoxicated with alcohol. [British slang, 1800s, Farmer and Henley]

take a shit to defecate. [U.S. collo-quial, 1900s or before]

take a turn in the stubble to copu-late. STUBBLE (*q.v.*) is the female pubic hair. [British slang, 1800s]

take a turn on shooter's hill to copulate. "Shoot" refers to ejacula-tion. [British slang, 1800s, Farmer and Henley]

take down to cool a man's sexual passion by satisfying him sexually. *Cf.* BRING DOWN BY HAND. [from *Romeo and Juliet* (Shakespeare)]

take his commission to castrate a man. [U.S., 1900s or before]

take in beef to receive a man sexual-ly, said of a woman. BEEF (sense 2) refers to the penis.

take in cargo (also **take on cargo**) to get drunk. [British, early 1800s, (Pierce Egan)]

take in cream for a woman to permit copulation. CREAM (sense 1) refers to semen. [British slang, 1800s, Farmer and Henley]

take it out in trade for a person to permit copulation in payment of a debt. [U.S. slang, early 1900s-pres., Monte-lone]

taken intoxicated or unconscious due to narcotics. For synonyms see TALL. [U.S. underworld, early 1900s]

take Nebuchadnezzar out to grass for a woman to permit copulation. The "grass" refers to GREENS (*q.v.*), "sex-ual pleasure." *Cf.* NEBUCHADNEZZAR. [British, 1800s, Farmer and Henley]

take oneself in hand to masturbate, said of a male. For synonyms see WASTE TIME. [U.S. slang, mid 1900s-pres.]

take one's snake for a gallop to urinate. *Cf.* BLACKSNAKE, ROCK PYTHON, SYPHON THE PYTHON. [British military, 1900s, *Dictionary of Slang and Un-conventional English*]

take on fuel to drink alcohol to ex-cess. For synonyms see PLAY CAMELS. [U.S. colloquial, 1900s]

take the long count (also **take the count**) to die. [U.S., early 1900s-pres.]

take the piss out of someone (also **knock the piss out of someone**) to deflate someone; to make a person (almost always a male) behave with less boasting and bravado. *Cf.* KNOCK THE SHIT OUT OF SOMEONE. [British and U.S., 1900s]

take the starch out of for a woman to copulate with a man. STARCH (sense 1) refers to stiffness and to semen. [British, 1800s, Farmer and Henley]

talk German to break wind audibly. Refers to the "guttural" sounds in German. For synonyms see GURK.

talking-load intoxication with alco-hol; a degree of alcoholic intoxication marked by talkativeness.

talk to the canoe driver to perform CUNNILINGUS (*q.v.*). The "canoe driv-er" is the clitoris. "Canoe" refers to the shape of the vulva or the *labia minora*. Based on "talk to the (bus) driver." *Cf.* LITTLE MAN IN THE BOAT. [U.S. slang, mid 1900s-pres.]

tall intoxicated with marijuana; under the effects of any RECREATIONAL DRUG (*q.v.*). Based on HIGH (sense 3). [U.S. drug culture, early 1900s] Similar terms: AMPED, BACKED-UP, BAKED, BASTED,

BEAMING, BELTED, BENNY, BENT, BLAST-
ED, BLIND, BLITZED, BLOCKED, BLOWED-
AWAY, BLOWN-AWAY, BLOWN-OUT,
BOGGY, BOMBED, BOXED-UP, BUZZ,
BUZZED, CAUGHT IN A SNOWSTORM,
COCAINIZED, COKED, CRISP, DEAD,
FLOATING, FLYING, FREAKED, FREAKED-
OUT, FRENCH-FRIED, FRIED, GEEZED,
GEEZED-UP, GOOFED-UP, GOWED-UP,
HIGH, HOPPED, HORSED, JOY-RIDE,
KEYED, KIF, LAID-OUT, LAYED, LIT,
LOADED, MOHASKY, OUT, PASTED,
PHAZED, POLLUTED, POTSVILLE, POTTED,
RACKED, RACKED-UP, RIPPED, SENT, SHOT-
UP, SMASHED, SMEARED, SNAPPED-UP,
SNOWED-UNDER, SPACED-OUT, STEAMED-
UP, STEPPING-HIGH, STRUNG-OUT, TAKEN,
TEAD-UP (marijuana), TRIPPED-OUT, TRIP-
PING, TURNED-ON, TWISTED, UNDER, UP,
WASTED, WIPED, WIPED-OUT, WIRED-UP,
WRECKED, ZONED, ZONKED, ZONKED-
OUT.

tallywhacker the penis. *Cf.* BUSH-
WHACKER. [U.S. colloquial, late 1800s-
pres.]

tamale a derogatory term for a Mexican girl, especially if attractive. [U.S.,
1900s or before]

tampered-with pertaining to a nonvirgin. Used especially in reference to
young males who seem likely to serve
as catamites. See CATAMITE. [U.S. underworld, 1900s, Goldin, O'Leary, and
Lipsius]

tan 1. a mulatto. For synonyms see
MAHOGANY. **2.** pertaining to a mulatto.
[both senses, U.S., 1900s]

T. and A. "tits and ass." pertaining
to magazines or any publicly available
material showing exposed or prominent
breasts and buttocks. *Cf.* B. AND B.,
SOFT-CORE (sense 1). [U.S., mid
1900s-pres.]

tanglefoot any alcoholic drink. Refers
to the effect alcohol can have on one's
ability to walk. From the common
name of a vining weed. For synonyms
see BOOZE. [colloquial, mid 1800s-pres.]

tanglefooted intoxicated with alcohol.
For synonyms see WOOFLED. [British
and U.S., mid 1800s-pres.]

tangle-leg any alcoholic drink. Used
specifically at various times and places
for beer, gin, rum, and whisky. [Brit-
ish and U.S., mid 1800s]

tanked-up (also **tanked**) intoxicated
with alcohol. [U.S. slang, early 1900s-
pres.]

tan-track the rectum and the anus.
[British euphemism, late 1800s]

tantrum the penis. [based on Latin
tentum; British jocular, late 1600s]

tap a nut which secures a bolt. A
euphemistic avoidance of "nut," meaning "testicle." See NUTS (sense 1).
[U.S. dialect, 1900s or before]

tape liquor, especially gin. *Cf.* BLUE
RIBBON, BLUE TAPE, WHITE TAPE. [cant,
early 1700s]

tap-shackled intoxicated with alcohol; chained to a cask of drink. [slang,
early 1600s]

tar opium. Opium used for smoking is
a blackish or dark brownish waxy substance. *Cf.* DREAM WAX. [U.S. underworld and drug culture, 1900s]

tarantula-juice very strong or infe-
rior liquor; rot-gut. For synonyms see
EMBALMING FLUID. [U.S. slang, 1900s,
Berrey and Van den Bark]

tar baby a Negro baby. *Cf.* TAR POT
(sense 1). [U.S. colloquial, mid
1800s-pres.]

TARFU "things are really fucked-up,"
said when everything is in a state of
confusion. See SNAFU for similar expressions. [British and U.S., World
War II]

tarnation damnation. [U.S. colloquial
since the 1700s]

tar pot 1. a Negro child or baby. *Cf.*
TAR BABY. [U.S., 1900s or before] **2.** a
sailor. From the sailor's use of tar in
caulking. [both senses, U.S., 1900s
and before]

tarse the penis of a human or a beast.
See synonyms at YARD. [from *c.* 1000
to the 1700s, *Oxford English Dictionary*]

tart 1. a wanton young woman; a
prostitute. [British and later U.S.,
1500s-pres.] **2.** any girl, especially a

sweet girl. *Cf.* CAKE (sense 3), PIE. [colloquial, 1800s-pres.]

TASFUIRA "things are so fucked-up it's really amazing," said when everything is in an amazingly confused mess. A contrived acronym. See SNAFU for similar expressions. [World War II]

tassel 1. a child's penis. [British, 1900s] **2.** the scrotum. [U.S., 1900s]

taste 1. to coit. *Cf.* FLAVOUR, SALT. [from *Othello* (Shakespeare)] **2.** copulation. Similar to BIT OF – or SOME (both *q.v.*). [U.S., mid 1900s-pres.]

taverned intoxicated with alcohol. For synonyms see WOOFLED. [British, 1800s or long before]

T.B. 1. "tired butt," said when one has grown tired of sitting. [U.S. slang, mid 1900s-pres.] **2.** "two beauts," said of well-proportioned or large breasts. Both are based on the abbreviation of "tuberculosis." [Australian, early 1900s, *Dictionary of Slang and Unconventional English*]

T.C.C.FU "typical coastal command fuck-up," the type of slip-up typically created by the coastal command. A mixture of initialism and acronym. See SNAFU for similar expressions. [British, World War II]

tea 1. alcoholic drink. [British, late 1600s, *Oxford English Dictionary*] **2.** urine. From its color. [euphemistic colloquial and slang, early 1700s-pres.] Synonyms for sense 2: ADDLE, APPLE AND PIP, CHAMBER-LYE, COUSIN SIS, EMICTION, GOLDEN SHOWER, LANT, LONG TEA, LYE, MICKEY BLISS, MIKE BLISS, NETTING, PEE-PEE, PIDDLE, PISS, SALT-WATER, SIG, SIS, STALE, TAIL-JUICE, TAIL-WATER, URINA, URINE, WASTE, WEE-WEE, YOU AND ME, ZIGG. **3.** marijuana. [U.S. drug culture, mid 1900s-pres.] **4.** marijuana brewed and drunk like tea. [U.S. drug culture, mid 1900s-pres.]

tea-blower a marijuana smoker. To BLOW (sense 7) is to smoke. [U.S. drug culture, mid 1900s-pres.]

teacups small human breasts. [U.S. slang, mid 1900s]

tead-up 1. intoxicated with marijuana. *Cf.* TEA (sense 3). [U.S. drug culture, mid 1900s] **2.** intoxicated with alcohol. *Cf.* TEA (sense 1). [U.S. slang, early 1900s]

teahound a marijuana smoker. [U.S. drug culture, mid 1900s-pres.]

tea-man 1. a seller of marijuana. **2.** a marijuana smoker. [both senses, U.S. drug culture, mid 1900s]

team-cream any type of group sex involving ejaculation; a "gang-rape." *Cf.* BUNCH-PUNCH, GANG-BANG. [U.S. slang and male homosexual use, 1900s]

tea party a party where marijuana is smoked or any occasion marked by the smoking of marijuana. *Cf.* PARTY. [U.S. slang and drug culture, mid 1900s-pres.]

teapot 1. a child's penis, from which comes TEA (sense 2). [U.S. dialect, 1800s, Green] **2.** a Negro. Possibly from the color black. Derogatory. For synonyms see EBONY. [British, 1800s] See also TEAPOT LID.

teapot lid (also **teapot**) **1.** a Jewish man or woman. Rhyming slang for "yid," a derogatory reference to a Jew. For synonyms see FIVE AND TWO. **2.** a child. Rhyming slang for "kid." [both senses, British, 1900s, *Dictionary of Slang and Unconventional English*]

tear 1. gonorrhea. "Tear" is pronounced "teer" in this sense. [British, late 1800s, *Dictionary of Slang and Unconventional English*] **2.** a drinking spree. "Tear" rhymes with "fare" in this sense. [U.S. slang, 1900s]

tear off a piece to copulate with a female. The "piece" is PIECE (sense 4), a woman considered as a source of sexual gratification. [widespread colloquial, 1800s-pres.]

tearoom a men's restroom, particularly a public restroom where homosexual activity is known to take place. *Cf.* COFFEE HOUSE. [U.S. homosexual use, mid 1900s-pres.]

tearoom queen a homosexual male who specializes in having sexual relations in public restrooms. See similar terms at QUEEN. *Cf.* HEAD QUEEN.

[U.S. homosexual use, mid 1900s-pres.]

teaser a sexually loose female; a VAMP (sense 1). *Cf.* COCK-TEASER. [U.S. slang, mid 1900s-pres.]

teat the nipple. Either one of those on the breasts or (later) a rubber one on a baby's bottle. [since before 1000, *Oxford English Dictionary*]

tecata (also **tecaba**) heroin. From the name of a town in Mexico. [U.S. drug culture, mid 1900s-pres.]

tecato a heroin or morphine addict. [U.S. drug culture, mid 1900s-pres., *Current Slang*]

teed-up (also **teed**) intoxicated with alcohol; the same as TEAD-UP (sense 2). For synonyms see WOOFLED. [U.S. slang, mid 1900s-pres.]

teeming gravid; pregnant when said of humans. Otherwise pertaining to abundant offspring. For synonyms see FRAGRANT. [since the early 1500s]

temple a privy; a bathroom. *Cf.* CHAPEL OF EASE. [U.S. slang, 1900s]

temple of convenience a privy. For synonyms see AJAX. [euphemistic, 1800s or before]

temple of low men the female genitals, especially the vagina. A play on "the temple of high men" (hymen). [British, 1800s, *Dictionary of Slang and Unconventional English*]

tendencies homosexual tendencies. Used in reference to a male thought to engage in homosexual practices. The term is used to avoid an accusation of homosexuality. [U.S. slang, mid 1900s-pres.]

tenderloin madam 1. a prostitute. For synonyms see HARLOT. **2.** a female keeper of a brothel. [both senses, U.S. underworld, early 1900s]

tender passion, the love. Usually in the emotional sense but also for sexual love. [1800s or before, (Halliwell)]

tenip a pint of beer or ale. Backslang for "pint." [British, mid 1800s, Hotten]

ten-one hundred urination; a stop along a highway to urinate. Mock-citizens band radio slang based on the "ten-code." [U.S., mid 1900s-pres.]

tens a type of amphetamine tablets. Refers to its strength in milligrams. [U.S. drug culture, mid 1900s-pres.]

tenterbelly a fat man; a glutton with a stretched belly. [British slang, 1600s]

ten-to-two a Jewish man or woman. Rhyming slang for "Jew." Not necessarily derogatory. For synonyms see FIVE AND TWO. [British, 1900s, *Dictionary of Slang and Unconventional English*]

tent-peg the penis. [British slang, 1800s, Farmer and Henley]

tenuc backslang for CUNT (*q.v.*). [British slang, 1800s, Farmer and Henley]

terms the menses; a woman's period. *Cf.* MONTHLY TERMS. For synonyms see FLOODS. [medical]

terrier a derogatory term for an Irishman. [U.S., 1900s]

testicles 1. the male gonads. The medical word-of-choice for these glands. [since the early 1400s, *Oxford English Dictionary*] **2.** oysters. A play on MOUNTAIN OYSTERS (*q.v.*), which refers to testicles eaten as food. [U.S. slang, early 1900s, Monteleone]

Testicles to you! a translation of ORCHIDS TO YOU! (*q.v.*), a mild curse; a version of BALLS TO YOU! (*q.v.*) [British, early 1900s]

testimonials the testicles. An intentional malapropism for a cognate of "testicles." *Cf.* CREDENTIALS. For synonyms see WHIRLYGIGS. [British military, early 1900s]

tetrahydrocannabinol the active ingredient of marijuana. *Cf.* CLARABELLE, CLAY. [U.S. drug culture, mid 1900s-pres.]

Texas tea marijuana. *Cf.* OIL, RED OIL, TEA (sense 3). [U.S. drug culture, mid 1900s-pres.]

T.G.I.F. "Thank God it's Friday!" or, in a milder form "Thank goodness it's Friday!"

T.G.I.F.-O.T.M.W.D.U.M. "Thank God it's Friday, only two more work days until Monday." An elaboration of T.G.I.F. (*q.v.*).

Thai sticks. 1. a marijuana cigarette coated with opium; marijuana. **2.** a grade of marijuana; the type of marijuana typically consumed by smoking. [both senses, U.S. drug culture, mid 1900s-pres.]

Thank Goodness! a mild oath or exclamation used in avoidance of "Thank God!"

that 1. the penis. **2.** the female genitals. For both, *cf.* IT (sense 2), THING (sense 2). [colloquial euphemism, 1800s-pres.] **3.** the hymen. For synonyms see BEAN [British, 1800s]

that and this urine; an act of urination; to urinate. Rhyming slang for "piss." [British, 1800s, *Dictionary of Rhyming Slang*]

thatch 1. the pubic hair. For synonyms see PLUSH. **2.** the female genitals. [both senses, British slang, late 1700s]

thatched house under the hill the female genitals. From a song title. [British slang, late 1700s]

that crime SODOMY (*q.v.*); sexual perversion. [U.S., 1900s, Berrey and Van den Bark]

that time the menses; the same as HER TIME (sense 2). [colloquial, 1900s or before]

that way 1. having one's menstrual period. **2.** homosexual. **3.** intoxicated with alcohol. **4.** pregnant. [all senses, 1900s]

thawed intoxicated with alcohol. From the dripping of melting ice. [U.S. slang, early 1700s, Ben Franklin]

T.H.C. 1. TETRAHYDROCANNABINOL (*q.v.*), the active ingredient in marijuana. A highly desirable substance among marijuana smokers. **2.** erroneously for the drug P.C.P. (*q.v.*), which is sometimes sold as T.H.C. [both senses, U.S. drug culture, mid 1900s-pres.]

thicklips a derogatory term for a Negro. [from *Othello* (Shakespeare)]

thimble and thumb rum; a glass of

rum. Rhyming slang for "rum." [British, 1900s, *Dictionary of Slang and Unconventional English*]

thing 1. the penis or the male genitals. **2.** the female genitals. See THINGSTABLE. *Cf.* IT, THAT. [senses 1 and 2 since the early 1600s or before] **3.** a homosexual male or an effeminate male. [U.S. slang, early 1900s] **4.** an illicit romance; an affair. [U.S. euphemism, 1900s] **5.** heroin. [U.S. drug culture, mid 1900s-pres.]

thing, old the female genitals. *Cf.* THING (sense 2). [British, 1800s, *Dictionary of Slang and Unconventional English*]

thing, the the menses. For synonyms see FLOODS. A euphemism of avoidance. See also THING.

thingamabob 1. a gadget. **2.** the penis. [both senses, slang, mid 1900s-pres.]

thingamy 1. the female genitals. **2.** the penis. **3.** a gadget. [all senses, colloquial, 1800s-1900s]

thingstable a "constable," an officer of the law. A jocular play on the British pronunciation "cunt-stable." *Cf.* THING (sense 2). [British slang, late 1700s, Grose]

third leg the penis. *Cf.* BEST LEG OF THREE. [U.S. slang, 1900s]

third sex 1. homosexuals; homosexual males. [U.S. slang, 1900s] **2.** eunuchs; males who have been neutered or who have not developed sexually. [early 1800s-pres.]

third-sexer a male or female homosexual. [U.S. slang, early 1900s]

thirstington a drunkard. *Cf.* LUSHINGTON, SWIPPINGTON. [British slang, 1800s]

thirteen marijuana. "M" is the thirteenth letter of the alphabet. [U.S. drug culture, mid 1900s-pres.]

thirty-first of May a fool; a dupe; a simpleton. Rhyming slang for "gay." See GAY (sense 3). [Australian, 1900s, *Dictionary of Rhyming Slang*]

thistle the penis. *Cf.* PRICK (sense 1),

PRICKLE. [double entendre from *Much Ado About Nothing (Shakespeare)*]

thithy an effeminate male. A lisping pronunciation of "sissy." For synonyms see FRIBBLE. [U.S. slang, 1900s]

Thomas the penis; a personification of the penis. From JOHN THOMAS (*q.v.*), a stereotypical name for a manservant. [British and some U.S. use, late 1700s-1900s, Grose]

thorn the penis *Cf.* PRICK (sense 1), PRICKLE, THISTLE. [literary euphemism and widespread recurrent nonce]

thorn-back1. the "stickle-back," a fish said to have aphrodisiac properties [colloquial] **2.** an old maid. [British, late 1600s, B.E.]

thorn-in-the-flesh the penis. *Cf.* PRICKLE, THORN. [British, 1800s, Farmer and Henley]

thoroughbred a skilled prostitute. A play on "breeding." [U.S. prostitute's jargon, James]

those days of the month the menses. *Cf.* MONTHLIES. For synonyms see FLOODS.

those difficult days the menstrual period. [U.S. advertising, mid 1900s]

thousand pities the human breasts. Rhyming slang for "titties." [British, 1800s, *Dictionary of Slang and Unconventional English*]

thread 1. to coit a woman. [British, 1800s] **2.** semen. For synonyms see METTLE. [British, 1800s]

thread the needle to coit a woman. [British, 1800s, Farmer and Henley]

three-by-two a Jewish man or woman. Rhyming slang for "Jew." For synonyms see FIVE AND TWO. [British, 1800s, *Dictionary of Rhyming Slang*]

three-dollar bill a homosexual male. Related to the expression "queer as a three-dollar bill." "Queer" in the 1600s-1800s meant "counterfeit." [U.S. slang, 1900s, Wentworth and Flexner]

three-F.s "fuck, fun, and a footrace," pertaining to a wild time or a lewd person. See FOUR-F.METHOD. [British slang, 1800s, Farmer and Henley]

three-legged beaver a homosexual male. In citizens band radio slang, a "beaver" is a "woman." The THIRD LEG (*q.v.*) is the penis. [U.S., mid 1900s-pres.]

three-letter man a homosexual male. From FAG. See FAG (sense 2). *Cf.* FOUR-LETTER MAN. [U.S. slang, 1900s]

threepenny bits 1. diarrhea. Rhyming slang for "shits." For synonyms see QUICKSTEP. **2.** the breasts. Rhyming slang for "tits." For synonyms see BOSOM. [Both senses, British, 1900s]

three sheets in the wind (also **three sheets to the wind**) intoxicated with alcohol. [originally nautical; British and U.S. slang, 1800s-pres.]

three-way sexual activity involving three people in any combination of sexes. *Cf.* CLUB SANDWICH. [attested as U.S. homosexual use, mid 1900s, Farrell]

thrill an orgasm. [British and U.S., early 1900s-pres.]

thrill dame a prostitute. [U.S. slang, early 1900s]

thrill pills barbiturate tablets. [U.S. drug culture, mid 1900s]

throne 1. a CHAMBER POT (*q.v.*). *Cf.* TIN THRONE. **2.** a toilet; a toilet seat. [both senses, U.S. colloquial, 1900s]

through-cough (also **thorough-cough**) a cough accompanied by the audible release of intestinal gas. *Cf.* SNEEZE. [British, late 1600s, B.E.]

throw to castrate a quadruped, usually a colt. [Australian and U.S. euphemism, 1900s or before]

throw a bird to give someone the FINGER (*q.v.*). *Cf.* FLIP THE BIRD. [U.S. slang, mid 1900s-pres.]

throw a leg over to coit a woman. *Cf.* BOARD, MOUNT. [British, 1700s-1800s]

throw a map to vomit. For synonyms see YORK. [Australian, 1900s or before, Baker]

throw one a hump to coit a woman, said of a male; to permit coition, said of a female. *Cf.* HUMP. [U.S. underworld, early 1900s, Goldin, O'Leary, and Lipsius]

throw up 1. to vomit. [colloquial since the early 1700s] **2.** vomitus. Usually hyphenated. [colloquial since the 1800s or before] **3.** to ejaculate. [British slang, 1800s, *Dictionary of Slang and Unconventional English*]

throw up one's accounts (also **cast up one's accounts**) to vomit. [British and some U.S. use, mid 1700s-early 1900s]

throw up one's toenails to vomit a lot. [U.S. slang, 1900s]

thrum to coit a woman. For synonyms see OCCUPY. [British, 1500s-1800s]

thrumster a lecher; a whoremonger. [British, early 1600s]

thrust 1. a pelvic thrust, said in reference to the movements of the male in copulation. The term is generally used in reference to any copulatory movements. [since the early 1600s or before] **2.** amphetamine tablets. See THRUSTERS. [U.S. drug culture, mid 1900s-pres.]

thrusters amphetamine tablets. From the space jargon term for a rocket engine. *Cf.* ROCKET, ROCKET-FUEL. [U.S. drug culture, mid 1900s-pres.]

thumb 1. to coit a woman. [British slang, 1700s] **2.** to feel or grope a woman. *Cf.* FINGER (senses 1 and 2). [British, 1800s, Farmer and Henley] **3.** a fat marijuana cigarette. [U.S. drug culture, mid 1900s-pres.]

thumb of love the penis. *Cf.* FOREFINGER, LITTLE FINGER, MIDDLE FINGER. This is one of the very few entries which Farmer and Henley mark "obscene." [euphemistic, 1800s]

thump to coit a woman. [from *A Winter's Tale* (Shakespeare)]

thunder!, By a mild oath or an exclamation. For synonyms see 'ZOUNDS! [since the early 1700s]

Thunderation! a euphemistic oath and an exclamation, "Damnation!" [U.S. colloquial, early 1800s-pres.]

thunder-box (also **thunder-bowl**) a toi-

let. Refers to the audible breaking of wind. See THUNDER-MUG.

thunder-cookie a marijuana cigarette. For synonyms see MEZZROLL. [U.S. drug culture, mid 1900s-pres.]

thunder-mug a CHAMBER POT (*q.v.*). Refers to the audible breaking of wind. *Cf.* MEMBER MUG, THUNDER-BOX. [colloquial, 1700s-1900s]

tib 1. a strumpet; a harlot; a woman considered sexually. Possibly backslang for "bit," but certainly the feminine counterpart of TOM (sense1). A specialized use of a "polite" term. [early 1500s] **2.** the anus. Backslang for "bit." [British colloquial, 1800s, Farmer and Henley]

ticket the drug L.S.D. (*q.v.*), a ticket for a TRIP (sense 3). [U.S. drug culture, mid 1900s-pres.]

tickle 1., sexually aroused. *Cf.* FLAVOUR, SALT. [1300s] **2.** to coit a woman. [slang, late 1500s] **3.** to feel or grope a woman. *Cf.* FINGER (sense 1). [colloquial and nonce, 1700s-pres.]

tickle-brain 1. strong alcoholic drink. [from *Henry IV*, Part One (Shakespeare)] **2.** a drunkard. [British slang, 1800s, Farmer and Henley]

tickle one's crack to masturbate, said of a woman. [British slang, 1800s, Farmer and Henley]

tickle-pitcher a drunkard. [British colloquial, 1800s or before]

tickler the penis. [British slang, 1800s, Farmer and Henley]

tickle-tail 1. a rod used for punishment, *i.e.*, for striking the buttocks. [British slang, late 1700s, Grose] **2.** the penis. [British slang, early 1800s, *Lexicon Balatronicum*] **3.** a wanton woman. [British slang, early 1800s or before]

tickle-text a clergyman. For synonyms see SKY-PILOT. [British colloquial, 1800s or before]

tickle-Thomas the female genitals. "Thomas" is JOHN THOMAS (*q.v.*), "penis." [British slang, 1800s, Farmer and Henley]

tickle-toby 1. a wanton woman. [British slang, 1600s] **2.** the female genitals. [British slang, 1800s, Farmer and Henley]

tickle-your-fancy a homosexual male; an effeminate male. Rhyming slang for NANCY (*q.v.*), a male homosexual. [British, 1900s, *Dictionary of Rhyming Slang*]

tiddled intoxicated with alcohol. Perhaps only slightly. [British slang, early 1900s, *Dictionary of Slang and Unconventional English*]

tiddly intoxicated with alcohol. [British and U.S., 1800s-1900s]

tie one on 1. to spree; to become intoxicated with alcohol. Also **tie the bag on.** [U.S. slang, 1900s] **2.** to become intoxicated with marijuana. [U.S. drug culture, mid 1900-pres.]

tie the true lover's knot to copulate. *Cf.* KNOT, VIRGIN-KNOT. [euphemistic, 1800s-1900s]

tie up 1. to impregnate a woman. For synonyms see STORK. [British, 1800s, *Dictionary of Slang and Unconventional English*] **2.** to render one constipated. [colloquial, 1800s-1900s]

tiffled intoxicated with alcohol. [U.S. slang, 1900s]

tiger a prostitute. [U.S. slang, late 1800s, Ware]

tiger juice strong alcoholic drink. Euphemistic for TIGER PISS (*q.v.*). *Cf.* PANTHER JUICE. [U.S., 1900s]

tiger milk strong alcoholic drink; any alcoholic drink. See TIGER JUICE. [U.S. slang, 1900s]

tiger piss inferior or weak beer or any alcoholic drink. *Cf.* SQUAW PISS. [slang, 1900s]

tiger sweat strong alcoholic drink; whisky. Euphemistic for TIGER PISS (*q.v.*). [U.S., slang, 1900s]

tight intoxicated with alcohol. Refers to being full enough to burst. [colloquial since the 1800s]

tight-arsed (also **tight-assed**) **1.** pertaining to a chaste woman. [British, 1800s, Farmer and Henley] **2.** prudish and overly alarmed by subjects like sex. [U.S. slang, 1900s]

tight as a brassiere intoxicated with alcohol, as drunk as a brassiere is tight. [U.S. slang, mid 1900s]

tight as a drum intoxicated with alcohol. The expression pertains to anything tight. [U.S. slang, 1900s]

tight as a fart intoxicated with alcohol. Refers to the tension required to prevent the breaking of wind. [British slang, early 1900s, *Dictionary of Slang and Unconventional English*]

tight as a goat intoxicated with alcohol. A mixture of "tight as a drum" and "stinking (drunk) as a goat." *Cf.* GOAT-DRUNK. [U.S. slang, 1900s]

tight as a mink intoxicated with alcohol. [U.S. slang, 1900s]

tight as a ten-day drunk intoxicated with alcohol; very drunk indeed. [U.S. slang, 1900s]

tight as a tick intoxicated with alcohol; as full of drink as a tick engorged with blood. *Cf.* DRUNK AS A TICK, FULL AS A TICK. For synonyms see WOOFLED. [British and U.S., 1900s]

tight as the bark on a tree very drunk. [U.S. slang, 1900s]

tight skirt a drunken woman. From TIGHT (*q.v.*) meaning "drunk" and SKIRT (*q.v.*) meaning "woman." [U.S. slang, 1900s, Berrey and Van den Bark]

till the female genitals. Directly from MONEY-BOX (*q.v.*). [British slang, 1800s, Farmer and Henley]

timbered 1. pertaining to a WELL-BUILT (sense 1) male. [colloquial, 1400s] **2.** MENTULATE (*q.v.*); pertaining to a male with large genitals. *Cf.* WELL-BUILT (sense 2).

timber-headed stupid; oafish. [U.S. slang, 1900s]

timdoddle a silly oaf; the same as TOM DOODLE (*q.v.*). [British colloquial, 1800s]

timer, old a skilled and successful prostitute. [U.S. prostitute's jargon, 1900s, James]

timothy 1. the penis, especially that of a child; a personification of the

penis. Sometimes capitalized. *Cf.*
PETER. [British colloquial dialect, 1800s]
2. a brothel. [Australian, early 1900s]

tin one ounce (one tobacco tin) of
marijuana. *Cf.* O.Z. [U.S. drug culture,
1900s]

tin hat (Also **tin hats**) intoxicated
with alcohol. Implying that one is wearing a tin hat that someone is beating
on. Also a slang term for a military helmet. [British military, late
1800s-mid 1900s]

tin-horn 1. a cheap gambler [U.S.
slang, 1900s or before] **2.** pertaining
to an insignificant and inexperienced
person, usually a male. The HORN
(sense 3) is a veiled reference to the
penis. *Cf.* GREENHORN. [British and
U.S., late 1800s-pres.]

tinkle 1. urine. For synonyms see TEA.
2. to urinate. Based on the sound of
urination into a vessel of water.
For synonyms see WHIZ. [originally and
primarily juvenile; both senses, British and U.S., 1900s or before]

tinkle-tinkle an effeminate male. For
synonyms see FRIBBLE. [Australian,
World War II, Baker]

tinned intoxicated with liquor. [British
slang, 1900s]

tin throne a CHAMBER POT (*q.v.*).
Cf. CAN (sense 1), THRONE. [U.S.
prison slang, 1900s]

tip 1. to coit with someone. *Cf.*
TUP. **2.** coition (both senses, U.S.,
1900s) **3.** to be unfaithful to someone. Also **tip out.** [U.S. slang,
mid 1900s-pres., Wentworth and
Flexner] **4.** a sexually attractive
woman. [U.S. slang, mid 1900s]

tipium grove, in intoxicated with
alcohol. Derived from "tipsy." [U.S.
slang, early 1700s, Ben Franklin]

tip-merry intoxicated with alcohol.
From tipping a glass or mug. [Brit-
ish, early 1600s]

tip out See TIP (sense 3).

tip over to die. [U.S. colloquial,
1900s or earlier]

tipple 1. any alcoholic beverage. **2.**
to drink an alcoholic beverage, espe-

cially to sip a little bit every now
and then. [both colloquial since the
1500s]

tippler 1. a tavern-keeper. [1300s]
2. a drunkard or a person who sips
drink all day. [since the mid 1500s]

tipsified intoxicated with alcohol.
For synonyms see WOOFLED. [British
slang, early 1800s]

tipsy (also **tipsey**) intoxicated with
alcohol, not necessarily deeply intoxicated. [colloquial since the 1500s]

tip the long one to coit a woman.
[British slang, 1800s, Farmer and
Henley]

tip the middle finger to engage
in sexual foreplay; to grope a woman.
See MIDDLE FINGER. *Cf.* BIT FOR THE
FINGER. [British slang, 1800s,
Farmer and Henley]

tip the velvet 1. to kiss with the
tongue entering the other's mouth.
Cf. FRENCH KISS. [British slang or
cant, 1600s-1700s] **2.** to perform CUN-
NILINGUS (*q.v.*). The VELVET (*q.v.*)
is the tongue. [British, late 1600s-
1800s]

tishy intoxicated with alcohol. *Cf.*
BOSHY, which is from BOSKY (*q.v.*).
[British, early 1900s, *Dictionary of
Slang and Unconventional English*]

tit 1. a horse, *i.e.*, a filly. No
negative connotations. [British, mid
1500s-1800s] **2.** a young woman.
From sense 1. *Cf.* TITTER (sense
1). [since the late 1500s] **3.** a harlot
or a prostitute. This is probably an
overstatement of sense 2. [late
1500s] **4.** a nipple. Based on "titty,"
which dates from the 1700s. **5.** a
human breast. Usually in the plural. [U.S. slang and colloquial, 1800s-
pres.] Synonyms for sense 5: BRACE
AND BIT, BUB, BUBBY, DIDDY, MAMMA,
TITTY, TRACY-BIT. See BOSOM for
a complete list. **6.** human milk. *Cf.*
TITTY (sense 2). **7.** to milk a cow.
[U.S. colloquial, 1900s or before]
8. the female genitals. [never in wide
use, 1900s] **9.** an exclamation. See
TITS!

tit-bag a brassiere. A play on "kit-bag." For synonyms see BRA. [widespread slang, 1900s]

tit-hammock a brassiere; the same as TIT-BAG (*q.v.*). For synonyms see BRA. [British, early 1900s, *Dictionary of Slang and Unconventional English*]

titiculture the appreciation of well-shaped human breasts; breast worship. Patterned on "agriculture." Partly jocular. See TIT-MAN. [1900s or before]

titley alcoholic drink. *Cf.* TITTERY. For synonyms see BOOZE. [British slang, mid 1800s]

tit-man a male who is attracted to women's breasts; a TITTER (sense 3). *Cf.* LEG-MAN. [British and U.S. slang, early 1900s-pres.]

tit-mouse (also **tytmose**) the female genitals. *Cf.* DORMOUSE. [British, mid 1600s]

Tits! an exclamation, "Great!" [U.S., 1900s and before]

tits for days pertaining to a woman with large or immensely large breasts. *Cf.* DOUBLE-DUGGED. [U.S. slang, mid 1900s-pres.]

titter 1. a young woman or girl. [slang since the 1800s] 2. an animal's teat. [British colloquial, 1800s or before] 3. a man who spends much time with girls or is highly attracted to them. *Cf.* TIT-MAN. [U.S. slang, early 1900s]

titty (also **diddy**) 2. the human breast. Usually in the plural. *Cf.* DIDDIES, TIT. [since the mid 1700s] 2. human breast milk. [colloquial, 1700s-early 1900s] 3. a girl or a woman. [since the late 1700s]

titty-bottle a baby-bottle; a nursing-bottle. [British colloquial, 1800s, Northall]

titty-oggy FELLATIO (*q.v.*). [British slang, 1800s, *Dictionary of Slang and Unconventional English*]

tivvy (also **tivy**) the female genitals. From "tantivy," meaning "at full gallop." [British, 1800s, Farmer and Henley]

T.N.T "two nifty tits." A reinterpretation of the initialism for "trinitrotoluene." [U.S. slang]

toady 1. to behave as a sycophant. From the lowly posture of the toad. 2. a sycophant. For synonyms see ACQUIESCE-MAN. [both since the early 1800s]

toast and butter (also **toast**) a drunkard. For synonyms see ALCHY. [1500s-1600s]

toby 1. the buttocks. [British slang, late 1600] 2. the female genitals. [British slang, late 1600s, Farmer and Henley] 3. a prostitute. *Cf.* TICKLE-TOBY (sense 1). [Australian, Baker]

tocks the posteriors. A truncation of "buttocks." [U.S. slang, mid 1900s, *Current Slang*]

toe-jam (also **toe-punk**) a real or imagined nasty substance found between the toes. *Cf.* GRONK. [U.S. slang, 1900s]

toe queen a homosexual male who obtains gratification through playing with the feet of another person. See related subjects at QUEEN. *Cf.* FOOT QUEEN, SHRIMP QUEEN. [U.S. homosexual use, 1900s]

toffer (also **toff**) a fashionable prostitute. Also a slang term for a showy gentleman. This refers perhaps to the type of harlot suitable for such gentlemen or a harlot who pursues such gentlemen. [British, mid 1800s]

toilet 1. a dressing room (late 1600s). By the early 1800s, a dressing room in which one could bathe. 2. a W.C.; a bathroom; a restroom. 3. a water-flush toilet bowl and its associated water reservoir. [1900s]

toilet mouth a person who uses obscene language illegally on citizens band radio. *Cf.* POTTY MOUTH. [U.S., mid 1900s-pres.]

toilet paper the same as TOILET TISSUE (*q.v.*). A common generic term for this matter in the U.S. For synonyms see T.P.

toilet tissue a type of thin (and sometimes absorbent) paper designed specifically for cleansing after elimination. Somewhat more polite than "toilet paper." [U.S., 1900s]

toilet-training the process of teaching a child to control bowels and bladder so that elimination is accomplished in private into a toilet.

tojo a derogatory term for a Japanese. The name of a Japanese general, 1885–1948. [English-speaking armed forces, World War II, and general slang, mid 1900s]

toke (also **toak**) **1.** to smoke a marijuana cigarette. **2.** a puff of a marijuana cigarette. [both senses, U.S. drug culture, mid 1900s-pres.] **3.** a cigarette made of tobacco. All senses are from "token." [U.S. slang, mid 1900s-pres.]

token 1. the female genitals. [early 1500s] **2.** the plague. [British, late 1600s, B.E.] **3.** venereal disease. [British slang or cant, late 1700s, Grose]

tokus (also **dokus**, **tochas**, **tockus**, **tokis**) **1.** the posteriors; the buttocks. **2.** the anus or rectum. [from Yiddish; both senses, British and U.S. since the early 1800s]

toll-hole the vagina of a prostitute; a prostitute. [U.S. nonce or synthetic slang, 1900s]

tol-lol happy and drunk. [British slang, late 1800s]

tom 1. the male of certain animals; a tomcat, tom turkey, or the male of other animals. Sometimes for a human male. No negative connotations. **2.** an UNCLE TOM (q.v.). Usually capitalized. [U.S., 1900s or before] **3.** a prostitute. [British and U.S.] **4.** to coit a woman. Cf. MAN (sense 1). [British slang, 1800s] **5.** a chamber pot; a close stool. [British colloquial, 1800s or before] **6.** a virago; a lesbian. [British, late 1800s, Ware] **7.** a gin. See TOM, OLD. For synonyms see RUIN. **8.** a girl or woman, [Australian and U.S., 1900s] **9.** the penis. See LONG TOM, MISTER TOM.

Tom, old gin. For synonyms see RUIN. [British slang, early 1800s]

tomato 1. an attractive girl or woman. [U.S. slang, 1900s] **2.** a prostitute. [U.S. underworld, early 1900s]

tomboy 1. a rude and sexually uncontrolled girl; a strumpet. There are numerous other meanings. [primarily British, 1500s-1800s] **2.** a boyish girl; a young girl who engages in boys sports. [U.S., 1900s and before]

tomcat 1. a sexually active male; a whoremonger. **2.** to prowl around searching for sex, said of a male. [Both senses, U.S. slang, 1900s]

tomfool (also **Tom Fool**) **1.** a fool or an oaf. [since the 1300s] **2.** a damn fool. A corruption of "damn fool." [slang since the early 1700s]

tommy 1. a fool; an oaf. Sometimes capitalized. See TOMMY-ROT. Cf. TOMFOOL. [British, 1800s, Farmer and Henley] **2.** the penis; a personification of the penis. From JOHN THOMAS (q.v.). Sometimes capitalized. For synonyms see YARD. [British 1800s] **3.** a British soldier. Usually capitalized. Also **Tommy Atkins.** [English-speaking armed forces, World War II]

tommy-buster a rapist; a sadist. Cf. TOMMY (sense 2). [U.S. underworld, early 1900s]

Tommy Rollocks the testicles. Rhyming slang for BALLOCKS (sense 1). [British slang, late 1800s, *Dictionary of Slang and Unconventional English*]

tommy-rot nonsense. From TOMMY (sense 1). [colloquial and slang, late 1800s-pres.]

tomrig a girl or woman, especially one who is sexually loose. See TOMBOY. [colloquial, early 1700s-1900s]

Tom Tart 1. one's girlfriend. Rhyming slang for "sweetheart." [Australian, late 1800s-1900s, Wilkes] **2.** a sexually loose woman. Rhyming slang for "tart." **3.** a release of intestinal gas. Rhyming slang for FART (q.v.). [senses 2 and 3 are U.S., 1900s]

Tom Thumb rum; a glass of rum. Rhyming slang for "rum." [British, 1900s, Fraser and Gibbons]

tom-tit dung; to defecate. Rhyming slang for SHIT (q.v.). [British slang, 1800s]

Tom Turdman (also **turdman**) the man who hauls away excrement; a cleaner of privies. Cf. HONEY-DIPPER, SHIT-SHARK. [British slang, late 1700s, Grose]

tonge the penis. For synonyms see YARD. [British military, early 1900s, Dictionary of Slang and Unconventional English]

tongue 1. to perform PENILINGUS (q.v.). **2.** to perform CUNNILINGUS (q.v.), especially in the expression "tongue a woman." [both senses, British and U.S., 1800s-pres.]

tongue bath a sexual act or the prelude to a sexual act wherein the genitals and the genital area are licked with the tongue; an act of licking the entire body. [1900s]

tongue-fuck 1. CUNNILINGUS (q.v.). **2.** PENILINGUS (q.v.). **3.** ANILINGUS (q.v.). [all senses, slang, 1900s or before]

tonsil bath a drink of an alcoholic beverage. [U.S. slang, mid 1900s]

tonsil paint an alcoholic drink. [U.S. slang, mid 1900s]

tonsils the human breasts. Cf. LUNGS. [U.S. jocular euphemism, 1900s]

tonsil-swabbing kissing and necking. See SWAB SOMEONE'S TONSILS.

tons of basket pertaining to extremely large male genitals. Cf. BASKET (sense 3), BASKET FOR DAYS. [U.S. homosexual use, mid 1900s, Farrell]

tons of meat pertaining to extremely large male genitals, especially a large penis. See MEAT (sense 4). Cf. BASKET FOR DAYS, MENTULATE, MIRACLE-MEAT. [U.S. homosexual use, mid 1900s]

too big for her clothes pregnant. Based on "too big for his britches," an expression describing an arrogant male. [U.S. colloquial, 1900s]

toodles a child's VIRILIA (q.v.). Cf. DOODLE (sense 3). [U.S. colloquial, 1800s, Green]

tooie Tuinal (trademark), a barbiturate; the same as TUIE (q.v.). For synonyms see BARB. [U.S. drug culture, mid 1900s-pres.]

tool 1. the penis. In the plural, the male genitals. [since the early 1600s] **2.** a dupe; someone easily tricked. [British and later, U.S., mid 1600s-pres.]

tool bag the scrotum or the scrotum and its contents. [colloquial and nonce] Synonyms: BAG, BALLOCK-COD, BALLOCKS, BASKET, BURSA VIRILIS, BURSULA TESTICUM, COD, JELLY BAG, LURN, POKE, PURSE, SACK, TASSEL.

tool-check a military inspection of the male genitals for venereal disease. Cf. POULTRY-SHOW. [British military, early 1900s, Dictionary of Slang and Unconventional English]

tool-chest the female genitals, especially the vagina. A place for the TOOL (sense 1).]British slang, 1800s, Farmer and Henley]

too many cloths in the wind intoxicated with alcohol. Nautically, a "sheet" is a rope. Cf. THREE SHEETS IN THE WIND. [British and U.S., 1800s]

too numerous to mention. intoxicated with alcohol. [British, late 1800s, Ware]

toot 1. to drink copiously. [British slang, late 1600s] **2.** a binge or a drinking spree. [U.S., late 1800s-pres.] **3.** a fool; an oaf. [British slang, late 1800s] **4.** the devil. Usually capitalized. [British, 1800s, Farmer and Henley] **5.** a W.C. Cf. THUNDER-BOX. [Australian, 1900s, Dictionary of Slang and Unconventional English] **6.** a breaking of wind. [U.S., 1900s] **7.** cocaine. A LINE (sense 5) of cocaine. [U.S. drug culture, mid 1900s-pres.] **8.** to inhale or SNORT (sense 2) cocaine. [U.S. drug culture, mid 1900s-pres.]

tooter a drunkard who frequently goes on a TOOT (sense 2). [British slang, early 1900s]

toothache an erection of the penis. From IRISH TOOTHACHE (q.v.). [British slang, 1800s]

tooth-carpenter a dentist. [British slang, 1800s, Farmer and Henley]

tooth-doctor a dentist. [U.S. colloquial, 1900s or before]

tootledum-pattick a fool; an oaf. [British dialect (Cornwall), 1800s or before]

tootsie 1. a Tuinal (trademark) capsule. [U.S. drug culture, mid 1900s-pres.] **2.** a lesbian. For synonyms see LESBYTERIAN. [Australian, 1900s, Baker]

top ballocks the human breasts. *Cf.* CHESTNUTS (sense 1), FORE-BUTTOCKS. [British military, late 1800s, *Dictionary of Slang and Unconventional English*]

top cow a bull. *Cf.* TOP (sense 1). For synonyms see BULL. [U.S. colloquial euphemism, 1900s or before]

top-diver an older, sexually experienced male. *Cf.* TOP (sense 1). [British slang or cant, late 1700s, Grose]

top-dressing a thin top layer of manure on a field. *Cf.* MEADOW DRESSING. [British and U.S., late 1700s-1800s]

top-heavy 1. intoxicated with alcohol. Refers to a swollen head, the inability to stand up, and a fullness in the stomach. [slang since the late 1600s] **2.** heavy-breasted; pertaining to a woman with large or pendulous breasts. [U.S. slang, 1900s]

top ones the human breasts. *Cf.* TOP BALLOCKS. [British slang, 1900s, *Dictionary of Slang and Unconventional English*]

toppy (also **topy**) intoxicated with alcohol. *Cf.* TOP HEAVY (sense 1). [British slang, late 1800s]

tops-and-bottoms copulation in expressions such as "play at tops-and-bottoms." See TOP (sense 3), "the breasts," and BOTTOM (sense 2), "female genitals." [British slang, 1800s, Farmer and Henley]

top sergeant a lesbian who takes the masculine role, literally, "on top." [U.S. slang, mid 1900s]

topsy-boozy intoxicated with alcohol. [British and U.S. slang, late 1800s]

topsy-turvy 1. head oever heels. [since the 1700s or before] **2.** intoxicated with alcohol. From sense 1. [U.S. slang, early 1700s, Ben Franklin]

tora-loorals a woman's breast. For synonyms see BOSOM. [British, late 1800s, Ware]

torche-cul (also **torch-cul**) toilet paper. *Cf.* CURL PAPER. [from French; British, 1600s-1800s]

torch of Cupid the penis. From the heat generated by passion. For synonyms see GARGANTUA'S PENIS. *Cf.* CUPID'S TORCH. [mid 1600s, (Urquhart)]

torch up to smoke marijuana. [U.S. drug culture, mid 1900s]

tore-up (also **torn-up**) intoxicated with alcohol. [U.S. slang, mid 1900s-pres.]

torpedo a marijuana cigarette. *Cf.* BOMBER. [U.S. drug culture, 1900s]

torrid 1. intoxicated with alcohol. [British, late 1700s] **2.** lustful, ardent, or passionate.

tosh the penis. [British, late 1800s, *Dictionary of Slang and Unconventional English*]

tossed intoxicated with alcohol. [British slang, 1800s, Farmer and Henley]

toss in the hay an act of copulation; the same as ROLL IN THE HAY (*q.v.*).

toss off (also **toss**) to masturbate. [slang, late 1700s-pres.]

toss one's cookies (also **toss one's lunch**) to vomit. *Cf.* SNAP ONE'S COOKIES. [U.S., 1900s]

toss-pot a drunkard. [slang and colloquial, mid 1500s-1900s]

toss-prick a worthless man. A derogatory term of address for a male. *Cf.* SPARE PRICK. [British, 1900s]

tostificated (also **tosticated**) intoxicated with alcohol. A corruption of "intoxicated." [British and U.S. slang, 1700s-early 1900s]

totalled intoxicated with alcohol; very drunk. From the term used to describe an automobile which has been demolished in a collision. [U.S. slang, mid 1900s-pres.]

tottie 1. a high-class prostitute; a harlot. [British, 1800s] **2.** a simple term of endearment for a woman. [British, 1800s]

touched (also **teched**) crazy or slightly crazy. [since the early 1600s]

touch-up 1. sexual foreplay; stimulation in preparation for copulation. *Cf.* RUB-UP. [British, 1700s] **2.** masturbation. [British 1800s]

tough cat a male who is very successful with women. Usually said in reference to a black male. *Cf.* TOMCAT (sense 1). [U.S. slang, mid 1900s-pres.]

Tough shit! "Tough luck!" or "Too bad!" [U.S., 1900s]

Tough titty! (also Hard titty!) a catch phrase meaning "Tough luck!" [slang, mid 1900s-pres.]

toupee 1. the female pubic hair. [British, 1700s] **2.** a MERKIN (sense 2). For both, see LADY'S LOW TOUPEE.

touristas (also **turistas**) diarrhea, especially when it occurs in American tourists in Mexico. *Cf.* AZTEC TWO-STEP. [U.S. slang, mid 1900s-pres.]

town bull (also **town rake, town stallion**) a lecher; a whoremonger. A reinterpretation of a term used for a bull kept in common by townspeople and used for breeding purposes. [colloquial, 1600s-pres.]

town pump a sexually loose woman; a woman who is known to copulate with anyone without much persuasion. A reinterpretation of the name of a water supply held in common by townspeople, similar to TOWN BULL (*q.v.*). [colloquial, 1900s and before]

town punch a sexually loose woman who permits copulation with any males who ask. *Cf.* PUNCHABLE [U.S. slang, mid 1900s-pres.]

towns and cities the breasts. Rhyming slang for "titties." *Cf.* BRISTOLS. For synonyms see BOSOM. [British, 1900s, *Dictionary of Rhyming Slang*]

toy 1. to play sexually; to engage in sexual foreplay. [since the early 1500s] **2.** the female genitals. [British and U.S., 1800s-pres.] **3.** the HYMEN (sense 2). [British, 1800s] **4.** the penis. *Cf.* TRIFLE (sense 3). [1800s-pres.]

toy-shop the female genitals, especially

the vagina. *Cf.* TOY (sense 2). [British, 1800s, Farmer and Henley]

toy-toy to urinate. For synonyms see WHIZ. [U.S. juvenile, 1900s or before]

T.P. 1. "toilet paper." [U.S., 1900s and before]. Synonyms: AMMUNITION, ARMY FORM BLANK, ASS-WIPE, BATHROOM ROLL, BIMPH, BUMF, BUM-FODDER, BUM WAD, BUNG-FODDER, BUTT-WIPE, CAN-PAPER, FODDER, JOE-WAD, LAVATORY ROLL, SANITARY PAPER, SIX-BY-FOUR, TAIL-TIMBER, TOILET TISSUE, TORCHE-CUL. **2.** to festoon the trees and shrubbery of a residential yard with toilet paper. A teenage prank. Also **teepee.** [U.S. slang, mid 1900s-pres.]

trade 1. a man or a woman considered sexually in a commercial sense. [U.S. slang, 1900s and probably considerably older] **2.** the occupation of prostitute, pimp, or bawd. **3.** to look for some type of sexual activity or ACTION (*q.v.*). **4.** a male (presumably homosexual) who is seeking another male as a sex partner. [U.S. homosexual use, mid 1900s-pres., Farrell]

trade, the prostitution. See TRADE (sense 2). [U.S. euphemism, 1900s]

trader a prostitute. *Cf.* TRADE (sense 1). [British, 1600s]

trading copulation with a prostitute. See TRADE (sense 2). [since the 1600s]

traffic 1. a prostitute. [1500s] **2.** coition. [1600s or before]

traffiker (also **trafficer**) a drug peddler. [U.S. drug culture, mid 1900s-pres.]

train Terrence on the terracotta to urinate, said of a male. *Cf.* POINT PERCY AT THE PORCELAIN. [Australian, 1900s]

trammeled intoxicated with alcohol. [U.S. slang, early 1700s, Ben Franklin]

tramp a sexually loose woman. For synonyms see LAY. [U.S. slang, early 1900s-pres.]

trams a woman's legs, especially if shapely. Rhyming slang for "gams." [British, early 1800s]

trance, in a intoxicated with alcohol. [U.S. slang, early 1700s, Ben Franklin]

trancs (also **tranks, tranx**) tranquilizer

tablets or capsules. [U.S. drug culture and now general slang, mid 1900s-pres.]

translated intoxicated with alcohol. For synonyms see WOOFLED. [British slang, late 1800s, Ware]

transsexual 1. a person who has an overwhelming desire to be of the opposite sex. **2.** a person whose sex has been changed by surgery. [both senses, medical, 1900s]

trap the female genitals. Primarily in CARNAL TRAP (*q.v.*). *Cf.* TOUCH-TRAP. [1600s]

trapes (also **traipes, traipse, trapse**) a slattern. For synonyms see TROLLYMOG [late 1600s-1800s]

trap-stick the penis. *Cf.* TRAP. [British slang, late 1600s]

trash 1. a slut; a sexually loose female who is worse than a TRAMP (*q.v.*). Also **trashmire**. [since the early 1600s] **2.** a promiscuous homosexual male. From sense 1. [U.S. homosexual use, mid 1900s, Farrell] **3.** to gossip; to slander. [U.S. slang, mid 1900s-pres.] See also POOR WHITE TRASH.

trat 1. an old lady. [1300s (Chaucer)] **2.** backslang for TART (*q.v.*). *Cf.* TROT (sense 2). [British slang, late 1800s]

treacle "honey" in the sense of "lovemaking." Also in "treacle-moon," meaning "honeymoon." [British, early 1800s-1900s]

tread 1. the copulation of fowls. [late 1500s-1800s] **2.** the copulation of turtles. **3.** any copulation including that of humans. [British and U.S. colloquial, 1800s-1900s]

trench the female genitals, particularly the PUDENDAL CLEAVAGE (*q.v.*). [written nonce; British, late 1700s]

trey bits 1. the breasts. Rhyming slang for "tits." [Australian, 1900s, Baker] **2.** diarrhea. Rhyming slang for "shits." Also **treys**. [Australian, mid 1900s, Wilkes]

triangles the DELIRIUM TREMENS (*q.v.*). Named for the ringing in the ears which accompanies this disorder. *Cf.* CLANKS. [British slang, mid 1800s]

trichet the female genitals. See TWITCHET. For synonyms see MONOSYLLABLE. [U.S. colloquial, 1900s or before]

trick 1. copulation [since the 1600s] **2.** an unpopular or disliked person. [U.S. slang, 1900s] **3.** a sexually attractive girl, as in "cute trick." [U.S. slang, 1900s] **4.** a sexual customer of a prostitute. [U.S., mid 1900s-pres.] **5.** a casual (nonpaying) male homosexual partner. *Cf.* TRADE. [U.S. homosexual use, mid 1900s-pres.] **6.** to seek out a male homosexual partner.

trick babe a prostitute. *Cf.* TRICK (sense 1). [U.S. slang, mid 1900s-pres.]

trick-flick a pornographic movie which depicts some type of sexual activity or copulation. [U.S. homosexual use, 1900s]

tricking-broad a prostitute. [U.S. underworld, early 1900s]

trickster a prostitute. [U.S. slang, 1900s]

trick-towel a towel used to clean up after intercourse. [U.S. homosexual use, mid 1900s-pres., Stanley]

trifle 1. to play, perhaps cruelly, with someone's affections. **2.** to play with someone sexually. *Cf.* TOY. For synonyms see FIRKY-TOODLE. **3.** the penis. *Cf.* BAUBLE (sense 1), TOY (sense 4). For synonyms see YARD. [all senses, 1800s-1900s]

trigger the penis. *Cf.* GUN. [slang, 1800s-1900s]

trim 1. to DEFLOWER (*q.v.*) a woman. *Cf.* UNTRIMMED. [British, 1500s-1700s] **2.** to copulate with a woman. [slang, 1500s-pres.] **3.** copulation, as in "get some trim." [U.S., 1900s and before] **4.** women considered sexually. For synonyms see TAIL. [U.S., 1900s] **5.** to castrate. See CUT (sense 1). [U.S. dialect and colloquial, 1800s-1900s] **6.** to cheat or beat. [cant and slang, early 1800s-1900s]

trim and buff 1. to deflower a woman. For synonyms see DEFLOWER. **2.** to copulate with a woman. *Cf.* TRIM (sense 2). [both senses, British, late 1700s]

trinket the female genitals or an act of

copulation; a sexual toy or favor. *Cf.*
TOY (sense 2). [recurrent nonce; British, early 1700s]

trip 1. a bastard in "make a trip,"
i.e., "have a bastard." [British, late
1700s, Grose] **2.** a prostitute. [cant,
1800s] **3.** a period of intoxication from
drugs. [U.S. drug culture, mid 1900s-
pres.]

tripe nonsense. From the low value of
TRIPES. For synonyms see ANIMAL. [British and U.S., late 1800s-pres.]

tripes (also **tripe**) intestines; guts. Sometimes jocular or emphatic for "guts" or
"courage." [since the early 1600s]

triple-W a "warm, wet womb," a
deeply satisfying act of copulation or a
sexually obliging woman. [U.S. slang,
mid 1900s, *Current Slang*]

tripped-out intoxicated with alcohol
or drugs or both. *Cf.* TRIP (sense 3).
[U.S. drug culture, mid 1900s-pres.]

tripping 1. intoxicated with drugs. **2.**
in the process of becoming drug intoxicated. **3.** enjoying drug intoxication; in
a daze from intoxicants. [all senses,
U.S. drug culture, mid 1900s-pres.]

trip up the Rhine an act of copulation. [British military, 1900s, *Dictionary of Slang and Unconventional English*]

tripweed a type of marijuana. *Cf.*
WEED (sense 1). [U.S. drug culture,
1900s]

trizzer a men's urinal; a W.C. *Cf.*
WHIZ-STAND. [onomatopoetic; Australian,
early 1900s]

trolley and truck to coit a woman;
copulation. Rhyming slang for "fuck."
[British, early 1900s, *Dictionary of Rhyming Slang*]

trolling a prostitute's prowling the
streets for a customer. From the fishing
technique. *Cf.* HOOKER. [British, early
1900s, *Dictionary of Slang and Unconventional English*]

trollops (also **trollop**) **1.** a coarse
and vulgar woman. [British and U.S.
colloquial, 1600s-1800s] **2.** a prostitute; a harlot. [British, 1600s]

trolly bags (also **trollybobs**) **1.** an
animal's intestines, specifically a sheep's
intestines. *Cf.* TRIPES. [British slang,
1800s, Farmer and Henley] **2.** a fat,
dirty, and uncouth person. [British
dialect.]

trollymog a slovenly woman; a slattern. [British, 1900s or before] Synonyms: BRUM, CLAMMUX, DAGGLE-TAIL,
DANGUS, DAWKIN, DIRTY PUZZLE, DISH-CLOUT, DOLLOP, DOLLUMS, DRABBLE-TAIL,
DRAGGLE-TAIL, DRAP, DRAPSOCK, DRASSOCK, DRATCHELL, DROOPY-DRAWERS,
DROSSEL, DROZEL, DROZZLE-TAIL, DULLY-TRIPE, FEAGUE, FEAK, FLAMTAG, FLOMMAX, GAD-ABOUT, HAGGAGE, MAB, MAUKS,
MAUNSEL, MAWKIN, MIDDEN, MOPSY,
MOX, MUCK-HEAP, MUCK-SCUTCHEON,
MUCK-SUCKLE, MULLOCKS, RAG DOLL,
RUBBACROCK, SLACK-TRACE, SLACKUMTRANS, SLAMKIN, SLAMMERKIN, SLATTERN, SLOMMOCKS, SLUMMOCKS, SLURRUP, SLUT, SOSS-BRANGLE, SOZZLE, STREEL,
SWASH-BUCKET, SWATCHEL, TRAPES,
TRASHMIRE, TROLLOPS, TRUB.

trolly-wags (also **trolly-wogs**) trousers; breeches. For synonyms see GALLIGASKINS. [British, late 1800s]

tromboning copulating. From the action of a trombone slide. Reinforced by
BONE (senses 2 and 3). [British slang,
late 1800s, Farmer and Henley]

trossy slatternly; slovenly. [British,
1900s, Fraser and Gibbons]

trot (also **trat**) **1.** a base and ugly
old woman. *Cf.* TRAT (sense 1). [early
1500s or before] **2.** a bawd; a harlot; an
old whore. A narrowing of sense 1.
[1500s-1600s] See also TROTS

trot out one's pussy (also **feed one's
pussy**) to receive a man sexually, said
of a woman. As one might trot out a
horse for approval. [British, 1800s,
Farmer and Henley]

trots diarrhea. *Cf.* BACK-DOOR TROTS,
MOVIES, RUNS. [British and U.S., late
1800s-pres.]

trottles sheep's dung. For synonyms
see DROPPINGS. [British rural colloquial, 1800s, or before, Halliwell]

trouble, in pregnant and unmarried.

Cf. DUTCH, IN. [colloquial, 1800s-pres.]

trouble-giblets (also **trouble-gusset**) the penis. *Cf.* GIBLETS (sense 2). [mid 1600s, (Urquhart)] See also JOIN GIBLETS.

trounce to coit a woman. From the meaning "beat." [British, 1800s, Farmer and Henley]

trouserloons trousers. A blend of "trousers" and "pantaloons." [U.S. slang, 1900s, Wentworth]

trub a short, squat woman; a slattern. [British colloquial, 1800s]

truck-driver 1. a masculine homosexual, either male or female. *Cf.* COW-BOY. [U.S. homosexual use, mid 1900s] **2.** a straight male, a nonhomosexual male. [U.S. underworld, early 1900s, Goldin, O'Leary, and Lipsius] **3.** an amphetamine tablet or capsule. From the use of amphetamines by cross-country truck drivers. [U.S. drug culture, mid 1900s-pres.]

trucks trousers. [British, mid 1800s]

trug (also **trugge, truk**) **1.** a prostitute; a low woman; a concubine. [cant or slang, late 1500s] **2.** a CATAMITE (*q.v.*). From sense 1. [British, early 1600s]

trugging-ken (also **trugging-house**) a brothel. [cant, 1800s, Farmer and Henley]

trugmoldy (also **trudmoldy, trugmouldy**) a prostitute. [British, early 1700s]

trull a prostitute or camp follower. *Cf.* STRULL, TROLLOPS. (early 1500s]

trump a breaking of wind. *Cf.* ARS MUSICA, BLOW THE HORN, TOOT (sense 6). For synonyms see GURK. [British slang, late 1700s]

try to get even for a man to switch from being a CATAMITE (*q.v.*) to acting as the inserting PEDERAST (*q.v.*). [U.S. underworld, early 1900s, Goldin, O'Leary, and Lipsius]

T.S. an abbreviation of "tough shit." Also euphemized as "tough situation." [from World War II; U.S. slang, mid 1900s-pres.]

tube 1. a very promiscuous girl. The "tube" is the vagina. [U.S. slang, mid 1900s, *Current Slang*] **2.** the penis. [nonce, 1900s and before]

tubed intoxicated with alcohol or drugs. Based on the expression "down the tubes." [U.S. slang, mid 1900s-pres.]

tube-steak 1. a frankfurter or a wiener. Based on "cube-steak." [U.S., 1900s] **2.** the penis. *Cf.* MEAT (sense 4). [U.S. slang, mid 1900s-pres.]

tub of guts (also **tub of lard**) a fat person. [U.S. colloquial, 1900s or before]

tucked-away dead and buried. From an expression meaning "put to bed." [1900s]

tuie a Tuinal (trademark) capsule, a specific barbiturate. For synonyms see BARB. [U.S. drug culture, mid 1900s-pres.]

TUIFU "the ultimate in fuck-ups," the worst conceivable confused mess. See SNAFU for similar expressions. [U.S., mid 1900s]

Tuinal the trademarked brand name of a barbiturate. See T.

tulip-sauce kissing. Based on "two lips." [British slang, 1800s]

tumble 1. to fondle or grope. [1600s] **2.** to coit a female. [since the early 1600s] **3.** a prostitute. [British slang, 1800s, Farmer and Henley]

tumble-down-the-sink (also **tumble-down**) a glass of gin, beer, or other alcoholic beverage. Rhyming slang for an alcoholic "drink." [Australian and British, late 1800s]

tumble in 1. to get into bed, presumably for sexual purposes. **2.** to copulate; to penetrate a woman. [both senses, British, 1800s, Farmer and Henley]

tumble-turd a dung beetle. [U.S. colloquial, 1900s and before]

tumbling-drunk intoxicated with alcohol; drunk and willing to copulate. See TUMBLE (sense 2). [British, 1800s or before]

tumbling-ripe pertaining to a female who is sufficiently aroused for copulation. *Cf.* BED-WORTHY, TOUCHABLE, TUMBLE (sense 2). [British, early 1600s]

tummy the stomach. For synonyms see BELLY. [colloquial, 1800s-1900s]

tummy-fuck simulated coition between males. *Cf.* PRINCETON RUB. [U.S. homosexual use, 1900s, Farrell]

tummy-tickler a lecher; a whoremonger. *Cf.* TICKLE (sense 2). [British slang, 1800s, Farmer and Henley]

tump to PUSH (sense 1); to copulate. Similar to "tamp." [British slang, 1800s, Farmer and Henley]

tum-tum the stomach. *Cf.* TUMMY. [U.S. juvenile, 1800s-1900s]

tuna 1. a disliked person. [U.S. slang, mid 1900s] 2. a girl or young woman; a sexually attractive woman. *Cf.* FISH (sense 1). [U.S. slang, mid 1900s]

tunnel the female genitals, specifically the vagina. *Cf.* CAVE OF HARMONY.

tup 1. a ram. No negative connotations. [1300s-1800s] 2. the ram's copulation with a ram. [British, early 1600s-1800s] 3. to seek copulation, said of ewes and of human males. [British, early 1600s] 4. human copulation. *Cf.* TIP (sense 1), TOP (sense 1). [British slang, early 1800s] 5. a CUCKOLD (*q.v.*). [British, early 1800s]

tup cat a tom cat. Literally, RAM CAT (*q.v.*). *Cf* TUP (sense 1). [British dialect, 1800s or before, Holland]

tupping-time breeding time for rams and ewes. [British dialect]

turd 1. a lump of excrement; a formed lump of excrement. This is one of the few terms for dung which can be made plural. 2. a rude nickname for a disliked person. From sense 1. [both senses, Anglo-Saxon; both since *c.* 1000]

turd-walloper the man who carts away dung from privies. [British, 1900s or before, *Dictionary of Slang and Unconventional English*]

turf-cutter a derogatory term for an Irishman. For synonyms see HARP. [British and U.S., 1900s or before.]

turk 1. any cruel and overbearing man. [slang, late 1700s-pres.] 2. an

active PEDERAST (*q.v.*); a SADIST (*q.v.*). [U.S., early 1900s] 3. an Irishman. Derogatory. [not widespread; U.S., 1900s]

turkey 1. to breathe the smoke of a marijuana cigarette. [U.S. drug culture, mid 1900s-pres.] 2. an oaf; a total jerk. [U.S. slang, early 1900s-pres.] See also HAVE A TURKEY ON ONE'S BACK.

Turkish medal an undone fly button. See YOUR MEDALS ARE SHOWING. For synonyms see X.Y.Z.

turn an act of copulation *Cf.* TAKE A TURN IN THE STUBBLE.

turnabouts amphetamine tablets. See L.A. TURNABOUTS. [U.S. drug culture, mid 1900s-pres.]

turn a trick 1. to commit a crime of any type. 2. to practice prostitution; to perform an act of male or female prostitution with a customer. 3. to perform a homosexual act. *Cf.* TRICK. [all senses, U.S. underworld, early 1900s]

turned-on 1. intoxicated with marijuana or other drugs. [U.S. colloquial, 1900s] 2. sexually aroused. See TURN ON (sense 1). *Cf.* TURN OFF. [U.S. colloquial, mid 1900s-pres.] 3. interested, alerted to, or made enthusiastic by some thing or person. [U.S. current slang]

turn gay 1. to become a prostitute, said of a woman *Cf.* GAY [British, late 1800s] 2. to become homosexual. [slang, mid 1900s-pres.]

turn off to prevent or terminate sexual desire or arousal. *Cf.* TURN ON. [U.S., mid 1900s-pres.]

turn on 1. to arouse someone sexually or to become sexually aroused; to turn someone on or to become turned on oneself. *Cf.* BRING ON. 2. to excite or entice. 3. to experience drug intoxication. *Cf.* TURNED-ON. 4. to persuade someone to use drugs. To "turn someone on to L.S.D." (*q.v.*) [all senses, U.S. slang and drug culture, mid 1900s-pres.]

turns the menses. *Cf.* COURSES. For synonyms see FLOODS. [U.S. colloquial, 1900s]

turn up to coit a woman. [British, 1800s, Farmer and Henley]

turn up one's toes (also **turn one's toes up**) to die. [British and U.S., mid 1800s]

turps (also **terps**) any alcoholic drink. From a nickname for turpentine. [slang, 1900s]

turtle 1. the female genitals. [British, 1800s] **2.** women considered sexually. *Cf.* NURTLE. **3.** a prostitute. For synonyms see HARLOT. [both senses, Australian, 1900s or before, Baker]

tush 1. a light-skinned Negro. Derogatory. [U.S., 1900s or before] **2.** the posteriors. See TUSHY. [from Yiddish] **3.** to defecate. For synonyms see EASE ONESELF. [Caribbean (Jamaican), Cassidy and Le Page]

tushy (also **tush, tushie**) the posteriors. [from Yiddish *tochis;* U.S. slang, 1900s or before]

tussey a low drunkard. *Cf.* TUZZY. [British, 1800s, Farmer and Henley]

tuzzy intoxicated with alcohol. This is most likely related to MUZZY (*q.v.*), and probably to TUZZY-MUZZY (*q.v.*), in its dialect sense, "nosegay." [British dialect, 1800s or before, Rye]

tuzzy-muzzy the female genitals. From an old term for "nosegay." [British slang, early 1700s-mid 1800s]

twaddle 1. to utter nonsense. **2.** nonsense. [both since the late 1700s]

twammy (also **twam**) the female genitals. For synonyms see MONOSYLLABLE. [British slang, 1900s, *Dictionary of Slang and Unconventional English*]

twang 1. to coit a female. *Cf.* STRUM. **2.** a term of contempt. [since the late 1500s] **3.** opium. [Australian, late 1800s-1900s, Wilkes]

twanger the penis. [slang since the 1500s]

twank 1. an effeminate male. For synonyms see FRIBBLE. **2.** a homosexual male. *Cf.* TWINK (sense 2). [early 1900s, *Dictionary of the Underworld*]

twat (also **twot**) **1.** the female genitals. Occasionally the British pronunciation

rhymes with "sat"; the U.S. pronunciation rhymes with "sot." [widespread, mid 1600s-pres.] **2.** the buttocks. Not widely known. [U.S. slang, 1900s]

twatchel (also **twachel, twachylle, twatchil, twatchit, twitchet, twittle**) the female genitals. For synonyms see MONOSYLLABLE. [British and some U.S. dialect use, 1600s-1900s]

twat-faker a lecher; a whoremonger; a pimp; a whore's bully. ["fake" is probably from a Gypsy word meaning "mend"; British, 1800s-1900s, Farmer and Henley]

twat-raking copulating; copulation. [British, 1600s]

twat-rug the female pubic hair. For synonyms see DOWNSHIRE. [British, late 1800s-1900s]

tweak 1. a prostitute. [British colloquial, 1600s] **2.** a whoremonger. For synonyms see LECHER. [British colloquial, 1700s]

twerp a jerk. For synonyms see OAF. [colloquial, 1900s]

twiddle to copulate. *Cf.* DIDDLE. [British slang, 1800s]

twiddle-diddles the testicles. [British slang, late 1700s, Grose]

twiddle-poop an effeminate male. See POOP (sense 1), TWIDDLE. For synonyms see FRIBBLE. [British slang, late 1700s, Grose]

twidget 1. a prostitute. **2.** a CATAMITE (*q.v.*). From sense 1. [both senses, U.S. underworld, mid 1900s, Goldin, O'Leary, and Lipsius]

twig and berries the penis and testicles of a child. *Cf.* PENCIL AND TASSEL. [British and U.S., 1900s]

twigger a wanton man or woman; a prostitute or a lecherous male. [slang, late 1500s]

twigle to copulate. *Cf.* NIGGLE (sense 1). For synonyms see OCCUPY. [British slang, 1800s, Farmer and Henley]

twilight a toilet. [corruption of the French *toilette;* British and U.S., 1800s-1900s, Barrère and Leland]

twin the female genitals. Possibly a

blend of "twat" and "quim" (Partridge). *Cf.* TRIM. [British, 1900s]

twink 1. any odd person. **2.** a homosexual male. *Cf.* TWANK. **3.** a JERK (sense 2). [all senses, U.S. slang, 1900s]

twin lovelies the human breasts. [euphemistic, 1900s or before]

twins 1. the testicles. [U.S. slang, 1900s] **2.** the human breasts. [U.S. 1900s]

twirl a woman; a girl. From TWIST AND TWIRL (*q.v.*). [U.S. slang, 1900s]

twiss a CHAMBER POT (*q.v.* at the bottom of which appeared the face of one Richard Twiss, who had published derogatory remarks about the Irish. The expression "Let everyone piss on lying Dick Twiss" was inscribed with the portrait of Twiss. [Irish use, late 1700s]

twist 1. to hand a man. [cant, early 1800s, Egan's Grose] **2.** a girl, especially a wanton girl; a SCREW (sense 4). From rhyming slang TWIST AND TWIRL (*q.v.*). [U.S. slang, early 1900s] **3.** a passive lesbian. [U.S. homosexual use, mid 1900s, Stanley] **4.** a drunken spree. [U.S., 1900s, Wentworth and Flexner] **5.** marijuana or a marijuana cigarette. [U.S. drug culture, mid 1900s-pres.] **6.** to copulate; to SCREW (sense 1). [U.S. slang, mid 1900s-pres.]

twist and twirl one's sweetheart; any woman. Rhyming slang for "girl." *Cf.* TWIRL, TWIST (sense 2).

twister a sexually perverted person; a TWISTY (sense 1) person. [slang, mid 1900s-pres.]

twisty 1. perverted; pertaining to a "perverted" person. **2.** a person who has a "perverted" sexual appetite. Both are from KINKY (sense 3). [both senses, slang, mid 1900s-pres.]

twit a miserable, contemptible person; a worthless nobody. [widespread slang, 1900s]

twitcher 1. a drug addict. From the trembling and twitching. *Cf.* SHAKER. [British, early 1900s, *Dictionary of the Underworld*] **2.** the female genitals; the vagina. *Cf.* SNAPPER (sense 3). [slang, mid 1900s]

twitchet (also **twitchit**) the female genitals. *Cf.* TRICHET, TWATCHEL. For synonyms see MONOSYLLABLE. [U.S. dialect or slang, 1800s-1900s]

twitchet-struck woman-crazy; enamored of females and sexual matters. *Cf.* PUSSY-SIMPLE. [U.S. dialect]

twitters (also **twitteration**) **1.** sexual excitement, especially that of a woman. [British, 1600s] **2.** excitement of any kind. [U.S. slang, 1900s]

twittle the female genitals. *Cf.* TWATCHEL [British slang, 1800s, Farmer and Henley]

twixter 1. an effeminate male. For synonyms see FRIBBLE. **2.** a masculine female. From "betwixt," meaning "between." For synonyms see AMAZON. [both senses, British slang, late 1800s, Ware]

two-bit hustler a cheap prostitute, male or female. [U.S. underworld, 1900s]

two-by-four a prostitute. Rhyming slang for "whore." [British, *Dictionary of Rhyming Slang*]

two-foot rule an oaf; a simpleton. Rhyming slang for "fool," a yardstick with something missing. [British slang, mid 1800s]

two sheets to the wind intoxicated with alcohol. *Cf.* BOTH SHEETS IN THE WIND, FOUR SHEETS TO THE WIND, THREE SHEETS IN THE WIND, TOO MANY CLOTHS IN THE WIND.

two stone underweight castrated. The STONES (sense 2) are the testicles. Body weight in Britain is measured in "stones." A stone is equal to fourteen pounds. *Cf.* UNPAVED. [British, 1800s, Farmer and Henley]

two-time to be (sexually) unfaithful to one's lover, as in "Don't you two-time me, buster!" [U.S. slang, 1900s]

two tin fucks a worthless bit of nothing in expressions such as "I don't give two tin fucks." *Cf.* FLYING-FUCK (sense 1). [British slang, 1900s, *Dictionary of Slang and Unconventional English*]

tytmose the female genitals. See TITMOUSE. For synonyms see MONOSYLLABLE.

U

ubble-gubble nonsense; gibberish. For synonyms see ANIMAL. [U.S. slang, mid 1900s-pres.]

uck-fay Pig Latin for "fuck." [U.S. slang, 1900s]

udder the mammary glands of an animal. Used jocularly for the human breasts. [since the 1700s]

'Uds a euphemism for "God's" found in the following mock and disguised oaths: 'Uds bluff!'' 'Uds bobblekens!, 'Uds bobs!, 'Uds bodkins!, 'Uds bows!, 'Uds bud!, 'Uds buddikins!, 'Uds death!, 'Uds foot!, 'Uds-my-life!, 'Uds niggers!, 'Uds niggs!, 'Uds noggers!, 'Uds wountlikins! [1600s]

uglies the DELIRIUM TREMENS (q.v.). For synonyms see ORK-ORKS. [British and U.S., late 1800s-1900s]

ugly fornication, especially in "the ugly." Cf. NAUGHTY. [U.S. dialect (Southern), 1900s]

ug-may a sucker; a dupe. Pig Latin for "mug." [U.S. underworld, early 1900s]

uh-huh (also **some uh-huh, the uh-huh**) copulation. For synonyms see SMOCKAGE. [U.S. slang, early 1900s, Rose]

ultimate favor, the copulation; the same as the FAVOR (q.v.). [literary euphemism; British, late 1600s]

um-bay a bum; a worthless oaf. Pig Latin for "bum." [U.S., early 1900s-pres.]

ump-chay a sucker; an oaf. Pig Latin for "chump." [U.S., early 1900s-pres.]

unattached 1. pertaining to an adult woman who is not married. Cf. ATTACHED. **2.** pertaining to a sexually or maritally available man or woman. [both senses, U.S. colloquial, 1900s]

unbleached American 1. an American Indian. For synonyms see REDSKIN. [jocular or derogatory; U.S. slang, 1800s] **2.** an American Negro. For synonyms see EBONY. [jocular or derogatory; U.S. slang, 1800s]

unchaste 1. defiled; having been deflowered involuntarily. See DEFLOWER. Cf. CHASTE. **2.** lascivious. [both senses, since the 1300s]

unclad naked. For synonyms see STARKERS. [since the early 1400s]

uncle 1. a privy. Especially in expressions such as "visit one's uncle." Cf. AUNT (sense 5). [British slang, late 1700s, Grose] **2.** a PEDERAST or a FELLATOR who is interested in young boys. Cf. AUNTIE, CHICKEN-HAWK. [U.S. underworld, early 1900s, Goldin, O'Leary, and Lipsius]

uncles and aunts trousers; pants. Rhyming slang for "pants." Cf. BULL ANTS.

Uncle Tom a Negro who is a traitor to racial causes. From the book *Uncle Tom's Cabin*, by Harriet Beecher Stowe, 1852. Derogatory. Cf. AUNT TOM. [U.S. slang, mid 1900s-pres.]

Uncle Tommyhawk an American Indian who is a traitor to militant Indian causes. Derogatory. Based on UNCLE TOM (q.v.). [U.S. slang, mid 1900s-pres.]

undamaged goods a virgin female. The opposite of DAMAGED GOODS (q.v.). Cf. CANNED GOODS. [U.S. slang, 1900s, Berrey and Van den Bark]

under 1. unconscious due to anesthesia. No negative connotations. [U.S., 1900s] **2.** intoxicated with narcotics. For synonyms see TALL. [drug culture, 1900s] **3.** intoxicated with alcohol. For synonyms see WOOFLED. [U.S. slang, 1900s] See also GONE UNDER.

under-cover man a homosexual male. Refers to his secrecy and is reinforced by a reference to bed-covers. [U.S. underworld, early 1900s, Montelone]

under-dimple the female genitals. For synonyms see MONOSYLLABLE. [British, 1800s, Farmer and Henley]

undergarments underwear; the clothing worn next to the skin. A specialization of a word referring to all but the outermost clothing. [this sense since the mid 1800s]

underparts the genitals, either male or female. See BACK PARTS, PARTS BELOW. [colloquial, 1800s or before]

unders 1. the female genitals. *Cf.* UNDERPARTS. [British colloquial, 1800s] 2. underpants. For synonyms see NETHER GARMENTS. [U.S. slang, 1900s]

under-side 1. death; the grave. [colloquial euphemism, 1800s] 2. the posteriors; the bottom. For synonyms see DUFF. [colloquial since the 1800s or before]

undertaker 1. someone who operates a funeral parlor; a man who makes his livelihood by performing burials. [British and U.S., early 1800s-pres.] Synonyms: BLACK COAT, BODY-SNATCHER, CARRION-HUNTER, COLD COOK, DEATH-HUNTER, GRAVE-DIGGER, LAND-BROKER, PLANTER. 2. the female genitals. *Cf.* UNDERS (sense 1). [British slang, 1800s, Farmer and Henley]

under the influence a truncation of "under the influence of alcohol." Euphemistic for "drunk." [U.S., 1900s]

under the table intoxicated with alcohol. Implying that someone has slid under the table. [U.S. slang, early 1900s-pres.]

under the weather 1. intoxicated with alcohol or having a hangover. [1800s-pres.] 2. pertaining to a woman who is menstruating. [U.S. slang, 1900s] 3. pertaining to any sick person. [U.S. colloquial, 1900s or before]

underthings women's underwear, especially underpants. For synonyms see NETHER GARMENTS. [U.S. advertising euphemism, mid 1900s]

underworld 1. hell; the region of departed souls. [since the early 1600s] 2. the world of thieves, prostitutes, tramps, sexual degenerates, and confidence men. [British and U.S., 1800s-pres.]

undies women's underpants. The singular, "undy," is rare. *Cf.* UNDERTHINGS. [U.S. slang, early 1900s-pres.] Syn-

onyms; LINGERIE, NEATHIE-SET, PULL-ONS, SCANTIES, SCANTY TROUSERS.

unfeed to defecate. For synonyms see EASE ONESELF. [U.S. dialect, 1900s or before]

unflushable an outdoor privy compared to a water-flush toilet bowl. [U.S. slang, early 1900s or before, *Current Slang*] See also OUTDOOR PLUMBING.

unfortunate women (also **unfortunates**) prostitutes in general. Also in the singular. [early 1800s]

un-fucking-conscious totally unconscious. [U.S., 1900s]

un-fucking-sociable extremely unsociable. [U.S., 1900s]

ungenitured without testicles; pertaining to a eunuch. [from *Measure for Measure* (Shakespeare)]

unhintables 1. trousers. For synonyms see GALLIGASKINS. [British jocular euphemism, 1800s] 2. women's underwear. [U.S., 1900s, Berrey and Van den Bark]

union 1. copulation; the sexual joining of a male and a female, said of all species of animals in which the male has an intromittent organ. [as early as the 1600s in *The Tempest* (Shakespeare)] 2. marriage. Usually with no undue focus on sexual copulation. [euphemistic]

unisex pertaining to a lack of distinction between the sexes. A fad (late 1960s, U.S.) and an occasional theme in the women's movements. The goals include (in varying degrees) identical dress, rights, and a dissolution of the traditional male-female division of labor.

unit 1. a gadget; a nameless object. 2. the penis. For synonyms see YARD. [both senses, U.S. slang, 1900s]

unkie morphine. For synonyms see MORPH. [U.S. drug culture, 1900s]

unknown birth, of illegitimate; bastard. [euphemistic]

unk-pay a chump or a dupe. Pig Latin for "punk." *Cf.* UMP-CHAY. [U.S. underworld, early 1900s]

unlawfully begotten pertaining to a bastard.

unmentionables 1. breeches; trousers. [colloquial, 1800s] **2.** women's underpants. [U.S. slang, early 1900s-pres.]

unmentionable vice SODOMY (*q.v.*) in general; an act of sexual perversion; the CRIMEN INNOMINATUM (*q.v.*). [euphemistic, 1800s-1900s]

unnatural connection SODOMY (*q.v.*), primarily PEDERASTY (*q.v.*). *Cf.* CARNAL CONNECTION. [euphemistic, 1800s-pres.]

unnatural sexual intercourse SODOMY (*q.v.*), in particular, PEDERASTY (*q.v.*). Includes any nonorthogenital sexual intercourse. [euphemistic, 1800s-pres.]

unnatural vice any nonorthogenital sexual act, including solitary masturbation; a euphemism for SODOMY. [1800s or before]

unpaved castrated. Literally, "without stones," *i.e.*, "without testicles." *Cf.* TWO STONE UNDERWEIGHT. [from *Cymbeline* (Shakespeare)]

unruly member the penis. *Cf.* MEMBER (sense 1), MEMBER FOR THE COCKSHIRE, PRIVY MEMBER. [British slang, late 1800s]

unseminared deprived of virility; castrated. A play on "unschooled" and "without semen" or the means for producing it. [from *Antony and Cleopatra* (Shakespeare)]

unsex 1. to castrate. [U.S., medical] **2.** to deprive either sex of its distinctive qualities. [from *Macbeth* (Shakespeare)]

unspeakables breeches or trousers. For synonyms see GALLIGASKINS. [British jocular euphemism, early 1800s]

upspit to vomit. [British euphemism, late 1800s]

unswallow to vomit. [British and U.S., early 1900s]

untrimmed pertaining to a virgin female. *Cf.* TRIM (sense 1), UNDEFLOWERED. (from *King John* (Shakespeare))

unutterables 1. trousers. [British slang, early 1800s] **2.** women's underwear. [U.S., 1900s, Berrey and Van den Bark]

unwell experiencing the menses. *Cf.* SICK (sense 1), UNDER THE WEATHER (sense 2). [U.S. colloquial, 1900s]

unwhisperables 1. trousers. [British and U.S., early 1800s, Farmer and Henley] **2.** women's underpants. [U.S., 1900s, Berrey and Van den Bark]

up 1. to coit a woman. [British and U.S. slang, 1800s-pres.] **2.** pertaining to the erect penis. *Cf.* GET IT UP. [U.S., 1900s or before] **3.** pertaining to the state of one who has consumed or abused drugs, especially amphetamines. A variation of HIGH (sense 3). [U.S. drug culture, mid 1900s-pres.] **4.** an amphetamine capsule or tablet; an UPPER (*q.v.*). [U.S. drug culture, mid 1900s-pres.]

up-and-coming pregnant. For synonyms see FRAGRANT. [U.S. dialect (Ozarks), Randolph and Wilson]

upchuck 1. to vomit. *Cf.* CHUCK UP. **2.** vomitus. [both senses, U.S. colloquial, 1900s]

upholstered 1. infected with venereal disease. [U.S. underworld, early 1900s] **2.** intoxicated with alcohol. [U.S. slang, 1900s]

Up it! a curse directing the cursed person to shove something up his anus, or her vagina or anus.

up-lifting sexually arousing, said of a male. Double entendre from the expression meaning "spiritually uplifting," *i.e.*, causing one (a male) to LIFT UP (*q.v.*). [U.S. slang, 1900s]

upped raped; having experienced coition. Usually said by men of women. [British and U.S., early 1900s-pres.]

upper amphetamine. *Cf.* UP (sense 4). For synonyms see AMP. (U.S. drug culture, mid 1900s-pres.)

upper-deck the human breasts. For synonyms see BOSOM. [widespread slang; attested as Australian, 1900s, *Dictionary of Slang and Unconventional English*]

upper-works the human breasts. In contrast to the underparts. [British slang, late 1800s]

uppie an amphetamine tablet or cap-

sule. *Cf.* UP (sense 4), UPPER. [U.S. drug culture, mid 1900s-pres.]

uppish intoxicated with alcohol. For synonyms see WOOFLED. [British slang, early 1700s-1900s]

upright an act of copulation performed standing up. [British, 1700s] Synonyms and related terms: FAST-FUCK, KNEE-TREMBLER, PERPENDICULAR, PERPENDICULAR CONJUNCTION, QUICKY, THREE-PENNY UPRIGHT, UPRIGHT GRAND.

upright grin the female genitals. From the image of the PUDENDAL CLEAVAGE (*q.v.*). *Cf.* FLASH THE UPRIGHT GRIN, LONG-EYE. For synonyms see MONOSYL-LABLE. [British slang, 1800s, Farmer and Henley]

upright wink the female genitals. From the image of the PUDENDAL CLEAV-AGE (*q.v.*). *Cf.* LONG-EYE, SQUINT, UP-RIGHT GRIN. [British euphemism, late 1800s, (Farmer)]

upshoot an ejaculation of semen. *Cf.* GET THE UPSHOOT. For synonyms see MELT. [from *Love's Labour's Lost* (Shakespeare)]

up the creek (also **up a creek**) See SHIT CREEK.

urinal of the planets a derogatory nickname for Ireland. Refers to the frequent rains. [British slang, 1600s]

urp 1. to vomit. **2.** vomit. See EARP.

use to copulate with, usually to coit a woman, See USE OF THE SEX. [since the 1500s]

used-beer department a toilet; a W.C., especially one in a tavern or saloon. For synonyms see W.C. [slang, 1900s]

used-up dead; killed in battle. For synonyms see DONE FOR. [U.S. slang, World War I]

use of the sex copulation. [British euphemism, 1800s, Farmer and Henley]

user someone who takes ''hard'' drugs, *i.e.* cocaine, morphine, heroin, L.S.D., and P.C.P. [U.S. underworld and drug culture, 1900s] Similar terms; GHOST, HAY-BURNER, HAY-HEAD, HEAD, JOY-POPPER, JOY-RIDER, KOKOMO, METH-FREAK, METH-HEAD, METH MONSTER, OPIUM-EATER, PILL-HEAD, PINHEAD, SCHNOZZLER, SCHOOL BOY, SNIFFER, SNOWDRIFTER, SNOW-FLOWER, SPEED-FREAK, ZONKER.

usher a PEDERAST (*q.v.*). Primarily the INSERTOR, but also the RECEIVER (both *q.v.*). From GENTLEMAN OF THE BACK DOOR (*q.v.*). *Cf.* BACK-DOOR WORK, BUR-GLAR (sense 1). [British slang, late 1700s-late 1800s]

U-trou (also **U-wear**) men's under-pants. From ''underwear.'' [U.S. slang, 1900s]

V

V. the tranquilizer "Valium" (trademark). [U.S. drug culture, mid 1900s-pres.]

vack an old woman. [attested as Australian, Baker]

vacuum the female genitals; the vagina. NATURE (sense 5), the male libido abhors a vacuum and seeks to fill it. [British, 1800s, Farmer and Henley]

vagina the sheath of flesh in the female which receives the penis. From the Latin word for "sheath." It is this sheath which receives the "gladius," the "sword" or penis. This is the word-of-choice for this organ. See PUDENDUM. For synonyms see PASSAGE. [from Latin; in English since the late 1600s]

valve the female genitals. A confusion of "vulva" and "valve," a synonym of "cock." [slang and nonce, 1800s-1900s]

vamp 1. a woman who uses her sexual charms to captivate men. **2.** to captivate a man with one's sexual charms, said of a woman. Both are from "vampire." [both senses, British and U.S., 1900s and before]

vampire 1. the spirit of a dead person in the form of a large, bloodsucking bat. [since the early 1700s] **2.** a seductive female. Cf. VAMP. [U.S., 1900s]

Vanishing American the American Indian. For synonyms see REDSKIN. [U.S., 1900s]

vapors 1. a sickness; a fainting spell; nausea. [colloquial euphemism, 1900s and before] **2.** the menses. [U.S. colloquial, 1900s]

varf to vomit. See BARF. [from German *werfen*, "throw," via Yiddish, 1900s]

varnished intoxicated with alcohol. Cf. SHELLACKED

varnish one's cane to copulate. From the male point of view. Cf. CANE (sense 2). [attested as Canadian, 1900s, *Dictionary of Slang and Unconventional English*]

varnish-remover (also **paint-remover**) an inferior grade of whisky or home-made whisky. [U.S. slang, 1900s or before]

Vatican roulette a jocular or sarcastic nickname for the RHYTHM METHOD (*q.v.*) of birth control. "Vatican" refers to "Vatican City," the seat of the Roman Catholic Church. Based on "Russian roulette." [U.S. slang, mid 1900s-pres.]

vault to copulate, especially when done illicitly. A literal translation of the Latin FORNIX (*q.v.*). [slang, late 1500s]

vaulting-school (also **vaulting-house**) a brothel. [British, early 1600s]

V-eight pertaining to a cold or unresponsive female. [U.S. slang, 1900s]

veiled twins the breasts. For synonyms see BOSOM. [British, 1800s]

velvet the tongue in expressions such as TIP THE VELVET (*q.v.*). [cant, late 1600s, B.E.]

venery 1. hunting of wild game. [late 1400s, *Oxford English Dictionary*] **2.** sexual delight and copulation; the world of prostitution. [British, 1800s]

vent 1. the waste opening in birds and fish. [since the late 1500s] **2.** to break wind. For synonyms see GURK. [1600s] **3.** the vagina. Possibly a misunderstanding, or from VENTER (sense 1). [slang, mid 1900s]

venter 1. the uterus; the womb. [late 1500s] **2.** the abdomen; the belly. [from French; 1900s and before.]

vent-renter a prostitute. See VENT (sense 3). U.S. synthetic slang or nonce, 1900s]

venturer a prostitute. [British, 1800s, Farmer and Henley]

Venus sexuality in general. The name of the Roman goddess of love. [since the 1500s]

Venus' glove the vagina. For synonyms see PASSAGE. [from *Troilus and Cressida* (Shakespeare)]

Venus's-cell the female genitals; the vagina. [early 1500s]

Venus's curse (also **Venus' curse**) a venereal disease, syphilis or gonorrhea. [British and U.S., 1800s-1900s]

Venus's honypot (also **Venus's honeypot**) 1. the female genitals. 2. copulation. [both senses, British, early 1700s] See also HONEY-POT.

verenda* the female genitals. See FEMALE VERENDA. For synonyms see MONOSYLLABLE.

verge 1. the penis. [from Latin VIRGA (*q.v.*), 1400s] 2. the male copulatory organ of certain insects.

Vermont green local variety of marijuana. For synonyms see MARI. [U.S. drug culture, mid 1900s-pres.]

vert 1. a sexual pervert. [British and U.S., 1800s-pres.] 2. to practice sexual perversion. [U.S. slang] See also PERVE.

vertical bathtub a wall-mounted men's urinal. [U.S. jocular slang, mid 1900s]

very uncomfortable place hell. [British euphemism, 1900s or before]

vestry-man the penis. For synonyms see YARD. [British slang, 1800s, Farmer and Henley]

vice prostitution. The term refers to any wrongdoing but is often used in this sense as a euphemism. [U.S., 1900s]

vice sister a prostitute. For synonyms see HARLOT. [U.S. slang, 1900s]

Victoria Monk semen. Rhyming slang for "spunk." [British, 1800s, *Dictionary of Slang and Unconventional English*]

vipe to crave a marijuana cigarette. [U.S. underworld, early 1900s, Deak]

viper 1. a dealer in marijuana. [U.S. drug culture, 1900s] 2. a marijuana smoker, especially one who has been at it for some years. [U.S. drug culture, early 1900s]

viper's weed marijuana. [U.S. drug culture, mid 1900s-pres.]

virga the penis. See VERGE. [latin for "rod"; euphemistic, 1800s-1900s]

virginhead 1. virginity. 2. the hymen. [both since the early 1600s]

virginity!, By my a mild oath and an exclamation. For synonyms see 'ZOUNDS!

virgin-knot (also **knot**) 1. virginity. 2. the hymen. [from *The Tempest* (Shakespeare)]

virgin queen a homosexual male who will not engage in coition until after MARRIAGE (sense 2). Based on the well-known nickname for Queen Elizabeth I. [U.S. homosexual use, 1900s, Farrell]

virgin-treasure the female genitals. For synonyms see MONOSYLLABLE. (British slang, early 1600s]

virile 1. masculine, said of men or women. 2. pertaining to the male sex. [both since the late 1400s]

virile member the penis; the erect penis. [translation of the Latin *membrum virile;* since the 1700s]

virilia the external male genitals, the penis and the scrotum containing the testicles. [Latin; medical] Synonyms: ADAM'S ARSENAL, AFFAIR, AFFAIRS, APPARATUS, BAG OF TRICKS, BALLS AND BAT, BASKET, BAT AND BALLS, BOX, BUSINESS, CODPIECE, CONCERN, CREDENTIALS, CROTCH, CROWN JEWELS, DINGBATS, DOHICKIES, DOJIGGERS, EQUIPMENT, FAMILY JEWELS, FANCY-WORK, GEAR, HAIRY WHEEL, JEWELRY, KIT, LADY-WARE, LOINS, LOT, LUGGAGE, MANLINESS, MATCH, MATE, MEAT AND TWO VEGETABLES, NATURA, NATURALIA, NECESSARIES, NETHERLANDS, OUTFIT, PENCIL AND TASSEL, POPERINE PEAR, PRACK, PRIDES, PRIVATE PARTS, PRIVATE PROPERTY, PRIVATES, PRIVITIES, RULE-OF-THREE, SHAPE, STICK AND BANGERS, TACKLE, TOODLES, TOOLS, VITALS, WARE, WATCH-AND-SEALS, WEDDING-KIT, WORKS.

virtue 1. female chastity. [since the late 1500s] 2. jocular for "vice," *i.e.*, drinking and womanizing. [British slang, 1800s, Farmer and Henley]

virtue after a prostitute. For synonyms see HARLOT. [U.S., 1800s, Matsell]

viscera the intestines or inner organs.

Used euphemistically for "guts." [since the mid 1600s] Synonyms: ALIMENTARY CANAL, ARSE-ROPES, BOWEL, CHITTER-LINGS, GUT, INNARDS, INSIDES, INTESTINAL FORTITUDE, INWARDS, PUDDING, TRANKLEMENTS, TRIPES, TROLLYBAGS.

visitors (also **visitor**) the menses. [U.S. slang, early 1900s or before, Montelone]

visit the sand-box to retire to urinate. With reference to a box of sand used for elimination by a cat. Cf. SAND-BOX. [jocular euphemism, 1900s]

vitals the genitals of both sexes; the male genitals; the testicles. [euphemistic, 1900s and before]

vital zone the male pubic area; the groin. [1900s]

vomick 1. to vomit. **2.** VOMITUS (q.v.). [U.S. dialect, 1900s or before]

vomit 1. to eject or release the contents of the stomach through the mouth. [since the 1300s] **2.** the contents of the stomach when brought up. See list at YORK.

vomitive (also **vomitory**) **1.** pertaining to VOMIT (sense 2) or the act of vomiting. **2.** an emetic; an agent causing vomiting. [both since the late 1500s]

vomitus the contents of the stomach when brought up; VOMIT (sense 2).

vonce marijuana. For synonyms see MARI. [U.S. drug culture, mid 1900s-pres.]

voodoo a type of sorcery found in the Southern U.S. and some Caribbean islands. [late 1800s-pres.]

voos the breasts. [U.S. slang, 1900s, Wentworth and Flexner]

votaries of pleasure prostitution. [British written nonce, early 1800s]

voyeur one who obtains sexual gratification from watching others undress, copulate, or engage in sexual activity. Masturbation may accompany or follow the viewing. See VOYEURISM. Cf. KEEK, PEEK-FREAK.

voyeurism the practice of obtaining sexual gratification by looking at sexual stimulants in private. See VOYEUR.

vrow-case a brothel. [British slang or cant, 1600s]

V.T.P. "voluntary termination of pregnancy," an abortion; a therapeutic abortion. [U.S. euphemism, 1970-1980]

vulcanized intoxicated. For synonyms see WOOFLED. [U.S. slang, early 1900s]

Vulgarian a derogatory nickname for a Bulgarian. [U.S., early 1900s]

vum!, I (also **I van!, I vow!, I vowny!, I vummy!, I vumpers!**) "I vow!" or "I swear!" [U.S., late 1700s-1800s]

W

W. a truncation of "water closet," a toilet or a bathroom. For synonyms see W.C. [British colloquial, 1800s]

wacky tabbacky marijuana. [U.S. drug culture and slang, mid 1900s-pres.]

wacky weed marijuana. *Cf.* WEED (sense 1). [U.S. drug culture and slang, mid 1900s-pres.]

wad 1. accumulated semen, as in SHOOT ONE'S WAD (*q.v.*). [U.S. slang, 1900s] **2.** an unpopular or disliked person. [U.S., 1900s] See also BUM WAD.

waddy contemptible; undesirable. From WAD (sense 2). *Cf.* BUM WAD. [U.S. slang, 1900s]

waffles an idle loafer; a good-for-nothing. [British slang, 1800s, Farmer and Henley]

wag 1. a buffoon; a jester; a joker. [slang since the late 1500s] **2.** the penis, especially that of a child. Also **wiggle.** [U.S., 1900s]

wagon, on the abstaining totally from alcohol. [U.S., 1900s and before]

wag one's bottom (also **wag one's tail**) to solicit for a sexual act; to be a prostitute. [British slang, 1800s]

wag-tail a wanton woman; a prostitute. [from *King Lear* (Shakespeare)]

waiter a male who waits in a public restroom for another male who has agreed to come there and perform a homosexual act. An extension of the TEAROOM (*q.v.*) theme. [U.S., 1900s]

wake-up an amphetamine tablet. Usually plural. *Cf.* EYE-OPENER. For synonyms see AMP. [U.S. drug culture, mid 1900s-pres.]

walking dandruff lice. [U.S., 1900s or before] Synonyms both singular and plural: ACTIVE CITIZEN, BOSOM CHUMS, BOSOM FRIEND, CHATTS, CHUM, COOTIES, CRABS, CREEPERS, FAMILIARS, GENTLEMAN'S COMPANION, LIGHT TROOPS, PANTS RABBITS. SCOTCH GREYS, SCOTCHMEN, SEAM-SQUIRREL.

walking-mort a streetwalking prostitute. [cant, 1500s, Harman]

walk-up a brothel. [U.S., 1900s]

walk-up fuck a woman who is agreeable to copulation, "just walk up and ask." See FUCK (sense 5). [Australian, 1900s, *Dictionary of Slang and Unconventional English*]

wall, off the pertaining to a strange or improbable person or situation. [U.S. slang, mid 1900s-pres.]

wall-eyed intoxicated with alcohol. [U.S. slang, 1900s]

walliyo a derogatory term for an Italian. For synonyms see SKY. [U.S., 1900s]

wallopies large breasts, not necessarily shapely ones. [U.S. slang, mid 1900s-pres.]

wallow to copulate. [U.S. slang, 1900s]

wallydraigle (also **wallydrag**) a male or female sloven; a slob. [British colloquial, 1500s-1800s]

wamble-cropped (also **womble-cropped**) intoxicated with alcohol. From a term for general anxiety. *Cf.* WOMBLE-TY-CROPT. [U.S. slang, 1700s, Ben Franklin]

wand the penis, especially in MAGIC WAND (*q.v.*). [attested as British slang, 1800s, Farmer and Henley]

wang the penis. See WHANG, WONG. For synonyms see YARD.

wank 1. a simpleton; an oaf. [British colloquial] **2.** to coit a woman. **3.** to masturbate. *Cf.* LEVY AND FRANK, WHANK OFF. [British slang, 1900s]

wank off masturbate. See WHANK OFF. For synonyms see WASTE TIME.

wapsed down intoxicated with alcohol. For synonyms see WOOFLED. [U.S. slang, 1900s]

war-baby 1. one of a large number of babies resulting from conceptions before or during wartime. **2.** an illegitimate baby born during wartime. [colloquial, 1900s]

warden a wife. [U.S. slang, 1900s] Synonyms: BALL AND CHAIN, BEST PIECE, BETTER HALF, BIT OF TRIPE, BITTER HALF, BRIDE, CARVING-KNIFE, CHEESE AND KISSES, COWS AND KISSES, DRUM AND FIFE, DUCHESS OF FIFE, FORK AND KNIFE, JOY OF MY LIFE, LAWFUL BLANKET, LAWFUL JAM, MARE, O.L., OLD LADY, O.W., PLATES AND DISHES, POKER-BREAKER, SQUAW, STRUGGLE AND STRIFE, TROUBLE AND STRIFE, WAR AND STRIFE, WEDDED-WENCH, WORRY AND STRIFE.

wardrobe 1. a privy. See GARDEROBE. [1300s, (Chaucer)] **2.** a bathroom. [vague and euphemistic]

ware 1. a general term for male and female genitals. [1400s-1900s] **2.** the female genitals. [British slang, 1800s] **3.** the male genitals; the VIRILIA (*q.v.*). *Cf.* LADY-WARE, STANDING-WARE. [British slang, 1700s] **4.** the breasts or other sexual characerics. Also **wares**. [British, 1700s]

war-horse an aggressive or determined woman; a BATTLE-AXE (*q.v.*). For synonyms see AMAZON. [U.S., 1900s]

warm bit (also **warm-baby**) a sexually attractive and COMING (*q.v.*) woman. Ware has "vigorous woman," which may be euphemistic. [British and U.S., 1800s-1900s]

warm member 1. a prostitute. [British slang, 1800s] **2.** a lecher or whoremonger. [British slang, 1800s] **3.** a wanton man or woman. [British, 1800s]

warm shop (also **warm show**) a brothel. From the "heat" of passion. [British slang, 1900s]

wart 1. a euphemism for a syphilitic CHANCRE (*q.v.*). [mid 1500s] **2.** a term of contempt for a small person or a disliked person. [U.S. slang, 1900s or before] **3.** a low-ranking member of the military. [British military, late 1800s] **4.** a breast. See WARTS.

warts the human breasts, particularly if small or unattainable. *Cf.* TEACUPS.

wash a Negro to do the impossible. [U.S., 1900s or before]

wash one's hands to retire to the bathroom; to eliminate waste. [widespread colloquial euphemism]

washroom a W.C.; a bathroom; a place to wash one's hands. For synonyms see W.C. [U.S. euphemism, 1800s or before]

wash up (also **wash**) to wash one's hands; to eliminate. *Cf.* WASHROOM. [British and U.S.]

WASP "white Anglo-Saxon Protestant," a stereotype of the white, middle-class, conservative bigot. Usually derogatory. [U.S., mid 1900s-pres.]

wasp a prostitute with venereal disease, especially gonorrhea, *i.e.*, a prostitute with a sting in her tail. [British slang, 1800s]

wassailer a heavy drinker or a drunkard. For synonyms see ALCHY. [since the early 1600s]

waste 1. products of elimination; urine and feces. **2.** to kill. [U.S. slang, mid 1900s-pres.]

wasted 1. dead. **2.** intoxicated with alcohol. [both senses, U.S. slang, mid 1900s-pres.] **3.** intoxicated with marijuana. [U.S. drug culture, mid 1900s-pres.]

waste-pipe the female genitals. For synonyms see MONOSYLLABLE. [British slang, 1800s, Farmer and Henley]

waste time to masturbate. [euphemistic, 1900s] These synonyms and related terms refer to males unless indicated otherwise: ABUSE, ABUSE ONESELF, BALL OFF, BAT, BEAT OFF, BEAT THE BISHOP, BEAT THE DUMMY, BEAT THE MEAT, BEAT THE PUP, BLANKET DRILL, BLOOCH, BOB, BOFF, BOX THE JESUIT, BOX THE JESUIT AND GET COCKROACHES, BRANDLE, BRING DOWN BY HAND, CHOKE THE CHICKEN, CHUFF, COME ONE'S MUTTON, COME ONE'S TURKEY, DIDDLE, DO-IT-YOURSELF, EAT COCKROACHES, EXPRESS A SECRET VICE, FAIRE ZAGUE-ZAGUE, FETCH METTLE, FIGHT ONE'S TURKEY, FIST-FUCK, FIVE AGAINST ONE, FLOG, FLOG ONE'S DONKEY, FLOG ONE'S MEAT, FLOG ONE'S SAUSAGE, FLOG THE BISHOP, FLONG ONE'S DONG, FONDLE ONE'S FIG, FRIG, FRIGGLE, FRIG ONESELF, FUCK OFF, FUCK ONE'S

FIST, GALLOP ONE'S ANTELOPE, GALLOP ONE'S MAGGOT, GET COCKROACHES, GET ONE'S NUTS OFF, GRIND, GRIP, HAND-JOB, HANDLE, HOT-ROD, JACK OFF, JAG OFF, JAZZ ONESELF, JERK OFF, JERK ONE'S GHERKIN, JERK ONE'S MUTTON, KEEP THE CENSUS DOWN, KNOB, LARK, LEVY AND FRANK, MANIPULATE ONE'S MANGO, MANUAL EXERCISE, MANUAL POLLUTION, MANUSTUPRATION, MASTURBATE, MEANS OF WEAKNESS AND DEBILITY, MOUNT A CORPORAL AND FOUR, ONANISM, PAW-PAW TRICKS, PLAY OFF, PLAY WITH ONESELF, PLUNK ONE'S TWANGER, POLLUTE, POLLUTION, PORTUGUESE PUMP, POUND OFF, POUND ONE'S POMEGRANATE, POUND THE MEAT, PULL ABOUT, PULL ONESELF OFF, PULL ONE'S PUD, PULL ONE'S PUDDING, PULL ONE'S WIRE, PUMP, PUMP ONESELF OFF, PUMP ONE'S PICKLE, PUMP ONE'S PYTHON, RUB-OFF, RUB UP, SCREW OFF, SECRET VICE, SELF-ABUSE, SELF-POLLUTION, SHAG, SHAKE, SHAKE UP, SIMPLE INFANTICIDE, SLING ONE'S JELLY, SLING ONE'S JUICE, SNAP THE RUBBER, SNAP THE WHIP, SOLDIER'S JOY, SOLITARY SIN, SQUEEZE THE LEMON, STROKE THE LIZARD, TAKE ONESELF IN HAND, TICKLE ONE'S CRACK (female), TOSS OFF, TOUCH-UP, WANK OFF, WHACK OFF, WHANG OFF, WHANK OFF, WHIP OFF, WHIP ONE'S WIRE, WHIP THE DUMMY, WORK OFF, YANK, YANK ONE'S STRAP, YANK ONE'S YAM.

watch-and-seals the penis and testicles. Gentlemen would often attach to their watch fobs objects used to seal letters. *Cf.* DUMB WATCH, SEALS. [British, 1800s, Farmer and Henley]

watchqueen. 1. a peeper; a voyeur. *Cf.* PEEK-FREAK, PEER-QUEER. • the nickname for a lookout in a public restroom where homosexual activities are performed. See TEAROOM. [both senses, U.S. homosexual use, mid 1900s]

water box (also **water-course, water-engine, water-gap, water-works**) the human genitals with reference to their urinary function. See WATERWORKS. [in various forms since the 1500s]

water closet 1. a chamber pot or a close stool with a water compartment to receive human excrement. See CLOSET STOOL. [British, 1700s] **2.** a room containing sanitary apparatus to receive, contain, and flush away human excrement. [since the 1700s]

water-logged intoxicated with alcohol; absolutely saturated. For synonyms see WOOFLED. [British and U.S. slang, early 1900s-pres.]

watermelons the human breasts, especially if large. *Cf.* HONEYDEW MELONS, MELONS. [U.S. slang, 1900s]

water-mill the female genitals. See WATER-BOX for similar terms. [British slang, 1800s]

water of life gin. For synonyms see RUIN. [British slang, early 1800s]

water one's pony (also **water one's nag**) to urinate; to retire to urinate. A variant of WATER THE HORSES (*q.v.*). For synonyms see RETIRE. [British slang, 1800s]

water-pipe 1. a pipe used for smoking marijuana, hashish, or opium. [U.S. drug culture, mid 1900s] **2.** the male or female urethra. *Cf.* WATER-BOX. [U.S. slang, 1900s or before]

waterspout the penis, especially if flaccid. *Cf.* SPOUT. [widespread slang, 1900s or before]

water tank the bladder. [U.S. colloquial, 1900s or before]

water the dragon for a male to urinate; the same as DRAIN THE DRAGON (*q.v.*). *Cf.* WATER THE HORSES. [slang, 1700s-1900s]

water the horses for a male to retire to urinate. An excuse for leaving the room. For synonyms see RETIRE. [widespread slang since the 1800s]

waterworks 1. the male or female urinary organs. *Cf.* PLUMBING, WATERBOX. [British slang, 1800s, Farmer and Henley] **2.** the eyes when used for crying. No negative connotations.

way, on the pregnant. For synonyms see FRAGRANT. [since the 1600s or before]

wazoo the penis; the anus or any unnamed area which can be tantalizingly hinted about. *Cf.* BAZOO. [U.S. slang,

1900s] **2.** the mouth. No negative connotations.

W.C. a "water closet," a bathroom or toilet [originally British; colloquial, mid 1800s-pres.] Synonyms: ALTAR, ALTAR ROOM, BATH, BIF, BIFFY, BOG, CABINET D'AISANCE, CARSEY, CASA, CASE, CHAMBER OF COMMERCE, CLOAKROOM, CLOSET OF DECENCY, CLOSET OF EASE, CLOSET STOOL, COLFABIAS, COMFORT ROOM, COMFORT STATION, CONVENIENCE, CRYSTAL, CUZ, DOMUS, DUBBY, EGYPT, GAB ROOM, GENTLEMEN'S ROOM, GENTLEMEN'S WALK, GROWLER, GULF, GUTTER-ALLEY, GUTTER-LANE, HEAD, HOLY OF HOLIES, HOUSE OF LORDS, INDOOR PLUMBING, JAKE, JAKEHOUSE, JAKES, JANE, JIM, JOE, JOHN, JOHNNIE, LADIES', LADIES' ROOM, LADIES' WALK, LAST RESORT, LAT, LAV, LAVATORY, LAVO, LAVVY, LAVY, LEAKERY, LIBRARY, LITTLE BOY'S ROOM, LITTLE GIRL'S ROOM, LOB, LOCUS, LOO, LULU, MARBLE PALACE, MAY, MEN'S JOHN, MEN'S ROOM, MINOR, MRS. JONES, MRS. JONES'S PLACE, MRS. MURPHY, NECESSARY CHAMBER, OLD SOLDIER'S HOME, PISSER, PISSHOUSE, PISSING-POST, PLACE, PLUMBING, POET'S CORNER, POT, POTTY, POWDER ROOM, PRIVATE OFFICE, PUBLIC COMFORT STATION, PUBLIC CONVENIENCE, RECEIVING-SET, RESTROOM, RETIRING ROOM, ROUND HOUSE, RUTH, SAND-BOX, SHITTER, SHOT TOWER, SMALLEST ROOM, STATE HOUSE, TEAROOM, TEMPLE, THE EXCUSE ME, THE GENT'S, THE GENT'S ROOM, THRONE, THUNDER-BOWL, THUNDER-BOX, TOOT, TRIZZER, TWILIGHT, USED-BEER DEPARTMENT, W., WASHROOM, WATER CLOSET, WEST-CENTRAL, WHERE THE QUEEN GOES ON FOOT, WHIZ-STAND, WIDOW JONES, WIZZER, X.

weaker-vessel a woman; females in general. [from *Love's Labour's Lost* (Shakespeare)]

weak-jointed intoxicated with alcohol. *Cf.* TANGLEFOOTED. [U.S., 1900s]

weak sister 1. a weakling or a coward. **2.** an effeminate male, possibly a homosexual male. [both senses, U.S., 1900s or before]

weapon the penis. *Cf.* CLUB. (sense 1).

GUN. [widespread nonce; since *c.* 1000, *Oxford English Dictionary*]

wearing a smile (also **wearing nothing but a smile**) to be completely naked. Refers to both sexes. May be from the UPRIGHT GRIN (*q.v.*). [U.S. slang, 1900s]

wearing the bustle wrong pregnant. [U.S. jocular slang, 1900s]

wear the kilt to act as a CATAMITE (*q.v.*). From the image of a man wearing a skirt. *Cf.* HIGH-KILTED. [British, 1900s]

weary intoxicated with alcohol, [British, late 1800s]

weathervane a wind direction indicator. A term sometimes used to avoid the "cock" in "weathercock." [British and U.S., mid 1800s-pres.]

wedded-wench one's wife; a wife. [U.S. slang, 1900s]

wedding bells acid the drug L.S.D. (*q.v.*). [U.S. drug culture, mid 1900s-pres.]

wedding-kit the male genitals. [British military, early 1900s, *Dictionary of Slang and Unconventional English*]

wedge 1. the penis. For synonyms see YARD [slang since the 1800s] **2.** backslang for "Jew." Usually considered derogatory. [British slang, 1800s] See also WEDGES.

wedged-up pregnant. *Cf.* WEDGE (sense 1). For synonyms see FRAGRANT. [British slang, 1800s, Farmer and Henley]

wedges (also **wedgies**) the drug L.S.D. (*q.v.*). *Cf.* CUBE (sense 2). [U.S. drug culture, mid 1900s-pres.]

weed 1. marijuana or a marijuana cigarette: From a term for tobacco. [U.S. slang and drug culture, 1900s] **2.** the drug P.C.P. (*q.v.*). sold as T.H.C. See T.H.C. [U.S. drug culture, mid 1900s-pres.]

weed monkey a cheap and lewd prostitute. See MONKEY (sense 1), the female genitals. [U.S. slang, 1900s]

weed tea marijuana. Sometimes in reference to a tea brewed from marijuana. [U.S. drug culture, 1900s]

weekend ho a "weekend whore," a part-time prostitute who usually only works on weekends or during conventions. [U.S. black use, mid 1900s-pres.]

weekend warrior a "weekend" or occasional prostitute; a WEEKEND HO (*q.v.*). From the nickname for members of the U.S. military reserves. [U.S., mid 1900s-pres.]

weenie 1. the penis, particularly if small or that of a child. *Cf.* PEENIE. [U.S. slang, 1900s] **2.** a jerk or an oaf. From sense **1.** [U.S. slang, 1900s]

wee-wee 1. to urinate. *Cf.* PEE-WEE sense 3). **2.** urine. [both senses, juvenile euphemism; British and U.S., 1800s-pres.]

weiner a jerk or an oaf. *Cf.* WEENIE (sense 2). [U.S. slang, mid 1900s-pres.]

weird pertaining to a homosexual male. [U.S. slang, 1900s]

weirdo (also **weirdy**) **1.** any unpleasant person, usually male; an oaf or jerk. [U.S. slang, mid 1900s] **2.** a homosexual male. See WEIRD. [both senses, U.S. slang, mid 1900s-pres.]

welfare pimp a pinp who collects the welfare checks due to his prostitutes. [U.S. underworld, mid 1900s-pres., James]

well-along pregnant; obviously pregnant. [U.S. colloquial, 1900s]

well-bottled intoxicated with alcohol. [British and U.S. slang, 1900s]

well-bred lewd; frequently copulated with; thoroughly copulated with. [double entendre and widespread recurrent nonce]

well-built 1. pertaining to a well-proportioned woman or a well-proportioned and well-muscled man. [colloquial, 1800s-pres.] **2.** euphemistic for "having large male genitals." *Cf.* MENTULATE. [British and U.S., 1800s-pres.]

well-developed 1. pertaining to a woman with qualities such as large, well-proportioned breasts and prominent hips and buttocks; pertaining to a woman who has reached sexual maturity. **2.** pertaining to a man with fully developed or large genitals, slim hips, broad shoulders, and a muscular body. **3.** pertaining to primary sexual characteristics.

well-endowed 1. pertaining to a woman with large or very large breasts or any other significantly large primary or secondary sexual characteristic. **2.** pertaining to a man with large or very large genitals or some other significant sexual characteristic. [both senses, British and U.S., 1900s or before]

well-favored by nature 1. having large male genitals, said of a man. **2.** having large breasts, said of a woman. [both senses, British euphemism, late 1800s, (Farmer)]

well-holed pertaining to a woman with satisfying sexual qualities. From the expression "well-heeled," meaning "wealthy." *Cf.* WELL-HUNG.

well-hung pertaining to a man with large or very large genitals. *Cf.* MENTULATE. [colloquial since the early 1800s] See also HUNG.

well-oiled intoxicated with alcohol. See OILED. [British and U.S. military, early 1900s-pres.]

well-sprung intoxicated with alcohol. For synonyms see WOOFLED. [British and U.S. slang, 1900s]

well-under intoxicated with alcohol. *Cf.* UNDER (sense 3). [Australian, 1900s]

welt a large penis. *Cf.* MENTULATE. [British military, 1900s, *Dictionary of Slang and Unconventional English*]

wench 1. a girl; a small child of the female sex. No negative connotations. [1200s, *Oxford English Dictionary*] **2.** a girl, especially a servant girl. [late 1500s] **3.** a girl, prostitute, or wanton woman. [since the 1300s] **4.** to chase after women; to seek prostitutes. [late 1500s] **5.** a black or mulatto woman or girl. [U.S., 1800s, Green]

wencher a man who seeks prostitutes. For synonyms see LECHER. [since the late 1500s]

Wesson party a form of sexual contact where the participants cover their bodies with liquid cooking oil and then perform various sexual activities; the same as MAZOLA PARTY (*q.v.*). From the trademarked brand name of a cooking oil. See GROUP SEX for related subjects. [U.S. slang, mid 1900s-pres.]

West-Central a reinterpretation of W.C. (*q.v.*), "water closet," a bathroom or privy. Based on one of the divisions of London. [British slang, 1800s-1900s]

West-Coast turnarounds amphetamines; the same as L.A. TURNABOUTS (*q.v.*). [U.S. drug culture, 1900s]

wet 1. intoxicated with alcohol. [slang since the early 1700s] **2.** pertaining to a woman who is sufficiently sexually aroused to produce vaginal lubrication. *Cf.* DRIPPING FOR IT, JUICY (sense 1), SLICK-CHICK. [since the 1700s] **3.** to urinate, especially in "wet one's pants," as said of a child. *Cf.* MAKE WATER. [U.S. slang, 1900s or before] **4.** a fool; an oaf, as in WET NOODLE (*q.v.*) or "wet behind the ears." [Australian, Baker]

wet a bottom (also **get a wet bottom**) to coit, from a woman's point of view. [British slang, 1800s]

wetback a derogatory term for a Mexican or Mexican American. The name referred originally to illegal Mexicans who were still wet from swimming across the Rio Grande. [U.S. slang and colloquial, 1900s]

wet deck a woman who has just finished copulating with one man and is ready for another, usually said of a prostitute. *Cf.* BUTTERED BUN. [British and U.S. slang, 1800s-1900s]

wet dream a nocturnal seminal emission. [British and U.S., 1800s-pres.]

wet duck the same as WET DECK (*q.v.*).

wet-goose an oaf or simpleton. For synonyms see OAF. [British, 1800s, Farmer and Henley]

wet-hand a drunkard. For synonyms see ALCHY. [British slang, late 1800s]

wether-head an oaf or dolt. [British colloquial, late 1600s]

wet noodle a dupe; an oaf; an effeminate male. [U.S. colloquial and slang, 1900s]

wet one (also **wet fart**) a strong breaking of wind containing fecal matter. [British slang, 1800s]

wet one's pants to urinate in one's pants from fear or other uncontrolled emotional situations. [colloquial, 1900s or before]

wet one's wick (also **wet one's end**) to copulate, from the male point of view. *Cf.* DIP ONE'S WICK, WICK. [U.S. slang, 1900s]

wet sock (also **wet rag**) an oaf; a useless jerk. *Cf.* RUBBER SOCK. [U.S., mid 1900s]

wetster a drunkard. [British and U.S. slang, 1800s-1900s]

wet-subject a drunkard. The opposite of a dry or dull subject. [British and U.S. slang, 1800s-1900s]

wet-'un 1. coition; an act of coition. **2.** a drunkard. See also WET ONE. This entry is eye-dialect and could be spelled "wet-one" just as well [both senses, British slang, 1800s, Farmer and Henley]

whack to cut or dilute a drug such as heroin or cocaine. [U.S. drug culture, mid 1900s-pres.]

whacker 1. the penis. *Cf.* BUSH-WHACKER (sense 2). **2.** a gadget. [both senses, U.S., 1900s]

whack it up to copulate. For synonyms see OCCUPY. [British slang, 1800s]

whack off (also **wack off**) to masturbate, said of a male. *Cf.* WHANK OFF. For synonyms see WASTE TIME. [U.S. slang, 1900s]

wham-bam-thank-you-ma'am a catch phrase used in reference to real or imagined extremely rapid copulation. *Cf.* BIP-BAM-THANK-YOU-MA'AM. [U.S. slang, late 1800s-pres.]

whang (also **wang**) **1.** the penis. Also **whangbone.** [British and U.S., 1900s] **2.** an oaf; a contemptible person. [U.S. slang, 1900s]

whangdoodle 1. a gadget. Also **whangydoodle. 2.** nonsense. [both senses, U.S., 1900s]

whanger the penis. For synonyms see YARD. [slang, 1900s]

whank off (also **wank, wank off, whang off, whank**) to masturbate, said of a male. *Cf.* WHACK OFF. [primarily British slang, 1800s-pres.]

whank-pit a bed; the place where a male "whanker" masturbates. See WHANK OFF.

what 1. the penis. For synonyms see YARD. **2.** the female genitals in expressions such as "What's-her-name?", "What's-its-name?", "The Lord-knows-what." [both senses, British euphemisms, 1800-pres.]

watchamacallit (also **whatcheema-callit**) **1.** a gadget. **2.** one of a large series of gadget names, many of which are avoidance terms for either the male or female genitals. Others are: watchma-callem, watchma-dad, watchma-daddy, watchma-diddle, watchma-dingle, watchma-doodle, watchma-gadget, watchma-hickey, watchma-jigger. [all senses, U.S. colloquial and slang, 1800s-pres.] See a full list at GADGET.

what Eve did with Adam copulation. *Cf.* ADAM-AND-EVE IT. [British euphemism, 1800s]

what mother did before me copulation. [British euphemism, 1800s]

what-nosed intoxicated with alcohol. For synonyms see WOOFLED. [British and U.S. slang, 1800s]

whatsis (also **whatsit, whatzit, whazzit**) any gadget or a name used for an object or person when the correct name is forgotten or to be avoided. [U.S., 1800s-1900s]

What's your bag? "What do you do or require?" Said among persons interested in performing nonorthogenital sex acts. *Cf.* QUEEN for examples. [U.S. homosexual use, mid 1900s]

whazooed (also **waa-zooed**) intoxicated with alcohol. From a slang term meaning "beat" or "worn down." [U.S. slang, mid 1900s-pres.] See also WAZOO.

wheat marijuana. For synonyms see MARI. [U.S. drug culture, mid 1900s-pres.]

whennymegs the testicles. From a colloquial term for "trinkets." [British dialect, 1800s or before]

whereabouts men's underpants. A pun on "wear-abouts" (Partridge). [Australian slang, early 1900s]

where the queen goes on foot the W.C.; the bathroom. [British euphemism, 1800s]

where uncle's doodle goes the vagina; the female genitals in general. *Cf.* DOODLE (sense 3). [British slang, 1800s, Farmer and Henley]

wheting-corne the female genitals. The opposite of a TOOL (*q.v.*), which is the erect penis. See GRINDSTONE, HONE. [British, 1800s or before]

Whickerbill 1. a worthless oaf or bumpkin. [U.S. slang, 1900s or before, Berrey and Van den Bark] **2.** the foreskin of the penis. [U.S. dialect (Ozarks), Randolph and Wilson]

whiffer 1. the nose. [U.S. slang, 1900s] **2.** a bad-smelling breaking of wind. *Cf.* BURNT CHEESE, S.B.D. [U.S. slang, 1900s]

whiffled intoxicated with alcohol. [British slang, early 1900s]

whiffles a relaxation of the scrotum. [British slang, late 1700s]

whim-wham (also **whim**) the female genitals. [British slang, early 1700s]

whin-bush the female pubic hair. [British slang, 1800s, Farmer and Henley]

whingding 1. a drunken spree; any wild time. [U.S., 1900s or before] **2.** a gadget. [U.S. colloquial, 1900s]

whip the penis. For synonyms see YARD. [slang, mid 1900s]

Whip it to me! 1. catch phrase encouraging the continuation of sexual advances or performance. **2.** a proposition for sexual intercourse. *Cf.* SOCK IT TO ME! [both senses, U.S. slang, mid 1900s-pres.]

whip off to masturbate. For synonyms see WASTE TIME. [U.S. slang, mid 1900s-pres.]

whip one's wire to masturbate. *Cf.*

PULL ONE'S WIRE, YANK ONE'S STRAP. [U.S. slang, 1900s]

whipped intoxicated with alcohol. For synonyms see WOOFLED. [U.S. slang, 1800s]

whipsey intoxicated with alcohol. [U.S. slang, 1900s]

whip the cat to vomit; the same as JERK THE CAT, SHOOT THE CAT (both *q.v.*). [British slang, 1600s]

whip the dummy to masturbate. *Cf.* DUMMY. [slang, 1900s]

whirlygigs the human testes. [British slang, 1600s-1700s] Synonyms: ALLS-BAY, APPLES, BALLICKS, BALLOCKS, BALLOCK-STONES, BALLS, BANGERS, BAUBLES, BEECHAM'S PILLS, BERRIES, BIRD'S-EGGS, BOBBLES, BOOBOOS, BULLETS, BUMBALLS, BUTTONS, CALLIBISTERS, CANNON BALLS, CHARLIES, CHESTNUTS, CLANGERS, CLAPPERS, CLOCK-WEIGHTS, COBBLER'S, COBBLER'S AWLS, COBBLER'S STALLS, COBS, CODS, COFFEE STALLS, COJONES, CUBES, CULLION, CULLS, DANGLERS, DIAMONDS, DUSTERS, FAMILY JEWELS, FLOWERS AND FROLICS, FUN AND FROLICS, FUTURE, GINGAMBOBS, GLANDS, GONADS, GOOLIES, GOOSEBERRIES, GROIN, JENNY HILLS, JEWELS, JIGGUMBOBS, JINGLEBERRIES, KANAKAS, KELKS, KNACKERS, KNOCKERS, LES ACCESSORIES, LOVE-APPLES, MALE-MULES, MAN-BALLS, MARBLES, MARSHMALLOWS, MOUNTAIN OYSTERS, NACKERS, NADS, NAGS, NARDS, NERTS, NIAGARA FALLS, NICKNACKS, NUTMEGS, NUTS, ORCHESTRA STALLS, ORKS, OYSTER, PEBBLES, PLUMS, POUNDERS, ROCKS, ROLLIES, ROLLOCKS, SEALS, SEEDS, SEX GLANDS, SLASHERS, SPUNKHOLDERS, STONES, SWINGERS, TALLYWAGS, TARRIWAYS, TESTICLES, TESTICULUS, TESTIMONIALS, THINGUMBOBS, THINGUMMY, TOMMY ROLLOCKS, TWIDDLE-DIDDLES, TWINS, VITALS, WHENNYMEGS.

whisker 1. a prostitute. **2.** a woman considered as a sex object. Refers to the pubic hair. *Cf.* BEARD. [both senses, U.S. slang, 1900s, Wentworth and Flexner]

whiskers 1. pertaining to sexually loose women. **2.** pertaining to sexually perverted men. An extreme instance of being HAIRY (sense 1). [both senses, U.S. underworld, 1900s, Goldin, O'Leary, and Lipsius]

whisker-splitter a whoremonger; a notorious copulator. It is highly probable that this term also meant "penis." *Cf.* BEARD-SPLITTER. [British slang, early 1800s, *Lexicon Balatronicum*]

whiskyfied intoxicated with alcohol. [U.S. slang, mid 1800s-pres.]

whisky-frisky intoxicated with alcohol. From an older term meaning "flighty." [U.S. slang, early 1900s]

whistle the penis, especially that of a child. Essentially a small FLUTE (sense 1). [British colloquial, 1800s, *Dictionary of Slang and Unconventional English*]

whistle-berries beans. *Cf.* ARS MUSICA, MUSICAL FRUIT. [U.S. slang, 1900s or before]

white 1. gin or any alcoholic beverage. *Cf.* WHITE MULE. [U.S. drug culture, 1900s] **2.** one of the powerful powdered narcotics, heroin or cocaine. [U.S. drug culture 1900s] **3.** a Caucasian.

white coffee illicit (bootleg) alcohol. [U.S. underworld, early 1900s]

white cross 1. cocaine. *Cf.* RED CROSS. (U.S. slang, 1900s] **2.** an amphetamine tablet. *Cf.* CARTWHEEL. [U.S. drug culture, mid 1900s-pres.]

white drugs cocaine. *Cf.* WHITE, WHITE STUFF. [U.S. drug culture, mid 1900s-pres.]

white girl cocaine. *Cf.* GIRL (sense 9). [U.S. drug culture, 1900s]

white honey semen. *Cf.* HIVE, HONEY. [British, late 1800s]

white lady cocaine. The "white" is from SNOW (sense 2). *Cf.* LADY SNOW. [U.S. drug culture, 1900s]

white lightning 1. whisky. *Cf.* LIGHTNING (sense 2). [U.S. colloquial, 1900s] **2.** the drug L.S.D. (*q.v.*) or L.S.D. mixed with other drugs, such as Methedrine (trademark). [U.S. drug culture, mid 1900s-pres.] **3.** a substance which produces a shock or a charge: alcohol or amphetamines. See LIGHTNING (sense 1)

white line alcohol. [U.S. slang, 1900s, Berrey and Van den Bark]

white meat 1. a white woman considered sexually by a non-white male. Cf. DARK MEAT. **2.** a white woman's genitals. Both are from the term used to describe the breast meat of the domestic chicken. [both are U.S. slang, 1900s]

white merchandise morphine and other powdered narcotics. [U.S. underworld, 1900s]

white mosquitoes cocaine. [U.S. underworld, mid 1900s, Berrey and Van den Bark]

white mule moonshine; powerful homemade liquor with a kick like a mule. Cf. DONK (sense 1), WHITE LIGHTNING (sense 1). [U.S. slang, early 1900s-pres.]

white Negro 1. an albino or mulatto Negro. Derogatory. **2.** a Negro who behaves in a way which will please white people. Derogatory. Cf. OREO, WHITE NIGGER. [both senses, U.S., 1900s]

white nigger 1. a term of contempt for whites who do menial tasks. Derogatory. [British and U.S., late 1800s] **2.** a Caucasian who works for Negro civil rights causes. Derogatory. [U.S., mid 1900s-pres.]

white nurse morphine or other drugs secretly passed to an inmate of a prison or a hospital. [U.S. underworld, 1900s or before]

whites 1. Benzedrine (trademark) tablets. [U.S. drug culture, mid 1900s-pres.] **2.** amphetamines in general. [U.S. drug culture, mid 1900s-pres.] **3.** LEUKORRHEA (q.v.). [British and U.S. colloquial, 1800s-pres.]

white satin (also **satin**) gin. For synonyms see RUIN. [British slang, 1800s or before]

white stuff 1. alcohol, especially illegal whisky. Cf. WHITE MULE. [U.S., 1900s] **2.** cocaine. From a nickname for SNOW (sense 2). Cf. SNOW STUFF.

[U.S. underworld, early 1900s] **3.** various hard drugs. The exact definition varies in time and place: heroin, morphine, and others. Cf. BLACK STUFF, SNOW STUFF. [U.S. drug culture, mid 1900s-pres.]

white tape gin. Similar to BLUE RIBBON and BLUE TAPE (both q.v.). [British slang, early 1700s-1800s]

white velvet gin. Cf. WHITE SATIN. [U.S. underworld, 1800s]

whitewash 1. to coit a female. Cf. LIME. [British slang, 1900s] **2.** liquor. [U.S., 1900s]

whitey (also **whitie**) **1.** a derogatory term for a Caucasian. [U.S. black use, 1900s] **2.** amphetamines. [U.S. drug culture, mid 1900s-pres.]

whittled intoxicated with alcohol. Cf. CUT (sense 2). [British and U.S., late 1500s-1700s]

whiz 1. to urinate. **2.** "urination" in expressions such as "take a whiz." Euphemistic for PISS (sense 2). Cf. WHIZ-STAND, WIZZER. [both senses, U.S. slang, mid 1900s-pres.] Synonyms and related terms for both senses: BURN THE GRASS, DICKY-DIDDLE, DO A RURAL, DRAIN, DRAIN ONE'S RADIATOR, DRAIN ONE'S SNAKE, DRAIN THE CRANKCASE, DRAIN THE DRAGON, DRAIN THE LIZARD, DRAIN THE SPUDS, DRAIN THE SUDS, DRAW OFF, EMICTION, EVACUATE THE BLADDER, GO TO THE BATHROOM, HAVE A RUN-OUT, HIT AND MISS, JERRY RIDDLE, JIM, JIMMY RIDDLE, KILL A SNAKE, KILL A TREE, LAG, LANT, LEAK, LET FLY, LOOK UPON A HEDGE, MAKE, MAKE A BRANCH, MAKE WATER, MICTURATE, NATURE STOP, NUMBER ONE, PASS URINE, PASS WATER, PEE-WEE, PERFORM THE WORK OF NATURE, PICK A DAISY, PIDDLE, PISS, POINT PERCY AT THE PORCELAIN, POTTY, PREEZE, PUMP, PUMP SHIP, RACK OFF, RUN OFF, SAY, SCATTER, SHAKE A SOCK, SHAKE HANDS WITH AN OLD FRIEND, SHAKE HANDS WITH THE BLOKE ONE ENLISTED WITH, SHAKE HANDS WITH WIFE'S BEST FRIEND, SHAKE THE DEW OFF THE LILY, SHOOT A LION, SLACK, SPLASH, SPRING A LEAK, SQUEEZE THE LEMON, SQUIRT, STIMBLE, STRAIN ONE'S TATERS, SYPHON OFF, SYPHON THE

PYTHON, TAKE A LEAK, TAKE A PISS, TAKE ONE'S SNAKE FOR A GALLOP, TINKLE, TOY-TOY, TRAIN TERRENCE ON THE TERRACOTTA, URINATE, VOID, WATER ONE'S NAG, WATER ONE'S PONY, WATER THE DRAGON, WATER THE HORSES, WEE-WEE, WET, WIDDLE, WRING ONE'S SOCK OUT, WRING THE DEW OFF THE BRANCH, WRING THE RATTLESNAKE.

whiz-bang a mixture of cocaine and morphine or other drugs. [U.S. drug culture, mid 1900s]

whiz-stand a urinal, usually a male urinal. [U.S. slang, mid 1900s-pres.]

wholemeal a lesbian term for a straight female. *Cf.* EAT. [mid 1900s *Dictionary of Rhyming Slang*]

wholly naked naked with the pelvic area uncovered. See NAKED. For synonyms see STARKERS.

whoopee-water champagne or other liquor. [U.S. slang, 1900s] Synonyms: BUBBLE-WATER, BUBBLY, CHAM, FIZZ, SHAMPOO.

whoops and jingles (also **whips and jingles**) severe DELIRIUM TREMENS (*q.v.*). For synonyms see ORK-ORKS. [U.S. slang, early 1900s]

whoops boy an effeminate male. A male who frequently says "Whoops!," which is supposedly a catch phrase used by homosexuals. [U.S. slang, mid 1900s]

whooshed intoxicated with alcohol. [U.S. slang, mid 1900s]

whore 1. a prostitute. [since the 1100s, *Oxford English Dictionary*] **2.** to utilize prostitutes; to consort with harlots. **3.** the queen in chess and playing cards. *Cf.* BITCH (sense 7). **4.** a promiscuous homosexual male. **5.** a term of contempt from one male to another. [1800s-1900s]

whore-bitch a prostitute. For synonyms see HARLOT. [U.S. colloquial dialect, 1900s and before]

whore-hopper a user of prostitutes; a whoremonger. [U.S. slang, 1900s]

whoremaster 1. a user of whores; a whoremonger. [since the 1500s] **2.** a

pimp; a procurer. Possibly in error. [both senses, British, early 1500s-1800s]

whoremonger a notorious user of whores; possibly a pimp. *Cf.* MUTTON-MONGER. [early 1500s]

whorephan an orphan child of a prostitute. [U.S. slang, early 1900s]

whore-pipe the penis with reference to copulation with prostitutes. [British slang, late 1700s-1800s]

whoreson 1. the bastard son of a whore. *Cf.* COWSON. **2.** a term of contempt for a male; the equivalent of bastard. [since the 1300s, *Oxford English Dictionary*]

whorez "Juarez," Mexico, a city notorious for vice. [U.S. slang, mid 1900s-pres.]

whozits a name for an object or person whose name is forgotten. *Cf.* WHATSIS. [U.S., 1900s]

wick the penis. Especially in the expressions, BURY ONE'S WICK, DIP ONE'S WICK, WET ONE'S WICK (all *q.v.*). [slang, 1900s]

widdle to urinate, usually said of a child. *Cf.* PIDDLE. [British, 1900s, *Dictionary of Slang and Unconventional English*]

widget a gadget. Recently, a generic term for a real or imaginary manufactured product. [U.S. colloquial, 1900s]

widow Jones a privy; a W.C. *Cf.* MRS. JONES'S PLACE. [U.S. dialect and slang, 1900s]

wife 1. a mistress or concubine. [slang, 1800s-1900s] **2.** a passive homosexual partner; a CATAMITE or FLUFF (both *q.v.*). [British and U.S. slang, 1800s-1900s] **3.** the more feminine partner in a homosexual marriage.

wiffle-woffles a stomachache or a depression. *Cf.* COLLYWOBBLES, MULLI-GRUBS. [British colloquial, 1900s]

wigga-wagga the penis. Named for a flexible walking cane (Partridge). [British slang, early 1900s]

wild hair the imaginary cause of impassioned or violent behavior. A truncation of "have a wild hair up one's asshole." [U.S. slang, mid 1900s-pres.]

wild mare's milk rot-gut liquor. [U.S. slang, 1900s, Berrey and Van den Bark]

wild oats 1. excitement and energy in youth. Usually considered to be sexual in the male. **2.** a youth; a male who sows wild oats. [both since the 1500s]

wild quirt diarrhea. *Cf.* SQUIRTS. [colloquial, 1600s]

will-jill 1. a sterile or impotent person. **2.** some type of HERMAPHRODITE (*q.v.*). [British dialect, 1800s and before]

willy the stereopype of a domestic Negro servant or slave; a HOUSE NIGGER (*q.v.*). [U.S., 1800s-1900s]

wilted intoxicated with alcohol. For synonyms see WOOFLED. [U.S., 1900s, Wentworth and Flexner]

wimble the penis. From a term for an auger. *Cf.* TOOL (sense 1). [British slang, 1800s]

wimp (also **whimp**) a spineless, whimpering, undesirable person. [U.S. slang, mid 1900s-pres.]

Winchester-goose (also **Winchester-pigeon**) a venereal BUBO (*q.v.*). [slang, late 1500s]

wind, in the intoxicated with alcohol. *Cf.* BOTH SHEETS IN THE WIND. [British slang, 1800s

windbag a chatterer and a boaster. [U.S. slang, 1900s and before]

wind-cheater one who breaks wind frequently. [British slang, 1900s]

winder a breaking of wind. For synonyms see GURK. [U.S. slang, 1900s]

wind-mill the anus. Refers to the breaking of wind. *Cf.* WATER-MILL. [British slang, early 1800s. *Lexicon Balatronicum*]

window pane the drug L.S.D. (*q.v.*). [U.S. drug culture, mid 1900s-pres.]

window-tapper (also **window-girl**) an inmate of a WINDOW TAPPERY (*q.v.*), a prostitute.

window tappery a brothel. Applies to the customer's tapping on a window as a signal to gain entrance or to a prostitute's tapping to attract customers. [U.S. underworld, 1900s]

wind up the clock to coit a woman.

Cf. CLOCK. [British slang, 1800s or before]

wind up with one's joint in one's hand to be put in jail with no sexual outlet but masturbation. *Cf.* JOINT (sense 1), [U.S. underworld, early 1900s, Goldin, O'Leary, and Lipsius]

windward passage the anus with reference to the breaking of wind. "To navigate the windward passage" is to commit PEDERASTY (*q.v.*). [British slang, late 1700s, Grose]

windy-puffs flatulence. For synonyms see GURK. [British colloquial, 1900s or before]

wineache a hangover from wine; severe intestinal pain resulting from overindulging in wine, especially cheap wine. [U.S., 1900s]

wine-bag a drunkard. For synonyms see ALCHY. [British slang, 1800s, Farmer and Henley]

winey intoxicated with alcohol. [British and U.S. slang, 1800s-1900s]

wing-ding (also **whing-ding**) **1.** a gadget. **2.** a drinking spree. **3.** an affair or sexual encounter. [all senses, U.S., 1900s]

wing-heavy intoxicated with alcohol to the degree that one is unable to move or navigate. [U.S. slang, 1900s, Wentworth and Flexner]

wings cocaine. *Cf.* ROCKET-FUEL, SKY-ROCKET. [U.S. underworld, early 1900s]

winkle a child's penis. [British juvenile, 1800s, *Dictionary of Slang and Unconventional English*]

wino someone who is a drunkard on wine. [U.S., 1900s]

winter coals syphilis. *Cf.* COALS. [British slang, 1800s, Farmer and Henley]

wipe to cleanse oneself after excreting. Usually "wipe oneself." [colloquial 1900s or before]

wiped-out (also **wiped**) drug or alcohol intoxicated. *Cf.* ELIMINATED. [U.S. slang and drug culture, 1900s]

wiped-over intoxicated with alcohol. For synonyms see WOOFLED. See WIPED-OUT.

wipe off to kill. See WIPE OUT.

wipe out (also **wipe off**) **1.** to kill a person. Also **rub out.** [U.S. underworld, early 1900s] **2.** to cleanse oneself after excreting. [U.S. slang, 1900s]

wire the penis. In expressions such as PULL ONE'S WIRE and WHIP ONE'S WIRE (both q.v.). [British and U.S. slang, 1900s or before]

wired-up (also **wired**) drug or alcohol intoxicated. [U.S. slang and drug culture, mid 1900s-pres.]

wiseacre a smart aleck or an oaf. [colloquial and slang since the late 1800s]

wise guy a stupid oaf or smart aleck. [U.S. slang and stereotypical underworld, 1900s]

wishy-washy pertaining to insipid or weak persons, actions, or ideas. [British and U.S. slang, mid 1700s-pres.]

witch hazel heroin. From the medicine name. [U.S. drug culture, 1900s]

witch-piss inferior liquor; weak beer. Cf. SQUAW PISS. [British slang, early 1900s]

withdrawal in copulation, the removal of the penis before ejaculation as a means of birth control.

without a paddle being in a very bad situation. A euphemism for "up shit creek without a paddle." Cf. SHIT CREEK [U.S. slang, 1900s]

with squirrel pregnant. For synonyms see FRAGRANT. [U.S. dialect (Ozarks), Randolph and Wilson]

with young pregnant, usually said of animals, jocularly said of humans. [U.S., 1900s]

wizzer (also **wizzy**) an act of urination. Probably developed independently from WHIZ (q.v.). [Scots juvenile (Partridge); British, 1800s]

wobbly intoxicated with alcohol. For synonyms see WOOFLED. [U.S. slang, 1900s]

wog gut diarrhea. For synonyms see QUICKSTEP. [Australian military, early 1900s, *Dictionary of Slang and Unconventional English*]

WOGS a derogatory term for "natives" of various countries, e.g. Indians, Arabs, Australian aborigines. Said to be based on "Wonderful Oriental Gentleman," "Westernized Oriental Gentleman," or "Wiley Oriental Gentleman." These are all reinterpretations of the acronym printed on WOGS' work uniforms, which stands for "Working on Government Services." There is also a tradition that "wog" is from "golliwog" or "polliwog." See GOLLY. [attested in some form in both World Wars and the Vietnamese War]

wolf 1. a chaser or seducer of women; a flirt. [U.S. slang, early 1900s-pres.] **2.** an aggressive or masculine lesbian. From sense 1. [U.S. mid 1900s] **3.** an active PEDERAST (q.v.); an INSERTOR (q.v.). The combative opposite of LAMB (sense 1), a CATAMITE (q.v.). From sense 1. [U.S., early 1900s]

wolfess jocular for a "seductress," a female flirt. [U.S. slang, mid 1900s]

woman 1. a rude term for a woman. **2.** a prostitute or concubine. [both since the 1600s] **3.** an effeminate male. For synonyms see FRIBBLE. [U.S. slang, mid 1900s]

woman, old. the female genitals. Cf. LADY, OLD. [British, 1800s, Farmer and Henley]

woman-chaser a male flirt or seducer of women. Cf. TOWN BULL, WOLF (sense 1). [U.S. slang, 1900s]

woman-flesh women considered sexually. Based on "horse-flesh." [colloquial since the 1600s or before]

womanhood the female genitals. Based on MANHOOD (sense 2), the male genitals. [U.S., mid 1900s]

womanize to chase women for sexual purposes; to coit women. [1800s-pres.]

womanizer a lecher; a woman-chaser; a whoremonger. [since the late 1800s or before]

woman of accommodating morals (also **woman of pleasure**) a sexually loose woman; a prostitute. [British, 1800s]

woman of a certain class (also

woman about town, woman of the town) a prostitute. [British euphemism, 1900s-pres.]

woman of easy virtue (also **lady of easy virtue**) a sexually loose woman; a prostitute. [widespread euphemism, 1800s-pres.]

woman of loose morals a sexually loose woman; a harlot. [U.S., 1900s]

woman's home companion the menses. From the name of a women's magazine. For synonyms see FLOODS. [U.S., 1900s]

womb 1. the belly. [c. 800s, Oxford English Dictionary] **2.** the belly and the bowels. [c. 1000, Oxford English Dictionary] **3.** the uterus.

womble-ty-crop (also **womble-cropped, womblety-crop**) intoxicated with alcohol and very sick; hungover. From an old term meaning "uncertain" or "uncomfortable," Cf. WAMBLE-CROPPED. [British slang, 1700s, New Canting Dictionary]

wong the penis. One of a number of spelling variants of WHANG (sense 1). For synonyms see YARD. [U.S. slang, mid 1900s-pres.]

wonk (also **wank**) **1.** a simpleton; an oaf. [slang, 1900s] **2.** a homosexual male. [Australian, mid 1900s-pres., Wilkes]

woo to flirt, court, neck, or persuade to copulate. [since c. 1100]

wood the penis, especially the erect penis. See WOODMAN. For synonyms see ERECTION. [colloquial since the 1700s]

woodcock a gullible fool; an oaf. From the ease with which a woodcock can be captured. [since the 1400s]

wooden-coat a coffin. [U.S. slang, mid 1800s]

wooden habeas a coffin made for a prisoner. [cant and slang, late 1700s]

woodenhead a blockhead; an oaf. For synonyms see OAF. [U.S. slang, 1900s or before]

wooden-kimona (also **wooden-kimono**) a coffin. [U.S. underworld, early 1900s]

wooden-overcoat a coffin. [underworld, mid 1800s-pres.]

wooden-shoe a Jewish man or woman. Rhyming slang for "Jew." Not necessarily derogatory. [British, 1900s or before, Dictionary of Rhyming Slang]

wooden spoon a dunce or an oaf. Cf. SPOON (sense 1), SPOONY (sense 1). [British and U.S. slang, 1800s]

wooden-suit a coffin. Cf. WOODEN-COAT, WOODEN-OVERCOAT. [U.S. dialect and slang, 1900s and before]

woodman a WENCHER (q.v.); a whoremonger. Cf. WOOD [British, 1800s, Farmer and Henley]

woodpecker of Mars the AMANITA MUSCARIA (q.v.), a hallucinogenic mushroom. [U.S. drug culture, mid 1900s-pres.]

woods-colt 1. a colt sired by an unknown stallion. No negative connotations. **2.** a bastard. Partly euphemistic. Cf. CATCH-COLT. [both senses, U.S. colloquial, late 1800s-1900s]

woofits a hangover, especially if notably unpleasant. [U.S. slang, 1900s]

woofled intoxicated with alcohol. [U.S. slang, 1900s] Synonyms: A BIT ON, ABOUT GONE, ABOUT RIGHT, ADDLED, ADRIP, AFFLICTED, AFLOAT, ALCOHOLIZED, ALECIE, ALKIED-UP, ALL AT SEA, ALL GONE, ALTOGETHERY, ANCHORED IN SOT'S BAY, APED, APPLE PALSY, ARF AN ARF, ARFARFANARF, AT ONE'S EASE, AT REST, AWASH, AWRY-EYED, BACCHI PLENUS, BAGGED, BALL-DOZED, BALMY, BAMBOOZLED, BAPTIZED, BARRELED, BARRELED-UP, BARREL-HOUSE DRUNK, BASTED, BATTED, BATTERED, BEARGERED, BEEN AT AN INDIAN FEAST, BEEN IN THE SUN, BEEN TO FRANCE, BEERIFIED, BEERY, BEHIND THE CORK, BELTED, BEMUSED, BENT, BENT OUT OF SHAPE, BEWITCHED, BIBACIOUS, BIBULOUS, BIFFY, BINGED, BLANKED, BLASTED, BLEARY-EYED, BLEWED, BLIMPED, BLIND, BLIND DRUNK, BLINDED, BLINDERS, BLINDO, BLIND STAGGERS, BLITHERED, BLITZED, BLOATED, BLOTTO, BLOWED-AWAY, BLOWN-AWAY, BLOWN-UP, BLUE, BLUED, BLUE-EYED, BOILED, BOILED AS AN OWL, BOILING DRUNK,

BOMBED, BONED, BONGO, BONGOED, BONKERS, BOOSY, BOOZEBLIND, BOOZED, BOOZED AS THE GAGE, BOOZED-UP, BOOZY, BOSHY, BOSKO ABSOLUTO, BOSKY, BOTH SHEETS IN THE WIND, BOTTLE-ACHE, BOTTLED, BOWZERED, BOXED, BOXED-UP, BRANDY-FACED, BREATH STRONG ENOUGH TO CARRY COAL WITH, BREEZY, BRIDGEY, BRIGHT IN THE EYE, BRUISED, BUBBY, BUDGY, BUFFY, BULL-DOZED, BUMPSY, BUNG, BUNGED, BUNGEY, BUNG-EYED, BUNGFU, BUNNED, BURIED, BURN WITH A LOW BLUE FLAME, BURST, BUZZ, BUZZED, BUZZEY, CAGED, CANDY, CANNED, CANNED-UP, CANON, CAN'T SEE A HOLE IN A LADDER, CAPERNOITED, CAP-SICK, CARRYING A HEAVY LOAD, CARRYING TWO RED LIGHTS, CAST, CATSOOD, CHERRY-MERRY, CHERUBIMICAL, CHICKORY, CHUCKED, CLEAR, CLOBBERED, COCKED, COCKEYED, COGNACKED, COGUEY, COMBOOZELATED, COMFORTABLE, CONCERNED, CONFLUMMOXED, COOKED, CORKED, CORKED-UP, CORKY, CORNED, CORNERED, CRACKED, CRAMPED, CRAZY, CREAMED, CROCKED, CRONK, CROSS-EYED, CRUMPED-OUT, CRUMP-FOOTED, CRYING DRUNK, DAGGED, DAMAGED, D. AND D., DEAD DRUNK, DEADS, DEAD TO THE WORLD, DECAYED, DECKS AWASH, DELEERIT, DINGED-OUT, DINKY, DIRTY-DRUNK, DISCOURAGED, DISCUMFUDDLED, DISGUISED, DISORDERLY, DITHERED, DIZZY AS A COOT, DIZZY AS A GOOSE, DONEOVER, DRAPED, DRENCHED, DRUNK, DRINKING, DRIPPING-TIGHT, DRUNK, DRUNK AS A BASTARD, DRUNK AS A BESOM, DRUNK AS A BOILED OWL, DRUNK AS A BREWER'S FART, DRUNK AS A BROOM, DRUNK AS A COOT, DRUNK AS A CUNT, DRUNK AS A FIDDLER, DRUNK AS A FLY, DRUNK AS A FOWL, DRUNK AS A LORD, DRUNK AS A MOUSE, DRUNK AS AN EARL, DRUNK AS AN OWL, DRUNK AS A PIPER, DRUNK AS A PISS-ANT, DRUNK AS A RAT, DRUNK AS A ROLLING FART, DRUNK AS A SKUNK, DRUNK AS A SOW, DRUNK AS A TAPSTER, DRUNK AS A TICK, DRUNK AS A TOP, DRUNK AS A WHEELBARROW, DRUNK AS A BACCHUS, DRUNK AS BUGGERY, DRUNK AS CHLOE, DRUNK AS DAVID'S SOW, DRUNK AS FLOEY, DRUNKY, DRUNOK, DULL IN THE EYE, EBRIOUS, EDGED, EGG, ELECTRIFIED, ELEPHANT'S

TRUNK, ELEVATED, ELIMINATED, EMBALMED, FACED, FALLING-DOWN DRUNK, FARAHEAD, FEARS NO MAN, FEATURED, FEELING GOOD, FEELING NO PAIN, FETTERED, FIDDLED, FIGHTING TIGHT, FIRED-UP, FISHY, FISHY ABOUT THE GILLS, FLAKERS, FLATCH KENNURD, FLAWED, FLOATING, FLOOEY, FLOORED, FLORID, FLUSH, FLUSHED, FLUSTERATED, FLUSTERED, FLUSTRATED, FLY-BLOWN, FLY-BY-NIGHT, FLY THE ENSIGN, FOGGED, FOGGY, FOGMATIC, FOLDED, FOOZLIFIED, FOU, FOUR SHEETS TO THE WIND, FOX-DRUNK, FOXED, FOXY, FRACTURED, FRAZZLED, FRESH, FRESHISH, FRIED, FRIED TO THE GILLS, FROZE HIS MOUTH, FROZEN, FUDDLED, FULL, FULL AS A BOOT, FULL AS A BULL, FULL AS A FIDDLE, FULL AS A GOAT, FULL AS A GOOG, FULL AS A LORD, FULL AS AN EGG, FULL AS A TICK, FULL TO THE BUNG, FULL TO THE GUARDS, FUNNY, FUZZLED, FUZZY, GAGED, GASSED, GAY, GEED-UP, GEEZED, GEEZED-UP, GENEROUS, GILDED, GINGERED-UP, GINNED, GINNED-UP, GLAD, GLASSY-EYED, GLAZED, GLAZED DRUNK, GLOBULAR, GLORIOUS, GLUED, GOATDRUNK, GONE, GOREY-EYED, GOT A BRASS EYE, GOT THE GLANDERS, GOT THE GOUT, GRAPE-SHOT, GRAVELLED, GREASED, GROATABLE, GROGGED, GROGGY, GUYED-OUT, GUZZLED, HAD ENOUGH, HALF AND HALF, HALF-BLIND, HALF-BULLED, HALF-CANNED, HALF-COCKED, HALF-CUT, HALF-GONE, HALF IN THE BAG, HALF-LIT, HALF-ON, HALF-PISSED, HALF-RATS, HALF-RINSED, HALF-SCREWED, HALF-SHAVED, HALF-SHOT, HAMMERED, HAMMERISH, HANCED, HAPPY, HARD-UP, HARDY, HARRY FLAKERS, HAVE A BUN ON, HAVE A DROP IN THE EYE, HAVE A GLOW ON, HAVE A JAG ON, HAVE A LOAD ON, HAVE A PACKAGE ON, HAVE A SKATE ON, HAVE A SLANT ON, HAVE A TURKEY ON ONE'S BACK, HAZY, HELPLESS, HET-UP, HICCIUS-DOCCIUS, HICKSIUS-DOXIUS, HIGH, HIGH AS A KITE, HIGHER THAN A KITE, HIPPED, HOARY-EYED, HOCKEY, HOCUS, HOCUS POCUS, HONKED, HOOCHED, HOOCHED-UP, HOODMAN, HOOTED, HOPPED, HORIZONTAL, HORSEBACK, HOT, HOT AS A RED WAGON, HOW-CAME-YOU-SO?, ILLUMINATED, IMPIXLOCATED, IN ARMOUR, IN A TRANCE, IN-COG, IN COLOR, IN DRINK,

INEBRIOUS, IN GOOD FETTLE, INKED, INKY, INKYPOO, IN LIQUOR, IN ONE'S AIRS, IN ONE'S ALTITUDES, IN ONE'S CUPS, INSO-BRIETY, INSPIRED, INTER POCULA, IN THE GUN, IN THE OZONE, IN THE PINK, IN THE SUDS, IN THE SUN, IN THE WIND, IN TIPIUM GROVE, INTOXED, INTOXICATED, INUN-DATED, IRRIGATED, ISHKIMMISK, JAGGED, JAMBLED, JAZZED, JAZZED-UP, JIGGERED, JINGLED, JOLLY, JUG-BITTEN, JUGGED, JUGGED-UP, JUG-STEAMED, JUICED, JUICED-UP, JUICY, JUNGLED, KEYED, KEYED TO THE ROOF, KEYED-UP, KISKY, KNAPT, KNOCKED-OUT, KNOCKED-UP, LAID-OUT, LAID TO THE BONE, LAPPY, LATHERED, LEAPING, LEARY, LEERY, LIGHT, LIKKERED-UP, LIMBER, LIMP, LINED, LION-DRUNK, LIQUEFIED, LIQUORED-UP, LIQUORISH, LIQUOR PLUG, LIQUOR-STRUCK, LIT, LIT TO THE GILLS, LIT-UP, LOADED, LOADED FOR BEAR, LOADED TO THE GILLS, LOADED TO THE GUNWALES, LOADED TO THE PLIM-SOLL MARK, LOGGED, LOOK LIVELY, LOOPED, LOOP-LEGGED, LOOSE IN THE HILT, LUBRICATED, LUMPY, LUSH, LUSHED, LUSHED-UP, LUSHY, MAGGOTY, MALTED, MARTIN-DRUNK, MASTOK, MAUDLIN DRUNK, MAULED, MAWBRISH, MELLOW, MELTED, MERRY. METHODISTICONATED, MICKEY FINISHED, MILLED, MIRACULOUS, MIZZLED, MOIST AROUND THE EDGES, MOONEY, MOON-EYED, MOONY, MOPPY, MOPS AND BROOMS, MORTAL MORTALLIOUS, MUCKI-BUS, MUDDLED, MUDDLED-UP, MUGG BLOTTS, MUGGED, MUGGED-UP, MUGGY, MULLED, MULLED-UP, MUZZY, NAPPY, NASE, NAZY, NEGRO DRUNK, NIMPTOP-SICAL, NODDY-HEADED, NOGGY, NOLO, N.Y.D., OBFUSCATED, OBFUSTICATED, OFF ONE'S NUT, OFF THE NAIL, OIL, OILED, ON, ON A JAG, ONE-OVER-EIGHT, ONE'S FLAG IS OUT, ON ONE'S ASS, ON ONE'S EAR, ON ONE'S FOURTH, ON SENTRY, ON THE FRITZ, ON THE GROG, ON THE RANTAN ON THE SAUCE, ON THE SKYTE, ORGAN-IZED, ORIE-EYED, OSSIFIED, OUT, OUT ON THE ROOF, OUT TO IT, OVERBOARD, OVER-COME, OVERSEAS, OVERSEEN, OVERSET, OVERSHOT, OVERSPARRED, OVER-TAKEN, OVER THE BAY, OVER THE MARK, OWLED, OWLY-EYED, OXYCROCIUM, PACKAGED, PAID, PALATIC, PALLED, PARALYTIC, PAR-ALYZED, PARBOILED, PASTED, PECKISH,

PEE-EYED, PEPST, PERKED, PERTISH, PET-RIFIED, PICKLED, PIE-EYED, PIFFED, PIF-FICATED, PIFFLED, PIFFLICATED, PIGEON-EYED, PILFERED, PINKED, PINKO, PIPPED, PIPPED-UP, PISSED, PISSED IN THE BROOK, PISSED-UP, PISSED UP TO THE EYEBROWS, PISSING-DRUNK, PISSY-ARSED, PIXILATED, PIZZICATO, PLASTERED, PLEASANTLY PLASTERED, PLONKED, PLOOTERED, PLOUGHED, PLOWED, PODDY, POGGLED, POGY, POLISHED, POLISHED-UP, POLLED-OFF, POLLUTED, POOPIED, POT, POT-SHOT, POT-SICK, POTTED, POTULENT, POWDERED, POWDERED-UP, PRESERVED, PRIMED, PRUNED, PUGGLED, PUGGY-DRUNK, PUNGEY, PUSHED, PUT TO BED WITH A SHOVEL, PYE-EYED, QUEER, QUEERED, QUISBY, RACKED, RACKED-UP, RADDLED, RAGGED, RAMMAGED, RAMPING MAD, RATTLED, RAUNCHY, REEKING, REELING, REELING RIPE, REELY, RELIGIOUS, RIGID, RILEYED, RIPE, RIPPED, ROARING-DRUNK, ROCKY, ROLLING-DRUNK, ROOSTERED, RORTY, ROSINED, ROSY, ROSY ABOUT THE GILLS, ROTTEN, ROYAL RUMMED, RUMMED-UP, SALT, SALTED, SALTED-DOWN, SALT JUNK, SALUBRIOUS, SAP HAPPY, SATUR-ATED, SAUCED, SAWED, SCAMMERED, SCHICKER, SCOOPED, SCORCHED, SCOTCH MIST, SCRAMBLED, SCRANCHED, SCRATCHED, SCREECHING, SCREWED, SCREWY, SCRONCHED, SCROOCHED, SCRO-OCHED-UP, SEE DOUBLE, SEEING SNAKES, SEE PINK ELEPHANTS, SEE TWO MOONS, SEMI-BOUSY, SENT, SERVED-UP, SEWED-UP, SHAVED, SHELLACKED, SHERBETTY, SHICER, SHICK, SHICKED, SHICKERED, SHIKKER, SHINED, SHINY, SHIPWRECKED, SHIT-FACED, SHOT, SHOT-AWAY, SHOT FULL OF HOLES, SHOT IN THE NECK, SHOT-UP, SKIMISHED, SLATHERED, SLEWED, SLEWY, SLIGHTLY-TIGHTLY, SLOPPED, SLOPPED-OVER, SLOPPED TO THE EARS, SLOPPY, SLOPPY-DRUNK, SLOSHED, SLOSHED TO THE EARS, SLOUGHED, SLUGGED, SLURKS, SLUSHED, SLUSHED-UP, SMASHED, SMEARED, SMEEKIT, SMOKED, SNAPPED, SNOCKERED, SNOOTED, SNOT-TED, SNOZZLED, SNUBBED, SNUFFY, SNUG, SO, SOAKED, SOAPY-EYED, SOGGY, SOSH-ED, SOTTISH, SOUPY, SOUSED, SOUSED TO THE GILLS, SOW-DRUNK, SOZZLED, SOZZLY, SPEECHLESS, SPIFFED, SPIFFLICATED,

SPIFFLO, SPOONY DRUNK, SPRUNG, SQUIF-
FY, STAGGERISH, STALE DRUNK, STAND-
ING TOO LONG IN THE SUN, STARCHY,
STATE OF ELEVATION, STEAMED-UP, STEEP-
ED, STEW, STEWED, STEWED TO THE GILLS,
STIFF, STIFFED, STIFFO, STINKING, STINKO,
STITCHED, STOLLED, STONE BLIND, STONED,
STONY BLIND, STOZZLED, STRIPED, STUB-
BED, STUCCOED, STUNG, STUNNED, STU-
PID, SUCKED, SUCKY, SUN IN THE EYES,
SUPERCHARGED, SWACKED, SWALLOWED
A HARE, SWAMPED, SWATCHED, SWAT-
TLED, SWAZZLED, SWEET, SWIGGED,
SWIGGLED, SWILLED, SWILLED-UP, SWINE-
DRUNK, SWINNY, SWIPED, SWIPY, SWIVEL-
LY, SWIZZLED, SWOZZLED, TACKY, TAKE
A SHARD, TANGLEFOOTED, TANKED,
TANKED-UP, TAP-SHACKLED, TAVERNED,
TEAD-UP, TEED, TEED-UP, TEMULENT, THAT
WAY, THAWED, THREE SHEETS IN THE
WIND, THREE SHEETS TO THE WIND,
TIDDLED, TIDDLY, TIFFLED, TIGHT, TIGHT
AS A BRASSIERE, TIGHT AS A DRUM, TIGHT
AS A FART, TIGHT AS A GOAT, TIGHT AS A
MINK, TIGHT AS A TEN-DAY DRUNK, TIGHT
AS A TICK, TIGHT AS THE BARK ON A
TREE, TIN HATS, TINNED, TIP-MERRY,
TIPPLY, TIPSIFIED, TIPSY, TIRED, TISHY,
TOASTED, TOL-LOL, TONGUE-TIED, TOO
MANY CLOTHS ON THE WIND, TOO NU-
MEROUS TO MENTION, TOP-HEAVY, TOP-
PED, TOPPY, TOPSY-BOOZY, TOPY, TORE-
UP, TORRID, TOSSED, TOSTIFICATED,
TOTALLED, TOXED, TOXY, TRAMMELED,
TRANSLATED, TUBED, TUMBLING-DRUNK,
TUNED, TUNED-UP, TWO SHEETS TO THE
WIND, UNDER, UNDER THE INFLUENCE,
UNDER THE TABLE, UNDER THE WEATH-
ER, UNK-DRAY, UNSOBER, UPHOLSTERED,
UPPISH, UP THE POLE, UP TO THE GILLS,
VARNISHED, VULCANIZED, WALL-EYED,
WAMBLE-CROPPED, WAPSED DOWN, WAST-
ED, WATER-LOGGED, WEAK-JOINTED,
WEARY, WELL-BOTTLED, WELL-FIXED,
WELL-OILED, WELL-SPRUNG, WELL-UNDER,
WET, WHAT-NOSED, WHAZOOD, WHIFFLED,
WHIPCAT, WHIPPED, WHIPSEY, WHISKY-
FIED, WHISKY-FRISKY, WHISTLE DRUNK,
WHITTLED, WHOOSHED, WILTED, WINEY,
WING-HEAVY, WIPED, WIPED-OUT, WIPED-
OVER, WIRED-UP, WOBBLY, WOMBLE-TY-
CROPT, WOOZY, WRECKED, YDRUNKEN,
ZAGGED, ZIG-ZAG, ZIG-ZAGGED, ZISSIFIED,
ZONED, ZONKED, ZONKED-OUT.

woolies 1. woolen underwear. [U.S.
colloquial, 1900s or before] **2.** the
DELIRIUM TREMENS (*q.v.*).]U.S. slang,
1900s]

wooly bear 1. a woman; a woman
considered sexually. **2.** a female police officer. [both senses, citizens band
radio slang, U.S., mid 1900s-pres.]

wooly-head (also **woolie-head**) a derogatory term for a Negro. [U.S. slang,
1800s and before]

wooly-wooly a woman; the same as
WOOLY BEAR (*q.v.*). *Cf.* FUR (sense 1).

woozy (also **woozey**) intoxicated with
alcohol. [U.S. slang, late 1800s-1900s]

wop 1. a derogatory term for an Italian.
One explanation of its origin is that it
is an acronym of "without a pass-
port," referring to immigration status.
Another explanation is that the term is
from Italian *guappo* (pronounced
"wappo"), "a large, handsome man."
[U.S. slang, late 1800s-pres.] **2.** a
prostitute. [Australian, Baker]

wop special macaroni or spaghetti
dishes. Not always derogatory. The
term "wop salad" is widely known
and is inoffensive to some people.
From WOP (sense 1). [U.S. slang, 1900s]

word!, My 1. a mild oath and an
exclamation. Also **Upon my word! 2.**
dung. Rhyming slang for "turd." [Brit-
ish, 1900s, *Dictionary of Rhyming
Slang*]

work 1. to coit a woman. *Cf.* DO A
WOMAN'S JOB FOR HER. **2.** copulation.
[senses 1 and 2 are both U.S. slang,
1900s] **3.** a euphemism for any sexual
activity. [colloquial, 1900s or before]
4. to solicit and perform sexual acts,
as in "work an area" in prostitution.
[U.S. underworld, mid 1900s or before]

working girl (also **working broad,
working woman**) a euphemism for
"prostitute." *Cf.* BUSINESS GIRL. [U.S.
slang, mid 1900s or before]

work off to masturbate. For synonyms
see WASTE TIME. [British colloquial or
slang, 1800s or before]

work out to coit. Borrowed from an athletic "workout." [U.S. slang, mid 1900s]

works 1. either the male or female genitals. In the sense of WATERWORKS (*q.v.*). **2.** copulation, "the works." From the male point of view. Referring to "giving" the female his WORKS (sense 1). **3.** the "third degree," a prolonged and supposedly violent period of questioning by the police. [all senses, slang, 1900s]

workshop the female genitals. See WORK (sense 1). [British slang, late 1800s, Farmer and Henley]

work the dumb oracle (also **work the hairy oracle**) to coit a woman. *Cf.* MOUTH-THANKLESS, MOUTH-THAT-CAN-NOT-BITE. [British slang, 1800s, Farmer and Henley]

worm 1. a low creep or jerk. From the lowness and sliminess of a worm. [U.S. slang, 1900s or before] **2.** the penis. [widespread nonce, 1800s-1900s]

worms spaghetti. For similar terms see DOG'S VOMIT. [colloquial since the early 1900s or before]

worms in blood spaghetti in tomato sauce. [U.S. jocular dysphemism, 1900s]

wound the female genitals. *Cf.* CUT, GASH, SLIT. [from *Cymbeline* (Shakespeare)]

wrecked alcohol or dug intoxicated. [U.S. slang and drug culture, mid 1900s-pres.]

wren. 1. a prostitute. For synonyms see QUAIL. [British slang, 1800s] **2.** a young woman or girl. [U.S. slang, 1900s]

wriggle to masturbate. [British slang, 1800s or before]

wriggle navels to copulate. [British slang, 1800s, Farmer and Henley]

wring one's sock out to urinate. There is an implication that one has waited too long to urinate. *Cf.* SHAKE A SOCK. For synonyms see WHIZ. [British slang, 1900s, *Dictionary of Slang and Unconventional English*]

wring the dew off the branch to urinate. A confusion of WRING ONE'S SOCK OUT (*q.v.*) and SHAKE THE DEW OFF THE LILY (*q.v.*). [U.S. slang, 1900s]

wring the rattlesnake to urinate. *Cf.* BLACKSNAKE, ROCK PYTHON. [Australian, 1900s or before]

wrinkle-room a bar patronized by aging homosexual males. [U.S. homosexual use, mid 1900s-pres.]

X

X. 1. a toilet or privy. For synonyms see AJAX. [U.S., 1900s] **2.** the Christus; Jesus Christ. Also **XP.**, **Xt.**

X.L. "ex-lady" friend; former lady friend. *Cf.* X.Y.L. [U.S. slang, mid 1900s-pres.]

X-rated the extreme end of a rating scale of sexual content and violence in the motion picture industry. X-rated films usually contain explicit sex acts. *Cf.* ADULT, FRANK. [U.S., mid 1900s-pres.]

X.Y.L. "ex-young lady," former girlfriend or former wife.

X.Y.Z. "examine your zipper," a catch phrase reminding a male that he has forgotten to zip up his trousers. [U.S. slang, 1900s] Synonyms: COWS AND HORSES WILL GET OUT, ONE O'CLOCK, ONE O'CLOCK AT THE WATERWORKS, YOUR MEDALS ARE SHOWING, YOUR NOSE IS BLEEDING.

Y

yack (also **yock, yuck, yuk**) a stupid fellow; an oaf. For synonyms see OAF. [U.S. slang, 1900s]

yak a derogatory nickname for a Pole or a person of Polish descent. *Cf.* YACK. [U.S. slang, 1900s]

yang the penis. *Cf.* JANG, YING-YANG. [U.S., 1900s]

yank one's strap (also **fondle one's fig, manipulate one's mango, pound one's pomegranate, yank, yank one's yam**) to masturbate. *Cf.* STRAP (sense 2). For synonyms see WASTE TIME. [slang, mid 1900s-pres.]

yap 1. an easy victim; a dupe. [U.S., 1900s] **2.** a fool or oaf; a hillbilly or bumpkin. [U.S. slang and dialect, 1900s] **3.** a Japanese. [1900s] **4.** nonsense. *Cf.* YAWP. [U.S. colloquial, 1900s]

yard 1. the penis. The word-of-choice for the penis between 1400s-1800. [primarily British, but also used in U.S. regional dialect and for literary effect, 1300s-pres.] Synonyms: AARON'S ROD, ABRAHAM, AFFAIR, ALMOND, ALMOND ROCK, ANGLE, ARBOR VITAE, ARM, ARSE-OPENER, ARSE-WEDGE, ATHENAEUM, AULD HORNIE, BABY-MAKER, BALD-HEADED HERMIT, BALD-HEADED MOUSE, BALONEY, BANANA, BAT, BATTERING-PIECE, BAUBLE, BAYONET, BEAK, BEAN, BEAN-TOSSER, BEEF, BELL-ROPE, BELLY, BELLY-RUFFIAN, BEST LEG OF THREE, BICHO, BINGY, BIRD, BLACKSNAKE, BLADE, BLOWTORCH, BLUDGEON, BLUESKIN, BOB TAIL, BODKIN, BONE, BONFIRE, BOW, BOW-SPRIT, BRACMARD, BROOM-HANDLE, BROOMSTICK, BUM-TICKLER, BUSH-BEATER, BUSHWHACKER, BUSK, BUTTER-KNIFE, BUTTON-HOLE WORKER, CADULIX, CALLIBISTRIS, CANDLE, CANE, CARK, CARNAL STUMP, CARROT, CATSO, CHANTI-CLEER, CHICKEN, CHILD-GETTER, CHINGUS, CHINK-STOPPER, CHOPPER, CHUM, CLAVA, CLOTHES PROP, CLUB, COCK, CODPIECE, COPPERSTICK, CORAL BRANCH, COREY, CRACK-HAUNTER, CRACK-HUNTER, CRACKSMAN, CRANNY-HUNTER, CREAM-STICK, CRIMSON-CHITTERLING, CROOK, CUCKOO, CULTY-GUN, DAGGER, DANG, DARD, DART OF LOVE, DEAREST MEMBER, DIBBLE, DICK, DICKORY DOCK, DICKY, DIDDLE, DILDO, DINGBAT, DING-DONG, DINGER, DINGLE-DANGLE, DINGUS, DIP-STICK, DIRK, DOCTOR JOHNSON, DODAD, DODADDY, DOFUNNY, DOHICKY, DO-HINGER, DOJIGGER, DOJOHNNIE, DOLLY, DONG, DOODLE, DOOFLICKER, DORK, DOWN-LEG, DRAGON, DRIBBLING DART OF LOVE, DROPPING MEMBER, DRUMSTICK, DUCY, DUMMY, EEL, END, ENEMY, ENOB, EYE-OPENER, FAG, FAMILY ORGAN, FATHER-CONFESSOR, FIDDLE-BOW, FIRE-BRAND, FISH, FISHING ROD, FLAPPDOODLE, FLAPPER, FLIP-FLAP, FLOATER, FOOL-STICKER, FOREFINGER, FOREMAN, FORNI-CATING-ENGINE, FORNICATING-MEMBER, FORNICATING-TOOL, FORNICATOR, FRIGA-MAJIG, FUCKER, GADGET, GADSO, GAP-STOPPER, GARDEN-ENGINE, GARDENER, GAYING INSTRUMENT, GENERATION TOOL, GENTLE-TITTLER, GIGGLE-STICK, GIG-GLING-PIN, GIRLOMETER, GLADIUS, GOO-BER, GOOSER, GOOSE'S-NECK, GRAVY-GIVER, GRAVY-MAKER, GRINDING-TOOL, GRISTLE, GULLY-RAKER, GUN, GUT-STICK, HAIR-DIVIDER, HAIR-SPLITTER, HAMBONE, HAMMER, HAMPTON WICK, HANDSTAFF, HANGING JOHNNY, HERMIT, HOE-HANDLE, HOLY POKER, HORN, HONEY-POT CLEAVER, HOOTCHEE, HORN, HOSE, HOT-ROD, HUNK OF MEAT, HUSBANDMAN OF NATURE, IM-PUDENCE, INSTRUMENT, INTROMITTENT ORGAN, IRISH ROOT, IT, JACK, JACK-IN-THE-BOX, JACK ROBINSON, JACOB, JACQUE'S, JANG, JAQUES, JARGONELLE, JEMMISON, JEMSON, JERKING-IRON, JEZ-EBEL, JIG, JIGGER, JIGGLING-BONE, JING-JANG, JOCK, JOCKAM, JOCKUM, JOCKY, JOCUM, JOHN, JOHNNIE, JOHNSON, JOHN THOMAS, JOHN WILLIE, JOINT, JONES, JOY KNOB, JOY PRONG, JOY-STICK. J.T., JULIUS CAESAR, JUSTUM, KEY, KIDNEY-SCRAPER, KIDNEY-WIPER, KING-MEMBER, KNOB, KNOCK, KNOCKER, KORI, KORO, LABOURER OF NATURE, LADIES' DELIGHT, LADIES' LOLLIPOP, LADIES' TREASURE,

LAMP OF LIFE, LANCE, LANCE OF LOVE, LANGOLEE, LARYDOODLE, LIFE-PRESERVER, LITTLE BROTHER, LITTLE DAVY, LITTLE FINGER, LITTLE WILLIE, LIVE RABBIT, LIVER-TURNER, LIVE SAUSAGE, LIZARD, LOB, LOB-COCK, LOBSTER, LOLLYPOP, LONG JOHN, LONG TOM, LOVE-DART, LOVE'S PICKLOCK, LUCY, LULLABY, LUNG-DISTURBER, MACHINE, MAD MICK, MAGIC WAND, MALE GENITAL ORGAN, MALE MEMBER, MALE PUDENDUM, MAN-ROOT, MAN THOMAS, MARROWBONE, MARROW-BONE-AND-CLEAVER, MARROW-PUDDING, MASCULINE PART, MASTER JOHN THURSDAY, MASTER MEMBER, MASTER OF CEREMONIES, MATRIMONIAL PEACEMAKER, MEAT, MEMBER, MEMBER FOR THE COCKSHIRE, MEMBRUM, MEMBRUM VIRILE, MENTULA, MENTULE, MERRYMAKER, MICKEY, MIDDLE FINGER, MIDDLE LEG, MIDDLE STUMP, MILKMAN, MISTER TOM, MODIGGER, MOUSE, MOWDIEWART, MUSCLE OF LOVE, MUTTON-DAGGER, MY BODY'S CAPTAIN, MY MAN THOMAS, NAG, NATURAL MEMBER, NATURE'S SCYTHE, NEBUCHADNEZZAR, NEEDLE, NERVOUS-CANE, NIMROD, NINE-INCH KNOCKER, NIPPY, NOONEY, NOSE, NUDINNUDO, OLD BLIND BOB, OLD HORNINGTON, OLD HORNY, OLD MAN, OLD SLIMY, ONE-EYED MILKMAN, ONE-EYED WORM, ORGAN, PAT AND MICK, PAX-WAX, PEACEMAKER, PECKER, PECNOSTER, PEENIE, PEE-WEE, PEEZEL, PEGO, PEN, PENCIL, PENDULUM, PENIS, PENIS DEPENDENS, PERCE, PERCH, PERCY, PESTLE, PETER, PICCOLO, PICKLOCK, PIKE, PIKESTAFF, PILE-DRIVER, PILGRIM'S STAFF, PILLICOCK, PIMPLE, PIN, PINGA, PINTLE, PIONEER OF NATURE, PIPE, PISSER, PISTOL, PISTON, PISTON ROD, PIZELL, PIZZLE, PLACKET-RACKET, PLAYTHING, PLENIPO, PLOWSHARE, PLUG, PLUGTAIL, PLUM-TREE SHAKER, P-MAKER, POINT, POINTER, POKER, POLE, POLL-AXE, POLYPHEMUS, PONDSNIPE, PONY, POONTANGER, POPERINE PEAR, PORK, PORK-SWORD, POST, POTATO-FINGER, POTENT REGIMENT, POWER, PRIAPUS, PRICK, PRICKLE, PRIDE AND JOY, PRINCOCK, PRIVY MEMBER, PRONG, PUD, PUDDING, PULSE, PUMP, PUMP-HANDLE, PUP, PUTZ, QUARTERMASTER, QUICKENING-PEG, QUIMSTAKE, QUIM-WEDGE, RADISH, RAM, RAMMER, RAMROD, RANGER, RAW MEAT, REAMER, RECTOR OF THE FEMALES, RED-CAP, RED-HOT POKER, RHUBARB, ROD, ROGER, ROGERRY, ROLLING-PIN, ROLY-POLY, ROOSTER, ROOT, RUBIGO, RUDDER, RUFFIAN, RUMP-SPLITTER, RUPERT, SAINT PETER, SCEPTRE, SCHLANGE, SCHLONG, SCHMOCK, SCHMUCK, SCHVANCE, SCHVONTZ, SCHWEEN, SCREWDRIVER, SENSITIVE PLANT, SENSITIVE-TRUNCHEON, SEXING-PIECE, SHAFT OF CUPID, SHE, SHMUCK, SHORT-ARM, SHORT-ARM TAIL, SHOVE-DEVIL, SHOVE-STRAIGHT, SILENT FLUTE, SIR MARTIN WAGSTAFF, SKIN FLUTE, SKYSCRAPER, SLUG, SMALL-ARM, SMELL-SMOCK, SNAKE, SNAKE IN THE GRASS, SNAPPER, SOLICITOR-GENERAL, SPIGOT, SPIKE-FAGGOT, SPINDLE, SPIT, SPLIT-ARSE MECHANIC, SPLIT-MUTTON, SPLIT-RUMP, SPONGE, SPOUT, STAFF, STAFF OF LIFE, STAFF OF LOVE, STAKE, STALLION, STAR-GAZER, STEMMER, STERN-POST, STICK, STING, STORMY DICK, STRAP, STRETCHER, STRUNT, STUFF, STUMP, SUCKER, SUGAR-STICK, SWEET-MEAT, SWIPE, SWIVER, SWORD, TACKET, TACKLE, TADGER, TAIL, TAIL-PIKE, TAIL-PIN, TAIL-PIPE, TAIL-TACKLE, TAIL-TREE, TALLY-WHACKER, TANTRUM, TARSE, TASSEL, TEAPOT, TENANT-IN-TAIL, TENT, TENT-PEG, TENTUM, THAT, THE BOY, THE OLD ADAM, THE OLD ROOT, THING, THINGAMA-BOB, THINGAMY, THINGUMMY, THIRD LEG, THISTLE, THOMAS, THORN, THORN-IN-THE-FLESH, THUMB OF LOVE, TICKLE-GIZZARD, TICKLER, TICKLE-TAIL, TIMOTHY, TOMMY, TONGUE, TOOL, TORCH OF CUPID, TOSH, TOUCH-TRAP, TOY, TRAP-STICK, TRIFLE, TRIGGER, TROUBLE-GIBLETS, TUBE, TUBE-STEAK, TUG-MUTTON, UNCLE DICK, UNIT, UNRULY MEMBER, VERGE, VESTRY-MAN, VIRGA, VIRILE MEMBER, VOMER, WAG, WAND, WANG, WATERSPOUT, WAZOO, WEAPON, WEDGE, WEENIE, WHACKER, WHANG, WHANG-BONE, WHANGER, WHAT, WHIP, WHISTLE, WHORE-PIPE, WICK, WIGGA-WAGGA, WILLIE, WIMBLE, WINKLE, WIRE, WONG, WORM, WRIGGLING-POLE, YANG, YARD MEASURE, YING-YANG, YOSH, YUM-YUM, ZUBRICK. **2.** to coit a woman. [1700s] **3.** to be unfaithful to one's lover. [U.S. slang, mid 1900s–pres.]

yard-child an illegitimate child; a bastard. Probably not from YARD (sense 1) above. [U.S. dialect, 1900s]

yard measure 1. the female genitals, specifically the vagina. From a name for a one-yard measuring stick (yardstick). A jocular reference to the penis and to the length implications of "yard." *Cf.* GIRLOMETER. [British slang, 1800s] **2.** the penis. [British, late 1800s-1900s]

yawp (also **yaup**) nonsense. *Cf.* YAP (sense 4). [U.S. colloquial, mid 1800s]

yazzihamper a term of contempt for a disliked person. [U.S., 1900s]

yeast-powder biscuit the female genitals, especially when swollen due to sexual stimulation. *Cf.* BISCUIT. [U.S. dialect (Boontling), late 1800s-early 1900s, Charles Adams]

Ye gods! an exclamation. From YE GODS AND LITTLE FISHES! (*q.v.*).

Ye gods and little fishes! (also **Ye gods!**) an exclamation or mock oath. [U.S. and British, 1800s-pres.]

Yehuda a Jewish man or woman. The plural is "Yehudim." For synonyms see FIVE AND TWO. [from Hebrew]

yeller 1. a mulatto. For synonyms see MAHOGANY. Derogatory. **2.** pertaining to mulattoes or light-skinned Negroes. Derogatory. [both senses, U.S., 1900s]

yeller-feller a light-skinned or racially mixed Australian aborigine. [Australian, 1800s or before, Baker]

yellow 1. a light-skinned Negro; a mulatto; the same as YELLER (*q.v.*). [U.S., early 1800s-1900s] **2.** the drug L.S.D. (*q.v.*). [U.S. drug culture, mid 1900s-pres.] **3.** a barbiturate, specifically Nembutal (trademark). Usually in the plural, "yellows." [U.S. drug culture, mid 1900s-pres.]

yellow angel a barbiturate, Nembutal (trademark). [U.S. drug culture, 1900s]

yellow-back a gob of phlegm. [Australian, 1900s, Baker]

yellowbelly 1. a coward. [U.S. colloquial, 1900s or before] **2.** a Chinese. [U.S., 1900s]

yellow-black a mulatto; a light-skinned Negro. Derogatory. [U.S., 1900s]

yellow boy a Chinese. For synonyms see JOHN CHINAMAN. [U.S., 1900s or before]

yellow bullets Nembutal (trademark) capsules; any barbiturate tablets or capsules. [U.S. drug culture, mid 1900s-pres.]

yellow-dog 1. a coward. [U.S. slang, 1900s] Synonyms: CANDY-ASS, CHICKEN, CHICKEN-HEART, COW-BABY, CRADDON, CRAVEN, DAFF, DASTARD, FUNKER, JELLY BELLY, LILY-LIVER, MILQUETOAST, MUDGER, PANSY, PANTYWAIST, PIKER, POLTROON, PUSSYCAT, QUAKEBUTTOCK, RABBIT, RECREANT, RING-TAIL, SHY-COCK, SISSY, SOOK, SOP, SQUIB, WEAK SISTER, WHEYFACE, YELLOWBELLY, YELLOW HEEL, YELLOW LIVER. **2.** a term of contempt. [both senses, U.S., 1800s-pres.]

yellow girl a female mulatto. [U.S. colloquial, mid 1800s-1900s]

yellow heel a coward. [U.S. slang, 1900s]

yellow-jacket a barbiturate tablet or capsule, usually Nembutal (trademark). From the common name of the insect. [U.S. drug culture, mid 1900s-pres.]

yellow peril 1. an Oriental of any nationality. Derogatory and sometimes jocular. **2.** the Mongoloid race in general. From the fear that they will overtake the earth due to their great numbers. [since the late 1800s]

yellow sunshine the drug L.S.D. (*q.v.*). *Cf.* ORANGE SUNSHINE, SUNSHINE. [U.S. drug culture, mid 1900s-pres.]

yen 1. sexual arousal or desire. [colloquial, 1900s] **2.** a craving for addictive drugs, especially opium or heroin. See PEN YEN. [U.S. drug culture, 1900s]

yen-chee (also **yen-shee**) **1.** the residue or "ash" left in an opium pipe. See YEN-SHE. **2.** heroin. Both are Chinese or mock-Chinese. [both senses, U.S. drug culture, 1900s]

yen-she opium ashes mixed with whisky; the same form as YEN-CHEE (*q.v.*). [Chinese or mock-Chinese; U.S. drug culture, 1900s]

yenta a gossip or a shrew, usually a woman. [Yiddish; U.S., 1900s]

yentz 1. to copulate or screw (*q.v.*). **2.** to cheat or deceive, *i.e.*, screw. [both senses, Yiddish, 1900s]

yentzer a man or woman who copulates frequently or obsessively. See YENTZ (sense 1).

yerba marijuana. [the Spanish cognate of HERB (*q.v.*); U.S. drug culture, mid 1900s-pres.]

yesca marijuana. [U.S. drug culture, 1900s]

yid a derogatory nickname for a Jewish man or woman. For synonyms see FIVE AND TWO. [U.S., late 1800s-1900s]

yiddle a Jewish man or woman. Derogatory, [British and U.S., 1900s]

yield one's favors for a female to agree to coition. [British euphemism, 1800s, Farmer and Henley]

ying-yang the penis. *Cf.* JING-JANG. [U.S. slang, 1900s]

yit a Jewish man or woman. From YID, YIDDLE (both *q.v.*). Derogatory. [British slang, 1800s]

yock a stupid oaf. *Cf.* YACK. [slang and colloquial, 1900s]

yodel to commit SODOMY (*q.v.*), possibly COITUS PER ANUM (*q.v.*). More likely FELLATIO (*q.v.*) with repeated movement of the tongue. *Cf.* CANYON-YODELING. [U.S. underworld, Berrey and Van den Bark]

yog backslang for GOY (*q.v.*), a non-Jew. Can be derogatory. [British, 1900s]

yokel 1. a bumpkin or an oaf. [British and U.S., 1800s-pres.] **2.** a Negro term of contempt for Caucasians. [U.S., mid 1900s]

yola a female mulatto. For synonyms see MAHOGANY.

yold (also **yuld**) a sucker or a dupe; someone easily fooled. [From Yiddish; U.S. underworld and slang, 1900s]

york 1. to vomit. **2.** vomitus. [both senses, U.S. slang and dialect, 1900s] Synonyms for both senses: ACCOUNTS, BARF, BECOME ILL, BLOW BEETS, BLOW LUNCH, BOFF, BRACK, BRAKE, BRING UP, CACK, CASCADE, CAST, CAST UP, CAT, CHUCK UP, CHUNDER, DEFOOD, DRAIN THE BILGE, DRIVE FRENCH HORSES, DUMP, EARP, FLASH, FLASH THE HASH, FLAY THE FOX, FLING UP, HAPPY RETURNS, HASH, HONK, JERK THE CAT, KECK, LOSE A MEAL, LOSE ONE'S COOKIES, MAKE A SALE, PARBREAK, PERK, PUKE, PUMP, PUMP SHIP, PURGE, PUT, PUT BIRDIE, QUOCKEN, RALPH, REECH, REGURGITATE, RETCH, SELL OUT, SHIT, SHOOT ONE'S COOKIES, SHOOT THE CAT, SHOOT THE WORKS, SICK, SICKS, SICK UP, SKIN A GOAT, SLING A CAT, SNAP ONE'S COOKIES, SPEW, THROW A MAP, THROW UP, THROW UP ONE'S ACCOUNTS, THROW UP ONE'S TOENAILS, TOSS ONE'S COOKIES, TOSS ONE'S LUNCH, UNSPIT, UNSWALLOW, UPCHUCK, URP, VARF, VOMICK, VOMIT, VOMITUS, WHIP THE CAT.

yosh the penis. For synonyms see YARD. [U S. slang, 1900s]

you and me urine; an act of urination; to urinate. Rhyming slang for "pee," *i.e.*, urine. [British, 1900s]

you know cocaine. Rhyming slang for SNOW (sense 2). [U.S. drug culture, 1900s]

you-know-what the female genitals. [colloquial since the mid 1600s]

young, in pregnant. Normally said of a sow and extended to humans. [euphemistic]

your brown!, Up a curse the equivalent of "Up your ass!" *Cf.* BROWN (sense 1). [U.S. slang, 1900s]

your medals are showing a disguised warning that one's fly is undone. The medals are fly buttons. See TURKISH MEDAL. For synonyms see X.Y.Z. [British slang, 1900s or before]

your nose is bleeding a disguised warning that one's fly is undone. [British slang, 1800s]

yours!, Up the same as UP IT! (*q.v.*). [U.S., 1900s]

yo-yo an oaf or jerk. For synonyms see OAF. [U.S. slang, 1900s]

yuckel a dull oaf; a slow-witted person. *Cf.* YACK, YOKEL (sense 1). [U.S. slang, 1900s or before]

yum-yum 1. the female genitals. **2.** the penis. [both senses, British slang, 1800s, Farmer and Henley]

Z

Z. one ounce of a narcotic or marijuana. From "oz.," the abbreviation of "ounce." *Cf.* LID, O.Z. [U.S. drug culture, 1900s]

Zacatecas purple marijuana from Zacatecas, Mexico. [U.S. drug culture, mid 1900s-pres.]

zagged intoxicated with alcohol. *Cf.* ZIG-ZAG. [U.S. slang, 1900s]

zap to kill, stun, or sterilize with an imaginary ray gun. [U.S., mid 1900-pres.]

zarf an ugly and undesirable male. [U.S. slang, mid 1900s]

zazzle 1. sexual desire. 2. exaggerated sexuality; sex appeal [both senses, U.S. slang, 1900s]

Zen the drug L.S.D. (*q.v.*). [U.S. drug culture, mid 1900s-pres.]

zent a pimple. See ZIT. For synonyms see BURBLE.

zero an insignificant person; a dull nobody. For synonyms see OAF. [U.S. slang, mid 1900s-pres.]

zhlub (also **schlub, shlub, zhlob**) an oaf or dolt. [from Yiddish; U.S., mid 1900s-pres.]

zib 1. a fool or sucker. 2. an oaf or nincompoop. [both senses, U.S. slang, 1900s]

zigaboo a derogatory term for a Negro; the same as JIGABOO (*q.v.*). [U.S. slang, 1900s]

zig-zag intoxicated with alcohol. From the staggering gait of the drinker. *Cf.* MAKE MS AND WS, ZAGGED. [British and U.S. slang, 1900s]

zig-zagged intoxicated with alcohol. [U.S., 1900s]

zig-zig 1. to copulate. 2. copulation. [both are widespread military slang; 1800s-1900s]

zings the DELIRIUM TREMENS (*q.v.*). [U.S. slang, early 1900s]

ZIP "zero intelligence potential," a derogatory term for Orientals. *Cf.*

WOGS. [U.S. military, mid 1900s-pres.]

zipper morals loose sexual morals, said of a man or a woman. [U.S. slang, mid 1900s-pres.]

zissified drunk. *Cf.* WHISKYFIED. [U.S. slang, 1900s, Berrey and Van den Bark]

zit a pimple. Usually in the plural. For synonyms see BURBLE. [U.S. slang, mid 1900s-pres.]

zob a worthless person; a nobody. See ZIB. [U.S. slang, 1900s]

zombie 1. a very stupid person; a dunce. 2. a weird and frightening person. 3. a dead body made to live by magic or some other force. The word and concepts are ultimately West African via West Indian voodoo. [all senses, U.S., 1900s]

zone a detached and giddy person; someone who is SPACED-OUT (*q.v.*). [U.S. slang, mid 1900s-pres.]

zoned drug or alcohol intoxicated. [U.S. drug culture and slang, mid 1900s-pres.]

zonk an oaf; a totally incompetent person. [U.S. slang, mid 1900s-pres.]

zonked-out (also **zonked**) 1. asleep or very sleepy. [U.S. slang, mid 1900s-pres.] 2. drug or alcohol intoxicated. [U.S. drug culture and slang, mid 1900s-pres.]

zonker a frequent user of drugs or a marijuana smoker. Based on ZONK (*q.v.*). *Cf.* ZONKED-OUT. [U.S. drug culture, mid 1900s-pres.]

zoo 1. a brothel with women of various types and nationalities. 2. a prison, especially if racially mixed. [both senses, U.S. underworld, 1900s]

Zoodikers! an oath and an exclamation, "By God's hookers!" "Hookers" are fingernails. For synonyms see 'ZOUNDS! [1600s]

zook (also **zucke**) a wretched and dilapidated prostitute. *Cf.* MADAMOIZOOK. [U.S. underworld, 1900s]

Zookers! an oath and an exclamation. "By His hookers!", "Hookers" are fingernails. [early 1600s]

zool an Italian, especially an Old World Italian. Derogatory. [U.S. underworld, 1900s]

zoom amphetamines, specifically Methedrine (trademark). [U.S. drug culture, mid 1900s-pres.]

'Zounds! an old oath and an exclamation now used primarily for effect, "By His wounds!" Perhaps the most widely-known of the ancient oaths. [late 1600s-pres.] Other oaths: ADAD!, ADOD!, ADZOOKS!, AGAD!, BEDAD!, BEGAD!, BEGORRA!, BEGOSH!, BEGUM!, BEJABERS!, BEJESUS!, BELEAKINS!, BLIMEY!, BLIND ME!, BLOOD-AN'-'OUNS!, BLOW ME DOWN!, BLUE-BOTTLES!, BLURT, BOB!, BODIKIN!, BODKINS!, BUDKIN!, BUDLIKINS!, BUMFAY!, BURBAGE!, BURN YOU!, BY CHRISAMIGHTY!, BY CHRIST'S FOOT!, BY COB'S BODY!, BY COCK-AND PIE!, BY CORPUS BONES!, BY CRACKY!, BY CRICKETY!, BY CRICKY!, BY DINGY!, BY GAD'S BUD!, BY GAR!, BY GARY!, BY GEE AND JAY!, BY GINGER!, BY GIS!, BY GODFREY!, BY GOD'S ARMS!, BY GOD'S BODIKEN!, BY GOD'S BODKIN!, BY GOD'S CORPUS!, BY GOD'S DIGGERS!, BY GOD'S DIGNITY!, BY GOD'S PITTIKINS!, BY GOD'S SANTY!, BY GOG!, BY GOG'S WOUNS!, BY GOLLY!, BY GORRAM!, BY GOSH!, BY GOSHDANG!, BY GRABS!, BY GRACIOUS!, BY GRANNY!, BY GRAVY!, BY GUINEA!, BY GUM!, BY GYS!, BY HOKEY!, BY JEHOSHAPHAT!, BY JERPS!, BY JINGO!, BY JINKS!, BY JOCKIES!, BY JOCKS!, BY JOE BEESWAX!, BY JOVE!, BY JUCKIES!, BY JUDAS!, BY JUPITER!, BY JYSSE!, BY KING!, BY MY CABBAGE-TREE!, BY MY FAY!, BY MY SAINTED AUNT!, BY NAILS AND BY BLOOD!, BY OUR LADY!, BY THE BLOOD OF CHRIST!, BY THE CROSS!, BY THE ELEVENS!, BY THE ETERNAL GOD!, BY THE FATHER OF LIGHT!, BY THE GREAT FATHER!, BY THE GREAT HORN SPOON!, BY THE GREAT JEHOVAH!, BY THE HOLY CROSS!, BY THE HOLY SACRAMENT!, BY THE LORD OF HEAVEN!, BY THE MASS!, BY THE MOUSE-FOOT!, BY THE SAINTS ABOVE!, BY THUNDER!, CARAMBA!, CAT'S NOUNS!, CATSO!, CHEESE AND CRUST!, CHRIST-ALL-BLEEDING-MIGHTY!, CHRIST-ALL-JESUS!, CHRIST-ALMIGHTY-WONDER!, CHRISTMAS!, CHRIST-ON-A-CRUTCH!, CODSFISH!, COKKES BODY!, COKKES BONES!, CONSARN!, CONSARN YE!, COO LUMMY!, CORKS!, CORKSCREW!, COR LUMMIE!, COT, COTZOOKS!, CREEPING JESUS!, CRIMENY SAKES ALIVE!, CRIM-INEY!, CRIMINITLY!, CRIPES!, CRIPUS!, DAMMIT TO HELL!, DAMN YOUR EYES!, DEAR GUSSIE!, DEAR ME!, DIG SWIGGER IT!, DING BUST IT!, DOB DARN!, DOG BITE ME!, DOG-BLINE-ME!, DOG'S WOUNDS!, DOG TAKE!, DONNER UND BLITZEN!, D'RABBIT!, DRAT!, DRAT IT!, ECOD!, EDÓD!, EGAD!, FEGS!, FISH!, FOR CHRISAKE!, FOR COCK'S BONES!, FOR CRIMP'S SAKE!, FOR CRYING OUT LOUD!, FOR GOSH SAKE!, FOR JESUS' FOOT!, FOR-SOOTH!, FOR THE LOVE OF MIKE!, FOR THE LOVE OF MUD!, GAD'S BUD!, GADSO!, GADSOBS!, GADZOOKS!, GARDENIA!, GARN IT!, GAWBLIMEY!, GAWDFER!, GEE-HOLLIKENS!, GEE-WHILLICATS!, GEE-WHILLIGINS!, GEE-WHILLIKERS!, GEE-WHISKERS!, GEE-WHITTAKERS!, GEE-WHIZ!, GEE-WHIZZARD!, GEE-WHOLLIKER!, GEEZ!, GODAMERCY!, GODAMIGHTY!, GOD BLESS AMERICA!, GOD BLIND ME, GOD BURN!, GOD DAMN ME!, GOD FORBID!, GODFREY DORMAN!, GODFREY MIGHTY!, GOD'S DEATH!, GOD'S HOOKS!, GODSO!, GOD SWORBET!, GOLBLAST!, GOM!, GONNOWS!, GOOD CHRISTMAS!, GOOD GOD!, GOOD GODFREY!, GOOD GODFREY DANIEL!, GOOD GRACIOUS!, GOOD GRIEF!, GOODNESS GRACIOUS!, GOODY GOODY GODDAMN!, GOODY GOODY GUMDROP!, GORAMITY!, GORBLIMEY!, GORDELPUS!, GOSH-ALL-LIGHT-NING!, GOSH ALMIGHTY!, GOSHAMIGHTY!, GOSHDAL!, GOSHWALADER!, GREAT CAESAR'S GHOST!, GREAT GUNS!, GREAT SCOTT!, GREAT SNAKES!, HANG IT!, HOLY CATS, HOLY CHRIST!, HOLY COW!, HOLY DOG CRAP!, HOLY DOG SHIT!, HOLY FUCK!, HOLY GEE!, HOLY GOD!, HOLY GUM-DROPS!, HOLY JERUSALEM!, HOLY JUMPING MOTHER OF JESUS!, HOLY JUMPING MOTHER OF MOSES!, HOLY KERIST!, HOLY

MACKEREL!, HOLY MITHER!, HOLY MOLY!, HOLY MOSES!, HOLY SMOKES!, HOLY SNOOKS!, HOLY SOCKS!, HOLY SUFFERING SNAKES!, HOLY SWISS CHEESE!, HOLY TOLEDO!, HONEST TO GOD!, HONEST-TO-GOODNESS!, HONEST-TO-GOTHAM!, HOT ALMIGHTY!, HOT-DAMN!, I DO VUM!, IGAD!, I'LL BE A DIRTY WORD!, I'LL BE A RING-TAILED POLECAT!, I'LL BE DING-BUSTED!, I'LL BE DUM SQUIZZLED!, I'LL BE FLABBERGASTED!, I'LL BE HANGED!, I'LL BE JIGGERED!, I'LL BE JIG-SWIGGERED!, I'LL BE JIM-SWIGGLED!, I'LL BE SWITCHED!, I SNOW!, I SNUM!, I SWAN!, I SWANNY!, I SWOW!, I VUM!, JEE!, JEES!, JEE-WHILLIKINS!, JEE-WHISKERS!, JEEZ!, JEEZE!, JEHOSHAPHAT!, JEMIMA!, JEMINY!, JERUSALEM!, JESUS!, JESUS H. CHRIST!, JEWHILLIKENS!, JIMINITLY!, JIMINY CRICKETS!, JUDAS PRIEST!, JUMPING JEHOSHAPHAT!, JUMPING JEW'S-HARPS!, JUMPING MOSES!, KE-RIST!, LAND OF GOSHEN!, LAND SAKES, LAWDY SAKES ALIVE!, LAWKS, LAW'S SAKES!, LAWSY!, LAWSY'S SAKES!, LIKE FUCK!, LIKE FUN!, LIKE HELL!, LIKE SIN!, LOD-A-MASSY!, LORD LOVE A DUCK, LORD SAKES ALIVE!, LORDY!, LORGAMIGHTY!, LORS!, MAY GOD BLIND ME!, MAY I GO TO HELL!, MERCY!, MIST ALCRITY!, MON DIEU!, MY ASS, MY BLOOD!, MY FOOT!, MY GAY!, MY GOD!, MY GOODNESS!, MY KING OATH!, MY OATH!, MYST ALL CRIKEY!, MYST ALL CRITEY!, MYST ALL KRITEY!, MY STARS ALIVE!, NICK TAKE ME!, NIGGERS!, NIGGERS-NOGGERS!, NOUNS, O CRIMES!, 'ODDS BOB!, 'ODDS BONES!, 'ODDS FISH!, 'ODDS WUCKS AND TAR!, 'OD ROT IT!, 'ODS BLOOD!, 'ODS-BODIKINS, 'ODS BODKINS!, 'ODSFLESH!, 'ODS FOOT!, 'ODS HARICOTS AND CUTLETS!, 'ODSKILDERKINS!, 'ODSOONS!, 'ODS WOOKERS!, ON MY TROTH!, PARDEE!, PERDITION!, SAKES ALIVE!, 'SBLID!, 'SBLOOD!, 'SBOBS, 'SBODKINS!, 'SBODY!, 'SBORES!, 'SBUD!, 'SDEATH!, 'SDEYNES!, 'SDIGGERS!, S'ELP ME GOD!, S'ELP ME GREENS!, S'FIRE!, 'SFLESH!, 'SFOOT!, S'GAD!, 'SHEART!, SHIDDLE-CUM-SHITE!, SHIT!, SHITTLE-CUM-SHAW!, SHITTLE-TIDEE!, SHIVER MY TIMBERS!, 'SLID!, 'SLIDIKINS!, 'SLIFE!, 'SLIGHT!, 'SLOOD!, 'SLUCK!, 'SLUD!, SMOLEY HOKE!, 'SNAILS!, 'SNEAKS!, 'SNIGGERS!, 'SNIGS!, 'SNOWNS!, SO 'ELP ME!, SO HELP ME GOD!, S'OONDS!, SPLIT MY WINDPIPE!, 'STREWTH!, STRIKE ME DEAD!, STRIKE ME DUMB!, STRIKE ME HANDSOME!, 'STRUTH!, SUFFERING CATS!, SUFFERING CHRIST!, SUFFERING SAINTS!, SUFFERING SASSAFRASS!, SUFFERING SEASERPENTS!, SUFFERING SEAWEED!, SUFFERING SNAKES!, 'SWILL!, SWOGGLE MY EYES!, 'SWORBOTE!, 'SWOUNDS!, THE HELL!, THE HELL YOU SAY!, THE MISCHIEF YOU SAY!, THE PODY CODY!, THUNDERATION!, UPON MY SOUL!, UPON MY WORD!, WOUNDS!, YE GODS!, YE GODS AND LITTLE FISHES!, 'ZBLOUD!, 'ZBUD!, 'ZDEATH!, Z-DZ!, ZOODIKERS!, ZOOKERS!, 'ZOOKS!, ZOWKS!

zubrick the penis. For synonyms see YARD. [Australian, 1900s, *Dictionary of Slang and Unconventional English*]

zulu (also **zoolo**) a Negro. From the name of an indigenous people of Southeast Africa. Derogatory. [U.S. slang, 1900s]

BIBLIOGRAPHY

Reference Works

The American College Dictionary. New York: Random House, 1957.

The American Heritage Dictionary of the English Language. Boston: Houghton Mifflin Company, 1976.

The Concise Oxford Dictionary. Sixth edition. Oxford, England: The Clarendon Press, 1976.

Dorland's Pocket Medical Dictionary. Philadelphia: W.B. Saunders Company, 1959.

Oxford English Dictionary. Oxford, England: Oxford University Press, 1933, and supplements.

Physicians' Desk Reference. Thirty-second edition. Oradell, New Jersey: Medical Economics Co., 1978.

The Random House Dictionary of the English Language. New York: Random House, 1966.

The Scribner-Bantam English Dictionary. New York: Charles Scribner's Sons, 1977.

Stedman's Medical Dictionary. Twenty-first edition. Baltimore, Maryland: The Williams and Wilkins Company, 1966.

Taber's Cyclopedic Medical Dictionary. Philadelphia: F.A. Davis Company, 1973.

Webster's New International Dictionary. Springfield, Massachusetts: G. & C. Merriam Company, 1881; second edition, 1934; third edition, 1961.

Webster's New Collegiate Dictionary. Seventh edition. Springfield, Massachusetts: G. & C. Merriam Company, 1963.

Other Works Consulted

Adams, Charles C. *Boontling, An American Lingo*. Austin: University of Texas Press, 1971.

Adams, Ramon F. *Western Words*. Second edition. Norman, Oklahoma: University of Oklahoma Press, 1968.

Anderson, Dennis. *The Book of Slang*. Middle Village, New York: Jonathan David Publishers, Inc., 1975.

Andrews, William. *Old Time Punishments*. Hull, England: W. Andrews and Company, 1890.

Anglicus, Ducange (pseud.). *The Vulgar Tongue*. London: Bernard Quaritch, 1857.

Anonymous. *Dictionary of Love*. 1733.

———. *New Canting Dictionary*. London, 1725.

———. *Sinks of London Laid Open*. London: J. Duncombe, 1848.

Axley, Lowry. " 'Drunk' Again." *American Speech*, Volume IV, Number 6 (1929).

Axon, W.E.A. *English Dialect in the Eighteenth Century*. Publication Number 41. English Dialect Society, 1883.

Babbitt, E.H. "College Words and Phrases." *Dialect Notes*, Volume II, Part I (1900).

Badcock, Jon (Jon Bee). *Dictionary*. 1823.

Bailey, Nathan. *Dictionarium Britannicum: Universal Etymological English Dictionary*. 1730. Reprinted by Georg Olms Verlage, 1969.

Baker, Sidney J. *The Australian Language*. Sydney: Angus and Robertson, Ltd., 1945.

———. *Australia Speaks*. Sydney: Shakespeare Head Press, 1953.

———. *The Drum*. Sydney: Currawong, 1959.

———. *A Popular Dictionary of Australian Slang*. Melbourne: Robertson and Mullens Limited, 1943.

———. *New Zealand Slang*. Christchurch: Whitcombe and Tombs Limited, 1941.

Baring-Gould, William S. *The Lure of the Limerick*. New York: Clarkson N. Potter Inc., 1967.

Barrère, Albert, and Charles G. Leland. *A Dictionary of Slang, Jargon, and Cant*. Two volumes. London: The Ballantyne Press, 1889-90.

Bartlett, John Russell. *Americanisms*. Boston: Little, Brown and Co., 1884.

B.E. *A New Dictionary of the Canting Crew*. 1690-1700.

Beath, Paul Robert. "More Crook Words." *American Speech*, Volume VI, Number 2 (1930).

Berger, Morroe. "Army Language." *American Speech*, Volume XX, Number 4 (1945).

Berrey, Lester V., and Melvin Van den Bark. *The American Thesaurus of Slang*. Second edition. New York: Thomas Y. Crowell Company, 1953.

Bierce, Ambrose. *The Devil's Dictionary*. New York: World Publishing Company, 1942.

Billups, Norman F. *American Drug Index*. Philadelphia: J. B. Lippincott Company, 1977.

Black, Henry Campbell. *Black's Law Dictionary*. Revised fourth edition. St. Paul, Minnesota: West Publishing Company, 1968.

Bolwell, Robert. "College Slang Words and Phrases." *Dialect Notes*, Volume IV, Part III (1915).

Brackbill, Hervey. "Midshipman Jargon." *American Speech*, Volume III, Number 6 (1928).

Brewer, E. Cobham. *The Dictionary of Phrase and Fable*. 1894. Reprinted by Avenel Books, 1978.

Brophy, John, and Eric Partridge. *The Long Trail*. New York: London House and Maxwell, 1965.

Carey, James T. *The College Drug Scene*. Englewood Cliffs, New Jersey: Prentice-Hall, Inc., 1968.

Cassidy, Frederic, G. *Jamaica Talk*. London: Macmillan & Co. Ltd., 1961.

Cassidy, F.G., and R.B. Le Page. *Dictionary of Jamaican English*. London: Cambridge University Press, 1967.

Chaplin, J.P. *Dictionary of Psychology*. New York: Dell Publishing Company, Inc., 1975.

Claerbaut, David. *Black Jargon in White America*. Grand Rapids, Michigan: William B. Eerdman's Publishing Company, 1972.

Coles, Elisha. *An English Dictionary*. London, 1696.

Cope, William H. *Hampshire Words and Phrases*. Publication Number 40. English Dialect Society, 1883.

Craigie, W.L., and R.J. Hulbert. *Dictionary of American English*. Chicago: University of Chicago Press, 1942.

Crowley, Ellen T., and Robert C. Thomas. *Reverse Acronyms, Initialisms, and Abbreviations Dictionary*. Fifth edition. Detroit, Michigan: Gale Research Company, 1976.

Dahlskog, Helen, editor. *A Dictionary of Contemporary and Colloquial Usage*. Chicago: The English-Language Institute of America, 1972.

Dartnell, G.E. *A Glossary of Wiltshire Words*. Publication Number 69, English Dialect Society, 1893.

Deak, Etienne, and Simone Deak. *Grand Dictionnaire d'Américanismes*. Paris: Editions Du Dauphin, 1956.

Dekker, Thomas. *The Gull's Hornbook*. 1609.

De Lannoy, William C., and Elizabeth Masterson. "Teen-Age Hophead Jargon." *American Speech*, Volume XXVII, Number 1 (1952).

Dennis, Paul, and Carolyn Barry. *The Marijuana Catalogue*. Chicago: Playboy Press, 1978.

Dill, Stephen H., and Donald E. Bebeau. *Current Slang*. Six volumes. University of South Dakota, 1966-1971.

Dillard, J.L. *All-American English*. New York: Random House, 1975.

————. *Black English*. New York: Random House, 1972.

Dills, Lanie. *CB Slanguage Language Dictionary*. Nashville, Tennessee: Lanie Dills, Publisher, 1976.

Dingus, L.R. "A Word-List from Virginia." *Dialect Notes,* Volume IV, Part III (1915).

Douglas, Norman. *Some Limericks*. Originally privately printed, 1928. Reprinted by Grove Press, Inc., 1967.

Easther, A., and Thomas Lees. *A Glossary of the Dialect of Almondbury and Huddersfield*. Publication Number 39. English Dialect Society, 1883.

Edwards, Gillian. *Uncumber and Pantaloons*. New York: E.P. Dutton, 1969.

Eliason, Norman E. *Tarheel Talk*. Chapel Hill, North Carolina: University of North Carolina Press, 1956.

English, Horace B., and Ava Champney English. *A Comprehensive Dictionary of Psychological and Psychoanalytical Terms*. New York: David McKay Co., Inc., 1958.

Espy, Willard R. *The Game of Words*. New York: Bramhall House, 1972.

————. *O Thou Improper, Thou Uncommon Noun*. New York: Clarkson N. Potter, Inc., 1978.

Evans, A.B. *The Dialect of Leicestershire*. Publication Number 31. English Dialect Society, 1881.

Evans, Bergen. *Comfortable Words*. New York: Random House, 1962.

Evans, Bergen, and Cornelia Evans. *A Dictionary of Contemporary American Usage*. New York: Random House, 1957.

Fairchild, Henry Pratt. *Dictionary of Sociology and Related Sciences*. Paterson, New Jersey: Littlefield Adams and Co., 1961.

Farb, Peter. *Word Play*. New York: Alfred A. Knopf, 1974.

Farmer, John S. *Americanisms*. London: Thomas Poulter and Sons, 1889.

Farmer, John Stephen, and W.E. Henley. *Slang and Its Analogs*. Seven volumes, 1890-1904. Reprinted by Kraus Reprint Co., 1974.

Farmer, John. *Vocabula Amatoria*. 1896. Reprinted by University Books, 1966.

Farrell, Ronald A. "The Argot of the Homosexual Subculture." *Anthropological Linguistics,* Volume 14, Number 3 (1972).

Flexner, Stuart Berg. *I Hear America Talking*. New York: Van Norstrand Reinhold, 1976.

Florio, John. *A Worlde of Words*. 1598.

Folb, Edith A. *A Comparative Study of Urban Black Argot*. Arlington, Virginia: ERIC Document Reproduction Service, 1972.

Fowler, H.W. *A Dictionary of Modern English Usage*. London: Oxford University Press, 1937.

Franklin, Benjamin. "The Drinker's Dictionary." *Pennsylvania Gazette*, January 6, 1737.

Franklyn, Julian. *Dictionary of Nicknames*. London: Hamish Hamilton, 1962.

―――. *A Dictionary of Rhyming Slang*. London: Routledge & Kegan Paul, 1961.

―――. *Which Witch?* Boston: Houghton Mifflin Co., 1966.

Fraser, Edward, and John Gibbons. *Soldier and Sailor Words and Phrases*. London: George Routledge and Sons, Ltd., 1925.

Fuller, Robert Sevier. *Duppies Is*. Georgetown, Cayman Islands: Cayman Authors Limited, 1967.

Funk, Wilfred. *Word Origins*. New York: Grosset and Dunlap, 1950.

Gibson, Walter B., and Litzka R. Gibson. *The Complete Illustrated Book of Divination and Prophesy*. Garden City, New York: Doubleday and Company, Inc., 1973.

Goldin, Hyman E., Frank O'Leary, and Morris Lipsius. *Dictionary of American Underworld Lingo*. New York: Twayne Publishers, Inc., 1950.

Granville, Wilfred. *Dictionary of Sailor's Slang*. London: Andre Deutsch, 1962.

Green, B.W. *Word-Book of Virginia Folk-Speech*. Richmond, Virginia: Wm. Ellis Jones, Inc., 1899.

Grose, Francis. *A Classical Dictionary of the Vulgar Tongue*. 1785; second edition, 1788; third edition, 1796.

―――. *A Classical Dictionary of the Vulgar Tongue*. Edited by Pierce Egan. London: Sherwood, Neely, and Jones, 1823.

―――. *A Classical Dictionary of the Vulgar Tongue*. Edited by Eric Partridge. London: The Scholartis Press, 1931.

―――. *Lexicon Balatronicum*. Edited by H. Clarke. London, 1811.

―――. *Provincial Glossary*. London: E. Jeffery, 1811.

Hall, B.H. *A Collection of College Words and Customs*. Cambridge, Massachusetts: John Bartlett, 1856.

Halliwell, James Orchard. *A Dictionary of Archaic and Provincial Words*. Fifth edition. London: Gibbings and Company, Limited, 1901.

Hamilton, Delbert W. "Pacific War Language." *American Speech*, Volume XXII, Number 1 (1947).

Hardin, Achsah. "Volstead English." *American Speech*, Volume IV, Number 2 (1931).

Hardy, Richard E., and John G. Cull. *Drug Language and Lore*. Springfield, Illinois: Charles C. Thomas, 1975.

Harman, Thomas. *A Caveat*. 1567.

Hayden, M.G. "Terms of Disparagement." *Dialect Notes*, Volume IV, Part III (1915).

Haywood, Charles. *Yankee Dictionary*. Lynn, Massachusetts: Jackson and Phillips, Inc., 1963.

Heifetz,Josefa. *Mrs. Byrne's Dictionary*. Secaucus, New Jersey: Citadel Press, 1976.

Heslop, R. Oliver. *Northumberland Words*. Publication Number 66, 68, 71. English Dialect Society. 1892-1894.

Hills, E.C. "Exclamations in American English." *Dialect Notes*, Volume V, Part VIII (1924).

Holland, Robert. *Glossary of Cheshire Words*. Publication Number 44 and 46. English Dialect Society, 1884-1885.

Hotten, John Camden. *The Slang Dictionary*. London, 1859; second edition, 1860; third edition, 1864; fourth editon, 1870; fifth edition, 1874.

Humphreys, Laud. *Tearoom Trade*. Chicago: Aldine Publishing Co., 1970.

Irwin, Godfrey. *American Tramp and Underworld Slang*. London: Scholartis Press, 1931.

James, Jennifer. "Two Domains of Streetwalker Argot." *Anthropological Linguistics*, Volume 14, Number 5 (1972).

Jamieson, John. *Dictionary of the Scottish Language*. Edited by John Johnstone. London: William P. Nimmo, 1885.

Joffe, Natalie. "The Vernacular of Menstruation." *Word*, Volume 4, Number 3 (1948).

Kane, Elisha K. "The Jargon of the Underworld." *Dialect Notes*, Volume V, Part X (1927).

Keller, Mark, and Mairi McCormick. *A Dictionary of Words About Alcohol*. New Brunswick, New Jersey: Rutgers Center for Alcohol Studies, 1968.

Kirshenblatt-Gimblett, Barbara, editor. *Speech Play*. Philadelphia: University of Pennsylvania Press, 1976.

Klein, Nicholas. "Hobo Lingo." *American Speech*, Volume I, Number 12 (1926).

Kolin, Philip C. "The Language of Nursing." *American Speech*, Volume 48, Numbers 3—4 (1973).

Kuethe, J. Louis. "Prison Parlance." *American Speech*, Volume IX, Number 1 (1934).

Lambton, Lucinda. *Temples of Convenience*. New York: St. Martin's Press, 1978.

Landy, Eugene E. *The Underground Dictionary*. New York: Simon and Schuster, 1971.

Lawrence, Jeremy. *Unmentionables and Other Euphemisms*. London: Gentry Books, 1973.

Leeds, Winifred. *Herefordshire Speech*. n.d.

Legman, G. *Rationale of the Dirty Joke: An Analysis of Sexual Humor*. New York: Bell Publishing Company, 1975.

Lester, David. *Unusual Sexual Behavior*. Springfield, Illinois: Charles C. Thomas, 1975.

Liddell, H.G., and Robert Scott. *A Greek-English Lexicon*. Oxford, England: Clarendon Press, 1940.

Lighter, Jonathan. "The Slang of the American Expeditionary Forces in Europe, 1917-1919." *American Speech*, Volume 47 (1972).

Lingeman, Richard R. *Drugs From A To Z: A Dictionary*. Second editon. New York: McGraw-Hill Book Company, 1974.

Fruit, J.P. "Kentucky Words." *Dialect Notes*, Volume I, Part V (1891).

Major, Clarence. *Dictionary of Afro-American Slang*. New York: International Publishers, 1970.

Manchon, Joseph. *Le Slang, Lexique de l'Anglais Familier et Vulgaire*. Paris, 1923.

Marckwardt, Albert H. *An Introduction to the English Language*. New York: Oxford University Press, 1942.

Marples, Morris. *University Slang*. London: Williams and Norgate, 1950.

Marshall, Mary. *Bozzimacoo: Origins and Meanings of Oaths and Swearwords*. London: M. & J. Hobbs, 1975.

Matsell, George W. *Vocabulum; or The Rogue's Dictionary*. New York: George W. Matsell & Co., 1859.

Matthews, Mitford M. *A Dictionary of Americanisms on Historical Principles*. Chicago: University of Chicago Press, 1951.

Maurer, David W. "The Argot of the Underworld." *American Speech*, Volume VII, Number 2 (1931).

———. "Argot of the Underworld Narcotics Addict." *American Speech*, Volume XI, Number 2, Part 1 (1936); Volume XIII, Number 3, Part 2 (1938).

———. " 'Australian' Rhyming Argot in the American Underworld." *American Speech*, Volume XIX, Number 3 (1944).

———. "The Lingo of the Good-People." *American Speech*, Volume X, Number 1 (1935).

Mawson, C.O. Sylvester. *Dictionary of Foreign Terms*. New York: Thomas Y. Crowell Company, 1934.

Mayhew, Henry. *Mayhew's London, Selections From "London Labour and the London Poor"*. Edited by P. Quennell. London: Spring Books, 1949.

McCulloch, Walter F. *Woods Words*. Oregon State College, Champoeg Press, 1958.

Mead, W.E., and G.D. Chase. "A Central Connecticut Word-List." *Dialect Notes,* Volume III, Part I (1905).

Mencken, H.L. *The American Language*. New York: Alfred A. Knopf, 1921.

————. *The American Language*. Supplement One. New York: Alfred A. Knopf, 1945.

————. *The American Language*. Supplement Two. New York: Alfred A. Knopf, 1948.

Meredith, Mamie. "Inexpressibles, Unmentionables, Unwhisperables, and other Verbal Delicacies of Mid-Nineteenth Century Americans." *American Speech,* Volume V, Number 4 (1930).

Milburn, George. " 'Convicts' Jargon." *American Speech,* Volume VI, Number 6 (1931).

Montelone, Vincent J. *Criminal Slang*. Revised edition. Boston: The Christopher Publishing House, 1949.

Montagu, Ashley. *The Anatomy of Swearing*. New York: Macmillian Publishing Company, 1967.

Morris, William, and Mary Morris. *Morris Dictionary of Word and Phrase Origins*. New York: Harper & Row, Publishers, 1977.

Mueller, Gerhard O.W. *Legal Regulation of Sexual Conduct*. New York: Oceana Publications, Inc., 1961.

Nares, Robert. *A Glossary of Words, Phrases, Names, and Allusions in Works of English Authors*. London: Reeves and Turner, 1888.

Nicholson, Margaret. *A Dictionary of American-English Usage*. New York: Oxford University Press, 1957.

Niemoeller, A.F. "A Glossary of Homosexual Slang." *Fact,* Volume 2, Number 1 (1965).

Nodal, J.H., and George Milner. *Glossary of the Lancashire Dialect*. Publication Number 35. English Dialect Society, 1882.

Northall, G.F. *A Warwickshire Word-Book*. Publication Number 79. English Dialect Society, 1896.

Opie, I., and P. Opie. *The Lore and Language of School Children*. Oxford, England: Clarendon Press, 1959.

————. *Children's Games in Street and Playground*. Oxford, England: Clarendon Press, 1969.

Orkin, Mark M. *Speaking Canadian English*. Toronto: General Publishing Company Limited, 1970.

Ottley, C.R. *Creole Talk, Trinibaganese*. Trinidad, Victory Printers, 1971.

Partridge, Eric. *A Dictionary of Catch Phrases*. New York: Stein and Day, 1977.

———. *Dictionary of Forces Slang*. London: Secker & Warburg, 1948.

———. *A Dictionary of R.A.F. Slang*. London: Michael Joseph Ltd., 1945.

———. *A Dictionary of Slang and Unconventional English*. Seventh edition. New York: Macmillian Publishing Co., 1970.

———. *A Dictionary of the Underworld*. New York: Macmillian Publishing Co., 1968.

———. *Origins*. London: Routledge and Kegan Paul, 1958.

———. *Shakespeare's Bawdy*. London: Routledge & Kegan Paul, 1968.

———. *Slang Today and Yesterday*. Fourth editon. New York: Barnes and Noble, Inc., 1970.

———. *Smaller Slang Dictionary*. London: Routledge and Kegan Paul, 1964.

Pederson, Lee. "An Approach to Urban Word Geography." *American Speech*, Volume 46, Numbers 1-2 (1971).

Pederson, Lee. "Chicago Words: The Regional Vocabulary." *American Speech*, Volume 46, Numbers 3-4 (1971).

Pegge, Samuel. *Two Collections of Derbicisms*. Publication Number 78, English Dialect Society, 1896.

Pei, Mario, and Salvatore Ramondino. *Dictionary of Foreign Terms*. New York: Dell Publishing Company, Inc., 1974.

Potter, Stephen, and Laurens Sargent. *Pedigree: The Origins of Words From Nature*. New York: Taplinger Publishing Company, 1974.

Pound, Louise. "American Euphemisms for Dying, Death, and Burial." *American Speech*, Volume XI, Number 3 (1936).

———. "Dialect Speech of Nebraska." *Dialect Notes*, Volume III, Part I (1905).

Prenner, Manuel. "Slang Synonyms for Drunk." *American Speech*, Volume IV, Number 2 (1928).

Pudney, John. *The Smallest Room*. London: Michael Joseph, 1954.

Pyles, Thomas. *The Origin and Development of the English Language*. Second edition. New York: Harcourt, Brace and Jovanovitch Inc., 1971.

Randolph, Vance. "Verbal Modesty in the Ozarks." *Dialect Notes*, Volume VI, Part I (1928).

———. "Wet Words in Kansas." *American Speech*, Volume IV, Number 5 (1929).

Randolph, Vance, and Carl Pingry. "Kansas University Slang." *American Speech*, Volume III, Number 3 (1928).

Randolph, Vance, and George P. Wilson. *Down in the Holler*. Norman, Oklahoma: University of Oklahoma Press, 1953.

Read, Allen Walker. "An Obscenity Symbol." *American Speech*, Volume IX (1934).

————. *Lexical Evidence from Folk Epigraphy in Western North America*. Printed privately in Paris in 1935. Reprinted as *Classical American Graffiti*. Waukesha, Wisconsin: Maledicta Press, 1977.

————. "Noah Webster as a Euphemist." *Dialect Notes*, Volume VI, Part VIII (1934).

Reynolds, Reginald. *Cleanliness and Godliness*. Garden City, New York: Doubleday and Company, Inc., 1943.

Roback, A.A. *A Dictionary of International Slurs*. Cambridge, Massachusetts: Sci-Art Publishers, 1944.

Rose, Howard N. *A Thesaurus of Slang*. New York: The Macmillian Company, 1934.

Ross, Alan S.C., and A.W. Moverley. *The Pitcairnese Language*. London: Andre Deutsch, 1964.

Rosten, Leo. *The Joys of Yiddish*. New York: McGraw-Hill Book Company, 1968.

Rye, Walter. *East Anglian Glossary*. Publication Number 75. English Dialect Society, 1895.

Sabbath, Dan, and Mandel Hall. *End Product: The First Taboo*. New York: Urizen Books, 1977.

Sagarin, Edward. *The Anatomy of Dirty Words*. New York: Lyle Stuart, Publisher, 1962.

Samolar, Charlie. "The Argot of the Vagabond." *American Speech*, Volume II, Number 9 (1927).

Saul, Vernon W. "The Vocabulary of Bums." *American Speech*, Volume IV, Number 5, (1929).

Schur, Norman W. *British Self-taught with Comments in American*. New York: Macmillan Publishing Company, Inc., 1973.

Seymour, Richard K. "Collegiate Slang: Aspects of Word Formation and Semantic Change." *Publication of the American Dialect Society*, Number 51 (April, 1969).

Shipley, Joseph T. *Dictionary of Early English*. New York: Philosophical Library, 1955.

Simons, Hi. "A Prison Dictionary (Expurgated)." *American Speech*, Volume VIII, Number 3 (1933).

Skeat, Walter, editor. *Fitzherbert's Book of Husbandry, 1534*. Publication Number 37. English Dialect Society, 1882.

Skeat, Walter. *Nine Specimens of English Dialect*. Publication Number 76. English Dialect Society.

Skinner, Henry Alan. *The Origin of Medical Terms.* Second edition. New York: Hafner Publishing Co., 1970.

Slovenko, Ralph. *Sexual Behavior and the Law.* Springfield, Illinois: Charles C. Thomas, 1965.

Sperling, Susan Kelz. *Poplollies and Bellibones: A Celebration of Lost Words.* New York: Clarkson N. Potter, 1977.

Stanley, Julia P. "Homosexual Slang." *American Speech,* Volume 45 (1970).

Steadman, J.M. "A Study of Verbal Taboos." *American Speech,* Volume X, Number 2 (1935).

Tak, Montie. *Truck Talk.* Philadelphia, Pennsylvania: Chilton Book Co., 1971.

Taylor, A. Marjorie. *The Language of World War II.* New York: H.W. Wilson Co., 1944.

Taylor, Sharon Henderson. "Terms for Low Intelligence." *American Speech,* Volume 49, Numbers 3-4 (1974).

Thornton, Richard H. *An American Glossary.* Philadelphia: J.B. Lippincott, 1912.

Underwood, Gary. "Razorback Slang." *American Speech,* Volume 50 (1975).

Untermeyer, Louis. *Lots of Limericks.* New York: Bell Publishing Company, 1959.

Ward, Harvey E. *Down Under Without Blunder.* Rutland, Vermont: Charles E. Tuttle Co., 1967.

Ware, J. Redding. *Passing English of the Victorian Era.* London: George Routledge & Sons, Limited, 1909.

Warnock, E.L. "Terms of Approbation and Eulogy." *Dialect Notes,* Volume IV, Part I (1913).

Weingarten, Joseph. *An American Dictionary of Slang and Colloquial Speech.* New York: 1954.

Wentworth, Harold. *American Dialect Dictionary.* New York: Thomas Y. Crowell Company, 1944.

Wentworth, Harold, and Stuart Berg Flexner. *Dictionary of American Slang.* Second supplemented edition. New York: Thomas Y. Crowell Company, 1975.

Weseen, Maurice H. *Dictionary of American Slang.* New York: Thomas Y. Crowell Company, 1934.

Whitman, Walt. *Leaves of Grass.* First published in 1855. Revised and expanded in various editions until 1891.

Wilkes, Gerald Alfred. *A Dictionary of Australian Colloquialisms.* London: Routledge & Kegan Paul, 1978.

Wilson, David. *Staffordshire Dialect Words.* Stafford, England: Moorland Publishing Co., 1974.

Wolfenstein, Martha. *Children's Humor: A Psychological Analysis*. Glencoe, Illinois: The Free Press, 1954.

Wright, Joseph, editor. *The English Dialect Dictionary*. London: Henry Frowde, 1900.

Wright, Lawrence. *Clean and Decent*. London: Routledge & Kean Paul, 1960.

Wright, Peter. *The Language of British Industry*. London: Macmillan Publishing Company, 1974.

Yenne, Herbert. "Prison Lingo." *American Speech,* Volume II, Number 6 (1927).

Young, Lawrence A., et al. *Recreational Drugs*. New York: Collier Macmillan Publishers, 1977.

Zandvoort, R.U. *Wartime English*. Groningen: J.B. Wolters, 1957.

Various works of the following authors were consulted:

Joseph Addison, Francis Beaumont, James Boswell, Robert Burns, Truman Capote, Thomas Carew, Thomas Carlyle, George Chapman, Geoffrey Chaucer, Samuel Clemens (Mark Twain), William Congreve, James Fenimore Cooper, Randle Cotgrave, Daniel Defoe, Charles Dickens, John Dryden, Thomas D'Urfrey, Pierce Egan, Henry Fielding, John Fletcher, Sigmund Freud, George Gordon (Lord Byron), Robert Graves, Zane Grey, Joseph Heller, William Ernest Henley, Robert Herrick, Washington Irving, James Joyce, Rudyard Kipling, William Langland, D.H. Lawrence, Jack London, Thomas Babington Macaulay, Thomas Malory, Thomas Middleton, John Stuart Mill, John Milton, Peter Anthony Motteux, Vladimir Nabokov, Thomas Nashe, George Orwell, Samuel Pepys, Alexander Pope, Phillip Roth, J.D. Salinger, Sir Walter Scott, William Shakespeare, George Bernard Shaw, Tobias George Smollett, Edmund Spenser, Richard Steele, Jonathan Swift, William Makepeace Thackery, Anthony Trollope, Nicholas Udall, Sir Thomas Urquhart, Edward (Ned) Ward, John Webster, Walt Whitman.